Lecture Notes in Artificial Intelligence   2821

Edited by J. G. Carbonell and J. Siekmann

Subseries of Lecture Notes in Computer Science

T0190014

Springer

Berlin
Heidelberg
New York
Hong Kong
London
Milan
Paris
Tokyo

Andreas Günter   Rudolf Kruse
Bernd Neumann (Eds.)

KI 2003:
Advances in
Artificial Intelligence

26th Annual German Conference on AI, KI 2003
Hamburg, Germany, September 15-18, 2003
Proceedings

 Springer

Series Editors

Jaime G. Carbonell, Carnegie Mellon University, Pittsburgh, PA, USA
Jörg Siekmann, University of Saarland, Saarbrücken, Germany

Volume Editors

Andreas Günter
HITeC e. V.
Universität Hamburg
Fachbereich Informatik
Vogt-Kölln-Str. 30, 22527 Hamburg, Germany
E-mail: guenter@informatik.uni-hamburg.de

Rudolf Kruse
OvG-Universität Magdeburg
Fakultät für Informatik
Universitätsplatz 2, 39106 Magdeburg, Germany
E-mail: kruse@iws.cs.uni-magdeburg.de

Bernd Neumann
Universität Hamburg
Fachbereich Informatik
Vogt-Kölln-Str. 30, 22527 Hamburg, Germany
E-mail: neumann@informatik.uni-hamburg.de

Cataloging-in-Publication Data applied for

A catalog record for this book is available from the Library of Congress.

Bibliographic information published by Die Deutsche Bibliothek
Die Deutsche Bibliothek lists this publication in the Deutsche Nationalbibliografie;
detailed bibliographic data is available in the Internet at <http://dnb.ddb.de>.

CR Subject Classification (1998): I.2

ISSN 0302-9743
ISBN 3-540-20059-2 Springer-Verlag Berlin Heidelberg New York

Springer-Verlag Berlin Heidelberg New York
a member of BertelsmannSpringer Science+Business Media GmbH

http://www.springer.de

© Springer-Verlag Berlin Heidelberg 2003
Printed in Germany

Typesetting: Camera-ready by author, data conversion by PTP-Berlin GmbH
Printed on acid-free paper   SPIN: 10953594   06/3142   5 4 3 2 1 0

Preface

The German Conference on Artificial Intelligence is a traditional and unique yearly event which brings together the German AI community and an increasing number of international guests. While not as old as IJCAI (which first took place in 1969), KI 2003 marks a tradition which officially began in 1975 with a workshop of the working group "Künstliche Intelligenz" of GI. Actually, there was one important AI conference in Germany before this, the "Fachtagung Cognitive Verfahren und Systeme" (Cognitive Methods and Systems) held in Hamburg in April 1973.

This volume contains the proceedings of the 26th Annual German Conference on Artificial Intelligence. For the technical program we had 90 submissions from 22 countries. Out of these contributions 18 papers were accepted for oral presentation and 24 papers for poster presentation. The acceptance criteria were set to meet high international standards. Poster presenters were given the additional opportunity to summarize their papers in three minute spotlight presentations. Oral, spotlight as well as the poster presentations were then scheduled in an interesting conference program, summarized in the book you have before you.

The contributions in this volume reflect the richness and diversity of artificial intelligence research and represent several important developments in the field. As a first highlight, we would like to mention work on multimodal information processing. Multimodal aspects are addressed in several contributions, for example, on information fusion, vision-language integration, dialogue control with integrated gesture, and facial expression analysis. The interest in multimodal information processing is a positive indicator for integration efforts across subfield boundaries. Another interesting development is the integration of cognitive modeling with AI engineering tasks. Advanced user interfaces provide an important motivation, as human cognitive mechanisms and constraints have to be considered when shaping human-computer interactions. The interest in cognitive modeling may also reflect a certain amount of frustration about more formal approaches to human-type reasoning. More and more advanced applications – for example in robotics, decision making, high-level vision, diagnosis, planning – ask for some sort of common-sense integration, which is still difficult to provide in a strictly formal framework. Hence, high-level cognitive empiricism is enjoying a revival. In addition to application-oriented work, this volume also features excellent contributions on formal foundations – one of the traditional strengths of German AI. As the Semantic Web and the demand for ontologies increase in importance, progress in formal knowledge representation, in particular in description logics, is quite appreciated.

The paper "Applied Connectionistic Methods in Computer Vision to Compare Segmented Images" by S. Bischoff (Fraunhofer Institute "Heinrich Hertz" in Berlin), D. Reuss, and F. Wysotzki (both Technical University of Berlin) was selected for the Springer Best Paper Award by the program committee. Congratulations to the authors for their excellent contribution.

This volume also contains contributions corresponding to the five invited talks at KI 2003. We were delighted that Nick Jennings (University of Southampton), Daniel Keim (University of Konstanz), Erik Sandewall (University of Linköping), Rudi Studer (University of Karlsruhe), and Wolfgang Wahlster (DFKI Saarbrücken) accepted our invitation to present keynote lectures on important AI topics.

Organizing a conference such as this one is not possible without the support of many individuals. As for the technical program, we thank all the authors who submitted papers to the conference. We are most grateful to the members of the program committee and all the additional reviewers for providing timely, qualified reviews and participating in the discussion during the paper selection process. We are very grateful to Christopher Habel, who served as the Workshop Chair, Wolfgang Menzel, who helped to organize the poster sessions, Bärbel Mertsching who was responsible for the industrial exhibition, and Thorsten Krebs who created the website.

Christian Döring has been the backbone on several electronic issues, starting from the electronic paper submission with the ConfMan system all the way to the assembly of the final proceedings.

July 2003   Andreas Günter, Rudolf Kruse, and Bernd Neumann

Organization

General Chair

Bernd Neumann — University of Hamburg

Program Committee

Kruse, Rudolf	University of Magdeburg (Chair)
André, Elizabeth	University of Augsburg
Baader, Franz	University of Dresden
Brauer, Wilfried	TU München
Bramer, Max	University of Portsmouth
Brewka, Gerhard	University of Leipzig
Buhmann, Joachim	University of Bonn
Burkhard, Hans-Dieter	HU Berlin
Bürckert, Hans-Jürgen	DFKI Saarbrücken
Dubois, Didier	IRIT Toulouse
Eklund, Peter	University of Queensland
Fensel, Dieter	University of Innsbruck
Freksa, Christian	University of Bremen
Görz, Gunter	University of Erlangen
Günter, Andreas	University of Hamburg
Habel, Christopher	University of Hamburg
Herzog, Otthein	University of Bremen
Jensen, Finn	University of Aalborg
Kirn, Stefan	TU Ilmenau
Köhler, Jana	IBM Research Laboratory, Zürich
Lakemeyer, Gerhard	RWTH Aachen
Mántaras, Ramon López de	University of Barcelona
Menzel, Wolfgang	University of Hamburg
Mertsching, Bärbel	University of Hamburg
Miksch, Silvia	TU Wien
Milne, Rob	Intelligent Applications, Livingston
Nagel, Hans Hellmut	University of Karlsruhe
Nauck, Detlef	BT Exact, Ipswich
Nebel, Bernhard	University of Freiburg
Neumann, Bernd	University of Hamburg
Niemann, Heinrich	University of Erlangen
Puppe, Frank	University of Würzburg
Ritter, Helge	University of Bielefeld
Rojas, Paul	University of Berlin
Rollinger, Claus	University of Osnabrück
Saitta, Lorenza	Università di Torino
Studer, Rudi	University of Karlsruhe
Wolkenhauer, Olaf	UMIST Manchester
Wrobel, Stefan	Fraunhofer AIS, Bonn
Wysotzki, Fritz	TU Berlin

Organization Chair
Andreas Günter   University of Hamburg

Workshop Chair
Christopher Habel   University of Hamburg

Poster Chairs
Wolfgang Menzel   University of Hamburg
Rudolf Kruse   Otto-von-Guericke-University of Magdeburg

Exhibition Chairs
Bärbel Mertsching   University of Hamburg
Wiebke Frauen   University of Hamburg

Publication Chair
Christian Döring   Otto-von-Guericke-University of Magdeburg

Additional Reviewers

Arroyo, Sinuhe   Klose, Aljoscha
Berka, David   Knoll, Alois
Bischoff, Stefan   Kocka, Tomas
Borgelt, Christian   Konev, Boris
Ding, Ying   Lausen, Holger
Dong, Tiansi   Leopold, Edda
Gärtner, Thomas   Lutz, Carsten
Gebhardt, Jörg   Monfroy, E.
Geibel, Peter   Nielsen, Thomas
Gips, Carsten   Pajot, B.
Gust, Helmar   Richter, Kai-Florian
Han, Sung-kook   Runkler, Thomas
Hernández, Daniel   Schmid, Ute
Hoffmann, Jörg   Spieß, Thurid
Jain, Brijnesh-Johannes   Stein, Klaus
Kühnberger, Kai-Uwe   Thielscher, Michael
Kindermann, Jörg   Wallgrün, Jan Oliver
Klawonn, Frank   Wolter, Diedrich

Table of Contents

Invited Paper

Logics and Ontologies

Cognitive Modeling

Reasoning Methods

Machine Learning

Neural Networks

Reasoning under Uncertainty

Planning and Constraints

Spatial Modeling

User Modeling

Agent Technology

Author Index

Towards Symmetric Multimodality: Fusion and Fission of Speech, Gesture, and Facial Expression

Wolfgang Wahlster

German Research Center for Artificial Intelligence (DFKI)
Stuhlsatzenhausweg 3
D-66123 Saarbrücken, Germany
`www.dfki.de/~wahlster`

Abstract. We introduce the notion of symmetric multimodality for dialogue systems in which all input modes (eg. speech, gesture, facial expression) are also available for output, and vice versa. A dialogue system with symmetric multimodality must not only understand and represent the user's multimodal input, but also its own multimodal output. We present the SmartKom system, that provides full symmetric multimodality in a mixed-initiative dialogue system with an embodied conversational agent. SmartKom represents a new generation of multimodal dialogue systems, that deal not only with simple modality integration and synchronization, but cover the full spectrum of dialogue phenomena that are associated with symmetric multimodality (including crossmodal references, one-anaphora, and backchannelling). We show that SmartKom's plug-an-play architecture supports multiple recognizers for a single modality, eg. the user's speech signal can be processed by three unimodal recognizers in parallel (speech recognition, emotional prosody, boundary prosody). Finally, we detail SmartKom's three-tiered representation of multimodal discourse, consisting of a domain layer, a discourse layer, and a modality layer.

1 Introduction

In-car electronics, dashboard computers, mobile devices (eg. PDAs, smartphones, wearables), and remote control systems for infotainment appliances are providing ever more functionality. However, along with greater functionality, the user must also come to terms with the greater complexity and a steeper learning curve. This complexity is compounded by the sheer proliferation of different devices lacking a standard user interface. Our SmartKom system (www.smartkom.org) is designed to support a wide range of collaborative and multimodal help dialogues, that allow users to intuitively and efficiently access the functionalities needed for their task. The application of the SmartKom technology is especially motivated in non-desktop scenarios, such as smart rooms, kiosks, or mobile environments. SmartKom features the situated understanding of possibly imprecise, ambiguous or incomplete multimodal input and the generation of coordinated, cohesive, and coherent multimodal presentations. SmartKom's interaction management is based on representing, reasoning, and exploiting models of the user, domain, task, context, and modalities. The system is ca-

A. Günter et al. (Eds.): KI 2003, LNAI 2821, pp. 1–18, 2003.

pable of real-time dialogue processing, including flexible multimodal turn-taking, backchannelling, and metacommunicative interaction.

Four major scientific goals of SmartKom were to:

- explore and design new symbolic and statistical methods for the seamless fusion and mutual disambiguation of multimodal input on semantic and pragmatic levels
- generalize advanced discourse models for spoken dialogue systems so that they can capture a broad spectrum of multimodal discourse phenomena
- explore and design new constraint-based and plan-based methods for multimodal fission and adaptive presentation layout
- integrate all these multimodal capabilities in a reusable, efficient and robust dialogue shell, that guarantees flexible configuration, domain independence and plug-and-play functionality

We begin by describing the notion of symmetric multimodality in section 2. In section 3, we introduce SmartKom as a flexible and adaptive multimodal dialogue shell and show in section 4 that SmartKom bridges the full loop from multimodal perception to physical action. SmartKom's distributed component architecture, realizing a multi-blackboard system, is described in section 5. Then in section 6 and 7, we describe SmartKom's methods for multimodal fusion and fission. Section 8 discusses the role of the three-tiered multimodal discourse model in SmartKom.

2   Towards Symmetric Multimodality

SmartKom provides full symmetric multimodality in a mixed-initiative dialogue system. Symmetric multimodality means that all input modes (speech, gesture, facial expression) are also available for output, and vice versa. A dialogue system with symmetric multimodality must not only understand and represent the user's multimodal input, but also its own multimodal output.

In this sense, SmartKom's modality fission component provides the inverse functionality of its modality fusion component, since it maps a communicative intention of the system onto a coordinated multimodal presentation (Wahlster 2002). SmartKom provides an anthropomorphic and affective user interface through an embodied conversational agent called Smartakus. This life-like character uses coordinated speech, gesture and facial expression for its dialogue contributions.

Thus, SmartKom supports face-to-face dialogic interaction between two agents that share a common visual environment: the human user and Smartakus, an autonomous embodied conversational agent. The "i"-shape of Smartakus is analogous to that used for information kiosks (see Fig. 1). Smartakus is modeled in 3D Studio Max. It is a self-animated interface agent with a large repertoire of gestures, postures and facial expressions. Smartakus uses body language to notify users that it is waiting for their input, that it is listening to them, that is has problems in understanding their input, or that it is trying hard to find an answer to their questions.

Most of the previous multimodal interfaces do not support symmetric multimodality, since they focus either on multimodal fusion (eg. QuickSet, see Cohen et al. 1977, or MATCH, see Johnston et al. 2002) or multimodal fission (eg. WIP, see Wahlster et al. 1993). But only true multimodal dialogue systems like SmartKom create a natural experience for the user in the form of daily human-to-human communication, by allowing both the user and the system to combine the same spectrum of modalities.

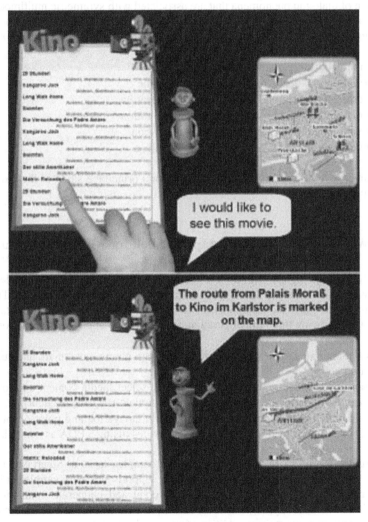

Fig. 1. Speech and Gesture for Input and Output

SmartKom is based on the situated delegation-oriented dialogue paradigm (SDDP): The user delegates a task to a virtual communication assistant (Wahlster et al. 2001). This cannot however be done in a simple command-and-control style for more complex tasks. Instead, a collaborative dialogue between the user and the agent elaborates the specification of the delegated task and possible plans of the agent to achieve the user's intentional goal. The user delegates a task to Smartakus and helps the agent, where necessary, in the execution of the task. Smartakus accesses various digital services and appliances on behalf of the user, collates the results, and presents them to the user.

SmartKom represents a new generation of multimodal dialogue systems, that deal not only with simple modality integration and synchronization, but cover the full spectrum of dialogue phenomena that are associated with symmetric multimodality.

One of the technical goals of our research in the SmartKom project was to address the following important discourse phenomena that arise in multimodal dialogues:

- mutual disambiguation of modalities
- multimodal deixis resolution and generation
- crossmodal reference resolution and generation
- multimodal anaphora resolution and generation
- multimodal ellipsis resolution and generation
- multimodal turn-taking and backchannelling

Symmetric multimodality is a prerequisite for a principled study of these discourse phenomena.

3 Towards a Flexible and Adaptive Shell for Multimodal Dialogues

SmartKom was designed with a clear focus on flexibility, as a transmutable system that can engage in many different types of tasks in different usage contexts. The same software architecture and components are used in various roles that Smartakus can play in the following three fully operational experimental application scenarios:

- a communication companion that helps with phone, fax, email, and authentca-tion tasks
- an infotainment companion that helps to select media content and to operate various TV appliances (using a tablet computer as a mobile client)
- a mobile travel companion that helps with navigation and point-of-interest in-formation retrieval in location-based services (using a PDA as a mobile client)

Currently, the user can delegate 43 types of complex tasks to Smartakus in multi-modal dialogues. The SmartKom architecture supports not only simple multimodal command-and-control interfaces, but also coherent and cooperative dialogues with mixed initiative and a synergistic use of multiple modalities. SmartKom's plug-and-play architecture supports easy addition of new application services.

Fig. 2 shows a three-camera configuration of SmartKom that can be used as a mul-timodal communication kiosk for airports, train stations, or other public places where people may seek information on facilities such as hotels, restaurants, and movie thea-tres. Users can also access their personalized webservices. The user's speech input is captured with a directional microphone. The user's facial expressions of emotion are captured with a CCD camera and their gestures are tracked with an infrared camera. A video projector is used for the projection of SmartKom's graphical output onto a horizontal surface. Two speakers under the projection surface provide the speech output of the life-like character. An additional camera that can automatically tilt and pan, is used to capture images of documents or 3D objects that the user would like to include in multimedia messages composed with the help of SmartKom.

As a resource-adaptive multimodal system, the SmartKom architecture supports a flexible embodiment of the life-like character, that is used as a conversational partner

Fig. 2. SmartKom's Multimodal Input and Output Devices

in multimodal dialogue. The Smartakus agent is visualized either simply as a talking head together with an animated hand, when screen space is scarce, or as a full-body character, when enough screen space is available (see Fig. 4). Thus, Smartakus is embodied on a PDA differently than on a tablet computer or on the large top-projected screen used in the public information kiosk.

4   Perception and Action under Multimodal Conditions

SmartKom bridges the full loop from multimodal perception to physical action. Since the multimodal interaction with Smartakus covers both communicative and physical acts, the mutual understanding of the user and the system can often be validated by checking whether the user and the system "do the right thing" for completing the task at hand.

In a multimodal dialogue about the TV program, the user may browse a TV show database, create a personalized TV listing, and finally ask Smartakus to switch on the

TV and tune to a specific program. Smartakus can also carry out more complex actions like programming a VCR to record the user's favourite TV show. Moreover, it can scan a document or a 3D object with its camera and then send the captured image to another person as an email attachment. Fig. 3 shows Dr. Johannes Rau, the German Federal President, using SmartKom's multimodal dialogue capabilities to scan the "German Future Award" trophy and send the scanned image via email to a colleague. This example shows that on the one hand, multimodal dialogue contributions can trigger certain actions of Smartakus. On the other hand, Smartakus may also ask the

user to carry out certain physical actions during the multimodal dialogue.

Fig. 3. The German Federal President E-mailing a Scanned Image with SmartKom's Help

For example, Smartakus will ask the user to place their hand with spread fingers on a virtual scanning device, or to use a write-in field projected on the screen for their signature, when biometric authentication by hand contour recognition or signature verification is requested by a security-critical application. Fig. 3 shows a situation in which Smartakus has found an address book entry for the user, after they have introduced themself by name. Since the address book entry, which is partially visualized by SmartKom on the left part of the display, requests hand contour authentication for this particular user, Smartakus asks the user to place their hand on the marked area of the projected display, so that the hand contour can be scanned by its camera (see Fig. 4).

Since quite complex tasks can be delegated to Smartakus, there may be considerable delays in replying to a request. Our WOZ experiments and user tests with earlier prototypes of SmartKom, showed clearly that users want a simple and fast feedback on the state of the system in such situations. Therefore, a variety of adaptive perceptual feedback mechanisms have been realized in SmartKom.

In the upper left corner of a presentation, SmartKom can display a "magic eye" icon, that lights up while the processing of the user's multimodal input is proceeding (see the left part of Fig. 5). "Magic eye" is the common name applied to the green-glow tubes used in 1930's radio equipment to visually assist the listener in tuning a radio station to the point of greatest signal strength. Although SmartKom works in real-time, there may be some processing delays caused by corrupted input or complex disambiguation processes.

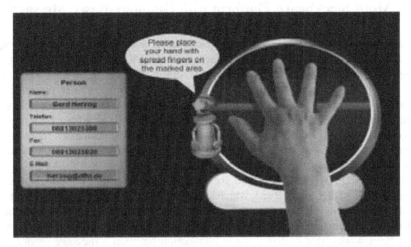

Fig. 4. Interactive Biometric Authentication by Hand Contour Recognition

An animated dashed line (see the left part of Fig. 5) circles the Smartakus character, while the system is engaged in an information retrieval task (e.g. access to maps, EPG, web sites). This type of feedback is used when screen space is scarce. When more screen space is available, an animation sequence that shows Smartakus working on a laptop is used for the same kind of feedback. When Smartakus is downloading a large file, it can show a progress bar to indicate to the user how the data transfer is going (see the right part of Fig. 5).

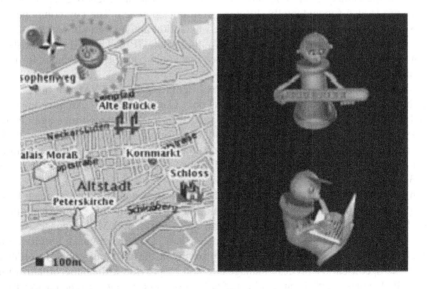

Fig. 5. Adaptive Perceptual Feedback on the System State

5 A Multi-blackboard Platform with Ontology-Based Messaging

SmartKom is based on a distributed component architecture, realizing a multi-blackboard system. The integration platform is called MULTIPLATFORM (Multiple Language Target Integration Platform for Modules, see Herzog et al. 2003) and is built on top of open source software. The natural choice to realize an open, flexible and scalable software architecture, is that of a distributed system, which is able to integrate heterogeneous software modules implemented in diverse programming languages and running on different operating systems. SmartKom includes more than 40 asynchronously running modules coded in four different programming languages: C, C++, Java, and Prolog.

The MULTIPLATFORM testbed includes a message-oriented middleware. The implementation is based on PVM, which stands for parallel virtual machine. On top of PVM, a message-based communication framework is implemented based on the so-called publish/subscribe approach. In contrast to unicast routing known from multi-agent frameworks, that realize a direct connection between a message sender and a known receiver, MULTIPLATFORM is based on the more efficient multicast addressing scheme. Instead of addressing one or several receivers directly, the sender publishes a notification on a named message queue, so that the message can be forwarded to a list of subscribers. This kind of distributed event notification makes the communication framework very flexible as it focuses on the data to be exchanged and it decouples data producers and data consumers. Compared with point-to-point messaging used in multi-agent frameworks like OAA (Martin et al. 1999), the publish/subscribe scheme helps to reduce the number and complexity of interfaces significantly.

GCSI, the Galaxy Communicator Software Infrastructure (Seneff et al. 1999) architecture is also fundamentally different from our approach. The key component of GCSI is a central hub, which mediates the interaction among various servers that realize different dialog system components. Within MULTIPLATFORM there exists no such centralized controller component, since this could become a bottleneck for more complex multimodal dialogue architectures.

In order to provide publish/subscribe messaging on top of PVM, we have added another software layer called PCA (Pool Communication Architecture). In MULTIPLATFORM, the term data pool is used to refer to named message queues. Every single pool can be linked with a pool data format specification in order to define admissible message contents. The messaging system is able to transfer arbitrary data contents, and provides excellent performance characteristics (see Herzog et al. 2003).

In SMARTKOM, we have developed M3L (Multimodal Markup Language) as a complete XML language that covers all data interfaces within this complex multimodal dialog system. Instead of using several quite different XML languages for the various data pools, we aimed at an integrated and coherent language specification, which includes all sub-structures that may occur on the different pools. In order to make the specification process manageable and to provide a thematic organization, the M3L language definition has been decomposed into about 40 schema specifications. The basic data flow from user input to system output continuously adds further processing results so that the representational structure will be refined, step-by-step.

The ontology that is used as a foundation for representing domain and application knowledge is coded in the ontology language OIL. Our tool OIL2XSD (Gurevych et al. 2003) transforms an ontology written in OIL (Fensel et al. 2001) into an M3L compatible XML Schema definition. The information structures exchanged via the various blackboards are encoded in M3L. M3L is defined by a set of XML schemas. For example, the word hypothesis graph and the gesture hypothesis graph, the hypotheses about facial expressions, the media fusion results, and the presentation goal are all represented in M3L. M3L is designed for the representation and exchange of complex multimodal content. It provides information about segmentation, synchronization, and the confidence in processing results. For each communication blackboard, XML schemas allow for automatic data and type checking during information exchange. The XML schemas can be viewed as typed feature structures. SmartKom uses unification and a new operation called overlay (cf. Alexandersson and Becker 2003) of typed feature structures encoded in M3L for discourse processing.

Application developers can generate their own multimodal dialogue system by creating knowledge bases with application-specific interfaces, and plugging them into the reusable SmartKom shell. It is particularly easy to add or remove modality analyzers or renderers, even dynamically while the system is running. This plug and play of modalities can be used to adjust the system's capability to handle different demands of the users, and the situative context they are currently in. Since SmartKom's modality analyzers are independent from the respective device-specific recognizers, the system can switch in real-time, for example, between video-based, pen-based or touch-based gesture recognition. SmartKom's architecture, its dialogue backbone, and its fusion and fission modules are reusable across applications, domains, and modalities.

MULTIPLATFORM is running on the SmartKom server that consists of 3 dual Xeon 2.8 GHz processors. Each processor uses 1.5 GB of main memory. One processor is running under Windows 2000, and the other two under Linux. The mobile clients (an iPAQ Pocket PC for the mobile travel companion and a Fujitsu Stylistic 3500X webpad for the infotainment companion) are linked to the SmartKom server via WaveLAN.

6 Reducing Uncertainty and Ambiguity by Modality Fusion

The analysis of the various input modalities by SmartKom is typically plagued by uncertainty and ambiguity. The speech recognition system produces a word hypothesis graph with acoustic scores, stating which word might have been spoken in a certain time frame. The prosody component generates a graph of hypotheses about clause and sentence boundaries with prosodic scores. The gesture analysis component produces a set of scored hypotheses about possible reference objects in the visual context. Finally, the interpretation of facial expressions leads to various scored hypotheses about the emotional state of the user. All the recognizers produce time-stamped hypotheses, so that the fusion process can consider various temporal constraints. The key function of modality fusion is the reduction of the overall uncertainty and the mutual disambiguation of the various analysis results. By fusing symbolic and statistical information derived from the recognition and analysis components for speech, prosody, facial expression and gesture, SmartKom can correct various recognition errors of its unimodal input components and thus provide a more robust dialogue than a unimodal system.

In principle, modality fusion can be realized during various processing stages like multimodal signal processing, multimodal parsing, or multimodal semantic processing. In SmartKom, we prefer the latter approach, since for the robust interpretation of possibly incomplete and inconsistent multimodal input, more knowledge sources become available on later processing stages. An early integration on the signal level allows no backtracking and reinterpretation, whereas the multimodal parsing approach has to pre-specify all varieties of crossmodal references, and is thus unable to cope robustly with unusual or novel uses of multimodality. However, some early fusion is also used in SmartKom, since the scored results from a recognizer for emotional prosody (see Batliner et al. 2000) are merged with the results of a recognizer for affective facial expression. The classification results are combined in a synergistic fashion, so that a hypothesis about the affective state of the user can be computed.

In SmartKom, the user state is used for example, in the dialogue-processing backbone to check whether the user is satisfied or not with the information provided by Smartakus. It is interesting to note that SmartKom's architecture supports multiple recognizers for a single modality. In the current system, prosody is evaluated by one recognizer for clause boundaries and another recognizer for emotional speech. This means that the user's speech signal is processed by three unimodal recognizers in parallel (speech recognition, emotional prosody, boundary prosody).

The time stamps for all recognition results are extremely important since the confidence values for the classification results may depend on the temporal relations between input modalities. For example, experiments in SmartKom have shown that the results from recognizing various facial regions (like eye, nose, and mouth area) can be merged to improve recognition results for affective states like anger or joy. However, while the user is speaking, the mouth area does not predict emotions reliably, so that the confidence value of the mouth area recognizer must be decreased. Thus, SmartKom's modality fusion is based on adaptive confidence measures, that can be dynamically updated depending on the synchronization of input modalities.

One of the fundamental mechanisms implemented in SmartKom's modality fusion component is the extended unification of all scored hypothesis graphs and the application of mutual constraints in order to reduce the ambiguity and uncertainty of the combined analysis results. This approach was pioneered in our XTRA system, an early multimodal dialogue system that assisted the user in filling out a tax form with a combination of typed natural language input and pointing gestures (Wahlster 1991). QuickSet uses a similar approach (Cohen et al. 1997).

In SmartKom, the intention recognizer has the task to finally rank the remaining interpretation hypotheses and to select the most likely one, which is then passed on to the action planner. The modality fusion process is augmented by SmartKom's multimodal discourse model, so that the final ranking of the intention recognizer becomes highly context sensitive. The discourse component produces an additional score that states how good an interpretation hypothesis fits to the previous discourse (Pfleger et. al. 2002).

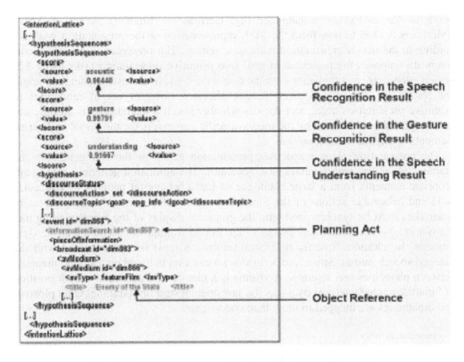

Fig. 6. M3L Representation of an Intention Lattice Fragment

As soon as the modality fusion component finds a referential expression that is not combined with an unambiguous deictic gesture, it sends a request to the discourse component asking for reference resolution. If the resolution succeeds, the discourse component returns a completely instantiated domain object.

Fig. 6 shows an excerpt from the intention lattice for the user's input "I would like to know more about this [deictic pointing gesture]". It shows one hypothesis sequence with high scores from speech and gesture recognition. A potential reference object for the deictic gesture (the movie title "Enemy of the State") has been found in the visual context. SmartKom assumes that the discourse topic relates to an electronic program guide and the intended action of Smartakus refers to the retrieval of information about a particular broadcast.

7   Plan-Based Modality Fission in SmartKom

In SmartKom, modality fission is controlled by a presentation planner. The input to the presentation planner is a presentation goal encoded in M3L as a modality-free representation of the system's intended communicative act. This M3L structure is generated by either an action planner or the dynamic help component, which can initiate clarification subdialogues. The presentation planning process can be adapted to various application scenarios via presentation parameters that encode user preferences (eg. spoken output is preferred by a car driver), output devices (eg. size of the display), or the user's native language (eg. German vs. English). A set of XSLT stylesheets is used to transform the M3L representation of the presentation goal, according to the actual presentation parameter setting. The presentation planner recursively decomposes the presentation goal into primitive presentation tasks using 121 presentation strategies that vary with the discourse context, the user model, and ambient conditions. The presentation planner allocates different output modalities to primitive presentation tasks, and decides whether specific media objects and presentation styles should be used by the media-specific generators for the visual and verbal elements of the multimodal output.

The presentation planner specifies presentation goals for the text generator, the graphics generator, and the animation generator. The animation generator selects appropriate elements from a large catalogue of basic behavioral patterns to synthesize fluid and believable actions of the Smartakus agent. All planned deictic gestures of Smartakus must be synchronized with the graphical display of the corresponding media objects, so that Smartakus points to the intended graphical elements at the right moment. In addition, SmartKom's facial animation must be synchronized with the planned speech output. SmartKom's lip synchronization is based on a simple mapping between phonemes and visemes. A viseme is a picture of a particular mouth position of Smartakus, characterized by a specific jaw opening and lip rounding. Only plosives and diphthongs are mapped to more than one viseme.

```
<presentationTask>
 <presentationGoal>
  <inform> <informFocus> <RealizationType>list </RealizationType> </informFocus> </inform>
  <abstractPresentationContent>
      <discourseTopic> <goal>epg_browse</goal> </discourseTopic>
      <informationSearch id="dim24"><tvProgram id="dim23">
         <broadcast><timeDeictic id="dim16">now</timeDeictic>
              <between>2003-03-20T19:42:32 2003-03-20T22:00:00</between>
            <channel><channel id="dim13"/> </channel>
            </broadcast></tvProgram>
        </informationSearch>
  <result> <event>
      <pieceOfInformation>
       <tvProgram id="ap_3">
         <broadcast> <beginTime>2003-03-20T19:50:00</beginTime>
                  <endTime>2003-03-20T19:55:00</endTime>
                <avMedium> <title>Today's Stock News</title></avMedium>
                <channel>ARD</channel>
         </broadcast>........</event>
  </result>
 </presentationGoal>
</presentationTask>
```

Fig. 7. A Fragment of a Presentation Goal, as specified in M3L

One of the distinguishing features of SmartKom's modality fission is the explicit representation of generated multimodal presentations in M3L. This means that Smart-Kom ensures dialogue coherence in multimodal communication by following the design principle "no presentation without representation". The text generator provides a list of referential items that were mentioned in the last turn of the system. The display component generates an M3L representation of the current screen content, so that the discourse modeler can add the corresponding linguistic and visual objects to the discourse representation. Without such a representation of the generated multimodal presentation, anaphoric, crossmodal, and gestural references of the user could not be resolved. Thus, it is an important insight of the SmartKom project that a multimodal dialogue system must not only understand and represent the user's multimodal input, but also its own multimodal output.

Fig. 7 shows the modality-free presentation goal that is transformed into the multimodal presentation shown in Fig. 8, by SmartKom's media fission component and unimodal generators and renderers. Please note that all the graphics and layout shown in Fig. 8 are generated on the fly and uniquely tailored to the dialogue situation, ie. nothing is canned or pre-programmed. The presentation goal shown in Fig. 7 is coded in M3L and indicates that a list of broadcasts should be presented to the user. Since there is enough screen space available and there are no active constraints on using graphical output, the strategy operators applied by the presentation planner lead to a graphical layout of the list of broadcasts. In an eyes-busy situation (eg. when the user is driving a car), SmartKom would decide that Smartakus should read the list of retrieved broadcasts to the user. This shows that SmartKom's modality fission process is highly context-aware and produces tailored multimodal presentations.

The presentation planner decides that the channel should be rendered as an icon, and that only the starting time and the title of the individual TV item should be mentioned in the final presentation.

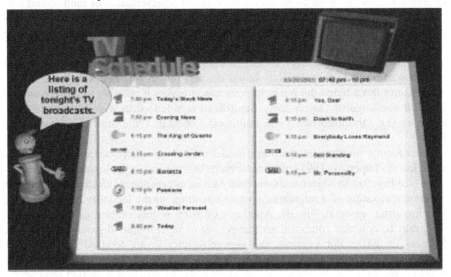

Fig. 8. A Dynamically Generated Multimodal Presentation based on a Presentation Goal

In the next section, we show how the visual, gestural and linguistic context stored in a multimodal discourse model can be used to resolve crossmodal anaphora. We will use the following dialogue excerpt as an example:

(1)   User: I would like to go to the movies tonight.
(2)   Smartakus: [displays a list of movie titles] This is a list of films showing in Heidelberg.
(3)   User: Hmm, none of these films seem to be interesting... Please show me the TV program.
(4)   Smartakus: [displays a TV listing] Here [points to the listing] is a listing of tonight's TV broadcasts. (see Fig. 7)
(5)   User: Please tape the third one!

8   A Three-Tiered Multimodal Discourse Model

Discourse models for spoken dialogue systems store information about previously mentioned discourse referents for reference resolution. However, in a multimodal dialogue system like SmartKom, reference resolution relies not only on verbalized, but also on visualized information. A multimodal discourse model must account for entities not explicitly mentioned (but understood) in a discourse, by exploiting the verbal, the visual and the conceptual context. Thus, SmartKom's multimodal discourse representation keeps a record of all objects visible on the screen and the spatial relationships between them.

An important task for a multimodal discourse model is the support of crossmodal reference resolution. SmartKom uses a three-tiered representation of multimodal discourse, consisting of a domain layer, a discourse layer, and a modality layer. The modality layer consists of linguistic, visual, and gestural objects, that are linked to the corresponding discourse objects. Each discourse object can have various surface realizations on the modality layer. Finally, the domain layer links discourse objects with instances of SmartKom's ontology-based domain model (cf. Loeckelt et al. 2002). SmartKom's three-tiered discourse representation makes it possible to resolve anaphora with non-linguistic antecedents. SmartKom is able to deal with multimodal one-anaphora (eg. "the third one") and multimodal ordinals ("the third broadcast in the list").

SmartKom's multimodal discourse model extends the three-tiered context representation of (Luperfoy, 1991) by generalizing the linguistic layer to that of a modality layer (see Fig. 9). An object at the modality layer, encapsulates information about the concrete realization of a referential object depending on the modality of presentation (eg. linguistic, gestural, visual). Another extension is that objects at the discourse layer may be complex compositions that consist of several other discourse objects (cf. Salmon-Alt 2001). For example, the user may refer to an itemized list shown on SmartKom's screen as a whole, or they may refer to specific items displayed in the list. In sum, Smartkom's multimodal discourse model provides a unified representation of discourse objects introduced by different modalities, as a sound basis for crossmodal reference resolution.

The modality layer of SmartKom's multimodal discourse model contains three types of modality objects:

- Linguistic Objects (LOs): For each occurrence of a referring expression in SmartKom's input or output, one LO is added .
- Visual Objects (VOs): For each visual presentation of a referrable entity, one VO is added.
- Gesture Objects (GOs) For each gesture performed either by the user or the system, a GO is added.

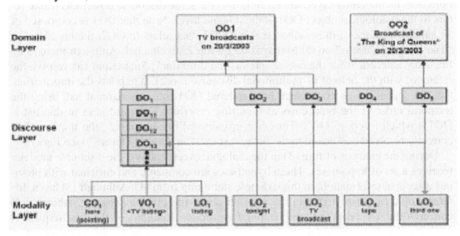

Fig. 9. An Excerpt from SmartKom's Multimodal Discourse Model

Each modality object is linked to a corresponding discourse object. The central layer of the discourse model is the discourse object layer. A Discourse Object (DO) represents a concept that can serve as a candidate for referring expressions, including objects, events, states and collections of objects. When a concept is newly introduced by a multimodal communicative act of the user or the system, a DO is created. For each concept introduced during a dialogue, there exists only one DO, regardless of how many modality objects mention this concept.

The compositional information for the particular DOs that represent collections of objects, is provided by partitions (Salmon-Alt, 2001). A partition provides information about possible decompositions of a domain object. Such partitions are based either on perceptual information (eg. a set of movie titles visible on the screen) or discourse information (eg. "Do you have more information about the first and the second movie" in the context of a list of movie titles presented on the screen). Each element of a partition is a pointer to another DO, representing a member of the collection. The elements of a partition are distinguishable from one another by at least one differentiation criterion like their relative position on the screen, their size, or color. For instance, the TV listing shown in Fig. 8 is one DO that introduces 13 new DOs corresponding to particular broadcasts.

The domain object layer provides a mapping between a DO and instances of the domain model. The instances in the domain model are Ontological Objects (OO) that provide a semantic representation of actions, processes, and objects. SmartKom's domain model is described in the ontology language OIL (Fensel et al. 2001).

Let us discuss an example of SmartKom's methodology for multimodal discourse modeling. The combination of a gesture, an utterance, and a graphical display that is generated by SmartKom's presentation planner (see Fig. 8) creates the gestural object GO1, the visual object VO1 and the linguistic object LO1 (see Fig. 9). These three objects at the modality layer, are all linked to the same discourse object DO1, that refers to the ontological object OO1 at the domain layer. Note that DO1 is composed of 13 subobjects. One of these subobjects is DO13, that refers to OO2, the broadcast of "The King of Queens" on 20 March 2003 on the ZDF channel. Although there is no linguistic antecedent for the one-anaphora "the third one", SmartKom can resolve the reference with the help of its multimodal discourse model. It exploits the information, that the spatial layout component has rendered OO1 into a horizontal list, using the temporal order of the broadcasts as a sorting criterion. The third item in this list is DO13, which refers to OO2. Thus, the crossmodal one-anaphora "the third one" is correctly resolved and linked to the broadcast of "The King of Queens" (see Fig. 9).

During the analysis of turn (3) in the dialogue excerpt above, the discourse modeler receives a set of hypotheses. These hypotheses are compared and enriched with previous discourse information, in this example stemming from (1). Although (3) has a different topic to (1) (it requests information about the cinema program, whereas (3) concerns the TV program), the temporal restriction (tonight) of the first request is propagated to the interpretation of the second request. In general, this propagation of information from one discourse state to another is obtained by comparing a current intention hypothesis with previous discourse states, and by enriching it (if possible) with consistent information. For each comparison, a score has to be computed reflecting how well this hypothesis fits in the current discourse state. For this purpose, the non-monotonic overlay operation (an extended probabilistic unification-like scheme, see Alexandersson and Becker 2003) has been integrated into SmartKom as a central computational method for multimodal discourse processing.

9   Conclusion

We have introduced the notion of symmetric multimodality for dialogue systems in which all input modes (eg. speech, gesture, facial expression) are also available for output, and vice versa. We have shown that a dialogue system with symmetric multimodality must not only understand and represent the user's multimodal input, but also its own multimodal output. We presented the SmartKom system, that provides full symmetric multimodality in a mixed-initiative dialogue system with an embodied conversational agent.

The industrial and economic impact of the SmartKom project is remarkable. Up to now, 51 patents concerning SmartKom technologies have been filed by members of the SmartKom consortium, in areas such as speech recognition (13), dialogue management (10), biometrics (6), video-based interaction (3), multimodal analysis (2), and emotion recognition (2).

In the context of SmartKom, 59 new product releases and prototypes have been surfacing during the project's life span. 29 spin-off products have been developed by the industrial partners of the SmartKom consortium at their own expense.

SmartKom's MULTIPLATFORM software framework (see section 5) is being used at more than 15 industrial and academic sites all over Europe and has been selected as the integration framework for the COMIC (COnversational Multimodal Interaction with Computers) project funded by the EU (Catizone et al. 2003).

The sharable multimodal resources collected and distributed during the SmartKom project will be useful beyond the project's life span, since these richly annotated corpora will be used for training, building, and evaluating components of multimodal dialogue systems in coming years. 448 multimodal Wizard-of-OZ sessions resulting in 1.6 terabytes of data have been processed and annotated (Schiel et al. 2002). The annotations contain audio transcriptions combined with gesture and emotion labeling.

Acknowledgements. The SmartKom project has been made possible by funding from the German Federal Ministry of Education and Research (BMBF) under grant 01 IL 905. I would like to thank my SmartKom team at DFKI: Jan Alexandersson, Tilman Becker, Anselm Blocher (project management), Ralf Engel, Gerd Herzog (system integration), Heinz Kirchmann, Markus Löckelt, Stefan Merten, Jochen Müller, Alassane Ndiaye, Rainer Peukert, Norbert Pfleger, Peter Poller, Norbert Reithinger (module coordination), Michael Streit, Valentin Tschernomas, and our academic and industrial partners in the SmartKom project consortium: DaimlerChrysler AG, European Media Laboratory GmbH, Friedrich-Alexander University Erlangen-Nuremberg, International Computer Science Institute, Ludwig-Maximilians University Munich, MediaInterface GmbH, Philips GmbH, Siemens AG, Sony International (Europe) GmbH, Stuttgart University for the excellent and very successful cooperation.

References

Alexandersson, A., Becker, T. (2003): The Formal Foundations Underlying Overlay. In: Proc. of the Fifth International Workshop on Computational Semantics (IWCS-5), Tilburg, The Netherlands, 2003, p. 22–36.

Batliner, A., Huber, R., Niemann, H., Nöth, E., Spilker, J., Fischer, K. (2000): The Recognition of Emotion. In: W. Wahlster (ed.): Verbmobil: Foundations of Speech-to-Speech Translations, Berlin, New York: Springer, p. 122–130.

Catizone, R., Setzer, A., Wilks, Y. (2003): Multimodal Dialogue Management in the COMIC Project, In: Workshop on 'Dialogue Systems: interaction, adaptation and styles of management', European Chapter of the Association for Computational Linguistics (EACL), Budapest, Hungary, April 2003.

Cohen, P. R., Johnston, M., McGee, D., Oviatt, S., Pittman, J., Smith, I., Chen, L., Clow, J. (1997): QuickSet: Multimodal interaction for distributed applications, In: Proc. of the Fifth International Multimedia Conference (Multimedia '97), ACM Press, p. 31–40.

Fensel, D., van Harmelen, F., Horrocks, I. McGuinness, D., Patel-Schneider, P. (2001): OIL: An Ontology Infrastructure for the Semantic Web. In: IEEE Intelligent Systems, 16(2), 2001. p. 38–45.

Gurevych, I., Merten, S., Porzel, R. (2003): Automatic Creation of Interface Specifications from Ontologies. In: Proc. of the HLT-NAACL'03 Workshop on the Software Engineering and Architecture of Language Technology Systems (SEALTS), Edmonton, Canada.

Herzog, G., Kirchmann, H., Merten S., Ndiaye, A. Poller, P. (2003): MULTIPLATFORM Testbed: An Integration Platform for Multimodal Dialog Systems. In: Proc. of the HLT-NAACL'03 Workshop on the Software Engineering and Architecture of Language Technology Systems (SEALTS), Edmonton, Canada.

Johnston, M., Bangalore, S., Vasireddy, G., Stent, A., Ehlen, P., Walker, M., Whittaker, S, Maloor, P. (2002): MATCH: An Architecture for Multimodal Dialogue Systems. In: Proc. of the 40th Annual Meeting of the Association for Computational Linguistics., Philadelphia, p. 376–383.

Löckelt, M., Becker, T., Pfleger, N., Alexandersson, J.: Making Sense of Partial. In: Bos, J., Foster, M., Matheson, C. (eds.): Proc. of the Sixth Workshop on the Semantics and Pragmatics of Dialogue (EDILOG 2002), Edinburgh, p. 101–107.

Luperfoy, S. (1991): Discourse Pegs: A Computational Analysis of Context-Dependent Referring Expressions. Ph.D. thesis, University of Texas at Austin.

Martin, D. L. , Cheyer, A. J., Moran, D.B. (1999): The Open Agent Architecture: A Framework for Building Distributed Software Systems. Applied Artificial Intelligence, 13(1–2), p. 91–128.

Pfleger, N., Alexandersson,J., Becker, T. (2002): Scoring Functions for Overlay and their Application in Discourse Processing. In: Proc. of KONVENS 2002, Saarbrücken, Germany, 2002, p. 139–146.

Salmon-Alt S. (2001): Reference Resolution within the Framework of Cognitive Grammar. In: Proc. of International Colloquium on Cognitive Science, San Sebastian, Spain, May 2001, p. 1–15.

Schiel, F., Steininger, S., Türk. U. (2002): The SmartKom Multimodal Corpus at BAS. In: Proc. of the 3rd Language Resources & Evaluation Conference (LREC) 2002, Las Palmas, Gran Canaria, Spain, p. 35–41.

Seneff, S., Lau, R., Polifroni, J. (1999): Organization, Communication, and Control in the Galaxy-II Conversational System. In: Proc. of Eurospeech' 99, Budapest, Hungary, p. 1271–1274.

Wahlster, W. (1991): User and Discourse Models for Multimodal Communication. In: Sullivan, J., Tyler, S. (eds.): Intelligent User Interfaces, New York: ACM Press, 1991, p. 45–67.

Wahlster, W., André, E., Finkler, W., Profitlich, H.-J., Rist, T. (1993).: Plan-Based Integration of Natural Language and Graphics Generation. In: Artificial Intelligence, 63, 1993, p. 387–427.

Wahlster, W., Reithinger N., Blocher, A. (2001): SmartKom: Multimodal Communication with a Life-Like Character. In: Proc. of Eurospeech 2001, 7th European Conference on Speech Communication and Technology, Aalborg, Denmark, September 2001, Vol. 3, p. 1547–1550.

Wahlster, W. (2002): SmartKom: Fusion and Fission of Speech, Gestures, and Facial Expressions. In: Proc. of the 1st International Workshop on Man-Machine Symbiotic Systems, Kyoto, Japan, 2002. p. 213–225.

Leveraging Metadata Creation for the Semantic Web with CREAM

Siegfried Handschuh[1], Steffen Staab[1,2], and Rudi Studer[1,2,3]

[1] Institute AIFB, University of Karlsruhe, 76128 Karlsruhe, Germany
{sha,sst,rst}@aifb.uni-karlsruhe.de,
http://www.aifb.uni-karlsruhe.de/WBS

[2] Ontoprise GmbH, 76131 Karlsruhe, Germany,
http://www.ontoprise.com/

[3] Forschungszentrum Informatik,
http://www.fzi.de/wim/

Abstract. The success of the Semantic Web crucially depends on the easy creation of ontology-based metadata by semantic annotation. We provide a framework, CREAM, that allows for the creation of semantic metadata about static and dynamic Web pages, i.e. for semantic annotation of the Shallow and the Deep Web. CREAM supports the manual and the semi-automatic annotation of static Web pages, the authoring of new web pages with the simultaneous creation of metadata, and the deep annotation of Web pages defined dynamically by database queries.

1 Introduction

The Semantic Web supports its users to find accurate information, to combine related pieces of information into an overarching picture and to compose new applications without programming knowledge. To achieve these objectives not only human readers have to understand the content of on a web page, software agents also must be able to interpret existing information. This is only possible when the relevant information is represented in a declarative and semantically precise way and when it is thus understandable for the computer. This need creates the necessity to provide semantically accurate, ontology-based metadata. We describe how the problem is tackled by means of our annotation framework, CREAM — CREAting Metadata for the Semantic Web. CREAM comprises methods for:

- Manual annotation: The transformation of existing syntactic resources (*viz.* textual documents) into interlinked knowledge structures that represent relevant underlying information.
- Authoring of documents: In addition to the annotation of existing documents the authoring mode lets authors create metadata — almost for free — while putting together the content of a document [11].
- Semi-automatic annotation: Efficient semi-automatic annotation based on information extraction that is trained to handle structurally and/or linguistically similar documents [13].

A. Günter et al. (Eds.): KI 2003, LNAI 2821, pp. 19–33, 2003.

– Deep annotation: Dynamic Web documents results in a semantic mapping to the underlying database if the database owner cooperates in the Semantic Web and allows for direct access to the database [14].

In the following we wrap up several previous contributions ([11,13,14]). We start to describe core requirements for semantic annotation. For a more concise description, we first define our terminology and give an example of the kind of metadata the generation of which we support by CREAM (Section 2). In Section 3 we derive the design of CREAM from the requirements elaborated before. In Section 4, we explain the major modes of interaction supported by CREAM. We briefly sketch the integration of CREAM with a learnable information extraction component in Section 5, before we outline the basic building blocks for deep annotation in Section 6.

2   Creating Metadata for the Semantic Web

CREAM is an annotation and authoring framework suited for the easy and comfortable creation of relational metadata. OntoMat-Annotizer (OntoMat for short) is its concrete implementation.

2.1   Requirements for CREAM

Given the problems with syntax, semantics and pragmatics in earlier experiences (e.g. KA2 [1]), we list here a set of requirements. Thereby, the principal requirements apply for *a-posteriori annotation* as well as for the *integration of web page authoring with metadata creation* as follows:

– **Consistency**: Semantic structures should adhere to a given ontology in order to allow for better sharing of knowledge. For example, it should be avoided that annotators use an attribute instance, whereas the ontology requires a concept instance.
– **Proper Reference**: Identifiers of instances, *e.g.* of persons, institutes or companies, should be unique. For instance, the metadata generated in the KA2 case study contained three different identifiers for our colleague Dieter Fensel. Thus, knowledge about him could not be grasped with a straightforward query.
– **Avoid Redundancy**: Decentralized knowledge provisioning should be possible. However, when annotators collaborate, it should be possible for them to identify (parts of) sources that have already been annotated and to reuse previously captured knowledge in order to avoid laborious redundant annotations.
– **Relational Metadata**: Like HTML information, which is spread on the Web, but related by HTML links, knowledge markup may be distributed, but it should be semantically related. Current annotation tools tend to generate template-like metadata, which is hardly connected, if at all. For example, annotation environments often support Dublin Core [5,6], providing means to state, e.g., the name of authors of a document, but not their IDs[1]. Thus,

---

[1] In the web context one typically uses the term 'URI' (uniform resource identifier) to speak of 'unique identifier'.

the only possibility to query for all publications of a certain person requires the querying for some attribute like fullname — which is very unsatisfying for frequent names like "John Smith".

- **Dynamic Documents**: A large percentage of the Web pages are not static documents. For dynamic web pages (e.g. ones that are generated from a database) it does not seem to be usefull to annotate every single page. Rather one wants to "annotate the database" in order to reuse it for its own Semantic Web purpose.
- **Maintenance**: Knowledge markup needs to be maintained. An annotation tool should support the maintenance task.
- **Ease of Use**: It is obvious that an annotation environment should be easy to use in order to be really useful. However, this objective is not easily achieved, because metadata creation involves intricate navigation of semantic structures, e.g. taxonomies, properties and concepts.
- **Efficiency**: The effort for the production of metadata is an important restraining threshold. The more efficiently a tool supports metadata creation, the more metadata users tend to produce. This requirement is related to the ease of use. It also depends on the automation of the metadata creation process, e.g. on the preprocessing of the document.
- **Multiple Ontologies**: HTML documents in the semantic web may contain information that is related to different ontologies. Therefore the annotation framework should cater for concurrent annotations with multiple ontologies.

Our framework CREAM that is presented here, targets a comprehensive solution for metadata creation during web page authoring and a-posteriori annotation. The objective is pursued by combining advanced mechanisms for inferencing, fact crawling, document management, meta ontology definitions, metadata re-recognition, content generation, and information extraction. These components are explained in the subsequent sections.

2.2   Relational Metadata

We elaborate the terminology here because many of the terms that are used with regard to metadata creation tools carry several, ambiguous connotations that imply conceptually important differences:

- **Ontology**: An ontology is a formal, explicit specification of a shared conceptualization of a domain of interest [10]. In our case it is constituted by statements expressing definitions of DAML+OIL classes and properties [8].
- **Annotations**: In our context an annotation is a set of instantiations attached to an HTML document. We distinguish *(i)* instantiations of DAML+OIL classes, *(ii)* instantiated properties from one class instance to a datatype instance — henceforth called attribute instance (of the class instance), and *(iii)* instantiated properties from one class instance to another class instance — henceforth called relationship instance.
  Class instances have unique URIs, e.g. like 'http://www.aifb.uni-karlsruhe.de/WBS/sst/#Steffen'. They frequently come with attribute instances, such as a human-readable label like 'Steffen'.

- **Metadata**: Metadata are data about data. In our context the annotations are metadata about the HTML documents.
- **Relational Metadata**: We use the term relational metadata to denote the annotations that contain relationship instances. Often, the term "annotation" is used to mean something like "private or shared note", "comment" or "Dublin Core metadata". This alternative meaning of annotation may be emulated in our approach by modelling these notes with attribute instances. For instance, a comment note "I like this paper" would be related to the URL of the paper via an attribute instance 'hasComment'.

  In contrast, relational metadata also contain statements like 'Siegfried cooperates with Steffen', *i.e.* relational metadata contain relationships between class instances rather than only textual notes.
- **Generic Annotations**: In a *generic annotation*, a piece of text that corresponds to a database field and that is annotated, is only considered to be a place holder. I.e. a variable must be generated for such an annotation. For example, a concept Institute in the client ontology may correspond to one generic annotation for the Organization identifier in the database. As a consequence, we will refer to detailed generic annotations as *generic class instances*, *generic attribute instances*, and *generic relationship instances*.

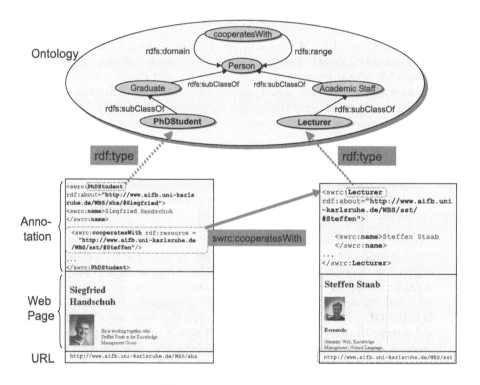

Fig. 1. Annotation example.

Figure 1 illustrates our use of the terms "ontology", "annotation" and "relational metadata". It depicts some part of the SWRC[2] (semantic web research community) ontology. Furthermore it shows two homepages, viz. pages about Siegfried and Steffen (`http://www.aif b.uni-karlsruhe.de/WBS/sha` and `http://www.aifb.uni-karlsruhe.de/WBS/sst`, respectively) with annotations given in an XML serialization of RDF facts. For the two persons there are instances denoted by corresponding URIs (`http://www.aifb.uni-karlsruhe.de/WBS/sst/#Steffen` and `http://www.aifb.uni-karlsruhe.de/WBS /sha/#Siegfried`). The swrc:name of `http: //www.aifb.uni-karlsruhe.de/WBS/sha/#Siegfried` is "Siegfried Handschuh".

In addition, there is a relationship instance between the two persons, *viz.* they cooperate. This cooperation information 'spans' the two pages.

The objective of CREAM is to allow for the easy generation of such a target representation irrespective of whether the major mode of interaction is a-posteriori annotation or web page authoring.

3   Design of CREAM

3.1   CREAM Modules

The difficulties sketched before directly feed into the design rationale of CREAM. The design rationale links the requirements with the CREAM modules. This results in a N:M mapping (neither functional nor injective). A tabular overview of the matrix can be found in [11].

– **Document Editor**: The document editor may be conceptually — though not practically — distinguished into a viewing component and the component for generating content:
  • **Document Viewer**: The document viewer visualizes the document contents. The annotator may easily provide new metadata by selecting pieces of text and aligning it with parts of the ontology. The document viewer should support various formats (HTML, PDF, XML, etc.). For some formats the following component for content generation may not be available.
  The document viewer highlights the existing semantic annotation and server-side markup the of web page. It distinguishes visually between semantic annotation and markup that describes the information structure of a underlaying database.
  • **Content Generation**: The editor also allows the conventional authoring of documents. In addition, instances already available may be dragged from a visualization of the content of the annotation inference server and dropped into the document. Thereby, some piece of text and/or a link is produced taking into account the information from the meta ontology (cf. module meta ontology).
  The newly generated content is already annotated and the meta ontology guides the construction of further information, e.g. further XPointers (cf. [3], [9]) are attached to instances.

---

[2] `http://ontobroker.semanticweb.org/ontos/swrc.html`

- **Ontology Guidance and Fact Browser**: The framework needs guidance from the ontology. In order to allow for sharing of knowledge, newly created annotations must be consistent with a community's ontology. If metadata creators instantiate arbitrary classes and properties the semantics of these properties remains void. Of course the framework must be able to adapt to multiple ontologies in order to reflect different foci of the metadata creators. In the case of concurrent annotation with multiple ontologies there is an ontology guidance/fact browser for each ontology.
- **Crawler:** The creation of relational metadata must take place *within* the Semantic Web. During metadata creation, subjects must be aware of which entities exist already in their part of the Semantic Web. This is only possible if a crawler makes relevant entities immediately available.
- **Annotation Inference Server**: Relational metadata, proper reference and avoidance of redundant annotation require querying for instances, i.e. querying whether and which instances exist. For this purpose as well as for checking of consistency, we provide an annotation inference server. The annotation inference server reasons on crawled and newly created instances and on the ontology. It also serves the ontological guidance and fact browser, because it allows to query for existing classes, instances and properties.
- **Meta Ontology**: The purpose of the meta ontology is the separation of ontology design and use. It is needed to describe how classes, attributes and relationships from the domain ontology should be used by the CREAM environment. Thus, the ontology describes how the semantic data should look like and the meta ontology connected to the ontology describes how the ontology is used by the annotation environment to actually create semantic data. It is specifically explained in [11].
- **Deep Annotation Module**: This module enables the deep annotation scenario. It manages the generation of mapping rules between the database and the client ontology. For this purpose, it combines the generic annotation stored in the annotation inference server and the server-side markup provided with the content (cf. Section 6). On demand it publishes the mapping rules derived from the generic annotations.
- **Document Management**: Considering the dynamics of HTML pages on the web, it is desirable to store foreign web pages one has annotated together with their annotations. Foreign documents for which modification is not possible may be remotely annotated by using XPointer (cf. [3], [9]) as a addressing meachanism.
- **Metadata Re-recognition & Information Extraction**: Even with sophisticated tools it is laborious to provide semantic annotations. A major goal thus is semi-automatic metadata creation taking advantage of information extraction techniques to propose annotations to metadata creators and, thus, to facilitate the metadata creation task. Concerning our environment we envisage three major techniques:
  1. First, metadata re-recognition compares existing metadata literals with newly typed or existing text. Thus, the mentioning of the name "Siegfried Handschuh" in the document triggers the proposal that URI, http://www.aifb.uni-karlsruhe.de/WBS/sha/#Siegfried is co-referenced at this point.

2. "Wrappers" may be learned from given markup in order to automatically annotate similarly structured pages.
3. Message extraction systems may be used to recognize named entities, propose co-reference, and extract some relationship from texts (cf., e.g., [15,19]).

This component has been realized by using the Amilcare information extraction system (cf. Section 5)[3], but it is not yet available in the download version of OntoMat.

Besides the requirements that constitute single modules, one may identify functions that cross module boundaries:

- **Storage**: CREAM supports two different ways of storage. The annotations will be stored inside the document that is in the document management component. Alternatively or simultaneously it is also possible to store them in the annotation inference server.
- **Replication**: We provide a simple replication mechanism by crawling annotations into our annotation inference server. Then inferencing can be used to rule out formal inconsistencies.

3.2 Architecture of CREAM

The architecture of CREAM is depicted in Figure 2. The Design of the CREAM framework pursues the idea to be flexible and open. Therefore, OntoMat, the implementation of the framework, comprises a plug-in structure, which is flexible with regard to adding or replacing modules.

The core OntoMat, which is downloadable, consists of an Ontology Guidance and Fact browser, a document viewer/editor, and a internal memory datastructure for the ontology and metadata. However, one only gets the full-fledged semantic capabilities (e.g. datalog reasoning or subsumption reasoning) when one uses a plug-in connection to a corresponding annotation inference server.

4   Modes of Interaction

The metadata creation process in OntoMat is actually supported by three types of interaction with the tool (also cf. Figure 2):

1. Annotation by Typing Statements: This involves working almost exclusively within the ontology guidance/fact browser.
2. Annotation by Markup: This mostly involves the reuse of data from the document editor/viewer in the ontology guidance/fact browser.
3. Annotation by Authoring Web Pages: This mostly involves the reuse of data from the fact browser in the document editor.

In order to clarify the different role of the three types of interaction, we here describe how they differ for generating three types of metadata: i) Generating instances of classes, ii) generating attribute instances, and iii) generating relationship instances.

---

[3] http://www.dcs.shef.ac.uk/~fabio/Amilcare.html

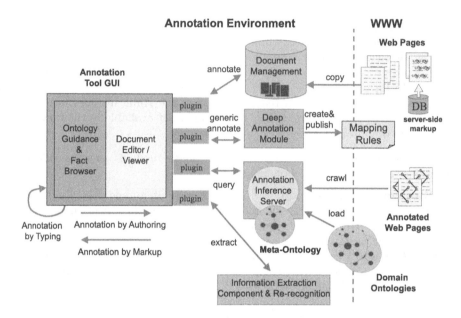

Fig. 2. Architecture of CREAM.

4.1 Annotation by Typing

Annotation by typing is almost purely based on the ontology guidance/fact browser (cf. Section 3). The user generates metadata (class instances, attribute instances, relationship instances) that are completely independent from the Web page currently viewed. In addition, the user may drag-and-drop around instances that are already in the knowledge base in order to create new relationship instances (cf. arrow #0 in Figure 3).

4.2 Annotation by Markup

The basic idea of annotation by markup is the usage of marked-up content in the document editor/viewer for instance generation.

1. Generating class instances: When the user drags a marked up piece of content onto a particular concept from the ontology, a new class instance is generated. A new URI is generated and a corresponding property is assigned the marked up text (cf. arrow #1 in Figure 3). For instance, marking "Siegfried Handschuh" and dropping this piece of text on the concept PhDStudent creates a new URI, instantiates this URI as belonging to PhDStudent and assigns "Siegfried Handschuh" to the swrc:name slot of the new URI.
2. Generating attribute instance: In order to generate an attribute instance the user drops the marked up content into the corresponding table entry (cf. arrow #2 in Figure 3). Depending on the setting the corresponding XPointer or the content itself is filled into the attribute.

3. Generating relationship instance: In order to generate a relationship instance the user simply drops the marked up content onto the relation of a pre-selected instance (cf. arrow #3 in Figure 3). Like in "class instance generation" a new instance is generated and connected with the pre-selected instance.

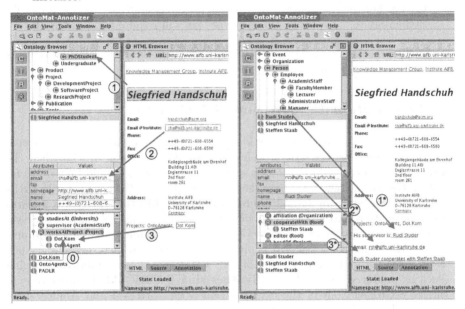

Fig. 3. Screenshot Annotation by Markup (left) and Annotation by Authoring (right).

4.3 Annotation by Authoring

The third major process is authoring Web pages and metadata together. There are two modi for authoring: *(i)*, authoring by using ontology guidance and fact browser for content generation and, *(ii)*, authoring with the help of metadata re-recognition or — more general — information extraction. As far as authoring is concerned, we have only implemented *(i)* so far. However, we want to point out that already very simple information extraction mechanisms, i.e. metadata re-recognition (cf. Section 3) may help the author to produce consistent metadata.
Authoring with Content Generation By inverting the process of markup (cf. Figure 3), we may reuse existing instance description, like labels or other attributes:

1. Class instances: Dropping class instances from the fact browser into the document creates text according to their labels and — if possible — links (cf. arrow #1* in Figure 3).
2. Attribute instances: Dropping attribute instances from the fact browser in the document (cf. arrow #2* in Figure 3) generates the corresponding text or even linked text.

3. Relationship instances: Dropping relationship instances from the fact browser in the document generates simple "sentences". For instance, the dropping of the relationship COOPERATESWITH between the instances corresponding to Rudi and Steffen triggers the creation of a small piece of text (cf. arrow #3* in Figure 3). The text corresponds to the instance labels plus the label of the relationship (if available), e.g. "Rudi Studer cooperates with Steffen Staab". Typically, this piece of text will require further editing.

Further mechanisms, like the creation of lists or tables from selected concepts (e.g. all Persons), still need to be explored.

5   Semi-automatic Creation of Metadata

Providing plenty of relational metadata by manual annotation, i.e. conceptual mark-up of text passages, is a laborious task. In Section 2 we described the idea that wrappers and information extraction components could be used to facilitate the work. Hence, we have developed S-CREAM (Semi-automatic CREAtion of Metadata), an annotation framework (cf. [13]) that integrates a learnable information extraction component (viz. Amilcare [2]). Amilcare is a system that learns information extraction rules from manually marked-up input. S-CREAM aligns conceptual markup, which defines relational metadata, (such as provided through OntoMat-Annotizer) with semantic and indicative tagging (such as produced by Amilcare). **Synthesizing S-CREAM:** In order to synthesize S-CREAM out of the existing frameworks CREAM and Amilcare, we consider their core processes in terms of input and output, as well as the process of S-CREAM. Figure 4 surveys the three processes. The first process is indicated by a circled M. It is manual annotation of metadata, which turns a document into relational metadata that corresponds to the given ontology. The second process is indicated by a circled A1. It is information extraction, e.g. provided by Amilcare. When comparing the desired relational metadata from manual markup and the semantic tagging provided by information extraction systems, one recognizes that the output of this type of systems is underspecified for the purpose of the Semantic Web. In particular, the nesting of relationships between different types of concept instances is undefined and, hence, more comprehensive graph structures may not be produced. In order to overcome this problem, we introduce a new processing component, viz. a lightweight module for discourse representation. This third process is indicated by the composition of A1, A2 and A3. It bridges from the tagged output of the information extraction system to the target graph structures via an explicit discourse representation. Our discourse representation is based on a very lightweight version of Centering.

6   On Deep Annotation

A large percentage of Web pages are not static documents. Rather the majority of Web pages are dynamic. For dynamic web pages (e.g. ones that are generated from the database that contains a catalogue of books) it does not seem

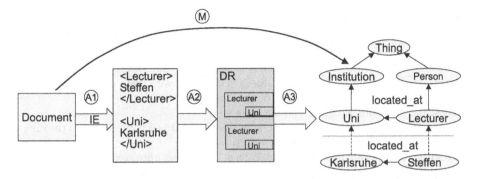

Fig. 4. Manual and Automatic Annotation

to be useful to annotate every single page. Rather one wants to "annotate the database" in order to reuse it for one's own Semantic Web purposes.

For this objective, approaches have been conceived that allow for the construction of wrappers by explicit definition of HTML or XML queries [17] or by learning such definitions from examples [2]. Thus, it has been possible to manually create metadata for a set of structurally alike Web pages. The wrapper approaches come with the advantage that they do not require cooperation by the owner of the database. However, their disadvantage is that the correct scraping of metadata is dependent to a large extent by data layout rather than by the structures underlying the data.

While for many web sites, the assumption of non-cooperativity may remain valid, we assume that many web sites will in fact participate in the Semantic Web and will support the sharing of information. Such web sites may present their information as HTML pages for viewing by the user, but they may also be willing to describe the structure of their information on the very same web pages.

Dynamic web sites with an cooperative owner may present their information as HTML pages for viewing by the user, but they may also be willing to describe the structure of their information on the very same web pages. Thus, they give their users the possibility to utilize: i) information proper, ii) information structures, and ii) information context.

A user may then exploit these three types of information in order to create mappings into his own information structures (e.g., his ontology) — which may be a lot easier than if the information a user gets is restricted to information structures [16] and/or information proper only [4].

We define "deep annotation" as an annotation process that utilizes information proper, information structures and information context in order to derive mappings between information structures. The mappings may then be exploited by the same or another user in order to query the database underlying a web site in order to retrieve semantic data — combining the capabilities of conventional annotation and databases.

6.1   Deep Annotation Process

The process of deep annotation consists of the following four steps:

Input: A Web site[4] driven by an underlying relational database.
Step 1: The database owner produces server-side web page markup according to the information structures of the database.
Result: Web site with server-side markup.
Step 2: The annotator produces client-side annotations conforming to the client ontology and the server-side markup.
Result: Mapping rules between database and client ontology
Step 3: The annotator publishes the client ontology (if not already done before) and the mapping rules derived from annotations.
Result: The annotator's ontology and mapping rules are available on the Web
Step 4: The querying party loads second party's ontology and mapping rules and uses them to query the database via the web service API.
Result: Results retrieved from database by querying party.

Obviously, in this process one single person may be the database owner and/or the annotator and/or the querying party. For example, the annotator might annotate an organization entry from ontoweb.org according to his own ontology. Then, he may use the ontology and corresponding mapping to instantiate his own syndication services by regularly querying for all recent entries the titles of which match to his list of topics.

6.2   Configuration and Roles

Our scenario for deep annotation consists of three major pillars corresponding to the three different roles (database owner, annotator, querying party) as described in the process.
Database and Web Site Provider. At the web site, we assume that there is an underlying database (cf. Figure 5) and a server-side scripting environment, like Zope, JSP or ASP, used to create dynamic Web pages. Furthermore, the web site may also provide a Web service API to third parties who want to query the database directly.
Annotator. The annotator uses an extended version of the OntoMat in order to manually create relational metadata, which correspond to a given client ontology, for some Web pages. The extended OntoMat takes into account problems that may arise from generic annotations required by deep annotation (see Section 6.3). With the help of OntoMat, we create mapping rules from such annotations that are later exploited by an inference engine.
Querying Party. The querying party uses a corresponding tool to visualize the client ontology, to compile a query from the client ontology and to investigate the mapping. In our case, we use OntoEdit [18] for those three purposes. In particular, OntoEdit also allows for the investigation, debugging and change of given mapping rules. For this purpose, OntoEdit integrates and exploits the Ontobroker [7] inference engine (see Figure 5).

---

[4] Cf. Section 7 on other information sources.

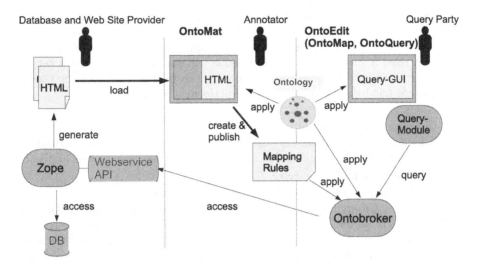

Fig. 5. Configuration for Deep Annotation

6.3 Annotation

To enable deep annotation one must consider an additional kind of annotation, viz. *generic annotation.* In a *generic annotation,* a piece of text that corresponds to a database field and that is annotated is only considered to be a place holder. I.e. a variable must be generated for such an annotation and the variable may have multiple relationships allowing for the description of general mapping rules.

Annotation Process: An annotation process of server-side markup (generic annotation) is supported by the user interface as follows:

1. The user opens in the browser a server-side marked up web page.
2. The server-side markup is handled individually by the browser, e.g. it provides graphical icons on the page wherever a markup is present, so that the user can easily identify values which come from a database.
3. The user can select one of the server-side markups to either create a new *generic instance* and map its database field to a generic attribute, or map a database field to a *generic attribute* of an existing *generic instance.*
4. The database information necessary to query the database in a later step is stored alongwith the *generic instance.*

The reader may note that *literal annotation* is still performed when the user drags a marked up piece of content, that is not a server-side markup.

Create Generic Instances of Classes: When the user drags a server-side markup onto a particular concept of the ontology, a new generic class instance is generated. The application displays a dialog for the selection of the instance name and the attributes to map the database value to. Attributes which resemble the column name are preselected. If the user clicks OK, database concept and instance checks are performed and the new generic instance is created. Generic instances will appear with a database symbol in their icon.

Create Generic Attribute Instances: In order to create a generic attribute instance the user simply drops the server-side markup into the corresponding table entry. Generic attributes which are mapped to database table columns will also show a special icon and their value will appear in italics. Such generic attributes cannot be modified, but their value can be deleted. When the generic attribute is filled the following steps are performed by the system:

1. Checking database definition integrity.
2. All attributes of the selected generic instance (except the generic attribute to be pasted to) are examined. The following conditions apply to each attribute:
   - The attribute is empty or
   - The attribute does not hold server-side markup or
   - The attribute holds markup, the database name and the query ID of the content on the current selection must be the same. This must be checked to ensure that result fields come from the same database and the same query. If this is not checked, unmatching information (e.g. publication titles and countries) could be queried for.
3. The generic attribute contains the information given by the markup, i.e. which column of the result tuple delivered by a query represents the value.

Create Generic Relationship Instances: To create a generic relationship instance the user drops the selected server-side markup onto the relation of a pre-selected instance. As in Section 6.3 a new generic instance is generated. The new generic instance is connected with the preselected generic instance.

6.4 Mapping and Querying

The results of the annotation are mapping rules between the database and the client ontology. The annotator publishes the client ontology and the mapping rules derived from annotations. This enables third parties (querying party) to access and query the database on the basis of the semantics that is defined in the ontology. The user of this mapping description might be a software agent or a human user.

7 Conclusion

CREAM is a comprehensive framework for creating semantic metadata, relational metadata in particular — the foundation of the Semantic Web. CREAM supports the annotation on the Shallow and the Deep Web. In order to avoid problems with syntax, semantics and pragmatics, CREAM employs a rich set of modules including inference services, crawler, document management system, ontology guidance/fact browser, and document editors/viewers. For a more elaborate comparison of related work the interested reader may turn to [11,14] as well as to the corresponding contributions in [12].

References

1. R. Benjamins, D. Fensel, and S. Decker. KA2: Building Ontologies for the Internet: A Midterm Report. *International Journal of Human Computer Studies*, 51(3):687–713, 1999.
2. F. Ciravegna. Adaptive information extraction from text by rule induction and generalisation. In *Proc. of the 17th IJCAI*, Seattle, Usa, August 2001.
3. S. DeRose, E. Maler, and R. Daniel. XML Pointer Language (XPointer). Technical report, W3C, 2001. Working Draft 16 August 2002.
4. A. Doan, J. Madhavan, P. Domingos, and A. Halevy. Learning to map between ontologies on the semantic web. In *Proc. of the WWW 2002*, pages 662–673. ACM Press, 2002.
5. Dublin core metadata initiative, April 2001. http://purl.oclc.org/dc/.
6. Dublin Core Metadata Template, 2001. http://www.ub2.lu.se/metadata/DC_creator.html.
7. D. Fensel, J. Angele, S. Decker, M. Erdmann, H.-P. Schnurr, S. Staab, R. Studer, and Andreas Witt. On2broker: Semantic-based access to information sources at the WWW. In *Proc. of WebNet 99, Honolulu, Hawaii, USA*, pages 366–371, 1999.
8. Reference description of the DAML+OIL (March 2001) ontology markup language, March 2001. http://www.daml.org/2001/03/reference.html.
9. C. Goble, S. Bechhofer, L. Carr, D. De Roure, and W. Hall. Conceptual Open Hypermedia = The Semantic Web? In S. Staab, S. Decker, D. Fensel, and A. Sheth, editors, *The Second International Workshop on the Semantic Web*, CEUR Proceedings, Volume 40, http://www.ceur-ws.org, pages 44–50, Hong Kong, May 2001.
10. T. R. Gruber. A Translation Approach to Portable Ontology Specifications. *Knowledge Acquisition*, 6(2):199–221, 1993.
11. S. Handschuh and S. Staab. Authoring and annotation of web pages in cream. In *Proc. of the 11th WWW 2002, Honolulu, Hawaii, May 7-11, 2002*, pages 462–473. ACM Press, 2002.
12. S. Handschuh and S. Staab, editors. *Annotation in the Semantic Web*. IOS Press, 2003.
13. S. Handschuh, S. Staab, and F. Ciravegna. S-CREAM — Semi-automatic CREAtion of Metadata. In *Proc. of EKAW02*, LNCS/LNAI 2473, pages 358–372, Sigüenza, Spain, October 2002. Springer.
14. S. Handschuh, S. Staab, and R. Volz. On deep annotation. In *Proc. of the WWW2003*, Budapest, HUNGARY, May 2003.
15. *MUC-7 — Proc. of the 7th Message Understanding Conference*, 1998. http://www.muc.saic.com/.
16. N. F. Noy and M. A. Musen. PROMPT: Algorithm and Tool for Automated Ontology Merging and Alignment. In *Proc. of AAAI-2000*, pages 450–455, 2000.
17. A. Sahuguet and F. Azavant. Building intelligent Web applications using lightweight wrappers. *Data and Knowledge Engineering*, 3(36):283–316, 2001.
18. Y. Sure, J. Angele, and S. Staab. Guiding Ontology Developement by Methodology and Inferencing. In K. Aberer and L. Liu, editors, *Proc. of ODBASE-2002. Irvine, CA, USA, Oct. 29-31, 2002*, LNCS, pages 1025–1222. Springer, 2002.
19. M. Vargas-Vera, E. Motta, J. Domingue, S. Buckingham Shum, and M. Lanzoni. Knowledge Extraction by using an Ontology-based Annotation Tool. In *Proc. of the Knowledge Markup and Semantic Annotation Workshop 2001 (at K-CAP 2001)*, pages 5–12, Victoria, BC, Canada, October 2001.

Negotiation Technologies

Nicholas R. Jennings

Dept. of Electronics and Computer Science
University of Southampton
Southampton SO17 1BJ, UK.
nrj@ecs.soton.ac.uk

Negotiation is a process by which a group of entities try and come to a mutually acceptable agreement on some matter. Because of its ubiquity in everyday encounters, it is a subject that has been extensively discussed in the game-theoretic, economic, and management science literatures. Recently, however, there has been a surge of interest in automated negotiation systems that are populated with artificial agents (see [1] for more details). This is due to both a technology push and an application pull. The technology push is mainly from a growing standardised communication infrastructure (*e.g.*, the Semantic Web, the Grid and Peer-to-Peer systems) which allows distributed and heterogeneous entities to interact flexibly. The application pull is from domains (*e.g.*, supply chain management, telecommunication network management, virtual organisations and electronic trading systems) that require self-interested software entities, representing different stakeholders, to interact in a flexible manner. In these applications, conflicts often arise because the agents represent distinct stakeholders with different perspectives and different preferences. Allied to this, is the fact that the agents act autonomously (*i.e.*, they decide for themselves what actions they should take, at what time, and under what terms and conditions). In such circumstances, the interaction between the agents can only proceed by the process of making proposals and/or trading offers, with the aim of finding a mutually acceptable agreement. In short, by *negotiation*.

The process of automating negotiations also opens up a number of new possibilities. In contrast to its manual counterpart, the potential advantages of automated negotiation are as follows:

1) Manual negotiation of contracts is time consuming and hence expensive. Thus, it tends to be carried out relatively infrequently. This inertia means that institutions tend to stay locked into contracts that may not be in either parties best interest. In contrast, by automating the process, negotiations can take place much more frequently, between many more partners, for much smaller value goods. This has the effect of making commerce much more frictionless and responsive to the prevailing circumstances which should make it more efficient.

2) Manual negotiation is often considered either too embarrassing or frustrating for ordinary consumers (even if it is in their best interest to do so). Automation removes these human sensibilities and can lead to more satisfactory outcomes. Moreover, complicated negotiation problems (perhaps

A. Günter et al. (Eds.): KI 2003, LNAI 2821, pp. 34–36, 2003.

involving multiple, inter-related goods) are often too difficult for many consumers to handle manually. In this case, automated negotiation systems can
help ordinary users perform like experts in complicated negotiations.

3) Automated negotiations do not require the participants to be colocated in
space or time. This means that the number of entities with which an agent
can negotiate is increased. This, in turn, should improve the likely outcome
for both buyers and sellers.

Table 1. Negotiation Landscape

Bilateral Negotiations

One service	One service	multiple services	multiple services
1 seller 1 buyer	many sellers many buyers	1 seller many buyers	1 seller many buyers
single institution	single institution	single institution	multiple institutions

Given this ubiquity, negotiation exists in many shapes and forms (see [2]
for a detailed typology). In this talk, however, the focus will be on negotiation
technologies that vary along the three main dimensions of number of services
being negotiated, numbers of buyers and sellers involved in the negotiation, and
number of institutions over which the negotiation takes place (see Table 1).

In more detail, the first column deals with various aspects of bi-lateral negotiation encounters in which the participants have minimal information about their
opponent and when there are deadlines by when the negotiation must finish [3,
4,5,6,7]. The second column deals with work on continuous double auctions in
which multiple buyers and multiple sellers trade simultaneously. In particular,
work is presented on developing a new bidding strategy for this type of auc-
tion based upon fuzzy techniques [8,9]. The third column deals with work on
combinatorial auctions in which an agent seeks to buy multiple inter-related
goods (in which there are substituteables and complementarities). Specifically,
the main foucs here is on developing winner determination algorithms that can
take the various bids and determine what allocation of goods should be made
(under various criteria) [10,11]. The final column deals with the development of
agents that can act across multiple auctions (institutions) and make informed
purchasing decisions across this space. In particular, work we have carried out
in the context of the trading agents competition will be discussed [12,13,14,15].

In summary, I believe the bureoning field of automated negotiation is likely to
have a major impact on the development of complex systems in a wide range of
applications. This is because such systems are increasingly being characterised in
terms of autonomous agents that offer services to one another in a institutional
setting [16,17] and in such circumstances the de facto mode of interaction will
be some form of negotiation.

References

1. Jennings, N.R., Faratin, P., Lomuscio, A.R., Parsons, S., Sierra, C., Wooldridge, M.: Automated negotiation: prospects, methods and challenges. Group Decision and Negotiation **10** (2001) 199–215
2. Lomuscio, A.R., Wooldridge, M., Jennings, N.R.: A classification scheme for negotiation in electronic commerce. Group Decision and Negotiation **12** (2003) 31–56
3. Fatima, S., Wooldridge, M., Jennings, N.R.: Optimal agendas for multi-issue negotiation. In: Proceedings of the Second International Joint Conference on Autonomous Agents and Multi-Agent Systems (AAMAS'03), Melbourne, Australia (2003)
4. Fatima, S., Wooldridge, M., Jennings, N.R.: An agenda based framework for multi-issues negotiation. Artificial Intelligence Journal (2003) To appear.
5. Fatima, S., Wooldridge, M., Jennings, N.R.: Bargaining with incomplete information. Annals of Mathematics and Artificial Intelligence (2003) To appear.
6. Luo, X., Jennings, N.R., Shadbolt, N., Leung, H., Lee, J.H.: A fuzzy constraint based model for bilateral multi-issue negotiations in semi-competitive environments. Artificial Intelligence Journal **148** (2003)
7. Faratin, P., Sierra, C., Jennings, N.R.: Using similarity criteria to make trade-offs in automated negotiations. Artificial Intelligence **142** (2002) 205–237
8. He, M., Jennings, N.R., Leung, H.: On agent-mediated electronic commerce. IEEE Transactions on Knowledge and Data Engineering **15** (2003) 985–1003
9. He, M., Jennings, N.R.: A fuzzy logic based bidding strategy for autonomous agents in continuous double auctions. IEEE Transactions on Knowledge and Data Engineering **15** (2003) To appear.
10. Dang, V.D., Jennings, N.R.: Polynomial algorithms for clearing multi-unit single item and multi-unit combinatorial reverse auctions. In: Proceedings of the 15th European Conference on Artificial Intelligence (ECAI02), Lyon, France (2003) 23–27
11. Dang, V.D., Jennings, N.R.: Optimal clearing algorithms for multi-unit single item and multi-unit combinatorial auctions with demand/suppy function bidding. In: Proceedings of the 5th International Conference on Electronic Commerce, Pittsburgh, USA (2003)
12. Anthony, P., Jennings, N.R.: Developing a bidding agent for multiple heterogeneous auctions. ACM Transactions on Internet Technology (TOIT) **3** (2003)
13. He, M., Jennings, N.R.: SouthamptonTAC: An adaptive autonomous trading agent. ACM Transactions on Internet Technology **3** (2003) To appear.
14. He, M., Jennings, N.R.: Designing a successful trading agent using fuzzy techniques. IEEE Transactions on Fuzzy Systems (2003) To appear.
15. Byde, A., Priest, C., Jennings, N.R.: Decision procedures for multiple auctions. In: Proceedings of the First International Joint Conference on Autonomous Agents & Multi-Agent Systems (AAMAS'02), Bologna, Italy, ACM Press (2002) 613–620
16. Jennings, N.R.: An agent-based approach for building complex software systems. Communications of the ACM **44** (2001) 35–41
17. Jennings, N.R.: On agent-based software engineering. Artificial Intelligence **117** (2000) 277–296

Pushing the Limit in Visual Data Exploration: Techniques and Applications*

Daniel A. Keim[1], Christian Panse[1], Jörn Schneidewind[1], Mike Sips[1], Ming C. Hao[2], and Umeshwar Dayal[2]

[1] University of Konstanz, Germany
{keim,panse,schneide,sips}@informatik.uni-konstanz.de

[2] Hewlett Packard Research Laboratories, Palo Alto, CA, USA
{ming_hao,dayal}@hp.hpl.com

Abstract. With the rapid growth in size and number of available databases, it is necessary to explore and develop new methods for analysing the huge amounts of data. Mining information and interesting knowledge from large databases has been recognized by many researchers as a key research topic in database systems and machine learning, and by many industrial companies as an important area with an opportunity of major revenues. Analyzing the huge amount (usually tera-bytes) of data obtained from large databases such as credit card payments, telephone calls, environmental records, census demographics, however, a very difficult task. *Visual Exploration* and *Visual Data Mining* techniques apply human visual perception to the exploration of large data sets and have proven to be of high value in exploratory data analysis. Presenting data in an interactive, graphical form often opens new insights, encouraging the formation and validation of new hypotheses to the end of better problem-solving and gaining deeper domain knowledge. In this paper we give a short overview of visual exploration techniques and present new results obtained from applying PixelBarCharts in sales analysis and internet usage management.

Keywords: Information Visualization, Visual Data Mining, Visual Exploration, Knowledge Discovery, Pixel Displays

1 Introduction

Progress in technology allows today's computer systems to store and exchange amounts of data that until very recently were considered extraordinarily vast. The automation of business activities produces an ever-increasing stream of data, because even simple transactions, such as the use of a credit card, shopping in e-commerce stores or telephone calls are typically recorded by a computer. The data is collected, because it is a potential source of valuable information, providing a competitive advantage to its holders. In addition, commercial databases, scientific and government databases are also rapidly growing. The data is often

---

* Portions of this article have previously appeared in [11,12,15].

A. Günter et al. (Eds.): KI 2003, LNAI 2821, pp. 37–51, 2003.

automatically recorded via sensors and monitoring systems. Usually many parameters are recorded, resulting in data with a high dimensionality. With today's data management systems, it is only possible to view quite small portions of this data. If the data is presented textually, the amount of data that can be displayed is in the range of some hundred data items. Having no possibility to adequately explore the large amounts of data that have been collected because of their potential usefulness, the data becomes useless and the databases become 'Data Dumps'. The computer science community is responding to both the scientific and practical challenges. The broad topic of knowledge discovery and automatic learning is inherently cross-disciplinary in nature - it falls right into the intersection of disciplines including Statistics, Artificial Intelligence (AI), Visualization and Data Mining. Applying machine learning techniques for knowledge discovery in large databases is a major research area in the field of Artificial Intelligence. Large databases consist of millions of transactions, and it is desirable to have machine learning algorithms, that can handle and analyze such large data sets. In this paper we present visual data exploration techniques, which are indispensable to solving the problem of exploring large data sets.

2   Visual Data Mining

For data mining to be effective, it is important to include the human in the data exploration process and combine the flexibility, creativity, and general knowledge of the human with the enormous storage capacity and the computational power of today's computer systems. Visual data exploration aims at integrating humans in the data exploration process, applying their perceptual abilities to the large data sets available in today's computer systems. The basic idea of visual data exploration is to present the data in some visual form, allowing the human to get insight into the data, draw conclusions, and directly interact with the data. Visual data mining techniques have proven to be of high value in exploratory data analysis and they also have a high potential for exploring large databases.

Visual Data Exploration usually follows a three step process: *Overview first, zoom and filter, and then details-on-demand* (which has been called the Information Seeking Mantra [22]). First, the user needs to get an overview of the data. In the overview, the user identifies interesting patterns or groups in the data and focuses on one or more of them. For analyzing these patterns, the user needs to drill-down and access details of the data. Visualization technology may be used for all three steps of the data exploration process. Visualization techniques are useful for showing an overview of the data, allowing the user to identify interesting subsets. In this process, it is important to keep the overview visualization while focusing on the subset using another visualization. An alternative is to distort the overview visualization in order to focus on the interesting subsets. This can be performed by dedicating a larger percentage of the display to the interesting subsets while decreasing the screen space of the uninteresting data. To further explore the interesting subsets, the user needs a drill-down capability in order to observe the details about the data. Note that visualization technology

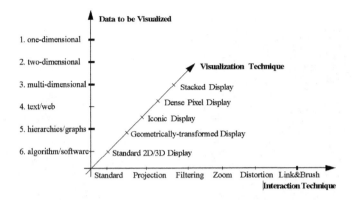

Fig. 1. Classification of visual data exploration techniques

does not only provide visualization techniques for all three steps but also bridges the gaps between them.

2.1   Classification of Visual Data Mining Techniques

There are a number of well known techniques for visualizing large data sets, such as x-y plots, line plots, and histograms. These techniques are useful for data exploration but are limited to relatively small and low dimensional data sets. Over the last years, a large number of novel information visualization techniques have been developed, allowing visualizations of multidimensional data sets without inherent two- or three-dimensional semantics. Nice overviews of the approaches can be found in a number of recent books [3] [20] [23] [26]. The techniques can be classified based on three criteria [10] (see also Figure 1):

– the data to be visualized
– the visualization technique
– and the interaction technique used

The **data type to be visualized** [22] may be *one-dimensional data*, such as temporal (time-series) data, *two-dimensional data*, such as geographical maps, *multidimensional data*, such as relational tables, *text and hypertext*, such as news articles and web documents, *hierarchies and graphs*, such as telephone calls, and *algorithms and software*.

The **visualization technique** used may be classified as: *Standard 2D/3D displays*, such as bar charts and x-y plots, *Geometrically transformed displays*, such as hyperbolic plane [24] and parallel coordinates (Figure 2(b)) [7], *Icon-based displays*, such as chernoff faces [4] and stick figures [18] [19], *pixel displays*, such as the recursive pattern [1] and circle segments [2], and *Stacked displays*, such as treemaps (Figure 2(a)) [8] [21] and dimensional stacking [25].

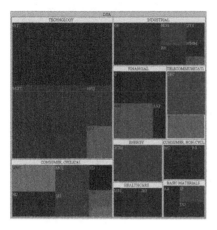 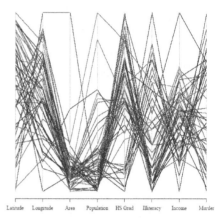

(a) Treemap visualization of stock market data. The area of each box corresponds to the volume of the stock trade and the color reflects the stock price changing.

(b) The Parallel Coordinates plot displays the US-Census data of the 50 states. Color is used to point out which party has won the 2000 US presidential election

Fig. 2. Examples for a hierarchical 2(a) and geometrical 2(b) visualization techniques.

The third dimension of the classification is the ***interaction technique*** used. Interaction techniques allow users to directly navigate and modify the visualizations, as well as select subsets of the data for further operations. Examples include: Dynamic Projection, Interactive Filtering, Interactive Zooming, Interactive Distortion, Interactive Linking and Brushing.

Note that the three dimensions of our classification - data type to be visualized, visualization technique, and interaction technique - can be assumed to be orthogonal. Orthogonality means that any of the visualization techniques may be used in conjunction with any of the interaction techniques for any data type. Note also that a specific system may be designed to support different data types and that it may use a combination of visualization and interaction techniques. More details can be found in [15].

3   Pixel Based Visualization Techniques

A special group of visual data mining techniques are the pixel-oriented techniques. The class of pixel-oriented techniques is an important class of visualization techniques for visualizing very large multidimensional data sets. The general idea of pixel oriented visualization techniques is to represent as many data objects as possible on the screen at the same time by mapping each data value to a pixel of the screen and arranging the pixels adequately. Many different pixel-oriented visualization techniques have been proposed in recent years and it has been shown that the techniques are useful for visual exploration of large databases in a number of different application contexts.

3.1 Basic Idea of Pixel-Display Techniques

The basic idea of pixel-oriented techniques is to map each data value to a colored pixel and present the data values belonging to one dimension (attribute) in a separate subwindow (see Figure 3).

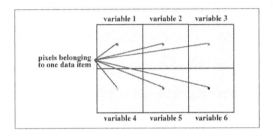

Fig. 3. Arrangement of Windows for Data with Six Variables

Since, in general, pixel display techniques use only one pixel per data value, the techniques allow us to visualize the largest amount of data which is possible on current displays (up to about $1,000,000$ data values). All pixel-display techniques partition the screen into multiple subwindows. For data sets with m dimensions (attribute), the screen is partitioned into m subwindows, one for each of the dimensions. Correlations, functional dependencies, and other interesting relationships between dimensions may be detected by relating corresponding regions in the multiple windows. To achieve that objective, a number of design problems have to be solved.

3.2 Design Issues for Pixel-Based Visualization Techniques

Color Mapping. The first problem is the mapping of data values to colors. A good color mapping is obviously very important, but has to be carefully engineered to be intuitive. The advantage of color over gray scales is that the number of Just Noticeable Differences (JND)[14] are much higher. Finding a path through a color space that maximizes the numbers of just noticeable difference, but at the same time, is intuitive for the application domain, however, is a difficult task. More information about color models and color mappings can be found in [5]

Arrangement of Pixels. As already mentioned, the basic idea of pixel-oriented visualization techniques is to present as many data values as possible at the same time with the number of data values being only limited by the number of pixels of the display. In dealing with arbitrary multivariate data without any 2D-or 3D-semantics, a major problem is to find meaningful arrangements of pixels on the screen. Even if the data has a natural ordering according to one variable, there are many arranging possibilities. One straightforward possibility is to arrange the data items from left to right in a line-by-line fashion. Another possibility is to arrange the data items top-dowm in a column-by-column fashion. If these arrangements are done pixelwise, in general, the resulting visualizations do not provide useful results. More useful are techniques which provide a better clustering of closely related data items and allow the user to influence the arrangement of the data. Techniques which support the clustering properties are screen filling curves or the Recursive Pattern technique.

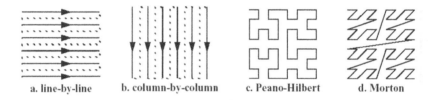

a. line-by-line   b. column-by-column   c. Peano-Hilbert   d. Morton

Fig. 4. Data Arrangements

The *screen-filling curves techniques* are based on the well-known space filling curve algorithms by Peano and Hilbert[6,17] and Morton[16]. The idea of these techniques is to provide a continuous curve which passes through every point of a regular spatial region. Space filling curves provide a mapping which preserves the spatial locality of the original image. In visualizing multivariate data, which is sorted according to one dimension, we can use space-filling curves to map the one dimensional distribution of data items onto the two dimensions of the screen. Space filling curves have the nice property that data items which are close together in the one dimensional distribution are likely to be close together in the two dimensional visual representation. This property of space-filling curves may help to discover patterns in the data which are difficult to discover otherwise. If each variable is visualized using the same arrangement, interesting properties of the data may be revealed including the distribution of variable values, correlations between variables, and clusters.

The *recursive pattern technique* is based on a generic recursive back-and-forth arrangement of the pixels and is particularly aimed at representing datasets with a natural order according to one attribute (e.g. time-series data). The user may specify parameters for each recursion level, and thereby control the arrangement of the pixels to form semantically meaningful substructures. The base element on each recursion level is a pattern of height h_i and width w_i as specified by the user. First, the elements correspond to single pixels that are arranged within a rectangle of height h_1 and width w_1 from left to right, then below backwards from right to left, then again forward from left to right, and so on. The same basic arrangement is done on all recursion levels with the only difference that the basic elements that are arranged on level i are the pattern resulting from the level $(i-1)$ arrangements. In Figure 5, an example recursive pattern visualization of financial data is shown. The visualization shows twenty years (January 1974 - April 1995) of daily prices of the 50 stocks contained in the Frankfurt Stock Index (FAZ).

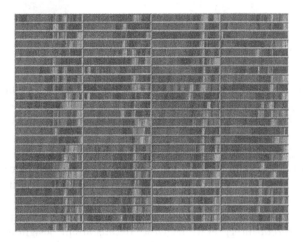

Fig. 5. Dense Pixel Displays: Recursive Pattern Technique showing 50 stocks in the Frankfurt Allgemeine Zeitung (Frankfurt Stock Index Jan 1975 - April 1995). The technique maps each stock value to a colored pixel; high values correspond to bright colors. ©IEEE

Shape of Subwindows. Another important question is whether there exists an alternative to the partitioning of the screen into rectangular subwindows. The rectangular shape of the subwindows allows a good screen usage, but at the other hand, the rectangular shape leads to a dispersal of the pixels belonging to one data object over the whole screen. Especially for data sets with many dimensions, the subwindows of each dimension are rather far apart, which prevent the user from detecting clusters, correlations, and interesting patterns. An alternative shape of the subwindows is the *Circle Segments technique* [2]. The basic idea of these technique is to display the data dimensions as segments of a circle, as shown in Figure 6.

Ordering of Dimensions. The next question to consider is the ordering of the dimensions. This problem is actually not just a problem of dense pixel displays, but a more general problem which arises for a number of other visualization techniques, such as the parallel coordinate plots, as well. The basic problem is

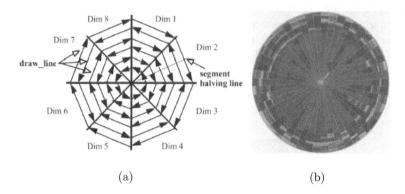

(a)   (b)

Fig. 6. Circle Segments: Figure (a) shows the circle segment technique for 8 dimensional data; Figure (b) visualizes twenty years (January 1974 - April 1995) of daily prices of the 50 stocks contained in the Frankfurt Stock Index (FAZ)

that the data dimensions have to be arranged in some one- or two dimensional ordering on the screen. The ordering of dimensions, however, has a major impact on the expressiveness of the visualization. If a different ordering of the dimensions is chosen, the resulting visualization becomes completely different and allows different interpretations. More details about designing pixel-oriented visualization techniques can be found in [9].

4   Pixel Bar Charts

In many cases simple presentation graphics, like bar charts or pie charts, are used to visualize large data sets, because these techniques are intuitive and easy-to-use. The disadvantage is, that they show only highly aggregated data and present only a very limited number of data values (as in the case of bar charts), and may have a high degree of overlap which may occlude a significant portion of the data values (as in the case of x-y plots). *Pixel Bar Charts*[13] solve these problems by presenting a pixel-oriented generalization of traditional bar charts and x-y-plots, which allows the visualization of large amounts of data. The basic idea is to use the pixels within the bars to present the detailed information of the data records. Pixel Bar Charts retain the intuitiveness of traditional bar charts while allowing very large data sets to be visualized in an effective way. Bar charts are widely used, very intuitive and easy to understand. Figure 7(a) illustrates the use of a regular bar chart to visualize customer distribution in an e-commerce sales transaction. The height of the bars represents the number of customers for 12 different product categories. Bar charts, however, require a high degree of data aggregation and actually show only a rather small number of data values (only 12 values are shown in Figure 7(a)). Therefore, they are of limited value for data exploration of large multidimensional data, and are not able to show important information such as:

– data distributions of multiple attributes
– local patterns, correlations, and trends
– detailed information, such as each customer profile data

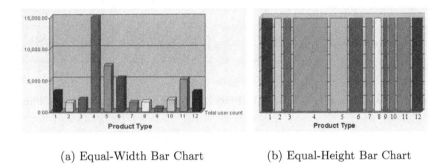

(a) Equal-Width Bar Chart   (b) Equal-Height Bar Chart

Fig. 7. Traditional Bar Charts

4.1 Basic Idea of Pixel Bar Charts

Pixel bar charts are derived from regular bar charts. The basic idea of a pixel bar chart is to present the data values directly instead of aggregating them into a few data values. The approach is to represent each data item (e.g. a customer) by a single pixel in the bar chart. The detailed information of one attribute of each data item is encoded into the pixel color and can be accessed and displayed as needed. One important question is: how are the pixels arranged within each bar? Our idea is to use one or two attributes to separate the data into bars and then use two additional attributes to impose an ordering within the bars. The general idea is shown in Figure 8(a). The pixel bar chart can therefore be seen as a combination of the traditional bar charts and the x-y diagrams. Now, we have a visualization in which one pixel corresponds to one customer. If the partitioning attribute is redundantly mapped to the colors of the pixels, we obtain the regular bar chart shown in Figure 7(a) (Figure 7(b) shows the equal-height-bar-chart", which we explain in the next section). Pixel bar charts, however, can be used to present large amounts of detailed information. The one-to-one correspondence between customer data and pixels allows us to use the color of the pixels to represent an additional attribute of the customer - for example, sales amount, number of visits, or sales quantity. In Figure 8, a pixel bar chart is used to visualize thousands of e-commerce sales transactions. Each pixel in the visualization represents one customer. The number of customers can be as large as the screen size (about 1.3 million). The pixel bar chart shown in Figure 8(b) uses product type as the partitioning attribute and dollar amount as the x and y ordering attributes. The color represents the dollar amount spent by the corresponding customer. High dollar amounts correspond to bright colors, low dollar amounts to dark colors

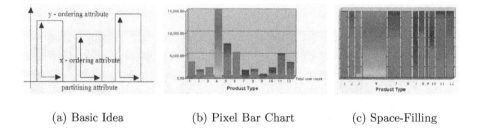

(a) Basic Idea   (b) Pixel Bar Chart   (c) Space-Filling

Fig. 8. Pixel Bar Charts

4.2 Space-Filling Pixel Bar Charts

One problem of traditional bar charts is that a large portion of the screen space is not used due to the differing heights of the bars. With very large data sets, we would like to use more of the available screen space to visualize the data. One idea that increases the number of displayable data values is to use equal-height instead of equal-width bar charts. In Figure 7(b), the regular bar chart of Figure 7(a) is shown as an equal-height bar chart. The area (width) of the bars corresponds to the attribute shown, namely the number of customers.

If we now apply our pixel bar chart idea to the resulting bar charts, we obtain space-filling pixel bar charts which use virtually all pixels of the screen to display customer data items. In Figure 8(c), we show an example of a space-filling pixel bar chart which uses the same partitioning, ordering, and coloring attributes as the pixel bar chart in Figure 8(b). In this way, each customer is represented by one pixel. Note that pixel bar charts generalize the idea of regular bar charts. If the partitioning and coloring attributes are identical, both types of pixel bar charts become scaled versions of their regular bar chart counterparts. The pixel bar chart can therefore be seen as a generalization of the regular bar charts but they contain significantly more information and allow a detailed analysis of large original data sets.

4.3 Multi-pixel Bar Charts

In many cases, the data to be analyzed consists of multiple attributes. With pixel bar charts we can visualize attribute values using multi-pixel bar charts which use different color mappings but the same partitioning and ordering attributes. This means that the arrangement of data items within the corresponding bars of multi-pixel bar charts is the same, i.e., the colored pixels corresponding to the different attribute values of the same data item have a unique position within the bars. Figure 9 shows an example of three pixel bar charts with product type as the partitioning attribute and number of visits and dollar amount as the x and y ordering attributes. The attributes which are mapped to color are dollar amount spent, number of visits, and sales quantity.

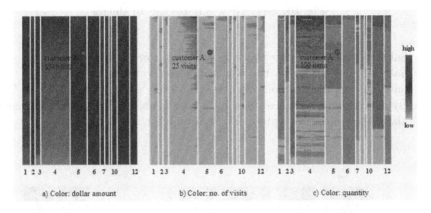

Fig. 9. Multi-pixel Bar Chart for Mining 405,000 Sales Transaction Records

4.4 Application of Pixel Bar Charts in Sales Analysis and Internet Usage

The pixel bar chart technique has been applied in two business service applications - Sales Analysis and Internet Duration Time Analysis at Hewlett Packard Laboratories. The applications show the wide applicability and usefulness of pixel bar charts.

Sales Analysis. The rapid growth of business on the Internet has led to the availability of large volumes of data. Business research efforts have been focused on how to turn raw data into actionable knowledge. In order to find and retain customers, business analysts need to improve their sales quality based on prior information. For sales analysis, sales specialists would like to discover new patterns and relationships in the invoice data. Common questions are 'What is the sales growth rate in recent months? ', 'Which product has the most sales? ', and 'Where do the sales come from?'.

In Figure 10, each pixel represents an invoice. Color represents sales amount. The red color indicates that the sales amount exceeds \$ 10.000. The width of a bar represents the sales volume. The analyst can find the following:

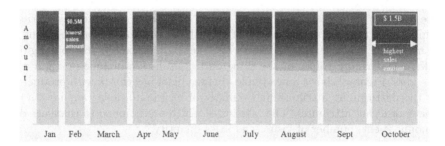

Fig. 10. Sales Growth Rate Over 10 Months

– Sales amount varies over time (shown by a growing color wave)
– Sales volume varies over time (shown by bar width)
– Sales amount distribution over time (shown by color)
– By clicking on an invoice (pixel), the user is able to find detail information about the transaction (products, location, time ...)

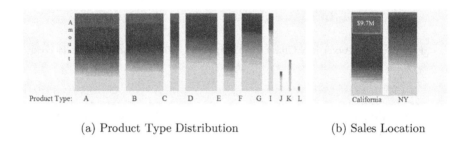

(a) Product Type Distribution   (b) Sales Location

Fig. 11. Drill down to show the October sales distribution 11(a) and to show that most sales come from California 11(b)

The analyst is further able to rubber-band an area inside a bar to display the total sales amount in the area. The sales amount represented by the rubber-band areas has grown from $0.5M (February) to $1.5B (October). Many important facts may be discovered in the layered drill-downs of Figure 11. The analyst may observe the following facts:

1. Sales distribution: From Figure 10, it becomes clear that October has the highest sales amount (less yellow, more burgundy and red). The analyst can drill down to the next level of hierarchy (products). A visualization of the drill-down to products is shown in Figure 11(a). Product 'A 'has the highest sales amount (less yellow, more blue, burgundy, and red) and highest sales volumes (widest bar).

2. Sales source: The analyst may continue drill-down to examine other interesting facts, for example, where the sale comes from which source/location. From Figure 11(b), it is clear that most sales comes from 'California'(more burgundy and red). The analyst can rubber-band area to display the total sales amount in the area (i.e. $ 9.7M).

Internet Usage Management Analysis. Pixel bar charts have been also used to explore Internet usage management. The pixels of the bar chart represent Internet events. In pixel bar charts, events with similar duration time are placed close to each other. A system analyst can use the visualization to rapidly discover event patterns and use those patterns to identify the latency and manage the Internet configuration.

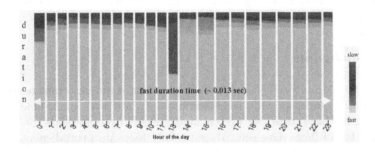

Fig. 12. Internet Event Duration Time Distribution

The pixel bar chart shown in Figure 12 illustrates the Internet event hourly duration time distribution. Each pixel represents an event record. It uses *hour* as the dividing attribute and *duration time* as the y-ordering attributes. The color represents the duration time value of an Internet event. The fast duration time corresponds to bright colors (yellow, green); the slow duration time corresponds to dark colors (blue, burgundy). From the data distribution, we can discover that a large number of fast Internet events occurred cross all 24 hours except hour 13. Hour 13 has highest average duration time (more blue, burgundy). It is crucial for analysts to realize that the number of events with high duration time in hour 13 is only half of the events processed in hour 13. The rest of events have short duration time (green). These valuable facts get lost in the aggregated data. As a result, the Internet analyst may make a wrong decision.

Figure 13 illustrates the correlations between the number of bytes and the number of pockets. The x-axis dividing attribute is hour and the y-axis ordering attribute is the number of bytes. The colors in the different bar charts represent number of pockets. The analysts can easily conclude that there is a close correlation between number of bytes and number of pockets. It shows that the high number of pockets are corresponding to the high number of bytes transferred

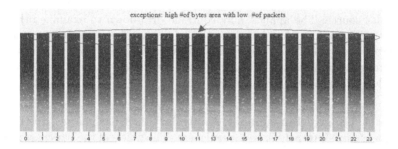

Fig. 13. Internet number of Bytes and number of Pockets Correlations

across all 24 hours (with the same patterns of yellow, green, blue, and burgundy colors) except several sprinkles (exceptional cases), such as there are several low number of pockets in the highest number of bytes areas as shown inside the red circle in Figure 13.

5   Conclusion

Visual Data Mining and Visual Data Exploration is an important research area. Many data sources provide large amounts of data with multidimensional attributes. In this article, we present an overview over methods for the Visual Exploration of large data sets. We especially focus on pixel display techniques which are able to visualize significantly more information then existing techniques. The application examples exemplify the potential of visual data exploration techniques.

References

1. M. Ankerst, D. A. Keim, and H.-P. Kriegel. Recursive pattern: A technique for visualizing very large amounts of data. In *Proc. Visualization '95, Atlanta, GA,* pages 279–286, 1995.
2. M. Ankerst, D. A. Keim, and H.-P. Kriegel. Circle segments: A technique for visually exploring large multidimensional data sets. In *Visualization '96, Hot Topic Session, San Francisco, CA,* 1996.
3. S. Card, J. Mackinlay, and B. Shneiderman. *Readings in Information Visualization.* Morgan Kaufmann, 1999.
4. H. Chernoff. The use of faces to represent points in k-dimensional space graphically. *Journal Amer. Statistical Association,* 68:361–368, 1973.
5. G. Herman and H. Levkowitz. Color scales for image data. *Computer Graphics and Applications,* pages 72–80, 1992.
6. D. Hilbert. Über stetige Abbildungen einer Linie auf einem Flächenstück. *Mathematische Annalen,* (78), 1891.
7. A. Inselberg and B. Dimsdale. Parallel coordinates: A tool for visualizing multi-dimensional geometry. In *Proc. Visualization 90, San Francisco, CA,* pages 361–370, 1990.

8. B. Johnson and B. Shneiderman. Treemaps: A space-filling approach to the visualization of hierarchical information. In *Proc. Visualization '91 Conf*, pages 284–291, 1991.
9. D. Keim. Designing pixel-oriented visualization techniques: Theory and applications. *Transactions on Visualization and Computer Graphics*, 6(1):59–78, Jan–Mar 2000.
10. D. Keim. Visual exploration of large databases. *Communications of the ACM*, 44(8):38–44, 2001.
11. D. A. Keim. Designing pixel-oriented visualization techniques: Theory and applications. *IEEE Transactions on Visualization and Computer Graphics (TVCG)*, 6(1):59–78, January–March 2000.
12. D. A. Keim, M. Hao, and U. Dayal. Hierarchical pixel bar charts. *IEEE Transactions on Visualization and Computer Graphics (TVCG)*, 8(3):255–269, July–September 2002.
13. D. A. Keim, M. C. Hao, J. Ladisch, M. Hsu, and U. Dayal. Pixel bar charts: A new technique for visualizing large multi-attribute data sets without aggregation. In *Visualization 2001, Los Angeles*, page 113, 2001.
14. D. A. Keim and H.-P. Kriegel. Issues in visualizing large databases. In *Proc. Conf. on Visual Database Systems (VDB'95), Lausanne, Schweiz, März 1995, in: Visual Database Systems*, pages 203–214. Chapman & Hall Ltd., 1995.
15. D. A. Keim and M. Ward. *Intelligent Data Analysis, an Introduction by D. Hand and M. Berthold*, chapter Visual Data Mining Techniques. Springer Verlag, 2 edition, 2002.
16. G. Morton. A computer oriented geodetic data base and a new technique in file sequencing. *IBM Ltd, Ottawa, Canada*, 1966.
17. G. Peano. Sur une courbe qui remplit toute une aire plane. *Mathematische Annalen*, (36), 1890.
18. R. M. Pickett. *Visual Analyses of Texture in the Detection and Recognition of Objects*. Academic Press, New York, 1970.
19. R. M. Pickett and G. G. Grinstein. Iconographic displays for visualizing multi-dimensional data. In *Proc. IEEE Conf. on Systems, Man and Cybernetics, IEEE Press, Piscataway, NJ*, pages 514–519, 1988.
20. H. Schumann and W. Müller. *Visualisierung: Grundlagen und allgemeine Methoden*. Springer, 2000.
21. B. Shneiderman. Tree visualization with treemaps: A 2D space-filling approach. *ACM Transactions on Graphics*, 11(1):92–99, 1992.
22. B. Shneiderman. The eye have it: A task by data type taxonomy for information visualizations. In *Visual Languages*, 1996.
23. B. Spence. *Information Visualization*. Pearson Education Higher Education publishers, UK, 2000.
24. J. Walter and H. Ritter. On interactive visualization of high-dimensional data using the hyperbolic plane. In *Proc. ACM SIGKDD International Conference on Knowledge Discovery and Data Mining*, pages 123–131, 2002.
25. M. O. Ward. Xmdvtool: Integrating multiple methods for visualizing multivariate data. In *Proc. Visualization 94, Washington, DC*, pages 326–336, 1994.
26. C. Ware. *Information Visualization: Perception for Design*. Morgen Kaufman, 2000.

Words at the Right Time: Real-Time Dialogues with the WITAS Unmanned Aerial Vehicle
Extended Abstract

Erik Sandewall[1], Patrick Doherty[1], Oliver Lemon[2], and Stanley Peters[3]

[1] Department of Computer and Information Science
Linköping University
S-58183 Linköping, Sweden

[2] School of Informatics
University of Edinburgh
Edinburgh EH8 9LW, Scotland

[3] Center for the Study of Language and Information
Stanford University
Stanford, Calif. 94305, USA

Abstract. The WITAS project addresses the design of an intelligent, autonomous UAV (Unmanned Aerial Vehicle), in our case a helicopter. Its dialogue-system subprojects address the design of a deliberative system for natural-language and graphical dialogue with that robotic UAV. This raises new issues both for dialogue and for reasoning in real time. The following topics have been particularly important for us in various stages of the work in these subprojects:
- spatiotemporal reference in the dialogue, including reference to past events and to planned or expected, future events
- mixed initiative in the dialogue architecture of a complex system consisting of both dialogue-related components (speech, grammar, etc) and others (simulation, event recognition, interface to robot)
and more recently as well
- identification of a dialogue manager that is no more complex than what is required by the application
- uniform treatment of different types of events, including the robot's own actions, observed events, communication events, and dialogue-oriented deliberation events
- a logic of time, action, and spatiotemporal phenomena that facilitates the above.

This paper gives a brief overview of the WITAS project as a whole, and then addresses the approaches that have been used and that are presently being considered in the work on two generations of dialogue subsystems.

1 The WITAS Project: Goals, Structure, and the WITAS System

The WITAS Unmanned Aerial Vehicle Project [14,15] is an ambitious, long-term basic research project whose main objectives are the development of an

A. Günter et al. (Eds.): KI 2003, LNAI 2821, pp. 52–63, 2003.
© Springer-Verlag Berlin Heidelberg 2003

integrated hardware/software VTOL (Vertical Take-Off and Landing) platform for fully autonomous missions and its future deployment in applications such as traffic monitoring and surveillance, emergency services assistance, photogrammetry and surveying. Basic and applied research in the project covers a wide range of topics that include both the development of traditional AI technologies, core functionalities and their pragmatic integration with other technologies in a prototype experimental UAV system.

The following is a non-exclusive list of some of the activities in the project:

- Development of a generic distributed deliberative/reactive software architecture for (aerial) robotic systems.
- Development of a helicopter control system with flight modes for stable hovering, takeoff and landing, trajectory following, and reactive flight modes for interception and tracking of vehicles.
- Development and integration of numerous AI technologies. These include both path and task-based planning systems, a chronicle recognition system for identifying complex vehicular patterns on the ground, and other high-level services for reasoning about action and change.
- Development and integration of numerous knowledge representation technologies. These include an on-board geographical information system; a dynamic object repository to anchor, manage and reason about dynamic objects such as vehicles discovered during mission execution; a qualitative signal processing framework for dynamic construction of trajectories and histories of world behavior with associated reasoning mechanisms; and development of knowledge structures for signal-to-symbol conversion and approximate reasoning in soft real-time.
- Development of an on-board dynamically programmable image processing system.
- Development of multi-modal interfaces (including dialogue) for ground operator/UAV communication with both speech generation and recognition capability.
- Development of simulation environments with hardware-in-the-loop for both testing and visualization of control, reaction and deliberation functionalities.

Each of these activities is expected to contribute both to the construction of the project's integrated demonstrator, and by development and publication of specialized basic research results in their respective areas. The main demonstrations of the integrated WITAS demonstrator are due before the end of 2003.

The VTOL platform used in the project is a slightly modified Yamaha RMAX helicopter manufactured by Yamaha Motor Company. It is commercially available in Japan as a radio-controlled platform. The RMAX is approximatively 2.7 x 0.7 meters, with a main rotor 3 meters in length.

The *WITAS System* is developed under the direction of Patrick Doherty. It includes on-board facilities for autonomous control, sensor data interpretation and integration, a system for reactive task procedures, trajectory planning, high-level action planning, ground-to-UAV communication, and others more. The *WITAS*

System uses a distributed architecture [15] that is based on real-time CORBA, and which facilitates reconfiguration of the system as well as integration of additional facilities and interface to other and remote services.

Although the development of the *WITAS System* requires the integration of a large number of subsystems and technologies, a few of the facilities for the intended final demonstrator are developed as separate subprojects while planning for eventual integration across well defined interfaces. This applies in particular for the advanced vision facilities that are being developed within the project by Gösta Granlund and his group, and for the natural-language dialogue facilities that are the topic of the present paper. The *WITAS Demonstrator* will consist of the *WITAS System* (its major part), a dialogue system, and optionally an augmented vision system.

The *WITAS System* has been tested in actual flights at a considerable number of occasions, but the integration of the other subsystems to form the *WITAS Demonstrator* is in progress at the time of writing (June, 2003) and has not yet been tested in flights.

Before proceeding to the dialogue system, a brief overview of the *WITAS System* is appropriate since it sets the context within which the dialogue is performed.

The first-generation *WITAS system* was developed during 1997 and 1998, and operated entirely in a simulation environment. After an intermediate period of analysis and redesign, work started in year 2000 on the present generation of WITAS system which is designed to be used in real flights, with the resulting requirements on reliability and on real-time performance.

A great deal of effort has gone into the development of a control system for the WITAS UAV which incorporates a number of different control modes and includes a high-level interface to the control system. This enables other parts of the architecture to call the appropriate control modes dynamically during the execution of the mission. The ability to switch modes contingently is a fundamental functionality in the architecture and can be programmed into the 'task procedures' associated with the reactive component of the architecture. At the time of writing we have developed the following control modes which are used in actual flights on a regular basis:

- hovering (H-mode)
- trajectory following (TF-mode)
- proportional navigation (PN-mode)

PN-mode is a reactive flight mode for interception and tracking. Additional take-off and landing modes are in an early testing stage at present.

A number of fully autonomous flights have been demonstrated successfully in tests during 2002 and 2003. These include stable hovering, predefined 3D trajectory following including 360 degrees banked turns, vehicle interception and road following. Acceleration and braking with no overshoot have been tested at speeds of 55 km/h, and coordinated banked turns have been tested with a turn rate of 20 degrees/second. We have completed autonomous missions of up to a duration of 20 minutes using a combination of control modes in addition to interaction with a ground operator.

One of the more sophisticated missions flown of this character is based on an emergency services scenario where a train carrying a bio-chemical ingredient has collided with a vehicle and contaminated a small region around the train which partially intersects a small town. The goal of the mission is to interactively fly to specific points in the contaminated region and provide initial video sequences of injured inhabitants at these points. Successful completion of the mission involves repeated use of H- and TF- modes, on-line trajectory planning to avoid colliding with building structures in the region, and command-mode communication from the ground to inform the UAV of new coordinates to fly to.

A number of knowledge representation techniques have also been developed which are currently being integrated with the UAV software architecture. These techniques have been developed to meet the specific constraints and needs associated with the type of missions flown by the UAV. These involve such issues as real-time querying of knowledge structures, integration of quantitative and qualitative representations, incremental refinement of existing knowledge structures through machine learning techniques and techniques for defining tolerance and similarity measures on primitive and complex data structures. Details concerning these and other knowledge representation related tools and techniques may be found in the following publications, [12,11,10,4,8,9,13].

2   Real-Time Dialogue in WITAS: First Stage

Although the WITAS project started in 1997, we did not begin to address the dialogue problem until in 2000. During the first three years the project was only focused on the problem of fully autonomous flight for achieving a goal that had been set for the UAV before the start of the flight.

The dialogue subproject was added to WITAS in response to both an obvious practical need in the applications being considered, and for purely scientific reasons. Natural-language and multimedia dialogue with an autonomous robot is a challenging research problem which introduces several important issues that are not present in, for example, dialogue with a database or a service provider such as an automated travel agency. Dialogue with an intelligent robot must be able to refer to phenomena along a time-line, including both what has happened in the robot's own actions and in its environment, what the robot plans to do, and what events can be predicted in the environment. The dialogue software must be able to interleave planning and execution-related dialogue threads, and needs to be able to coordinate several simultaneous tasks of the robot (see [22]).

Furthermore, the dialogue itself is located on the same time-line as the robot's actions, so that speedy and concise expressions, break-ins, and other time-aware aspects of dialogue are not only important for user convenience, they are in fact essential for the success of the dialogue and, eventually, of the robot's mission. Meeting these demands sets strong requirements on both the representational power, the deliberative capability, and the computational performance of the dialogue system.

During three years, 2000 to 2002, the dialogue subproject of WITAS was conducted by Stanley Peters and Oliver Lemon at the Center for the Study of Language and Information (CSLI) at Stanford university. Oliver Lemon was the technical project leader. This group developed a first-generation *WITAS Dialogue System*, a stand-alone system that conducts a spoken dialogue with a simulated UAV performing a flight mission over a small town.

The system supports dialogues about tasks such as locating and following vehicles, delivering objects to locations, and flying to locations. It allows specification of local and global constraints on tasks (e.g. "always fly high" and negotiation subdialogues about constraint violations (e.g. "I am supposed to always fly high. Shall I fly to the lake at low altitude anyway?"). It uses open-microphone speech recognition in an asynchronous architecture and has the ability to resolve multimodal inputs (e.g. "Fly here" [user points to map location]). Speech recognition language models are set dynamically, depending on dialogue state, resulting in significant improvements in recognition and concept error rates.

Dialogue management is based on the "Information State Update" approach (see e.g. Bohlin et al., [2]) with a clean separation of task and dialogue knowledge. The following are the components of the information state of this system:

- A *dialogue move tree* that represents the structure of the dialogue by way of conversational 'threads', composed of the dialogue moves of both participants (e.g. *command, wh-question*), and their relations;
- An *activity tree* that represents hierarchically decomposed tasks and plans of the UAV, and their states (e.g. planned, current, failed, suspended, cancelled);
- A *system agenda* that represents the planned dialogue contributions of the system and their priorities (e.g. report task failure, ask clarification question);
- A *pending list* that represents open questions raised in the dialogue;
- A *salience list* that contains a priority-ordered list of objects that have been mentioned in the dialogue, and a record of how they have been referred to. It is used for identifying the referents of anaphoric and deictic expressions and for *generation* of contextually appropriate referring expressions (see [21]);
- A *modality buffer* which records gesture inputs from the user (in the form of mouse clicks) for multimodal fusion with linguistic referring expressions.

This design uses domain-independent dialogue move classes and is intended to be applicable in general for dialogues between humans and autonomous real-world systems. Central components of the system have been reused in other domains and genres, for example tutorial dialogues [3].

The WITAS project uses the Revinge training area as its standard flight-test area for advanced flights; Revinge is small town of about 0.6 x 0.8 km which is operated by the Swedish Civil Rescue Service as a training grounds. The flight simulations in the *WITAS Dialogue System* were conducted in a simulation of Revinge which had been prepared in the main (Linköping) part of the project.

This stage of the project developed a system with the dialogue management architecture that has been briefly outlined here, with facilities for:

- multitasking
- interleaved task planning and execution
- constraint negotiation
- revision and repair utterances
- multimodal interpretation and generation
- dynamic language models
- domain-specific task models, reusability

The dialogue competence of the system includes also a number of situation types that the actual UAV can not perform at present, in particular because of the restricted image interpretation capability.

An evaluation of the system was conducted, measuring task completion rates for novice users with no training (see Hockey et al, [17] for full details). We found that 55% of novice users where able to complete their first task successfully, rising to 80% by the fifth task. (An example task is "There is a red car near the warehouse. Use the helicopter to find it. Then land the helicopter in the parking lot." - note that the user can not simply read these task statements out to the system). Performance was significantly improved via the use of a targeted help system in the dialogue interaction.

Besides the normal international publications of these results, the system has also been demonstrated to a variety of audiences. See Lemon et al in [20,22,17, 21] for full details.

These results having been achieved, the next step for the project was to integrate the dialogue system with the *WITAS System* that was described in section 1, in order to realize a demonstrator capable of flight control with high-level autonomy, computer vision, and natural-language dialogue between operator and UAV. The integration is done in the Linköping section of the project. It is first of all a practical software challenge, but actually it has raised some more principled issues as well, having to do with the precise treatment of time in a dialogue system. The rest of the present paper is devoted to a report of our current, on-going work in that respect.

3   Reasoning about Action and Change in WITAS

Two of the present authors (Sandewall and Doherty) have been active in research on reasoning about actions and change since many years. When we started the WITAS project in 1997 we expected that this background would become an important technique on the deliberative level in the eventual WITAS demonstrator. However, many other problems had to be dealt with first, in both the first and the second generation of the WITAS system, and the research on actions and change has been a concurrent activity in the project whose integration is only beginning to take place.

Patrick Doherty and his group have developed TALplanner, a forward-chaining planner that relies on domain knowledge in the form of temporal logic formulas in order to prune irrelevant parts of the search space. Details concerning TALplanner may be found in the following publications: [5,18,6,7]. The core engine used in TALplanner is currently being extended for use as both a predictive component and an on-line execution monitor in the UAV architecture.

Although the dramatic improvement in performance of the planner is the most striking aspect of the TALplanner work, there have also been several other developments that are as well important for the overall project. Jonas Kvarnström has developed systematic domain analysis techniques for domain-dependent control [19]. Joakim Gustafsson and Jonas Kvarnström have extended the basic TAL formalism with constructs for object-orientation and shown how they provide elaboration tolerance in several standard testing domains in the literature [16]. Tests using the research software tool VITAL (which is related to TALplanner) showed performance that was much better, often by one or more orders of magnitude, compared with another published tool, the Causal Calculator of Vladimir Lifschitz and his group [1].

During the same period, Erik Sandewall has worked on semantic issues for RAC and, in particular, on the semantic relationship between the world where actions and change take place on one hand, and the logic formulas the represent that action and change on the other hand. In [26] he described an idealized architecture for a cognitive robot that relates actions and change with the formulas describing them, in two ways: the architecture uses such formulas as its data objects, and the formulas characterize what happens when the architecture executes. (This abstract architecture must not be confounded with the actual architecture in the *WITAS System* as described in [15]; they are different things and serve different purposes).

Continuing the same track, [27] proposed a formal characterization of the act of decision, that is, the transition from a situation where an agent has deliberated over several possible courses of action for the future, to the situation where the agent has chosen one of them and it has become a part of its intentions for the immediate future.

Sandewall's work has been using a logic of actions and change called CRL (for Cognitive Robotics Logic) [25] which is similar to TAL (for Time and Action Logic). They have a common ancestry in the analysis of nonmonotonic entailment methods for actions and change in 'Features and Fluents' [24].

4   Real-Time Dialogue in WITAS: Second Stage

During the year 2003 we are integrating the results from the Stanford subproject so that it can operate in conjunction with the *WITAS System*. At the same time, Erik Sandewall and his group is building a next-generation dialogue system called the *DOSAR system* that builds on the experience and the design from the first generation. However, the new system uses a different approach to representing time and action which is based on a formal logic of time and action, and which is closely related to a high-level simulator of helicopter actions. The group also hopes to further improve the robustness of the dialogue so that misunderstandings occur less frequently and so that they can be resolved efficiently. This work makes use of the background on reasoning about actions and change that was described above.

The acronym 'DOSAR' stood originally for 'Dialogue-Oriented Simulation And Reasoning' since it started as a logic-based simulator. It was first written in order to provide an environment in which to test the WITAS dialogue system in its early stages of development, and as an experimental implementation of the double helix architecture [26]. However, we found after a while that the task structuring and the time management capabilities of this simulator were also useful as a platform for a dialogue manager.

Our approach is to represent several kinds of actions in a uniform manner and using Cognitive Robotics Logic, namely:

- physical actions by the helicopter as a whole (take off, land, fly to X, etc) and by its various components such as its video camera system
- speech acts and other communication acts, as performed by both the operator and the dialogue system
- cognitive acts, such as parsing a sentence, or deciding what to say next.

One reason for representing these types of actions in a uniform way is for conceptual economy, in particular since similar logical constructs arise for all of them. Another reason is to prepare for dialogue where the user makes combined reference to several types of actions, for example "where were you when I told you to fly to the parking garage?"

All these types of actions may fail, and such failure is important for the dialogue management. Actual or potential failure of physical actions is obviously a topic of discussion. Failure of the cognitive acts is equally relevant since it typically leads to misunderstandings that need to be resolved in the further dialogue. In order to analyze and characterize the failure of these cognitive actions, they have to be decomposed into more elementary subactions that represent successive steps in the actual software, for example, a simple sequence of speech understanding, parsing, and so forth. Each of these steps may fail, and each kind of failure will be reflected in the continued dialogue.

The *WITAS Dialogue System* demonstrated the importance of properly managing faults in the cognitive actions that are involved in the dialogue. The *DOSAR System* therefore takes a further step and introduces the use of a logic of actions and change for characterizing these faults. The Cognitive Robotics Logic (CRL) which it uses, provides a concise representation for the succeed/fail distinction. It is used there for a formal characterization of goal-directed behavior in the sense of "if one method or plan for achieving the goal fails, then try another one". These aspects of the logic are part of the reasons why it was chosen as the representation language for the DOSAR dialogue system.

Although it is conceptually attractive to use a uniform representation for different kinds of actions, there are also significant differences between different types of actions, and these differences have to be reflected by the knowledge represenation. Consider, in particular, the following classification of action types:

- the *speech act proper*, that is, the period of time where the phrase is actually uttered
- the *understanding of the phrase*, which may consist of sub-actions such as speech understanding (speech to text), parsing, identification and screening of semantic content, etc.
- the *decision how to react*, where the reaction may be, for example, to answer a question, to send a command to the helicopter, or to verify that a command has been correctly understood before it is sent to the helicopter.

Both our generations of dialogue systems use a classification more or less along these lines. All of these steps are specific to the particular received sentence. In terms of the information-state structure that was described above, the third step also includes attaching the current phrase, or its 'semantic' representation, to the dialogue move tree. In some cases the phrase or its derivatives are attached to other parts of the information state as well.

However, these types of actions are also different in two important aspects. First, the time scale: physical actions in a helicopter take from a few seconds to tens of seconds (rarely more, in our confined testing area). The speech acts proper often take several seconds as well. However, the understanding of the phrase, and even more its distinct subactions is performed more quickly than that, which of course is a necessity since a delay of several seconds between successive dialogue moves would be very annoying. The same applies for the decision how to react, although of course the decision may have been anticipated in deliberations that took place earlier in the course of the dialogue. This requires the representation of actions to work with two different time scales.

The other difference concerns the effects of actions. Physical actions have effects on the state of the world, which is modeled using objects and features (properties) of objects in our system. The cognitive actions, on the other hand, can better be thought of as transformers that convert one symbolic expression (for example, a parse tree) to another symbolic expression, of another kind. Traditional formalisms for actions and change are not well adapted to represent actions of this kind.

We are extending the CRL formalism in order to cope with these new demands. Since our goal here is to give an overview of the project, and due to the format of the present conference proceedings, it is not possible to describe the specifics of the chosen formal system, and we have to refer to forthcoming, more extensive publications. Please use the WITAS webpage www.ida.liu.se/ext/witas for an up-to-date list of publications.

5   Connections between Dialogue System and UAV

Both generations of dialogue managers (the one developed at Stanford, and the one presently developed at Linköping) will be connected to the *WITAS system* for the demonstrations. However, for safety reasons this can not be a direct connection, and there must be checkpoints in-between. Technically, it works as follows. The UAV communicates with a *UAV ground station* using three independent communication channels. First, there is a basic control channel for direct remote-control of the UAV, which is provided by the manufacturer and which is essential for safety reasons as a backup. Secondly, there is a two-directional data link for downloading measurement data and for uploading commands to the helicopter. Thirdly, there is a video downlink so that a person on the ground can see what the helicopter sees. (The computer vision system of the UAV is on board, however, like all its other control systems).

The dialogue system, on the other hand, consists of a *mobile terminal* that the operator can carry with him or her, and a *dialogue ground station* that is located adjacent to the UAV ground station. The mobile terminal is a laptop or tablet running the dialogue system software, which may be both the *WITAS Dialogue System* from Stanford and the more recent *DOSAR system*, together with the necessary audio and radio equipment and power supply. The dialogue ground station is a cart carrying two computers, one for real-time video recording and one for interfacing and for supervision of experiments.

When the operator issues a command to the helicopter, then the command phrase is interpreted in the mobile terminal; a command message is sent to the dialogue ground station, from there on to the UAV ground station where it is checked by a supervisor, and only if it passes that check is it actually transmitted to the UAV for execution.

The downloaded video signal is recorded in the dialogue ground station, in such a way that it can be referred to in the subsequent dialogue; the operator can request to see the video segment containing a particular event that is referred to verbally.

This relatively complex configuration is required in order to deal first of all with the application as such and the safety issues during test flights, but also because of the diversity of signal types and the bandwidth limitations. It leads to several interesting problems of synchronization and other time management, in particular in the continued development of the dialogue system. Consider, for example, the situation where an operator wishes to identify a moving object by pointing into a running video that is shown on the display screen.

Besides the transmission of commands from the dialogue system to the UAV, there are also several other facilities in the interface between the *WITAS system* and the dialogue systems. These are presently being implemented for the interface to the *DOSAR System*, and the interface to the *WITAS Dialogue System* will follow. There is a flow of observations from the UAV to the dialogue manager which uses the same communication lines as the commands, but in the opposite direction. Also, some of the knowledge representation technologies that were mentioned in section 1, are made accessible to the dialogue managers via the interface. This applies, in particular, for the specialized, real-time GIS system, but also for the dynamic object repository (DOR). The DOR contains dynamically updated descriptions and properties of objects on the ground that are observed by the helicopter, and may also be used for storing properties of the camera system and other subsystems within the helicopter itself.

6   Future Plans

The first author of this article foresees two important tasks in the continued work on the DOSAR dialogue system for WITAS, besides completing the integration and the final project demonstration. The continued modeling of paradigmatic dialogue situations and how they relate to the application model is a major consideration. In the architecture used by these systems, incoming phrases have to be attached to the dialogue move tree which in turn is used for determining the system's responses. The attachment rules for the Stanford system have been published in [22]. The structure of these attachment rules will be a topic of further study.

Our second goal is methodological. For continued progress in this research area, it will be important to have a means of comparing the architectures and approaches that are used in different systems, as implemented by different research groups. The techniques that have been developed for comparing and assessing different approaches to reasoning about actions and change [24] may be applicable for this domain as well.

Acknowledgements. The research reported here was supported by the Knut and Alice Wallenberg Foundation. We acknowledge the contributions of the following persons who have participated in the work on the WITAS dialogue systems,

at Stanford: Anne Bracy, Alexander Gruenstein, and Laura Hiatt;

in Linköping: Malin Alzén, Peter Andersson, Genevieve Correll, Karolina Eliasson, Coynthia Hernandez, Tomas Johansson, Felix Koch, Susanna Monemar, Egil Möller, Krister Nilsson, and Tobias Nurmiranta.

References

1. V. Akman, S. Erdogan, J. Lee, V. Lifschitz, and H. Turner. Representing the zoo world and the traffic world in the language of the causal calculator (to appear). *Artificial Intelligence*, 2003.
2. Peter Bohlin, Robin Cooper, Elisabet Engdahl, and Staffan Larsson. Information states and dialog move engines. *Electronic Transactions in AI*, 3(9), 1999. Website with commentaries: `www.etaij.org`.
3. Brady Clark, Oliver Lemon, Alexander Gruenstein, Elizabeth Owen Bratt, John Fry, Stanley Peters, Heather Pon-Barry, Karl Schultz, Zack Thomsen-Gray, and Pucktada Treeratpituk. A general purpose architecture for intelligent tutoring systems. In *Natural, Intelligent and Effective Interaction in Multimodal Dialogue Systems*. Kluwer, 2003.
4. P. Doherty, J. Kachniarz, and A. Szałas. Using contextually closed queries for local closed-world reasoning in rough knowledge databases. In *[23]*. 2002.
5. P. Doherty and J. Kvarnström. TALplanner: An empirical investigation of a temporal logic-based forward chaining planner. In *Proceedings of the 6th International Workshop on Temporal Representation and Reasoning (TIME'99)*, 1999.
6. P. Doherty and J. Kvarnström. TALplanner: A temporal logic based forward chaining planner. *Annals of Mathematics and Artificial Intelligence*, 30:119–169, 2001.
7. P. Doherty and J. Kvarnström. TALplanner: A temporal logic based planner. *Artificial Intelligence Magazine*, Fall Issue 2001.
8. P. Doherty, W. Łukaszewicz, A. Skowron, and A. Szałas. Combining rough and crisp knowledge in deductive databases. In *[23]*. 2003.
9. P. Doherty, W. Łukaszewicz, and A. Szałas. Computing strongest necessary and weakest sufficient conditions of first-order formulas. *International Joint Conference on AI (IJCAI'2001)*, pages 145–151, 2000.
10. P. Doherty, W. Łukaszewicz, and A. Szałas. Efficient reasoning using the local closed-world assumption. In A. Cerri and D. Dochev, editors, *Proc. 9th Int. Conference AIMSA 2000*, volume 1904 of *LNAI*, pages 49–58. Springer-Verlag, 2000.

11. P. Doherty, W. Łukaszewicz, and A Szałas. Cake: A computer-aided knowledge engineering technique. In F. van Harmelen, editor, *Proc. 15th European Conference on Artificial Intelligence, ECAI'2002*, pages 220–224, Amsterdam, 2002. IOS Press.
12. P. Doherty, W. Łukaszewicz, and A Szałas. On mutual understanding among communicating agents. In B. Dunin-Keplicz and R. Verbrugge, editors, *Proceedings of Workshop on Formal Approaches to Multi-agent Systems (FAMAS'03)*, pages 83–97, 2003.
13. P. Doherty, W. Łukaszewicz, and A. Szałas. Tolerance spaces and approximative representational structures. In *26th German Conference on Artificial Intelligence*. Springer-Verlag, 2003.
14. Patrick Doherty et al. The WITAS unmanned aerial vehicle project. In *Proc. 14th European Conference on Artificial Intelligence, ECAI'2000*, pages 220–224. Wiley, 2000.
15. Patrick Doherty et al. A distributed architecture for intelligent unmanned aerial vehicle experimentation (to appear). 2003.
16. Joakim Gustafsson and Jonas Kvarnström. Elaboration tolerance through object-orientation. *Artificial Intelligence*, 2003.
17. Beth-Ann Hockey, Oliver Lemon, Ellen Campana, Laura Hiatt, Gregory Aist, Jim Hieronymus, Alexander Gruenstein, and John Dowding. Targeted help for spoken dialogue systems: intelligent feedback improves naive users' performance. In *Proceedings of European Association for Computational Linguistics (EACL 03)*, pages 147–154, 2003.
18. J. Kvarnström, P. Doherty, and P. Haslum. Extending TALplanner with concurrency and resources. In *Proceedings of the 14th European Conference on Artificial Intelligence*, pages 501–505, 2000.
19. Jonas Kvarnström. Applying domain analysis techniques for domain-dependent control in tal-planner. In *Proceedings of the Sixth International Conference on Artificial Intelligence Planning and Scheduling (AIPS-2002)*, pages 147–154, 2002.
20. Oliver Lemon, Anne Bracy, Alexander Gruenstein, and Stanley Peters. Information states in a multi-modal dialogue system for human-robot conversation. In Peter Kühnlein, Hans Reiser, and Henk Zeevat, editors, *5th Workshop on Formal Semantics and Pragmatics of Dialogue (Bi-Dialog 2001)*, pages 57–67, 2001.
21. Oliver Lemon, Alexander Gruenstein, Randolph Gullett, Alexis Battle, Laura Hiatt, and Stanley Peters. Generation of collaborative spoken dialogue contributions in dynamic task environments. In *AAAI Spring Symposium on Natural Language Generation in Spoken and Written Dialogue*, Technical Report SS-03-07, Menlo Park, CA, 2003. AAAI Press.
22. Oliver Lemon, Alexander Gruenstein, and Stanley Peters. Collaborative activities and multi-tasking in dialogue systems. *Traitement Automatique des Langues (TAL)*, 43(2):131–154, 2002. Special Issue on Dialogue.
23. S.K. Pal, L. Polkowski, and A. Skowron, editors. *Rough-Neuro Computing: Techniques for Computing with Words*. Springer–Verlag, Heidelberg, 2003.
24. Erik Sandewall. *Features and Fluents*. Oxford University Press, 1994.
25. Erik Sandewall. Cognitive robotics logic and its metatheory: Features and fluents revisited. *Electronic Transactions on Artificial Intelligence*, 2:307–329, 1998.
26. Erik Sandewall. Use of cognitive robotics logic in a double helix architecture for autonomous systems. In M. Beetz, J. Hertzberg, M. Ghallab, and M. Pollack, editors, *Plan-based Control of Robotic Agents*. Springer, 2002.
27. Erik Sandewall. What's in a decision. 2002. Submitted for publication.

The Instance Problem and the Most Specific Concept in the Description Logic $\mathcal{EL}$ w.r.t. Terminological Cycles with Descriptive Semantics

Franz Baader*

Theoretical Computer Science, TU Dresden, D-01062 Dresden, Germany
baader@inf.tu-dresden.de

Abstract. Previously, we have investigated both standard and non-standard inferences in the presence of terminological cycles for the description logic $\mathcal{EL}$, which allows for conjunctions, existential restrictions, and the top concept. The present paper is concerned with two problems left open by this previous work, namely the instance problem and the problem of computing most specific concepts w.r.t. descriptive semantics, which is the usual first-order semantics for description logics. We will show that—like subsumption—the instance problem is polynomial in this context. Similar to the case of the least common subsumer, the most specific concept w.r.t. descriptive semantics need not exist, but we are able to characterize the cases in which it exists and give a decidable sufficient condition for the existence of the most specific concept. Under this condition, it can be computed in polynomial time.

1 Introduction

Early description logic (DL) systems allowed the use of value restrictions ($\forall r.C$), but not of existential restrictions ($\exists r.C$). Thus, one could express that all children are male using the value restriction ∀child.Male, but not that someone has a son using the existential restriction ∃child.Male. The main reason was that, when clarifying the logical status of property arcs in semantic networks and slots in frames, the decision was taken that arcs/slots should be read as value restrictions (see, e.g., [12]). Once one considers more expressive DLs allowing for full negation, existential restrictions come in as the dual of value restrictions [14]. Thus, for historical reasons, DLs that allow for existential, but not for value restrictions, were until recently mostly unexplored.

The recent interest in such DLs has at least two reasons. On the one hand, there are indeed applications where DLs without value restrictions appear to be sufficient. For example, SNOMED, the Systematized Nomenclature of Medicine [16,15] employs the DL $\mathcal{EL}$, which allows for conjunctions, existential restrictions, and the top concept. On the other hand, non-standard inferences in DLs [11],

---

* Partially supported by the DFG under grant BA 1122/4-3.

A. Günter et al. (Eds.): KI 2003, LNAI 2821, pp. 64–78, 2003.

like computing the least common subsumer, often make sense only for DLs that do not allow for full negation. Thus, the decision of whether to use DLs with value restrictions or with existential restrictions becomes again relevant.

Non-standard inferences were introduced to support building and maintaining large DL knowledge bases. For example, computing the most specific concept of an individual and the least common subsumer of concepts can be used in the bottom-up construction of description logic knowledge bases. Instead of defining the relevant concepts of an application domain from scratch, this methodology allows the user to give typical examples of individuals belonging to the concept to be defined. These individuals are then generalized to a concept by first computing the most specific concept of each individual (i.e., the least concept description in the available description language that has this individual as an instance), and then computing the least common subsumer of these concepts (i.e., the least concept description in the available description language that subsumes all these concepts). The knowledge engineer can then use the computed concept as a starting point for the concept definition.

The most specific concept (msc) of a given ABox individual need not exist in languages allowing for existential restrictions or number restrictions. For the DL $\mathcal{ALN}$ (which allows for conjunctions, value restrictions, and number restrictions), it was shown in [6] that the most specific concept always exists if one adds cyclic concept definitions with greatest fixpoint semantics. If one wants to use this approach for the bottom-up construction of knowledge bases, then one must also be able to solve the standard inferences (the subsumption and the instance problem) and to compute the least common subsumer in the presence of cyclic concept definitions. Thus, in order to adapt the approach also to the DL $\mathcal{EL}$, the impact on both standard and non-standard inferences of cyclic definitions in this DL had to be investigated first.

The paper [5] considers cyclic terminologies in $\mathcal{EL}$ w.r.t. the three types of semantics (greatest fixpoint, least fixpoint, and descriptive semantics) introduced by Nebel [13], and shows that the subsumption problem can be decided in polynomial time in all three cases. This is in strong contrast to the case of DLs with value restrictions. Even for the small DL $\mathcal{FL}_0$ (which allows for conjunctions and value restrictions only), adding cyclic terminologies increases the complexity of the subsumption problem from polynomial (for concept descriptions) to PSPACE [1]. The main tool in the investigation of cyclic definitions in $\mathcal{EL}$ is a characterization of subsumption through the existence of so-called simulation relations, which can be computed in polynomial time [9]. The results in [5] also show that cyclic definitions with least fixpoint semantics are not interesting in $\mathcal{EL}$. For this reason, all the extensions of these results mentioned below are concerned with greatest fixpoint (gfp) and descriptive semantics only.

The characterization of subsumption in $\mathcal{EL}$ w.r.t. gfp-semantics through the existence of certain simulation relations on the graph associated with the terminology is used in [4] to characterize the least common subsumer via the product of this graph with itself. This shows that, w.r.t. gfp semantics, the lcs always exists, and the binary lcs can be computed in polynomial time. (The n-ary lcs may grow exponentially even in $\mathcal{EL}$ without cyclic terminologies [7].) For cyclic terminologies in $\mathcal{EL}$ with descriptive semantics, the lcs need not exist. In [2], possible candidates P_k $(k \geq 0)$ for the lcs are introduced, and it is shown that the lcs exists iff one of these candidates is the lcs. In addition, a sufficient condition for the existence of the lcs is given, and it is shown that, under this condition, the lcs can be computed in polynomial time.

In [4], the characterization of subsumption w.r.t. gfp-semantics is also extended to the instance problem in $\mathcal{EL}$. This is then used to show that, w.r.t. gfp-semantics, the instance problem in $\mathcal{EL}$ can be decided in polynomial time and that the msc in $\mathcal{EL}$ always exists, and can be computed in polynomial time.

Given the positive results for gfp-semantics regarding both standard inferences (subsumption and instance) and non-standard inferences (lcs and msc), one might be tempted to restrict the attention to gfp-semantics. However, existing DL systems like FaCT [10] and RACER [8] allow for terminological cycles (even more general inclusion axioms), but employ descriptive semantics. In some cases it may be desirable to use a semantics that is consistent with the one employed by these systems even if one works with a DL that is considerably less expressive than then one available in them. For example, non-standard inferences that support building DL knowledge bases are often restricted to rather inexpressive DLs (either because they do not make sense for more expressive DLs or because they can currently only be handled for such DLs). Nevertheless, it may be desirable that the result of these inferences (like the msc or the lcs) is again in a format that is accepted by systems like FaCT and RACER. This is not the case if the msc algorithm produces a cyclic terminology that must be interpreted with gfp-semantics.

The subsumption problem and the problem of computing least common subsumers in $\mathcal{EL}$ w.r.t cyclic terminologies with descriptive semantics have already been tackled in [5] and [2], respectively. In the present paper we address the instance problem and the problem of computing the most specific concept in this setting. We will show that the instance problem is polynomial also in this context. Unfortunately, the most specific concept w.r.t descriptive semantics need not exist, but—similar to the case of the least common subsumer—we are able to characterize the cases in which it exists and give a decidable sufficient condition for the existence of the most specific concept. Under this condition, it can be computed in polynomial time.

2   Cyclic Terminologies and Most Specific Concepts in $\mathcal{EL}$

Concept descriptions are inductively defined with the help of a set of *constructors*, starting with a set N_C of *concept names* and a set N_R of *role names*. The constructors determine the expressive power of the DL. In this paper, we restrict the attention to the DL $\mathcal{EL}$, whose concept descriptions are formed using the constructors top-concept ($\top$), conjunction ($C \sqcap D$), and existential restriction ($\exists r.C$). The semantics of $\mathcal{EL}$-concept descriptions is defined in terms of an *interpretation* $\mathcal{I} = (\Delta^{\mathcal{I}}, \cdot^{\mathcal{I}})$. The domain $\Delta^{\mathcal{I}}$ of $\mathcal{I}$ is a non-empty set of individuals

Table 1. Syntax and semantics of $\mathcal{EL}$

name of constructor	Syntax	Semantics
concept name $A \in N_C$	A	$A^{\mathcal{I}} \subseteq \Delta^{\mathcal{I}}$
role name $r \in N_R$	r	$r^{\mathcal{I}} \subseteq \Delta^{\mathcal{I}} \times \Delta^{\mathcal{I}}$
top-concept	$\top$	$\Delta^{\mathcal{I}}$
conjunction	$C \sqcap D$	$C^{\mathcal{I}} \cap D^{\mathcal{I}}$
existential restriction	$\exists r.C$	$\{x \in \Delta^{\mathcal{I}} \mid \exists y : (x,y) \in r^{\mathcal{I}} \wedge y \in C^{\mathcal{I}}\}$
concept definition	$A \equiv D$	$A^{\mathcal{I}} = D^{\mathcal{I}}$
individual name $a \in N_I$	a	$a^{\mathcal{I}} \in \Delta^{\mathcal{I}}$
concept assertion	$A(a)$	$a^{\mathcal{I}} \in A^{\mathcal{I}}$
role assertion	$r(a,b)$	$(a^{\mathcal{I}}, b^{\mathcal{I}}) \in r^{\mathcal{I}}$

and the interpretation function $\cdot^{\mathcal{I}}$ maps each concept name $A \in N_C$ to a subset $A^{\mathcal{I}}$ of $\Delta^{\mathcal{I}}$ and each role $r \in N_R$ to a binary relation $r^{\mathcal{I}}$ on $\Delta^{\mathcal{I}}$. The extension of $\cdot^{\mathcal{I}}$ to arbitrary concept descriptions is inductively defined, as shown in the third column of Table 1.

A *terminology* (or *TBox* for short) is a finite set of concept definitions of the form $A \equiv D$, where A is a concept name and D a concept description. In addition, we require that TBoxes do not contain *multiple definitions*, i.e., there cannot be two distinct concept descriptions D_1 and D_2 such that both $A \equiv D_1$ and $A \equiv D_2$ belongs to the TBox. Concept names occurring on the left-hand side of a definition are called *defined concepts*. All other concept names occurring in the TBox are called *primitive concepts*. Note that we allow for cyclic dependencies between the defined concepts, i.e., the definition of A may refer (directly or indirectly) to A itself. An interpretation $\mathcal{I}$ is a model of the TBox $\mathcal{T}$ iff it satisfies all its concept definitions, i.e., $A^{\mathcal{I}} = D^{\mathcal{I}}$ for all definitions $A \equiv D$ in $\mathcal{T}$.

An *ABox* is a finite set of assertions of the form $A(a)$ and $r(a,b)$, where A is a concept name, r is a role name, and a, b are individual names from a set N_I. Interpretations of ABoxes must additionally map each individual name $a \in N_I$ to an element $a^{\mathcal{I}}$ of $\Delta^{\mathcal{I}}$. An interpretation $\mathcal{I}$ is a model of the ABox $\mathcal{A}$ iff it satisfies all its assertions, i.e., $a^{\mathcal{I}} \in A^{\mathcal{I}}$ for all concept assertions $A(a)$ in $\mathcal{A}$ and $(a^{\mathcal{I}}, b^{\mathcal{I}}) \in r^{\mathcal{I}}$ for all role assertions $r(a,b)$ in $\mathcal{A}$. The interpretation $\mathcal{I}$ is a model of the ABox $\mathcal{A}$ together with the TBox $\mathcal{T}$ iff it is a model of both $\mathcal{T}$ and $\mathcal{A}$.

The semantics of (possibly cyclic) $\mathcal{EL}$-TBoxes we have defined above is called *descriptive semantic* by Nebel [13]. For some applications, it is more appropriate to interpret cyclic concept definitions with the help of an appropriate fixpoint semantics. However, in this paper we restrict our attention to descriptive semantics (see [5,4] for definitions and results concerning cyclic terminologies in $\mathcal{EL}$ with fixpoint semantics).

Definition 1. *Let $\mathcal{T}$ be an $\mathcal{EL}$-TBox and $\mathcal{A}$ an $\mathcal{EL}$-ABox, let C, D be concept descriptions (possibly containing defined concepts of $\mathcal{T}$), and a an individual name occurring in $\mathcal{A}$. Then,*

- C *is subsumed by* D *w.r.t. descriptive semantics* $(C \sqsubseteq_{\mathcal{T}} D)$ *iff* $C^{\mathcal{I}} \subseteq D^{\mathcal{I}}$
  holds for all models $\mathcal{I}$ *of* $\mathcal{T}$.
- a *is an instance of* C *w.r.t. descriptive semantics* $(\mathcal{A} \models_{\mathcal{T}} C(a))$ *iff* $a^{\mathcal{I}} \in C^{\mathcal{I}}$
  holds for all models $\mathcal{I}$ *of* $\mathcal{T}$ *together with* $\mathcal{A}$.

On the level of concept descriptions, the most specific concept of a given ABox individual a is the least concept description E (of the DL under consideration) that has a as an instance. An extensions of this definition to the level of (possibly cyclic) TBoxes is not completely trivial. In fact, assume that a is an individual in the ABox $\mathcal{A}$ and that $\mathcal{T}$ is a TBox. It should be obvious that taking as the msc of a the least defined concept A in $\mathcal{T}$ such that $\mathcal{A} \models_{\mathcal{T}} A(a)$ is too weak since the lcs would then strongly depend on the defined concepts that are already present in $\mathcal{T}$. However, a second approach (which might look like the obvious generalization of the definition of the msc in the case of concept descriptions) is also not quite satisfactory. We could say that the msc of a is the least concept description C (possibly using defined concepts of $\mathcal{T}$) such that $\mathcal{A} \models_{\mathcal{T}} C(a)$. The problem is that this definition does not allow us to use the expressive power of cyclic definitions when constructing the msc.

To avoid this problem, we allow the original TBox to be extended by new definitions when constructing the msc. We say that the TBox $\mathcal{T}_2$ is a *conservative extension* of the TBox $\mathcal{T}_1$ iff $\mathcal{T}_1 \subseteq \mathcal{T}_2$ and $\mathcal{T}_1$ and $\mathcal{T}_2$ have the same primitive concepts and roles. Thus, $\mathcal{T}_2$ may contain new definitions $A \equiv D$, but then D does not introduce new primitive concepts and roles (i.e., all of them already occur in $\mathcal{T}_1$), and A is a new concept name (i.e., A does not occur in $\mathcal{T}_1$). The name "conservative extension" is justified by the fact that the new definitions in $\mathcal{T}_2$ do not influence the subsumption relationships between defined concepts in $\mathcal{T}_1$ (see [4] for details).

Definition 2. *Let* $\mathcal{T}_1$ *be an* $\mathcal{EL}$*-TBox and* $\mathcal{A}$ *an* $\mathcal{EL}$*-ABox containing the individual name* a, *and let* $\mathcal{T}_2$ *be a conservative extension of* $\mathcal{T}_1$ *containing the defined concept* E.[1] *Then* E *in* $\mathcal{T}_2$ *is a* most specific concept *of* a *in* $\mathcal{A}$ *and* $\mathcal{T}_1$ *w.r.t. descriptive semantics* (msc) *iff the following two conditions are satisfied:*

1. $\mathcal{A} \models_{\mathcal{T}_2} E(a)$.
2. *If* $\mathcal{T}_3$ *is a conservative extension of* $\mathcal{T}_2$ *and* F *a defined concept in* $\mathcal{T}_3$ *such that* $\mathcal{A} \models_{\mathcal{T}_3} F(a)$, *then* $E \sqsubseteq_{\mathcal{T}_3} F$.

In the case of concept descriptions, the msc is unique up to equivalence. In the presence of (possibly cyclic) TBoxes, this uniqueness property also holds, though its formulation is more complicated (see [4] for details).

---

[1] Without loss of generality we assume that the msc is given by a defined concept rather than a concept description since one can always introduce an appropriate definition for the description. For the same reason, we can in the following restrict the instance problem and the subsumption problem to defined concepts.

3   Characterizing Subsumption in Cyclic $\mathcal{EL}$-TBoxes

In this section, we recall the characterizations of subsumption w.r.t. descriptive semantics developed in [5]. To this purpose, we must represent TBoxes by description graphs, and introduce the notion of a simulation on description graphs. Before we can translate $\mathcal{EL}$-TBoxes into description graphs, we must normalize the TBoxes. In the following, let $\mathcal{T}$ be an $\mathcal{EL}$-TBox, N_{def} the defined concepts of $\mathcal{T}$, N_{prim} the primitive concepts of $\mathcal{T}$, and N_{role} the roles of $\mathcal{T}$. We say that the $\mathcal{EL}$-TBox $\mathcal{T}$ is *normalized* iff $A \equiv D \in \mathcal{T}$ implies that D is of the form

$$P_1 \sqcap \ldots \sqcap P_m \sqcap \exists r_1.B_1 \sqcap \ldots \sqcap \exists r_\ell.B_\ell,$$

for $m, \ell \geq 0$, $P_1, \ldots, P_m \in N_{prim}$, $r_1, \ldots, r_\ell \in N_{role}$, and $B_1, \ldots, B_\ell \in N_{def}$. If $m = \ell = 0$, then $D = \top$.

As shown in [5], one can (without loss of generality) restrict the attention to normalized TBox. In the following, we thus assume that all TBoxes are normalized. Normalized $\mathcal{EL}$-TBoxes can be viewed as graphs whose nodes are the defined concepts, which are labeled by sets of primitive concepts, and whose edges are given by the existential restrictions. For the rest of this section, we fix a normalized $\mathcal{EL}$-TBox $\mathcal{T}$ with primitive concepts N_{prim}, defined concepts N_{def}, and roles N_{role}.

Definition 3. *An $\mathcal{EL}$-description graph is a graph $\mathcal{G} = (V, E, L)$ where*

- *V is a set of nodes;*
- *$E \subseteq V \times N_{role} \times V$ is a set of edges labeled by role names;*
- *$L\colon V \to 2^{N_{prim}}$ is a function that labels nodes with sets of primitive concepts.*

The normalized TBox $\mathcal{T}$ can be translated into the following $\mathcal{EL}$-description graph $\mathcal{G}_{\mathcal{T}} = (N_{def}, E_{\mathcal{T}}, L_{\mathcal{T}})$:

- *the nodes of $\mathcal{G}_{\mathcal{T}}$ are the defined concepts of $\mathcal{T}$;*
- *if A is a defined concept and $A \equiv P_1 \sqcap \ldots \sqcap P_m \sqcap \exists r_1.B_1 \sqcap \ldots \sqcap \exists r_\ell.B_\ell$ its definition in $\mathcal{T}$, then*
  - *$L_{\mathcal{T}}(A) = \{P_1, \ldots, P_m\}$, and*
  - *A is the source of the edges $(A, r_1, B_1), \ldots, (A, r_\ell, B_\ell) \in E_{\mathcal{T}}$.*

Simulations are binary relations between nodes of two $\mathcal{EL}$-description graphs that respect labels and edges in the sense defined below.

Definition 4. *Let $\mathcal{G}_i = (V_i, E_i, L_i)$ $(i = 1, 2)$ be two $\mathcal{EL}$-description graphs. The binary relation $Z \subseteq V_1 \times V_2$ is a simulation from $\mathcal{G}_1$ to $\mathcal{G}_2$ iff*

(S1) *$(v_1, v_2) \in Z$ implies $L_1(v_1) \subseteq L_2(v_2)$; and*

(S2) *if $(v_1, v_2) \in Z$ and $(v_1, r, v_1') \in E_1$, then there exists a node $v_2' \in V_2$ such that $(v_1', v_2') \in Z$ and $(v_2, r, v_2') \in E_2$.*

We write $Z\colon \mathcal{G}_1 \overset{\rightarrow}{\sim} \mathcal{G}_2$ to express that Z is a simulation from $\mathcal{G}_1$ to $\mathcal{G}_2$.

$$B = B_0 \overset{r_1}{\to} B_1 \overset{r_2}{\to} B_2 \overset{r_3}{\to} B_3 \overset{r_4}{\to} \cdots$$
$$Z\downarrow \quad Z\downarrow \quad Z\downarrow \quad Z\downarrow$$
$$A = A_0 \overset{r_1}{\to} A_1 \overset{r_2}{\to} A_2 \overset{r_3}{\to} A_3 \overset{r_4}{\to} \cdots$$

Fig. 1. A (B, A)-simulation chain.

$$B = B_0 \overset{r_1}{\to} B_1 \overset{r_2}{\to} \cdots \overset{r_{n-1}}{\to} B_{n-1} \overset{r_n}{\to} B_n$$
$$Z\downarrow \quad Z\downarrow \qquad\qquad Z\downarrow$$
$$A = A_0 \overset{r_1}{\to} A_1 \overset{r_2}{\to} \cdots \overset{r_{n-1}}{\to} A_{n-1}$$

Fig. 2. A partial (B, A)-simulation chain.

W.r.t. gfp-semantics, A is subsumed by B iff there is a simulation $Z: \mathcal{G}_T \overset{\sim}{\to} \mathcal{G}_T$ such that $(B, A) \in Z$ (see [5]). W.r.t. descriptive semantics, the simulation Z must satisfy some additional properties for this equivalence to hold. To define these properties, we must introduce some notation.

Definition 5. *The path p_1: $B = B_0 \overset{r_1}{\to} B_1 \overset{r_2}{\to} B_2 \overset{r_3}{\to} B_3 \overset{r_4}{\to} \cdots$ in $\mathcal{G}_T$ is Z-simulated by the path p_2: $A = A_0 \overset{r_1}{\to} A_1 \overset{r_2}{\to} A_2 \overset{r_3}{\to} A_3 \overset{r_4}{\to} \cdots$ in $\mathcal{G}_T$ iff $(B_i, A_i) \in Z$ for all $i \geq 0$. In this case we say that the pair (p_1, p_2) is a (B, A)-simulation chain w.r.t. Z (see Figure 1).*

If $(B, A) \in Z$, then (S2) of Definition 4 implies that, for every infinite path p_1 starting with $B_0 := B$, there is an infinite path p_2 starting with $A_0 := A$ such that p_1 is Z-simulated by p_2. In the following we construct such a simulating path step by step. The main point is, however, that the decision which concept A_n to take in step n should depend only on the partial (B, A)-simulation chain already constructed, and *not* on the parts of the path p_1 not yet considered.

Definition 6. *A partial (B, A)-simulation chain is of the form depicted in Figure 2. A selection function S for A, B and Z assigns to each partial (B, A)-simulation chain of this form a defined concept A_n such that (A_{n-1}, r_n, A_n) is an edge in $\mathcal{G}_T$ and $(B_n, A_n) \in Z$. Given a path $B = B_0 \overset{r_1}{\to} B_1 \overset{r_2}{\to} B_2 \overset{r_3}{\to} B_3 \overset{r_4}{\to} \cdots$ and a defined concept A such that $(B, A) \in Z$, one can use a selection function S for A, B and Z to construct a Z-simulating path. In this case we say that the resulting (B, A)-simulation chain is S-selected.*

Definition 7. *Let A, B be defined concepts in T, and $Z: \mathcal{G}_T \overset{\sim}{\to} \mathcal{G}_T$ a simulation with $(B, A) \in Z$. Then Z is called (B, A)-synchronized iff there exists a selection function S for A, B and Z such that the following holds: for every infinite S-selected (B, A)-simulation chain of the form depicted in Figure 1 there exists an $i \geq 0$ such that $A_i = B_i$.*

We are now ready to state the characterization of subsumption w.r.t. descriptive semantics from [5].

Theorem 1. *Let $\mathcal{T}$ be an $\mathcal{EL}$-TBox, and A, B defined concepts in $\mathcal{T}$. Then the following are equivalent:*

1. *$A \sqsubseteq_{\mathcal{T}} B$.*
2. *There is a (B, A)-synchronized simulation $Z \colon \mathcal{G}_{\mathcal{T}} \overset{\rightharpoonup}{\sim} \mathcal{G}_{\mathcal{T}}$ such that $(B, A) \in Z$.*

In [5] it is also shown that, for a given $\mathcal{EL}$-TBox $\mathcal{T}$ and defined concepts A, B in $\mathcal{T}$, the existence of a (B, A)-synchronized simulation $Z \colon \mathcal{G}_{\mathcal{T}} \overset{\rightharpoonup}{\sim} \mathcal{G}_{\mathcal{T}}$ with $(B, A) \in Z$ can be decided in polynomial time, which shows that the subsumption w.r.t. descriptive semantics in $\mathcal{EL}$ is tractable.

4   The Instance Problem

Assume that $\mathcal{T}$ is an $\mathcal{EL}$-TBox and $\mathcal{A}$ an $\mathcal{EL}$-ABox. In the following, we assume that $\mathcal{T}$ is fixed and that all instance problems for $\mathcal{A}$ are considered w.r.t. this TBox. In this setting, $\mathcal{A}$ can be translated into an $\mathcal{EL}$-description graph $\mathcal{G}_{\mathcal{A}}$ by viewing $\mathcal{A}$ as a graph and extending it appropriately by the graph $\mathcal{G}_{\mathcal{T}}$ associated with $\mathcal{T}$. The idea is then that the characterization of the instance problem should be similar to the statement of Theorem 1: the individual a is an instance of A in $\mathcal{A}$ and $\mathcal{T}$ iff there is an (A, a)-synchronized simulation $Z \colon \mathcal{G}_{\mathcal{T}} \overset{\rightharpoonup}{\sim} \mathcal{G}_{\mathcal{A}}$ such that $(A, a) \in Z$.[2] The formal definition of the $\mathcal{EL}$-description graph $\mathcal{G}_{\mathcal{A}}$ associated with the ABox $\mathcal{A}$ and the TBox $\mathcal{T}$ given below was also used in [4] to characterize the instance problem in $\mathcal{EL}$ w.r.t. gfp-semantics.

Definition 8. *Let $\mathcal{T}$ be an $\mathcal{EL}$-TBox, $\mathcal{A}$ an $\mathcal{EL}$-ABox, and $\mathcal{G}_{\mathcal{T}} = (V_{\mathcal{T}}, E_{\mathcal{T}}, L_{\mathcal{T}})$ be the $\mathcal{EL}$-description graph associated with $\mathcal{T}$. The $\mathcal{EL}$-description graph $\mathcal{G}_{\mathcal{A}} = (V_{\mathcal{A}}, E_{\mathcal{A}}, L_{\mathcal{A}})$ associated with $\mathcal{A}$ and $\mathcal{T}$ is defined as follows:*

- *the nodes of $\mathcal{G}_{\mathcal{A}}$ are the individual names occurring in $\mathcal{A}$ together with the defined concepts of $\mathcal{T}$, i.e.,*

$$V_{\mathcal{A}} := V_{\mathcal{T}} \cup \{a \mid a \text{ is an individual name occurring in } \mathcal{A}\};$$

- *the edges of $\mathcal{G}_{\mathcal{A}}$ are the edges of $\mathcal{G}$, the role assertions of $\mathcal{A}$, and additional edges linking the ABox individuals with defined concepts:*

$$E_{\mathcal{A}} := E_{\mathcal{T}} \cup \{(a, r, b) \mid r(a, b) \in \mathcal{A}\} \;\cup$$
$$\{(a, r, B) \mid A(a) \in \mathcal{A} \text{ and } (A, r, B) \in E_{\mathcal{T}}\};$$

- *if $u \in V_{\mathcal{A}}$ is a defined concept, then it inherits its label from $\mathcal{G}_{\mathcal{T}}$, i.e.,*

$$L_{\mathcal{A}}(u) := L_{\mathcal{T}}(u) \quad \text{if } u \in V_{\mathcal{T}};$$

otherwise, u is an ABox individual, and then its label is derived from the concept assertions for u in $\mathcal{A}$. In the following, let P denote primitive and A denote defined concepts.

$$L_{\mathcal{A}}(u) := \{P \mid P(u) \in \mathcal{A}\} \cup \bigcup_{A(u) \in \mathcal{A}} L_{\mathcal{T}}(A) \quad \text{if } u \in V_{\mathcal{A}} \setminus V_{\mathcal{T}}.$$

---

[2] The actual characterization of the instance problem turns out to be somewhat more complex, but for the moment the above is sufficient to gives the right intuition.

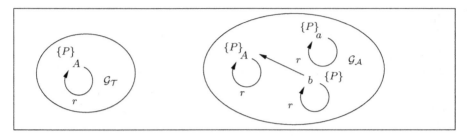

Fig. 3. The $\mathcal{EL}$-description graphs $\mathcal{G}_{\mathcal{T}}$ and $\mathcal{G}_{\mathcal{A}}$ of the example.

We are now ready to formulate our characterization of the instance problem w.r.t. descriptive semantics (see [3] for the proof).

Theorem 2. *Let $\mathcal{T}$ be an $\mathcal{EL}$-TBox, $\mathcal{A}$ an $\mathcal{EL}$-ABox, A a defined concept in $\mathcal{T}$ and a an individual name occurring in $\mathcal{A}$. Then the following are equivalent:*

1. *$\mathcal{A} \models_{\mathcal{T}} A(a)$.*
2. *There is a simulation $Z: \mathcal{G}_{\mathcal{T}} \overset{\rightharpoonup}{\sim} \mathcal{G}_{\mathcal{A}}$ such that*
   - *$(A, a) \in Z$.*
   - *Z is (B, u)-synchronized for all $(B, u) \in Z$.*

As an example, we consider the following TBox and ABox:

$$\mathcal{T} := \{A \equiv P \sqcap \exists r.A\} \text{ and } \mathcal{A} := \{P(a), r(a, a), A(b), r(b, b)\}.$$

It is easy to see that there is no simulation satisfy the conditions of Theorem 2 for A and a. In contrast, the simulation $Z := \{(A, A), (A, b)\}$ satisfies these conditions for A and b (see also Figure 3).

Since the existence of a synchronized simulation relation satisfying the conditions stated in (2) of Theorem 2 can be decided in polynomial time (see [3]), the instance problem w.r.t. descriptive semantics is tractable.

Corollary 1. *The instance problem w.r.t. descriptive semantics in $\mathcal{EL}$ can be decided in polynomial time.*

5   The Most Specific Concept

In this section, we will first show that the most specific concept w.r.t. descriptive semantics need not exist. Then, we will show that the most specific concept w.r.t. gfp-semantics (see [4]) coincides with the most specific concept w.r.t. descriptive semantics iff the ABox satisfies a certain acyclicity condition. This yields a sufficient condition for the existence of the msc, which is, however, not a necessary one. We will then characterize the cases in which the msc exists. Unfortunately, it is not yet clear how to turn this characterization into a decision procedure for the existence of the msc.

5.1   The msc Need Not Exist

Theorem 3. *Let* $\mathcal{T}_1 = \emptyset$ *and* $\mathcal{A} = \{r(b,b)\}$. *Then* b *does not have an msc in* $\mathcal{A}$ *and* $\mathcal{T}_1$.

Proof. Assume to the contrary that $\mathcal{T}_2$ is a conservative extension of $\mathcal{T}_1$ such that the defined concept E in $\mathcal{T}_2$ is an msc of b. Let $\mathcal{G}_\mathcal{A}$ be the $\mathcal{EL}$-description graph corresponding to $\mathcal{A}$ and $\mathcal{T}_2$, as introduced in Definition 8. Since b is an instance of E, there is a simulation $Z: \mathcal{G}_{\mathcal{T}_2} \stackrel{\rightarrow}{\sim} \mathcal{G}_\mathcal{A}$ such that $(E,b) \in Z$ and Z is (B,u)-synchronized for all $(B,u) \in Z$.

Since $\mathcal{T}_1 = \emptyset$, there is no edge in $\mathcal{G}_\mathcal{A}$ from b to a defined concept in $\mathcal{T}_2$. Thus, the fact that Z is (E,b)-synchronized implies that there cannot be an infinite path in $G_{\mathcal{T}_2}$ (and thus $\mathcal{G}_\mathcal{A}$) starting with E. Consequently, there is an upper-bound n_0 on the length of the paths in $G_{\mathcal{T}_2}$ (and thus $\mathcal{G}_\mathcal{A}$) starting with E. Now, consider the TBox $\mathcal{T}_3 = \{F_n \equiv \exists r.F_{n-1}, \dots, F_1 \equiv \exists r.F_0, F_0 \equiv \top\}$. It is easy to see that $\mathcal{T}_3$ is a conservative extension of $\mathcal{T}_2$ (where we assume without loss of generality that $F_0, \dots, F_n$ are concept names not occurring in $\mathcal{T}_2$) and that $\mathcal{A} \models_{\mathcal{T}_3} F_n(b)$. Since E is an msc of b, this implies that $E \sqsubseteq_{\mathcal{T}_3} F_n$. Thus, there is an (F_n, E)-synchronized simulation $Y: \mathcal{G}_{\mathcal{T}_3} \stackrel{\rightarrow}{\sim} \mathcal{G}_{\mathcal{T}_3}$ such that $(F_n, E) \in Y$. However, for $n > n_0$, the path

$$F_n \xrightarrow{r} F_{n-1} \xrightarrow{r} \cdots \xrightarrow{r} F_0$$

cannot be simulated by a path starting from E. $\square$

5.2   A Sufficient Condition for the Existence of the msc

Let $\mathcal{T}_1$ be an $\mathcal{EL}$-TBox and $\mathcal{A}$ an $\mathcal{EL}$-ABox containing the individual name a. Let $\mathcal{G}_\mathcal{A} = (V_\mathcal{A}, E_\mathcal{A}, L_\mathcal{A})$ be the $\mathcal{EL}$-description graph corresponding to $\mathcal{A}$ and $\mathcal{T}_1$, as introduced in Definition 8. We can view $\mathcal{G}_\mathcal{A}$ as the $\mathcal{EL}$-description graph of an $\mathcal{EL}$-TBox $\mathcal{T}_2$, i.e., let $\mathcal{T}_2$ be the TBox such that $\mathcal{G}_\mathcal{A} = \mathcal{G}_{\mathcal{T}_2}$. It is easy to see that $\mathcal{T}_2$ is a conservative extension of $\mathcal{T}_1$. By the definition of $\mathcal{G}_\mathcal{A}$, the defined concepts of $\mathcal{T}_2$ are the defined concepts of $\mathcal{T}_1$ together with the individual names occurring in $\mathcal{A}$. To avoid confusion we will denote the defined concept in $\mathcal{T}_2$ corresponding to the individual name b in $\mathcal{A}$ by C_b.

In [4] it is shown that, w.r.t. gfp-semantics, the defined concept C_a in $\mathcal{T}_2$ is the most specific concept of a in $\mathcal{A}$ and $\mathcal{T}_1$. W.r.t. descriptive semantics, this is only true if $\mathcal{A}$ does not contain a cycle that is reachable from a.

Definition 9. *The ABox* $\mathcal{A}$ *is called* a-acyclic *iff there are no* $n \geq 1$ *and individuals* $a_0, a_1, \dots, a_n$ *and roles* $r_1, \dots, r_n$ *such that*

- $a = a_0$,
- $r_i(a_{i-1}, a_i) \in \mathcal{A}$ *for* $1 \leq i \leq n$,
- *there is a* $j, 0 \leq j < n$ *such that* $a_j = a_n$.

Theorem 4. *Let* $\mathcal{T}_1, \mathcal{A}, a,$ *and* $\mathcal{T}_2$ *be defined as above. Then the following are equivalent:*

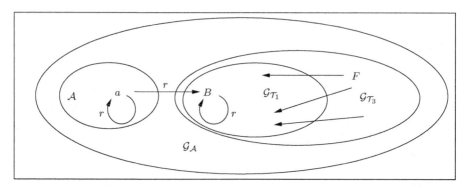

Fig. 4. The $\mathcal{EL}$-description graph $\mathcal{G}_\mathcal{A}$ in the proof of Proposition 1.

1. *The defined concept C_a in $\mathcal{T}_2$ is the msc of a in $\mathcal{A}$ and $\mathcal{T}_1$.*
2. *$\mathcal{A} \models_{\mathcal{T}_2} C_a(a)$.*
3. *$\mathcal{A}$ is a-acyclic.*

A proof of this theorem can be found in [3]. Given $\mathcal{T}$ and an a-acyclic ABox $\mathcal{A}$, the graph $\mathcal{G}_\mathcal{A}$ can obviously be computed in polynomial time, and thus the msc can in this case be computed in polynomial time.

Corollary 2. *Let $\mathcal{T}_1$ be an $\mathcal{EL}$-TBox and $\mathcal{A}$ an $\mathcal{EL}$-ABox containing the individual name a such that $\mathcal{A}$ is a-acyclic. Then the msc of a in $\mathcal{T}_1$ and $\mathcal{A}$ always exists, and it can be computed in polynomial time.*

The a-acyclicity of $\mathcal{A}$ is thus a sufficient condition for the existence of the msc. The following proposition states that this is not a necessary condition.

Proposition 1. *There exists an $\mathcal{EL}$-TBox $\mathcal{T}_1$ and an $\mathcal{EL}$-ABox $\mathcal{A}$ containing the individual name a such that the msc of a in $\mathcal{T}_1$ and $\mathcal{A}$ exists, even though $\mathcal{A}$ is not a-acyclic.*

Proof. Let $\mathcal{T}_1 = \{B \equiv \exists r.B\}$ and $\mathcal{A} = \{r(a,a), B(a)\}$. We show that B in $\mathcal{T}_1$ is the msc of a in $\mathcal{A}$ and $\mathcal{T}_1$. Since $\mathcal{A}$ is obviously not a-acyclic, this shows that a-acyclicity of $\mathcal{A}$ is not a necessary condition for the existence of the msc.

The instance relationship $\mathcal{A} \models_{\mathcal{T}_1} B(a)$ is trivially true since $B(a) \in \mathcal{A}$. Now, assume that $\mathcal{T}_3$ is a conservative extension of $\mathcal{T}_1$, and that the defined concept F in $\mathcal{T}_3$ satisfies $\mathcal{A} \models_{\mathcal{T}_3} F(a)$. Let $\mathcal{G}_\mathcal{A}$ be the $\mathcal{EL}$-description graph corresponding to $\mathcal{A}$ and $\mathcal{T}_3$, as introduced in Definition 8 (see Figure 4). Since $\mathcal{A} \models_{\mathcal{T}_3} F(a)$, there is a simulation $Z \colon \mathcal{G}_{\mathcal{T}_3} \overset{\rightarrow}{\sim} \mathcal{G}_\mathcal{A}$ such that $(F,a) \in Z$ and Z is (C,u)-synchronized for all $(C,u) \in Z$.

We must show that $B \sqsubseteq_{\mathcal{T}_3} F$, i.e., there is an (F,B)-synchronized simulation $Y \colon \mathcal{G}_{\mathcal{T}_3} \overset{\rightarrow}{\sim} \mathcal{G}_{\mathcal{T}_3}$ such that $(F,B) \in Y$. We define Y as follows:

$$Y := \{(u,v) \mid (u,v) \in Z \text{ and } v \text{ is a defined concept in } \mathcal{T}_3\} \cup$$
$$\{(u,B) \mid (u,a) \in Z\}.$$

Since $(F,a) \in Z$ we have $(F,B) \in Y$. Next, we show that Y is a simulation.

(S1) is trivially satisfied since $\mathcal{T}_1$ (and thus also $\mathcal{T}_3$) does not contain primitive concepts. Consequently, all node labels are empty.

(S2) Let $(u, v) \in Y$ and (u, r, v) be an edge in $\mathcal{G}_{\mathcal{T}_3}$.[3]

First, assume that v is a defined concept in $\mathcal{T}_3$ and $(u, v) \in Z$. Since Z is a simulation, there exists a node v' in $\mathcal{G}_{\mathcal{A}}$ such that (v, r, v') is an edge in $\mathcal{G}_{\mathcal{A}}$ and $(u', v') \in Z$. By the definition of $\mathcal{G}_{\mathcal{A}}$, this implies that also v' is a defined concept in $\mathcal{T}_3$, and thus (v, r, v') is an edge in $\mathcal{G}_{\mathcal{T}_3}$ and $(u', v') \in Y$.

Second, assume that $v = B$ and $(u, a) \in Z$. Since Z is a simulation, there exists a node v' in $\mathcal{G}_{\mathcal{A}}$ such that (a, r, v') is an edge in $\mathcal{G}_{\mathcal{A}}$ and $(u', v') \in Z$. Since there are only two edges with source a in $\mathcal{G}_{\mathcal{A}}$, we know that $v' = a$ or $v' = B$. If $v' = B$, then v' is a defined concept in $\mathcal{T}_3$, and thus (v, r, v') is an edge in $\mathcal{G}_{\mathcal{T}_3}$ and $(u', v') \in Y$. If $v' = a$, then (B, r, B) is an edge in $\mathcal{G}_{\mathcal{T}_3}$ and $(u', a) \in Z$ yields $(u', B) \in Y$.

Thus, we have shown that Y is indeed a simulation from $\mathcal{G}_{\mathcal{T}_3}$ to $\mathcal{G}_{\mathcal{T}_3}$. It remains to be shown that it is (F, B)-synchronized. Since (B, r, B) is the only edge in $\mathcal{G}_{\mathcal{T}_3}$ with source B, the selection function always chooses B. Thus, it is enough to show that any infinite path starting with F in $\mathcal{G}_{\mathcal{T}_3}$ eventually leads to B. This is an easy consequence of the fact that Z is (F, a)-synchronized and that the only node in $\mathcal{G}_{\mathcal{T}_3}$ reachable in $\mathcal{G}_{\mathcal{A}}$ from a is B. □

5.3   Characterizing When the msc Exists

The example that demonstrates the non-existence of the msc given above (see Theorem 3) shows that cycles in the ABox are problematic. However, Proposition 1 shows that not all cycles cause problems. Intuitively, the reason for some cycles being harmless is that they can be simulated by cycles in the TBox. For this reason, it is not really necessary to have them in $\mathcal{G}_{\mathcal{A}}$. In order to make this more precise, we will introduce acyclic versions $\mathcal{G}_{\mathcal{A}}^{(k)}$ of $\mathcal{G}_{\mathcal{A}}$, where cycles are unraveled into paths up to depth k starting with a (see Definition 10 below). When viewed as the $\mathcal{EL}$-description graph of an $\mathcal{EL}$-TBox, this graph contains a defined concept that corresponds to the individual a. Let us call this concept P_k. We will see below that the msc of a exists iff there is a k such that P_k is the msc.[4] Unfortunately, it is not clear how this condition can be decided in an effective way.

Definition 10. Let $\mathcal{T}_1$ be a fixed $\mathcal{EL}$-TBox with associated $\mathcal{EL}$-description graph $\mathcal{G}_{\mathcal{T}_1} = (V_{\mathcal{T}_1}, E_{\mathcal{T}_1}, L_{\mathcal{T}_1})$, $\mathcal{A}$ an $\mathcal{EL}$-ABox, a a fixed individual in $\mathcal{A}$, and $k \geq 0$. Then the graph $\mathcal{G}_{\mathcal{A}}^{(k)} := (V_k, E_k, L_k)$ is defined as follows:

$$V_k := V_{\mathcal{T}_1} \cup \{a^0\} \cup \{b^n \mid b \text{ is an individual in } \mathcal{A} \text{ and } 1 \leq n \leq k\},$$

where a^0 and b^n are new individual names;

---

[3] Since r is the only role occurring in $\mathcal{T}_1$, it is also the only role occurring in the conservative extension $\mathcal{T}_3$ of $\mathcal{T}_1$.

[4] This result is similar to the characterization of the existence of the lcs w.r.t. descriptive semantics given in [2].

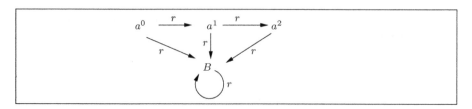

Fig. 5. The $\mathcal{EL}$-description graph $\mathcal{G}_{\mathcal{A}}^{(2)}$ of the example in the proof of Proposition 1.

$$E_k := E_{\mathcal{T}_1} \cup$$
$$\{(b^i, r, c^{i+1}) \mid r(b, c) \in \mathcal{A}, b^i, c^{i+1} \in V_k \setminus V_{\mathcal{T}_1}\} \cup$$
$$\{(b^i, r, B) \mid A(b) \in \mathcal{A}, b^i \in V_k \setminus V_{\mathcal{T}_1}, (A, r, B) \in E_{\mathcal{T}_1}\};$$

If u is a node in $V_{\mathcal{T}_1}$, then
$$L_k(u) := L_{\mathcal{T}_1}(u);$$

and if $u = b^i \in V_k \setminus V_{\mathcal{T}_1}$, then

$$L_k(u) := \{P \mid P(b) \in \mathcal{A}\} \cup \bigcup_{A(b)\in\mathcal{A}} L_{\mathcal{T}_1}(A),$$

where P denotes primitive and A denotes defined concepts.

As an example, consider the TBox $\mathcal{T}_1$ and the ABox $\mathcal{A}$ introduced in the proof of Proposition 1. The corresponding graph $\mathcal{G}_{\mathcal{A}}^{(2)}$ is depicted in Figure 5 (where the empty node labels are omitted).

Let $\mathcal{T}_2^{(k)}$ be the $\mathcal{EL}$-TBox corresponding to $\mathcal{G}_{\mathcal{A}}^{(k)}$. In this TBox, a^0 is a defined concept, which we denote by P_k. For example, the TBox corresponding to the graph $\mathcal{G}_{\mathcal{A}}^{(2)}$ depicted in Figure 5 consists of the following definitions (where nodes corresponding to individuals have been renamed[5]):

$$P_2 \equiv \exists r.A_1 \sqcap \exists r.B, \quad A_1 \equiv \exists r.A_2 \sqcap \exists r.B, \quad A_2 \equiv \exists r.B, \quad B \equiv \exists r.B.$$

Any msc of a must be equivalent to one of the concepts P_k:

Theorem 5. *Let $\mathcal{T}_1$ be an $\mathcal{EL}$-TBox, $\mathcal{A}$ an $\mathcal{EL}$-ABox, and a an individual in $\mathcal{A}$. Then there exists an msc of a in $\mathcal{A}$ and $\mathcal{T}_1$ iff there is a $k \geq 0$ such that P_k in $\mathcal{T}_2^{(k)}$ is the msc of a in $\mathcal{A}$ and $\mathcal{T}_1$.*

This theorem, whose proof can be found in [3], is an easy consequence of the following two lemmas. The first lemma states that a is an instance of the concepts P_k.

Lemma 1. $\mathcal{A} \models_{\mathcal{T}_2^{(k)}} P_k(a)$ *for all $k \geq 0$.*

---

[5] This renaming is admissible since these nodes cannot occur on cycles

The second lemma says that every concept that has a as an instance also subsumes P_k for an appropriate k. To make this more precise, assume that $\mathcal{T}_2$ is a conservative extension of $\mathcal{T}_1$, and that F is a defined concept in $\mathcal{T}_2$ such that $\mathcal{A} \models_{\mathcal{T}_2} F(a)$. Let $k := n \cdot (n+m)$ where n is the number of defined concepts in $\mathcal{T}_2$ and m is the number of individuals in $\mathcal{A}$. In order to have a subsumption relationship between P_k and F, both must "live" in the same TBox. For this, we simply take the union $\mathcal{T}_3$ of $\mathcal{T}_2^{(k)}$ and $\mathcal{T}_2$. Note that we may assume without loss of generality that the only defined concepts that $\mathcal{T}_2^{(k)}$ and $\mathcal{T}_2$ have in common are the ones from $\mathcal{T}_1$. In fact, none of the new defined concepts in $\mathcal{T}_2^{(k)}$ (i.e., the elements of $V_k \setminus V_{\mathcal{T}_1}$) lies on a cycle, and thus we can rename them without changing the meaning of these concepts. (Note that the characterization of subsumption given in Theorem 1 implies that only for defined concepts occurring on cycles their actual names are relevant.) Thus, $\mathcal{T}_3$ is a conservative extension of both $\mathcal{T}_2^{(k)}$ and $\mathcal{T}_2$.

Lemma 2. *If $k := n \cdot (n+m)$ where n is the number of defined concepts in $\mathcal{T}_2$ and m is the number of individuals in $\mathcal{A}$, then $P_k \sqsubseteq_{\mathcal{T}_3} F$.*

In the following, we assume without loss of generality that the TBoxes $\mathcal{T}_2^{(k)}$ ($k \geq 0$) are renamed such that they share only the defined concepts of $\mathcal{T}_1$.

Lemma 3. *Let $\mathcal{T} := \mathcal{T}_2^{(k)} \cup \mathcal{T}_2^{(k+1)}$. Then $P_{k+1} \sqsubseteq_{\mathcal{T}} P_k$.*

Thus, the concepts P_k form a decreasing chain w.r.t. subsumption. The individual a has an msc iff this chain becomes stable.

Corollary 3. *P_k is the msc of a iff it is equivalent to P_{k+i} for all $i \geq 1$.*

As an example, consider the TBox $\mathcal{T}_1$ and the ABox $\mathcal{A}$ introduced in the proof of Proposition 1 (see also Figure 5). It is easy to see that in this case P_0 is equivalent to P_k for all $k \geq 1$, and thus P_0 is the msc of a in $\mathcal{T}_1$ and $\mathcal{A}$.

6 Conclusion

The impact of cyclic definitions in $\mathcal{EL}$ on both standard and non-standard inferences in now well-investigated. The only two questions left open are how to give a decidable characterization of the cases in which the lcs/msc exists w.r.t. descriptive semantics, and to determine whether it can then be computed in polynomial time.

Though the characterizations of the existence of the lcs/msc given in [2] and in this paper do not provide us with such a decision procedure, they can be seen as a first step in this direction. In addition, these characterizations can be used to compute approximations of the lcs/msc.

References

1. Franz Baader. Using automata theory for characterizing the semantics of terminological cycles. *Ann. of Mathematics and Artificial Intelligence*, 18:175–219, 1996.
2. Franz Baader. Computing the least common subsumer in the description logic $\mathcal{EL}$ w.r.t. terminological cycles with descriptive semantics. In *Proceedings of the 11th International Conference on Conceptual Structures*, Lecture Notes in Artificial Intelligence. Springer-Verlag, 2003. To appear.
3. Franz Baader. The instance problem and the most specific concept in the description logic $\mathcal{EL}$ w.r.t. terminological cycles with descriptive semantics. LTCS-Report LTCS-03-01, Chair for Automata Theory, Institute for Theoretical Computer Science, Dresden University of Technology, Germany, 2003. See http://lat.inf.tu-dresden.de/research/reports.html.
4. Franz Baader. Least common subsumers and most specific concepts in a description logic with existential restrictions and terminological cycles. In *Proceedings of the 18th International Joint Conference on Artificial Intelligence*, 2003. To appear.
5. Franz Baader. Terminological cycles in a description logic with existential restrictions. In *Proceedings of the 18th International Joint Conference on Artificial Intelligence*, 2003. To appear.
6. Franz Baader and Ralf Küsters. Computing the least common subsumer and the most specific concept in the presence of cyclic $\mathcal{ALN}$-concept descriptions. In *Proc. of the 22nd German Annual Conf. on Artificial Intelligence (KI'98)*, volume 1504 of *Lecture Notes in Computer Science*, pages 129–140. Springer-Verlag, 1998.
7. Franz Baader, Ralf Küsters, and Ralf Molitor. Computing least common subsumers in description logics with existential restrictions. In *Proc. of the 16th Int. Joint Conf. on Artificial Intelligence (IJCAI'99)*, pages 96–101, 1999.
8. Volker Haarslev and Ralf Möller. High performance reasoning with very large knowledge bases: A practical case study. In *Proc. of the 17th Int. Joint Conf. on Artificial Intelligence (IJCAI 2001)*, 2001.
9. Monika R. Henzinger, Thomas A. Henzinger, and Peter W. Kopke. Computing simulations on finite and infinite graphs. In *36th Annual Symposium on Foundations of Computer Science*, pages 453–462, Milwaukee, Wisconsin, 1995. IEEE Computer Society Press.
10. Ian Horrocks. Using an expressive description logic: FaCT or fiction? In *Proc. of the 6th Int. Conf. on Principles of Knowledge Representation and Reasoning (KR'98)*, pages 636–647, 1998.
11. Ralf Küsters. *Non-standard Inferences in Description Logics*, volume 2100 of *Lecture Notes in Artificial Intelligence*. Springer-Verlag, 2001.
12. Bernhard Nebel. *Reasoning and Revision in Hybrid Representation Systems*, volume 422 of *Lecture Notes in Artificial Intelligence*. Springer-Verlag, 1990.
13. Bernhard Nebel. Terminological cycles: Semantics and computational properties. In John F. Sowa, editor, *Principles of Semantic Networks*, pages 331–361. Morgan Kaufmann, Los Altos, 1991.
14. Manfred Schmidt-Schauß and Gert Smolka. Attributive concept descriptions with complements. *Artificial Intelligence*, 48(1):1–26, 1991.
15. K.A. Spackman. Normal forms for description logic expressions of clinical concepts in SNOMED RT. *J. of the American Medical Informatics Association*, pages 627–631, 2001. Symposium Supplement.
16. K.A. Spackman, K.E. Campbell, and R.A. Cote. SNOMED RT: A reference terminology for health care. *J. of the American Medical Informatics Association*, pages 640–644, 1997. Fall Symposium Supplement.

Satisfiability and Completeness of Converse-PDL Replayed

Martin Lange

Institut für Informatik, University of Munich
mlange@informatik.uni-muenchen.de

Abstract. This paper reinvestigates the satisfiability problem and the issue of completeness for Propositional Dynamic Logic with Converse. By giving a game-theoretic characterisation of its satisfiability problem using focus games, an axiom system that is extracted from these games can easily be proved to be complete.

1   Introduction

Complete axiomatisations are essential for automated reasoning with logics. Propositional Dynamic Logic, PDL, was first introduced in [2] for program verification purposes. In [5] completeness of an axiom system for PDL proposed in [10] was proved. A different proof was given in [8].

The key to proving completeness is to establish that a finite consistent set of formulas is satisfiable. The default way to do this is of course to construct a model for this set. Other methods appeal to canonical structures of maximal consistent sets or to filtrations. Although automata-theory has been very successful for deciding satisfiability of various logics including PDL (cf. [13,12]) it is in general not known how to use automata-theoretic algorithms in order to establish completeness.

Together with PDL, Fischer and Ladner introduced Converse-PDL, CPDL for short, [2]. It extends PDL by allowing formulas to speak about the backwards execution of a program. Computationally, CPDL is not harder than PDL: model checking can be done in linear time for both logics, satisfiability is EXPTIME-complete and both have the finite model property. However, conceptually the satisfiability problem for CPDL seems to be slightly harder than the one for PDL because of the way how formulas speaking about the forwards and backwards execution of the same program influence each other.

In recent years propositional dynamic logics have become interesting again because of their close connection to description logics, cf. [14,3]. In this paper we characterise the satisfiability problem for CPDL in terms of simple two-player games. The naive tableau method that eliminates conjuncts and branches at disjuncts does not work because it does not capture the regeneration of least fixed point constructs correctly. To overcome this we employ an additional structure on sets called focus. This approach was first used in [6] to solve the model checking problem for the temporal logics LTL and CTL* in a game-based way.

A. Günter et al. (Eds.): KI 2003, LNAI 2821, pp. 79–92, 2003.

In [7] it was shown how this technique is also helpful for solving the satisfiability problem of the temporal logics LTL and CTL, and at the same time led to simple completeness proofs. It is, as this paper shows, also applicable to CPDL. The axiom system can easily be extracted from the satisfiability games. Thus, it is divided into those axioms justifying the game rules and those capturing winning strategies for one of the players.

2   Syntax and Semantics

Let $\mathcal{A} = \{a, b, \dots\}$ be a set of atomic programs and $\mathcal{P}$ be a set of propositional constants including *true* and *false*. We assume $\mathcal{P}$ to be closed under complementary propositions, i.e. $\mathcal{P} = \{\text{tt}, \text{ff}, q_1, \overline{q_1}, \dots\}$ where $\overline{\overline{q}} = q$ and $\overline{\text{tt}} = \text{ff}$. A labelled *transition system* $\mathcal{T}$ is a tuple $(S, \{\xrightarrow{a} | a \in Prog\}, L)$ with state set S. $L : S \to 2^{\mathcal{P}}$ labels the states, such that for all $s \in S$: $\text{tt} \in L(s)$, $\text{ff} \notin L(s)$ and $q \in L(s)$ iff $\overline{q} \notin L(s)$. We will write $s \xrightarrow{a} t$ if $s, t \in S$, and $(s, t) \in \xrightarrow{a}$.

Formulas φ and programs α of CPDL are defined in the following way.

$$\varphi \quad ::= \quad q \mid \varphi \vee \varphi \mid \varphi \wedge \varphi \mid \langle \alpha \rangle \varphi \mid [\alpha]\varphi$$
$$\alpha \quad ::= \quad a \mid \alpha; \alpha \mid \alpha \cup \alpha \mid \alpha^* \mid \overline{\alpha} \mid \varphi?$$

where q ranges over $\mathcal{P}$, and a over $\mathcal{A}$. Greek letters from the end of the alphabet will denote formulas while those from the beginning will stand for programs.

Although formulas are presented in positive form to be suitable for games, negation is needed as a syntactical operation to handle formulas of the form $[\psi?]\varphi$. It is introduced and eliminated using deMorgan's laws, and the equivalences $\neg q \equiv \overline{q}$, $\neg \langle \alpha \rangle \varphi \equiv [\alpha]\neg \varphi$, $\neg \neg \varphi \equiv \varphi$. With $\overline{\varphi}$ we denote the unique formula that results from $\neg \varphi$ when negation is eliminated using these rules.

The set $Sub(\varphi)$ of subformulas of a given φ is defined in the usual way for atomic propositions and boolean connectives. For formulas with modalities the subformula set depends on the program inside, e.g.

$$
\begin{aligned}
Sub(\langle a \rangle \varphi) \quad &= \{\langle a \rangle \varphi\} \cup Sub(\varphi) \\
Sub(\langle \alpha; \beta \rangle \varphi) \quad &= \{\langle \alpha; \beta \rangle \varphi\} \cup Sub(\langle \alpha \rangle \langle \beta \rangle \varphi) \\
Sub(\langle \alpha \cup \beta \rangle \varphi) &= \{\langle \alpha \cup \beta \rangle \varphi\} \cup Sub(\langle \alpha \rangle \varphi) \cup Sub(\langle \beta \rangle \psi) \\
Sub(\langle \alpha^* \rangle \varphi) \quad &= \{\varphi \vee \langle \alpha \rangle \langle \alpha^* \rangle \varphi, \langle \alpha \rangle \langle \alpha^* \rangle \varphi, \langle \alpha^* \rangle \varphi\} \cup Sub(\varphi) \\
Sub([\alpha^*]\varphi) \quad &= \{\varphi \wedge [\alpha][\alpha^*]\varphi, [\alpha][\alpha^*]\varphi, [\alpha^*]\varphi\} \cup Sub(\varphi) \\
Sub(\langle \psi? \rangle \varphi) \quad &= \{\langle \psi? \rangle \varphi\} \cup Sub(\psi) \cup Sub(\varphi) \\
Sub([\psi?]\varphi) \quad &= \{[\psi?]\varphi\} \cup Sub(\overline{\psi}) \cup Sub(\varphi) \\
Sub(\langle \overline{\alpha \cup \beta} \rangle)\varphi &= Sub(\langle \overline{\alpha} \cup \overline{\beta} \rangle \varphi) \\
Sub(\langle \overline{\alpha; \beta} \rangle)\varphi \quad &= Sub(\langle \overline{\beta}; \overline{\alpha} \rangle \varphi) \\
Sub(\langle \overline{\alpha^*} \rangle)\varphi \quad &= Sub(\langle \overline{\alpha}^* \rangle \varphi) \\
Sub(\langle \overline{\psi?} \rangle)\varphi \quad &= Sub(\langle \psi? \rangle \varphi)
\end{aligned}
$$

The remaining $[\alpha]\varphi$ cases are similar to the corresponding $\langle \alpha \rangle \varphi$ cases. The notion of a *subprogram* is defined in the same way. For a set Φ of CPDL formulas we set $Sub(\Phi) := \bigcup \{ Sub(\varphi) \mid \varphi \in \Phi \}$. Note that $|Sub(\Phi)| = O(|\Phi|)$.

Sets Φ of formulas will be interpreted conjunctively, i.e. $\varphi \vee \Phi$ for example is to be read as $\varphi \vee (\bigwedge_{\psi \in \Phi} \psi)$. We will use the following abbreviation: $\Phi^{[\alpha]} := \{\varphi \mid [\alpha]\varphi \in \Phi\}$.

CPDL formulas are interpreted over transition systems. The semantics of a CPDL formula is explained mutually recursively with an extension of the accessibility relation $\xrightarrow{a}$ to full programs α.

$$
\begin{aligned}
s \xrightarrow{\alpha;\beta} t \quad &\text{iff} \quad \exists u \in S \text{ s.t. } s \xrightarrow{\alpha} u \text{ and } u \xrightarrow{\beta} t \\
s \xrightarrow{\alpha \cup \beta} t \quad &\text{iff} \quad s \xrightarrow{\alpha} t \text{ or } s \xrightarrow{\beta} t \\
s \xrightarrow{\alpha^*} t \quad &\text{iff} \quad \exists n \in \mathbb{N}, s \xrightarrow{\alpha^n} t \text{ where} \\
&\qquad \forall s, t \in S : s \xrightarrow{\alpha^0} s, \text{ and } s \xrightarrow{\alpha^{n+1}} t \text{ iff } s \xrightarrow{\alpha;\alpha^n} t \\
s \xrightarrow{\overline{\alpha}} t \quad &\text{iff} \quad t \xrightarrow{\alpha} s \\
s \xrightarrow{\varphi?} s \quad &\text{iff} \quad s \models \varphi
\end{aligned}
$$

We define equivalences of programs $\alpha \equiv \beta$ as $s \xrightarrow{\alpha} t$ iff $s \xrightarrow{\beta} t$ for all s, t of all transition systems. Complementation of programs $\overline{\alpha}$ can be assumed to be applied to atomic progams solely because of $\overline{\alpha;\beta} \equiv \overline{\beta};\overline{\alpha}$, $\overline{\alpha \cup \beta} \equiv \overline{\alpha} \cup \overline{\beta}$, $\overline{\alpha^*} \equiv \overline{\alpha}^*$, and $\overline{\varphi?} \equiv \varphi?$. We set $\mathcal{A}^+ := \mathcal{A} \cup \{\overline{a} \mid a \in \mathcal{A}\}$, and $\overline{\overline{a}} = a$ for every $a \in \mathcal{A}^+$.

Again, assuming a transition system $\mathcal{T}$ to be fixed we define the semantics of a formula φ just as $s \models \varphi$ instead of $\mathcal{T}, s \models \varphi$.

$$
\begin{aligned}
s \models q \quad &\text{iff} \quad q \in L(s) \\
s \models \varphi \vee \psi \quad &\text{iff} \quad s \models \varphi \text{ or } s \models \psi \\
s \models \varphi \wedge \psi \quad &\text{iff} \quad s \models \varphi \text{ and } s \models \psi \\
s \models \langle \alpha \rangle \varphi \quad &\text{iff} \quad \exists t \in S \text{ s.t. } s \xrightarrow{\alpha} t \text{ and } t \models \varphi \\
s \models [\alpha]\varphi \quad &\text{iff} \quad \forall t \in S : s \xrightarrow{\alpha} t \text{ implies } t \models \varphi
\end{aligned}
$$

A formula φ is called *satisfiable* if there is a transition system $\mathcal{T} = (S, \{\xrightarrow{a} \mid a \in Prog\}, L)$ and a state $s \in S$, s.t. $\mathcal{T}, s \models \varphi$. A set Φ is satisfiable if $\bigwedge \Phi$ is so. A formula φ is called *valid*, written $\models \varphi$, if it is true in every state of every transition system. Note that $\not\models \varphi$ iff $\neg \varphi$ is satisfiable.

3   Satisfiability Games

A satisfiability game $\Gamma(\Phi_0)$ on a set Φ_0 of CPDL formulas is played by two players, called $\forall$ and $\exists$. It is player $\exists$'s task to show that Φ_0 is satisfiable, whereas player $\forall$ attempts to show the opposite. A *play* is a sequence $C_0, C_1, \ldots, C_n$ of *configurations* where $C_i \in Sub(\Phi_0) \times 2^{Sub(\Phi_0)}$ for all $i = 0, \ldots, n$. Configurations are more than non-empty sets of formulas. In every configuration, one particular formula is highlighted. This formula is said to be *in focus*, indicated by big square brackets.

Every play of $\Gamma(\Phi_0)$ starts with $C_0 = \left[\bigwedge \Phi_0 \right]$. Transitions from C_i to C_{i+1} are instances of *game rules* which may require one of the players to make a choice on a formula in C_i. Game rules are written

$$\frac{\boxed{\varphi}, \Phi}{\boxed{\varphi'}, \Phi'} \ p \ c$$

where C_i is the upper configuration, C_{i+1} the lower one. The player p is either $\forall$ or $\exists$, or empty if the rule does not require a player to take a choice. The choice c describes what p has to select. We will write

$$\frac{\underset{\llcorner\lrcorner}{\ulcorner\urcorner}\varphi\ , \Phi}{\underset{\llcorner\lrcorner}{\ulcorner\urcorner}\varphi'\ , \Phi'} \ p \ c$$

in order to abbreviate two rules of the form

$$\frac{\boxed{\varphi}, \Phi}{\boxed{\varphi'}, \Phi'} \ p \ c \qquad \text{and} \qquad \frac{\boxed{\psi}, \varphi, \Phi}{\boxed{\psi}, \varphi', \Phi'} \ p \ c$$

It might be that in the latter case the role of the choosing player becomes redundant. A class of games has the *subformula property* if the formulas in the premise (lower) of any rule are subformulas of the one in the conclusion (upper).

The CPDL game rules are presented in Figure 1. A disjunction is satisfiable iff one of its disjuncts is satisfiable. Therefore, player $\exists$ chooses one with rule $(\vee)$. Conjunctions are preserved, but player $\forall$ can decide with conjunct to keep in focus with rule $(\wedge)$. Rules $(\langle?\rangle)$, $([?])$, $(\langle;\rangle)$, $([;])$, $(\langle\cup\rangle)$ and $([\cup])$ apply equivalences for programs to reduce the size of the program in the outermost modality. Rules $(\langle*\rangle)$ and $([*])$ unfold the fixed point constructs of CPDL.

At any moment, player $\forall$ can play rule (FC) to move the focus to another formula in the actual configuration. This is particularly necessary if the formula in focus is atomic or the unfolding of a $\langle\alpha^*\rangle\varphi$ which player $\exists$ has just fulfilled. In the first case, the play could not proceed without a focus change. In the second case the new formula in focus might not enable player $\forall$ to win the play anymore. This is because the focus is used by player $\forall$ to track a least fixed point construct, i.e. a formula of the form $\langle\alpha^*\rangle\varphi$, via its unfoldings and to show that it never gets fulfilled.

In the remaining rules $(\langle a\rangle)$ and $([a])$, a can be an arbitrary atomic program or its complement: $a \in \mathcal{A}^+$. Moreover, these rules are only applicable if the set of sideformulas Φ satisfies the following condition: if $\varphi \in \Phi$ then $\varphi \in \mathcal{P}$, or $\varphi = \langle b\rangle\psi$ or $\varphi = [b]\psi$ for a $b \in \mathcal{A}^+$. Note that applying all the other rules will necessary result in such a configuration unless one of the following winning conditions applies beforehand.

Let $C_0, \ldots, C_n$ be a play of the game $\Gamma(\Phi_0)$. Player $\forall$ wins this play if

1. $C_n = \boxed{q}, \overline{q}, \Phi$ or $C_n = \boxed{\text{ff}}, \Phi$, or

2. there is an $i < n$ s.t. $C_i = \boxed{\langle\alpha^*\rangle\varphi}, \Phi$ and $C_n = \boxed{\langle\alpha^*\rangle\varphi}, \Phi'$, and $Sub(\Phi_0) \cap \Phi = Sub(\Phi_0) \cap \Phi'$, and between C_i and C_n player $\forall$ has not used rule (FC).

$$(\vee)\ \frac{\ulcorner \varphi_0 \vee \varphi_1 \urcorner, \Phi}{\ulcorner \varphi_i \urcorner, \Phi}\ \exists i \qquad (\wedge)\ \frac{\ulcorner \varphi_0 \wedge \varphi_1 \urcorner, \Phi}{\ulcorner \varphi_i \urcorner, \varphi_{1-i}, \Phi}\ \forall i \qquad (\langle ? \rangle)\ \frac{\ulcorner \langle \psi? \rangle \varphi \urcorner, \Phi}{\psi, \ulcorner \varphi \urcorner, \Phi}$$

$$([?])\ \frac{\ulcorner [\psi?]\varphi \urcorner, \Phi}{\ulcorner \overline{\psi} \vee \varphi \urcorner, \Phi} \qquad (\langle ; \rangle)\ \frac{\ulcorner \langle \alpha;\beta \rangle \varphi \urcorner, \Phi}{\ulcorner \langle \alpha \rangle \langle \beta \rangle \varphi \urcorner, \Phi} \qquad ([;])\ \frac{\ulcorner [\alpha;\beta]\varphi \urcorner, \Phi}{\ulcorner [\alpha][\beta]\varphi \urcorner, \Phi}$$

$$(\langle \cup \rangle)\ \frac{\ulcorner \langle \alpha_0 \cup \alpha_1 \rangle \varphi \urcorner, \Phi}{\ulcorner \langle \alpha_i \rangle \varphi \urcorner, \Phi}\ \exists i \qquad ([\cup])\ \frac{\ulcorner [\alpha_0 \cup \alpha_1]\varphi \urcorner, \Phi}{\ulcorner [\alpha_i]\varphi \urcorner, [\alpha_{1-i}]\varphi, \Phi}\ \forall i$$

$$(\langle * \rangle)\ \frac{\ulcorner \langle \alpha^* \rangle \varphi \urcorner, \Phi}{\ulcorner \varphi \vee \langle \alpha \rangle \langle \alpha^* \rangle \varphi \urcorner, \Phi} \qquad ([*])\ \frac{\ulcorner [\alpha^*]\varphi \urcorner, \Phi}{\ulcorner \varphi \wedge [\alpha][\alpha^*]\varphi \urcorner, \Phi} \qquad (\text{FC})\ \frac{\ulcorner \varphi \urcorner, \psi, \Phi}{\varphi, \ulcorner \psi \urcorner, \Phi}\ \forall$$

$$(\langle a \rangle)\ \frac{\ulcorner \langle a \rangle \varphi \urcorner, \Phi}{\ulcorner \varphi \urcorner, \Phi^{[a]}, \langle \overline{a} \rangle (\Phi - \Phi^{[a]})} \qquad ([a])\ \frac{\ulcorner [a]\varphi \urcorner, \Phi}{\ulcorner \varphi \urcorner, \psi, \Phi^{[a]}, \langle \overline{a} \rangle (\Phi - \{\psi\} - \Phi^{[a]})}\ \forall \langle a \rangle \psi \in \Phi$$

Fig. 1. The satisfiability game rules for CPDL.

Player $\exists$ wins this play if

3. $C_n = \ulcorner q_1 \urcorner, \dots, q_k$ and $\{q_1, \dots, q_k\}$ is satisfiable, or
4. there is an $i < n$ s.t. $C_i = \ulcorner [\alpha^*]\varphi \urcorner, \Phi$ and $C_n = \ulcorner [\alpha^*]\varphi \urcorner, \Phi'$, and $Sub(\Phi_0) \cap \Phi = Sub(\Phi_0) \cap \Phi'$, and between C_i and C_n player $\forall$ has not used rule (FC).
5. there is an $i < n$ s.t. $C_i = \ulcorner \varphi \urcorner, \Phi$ and $C_n = \ulcorner \varphi \urcorner, \Phi'$, and $Sub(\Phi_0) \cap \Phi = Sub(\Phi_0) \cap \Phi'$, and between C_i and C_n player $\forall$ has used rule (FC).

A player p has a *winning strategy* for, or simply *wins* the game $\Gamma(\Phi_0)$ if they can enforce a play that is winning for themselves. The *game tree* for player p is a representation of player p's winning strategy and can be obtained from the tree of all plays of the underlying game in the following way. At nodes which require p to make a choice include exactly one successor configuration from which on player p can still win the remaining game. At other nodes retain all successors. Thus, every full path in player p's game tree is a winning play for p.

Example 1. Take the satisfiable CPDL-formula $\varphi = \overline{q} \wedge \langle \overline{a}^* \rangle q$. A simple model for φ consists of two states s and t with $s \xrightarrow{a} t$, $L(s) = \{q\}$ and $L(t) = \{\overline{q}\}$. Then $t \models \varphi$. A play won by player $\exists$ of the game $\Gamma(\varphi)$ is shown in Figure 2.

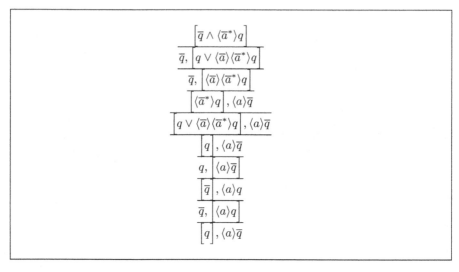

Fig. 2. A winning play for player ∃.

When the $\langle \overline{a}^* \rangle q$ becomes unfolded she does not choose q in the first place since this would result in a win for player ∀. However, after the first application of rule $(\langle \overline{a} \rangle)$ she can fulfil this subformula. From then on, player ∀ has to change focus away from atomic propositions so that the play can continue until eventually winning condition 5 applies.

Lemma 1. *Every game $\Gamma(\Phi_0)$ has a unique winner.*

Proof. Note that rules $(\vee) - ([\cup])$, $(\langle a \rangle)$ and $([a])$ reduce the size of the formula in focus or the size of the actual configuration. Hence, it is possible for a play to reach a configuration $\boxed{q}, \Phi$. If $\Phi = \emptyset$ then the winner is determined by condition 1 or 3 depending on whether $q = \mathbf{ff}$ or not. If $\Phi \neq \emptyset$ and condition 1 does not apply then player ∀ can use rule (FC) to set the focus to a bigger formula. The argument is iterated with this new formula until a configuration is reached that consists of atomic propositions only. Again, conditions 1 and 3 determine the winner uniquely.

This is not necessarily the case if rule $(\langle * \rangle)$ or $([*])$ is played at some point since they increase the size of the actual configuration and possibly the formula in focus. But then eventually there must be a C_i and a C_n s.t. $Sub(\Phi_0) \cap C_i = Sub(\Phi_0) \cap C_n$. Suppose this was not the case. Then there would infinitely many configurations that differ from each other in the set of subformulas of Φ_0. But $|Sub(\Phi_0)| < \infty$.

There are two possibilities for player ∀: either he has used rule (FC) between C_i and C_n. Then player ∃ wins with her winning condition 5. Or he has not. But then between C_i and C_n some rules that increase and some rules that decrease the size of the actual configuration must have been played, and a repeat is only possible if this applies to the formula in focus, too. Therefore, this must have been a $\langle \alpha^* \rangle \varphi$ or a $[\alpha^*]\varphi$ and, most importantly, it is a subformula of Φ_0. Note that any configuration C satisfies: if $\varphi \in C - Sub(\Phi_0)$ then $\varphi = \langle a \rangle \psi$ for some ψ and some $a \in \mathcal{A}^+$. This is because only rules $(\langle a \rangle)$ and $([a])$ violate the subformula property but the created formulas are always prefixed by a $\langle a \rangle$.

But then the winner is determined by winning conditions 2 or 4 depending on which formula and its unfoldings stayed in focus. Note that CPDL is non-alternating, i.e. this formula is unique.   □

Theorem 1. (Soundness)   *If player* $\exists$ *wins* $\Gamma(\Phi_0)$ *then* Φ_0 *is satisfiable.*

Proof. Suppose player $\forall$ uses his best strategy but player $\exists$ still wins against it. Then there is a successful game tree for player $\exists$. We use this to construct a tree-like model $\mathcal{T}$ for Φ_0. States of this model are equivalence classes $[C_i]$ of configurations under the following equivalence relation

$$C_i \sim C_j \quad \text{iff} \quad C_i \text{ and } C_j \text{ are on the same path and between}$$
$$C_i \text{ and } C_j \text{ there is no application of rule } (\langle a \rangle) \text{ or } ([a])$$

Transitions in this model are given for some $a \in \mathcal{A}^+$ by

$$[C_i] \xrightarrow{a} [C_j] \quad \text{iff} \quad C_i \not\sim C_j, \text{ but there is a } C_k \text{ s.t. } C_i \sim C_k \text{ and } C_{k+1} \sim C_j$$
$$\text{and between } C_k \text{ and } C_{k+1} \text{ rule } (\langle a \rangle) \text{ or } ([a]) \text{ was played}$$

Finally, the labellings on the states are given by the atomic propositions that occur in a corresponding configuration:

$$q \in L([C_i]) \quad \text{if} \quad \text{there is a } C_j \text{ with } C_i \sim C_j \text{ and } q \in C_j$$

It remains to be seen that $\mathcal{T}, [C_0] \models \Phi_0$. Indeed, the following stronger fact holds: if $\varphi \in C_i$ then $\mathcal{T}, [C_i] \models \varphi$. We prove this by induction on φ. For atomic formulas $\varphi = q$ this is true by the construction of the labellings. Note that an inconsistent labelling is not possible because in such a case player $\forall$ would have won the corresponding play with his winning condition 1 which is excluded by assumption. Moreover, a consistent labelling can easily be extended to a maximal one without changing the truth values of the formulas involved.

For disjunctions and conjunctions it is true because of the way rules $(\vee)$ and $(\wedge)$ are defined. It is trivially true for all constructs for which there is a deterministic rule as they replace formulas by equivalent ones.

The only interesting cases are those of the form $\varphi = \langle \alpha^* \rangle \psi$ and $\varphi = [\alpha^*]\psi$. It locally holds for these cases, too, since there is a deterministic rule which replaces φ with its logically equivalent unfolding. However, in the case of $\varphi = \langle \alpha^* \rangle \psi$ one has to ensure that global correctness holds, too. I.e. the least fixed point must eventually get fulfilled.

Suppose this was not the case, i.e. there was no moment in which player $\exists$ could have chosen the disjunct ψ after $\langle \alpha^* \rangle \psi$ was unfolded. But then player $\forall$

could have easily won the corresponding play by setting the focus to φ at some point and leaving it there. The only reason why he would not have done so would be another $\langle \beta^* \rangle \chi$ which did not get fulfilled and which he left the focus on. In any case, such a play is not possible in player $\exists$'s game tree. $\qquad \square$

Lemma 2. *If $\Phi \wedge \langle \alpha^* \rangle \varphi$ is satisfiable then so is $\Phi \wedge (\varphi \vee \langle \alpha \rangle \langle (\neg \Phi?; \alpha)^* \rangle (\varphi \wedge \neg \Phi))$.*

Proof. Assume

1. $\Phi \wedge \langle \alpha^* \rangle \varphi$ has a model $\mathcal{T}, s_0$, but
2. $\models \Phi \to (\neg \varphi \wedge [\alpha][(\neg \Phi?; \alpha)^*](\neg \varphi \vee \Phi))$ is true.

By (1) there is a sequence $s_0, \dots, s_n$ of states s.t. $s_0 \models \Phi$, $s_n \models \varphi$, and $s_i \xrightarrow{\alpha} s_{i+1}$ for all $i = 0, \dots, n-1$. Take the least such n, i.e. $s_i \not\models \varphi$ for all $i = 0, \dots, n-1$. We have $n > 0$ because of (2). Again by (2): $s_0 \models [\alpha][(\neg \Phi?; \alpha)^*](\neg \varphi \vee \Phi)$ and therefore $s_1 \models [(\neg \Phi?; \alpha)^*](\neg \varphi \vee \Phi)$. Note that

$$
\begin{aligned}
[(\neg \Phi?; \alpha)^*](\neg \varphi \vee \Phi) \ &\equiv \ (\neg \varphi \vee \Phi) \wedge [\neg \Phi?; \alpha][(\neg \Phi?; \alpha)^*](\neg \varphi \vee \Phi) \\
&\equiv \ (\neg \varphi \vee \Phi) \wedge (\Phi \vee [\alpha][(\neg \Phi?; \alpha)^*](\neg \varphi \vee \Phi)) \\
&\equiv \ (\neg \varphi \wedge \Phi) \ \vee \ \Phi \ \vee \\
&\quad\ (\neg \varphi \wedge [\alpha][(\neg \Phi?; \alpha)^*](\neg \varphi \vee \Phi)) \ \vee \\
&\quad\ (\Phi \wedge [\alpha][(\neg \Phi?; \alpha)^*](\neg \varphi \vee \Phi))
\end{aligned}
$$

Regardless of which of the four disjuncts is fulfilled in s_1, because of (2) we have $s_1 \not\models \varphi$ and $s_1 \models [\alpha][(\neg \Phi?; \alpha)^*](\neg \varphi \vee \Phi)$. This argument can be iterated down the sequence $s_2, s_3, \dots$ until s_n is reached to show $s_n \not\models \varphi$ which contradicts the assumption. $\qquad \square$

Alternatively, this lemma can be proved by translation into fixed point logic and by using Park's fixed point principle (1) and the fact that a fixed point is equivalent to its unfolding (2).

$$
\begin{aligned}
&\text{if} \ \models \varphi\{\psi/Y\} \to \psi \ \text{then} \ \models \mu Y.\varphi \to \psi & (1) \\
&\models \mu Y.\varphi \leftrightarrow \varphi\{\mu Y.\varphi/Y\} & (2)
\end{aligned}
$$

This has been done for general fixed point logic, cf. [4,11].

Corollary 1. $\models \psi \to \varphi \wedge [\alpha][(\neg \psi; \alpha)^*](\varphi \vee \psi)$ *implies* $\models \psi \to [\alpha^*]\varphi$

Proof. By contraposition of Lemma 2. $\qquad \square$

Lemma 3. *If $[\alpha]\varphi \wedge \langle \alpha \rangle \psi \wedge \Phi$ is satisfiable then $\varphi \wedge \psi \wedge \Phi^{[\alpha]} \wedge \langle \overline{\alpha} \rangle \Phi$ is satisfiable.*

Proof. Suppose there is a transition system with a state s s.t. $s \models [\alpha]\varphi \wedge \langle \alpha \rangle \psi \wedge \Phi$. Then there is another state t with $s \xrightarrow{\alpha} t$ and $t \models \varphi \wedge \psi \wedge \Phi^{[\alpha]}$. Furthermore, because of $t \xrightarrow{\overline{\alpha}} s$ we have $t \models \langle \overline{\alpha} \rangle \Phi$ and, hence, $t \models \varphi \wedge \psi \wedge \Phi^{[\alpha]} \wedge \langle \overline{\alpha} \rangle \Phi$, i.e. this formula is satisfiable. $\qquad \square$

Theorem 2. (Completeness) *If Φ_0 is satisfiable then player $\exists$ wins the game $\Gamma(\Phi_0)$.*

Proof. Assuming that Φ_0 is satisfiable we show what player $\exists$'s winning strategy has to look like. All of player $\forall$'s moves preserve satisfiability. That is trivial for the boolean $\wedge$ and for rule (FC). Preservation of satisfiability in the modality rules is proved in Lemma 3. Player $\exists$ always has the chance to make a choice which preserves satisfiability, i.e. if $\Phi \wedge (\varphi_0 \vee \varphi_1)$ is satisfiable, then so is $\Phi \wedge \varphi_i$ for some $i \in \{0, 1\}$.

If a play reaches a position $\left[\langle \alpha^* \rangle \varphi\right], \Phi$ then player $\exists$ takes a note of the context Φ in the index of the modal formula when it is unfolded to

$$\left[\varphi \vee \langle \alpha \rangle \langle \alpha^* \rangle_{\neg \Phi} \varphi\right], \Phi$$

A formula $\langle \alpha^* \rangle_{\neg \Phi} \varphi$ is interpreted as $\langle (\neg \Phi?; \alpha)^* \rangle (\varphi \wedge \neg \Phi)$. Lemma 2 shows that satisfiability is still preserved. This is done for as long as $\langle \alpha^* \rangle \varphi$ is in focus. Subscripting of already subscripted formulas is allowed, i.e. $\langle \alpha^* \rangle_{\neg \Phi_1, \ldots, \neg \Phi_k} \varphi$ is interpreted as

$$\langle (\neg \Phi_1?; \ldots; \neg \Phi_k?; \alpha)^* \rangle (\varphi \wedge \neg \Phi_1 \wedge \ldots \wedge \neg \Phi_k)$$

Once player $\forall$ removes the focus from it, player $\exists$ drops the indices that have been collected so far.

Player $\forall$ cannot win a single play of $\Gamma(\Phi_0)$ with winning condition 1 because this requires him to reach a propositionally unsatisfiable configuration which is excluded by the preservation of satisfiability. He cannot win with condition (2) either because he would enforce a play that ends on $\left[\langle \alpha^* \rangle_{\neg \Phi, \ldots, \neg \Phi'} \varphi\right], \Phi$. But such a configuration is also unsatisfiable because of

$$\langle \alpha^* \rangle_{\neg \Phi, \ldots, \neg \Phi'} \varphi \equiv \neg \Phi \wedge \ldots \wedge \neg \Phi' \wedge (\varphi \vee \langle \alpha \rangle \langle \alpha^* \rangle_{\neg \Phi, \ldots, \neg \Phi'} \varphi)$$

Finally, Lemma 1 shows that player $\exists$ must win $\Gamma(\Phi_0)$. $\square$

Corollary 2. *CPDL has the finite model property.*

Proof. Suppose $\varphi \in$ CPDL is satisfiable. According to Theorem 2, player $\exists$ has a winning strategy for $\Gamma(\varphi)$. The proof of Theorem 1 shows that a finite model can be extracted from this winning startegy. $\square$

We will show that the winner of $\Gamma(\Phi_0)$ can be decided using exponential time. This matches the known lower and upper bounds for deciding satisfiability of CPDL formulas, [9]. Before that, we need to prove a technical lemma.

Lemma 4. *It suffices to explore the part of the game $\Gamma(\Phi_0)$ that consists of subformulas of Φ_0 only.*

Proof. Assume player p wins $\Gamma(\Phi_0)$. Take their game tree T. First, let $p = \exists$. If every application of rules $(\langle a \rangle)$ or $([a])$ is replaced by

$$\frac{\left[\langle a \rangle \varphi\right], \Phi}{\left[\varphi\right], \Phi^{[a]}} \qquad \frac{\left[[a]\varphi\right], \Phi}{\left[\varphi\right], \psi, \Phi^{[a]}} \;\forall \langle a \rangle \psi \in \Phi$$

then T can be transformed into another game tree T' for player $\exists$. Note that her winning conditions 3 and 4 are not effected by the removal of formulas of the form $\langle \overline{a} \rangle \psi$. Now take a play in T which is won with condition 5. I.e. there are configurations C_i and C_n s.t. $Sub(\Phi_0) \cap C_i = Sub(\Phi_0) \cap C_n$ and $\left[\varphi\right] \in C_i \cap C_n$. Moreover, player $\forall$ has changed focus between C_i and C_n. If $\varphi \in Sub(\Phi_0)$ then removing formulas not in $Sub(\Phi_0)$ results in a shorter play because there are fewer possibilities for player $\forall$ to set the focus to. If $\varphi \notin Sub(\Phi_0)$ then, with the new game rules, the focus must have been on a different formula. But then player $\forall$ cannot win the new play either since removing formulas does not give him new chances to win. According to Lemma 1, player $\exists$ still wins the new play.

Now let $p = \forall$. Note that all he does is position the focus and choose formulas of the form $\langle a \rangle \psi$ with rule $([a])$. We describe an optimal strategy for player $\forall$, i.e. if he can win and he uses this strategy then he will win. Regarding the focus, this strategy will only make use of subformulas of Φ_0.

Note that in a game tree for player $\forall$, all occurring configurations are unsatisfiable. But the converse holds, too. Thus, a significant part of his strategy, namely what he does in rule $([a])$, is to preserve unsatisfiability with his choices. But with the new rule above where no $\langle \overline{a} \rangle (\Phi - \Phi^{[a]})$ is included, he can still preserve unsatisfiability.

It remains to be seen what he does with the position of the focus. He maintains a list of all formulas of the form $\langle \alpha^* \rangle \psi$ in decreasing order of size. At the beginning he sets the focus to the $\langle \alpha^* \rangle \psi$ which is earliest in the list or a superformula of it, and keeps it there until player $\exists$ fulfils it after it has been unfolded. Then he deletes it from the list, adds ψ to its end and changes focus to the next formula which is present and earliest in the list. At any moment he checks whether he can win with condition 1 by changing focus to an atomic proposition.

This strategy guarantees him to win if he can because he will not miss out atomic propositions and if there is a $\langle \alpha^* \rangle \psi$ that does not get fulfilled, he will eventually set the focus to it. Note that by adding formulas to the end of the list he avoids creating a repeat for as long as possible.

Most importantly, player $\forall$ never needs to put the focus onto a formula which is not a subformula of Φ_0. Thus, he can also win $\Gamma(\Phi_0)$ with the amended rules. $\square$

Theorem 3. *Deciding the winner of $\Gamma(\Phi_0)$ is in EXPTIME.*

Proof. An alternating algorithm can be used to decide the winner of $\Gamma(\Phi_0)$. Lemma 4 shows that only subformulas of Φ_0 need to be taken into consideration when player $\forall$'s strategy is partially determinised using a priority list to establish the position of the focus.

A single play can easily be played using polynomial space only. The algorithm needs to store the actual configuration and one that player $\forall$ thinks will occur again. The actual one gets overwritten each time a rule is played. If the focus is changed then player $\forall$'s configuration gets deleted. To validate the guesses and to disable infinite plays, the algorithm also needs to store a counter to measure the length of the play which is restarted with a different stored configuration when no repeat has been found. The size of the counter is $O(|\Phi_0| + \log|\Phi_0|)$ because there are only $|\Phi_0| \cdot 2^{|\Phi_0|}$ many different configurations when subformulas of Φ_0 are considered only.

Finally, alternating polynomial space is the same as deterministic exponential time according to [1]. $\qquad\square$

4 A Sound and Complete Axiomatisation

Using the same technique as in the completeness proof of the satisfiability games it is easy to prove completeness of an axiom system that can be extracted from the games.

Definition 1. An axiom system A is a finite set of axioms of the form $\vdash \varphi$ and rules of the form "if $\vdash \varphi \ldots$ then $\vdash \psi$". A proof is a finite sequence of formulas s.t. every member of this sequence is an instance of an axiom in A or follows from earlier ones by an application of a rule in A. If there is a proof of φ in A we write $\vdash_A \varphi$ and often for short just $\vdash \varphi$.

Given an axiom system A, a formula φ is called A-*consistent* if its negation is not derivable, i.e. $\nvdash_A \neg\varphi$. A is called *sound* if $\vdash_A \varphi$ implies $\models \varphi$ for any φ, and *complete* if the converse is true, i.e. $\models \varphi$ implies $\vdash_A \varphi$. Completeness can be reformulated as: if φ is A-consistent then φ is satisfiable.

Completeness of an axiom system can be shown by the help of the satisfiability games in the following way.

Proposition 1. *If for any* A-*consistent* φ *player* $\exists$ *wins* $\Gamma(\varphi)$ *then* A *is complete for CPDL.*

The axiom system A that has been constructed with respect to the satisfiability games is shown in Figure 3. Note that the axioms and rules are to be taken as schemes where φ and ψ can be any formula of CPDL, α and β can be any program, and a can be any atomic program or the complement thereof. Remember that $\bar{\bar{a}} \equiv a$ for any $a \in \mathcal{A}^+$.

Lemma 5. *The rules of the satisfiability games preserve* A-*consistency.*

Proof. Suppose Φ is A-consistent. We show that every move taken by player $\forall$ results in a configuration Φ' that is also A-consistent, and that player $\exists$ can always make a choice that preserves consistency.

Axioms

1. any tautology of propositional logic
2. $\neg\langle\alpha\rangle\varphi \leftrightarrow [\alpha]\neg\varphi$
3. $\langle\alpha \cup \beta\rangle\varphi \leftrightarrow \langle\alpha\rangle\varphi \vee \langle\beta\rangle\varphi$
4. $\langle\alpha;\beta\rangle\varphi \leftrightarrow \langle\alpha\rangle\langle\beta\rangle\varphi$
5. $\langle\alpha^*\rangle\varphi \leftrightarrow \varphi \vee \langle\alpha\rangle\langle\alpha^*\rangle\varphi$
6. $\langle\psi?\rangle\varphi \leftrightarrow \psi \wedge \varphi$
7. $\langle\overline{\alpha \cup \beta}\rangle\varphi \leftrightarrow \langle\overline{\alpha} \cup \overline{\beta}\rangle\varphi$
8. $\langle\overline{\alpha;\beta}\rangle\varphi \leftrightarrow \langle\overline{\beta};\overline{\alpha}\rangle\varphi$
9. $\langle\overline{\alpha^*}\rangle\varphi \leftrightarrow \langle\overline{\alpha}^*\rangle\varphi$
10. $\langle\overline{\psi?}\rangle\varphi \leftrightarrow \langle\psi?\rangle\varphi$
11. $[a]\varphi \wedge [a]\psi \rightarrow [a](\varphi \wedge \psi)$
12. $[a](\varphi \rightarrow \psi) \rightarrow ([a]\varphi \rightarrow [a]\psi)$
13. $\varphi \rightarrow [a]\langle\overline{a}\rangle\varphi$

Rules

MP   if $\vdash \varphi$ and $\vdash \varphi \rightarrow \psi$ then $\vdash \psi$

Gen   if $\vdash \varphi$ then $\vdash [a]\varphi$ for any $a \in \mathcal{A}^+$

Rel   if $\vdash \psi \rightarrow \varphi \wedge [\alpha][\alpha^*](\varphi \vee \psi)$ then $\vdash \psi \rightarrow [\alpha^*]\varphi$

Fig. 3. A complete axiomatisation for CPDL.

The rules for conjuncts and (FC) obviously preserve consistency. If $\Phi, \varphi_0 \vee \varphi_1$ is A-consistent then Φ, φ_i is A-consistent for some $i \in \{0,1\}$ by axiom 1 and rule MP. Player $\exists$ can select this φ_i.

Axioms 2–6 show that the game rules for modalities and non-atomic programs preserve consistency. Axioms 7–10 do the same for the equivalences for programs which we could have formulated as game rules instead of requiring complementation to be pushed inwards in the first place.

The case of subscripting a $\langle\alpha^*\rangle\varphi$ is dealt with by rule REL.

The interesting case is rule ($\langle a\rangle$) or ($[a]$). Note that they only differ in the position of the focus, which does not effect consistency. Thus, they can be dealt with in one case. Suppose $\varphi \wedge \Phi \wedge \langle\overline{a}\rangle\Phi'$ is inconsistent, i.e. $\vdash \Phi \wedge \langle\overline{a}\rangle\Phi' \rightarrow \neg\varphi$. By axioms 11,12,2 and rule MP we have $\vdash [a]\Phi \wedge [a]\langle\overline{a}\rangle\Phi' \rightarrow \neg\langle a\rangle\varphi$. By axiom 1 and rule MP, this can be transformed into $\vdash \neg[a]\Phi \vee \neg[a]\langle\overline{a}\rangle\Phi' \vee \neg\langle a\rangle\varphi$.

Axiom 13 can be instantiated and inverted by 1 and MP to $\vdash \neg[a]\langle\overline{a}\rangle\Phi' \rightarrow \neg\Phi'$. Again, by 1 and MP this can be used to obtain $\vdash \neg[a]\Phi \vee \neg\Phi' \vee \neg\langle a\rangle\varphi$, resp. $\vdash [a]\Phi \wedge \Phi' \rightarrow \neg\langle a\rangle\varphi$ which shows that the conclusion of rule ($\langle a\rangle$) or ($[a]$) would be inconsistent as well. □

Theorem 4. *The axiom system* A *is sound and complete for* CPDL.

Proof. Soundness of A is straightforward since all the axioms are valid and the rules preserve validity. The only interesting case is the rule **Rel** whose correctness is proved in Corollary 1.

The proof of completeness of A is similar to the one of Theorem 2. Suppose Φ_0 is A-consistent. Player $\forall$ is not able to win a play of $\Gamma(\Phi_0)$ with winning condition 1 since this would contradict Lemma 5. He is also unable to win a play with condition 2 because a configuration $\langle \alpha^* \rangle_{\neg\Phi,\dots,\neg\Phi'}\varphi, \Phi$ is inconsistent by propositional reasoning.

By Lemma 1 player $\exists$ must win $\Gamma(\Phi_0)$ and by Proposition 1 the axiom system A is complete. $\square$

A differs from the Segerberg axioms S (cf. [5,10]) for PDL in the use of rule REL instead of the induction axiom I:

$$\vdash \varphi \wedge [\alpha^*](\varphi \to [\alpha]\varphi) \to [\alpha^*]\varphi$$

To show that REL really replaces I in A, one can consider its negation $\neg I$ and the way player $\forall$ wins $\Gamma(\neg I)$. Depending on the exact structure of φ and α, the resulting play looks like

$$
\frac{
\varphi, [\alpha^*](\neg\varphi \vee [\alpha]\varphi), \left[\langle \alpha^* \rangle \neg\varphi\right]
}{
\dfrac{
\varphi, (\neg\varphi \vee [\alpha]\varphi) \wedge [\alpha][\alpha^*](\neg\varphi \vee [\alpha]\varphi), \boxed{\neg\varphi \vee \langle\alpha\rangle\langle\alpha^*\rangle_{\neg\Phi}\neg\varphi}
}{
\dfrac{
\varphi, [\alpha]\varphi, [\alpha][\alpha^*](\neg\varphi \vee [\alpha]\varphi), \boxed{\langle\alpha\rangle\langle\alpha^*\rangle_{\neg\Phi}\neg\varphi}
}{
\varphi, [\alpha^*](\neg\varphi \vee [\alpha]\varphi), \left[\langle\alpha^*\rangle_{\neg\Phi}\neg\varphi\right]
}
}
}
$$

where $\Phi = \varphi \wedge [\alpha]\varphi \wedge [\alpha][\alpha^*](\neg\varphi \vee [\alpha]\varphi)$. Player $\forall$ wins with his winning condition 2 since he is able to keep the focus on $\langle\alpha^*\rangle\neg\varphi$ which gets subscripted with the context. Subscripting is captured by rule REL.

References

1. A. K. Chandra, D. C. Kozen, and L. J. Stockmeyer. Alternation. *Journal of the ACM*, 28(1):114–133, January 1981.
2. M. J. Fischer and R. E. Ladner. Propositional dynamic logic of regular programs. *Journal of Computer and System Sciences*, 18(2):194–211, April 1979.
3. G. de Giacomo and F. Massacci. Combining deduction and model checking into tableaux and algorithms for Converse-PDL. *Information and Computation*, 162:117–137, 2000.
4. D. Kozen. Results on the propositional μ-calculus. *TCS*, 27:333–354, December 1983.
5. D. Kozen and R. Parikh. An elementary proof of the completeness of PDL (note). *TCS*, 14:113–118, 1981.
6. M. Lange and C. Stirling. Model checking games for CTL*. In *Proc. Conf. on Temporal Logic, ICTL'00*, pages 115–125, Leipzig, Germany, October 2000.
7. M. Lange and C. Stirling. Focus games for satisfiability and completeness of temporal logic. In *Proc. 16th Symp. on Logic in Computer Science, LICS'01*, Boston, MA, USA, June 2001. IEEE.
8. V. R. Pratt. A practical decision method for propositional dynamic logic. In *Proc. 10th Symp. on Theory of Computing, STOC'78*, pages 326–337, San Diego, California, May 1978.

9. V. R. Pratt. Models of program logics. In *Proc. 20th Symp. on Foundations of Computer Science, FOCS'79*, pages 115–122. IEEE, 1979.

10. K. Segerberg. A completeness theorem in the modal logic of programs. *Notices of the AMS*, 24(6):A–552, October 1977.

11. C. Stirling. Modal and temporal logics. In S. Abramsky, D. M. Gabbay, and T. S. E. Maibaum, editors, *Handbook of Logic in Computer Science*, volume 2 (Background: Computational Structures), pages 477–563. Clarendon Press, Oxford, 1992.

12. R. S. Streett. Propositional dynamic logic of looping and converse is elementarily decidable. *Information and Control*, 54(1/2):121–141, July 1982.

13. M. Y. Vardi and P. Wolper. Automata-theoretic techniques for modal logic of programs. *Journal of Computer and System Sciences*, 32:183–221, 1986.

14. W. A. Woods and J. G. Schmolze. The KL-ONE family. In Fritz Lehmann, editor, *Semantic Networks in Artificial Intelligence*, pages 133–177. Pergamon Press, Oxford, 1992.

Optimality Theory through Default Logic

P. Besnard[1]*, R.E. Mercer[2], and T. Schaub[3]

[1] IRIT-CNRS, Université Paul Sabatier
118 route de Narbonne, F-31062 Toulouse cedex, France
besnard@irit.fr
[2] Computer Science Department, Middlesex College
The University of Western Ontario, London Ont. N6A 5B7, Canada
mercer@csd.uwo.ca
[3] Institut für Informatik, Universität Potsdam
Postfach 900327, D-14439 Potsdam, Germany
torsten@uni-potsdam.de

Abstract. Optimality Theory is an approach to linguistic problems which is based on rules with exceptions, resorting to a ranking among rules to resolve conflicts arising from competing rules.

In such a way, dealing with linguistic problems amounts to applying rules with exceptions: That is reasoning. A related issue is then about a formalization of the logic at work. An immediate candidate is Default Logic which is dedicated to reasoning from rules with exceptions. Moreover, there are versions of default logic with priorities.

We show that Default Logic is well-suited as a specification language capturing Optimality Theory and suggests that implementations of default logic can be applied to run experiments with grammatical interaction in the sense of Optimality Theory and beyond.

Keywords: Application to Natural Language, Default Logic.

1   Introduction

Optimality Theory is a grammatical architecture that was invented in phonology [Prince & Smolensky 1993] but managed to spread into the other subdisciplines of linguistics quite successfully. In its standard version, Optimality Theory (cf [Kager 1999] for instance) is a representational rather than a derivational account of grammatical facts: It comprises of a set of grammatical constraints that evaluate the quality of candidate structures (or, say, representations), but it does not care how these candidate structures are generated.

In this respect, Optimality Theory only needs a component that decides which structures are compared with each other. The grammatical description of Optimality Theory is thus anchored with an input component. Inputs could be strings of sounds (in phonology), sets of morphemes (in morphology) or predicate-argument structures (in syntax). They are subjected to a GEN component that generates the candidate set on the basis of the input by very general

---

* Contributed while at Institut für Informatik, Universität Potsdam.

A. Günter et al. (Eds.): KI 2003, LNAI 2821, pp. 93–104, 2003.
© Springer-Verlag Berlin Heidelberg 2003

grammatical processes. The candidate set is passed on to the EVAL component (EVAL stands for evaluation) that is in charge of selecting the optimal candidate according to the language at hand, using the grammatical constraints.

Optimality Theory assumes that the grammatical constraints are simple and universal (all languages work with the same set of constraints): "syllables have an onset", "sentences have a subject" are examples of what could be a constraint.

The grammatical constraints may imply incompatible requirements for certain structures. E.g., objects should follow the verb (compare *John loves Mary* with *John Mary loves) but questions should begin with the question word (*how did she say this* vs. **she said this how*). For an object question, the two principles make different predictions (*what did she say* vs. *she said what), and we see that the conflict between the two principles is resolved in favor of the question principle.

In Optimality Theory, the grammatical constraints are organized in a hierarchy. When two options compete, the one with the better violation profile wins: A candidate structure S is grammatical if and only if there is no competitor S' such that the highest constraint on which S and S' differ incurs less violations from S' than from S.

Conflict resolution is lexicographic: The numbers of violations of a candidate with respect to each constraint form a vector (constraints are considered in decreasing order).

Here is an example. The highest constraint is "the question word occurs first", the next highest constraint is "the verb group comes second", and the lowest constraint is "any non-subject item occurs after the subject". Consider the candidates: (1) **where she is now?*, (2) **she is where now?*, (3) *where is she now?*, (4) **where is now she?* The first constraint rules out (2) that is the only candidate to violate it, and then similarly for (1) with respect to the second constraint. The last constraint is violated thrice by (4) but only twice by (3) that is thus the best candidate (the fact that (2) does not violate the last constraint is irrelevant: (2) was already out of the competition).

In Optimality Theory, this is often visualized in a two-dimensional table as follows. Rewriting the candidates (1) to (4) as x_1 to x_4 and abbreviating the three constraints (from higher to lower) by c_1 to c_3, we obtain the configuration depicted in Table 1:

Table 1. A constraint tableau in Optimality Theory (optimal candidate: x_3).

	c_1	c_2	c_3
x_1: **where she is now?*		*	
x_2: **she is where now?*	*		
x_3: *where is she now?*			**
x_4: **where is now she?*			***

The ranking among the contraints is reflected by their decreasing importance from left to right. With the exception of grey cells, Table 1 displays to what extent each candidate (dis)agrees with each constraint. E.g., the violation of c_1 by x_2 is indicated by $*$ while the triple violation of c_3 by x_4 is represented by $***$. Grey cells denote data that are not taken into account (for instance, the cell $x_2 \times c_3$ is grey to reflect the aforementioned fact that no matter how well (2) fares with respect to the last constraint it is irrelevant because (2) is out by virtue of the first constraint).

Constraints in Optimality Theory turn out to be rules with exceptions: They are universal but they are *not* universally valid (e.g., there are syllables in English that have no onset). Indeed, Optimality Theory provides a methodology to apply rules with exceptions. As Default Logic was motivated by the need to deal with such rules, it seems natural to investigate whether Optimality Theory conforms with Default Logic.

2   Interaction in a Linear Hierarchy of Constraints

Consider the case where the candidates involve no calculation: The list of candidates in final form $a, b, \ldots$ is available and the status (whether[1] absolute or relative to any other candidate) of each candidate with respect to every constraint is decided.

2.1   Harmonic Parallel Approach

Logic relations and defaults. The status of candidates with respect to constraints is to be encoded by means of $c_i\, defeats(a, b)$ relations over candidates and suboptimality (i.e., failure for a candidate to be a correct output) is encoded as $suboptimal(a)$.

The relation $c_i\, defeats(a, b)$ captures the case of non-binary constraints as well as the case of binary constraints (cf page 69 onwards in [7]).

That suboptimality is determined from the status of the candidates is rendered through defaults:

$$(c_i) \quad \frac{c_i\, defeats(a, b) \; : \; \neg suboptimal(a)}{suboptimal(b)}$$

that should be read (after [7] on page 74) as follows:

> *if b is less harmonic than a with respect to the constraint c_i*
> *then b is suboptimal*
> *unless a is itself suboptimal*

While the set of all candidates is simply assumed to be finite, the set of constraints is assumed to be both finite and totally ordered: $C = \{c_1, c_2, \ldots\}$ where

---

[1] Depending on each particular constraint.

c_1 ranks highest then c_2 and so on. So, the above defaults for optimality theory are ordered accordingly:

$$c_i < c_j \quad \text{iff} \quad j \geq i \text{ and } i \neq j$$

Hence, let us consider default logic with priorities (adapted from [2]):

Definition 1. *Let $(W, D, <)$ be a default theory where $<$ is a total order over D. Define*

- $E_0 = W$
- *for $n \geq 0$, $E_{n+1} = \mathrm{Th}(E_n \cup \{cons(\delta)\})$*
  where δ ranks highest among all defaults $\frac{\alpha:\beta}{\gamma}$ in D that satisfy the conditions[2] $\alpha \in E_n$ and $\neg\beta \notin E_n$ while $\gamma \notin \mathrm{Th}(E_n)$; if no such default exist, $\{cons(\delta)\} = \emptyset$.

Then, $E = \cup_{n \geq 0} E_n$ is the extension of $(W, D, <)$.

A correct output is then any candidate for which there exists an extension in which it is *not* proven suboptimal.[3]

Example 1. The language is a dialect of Berber and the item to be parsed is /txznt/. Two constraints (the one denoted c_1 ranks higher than the one denoted c_2) are examined:

(c_1) ONS (Syllables must have onsets)
(c_2) HNUC (Higher sonority nucleus is more harmonic)

For this example, [7] consider the following three candidates:

> .txź.ńt.   .tx́.zńt.   .t́x.zńt.

With a and b ranging over the candidate set $\{.txź.ńt., .tx́.zńt., .t́x.zńt.\}$, defaults are:

$$(c_1) \quad \frac{c_1 \, defeats(a, b) \; : \; \neg suboptimal(a)}{suboptimal(b)}$$

(requiring $a \neq b$ yields six such defaults) [4]

$$(c_2) \quad \frac{c_2 \, defeats(a, b) \; : \; \neg suboptimal(a)}{suboptimal(b)}$$

(requiring $a \neq b$ yields six such defaults) [4]

---

[2] Or equivalently, δ is such that $\neg jus(\delta') \notin \mathrm{Th}(E_n \cup \{cons(\delta)\})$ for all defaults δ' selected prior to δ. (i.e., for some $m < n$, δ' ranking highest such that $\alpha' \in E_m$ and $\neg\beta' \notin E_m$ while $\gamma' \notin \mathrm{Th}(E_m)$).

[3] The reader should not worry about matters of uniqueness and non-uniqueness, which are unproblematic even though the existence of exactly one extension for $(W, D, <)$ does not preclude the existence of more than one optimal output. By contrast, it is an absolute requirement that the order of defaults be total and this means that *instances* of the *same* constraint c_i have to be ordered (or $c_i \, defeats(a, b)$ must be antisymmetric, as well as irreflexive of course).

[4] An arbitrary total order is assumed among these six defaults (cf the previous footnote).

Taking $.txź.ńt.$ to be less behaved than the other two candidates regarding ONS,

$$c_1\,defeats(.tx̂.zńt., .txź.ńt.) \in W,$$

$$c_1\,defeats(.t́x.zńt., .txź.ńt.) \in W,$$

and taking $.t́x.zńt.$ to be less behaved than $.tx̂.zńt.$ regarding HNUC,

$$c_2\,defeats(.tx̂.zńt., .t́x.zńt.) \in W,$$

the resulting default theory has exactly one extension E:

$$E = \mathrm{Th}(W \cup \{suboptimal(.txź.ńt.), suboptimal(.t́x.zńt.)\})$$

The only candidate which is not proven suboptimal in the extension is $.tx̂.zńt.$, this is the unique optimal candidate (the correct output).

The outcome would be the same, should $c_1\,defeats(.t́x.zńt., .txź.ńt.)$ not be in W. This is an instance of the property which ensures that those $c_i\,defeats(a, \cdot)$ items are enough to get the correct output(s), where a ranges over the optimal candidate(s) while c_i ranges over all constraints such that $i > j$ where j is the highest ranking constraint violated by the optimal candidate(s).

It would also make no difference if HNUC had $.t́x.zńt.$ less behaved than $.txź.ńt.$

Although the underlying idea is the same, using $c_i\,defeats$ relations is more general than the mark approach in [7] (cf page 68 onwards) which can be captured (as $c_i\,defeats$ can be defined in virtually any way in W) as follows.

$\forall a, b, m_a, m_b \ \ Ons(a, m_a) \wedge Ons(b, m_b) \wedge m_a \succ_{Ons} m_b \rightarrow c_1\,defeats(a, b)$

$\forall a, b, m_a, m_b \ \ FM(m_a) \succ_{Ons} FM(m_b) \rightarrow m_a \succ_{Ons} m_b$

$\forall a, b, m_a, m_b \ \ FM(m_a) \approx_{Ons} FM(m_b) \wedge Rest(m_a) \succ_{Ons} Rest(m_b) \rightarrow$
$$m_a \succ_{Ons} m_b$$

$Ons(c, m_c)$ means that ONS assigns a list m_c of violation marks to every candidate c. Then, $FM(m_a) \succ_{Ons} FM(m_b)$ always holds when m_a is empty while m_b is not. Also, $FM(m_a) \approx_{Ons} FM(m_b)$ always holds when m_a and m_b are both non-empty. Lastly, $Rest(m_c)$ denotes the list m_c deprived of its first mark.

$\forall a, b, m_a, m_b \ \ Hnuc(a, m_a) \wedge Hnuc(b, m_b) \wedge m_a \succ_{Hnuc} m_b \rightarrow$
$$c_2\,defeats(a, b)$$

$\forall a, b, m_a, m_b \ \ FM(m_a) \succ_{Hnuc} FM(m_b) \rightarrow m_a \succ_{Hnuc} m_b$

$\forall a, b, m_a, m_b \ \ FM(m_a) \approx_{Hnuc} FM(m_b) \wedge Rest(m_a) \succ_{Hnuc} Rest(m_b) \rightarrow$
$$m_a \succ_{Hnuc} m_b$$

Similarly to ONS, this assumes HNUC ([7] page 72) to provide:

- a list of marks m_c sorted from most to least sonorous[5] for every candidate c (as is required in the first formula)

---

[5] Harmonic, if we identify the mark with the nucleus it stands for (p. 72 [7]).

- an assessment for every pair of marks where one is more sonorous than the other
  (as is required in the second formula)
- an assessment for every pair of equally sonorous marks
  (as is required in the third formula)

All this assumes further that W contains the usual axioms for equality (for instance, $Rest(Rest(Rest(m_c)))$ must be provably equal with the list obtained by deleting the first three marks in m_c). There are other formulations, getting rid of FM and $Rest$, such that the axioms of equality can be dispensed with.

As to a different kind of an example, consider NONFINALITY in a version where it is a binary constraint that does not apply multiply ([7] page 43)

$$\forall a, b \ \ Nonfinality(a) \wedge \neg Nonfinality(b) \rightarrow c_i defeats(a,b)^6$$

where i is the rank of NONFINALITY and for every candidate c, $Nonfinality(c)$ holds when the head foot of the prosodic word is not final.

2.2   Harmonic Sequential Approach

Now, it is no longer the case that the candidates are available right from the start. They are to form step by step, some of them getting discarded even before they develop to final form (this is the difference with the parallel approach).

Logic relations and defaults. Generation of (partial) candidates is encoded by means of the $gen(a,b)$ relation indicative of a derivation step from a to b. That a representation in the derivation currently counts as a candidate is encoded by means of $current(a)$. Steps in generation are rendered through the default[7]

$$(Gen) \quad \frac{current(a) \wedge gen(a,b) \ : \ \neg suboptimal(b)}{current(b)}$$

that reads

> if a counts as a candidate and there is a step in derivation
> turning a into b
> then b counts as a candidate unless b is suboptimal

Importantly, this default[8] ranks lower than all the ones representing constraints:

$$(c_i) \quad \frac{c_i defeats(a,b) \ : \ \neg suboptimal(a)}{suboptimal(b)}$$

---

[6] This formula makes $c_i defeats(a,b)$ to be antisymmetric. Also, if all candidates fail NONFINALITY then $c_i defeats(a,b)$ holds for no a and b.

[7] Singular is used here, although improperly, as the specific values of a and b are unimportant.

[8] Again, singular is improperly used. As a further motive, it can be pointed out that the highest ranking among all defaults of that form ranks lower than any default representing a constraint.

These defaults are exactly as in the parallel approach[9] (making the sequential approach a generalization of it).

$$\forall x \ input(x) \rightarrow current(x) \in W$$

If that is desired, a more detailed formulation is possible where changed elements are explicited as it only takes including in W the following formulas for all relevant a, b, c:

$change(a, e_a)$
$gen(a, b) \wedge gen(a, c) \wedge change(b, e_b) \wedge change(c, e_c) \wedge$
$$c_i \, defeats(e_b, e_c) \rightarrow c_i \, defeats(b, c)$$

The former formulas indicate that e_a is the changed element in a and the latter formulas state that defeat among candidates is ruled by defeat among changed elements.

Digression. A subtlety is that antisymmetry is required for $c_i \, defeats$ if its arguments are changed elements (i.e., $c_i \, defeats(e_b, e_c)$ and $c_i \, defeats(e_c, e_b)$ are incompatible). Such a requirement is *not* needed for $c_i \, defeats$ if its arguments are partial candidates (that is, of concern here is symmetry through $c_i \, defeats(b, c)$ and $c_i \, defeats(c, b)$). How can this be? Well, b and c differ from each other by at least one changed element. Now, one of these must occur before the other and therefore *rules out* the other candidate.

Example 2. In the same dialect of Berber, the item to be parsed is /ratlult/ so that

$$input(ratlult) \in W$$

The following formulas are also in W:

$gen(ratlult, \{rA\}tlult)$
$gen(\{rA\}tlult, \{rA\}t\{lu\}lt)$
$gen(\{rA\}tlult, \{rAt\}lult)$

Distinctively from the parallel approach (cf [7]), the ordering of constraints[10] is:

(c_1) −COD (Syllables do not have codas)
(c_2) HNUC (Higher sonority nucleus is more harmonic)

such that

$$c_2 \, defeats(\{rAt\}lult, \{rA\}t\{lu\}lt) \in W$$

$$c_1 \, defeats(\{rA\}t\{lu\}lt, \{rAt\}lult) \in W$$

The resulting default theory has exactly one extension E:

$$E = \text{Th}(W \cup \{current(\{rAt\}lult),$$
$$suboptimal(\{rAt\}lult), current(\{rA\}t\{lu\}lt)\})$$

---

[9] Even though they need *not* obey the same order: see footnote 49 in [7].
[10] Where −COD is introduced on page 34 in [7].

The above data are partial, they only describe an initial part of the process of selecting the correct output. Yet, they suffice to indicate that $\{rA\}t\{lu\}lt$ is the line to be developed but not $\{rAt\}lult$. Should more data be taken into account, the result goes further.

If the changed elements are to be explicited, the following formulas have to be in W:

$$gen(ratlult, \{rA\}tlult) \rightarrow change(\{rA\}tlult, \{rA\})$$
$$gen(\{rA\}tlult, \{rA\}t\{lu\}lt) \rightarrow change(\{rA\}t\{lu\}lt, \{lu\})$$
$$gen(\{rA\}tlult, \{rAt\}lult) \rightarrow change(\{rAt\}lult, \{rAt\})$$
$$c_2 defeats(\{rAt\}, \{lu\}) \quad \wedge \quad c_1 defeats(\{lu\}, \{rAt\})$$
$$c_2 defeats(\{rAt\}, \{lu\}) \rightarrow c_2 defeats(\{rAt\}lult, \{rA\}t\{lu\}lt)$$
$$c_1 defeats(\{lu\}, \{rAt\}) \rightarrow c_1 defeats(\{rA\}t\{lu\}lt, \{rAt\}lult)$$

Of course, the outcome is exactly the same.

3   Interaction in an Arbitrary Hierarchy of Constraints

3.1   Harmonic Parallel Approach

Footnote 31 in [7] acknowledges the possibility that a grammar should recognize nonranking pairs of constraints (although the authors make it clear that they found no evidence of crucial nonranking). Non-linear hierarchies of constraints may further seem invited from the view stated on page 88 in [7], that a category of constraints dominated by others fixed in superordinate position may be relatively ranked in any dominance order in a particular language. [11]

Logic relations and defaults. Logic relations and defaults are still as described above. The set of constraints is still finite but need no longer to be totally ordered: Therefore, it is still the case that $c_i < c_j$ for some c_i and c_j in $C = \{c_1, c_2, \ldots\}$ but this no longer relates to $j \geq i$. Accordingly, let us now consider default logic with non-linear priorities (adapted from [1]):

Definition 2. *Let $(W, D, <)$ be a default theory where $<$ is a partial order over D. Then, E is an extension for $(W, D, <)$ iff $E = \cup_{n \geq 0} E_n$ such that*

- $E_0 = W$
- *for $n \geq 0$,*

$$E_{n+1} = \text{Th}(E_n \cup Cons(\{\delta_1, \ldots, \delta_k\}))$$

where $\delta_1 \ldots \delta_k$ have priority[12] among all defaults in D that are active[13] in E_n

---

[11] Not: . . . are relatively ranked in some dominance order . . .

[12] The precise definition depends on what variant of default logic is selected.

[13] Again, there is a choice of definitions here and $Cons(\{\delta_1, \ldots, \delta_k\}) = \emptyset$ by convention when no default is active.

An example [7] not requiring a linear hierarchy of constraints:

Example 3. The language is Latin. Three constraints are considered:

(c_1) FTBIN (Feet are binary at some level of analysis)
(c_2) LX≈PR (A member of a certain morphological category corresponds to a PRWD)
(c_3) NONFINALITY (The head foot of the prosodic word is not final)

Consider the following three candidates:

.a.qua.
($á$) L
($á.qua$)

With u and v ranging over the set of candidates $\{.a.qua., (á)\,L, (á.qua)\}$, defaults are:

$$(c_1) \quad \frac{c_1\,defeats(u,v) \ : \ \neg suboptimal(u)}{suboptimal(v)}$$

$$(c_2) \quad \frac{c_2\,defeats(u,v) \ : \ \neg suboptimal(u)}{suboptimal(v)}$$

$$(c_3) \quad \frac{c_3\,defeats(u,v) \ : \ \neg suboptimal(u)}{suboptimal(v)}$$

c_3 ranks lowest of all but neither c_1 ranks higher than c_2 nor c_2 ranks higher than c_1. The other data are

$$\forall u \ c_1\,defeats(u,(á)\,L) \in W$$

$$\forall u \ c_2\,defeats(u,.a.qua.) \in W$$

$$\forall u \ c_3\,defeats(u,(á.qua)) \in W$$

The outcome is that the default theory at hand has a single extension

$$E = \mathrm{Th}(W \cup \{suboptimal(á)\,L), suboptimal(.a.qua.)\})$$

The optimal candidate is ($á.qua$), there was no need for a linear ordering of constraints.

The existence of a unique optimal candidate coincides with the existence of a greatest element in the induced[14] ordering.

For lack of space, the non-linear case of the sequential approach is not addressed here.

---

[14] Induced by c_i's ordering.

4   Logic Programming

As for harmonic parallelism, the case of a linear hierarchy of constraints is efficiently tackled using logic programming, in a guise e.g.
[3] where preferences can be expressed so that preemption among constraints is resolved:

```
suboptimal(b) :- name(i(a,b)), c-i-defeats(a,b),
                            not suboptimal(a).
```

For all $j < k$ (i.e., constraint j ranks higher than constraint k), one need the clauses:

```
(j(_,_) < k(_,_)).
```

Example 4. (Back to the Berber example.) The predicate `missing-ons(c,r)` assigns the missing onsets in the candidate c to the variable r whereas `s-nuclei(c,r)` assigns the nuclei in the candidate c (sorted from most to least sonorous) to the variable r.

```
c-1-defeats(a,b) :- missing-ons(a,p), missing-ons(b,q),
                            better-ons(p,q).
c-2-defeats(a,b) :- s-nuclei(a,p), s-nuclei(b,q),
                            better-hnuc(p,q).
better-ons([],[z|t]).
better-ons([x|r],[y|s]) :- better-ons(r,s).
better-hnuc([x|r],[y|s]) :- more-sonorous(x,y).
better-hnuc([x|r],[x|s]) :- better-hnuc(r,s).
```

Entering the data,

```
missing-ons(".txZ.Nt.",[2nd-syll]).
missing-ons(".tX.zNt.",[]).
missing-ons(".Tx.zNt.",[]).
s-nuclei(".txZ.Nt.",["N","Z"]).
s-nuclei(".tX.zNt.",["N","X"]).
s-nuclei(".Tx.zNt.",["N","T"]).
more-sonorous("X","T").
```

the outcome is that the goals `suboptimal(".txZ.Nt.")` and `suboptimal(".Tx.zNt.")` succeed while `suboptimal(".tX.zNt.")` fails, meaning that `".tX.zNt."` is optimal.

For lack of space, various other aspects are not dealt with here.

5   Summary of Method

The method introduced here can be described as follows:

1. *Include in W the status of candidates with respect to constraints:*

   $$C_\lambda \to c_i\,defeats(\varphi, \sigma)$$

   $$\vdots$$

   where the conditions C_λ are basically tautological in the parallel approach[15] *—in which case the above formulas then simplify to $c_i\,defeats(\varphi, \sigma)$.*

2. *Include in D the effect of constraints towards suboptimality:*

   $$\frac{c_i\,defeats(\varphi, \sigma) \; : \; \neg suboptimal(\varphi)}{suboptimal(\sigma)}$$

3. *Specify the ordering $<$ between constraints.*
4. *In view of the resulting default theory $(W, D, <)$, look for any candidate c such that $suboptimal(c)$ is not in an extension. Such a candidate is a correct output.*

As we have seen, the above scheme can be extended when dealing with special cases such as the sequential approach and so on:

$$gen(\chi, \kappa)$$

$$\vdots$$

$$change(\kappa, \epsilon_\kappa)$$

$$\vdots$$

$$gen(\varphi, \sigma) \wedge gen(\varphi, \rho) \wedge change(\sigma, \epsilon_\sigma) \wedge change(\rho, \epsilon_\rho) \wedge$$
$$c_i\,defeats(\epsilon_\sigma, \epsilon_\rho) \to c_i\,defeats(\sigma, \rho)$$

$$\vdots$$

Expressing optimality theory in default logic without priority is also possible, with defaults that are no more complex than above. However, modularity as well as independence of defaults from constraint ranking are lost.

Acknowledgements. This research has been partially supported by the German Science Foundation (DFG) under grant FOR 375/1-1, TP C.

---

[15] Reduplication of the mark approach is a good example showing that the conditions C_λ can take various forms, all of them amount to tautologies.

References

1. F. Baader and B. Hollunder. Priorities on defaults with prerequisites. *Journal of Automated Reasoning* 15:41–68, 1995.
2. G. Brewka. Adding priorities and specificity to default logic. In L. Pereira and D. Pearce, editors, *4th European Workshop on Logics in Artificial Intelligence (JELIA-94)*, pp. 247–260, 1994.
3. J. Delgrande, T. Schaub, and H. Tompits. A compiler for logic programs with preferences. 2000.
   http://www.cs.uni-potsdam.de/~torsten/plp/
4. J. Delgrande, T. Schaub, and H. Tompits. A compiler for ordered logic programs. *8th International Workshop on Non-Monotonic Reasoning (NMR-2000)*, Breckenridge, CO, 2000.
5. J. Delgrande, T. Schaub, and H. Tompits. Logic programs with compiled preferences. *8th European Conference on Artificial Intelligence (ECAI-2000)*, Berlin, Germany, 2000.
6. R. Kager. *Optimality Theory*. Cambridge Textbooks in Linguistics. Cambridge University Press. 1999.
7. A. Prince and P. Smolensky. *Optimality Theory*. Technical Report, Rutgers University, New Brunswick (NJ), and Computer Science Department, University of Colorado, Boulder. 1993.

Towards a Systematic Account of Different Logic Programming Semantics

Pascal Hitzler

Department of Computer Science, Dresden University of Technology
www.wv.inf.tu-dresden.de/~pascal/
phitzler@inf.tu-dresden.de

Abstract. In [1,2], a new methodology has been proposed which allows to derive uniform characterizations of different declarative semantics for logic programs with negation. One result from this work is that the well-founded semantics can formally be understood as a stratified version of the Fitting (or Kripke-Kleene) semantics. The constructions leading to this result, however, show a certain asymmetry which is not readily understood. We will study this situation here with the result that we will obtain a coherent picture of relations between different semantics.

1 Introduction

Within the past twenty years, many different declarative semantics for logic programs with negation have been developed. Different perspectives on the question what properties a semantics should foremost satisfy, have led to a variety of diverse proposals. From a knowledge representation and reasoning point of view it appears to be important that a semantics captures established non-monotonic reasoning frameworks, e.g. Reiters default logic [3], and that they allow intuitively appealing, i.e. "common sense", encodings of AI problems. The semantics which, due to common opinion by researchers in the field, satisfy these requirements best, are the least model semantics for definite programs [4], and for normal programs the stable [5] and the well-founded semantics [6]. Of lesser importance, albeit still acknowledged in particular for their relation to resolution-based logic programming, are the Fitting semantics [7] and approaches based on stratification [8,9].

The semantics just mentioned are closely connnected by a number of well- (and some lesser-) known relationships, and many authors have contributed to this understanding. Fitting [10] provides a framework using Belnap's four-valued logic which encompasses supported, stable, Fitting, and well-founded semantics. His work was recently extended by Denecker, Marek, and Truszczynski [11]. Przymusinsky [12] gives a version in three-valued logic of the stable semantics, and shows that it coincides with the well-founded one. Van Gelder [13] constructs the well-founded semantics unsing the Gelfond-Lifschitz operator originally associated with the stable semantics. Dung and Kanchanasut [14] define the notion of fixpoint completion of a program which provides connections between the

A. Günter et al. (Eds.): KI 2003, LNAI 2821, pp. 105–119, 2003.
© Springer-Verlag Berlin Heidelberg 2003

supported and the stable semantics, as well as between the Fitting and the well-founded semantics, studied by Fages [15] and Wendt [16]. Hitzler and Wendt [1, 2] have recently provided a unifying framework using level mappings, and results which amongst other things give further support to the point of view that the stable semantics is a formal and natural extension to normal programs of the least model semantics for definite programs. Furthermore, it was shown that the well-founded semantics can be understood, formally, as a stratified version of the Fitting semantics.

This latter result, however, exposes a certain asymmetry in the construction leading to it, and it is natural to ask the question as to what exactly is underlying it. This is what we will study in the sequel. In a nutshell, we will see that formally this asymmetry is due to the well-known preference of falsehood in logic programming semantics. More importantly, we will also see that a "dual" theory, obtained from prefering truth, can be stablished which is in perfect analogy to the close and well-known relationships between the different semantics mentioned above. We want to make it explicit from the start that we do not intend to provide new semantics for practical purposes[1]. We rather want to focus on the deepening of the theoretical insights into the relations between different semantics, by painting a coherent and complete picture of the dependencies and interconnections. We find the richness of the theory very appealing, and strongly supportive of the opinion that the major semantics studied in the field are founded on a sound theoretical base.

The plan of the paper is as follows. In Section 2 we will introduce notation and terminology needed for proving the results in the main body of the paper. We will also review in detail those results from [1,2] which triggered and motivated our investigations. In Section 3 we will provide a variant of the stable semantics which prefers truth, and in Section 4 we will do likewise for the well-founded semantics. Throughout, our definitions will be accompanied by results which complete the picture of relationships between different semantics.

2   Preliminaries and Notation

A (*normal*) *logic program* is a finite set of (universally quantified) *clauses* of the form $\forall (A \leftarrow A_1 \wedge \cdots \wedge A_n \wedge \neg B_1 \wedge \cdots \wedge \neg B_m)$, commonly written as $A \leftarrow A_1, \ldots, A_n, \neg B_1, \ldots, \neg B_m$, where A, A_i, and B_j, for $i = 1, \ldots, n$ and $j = 1, \ldots, m$, are atoms over some given first order language. A is called the *head* of the clause, while the remaining atoms make up the *body* of the clause, and depending on context, a body of a clause will be a set of literals (i.e. atoms or negated atoms) or the conjunction of these literals. Care will be taken that this identification does not cause confusion. We allow a body, i.e. a conjunction, to be empty, in which case it always evaluates to true. A clause with empty body is called a *unit clause* or a *fact*. A clause is called *definite*, if it contains no negation symbol. A program is called *definite* if it consists only of definite

---

[1] Although there may be some virtue to this perspective, see [17].

clauses. We will usually denote atoms with A or B, and literals, which may be atoms or negated atoms, by L or K.

Given a logic program P, we can extract from it the components of a first order language, and we always make the mild assumption that this language contains at least one constant symbol. The corresponding set of ground atoms, i.e. the *Herbrand base* of the program, will be denoted by B_P. For a subset $I \subseteq B_P$, we set $\neg I = \{\neg A \mid A \in B_P\}$. The set of all ground instances of P with respect to B_P will be denoted by $\mathsf{ground}(P)$. For $I \subseteq B_P \cup \neg B_P$, we say that A is *true with respect to* (or *in*) I if $A \in I$, we say that A is *false with respect to* (or *in*) I if $\neg A \in I$, and if neither is the case, we say that A is *undefined with respect to* (or *in*) I. A (*three-valued* or *partial*) *interpretation* I for P is a subset of $B_P \cup \neg B_P$ which is *consistent*, i.e. whenever $A \in I$ then $\neg A \notin I$. A body, i.e. a conjunction of literals, is true in an interpretation I if every literal in the body is true in I, it is false in I if one of its literals is false in I, and otherwise it is undefined in I. For a negated literal $L = \neg A$ we will find it convenient to write $\neg L \in I$ if $A \in I$. By I_P we denote the set of all (three-valued) interpretations of P. Both I_P and $B_P \cup \neg B_P$ are complete partial orders (cpos) via set-inclusion, i.e. they contain the empty set as least element, and every ascending chain has a supremum, namely its union. A *model* of P is an interpretation $I \in I_P$ such that for each clause $A \leftarrow \mathsf{body}$ we have that $\mathsf{body} \subseteq I$ implies $A \in I$. A *total* interpretation is an interpretation I such that no $A \in B_P$ is undefined in I.

For an interpretation I and a program P, an I-*partial level mapping* for P is a partial mapping $l : B_P \to \alpha$ with domain $\mathsf{dom}(l) = \{A \mid A \in I \text{ or } \neg A \in I\}$, where α is some (countable) ordinal. We extend every level mapping to literals by setting $l(\neg A) = l(A)$ for all $A \in \mathsf{dom}(l)$. A (*total*) *level mapping* is a total mapping $l : B_P \to \alpha$ for some (countable) ordinal α.

Given a normal logic program P and some $I \subseteq B_P \cup \neg B_P$, we say that $U \subseteq B_P$ is an *unfounded set* (*of* P) *with respect to* I if each atom $A \in U$ satisfies the following condition: For each clause $A \leftarrow \mathsf{body}$ in $\mathsf{ground}(P)$ (at least) one of the following holds.

(Ui) Some (positive or negative) literal in body is false in I.
(Uii) Some (non-negated) atom in body occurs in U.

Given a normal logic program P, we define the following operators on $B_P \cup \neg B_P$. $T_P(I)$ is the set of all $A \in B_P$ such that there exists a clause $A \leftarrow \mathsf{body}$ in $\mathsf{ground}(P)$ such that body is true in I. $F_P(I)$ is the set of all $A \in B_P$ such that for all clauses $A \leftarrow \mathsf{body}$ in $\mathsf{ground}(P)$ we have that body is false in I. Both T_P and F_P map elements of I_P to elements of I_P. Now define the operator $\Phi_P : I_P \to I_P$ by

$$\Phi_P(I) = T_P(I) \cup \neg F_P(I).$$

This operator is due to [7] and is well-defined and monotonic on the cpo I_P, hence has a least fixed point by the Knaster-Tarski[2] fixed-point theorem, and we can obtain this fixed point by defining, for each monotonic operator F, that

---

[2] We follow the terminology from [18]. The Knaster-Tarski theorem is sometimes called Tarski theorem and states that every monotonic function on a cpo has a least fixed

$F \uparrow 0 = \emptyset$, $F \uparrow (\alpha + 1) = F(F \uparrow \alpha)$ for any ordinal α, and $F \uparrow \beta = \bigcup_{\gamma < \beta} F \uparrow \gamma$ for any limit ordinal β, and the least fixed point of F is obtained as $F \uparrow \alpha$ for some ordinal α. The least fixed point of Φ_P is called the *Kripke-Kleene model* or *Fitting model* of P, determining the *Fitting semantics* of P.

Now, for $I \subseteq B_P \cup \neg B_P$, let $U_P(I)$ be the greatest unfounded set (of P) with respect to I, which always exists due to [6]. Finally, define

$$W_P(I) = T_P(I) \cup \neg U_P(I)$$

for all $I \subseteq B_P \cup \neg B_P$. The operator W_P, which operates on the cpo $B_P \cup \neg B_P$, is due to [6] and is monotonic, hence has a least fixed point by the Knaster-Tarski[2] fixed-point theorem, as above for Φ_P. It turns out that $W_P \uparrow \alpha$ is in I_P for each ordinal α, and so the least fixed point of W_P is also in I_P and is called the *well-founded model* of P, giving the *well-founded semantics* of P.

In order to avoid confusion, we will use the following terminology: the notion of *interpretation*, and I_P will be the set of all those, will by default denote consistent subsets of $B_P \cup \neg B_P$, i.e. interpretations in three-valued logic. We will sometimes emphasize this point by using the notion *partial interpretation*. By *two-valued interpretations* we mean subsets of B_P. Both interpretations and two-valued interpretations are ordered by subset inclusion. Each two-valued interpretation I can be identified with the partial interpretation $I' = I \cup \neg(B_P \setminus I)$. Note however, that in this case I' is always a maximal element in the ordering for partial interpretations, while I is in general not maximal as a two-valued interpretation[3]. Given a partial interpretation I, we set $I^+ = I \cap B_P$ and $I^- = \{A \in B_P \mid \neg A \in I\}$.

Given a program P, we define the operator T_P^+ on subsets of B_P by $T_P^+(I) = T_P(I \cup \neg(B_P \setminus I))$. The pre-fixed points of T_P^+, i.e. the two-valued interpretations $I \subseteq B_P$ with $T_P^+(I) \subseteq I$, are exactly the models, in the sense of classical logic, of P. Post-fixed points of T_P^+, i.e. $I \subseteq B_P$ with $I \subseteq T_P^+(I)$ are called *supported interpretations* of P, and a supported model of P is a model P which is a supported interpretation. The supported models of P thus coincide with the fixed points of T_P^+. It is well-known that for definite programs P the operator T_P^+ is monotonic on the set of all subsets of B_P, with respect to subset inclusion. Indeed it is Scott-continuous [4,20] and, via the Tarski-Kantorovich[2] fixed-point theorem, achieves its least pre-fixed point M, which is also a fixed point, as the supremum of the iterates $T_P^+ \uparrow n$ for $n \in \mathbb{N}$. So $M = \mathsf{lfp}\left(T_P^+\right) = T_P^+ \uparrow \omega$ is *the least two-valued model* of P. Likewise, since the set of all subsets of B_P is

---

point, which can be obtained by transfinitely iterating the bottom element of the cpo. The Tarski-Kantorovitch theorem is sometimes refered to as the Kleene theorem or the Scott theorem (or even as "the" fixed-point theorem) and states that if the function is additionally Scott (or order-) continuous, then the least fixed point can be obtained by an iteration which is not transfinite, i.e. closes off at ω, the least infinite ordinal. In both cases, the least fixed point is also the least pre-fixed point of the function.

[3] These two orderings in fact correspond to the knowledge and truth orderings as discussed in [19].

a complete lattice, and therefore has greatest element B_P, we can also define $T_P^+ \downarrow 0 = B_P$ and inductively $T_P^+ \downarrow (\alpha + 1) = T_P^+(T_P^+ \downarrow \alpha)$ for each ordinal α and $T_P^+ \downarrow \beta = \bigcap_{\gamma < \beta} T_P^+ \downarrow \gamma$ for each limit ordinal β. Again by the Knaster-Tarski fixed-point theorem, applied to the superset inclusion ordering (i.e. reverse subset inclusion) on subsets of B_P, it turns out that T_P^+ has a greatest fixed point, $\mathsf{gfp}\,(T_P^+)$.

The stable model semantics due to [5] is intimately related to the well-founded semantics. Let P be a normal program, and let $M \subseteq B_P$ be a set of atoms. Then we define P/M to be the (ground) program consisting of all clauses $A \leftarrow A_1, \ldots, A_n$ for which there is a clause $A \leftarrow A_1, \ldots, A_n, \neg B_1, \ldots, \neg B_m$ in $\mathsf{ground}(P)$ with $B_1, \ldots, B_m \notin M$. Since P/M does no longer contain negation, it has a least two-valued model $T_{P/M}^+ \uparrow \omega$. For any two-valued interpretation I we can therefore define the operator $\mathrm{GL}_P(I) = T_{P/I}^+ \uparrow \omega$, and call M a *stable model* of the normal program P if it is a fixed point of the operator GL_P, i.e. if $M = \mathrm{GL}_P(M) = T_{P/M}^+ \uparrow \omega$. As it turns out, the operator GL_P is in general not monotonic for normal programs P. However it is *antitonic*, i.e. whenever $I \subseteq J \subseteq B_P$ then $\mathrm{GL}_P(J) \subseteq \mathrm{GL}_P(I)$. As a consequence, the operator GL_P^2, obtained by applying GL_P twice, is monotonic, and hence has a least fixed point L_P and a greatest fixed point G_P. In [13] it was shown that $\mathrm{GL}_P(L_P) = G_P$, $L_P = \mathrm{GL}_P(G_P)$, and that $L_P \cup \neg(B_P \setminus G_P)$ coincides with the well-founded model of P. This is called the *alternating fixed point characterization* of the well-founded semantics.

Some Results

The following is a straightforward result which has, to the best of our knowledge, not been noted before. It follows the general approach put forward in [1,2].

Theorem 1. *Let P be a definite program. Then there is a unique two-valued model M of P for which there exists a (total) level mapping $l : B_P \to \alpha$ such that for each atom $A \in M$ there exists a clause $A \leftarrow A_1, \ldots, A_n$ in $\mathsf{ground}(P)$ with $A_i \in M$ and $l(A) > l(A_i)$ for all $i = 1, \ldots, n$. Furthermore, M is the least two-valued model of P.*

Proof. Let M be the least two-valued model $T_P^+ \uparrow \omega$, choose $\alpha = \omega$, and define $l : B_P \to \alpha$ by setting $l(A) = \min\{n \mid A \in T_P^+ \uparrow (n + 1)\}$, if $A \in M$, and by setting $l(A) = 0$, if $A \notin M$. From the fact that $\emptyset \subseteq T_P^+ \uparrow 1 \subseteq \ldots \subseteq T_P^+ \uparrow n \subseteq \ldots \subseteq T_P^+ \uparrow \omega = \bigcup_m T_P^+ \uparrow m$, for each n, we see that l is well-defined and that the least model $T_P^+ \uparrow \omega$ for P has the desired properties.

Conversely, if M is a two-valued model for P which satisfies the given condition for some mapping $l : B_P \to \alpha$, then it is easy to show, by induction on $l(A)$, that $A \in M$ implies $A \in T_P^+ \uparrow (l(A) + 1)$. This yields that $M \subseteq T_P^+ \uparrow \omega$, and hence that $M = T_P^+ \uparrow \omega$ by minimality of the model $T_P^+ \uparrow \omega$.

The following result is due to [15], and is striking in its similarity to Theorem 1.

Theorem 2. *Let P be normal. Then a two-valued model $M \subseteq B_P$ of P is a stable model of P if and only if there exists a (total) level mapping $l : B_P \to \alpha$ such that for each $A \in M$ there exists $A \leftarrow A_1, \ldots, A_n \neg B_1, \ldots, \neg B_m$ in* $\mathsf{ground}(P)$ *with $A_i \in M$, $B_j \notin M$, and $l(A) > l(A_i)$ for all $i = 1, \ldots, n$ and $j = 1, \ldots, m$.*

We next recall the following alternative characterization of the Fitting model, due to [1,2].

Definition 1. *Let P be a normal logic program, I be a model of P, and l be an I-partial level mapping for P. We say that P satisfies (F) with respect to I and l, if each $A \in \mathsf{dom}(l)$ satisfies one of the following conditions.*

(Fi) *$A \in I$ and there exists a clause $A \leftarrow L_1, \ldots, L_n$ in* $\mathsf{ground}(P)$ *such that $L_i \in I$ and $l(A) > l(L_i)$ for all i.*

(Fii) *$\neg A \in I$ and for each clause $A \leftarrow L_1, \ldots, L_n$ in* $\mathsf{ground}(P)$ *there exists i with $\neg L_i \in I$ and $l(A) > l(L_i)$.*

Theorem 3. *Let P be a normal logic program with Fitting model M. Then M is the greatest model among all models I, for which there exists an I-partial level mapping l for P such that P satisfies (F) with respect to I and l.*

Let us recall next the definition of a (locally) stratified program, due to [8,9]: A normal logic program is called *locally stratified* if there exists a (total) level mapping $l : B_P \to \alpha$, for some ordinal α, such that for each clause $A \leftarrow A_1, \ldots, A_n, \neg B_1, \ldots, \neg B_m$ in $\mathsf{ground}(P)$ we have that $l(A) \geq l(A_i)$ and $l(A) > l(B_j)$ for all $i = 1, \ldots, n$ and $j = 1, \ldots, m$. The notion of (locally) stratified program was developed with the idea of preventing *recursion through negation*, while allowing recursion through positive dependencies. (Locally) stratified programs have total well-founded models.

There exist locally stratified programs which do not have a total Fitting semantics and vice versa — just consider the programs consisting of the single clauses $p \leftarrow p$, respectively, $p \leftarrow \neg p, q$. In fact, condition (Fii) requires a strict decrease of level between the head and a literal in the rule, independent of this literal being positive or negative. But, on the other hand, condition (Fii) imposes no further restrictions on the remaining body literals, while the notion of local stratification does. These considerations motivate the substitution of condition (Fii) by the condition (Cii), as done for the following definition.

Definition 2. *Let P be a normal logic program, I be a model of P, and l be an I-partial level mapping for P. We say that P satisfies (WF) with respect to I and l, if each $A \in \mathsf{dom}(l)$ satisfies (Fi) or the following condition.*

(Cii) *$\neg A \in I$ and for each clause $A \leftarrow A_1, \ldots, A_n, \neg B_1, \ldots, \neg B_m$ contained in* $\mathsf{ground}(P)$ *(at least) one of the following conditions holds:*
   (Ciia) *There exists $i \in \{1, \ldots, n\}$ with $\neg A_i \in I$ and $l(A) \geq l(A_i)$.*
   (Ciib) *There exists $j \in \{1, \ldots, m\}$ with $B_j \in I$ and $l(A) > l(B_j)$.*

So, in the light of Theorem 3, Definition 2 should provide a natural "stratified version" of the Fitting semantics. And indeed it does, and furthermore, the resulting semantics coincides with the well-founded semantics, which is a very satisfactory result from [1,2].

Theorem 4. *Let P be a normal logic program with well-founded model M. Then M is the greatest model among all models I, for which there exists an I-partial level mapping l for P such that P satisfies (WF) with respect to I and l.*

For completeness, we remark that an alternative characterization of the weakly perfect model semantics [21] can also be found in [1,2].

The approach which led to the results just mentioned, originally put forward in [1,2], provides a methodology for obtaining uniform characterizations of different semantics for logic programs.

3   Maximally Circular Stable Semantics

We note that condition (Fi) has been reused in Definition 2. Thus, Definition 1 has been "stratified" only with respect to condition (Fii), yielding (Cii), but not with respect to (Fi). Indeed, also replacing (Fi) by a stratified version such as the following seems not satisfactory at first sight.

(Ci) $A \in I$ and there exists a clause $A \leftarrow A_1, \ldots, A_n, \neg B_1, \ldots, \neg B_m$ in ground(P) such that $A_i, \neg B_j \in I$, $l(A) \geq l(A_i)$, and $l(A) > l(B_j)$ for all i and j.

If we replace condition (Fi) by condition (Ci) in Definition 2, then it is not guaranteed that for any given program there is a greatest model satisfying the desired properties, as the following example from [1,2] shows.

Example 1. Consider the program consisting of the two clauses $p \leftarrow p$ and $q \leftarrow \neg p$, and the two (total) models $M_1 = \{p, \neg q\}$ and $M_2 = \{\neg p, q\}$, which are incomparable, and the level mapping l with $l(p) = 0$ and $l(q) = 1$.

In order to arrive at an understanding of this asymmetry, we consider the setting with conditions (Ci) and (Fii), which is somehow "dual" to the well-founded semantics which is characterized by (Fi) and (Cii).

Definition 3. *Let P be a normal logic program, I be a model of P, and l be an I-partial level mapping for P. We say that P satisfies (CW) with respect to I and l, if each $A \in$ dom(l) satisfies (Ci) or (Fii).*

By virtue of Definition 3 we will be able to develop a theory which complements the restults from Section 2. We will first characterize the greatest model of a definite program analogously to Theorem 1.

Theorem 5. *Let P be a definite program. Then there is a unique two-valued supported interpretation M of P for which there exists a (total) level mapping $l : B_P \to \alpha$ such that for each atom $A \notin M$ and for all clauses $A \leftarrow A_1, \ldots, A_n$ in $\mathsf{ground}(P)$ there is some $A_i \notin M$ with $l(A) > l(A_i)$. Furthermore, M is the greatest two-valued model of P.*

Proof. Let M be the greatest two-valued model of P, and let α be the least ordinal such that $M = T_P^+ \downarrow \alpha$. Define $l : B_P \to \alpha$ by setting $l(A) = \min\{\gamma \mid A \notin T_P^+ \downarrow (\gamma + 1)\}$ for $A \notin M$, and by setting $l(A) = 0$ if $A \in M$. The mapping l is well-defined because $A \notin M$ with $A \notin T_P^+ \downarrow \gamma = \bigcap_{\beta < \gamma} T_P^+ \downarrow \beta$ for some limit ordinal γ implies $A \notin T_P^+ \downarrow \beta$ for some $\beta < \gamma$. So the least ordinal β with $A \notin T_P^+ \downarrow \beta$ is always a successor ordinal. Now assume that there is $A \notin M$ which does not satisfy the stated condition. We can furthermore assume without loss of generality that A is chosen with this property such that $l(A)$ is minimal. Let $A \leftarrow A_1, \ldots, A_n$ be a clause in $\mathsf{ground}(P)$. Since $A \notin T_P^+ (T_P^+ \downarrow l(A))$ we obtain $A_i \notin T_P^+ \downarrow l(A) \supseteq M$ for some i. But then $l(A_i) < l(A)$ which contradicts minimality of $l(A)$.

Conversely, let M be a two-valued model for P which satisfies the given condition for some mapping $l : B_P \to \alpha$. We show by transfinite induction on $l(A)$ that $A \notin M$ implies $A \notin T_P^+ \downarrow (l(A) + 1)$, which suffices because it implies that for the greatest two-valued model $T_P^+ \downarrow \beta$ of P we have that $T_P^+ \downarrow \beta \subseteq M$, and therefore $T_P^+ \downarrow \beta = M$. For the inductive proof consider first the case where $l(A) = 0$. Then there is no clause in $\mathsf{ground}(P)$ with head A and consequently $A \notin T_P^+ \downarrow 1 = T_P^+(B_P)$. Now assume that the statement to be proven holds for all $B \notin M$ with $l(B) < \alpha$, where α is some ordinal, and let $A \notin M$ with $l(A) = \alpha$. Then each clause in $\mathsf{ground}(P)$ with head A contains an atom B with $l(B) = \beta < \alpha$ and $B \notin M$. Hence $B \notin T_P^+ \downarrow (\beta + 1)$ and consequently $A \notin T_P^+ \downarrow (\alpha + 1)$.

The following definition and theorem are analogous to Theorem 2.

Definition 4. *Let P be normal. Then $M \subseteq B_P$ is called a maximally circular stable model (maxstable model) of P if it is a two-valued supported interpretation of P and there exists a (total) level mapping $l : B_P \to \alpha$ such that for each atom $A \notin M$ and for all clauses $A \leftarrow A_1, \ldots, A_n, \neg B_1, \ldots, \neg B_m$ in $\mathsf{ground}(P)$ with $B_1, \ldots, B_m \notin M$ there is some $A_i \notin M$ with $l(A) > l(A_i)$.*

Theorem 6. *$M \subseteq B_P$ is a maxstable model of P if and only if $M = \mathsf{gfp}\left(T_{P/M}^+\right)$.*

Proof. First note that every maxstable model is a a supported model. Indeed supportedness follows immediately from the definition. Now assume that M is maxstable but is not a model, i.e. there is $A \notin M$ but there is a clause $A \leftarrow A_1, \ldots, A_n$ in $\mathsf{ground}(P)$ with $A_i \in M$ for all i. But by the definition of maxstable model we must have that there is $A_i \notin M$, which contradicts $A_i \in M$.

Now let M be a maxstable model of P. Let $A \notin M$ and let $T^+_{P/M} \downarrow \alpha = \mathsf{gfp}\left(T^+_{P/M}\right)$. We show by transfinite induction on $l(A)$ that $A \notin T^+_{P/M} \downarrow (l(A)+1)$ and hence $A \notin T^+_{P/M} \downarrow \alpha$. For $l(A) = 0$ there is no clause with head A in P/M, so $A \notin T^+_{P/M} \downarrow 1$. Now let $l(A) = \beta$ for some ordinal β. By assumption we have that for all clauses $A \leftarrow A_1, \ldots, A_n, \neg B_1, \ldots, \neg B_m$ with $B_1, \ldots, B_m \notin M$ there exists $A_i \notin M$ with $l(A) > l(A_i)$, say $l(A_i) = \gamma < \beta$. Hence $A_i \notin T^+_{P/M} \downarrow (\gamma+1)$, and consequently $A \notin T^+_{P/M} \downarrow (\beta+1)$, which shows that $\mathsf{gfp}\left(T^+_{P/M}\right) \subseteq M$.

So let again M be a maxstable model of P and let $A \notin \mathsf{gfp}\left(T^+_{P/M}\right) = T^+_{P/M} \downarrow \alpha$ and $l(A) = \beta$. Then for each clause $A \leftarrow A_1, \ldots, A_n$ in P/M there is A_i with $A_i \notin T^+_{P/M} \downarrow \alpha$ and $l(A) > l(A_i)$. Now assume $A \in M$. Without loss of generality we can furthermore assume that A is chosen such that $l(A) = \beta$ is minimal. Hence $A_i \notin M$, and we obtain that for each clause in P/M with head A one of the corresponding body atoms is false in M. By supportedness of M this yields $A \notin M$, which contradicts our assumption. Hence $A \notin M$ as desired.

Conversely, let $M = \mathsf{gfp}\left(T^+_{P/M}\right)$. Then as an immediate consequence of Theorem 5 we obtain that M is maxstable.

4 Maximally Circular Well-Founded Semantics

Maxstable models are formally analogous[4] to stable models in that the former are fixed points of the operator $I \mapsto \mathsf{gfp}\left(T^+_{P/I}\right)$, while the latter are fixed points of the operator $I \mapsto \mathsf{lfp}\left(T^+_{P/I}\right)$. Further, in analogy to the alternating fixed point characterization of the well-founded model, we can obtain a corresponding variant of the well-founded semantics, which we will do next. Theorem 6 suggests the defininition of the following operator.

Definition 5. *Let P be a normal program and I be a two-valued interpretation. Then define* $\mathrm{CGL}_P(I) = \mathsf{gfp}\left(T^+_{P/I}\right)$.

Using the operator CGL_P, we can define a "maximally circular" version of the alternating fixed-point semantics.

Proposition 1. *Let P be a normal program. Then the following hold.*

(i) CGL_P is antitonic and CGL_P^2 is monotonic.
(ii) $\mathrm{CGL}_P\left(\mathsf{lfp}\left(\mathrm{CGL}_P^2\right)\right) = \mathsf{gfp}\left(\mathrm{CGL}_P^2\right)$ and $\mathrm{CGL}_P\left(\mathsf{gfp}\left(\mathrm{CGL}_P^2\right)\right) = \mathsf{lfp}\left(\mathrm{CGL}_P^2\right)$.

Proof. (i) If $I \subseteq J \in B_P$, then $P/J \subseteq P/I$ and consequently $\mathrm{CGL}_P(J) = \mathsf{gfp}\left(T^+_{P/J}\right) \subseteq \mathsf{gfp}\left(T^+_{P/I}\right) = \mathrm{CGL}_P(I)$. Monotonicity of CGL_P^2 then follows trivially.

---

[4] The term *dual* seems not to be entirely adequate in this situation, although it is intuitively appealing.

(ii) Let $L_P = \mathsf{lfp}\left(\mathrm{CGL}_P^2\right)$ and $G_P = \mathsf{gfp}\left(\mathrm{CGL}_P^2\right)$. Then we can calculate $\mathrm{CGL}_P^2(\mathrm{CGL}_P(L_P)) = \mathrm{CGL}_P\left(\mathrm{CGL}_P^2(L_P)\right) = \mathrm{CGL}_P(L_P)$, so $\mathrm{CGL}_P(L_P)$ is a fixed point of CGL_P^2, and hence $L_P \subseteq \mathrm{CGL}_P(L_P) \subseteq G_P$. Similarly, $L_P \subseteq \mathrm{CGL}_P(G_P) \subseteq G_P$. Since $L_P \subseteq G_P$ we get from the antitonicity of CGL_P that $L_P \subseteq \mathrm{CGL}_P(G_P) \subseteq \mathrm{CGL}_P(L_P) \subseteq G_P$. Similarly, since $\mathrm{CGL}_P(L_P) \subseteq G_P$, we obtain $\mathrm{CGL}_P(G_P) \subseteq \mathrm{CGL}_P^2(L_P) = L_P \subseteq \mathrm{CGL}_P(G_P)$, so $\mathrm{CGL}_P(G_P) = L_P$, and also $G_P = \mathrm{CGL}_P^2(G_P) = \mathrm{CGL}_P(L_P)$.

We will now define an operator for the maximally circular well-founded semantics. Given a normal logic program P and some $I \in I_P$, we say that $S \subseteq B_P$ is a *self-founded set (of P) with respect to I* if $S \cup I \in I_P$ and each atom $A \in S$ satisfies the following condition: There exists a clause $A \leftarrow \mathsf{body}$ in $\mathsf{ground}(P)$ such that one of the following holds.

(Si) body is true in I.
(Sii) Some (non-negated) atoms in body occur in S and all other literals in body are true in I.

Self-founded sets are analogous[5] to unfounded sets, and the following proposition holds.

Proposition 2. *Let P be a normal program and let $I \in I_P$. Then there exists a greatest self-founded set of P with respect to I.*

Proof. If $(S_i)_{i \in \mathcal{I}}$ is a family of sets each of which is a self-founded set of P with respect to I, then it is easy to see that $\bigcup_{i \in \mathcal{I}} S_i$ is also a self-founded set of P with respect to I.

Given a normal program P and $I \in I_P$, let $S_P(I)$ be the greatest self-founded set of P with respect to I, and define the operator CW_P on I_P by

$$\mathrm{CW}_P(I) = S_P(I) \cup \neg F_P(I).$$

Proposition 3. *The operator CW_P is well-defined and monotonic.*

Proof. For well-definedness, we have to show that $S_P(I) \cap F_P(I) = \emptyset$ for all $I \in I_P$. So assume there is $A \in S_P(I) \cap F_P(I)$. From $A \in F_P(I)$ we obtain that for each clause with head A there is a corresponding body literal L which is false in I. From $A \in S_P(I)$, more precisely from (Sii), we can furthermore conclude that L is an atom and $L \in S_P(I)$. But then $\neg L \in I$ and $L \in S_P(I)$ which is impossible by definition of self-founded set which requires that $S_P(I) \cup I \in I_P$. So $S_P(I) \cap F_P(I) = \emptyset$ and CW_P is well-defined.

For monotonicity, let $I \subseteq J \in I_P$ and let $L \in \mathrm{CW}_P(I)$. If $L = \neg A$ is a negated atom, then $A \in F_P(I)$ and all clauses with head A contain a body literal which is false in I, hence in J, and we obtain $A \in F_P(J)$. If $L = A$ is an atom, then $A \in S_P(I)$ and there exists a clause $A \leftarrow \mathsf{body}$ in $\mathsf{ground}(P)$ such

---

[5] Again, it is not really a duality.

that (at least) one of (Si) or (Sii) holds. If (Si) holds, then body is true in I, hence in J, and $A \in S_P(J)$. If (Sii) holds, then some non-negated atoms in body occur in S and all other literals in body are true in I, hence in J, and we obtain $A \in S_P(J)$.

The following theorem relates our previous observations to Definition 3, in perfect analogy to the correspondence between the stable model semantics, Theorem 1, Fages's characterization from Theorem 2, the well-founded semantics, and the alternating fixed point characterization.

Theorem 7. *Let P be a normal program and $M_P = \mathsf{lfp}(\mathrm{CW}_P)$. Then the following hold.*

(i) *M_P is the greatest model among all models I of P such that there is an I-partial level mapping l for P such that P satisfies (CW) with respect to I and l.*

(ii) *$M_P = \mathsf{lfp}\left(\mathrm{CGL}_P^2\right) \cup \neg \left(B_P \setminus \mathsf{gfp}\left(\mathrm{CGL}_P^2\right)\right)$.*

Proof. (i) Let $M_P = \mathsf{lfp}(\mathrm{CW}_P)$ and define the M_P-partial level mapping l_P as follows: $l_P(A) = \alpha$, where α is the least ordinal such that A is not undefined in $\mathrm{CW}_P {\uparrow} (\alpha + 1)$. The proof will be established by showing the following facts: (1) P satisfies (CW) with respect to M_P and l_P. (2) If I is a model of P and l is an I-partial level mapping such that P satisfies (CW) with respect to I and l, then $I \subseteq M_P$.

(1) Let $A \in \mathsf{dom}(l_P)$ and $l_P(A) = \alpha$. We consider two cases.

(Case i) If $A \in M_P$, then $A \in S_P(\mathrm{CW}_P \uparrow \alpha)$, hence there exists a clause $A \leftarrow \text{body}$ in $\mathsf{ground}(P)$ such that (Si) or (Sii) holds with respect to $\mathrm{CW}_P {\uparrow} \alpha$. If (Si) holds, then all literals in body are true in $\mathrm{CW}_P {\uparrow} \alpha$, hence have level less than $l_P(A)$ and (Ci) is satisfied. If (Sii) holds, then some non-negated atoms from body occur in $S_P(\mathrm{CW}_P {\uparrow} \alpha)$, hence have level less than or equal to $l_P(A)$, and all remaining literals in body are true in $\mathrm{CW}_P {\uparrow} \alpha$, hence have level less than $l_P(A)$. Consequently, A satisfies (Ci) with respect to M_P and l_P.

(Case ii) If $\neg A \in M_P$, then $A \in F_P(\mathrm{CW}_P {\uparrow} \alpha)$, hence for all clauses $A \leftarrow \text{body}$ in $\mathsf{ground}(P)$ there exists $L \in \text{body}$ with $\neg L \in \mathrm{CW}_P {\uparrow} \alpha$ and $l_P(L) < \alpha$, hence $\neg L \in M_P$. Consequently, A satisfies (Fii) with respect to M_P and l_P, and we have established that fact (1) holds.

(2) We show via transfinite induction on $\alpha = l(A)$, that whenever $A \in I$ (respectively, $\neg A \in I$), then $A \in \mathrm{CW}_P \uparrow (\alpha + 1)$ (respectively, $\neg A \in \mathrm{CW}_P \uparrow (\alpha + 1)$). For the base case, note that if $l(A) = 0$, then $\neg A \in I$ implies that there is no clause with head A in $\mathsf{ground}(P)$, hence $\neg A \in \mathrm{CW}_P \uparrow 1$. If $A \in I$ then consider the set S of all atoms B with $l(B) = 0$ and $B \in I$. We show that S is a self-founded set of P with respect to $\mathrm{CW}_P \uparrow 0 = \emptyset$, and this suffices since it implies $A \in \mathrm{CW}_P \uparrow 1$ by the fact that $A \in S$. So let $C \in S$. Then $C \in I$ and C satisfies condition (Ci) with respect to I and l, and since $l(C) = 0$, we have that there is a definite clause with head C whose body atoms (if it has any) are all of level 0 and contained in I. Hence condition (Sii) (or (Si)) is satisfied for this clause and S is a self-founded set of P with respect to I. So assume now that

the induction hypothesis holds for all $B \in B_P$ with $l(B) < \alpha$, and let A be such that $l(A) = \alpha$. We consider two cases.

(Case i) If $A \in I$, consider the set S of all atoms B with $l(B) = \alpha$ and $B \in I$. We show that S is a self-founded set of P with respect to $\mathrm{CW}_P \uparrow \alpha$, and this suffices since it implies $A \in \mathrm{CW}_P \uparrow (\alpha + 1)$ by the fact that $A \in S$. First note that $S \subseteq I$, so $S \cup I \in I_P$. Now let $C \in S$. Then $C \in I$ and C satisfies condition (Ci) with respect to I and l, so there is a clause $A \leftarrow A_1, \ldots, A_n, \neg B_1, \ldots, \neg B_m$ in $\mathsf{ground}(P)$ such that $A_i, \neg B_j \in I$, $l(A) \geq l(A_i)$, and $l(A) > l(B_j)$ for all i and j. By induction hypothesis we obtain $\neg B_j \in \mathrm{CW}_P \uparrow \alpha$. If $l(A_i) < l(A)$ for some A_i then we have $A_i \in \mathrm{CW}_P \uparrow \alpha$, also by induction hypothesis. If there is no A_i with $l(A_i) = l(A)$, then (Si) holds, while $l(A_i) = l(A)$ implies $A_i \in S$, so (Sii) holds.

(Case ii) If $\neg A \in I$, then A satisfies (Fii) with respect to I and l. Hence for all clauses $A \leftarrow \mathsf{body}$ in $\mathsf{ground}(P)$ we have that there is $L \in \mathsf{body}$ with $\neg L \in I$ and $l(L) < \alpha$. Hence for all these L we have $\neg L \in \mathrm{CW}_P \uparrow \alpha$ by induction hypothesis, and consequently for all clauses $A \leftarrow \mathsf{body}$ in $\mathsf{ground}(P)$ we obtain that body is false in $\mathrm{CW}_P \uparrow \alpha$ which yields $\neg A \in \mathrm{CW}_P \uparrow (\alpha + 1)$. This establishes fact (2) and concludes the proof of (i).

(ii) We first introduce some notation. Let

$$
\begin{aligned}
L_0 &= \emptyset, & G_0 &= B_P, \\
L_{\alpha+1} &= \mathrm{CGL}_P(G_\alpha), & G_{\alpha+1} &= \mathrm{CGL}_P(L_\alpha) & \text{for any ordinal } \alpha, \\
L_\alpha &= \bigcup_{\beta<\alpha} L_\beta, & G_\alpha &= \bigcap_{\beta<\alpha} G_\beta & \text{for limit ordinal } \alpha, \\
L_P &= \mathsf{lfp}(\mathrm{CGL}_P^2), & G_P &= \mathsf{gfp}(\mathrm{CGL}_P^2).
\end{aligned}
$$

By transfinite induction, it is easily checked that $L_\alpha \subseteq L_\beta \subseteq G_\beta \subseteq G_\alpha$ whenever $\alpha \leq \beta$. So $L_P = \bigcup L_\alpha$ and $G_P = \bigcap G_\alpha$.

Let $M = L_P \cup \neg(B_P \setminus G_P)$. We intend to apply (i) and first define an M-partial level mapping l. We will take as image set of l, pairs (α, γ) of ordinals, with the lexicographic ordering. This can be done without loss of generality since any set of such pairs, under the lexicographic ordering, is well-ordered, and therefore order-isomorphic to an ordinal. For $A \in L_P$, let $l(A)$ be the pair $(\alpha, 0)$, where α is the least ordinal such that $A \in L_{\alpha+1}$. For $B \notin G_P$, let $l(B)$ be the pair (β, γ), where β is the least ordinal such that $B \notin G_{\beta+1}$, and γ is least such that $B \notin T_{P/L_\beta} \downarrow \gamma$. It is easily shown that l is well-defined, and we show next by transfinite induction that P satisfies (CW) with respect to M and l.

Let $A \in L_1 = \mathsf{gfp}\left(T_{P/B_P}^+\right)$. Since P/B_P contains exactly all clauses from $\mathsf{ground}(P)$ which contain no negation, we have that A is contained in the greatest two-valued model of a definite subprogram of P, namely P/B_P. So there must be a definite clause in $\mathsf{ground}(P)$ with head A whose corresponding body atoms are also true in L_1, which, by definition of l, must have the same level as A, hence (Ci) is satisfied. Now let $\neg B \in \neg(B_P \setminus G_P)$ such that $B \in (B_P \setminus G_P) = B_P \setminus \mathsf{gfp}\left(T_{P/\emptyset}^+\right)$. Since $P/\emptyset$ contains all clauses from $\mathsf{ground}(P)$ with all negative literals removed, we obtain that B is not contained in the greatest two-valued model of the definite program $P/\emptyset$, and (Fii) is satisfied by Theorem 5 using a simple induction argument.

Assume now that, for some ordinal α, we have shown that A satisfies (CW) with respect to M and l for all $A \in B_P$ with $l(A) < (\alpha, 0)$.

Let $A \in L_{\alpha+1} \setminus L_\alpha = \mathsf{gfp}\left(T^+_{P/G_\alpha}\right) \setminus L_\alpha$. Then $A \in \left(T^+_{P/G_\alpha} \downarrow \gamma\right) \setminus L_\alpha$ for some γ; note that all (negative) literals which were removed by the Gelfond-Lifschitz transformation from clauses with head A have level less than $(\alpha, 0)$. Then A satisfies (Ci) with respect to M and l by definition of l.

Let $A \in (B_P \setminus G_{\alpha+1}) \cap G_\alpha$. Then $A \notin \mathsf{gfp}\left(T^+_{P/L_\alpha}\right)$ and we conclude again from Theorem 5, using a simple induction argument, that A satisfies (CW) with respect to M and l.

This finishes the proof that P satisfies (CW) with respect to M and l. It remains to show that M is greatest with this property.

So assume that $M_1 \supset M$ is the greatest model such that P satisfies (CW) with respect to M_1 and some M_1-partial level mapping l_1. Assume $L \in M_1 \setminus M$ and, without loss of generality, let the literal L be chosen such that $l_1(L)$ is minimal. We consider two cases.

(Case i) If $L = \neg A \in M_1 \setminus M$ is a negated atom, then by (Fii) for each clause $A \leftarrow L_1, \ldots, L_n$ in $\mathsf{ground}(P)$ there exists i with $\neg L_i \in M_1$ and $l_1(A) > l_1(L_i)$. Hence, $\neg L_i \in M$ and consequently for each clause $A \leftarrow \mathsf{body}$ in P/L_P we have that some atom in body is false in $M = L_P \cup \neg(B_P \setminus G_P)$. But then $A \notin \mathsf{CGL}_P(L_P) = G_P$, hence $\neg A \in M$, contradicting $\neg A \in M_1 \setminus M$.

(Case ii) If $L = A \in M_1 \setminus M$ is an atom, then $A \notin M = L_P \cup \neg(B_P \setminus G_P)$ and in particular $A \notin L_P = \mathsf{gfp}\left(T^+_{P/G_P}\right)$. Hence $A \notin T^+_{P/G_P} \downarrow \gamma$ for some γ, which can be chosen to be least with this property. We show by induction on γ that this leads to a contradiction, to finish the proof.

If $\gamma = 1$, then there is no clause with head A in P/G_P, i.e. for all clauses $A \leftarrow \mathsf{body}$ in $\mathsf{ground}(P)$ we have that body is false in M, hence in M_1, which contradicts $A \in M_1$.

Now assume that there is no $B \in M_1 \setminus M$ with $B \notin T^+_{P/G_P} \downarrow \delta$ for any $\delta < \gamma$, and let $A \in M_1 \setminus M$ with $A \notin T^+_{P/G_P} \downarrow \gamma$, which implies that γ is a successor ordinal. By $A \in M_1$ and (Ci) there must be a clause $A \leftarrow A_1, \ldots, A_n \neg B_1, \ldots, \neg B_m$ in $\mathsf{ground}(P)$ with $A_i, \neg B_j \in M_1$ for all i and j. However, since $A \notin T^+_{P/G_P} \downarrow \gamma$ we obtain that for each $A \leftarrow A_1, \ldots, A_n$ in P/G_P, hence for each $A \leftarrow A_1, \ldots, A_n, \neg B_1, \ldots, \neg B_m$ in $\mathsf{ground}(P)$ with $\neg B_1, \ldots, \neg B_m \in \neg(B_P \setminus G_P) \subseteq M \subseteq M_1$ there is A_i with $A_i \notin T^+_{P/G_P} \downarrow (\gamma - 1) \subseteq M$, and by induction hypothesis we obtain $A_i \notin M_1$. So $A_i \in M_1$ and $A_i \notin M_1$, which is a contradiction and concludes the proof.

Definition 6. *For a normal program P, we call $\mathsf{lfp}(\mathrm{CW}_P)$ the maximally circular well-founded model (maxwf model) of P.*

5   Conclusions and Further Work

We have displayed a coherent picture of different semantics for normal logic programs. We have added to well-known results new ones which complete the formerly incomplete picture of relationships. The richness of theory and relationships turns out to be very appealing and satisfactory. From a mathematical perspective one expects major notions in a field to be strongly and cleanly interconnected, and it is fair to say that this is the case for declarative semantics for normal logic programs.

The situation becomes much more difficult when discussing extensions of the logic programming paradigm like disjunctive [22], quantitative [23], or dynamic [24] logic programming. For many of these extensions it is as yet to be determined what the best ways of providing declarative semantics for these frameworks are, and the lack of interconnections between the different proposals in the literature provides an argument for the case that no satisfactory answers have yet been found.

We believe that successful proposals for extensions will have to exhibit similar interrelationships as observed for normal programs. How, and if, this can be achieved, however, is as yet rather uncertain. Formal studies like the one in this paper may help in designing satisfactory semantics, but a discussion of this is outside the scope of our exhibition, and will be pursued elsewhere.

References

1. Hitzler, P., Wendt, M.: The well-founded semantics is a stratified Fitting semantics. In Jarke, M., Koehler, J., Lakemeyer, G., eds.: Proceedings of the 25th Annual German Conference on Artificial Intelligence, KI2002, Aachen, Germany, September 2002. Volume 2479 of Lecture Notes in Artificial Intelligence., Springer, Berlin (2002) 205–221
2. Hitzler, P., Wendt, M.: A uniform approach to logic rogramming semantics. Technical Report WV–02–14, Knowledge Representation and Reasoning Group, Artificial Intelligence Institute, Department of Computer Science, Dresden University of Technology, Dresden, Germany (2002) Submitted.
3. Reiter, R.: A logic for default reasoning. Artificial Intelligence **13** (1980) 81–132
4. Lloyd, J.W.: Foundations of Logic Programming. Springer, Berlin (1988)
5. Gelfond, M., Lifschitz, V.: The stable model semantics for logic programming. In Kowalski, R.A., Bowen, K.A., eds.: Logic Programming. Proceedings of the 5th International Conference and Symposium on Logic Programming, MIT Press (1988) 1070–1080
6. van Gelder, A., Ross, K.A., Schlipf, J.S.: The well-founded semantics for general logic programs. Journal of the ACM **38** (1991) 620–650
7. Fitting, M.: A Kripke-Kleene-semantics for general logic programs. The Journal of Logic Programming **2** (1985) 295–312
8. Apt, K.R., Blair, H.A., Walker, A.: Towards a theory of declarative knowledge. In Minker, J., ed.: Foundations of Deductive Databases and Logic Programming. Morgan Kaufmann, Los Altos, CA (1988) 89–148

9. Przymusinski, T.C.: On the declarative semantics of deductive databases and logic programs. In Minker, J., ed.: Foundations of Deductive Databases and Logic Programming. Morgan Kaufmann, Los Altos, CA (1988) 193–216

10. Fitting, M.: Fixpoint semantics for logic programming — A survey. Theoretical Computer Science **278** (2002) 25–51

11. Denecker, M., Marek, V.W., Truszczynski, M.: Approximating operators, stable operators, well-founded fixpoints and applications in non-monotonic reasoning. In Minker, J., ed.: Logic-based Artificial Intelligence. Kluwer Academic Publishers, Boston (2000) 127–144

12. Przymusinski, T.C.: Well-founded semantics coincides with three-valued stable semantics. Fundamenta Informaticae **13** (1989) 445–464

13. van Gelder, A.: The alternating fixpoint of logic programs with negation. In: Proceedings of the Eighth ACM SIGACT-SIGMOD-SIGART Symposium on Principles of Database Systems, Philadelphia, Pennsylvania, ACM Press (1989) 1–10

14. Dung, P.M., Kanchanasut, K.: A fixpoint approach to declarative semantics of logic programs. In Lusk, E.L., Overbeek, R.A., eds.: Logic Programming, Proceedings of the North American Conference 1989, NACLP'89, Cleveland, Ohio, MIT Press (1989) 604–625

15. Fages, F.: Consistency of Clark's completion and existence of stable models. Journal of Methods of Logic in Computer Science **1** (1994) 51–60

16. Wendt, M.: Unfolding the well-founded semantics. Journal of Electrical Engineering, Slovak Academy of Sciences **53** (2002) 56–59 (Proceedings of the 4th Slovakian Student Conference in Applied Mathematics, Bratislava, April 2002).

17. Hitzler, P.: Circular belief in logic programming semantics. Technical Report WV–02–13, Knowledge Representation and Reasoning Group, Artificial Intelligence Institute, Department of Computer Science, Dresden University of Technology, Dresden, Germany (2002)

18. Jachymski, J.: Order-theoretic aspects of metric fixed-point theory. In Kirk, W.A., Sims, B., eds.: Handbook of Metric Fixed Point Theory. Kluwer Academic Publishers, Dordrecht, The Netherlands (2001) 613–641

19. Fitting, M.: Bilattices and the semantics of logic programming. The Journal of Logic Programming **11** (1991) 91–116

20. Abramsky, S., Jung, A.: Domain theory. In Abramsky, S., Gabbay, D., Maibaum, T.S., eds.: Handbook of Logic in Computer Science. Volume 3. Clarendon, Oxford (1994)

21. Przymusinska, H., Przymusinski, T.C.: Weakly stratified logic programs. Fundamenta Informaticae **13** (1990) 51–65

22. Wang, K.: A comparative study of well-founded semantics for disjunctive logic programs. In Eiter, T., Faber, W., Truszczynski, M., eds.: Logic Programming and Nonmonotonic Reasoning, 6th International Conference, LPNMR 2001, Vienna, Austria, September 17–19, 2001, Proceedings. Volume 2173 of Lecture Notes in Artificial Intelligence., Springer (2001) 133–146

23. Mateis, C.: Quantitative disjunctive logic programming: Semantics and computation. AI communications **13** (2000) 225–248

24. Leite, J.A.: Evolving Knowledge Bases. Volume 81 of Frontiers of Artificial Intelligence and Applications. IOS Press (2003)

How to Build a Foundational Ontology
The Object-Centered High-Level Reference Ontology OCHRE

Luc Schneider

Institute for Formal Ontology and Medical Information Science,
University of Leipzig, Härtelstrasse 16-18, D–4107 Leipzig
luc.schneider@ifomis.uni-leipzig.de

Abstract. Foundational ontologies are axiomatic accounts of high-level
domain-independent categories about the real world. They constitute
toolboxes of reusable information modeling primitives for building application ontologies in specific domains. As such, they enhance semantic interoperability between agents by specifying descriptively adequate
shared conceptualisations. The design of foundational ontologies gives
rise to completely new challenges in respect of their content as well
as their formalisation. Indeed, their underlying modeling options correspond to the ontological choices discussed in classical metaphysics as
well as in the research on qualitative reasoning. Building a foundational
ontology is thus an eminently interdisciplinary task. As a case study,
this article sketches the formalisation of the Object-Centered High-level
REference ontology OCHRE, emphasising in particular the problem of
achieving formal simplicity within the limits of descrip tive adequacy.

1 Introduction

Foundational ontologies are axiomatic theories about domain-independent top-
level categories such as *object, attribute, event, parthood, dependence* and *spatio-
temporal connection*. They amount to repositories of highly general information
modeling concepts that can be reused in the design of application ontologies for
all kinds of domains (Gangemi et al. 2002). By providing toolboxes of standardised knowledge representation primitives, foundational ontologies also enhance
the semantic interoperability between the communicating agents (ibid.).

According to received AI wisdom, an ontology is nothing other than the
formal statement of a shared conceptualisation (Gruber 1991, Guarino 1998).
However, it is not sufficient for an ontology to be merely consensual. The fact
that ontologies, whether in the medical field or in the area of business operations, have to be updated and revised, reveals the need for acknowledging the
constraint of *descriptive adequacy*. Ontologies which are designed to describe
a certain domain adequately, will be called *reference ontologies* (Smith 2003).
Foundational ontologies are top-level reference ontologies; though their starting
point is the set of common-sense intuitions that make up the human conceptualisation of reality, they ultimately aim at describing the categorial structure of
the world as a whole.

A. Günter et al. (Eds.): KI 2003, LNAI 2821, pp. 120–134, 2003.
© Springer-Verlag Berlin Heidelberg 2003

The challenges of building foundational ontologies are unfamiliar to most knowledge engineers. Indeed, the design options for top-level ontologies are identical to the ontological choices discussed in the branch of philosophy called *metaphysics* as well as in the research on qualitative reasoning. Although down-to-earth pragmatical considerations regarding simplicity and contextual applicability help to avoid getting bogged down in spurious details, a good knowledge of the recent advances in metaphysics as well as in qualitative reasoning is still necessary to gauge different ontological positions and approaches. Building foundational ontologies is thus an eminently interdisciplinary task.

As an illustration of current approaches to the design of foundational ontologies, the present paper outlines the formalisation of the Object-Centered High-level REference ontology OCHRE, elucidating and motivating its basic modeling decisions. The purpose of this article is not only to present a particular basic ontological framework, but also to demonstrate how the quality of a foundational ontology depends on maximal formal elegance and transparency in the limits of descriptive adequacy.

The paper is structured as follows. Section 2 treats the theory of parts and wholes, presenting a simple algebraic framework for mereology. Section 3 defends a qualitative account of objects as bundles of attributes and defines the relation of similarity between individual features. Section 4 outlines a theory of dependence grounding the ontological priority of objects over other entities. Section 5 discusses the problem of change, contending a distinction between objects and their short-lived stages, and axiomatises spatio-temporal connection between such stages of objects. Section 6 analyses the relations between attributes and objects and addresses the issue of constitution by a theory of guises. Section 7 formalises the relation of temporal succession between object-stages and offers an account of events in terms of ensuing object-stages.

It should be pointed out that the axioms (**XA n**), theorems (**XT n**), and definitions (**XD n**) given in this paper only aim at a minimal formal characterisation of the ontological primitives. The meaning of these primitives can only be constrained by referring to the ontological intuitions underlying human world knowledge. The informal parts of this essay are intended to clarify these intuitions and thus form an integral part of the specification of OCHRE.

2 Parts and Wholes

Mereology, the formal theory of parthood, has grown out of early-20th-century mathematical research into a calculus of individuals capturing relations between set-theoretical *urelemente* (Leonard and Goodman 1940). Classical mereology, namely *General Extensional Mereology (GEM)*, amounts to a Boolean algebra without a null element (Simons 1987, chap. 1; Casati and Varzi 1999, chap. 3). In particular, OCHRE is based on the atomistic version of GEM.

The *parthood* relation is reflexive, antisymmetric and transitive.

MA 1. Pxx *(reflexivity)*

MA 2. $(Pxy \wedge Pyx) \rightarrow x = y$ *(antisymmetry)*

MA 3. $(Pxy \wedge Pyz) \rightarrow Pxz$ *(transitivity)*

As a direct consequence of the reflexivity of parthood (**MA 1**), identity implies mutual parthood. In other words, parthood is partial identity (Armstrong 1997, p. 17; Lewis 1991, pp. 81–82).

MA 4. $x = y \rightarrow (Pxy \wedge Pyx)$ *(parthood is partial identity)*

The irreflexive variant of parthood is called *proper parthood*.

MD 1. $PPxy \equiv_{df} Pxy \wedge \neg x = y$ *(proper parthood)*

Two individuals *overlap* iff they have common parts.

MD 2. $Oxy \equiv_{df} \exists z (Pzx \wedge Pzy)$ *(overlap)*

An *atom* is an entity that has no proper parts.

MD 3. $\mathcal{A}x \equiv_{df} \neg \exists y\, PPyx$ *(atom)*

An atomistic mereology is based on the thesis that everything has atomic parts:

MA 5. $\exists y (\mathcal{A}y \wedge Pyx)$ *(atomicity)*

Parthood is assumed to be extensional, i.e. an individual is part of another if every atomic part of the first is also a part of the second.

MA 6. $((\mathcal{A}z \wedge Pzx) \rightarrow Pzy) \rightarrow Pxy$ *(extensionality)*

The basic mereological operation is the *(generalised) sum* or *fusion* of all φ-ers which yields the individual containing the atomic parts of entities satisfying the condition φ.

MD 4. $SM(x, \lambda y \varphi y) \equiv_{df} \forall z (\mathcal{A}z \rightarrow (Pzx \leftrightarrow \exists w (\varphi w \wedge Pzw)))$ *(sum)*

The *General Sum Principle* stipulates that, for every satisfiable condition φ, there is a unique sum of all φ-ers.

MA 7. $\exists x \varphi x \leftrightarrow \exists! y\, SM(y, \lambda z \varphi z)$ *(general sum principle)*

As a consequence, there is a least upper bound for parthood, some entity of which everything is a part, namely the fusion of all self-identical entities.

MD 5. $\mathcal{U}x \equiv_{df} SM(x, \lambda y (y = y))$ *(least upper bound)*

The mereological operations of *(binary) sum*, *product* and *difference* correspond to the set-theoretic operations of union, intersection and set difference:

MD 6. $SM(x, y, z) \equiv_{df} SM(x, \lambda w (Pwy \vee Pwz))$ *(binary sum)*

MD 7. $PR(x, y, z) \equiv_{df} SM(x, \lambda w (Pwy \wedge Pwz))$ *(product)*

MD 8. $DF(x, y, z) \equiv_{df} SM(x, \lambda w (Pwy \wedge \neg Owz))$ *(difference)*

This concludes the axiomatisation of Atomistic General Extensional Mereology, which has the advantage of being both formally elegant and simple.

3   Similarity

Repeatable and Non-repeatable Properties. A fundamental ontological choice in an atomistic mereology pertains to the nature of the building blocks of reality. Ontologists agree that the denizens of reality fall into three main categories: *objects* (like quarks, tables, stones, companies, and solar systems), *attributes* or particular properties and relations (like the various shades of colour on a soap bubble, the mass and velocity of a bullet, your intelligence, and your relationship with your parents), as well as *events* (like runnings, hugs, bank transfers, perceptions, and thinkings). In the final section of this paper, events will be reconstructed as successions of attribute bundles.

A descriptively adequate ontology like OCHRE has to account for both *objects* and *attributes*. This does not contradict considerations of conceptual economy that motivate defining references to entities of one category in terms of references to entities of the other. The so-called *Qualitative Account* of objects as bundles of attributes is favoured by many ontologists, such as e.g. Williams (1953), Campbell (1990), Denkel (1996), and Simons (1994), since it avoids the problematic notion of objects as unscrutable blobs which attributes somehow adhere to. Nevertheless, as Denkel (1996, pp. 16–17) rightly emphasises, it is also true that objects are more than mere sums of their properties: a descriptively adequate ontology has to explain the completeness, independence and spatio-temporal bulk that objects enjoy in contrast to arbitrary sums of attributes.

Attributes can be regarded either as *repeatables* or as *non-repeatables* (Armstrong 1997, p. 31). Repeatables, also called *universals*, apply to more than one case; by contrast, non-repeatables, commonly referred to as *property-instances* or *tropes* (Williams 1953; Campbell 1990), are single characteristics of individuals. OCHRE endorses the claim of Williams, Campbell, and Denkel that the atoms of mereology are all non-repeatables. So if two stones resemble each other with respect to mass or density, then they contain similar, but distinct mass- or density-instances. Note however, that not every non-repeatable has to be atomic: as we shall see, some non-repeatable properties (like colours) and in fact *all* non-repeatable relations (like family relationships) may be regarded as composite. In this paper, the term *trope* will denote atomic property-instances only.

Obviously, OCHRE has to acknowledge repeatable properties or relations, too, if only the *formal universals* that are the subject matter of every foundational ontology, such as *object, trope, parthood, dependence,* or *similarity.* References to formal properties and relations are made through (lambda-abstractions of) the respective predicates. Semantically, predicates can be interpreted as sets; ontologically, however, there is no need to regard a universal as something outside or above the entities that instantiate it. In point of fact, OCHRE embraces the stance of *Aristotelian realism,* according to which repeatable properties and relations are given or present in their very exemplifications (Aristotle, *Met.*: 1023b; Armstrong 1997, p. 22). For example, in order to know whether an individual is part of another, it suffices to inspect both of them.

Furthermore, formal universals apply to their exemplifications directly, without any further mediating relations. This is just a consequence of their being the top-level categories of reality. In other words, the nexus between a formal universal and its instances, in particular that between a formal relation and its relata, is ontologically unanalysable, lest there be an infinite regress. Nonetheless, the nexus of instantiation can be described on the level of model-theoretic semantics as the membership relation between a single instance or a tuple of relata and the class representing the extension of the universal. Set-theory, it should be noted, is not regarded here as a part of the ontology, which is assumed to deal with *urelemente* exclusively, but as belonging to the meta-ontological machinery of Tarskian semantics.

Intensity, Comparability and Similarity. Tropes, as well as their mereological sums, constitute families whose members can be compared with each other and ordered in terms of their *intensity*. Qualities like mass or density, relations like being-in-love, and dispositions like intelligence or brittleness may vary according to degrees. And though individual marriages and tropes of magnetic polarity admit no such degrees, they are nonetheless comparable. But there is no way to collate hues and tastes, or masses and electrical charges.

The relation of *being more or equally intense* (in symbols: "Ixy") is a reflexive and transitive relation defined over tropes (atoms).

SA 1. $Ixy \rightarrow (Ax \wedge Ay)$ $\hfill$ (restriction)

SA 2. $Ax \rightarrow Ixx$ $\hfill$ (reflexivity)

SA 3. $(Ixy \wedge Iyz) \rightarrow Ixz$ $\hfill$ (transitivity)

Multidimensional variability of intensity as in the case of colours indicates that the attribute in question is indeed composite; colours, for instance, can be resolved into tropes of saturation, brightness, and hue.

Two tropes are *comparable* iff they can be ordered in terms of their intensity.

SD 1. $CMxy \equiv_{df} Ixy \vee Iyx$ $\hfill$ (comparability)

Two tropes x and y are *similar* iff x and y are equally intense. Note that similarity is to be understood as *exact*, not *approximative* similarity.

SD 2. $Sxy \equiv_{df} Ixy \wedge Iyx$ $\hfill$ (similarity)

Two non-atomic individuals x and y are (exactly) similar iff their respective component tropes can be associated one-to-one such that to every trope of x there corresponds one (exactly) similar trope of y and vice-versa.

References to *material universals*, i.e. kinds of tropes (or trope-bundles), such as *Mass*, *Colour*, or *Humanity* are inevitable in every-day discourse and thus have to be allowed for by a descriptively adequate ontology. In particular, the *genus* of any conventionally chosen trope x is defined as the property of being comparable to x and its *species* as the property of being similar to x (cf. Campbell 1990, pp. 83–85). As similarity implies comparability, the genus of a trope (e.g. *Mass*) subsumes its species (e.g. *15 kg*).

SD 3. $GE_xy \equiv_{df} \lambda y\, CMyx$ *(genus)*

SD 4. $SP_xy \equiv_{df} \lambda y\, Syx$ *(species)*

These definitions can be extended to aggregate comparability and similarity relations between trope-bundles. In practice, it is not necessary to define every type explicitly through a comparability or similarity relation. The mere *possibility* of such a definition should be sufficient for ontology engineering purposes.

4   Dependence

Though tropes are the basic building blocks of reality, they cannot be conceived of as separate from the objects they characterise. Each trope (e.g. a mass) is *dependent* on a specific object (e.g. a bullet). According to Strawson (1959, pp. 16–17), dependence can be understood in terms of *identification*. An individual x is identificationally dependent on an individual y – in symbols: "Dxy" – if, and only if, in order to identify x, one has to single out y first. In a certain sense, the entites on which something is dependent are part of its very definition or identity (Fine 1994/1995, p. 275).

The difference between objects (like cars, tables, body organs, persons, companies, constellations, and quarks) and dependent entities (i.e. tropes like masses, velocities, colours, flavours, or processes like orbital movements, heart contractions, and bank transfers) consists in the fact that the former can be singled out on their own, while the latter have to be individuated relatively to some object. Hence, objects can be defined as identificationally self-dependent entities; furthermore, I assume that no object is atomic, that is, a single trope:

DD 1. $Ox \equiv_{df} Dxx$ *(objects)*

DA 1. $Ox \rightarrow \neg Ax$ *(non-atomicity of objects)*

In the next section, these self-dependent trope-bundles will be identified with so-called *thin objects*, the mereological sums of the essential features of every-day *thick* objects. Being self-dependent, objects are not dependent on other entities.

DA 2. $Ox \rightarrow (\, Dxy \rightarrow x = y\,)$ *(objects are independent)*

Objects have ontological priority over other particulars since they constitute a framework of reference that serves as a basis for identification. It is an open question to which degree the ultimate framework of reference is based on convention, and hence involves vagueness, since conventions are usually only partially defined and are liable to compete with each other (cf. Heller 1990, pp. 47–49). But the conventionality and vagueness of divisions of reality are properly dealt with in the particular contexts of application and thus on the level of single *domain* ontologies.

Nothing can depend on an entity that is not self-dependent.

DA 3. $Dxy \rightarrow \mathcal{O}y$ *(everything depends on objects)*

Every trope that is part of an object is dependent on the latter.

DA 4. $(\mathcal{O}x \wedge Ay \wedge Pyx) \rightarrow Dyx$ *(dependent atomic parts of objects)*

If something is not self-dependent, then it depends on anything that one of its atomic parts is dependent on. Hence by dealing with the dependences of tropes, we determine the dependences of every entity that is not an object.

DA 5. $(\neg \mathcal{O}x \wedge Ay \wedge Pyx \wedge Dyz) \rightarrow Dxz$ *(dependence of non-objects)*

Now, every trope is assumed to depend on exactly one object (note that by **DA 2**, this holds for objects, too). In other words, each trope is a non-repeatable attribute of one single individual. Thus each physical object has its own mass, velocity, and so on.

DA 6. $Ax \rightarrow \exists! y\, Dxy$ *(a trope is dependent on one object)*

Non-repeatable relations (e.g. individual loves, kinships, and ownerships) have been defined as multiply dependent attributes in the literature on ontology (Simons 1995, Mulligan and Smith 1986). Since tropes as atomic attributes are dependent on one object, non-repeatable relations have to be mereological sums of tropes.

The theory according to which relations supervene on monadic properties of their relata, such that there are no relational differences without qualitative ones, is called *foundationism* (Campbell 1990, pp. 101, 113). OCHRE endorses foundationism only as far as non-repeatables are concerned. In fact, an individual marriage just amounts to the mereological sum of the particular rights and duties of the husband and the wife. Similarly, a biological kinship is based on the particular DNA of each member of a family. Foundationism is obviously false with respect to repeatable relations, i.e. formal relations as well as their combinations and restrictions. So, following a proposal by Mulligan (1998, p. 327), OCHRE adopts monadism for atomic non-repeatables, but assumes irreducible repeatable relations like the formal relations of parthood and dependence.

5   Connection

The Problem of Change; Thin and Thick Objects. The thesis that objects form the basic framework of reference seems to be undermined by the pervading character of change. Objects apparently lose and gain parts, move around, and exhibit uncompatible properties and relations over time. A solution favoured by many ontologists, e.g. Quine (1960, p. 171), Heller (1990), and Armstrong (1997, pp. 99–107), is to regard objects as space-time worms: incompatible facts just pertain to different phases of such fourdimensional entities. This approach is elegant, but rejects the intuitive distinction between objects and processes.

Alternatively, one can stick to the intuition of objects as three-dimensional entities and temporalise the *assertions* about objects instead. Formal properties and relations, especially parthood, have to receive a time-stamp, an additional temporal parameter. This has been proposed, amongst others, by Thomson (1983, pp. 214–218), Johnston (1984, p. 129), Simons (1987, chap. 5) and Haslanger (1989, pp. 120f). Temporalisation, however, makes reasoning about formal universals like parthood rather intricate.

The problem of change reveals an ambiguity of the ontological category of object. Varying the terminology of Armstrong (1997, pp. 123–126) and developing intuitions from Simons (1994) and Denkel (1996, p. 108), one has to distinguish between an evanescent whole, the *thick object* and a core of enduring characteristics, the *thin object.* Thick objects have spatio-temporal bulk and undergo change. Change consists in the succession of temporary aggregations of tropes shaped by relations of spatio-temporal connection. Thin objects, as the enduring cores of thick objects, constitute the ultimate referential framework of independent entities, the ontological backbone of reality. Thick objects, on the contrary, are dependent entities; successions of thick objects are held together by thin objects common to all elements in these chains, as for example by bundles of essential functions in the case of artifacts or organisms.

Our approach to the problem of change is akin to the stage theory proposed by Sider (2001, pp. 1–10, pp. 188–208), Hawley (2001, chap. 2), and Denkel (1996, pp. 101–109), with the main difference that thick objects as stages of thin objects are considered to be dependent entities. Successive incompatible states of affairs hold of distinct elements in a chain of succeeding thick objects that share the same thin object as a common core. The exchange of colour-tropes in a ripening tomato just pertains to different evanescent wholes centered around the bundle of core characteristics, amongst them the tomato's DNA. That one speaks of the same object through change is grounded in the existence of thin objects. Every seemingly temporal attribution of properties and relations to a thin object really is just the atemporal attribution of these attributes to succeeding thick objects that are stages of the thin object.

Connection. As thin objects are nodes in a pervading network of dependences, thick objects are nodes in a comprehensive grid of spatio-temporal connections. The formal ontological theory of spatio-temporal connection is called *topology*; topology constraints mereology and both together constitute the formal-ontological framework of *mereotopology* (Casati and Varzi 1999, chap. 4).

The primitive of topology is *connection*, a symmetric and intransitive relation that is reflexive in all cases it applies at all. Its underlying intuition is that of immediate neighbourhood in space and time. E.g., France is connected to Germany and Germany to Poland, but France is not connected to Poland.

CA 1. $Cxy \rightarrow Cxx$ *(reflexivity)*

CA 2. $Cxy \rightarrow Cyx$ *(symmetry)*

Thick objects ("O^*x") are bundles of tropes exhibiting spatio-temporal connections. No thick object is a self-dependent entity or *thin object* ("Ox").

CD 1. $O^*x \equiv_{df} \exists y\, Cxy$ *(thick object)*

CA 3. $O^*x \rightarrow \neg Ax \wedge \neg Ox$ *(thick objects are dependent trope-bundles)*

Parthood between thick objects is called *thick parthood*.

CD 2. $TPxy \equiv_{df} O^*x \wedge O^*y \wedge Pxy$ *(thick parthood)*

Thick parthood will be linked to connection through the topological relation of *enclosure*. A thick object is enclosed in another if, and only if, everything which is connected to the first is also connected to the second. A heart is contained in a chest, a fish in a lake, and so on.

CD 3. $Exy \equiv_{df} \forall z\,(Czx \rightarrow Czy)$ *(enclosure)*

Mutual enclosure implies identity. In other words: distinct thick objects cannot be co-located, they compete for space. Thus there is no need to distinguish between a thick object and the region in which it is located. Indeed, a thick object can be seen as a qualitatively enriched spatio-temporal region.

CA 4. $(Exy \wedge Eyx) \rightarrow x = y$ *(mutual enclosure entails identity)*

The formal link between mereology and topology is the axiom of monotonicity (Casati and Varzi 1999, p. 54): thick parthood entails enclosure, but not vice-versa. Since a heart is part of a chest, it is also enclosed in the latter. However, a fish is enclosed in, but is not part of a lake.

CA 5. $TPxy \rightarrow Exy$ *(monotonicity)*

There is no commitment to regions of space and time as a distinct category of particulars in OCHRE. Space and time are considered as universals, namely as (formal) spatio-temporal relations that are exemplified by thick objects.

6 Inherence

Direct Parthood and Essence. The formal relation between (thin or thick) objects and their attributes that has traditionally been called *inherence* can be accounted for in terms of dependence and parthood. Since a thick object may have other thick objects as parts, one has to specify whether a trope or a thin object is associated with that thick object or one of its thick parts. For example, one would like to distinguish the weight of a body and the weight of its heart.

Such distinctions can be done through the relation of *direct parthood*. An individual x is a direct part of an entity y iff x is a proper part of y, y is a thick object, and there is no thick proper part z of y such that x overlaps with z.

ID 1. $DPxy \equiv_{df} PPxy \wedge O^*y \wedge \neg \exists z\,(TPzy \wedge \neg z = y \wedge Oxz)$ *(direct parthood)*

Direct parts cannot be thick objects. In the words of Williams (1953, p. 6), they are *fine* or *abstract* parts, as opposed to *gross* or *concrete* parts, of thick objects.

Every trope is a direct part of some thick object; there are no homeless tropes.

IA 1. $Ax \rightarrow \exists y\, DPxy$ *(no homeless tropes)*

No two comparable tropes may be both direct parts of the same thick object. E.g. a thick object cannot have more than one mass or kinetic energy.

IA 2. $(DPyx \wedge DPzx \wedge CMyz) \rightarrow y = z$ *(comparability and direct parthood)*

A thin object x that is a direct part of a thick object y is an *essence* of y.

ID 2. $ESxy \equiv_{df} \mathbb{O}x \wedge DPxy$ *(essence)*

Each thick object has at least one essence. It seems counterintuitive that a thick object may have more than one essence, but this is the case for most every-day objects such as artifacts (or organisms) and the amount of material they are made of.

IA 3. $\mathbb{O}^*x \rightarrow \exists y\, ESyx$ *(existence of essences)*

In order to fully specify the dependence of entities that are not self-dependent, one further constraint on the dependence of tropes is needed (cf. **DA 5**). Indeed, the so-called *inherence principle* links atomic direct parthood and dependence by stipulating that, for any trope x, thin object y, and thick object z, if x depends on y and is a direct part of z, then y is an essence of z.

IA 4. $(Ax \wedge Dxy \wedge DPxz) \rightarrow ESyz$ *(inherence principle)*

Since a) each thin object has tropes as parts (by **DA 1**), b) each atomic part of a thin object is dependent on the latter (by **DA 4**), and c) each trope is a direct part of some thick object (by **IA 1**), it follows that every thin object is an essence of some thick object (by **IA 4**; see also **TA 16**). The presence of a thin object in a thick object does not imply the presence of *all* its dependent tropes.

Coincidence and Guises. Common-sense allows for numerically distinct objects to be spatio-temporally co-located, or *coincident*, e.g., a terracotta statue and the clay it is made of, or a person and her body. Some ontologists, like Simons (1987, chap. 6), assume such entities to be distinct physical objects of which one (e.g. the clay) *constitutes* the other (e.g. the statue). In OCHRE, there is no need to allow for *constitution* as an additional non-extensional composition.

Thick objects cannot be co-located, since they have spatio-temporal bulk and thus compete for space. Instead, I consider coincident entities to be *direct parts* of the same thick object. Thick objects may have more than one essence, each of which has its own periphery of dependent tropes. The mereological sum of a thin object and all the tropes dependent on it represents a qualitative aspect of the thick object, which I call a *guise*, after Castañeda (1985/1986). Formally, some x is a guise of a thick object y with respect to some essence z of y iff x is the mereological sum of all atomic direct parts of y which are dependent on z.

ID 3. $G_zxy \equiv_{df} ESzy \wedge SM(x, \lambda w\,(Aw \wedge DPwy \wedge Dwz))$ *(guise)*

A particular thick object that we identify as a terracotta statue made of clay contains two sub-bundles of tropes, namely the statue and the amount of clay, each centered on a particular thin object: the functions of the artifact and the chemical characteristics of the material. These trope bundles are *fine* or *abstract* parts of the same thick object and represent different aspects of the latter.

7 Temporal Order

Temporal Anteriority and Essential Succession. As stages of thin objects, thick objects are not only spatio-temporally connected, but also succeed each other in time. Since any computer representation of time has to be granular, time may be regarded as a *discrete* series of atomic intervals.

The theory of temporal order is based on two primitive relations: *direct anteriority* and *simultaneity*, both defined over thick objects. Direct anteriority is irreflexive, asymmetric and intransitive.

TA 1. $DAxy \rightarrow (\mathcal{O}^*x \wedge \mathcal{O}^*y)$ *(restriction)*

TA 2. $\neg DAxx$ *(irreflexivity)*

TA 3. $DAxy \rightarrow \neg DAyx$ *(asymmetry)*

Simultaneity is, of course, an equivalence relation.

TA 4. $SIxy \rightarrow (\mathcal{O}^*x \wedge \mathcal{O}^*y)$ *(restriction)*

TA 5. $\mathcal{O}^*x \rightarrow SIxx$ *(reflexivity)*

TA 6. $SIxy \rightarrow SIyx$ *(symmetry)*

TA 7. $(SIxy \wedge SIyz) \rightarrow SIxz$ *(transitivity)*

Thick parthood only holds between simultaneous thick objects.

TA 8. $TPxy \rightarrow SIxy$ *(thick parthood implies simultaneity)*

Thick objects do not temporally overlap, but form discrete and synchronised series of stages that are instantaneous with respect to a certain granularity of time. This is ensured by postulating that all direct temporal antecessors, as well as all direct temporal successors, of a thick object are simultaneous.

TA 9. $(DAyx \wedge DAzx) \rightarrow SIyz$ *(simultaneity of direct temporal antecessors)*

TA 10. $(DAxy \wedge DAxz) \rightarrow SIyz$ *(simultaneity of direct temporal successors)*

The temporal relation of *(indirect) anteriority* is defined by recursion:

TA 11. $DAxy \rightarrow Axy$ *(indirect anteriority: base case)*

TA 12. $(DAxy \wedge Ayz) \rightarrow Axz$ *(indirect anteriority: recursive step)*

Any two thick objects x and y can be temporally compared in the sense that either x is an indirect temporal antecessor of y, or y is an indirect temporal antecessor of x, or x and y are simultaneous:

TA 13. $(\mathcal{O}^*x \wedge \mathcal{O}^*y) \rightarrow (Axy \vee Ayx \vee SIxy)$ *(temporal comparability)*

Successive thick objects that are stages of the same thin object stand in a peculiar relation of loose identity: they are not identical, but everything that is true of them is also true, in a temporal sense, of the common thin object. In the following I develop the idea of stage-successions, which is related to Chisholm's (1976, pp. 97–104) account of change in terms of consecutive entities.

A thick object x is the *direct essential successor* of some thick object y *with respect to a thin object* z iff y is directly anterior to x, x and y are spatio-temporally connected, and z is a common essence of x and y.

TD 1. $DS_z xy \equiv_{df} DAyx \land Cxy \land ESzx \land ESzy$ *(direct essential succession)*

Direct essential succession is linear. In other words, no thick object can be the direct essential successor of more than one other thick object, nor may distinct thick objects share the same direct essential successor.

TA 14. $(DS_z yx \land DS_z wx) \rightarrow y = w$ *(unicity on the left)*

TA 15. $(DS_z xy \land DS_z xw) \rightarrow y = w$ *(unicity on the right)*

In order to exclude that thin objects have instantaneous lives, I postulate for each thin object x there are at least two thick objects that are in direct essential succession with respect to x.

TA 16. $Ox \rightarrow \exists yz \, DS_x yz$ *(non-instantaneity of thin objects)*

Finally, the relation of indirect essential succession with respect to a thin object can be characterised recursively in terms of direct essential succession:

TA 17. $DS_z xy \rightarrow SC_z xy$ *(indirect essential succession: 1)*

TA 18. $(DS_z xy \land SC_z yw) \rightarrow SC_z xw$ *(indirect essential succession: 2)*

Note that, by extensionality of parthood, there must be at least one atomic part that is not shared between distinct stages of a thin object. Hence there cannot be successive stages with exactly the same proper parts: things change constantly.

Endurants and Perdurants. In everyday discourse, we distinguish between objects and processes, or, as the philosophical jargon has it, between *endurants* and *perdurants*. Perdurants consist of different *phases*, or *temporal parts*, at different times. Endurants, on the contrary, have no temporal parts, but are present as a whole at each instant they are present at all. (Lewis 1986, p. 202).

It is crucial for a descriptively adequate ontology to acknowledge this distinction. However, this does not mean that both categories have to be considered as primitive. According to the informal definition of endurants, tropes, as well as thin and thick objects, turn out to be endurants. Thin objects are wholly present in each of the thick objects they are part of, and the same holds for tropes, i.e. for atoms. And since a thick object as well as its thick parts are only present in one instant, they are trivially endurants. Perdurants can be regarded as successions of thick objects, i.e. endurants.

The basic perdurants are events as changes or state-transitions: the change of a tomato's colour from green to red amounts to the succession of a red tomato-stage to a green tomato-stage. The change of a memory cell from 0 to 1 is the succession of a charged cell-stage to an uncharged one. Some x is an *event in* a thin object y iff x is the sum of two thick objects that are directly essentially succeeding with respect to y; we also say that y is the *substrate* of x.

TD 2. $EVxy \equiv_{df} \exists wz\,(\,SM(x,w,z) \wedge DS_y wz\,)$ *(event in)*

TD 3. $\mathcal{E}x \equiv_{df} \exists y\,EVxy$ *(event)*

The definition implies that there are no instantaneous events, which is consistent with the doctrine that perdurants have at least two distinct temporal parts. The instantaneous left and right boundaries of perdurants are endurants, namely thick objects. Hence the *events* that represent the beginning and the ending of a perdurant cannot be instantaneous and always have to involve at least two object-stages.

Perdurants are arbitrary mereological sums of events; they can be recursively characterised with single events as a base case.

TA 19. $\mathcal{E}x \rightarrow \mathcal{P}x$ *(perdurant: base case)*

TA 20. $(\,\mathcal{E}x \wedge \mathcal{P}y \wedge SM(z,x,y)\,) \rightarrow \mathcal{P}z$ *(perdurant: recursive step)*

In particular, the life of a thin object is the perdurant that is the sum of all events in this thin object:

TD 4. $Lxy \equiv_{df} SM(x, \lambda z\,EVzy\,)$ *(life)*

The relation between perdurants and the (thin) objects involved in them is called *participation*. OCHRE's particular account of perdurants in terms of endurants allows for participation to be defined as a special case of parthood. Indeed, a thin object x *participates in* a process y, iff x is the substrate of an event that is part of y.

TD 5. $PCxy \equiv_{df} Ox \wedge \mathcal{P}y \wedge \exists z\,(\,EVzx \wedge Pzy\,)$ *(participation)*

Thus OCHRE acknowledges the distinction between endurants and perdurants without assuming two separate domains of objects and processes organised by two different parthood and dependence relations.

8 Conclusions

Building a foundational ontology involves challenges that are unusual to common knowledge representation practice. On the one hand, the need for descriptive adequacy requires a considerable subtlety of conceptual analysis based on a solid philosophical background. On the other hand, the usability of foundational ontologies depends on the greatest possible formal simplicity and transparency.

This paper places a strong emphasis on a clear and elegant mereological framework that gives a straightforward account of parthood relations between individuals. I have tried to illustrate this point by sketching the formalisation of the ontology OCHRE and by elucidating its underlying ontological choices.

Part-whole reasoning in Atomistic General Extensional Mereology, the basis of OCHRE, is quite simple, since the parthood structure is considered to be a Boolean algebra (without a null element). The problem of the identity of objects through change motivates many ontologists to reject extensional mereology and to recur to an opaque temporalisation of properties and relations, amongst them parthood itself. Furthermore, the apparent coincidence of objects is often tackled by introducing a non-mereological relation of constitution between objects. All in all, these modeling choices involve many superfluous complications.

OCHRE maintains the descriptively correct distinctions of common-sense while avoiding formal intricacies. To account for change in objects, OCHRE emphasises the ambiguity of references to objects and distinguishes between thin objects and thick objects as their evanescent stages. Temporal statements about thin objects are translated into atemporal statements about their stages. Events are accounted for in terms of succeeding object-stages. And co-located distinct entities are reconstructed as qualitative aspects or guises of the same thick object. Classical extensional mereology can be preserved throughout, assuming attributes as atoms out of which thick and thin objects are ultimately composed, leaving no space for propertyless substrates.

This essay should be considered a case study which attempts to highlight the particularities of building a foundational ontology. Once these particularities are better understood, more theoretical investigations into measuring the quality of the design of top-level ontologies will be possible.

Acknowledgements. This paper is based on work supported by the Alexander von Humboldt Foundation under the auspices of its Wilhelm Paul Programme. The author is deeply indebted to Pierre Grenon (IFOMIS, Leipzig/Germany), Brandon Bennett (School of Computing, University of Leeds/UK), Claudio Masolo (ISTC-CNR, Trento/Italy), as well as two anonymous reviewers for many helpful suggestions regarding a previous version of this paper.

References

Aristotle. *Metaphysics.*

Armstrong, D. M. 1997. *A World of States of Affairs.* Cambridge: Cambridge University Press.

Campbell, K. 1990. *Abstract Particulars.* Oxford: Blackwell.

Casati, R., Varzi, A. 1999. *Parts and Places. The Structures of Spatial Representation.* Cambridge/MA., London: MIT Press.

Castañeda, H. N. 1985/1986. "Objects, Existence and Reference. A Prolegomenon to Guise Theory". *Grazer Philosophische Studien 25/26*: 31–66.

Chisholm, R. 1976. *Person and Object. A Metaphysical Study.* Chicago, La Salle /Ill.: Open Court.

Denkel, A. 1996. *Object and Property.* Cambridge: Cambridge University Press.

Fine, K. 1994/1995. "Ontological Dependence". *Proceedings of the Aristotelian Society* 95: 269–290.

Gangemi A., Guarino N., Masolo C., Oltramari, A., Schneider L., 2002. "Sweetening Ontologies with DOLCE". In Gómez-Pérez, A., Benjamins, V.R., (eds.), *Knowledge Engineering and Knowledge Management. Ontologies and the Semantic Web. Proceedings of the 13th International Conference (EKAW 2002). Lecture Notes in Computer Science 2473.* Heidelberg: Springer, 166–181.

Gruber, T. 1991. "The Role of Common Ontology in Achieving Sharable, Reusable Knowledge Bases". *Principles of Knowledge Representation and Reasoning: Proceedings of the Second International Conference.* Morgan Kaufmann, San Mateo/CA.

Guarino N. 1998. "Formal Ontology and Information Systems". In Guarino, N. (ed.), *Formal Ontology in Information Science. Proceedings of FOIS'98, Trento, Italy* Amsterdam: IOS Press, 3–15.

Haslanger, S. 1989. "Endurance and Temporary Intrinsics". *Analysis 49*: 119–125.

Hawley, K. 2001. *How Things Persist.* Oxford: Clarendon Press.

Heller, M. 1990. *The Ontology of Physical Objects.* Cambridge: Cambridge University Press.

Johnston, M. 1984. "Is There a Problem About Persistence ?" *Proceedings of the Aristotelian Society, suppl. vol. 61*: 107–135.

Leonard, H. S., Goodman N., 1940. "The Calculus of Individuals and Its Uses". *Journal of Symbolic Logic 5*: 45–55.

Lewis, D. 1986. *On the Plurality of Worlds.* Oxford: Blackwell.

Lewis, D. 1991. *Parts of Classes.* Oxford: Blackwell.

Mulligan, K., Smith, B. 1986. "A Relational Theory of the Act". *Topoi 5*: 115–130.

Mulligan, K. 1998. "Relations – through thick and thin". *Erkenntnis 48*: 325–353.

Quine, W. O. 1960. *Word and Object.* Cambridge/MA: MIT Press.

Sider, T. 2001. *Four-Dimensionalism. An Ontology of Persistence and Time* Oxford: Clarendon Press.

Simons, P. 1987. *Parts. A Study in Ontology..* Oxford: Clarendon.

Simons, P. 1994. "Particulars in Particular Clothing: Three Trope Theories of Substance". *Philosophy and Phenomenological Research 65*: 553–575.

Simons, P. 1995. "Relational Tropes". In Haefliger, G., Simons, P. (eds.), *Analytic Phenomenology: Essays in Honor of Guido Küng.* Dordrecht: Kluwer.

Smith, B, 2003. "Ontology". Forthcoming in Floridi, L. (ed.), *The Blackwell Guide to the Philosophy of Information and Computing.* Oxford: Blackwell.

Strawson, P. 1959. *Individuals. An Essay in Descriptive Methaphysics.* London: Routledge.

Thomson, J. J. 1983. "Parthood and Identity Across Time". *Journal of Philosophy 80*: 201–220.

Williams, D. C. 1953. "On the elements of being". *Review of Metaphysics 7*: 3–18, 171–192.

The Universal Medical Language System and the Gene Ontology: Some Critical Reflections

Anand Kumar[1] and Barry Smith[2,3]

[1] Laboratory of Medical Informatics, Department of Computer Science,
University of Pavia, Italy

[2] Institute for Formal Ontology and Medical Information Science,
University of Leipzig, Germany
[3] Department of Philosophy, University at Buffalo, New York, USA

Abstract. The Unified Medical Language System and the Gene Ontology are among the most widely used terminology resources in the biomedical domain. However, when we evaluate them in the light of simple principles for well-constructed ontologies we find a number of characteristic inadequacies. Employing the theory of granular partitions, a new approach to the understanding of ontologies and of the relationships ontologies bear to instances in reality, we provide an application of this theory in relation to an example drawn from the context of the pathophysiology of hypertension. This exercise is designed to demonstrate how, by taking ontological principles into account we can create more realistic biomedical ontologies which will also bring advantages in terms of efficiency and robustness of associated software applications.

1 Introduction

1.1 The Unified Medical Language System

The integration of standard terminology systems into a unified knowledge representation system for biomedicine has formed a key area of research in recent years. The Unified Medical Language System (UMLS), designed by the National Library of Medicine in Bethesda MD, is one major effort in this direction, combining a large number of distinct terminologies into a single platform [1,2].

Semantic Networks are one means to find our way around vast terminological edifices such as are represented by UMLS. The January 2003 version of the UMLS Semantic Network consists of 134 Semantic Types together with 54 possible links between these types. These can be arranged in the form of a graph whose vertices are the Semantic Types and whose edges are the links between them. The result represents a high-level abstraction from the Metathesaurus, which is the total UMLS concept repository. The UMLS Semantic Network is a graph containing more than 6000 edges organized into a double tree structure which divides all items in the UMLS universe into two superclasses of *Entities* and *Events*. *Entity* is defined as "A broad type for grouping physical and conceptual entities". *Event* is defined as "A broad type for grouping activities, processes and states".

A. Günter et al. (Eds.): KI 2003, LNAI 2821, pp. 135–148, 2003.
© Springer-Verlag Berlin Heidelberg 2003

1.2   The Gene Ontology

The Gene Ontology project seeks to provide a hierarchical controlled vocabulary for the description of genes and gene products. Currently, efforts are underway to imcorporate GO into UMLS. GO's compilers have endeavored to develop a standardized cross-species biological vocabulary that can be used by multiple databases to annotate them in a consistent way [3,4,5]. As of June 2003, GO takes the form of a list of some 14,000 common biological terms together with text intended to convey definitions of many of the terms listed. Terms are organized in parent-child hierarchies, indicating that one term is *more general than* another. Additional information is provided where the entity denoted by one term is *part of* the entity denoted by another. Terms are divided into three disjoint trees, with roots: *Cellular Component*, *Molecular Function* and *Biological Process*. The result is meant to facilitate communication among biologists. The GO reference vocabulary is intended to ensure terminological standardization and thus to increase efficiency and reliability, for example in the process of searching for common concepts across large genetic databases.

1.3   Some Basic Formal-Ontological Distinctions

Unfortunately, both UMLS and GO are marked in their top-level categorial organization by certain ontological inadequacies. To see why this is so, we begin by drawing attention to two distinctions drawn by philosophers across the ages: a) between *Continuant* and *Occurrent* entities, and b) between *Dependent* and *Independent* entities [6].

Continuants, as the name implies, are entities which continue to exist through time. Organisms, cells, chromosomes are all continuants: they preserve their identity from one moment to the next even while undergoing a variety of different sorts of changes. Occurrents, in contrast, are never such as to exist in full in any single instant of time. Rather, they are such as to unfold themselves through time, in the way in which, for example, an intravenous drug infusion unfolds itself in successive temporal phases. The continuant/occurrent opposition corresponds in first approximation to the distinction between *Entity* and *Event* drawn by UMLS and to the distinction between *Components* and *Functions/Processes* drawn by GO. It corresponds also to the familiar medical distinction between *anatomy* and *physiology*.

To say that an entity is *independent* is to assert that it has an inherent ability to exist without reference to other entities – examples are: cells and molecules, organs and organisms – as contrasted with entities that require a support from other entities in order to exist, for example, in the case of cellular motion, temperature or mass. Cellular motion requires reference to a cell which moves; each case of viral infection, requires reference to some organism which is its subject or carrier. Because occurrents, at least on those levels of granularity which are of concern to us here, are always changes or movements *of* some enduring entity or entities, it follows that occurrents are always dependent entities. Thus of the

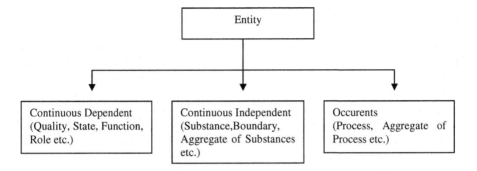

Fig. 1. A tripartite taxonomy

four abstractly possible combinations yielded by the two divisions of continu-ants/occurrents and dependence/independence, only three are instantiated:

We shall use this tripartite ontology in what follows in order to bring to light certain problems and irregularities in the UMLS and GO semantic networks. Note that we have to include under continuants not only substances (such as you and me, this cell, that molecule), but also *qualities* (your height, your skin-color), *states or conditions* (your diabetes, your state of high blood pressure), *roles* (your role as student, as doctor), and *functions* (of a drug, of a machine). This is because, like their bearers, qualities, states, roles and functions endure self-identically through time. The *realizations* of roles and functions,in contrast – for example, the *course* of a disease, the *performance* of a role, the *execution* of a program, are all *processes*, which means that they fall under the heading of occurrents.

1.4   The Theory of Granular Partitions

When human beings classify the entities in the domain of medicine by means of one or other of the standardized terminologies, then they *partition* reality into *cells* of various sorts. The Theory of Granular Partitions (TGP) is a theory of such partitions, which provides a set of simple conditions which partitions must satify together with a set of tools for their manipulation [7,8,9]. TGP deals primarily with transparent (veridical) partitions, that is with partitions which are the products of successfully demarcating some independently existing subject-domain. However, TGP also has the resources to deal with various sorts of partition *failure* and *incompleteness*, and it provides an elaborate machinery for dealing with the *vagueness* involved in many of our partitions of reality.

Perhaps the most important feature of TGP is that it recognizes that dif-ferent partitions may represent cuts through the same reality at different levels, and even cuts through reality which are skew to each other. It thus provides a framework within which we can formulate ontologies of a given domain which are at one and the same time realist and also do justice to the existence of a plurality of veridical representations of given domains of reality, as when we partition the human organism successively in terms of molecules, cells or organs. Each partition consists of cells and subcells (terms which are used here in a formal sense, freed from all connotations of the biological concept of 'cell'), the latter being nested within the former. The simplest type of partition is a mere list. This consists of just one layer of subcells (corresponding to the items on the list), together with one all-inclusive maximal cell (corresponding to the list as a whole). Other partitions are hierarchical: they consist of many layers of cells and subcells (for example, in the animal kingdom, the layers of species, genus, family, order, class, phylum and kingdom). The lowest layer of subcells corresponds to the finest grain of objects recognized by the partition in question.

2   UMLS Semantic Network

As mentioned above, there are certain problems which become apparent when we consider how the two dichotomies of occurrent/continuant and dependent/independent should be applied to the classification presupposed by the UMLS Semantic Network [2].

2.1   UMLS Semantic Tree with Root

Entity

The most problematic sub-class under *Entity* in the UMLS hierarchy is: *Conceptual Entity*. This has subclasses:

Organism Attribute	*Finding*
Idea or Concept	*Occupation or Discipline*
Organization	*Group*
Group Attribute	*Intellectual Product*
Language	

(see Figure 2 below).

The problem pertains first of all to the wide formal-ontological diversity of the items included in this list. It turns secondly on the fact that concepts, as we understand them, are dependent on minds, and thus, we assume that the same holds also for Conceptual Entities, too, are dependent entities. This explains why *Finding, Idea or Concept, Language* and *Intellectual Product* are listed as subclasses of *Conceptual Entity*. But what of *Organism Attributes*? These can however exist without a mind: there were organism attributes before there were concepts, not least the attributes of all those organisms which evolved before concept-using organisms existed. Hence, *Organism Attribute* cannot be a *Conceptual Entity*. A similar problem arises also in relation to *Group* (for example groups of macac monkeys), and to geographical regions (for example, Hambug), which are classified under *Idea or Concept* in the UMLS Semantic Network.

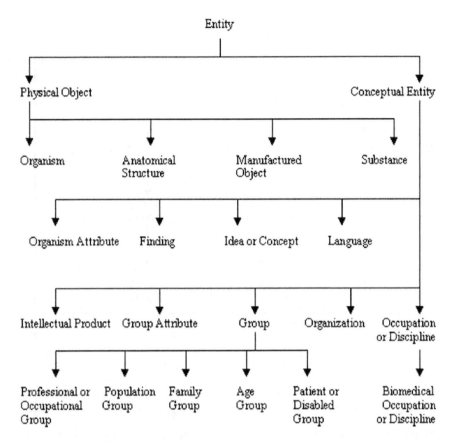

Fig. 2. A portion of the subsumption hierarchy of UMLS Semantic Types with root. Entity *(for the sake of clarity, not all nodes have been expanded)*

2.2   UMLS Semantic Tree with Root

Event

The tree starting from *Event* has subclasses, *Activity* and *Phenomenon or Process*.

Among the subclasses of *Phenomenon or Process* is *Natual Phenomenon or Process*, with subclass *Biologic Function*, which in turn has *Physiologic Function* and *Pathologic Function* as subclasses.

Here, unfortunately, functions, which are continuants, are run together with processes, which are occurrents. What is almost certainly meant by *Biologic Function* as a sublass of *Natural Phenomenom or Process* is the *exercise* of a function at some given time and place. UMLS hereby runs together *function* with *functioning*; it confuses what exists dispositionally in a thing, a certain power or potential which is the product of evolution or design, with what the thing *does* episodically, which is the product of intentionality or local causal influence.

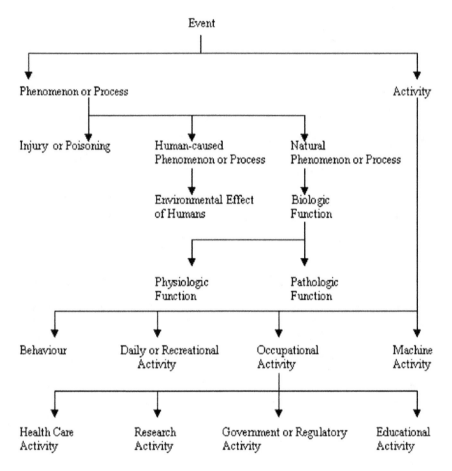

Fig. 3. A portion of the subsumption hierarchy of UMLS Semantic Types with root Event

The importance of this distinction becomes clear when we recognise that there are dormant functions and functions which for some other reason do not become expressed in any process.

3   Basic Formal Ontology

Basic Formal Ontology (BFO) is a reference ontology currently being developed in Leipzig for purposes of application in the medical domain. It consists of a series of sub-ontologies, the most important of which are the various SnapBFO and SpanBFO sub-ontologies developed at different levels of granularity within the framework of the Theory of Granular Partitions. SnapBFO is constituted by a series of *snapshot* ontologies indexed by times; SpanBFO is a single videoscopic ontology which apprehends the world in terms of the processes unfolding within it. SNAP is the ontology of continuants in our terminology above; SPAN the ontology of occurrents [10,11,12].

3.1 BFO Hierarchy with Root Continuant Entity

The outline category system of SnapBFO is shown in Figure 4. It consists of *Continuant Entity* as root, under which are the subclasses *Dependent Entity, Independent Entity* and *Spatial Region*. *Dependent Entity* consists of qualities, states, functions, roles, powers, etc. while *Independent Entity* consists of *Substances*, their aggregates, boundaries, fiat parts and so forth.

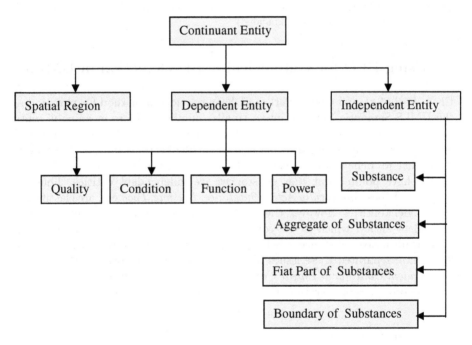

Fig. 4. SnapBFO: The Basic Formal Ontology with root *Continuant Entity* (for the sake of clarity, not all nodes have been expanded) [10]

3.2 BFO Hierarchy with Root Occurent Entity

SpanBFO, as shown in Figure 5, consists of *processes*, with *Occurrent Entity* as root.More precisely, it divides occurrent entities into the two sub-categories of *Processual Entities* and *Spatiotemporal Regions*. The category *Processual Entity* is sub-divided into processes, aggregates of processes, fiat parts of processes, and boundaries of processes [11].

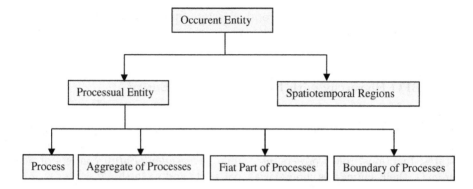

Fig. 5. SpanBFO: Basic Formal Ontology with root *Occurrent Entity* (for the sake of clarity, not all nodes have been expanded)

4   Using BFO for Ontological Error-Detection in UMLS

Chen, Perl *et al.* and Geller, Perl *et al.* have provided a method for partitioning the UMLS Semantic Network into a smaller number of more meaningful units, called Semantic Type Collections. In Tables 1 and 2 we used BFO in order to analyze the classifications incorporated in such collections in order to bring to light what we believe are the classification errors in the Network itself.

We have pointed out that substances are independent entities. Thus the Semantic Types *Biologically Active Substance, Enzyme, Food* etc. are classified as independent entities. However, there is for each of these types a closely associated dependent entity, which is the corresponding role, for example, the role of a biologically active substance of being precisely biologically active. In Tables 1 and 2, we have separated these issues based on BFO and categorised substances as *Independent Continuant Entities*, roles and functions are *Dependent Continuants* and the processes of exercising those functions as *Occurrents*.

5   Gene Ontology

The Gene Ontology is an inert hierarchy of terms, that is focused not on reasoning power or on supporting software implementations but rather on providing a robust framework for the annotations that are applied by biologists to organism gene products.

The vocabulary is divided into three parts, called the cellular component ontology, the molecular function ontology, and the biological process ontology (Figure 6). This corresponds, superficially at least, to the tripartite structure of independent continuants, dependent continuants (functions), and occurrents (processes) underlying BFO.

Table 1. UMLS Semantic Types analyzed using BFO classifications; ICE = Independent Continuant Entities and their parts and aggregates; PE = Processual Entities; DCE = Dependent Continuant Entities; * signifies an ontologically incoherent composite of different classes

Collection	UMLS Semantic Types in Collection	BFO
Anatomical Abnormality	Anatomical Abnormality; Acquired Abnormality; Congenital Abnormality	DCE (Qualities, etc.)
Anatomical Structure	Anatomical Structure; Embryonic Structure	ICE (Fiat Part/Boundary)
Animal	Animal; Invertebrate; Vertebrate; Amphibian; Bird; Fish; Reptile; Mammal; Human	ICE (Substance)
Behaviour	Behaviour; Social Behaviour; Individual Behaviour	PE
Biologic Function	Biologic Function	DCE (Function)
Biologically Active Substance	Biologically Active Substance; Receptor; Vitamin; Enzyme; Neuroreactive Substance or Biogenic Amine; Hormone; Immunologic Factor	ICE (Substance)
Chemical	Chemical; Chemical Viewed Structurally; Chemical Viewed Functionally; Hazardous or Poisonous Substance; Inorganic Chemical; Biomedical or Dental Material; Element, Ion or Isotope; Indicator, Agent or Diagnostic Aid; Carbohydrate; Organic Chemical; Organophosphorus Compound; Steroid; Eicosanoid; Amino Acid, Peptide or Protein; Lipid; Nucleic Acid, Nucleoside or Nucleotide	ICE (Substance)
Entity	Entity; Physical Object; Conceptual Entity; Group Attribute; Language; Intellectual Product; Classification; Regulation or Law	* (a conglomerate of ICE and DCE)
Event	Event; Activity; Daily or Recreation Activity; Machine Activity	PE
Finding	Finding; Lab or Test Result; Sign or Symptom	DCE (Quality, Condition)
Fully Formed Anatomical Structure	Fully Formed Anatomical Structure; Cell; Cell Component; Tissue; Gene or Genome; Body Part, Organ or Organ Component	ICE (Substance, Fiat part, Boundary etc.)
Group	Group; Professional or Occupational Group; Population Group; Family Group; Age Group; Patient or Disabled Group	ICE (Aggregate)
Health Care Activity	Health Care Activity; Diagnostic Procedure; Laboratory Procedure; Therapeutic or Preventive Procedure	PE
Idea or Concept	Idea or Concept; Functional Concept; Body System; Temporal Concept; Qualitative Concept; Quantitative Concept; Spatial Concept; Geographic Area; Body Location or Region; Molecular Sequence; Carbohydrate Sequence; Amino Acid Sequence; Body Space or Junction; Nucleotide Sequence	* (a conglomerate of ICE, DCE and spatial region)
Manufactured Object	Manufactured Object; Medical Device; Research Device; Clinical Drug	ICE (Substance)
Natural Phenomenon or Process	Natural Phenomenon or Process	PE
Occupation or Discipline	Occupation or Discipline; Biomedical Occupation or Discipline	PE
Occupation Activity	Occupation Activity; Educational Activity; Governmental or Regulatory Activity	PE

5.1   The Cellular Component Ontology

The GO definition for the term "Cell Component" is: "subcellular structures, locations, and macromolecular complexes; examples include nucleus, telomere, and origin recognition complex".

Table 2. UMLS Semantic Types analyzed using BFO classifications (cont.)

Collection	UMLS Semantic Types in Collection	BFO
Organism	Organism; Archaeon; Virus; Bacterium; Fungus; Rickettsia or Chlamydia	ICE (Substance)
Organism At-tribute	Organism Attribute; Clinical Attribute	DCE (Quality, Condition)
Organization	Organization; Health Care Related Organization; Professional Society; Self-help or Relief Organization	ICE (Aggregate)
Pathologic Function	Pathologic Function; Experimental Model of Disease; Cell or Molecular Dysfunction; Cell or Molecular Dysfunction; Disease or Syndrome; Mental or Behavioral Dysfunction	* (a conglomerate of DCE, ICE and PE)
Pharmacologic Substance	Pharmacologic Substance; Antibiotic	ICE (Substance)
Phenomenon or Process	Phenomenon or Process; Injury or Poisoning; Human-caused Phenomenon or Process; Environmental Effect of Humans	PE
Physiologic Function	Physiologic Function; Organ or Tissue Function; Mental Process; Molecular Function; Genetic Function; Cell Function	* (a conglomerate of DCE and PE)
Plant	Plant; Alga	ICE (Substance)
Research Activ-ity	Research Activity; Molecular Biology Research Technique	* (a conglomerate of DCE and PE)
Substance	Substance; Body Substance; Food	ICE (Substance, Aggregate of Substances)

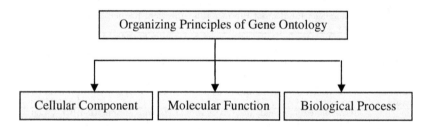

Fig. 6. The Tripartite Organization of the Gene Ontology.

Cellular components are physical objects, or the *substances* or parts or aggregates of substances in the BFO terminology: thus they are instances of *Independent Continuant Entity*. Cells themselves are subsumed by GO under *cellular component*.

5.2   The Molecular Function Ontology

The GO definition of the term "Molecular Function" is: "the tasks performed by individual gene products; examples are transcription factor and DNA helicase." The term 'task' is unfortunately ambiguous and GO, like the UMLS Semantic Types, correspondingly incorporate some confusions in the distinction between *functions* and their *functioning*. Until recently this confusion was compunded by the fact that the molecular function hierarchy includes terms such as *anticoagulant* (defined as: "a substance that retards or prevents coagulation") and *enzyme* (defined as: "a substance & that catalyzes") which refer neither to functions nor to actions but rather to substances. This problem was remedied by a policy change effective as of March 1, 2003 whereby GO molecular function term names are to be appended with the word "activity". Because, however, the change was *not* applied to the parent term "Molecular Function", and because associated defintions were not overhauled in the light of the new policy, some confusion as between "function" and "activity" still remains.

5.3 The Biological Process Ontology

A "Biological Process" is defined in GO, somewhat unclearly, as: "A phenomenon marked by changes that lead to a particular result, mediated by one or more gene products". Biological process terms include *glycolysis*. As far as one can tell, *biological processes* are compounds or aggregates of molecular functions, the latter being identified as tasks (actions) performed by individual gene products together with the processes set in motion in their wake. However, this means that there is a parthood relationship between functions and processes, which contradicts GO's sections to the effect that its three term hierarchies are strictly disjoint from each other.

6   A Biomedical Example

In order to show the relevance of the above, we will discuss the use of the BFO ontology in giving a realistic analysis of a specific biomedical example drawn from the pathophysiology of hypertension and of antihypertensive treatment [13,14].

6.1   Regulation of Blood Pressure

The diagnosis of hypertension depends primarily on the measurement of blood pressure. According to the UMLS Metathesaurus, hypertension is a *Disease or Syndrome* or a *Sign or Symptom* and blood pressure is an *Organism Function*. All of these Semantic Types correspond to *Dependent Continuant Entities* according to BFO. That is, they endure identically for a certain period of time and they depend for their existence on the organism which is their bearer.

According to the hydraulic equation: BP = CO*PVR, arterial blood pressure is directly proportional to the product of blood flow (cardiac output, CO) and peripheral vascular resistance (PVR).

According to the UMLS Metathesaurus, blood flow is an *Organism Function*, cardiac output is a *Laboratory or Test Result* or *Diagnostic Procedure*. In BFO, *Organism Function* and *Laboratory or Test Result* are *Dependent Continuant Entities*, a *Diagnostic Procedure* is an *Occurrent*, or in other words it is a process that unfolds itself through time. This leads to a conflict because the same term "cardiac output" embraces both continuant and occurrent entities. It harbors confusion also since it implies that blood pressure is proportional either to a laboratory or test result or to a diagnostic procedure, where in fact of course the relationship of proportionality applies to the underlying biomedical phenomena of which the latter are measures.

UMLS, as we might say, confuses epistemology with ontology; that is, it runs together the results of our attempts to gain knowledge about specific phenomena of the organism (functions, attributes, processes) with those phenomena themselves. This is seen already in the classification of cardiac output and of peripheral vascular resistance as *Findings*.

6.2   The Ontology of Antihypertensives and the Theory of Granular Partitions

Antihypertensives are a class of drugs used in the treatment of acute or chronic hypertension via a range of pharmacological mechanisms. These include diuretics, adrenergic Beta-antagonists, adrenergic alpha-antagonists, angiotensin converting-enzyme inhibitors, calcium channel blockers, ganglionic blockers and vasodilator agents.

We can classify such a family from a range of different perspectives. Our concerns might be biochemical, pharmacological, clinical, physiological etc., and even within each of these perspectives there can be subdivisions. For example, an antihypertensive could have a clinical role in relation not only to hypertension but also to cardiac failure, diabetes, and so on. The Theory of Granular Partitions is designed, now, to provide a framework within which precisely such differences of perspective on the same subject-matter can be comprehended within a single framework.

Beta receptor antagonists (or beta blockers) are one of the major drug families used in the management of hypertension. In Table 3 we take one prototypical example from this drug family – Propranolol – to show the different partitions being applied.

There is no doubt that these partitions are related to each other. Each provides a different window onto the same reality. Only a framework which can do justice to the existence of such distinct views on reality can allow us to formulate an adequate ontology of the domain in hand.

7   Conclusion

The vast amounts of knowledge currently being accumulated in the biomedical domain demand ontological resources based on clear and tested principles. The semantic types underlying UMLS and the organizing principles of the Gene Ontology both manifest a number of significant problems in this respect. We have apply the principles underlying Basic Formal Ontology and the Theory of Granular Partitions which brings not clarity to such terminology-based classifications and could provide a framework within which divergent classifications can be unified in a robust and realistic fashion.

Acknowledgement. Work on this paper was supported by the Wolfgang Paul Program of the Alexander von Humboldt Foundation.

Table 3. Partitions of Antihypertensive Agents with propranolol as example

Partition	Explanation of Classification	Illustration: Propranolol
General Therapeutic Partition	Actions of the drug which are significant at a symptomatic clinical level.	Management of hypertension; management of angina; management of life-threatening arrhythmia.
Causative Clinical Partition	Roles played by the drug in a specific pathological state, for example, based on a clinical practice guideline.	For the treatment of hypertension, the initial oral dose of propranolol is generally 40 to 80 mg per day.
Collateral Clinical Partition	Other effects the drug can have while being used in relation to a specific clinical condition.	Adverse effects (including effects of overdose). For example, dizziness, decreased heart rate, nausea.
Pharmaco-kinetic Partition	Effects of the different body systems on the drug, for example its absorption, metabolism, excretion, etc.	Complete oral absorption, 75% metabolism in first passage through the portal circulation, large volume of distribution, etc.
Pharmaco-dynamic Partition	Effects of the drug on different body systems from the pathophysiological point of view, with a granularity lower than that of the clinical level.	Slowing of the heart rate, decrease in myocardial contractility, decrease in cardiac output, increase in peripheral resistance, etc.
Biochemical Partition	Chemical attributes of the drug (according to its chemical family, chemical structure, etc.)	A benzene ring with an ethylamide side chain. Substitution of an isopropyl group favours interaction with beta-adrenergic receptors.
Product Partition	Commercially available products containing the drug as active principle (reflecting differences in physical form, mode of administration, etc.)	Propranolol HCl available as 10 mg, 20 mg, 40 mg, 60 mg, and 80 mg tablets for oral administration and as a 1 mg/ml sterile injectible solution for intravenous administration.

References

1. Humphreys BL, Lindberg DA, Schoolman HM, Barnett. The Unified Medical Language System: an informatics research collaboration. *J Am Med Inform Assoc.* 1998 Jan-Feb; 5(1): 1–11.
2. UMLS website http://www.nlm.nih.gov/research/umls/
3. The Gene Ontology Consortium. Gene Ontology: tool for the unification of biology. *Nature Genet.* 2000; 25: 25–29
4. Gene Ontology Consortium. Creating the Gene Ontology Resource: Design and Implementation. *Genome Res.* 2001; 11: 1425–1433
5. Gene Ontology website http://www.geneontology.org

6. Smith B, Williams J and Schulze-Kremer S. The Ontology of the Gene Ontology. *Proc AMIA Symp.* 2003.
7. Bittner T and Smith B. A Theory of Granular Partitions. *Foundations of Geographic Information Science*, M. Duckham, M. F. Goodchild and M. F. Worboys (eds.), London: Taylor & Francis, 117–151, 2003.
8. Bittner T. and Smith, B. Granular Spatio-Temporal Ontologies. *Proceedings of the AAAI Spring Symposium on Foundations and Applications of Spatio-Temporal Reasoning* (FASTR), 2003.
9. Bittner T and Smith B. 'Vague Reference and Approximating Judgements', *Spatial Cognition and Computation* (forthcoming).
10. Basic Formal Ontology. http://ontology.buffalo.edu/bfo/
11. Smith B. "Fiat Objects", *Topoi*, 20: 2, September 2001, 131–148
12. Bittner T and Smith B. Formal ontologies of space and time. http://ontology.buffalo.edu/geo/sto.pdf
13. Katzung BG. *Basic and Clinical Pharmacology.* 8th edn. Place: Lange/McGraw-Hill. 155–157.
14. Hardman JG, Limbird LE. *Goodman and Gilman's The Pharmacological Basis of Therapeutics.* 9th edition. Place: McGraw-Hill.

Behavioral Knowledge Representation for the Understanding and Creation of Video Sequences

Michael Arens and Hans-Hellmut Nagel

Institut für Algorithmen und Kognitive Systeme,
Fakultät für Informatik der Universität Karlsruhe (TH),
76128 Karlsruhe, Germany
{arens|nagel}@iaks.uni-karlsruhe.de

Abstract. The algorithmic generation of textual descriptions of *real world* image sequences requires conceptual knowledge. The algorithmic generation of *synthetic* image sequences from textual descriptions requires conceptual knowledge, too. An explicit representation formalism for behavioral knowledge based on formal logic is presented which can be utilized in both tasks – *Understanding* and *Creation* of video sequences. Common sense knowledge is represented at various abstraction levels in a *Situation Graph Tree*. This form of representation is exploited in order to fill in missing details in a natural language text describing developments for an image sequence to be synthesized.

1 Introduction

An (artifical) *cognitive* vision system is supposed to not only extract numerical results from input images or image sequences. It rather has to associate those quantitative results obtained by machine vision with primitive qualitative concepts which then can be aggregated into more complex concepts [6,10]. These complex concepts might then be transformed into a (natural language) textual description of what the computer vision system *recognized* in the depicted scene. In this sense, *Cognitive Vision* (CogV) constitutes an algorithmic link between visual and textual representations of information about the same discourse [16]. Examples from image sequences of innercity road traffic [9] and of vehicle maneuvers at a filling station [7] have shown that each step in this algorithmic linkage incorporates a–priori knowledge into the overall vision system.

The generation of synthetic image sequences from a (natural language) textual description of a time–varying scene might be seen as an inversion of CogV as described above: complex concepts mentioned in the input text have to be broken down into primitive concepts [16,5,2]. These primitive concepts have to be associated with (time–varying) geometric body configurations [16,12,14], which then can be visualized by standard computer graphic algorithms. The steps necessary for image sequence generation require knowledge very similar to the knowledge utilized in the CogV task. Such additional knowledge is definitely needed in cases where certain constraining information had not been incorporated into the

A. Günter et al. (Eds.): KI 2003, LNAI 2821, pp. 149–163, 2003.

input text due to the fact that a human reader can assume certain global constraints utilizing his *commonsense knowledge*. A good example for such *implicit* constraints is given in [4]. Thus, a–priori knowledge can control the (probably) vast amount of possible image sequences compatible with the input text. This kind of knowledge–supported image sequence generation is referred to, therefore, as *Controlled Imagery Generation* (CIG) in the following.

Accepting that CogV and CIG are inverse processes as motivated above, the question arises wether or not knowledge represented for one process can be utilized easily in the inverse process. This would not only minimize the effort of knowledge engineering or acquisition, but also would introduce the ability of feedback loops between both processes: the conceptual or textual description of image sequences produced by a vision system might be re–visualized. Differences between the original and the synthetic image sequence point out errors or short-comings in the knowledge deployed [17] or might even be used to re–formulate the output of the vision system in order to impose the correct 'mental image' to a human listener, as it is named in [3]. Analogously, a synthetic image sequence generated from an input text might be analyzed by a vision system. Again, differences between the original text and the text produced by the vision system might indicate deficiencies in the utilized knowledge or associated processing steps.

In the sequel, Section 2 refines the view of a cognitive vision system as a layered system of separable transformation steps. The knowledge employed in each of these steps will be described with special emphasis on conceptual, in particular behavioral knowledge. Section 3 outlines a possible approach to CIG as an inverted CogV task, focusing on the usability of the *same* behavioral knowledge.

2   Cognitive Vision

Fig. 1 depicts a layered model of a cognitive vision system. Each white rectangle in this figure stands for one representation form of information processed by the vision system. Filled rectangles surrounding one or more layers represent more encompassing sub–systems of the overall vision system. The left lower sub–system (middle–gray) comprises layers which process quantitative information. The upper (light–gray) sub–system contains layers processing conceptual information. The right lower sub–system (dark–gray) contains only one layer (so far): here, natural language information is processed. Arrows between layers indicate the flow of information between two layers, implying appropriate transformation steps. Dashed arrows show the direction in which information is passed during a CogV task, while solid arrows indicate the opposite direction to be taken by a video creation task.

The sub–system concerned with quantitative information (middle–gray in Fig. 1, comprising SAL, ISL, PDL and SDL) obtains signals from a camera configuration, converts these signals into images, and analyzes these images with respect to information about the depicted scene. The knowledge employed in these transformation steps includes knowledge about the *meaning* of two–dimensional

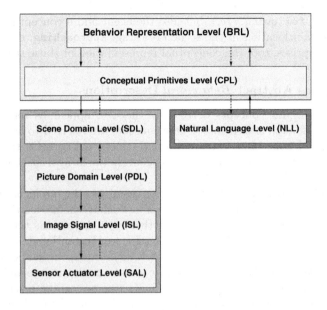

Fig. 1. Layer model of a Cognitive Vision System (adapted from [13]). Further explanation in the text.

image cues (as edges, optical flow, etc.), but in addition knowledge concerned with the projection from 3D scenes to the two–dimensional image plane. The vision system comprises, moreover, discourse–specific knowledge: in the case of image sequences of road traffic scenes, vehicle models, motion models, illumination models, and geometric models representing the static components of the depicted scene like the lane structure or other static objects are taken into account. The results obtained by this sub–system are converted into *conceptual primitives* and are passed up to the sub–system concerned with conceptual information (light–gray in Fig. 1, comprising CPL and BRL). These conceptual primitives contain the state of each depicted agent, which the quantitative sub–system was able to *recognize*, including, e.g., the agent's position and orientation in the scene and its linear and angular velocity.

2.1   Towards Primitive Conceptual Descriptions

Based on the state–information passed up from the quantitative sub–system, the *Conceptual Primitives Layer* (CPL) can derive more complex concepts by employing a *Fuzzy Metric Temporal Horn Logic* (FMTHL see [15]) on an a–priori given *terminology*. This terminology consists of logic–rules and facts which define from which (combination of) conceptual primitives a certain more complex concept can be derived [8]. Such complex concepts may regard the agent itself (standing, moving, accelerating, turning, etc.), the agent and another object (`overtaking`, `following`, etc.), but also the agent and a conceptual repesentation of a certain location in the scene (`leaving`, `approaching`, etc.). The CPL therefore comprises, too, the conceptual representation of static scene objects.

2.2   Towards Abstract *Behavioral* Descriptions

So far, the complex concepts derived by the CPL appear as temporally and conceptually isolated statements. These concepts are referred to as *occurrences*. To embed occurrences into a temporal and conceptual context, the next layer (BRL) describes the expected behavior of agents in the form of so–called *Situation Graph Trees* (SGTs).

SGTs [15,1] describe the behavior of an agent in a hierarchical manner: the basic unit of any SGT is the *situation scheme*. Such a scheme describes the state of an agent in terms of occurrencies together with the actions the agent is expected to carry out whenever the situation scheme is instantiated. Directed edges between situation schemes (called *prediction edges*) define a temporal successor relation on situation schemes. Thus, single situation schemes are embedded into (temporal) sequences of other schemes. Single schemes can be marked as start–situation and/or end–situation of such sequences. Situation schemes together with prediction edges build so–called *situation graphs*. These situation graphs can particularize superordinated situation schemes. This is done by connecting the situation scheme to be particularized with a situation graph by so–called *particularization edges*. The situation graph is said to *particularize* the situation scheme, which means it describes the particularized situation in a conceptually or temporally more detailed way. Thus, particularization edges define a partial order on situation schemes: situation schemes inside a situation graph which do not particularize any other scheme are called '*most general situations*' (the graph is called *root graph* of the SGT). Schemes inside any graph reachable by a particularization edge from inside this root graph are *more particularized*, and so on. Circles inside the SGT due to particularization edges are not allowed. Thus, schemes inside situation graphs together with particularization edges connecting schemes with particularizing graphs build tree–like structures, the *situation graph trees* [9,1].

In a CogV task, SGTs are utilized to recognize situations which can be instantiated for the observed agent by applying a graph traversal on a suitable SGT. For further details on this graph–traversal, see [15,9,1]. SGTs are incorporated into the vision system by their algorithmic transformation into FMTHL–logic programs. This allows easy modifications and even the exchange of the complete behavioral knowledge incorporated into the vision system if necessary. In addition, this formulation directly cooperates with the other conceptual knowledge sources such as the terminology and the conceptual representation of static scene objects. The complete conceptual sub–system of the vision system is based, therefore, on formal logic inference.

An example–SGT can be seen in Fig. 2. This SGT is presently used for the textual description of image sequences showing vehicle maneuvers at a filling station. Situation schemes are depicted as rectangles comprising the name

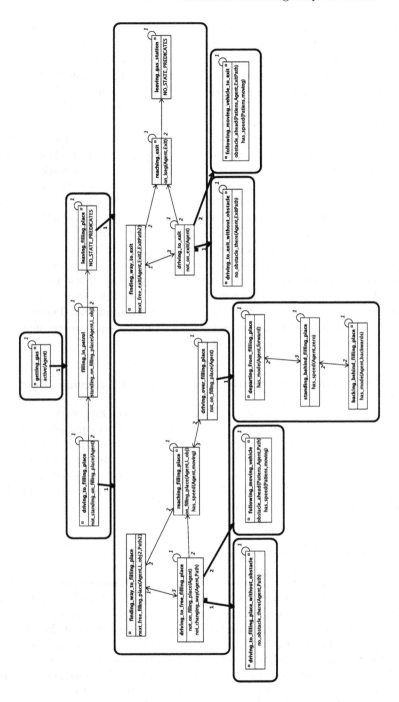

Fig. 2. (Part of an) SGT modelling the expected behavior of (vehicular) agents at a filling station. Further explanation in the text.

of the scheme and all occurrences which have to be evaluated to instantiate this scheme (note that actions normally associated with situation schemes have been omitted in Fig. 2 due to space limitations). Situation graphs are shown as rounded rectangles. Thin arrows denote prediction edges, while thick arrows indicate particularization edges. Note that small circles in the right upper corner of situation schemes depict predictions from one scheme to itself. These predictions are called *self–predictions*. The root graph (compare Fig. 2) comprises only one situation scheme, namely getting_gas. This scheme is particularized by another situation graph, comprising three schemes (driving_to_filling_place, filling_in_petrol, and leaving_filling_place), whereby the first of these schemes is marked as start–situation and the last one as end–situation (small squares to the left or to the right of situation names indicate start–schemes or end–schemes, respectively). Two of these schemes are particularized further. Note that multiple particularizations are allowed (compare Fig. 2: driving_to_free_filling_place). If multiple particularizations or multiple predictions occur in an SGT, these edges have to be ordered (small numbers in Fig. 2 show the order between particularizations and predictions from any scheme). The traversal algorithm mentioned above tests for further scheme instantiations in this order. Note that some particularizing graphs have been omitted in Fig. 2 due to space limitations. These omissions are indicated by small filled squares beneath situation schemes (compare Fig. 2: driving_to_free_filling_place and driving_to_exit).

2.3   From Behavioral Descriptions to Natural Language Text

The graph–traversal in BRL based on the employed SGT and on the occurrencies derived in the CPL instantiates one situation for each image frame and each recognized agent in the observed scene. The sequence of these situations can be used in the *Natural Language Layer* (NLL) to formulate a natural language text describing the scene as *seen* by the cognitive vision system [7]. The text generation conducted in NLL is based on the *Discourse Representation Theory* (DRT) treated by Kamp & Reyle [11].

3   Controlled Imagery Generation

The overall task in CIG is to generate *one plausible* image sequence which visualizes the scene characterized by a textual description. Considering CIG as an inverted CogV task, the first step of imagery generation includes the analysis of the input text in order to construct a conceptual description of the scene mentioned there (NLL to CPL in Fig. 1). Natural language processing (NLP) steps along the lines of the DRT as required for CIG have been reported in [2].

The next step towards the generation of a synthetic image sequence is the recognition of situations which have to be instantiated for any agent mentioned in the text (CPL to BRL in Fig. 1). Supposing that appropriate concepts were derived from the text, this instantiation of situation schemes is (at least) comparable to situation instantiation within the CogV task. It therefore is assumed in the following that a sequence of isolated situations for every agent mentioned in the input text has been derived after these two transformation steps.

One problem arises due to the fact that natural language texts are aimed at a human reader: not every fact has to be included into the text, because the reader is supposed to *assume* certain global facts on the basis of his commonsense knowledge. A text describing a vehicle at a filling station as *reaching* a certain filling place (reaching_filling_place in Fig. 2), would surely make the reader assume that this vehicle was driving towards that (previously vacant) filling place for some preceding time instances (see driving_to_free_filling_place in Fig. 2). The reader can obviously *embed* single situations into *plausible* situation sequences.

In addition to the above–mentioned problem of situation–embedding, a second type of potentially incomplete specification arises in association with most natural language texts: usually, a human observer describing, e.g., vehicle maneuvers at a filling station would formulate at a certain level of detail what he sees. For some purposes, it might be sufficient to describe a vehicle as driving to a filling place (driving_to_filling_place), without stating that the vehicle (i.e. the driver) first decides for a vacant filling place (finding_way_to_free_filling_place), drives towards it (driving_to_free_filling_place), and at last reaches that place (reaching_filling_place). Again, the human reader can be supposed to assume this more detailed description of what really happened in the scene on the basis of his commonsense knowledge.

3.1 Derivation of Plausible Behaviors from Situation Sequences

A single algorithm for both task – the embedding of situations and the derivation of *most detailed* descriptions – can draw advantage from the fact that the knowledge necessary for both task is already stored in form of SGTs: on one hand, every situation recognized in the input text will appear inside a situation graph, upon a path from some start–situation to some end–situation. Moreover, this situation graph might particularize another, more general situation: again, this particularized situation is not isolated, but may imply an entire sequence of situations, and so on. Thus, the embedding of given situations can be derived.

On the other hand, most situations might be superordinated to particularizing graphs. Each path from a start–situation to an end–situation in such a particularizing graph comprises a more detailed description of the initial situation. Situations occurring in that path might again be particularized by other graphs, and so on. Therefore, the particularization of given situations is also derivable. These relationships will be characterized more precisely in the following six definitions, prior to the description of an algorithm which solves both problems mentioned above.

Definition 1 (SGT–episode). *Any sequence E of situations inside one situation graph G which constitutes a path from any start–situation to any end–situation along prediction edges is denoted as an* SGT–episode *described by G. If G is particularizing a situation scheme* S, *E is called* particularizing SGT–episode *of* S.

Definition 2 (behavior). *Given an SGT $\mathcal{B}$, a behavior is recursively defined as follows:*

- *each SGT–episode E described by the root graph of $\mathcal{B}$ is a behavior.*
- *Given a behavior E, another behavior can be obtained by replacing one situation S in E with a particularizing SGT–episode of S.*

Definition 3 (particularizing behavior). *Given an SGT $\mathcal{B}$ and a behavior E, any behavior E' is denoted as a particularizing behavior of E, iff E' can be obtained by (recursively) replacing situations in E with particularizing SGT–episodes.*

Definition 4 (maximal behavior). *Given an SGT $\mathcal{B}$, any behavior E is called a maximal behavior, iff no situation S in E can be replaced by a particularizing SGT–episode of S.*

Definition 5 ($\mathcal{B}$–compatible behavior). *Given an SGT $\mathcal{B}$ and a situation sequence S, any behavior $\widehat{S}$ is called $\mathcal{B}$–compatible with S, iff*

- *each element of S is also element of $\widehat{S}$ and*
- *for each pair (s_i, s_j) of elements of S, where s_i lies before s_j in the sequence S, s_i lies before s_j in the sequence $\widehat{S}$.*

Definition 6 (maximized $\mathcal{B}$–compatible behavior). *Given an SGT $\mathcal{B}$ and a situation sequence S, any behavior M is called maximized $\mathcal{B}$–compatible with regard to S, iff*

- *M is a maximal behavior and*
- *M is a particularizing behavior of some behavior $\widehat{S}$ which is $\mathcal{B}$–compatible with S.*

The algorithmic solution for situation–embedding and situation–particularization takes an SGT $\mathcal{B}$ and a situation sequence S as input. It derives the desired *maximized $\mathcal{B}$–compatible behavior* in two recursive sub–processes: first, a $\mathcal{B}$–compatible behavior is searched for the given input sequence (compare Def. 5). This sub–process embeds the given situation sequence into a possible behavior as described by $\mathcal{B}$. Then, this $\mathcal{B}$–compatible behavior will be particularized until a maximized $\mathcal{B}$–compatible behavior (compare Def. 6) is found. This second sub–process thus derives a most–detailed description of the desired behavior.

To prepare the first recursion, the algorithm determines an *abstraction path* for each situation in S. These paths lead from the given situation up to a situation inside the root graph of $\mathcal{B}$. The paths are unique, because every situation can only be part of one graph and each graph can only particularize one or – in case of the root graph of $\mathcal{B}$ – no situation. The abstraction paths are used in the first recursion to restrict the search space for $\mathcal{B}$–compatible behaviors. The initial behavior S_0 for this search is given by any SGT–episode (compare Def. 1)

Input
  – SGT $\mathcal{B}$, situation sequence S

Preparation
  – determine abstraction path for each situation in S
  – build list L_0 of last elements of those paths in the order given by S
  – **determine SGT–episode** S_0 in root–graph containing all elements of L_0
  – delete last elements of abstraction paths
  – continue with **Recursion 1**

Recursion 1 /∗ derive $\mathcal{B}$–compatible behavior ∗/
  – build list L_i of last elements of abstraction paths
  – determine graph membership partition P_i of L_i
  – **determine list** E_i **of SGT–episodes** for each element of P_i
  – **replace** situations in S_{i-1} with particularizing SGT–episode from E_i
  – delete last elements of abstraction paths
  – all abstraction paths empty ?
  YES: ∗ continue with **Recursion 2**
   NO: ∗ goto **Recursion 1**

Recursion 2 /∗ extend to maximized $\mathcal{B}$–compatible behavior ∗/
  – **determine particularizing SGT–episode** for one situation in S_i
  – SGT–episode found ?
  YES: ∗ create S_{i+1} by substitution of SGT–episode for situation in S_i
         ∗ goto **Recursion 2**
   NO: ∗ continue with **Output**

Output
  – set $M = S_i$, return M

Fig. 3. The algorithm deriving plausible situation sequences in pseudo-code. Steps of the algorithm which might lead to multiple solutions are marked in **bold face**.

inside the root graph (as an initial behavior following Def. 2), which contains all *last* elements of the abstraction paths in correct order. The last elements of all abstraction paths are then deleted by the algorithm. The first recursive sub–process then particularizes the obtained initial behavior (compare Def. 3). Again, the remaining abstraction paths restrict this particularization: only those particularizing behaviors are investigated which contain the last elements of these abstraction paths. Therefore, a list of those last elements is constructed. This list is partitioned according to the graph membership of comprised consecutive situations. This is necessary for the following reason: in distinction to the initial step, where all last elements of the abstraction paths could be found within the root graph of $\mathcal{B}$, subsequent steps might lead to lists of last elements which lie in different graphs. If two or more consecutive situations lie within one graph, only one SGT–episode in that graph is searched which contains all these situations in the correct order. Thus, for each partition of the current last elements of the abstraction paths, one SGT–episode is searched for particularization. In each recursion step i, the algorithm constructs a particularizing behavior S_i from the result S_{i-1} obtained during the preceding recursion step. The last elements of

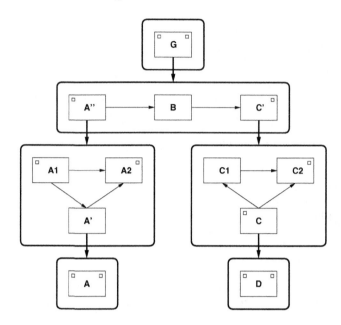

Fig. 4. Example SGT. Situation schemes are depicted as rectangles, situation graphs are shown as rectangles with rounded corners. Small squares in the left (right) upper corner of situation schemes mark them as start–situations (end–situations). Prediction edges are depicted as thin, particularization edges as thick arrows.

each (not empty) abstraction path are deleted until all these paths are empty. The resulting behavior is – due to its construction – $\mathcal{B}$–*compatible* with the initially given sequence S.

The second recursive sub–process of the algorithm takes the previously constructed $\mathcal{B}$–compatible behavior and particularizes this behavior until the resulting behavior is maximal (following Def. 6).

Note that the algorithm described above does not necessarily yield a unique solution. Depending on the SGT and the input situation sequence, the algorithm rather constructs *all possible* maximized $\mathcal{B}$–compatible behaviors with respect to the SGT and the input sequence. The order in which these possible solutions are obtained by the algorithm is defined by the order on prediction edges and particularization edges mentioned in Section 2.2. The following example will illustrate the application of the algorithm and the construction of multiple possible solutions, see Fig. 3 for a pseudo–code formulation of the algorithm outlined above.

3.2   An Example

Suppose we describe the possible behavior of agents with the SGT $\mathcal{B}$ depicted in Fig. 4. Suppose further that the text–analysis and subsequent situation instantiation yielded the initial situation sequence $S = \langle \texttt{A,B,C} \rangle$. Thus the following three abstraction paths result:

$$g_A = \langle \mathtt{A}, \mathtt{A'}, \mathtt{A''}, \mathtt{G} \rangle,$$
$$g_B = \langle \mathtt{B}, \mathtt{G} \rangle,$$
$$g_C = \langle \mathtt{C}, \mathtt{C'}, \mathtt{G} \rangle$$

according to the three situations of S. Notice that the last element of each path (i.e. $\mathtt{G}$) lies within the root graph of $\mathcal{B}$. Thus, building the list of last elements of all abstraction paths (whereby multiple appearances of the same situation are kept only once) the algorithm produces

$$L_0 = \langle \mathtt{G} \rangle$$

as the list of last elements. Due to the construction of abstraction paths, all elements of L_0 (only $\mathtt{G}$ in this example) lie within the root graph of $\mathcal{B}$. An SGT–episode in this graph is searched, therefore, which contains all elements of L_0 in the order given there, yielding simply

$$S_0 = \langle \mathtt{G} \rangle.$$

We thus proceed with the sequence $S_0 = \langle \mathtt{G} \rangle$. Because all last elements of the abstraction paths have been processed, these elements are deleted. The remaining paths have the form

$$g_A = \langle \mathtt{A}, \mathtt{A'}, \mathtt{A''} \rangle,$$
$$g_B = \langle \mathtt{B} \rangle,$$
$$g_C = \langle \mathtt{C}, \mathtt{C'} \rangle.$$

The first recursion starts with the determination of the list of last elements of the remaining abstraction paths: This yields

$$L_1 = \langle \mathtt{A''}, \mathtt{B}, \mathtt{C'} \rangle.$$

Partitioning according to graph membership of comprised situations leads to

$$P_1 = \langle \langle \mathtt{A''}, \mathtt{B}, \mathtt{C'} \rangle \rangle,$$

because all three situations belong to one graph. The search for SGT–episodes in that graph containing all three situations in the correct order produces a single tuple

$$E_1 = \langle \langle \langle \mathtt{A''}, \mathtt{B}, \mathtt{C'} \rangle \rangle \rangle.$$

We thus obtain one particularizing behavior, namely by replacing the situation $\mathtt{G}$ in S_0 by the sequence $\langle \mathtt{A''}, \mathtt{B}, \mathtt{C'} \rangle$ and by deleting every last element in each abstraction path, yielding $S_1 = \langle \mathtt{A''}, \mathtt{B}, \mathtt{C'} \rangle$ as new behavior and

$$g_A = \langle \mathtt{A}, \mathtt{A'} \rangle,$$
$$g_C = \langle \mathtt{C} \rangle$$

as remaining paths. Notice that the path g_B initially determined for the situation $\mathtt{B}$ is empty now and no longer affects the processing. The next iteration starts with

$$L_2 = \langle \mathtt{A'}, \mathtt{C} \rangle$$

as list of last elements and

$$P_2 = \langle\langle \mathtt{A}'\rangle, \langle \mathtt{C}\rangle\rangle$$

as the partition of that list. In this case, we obtain a partition comprising two elements, one containing elements of one graph on the abstraction path initially determined for A, the other containing elements of a graph on the abstraction path for C. Thus, determining possible SGT–episodes (compare Def. 1) in both of these graphs yields

$$E_2 = \langle\langle\langle \mathtt{A1}, \mathtt{A}', \mathtt{A2}\rangle\rangle, \langle\langle \mathtt{C}, \mathtt{C2}\rangle, \langle \mathtt{C}, \mathtt{C1}, \mathtt{C2}\rangle\rangle\rangle.$$

The first element of E_2 contains only one SGT–episode $\langle \mathtt{A1},\mathtt{A}',\mathtt{A2}\rangle$ because this is the only SGT–episode in the graph containing A′. The second element of E_2 contains two SGT–episodes: in the corresponding graph, two SGT–episodes can be found which both comprise the situation C (compare Fig. 4). We thus obtain two possible next particularizing behaviors

$$S_2 = \langle \mathtt{A1}, \mathtt{A}', \mathtt{A2}, \mathtt{B}, \mathtt{C}, \mathtt{C2}\rangle,$$
$$S_2' = \langle \mathtt{A1}, \mathtt{A}', \mathtt{A2}, \mathtt{B}, \mathtt{C}, \mathtt{C1}, \mathtt{C2}\rangle$$

by replacing the situations A″ and C′ in S_1 by the possible paths from E_2. The only remaining abstraction path after deletion then is

$$g_A = \langle \mathtt{A}\rangle.$$

A last iteration yields the list of last elements

$$L_3 = \langle \mathtt{A}\rangle,$$

the partition

$$P_3 = \langle\langle \mathtt{A}\rangle\rangle,$$

and resulting possible SGT–episodes

$$E_3 = \langle\langle\langle \mathtt{A}\rangle\rangle\rangle.$$

The only possible SGT–episode for replacing A′ in S_2 and S_2' is therefore $\langle \mathtt{A}\rangle$, yielding the particularizing behaviors

$$S_3 = \langle \mathtt{A1}, \mathtt{A}, \mathtt{A2}, \mathtt{B}, \mathtt{C}, \mathtt{C2}\rangle$$
$$S_3' = \langle \mathtt{A1}, \mathtt{A}, \mathtt{A2}, \mathtt{B}, \mathtt{C}, \mathtt{C1}, \mathtt{C2}\rangle.$$

Because all abstraction paths are empty after this step, the first sub–process of the algorithm terminates here. Notice that both situation sequences S_3 and S_3' are $\mathcal{B}$–compatible behaviors with respect to S. Nevertheless, the two sequences S_3 and S_3' do not describe the behavior of the mentioned agent in the most detailed way obtainable by $\mathcal{B}$: the situation C as part of both behaviors possesses a particularizing graph – consisting only of the situation scheme D (compare Fig. 4). The most particularized description is obtained, however, by the second sub–process of the algorithm: the $\mathcal{B}$–compatible behaviors obtained so far are particularized until a maximal $\mathcal{B}$–compatible behavior is reached. In the example above, only one situation (i.e. C) comprised in both behaviors possesses a

Table 1. Example for the computation of plausible situation sequences. For explanations see the text in Section 3.2.

Input: $\mathcal{B}$, $S = \langle \text{A}, \text{B}, \text{C} \rangle$	
$g_A = \langle \text{A}, \text{A}', \text{A}'', \text{G} \rangle$	
$g_B = \langle \text{B}, \text{G} \rangle$	
$g_C = \langle \text{C}, \text{C}', \text{G} \rangle$	
$L_0 = \langle \text{G} \rangle$	
$S_0 = \langle \underline{\text{G}} \rangle$	
$g_A = \langle \text{A}, \text{A}', \text{A}'' \rangle$	
$g_B = \langle \text{B} \rangle$	
$g_C = \langle \text{C}, \text{C}' \rangle$	
$L_1 = \langle \text{A}'', \text{B}, \text{C}' \rangle \;\Rightarrow\; P_1 = \langle\langle \text{A}'', \text{B}, \text{C}' \rangle\rangle \;\Rightarrow\; E_1 = \langle\langle\langle \text{A}'', \text{B}, \text{C}' \rangle\rangle\rangle$	
$S_1 = \langle \text{A}'', \text{B}, \text{C}' \rangle$	
$g_A = \langle \text{A}, \text{A}' \rangle$	
$g_B = \langle \; \rangle \surd$	
$g_C = \langle \text{C} \rangle$	
$L_2 = \langle \text{A}', \text{C} \rangle \;\Rightarrow\; P_2 = \langle\langle \text{A}' \rangle, \langle \text{C} \rangle\rangle \;\Rightarrow\; E_2 = \langle\langle\langle \text{A1}, \text{A}', \text{A2} \rangle\rangle, \langle\langle \text{C}, \text{C2} \rangle, \langle \text{C}, \text{C1}, \text{C2} \rangle\rangle\rangle$	
$S_2 = \langle \text{A1}, \text{A}', \text{A2}, \text{B}, \underline{\text{C}}, \text{C2} \rangle$	$S_2' = \langle \text{A1}, \text{A}', \text{A2}, \text{B}, \underline{\text{C}}, \text{C1}, \text{C2} \rangle$
$g_A = \langle \text{A} \rangle$	$g_A = \langle \text{A} \rangle$
$g_B = \langle \; \rangle \surd$	$g_B = \langle \; \rangle \surd$
$g_C = \langle \; \rangle \surd$	$g_C = \langle \; \rangle \surd$
$L_3 = \langle \text{A} \rangle \;\Rightarrow\; P_3 = \langle\langle \text{A} \rangle\rangle \;\Rightarrow\; E_3 = \langle\langle\langle \text{A} \rangle\rangle\rangle$	$L_3 = \langle \text{A} \rangle \;\Rightarrow\; P_3 = \langle\langle \text{A} \rangle\rangle \;\Rightarrow\; E_3 = \langle\langle\langle \text{A} \rangle\rangle\rangle$
$S_3 = \langle \text{A1}, \underline{\text{A}}, \text{A2}, \text{B}, \text{C}, \text{C2} \rangle$	$S_3 = \langle \text{A1}, \underline{\text{A}}, \text{A2}, \text{B}, \text{C}, \text{C1}, \text{C2} \rangle$
$g_A = \langle \; \rangle \surd$	$g_A = \langle \; \rangle \surd$
$g_B = \langle \; \rangle \surd$	$g_B = \langle \; \rangle \surd$
$g_C = \langle \; \rangle \surd$	$g_C = \langle \; \rangle \surd$
$M = \langle \text{A1}, \text{A}, \text{A2}, \text{B}, \underline{\text{D}}, \text{C2} \rangle$	$M = \langle \text{A1}, \text{A}, \text{A2}, \text{B}, \underline{\text{D}}, \text{C1}, \text{C2} \rangle$
Output: $M = \langle \text{A1}, \text{A}, \text{A2}, \text{B}, \text{D}, \text{C2} \rangle$	Output: $M = \langle \text{A1}, \text{A}, \text{A2}, \text{B}, \text{D}, \text{C1}, \text{C2} \rangle$

particularizing graph. In that graph, only one SGT–episode $\langle \text{D} \rangle$ can be found. Thus, for the example discussed above, this operation yields the final result(s)

$$M = \langle \text{A1}, \text{A}, \text{A2}, \text{B}, \text{D}, \text{C2} \rangle$$
$$M' = \langle \text{A1}, \text{A}, \text{A2}, \text{B}, \text{D}, \text{C1}, \text{C2} \rangle.$$

Table 1 recapitulates the example described above.

3.3 From Maximal $\mathcal{B}$–Compatible Behavior to Synthetic Image Sequences

Of course, the task of CIG is not finished by deriving plausible situation sequences in BRL (compare Fig. 1). The next step would be to transform these situations first into complex and then into primitive concepts in CPL. Subsequently, these primitive concepts have to be transformed into quantitative descriptions of body configurations in the described 3D-scene (SDL). These configurations then have to be visualized.

4   Conclusion

In this article, a view of *Cognitive Vision* and *Controlled Imagery Generation* as inverse processes has been motivated. Moreover, it was suggested to use *one* knowledge base for *both* processes in order to minimize knowledge engineering efforts and in order to allow feedback loops between both processes. Special emphasis was placed on the representation of *behavioral* knowledge. Here it has been shown that SGTs – behavioral representation formalisms developed for Cognitive Vision – can also be used for the derivation of plausible situation sequences as a starting point for the generation of synthetic video sequences.

An algorithm was explained which derives plausible situation sequences by not only particularizing given information – as described, e.g., in [16,17] – but also incorporates knowledge about plausible behavioral contexts into which the given information can be embedded.

5   Future Work

The algorithmic determination of plausible situation sequences presented in this article is only one step of the process of Controlled Imagery Generation. The extraction of concepts from an input text and their association with situation schemes in a given SGT still will profit from further investigations.

The same knowledge representation formalisms employed in the CogV task will be used to facilitate the transformation of situation schemes into conceptual primitives, including the terminology and a conceptual representation of static scene objects. Further steps will have to transform these conceptual primitives into numerical representations, using again the same quantative knowledge as employed in the CogV task, e.g., the illumination model and motion models for vehicles.

References

1. M. Arens and H.–H. Nagel: *Representation of Behavioral Knowledge for Planning and Plan–Recognition in a Cognitive Vision System.* In: M. Jarke et al. (Eds.): Proc. of the 25th German Conf. on Artificial Intelligence (KI-2002), 16–20 September 2002, Aachen, Germany. LNAI 2479, Springer-Verlag: Berlin·Heidelberg·New York/NY 2002, pp. 268-282.
2. M. Arens, A. Ottlik, and H.–H. Nagel: *Natural Language Texts for a Cognitive Vision System.* In: F. van Harmelen (Ed.): Proc. of the 15th European Conf. on Artificial Intelligence (ECAI–2002), 21–26 July 2002, Lyon, France, IOS Press: Amsterdam 2002, pp. 455–459.
3. A. Blocher and J. R. J. Schirra: *Optional Deep Case Filling and Focus Control with Mental Images: ANTLIMA–KOREF.* In: C. S. Mellish (Ed.): Proc. of the 14th Int. Joint Conf. on Artificial Intelligence (IJCAI–95), Montréal, Canada, 20–25 August 1995, pp. 417–423.
4. B. Coyne and R. Sproat: *WordsEye: An Automatic Text–to–Scene Conversion System.* In: Proc. of the 28th Annual Conf. on Computer Graphics and Interactive Techniques (SIGGRAPH 2001), 12–17 August 2001, Los Angeles, CA, pp. 487–496.

5. A. Egges, A. Nijholt, and P. Nugues: *Generating a 3D Simulation of a Car Accident from a Formal Description: the CarSim System.* In: V. Giagourta and M. G. Strintzis (Eds.): Proc. of the Int. Conf. on Augmented, Virtual Environments and Three–Dimensional Imaging (ICAV3D), Mykonos, Greece, May 2001, pp. 220–223.

6. J. Fernyhough, A. G. Cohn, and D. C. Hogg: *Constructing qualitative event models automatically from video input.* Image and Vision Computing **18**:2 (2000) 81–103.

7. R. Gerber: *Natürlichsprachliche Beschreibung von Straßenverkehrsszenen durch Bildfolgenauswertung.* Dissertation, Fakultät für Informatik der Universität Karlsruhe (TH), Januar 2000; see: http://www.ubka.uni-karlsruhe.de/cgi-bin/psview?document=2000/informatik/8 (in German).

8. R. Gerber and H.–H. Nagel: *Occurrence Extraction from Image Sequences of Road Traffic Scenes.* In: L. van Gool and B. Schiele (Eds.): Proc. of the Workshop on Cognitive Vision, 19–20 September 2002, ETH Zurich, Switzerland; pp. 1–8, see: http://www.vision.ethz.ch/cogvis02/finalpapers/gerber.pdf .

9. M. Haag and H.-H. Nagel: *Incremental Recognition of Traffic Situations from Video Image Sequences.* Image and Vision Computing **18**:2 (2000) 137–153.

10. R. J. Howarth and H. Buxton: *Conceptual descriptions from monitoring and watching image sequences.* Image and Vision Computing **18**:2 (2000) 105–135.

11. H. Kamp and U. Reyle: *From Discourse to Logic.* Kluwer Academic Publishers: Dordrecht, The Netherlands 1993.

12. A. Mukerjee, K. Gupta, S. Nautiyal, M.P. Singh, and N. Mishra: *Conceptual description of visual scenes from linguistic models.* Image and Vision Computing **18**:2 (2000) 173–187.

13. H.–H. Nagel: *Image Sequence Evaluation: 30 Years and Still Going Strong.* In: A. Sanfeliu et al. (Eds.): Proc. 15th Int. Conf. on Pattern Recognition (ICPR–2000), Barcelona/Spain, 3–7 September 2000, Vol. 1, IEEE Computer Society: Los Alamitos, CA 2000, pp. 149–158.

14. H. H. Nagel, M. Haag, V. Jeyakumar, and A. Mukerjee: *Visualisation of Conceptual Descriptions Derived from Image Sequences.* Mustererkennung 1999, 21. DAGM–Symposium, Bonn, 15–17 September 1999, Springer–Verlag: Berlin·Heidelberg·New York/NY 1999, pp. 364–371.

15. K. H. Schäfer: *Unscharfe zeitlogische Modellierung von Situationen und Handlungen in Bildfolgenauswertung und Robotik.* Dissertation, Fakultät für Informatik der Universität Karlsruhe (TH), Juli 1996; Dissertationen zur Künstlichen Intelligenz (DISKI) **135**; infix–Verlag: Sankt Augustin 1996 (in German).

16. J. R. J. Schirra: *Bildbeschreibung als Verbindung von visuellem und sprachlichem Raum.* Dissertation, Fakultät für Informatik der Universität des Saarlandes, Saarbrücken, April 1994; Dissertationen zur Künstlichen Intelligenz (DISKI) **71**; infix–Verlag: Sankt Augustin 1994 (in German).

17. V. T. Vu, F. Brémond, and M. Thonnat: *Human Behaviour Visualisation and Simulation for Automatic Video Understanding.* In: Proc. of the 10th Int. Conf. in Central Europe on Computer Graphics, Visualization and Computer Vision (WSCG–2002), Plzen–Bory, Czech Republic, 2002, pp. 485–492.

Designing Agents with MicroPsi Node Nets

Joscha Bach and Ronnie Vuine

Institut für Informatik, Humboldt-Universität zu Berlin
Unter den Linden 6, 10099 Berlin, Germany
{bach,vuine}@informatik.hu-berlin.de

Abstract. The MicroPsi agent architecture, which is based mainly on the Psi theory of Dietrich Dörner, describes the interaction of emotion, motivation and cognition of situated agents. The underlying theory has been formulated within the context of psychology but captures numerous aspects of interest for cognitive science, psychological modeling, social simulation and human-machine interaction. MicroPsi is an attempt to formulate this theory in a more abstract and formal way and to make necessary extensions to allow for the implementation of agents for a range of applications. This contribution describes some components of the architecture and introduces a node net formalism, which serves as the primary means of representation, behavior control and modeling of MicroPsi agents.

1 Introduction

To build agents that implement theories on human and animal cognition, perception, motivation and emotion (for instance for cognitive modeling, social simulation, human-computer interaction) we need psychological concepts that are detailed, comprehensive and formal at the same time. Unfortunately, there are not many theories around that meet this demand, which is apparently due to the fact that contemporary psychological methodology does not encourage the formulation of comprehensive functional theories [20].

A very interesting and inspiring aspirant, however, may be the *Psi theory* by psychologist Dietrich Dörner [9,11]. The theory makes attempts at addressing issues like perception, imagination, emotion, planning and memory in often very original ways, and has even partly been implemented by its author as a software agent. But since most aspects of the theory have never been published within the context of AI and the formulation is sometimes loose, informal and incomplete, its impact on computer science has so far been somewhat limited.

The MicroPsi architecture [3,4,5], is an agent architecture that incorporates many ideas from the Psi theory; in some way, it is meant to be a structured implementation of the original theory and a step towards its formulation within the context of computer science. The result is the description of a cognitive framework for autonomous, situated agents. Unlike in the successful (and more mature) architectures ACT [1] and SOAR [18], which concentrate mainly on cognition, a special focus is laid on motivation, emotion and flexible acquisition

A. Günter et al. (Eds.): KI 2003, LNAI 2821, pp. 164–178, 2003.

of object and action representations through interaction with the environment. MicroPsi is following a 'broad and shallow' approach, as suggested for instance by Bates, Loyall and Reilly [6].

Because the agent has no verbal ability beyond the association of acquired concepts with arbitrary names, many aspects of human problem solving can not be modeled yet. (This is a current line of research of Dörner's group [17]). Another limitation consists in the lack of social behavior, partly because social motivation and the perception of social aspects of the environment, namely a theory of mind (i.e. the attribution of intentional states to other agents) are still missing.

Many concepts of MicroPsi are more abstract and formal than the Psi theory. In its formulation as an architecture, it makes use of ideas from BDI [7, 21], but unlike common formulations of the BDI paradigm like PRS [14] and dMARS [8], it concentrates on modeling perception, emotion and interaction and incorporates notions from Sloman's theory of Cognition and Affect [24,25]. MicroPsi is not primarily meant to be a toolkit for cognitive or social modeling (like e.g. PECS [22]), but sets out to serve as an experimental platform that allows for the discussion of phenomena of human and animal cognition, similar to the 'Conscious Agents' of S. Franklin [13].

Extensions of MicroPsi, compared to the original theory, took place on two levels. On the agent design level, MicroPsi possesses a more structured, partly parallel process layout, a divided memory and more general internal representations. On the level of the theory, methods for category building and for attention based processing have been added, but implementation of these is still in an early stage. The original low level perception mechanism of the Psi agents, which is based on a simple image recognition method, is currently not a part of MicroPsi.

The following section gives a very brief overview of some of the main concepts of the MicroPsi architecture (for a more detailed introduction, see Bach 2003 [4]). This is followed by a short tour of MicroPsi Node Nets. These networks act as a unified representation of sensoric data, abstract representation, behavior and control scripts. The data structures of node nets may act as neural nets, Bayesian networks, hierarchical plan and script representations, and they may also encapsulate code in a native programming language to speed up processing. Section 4 explains how node nets are applied within MicroPsi agents.

2   The MicroPsi Architecture

2.1   Overview

MicroPsi agents are connected to their environment by external sensors and a set of somatic parameters (like 'intactness', 'energy level', and so on). From these, 'physiological' desires ('urges'), immediate percepts and *modulators* are automatically derived. The activity of the agent consists of a number of internal and external behavior modules. While the former act within the cognitive structures of the agent, the latter send sequences of actuator commands to the environment. The representations that can be derived from external percepts (based on

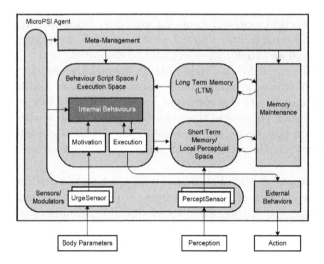

Fig. 1. Overview of Architecture

knowledge that has been acquired earlier) are stored in the agent's access memory. The agent also possesses a long term memory that holds its history and concepts that have been derived from interaction with the environment. The exchange between long term and access memory takes place through a set of autonomous memory maintenance processes, which also handle memory decay, concept generation and so on. The agent's internal behaviors are meant to handle its higher cognitive processes. They are triggered by motivations and modified by a set of modulators, which lead to emotional configurations in accordance with Dörner's theory of emotion. The management of processing resources between the internal behaviors and the memory maintenance mechanisms is handled by the meta-management module.

2.2   Main Concepts

We can not give a thorough description of the MicroPsi architecture here, but will list some of the main concepts:

Representation: Objects, situations, categories, actions, episodes and plans are all represented as hierarchical networks of nodes. Nodes may be expanded into weighted conjunctions or disjunctions of subordinated node nets, and ultimately 'bottom out' in references to sensors and actuators. Thus, the semantics of all acquired representations result from interaction with the environment or from somatic responses of the agent to external or internal situations. (For communicating agents, they may potentially be derived from explanations, where the interaction partner–another software agent or a human teacher–refers to such experiences or previously acquired concepts.)

Memory: Node nets act as universal data structures for perception, memory and planning. (See fig. 3 for a simple sensoric schema.) Even though the Psi theory does not distinguish between different types of memory, we have found that differentiating special areas (node spaces) helps to clarify the different stages of cognitive processing. The main distinction that has been introduced into MicroPsi is the split into long term memory and workspace. This enables agents to represent and manipulate data quickly according to a given context, and to establish and test new hypotheses without compromising established long term memory. Main kinds of information in the short term memory include the actual

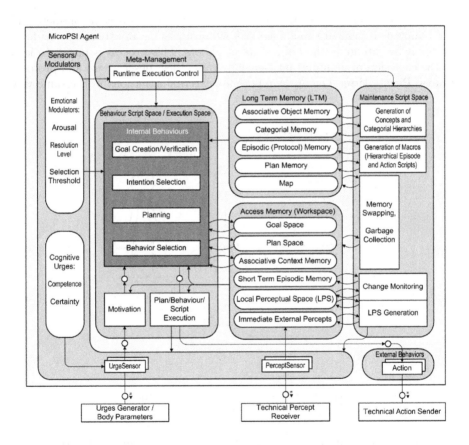

Fig. 2. Main components

situation, the current course of events, a contextual background for objects in the current situation, as well as currently active goals and plans. The long term memory stores information about individual objects, categories derived from these objects (both declarative memory), a biography of the agent (protocol memory), a library of plans and plan-components, and a map of the environment.

The links between nodes decay over time (as long as the strength of the links does not exceed a certain level that guarantees not to forget vital information). The decay is much stronger in short term memory, and is counterbalanced by two mechanisms:

- usage strengthens the links, and
- events that are strongly connected to a positive or negative influence on the urges of the agent (such as the discovery of an energy source or the suffering of an accident) lead to a retro gradient connection increase of the preceding situations.

If a link deteriorates completely, individual isolated nodes become obsolete and are removed. If gaps are the result of such an incision, an attempt is made to bridge it by extending the links of its neighbors. This process is meant to lead to the exclusion of unimportant elements from object descriptions and protocol chains. **Perception**: The agent represents external situations in the same way

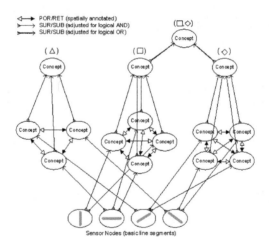

Fig. 3. 'Sensoric schema' for simple objects

as hypotheses or acquired knowledge; this is done in the *local perceptual space*. To this end, the agent retrieves hypotheses from previous content in the local perceptual space or from its long term memory and tests the immediate external percepts against them. This is called 'hypothesis based perception', or *hypercept*. If the expectations of the agent fail, and no theory about the perceived external phenomena can be found, a new object schema is acquired by a scanning process ('*accommodation*') that leaves the agent with a hierarchical node net. Abstract concepts that may not be directly observed (for instance classes of transactions or object categories) are defined by referencing multiple schemas in such a way that their commonalities, differences or process structure become the focus of attention.

Hierarchical categories: The similarity of node schemas can be established by a complete or a partial match. By constraining the depth of the comparison, the agent may notice *structural similarity*, for instance between a human face and a cartoon face. However, the key to structural similarity is the organization of node schemas into hierarchies (where an abstract face schema may consist of eye, nose and mouth schemas in a certain arrangement, and can thus be similar to a 'smiley'). Furthermore, many objects can *only* be classified using abstract hierarchies. Such hierarchies can be derived mainly in three ways: by identifying prominent elements of objects (that is, structures that are easy to recognize by interaction or perception and also good predictors for the object category), by guessing, and by communication. [2]

Emotion: In Dörner's framework, emotion is a set of configurations of the cognitive system of an individual. Cognitive processes are embedded into the emotional sub-system, and so emotional configurations influence how an agent perceives, plans, memorizes, selects intentions, acts etc. Main components of the emotional system are parameters that represent cognitive urges, situation evaluation and the *modulators*, like *arousal, resolution level* and *selection threshold*. They control the usage of semantic schemata during perception, retrieval etc., for instance by limiting search depth and width. The emotional modulation is designed to allocate mental resources in way that is suitable to a given situation and reduce the computational complexity of the current task. [10]

Motivation: The agent possesses a number of innate desires (urges) that are the source of its motives. Events that raise these desires are interpreted as negative reinforcement signals, whereas a satisfaction of a desire creates a positive signal. Currently, there are urges for intactness, energy (food and water), affiliation, competence and reduction of uncertainty. The levels of energy and social satisfaction (affiliation) are self-depleting and need to be raised through interaction with the environment. The cognitive urges (competence and reduction of uncertainty) lead the agent into exploration strategies, but limit these into directions, where the interaction with the environment proves to be successful. The execution of internal behaviors and the evaluation of the uncertainty of externally perceivable events create a feedback on the modulators and the cognitive urges of the agent.

Action: The agents may have an effect on their environment or their internal representations using a basic set of actor nodes. These may be arranged in sequences or alternatives and organized in hierarchies, thus creating more abstract actions–macros and scripts. The execution of these scripts may be controlled with sensor nodes, which serve as pre-conditions, post-conditions or suitability measures. Sensors may be grouped into hierarchies to, thereby representing more abstract situations and objects. Often, such a sense macro will contain actions and vice versa. Because active and sensoric schemata are represented as node nets, the agents have access to them and may thus rewrite their own behavior scripts.

Planning: The planning algorithms given in the current MicroPsi are very simple: given a goal (derived from a motivational process), the agent tries to find a chain of actions that has lead in the past from the given situation to the goal situation. If no such automatism is remembered, its construction is attempted by combining actions. Here, depth and width of the search are controlled by the modulators.

Meta-management and Alarms: It is quite possible that the allocation of processing resources of the agent does not meet the demands of the changing environment. This is the task of the meta-management. Because this module is not called very frequently, the agent may fail to adapt quickly to dramatical events. Dörner has proposed a 'securing behavior' that should be executed by the agent in regular intervals, while Sloman describes a system which he terms 'alarms', with the same purpose: to quickly disrupt current cognitive processes if the need arises. There is no alarm system in MicroPsi yet.

Shortcomings of the agent include a very limited potential for social behavior, mainly because means for the assessment of social situations (such as representations about mental states of other agents) are missing, and MicroPsi does not possess urges that would result in dominant, accepting, socially possessive or altruistic behaviors.

3   Node Nets

3.1   Representation with Nodes

The Psi theory suggests the use of a kind of neural network for the representation of control structures, declarative and protocol memory. [9] In Dörner's original concept, this is handled by assemblies of five neurons (such a group is called Ôquad'). Nonetheless, these networks should not be confused with biological neural structures and can be described more accurately as influence or belief networks [23]. (Dörner's implementation makes mostly use of iterative pointer lists). In MicroPsi agents, these representations are directional spreading activation networks that we call node nets, and quads are replaced by **concept nodes**. These nodes have nine different gates: general activation (*gen*), links for causal relations forwards (*por*) and backwards (*ret*), for part-of and contains relations (*sur*, *sub*), for membership (*cat*, *exp*), and for naming (*sym*, *ref*). Of these, *por*, *ret*, *sur* and *sub* are part of the original description of the Psi theory and derived from a theory of representation by Klix [16]; the others have been added to simplify the implementation and notation. Usually, nodes are symmetrically linked (i.e. for every *ret* link, there is a *por* link in the opposite direction, and so on.)

Concept nodes may be connected to special nodes, so-called **directional activators** which are connected to all individual gates of a certain type. Gates may only transmit an activation, if their corresponding activator is active, which allows for a *spreading activation* mechanism. A set of nodes that is connected to the same set of directional activators is called a *node space*.

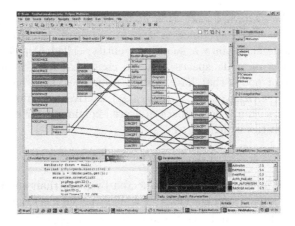

Fig. 4. Graphical editor for node nets.

By choosing appropriate weights and thresholds, links between nodes can express logical AND and OR terms. It can be demonstrated that this notation is suitable to express first order logic [11]. On the other hand, information retrieval with node spaces is very similar to using hierarchical Case Retrieval Networks with directional activation [19].

The current implementation of MicroPsi comes with a graphical front-end that allows to define, maintain and execute node nets (see fig. 4). The resulting networks can be saved in XML format.

3.2   Definition of Node Nets

Node nets consist of sets of net entities U, *nodes* and *modules*, connected to each other by links V and to the agent environment by a vector of *DataSources* and *DataTargets*.

$$NN = \{U, V, DataSources, DataTargets, f_{net}\} \qquad (1)$$

where f_{net} is a propagation function calculating the transition from one state of the node net to the next.

$$U = \{(id, type, I, O, \alpha, f_{act}, f_{node})\} \qquad (2)$$

Generally speaking, a net entity $u \in U$ consists of a vector I of slots, a vector O of gates, an activation α, an activation function $f_{act} : I \rightarrow \alpha$ and a node function $f_{node} : NN \rightarrow NN$ (there are no real limits to what the node function can do to the net). The *id* makes it possible to uniquely identify a net entity.

Entities come about in different *types*, such as register nodes, concept nodes and so on, which will be explained below. Nodes may be grouped into *node spaces*:

$$S = \left\{U^S, DataSources^S, DataTargets^S, f_{net}^S\right\} \qquad (3)$$

By mapping the $DataSources^S$ of a node space to slots, the $DataTargets^S$ to gates and the local net function f_{net}^S to an entity function, it is possible to embed a node space into a single net entity, called a *node space module*. Thus, hierarchies of node spaces may be created. Often, node spaced contain a number of nodes that have special properties, such as $Activators^S \subset U^S$; $Activators^S = \{u_{gateType_1}, ..., u_{gateType_n}\}$. Activators influence the way activation spreads within a node space and are explained later on. The vector of links between entities is defined as:

$$V = \left\{ \left(o_i^{u_1}, i_j^{u_2}, w, c, st \right) \right\} \tag{4}$$

Note that nodes u_1 and u_2 can be connected by more than one link. Links are defined by the gate $o_i^{u_1}$ and the slot $i_j^{u_2}$, which they connect, and are annotated by a weight $w \in \mathbb{R}_{[-1,1]}$ and a vector $st \in \mathbb{R}^4$; $st = (x, y, z, t)$ containing spatial-temporal values.

$$O = \{(gateType, out, \theta, amp, min, max, f_{out})\} \tag{5}$$

Gates provide the output of net entities and consist of an output activation $out \in \mathbb{R}$, a threshold θ, an amplification factor amp, upper and lower boundaries on the activation (min and max), and an output activation function f_{out} : $\alpha \times O \times Activators \rightarrow out$ that calculates the values of the gates, usually by:

$$out = \begin{cases} \min\left(\max\left(amp \cdot \alpha \cdot act_{gateType_o}, min\right), max\right), \text{if } \alpha \cdot act_{gateType_o} > \theta \\ 0, \text{else} \end{cases} \tag{6}$$

where $act_{gateType_o}$ is the output activation out of the activator node $u_{gateType_o} \in Activators^S$ of the respective node space. By triggering an activator, the spreading of activation from gates of the particular gate type is enabled.

Input to the entities is provided using an array of slots:

$$I = \{(slotType, in)\} \tag{7}$$

The value of each slot i_j^u is calculated using f_{net} as the sum of its inputs. Let $(v_1, ..., v_k)$ be the vector of links that end in a slot i_j^u to other nodes, and $(out_1, ..., out_k)$ be the output activations of the respective connected gates:

$$in_{i_j^u} = \frac{1}{k} \sum_{n=1}^{k} w_{v_n} c_{v_n} out_n \tag{8}$$

3.3   Specific Node Types

Concept Nodes are the typical building blocks of MicroPsi node nets. They consist of a single slot of the type *gen* (for 'generic') and their node activation is identical with their input activation: $\alpha = in_{gen}$. Dörner's representations make use of the link types *por, ret, sub* and *sur*, which are represented by gates. Additionally, concept nodes have the gates *cat, exp* (for 'category', denoting membership, and 'exemplar', pointing to members) and *sym*, *ref* (for symbols and referenced concepts). Finally, concept nodes contain a gate *gen*, which makes the input activation available if it is above the threshold θ_{gen} –there is no *gen* activator.

Register nodes are the most basic node type. They consist of a single slot and gate, both of type *gen*, and like in concept nodes, their output activation amounts to $out_{gen} = [amp \cdot \alpha]_{min}^{max}$, if $\alpha > \theta, 0$, else; $\alpha = in_{gen}$.

Sensor nodes are similar to register nodes, however, their activation out_{gen} is computed from an external variable $datasource \in DataSources^S$: $out_{gen} = [amp \cdot \alpha]_{min}^{max}$, if $\alpha > \theta, 0$, else; $\alpha = in_{gen} \cdot dataSource$.

Actor nodes are extensions to sensor nodes. Using their node function, they give their input activation in_{gen} to an external variable $dataTarget \in DataTargets^S$. The external value may be available to other node spaces, or, via the technical layer of the agent, to the agent environment (e.g. the world server). In return, an input value is read that typically represents failure (-1) or success (1) of the action returned as a sensor value to out_{gen} . Concept, register,

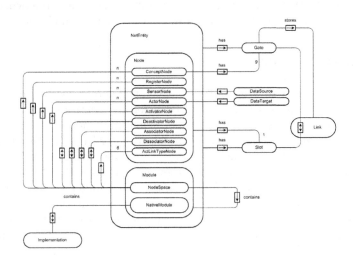

Fig. 5. ER definition of node nets.

sensor and actor nodes are the 'bread and butter' of node net representations. To *control* node nets, a number of specific register nodes have been introduced on top of that:

Activators are special registers that exist in correspondence to the gate types (*por*, *ret*, *sub*, *sur*, *cat*, *exp*, *sym* and *ref*) of concept nodes of a node space. Their output is read by the output activation function of the respective gate of their nodespace. By setting activators to zero, no activation can spread through the corresponding gates.

General activation nodes are special nodes with a single slot and gate of type *gen*, and when active, they increase the activation α of all nodes in the same node space.

General deactivation nodes are the counterpart of general activation nodes; they dampen the activation of all nodes within the same node space. They are mainly used to gradually reduce activity in a node space until only the most activated structures remain, or to end activity altogether.

Associator nodes are used to establish links between nodes in a node space. This happens by connecting all nodes with a gate activity different from zero, using a weight

$$w^t_{u^i_1 u^j_2} = \sqrt{w^{t-1}_{u^i_1 u^j_2}} + \alpha_{\text{associator}} \cdot associationFactor^S \cdot \alpha_{u_1} \cdot \alpha_{u_2} \qquad (9)$$

where t is the current time step, and $associationFactor^S \in \mathbb{R}_{[0,1]}$ a node space specific constant.

Disassociator nodes are the counterpart of associator nodes; they decrease or remove links between currently active nodes in the same node space.

Additionally, there is functionality for adding, copying and removing entities and links, provided as a programming interface for native modules.

4   Native Modules

It is perfectly possible to write and execute complete programs with node nets. In theory, they are sufficient to set up all behavior and control scripts of MicroPsi agents. However, the execution of scripts made up of nodes is slow, and they are hard to maintain, even using a graphical editor. This makes it desirable to add more nodes for specific tasks, and to encapsulate long scripts. This is where native modules come into play; they are entities with arbitrary numbers of slots and gates. In their node function f_{node}, they hide program code written in a native computer language. In the current implementation, native modules contain Java code and can perform any kind of manipulation on the node net. By integrating Java IDE, graphical node net editor and agent runtime environment, the extension of the agents becomes quite comfortable. For the basic functions of MicroPsi agents, a number of native modules have been added, of which two will be explained here:

4.1   ScriptExecution

Node scripts consist of chains of concept nodes that are connected by *por/ret* links. With *sub/sur* links, macros and hierarchies are defined. This may be read as: after 'step 1' follows 'step 2' (*por*), and 'step 1' consists of 'part 1', 'part 2', 'part 3' and so on. 'Part 1' is can again be the beginning of a chain or network of *por-linked* nodes. The linking of the 'parts' determines whether they are alternatives or conjunctions. The lowest level of these hierarchies is always formed by sensor and actor nodes. Because of these structures, it is possible to execute hierarchical plans with thousand of basic actions at the lowest level and few abstract elements on the highest levels and thus reduce the computational complexity of plan construction. Such hierarchical scripts can be run using the native module ScriptExecution.

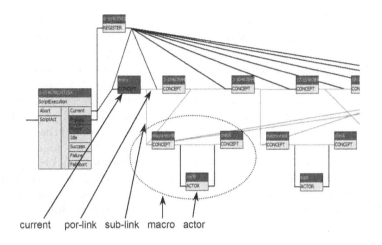

current   por-link sub-link macro actor

Fig. 6. Script execution

ScriptExecution has two slots–*Abort* and *ScriptActivation*–and seven gates: *Current, ProgramRegister, Macro, Idle, Success, Failure* and *FailAbort*. Initially, the script is retrieved and linked to a register on its highest level of hierarchy. This register is connected to the ScriptExection module. The execution starts by connecting *Idle* (which is active by default and thus susceptible to the *associator*) to the first concept node of the script. ScriptExecution first deactivates and unlinks *Idle*, and the first element is linked to *Current*. Now, in every step, the connected concept node is activated with the value of *ScriptActivation*. If this node is the parent of a macro, that is, if it has *sub* links, then the *sub*-linked concept node with the highest activation is chosen as new current node. (Using this pre-activation mechanism, scripts can be configured to follow certain paths before execution or even during execution.) If one of the *sub*-linked macros was successfully executed or there are no macros at all, the *por*-linked node with the highest activation becomes the new current node–if none of the *por*-linked nodes is active, ScriptExecution waits until one of the following happens:

- a *por*-linked node becomes active, causing it to become the new current node,
- a *por*-linked node becomes active with negative activation, causing failure,
- a timeout occurs, also causing the macro to fail.

When a macro just failed or was executed successfully, the entry point to this macro will again become the current node; ScriptExecution then decides how to go on in the manner given above. Macro success and failure are signaled at the *Success* and *Failure* gates. Fig. 6 shows a very simple script with just two levels of hierarchy.

4.2   EmotionalRegulation

This module calculates the emotional parameters from urges, relevant signals and values from the previous step. The module maintains the following internal states: *competence, arousal, certainty*, resolution level (*resLevel*) and selection threshold (*selThreshold*). These values are directly visible at the module's gates. Any subsystem of the agent that is subject to emotional regulation is linked to these gates, receiving the current emotional parameters via f_{net}. Additional gates signal the 'cognitive urges': *certaintyU* and *efficiencyU*, which are calculated every step simply as difference between a target value and the actual value. At the slots, the module receives the values of the 'physiological urges' (*extU1..3*) and the amount of change that is to be made to certainty and competence, if some event occurs that influences the system's emotional state (slots *certaintyS* and *efficiencyS*). The way we use these values is very similar to Dörner's 'EmoRegul' mechanism [9,11]. At every time step t the module performs the following calculations:

$$competence_t = \max \left(\min \left(competence_{t-1} + in_t^{efficiencyS}, 0 \right), l^{competence} \right) \tag{10}$$

$$certainty_t = \max \left(\min \left(certainty_{t-1} + in_t^{certaintyS}, 0 \right), l^{certainty} \right) \tag{11}$$

($l^{competence}$ and $l^{certainty}$ are constants to keep the values in range)

$$efficiencyU_t = target^{competence} - competence_t \tag{12}$$

$$certaintyU_t = target^{certainty} - certainty_t \tag{13}$$

($target^{competence}$ and $target^{certainty}$ are target values representing the optimum levels of competence and certainty for the agent.)

$$arousal_t = \max \left(certaintyU_t, efficiencyU_t, in_t^{extU} \right) - competence_t \tag{14}$$

$$resLevel_t = 1 - \sqrt{arousal_t} \tag{15}$$

$$selThreshold_t = selThreshold_{t-1} arousal_t \tag{16}$$

In a similar way, native modules for protocol generation, motivation, goal selection, event evaluation, simple planning, focus control, simple hypothesis based perception ('*hypercept*'), instance creation and so on have been defined. This toolbox enables the agent to explore its environment, memorize its experiences, attempt try-and-error strategies to satisfy its urges, learn from the results and to follow little plans.

5   Outlook

MicroPsi is still in an early stage of implementation, and many aspects of the original Psi theory and of several planned extensions have not been realized yet. The current architecture consists of a server that connects to both a set of agents, a simulated world and a set of user interfaces. A timer component can be used to control the speed of the simulation. The visualization of the simulated world using a 3D engine is planned for a later stage. Planned experiments with MicroPsi agents concern especially category and hierarchy generation, communication and social behavior. The current agent version does not feature social urges, apart from an affiliation urge, and its mental states are not complex enough to result in dominant, aggressive, accepting, possessive or altruistic behavior. Another interesting question concerns the results of emotional modulation on the agent's performance in environments of different complexity.

References

1. Anderson, J. R., & Lebière, C. (1998) Atomic Components of Thought. Hillsdale, NJ: Lawrence Erlbaum.
2. Bach, J. (2002). Enhancing Perception and Planning of Software Agents with Emotion and Acquired Hierarchical Categories. In Proceedings of MASHO 02, German Conference on Artificial Intelligence KI2002, (pp. 3–12)
3. Bach, J. (2003). Emotionale Virtuelle Agenten auf der Basis der Dörnerschen Psi-Theorie. In Burkhard, H.-D., Uthmann, T., Lindemann, G. (Eds.): ASIM 03, Workshop Modellierung und Simulation menschlichen Verhaltens, Berlin, Germany (pp. 1–10)
4. Bach, J. (2003). The MicroPsi Agent Architecture. To appear at ICCM 03, International Conference on Cognitive Modeling, Bamberg, Germany
5. Bach, J. (2003). Artificial Emotion Project/MicroPsi Home Page: http://www.artificial-emotion.de
6. Bates, J., Loyall, A. B., & Reilly, W. S. (1991). Broad agents. AAAI spring symposium on integrated intelligent architectures. Stanford, CA: Sigart Bulletin, 2(4), Aug. 91, pp 38–40
7. Bratman, M. E. (1987). Intention, Plans, and Practical Reason. Harvard University Press, Cambridge, Mass.
8. d'Iverno, M., Kinny, D., Luck, & M. Wooldridge, M. (1998). A Formal Specification of dMARS. Proceedings of the Fourth International Workshop on Agent Theories, Architectures and Language, LNAI 1365, 155–176: Springer
9. Dörner, D. (1999). Bauplan für eine Seele. Reinbeck: Rowohlt
10. Dörner, D., & Schaub, H. (1998). Das Leben von PSI. Über das Zusammenspiel von Kognition, Emotion und Motivation. http://www.uni-bamberg.de/ppp/insttheopsy/psi-literatur.html
11. Dörner, D., Bartl, C., Detje, F., Gerdes, J., Halcour, D., Schaub, H., & Starker, U. (2002). Die Mechanik des Seelenwagens. Eine neuronale Theorie der Handlungsregulation. Bern, Göttingen, Toronto, Seattle: Verlag Hans Huber.
12. Feldman, J. A., & Bailey, D. (2000). Layered Hybrid Connectionist Models for Cognitive Science. In Wermter,S., & Sun, R. (eds.): Hybrid Neural Systems 1998, LNCS 1778, 14–27: Springer

13. Franklin, S. (1999). Action Selection and Language Generation in 'Conscious' Software Agents. Proc. Workshop on Behavior Planning for Life-Like Characters and Avatars, i3 Spring Days '99, Sitges, Spain
14. Georgeff, M.P., & Ingrand, F.F. (1988). Research on Procedural Reasoning Systems. Technical Report, AI Center, SRI International, Menlo Park, CA Good, I. J. (1961). A Causal Calculus. British Journal of the Philosophy of Science, 11:305–318
15. Goldberg, A. E. (1995). Constructions: A Construction Grammar Approach to Argument Structure. Chicago: University of Chicago Press.
16. Klix, F. (1984). Über Wissensrepräsentation im Gedächtnis. In F. Klix (Ed.): Gedächtnis, Wissen, Wissensnutzung. Berlin: Deutscher Verlag der Wissenschaften.
17. Künzel, J. (2003) PSI-Lingua, Erste Schritte zur Sprachentwicklung bei einem künstlichen Agenten. In Burkhard, H.-D., Uthmann, T., Lindemann, G. (Eds.): ASIM 03, Workshop Modellierung und Simulation menschlichen Verhaltens, Berlin, Germany (pp. 68–76)
18. Laird, J. E., Newell, A., & Rosenbloom, P. S. (1987). SOAR: An Architecture for General Intelligence. Artificial Intelligence, 33: 1–64
19. Lenz, M., Burkhard, H.-D. (1998). Case retrieval nets: Basic ideas and extensions. Technical report, Humboldt University, Berlin
20. Newell, A. (1990). Unified Theories of Cognition. Cambridge, Mass.: Harvard University Press
21. Rao, A.S., & Georgeff, M.P. (1998). Decision procedures for BDI logics. Journal of Logic and Computation, 8
22. Schmidt, B. (2000): PECS. Die Modellierung menschlichen Verhaltens. SCS-Europe Publishing House, Ghent
23. Shachter, R. D. (1986). Evaluating influence diagrams. Operations Research, 34:871–882
24. Sloman, A. (1992). Towards an information processing theory of emotions. http://www.cs.bham.ac.uk/~axs/cog_affect/ Aaron.Sloman_IP.Emotion.Theory.ps.gz
25. Sloman, A. (1994). Semantics in an intelligent control system. Philosophical Transactions of the Royal Society: Physical Sciences and Engineering. Vol 349, 1689, 43–58

Conscious Behavior through Reflexive Dialogs

Pierre Bonzon

HEC, University of Lausanne
1015 Lausanne, Switzerland
pierre.bonzon@unil.ch

Abstract. We consider the problem of executing conscious behavior i.e., of driving an agent's actions and of allowing it, at the same time, to run concurrent processes reflecting on these actions. Toward this end, we express a single agent's plans as *reflexive* dialogs in a multi-agent system defined by a virtual machine. We extend this machine's planning language by introducing two specific operators for reflexive dialogs i.e., *conscious* and *caught* for monitoring beliefs and actions, respectively. The possibility to use the same language both to drive a machine and to establish a reflexive communication within the machine itself stands as a key feature of our model.

1   Introduction

Intelligent behavior, presumably, is strongly related to the concept of consciousness. In order to achieve true machine intelligence, one ought therefore to address the issue of modeling and executing *conscious behavior*. In the absence of a commonly agreed meaning for this term, we use it here in a somehow restricted sense i.e., to refer to the goal of "driving an agent's actions and of allowing it, at the same time, to run concurrent processes reflecting on these actions". We shall therefore not attempt to model the truly reflexive concept of "conscious to be conscious", which would be required for instance to capture the concept of "consciousness of having beliefs".

When compared to classical AI problems, such as automatic planning and/or reasoning, the amount of research devoted so far to this subject is rather limited. Surprisingly, we could hardly find more than a few references pertaining to recent work done in this area [5] [8] [15]. Provided that consciousness essentially functions as a mirror, the lack of formal models for the intelligence itself suggests that models of conscious behavior could not have anything to reflect upon. Furthermore, as this reflection seems to rely on internal linguistic representations relating beliefs and mental attitudes [6] [7], the lack of adequate formal languages for this purpose indicates why conscious behavior cannot be easily reproduced.

Comprehensive *agent* models, if available, could however well replace disembodied intelligence theories as the basis for modeling conscious behavior. More precisely, we envision that any system capable of mechanizing an agent's behavior could be first extended to reflect its selection of actions i.e., to somehow notify the agent of its choices. The language used by the system itself to plan actions should then be extended to use in turn these internal notifications. For an agent to be conscious would then simply mean being able to recognize and acknowledge internal

A. Günter et al. (Eds.): KI 2003, LNAI 2821, pp. 179–193, 2003.

notifications at will. This overall process could be iterated to represent the concept of "conscious to be conscious", and so on. Consciousness, taken as a whole, could thus be considered as the resulting "closure relation". As already indicated, we shall however refrain ourselves from exploring this concept, and be content with a possible implementation of the first iteration only.

Our recent proposal, that introduces formal communication primitives within a multi-agent system [3] and defines a language for agent *dialogs* [4], is an example of an agent model that can be used for this purpose. In this approach, consciousness will primarily function as a *monitor* of actions and beliefs (in the weak sense of the word and not in Hoare's strict sense) that allows for the triggering of new actions. As such, this concept of consciousness is truly reminiscent of previously introduced artifacts, such as *demons*[1]. Our basic idea that departs from these earlier attempts is as follows: in order to catch internal notifications, any conscious agent will engage in *multiple* ongoing conversations *with itself*. The way for an agent to engage in multiple conversations with other agents have already been discussed in [4], and will be reviewed below. As a result, each communicating agent will be considered as a multithreaded entity interleaving concurrent conversations. The introduction of *reflexive* dialogs (in a non-traditional sense i.e., of having a dialog "with oneself" instead of "about itself") then simply requires an extension of their synchronization processes. From there, any agent's plan will be represented as a *reflexive* dialog.

This model, which will be thoroughly developed in this paper, definitively reflects a "static" capability i.e., that of *being* conscious of explicit beliefs and of actions performed in full awareness. Different approaches might be possible. As an example, Baars [1] develops a concept of consciousness very much akin to a form of discovery and learning i.e., the "dynamic" process of *getting* conscious of facts resulting from myriads of sensations. We shall further relate these two approaches in our conclusion.

Let us further point out here the differential aspects pertaining to the consciousness of beliefs, on one hand, and of actions, on the other. As an agent's beliefs are considered part of his local state, they can be represented by logical formulas that are stored in his memory. The consciousness of an agent's beliefs is therefore *persistent* i.e., can be solicited at any time. In contrast, any action that he chooses to perform either have an effect on the environment or lead to an updating of his local state, and usually has no direct trace in his memory (unless, of course, it gives rise to an ad hoc new belief, as will be shown at the end of this paper). As such the consciousness of an agent's actions is *volatile* i.e., must be caught *"on the fly"* when these actions occur. The differentiation just made will lead us to the definition of two distinct operators i.e., *conscious* and *caught* for monitoring beliefs and actions, respectively.

The rest of this paper is organized as follows: in section 2, we review previously published material in order to provide the reader with a basic understanding of our concept of agents dialog and its associated virtual machine. Section 3 shows how to represent any single agent's plans as a reflexive dialog. Section 4 proposes the language extension allowing for the agent to reflect on his actions. Finally section 5 introduces the virtual machine extensions needed to notify an agent of his actions.

---

[1] « a procedure that watches for some condition to become true and then activates an associated process »[14]

2 A Model of Social Agents with Reactive and Proactive Capabilities

In this section, we review the agent model introduced in [3] [4].

2.1 A Language for Agent Dialogs

In order to get, first, an intuitive feeling for the language introduced in [4], let us consider the solution of the *two-agent meeting-scheduling* problem presented in [11]. In this problem, one agent is designated as the *host* and the other one as the *invitee*. Both agents have free time slots to meet e.g., if l^i refers to agent's i local state

l^{host} ⊢ *meet(13)* ∧ *meet(15)* ∧ *meet(17)*

$l^{invitee}$ ⊢ *meet(14)* ∧ *meet(16)* ∧ *meet(17)*

and they must find their earliest common slot (in this case, *17*). We use a predicate *epmeet(T1,T)* meaning *"T1 is the earliest possible meeting time after T"*, defined as

$\forall T1 \forall T \forall T'(\ meet(T1) \wedge (T1{>}{=}T) \wedge \neg(meet(T') \wedge (T'{>}{=}T) \wedge (T'{<}T1))\ \Rightarrow\ epmeet(T1,T))$

The solution involves successive negotiation *cycles*. The host has the responsibility of starting each cycle with a given lower time bound *T*. A cycle comprises three steps, each step involving an exchange of messages. In the first step, the host initializes a *call/return* exchange calling on the invitee to find out his earliest meeting slot *T1* after *T*. In the second step, roles are swapped: the invitee initializes a *call/return* calling on the host to find out his earliest meeting slot *T2* after *T1*. In the third step, the host either confirms an agreement on time *T2* (if *T1=T2*) by initializing a *tell/ask* exchange, or starts a new cycle with *T2* as his new lower bound.

This solution can be informally expressed as follows:

"start with a *call/return* exchange,

proceed with a *return/call* exchange,

conclude with a *tell/ask* exchange and *save* the meeting time or *resume*"

The corresponding, implicitly synchronized *dialogs* are then

dialog(invite(Invitee, T),   [T1,T2],

                                     [**call**(Invitee,epmeet(T1,T)),

                                      return(Invitee,epmeet(T2,T1)),

                                      ((T1=T2 | [**tell**(Invitee,confirm(T2)),

                                                        execute(save(meeting(T2))))]);

                                        (T1\=T2| [**resume**(invite(Invitee,T2))]))])

dialog(reply(Host),   [T,T1,T2],

                                       [**return**(Host,epmeet(T1,T)),

                                      call(Host,epmeet(T2,T1)),

                                      ((T1=T2 | [**ask**(Host,confirm(T2)),

                                                         execute(save(meeting(T2))))]);

                                        (T1\=T2| [**resume**(reply(Host))]))])

where "," and ";" are sequence (or conjunctive) and alternative (or disjunctive) operators, respectively. Variables start with capital letters, and variables that are local to a dialog are listed before the messages. As it can be seen in this example, each dialog consists of a *branching sequence* of messages i.e., a *sequence* with an *end alternative* containing *guarded messages*. Similarly to lists, branching sequences can have an embedded structure. Unless they are resumed (with a *resume* message), dialogs are exited at the end of each embedded branching sequence (e.g. the above example, after the *execute* messages). Actions interleaved with messages can be executed with an *execute* message. Sub-dialogues can be entered with an *enter* message, similarly to ordinary procedures (for an example, see section 2.4). The corresponding BNF syntax is given below in Fig. 1

```
<dialog>      ::= dialog(<dialogName>(<dialogParams>),<varList>,<branchSeq>)
<varList>     ::= [] || [<varName>|<varList>]
<branchSeq>   ::= [] || [<alt>] || <seq>
<alt>         ::= <guardMes> || (<guardMes>;<alt>)
<seq>         ::= [<mes>|<branchSeq>]
<guardMes>    ::= (<guard>|<branchSeq>)
<mes>         ::= <messageName>(<messageParams>)
<messageName> ::= ask || tell || call || return || execute || enter || resume
```

Fig. 1. BNF productions

As usual, "|" separates the head and tail of a list i.e., $[m_1|[m_2|...[]]]=[m_1,m_2,...]$. We also use "|" to isolate the guard in a guarded message. To avoid confusion, we use "||" as metasymbol for representing choices. We leave out the definitions for *names*, *parameters*, and *guards*, these being identifiers, first order terms and expressions, respectively. Branching sequences permit end alternatives, but do not allow for starting or middle alternatives i.e., cannot contain the list pattern *[<alt>|<branchSeq>]*.

2.2 A Virtual Machine for Executing Dialogs

As thoroughly developed in [4], the language introduced in section 2.1 can be compiled and executed on a *virtual* machine. This compilation amounts to *rewriting* each dialog into a non-deterministic *plan* (see below), and at the same time generates the necessary conditions to ensure its sequential execution. The abstract machine itself defines the run of a class of agents as a loop interleaving individual agent run cycles. It is given by the following procedure

procedure $run^{Class}(e,l)$
   loop
      for all i **such that** $l^{Class} \vdash agent(i)$ **do**
         $sense(l^i,e);$
         if $l^i \vdash plan(p_0^i)$
         then $react(e,l,p_0^i);$
         if $l^{Class} \vdash priority(n_0)$
         then $process^{Class}(e,l,n_0)$

where e represents the state of the environment, l the *local state* of a class of agents defined by a vector $l = [l^{Class}, l^1...l^n]$, and the components l^{Class} and l^i are the local state of the class and its members identified by an integer $i=1...n$, respectively. We assume that predicate *agent* is such that $l^{Class} \vdash agent(i)$ whenever agent i belongs to the class. The language defining each l^i includes a set P of non-deterministic plan names (*nd-plan* in short) and four predicates *plan, priority, do* and *switch*. For each agent i, its current nd-plan $p^i \in P$ refers to a set of implications "*conditions*" $\Rightarrow do(p^i, a)$ or "*conditions*" $\Rightarrow switch(p^i, p^{i'})$, where a is an action (for an example, see section 2.4). Similarly to plans, *processes* of explicit priority n encompass implications "*conditions*" $\Rightarrow do(n, a)$. We further assume that each agent's initial nd-plan p_0^i and the class highest priority n_0 can be deduced from l i.e., that $l^i \vdash plan(p_0^i)$ and $l^{Class} \vdash priority(n_0)$, respectively.

In each *run* cycle, initial plans p_0^i are activated by a procedure *react*. Synchronization of message pairs occurs globally through a procedure *process*^{Class}. These procedures are defined as:

procedure $react^i(e,l,p^i)$
if $l^i \vdash do(p^i, a)$
then $(e,l) \leftarrow \tau^i(e,l,a)$
else if $l^i \vdash switch(p^i, p^{i'})$
 then $react^i(e,l,p^{i'})$

procedure $process^{Class}(e,l,n)$
if $l^{Class} \vdash do(n, a)$
then $(e,l) \leftarrow \tau^{Class}(e,l,a);$
 $process^{Class}(e,l,n)$
else if $n > 0$
 then $process^{Class}(e,l,n-1)$

In these procedures, the state transformer functions τ^i and τ^{Class} are used to interpret actions and synchronize operations, respectively. As their names imply, nd-plans are not executed sequentially. At each run cycle, procedure $react^i$ will be called with the (possibly variable) initial plan p_0^i deduced for each agent. In each recursive $react^i$ call, the agent's first priority is to deduce and carry out an action a from its current plan p^i. Otherwise, it may switch from p^i to $p^{i'}$. If the *switch* predicate defines decision trees rooted at each p_0^i, then $react^i$ will go down this decision tree. This mechanism allows an agent to adopt a new plan whenever a certain condition occurs, and then to react with an appropriate action. As a result, actions will be chosen one at a time. In contrast to nd-plans, dialogs must be executed sequentially. Towards this end, the rewriting of dialogs into nd-plans generates implications of the form "*conditions*" $\Rightarrow do(p^i, a)$ only. In other words, there will be no switching of plans, and the state transformer function τ associated with the message *enter* (for entering sub-dialogs) will use instead a stack to reflect the dynamic embedding of dialogs. The *conditions* in each implication include both a synchronization and a sequencing condition (for further details, see [4]), and the action a always incorporate a predefined message together with some updating operations related to the conditions. As a result, a sequential execution of dialogs will be emulated, though actually each action will still be deduced one at the time using the mechanism defined for nd-plans.

As for procedure *process*^{Class}, it will execute, in descending order of priorities, all processes whose conditions are satisfied. Processes will be used for the purpose of synchronizing message pairs. Synchronization occurs when the two messages forming a pair (i.e., *tell(r, φ)/ask(s, ψ)* or *call(r, φ)/return (s, ψ)* issued by sender *s* and receiver *r*) are acknowledged. It is triggered by two processes defined as

$$ack(s, tell(r, \varphi)) \wedge ack(r, ask(s, \psi))) \quad \Rightarrow \quad do(2, tellAsk(s, r, \varphi, \psi))$$
$$ack(s, call(r, \varphi)) \wedge ack(r, return(s, \psi)) \quad \Rightarrow \quad do(1, callReturn(s, r, \varphi, \psi))$$

where the acknowledgment flag *ack(i,message)* is raised in l^{Class} when the *message* issued by agent *i* is interpreted using function t^i (for further details, see [3]). Similarly to actions, the synchronizing operations *tellAsk* and *callReturn* are interpreted by state transformer functions τ^{Class} that uses l^{Class} as a blackboard.

2.3 Engaging in Multiple Conversations

Agents should be allowed to engage in multiple conversations. A possible solution is to define a parallel operator that can be used at the message level i.e., to interleave possible concurrent messages [10] [11]. We favor the simpler solution whereby each agent is a multi-threaded entity interleaving concurrent conversations. In this extended model, dialogs are now syntactic entities that, once compiled into plans, can be associated with multiple conversations implemented as concurrent threads. Just as our multi-agent system was implemented as a multi-threaded entity of agents using predicate *agent*, our multi-threaded agent will be implemented as a multi-threaded entity of conversations using an additional predicate *conversation* as follows

procedure $run^{Class}(e, l)$
   loop
      for all *i* **such that** $l^{Class} \vdash agent(i)$ **do**
        $sense(l^i, e)$;
        for all *j* **such that** $l^i \vdash conversation(j)$ **do**
          if $l^i \vdash plan(p_0^{ij})$
          then $react^i(e, l, p_0^{ij})$;
          if $l^{Class} \vdash priority(n_0)$
          then $process^{Class}(e, l, n_0)$

where $l^i \vdash conversation(j)$ means "conversation thread *j* is attached to agent *i* " and p_0^{ij} is the initial compiled plan associated with thread *j* of agent *i*. An additional primitive message *concurrent* can then be used in any dialog to create a new conversation thread when required (for an example, see the end of section 2.4). The synchronization processes must be redefined accordingly as follows

$$ack(s^j, tell(r, \varphi)) \wedge ack(r^k, ask(s, \psi))) \quad \Rightarrow \quad do(2, tellAsk(s^j, r^k, \varphi, \psi))$$
$$ack(s^j, call(r, \varphi)) \wedge ack(r^k, return(s, \psi)) \quad \Rightarrow \quad do(1, callReturn(s^j, r^k, \varphi, \psi))$$

where the acknowledgment flag $ack(t^i, message)$ is raised when the message issued by conversation thread *j* of agent *i* is interpreted. Note that messages are still addressed to a given agent rather than to a specific thread of that agent.

As dialogs can include *execute* messages that allow in turn for the execution of any action, the language just reviewed constitutes a general model of social agents with sensing, reactive and proactive capabilities [16] (this latter capability deriving from the deduction of variable initial plans p_0^i). Its "operational semantics" is defined by the virtual machine together with the compiling functions contained in [4].

2.4 Example: A Vacuum Cleaner Robot

To illustrate the concepts just reviewed, let us consider a vacuum cleaner robot that can choose either to *work* i.e., *move* and *suck* any dirt on sight, or to go back *home* and wait. Let us further assume that the robot must *stop* whenever an *alarm* condition is raised. These three behaviors correspond to three possible *nd-plans*, i.e. *work*, *home*, and *pause*. The robot's overall behavior can be represented by a decision tree rooted at a single *initial* plan and defined by the following implications, where the predicate *in(X,Y)* and *dirt(X,Y)* are used to mean "*the agent is located at (x,y)*" and "*there is dirt at (x,y)*", respectively, and the action *stop*, *move*, *back*, and *suck* have the obvious corresponding meaning:

alarm	$\Rightarrow$ **switch**(initial,pause)
¬alarm	$\Rightarrow$ **switch**(initial,start)
true	$\Rightarrow$ **do**(pause,stop)
dirt(_,_)	$\Rightarrow$ **switch**(start,work)
¬dirt(_,_)	$\Rightarrow$ **switch**(start,home)
in(X,Y)∧ dirt(X,Y)	$\Rightarrow$ **do**(work,suck(X,Y))
in(X,Y)∧ ¬dirt(X,Y)	$\Rightarrow$ **do**(work,move(X,Y))
in(X,Y)	$\Rightarrow$ **do**(home,back(X,Y))

These implications can be directly interpreted on the virtual machine of section 2.2. Each run cycle will be initiated with the single *initial* plan and then go down the decision tree. Each action will be deduced "just on time", thus ensuring a truly reactive behavior. Equivalently, this robot can be specified by the following dialogs (that, at this point, do not involve any communication):

dialog(initial,   [],
              [((alarm | [**enter**(pause)]);
               (not alarm | [**enter**(start)]))])

dialog(pause,   [],
              [**execute**(stop)])

dialog(start,   [],
              [((dirt(_,_) | [**enter**(work)]);
               (not dirt(_,_) | [**enter**(home)]))])

dialog(work,   [X,Y],
              [((in(X,Y),dirt(X,Y) | [**execute**(suck(X,Y)),
                                         resume(initial)]);
              (in(X,Y),not dirt(X,Y) | [**execute**(move(X,Y)),
                                         resume(initial)]))])

dialog(home,   [X,Y],
              [((in(X,Y) | [**execute**(back(X,Y)),
                                         resume(initial)]))])

The rewriting of dialogs into nd-plans generate conditions that will ensure their sequential execution, similarly to that of ordinary procedures (e.g., after entering *start* from *initial*, the control will be transferred to either *work* or *home*, and so on). Unless explicitly directed to resume at some point, dialogs are exited at the end of each embedded branching sequence, and the dialog that was left on entering is then resumed by default. In the above example, the *initial* dialog is explicitly resumed after the execution of each action, thus enforcing the same reactive behavior as before.

As it can be seen in the above examples, the conditions in the implications defining nd-plans are identical to the guards in the guarded messages of the corresponding dialog. Furthermore, the *do* and *switch* predicates are used for the same purpose as the *execute* and *enter* messages, respectively. Intuitively then, a non-deterministic plan can thus be represented by a non-communicating dialog. Reversibly, any dialog can be compiled back into a nd-plan that do not contain any *switch* predicate. As already indicated, this arises because the state transformer functions for interpreting messages uses a stack to reflect the dynamic embedding of dialogs resulting from successive *enter* messages.

As a first step towards allowing an agent to reflect on his behavior, let us now try and express possible parallel tasks in dialogs. Recalling from the end of section 2.2 the possibility for a dialog to create *concurrent* conversation threads, our robot behavior can be further represented by the following dialogs

dialog(initial,   [],
                [**concurrent**(pause),
                [**concurrent**(start)])

dialog(pause,   [],
                [(((alarm | [**execute**(stop)])))])

dialog(start,   [],
                [(((not alarm | [**concurrent**(work),
                                concurrent(home)])))])

dialog(work,   [X,Y],
                [(((dirt(_,_),in(X,Y),dirt(X,Y) | [**execute**(suck(X,Y)),
                                                        resume(work)]);

                (dirt(_,_),in(X,Y),not dirt(X,Y) | [**execute**(move(X,Y)),
                                                        resume(work)])))])

dialog(home,   [X,Y],
                [(((not dirt(_,_),in(X,Y) | [**execute**(back(X,Y)),
                                                        resume(home)])))])

where concurrent guards are pushed one level "below" (i.e., the guards of concurrent conversation threads are checked on entry in these threads). Dialogs *work* and *home* can now resume *themselves*, as they are now concurrent together with dialog *pause* waiting for an eventual alarm. Let us further note that these two dialogs actually *must* resume themselves: if the *initial* dialog were to be resumed instead, as in the preceding example, superfluous new concurrent threads would then be created.

Before proceeding, it is noteworthy to point out here the role of guards in guarded messages. If a guard does not get satisfied (e.g., as in the case of the *pause* dialog, when no alarm has been received yet), the associated message is not sent. If there are no other alternatives, the dialog gets simply suspended until the guard gets satisfied. The guarded message as a whole thus acts as a *monitor* or *demon* i.e., it will stand alive, watch and wait until its associated message can eventually be sent.

3   Representing Agent Plans as Reflexive Dialogs

According to their intuitive meaning (and as defined by their compiling functions in which guarded messages are rewritten into implications), guards are required to be deductible from the agent local state. Let us now recall our introductory discussion about the *persistence* of beliefs v/s the *volatility* of action consciousness. We thus have to conclude that, in contrast to the monitoring of beliefs illustrated in the preceding example, guarded commands cannot be used to monitor actions. Looking for an alternative and general solution that will apply to both cases, our basic idea is to try and catch internal notifications by allowing any agent to engage in *multiple* conversations *with itself*. Towards this end, we first need to be able to process *reflexive* dialogs (in a non-traditional sense of the word i.e., a dialog "with oneself"). An ad hoc extension of the synchronization processes presented in section 2.2 simply requires two additional synchronization processes, defined as follows:

$$ack(s^j, tell(k, \varphi)) \wedge ack(s^k, ask(j, \psi))) \quad \Rightarrow \quad do(2, tellAsk(s^j, s^k, \varphi, \psi))$$
$$ack(s^j, call(k, \varphi)) \wedge ack(s^k, return(j, \psi)) \quad \Rightarrow \quad do(1, callReturn(s^j, s^k, \varphi, \psi))$$

where the sender and the receiver are the threads j and k attached to agent s. Reflexive messages are thus sent by and addressed to specific threads of a given agent.

To illustrate this, let us now define a generic dialog *conscience* as follows:

dialog(conscience(P),   [Thread],
                     [((P | [**return**(Thread,P)])])])

Suppose that this dialog has been attached to a given agent, and receives the message **call**(conscience(P),P) sent by a concurrent conversation (named *Thread*) attached to the same agent. This dialog will then either *return* the belief P and exit, if this belief holds in the agent's local state, or wait, in the contrary case. Let us further consider a new message *conscious* that can be macro expanded as follows

conscious(P) ==> (**concurrent**(conscience(P)), **call**(conscience(P),P))

This message will first create a conscience thread and then work as described above i.e., like a monitor for beliefs that will stand alive, watch and wait until expected beliefs are effective. If we assume that reflexive dialogs are precompiled to macro expand *conscious* messages and to include the generic dialog *conscience,* then our last example of section 2.4 can be rewritten as follows:

reflexive(initial,   [],
                  [**concurrent**(pause),
                   concurrent(start)])

reflexive(pause, [],
                  [**conscious**(alarm),
                   execute(stop)])

reflexive(start,   [],
                  [**conscious**(not alarm),
                   concurrent(work),
                   concurrent(home)])

reflexive(work,   [X,Y],
                  [**conscious**(dirt(_,_)),
                   conscious(in(X,Y)),
                   ((dirt(X,Y) | [**execute**(suck(X,Y)),
                                          resume(work)]]);

```
                    (not dirt(X,Y)    | [execute(move(X,Y)),
                                         resume(work)])])])
reflexive(home,   [X,Y,]
                  [conscious(not dirt(_,_)),
                   conscious(in(X,Y)),
                   execute(back(X,Y)),
                   resume(home)])
```

Let us stress here that this solution leads to the same behavior as before. In other words, in this example, the monitoring of individual beliefs using reflexive dialogs instead of guarded messages does not bring anything new. The explicit modeling of conscience threads does however open the door to more complex consciousness models relying on mental attitudes e.g., could lead to model such things as a troubled, selective or biased conscience. A similar scheme, introduced in the next section, will allow for the monitoring of actions.

The verification of dialog protocols expressed as concurrent reentrant threads guarded with **conscious** monitors could be quite an intricate task. In order to prevent concurrent threads to get "stuck", their monitors should not get bound by external variables. In the above example, the monitors of concurrent threads *work* and *home* get bound by local variables X and Y. In contrast, actions *suck(X,Y)* and *move(X,Y)* cannot be expressed as concurrent reentrant threads because their monitor would be bound by external variables X and Y.

4 Executing Conscious Behavior by Reflecting on One's Own Actions

As alluded to in our introductory discussion, the consciousness of an agent's actions is *volatile* i.e., must be caught *"on the fly"* when these actions actually occur. What we need to implement now is a mechanism whereby an agent will first be notified of, and then reflect on each of its actions individually. Once again, our language for agent dialogs will be used for this purpose. In contrast to the consciousness of an agent's beliefs, the sender of the notifications cannot be the agent itself, who will be solely the receiver, and the notifications will be sent by the underlying virtual machine. Towards this end, let us define a generic dialog *reflect* as follows

```
dialog(reflect(P), [Thread],
              [ask(react,P),
               tell(Thread,P)])
```

As before, suppose that this dialog has been attached to a given agent and receives the message **ask(reflect(P),P)** sent by a concurrent thread attached to the same agent. This dialog will first send the message **ask(react,P)** to a pseudo thread *react* representing the machine itself (or, more precisely, the *react* procedure of an extended virtual machine, as it will be explained in the next section) and then wait for an answer. Upon receiving a notification, it will in turn answer the asking thread by sending the message **tell(Thread,P)**. Let us further consider a new message *caught* that can be macro expanded as follows

```
caught(P) ==> (concurrent(reflect(P)), ask(reflect(P),P))
```

This message will first create a *reflect* thread and then work as described above i.e., will monitor the notification of actions. If we assume that reflexive dialogs are precompiled to macro expand *caught* messages and to include the dialog *reflect,* then any behavior could be directed to reflect on his own actions, using a concurrent reflexive dialog *introspect* saving ad hoc new beliefs *done(P)* as follows:

reflexive(initial,   [],
       [**concurrent**("any behavior"),
       concurrent(introspect)])

reflexive (introspect, [P],
        [**caught**(execute(P)),
         execute(save(done(P))),
         resume(introspect)])

reflexive ("any behavior", [P],
         [...
         conscious(done(P)),
         ...])

The monitoring of actions just presented represents a first step towards modeling conscious behavior. As illustrated by the *introspect* thread, any number of concurrent threads could similarly be designed to reflect in various ways on the execution of actions. For example, the ad hoc new beliefs *done(P)* created by the *introspect* thread could be monitored in turn to relate the consciousness of *previous* actions to that of the *current* action, and so on.

5 An Extended Virtual Machine for Sending Notifications

In order to complete the model, the virtual machine presented in section 2.2 must be extended to send internal notifications, when required. This extended virtual machine can be defined as follows:

procedure $run^{Class}(e,l)$
 loop
   for all i **such that** $l^{Class} \vdash agent(i)$ **do**
    $sense(l^i,e)$;
    for all j **such that** $l^i \vdash conversation(j)$ **and** $j \neq reflect(\_)$ **do**
     if $l^i \vdash plan(p_0^{ij})$
     then $react^i(e,l,p_0^{ij})$;
      $reflect^i(e,l)$;
      if $l^{Class} \vdash priority(n_0)$
      then $process^{Class}(e,l,n_0)$

In order to avoid infinite recursion, this machine is prevented from sending notifications about notifications (in other words, the consciousness is not iterated to represent the concept of "being conscious to be conscious", and so on). The *reflect* threads are thus not interleaved with other threads, but are executed separately in each cycle using procedure $reflect^i(e,l)$. This procedure is defined in turn as follows:

procedure $reflect^i(e,l)$
 if $l^i \vdash conversation(reflect(r))$
  and $l^i \vdash do(reflect(r), a)$
 then $(e,l) \leftarrow t^i(e,l,a)$;
  $reflect^i(e,l)$

As a result of the end recursive call *reflect*^{i}*(e,l)*, all ready messages of all concurrent *reflect* threads attached to agent *i* will be sent without delay. The actual notification takes place within an extended procedure *react*^{i}*(e,l,p*^{ij}*)* defined as follows:

> ***procedure*** *react*^{i}*(e,l,p*^{ij}*)*
> ***if*** *l*^{i} $\vdash$ *do(p*^{ij}*, a)*
> ***then*** *(e,l)* $\leftarrow$ τ^i*(e,l,a);*
>   ***if*** *l*^{i} $\vdash$ *conversation(reflect(r))*
>   ***and*** *a= (save(_,_),save(_,_),r)*
>   ***then*** *ack(i*^{react}*,tell(reflect(r),r)* $\leftarrow$ *true*
> ***else if*** *l*^{i} $\vdash$ *switch(p*^{ij}*, p*$^{ij'}$*)*
>   ***then*** *react*^{ij}*(e,l,p*$^{ij'}$*)*

Any action *a* resulting from the compilation of dialogs has the form of a triplet *a=(save(_,_),save(_,_),r)*, where *r* is one of the predefined message. After executing an action *a*, this extended procedure will check if the message *r* just processed can be matched with a *reflect(r)* thread attached to agent *i*. If so, it will raise an acknowledgment flag *ack(i*^{react}*,tell(reflect(r),r))* that in turn will be paired for synchronization with the acknowledgement flag *ack(i*$^{reflect(r)}$*,ask(react,r))* raised by message **ask**(react,r) from thread *reflect(r)*. As the thread *react* actually does not exist, this amounts to emulating communication between the machine and the agent *i*.

This overall process can be represented by the following picture that elaborates on the abstract, top-level view of an agent as given in Wooldridge's reference paper [16]:

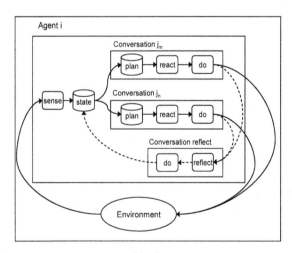

Fig. 2.

6   Related and Further Work

Previous proposals for representing consciousness either lack an explicit formal model [8] [9], functional specifications towards a possible implementation [5], or both

[15]. Using the same language to drive a machine and to reflexively communicate within the machine itself stands as a key feature of our own model. As consciousness basically works as a mirror, we view this duality to be an essential characteristics.

As already pointed out in the introduction, our model definitely reflects a "static" capability i.e., that of *being* conscious of explicit beliefs and of actions performed in full awareness. Baars [1] develops a concept of consciousness very much akin to a "dynamic" process of discovery and learning i.e., that of *getting* conscious of implicit facts resulting from sensations. Intuitively, Baars sees the human brain as being populated by myriads of parallel *unconscious processors* that compete for access into a *global workspace*. This workspace functions as a serial channel of limited capacity that can broadcast information to the unconscious processors. In various (possibly embedded) *contexts,* unconscious processors may form *coalitions* that will then force their way into the global workspace. Baars' theory is only described in general terms, and captured graphically in sets of diagrams of the type given below:

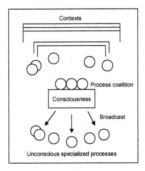

Fig. 3.

Although Baars himself once wrote "we now have a number of computational formalisms that can be used to make the current theory more explicit and testable", we do not know of any attempt to develop the corresponding formalization. These ideas however have already found their way into practical applications [8]. Unfortunately, as in many other artificial intelligence models, the "theory is the program" i.e., theoretical concepts are buried into ad hoc implementations that alone cannot qualify as a formalization of the theory.

Similarities do exist between Baars' theory involving a distributed system of parallel unconscious processors and our model of concurrent threads in a multi-agent system. First, our use of a blackboard for synchronizing messages is similar to Baars' workspace for broadcasting conscious messages. Other analogies to be found include:

serial information broadcast v/s our *blocking* communication primitives
goal *hierarchies* v/s our plan *decision trees*
dominant goal v/s our *initial* plan deduction
and (possibly) *process coalition* v/s *theory lifting*.

This last point is a mere conjecture that deserves an explanation. The concept of *theory lifting* was introduced by J. McCarthy in his attempt at formalizing contexts [12]. An executable account of this concept was given in [2]. We now suspect, and will try and formalize the hypothesis, that theory lifting can be used to model process coalition. As an example of a "Gedanken" experiment [8] that may be attempted, "a white square" should be recognized as "a sail" or "a hanging bed sheet" by lifting contextual knowledge associated with the surrounding landscape.

7 Conclusions

The explicit modeling of conscience threads, introduced in section 3, together with the possible reflection on one's own actions presented in section 4, opens the door to more complex consciousness models that should go beyond the simple monitoring of beliefs illustrated in this paper.

From a technical point of view, it is interesting to note that the *conscious* operator was defined using a *call(r, φ)/return(s, ψ)* pair of communication primitives, where $\varphi\theta=\psi\theta$ and $l^r \vdash \psi\theta$, with l^r referring to the agent's local state holding his beliefs. In contrast, the *caught* operator was defined using a *ask(s, ψ)/tell(r, φ)* pair involving a simplified $\varphi \vdash \psi\theta$ operation (because the agent's local state cannot be of any use in this case). Somehow, this a posteriori justifies the choice of communication primitives we made in [3].

We are well aware of the formal inconsistencies that arise when trying to model self referential sentences using a single uniform language, as discovered by Montague [13]. To escape from these pitfalls, we adopted a *constructivist* point of view i.e., similarly to nature itself, we grounded our concept of consciousness on successive, distinct operational layers, as summarized in the following pictures:

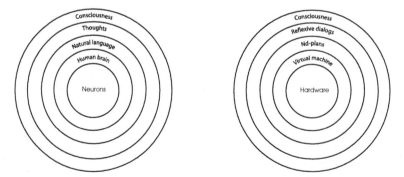

Fig. 4. Natural consciousness v/s simulated consciousness

Whereas inner layers interact with neighbors only (i.e., the virtual machine executes on the hardware, nd-plans are interpreted by this machine, dialogs are compiled into nd-plans, etc.), outer consciousness does rely on a direct access to a deeper underlying layer i.e., the virtual machine represented by the pseudo thread *react*. We are tempted to postulate that similar things happen in the working of natural consciousness.

Acknowledgment. We are indebted to an anonymous referee for his careful reading of this paper.

References

1. B.J. Baars, *A Cognitive Theory of Consciousness*, Cambridge University Press (1988)
2. P. Bonzon, A Reflexive Proof System for Reasoning in Context, *Proc. 14th Nat'l Conf. On AI , AAAI97* (1997)
3. P. Bonzon, An Abstract Machine for Communicating Agents Based on Deduction, in: J.-J. Meyer & M.Tambe (eds), *Intelligent Agents VIII*, LNAI vol. 2333, Springer Verlag (2002)
4. P. Bonzon, Compiling Dynamic Agent Conversations, in: M.Jarke, J.Koehler & G.Lakemeyer (eds), *Advances in Artificial Intelligence*, LNAI vol. 2479, Springer Verlag (2002)
5. J. Cunningham, Towards an Axiomatic Theory of Consciousness, Logic Journal of the IGPL, vol. 9, no 2 (2001)
6. D.C. Dennett, *Consciousness Explained*, Little Brown (1991)
7. O. Flanagan, *Consciousness Reconsidered*, MIT Press (1992)
8. S. Franklin & A. Graesser, A Software Agent Model of Consciousness, *Consciousness and Cognition*, vol. 8 (1999)
9. S. Franklin, Modeling Consciousness and Cognition in Software Agents, in: N. Taatgen, (ed.), *Proceedings of the International Conference on Cognitive Modeling*, Groeningen (2000)
10. G. de Giacomo, Y.Lespérance and H. Levesque, ConGolog, a Concurrent Programming Language Based on the Situation Calculus, *Artificial Intelligence*, vol. 121 (2000)
11. K.V. Hendricks, F.S. de Boer, W.van der Hoek and J.-J. Meyer, Semantics of Communicating Agents Based on Deduction and Abduction, in: F.Dignum & M.Greaves (eds), *Issues in Agent Communication*, LNAI vol. 1916, Springer Verlag (2000)
12. J. McCarthy, Notes on Formalizing Context, *Proc.13th Joint Conf. on Artificial Intelligence IJCAI93* (1993)
13. R. Montague, Syntactical treatment of modalities, with corollaries on reflexion principles and finite axiomatizability, Acta Philosophica Fennica, vol. 16 (1963)
14. E. Rich, *Artificial Intelligence*, McGraw-Hill (1983)
15 A. Sloman & R. Chrisley, Virtual Machines and Consciousness, submitted (2002)
16. M.Wooldridge, Intelligent Agents, in:G.Weiss (ed.), *Multiagent Systems*, MIT Press (1999)

What Observations Really Tell Us

Gero Iwan and Gerhard Lakemeyer

Department of Computer Science V
Aachen University
52056 Aachen, Germany
{iwan,gerhard}@cs.rwth-aachen.de

Abstract. When agents like mobile robots make observations while carrying out a course of actions, a formalization of the observed information is needed in order to reason about it. When doing so in the situation calculus, a seemingly straightforward approach turns out to be inappropriate since it leads to unintended results and has an unfortunate sensitivity with respect to different forms of successor state axioms. In this paper we suggest how to properly encode observed information in order to avoid both of these problems.

1 Introduction

When agents like mobile robots make observations while carrying out a course of actions, this information is of use when reasoning about the future as in planning, but also when reasoning about the past, which is necessary, for example, when diagnosing execution failures. Here we are considering formalizing actions and observations in the situation calculus [1,2,3].

At first glance, it seems to be quite clear what knowledge observations provide the agent with, namely that a certain statement about the world is true at a given point during its course of actions. However, when we began extending Iwan's work on the diagnosis of plan execution failures [4] to the case that observations can be made during a course of actions, we realized that a seemingly straightforward formalization of the information provided by the observations may lead to unintended and/or unintuitive results when drawing conclusions from these observations. Moreover, in this case different forms of the so-called successor state axioms which describe the effect and non-effects of actions yield different results although switching between these different forms was thought to be innocuous. We will suggest how to properly formalize the information provided by observations in order to avoid both of these problems.

We will illustrate the problem and our solution by way of the following simple scenario. Suppose an autonomous robot is acting in a typical office environment with rooms $R1, R2, R3, \ldots, Rm$ each of which is connected by a door to a hallway H. Starting from the hall in the initial situation, as the first action in a course of actions, the robot wants to enter room $R1$ and initiates navigating towards room $R1$.[1] But then, after arriving at the room, it finds out that it is

---

[1] We assume a navigation software as in [5] which usually, but not always, leads to successful navigation from one location to another.

A. Günter et al. (Eds.): KI 2003, LNAI 2821, pp. 194–208, 2003.

not *R1*. A reasonable diagnosis of this plan execution failure would be that the robot entered a room different from *R1*. In order to figure out what actually happened it would be helpful to determine the rooms for which it was possible to enter them in the initial situation. Assume that it is possible to enter a room from the hall iff the door of the room is open. Let us consider three cases:

1. Suppose that nothing is known about the state of the doors in the initial situation except that the door of room *R1* was open. Without any further information, one can only infer that it was possible to enter room *R1* and that it was at best *potentially* possible to enter any other room.
2. If the robot is capable of inquiring about the state of the doors (e. g., from a door control system) it can obtain new information. For example, let the answer to the request be: rooms *R1*, *R2*, *R3* are open, all other rooms are closed. From this information one should be able to infer that it was possible to enter rooms *R2*, *R3* instead of *R1*, but no other room.
3. Instead of requesting the door states from an outside source, suppose the robot uses its own sensors and observes, for example, that it is in a room whose door is open. In a sense, this seems like a rather trivial observation because having just entered a room should already imply that the door to this room is open. Thus from this redundant observation one should not be able to infer more than in the case where no observation was made.

As we will see below, there are surprisingly subtle issues that arise when attempting to formalize such scenarios. We remark that a preliminary version of this paper appeared, under the same title, at [6].

The rest of the paper is organized as follows. In the next section, we briefly introduce the situation calculus, followed by a first attempt at formalizing and reasoning about observations using the robot example. In Section 4, we analyze the problems with this approach and discuss our solution. In Section 5, we look at the more general picture of projecting both forward and backward in time. Finally, we end the paper with a section on related work and a brief summary.

2   The Situation Calculus

In this section we briefly go over the situation-as-histories variant [2,3,7] of the *situation calculus* [1,8] and, as we go along, give a formal account of our robot scenario in this framework. We adopt the convention that free variables are implicitly universally quantified unless otherwise stated. $\Phi[x_1, \ldots, x_n]$ indicates that the free variables of formula Φ are among $x_1, \ldots, x_n$.

The language of the situation calculus has three disjoint sorts: *situation*, *action*, *object*. There are two function symbols of sort *situation*: the constant S_0, which denotes the initial situation, and the binary function symbol *do*, where $do(\alpha, \sigma)$ denotes the situation that is reached after executing action α in situation σ. There are several domain-independent foundational axioms which, among other things, characterize the predicate $\sqsubset$ which denotes the predecessor relation between situations: $s' \sqsubset s$ means that s can be reached from s' by a sequence of actions. The abbreviation $s' \sqsubseteq s$ stands for $s' \sqsubset s \vee s' = s$.

An action is a term $A(t_1, \ldots, t_n)$, where A is a n-ary action function. The action functions used here are *enter* and *leave* for entering and leaving a room, *open*, *close* and *lock* for opening and locking doors. In the example, the rooms and the hall are denoted by the object constants $R1, R2, R3, \ldots, Rm$ and H. Properties of situations are represented using so-called fluents. Here we confine ourselves to relational fluents, which are predicates whose last argument is of sort *situation*, e. g., $Locked(r, s)$, $Open(r, s)$ and $RoLoc(l, s)$, whose meaning is "The (door of) room r is locked in situation s", "The (door of) room r is open in situation s" and "The robot is at location l in situation s", respectively. For each fluent there is a successor state axiom of the form

$$F(x_1, \ldots, x_n, do(a, s)) \equiv \Phi_F[x_1, \ldots, x_n, a, s] \tag{SSA}$$

which states under which condition, Φ_F, the property $F(x_1, \ldots, x_n, \_)$ holds in the successor situation $do(a, s)$ of situation s after executing action a, e. g.,

$$
\begin{aligned}
Locked(r, do(a, s)) \equiv \quad & a = lock(r) \\
& \vee\ Locked(r, s)
\end{aligned}
$$

$$
\begin{aligned}
Open(r, do(a, s)) \equiv \quad & a = open(r) \\
& \vee\ [Open(r, s) \wedge \neg[a = close(r) \vee a = lock(r)]\,]
\end{aligned}
$$

$$
\begin{aligned}
RoLoc(l, do(a, s)) \equiv \quad & a = enter(l) \\
& \vee\ [a = leave \wedge l = H] \\
& \vee\ [RoLoc(l, s) \wedge \neg[\exists r\ a = enter(r) \vee a = leave]\,]
\end{aligned}
$$

Axioms describing the initial situation and situation independent facts form the initial database, e. g.,

$$
\begin{aligned}
& RoLoc(H, S_0)\ \wedge\ Open(R1, S_0) \\
& \neg[Locked(r, S_0) \wedge Open(r, S_0)] \\
& [Open(r, S_0) \vee Locked(r, S_0)] \supset Room(r) \\
& Room(r) \equiv r = R1 \vee r = R2 \vee \cdots \vee r = Rm \\
& \text{unique names axioms for } R1, \ldots, Rm \text{ and } H
\end{aligned}
$$

Action precondition axioms of the form

$$Poss(A(x_1, \ldots, x_n), s) \equiv \Pi_A[x_1, \ldots, x_n, s]$$

are used to state under which condition, Π_A, it is possible to execute action $A(x_1, \ldots, x_n)$ in situation s, e. g.,

$$Poss(lock(r), s) \equiv Room(r) \wedge [RoLoc(r, s) \vee RoLoc(H, s)]$$

$$Poss(close(r), s) \equiv Room(r) \wedge [RoLoc(r, s) \vee RoLoc(H, s)]$$

$$Poss(open(r), s) \equiv Room(r) \wedge [RoLoc(r, s) \vee RoLoc(H, s)] \wedge \neg Locked(r, s)$$

$$Poss(enter(r), s) \equiv RoLoc(H, s) \wedge Open(r, s)$$

$$Poss(leave, s) \equiv \exists r \, [RoLoc(r, s) \wedge Open(r, s)]$$

A situation is said to be *executable* if, starting in the initial situation, it is possible to execute all the actions that lead to the situation. Formally:

$$Exec(s) \doteq \forall a', s' \, [do(a', s') \sqsubseteq s \supset Poss(a', s')]$$

As discussed in detail in [7], a basic action theory $\mathcal{D}$ describes the initial state of the world and how the world evolves under the effects of actions. It consists of foundational axioms for situations, unique names axioms for actions, an action precondition axiom for each action function, a successor state axiom for each fluent, and axioms describing the initial situation and situation independent facts.[2]

In what follows we also need the notion of *situation-suppressed formulas*, i. e., formulas where all occurrences of situation terms are "deleted" (details omitted). If ϕ is a situation-suppressed formula then $\phi[\sigma]$ denotes the situation calculus formula obtained after restoring suppressed situation arguments by "inserting" the situation σ where necessary, e. g., if $\phi = \exists x \, (Room(x) \wedge RoLoc(x) \wedge Open(x))$ then restoring σ yields $\phi[\sigma] = \exists x \, (Room(x) \wedge RoLoc(x, \sigma) \wedge Open(x, \sigma))$.

In contrast to the form of successor state axioms used above the form

$$Poss(a, s) \supset \big(F(x_1, \ldots, x_n, do(a, s)) \equiv \Phi_F\lceil x_1, \ldots, x_n, a, s \rceil \big) \qquad \text{(PSSA)}$$

is also found in the literature (e. g., in [9,10,11]) and is in fact the "original" form from [9]. We refer to it as the *Poss*-guarded form, and it only allows to infer effects of executable actions. Note that the unguarded form is logically equivalent to the *True*-guarded form

$$True \supset \big(F(x_1, \ldots, x_n, do(a, s)) \equiv \Phi_F\lceil x_1, \ldots, x_n, a, s \rceil \big) \qquad \text{(TSSA)}$$

Hence, from now on, we will write $\mathcal{D}_{True}$ for basic action theory using the unguarded form (or the *True*-guarded form) and $\mathcal{D}_{Poss}$ for basic action theory using the *Poss*-guarded form.

$\mathcal{D}_{True}$ and $\mathcal{D}_{Poss}$ are equivalent w. r. t. planning and projection for executable situations, strictly speaking *projection into the future* which means reasoning forward (in time) (cf. Section 5). But the example in the next section seems to suggest that they are not equivalent w. r. t. *projection into the past*, that is, reasoning backward in time. Worse yet, both forms suddenly seem inappropriate. However, Sections 4 and 5 will show how both problems can be avoided by accurately formalizing the information contained in observations.

---

[2] Note that with the given action theory $\mathcal{D}$ for the robot example, e. g.,
$\mathcal{D} \models \forall r, s \, [Exec(s) \supset \neg[Locked(r, s) \wedge Open(r, s)]]$ and
$\mathcal{D} \models \forall r, s \, [Exec(s) \supset ([Open(r, s) \vee Locked(r, s)] \supset Room(r))]$.

3   The Robot Example Revisited

With the situation-calculus account of the robot example given in the previous section, let us now reconsider the situation where the robot planned to perform the action $enter(R1)$ but fails. According to [4], $enter(\varrho)$ is a diagnosis of this plan execution failure for any $\varrho \in \{R2, \ldots, Rm\}$ provided the executability of $enter(\varrho)$ can be proved. Let ϕ be a situation-suppressed closed formula representing the observation that was made after performing the action $enter(\varrho)$. Then $\phi[do(enter(\varrho), S_0)]$ is the additional information provided by this observation. Since we want to determine whether it was possible to enter room ϱ in the initial situation we consider the sets of rooms $\mathsf{R}_1^{\oplus}(\mathcal{D}, \phi)$ and $\mathsf{R}_1^{\ominus}(\mathcal{D}, \phi)$ *intended* to be the sets of rooms different from $R1$ for which we are able to infer that it was possible or impossible to enter them respectively:[3]

$$\mathsf{R}_1^{\oplus}(\mathcal{D}, \phi) = \{\varrho \in \{R2, \ldots, Rm\} \mid \mathcal{D} \wedge \phi[do(enter(\varrho), S_0)] \models Open(\varrho, S_0)\}$$

$$\mathsf{R}_1^{\ominus}(\mathcal{D}, \phi) = \{\varrho \in \{R2, \ldots, Rm\} \mid \mathcal{D} \wedge \phi[do(enter(\varrho), S_0)] \models \neg Open(\varrho, S_0)\}$$

Note that $Poss(enter(\varrho), S_0) \equiv Open(\varrho, S_0)$ can be inferred from the action precondition axiom for $enter$ together with $RoLoc(H, S_0)$, no matter which form of successor state axioms is used.

The three cases regarding the information about the door states can be represented as follows:

$$\phi_{NoInfo} = True,$$
$$\phi_{Rooms123} = \forall r \, [Open(r) \equiv r = R1 \vee r = R2 \vee r = R3]$$
$$\phi_{LocOpen} = \exists r \, [Room(r) \wedge RoLoc(r) \wedge Open(r)]$$

where ϕ_{NoInfo} expresses that no observation was made, $\phi_{Rooms123}$ corresponds to the case where the agent was told that only the first three rooms are open, and $\phi_{LocOpen}$ corresponds to the case where the agent itself is able to figure out that the door to the room it just entered is open.

Let $\mathsf{R}^{\oplus}(\phi)$ and $\mathsf{R}^{\ominus}(\phi)$ denote the intended results for an observation ϕ. The argument given in the introduction suggests the following values for $\mathsf{R}^{\oplus}(\phi)$ and $\mathsf{R}^{\ominus}(\phi)$, respectively:

$$\mathsf{R}^{\oplus}(\phi_{Rooms123}) = \{R2, R3\} \qquad \mathsf{R}^{\oplus}(\phi_{LocOpen}) = \emptyset \qquad \mathsf{R}^{\oplus}(\phi_{NoInfo}) = \emptyset$$
$$\mathsf{R}^{\ominus}(\phi_{Rooms123}) = \{R4, \ldots, Rm\} \qquad \mathsf{R}^{\ominus}(\phi_{LocOpen}) = \emptyset \qquad \mathsf{R}^{\ominus}(\phi_{NoInfo}) = \emptyset$$

However, depending on whether we use *Poss-* or *True*-guarded successor state axioms, we sometimes get surprisingly different results as shown in the following table:

---

[3] In a slight abuse of notation, we often write $\mathcal{D} \wedge \Phi$ instead of $\mathcal{D} \cup \{\Phi\}$.

ϕ	$\phi_{Rooms123}$	$\phi_{LocOpen}$	ϕ_{NoInfo}
$R_1^{\oplus}(\mathcal{D}_{True}, \phi)$	$\{R2, R3\}$	$\{R2, \ldots, Rm\}$	$\emptyset$
$R_1^{\ominus}(\mathcal{D}_{True}, \phi)$	$\{R4, \ldots, Rm\}$	$\emptyset$	$\emptyset$
$R_1^{\oplus}(\mathcal{D}_{Poss}, \phi)$	$\emptyset$	$\emptyset$	$\emptyset$
$R_1^{\ominus}(\mathcal{D}_{Poss}, \phi)$	$\{R4, \ldots, Rm\}$	$\emptyset$	$\emptyset$

Thus for the observation $\phi_{Rooms123}$, $\mathcal{D}_{Poss}$ is too weak but $\mathcal{D}_{True}$ gives the intended results, whereas for $\phi_{LocOpen}$, $\mathcal{D}_{Poss}$ gives the intended results and $\mathcal{D}_{True}$ gives a completely counter-intuitive result.

This result can be meliorated by a more careful formulation of the sets $R_1^{\oplus}(\mathcal{D}, \phi)$ and $R_1^{\ominus}(\mathcal{D}, \phi)$:

$$R_2^{\oplus}(\mathcal{D}, \phi) = \{\xi \in \{R2, \ldots, Rm\} \mid \mathcal{D} \wedge \phi[do(enter(\varrho), S_0)] \models Open(\xi, S_0)\}$$
$$R_2^{\ominus}(\mathcal{D}, \phi) = \{\xi \in \{R2, \ldots, Rm\} \mid \mathcal{D} \wedge \phi[do(enter(\varrho), S_0)] \models \neg Open(\xi, S_0)\}$$

Here we distinguish between the room $\varrho \neq R1$ which is assumed to be entered and the room ξ for which we are able to infer that it was possible or impossible to enter it. Determining the sets of rooms yields the same results except that (1.) for observation $\phi_{Rooms123}$, $\mathcal{D}_{Poss}$ becomes even weaker since $R_2^{\ominus}(\mathcal{D}_{Poss}, \phi_{Rooms123}) = \emptyset$ if $\varrho \in \{R2, R3\}$ and $R_2^{\ominus}(\mathcal{D}_{Poss}, \phi_{Rooms123}) = \{\varrho\}$ if $\varrho \in \{R4, \ldots, Rm\}$, and (2.) for the other observation, $R_2^{\oplus}(\mathcal{D}_{True}, \phi_{LocOpen}) = \{\varrho\}$:

	ϕ	$\phi_{Rooms123}$	$\phi_{LocOpen}$	ϕ_{NoInfo}
	$R_2^{\oplus}(\mathcal{D}_{True}, \phi)$	$\{R2, R3\}$	$\{\varrho\}$	$\emptyset$
	$R_2^{\ominus}(\mathcal{D}_{True}, \phi)$	$\{R4, \ldots, Rm\}$	$\emptyset$	$\emptyset$
	$R_2^{\oplus}(\mathcal{D}_{Poss}, \phi)$	$\emptyset$	$\emptyset$	$\emptyset$
$\varrho \in \{R2, R3\}$:	$R_2^{\ominus}(\mathcal{D}_{Poss}, \phi)$	$\emptyset$	$\emptyset$	$\emptyset$
$\varrho \in \{R4, \ldots, Rm\}$:	$R_2^{\ominus}(\mathcal{D}_{Poss}, \phi)$	$\{\varrho\}$	$\emptyset$	$\emptyset$

Given the intuition that $R^{\oplus}(\phi_{LocOpen}) = \emptyset$ (i.e., $\phi_{LocOpen}$ is a redundant observation) the result $R_2^{\oplus}(\mathcal{D}_{True}, \phi_{LocOpen}) = \{\varrho\}$ is "less counter-intuitive" but nevertheless strange because it is trivial that the robot can leave a room it just entered. Thus, the robot should not gain any information from the observation $\phi_{LocOpen}$ after an $enter$-action. Let us consider the argument for $\mathcal{D}_{True}$ and $\phi_{LocOpen}$ in a bit more detail:

1. An effect of the execution of $enter(\varrho)$ is that $RoLoc(r) \equiv r = \varrho$, i.e., the location of the robot is ϱ [by the (unguarded) successor state axiom for $RoLoc$].
2. If the location of the robot is ϱ then observation $\phi_{LocOpen}$ is equivalent to $Open(\varrho)$ [w.r.t. the axioms], i.e., room ϱ is open.

3. If room ϱ is open after action $enter(\varrho)$ then room ϱ must have been open before action $enter(\varrho)$ [by the (unguarded) successor state axiom for $Open$].
4. If room ϱ is open before $enter(\varrho)$ then $enter(\varrho)$ is executable (since the location was the hallway before) [by the action precondition axiom for $enter$].

So we have a kind of circular argument here: "An effect of the execution of $enter(\varrho)$ is that ... $enter(\varrho)$ is executable." The crucial point in this circular argument is the first one which is considering effects of actions that are not known to be executable.

This discovery leads us to a defect of the formalization of observed information so far: we consider observations made in situations which are not known to be executable. But this seems absurd: if we make an observation in some situation then we have reached this situation, and if we have reached some situation then the actions leading to this situation must have been executable. So it is revealed now that the intuition $\mathsf{R}^{\oplus}(\phi_{LocOpen}) = \emptyset$ was wrong if we assume that a room ϱ was entered. The right intuition should have been $\mathsf{R}^{\oplus}(\phi_{LocOpen}) = \{\varrho\}$. Does the unintended results vanish if the intuition is corrected that way? No, they don't:

Generally, $\varrho \in \mathsf{R}^{\oplus}(\ldots)$ must hold if we assume that ϱ was entered. For ϕ_{NoInfo} this brings $\mathsf{R}^{\oplus}(\phi_{NoInfo}) = \{\varrho\}$, but it is $\mathsf{R}_2^{\oplus}(\mathcal{D}, \phi_{NoInfo}) = \emptyset$ for both $\mathcal{D} = \mathcal{D}_{True}$ and $\mathcal{D} = \mathcal{D}_{Poss}$. Furthermore, since $\mathsf{R}^{\ominus}(\phi_{Rooms123}) = \{R4, \ldots, Rm\}$ (i.e., after observing $\phi_{Rooms123}$ it should be known that $R4, \ldots, Rm$ were closed in S_0) $\mathcal{D} \wedge \phi_{Rooms123}[do(enter(\varrho), S_0)]$ should turn out to be inconsistent for $\varrho \in \{R4, \ldots, Rm\}$ (because in this case $enter(\varrho)$ was not executable in S_0 at all). This is not the case: $\mathcal{D} \wedge \phi_{Rooms123}[do(enter(\varrho), S_0)]$ is consistent. Even worse, if $\varrho \in \{R4, \ldots, Rm\}$ then $\mathcal{D} \wedge \phi_{Rooms123}[do(enter(\varrho), S_0)] \models \neg Open(\varrho, S_0)$. But this means that $enter(\varrho)$ was not executable, contradicting the assumption that ϱ was entered. To resolve these problems, we need to be more careful in representing what observations really tell us.

4   What Observations Really Tell Us

We define an *observation* as a situation-suppressed closed formula. In order to obtain the information provided by an observation one has to restore an appropriate situation, namely the situation where the observation was made. When an agent, while carrying out a course of actions, makes several observations $\phi_1, \ldots, \phi_n$ in sequence the *basic information* contained in this sequence of observations is

- For each observation ϕ_i there is a situation s_i where it was made.
- There is a situation s_* which is the current situation and therefore is executable.
- The sequence $s_1, \ldots, s_n, s_*$ provides us with a natural ordering of the situations.

This is captured by the formula $\overline{\exists}\, \Omega[\phi_1, \ldots, \phi_n]$ where

$$\Omega[\phi_1, \ldots, \phi_n] \ \doteq\ s_1 \sqsubseteq \ldots \sqsubseteq s_n \sqsubseteq s_* \wedge Exec(s_*) \wedge \phi_1[s_1] \wedge \cdots \wedge \phi_n[s_n]$$

Here $s_1 \sqsubseteq \ldots \sqsubseteq s_n \sqsubseteq s_*$ abbreviates $s_1 \sqsubseteq s_2 \wedge \cdots \wedge s_{n-1} \sqsubseteq s_n \wedge s_n \sqsubseteq s_*$. Note that, as a consequence of the foundational situation calculus axioms, $s \sqsubseteq s_* \wedge Exec(s_*)$ implies $Exec(s)$.

The message then is that the sole information as given by the observation formulas is not enough to draw the right conclusions, but that we also need to take into account the history and, in particular, the fact that it is executable.

In the robot example, the basic information contained in $\phi_{LocOpen}$ is no new information because, e.g., with $\sigma_1 = \sigma_* = do(enter(R1), S_0)$, $\mathcal{D}_{True}$ and $\mathcal{D}_{Poss}$ both entail $\exists\, \Omega[\phi_{LocOpen}]$ since $\sigma_1 \sqsubseteq \sigma_* \wedge Exec(\sigma_*) \wedge \phi_{LocOpen}[\sigma_1]$ is entailed. In general, the basic information may contain new information. For instance, for both $\mathcal{D} = \mathcal{D}_{True}$ and $\mathcal{D} = \mathcal{D}_{Poss}$

$$\mathcal{D} \wedge \exists\, \Omega[\phi_{Rooms123}] \models \neg Locked(R2, S_0) \wedge \neg Locked(R3, S_0)$$

Without this information we have[4] $\mathcal{D} \models \neg Locked(R1, S_0)$ but

$$\mathcal{D} \not\models \neg Locked(R2, S_0) \qquad \text{and} \qquad \mathcal{D} \not\models \neg Locked(R3, S_0)$$

However, mostly we have some additional assumptions about the action history. In the robot example, s_1 was assumed to be the situation reached after performing $enter(\varrho)$ in the initial situation (with $\varrho \in \{R2, \ldots, Rm\}$), i.e., the additional assumption was $s_1 = do(enter(\varrho), S_0)$. Let this formula be named Θ_ϱ:

$$\Theta_\varrho \;\doteq\; s_1 = do(enter(\varrho), S_0)$$

In general, a *history assumption* for $\Omega[\phi_1, \ldots, \phi_n]$ can be expressed by a formula $\Theta[s_1, \ldots, s_n, s_*]$ (i.e., by a formula Θ with free variables among $s_1, \ldots, s_n, s_*$) where $s_1, \ldots, s_n, s_*$ are the situation variables chosen in $\Omega[\phi_1, \ldots, \phi_n]$. The basic information together with the history assumption then is $\exists\, [\Omega[\phi_1, \ldots, \phi_n] \wedge \Theta]$.

We accordingly redefine the sets $\mathsf{R}_2^\oplus(\mathcal{D}, \phi)$ and $\mathsf{R}_2^\ominus(\mathcal{D}, \phi)$ from the previous section:

$$\mathsf{R}_\varrho^\oplus(\mathcal{D}, \phi) = \{\xi \in \{R2, \ldots, Rm\} \mid \mathcal{D} \wedge \exists\, [\Omega[\phi] \wedge \Theta_\varrho] \models Open(\xi, S_0)\}$$

$$\mathsf{R}_\varrho^\ominus(\mathcal{D}, \phi) = \{\xi \in \{R2, \ldots, Rm\} \mid \mathcal{D} \wedge \exists\, [\Omega[\phi] \wedge \Theta_\varrho] \models \neg Open(\xi, S_0)\}$$

Note that $\exists\, [\Omega[\phi] \wedge \Theta_\varrho]$ is equivalent to

$$Poss(enter(\varrho), S_0) \wedge \phi[do(enter(\varrho), S_0)]$$

(since $Exec(do(a, S_0)) \equiv Poss(a, S_0)$ is implied by the foundational situation calculus axioms). $\mathcal{D} \wedge \exists\, [\Omega[\phi_{Rooms123}] \wedge \Theta_\varrho]$ is inconsistent if $\varrho \notin \{R1, R2, R3\}$.

---

[4] We have $\mathcal{D} \models Open(R1, S_0) \wedge \forall r \, \neg[Locked(r, S_0) \wedge Open(r, S_0)]$ because of the axioms describing the initial situation.

Therefore the $\phi_{Rooms123}$-results are only reported for $\varrho \in \{R2, R3\}$ ($\varrho \neq R1$ was presupposed):

ϕ	$\phi_{Rooms123}$ ($\varrho \in \{R2, R3\}$)	$\phi_{LocOpen}$	ϕ_{NoInfo}
$\mathsf{R}_\varrho^\oplus(\mathcal{D}_{True}, \phi)$	$\{R2, R3\}$	$\{\varrho\}$	$\{\varrho\}$
$\mathsf{R}_\varrho^\ominus(\mathcal{D}_{True}, \phi)$	$\{R4, \ldots, Rm\}$	$\emptyset$	$\emptyset$
$\mathsf{R}_\varrho^\oplus(\mathcal{D}_{Poss}, \phi)$	$\{R2, R3\}$	$\{\varrho\}$	$\{\varrho\}$
$\mathsf{R}_\varrho^\ominus(\mathcal{D}_{Poss}, \phi)$	$\{R4, \ldots, Rm\}$	$\emptyset$	$\emptyset$

So for each of the three observations both $\mathcal{D}_{True}$ and $\mathcal{D}_{Poss}$ give the intended results that were discussed at the end of the previous section (including the inconsistence for observation $\phi_{Rooms123}$ if $\varrho \in \{R4, \ldots, Rm\}$).

Of course, in contrast to the previous section, here the statement that $enter(\varrho)$ is executable in the initial situation is given additionally. This was not done in the previous section. But the absence of this premise was exactly the shortcoming of the formalization of observed information in the previous section. Note that the premise $Poss(enter(\varrho), S_0)$ does not originate from the basic information contained in the observation but from the assumption about the action history (together with the basic information).

> The explicit distinction between the basic information contained in the observations on the one hand and the *assumption* about the history on the other hand is a valuable quality of the approach to observation information presented here.

Instead of explicitly introducing the entered room ϱ we could have used a history assumption where only the existence of an appropriate room is stated.[5] This is closer to what we wanted to express actually. Let the corresponding formula be named $\Theta_\exists$:

$$\Theta_\exists \doteq \exists r \, [Room(r) \wedge r \neq R1 \wedge s_1 = do(enter(r), S_0) \wedge s_* = s_1]$$

Using this formula within $\mathsf{R}_\varrho^\oplus(\mathcal{D}, \phi)$ and $\mathsf{R}_\varrho^\ominus(\mathcal{D}, \phi)$ instead of Θ_ϱ yields:

$$\mathsf{R}_\exists^\oplus(\mathcal{D}, \phi) = \{\xi \in \{R2, \ldots, Rm\} \mid \mathcal{D} \wedge \exists [\Omega[\phi] \wedge \Theta_\exists] \models Open(\xi, S_0)\}$$
$$\mathsf{R}_\exists^\ominus(\mathcal{D}, \phi) = \{\xi \in \{R2, \ldots, Rm\} \mid \mathcal{D} \wedge \exists [\Omega[\phi] \wedge \Theta_\exists] \models \neg Open(\xi, S_0)\}$$

Note that $\exists [\Omega[\phi] \wedge \Theta_\exists]$ is equivalent to

$$\exists r \, [Room(r) \wedge r \neq R1 \wedge Poss(enter(r), S_0) \wedge \phi[do(enter(r), S_0)] \,]$$

---

[5] Note that w.r.t. $\mathcal{D}$ $Room(r) \wedge r \neq R1$ is equivalent to $r = R2 \vee \cdots \vee r = Rm$ (i.e., $r \in \{R2, \ldots, Rm\}$) because of the situation independent facts.

Furthermore $\mathcal{D} \wedge \overline{\exists} \, [\Omega[\phi_{Rooms123}] \wedge \Theta_{\exists}]$ is consistent. The results now are:

ϕ	$\phi_{Rooms123}$	$\phi_{LocOpen}$	ϕ_{NoInfo}
$\mathsf{R}_{\exists}^{\oplus}(\mathcal{D}_{True}, \phi)$	$\{R2, R3\}$	$\emptyset$	$\emptyset$
$\mathsf{R}_{\exists}^{\ominus}(\mathcal{D}_{True}, \phi)$	$\{R4, \ldots, Rm\}$	$\emptyset$	$\emptyset$
$\mathsf{R}_{\exists}^{\oplus}(\mathcal{D}_{Poss}, \phi)$	$\{R2, R3\}$	$\emptyset$	$\emptyset$
$\mathsf{R}_{\exists}^{\ominus}(\mathcal{D}_{Poss}, \phi)$	$\{R4, \ldots, Rm\}$	$\emptyset$	$\emptyset$

So for each of the three observations both $\mathcal{D}_{True}$ and $\mathcal{D}_{Poss}$ give what we expect to be the intended results as initially stated at the beginning of the previous section.

Our robot example is a projection problem into the past where the form of successor state axioms does not matter. In the next section we will see that with our approach to observation information this is true in a rather general sense (correcting the impression that was given in Section 3).

5 Planning and Projection with Observations

In the last section, we used inferences like $\mathcal{D} \wedge \overline{\exists} \, [\Omega[\phi_1, \ldots, \phi_n] \wedge \Theta] \models \Psi$. This can be rephrased as

$$\mathcal{D} \models \overline{\forall} \, [(\Omega[\phi_1, \ldots, \phi_n] \wedge \wr\Theta) \supset \Psi] \qquad (\star)$$

where $\wr\Theta$ is obtained from Θ by removing all existential quantifiers from the front of Θ (so $\Theta = \overline{\exists} \wr\Theta$). Note though that $(\star)$ is more general since Ψ may refer to the free variables of $\Omega[\phi_1, \ldots, \phi_n] \wedge \wr\Theta$. This feature is needed, e. g., for general reachability, (re-)planning and projection problems.

For instance, $\wr\Theta_{\exists}$ is

$$Room(r) \wedge r \neq R1 \wedge s_* = s_1 = do(enter(r), S_0)$$

and we can ask for properties of r, e. g., whether r is currently open (which is obviously true since the robot just entered r): $\mathcal{D} \models \overline{\forall} \, [(\Omega[\phi] \wedge \wr\Theta_{\exists}) \supset Open(r, s_*)]$. Note that this could not be inferred if $\Theta_{\exists}$ would not contain $s_* = s_1$. Likewise, if we would like to know whether it is possible to recover from error in our robot example we have to check whether the original goal, Γ, of the robot can be reached from the current situation. This is a reachability problem. Its general form is

$$\mathcal{D} \models \overline{\forall} \, [(\Omega[\phi_1, \ldots, \phi_n] \wedge \wr\Theta) \supset \exists s \, [s_* \sqsubseteq s \wedge Exec(s) \wedge \Gamma(s)] \,] \quad \textbf{(reachability)}$$

where s_* is the variable referring to the current situation in $\Omega[\phi_1, \ldots, \phi_n]$.

(Re-)Planning means: Find an action sequence $\alpha_1, \ldots, \alpha_m$ and check that it is executable in the current situation and achieves a given goal, Γ.[6] The general form therefore is with $\sigma_\triangleright = do(\alpha_m, \ldots do(\alpha_1, s_*) \ldots)$

$$\mathcal{D} \models \overline{\forall} \left[(\Omega[\phi_1, \ldots, \phi_n] \wedge \wr\Theta) \supset [Exec(\sigma_\triangleright) \wedge \Gamma(\sigma_\triangleright)] \right] \qquad \textbf{(planning)}$$

Projection into the future means: Check whether a given action sequence $\alpha_1, \ldots, \alpha_m$ achieves a given goal, Γ, if it is performed in the current situation. So it refers to the given future situation $\sigma_\triangleright$ and asks whether a certain property (the goal) will hold in $\sigma_\triangleright$. Projection into the past instead refers to a given past situation $\sigma_\triangleleft$ (S_0 in our robot example) and asks whether a certain property (the goal) held in $\sigma_\triangleleft$. The general form for projection is

$$\mathcal{D} \models \overline{\forall} \left[(\Omega[\phi_1, \ldots, \phi_n] \wedge \wr\Theta) \supset \Gamma(\sigma) \right] \qquad \textbf{(projection)}$$

Note that plan checking (i.e., checking whether an action sequence is a plan) and reachability testing can be viewed as special cases of projection. If σ is not a bygone situation, i.e., $\mathcal{D} \not\models \overline{\forall} [(\Omega[\phi_1, \ldots, \phi_n] \wedge \wr\Theta) \supset \sigma \sqsubset s_*]$, then projection is *hypothetical reasoning*. Since they refer to future situations, plan checking and reachability testing are hypothetical reasoning, too.

If there are no observations (i.e.: $n = 0$) and the current situation is the initial situation (i.e.: Θ simply is $s_* = S_0$) then any occurrence of s_* in Γ can be replaced by S_0 and reachability, planning and projection (into the future) reduce to their standard forms

$$\mathcal{D} \models \exists s \, [Exec(s) \wedge \Gamma(s)] \qquad \text{(reachability)}$$
$$\mathcal{D} \models Exec(\sigma') \wedge \Gamma(\sigma') \qquad \text{(planning)}$$
$$\mathcal{D} \models \Gamma(\sigma') \qquad \text{(projection)}$$

with $\sigma' = do(\alpha_m, \ldots do(\alpha_1, S_0) \ldots)$ for variable-free actions $\alpha_1, \ldots, \alpha_m$. Note that the standard forms are hypothetical reasoning (since the foundational situation calculus axioms imply $\neg(\sigma' \sqsubset S_0)$).

Of course, the given general forms do not automatically guarantee that the form of the successor state axioms does not matter. For instance, if

$$\Theta' = \phi_{LocOpen} \big[do(enter(\varrho), S_0) \big]$$

then $\overline{\forall} [(\Omega[\phi_{Rooms123}] \wedge \wr\Theta') \supset Open(\varrho, S_0)]$ is equivalent to $\Theta' \supset Open(\varrho, S_0)$ w.r.t. both $\mathcal{D}_{True}$ and $\mathcal{D}_{Poss}$, but

$$\mathcal{D}_{True} \wedge \Theta' \models Open(\varrho, S_0)$$
$$\mathcal{D}_{Poss} \wedge \Theta' \not\models Open(\varrho, S_0)$$

(cf. Section 3). The crucial point here is that nothing is known about the executability of $do(enter(\varrho), S_0)$. If $do(enter(\varrho), S_0)$ were claimed to be executable,

---

[6] That is in a way: Check whether $s = \sigma_\triangleright$ yields an instance of the reachability problem.

either directly, e.g., by $Exec(do(enter(\varrho), S_0))$ or $Poss(enter(\varrho), S_0)$, or indirectly, e.g., by $do(enter(\varrho), S_0) = s_1$ or $do(enter(\varrho), S_0) \sqsubseteq s_*$, both $\mathcal{D}_{True}$ and $\mathcal{D}_{Poss}$ would give the same answer. For example, if instead of Θ' we use

$$\Theta'' = \phi_{LocOpen}[do(enter(\varrho), S_0)] \wedge do(enter(\varrho), S_0) \sqsubseteq s_*$$

then for both $\mathcal{D} = \mathcal{D}_{True}$ and $\mathcal{D} = \mathcal{D}_{Poss}$

$$\mathcal{D} \models \overline{\forall}\,[(\Omega[\phi_{Rooms123}] \wedge \wr\Theta'') \supset Open(\varrho, S_0)]$$

An appropriate definition of *claimed executable* would give us the following theorem:

If all situations are claimed executable within $\Omega[\dots]$, Θ and Ψ then

$$\mathcal{D}_{True} \models \overline{\forall}\,[(\Omega[\phi_1, \dots, \phi_n] \wedge \wr\Theta) \supset \Psi]$$
$$\text{iff} \quad \mathcal{D}_{Poss} \models \overline{\forall}\,[(\Omega[\phi_1, \dots, \phi_n] \wedge \wr\Theta) \supset \Psi].$$

It is a topic under investigation to formulate a precise (yet as comprehensive as possible) syntactic criterion for "all situations are claimed executable within ...." However, reasonable formula are likely to comply with this condition as can be seen from the following considerations.

For reachability and planning, s and $\sigma_{\triangleright}$ are explicitly claimed executable by $Exec(s)$ and $Exec(\sigma_{\triangleright})$ respectively.[7] Since reasoning about non-executable actions does not make much sense, for projection into the future Θ should contain $Exec(\sigma_{\triangleright})$, i.e., we assume that the action sequence $\alpha_1, \dots, \alpha_m$ is executable in the current situation. Likewise, for projection into the past it is safe to have $\sigma_{\triangleleft} \sqsubseteq s_*$ contained in Θ as the previous situation $\sigma_{\triangleleft}$ lies before the current situation s_*. Also, if the history assumption Θ mentions previous situations it can contain $\sigma \sqsubseteq s_*$ for each of these situations σ. Yet, Θ may also refer to the future, e.g., if we assume that the current situation is so that after performing some actions $\alpha_1', \dots, \alpha_k'$ a situation will be reached which has some property ψ, i.e., Θ contains $\psi[do(\alpha_k', \dots do(\alpha_1', s_*) \dots)]$. But if we think that we are able to reach $do(\alpha_m, \dots do(\alpha_1, s_*) \dots)$ then $Exec(do(\alpha_m, \dots do(\alpha_1, s_*) \dots))$ should be contained in Θ, too. Similar considerations can be made for situations in $\Gamma(s)$. However, often s will be the only situations mentioned in $\Gamma(s)$ in which case no problem arises from $\Gamma(s)$.

6   Related Work

As we already remarked at the beginning of this paper, this work grew out of Iwan's investigations into diagnosing plan execution failures [4]. There, as well as

---

[7] The fact that $Exec(\sigma_{\triangleright})$ occurs on the right side of the implication does not cause trouble since, e.g., $Exec(do(\alpha', do(\alpha, s_*)))$ is an abbreviation equivalent to $Poss(\alpha, s_*) \wedge Poss(\alpha', do(\alpha, s_*))$. So the first $Poss$-atom claims $do(\alpha, s_*)$ executable (because s_* is executable) and the second $Poss$-atom then claims $do(\alpha', do(\alpha, s_*))$ executable.

in McIlraith's earlier work on diagnosis [11], observations similar to those used in this paper, play a central role. Although we make no commitment as to how observations come about, they are often a result of sensing actions performed by the agent. Sensing in the framework of the situation calculus is considered, for example, in [12,13]. McIlraith and Scherl recently addressed the question what sensing tells us [14]. However, they are mainly concerned with knowledge, ramifications, and the notion of tests, issues which are orthogonal to those addressed in this paper.

There are also interesting connections between observations and narratives. Just as narratives talk about what *actually* happened in the past, so do observations.[8] Narratives were formalized in the situation calculus in [15,16].[9] We remark that the models of time considered in these approaches can easily be added to our framework as well. An interesting approach to modeling narratives in an action language different from the situation calculus is discussed in [18]. There the language $\mathcal{L}_1$ is proposed, which extends the language $\mathcal{A}$ [19,20,21] by adding the notions of actually occurring actions and observations to capture narratives. In the next paragraph, we take a closer look at this work.

To start with, $\mathcal{L}_1$ is a propositional language, just like $\mathcal{A}$. The constants S_i that are used to denote actual situations (in contrast to hypothetical situations) roughly correspond to our situation variables s_i in $\Omega \wedge \wr \Theta$. The *causal laws* (A causes F if ψ) correspond to effect axioms $\forall s \, [\psi [s] \supset F(do(A, s))]$ in the situation calculus and can be encoded by successor state axioms (cf. [9]; the necessary completeness assumption is also part of the semantics of $\mathcal{L}_1$). Observations are expressed by *fluent facts* (ϕ at S_i) which correspond to $\phi[s_i]$; *precedence facts* (S_j precedes S_i) correspond to $s_j \sqsubset s_i$; *occurrence facts* (A occurs_at S_i) translate to $do(A, s_i) \sqsubset s_*$; and *hypotheses* (ϕ after $[A_1, \ldots, A_n]$ at S_i) correspond to $\phi[do(A_n, \ldots do(A_1, s_i) \ldots)]$. Domain descriptions are collections of laws and facts and can be translated into successor state axioms (laws) and an observations-plus-history-assumption formula $\Omega \wedge \wr \Theta$ (facts). $\mathcal{L}_1$ has no notion of executability of actions, which means that $\forall s \, [Poss(A, s) \equiv True]$ for all actions A. Therefore, of course, problems regarding *Poss*- or *True*-guarded laws do not arise in $\mathcal{L}_1$ at all. (There are extensions of $\mathcal{L}_1$ containing executability conditions, e. g., in [17] where, applying our terminology, the causal laws are *True*-guarded.) The semantics of $\mathcal{L}_1$ imposes a minimality condition on the occurrence of actions leading to the current situation. It is an interesting question whether and how the same minimality property can be achieved within the situation calculus. Then $\mathcal{L}_1$ may be emulated in the situation calculus using our approach to observations with history assumptions.

Another extension of $\mathcal{A}$ is the language $\mathcal{B}$ in which *static laws* (F if ψ) are available [21]. In [22] a variant of $\mathcal{B}$ is used in a diagnostic setting. In this approach, observations are recorded by statements of the form obs(ϕ, i) where $i < n$ is a natural number indicating that ϕ was observed after the occurrence of i ac-

---

[8] Of course, in general observations could be mistaken, an issue we have ignored here altogether.

[9] See also [17], where the connection between diagnosis and narratives is investigated.

tions in sequence. Actions are sets of *elementary actions*, and statements of the form $\mathsf{hpd}(\gamma, i)$ record that elementary action γ happened after the occurrence of i actions in sequence. Using our notation, $\mathsf{obs}(\phi, i)$ is represented by $\phi[s_i]$, and the hpd-statements can be represented by $s_{i+1} = do(\alpha_i, s_i)$ for all $i < n$ where α_i is the action corresponding to the set $\{\gamma \mid \mathsf{hpd}(\gamma, i)$ is given$\}$ of elementary actions.[10] Furthermore, actions are defined to be executable in consistent recorded histories. So the trouble with formalizing the information provided by observations does not arise in [22] because the concepts underlying the solution we found for the situation calculus (namely observations-plus-history-assumption formulas $\Omega \wedge \wr\Theta$) are simply already implicit in the syntax of the languages used in [22]. This also is the case in [18] and probably in many other approaches not having observation-formalization troubles. However, without any special *observation expressions* (which, of course, could be introduced) in the situation calculus one needs to be attentive when representing what observations really tell us.

7 Summary

Our concern has been to answer the question "What do observations really tell us?" This question arose from examples where an unsophisticated formalization within the situation calculus led to unintended and unintuitive results when drawing conclusions and where the use of either unguarded or *Poss*-guarded successor state axioms unwantedly yields different results. So there was the need for a closer look on how to formalize information provided by observations. We found that the information can (and should) be divided into the *basic information* which only reflects the sequence of observations (up to the current situation) and an *assumption* about the history (including the current situation and possibly assumption about potential future evolutions). With this formalization at hand, we revised the general form of planning and projection (now into the future and into the past) in the presence of observations and argued that unguarded and *Poss*-guarded successor state axioms will behave equivalently.

References

1. McCarthy, J.: Situations, actions and causal laws. Stanford Artificial Intelligence Project: Memo 2 (1963) Reprinted in: M.L. Minsky, editor. *Semantic Information Processing*. MIT Press, 1968.
2. Levesque, H., Pirri, F., Reiter, R.: Foundations for the situation calculus. Electronic Transactions on Artificial Intelligence **2** (1998)
3. Reiter, R., Pirri, F.: Some contributions to the metatheory of the situation calculus. Journal of the ACM **46** (1999)
4. Iwan, G.: History-based diagnosis templates in the framework of the situation calculus. AI Communications **15** (2002)

---

[10] Note that $s_{i+1} = do(\alpha_i, s_i)$ implies $s_i \sqsubset s_{i+1}$.

5. Burgard, W., Cremers, A., Fox, D., Hähnel, D., Lakemeyer, G., Schulz, D., Steiner, W., Thrun, S.: Experiences with an interactive museum tour-guide robot. Artificial Intelligence **114** (1999)

6. Iwan, G., Lakemeyer, G.: What observations really tell us. In: Proceedings of the 3rd International Cognitive Robotics Workshop. (2002)

7. Reiter, R.: Knowledge in Action: Logical Foundations for Specifying and Implementing Dynamical Systems. MIT Press (2001)

8. McCarthy, J., Hayes, P.: Some philosophical problems from the standpoint of artificial intelligence. In Meltzer, B., Michie, D., eds.: Machine Intelligence 4. Edinburgh University Press (1969)

9. Reiter, R.: The frame problem in the situation calculus: A simple solution (sometimes) and a completeness result for goal regression. In Lifschitz, V., ed.: Artificial Intelligence and Mathematical Theory of Computation: Papers in Honor of John McCarthy. Academic Press (1991)

10. Levesque, H., Reiter, R., Lespérance, Y., Lin, F., Scherl, R.: GOLOG: A logic programming language for dynamic domains. Journal of Logic Programming **31** (1997)

11. McIlraith, S.: Explanatory diagnosis: Conjecturing actions to explain observations. In: Proceedings of the 6th International Conference on Principles of Knowledge Representation and Reasoning. (1998)

12. De Giacomo, G., Levesque, H.: An incremental interpreter for high-level programs with sensing. In Levesque, H.J., Pirri, F., eds.: Logical Foundation for Cognitive Agents: Contributions in Honor of Ray Reiter. Springer (1999)

13. De Giacomo, G., Levesque, H.: Projection using regression and sensors. In: Proceedings of the 16th International Joint Conference on Artificial Intelligence. (1999)

14. McIlraith, S., Scherl, R.: What sensing tells us: Towards a formal theory of testing for dynamical systems. In: Proceedings of the 17th National Conference on Artificial Intelligence. (2000)

15. Pinto, J.: Occurrences and narratives as constraints in the branching structure of the situation calculus. Journal of Logic and Computation **8** (1998)

16. Miller, R., Shanahan, M.: Narratives in the situation calculus. Journal of Logic and Computation **4** (1994)

17. Baral, C., McIlraith, S., Son, T.: Formulating diagnostic problem solving using an action language with narratives and sensing. In: Proceedings of the 7th International Conference on Principles of Knowledge Representation and Reasoning. (2000)

18. Baral, C., Gelfond, M., Provetti, A.: Representing actions: Laws, observations and hypotheses. Journal of Logic Programming **31** (1997)

19. Gelfond, M., Lifschitz, V.: Representing actions in extended logic programming. In: Proceedings of the Joint International Conference and Symposium on Logic Programming. (1992)

20. Gelfond, M., Lifschitz, V.: Representing action and change by logic programs. Journal of Logic Programming **17** (1993)

21. Gelfond, M., Lifschitz, V.: Action languages. Electronic Transactions on Artificial Intelligence **2** (1998)

22. Gelfond, M., Watson, R.: Diagnostics with answer sets: Dealing with unobservable fluents. In: Proceedings of the 3rd International Cognitive Robotics Workshop. (2002)

A Formal Assessment Result for Fluent Calculus Using the Action Description Language $\mathcal{A}_k{}^\star$

Ozan Kahramanoğulları and Michael Thielscher

Department of Computer Science
Dresden University of Technology

Abstract. Systematic approaches like the family of *Action Description Languages* have been designed for the formal assessments of action calculi. We assess the fluent calculus for knowledge and sensing with the help of the recently developed, high-level action language $\mathcal{A}_k$. As the main result, we present a provably correct embedding of this language into fluent calculus, excluding the while loops in the query language. As a spin-off, the action programming language FLUX, which is based on fluent calculus, provides a system for answering queries to $\mathcal{A}_k$ domains. Conversely, the action description language may serve as a high-level surface language for specifying action domains in FLUX.

1 Introduction

An unsatisfactory aspect of research into reasoning about actions is the co-existence of a variety of different approaches, which are difficult to assess and compare. Systematic approaches such as [11] or the Action Description Language $\mathcal{A}$ [2] have been developed to help eliminate this deficiency. Providing a high-level but formal semantics, these approaches are intended to be used to prove correctness of different action calculi for well-defined problem classes. A formal evaluation is particularly important when it comes to modeling complex phenomena such as knowledge and sensing actions.

In this paper, we follow this systematic approach and assess the fluent calculus for knowledge and sensing [12]. To this end, we use the extended Action Description Language $\mathcal{A}_k$ developed in [9] as a minimal extension of the action description language $\mathcal{A}$ [2] to handle non-deterministic actions, knowledge, and sensing. We present a mapping from $\mathcal{A}_k$ domains and queries (without loops) into fluent calculus and, as the main result, prove soundness and completeness wrt. the high-level semantics. Doing so, we show that fluent calculus can express an intricate commonsense phenomena of sensing captured by $\mathcal{A}_k$, namely, the unknown preconditions of a sensing action being learned during sensing. In addition, we have developed a logic programming realization of this translation into the action programming language FLUX—the F̲luent E̲x̲ecutor [13]. Our achievement is three-fold:

$\star$ A preliminary version of this paper has been presented at the 2003 AAAI Spring Symposium on Logical Formalizations of Commonsense Reasoning.

A. Günter et al. (Eds.): KI 2003, LNAI 2821, pp. 209–223, 2003.

1. The result shows that fluent calculus for knowledge and sensing is correct wrt. the problem class defined by $\mathcal{A}_k$.
2. Augmented by the translation program, FLUX provides a system for answering queries to $\mathcal{A}_k$ domains.
3. The syntax of $\mathcal{A}_k$ can serve as a high-level surface language for specifying action domains in FLUX.

The rest of the paper is organized as follows. We begin by recapitulating basic notions and notations of $\mathcal{A}_k$ and fluent calculus, respectively. We then present a provably correct translation of domain descriptions in $\mathcal{A}_k$ into fluent calculus axiomatizations. Thereafter, we extend the translation to queries in $\mathcal{A}_k$ so that query entailment in fluent calculus is sound and complete wrt. the high-level semantics. We conclude with a sketch of the logic programming realization of our translation using FLUX, followed by a brief discussion and outlook.

2   The Action Description Language $\mathcal{A}_k$

The language $\mathcal{A}_k$ [9] is the minimal extension of the action description language $\mathcal{A}$ [2] to handle non-deterministic actions, knowledge, and sensing. Domain descriptions in $\mathcal{A}_k$ allow one to answer queries about what will hold after executing a sequence of actions of that domain description.

2.1   Syntax of the Domain Language

The language of $\mathcal{A}_k$ consists of two non-empty disjoint sets of symbols **F**, **A**. They are called *fluents* and *actions*, respectively. The set **A** consists of two disjoint sets of actions: *Sensing* actions and *non-sensing* actions. Actions will be generically denoted by a, possibly indexed. A *fluent literal* is an element from the set of fluents that is possibly preceded by a $\neg$ sign. Fluents will be denoted by f or g and fluent literals by ℓ, p, or q, all possibly indexed.

There are three kinds of propositions in $\mathcal{A}_k$: A *value proposition* is an expression of the form

$$\textbf{initially } \ell \tag{1}$$

where ℓ denotes a fluent literal. Value propositions describe the initial knowledge the agent has about the world.

Effect propositions are expressions of the form

$$a \textbf{ causes } \ell \textbf{ if } p_1, \ldots, p_n \tag{2}$$

$$a \textbf{ may affect } f \textbf{ if } p_1, \ldots, p_n \tag{3}$$

where a is a non-sensing action, ℓ and $p_1, \ldots, p_n$ $(n \geq 0)$ are fluent literals, and f is a fluent. Intuitively, the first expression above mean that in a state where $p_1, \ldots, p_n$ are true, the execution of a causes ℓ to become true. The second expression says that the truth value of f may indeterminately change if a is executed in a state where $p_1, \ldots, p_n$ are true.

Sensing actions are described by *knowledge laws*:

$$a_s \text{ causes to know } f \text{ if } p_1, \ldots, p_n \tag{4}$$

where a_s is a sensing action, f is a fluent and $p_1, \ldots, p_n$ are preconditions as in (2) and (3). This expression says that if $p_1, \ldots, p_n$ are true, then the execution of a_s causes the agent to realize the current value of f in the world. Sensing actions are not allowed to occur in any effect proposition. A collection of the above propositions and laws is called a *domain description*.

Example Consider a robot that faces the door of the room but does not know if the door is open or not. The robot can execute the sensing action *Look*, which makes it realize the door's being open or closed, provided it is facing the door. The robot can also execute the action *SendId*, which is the action of sending the electronic signal of the door. This action causes the door to open if it is closed, and to close if it is open:

$$D_1 = \begin{cases} r_1 : \textbf{initially } FacingDr \\ r_2 : SendId \textbf{ causes } DrOpn \textbf{ if } \neg DrOpn \\ r_3 : SendId \textbf{ causes } \neg DrOpn \textbf{ if } DrOpn \\ r_4 : Look \textbf{ causes to know } DrOpn \textbf{ if } FacingDr \end{cases}$$

2.2 Semantics of the Domain Language

The semantics of $\mathcal{A}_k$ explains how an agent's knowledge changes according to the effects of the actions defined by a domain description. A *state* is a set of fluents. A set of states represents a *situation*. This way, incomplete descriptions of the world are captured.[1] The knowledge of the robot is represented by a set of (possibly incomplete) worlds (i.e., situations) in which the agent believes that it can be. Such a set is called an *epistemic state*. For example, the epistemic state (a) in Figure 1 represents that the robot knows $FacingDr$ but is ignorant of whether or not $DrOpn$ holds. In contrast, in the epistemic state (b) the robot knows *whether* the door is open: In situation Σ_1 fluent $DrOpn$ is false in all states. Conversely, in situation Σ_2 fluent $DrOpn$ is true in all states. Hence, in all situations of epistemic state (b) the status of $DrOpn$ is known.

A fluent f holds in a state σ iff $f \in \sigma$ (denoted by: $\sigma \models_{\mathcal{A}_k} f$). A fluent f does not hold in a state σ iff $f \notin \sigma$ (denoted by: $\sigma \not\models_{\mathcal{A}_k} f$). The truth of a formula φ made of fluents and the standard logical connectives in a state is recursively defined as usual. A formula φ is true in a situation Σ (denoted by: $\Sigma \models_{\mathcal{A}_k} \varphi$) if the formula is true in every state in Σ; it is false if $\neg \varphi$ is true in every state in Σ. A formula is true in an epistemic state if it is true in every situation in the epistemic state; it is false if its negation is true. A situation is *consistent* if it is non-empty, otherwise it is *inconsistent*. A situation is *complete* if it contains only one state, otherwise it is *incomplete*.

---

[1] Unfortunately, the inventors of $\mathcal{A}_k$ decided to use the term *situation* to denote something very different from what is normally called a situation in action calculi, namely, a sequence of actions. The reader should not be confused by this clash of names.

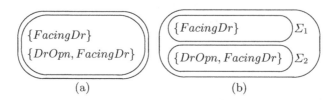

Fig. 1. Two epistemic states.

Interpretations for $\mathcal{A}_k$ are transition functions that map pairs of actions and situations into situations. In order to interpret the effects of the actions at state level, *0-interpretations* map actions a and states σ into sets of states $\Phi_0(a, \sigma)$. Each state in $\Phi_0(a, \sigma)$ represents a possible result of performing a in σ; this is how nondeterministic actions are dealt with.

Definition 1 *A 0-interpretation Φ_0 is a 0-model of a domain description D iff for every state σ and action a, $\Phi_0(a, \sigma)$ is the set that contains every state σ' such that:*

1. *For a fluent f of any effect proposition of the form 'a **causes** f **if** $p_1, \ldots, p_n$ ' in D, the fluent f holds in σ' if the preconditions $p_1, \ldots, p_n$ hold in σ;*
2. *For a fluent literal $\neg f$ of any effect proposition of the form 'a **causes** $\neg f$ **if** $p_1, \ldots, p_n$ ' in D, the fluent f does not hold in σ' if the preconditions $p_1, \ldots, p_n$ hold in σ;*
3. *For a fluent f such that there are no effect propositions of the above types, $f \in \sigma'$ iff $f \in \sigma$ unless there is a non-deterministic effect proposition of the form 'a **may affect** f **if** $p_1, \ldots, p_n$' for which $p_1, \ldots, p_n$ hold in σ.*

According to item 3, if there is no applicable deterministic effect proposition, then f keeps its truth-value unless there is an applicable non-deterministic effect proposition concerning f, in which case f can take on either truth-value in σ', thus giving rise to several possible resulting states.

Knowledge laws are interpreted according to the following definitions. An important aspect of the definition of sensing in $\mathcal{A}_k$ is that the *conditions* under which a fluent can be sensed will become known to the agent if the value of the fluent being sensed is previously unknown. For example, if our robot truly learns whether the door is open by performing the sensing action *Look*, then it also realizes that it is facing the door.

Definition 2 *Let Σ be a consistent situation, f a fluent, and φ a disjunction of conjunctions of fluent literals (preconditions). A consistent situation Σ' is 'f, φ — compatible' with Σ iff the following holds.*

- *If f is either true or false in Σ then $\Sigma' = \Sigma$.*
- *If f is unknown (neither true nor false) in Σ then Σ' must satisfy one of the following conditions:*
    1. *$\Sigma' = \{\sigma \in \Sigma \mid \varphi$ is not true in $\sigma\}$*
    2. *$\Sigma' = \{\sigma \in \Sigma \mid \varphi$ is true in σ, $f \notin \sigma\}$*
    3. *$\Sigma' = \{\sigma \in \Sigma \mid \varphi$ is true in σ, $f \in \sigma\}$*

In other words, if the fluent being sensed is unknown, then the sensing action splits situation Σ into three situations: One in which φ is false, one in which φ is true and f is false, and one in which φ is true and f is true. These situations are the worlds that are considered possible after the execution of the sensing action. Then the set containing all these situations is the epistemic state.

Definition 3 *A fluent f is a* potential sensing effect *of a sensing action a_s in a domain D if there is a knowledge law of the form a_s **causes to know** f **if** φ in D. The knowledge precondition of a fluent f with respect to a sensing action a_s in a domain D is $\varphi_1 \vee \ldots \vee \varphi_n$ where*

$$\{a_s \text{ **causes to know** } f \text{ **if** } \varphi_1, \ldots, a_s \text{ **causes to know** } f \text{ **if** } \varphi_n\}$$

are the knowledge laws with action a_s and potential sensing effect f.

Definition 4 *Given an interpretation Φ of $\mathcal{A}_k$, Φ is a model of domain description D, if and only if it satisfies the following: $\Phi(a, \Sigma) = \emptyset$ if Σ inconsistent, and for any consistent situation Σ:*

1. *There exists a 0-model Φ_0 of D, such that for any non-sensing action a, $\Phi(a, \Sigma) = \bigcup_{\sigma \in \Sigma} \Phi_0(a, \sigma)$.*
2. *For each sensing action a_s, let $f_1, \ldots, f_n$ be the potential sensing effects of a_s and φ_i the knowledge precondition of f_i with respect to a_s. Then $\Phi(a_s, \Sigma)$ must be consistent, and if $n = 0$ then $\Phi(a_s, \Sigma) = \Sigma$ otherwise $\Phi(a_s, \Sigma) = \bigcap_{i \in [1..n]} \Sigma_i$, such that each Σ_i is a situation f_i, φ_i − compatible with Σ.*

Definition 5 *A state is called* initial state *of a domain description D iff for every value proposition of the form 'initially ℓ' in D, ℓ is true in σ. The initial situation Σ_0 of D is the set of all the initial states of D.*

2.3   The Query Language

Queries in $\mathcal{A}_k$ are of the form φ **after** α where φ is a conjunction of fluent literals and α is a plan, which is inductively defined as follows: The empty sequence $[\,]$ is a plan. If a is an action and α is a plan then the concatenation $[a|\alpha]$ is a plan. If φ is a conjunction of fluent literals and α, α_1, and α_2 are plans then $[\text{ **if** } \varphi \text{ **then** } \alpha_1 \mid \alpha]$ and $[\text{ **if** } \varphi \text{ **then** } \alpha_1 \text{ **else** } \alpha_2 \mid \alpha]$ are (conditional) plans.[2]

Definition 6 *The plan evaluation function Γ_Φ of an interpretation Φ is a function such that for any situation Σ:*

1. *$\Gamma_\Phi([\,], \Sigma) = \Sigma$.*
2. *$\Gamma_\Phi([a|\alpha], \Sigma) = \Gamma_\Phi(\alpha, \Phi(a, \Sigma))$ for any action a.*

---

[2] The full query language of $\mathcal{A}_k$ includes plans with loops, which we do not consider in this paper.

3. $\Gamma_\Phi([$ **if** φ **then** $\alpha_1 \mid \alpha], \Sigma) = \Gamma_\Phi(\alpha, \Sigma')$, where

$$\Sigma' = \begin{cases} \Gamma_\Phi(\alpha_1, \Sigma) & \text{if } \varphi \text{ is true in } \Sigma \\ \Sigma & \text{if } \varphi \text{ is false in } \Sigma \\ \emptyset & \text{otherwise} \end{cases}$$

4. $\Gamma_\Phi([$ **if** φ **then** α_1 **else** $\alpha_2 \mid \alpha], \Sigma) = \Gamma_\Phi(\alpha, \Sigma')$, where

$$\Sigma' = \begin{cases} \Gamma_\Phi(\alpha_1, \Sigma) & \text{if } \varphi \text{ is true in } \Sigma \\ \Gamma_\Phi(\alpha_2, \Sigma) & \text{if } \varphi \text{ is false in } \Sigma \\ \emptyset & \text{otherwise} \end{cases}$$

Definition 7 *A query 'φ* **after** *α' is entailed by a domain description D (written as: $D \models_{A_k} \varphi$* **after** *α) iff for every model Φ of D, φ is true in $\Gamma_\Phi(\alpha, \Sigma_0)$ where Σ_0 is the initial situation of D.*

Example (continued) As shown in detail in [9], D_1 entails[3]

$$DrOpn \textbf{ after } [Look, \textbf{if } \neg DrOpn \textbf{ then } [SendId]] \tag{5}$$

3   Fluent Calculus

Fluents and states. A many-sorted predicate logic language, fluent calculus extends the classical situation calculus by the concept of a state. Its signature includes the standard sorts FLUENT and STATE. The intuition is that a state is characterized by the fluents that hold in it. Formally, every term of sort FLUENT also belongs to sort STATE, and the signature contains the two standard functions $\emptyset :$ STATE (denoting the empty state) and $\circ :$ STATE $\times$ STATE $\mapsto$ STATE (written in infix notation and denoting the union of two states). Let $Holds(f, z)$ be an abbreviation for the equational formula $(\exists z') z = f \circ z'$, then the *foundational axioms* of fluent calculus are:[4]

$$(z_1 \circ z_2) \circ z_3 = z_1 \circ (z_2 \circ z_3) \qquad\qquad z_1 \circ z_2 = z_2 \circ z_1$$
$$\neg Holds(f, \emptyset) \qquad\qquad\qquad\qquad Holds(f, g) \supset f = g$$
$$Holds(f, z_1 \circ z_2) \supset Holds(f, z_1) \vee Holds(f, z_2)$$
$$(\forall f)\, (Holds(f, z_1) \equiv Holds(f, z_2)) \supset z_1 = z_2$$
$$(\forall P)(\exists z)(\forall f)\, (Holds(f, z) \equiv P(f))$$

The very last axiom, with P being a second-order predicate variable of sort FLUENT, stipulates the existence of a state for any set of fluents.

Actions and situations. The sorts ACTION and SIT (for situations) are inherited from situation calculus along with the standard functions $S_0 :$ SIT (denoting

---

[3] For the sake of readability, we use the standard Prolog list syntax where $[a_1, \ldots, a_n]$ is $[a_1 \mid \ldots [a_n \mid [\,]]]$.

[4] Below, f, g are FLUENT variables while z_1, z_2, z_3 are STATE variables. Free variables are universally quantified.

the initial situation) and Do : ACTION $\times$ SIT $\mapsto$ SIT (denoting the successor situation of performing an action). In addition, fluent calculus includes the special function $State$: SIT $\mapsto$ STATE to denote the state of the world in a situation. With this, the basic predicate $Holds(f, s)$ of situation calculus is modeled as a mere macro in fluent calculus which stands for $Holds(f, State(s))$. For example, the statement $Holds(FacingDr, S_0)$ means

$$(\exists z)\, State(S_0) = FacingDr \circ z \tag{6}$$

State update axioms. Fluent calculus provides a solution to the fundamental frame problem in classical logic. The key is a purely axiomatic characterization of removal and addition of fluents to states. Let z_1, z_2 be states and f a fluent, then the expression $z_1 - f = z_2$ (denoting removal of f from z_1) is defined as an abbreviation for the formula

$$[z_2 = z_1 \lor z_2 \circ f = z_1] \land \neg Holds(f, z_2)$$

Let $\vartheta^- = f_1 \circ \ldots \circ f_n$ $(n \geq 0)$, then an inductive extension of this macro defines $z_1 - (\vartheta^- \circ f) = z_2$ as $(\exists z)\,(z_1 - \vartheta^- = z \land z - f = z_2)$. Finally, the definition of the *update equation* $z_2 = z_1 - \vartheta^- + \vartheta^+$, where $\vartheta^+ = g_1 \circ \ldots \circ g_m$ $(m \geq 0)$, is given by $(\exists z)\,(z_1 - \vartheta^- = z \land z_2 = z \circ \vartheta^+)$. The frame problem is then solved by *state update axioms*, which use update equations to specify the effects of an action. For example, the following state update axiom specifies the (conditional) effect of $SendId$ for all situations s:[5]

$$\neg Holds(DrOpn, s) \land State(Do(SendId, s)) = State(s) + DrOpn$$
$$\lor\ \ Holds(DrOpn, s) \land State(Do(SendId, s)) = State(s) - DrOpn \tag{7}$$

Representing knowledge. Basic fluent calculus has been extended in [12] by the foundational predicate $KState$: SIT $\times$ STATE to allow for both representing state knowledge and reasoning about actions which involve sensing. An instance $KState(s, z)$ means that, according to the knowledge of the agent, z is a *possible* state in situation s. For example, the initial knowledge of our robot can be specified by this axiom:

$$(\forall z)\,(KState(S_0, z) \equiv Holds(FacingDr, z)) \tag{8}$$

That is to say, all states which satisfy the initial specification are to be considered possible by the robot. In particular, it is unknown whether or not the door in question is open. Generally, a fluent is known to hold in a situation (not to hold, respectively) just in case it is true (false, respectively) in all possible states:

$$Knows(f, s) \overset{\text{def}}{=} (\forall z)\,(KState(s, z) \supset Holds(f, z))$$
$$Knows(\neg f, s) \overset{\text{def}}{=} (\forall z)\,(KState(s, z) \supset \neg Holds(f, z))$$
$$Unknown(f, s) \overset{\text{def}}{=} \neg Knows(f, s) \land \neg Knows(\neg f, s)$$

---

[5] For the sake of simplicity, we ignore the concept of action preconditions in this paper, since actions in $\mathcal{A}_k$ are always executable. Empty positive and negative effects of actions in update equations are simply omitted.

The frame problem for knowledge is solved by axioms that determine the relation between the possible states before and after an action, be it sensing or not. An example of such a *knowledge update axiom* is

$$
\begin{aligned}
KState(Do(Look, s), z) \equiv & \\
(KState(s, z) \wedge & \\
[Holds(FacingDr, s) \supset (Holds(DrOpn, z) \equiv Holds(DrOpn, s))] \wedge & \\
[Unknown(DrOpn, s) \supset (Holds(FacingDr, z) \equiv Holds(FacingDr, s))])
\end{aligned}
\tag{9}
$$

Put in words, if the robot faces the door, then all possible states in the resulting situation agree with the actual situation on whether *DrOpn* holds. Moreover, if it is unknown whether the door is open, then a side-effect of the sensing action is that the robot learns the condition of the conditional effect, that is, whether or not *FacingDr* holds. A pure sensing action, *Look* strictly reduces the set of possible states according to axiom (9). In general, however, knowledge update axioms may define arbitrary changes in the set of possible states, so that knowledge may also get lost after performing the action, e.g., in case of non-deterministic actions.

4   From $\mathcal{A}_k$ Domains to Fluent Calculus

In this section, we present a translation function which maps an $\mathcal{A}_k$ domain description D into a set of fluent calculus axioms $\Pi(D)$. To begin with, the fluents $\{f_1, \ldots, f_n\}$ and actions $\{a_1, \ldots, a_m\}$ in D determine the *unique-name axioms* $\Pi_{una}(D) = \{\bigwedge_{i \neq j} f_i \neq f_j \, , \, \bigwedge_{i \neq j} a_i \neq a_j\}$.

4.1   Translating the Value Propositions

The axioms for the initial state and the initial knowledge state, respectively, are determined by the value propositions: Let

$$
\left\{
\begin{array}{l}
\textbf{initially } f_1, \ldots, \textbf{initially } f_n, \\
\textbf{initially } \neg g_1, \ldots, \textbf{initially } \neg g_m
\end{array}
\right\}
$$

be the set of all the value propositions of D, then the set $\Pi_{init}(D)$ contains these two axioms:

$$
\begin{aligned}
(\exists z)\, (State(S_0) = f_1 \circ \ldots \circ f_n \circ z \wedge & \\
\neg Holds(g_1, z) \wedge \ldots \wedge \neg Holds(g_m, z)) & \\
KState(S_0, z) \equiv Holds(f_1, z) \wedge \ldots \wedge Holds(f_n, z) & \\
\wedge \neg Holds(g_1, z) \wedge \ldots \wedge \neg Holds(g_m, z) &
\end{aligned}
$$

Example (continued) The domain description D_1 contains only one value proposition, which determines the set $\Pi_{init}(D_1)$ as the fluent calculus axioms (6) and (8) mentioned earlier.

4.2   Translating the Effect Propositions

The translation handles each action a of an $\mathcal{A}_k$ domain description separately. Since sensing actions are not allowed to occur in any effect proposition, effect propositions are translated independently from the knowledge laws. As the first step for translating the effect propositions, we define a set which summarizes the effects of a non-sensing action of an $\mathcal{A}_k$ domain description:

Definition 8 *Let D be an $\mathcal{A}_k$ domain description. Let*

$$\left\{ \begin{array}{l} a \textbf{ causes } \ell_1 \textbf{ if } \varphi_1, \; \ldots, \; a \textbf{ causes } \ell_m \textbf{ if } \varphi_m, \\ a \textbf{ may affect } f_1 \textbf{ if } \phi_1, \; \ldots, \; a \textbf{ may affect } f_n \textbf{ if } \phi_n \end{array} \right\}$$

be the set of all effect propositions for the action a in D, where each ℓ_i is a fluent literal, each f_j is a fluent, each φ_i and ϕ_j is a sequence of fluent literals $(1 \leq i \leq m, 1 \leq j \leq n)$. The effect bag of action a (denoted by $\mathcal{B}_a$) is the set

$$\begin{aligned} \mathcal{B}_a = \{ & (\ell_1, S_1, dt), \ldots, (\ell_n, S_m, dt), \\ & (f_1, S_{m+1}, nd), \ldots, (f_m, S_{n+m}, nd) \}, \end{aligned}$$

where $S_i = \{p_1, \ldots, p_k\}$ for each sequence of fluent literals φ_i, and ϕ_j of the form $p_1, \ldots, p_k$. The tags 'dt' and 'nd' signify the deterministic effect and the non-deterministic effect, respectively.

The next step is to consider all combinations of preconditions of a. Given the effect bag $\mathcal{B}_a = \{(\ell_1, S_1, dt), \ldots, (\ell_n, S_n, nd)\}$, let Θ_a be all fluent literals that occur in some precondition S_i $(1 \leq i \leq n)$. Let $\mathcal{P}_a = \{P_1, \ldots, P_n\}$ be the power-set of Θ_a, and for each P_i let $\Theta_a \setminus P_i = \{f_{i,1}, \ldots, f_{i,k}\}$. Then the *condition set* of an action a of an $\mathcal{A}_k$ domain description is the set $\mathcal{C}_a = \{C_1, \ldots, C_n\}$, where for each $i = 1 \ldots n$

$$C_i = P_i \cup \{\neg f_{i,1}, \ldots, \neg f_{i,k}\}$$

The condition set $\mathcal{C}_a$ contains all the combinations of fluent literals under which the execution of the action a has an effect. Then, for each element C_i of $\mathcal{C}_a$, the sets $\mathcal{F}_i^{dt}$ and $\mathcal{F}_i^{nd}$ shall contain the fluents that are affected or that may be affected, respectively, by the execution of action a under the condition C_i:

$$\begin{aligned} \mathcal{F}_i^{dt} &= \{ f_k \mid (f_k, S_k, dt) \in \mathcal{B}_a, S_k \subseteq C_i \} \\ \mathcal{F}_i^{nd} &= \{ f_k \mid (f_k, S_k, nd) \in \mathcal{B}_a, S_k \subseteq C_i \} \end{aligned}$$

The set of fluent literals that represents the deterministic effects of the action a under the condition C_i, viz. $\mathcal{F}_i^{dt}$, can be partitioned into two sets of positive and negative effects. That is, if $\mathcal{F}_i^{dt} = \{f_1, \ldots, f_n, \neg g_1, \ldots, \neg g_m\}$, then

$$\mathcal{F}_i^+ = \{f_1, \ldots, f_n\} \quad \text{and} \quad \mathcal{F}_i^- = \{g_1, \ldots, g_m\}$$

Definition 9 *A pre-update Λ_a for an action a of an $\mathcal{A}_k$ domain description D is the set*

$$\Lambda_a = \{(C_1, \mathcal{F}_1^+, \mathcal{F}_1^-, \mathcal{F}_1^{nd}), \ldots, (C_n, \mathcal{F}_n^+, \mathcal{F}_n^-, \mathcal{F}_n^{nd})\}$$

A pre-update Λ_a of an action a contains all effects of the action a under the different conditions. However, the non-deterministic effects of actions have been treated separately so far. In the next step, we introduce the recursive function μ that allows branching for a non-deterministic effect of an action. That is, given that a fluent f is a non-deterministic effect of an action a under precondition C_i, if f does not occur in the positive effects $\mathcal{F}_n^+$ nor in the negative effects $\mathcal{F}_n^-$, then there will be two possible effects for this action under precondition C_i: One in which f becomes a positive effect and one in which f becomes a negative effect.

Definition 10 *Let* $\mu(C_i, \mathcal{F}_i^+, \mathcal{F}_i^-, \mathcal{F}_i^{nd})$ *be defined as*

$$
\begin{cases}
\{(C_i, \mathcal{F}_i^+, \mathcal{F}_i^-)\} \\
\qquad \text{if} \quad \mathcal{F}_i^{nd} = \emptyset \\
\mu((C_i, \mathcal{F}_i^+, \mathcal{F}_i^-, \mathcal{F}_i^{nd} \setminus \{f\})) \\
\qquad \text{if} \quad f \in \mathcal{F}_i^{nd}, \text{ and either } f \in \mathcal{F}_i^+ \text{ or } f \in \mathcal{F}_i^-) \\
\mu((C_i, \mathcal{F}_i^+ \cup \{f\}, \mathcal{F}_i^-, \mathcal{F}_i^{nd} \setminus \{f\})) \\
\quad \cup \mu((C_i, \mathcal{F}_i^+, \mathcal{F}_i^- \cup \{f\}, \mathcal{F}_i^{nd} \setminus \{f\})) \\
\qquad \text{if} \quad f \in \mathcal{F}_i^{nd}, \ f \notin \mathcal{F}_i^+, \text{ and } f \notin \mathcal{F}_i^-
\end{cases}
$$

Then, given a pre-update $\Lambda_a = \{\gamma_1, \ldots, \gamma_n\}$, *an* update *for an action* a *is the set* $\Omega_a = \bigcup_{i=1}^n \mu(\gamma_i)$.

An update Ω_a of a non-sensing action a of an $\mathcal{A}_k$ domain description contains all the information to construct the fluent calculus state update and knowledge update axioms for this action. Before, we proceed with constructing these axioms from an update Ω_a, below we illustrate the translation up to this point on the domain description D_1.

Example (continued) The effect bag $\mathcal{B}_{SendId}$ is

$$\{(DrOpn, \{\neg DrOpn\}, dt), (\neg DrOpn, \{DrOpn\}, dt)\}$$

Then $\Theta_{SendId} = \{DrOpn\}$, which is the set of all the fluents that appear in the conditions of the effect propositions for action $SendId$; hence, $\mathcal{P}_{SendId} = \{\{\}, \{DrOpn\}\}$. From this we obtain the *condition set*

$$\mathcal{C}_{SendId} = \{\{\neg DrOpn\}, \{DrOpn\}\}$$

After getting the *pre-update*

$$\Lambda_{SendId} = \{(\{\neg DrOpn\}, \{DrOpn\}, \{\}, \{\}), (\{DrOpn\}, \{\}, \{DrOpn\}, \{\})\}$$

according to Definition 9, plugging all the elements of it into function μ, and taking their union, we obtain the *update* Ω_{SendId} according to Definition 10:

$$\Omega_{SendId} = \{(\{\neg DrOpn\}, \{DrOpn\}, \{\}), \\ (\{DrOpn\}, \{\}, \{DrOpn\})\}. \tag{10}$$

From Ω_a to State and Knowledge Update Axioms. In $\mathcal{A}_k$ it is not possible to differentiate between the actual effects of actions and what an agent knows of the effects of an action. Hence, in our translation state update axioms and knowledge update axioms coincide as far as non-sensing actions are concerned.

Let Ω_a be the update of a non-sensing action a of an $\mathcal{A}_k$ domain description D. The translation algorithm generates the state update axiom and the knowledge update axiom of action a from the update Ω_a as follows.

Let $\Omega_a = \{(C_1, \mathcal{F}_1^+, \mathcal{F}_1^-), \ldots, (C_n, \mathcal{F}_n^+, \mathcal{F}_n^-)\}$, where for each $i = 1 \ldots n$,

$$
\begin{aligned}
C_i &= \{p_{i,1}, \ldots, p_{i,m_i}\} \\
\mathcal{F}_i^+ &= \{f_{i,1}, \ldots, f_{i,k_i}\} \\
\mathcal{F}_i^- &= \{g_{i,1}, \ldots, g_{i,l_i}\}
\end{aligned}
$$

These are the resulting state and knowledge update axioms for action a in $\Pi_{update}(D)$:

$$
\begin{aligned}
&HOLDS(p_{1,1} \wedge \ldots \wedge p_{1,m_1}, s) \wedge \\
&\quad State(Do(a,s)) = (State(s) - g_{1,1} \circ \ldots \circ g_{1,l_1}) \\
&\hspace{6em} + f_{1,1} \circ \ldots \circ f_{1,k_1} \\
&\vee \ldots \vee \\
&HOLDS(p_{n,1} \wedge \ldots \wedge p_{n,m_n}, s) \wedge \\
&\quad State(Do(a,s)) = (State(s) - g_{n,1} \circ \ldots \circ g_{n,l_n}) \\
&\hspace{6em} + f_{n,1} \circ \ldots \circ f_{n,k_n}
\end{aligned}
$$

$$
\begin{aligned}
&KState(Do(a,s),z) \equiv (\exists z')(KState(s,z') \wedge \\
&\quad [\, HOLDS(p_{1,1} \wedge \ldots \wedge p_{1,m_1}, z') \wedge \\
&\quad\quad z = (z' - g_{1,1} \circ \ldots \circ g_{1,l_1}) + f_{1,1} \circ \ldots \circ f_{1,k_1} \\
&\quad \vee \ldots \vee \\
&\quad Holds(p_{n,1} \wedge \ldots \wedge p_{n,m_n}, z') \wedge \\
&\quad\quad z = (z' - g_{n,1} \circ \ldots \circ g_{n,l_n}) + f_{n,1} \circ \ldots \circ f_{n,k_n} \,]))
\end{aligned}
$$

where $HOLDS(\varphi, s)$ and $HOLDS(\varphi, z)$, respectively, is obtained from φ by substituting each occurrence of a fluent f by $Holds(f, s)$ and $Holds(f, z)$, respectively.

Example (continued) Given the update Ω_{SendId} of equation (10), as the state update axiom for $SendId$ we obtain formula (7) mentioned earlier, while the knowledge update axiom is

$$
\begin{aligned}
&KState(Do(SendId, s), z) \equiv (\exists z')(KState(s, z') \wedge \\
&\quad [\, \neg Holds(DrOpn, z') \wedge z = z' + DrOpn \vee \\
&\quad Holds(DrOpn, z') \wedge z = z' - DrOpn \,])
\end{aligned}
$$

4.3   Translating the Knowledge Laws

We begin the translation of the knowledge laws by defining a set which contains all the effects of a sensing action.

Definition 11 *Let D be an $\mathcal{A}_k$ domain description. Let*

$$
\left\{
\begin{array}{l}
a \text{ causes to know} f_1 \text{ if } P_{1,1} \\
\quad\vdots \\
a \text{ causes to know} f_1 \text{ if } P_{1,n_1} \\
\quad\vdots \\
a \text{ causes to know } f_m \text{ if } P_{m,1} \\
\quad\vdots \\
a \text{ causes to know } f_m \text{ if } P_{m,n_m}
\end{array}
\right\}
$$

be the set of all the knowledge laws for the sensing action a in D, where each f_i is a fluent, and each $P_{i,j}$ is sequence of fluent literals $(1 \leq i \leq m; 1 \leq j \leq n_i)$. The knowledge bag *of sensing action a (denoted by $\mathcal{K}_a$) is the set*

$$
\mathcal{K}_a = \{(f_1, \varphi_1), \dots, (f_m, \varphi_m)\} \tag{11}
$$

where for each $i = 1 \dots m$, $\varphi_i = C_{i,1} \vee \dots \vee C_{i,n_i}$ such that for each $j = 1 \dots n_i$, $C_{i,j}$ is the conjunction of the fluent literals that appear in $P_{i,j}$.

From $\mathcal{K}_a$ to Update Axioms. Since sensing does not affect the world state, the state update axiom of a sensing action a is independent of the knowledge bag of this action:

$$
(\forall s)\, State(Do(a, s)) = State(s)
$$

The knowledge update axiom for sensing action a is determined by knowledge bag $\mathcal{K}_a = \{(f_1, \varphi_1), \dots, (f_m, \varphi_m)\}$ as follows:

$$
\begin{aligned}
&(\forall s)(\forall z)(KState(Do(a, s), z) \equiv \\
&\qquad (KState(s, z) \wedge \\
&[HOLDS(\varphi_1, s) \supset (Holds(f_1, z) \equiv Holds(f_1, s))] \wedge \\
&[Unknown(f_1, s) \supset \\
&\qquad (HOLDS(\varphi_1, z) \equiv HOLDS(\varphi_1, s))] \\
&\wedge \dots \wedge \\
&[HOLDS(\varphi_m, s) \supset (Holds(f_m, z) \equiv Holds(f_m, s))] \wedge \\
&[Unknown(f_m, s) \supset \\
&\qquad (HOLDS(\varphi_m, z) \equiv HOLDS(\varphi_m, s))]))
\end{aligned}
$$

A side-effect of sensing in $\mathcal{A}_k$ is that the conditions of a sensing action become known to the agent, if the potential sensing effect of this action is previously unknown. To reflect this, we have defined the knowledge update axiom in such a way that a sensing action's precondition φ of a potential sensing effect f will be known in the successor situation if f is previously unknown.

Example (continued) The knowledge bag of the sensing action *Look* of D_1 is $\mathcal{K}_{Look} = \{ (DrOpn, FacingDr)\}$. Then as the state and knowledge update axiom for *Look* we obtain, respectively, $(\forall s)\, State(Do(Look, s)) = State(s)$ and axiom (9) mentioned earlier.

5   Query Translation

The query translation function Π_Q translates an $\mathcal{A}_k$ query into a fluent calculus formula. The translation uses the recursive function τ that maps any $\mathcal{A}_k$ plan into a formula in fluent calculus.

Definition 12 *Let* α, α_1, α_2 *be* $\mathcal{A}_k$ *plans, a be an action, and ℓ be a fluent literal. The plan translation function τ is a function such that for any fluent calculus situation constant S_i, where S_{Final} denotes the final situation reached after executing the plan,*[6]

$$\tau([\,], S_i) \stackrel{\text{def}}{=} [\ S_i = S_{Final}\ ]$$

$$\tau([a|\alpha], S_i) \stackrel{\text{def}}{=} [\ S_{i+1} = Do(a, S_i)\ ]\ \wedge\ \tau(\alpha, S_{i+1})$$

$$\tau([\mathbf{if}\ \ell\ \mathbf{then}\ \alpha_1|\alpha], S_i) \stackrel{\text{def}}{=}$$
$$[\,(Knows(\ell, S_i) \supset \tau(\alpha_1; \alpha, S_i))\ \wedge$$
$$(Knows(\neg\ell, S_i) \supset \tau(\alpha, S_i))\,]$$

$$\tau([\mathbf{if}\ \ell\ \mathbf{then}\ \alpha_1\ \mathbf{else}\ \alpha_2|\alpha], S_i) \stackrel{\text{def}}{=}$$
$$[\,(Knows(\ell, S_i) \supset \tau(\alpha_1; \alpha, S_i))\ \wedge$$
$$(Knows(\neg\ell, S_i) \supset \tau(\alpha_2; \alpha, S_i))\,]$$

Given an $\mathcal{A}_k$ *query of the form 'ℓ after α',*

$$\Pi_Q(\ell\ \mathbf{after}\ \alpha) \stackrel{\text{def}}{=} \tau(\alpha, S_0) \supset Knows(\ell, S_{Final})$$

Example (continued) Query (5) is translated as follows:

$$\tau([Look, \mathbf{if}\ldots], S_0)$$

$$\equiv S_1 = Do(Look, S_0)\ \wedge$$
$$\tau([\mathbf{if}\ \neg DrOpn\ \mathbf{then}\ [SendId]], S_1)$$

$$\equiv S_1 = Do(Look, S_0)\ \wedge$$
$$[\ Knows(\neg DrOpn, S_1) \supset \tau([SendId], S_1)]\ \wedge$$
$$[Knows(\neg\neg DrOpn, S_1) \supset \tau([\,], S_1)]$$

$$\equiv S_1 = Do(Look, S_0)\ \wedge$$
$$[\ Knows(\neg DrOpn, S_1) \supset S_2 = Do(SendId, S_1)\ \wedge$$
$$S_2 = S_{Final}]$$
$$\wedge\ [Knows(DrOpn, S_1) \supset S_1 = S_{Final}]$$

Let Δ be the resulting formula, then the translated query is

$$\Delta \supset Knows(DrOpn, S_{Final})$$

---

[6] Below, $\alpha_1; \alpha_2$ is a macro denoting the concatenation of two plans α_1 and α_2.

which can be shown to be a logical consequence of the fluent calculus axiomatization $\Pi(D_1)$ for our running example domain.

The following main result of our work says that fluent calculus is sound and complete wrt. the semantics of $\mathcal{A}_k$.

Theorem 1 *Given a consistent $\mathcal{A}_k$ domain description D, a plan α, and a fluent literal ℓ. Then*

$$D \models_{\mathcal{A}_k} \ell \text{ after } \alpha \quad \text{iff} \quad \Pi(D) \models \Pi_Q(\ell \text{ after } \alpha)$$

Proof (sketch) The 0-models coincide with the models for the translated update axioms for non-sensing actions, and the epistemic state resulting from performing a single sensing action coincides with the models for the successor knowledge state determined by the translated knowledge update axioms. By induction, this equivalence can be generalized to sequences of actions and complex plans.

Space restrictions do not permit us to give the complete proof of this theorem; we refer to [5].

6   Query Answering in $\mathcal{A}_k$ Using FLUX

The programming language FLUX is a recent implementation of fluent calculus based on Constraint Logic Programming [13]. Its distinguishing feature is to support incomplete states, whereby negative and disjunctive information is encoded by constraints. The kernel of FLUX, which includes a declarative constraint solver, has been formally verified against the foundational axioms of fluent calculus [14]. We have extended this kernel by an implementation of our translation function, mapping an $\mathcal{A}_k$ domain descriptions into a FLUX program and an $\mathcal{A}_k$ query into a FLUX query. As a result, FLUX provides a query answering mechanism for the Action Description Language $\mathcal{A}_k$. A complementary use of the translation function can be to employ $\mathcal{A}_k$ as a high-level surface language for specifying action domains in FLUX when this system is used as a high-level programming method for cognitive agents that reason about their actions and plan [13].

Both the translation function as well as the FLUX kernel along with some examples are available at `www.cl.inf.tu-dresden.de/~ozan/ papers.html`.

7   Discussion

In being correct with respect to full $\mathcal{A}_k$ except for queries including loops, fluent calculus, as well as FLUX, is more expressive than most existing systems for reasoning about actions and planning with sensing actions, such as [4,1,8,3]. These approaches use restricted notions of incomplete states, which do not allow for handling any kind of disjunctive information or reasoning about cases as required, for example, if an action is described in $\mathcal{A}_k$ to have conditional effects depending on whether some unknown fluent is true or false, but where a query can be proved under both conditional effects [1]. A general solution to the frame problem for knowledge is realized in the systems [6,10], both of which are based on GOLOG [7]. However, an important restriction of these systems compared to the underlying situation calculus, is that they do not provide ways of actually deriving whether something is known after a sequence of actions.

Future work will include to extend our translation to cover loops in $\mathcal{A}_k$ queries. While a loop can be easily formalized by a second-order closure axiom in fluent calculus, it remains an open question how the effect of a loop can be actually inferred in a logic programming system like FLUX.[7]

References

1. C. Baral and T. Son. Approximate reasoning about actions in presence of sensing and incomplete information. In J. Maluszynski, ed., *Proc. of ILPS*, 387–401, 1997. MIT Press.
2. M. Gelfond and V. Lifschitz. Representing action and change by logic programs. *J. of Log. Prog.*, 17:301–321, 1993.
3. Giuseppe De Giacomo, Luca Iocchi, Daniele Nardi, and Riccardo Rosati. Planning with sensing for a mobile robot. In *Proc. of ECP*, vol. 1348 of *LNAI*, 158–170. Springer 1997.
4. K. Golden and D. Weld. Representing sensing actions: The middle ground revisited. In L. C. Aiello, J. Doyle, and S. Shapiro, ed.s, *Proc. of KR*, 174–185, 1996.
5. O. Kahramanoğulları. A translation from the action description language $\mathcal{A}_k$ to the fluent calculus. Master's thesis, Department of Computer Science, Dresden University of Technology, 2002. URL: www.cl.inf.tu-dresden.de/ozan/papers.html.
6. G. Lakemeyer. On sensing and off-line interpreting GOLOG. In H. Levesque and F. Pirri, ed.s, *Logical Foundations for Cognitive Agents*, 173–189. Springer, 1999.
7. H. Levesque, R. Reiter, Y. Lespérance, F. Lin, and R. Scherl. GOLOG: A logic programming language for dynamic domains. *J. of Log. Prog.*, 31(1–3):59–83, 1997.
8. J. Lobo. COPLAS: A conditional planner with sensing actions. In *Cognitive Robotics*, vol. FS–98–02 of *AAAI Fall Symposia*, 109–116. AAAI Press 1998.
9. J. Lobo, G. Mendez, and S. Taylor. Knowledge and the action description language $\mathcal{A}$. *Theory and Practise of Log. Prog.*, 1(2):129–184, 2001.
10. R. Reiter. On knowledge-based programming with sensing in the situation calculus. *ACM Transactions on Computational Logic*, 2(4):433–457, 2001.
11. E. Sandewall. *Features and Fluents. The Representation of Knowledge about Dynamical Systems*. Oxford University Press, 1994.
12. M. Thielscher. Representing the knowledge of a robot. In A. Cohn, F. Giunchiglia, and B. Selman, ed.s, *Proc. of KR*, 109–120, 2000. Morgan Kaufmann.
13. M. Thielscher. Programming of reasoning and planning agents with FLUX. In D. Fensel, D. McGuinness, and M.-A. Williams, ed.s, *Proc. of KR*, 435–446, 2002. Morgan Kaufmann.
14. M. Thielscher. Reasoning about actions with CHRs and finite domain constraints. In P. Stuckey, ed., *Proc. of ICLP*, vol. 2401 of *LNCS*, 70–84, 2002. Springer.

---

[7] The concept of loops in GOLOG is too restricted to this end, because GOLOG supports nondeterministic choice of actions but not the specification of actions that have nondeterministic effects, as in $\mathcal{A}_k$.

Computing Minimum-Cardinality Diagnoses Using OBDDs

Pietro Torasso and Gianluca Torta

Dipartimento di Informatica, Università di Torino
Torino (Italy)
{torasso, torta}@di.unito.it

Abstract. The paper addresses the problem of solving diagnostic problems by exploiting OBDDs (Ordered Binary Decision Diagrams) as a way for compactly representing the set of alternative diagnoses. In the MBD (Model Based Diagnosis) community it is indeed well known that the number of diagnoses can be exponential in the system size even when restricted to preferred diagnoses (e.g. minimal diagnoses). In particular, the paper presents methods and heuristics for efficiently encoding the domain theory of the system model in terms of an OBDD. Such heuristics suggest suitable ordering of the OBDD variables which prevents the explosion of the OBDD size for some classes of domain theories. Moreover, we describe how to solve specific diagnostic problems represented as OBDDs and report some results on the computational complexity of such process. Finally, we introduce a mechanism for extracting diagnoses with the minimum number of faults from the OBDD which represents the entire space of diagnoses. Experimental results are collected and reported on a model representing a simplified propulsion subsystem of a spacecraft.[1]

1 Introduction

Model-based reasoning has become the most relevant approach to diagnosis in the past 15 years. A problem recognized very early in the reaserch on model-based diagnosis concerns the potential huge number of alternative diagnoses and consequently the need of compactly representing them ([8]); in general, indeed, the number of solutions to a diagnostic problem can be exponential in the size of the problem (i.e. number of system components) even if one is only interested in representing minimal diagnoses w.r.t. set inclusion.

Many works have aimed at addressing this problem. Some of them have proposed representations that exploit properties of the system structure or behavior (e.g. *kernel diagnoses* ([8]), *consequences* ([7]), *scenarios* ([16])) in order to efficiently compute and encode diagnoses for restricted but practically relevant classes of systems.

---

[1] This research has been partially funded by ASI under project Diagnostic Systems for Autonomous Robots in Space and by MIUR under project RoboCare. We would also like to acknowledge the contribution of Stefano Ravizza in the implementation and experimental evaluation of the diagnostic system

A. Günter et al. (Eds.): KI 2003, LNAI 2821, pp. 224–238, 2003.

Others have aimed at exploiting hierarchical information on the system model (e.g. [14], [10]) or the limited observability of the system (e.g. [17], [22]) and produce abstract diagnoses that express the same diagnostic information as many more detailed-level diagnoses.

As the model-based diagnosis field has evolved, and the problem of diagnosing systems evolving over time has started to be addressed, a new dimension (i.e. time) has been added to the space of diagnoses, leading to an even more dramatic explosion of its size (e.g. [9], [13]).

Since a long-time tradition exists in representing, simulating and analyzing dynamic systems by modeling them as *discrete event systems* (DES), some MBD researchers have recently started to transfer representations, techniques and tools developed in the DES area (e.g. simulation, model-checking) to tasks as assessment of system diagnosability and computation of diagnoses (e.g. [6], [5]) of dynamic systems.

In this paper we explore the use of OBDDs (Ordered Binary Decision Diagrams) for the representation and computation of diagnoses of static systems. OBDDs (see [3]) are a well-known mathematical tool used in several areas of computing (including AI) for efficiently representing large state spaces and perform model-checking (e.g. [1], [12], [20]) [2].

A first proposal for applying OBDDs to diagnosis is reported in [21] where the authors sketch how to code a set of automata representing a discrete system into an OBDD. In our work we aim at addressing some relevant topics beside the issue of encoding a system model as an OBDD. In particular:

- how to choose a suitable ordering of the variables [3]
- how to solve specific diagnostic problems (by considering also the computational complexity of diagnosis)
- how to extract individual alternative diagnoses starting from the OBDD representing them (with particular attention to the extraction of preferred diagnoses)

In the present paper we investigate these issues in the context of the diagnosis of static systems [4]. As a next step, in future work we will look at extending our results to *time-varying systems* ([2]), in which components behavioral modes can change spontaneously across time, while the dynamic behavior of the system itself is not taken into account. In order to lay the ground for such extension, definitions in section 2 are already formulated in terms of time-varying systems.

---

[2] Binary logical operations can be performed on OBDDs in $O(sz1 \times sz2)$ where $sz1$, $sz2$ are the sizes of the two operand OBDDs; moreover the *restrict* operator substitutes a constant to a variable in time linear on the size of the OBDD. See [3] for more details

[3] Variable ordering choice is a preminent issue when encoding a logical theory as an OBDD (in [3], e.g., Bryant shows a theory whose OBDD encoding size varies from linear to exponential just because of different choices in variable ordering)

[4] Note that this covers a significant number of real-world problems, since in many cases dynamic systems can be diagnosed using state-based techniques, e.g. [19]

The paper is structured as follows. In section 2 we give formal definitions of the main concepts on which our work is based and present, as a motivating example, the model of a spacecraft propulsion system that will be used throughout the paper to clarify and validate our results.

In section 3 we show how to efficiently encode a system description using OBDDs, how diagnostic problems can be solved from this representation and how computationally complex the diagnostic process turns out to be. In section 4 we deal with extraction of diagnoses from their OBDD encoding, with particular focus on extracting only diagnoses which are preferred according to minimum fault-cardinality criterion.

Finally, in section 5 we analyze related work, discuss future directions and make some concluding remarks.

2 Diagnosis of Time-Varying Systems

2.1 Definition of Diagnosis

We represent a system through a model consisting of a set of variables, a domain theory expressed as a set of logical formulas and a set of transition graphs which model the time-varying dimension of components.

Definition 1. *A* Time-Varying System Description *(TSD) is a 3-tuple* $\langle \mathcal{SV}, DT, MTG \rangle$ *where:*

- *$\mathcal{SV}$ is a set of discrete system variables partitioned in the following sorts: CXT (system inputs and commands), $COMPS$ (components), $STATES$ (endogenous variables); we denote with OBS the subset of variables in $STATES$ that are observable; $DOM(V)$ is the finite domain of variable $V \in \mathcal{SV}$. In particular, for each $C \in COMPS$, $DOM(C)$ contains a set of behavioral modes, one corresponding to the nominal mode (OK) and the others to faulty behaviors*
- *DT (Domain Theory) is an acyclic set of Horn clauses defined over $\mathcal{SV}$ representing the behavior of the system (under normal and abnormal conditions); variables in $COMPS$ and CXT never appear in the head of a clause*
- *MTG is a set of directed transition graphs $mtg(C)$ associated to component variables (i.e. $C \in COMPS$). The nodes of $mtg(C)$ represent the behavioral modes of C and an arc between node bm_i and node bm_j means that the system can spontaneously move from behavioral mode bm_i to bm_j; arcs can be labeled with the quantitative or qualitative probability of the transition to happen in any given instant*

If we are not interested in the time-varying behavior of a system but just in its behavior in a single instant, it is sufficient to consider the System Description *$SD = \langle \mathcal{SV}, DT \rangle$.*

Given a model of the system, we are interested in describing (temporal) diagnostic problems over it. This is formalized in the following definition.

Definition 2. *A temporal diagnostic problem is a 3-tuple* $TDP = \langle TSD,$ **OBS, CXT**$\rangle$ *where* TSD *is the Time-Varying System Description,* **OBS** *is a list* (**OBS**$_0, \ldots,$ **OBS**$_\mathbf{k}$) *of instantiations of* OBS *variables at times* $0, \ldots, k$ *and* **CXT** *is a list* (**CXT**$_0, \ldots,$ **CXT**$_\mathbf{k}$) *of instantiations of* CXT *variables at times* $0, \ldots, k$

Often it is useful to consider a temporal diagnostic problem TDP as a sequence of *atemporal diagnostic problems* $DP_i = \langle SD, \mathbf{OBS_i}, \mathbf{CXT_i} \rangle$, compute their solution sets SOL_i and then compose such solution sets into a set of temporal solutions consistent with MTG (see e.g. [4]).
In the following two definitions, we first introduce the notion of atemporal diagnosis (i.e. solution to an atemporal diagnostic problem) and then extend it to the notion of temporal diagnosis.

Definition 3. *Let* $DP = \langle SD, \mathbf{OBS}, \mathbf{CXT} \rangle$ *be an atemporal diagnostic problem. We say that an instantiation* $D = \{C_1(bm_1), \ldots, C_n(bm_n)\}$ *of* $COMPS$ *is a* consistency-based diagnosis *for* DP *iff:*
$$DT \cup \mathbf{CXT} \cup \mathbf{OBS} \cup D \not\vdash \perp$$

Definition 4. *Let* $TDP = \langle TSD, \mathbf{OBS}, \mathbf{CXT} \rangle$ *be a temporal diagnostic problem and* $DP_0, \ldots, DP_k$ *the associated atemporal diagnostic problems. We say that a list* $(D_0, \ldots, D_k)$ *of instantiations of* $COMPS$ *is a* consistency-based temporal diagnosis *for* TDP *iff:*

- D_i *is an atemporal diagnosis for* DP_i
- *if* $C_j(bm_j) \in D_i$ *and* $C_j(bm'_j) \in D_{i+1}$ *then, in MTG, there is an arc directed from* bm_j *to* bm'_j

2.2 A Motivating Example

Figure 1 shows an idealized schematic of the main engine subsystem of the Cassini spacecraft (adapted from [13]); this example system was used by NASA to validate the performance of Livingstone, the MIR (Mode Identification and Reconfiguration) module of the core autonomy architecture of the Remote Agent experiment ([15]). The system consists of an oxidizer tank, a fuel tank, a set of valves and two engines plus pipes and pipe junctions. The system description variables $\mathcal{SV}$ consist in the following sets (we do not model pipes):

- $COMPS = V_{11}, \ldots, V_{28}$ (valves), E_1, E_2 (engines), T_1 (oxydizer tank), T_2 (fuel tank)
  $DOM(V_{ij}) = ok, so$ (stuck open), sc (stuck closed)
  $DOM(E_i) = ok, br$ (broken)
  $DOM(T_i) = full, empty$
- $CXT = CMD_{11}, \ldots, CMD_{28}$ (commands issued to valves)
  $DOM(CMD_{ij}) = open, close$

- $STATES = IV_{11}, \ldots, IV_{28}$ (input flows to valves), $OV_{11}, \ldots, OV_{28}$ (output flows from valves), $IJL_{11}, \ldots, IJL_{22}, IJR_{11}, \ldots, IJR_{22}$ (left and right input flows to junctions), $OJ_{11}, \ldots, OJ_{22}$ (output flow from junctions), OT_1, OT_2 (output flows from tanks), $IEL_1, IEL_2, IER_1, IER_2$ (left and right input flows to engines), OE_1, OE_2 (output thrust from engines)
  $DOM(IV_{ij}) = DOM(OV_{ij}) = DOM(IJL_{ij}) = DOM(IJR_{ij}) = DOM(OJ_{ij}) = DOM(OT_i) = DOM(IEL_i) = DOM(IER_i) = f$ (flow), nf (noflow)
  $DOM(OE_i) = thrust, nothrust$
- $OBS = OE_1, OE_2, OT_1, OT_2$

In table 1 we report portions of the Domain Theory representing the behavior of valves, joints, tanks and engines. The group of formulas describing valves behavior shows that the output flow OV_{ij} of valve V_{ij} depends, beside from the behavioral mode of V_{ij} itself, from the input flow IV_{ij} and from the current command CMD_{ij} issued to the valve.

Joints are not explicitly modeled as components. On the contrary, to each joint is associated a set of formulas relating the two input flows (IJL_{ij}, IJR_{ij}) to the output flow (OJ_{ij}). Finally, the thrust OE_i produced by an engine E_i is influenced by the behavioral mode of E_i and by the input flows of oxidizer (IEL_i) and fuel (IER_i).

Table 2 shows the $mtgs$ associated to the system components [5]. For instance, the valves mtg allows the ok mode to either change to so and sc or persist.

Let's now consider the system status depicted in figure 1, where black valves are closed (i.e. $CMD_{ij}(close)$) and white ones are open (i.e. $CMD_{ij}(open)$). Moreover suppose that the tanks are both full $(OT_1(f), OT_2(f))$ and that thrust is not observed at either engine $(OE_1(nothrust), OE_2(nothrust))$. We denote this diagnostic case as **DC1** for later reference.

It is easy to see that 7 single fault diagnoses are possible, respectively involving a fault in $V_{11}, V_{12}, V_{14}, V_{16}, V_{17}, V_{18}$ and E_1. Many more diagnoses exist, obviously, with two or more faults, but we regard them as less likely.

The number of diagnoses grows much larger if we consider that open paths also exist from the tanks to E2 (e.g. $V_{21}, V_{22}, V_{24}, V_{26}, V_{27}, V_{28}$ are all open), but still we observe no thrust at either engine (diagnostic case **DC2**). In this case the number of minimum-fault diagnoses (all involving two faults) is $7 \times 7 = 49$. Just from this simple example , it is apparent the need for representing in a compact way large numbers of alternative diagnoses.

3   Solving Atemporal Diagnostic Problems Using OBDDs

In this section we describe how atemporal diagnostic problems can be encoded and then solved using OBDDs. Some preliminary observations on how the presented techniques could be extended to deal with time-varying systems are given in section 5.

---

[5] Transitions may be further annotated with quantitative/qualitative probabilities of being taken at any given instant

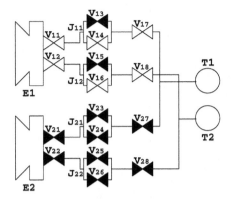

Fig. 1. Propulsion system

3.1 System Description Encoding

In order to use OBDDs for diagnostic problem solving, we first need to encode the System Model SD (definition 1) as an OBDD (that we will denote as $OBDD_{SD}$). Since OBDDs handle only propositional variables (whose value is either *true* or *false*), a generic variable $V \in \mathcal{SV}$ with domain $DOM(V) = \{val_1, \ldots, val_k\}$ is mapped to the set of boolean variables $\{V_{val_1}, \ldots, V_{val_k}\}$ [6]. Moreover, we need to express that, at any given time point, our multi-valued variable V must assume exactly one value; this can be enforced by a *completeness* formula (i.e. $V_{val_1} \vee \ldots \vee V_{val_k}$) and a set of *mutual-exclusion* formulas (i.e. $\sim (V_{val_i} \wedge V_{val_j}) \ \forall i \neq j$). These are propositional formulas that can be directly added to $OBDD_{SD}$ [7].

The formulas in DT need to be rewritten by substituting the instances of multi-valued variables with the associated propositional variables; thus, formula: $N1(val_1) \wedge \ldots \wedge Nk(val_k) \Rightarrow M(val)$ becomes $N1_{val_1} \wedge \ldots \wedge Nk_{val_k} \Rightarrow M_{val}$. Once they have been rewritten in this form, they can be directly added to $OBDD_{SD}$.

3.2 Variables Ordering for Causal Networks

As noted in the introduction, one major concern in encoding any propositional theory as an OBDD regards the choice of variables ordering ([3]). In order to present some heuristics we have developed to deal with this issue, we first introduce the notion of causal networks associated to system descriptions.

Definition 5. *Given $SD = \langle \mathcal{SV}, DT \rangle$ the associated* system causal network *$\mathcal{N}$ is a DAG whose nodes are in $\mathcal{SV}$ representing the causal structure of the system;*

---

[6] In general, we denote with $\mathcal{S}_B$ the set of boolean variables representing the set $\mathcal{S}$ of multi-valued variables

[7] Adding a formula to $OBDD_{SD}$ means to build an OBDD for the formula and intersecting it with $OBDD_{SD}$; clearly, $OBDD_{SD}$ is initialized to *true*

Table 1. Qualitative model of valves (V_{ij}), joints (J_{ij}), tanks (T_i) and engines (E_i)

$$V_{ij}(ok) \wedge IV_{ij}(f) \wedge CMD_{ij}(open) \Rightarrow OV_{ij}(f)$$
$$V_{ij}(ok) \wedge IV_{ij}(f) \wedge CMD_{ij}(close) \Rightarrow OV_{ij}(nf)$$
$$V_{ij}(ok) \wedge IV_{ij}(nf) \wedge CMD_{ij}(open) \Rightarrow OV_{ij}(nf)$$
$$V_{ij}(ok) \wedge IV_{ij}(nf) \wedge CMD_{ij}(close) \Rightarrow OV_{ij}(nf)$$
$$V_{ij}(so) \wedge IV_{ij}(f) \wedge CMD_{ij}(open) \Rightarrow OV_{ij}(f)$$
$$V_{ij}(so) \wedge IV_{ij}(f) \wedge CMD_{ij}(close) \Rightarrow OV_{ij}(f)$$
$$V_{ij}(so) \wedge IV_{ij}(nf) \wedge CMD_{ij}(open) \Rightarrow OV_{ij}(nf)$$
$$V_{ij}(so) \wedge IV_{ij}(nf) \wedge CMD_{ij}(close) \Rightarrow OV_{ij}(nf)$$
$$V_{ij}(sc) \wedge IV_{ij}(f) \wedge CMD_{ij}(open) \Rightarrow OV_{ij}(nf)$$
$$V_{ij}(sc) \wedge IV_{ij}(f) \wedge CMD_{ij}(close) \Rightarrow OV_{ij}(nf)$$
$$V_{ij}(sc) \wedge IV_{ij}(nf) \wedge CMD_{ij}(open) \Rightarrow OV_{ij}(nf)$$
$$V_{ij}(sc) \wedge IV_{ij}(nf) \wedge CMD_{ij}(close) \Rightarrow OV_{ij}(nf)$$
$$IJL_{ij}(f) \wedge IJR_{ij}(f) \Rightarrow OJ_{ij}(f)$$
$$IJL_{ij}(f) \wedge IJR_{ij}(nf) \Rightarrow OJ_{ij}(f)$$
$$IJL_{ij}(nf) \wedge IJR_{ij}(f) \Rightarrow OJ_{ij}(f)$$
$$IJL_{ij}(nf) \wedge IJR_{ij}(nf) \Rightarrow OJ_{ij}(nf)$$
$$T_i(full) \Rightarrow OT_i(f)$$
$$T_i(empty) \Rightarrow OT_i(nf)$$
$$E_i(ok) \wedge IEL_i(f) \wedge IER_i(f) \Rightarrow OE_i(thrust)$$
$$E_i(ok) \wedge IEL_i(f) \wedge IER_i(nf) \Rightarrow OE_i(nothrust)$$
$$E_i(ok) \wedge IEL_i(nf) \wedge IER_i(f) \Rightarrow OE_i(nothrust)$$
$$E_i(ok) \wedge IEL_i(nf) \wedge IER_i(nf) \Rightarrow OE_i(nothrust)$$
$$E_i(br) \wedge IEL_i(f) \wedge IER_i(f) \Rightarrow OE_i(nothrust)$$
$$E_i(br) \wedge IEL_i(f) \wedge IER_i(nf) \Rightarrow OE_i(nothrust)$$
$$E_i(br) \wedge IEL_i(nf) \wedge IER_i(f) \Rightarrow OE_i(nothrust)$$
$$E_i(br) \wedge IEL_i(nf) \wedge IER_i(nf) \Rightarrow OE_i(nothrust)$$

whenever a formula $N_1(val_1) \wedge \ldots \wedge N_k(val_k) \Rightarrow M(val)$ appears in DT, nodes N_1 through N_k are parents of M in $\mathcal{N}$

The most straightforward case is represented by a causal network consisting of one or more disjoint trees so that we can encode each such tree independently. Note that the leaves of such trees represent variables in $COMPS$ and CXT (i.e. primitive causes) and thus edges are directed from the leaves towards the root (see figure 2).

For this type of causal networks, we have experimentally demonstrated that the combination of the following heuristics can be quite effective in limiting the explosion of the OBDD size as the number of variables grows:

– $H1$: the propositional variables representing the values in the domain of a system variable are ordered in sequence (e.g. if $DOM(V) = \{val_1, \ldots, val_k\}$ then variables $V_{val_1}, \ldots, V_{val_k}$ have indexes i to $(i + k - 1)$ in the ordering)
– $H2$: always index parent variables in families of the causal network $\mathcal{N}$ [8] before the child variable

---

[8] A family contains a node and its parents

Table 2. MTG for valves (V_{ij}), tanks (T_i) and engines (E_i)

$(V_{ij}^t(ok) \Rightarrow V_{ij}^{t+1}(ok)) \vee (V_{ij}^t(ok) \Rightarrow V_{ij}^{t+1}(so)) \vee (V_{ij}^t(ok) \Rightarrow V_{ij}^{t+1}(sc))$
$(V_{ij}^t(so) \Rightarrow V_{ij}^{t+1}(so)) \vee (V_{ij}^t(so) \Rightarrow V_{ij}^{t+1}(ok))$
$(V_{ij}^t(sc) \Rightarrow V_{ij}^{t+1}(sc))$

$(T_i^t(full) \Rightarrow T_i^{t+1}(full)) \vee (T_i^t(full) \Rightarrow T_i^{t+1}(empty))$
$(T_i^t(empty) \Rightarrow T_i^{t+1}(empty))$

$(E_i^t(ok) \Rightarrow E_i^{t+1}(ok)) \vee (E_i^t(ok) \Rightarrow E_i^{t+1}(br))$
$(E_i^t(br) \Rightarrow E_i^{t+1}(br))$

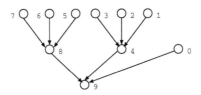

Fig. 2. Sample tree causal net with variables indexed according to heuristics $H1$ through $H3$

- $H3$: index variables in the same family of the causal network $\mathcal{N}$ as close as possible

The ordering **O1** which satisfies all three heuristics is obtained by visiting $\mathcal{N}$ depth first (ignoring arcs directions), assigning index $(|\mathcal{SV}| - 1)$ to the root and decreasing it at each visited node (see the numbering of nodes in figure 2). Once the multi-valued system variables have been ordered in this way it is sufficient to sequentially index the propositional variables starting at the ones associated with behavioral modes of system variable 0 (i.e. the last one visited by the depth-first algorithm) and moving up towards system variable $(|\mathcal{SV}| - 1)$ (i.e. the root).

It is worth noting that this result is in accordance with analogous results obtained by the digital circuit design/verification community (e.g. [18]) for a similar even if slightly different system modeling problem.

Experimental results 31 *In order to show the benefits of adopting the described heuristics for ordering the variables we have compared ordering **O1** with two alternative strategies:*

- **O2**: *visit the tree depth-first assigning index 0 to the root and increasing it at each visited node (violates H2 since it orders children before parents)*
- **O3**: *visit the tree breadth-first assigning index $(|\mathcal{SV}| - 1)$ to the root and decreasing it at each visited node (violates H3 since it groups variables at the same depth instead of the same family)*

*In particular, table 3 reports the results obtained for artificially generated systems of increasing complexity. System S_1 is depicted in figure 3 **(a)**; figure 3 **(b)** shows how system S_{i+1} is recursively built from system S_i. Note that each system variable was assigned a domain of 4 different values.*

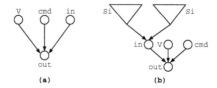

Fig. 3. Recursively defined test systems of increasing complexity

*Strategy **O1** significantly outperforms both **O2** and **O3**, being also able to deal
with system complexities that made **O3** fail on our test system (N/A values in
the table represent computations that run out-of-memory).*

Table 3. OBDD sizes for different systems applying different ordering strategies

system	Num of Variables	O1	O2	O3
S_1	3	21	27	21
S_2	9	108	134	143
S_3	21	517	1204	2367
S_4	45	2550	11904	572735
S_5	93	12703	118904	N/A

Clearly, the case when $\mathcal{N}$ is a pure tree only occurs rarely in practice; often
$\mathcal{N}$ will be a single graph with multiple "roots", and there may exist more than
one directed path between pairs of nodes . Our method still works well when the
causal network is a (set of) nearly-tree structures, meaning that edges departing
from the main tree-structure link to small structures.

If this is not the case there is no guarantee that our heuristics still work
well, since the assumptions behind $H2$ and $H3$ no longer hold.

One of such cases is represented by the causal network, shown in figure 4,
for the sample system of figure 1. It is apparent that there are two trees
interconnected with one another in such a way that we cannot identify one of
them as the "main tree" and the other as a small deviation from it.

Since the two trees share a small number of nodes, one possibility is to duplicate
the shared nodes (i.e. system variables) so that the non-tree structure is
transformed into two trees; clearly, after diagnoses are independently computed
for such trees, they must be joined by asserting the equivalence of duplicates
of the same variable, but this is usually done when the trees have been
greatly simplified by asserting context and observations and eliminating the
non-component variables (see paragraph 3.3).

Experimental results 32 *OBDD sizes obtained by encoding the causal net of
figure 4 as a single structure (denoted **SS**) and as two separate trees resulting*

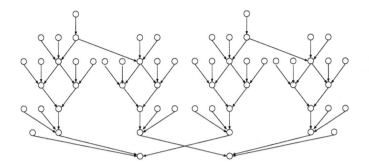

Fig. 4. Propulsion system causal net

*by the duplication of some of the variables (denoted **DUP**) are respectively 1587 and 968. In both cases we have used strategy **O1** to order the variables.*
For this sample system, where the number of duplicated variables is relatively small and the causal net structure significantly deviates from a tree, duplication leads to substantial reduction in the OBDD size.

3.3   Computation of the Solutions

Encoding a specific diagnostic problem DP given $OBDD_{SD}$ simply consists in adding to it the observations **OBS** $= \{M1(val_1), \ldots, Mk(val_k)\}$ and contexts **CXT** $= \{I1(val_1), \ldots, Il(val_l)\}$:

$OBDD_{DP} = OBDD_{SD}$
$OBDD_{DP} = restrict(OBDD_{DP}, Mi_{val_i}), i = 1, \ldots, k$
$OBDD_{DP} = restrict(OBDD_{DP}, Ii_{val_i}), i = 1, \ldots, l$

where $restrict(obdd, v)$ is the standard OBDD algorithm which substitutes *true* to the occurences of v in $obdd$.
At this point $OBDD_{DP}$ already contains implicitly all and only the consistency-based diagnoses for DP.

Theorem 1. *Let DP be a diagnostic problem, $OBDD_{DP}$ its OBDD encoding and $\mathcal{P}$ the set of paths in $OBDD_{DP}$ starting at the root and ending in the* true *node. Then the consistency based diagnoses for DP are all and only the projections of the paths in $\mathcal{P}$ over the component variables $COMPS$*

Proof. (sketch) By the definition of OBDDs we know that a path from the root to the *true* node represents an instantiation of the variables which makes *true* the boolean function represented by the OBDD.
Given the boolean encoding of the multi-valued variables and the formulas in SD described above, $OBDD_{DP}$ represents a boolean function B_{DP} over the boolean variables corresponding to $COMPS$ and $STATES \backslash OBS$ variables. Note that B_{DP} is *true* only if exactly one value is assigned to a $COMPS$ or $STATES$ variable.

Function Eliminate($OBDD_{DP}$)
    $OBDD_{DIAG} = OBDD_{DP}$
    For Each $V_B \in VS_B \backslash COMPS_B$
        $OBDD_{DIAG} = $ union(restrict($OBDD_{DIAG}, V_B$), restrict($OBDD_{DIAG}, \sim V_B$))
    Next
    Return $OBDD_{DIAG}$
EndFunction

Fig. 5. Eliminating non-component variables from $OBDD_{DP}$

Let's consider the restriction $B_{DP,D}$ of B_{DP} imposed by an assignment D to $COMPS$ variables (which is itself a boolean function in the $STATES \backslash OBS$ variables). It is easy to see that:

$$B_{DP,D} \equiv false \Leftrightarrow DT \cup \mathbf{CXT} \cup \mathbf{OBS} \cup D \vdash \bot$$

But $B_{DP,D} \not\equiv false$ exactly if D's atoms lie on paths that go to $true$, thus D is a diagnosis if and only if it is the projection over $COMPS$ of a path which goes to $true$.

Note that the previous theorem proves that the simple algorithm given above for computing diagnoses from $OBDD_{SD}$ is both correct and complete w.r.t. consistency-based diagnoses.

At the end of the diagnostic process it can be worth eliminating all the propositional variables that are not associated to variables in $COMPS$; this can be accomplished by repeatedly using the $restrict()$ operator as shown in figure 5.

Experimental results 33 *We have solved a number of diagnostic problems by using the* **SS** *encoding of SD (see experimental results 32). In particular, we have considered three batches* **TS1**, **TS2** *and* **TS3** *of 25 test cases each where 1,2 and 3 faults were injected in every case respectively.*
Our implementation of the diagnostic agent has been written in Java 2 (JDK 1.3) and run on a laptop machine equipped with Pentium III CPU at 933MHz and 256MB RAM. The OBDD functions were provided by the BuDDy *C++ package (*www.itu.dk/research/buddy/index.html*) via the JBDD interface (*www.chl.chalmers.se/ vahidi/bdd/bdd.html*).*
Results are reported in table 4. Both the $OBDD_{DIAG}$ *average size and the average time for solving a diagnostic problem are small even for the triple-fault diagnostic cases.*

3.4   Some Complexity Results

Since the $restrict()$ operator is linear in the size of the OBDD ([3]), it is easy to see that the computation of diagnoses (i.e. $OBDD_{DP}$) from $OBDD_{SD}$ has complexity:

Table 4. Average sizes of $OBDD_{DIAG}$ and diagnosis times (confidence 95%)

TS1		TS2		TS3	
size	time (msec)	size	time (msec)	size	time (msec)
118.6 ± 5.4	13.6 ± 3.3	126.5 ± 8.0	17.3 ± 10.2	125.1 ± 7.6	24.4 ± 20.2

$$O((|OBS| + |CXT|) \times size(OBDD_{SD}))$$

Indeed, we apply the $restrict()$ operator to $OBDD_{SD}$ once per atom in OBS and CXT.

As for the elimination of non-component variables (algorithm $Eliminate()$), the complexity could be in the worst case exponential, since $union(obdd1, obdd2)$ has complexity $O(|obdd1| \times |obdd2|)$ and can in principle produce a new OBDD of size $O(|obdd1| \times |obdd2|)$. However this was not the case in our experiments (both on tree and non-tree structure), since the size of $OBDD_{DIAG}$ in $Eliminate()$ almost steadily decreased instead of growing exponentially larger. At the end of the execution of $Eliminate()$, $OBDD_{DIAG}$ was significantly smaller than $OBDD_{DP}$, as expected.

These results show that the computation of diagnoses and the elimination of non-component variables can be efficient as far as $size(OBDD_{SD})$ is not large. Techniques described in paragraph 3.2 have thus a major impact on the time complexity of the diagnostic process.

4   Extracting Minimum-Cardinality Diagnoses

Extracting diagnoses from $OBDD_{DIAG}$ is pretty straightforward. It is sufficient, indeed, to visit all the paths from the root of the OBDD to the $true$ node. This approach takes time linear in the size of the set of diagnoses, and is therefore perfectly reasonable.

However in most diagnostic systems, especially when the set of returned diagnoses can be very large, we are interested only in the preferred diagnoses, according to some particular preference criterion. We now show how preferred diagnoses can be efficiently extracted from $OBDD_{DIAG}$ when the selected preference criterion is to minimize the number of faults.

Our extraction algorithm will be required to extract all the diagnoses with the minimum number of faults found in any diagnosis. Figure 6 shows the algorithm $ComputeFaultCardinalityMasks()$ to be run offline for computing the complete set of *fault cardinality masks*. Mask $FCMask_i$ is an OBDD representing all and only the instantiations of $COMPS$ variables containing exactly i faulty components.

Equipped with fault cardinality masks it is easy to implement an extraction algorithm $ExtractMinimumCardinalityDiagnoses()$ with the characteristics described above (figure 6).

Experimental results 41 *With reference to the sample propulsion system, the mask sizes for 0, 1, 2 and 3 faults are as follows:*

Function ComputeFaultCardinalityMasks($COMPS_B$, n)
  FCMask[0] = OBDD($C1_{normal} \wedge \ldots \wedge Cn_{normal}$)
  For i=1 To n
    FCMask[i] = OBDD($false$)
    For j=1 To n
      TMask = intersect(restrict(FCMask[i-1], Ci_{normal}), OBDD($\sim Ci_{normal}$)
      FCMask[i] = union(FCMask[i], TMask)
    Next
  Next
  Return FCMask[]
EndFunction

Function ExtractMinimumCardinalityDiagnoses($OBDD_{DIAG}$, n, FCMask[])
  $OBDD_{PREF}$ = OBDD($false$)
  For i=0 To n
    $OBDD_{TMP}$ = intersect($OBDD_{DP}$, FCMASK[i])
    If ($OBDD_{TMP} \not\equiv false$)
      $OBDD_{PREF} = OBDD_{TMP}$
      Exit For
    End If
  Next
  Return $OBDD_{PREF}$
EndFunction

Fig. 6. Computing the fault cardinality masks and extracting minimum-fault diagnoses

$size(FCMask_0) = 20$ $size(FCMask_2) = 56$
$size(FCMask_1) = 39$ $size(FC_Mask3) = 71$

We have performed experiments with both OBDD representations of the system description derived in experimental results 32 (i.e. single-structure **SS** *and pair of trees* **DUP***) on the two diagnostic cases* **DC1** *and* **DC2***. The resulting sizes of $OBDD_{DP}$ and $OBDD_{DIAG}$ are larger for the* **DUP** *system encoding both for* **DC1** *(758 vs 578 for $OBDD_{DP}$ and 269 vs 176 for $OBDD_{DIAG}$) and* **DC2** *(781 vs 580 for $OBDD_{DP}$ and 278 vs 181 for $OBDD_{DIAG}$). This contrasts with the results in experimental section 32 where we showed that the duplication reduced the size of the system encoding; there is thus a trade-off depending e.g. on how many operations have to be performed on the OBDD representing the system encoding and the OBDD representing the diagnostic problem solutions.*

By applying $FCMask_1$ to the $OBDD_{DIAG}$ of the **DC1** *case computed on the single structure (***SS***) we obtain an $OBDD_{DIAG1}$ of size 90, representing the diagnoses involving one fault (which we know to be 7 from paragraph 2.2). By applying $FCMask_2$ to the $OBDD_{DIAG}$ of the* **DC2** *case computed on the same system model we obtain an $OBDD_{DIAG2}$ of size 125, representing the diagnoses involving two faults (which we know to be 49).*

5   Conclusions

5.1   Towards Time-Varying Systems

Encouraging preliminary results for static diagnosis stimulate the extension of our approach to the case of time-varying systems. The coding of the *mtg*s as a set of propositional formulas is quite natural (see table 2). Additional criteria for the ordering of the variables have to be defined in order to deal with the problem of representing the same variable at different time instances; we are starting to investigate an approach that avoids the introduction of as many copies of a variable as the number of time instants within the diagnostic time window.
The fault cardinality masks introduced in section 4 can be exploited in singling-out the preferred diagnoses in each time instant.

Beside minimum fault-cardinality other preference criteria have been used for ranking diagnoses in preference order, e.g. minimality w.r.t. set inclusion, quantitative probability and ranks. One of the challenges of the extension of our work to time-varying systems concerns the capability of extracting the preferred trajectories instead of instantaneous diagnoses. Existing methods (such as the one proposed in [13]) have resorted to a number of simplifications in order to handle the huge space of possible trajectories. We believe that it is worth investigating to what extent a principled approach to the encoding of time-varying systems descriptions as OBDDs can make such trajectory spaces more manageable.

5.2   Discussion

In the present paper we have investigated the problem of solving diagnostic problems by using OBDDs. Such a formalism has been successfully used in different areas of computing and AI especially when the solution space is quite large. The problem of computing and representing a large set of solutions is relevant also within the model-based approach to diagnosis. However, the use of OBDDs is not a panacea per se since only a careful analysis on how to encode the domain model prevents the OBDD size to explode.
In our opinion the heuristics and techniques introduced in section 3 represent a step ahead in comparision with previous work suggesting the use of OBDDs ([21]) or of generic model-checking tools (e.g. [6]) for diagnostic problem solving.

Controlling the size of the OBDD encoding the model of the system to be diagnosed is particularly relevant since the solution of diagnostic problems involves operations whose computational complexity is in most cases linear or polynomial w.r.t. the size of the OBDD (paragraph 3.4). Similarly, the computational effort for extracting diagnoses involving a minimum number of faults, depends on the size of the OBDD encoding the entire space of solutions.
Experimental data we have collected on a non-trivial domain (i.e. the simplified model of the propulsion subsystem of a spacecraft) show that our techniques are able to keep the sizes of both the system model OBDD and the solutions space OBDD under control.

References

1. Bertoli, P., Cimatti, A., Roveri, M., Traverso, P.: Planning in Nondeterministic Domains under Partial Observability via Symbolic Model Checking. Proc. IJCAI01 (2001) 473–478
2. Brusoni, V., Console, L., Terenziani, P., Theseider Dupré, D.: A spectrum of definitions for temporal model-based diagnosis. Artificial Intelligence **102** (1998) 39–79
3. Bryant, R.: Symbolic boolean manipulation with Ordered Decision Diagrams. ACM Computing Surveys **24** (1992) 293–318
4. Console, L., Portinale, L., Theseider Dupré, D., Torasso, P.: Diagnosing time-varying misbehavior: an approach based on model decomposition. Annals of Mathematics and AI **11** (1994) 381–398
5. Console, L., Picardi, C., Ribaudo, M.: Process algebras for system diagnosis. Artificial Intelligence **142**(1) (2002) 19–51
6. Cordier, M.-O., Largouet, C.: Using model-checking techniques for diagnosing discrete-event systems. Proc. DX01 (2001) 39–46
7. Darwiche, A.: Model-based diagnosis using structured system descriptions. Journal of Artificial Intelligence Research **8** (1998) 165–222
8. de Kleer, J., Mackworth, A., Reiter, R.: Characterizing Diagnoses and Systems. Artificial Intelligence **56**(2–3) (1992) 197–222
9. Dvorak, D., Kuipers, B.: Model-Based Monitoring of Dynamic Systems. Proc. IJCAI89 (1989) 1238–1243
10. Friedrich, G.: Theory Diagnoses: A Concise Characterization of Faulty Systems. Proc. IJCAI93 (1993) 1466–1471
11. Goldszmidt, M., Pearl, J.: Rank-based systems: a simple approach to belief revision, belief update, and reasoning about evidence and actions. Proc. KR92 (1992) 661–672
12. Jensen, R. M.,Veloso, M. M.: Obdd-based universal planning: Specifying and solving planning problems for synchronized agents in nondeterministic domains. Lecture Notes in Computer Science **1600** (1999) 213–248
13. Kurien, J., Nayak, P. Pandurang: Back to the Future for Consistency-Based Trajectory Tracking. Proc. AAAI (2000) 370–377
14. Mozetič, I.: Hierarchical Model-Based Diagnosis. Int. Journal of Man-Machine Studies **35**(3) (1991) 329–362
15. Muscettola, N., Nayak, P., Pell, B., Williams, B.: Remote Agent: to Boldly Go Where No AI System has Gone Before. Artificial Intelligence **103** (1998) 5–47
16. Portinale, L., Torasso, P.: Diagnosis as a Variable Assignment Problem: a Case Study in a Space Robot Fault Diagnosis. Proc. IJCAI99 (1999) 1087–1093
17. Sachenbacher, M., Struss, P.: AQUA: A Framework for Automated Qualitative Abstraction. Proc. QR01 (2001)
18. Sauerhoff, M., Wegener, I., Werchner, R.: Optimal Ordered Binary Decision Diagrams for Fanout-Free Circuits. Proc. SASIMI (1996) 197–204
19. Struss, P.: Fundamentals of model-based diagnosis of dynamic systems. Proc. IJCAI97 (1997) 480–485
20. Struss, P., Rehfus, B., Brignolo, R., Cascio, F., Console, L., Dague, P., Dubois, P., Dressler, P., Millet, D.: Model-based Tools for the Integration of Design and Diagnosis into a Common Process – A Project Report. Proc. DX02 (2002)
21. Sztipanovits, J., Misra, A. Diagnosis of discrete event systems using Ordered Binary Decision Diagrams. Proc. DX96 (1996)
22. Torta, G., Torasso, P.: Automatic abstraction in component-based diagnosis driven by system observability. Proc. IJCAI (2003) *to appear*

Presenting Sets of Problem Solutions Concisely

Helmut Horacek

Universität des Saarlandes, FB 6.2 Informatik, Postfach 151150
D-66041 Saarbrücken, Germany
horacek@cs.uni-sb.de

Abstract. Improvements in formal reasoning systems enable these systems to produce large sets of solutions that may grow rather complex. However, automatically generated presentations of these data lack a sufficient degree of conciseness. In order to improve the presentation of problem solutions that can be casted in terms of sets of ground atoms, we adapt linguistic aggregation techniques to specificities of formal problems. We define novel constructs that can express sets of propositions with highly regular alternations on predicate argument values concisely, including special forms of disjunctions and versions for formulas. We demonstrate applications to model generation and to categorization proofs. The presentations obtained highlight commonalities among and differences across solution parts in a much better way than previous approaches do, thereby supporting the inspection of properties holding across several solutions, and the discovery of flaws in problem specifications.

1 Introduction

Improvements in formal reasoning systems enable these systems to produce large sets of solutions that may grow rather complex. Handling these results may require the inspection of the generated solutions for critical information, which is insufficiently supported by current presentation methods, including techniques from the field of natural language generation (NLG).

In order to improve the presentation of problem solutions that can be casted in terms of sets of ground atoms which are expressible in natural language or mathematical formulas, we adapt linguistic aggregation techniques to specificities of formal problems. We define novel constructs that can express sets of propositions with highly regular alternations on predicate argument values concisely, including special forms of disjunctions and versions for formulas. We demonstrate applications to model generation and to categorization proofs. The presentations obtained highlight commonalities among and differences across solution parts in a much better way than previous approaches do, thereby supporting the inspection of properties holding across several solutions, and the discovery of flaws in problem specifications.

The paper is organized as follows. We motivate the use of aggregation techniques and review previous methods. Then we define new constructs that allow the formation of compact expressions. Next, we describe the kernel of a procedure for making use of these operators. We follow with application-specific extensions to the basic procedure, some for addressing disjunctions, others addressing particularities of formulas. Finally, we discuss impacts and applications of our techniques.

A. Günter et al. (Eds.): KI 2003, LNAI 2821, pp. 239–253, 2003.
© Springer-Verlag Berlin Heidelberg 2003

2 Background and Motivation

Presenting multiple solutions to some problem effectively requires elaborating commonalities and differences among individual parts in a systematic way by using compact expressions (see the reports about the behavior of technical systems in [15]). In typical cases, that is, commonalities with minor differences, compact expressive means exist not only in natural language, but also in terms of formulas. With formulas, commonalities can be expressed within the structure of a formula, while differences can be captured by the values assigned to the variables contained. Similarly, repetition of the common parts is avoided in dedicated natural language expressions, while the components that make up the differences appear in *coordinated structures*. Building such coordinated structures is called *aggregation* in the field of NLG.

The term *aggregation* was first used by Mann and Moore [11]. Aggregation is a broadly used concept in NLG, relevant in all processing phases [14]. Its most common form, structural aggregation, concerns compositions of several logical assertions that *share information* into a single natural language utterance with coordinated or omitted parts, associated with a number of linguistic coordination phenomena including *conjunction reduction* ("*Foxes* and *wolves* are animals") and *ellipsis* or *gapping* ("*Foxes* are larger than birds and _ smaller than wolves").

Aggregation techniques have been incorporated in early systems, such as KDS [12]. Aggregation is a general concept that has also been applied in the area of automated theorem proving for several purposes, including mathematical discovery to find conjectures [2], abstract theorem proving to find proofs by aggregated steps [7], and the presentation of mathematical proofs [3, 4]. Even a linguistically motivated aggregation procedure, similar to [5], has been incorporated in proof presentation system [9]. However, almost all approaches to text presentation apply aggregation operators opportunistically, as one of several measures in a heterogeneous process. In contrast, Shaw [15, 16] applies aggregation techniques globally for settings in which aggregation is really the dominant concept for obtaining improvements, a similar situation as ours. Since his procedure is the only systematic and reasonably efficient method for handling aggregation in view of larger sets of data, we take it as a starting point. We briefly introduce the functionality of this algorithm, and we later will motivate adaptations and extensions to the particularities of our environment.

Shaw's algorithm operates on sets of propositions which are represented as attribute-value structures. Each proposition has several arguments including a verb, obligatory case role fillers according to the case frame of the verb, and modifiers, such as temporal and local specifications. Each argument, in turn, consists of attributes expressing the proper predicate, typically by a word stem, the semantic type, and word-class specific information, such as tense for verbs, and determiner specifications for nouns. For our purposes, it is sufficient to abstract these representations into a list of arguments each consisting of the proper predicate only. These specifications can be recasted into ground atoms with some dummy predicate p, where the argument type is encoded positionally. An example with four ground atoms, adapted from [16], is given in Figure 1 at various processing stages of Shaw's algorithm. The arguments represent an action, the agent of that action, the patient or object, the beneficent of the action, and the occurrence time, in precisely that order.

Shaw's algorithm uses two aggregation operations, one for propositions that differ in one argument, and another one for propositions that differ in multiple arguments. Propositions that differ in only one argument can be collapsed into a single proposition with a conjoined subexpression, such as building "Alice installed *Excel and Latex* for John on Monday", from the first and the third proposition in Figure 1, top left. For propositions that differ in multiple arguments, recurring elements can be deleted – in forward or backward direction, depending on grammatical conditions. For example, the fourth and the second proposition in Figure 1, top left can be expressed as "Cindy removed Access [for John] on Monday, and Bob [removed] Latex for John on Tuesday", including both deletion types. The algorithm has four stages:

1. Group propositions and order them according to their similarities while satisfying pragmatical constraints, e.g., chronological order among argument values. Primarily, ordering is based on the number of distinct values for each argument.
2. Determine recurring elements in the ordered propositions that will be combined. This is done incrementally, starting with the first two propositions, then with the third and the second or a combined proposition built out of the first two, etc.
3. Create a sentence boundary when the combined clause reaches a given threshold.
4. Determine which recurring elements are redundant and should be deleted – carrying out this operation requires grammatical knowledge about the target language.

In the example, reordering is applied to the initial representation in the top left of Figure 1 and leads to the representation on the top right. Then recurrence marking is applied to the first two propositions, which have one distinct argument (marked by '1' in the bottom left). Subsequently, recurrence marking is applied to the combined proposition and the third one, which are multiple distinct (marked by '2'). Due to the threshold used, a sentence boundary is created prior to considering the last proposition, yielding recurrence markings as shown in the bottom left of Figure 1. The combined clauses appear on the bottom right of Figure 1. A suitable wording, also considering tense, a preposition for dates ("on") and determiner specifications (all nouns except the days are proper names), is "On Monday, Alice installed Excel and Latex and Cindy removed Access for John. Bob removed Word for John on Tuesday".

Initial representation	*Representation after ordering (stage 1)*
p(install,Alice,Excel,John,Monday)	p(install,Alice,Excel,John,Monday)
p(remove,Bob,Word,John,Tuesday)	p(install,Alice,Latex,John,Monday)
p(install,Alice,Latex,John,Monday)	p(remove,Cindy,Access,John,Monday)
p(remove,Cindy,Access,John,Monday)	p(remove,Bob,Word,John,Tuesday)
Recurrence markings performed (stage 2 & 3)	*Deletions and coordination done (stage 4)*
p(install[1],Alice[1],Excel,John[1,2],Monday[1,2])	{p(install,Alice,<Excel,
p(install[1],Alice[1],Latex,John[1,2],Monday[1,2])	Latex>, – ,Monday),
p(remove,Cindy,Access,John[2],Monday[2])	p(remove,Cindy,Access,John, –)}
p(remove,Bob,Word,John,Tuesday)	p(remove,Bob,Word,John,Tuesday)

Fig. 1. Representations of aggregated propositions at different stages of processing

x-y	$2*x$-y	$2*x$-$(y+1)$	$3*x$-$(y+1)$	$2*x+(y+1)$	$3*x+(y+1)$	$(x$-$y)+1$	$(2*x)+(3*y)$
	$3*x$-y	$2*x$-$(y+2)$	$3*x$-$(y+2)$	$2*x+(y+2)$	$3*x+(y+2)$	$(x$-$y)+2$	$(3*x)+(2*y)$
	$2*x+y$	$2*x$-$(y+3)$	$3*x$-$(y+3)$	$2*x+(y+3)$	$3*x+(y+3)$	$(x$-$y)+3$	$2*(x$-$y)$
	$3*x+y$	$2*x$-$(y+4)$	$3*x$-$(y+4)$	$2*x+(y+4)$	$3*x+(y+4)$	$(x$-$y)+4$	$3*(x$-$y)$

Fig. 2. Formulas representing operations of residue classes modulo 5 (the quasi-groups)

3 Running Examples

In order to explain our techniques, we use two examples covering complementary aspects. The first one relates to sets of formulas that represent algebraic operations. In order to ease their inspection, compact representations of these formulas in terms of mathematical expressions, through aggregating sets of constants and operators from otherwise identical expressions, are desirable. We have encountered such a problem in the context of examining algebraic properties of sets of residue classes for composed operations. Through extensive use of the proof development environment $\Omega MEGA$ [17], these algebraic structures have been categorized into groups, semi-groups, quasi-groups, magmas, monoids, abelian and non-abelian [13], yielding sets of operations for each category (we used a maximum of three operators out of the set $\{*, +, -\}$, and a maximum nesting of 1). An example is given in Figure 2, which shows the 29 expressions for residue classes modulo 5, categorized as non-abelian quasi-group. Subsequently, the structures categorized this way are subject to expensive isomorphy proofs, whose intelligible organization demands the inspection of these expressions.

The second example is a *puzzle*: "There are four people: Roberta, Thelma, Steve, and Pete. Among them they hold eight different jobs, each exactly two. The jobs are: chef, guard, nurse, telephone operator, police officer, teacher, actor, and boxer. The job of the nurse is held by a male. The husband of the chef is the telephone operator. Roberta is not a boxer. Pete has no education past the ninth grade. Roberta, the chef, and the police officer went golfing together. Who holds which jobs?" This is a fully regular assignment problem. 16 solution variants consist of eight assignments each, which amounts to 128 propositions if unaggregated. In the representation of the assignments in Figure 3, the solution variants are referred to by numbers, realized as a special argument in the last position. In logical terms, it must hold that all propositions with the same value of this argument must be true at the same time, those with different values hold alternatively. To save space, facts holding in several variants are aggregated into single facts, with variant values enclosed between '<' and '>'.

be(Pete,boxer,<2,4,5,7,9-11,13-16>)   be(Steve,actor,<3,5,13>)   be(Thelma,actor,<4,8-10,15>)
be(Pete,guard,<1,3,6,8,12,15,16>)   be(Steve,boxer,<8,12>)   be(Thelma,boxer,<1,3,6>)
be(Pete,operator,<1-14>)   be(Steve,guard,<9,14>)   be(Thelma,chef,<1-16>)
be(Roberta,actor,<1,2,6,7,11,12,14,16>) be(Steve,nurse,<1-16>)   be(Thelma,guard,<2,5,7>)
be(Roberta,guard,<4,10,11,13>)   be(Steve,officer,<6,7,10,11>)be(Thelma,teacher,<11-14,16>)
be(Roberta,officer,<1-5,8,9,12-16>)   be(Steve,operator,<15,16>)
be(Roberta,teacher,<3,5-10,15>)   be(Steve,teacher,<1,2,4>)

Fig. 3. Solutions to a puzzle – alternative sets of assignments of persons to jobs

4 New Aggregation Constructs

High degrees of similarity of variable combinations in both examples suggest a good aggregation potential for illustrating commonalities. This is typical for logical problems, differing from situations in narratives in the following respects:

- While these commonalities arise somehow opportunistically in narrative texts, they arise regularly over parts of solutions to logical problems as consequences of underlying problem definitions and interdependencies holding among them.
- Unlike in narratives, complete subsets of possible value combinations may appear in solutions to these problems.
- The number of predicate arguments in typical problem specifications are rarely more than 2 (aiming at efficiency), as opposed to case frames with complements.

Consequently, there is a demand for specific aggregation operations, which we meet by novel *"2-dimensional"* coordinations that can be expressed in natural language and by formulas concisely. Normally, *coordination* is done in a *pairwise* fashion, as in the formula $i*x-(y+i)$, $i=2,3$ and in the example sentences in the Section 2. In the new constructs, aggregation is done by building the *cross product* of the values of two arguments, with special forms of disjunctions for commonalities across variants:

- The *Permut* construct
  It expresses a set of predications in which the values of two arguments are varied by building all combinations out of the two sets of argument fillers, within the same variant. An example sentence is "Each of Pete, Steve, and Thelma can be boxer and guard," expressing six of the facts in Figure 3, when abstracting from the variant. Similarly, the formulas in the third and the fourth columns from the left in Figure 3 can be expressed concisely by $i*x-(y+j)$, $i=2,3$, $j=1,...,4$.
- The *Choice* construct (and the *Except* construct) – a disjunctive construct
  It expresses an assignment of one individual to several others, each in a different variant. An example sentence is "Thelma holds *one of* the jobs actor, guard, and teacher," comprising job assignments of Thelma other than that to chef in variants 7, 10, and 11 (see Figure 3). An *Except* construct complements each variant of the *Choice* construct by the other assignments, holding for one other individual. For example, the text "and Roberta holds the *remaining* positions," the job assignments of Roberta in these variants, can follow (see Figure 3).
- The *Assign* construct – another disjunctive construct
  It comprises a specific set of *Choice* constructs which together express the set of all bijective functions between the two sets of individuals, each in one variant, without repetitions. An example sentence is "Roberta, Steve, and Thelma *each* hold *one distinct* job *out of the set* actor, guard, and teacher," expressing their job assignments in variants 2, 4, 5, 9, 13, and 14 (see Figure 3).

In order to define these constructs, we apply λ-expressions with some special notations (see Figure 4). Assertions can be reexpressed with the predicate as an additional argument (1), to allow the building of λ-expressions, that is, the extraction of

(1) base(P,a_1,...,a_n) ::= P(a_1,...,a_n)

(2) $<A_{in}>$ ::= $<a_{i1}$,...,$a_{in}>$

(3) $Coord$(base(...,$<A_{in}>$,...,$<A_{jn}>$,...)) ::= $\forall k(1{\leq}k{\leq}n)$: ($\lambda x_i,x_j$. base(...,$x_i$,...,$x_j$,...)) $a_{ik}\,a_{jk}$

(4) $Permut$(base(...,$<A_{in}[/a_{id}]>$,...,$<A_{jm}[/a_{je}]>$,...,a_c)) ::=
   $\forall k,l(1{\leq}k{\leq}n,1{\leq}l{\leq}m; (k,l){\neq}(d,e))$: ($\lambda x_i,x_j$. base(...,$x_i$,...,$x_j$,...,$a_c$)) $a_{ik}\,a_{jl}$

(5) $Choice$(base(...,a,...,$<A_{in}>$,...,$<A_{jn}>$)) ::=
   $\forall k(1{\leq}k{\leq}n)$: ($\lambda x_i,x_j$. base(...,$a$,...,$x_i$,...,$x_j$)) $a_{ik}\,a_{jk}$

(6) $Except$(base(...,a,...,$<A_{in}>$,...,$<A_{jn}>$)) ::=
   $\forall k,l(1{\leq}k,l{\leq}n,k{\neq}l)$: ($\lambda x_i,x_j$. base(...,$a$,...,$x_i$,...,$x_j$)) $a_{ik}\,a_{jl}$

(7) $Assign$(base(...,$<A_{in}[/a_{id}]>$,...,$<A_{jn}[/a_{je}]>$,...,$<A_{kn}>$)) ::=
   $\forall l,m(1{\leq}l,m{\leq}n; (l,m){\neq}(d,e))\ \forall p(1{\leq}p{\leq}n!)$: $Choice$(base(...,$<A_{il}>$,...,$<A_{jm}>$,...,$<A_{kp}>$))
   where jm = f(il,kp) with f(x,z) $\neq$ f(y,z) (mutually exclusive)

Fig. 4. Formal definitions of aggregation constructs

variables bound by λ, for which constants can be substituted. Moreover, arguments can be filled by lists, expressed by capital letters. The first index indicates the argument position, and the second the number of elements in the list (2). Moreover, square brackets indicate optionality, and a dash marks an element as an exception. Based on that, operators are used to express the way composition is done in each case, defined by implicitly conjoined λ-expressions – for formulas, we abstract from the nesting, assuming identical nesting in coordinated structures. The *Coord* operator handles pairwise coordination where the substitutions run over the same index, defined for two arguments in (3). The *Permut* operator is similar, but both indexes are varied separately, within one variant a_c (4). In addition, one specific combination can be excluded optionally (the pair a_{id} and a_{je}). The *Choice* operator is identical to *Coord*, but for the fact that the variant argument is aggregated (5); for *Choice*, however, aggregated assertions hold *alternatively* and not *simultaneously*. The complementing *Except* operator (6) is defined analoguously, so that precisely the index combinations covered by the *Choice* operator are excluded. The *Assign* operator is defined as a specific composition of *Choice* operators, and a specific assignment optionally excluded (7). Figure 5 shows examples of *Coord* constructs for text and for formulas, and examples for the new constructs covering formulas from Figure 2 and example sentences from this section.

(8a) $Coord$(be($<$Steve,Thelma$>$,$<$nurse,chef$>$,all))

(8b) $Coord$(x,-,y,+,$<$1,2,3,4$>$)   (abstracting from nesting)

(9a) $Permut$(be($<$Pete,Steve,Thelma$>$,$<$boxer,guard$>$))   (abstracting from variants)

(9b) $Permut$($<$2,3$>$,*,x,-,y,+,$<$1,2,3,4$>$)   (abstracting from nesting)

(10) $Choice$(be(Thelma,$<$actor,guard,teacher$>$,$<$10,7,11$>$))

(11) $Except$(be(Roberta,$<$actor,guard,teacher$>$,$<$10,7,11$>$))

(12) $Assign$(be($<$Roberta,Steve,Thelma$>$,$<$actor,guard,teacher$>$,$<$2,4,5,9,13,14$>$))

Fig. 5. Aggregation constructs built from the running examples

5 A Procedure for Aggregation

For exploiting the aggregation potential in presenting a set of ground atoms, we use a staged process with internal recursions. In contrast to Shaw, we compose stages 2 to 4 of his algorithm into a single subprocess, since we do not apply sentence boundary limitations, and our syntactic coverage is much simpler – we merely build lists of argument values rather than combining forward and backward deletion. However, *one-argument distinct* and *two-argument distinct* coordinations are treated in separate stages, since building complex coordinations such as the *Permut* construct requires an incremental construction. The basic algorithm comprises: (1) Propositions are ordered (Section 5.1), (2) structures with single coordinations are built (Section 5.2), (3) multiple coordinations are built out of these intermediate structures (Section 5.3), (4) results are reorganized as specifications for realization in natural language or formulas (Section 8). Moreover, there is a facility for dealing with disjunctions, used after step (2): (2a) Expressing all variants unambiguously is attempted (Section 6.1). (2b) If unsuccessful, the set of variants is splitted, and step (2a) is repeated for each subset (Section 6.2). Formulas impose further demands for organizing stages (2) and (3) (Section 7.1), and measures outside the scope of proper aggregation (Section 7.2).

5.1 Ordering Propositions

Propositions are ordered by heuristics that aim at maximal compactness in the context of solutions to formal problems. The variant argument is the last one sorted, to favor aggregation across variants. Since the behavior of individual predicates usually is of more interest in the kinds of applications we are considering than the behavior of individuals, we start ordering with the argument predicate, which leads to a relation-oriented view as opposed to object-oriented views usually adopted for narratives [5]. The remaining arguments are sorted by starting from the element with the *least* number of distinct values, which tends to keep together "regular" substructures in densely populated parts of the space of predicate-value combinations. This measure contrasts with the heuristic applied by Shaw, which leads to grouping together a few propositions that are identical in as many arguments as possible.

5.2 Coordination with a Single Difference

Coord constructs are built across propositions that differ in a single argument value only (*one-argument distinct*). This is done by comparing the first two propositions, and, in case all but one of their arguments have the same values, a *Coord* construct is built by forming a list out of the arguments with non-equal values. This is repeated for the next pair of adjacent propositions, or with the *Coord* construct just built and the proposition following. If a set contains all individuals in the given context, it is replaced by 'all'. For the formulas, this measure yields single expressions for each of the columns in Figure 2, except to the two leftmost and the rightmost ones. Moreover, two pairs of formulas in the leftmost column, distinguished only by occurrences of the constants 2 and 3, and one such pair in the rightmost column are aggregated into single expressions each, reducing the originally 29 formulas into 11 at this intermediate stage. For the puzzle, aggregation is done across variants, which yields exactly the propositions in Figure 3 within the scope of *Coord* operators.

5.3 Coordination with Differences in Two Arguments

Within subsets of variants, it is attempted to compose facts that hold across all of these variants into larger structures, preferably *Permut* constructs or at least *Coord* constructs with *two-argument distinct* facts. Building *Permut* constructs is done by composing *Coord* constructs that have identical lists $<A_{in}>$ in position i, non-equal atomic values a_{jk} in position j (k indexing m *Coord* constructs), and identical atomic values in other positions, to yield *Permut*(base(...,$<A_{in}>$,..., $<A_{jm}>$, ...)). At most once, one value a_x from $<A_{in}>$ may be missing, yielding *Permut*(base(...,$<A_{in}[/a_x]>$,...,$<A_{jm}$ [/a_y]>,...)) for a *Coord* construct with a_y in position j. For the remaining facts and *one-argument distinct Coord* constructs, aggregation into *two-argument distinct Coord* constructs is attempted. This is done similarly to the building of *one-argument distinct Coord* constructs, but two arguments can have distinct values, and lists are built in the positions of each argument. If a *one-argument distinct Coord* construct is incorporated, the atomic value in the other argument is copied as many times as the list in the argument with distinct values has elements. Repetitions in one of the arguments lead to *mixed* coordinations in the linguistic realization, where coordinated conjunctions are combined with predicate gapping. This constitutes an advance over previous approaches, due to our staged coordination procedure. However, the price to pay is the restriction to two-argument distinct coordinations.

For the formulas in Figure 3, *Coord* structures are further aggregated: those in the second column from the left yield *Permut*($<2,3>$,*,x,$<+,->$,y) by joining the operators '+' and '-'. Moreover, formulas from the third and the fourth column from the left are aggregated into *Permut*($<2,3>$,*,x,-,y,+,$<1,4>$), joining the constants 2 and 3. An analoguous expression is built out of the formulas in the two adjacent columns.

6 Extensions for Handling Disjunctions

6.1 Aggregating Disjunctions

In order to express a set of facts holding in several variants, coordinations must be built that convey all relations among these variants unambiguously. A subset of the propositions must be aggregated into one construct expressing disjunctions – either a *Choice* construct optionally complemented with an *Except* construct, or an *Assign* construct. The remaining propositions must be independent of the variants considered: they must be aggregated into *Coord* constructs covering these variants. In order to test whether this is possible, *Choice* constructs are built by aggregating adjacent propositions that differ by their variant argument only. Depending on the number of *Choice* constructs, there are three possible cases (in all other cases, the variants are splitted and each subset is processed separately; examples appear under variant subsets in which the set of propositions is partitioned and marked as cases in Figure 6):

- There are two *Choice* constructs, which are of the form *Choice*(x,$<a_1,a_2>$,$<i_1,i_2>$) and *Choice*(y,$<a_2,a_1>$,$<i_1,i_2>$). They are aggregated into an *Assign* construct of the form *Assign*($<x,y>$,$<a_1,a_2>$,$<i_1,i_2>$). In the puzzle, this operation applies to the pairs 'Roberta' and 'Thelma' and 'actor' and 'teacher', variants 15 and 16 (case 1).
- There is one *Choice* construct, *Choice*(x,$<A_n>$,$<I_n>$). If no further propositions

are left, or there are n *Coord* constructs of the form $Coord(y,a_i,<I_m>)$, where I_m is equal to I_n with i_i missing, then these *Coord* constructs are aggregated into an *Except* construct of the form $Except(y,<A_n>,<I_n>)$. In the puzzle, this measure applies to assigning 'Thelma' to 'actor', 'guard', and 'teacher' in variants 7, 10, and 11, and 'Roberta' to the remaining positions in each variant (case 2.1.2).

- There is no *Choice* construct. In this case, a specific set of *Coord* constructs must be present so that they can be aggregated into an *Assign* construct. This is an effective way to compose an *Assign* construct, the alternative one in Figure 4 being more convenient for defining it. To start with, there must be exactly $n!$ or $n!-(n-1)!$ variants for some n, and exactly n individuals in the arguments varied (without the variant argument) in n^2 or n^2-1 *Coord* constructs. With indexing over individuals, checking the conditions is cheap. Only in case of success, expensive conditions for building an *Assign* construct must be checked. For each i of n (or $n-1$) *Coord* constructs $Coord(x,a_i,<I_m>)$, the sets of variants must be pairwise disjoint, which means that each x is assigned to exactly one individual in each variant. Similarly, in each i of the n (or $n-1$) *Coord* constructs $Coord(x_i,a,<I_m>)$, the sets of variants must be pairwise disjoint, too, so that each x_i is assigned differently in each variant. If all this is fulfilled, an *Assign* construct comprising all individuals and variants locally considered is built. In case the number of intermediate *Coord* constructs is $n!-(n-1)!$ and not $n!$, the missing fact must be incorporated in the *Assign* construct as an exclusion case. It is precisely the combination of individuals not covered by the *Coord* constructs. In the puzzle, such a case occurs twice, in some subsets of variants and propositions. In variants 1, 3, 8, and 12 (4 = 3!-2! variants), all combinations of assigning 'Roberta', 'Steve', and 'Thelma' to 'actor', 'boxer', and 'teacher' occur, except to the fact that 'Thelma' is not assigned to 'boxer' (case 2.2.1). Similarly, variants 2, 4, 5, 9, 13, and 14 (6 = 3! 6 variants) contain all combinations of assigning 'Roberta', 'Steve', and 'Thelma' to 'actor', 'guard', and 'teacher' (case 2.2.2).

```
Coord(be(<Steve,Thelma>,<nurse,chef>,all))
case 1 (variants are <15,16>): be(Steve,operator,all)
 Coord(be(<Pete,Pete,Roberta>,<boxer,guard,officer>,all))
 Assign(be(<Roberta,Thelma>,<actor,teacher>,all))
case 2(variants are <1-14>): be(Pete,operator,all)
  case 2.1(variants are <6,7,10,11>): be(Steve,officer,all)
    case 2.1.1(variant is 6): be(Thelma,boxer,6)
      Coord(be(<Pete,Roberta,Roberta>,<guard,teacher,actor>,6))
    case 2.1.2(variants are <7,10,11>): be(Pete,boxer,all):
      Choice(be(Thelma,<actor,guard,teacher>,all))
      Except(be(Roberta,<actor,guard,teacher>,all))
  case 2.2(variants are <1-5,8,9,12-14>): be(Roberta,officer,all)
    case 2.2.1(variants are <1,3,8,12>): be(Pete,guard,all)
      Assign(be(<actor,boxer,teacher/boxer>,<Roberta,Steve,Thelma/Roberta>,all))
    case 2.2.2(variants are <2,4,5,9,13,14>): be(Pete,boxer,all)
      Assign(be(<actor,guard,teacher>,<Roberta,Steve,Thelma>,all))
```

Fig. 6. Aggregation constructs for the puzzle from Figure 2

6.2 Splitting Sets of Variants

If propositions holding in some set of variants cannot be expressed compactly, these variants are splitted into subsets. After *Coord* constructs that hold across all variants are extracted, splitting is done along a set of predications that are *two-argument distinct* from one another and appear in each variant exactly once. Due to the ordering imposed, finding such a set can be done locally. If there is none, no splitting is attempted, since finding one would be expensive and might appear unmotivated – each variant is then presented separately. If there are several candidates, a good selection is made according to the following criteria: (1) The candidate consisting of the smallest set of facts is chosen to minimize the number of cases; if there is a tie, (2) the candidate that distributes variants most *unevenly* is taken. The motivation for this measure is that particularities through interference of conditions are filtered out, so that the remaining parts are likely to be more regular, which enables the attainment of compact presentations; if there is still a tie, (3) the candidate is chosen that splits as few as possible facts aggregated over variants when building subsets.

In the puzzle, the propositions holding in all variants are extracted yielding the "fixed" jobs 'chef' and 'nurse'. For the first splitting into cases 1 and 2, 'operator' and 'officer' yield binary partitions, 'operator' leading to a more uneven partitioning. Case 2 is splitted again, according to the assignment variants for 'officer'. The first partition after this splitting, case 2.1, is splitted further. Among the candidates that yield binary splits, 'boxer' is chosen because it requires only two aggregated facts to be splitted instead of three for 'actor' and 'teacher'. The other partition resulting after the second split, case 2.2, is splitted again, the only binary choice are the jobs by Pete.

7 Extensions for Handling Formulas

7.1 Coordination of Formulas

The limited effect of the general method in aggregating formulas is hardly surprising, since nesting and the larger number of arguments increases the potential and the variety for applying aggregation operators. This has consequences on ordering criteria, and the sequence of data is processed several times instead of doing this only twice.

Ordering is critical for formulas, since it is not sensible to orient the criteria on the number of distinct argument values, in particular when arguments being adjacent in the ordering priority list belong to different substructures. Rather, the structuring imposed by the nesting, the number of operators, as well as the number and positions of variables are decisive factors. Ordering is set up in such a way that each pass over the data set yields most effective compactification for the pass following. To achieve that, adjacent expressions should be different in their inner subexpressions, rather than in their top level operators. In concrete, the first criterion is the number of operators and variables in each subexpression, to group expressions with the same structural pattern closely together. This is followed by making distinctions according to the top level operator, followed by the operators of the subexpressions, and by the operands.

In the natural language context, multiple coordinations expressed by the *Permut* construct are restricted to two arguments, otherwise the resulting texts tend to be cumbersome and difficult to understand. With formulas, such a restriction need not be maintained, since multiple indexes and operator alternation (such as '±'), including combination of both, are quite common in mathematical expressions. Consequently, several passes of aggregation operations running over the entire data set are carried out, putting more-dimensional *Permut* constructs together incrementally.

In the first pass, only the atomic operands, the constants, are aggregated, yielding simple coordinations such as $Coord(x,-,y,+,<1,2,3,4>)$ (see Figure 2, second column from the right). Next, aggregation with this focus is repeated in a second pass. These two passes yield, for example, $Permut(<2,3>,*,x,-,y,+,<1,4>)$ out of the third and fourth column from the left in Figure 2. In a third pass, coordination of expressions with *two-distinct* arguments is performed, which is not carried out earlier because it might interfere with a preferable *one-distinct* argument coordination with the expression following. Through a *two-distinct* argument coordination, the two expressions in the top right corner of Figure 2 are composed to $Coord(<2,3>,*,x,+, <3,2>, *,y)$. Next, coordination is done along the embedded operators, ultimately followed by the top level operator. The last step yields the construct $Permut(<2,3>,*,x,<+,->,y)$ out of two intermediate *Coord* expressions distinguished by their second operators.

Due to the large number of arguments in the nested expressions, further compactification may be possible, but cannot be obtained with the given ordering. This may be the case for expressions that are identical except to one operator, since expressions differing only in terms of operands may interfere. For example, expressions (13) to (16) appear in the order indicated, which inhibits the aggregation of the expressions (13) with (15) and (14) with (16). In order to enable aggregation along operators in such cases, the data is reordered twice, once for focusing on embedded operators, once for the top level operator, and aggregation is repeated for each modified ordering.

(13) $Coord(2,*,x,*,x,+,<1,3,4>)$	if reordered, further
(14) $Coord(3,*,x,*,x,+,<2,4>)$	aggregation yields
(15) $Coord(2,*,x,*,x,-,<1,3,4>)$	(13+15) $Permut(2,*,x,*,x,±,<1,3,4>)$
(16) $Coord(3,*,x,*,x,-,<2,4>)$	(14+16) $Permut(3,*,x,*,x,±,<2,4>)$

7.2 Embedding of Formula Coordination

Since formulas can appear in a variety of equivalent forms, the way their coordination into aggregated expressions is handled is largely influenced by the purpose underlying this operation. If, as in our case, the concrete form of a formula is not of interest, but a high degree of compactification is desirable, the sets of formulas are subject to two kinds of modifications prior to proper aggregation: *simplification* and *norming*.

Concerning simplification, standard operations exploiting zero and unit elements (e.g., $x+0$ and $x*1$ yield x) are performed for subexpressions, and the number of variable occurrences is minimized (e.g., $x+x$ is replaced by $x*2$). Proper norming concerns a uniform ordering of subexpression in commutative operations, and exploiting symmetries between variables. Some operations particular to residue class operations are applied, motivated by mathematical conventions or by the suitability for finding aggregations. For example, for a residue class modulo n, expressions of the form $x-c$, c being a constant, are modified into $x+(n-c)$. Moreover, subexpressions of the form $0-x$ and $(n-1)*x$ are opportunistcally interchanged, depending on the top level operator.

For a multiplication, the second form is chosen, otherwise it is the first form – with the chosen variants, finding simplifications in the entire expression is favored.

Further aggregattion of formulas can be obtained by applying measures other than proper aggregation operations. One operation which is quite common in mathematics is the embedding of a subexpression in a larger formula, so that both expressions can be expressed compactly by marking the unique components of the larger expression as optional. A typical example is the expression $x+y[+c]$, which is the compact form of the operations that make a residue class an abelian group. For the residue class modulo 5, we compose this expression out of two formulas: $x+y$, and the construct $Coord(x,+,y,+,<1,2,3,4>)$. Performing such an add-on for the aggregation operations is done for two candidate expressions e_1 and e_2 of the following form (without loss of generality, let e_1 be the 'larger' and e_2 the 'smaller' expression): either e_1 has one of the forms $e_2+<c>$ or $e_2*<c>$, where $<c>$ is a list of constants, or e_1 and e_2 are identical except to a subexpression, which is of the form s in e_2 and of one of the forms $s+<c>$ or $s*<c>$ in e_1. If such a pair of expressions has been found, the 'smaller' expression, e_2, is omitted, and the larger one, e_1, is modified by inserting into the subexpression $<c>$ the unit element consistent with the operator preceeding, unless this constant appears already in $<c>$. In our running example, applying this optionality feature causes the expression $x-y$ being embedded in the construct $Coord(x,-,y,+,<1,2,3,4>)$, yielding expression (18), and the construct $Permut(<2,3>,*,x,<+,->,y)$ is embedded into $Permut(<2,3>,*,x,<+,->,y,+,<1,2,3,4>)$ yielding expression (20). Altogether, the 29 formulas in Figure 2 are aggregated into the 4 expressions listed below.

(17) $Permut(<2,3>,*,x,<+,->,y)$ (19) $Coord(<2,3>,*,x,+,<3,2>,*,y)$

(18) $Coord(x,-,y,+,<0,1,2,3,4>)$ (20) $Permut(<2,3>,*,x,<+,->,y,+,<0,1,2,3,4>)$

8 Realization in Terms of Natural Language Text or Formulas

In order to express the representation constructs obtained by natural language text, we process them as an application of the linguistic realization component TG/2 [1]. The most unique capability of this tool is to process specifications from several levels of linguistic elaboration, integrating canned text, template techniques and context-free grammars into a single formalism, following a recent trend in the field. This enables us to model the linguistically complex coordination phenomena by defining simplified grammar rules for schematic sentence patterns, but maintaining generalities in other language concepts, such as verb phrases. The relevant natural language fragment has been elaborated for English, German, and Arabic [6]. This includes building a lexicon for the argument values (e.g., the verb "to be" and the phrasing "take a position" for the relation 'be' in the puzzle), and specifying default features, e.g., for tense. Augmenting the TG/2 control mechanism, phrase expansion is separated from ordering, which supports modeling commonalities and differences across languages.

Applying TG/2 is preceded by a procedure that reexpresses the position-based encodings in terms of predicate-argument structures. In addition, specifications with case splits are reorganized. For example, nested cases are converted into flat lists where each case is labeled explicitly, except to subcases expressible by a single sentence. TG/2 maps aggregation constructs via rules onto sentence patterns, such as

$<ASSIGN(P,A1,A2)> \rightarrow <SUBJ (A1)> <ASSIGN-VP(P,A2)> [<EXCLUDE (X(A1),X(A2))>]$

Steve is the nurse and Thelma the chef. Then we have three cases to consider.

Case 1: Steve is the operator.

Then Pete is the boxer and the guard, and Roberta the officer. Moreover, Roberta is the actor and Thelma the teacher, or vice-versa.

Case 2: Pete is the operator and Steve the officer.

One alternative here is that Thelma is the boxer. Then Roberta is the teacher and the actor, and Peter the guard.

The other alternative is that Pete is the boxer. Then Thelma takes one of the positions teacher, guard, and actor, and Roberta the remaining positions.

Case 3: Pete is the operator and Roberta the officer.

One alternative here is that Pete is the guard. Then Roberta, Thelma, and Steve each take one distinct position out of the set teacher, actor, and boxer, but Roberta is not the boxer.

The other alternative is that Pete is the boxer. Then Roberta, Thelma, and Steve each take one distinct position out of the set guard, teacher, and actor.

Fig. 7. Natural language text for the puzzle

which expands an *Assign* construct into a grammatical subject (SUBJ), a dedicated verb phrase (ASSIGN-VP), and an optional exception (EXCLUDE), and percolates relevant components to these substructures (e.g., X(A1), the exception value of the first of the two lists). The dedicated verb phrase (ASSIGN-VP) can further be expanded into

<ASSIGN-VP(P,A2)> → <FU-PRED (P)> <MARKER> <COMPL-ASSIGN(P,A2)>

where the proper predicate is the function verb (FU-PRED) in the phrasing expressing the underlying semantic relation P (here: "take" from the phrase "take a position"), a disambiguation <MARKER>, and a dedicated sentence complement (COMPL-ASSIGN). The former is expanded into "each" for English, and the latter into

<COMPL-ASSIGN(P,A2)> → "one distinct" <FU-NOUN (P)> "out of the set" <OBJ (A2)>

combining canned text that expresses the meaning of *Assign* with the noun part of the phrasing expressing P (here: "position") and the sentence object (OBJ).

In similar ways, most constructs are mapped onto a single sentence, only *Except* and exceptions are joined to their related constructs. A remarkable feature is the treatment of the 'mixed' coordinations in *Coord* constructs. Repetitions of elements are eliminated, and the corresponding elements in the other argument are aggregated into a sublist. This measure may require a local reordering, to group together sublists that later appear in subject positions, since the predicate must be repeated when plural changes to singular or vice-versa (see Figure 7, first sentence under Case 1).

For handling the formulas, only handling the lists of constants enclosed by '<' and '>' is not straightforward. Within a *Permut* construct, each list is replaced by a unique variable, and enumerations for the values associated with each of them follow

$Coord(<2,3>,*,x,+,<3,2,*,y)$	$i*x+(5-i)*y,\ i=2,3$
$Coord(x,-,y,+,<0,1,2,3,4>)$	$x-y[+i],\ i=1,\ldots,4$
$Permut(<2,3>,*,x,<+,->,y)$	$i*(x\pm y),\ i=2,3$
$Permut(<2,3>,*,x,<+,->,y,+,<0,1,2,3,4>)$	$i*x\pm y[+j],\ i=2,3,\ j=1\ldots4$

Fig. 8. Mathematical expressions for the operations of quasi-groups modulo 5

number of	abelian					non-abelian		
expressions	Groups	Magmas	Monoids	Quasi-gr.	Semi-gr.	Magmas	Quasi-gr.	Semi-gr.
mod 5, original	5	19	6	8	5	343	29	2
mod 5, aggregated	1	7	2	2	1	51	4	2
mod 6, original	6	23	5	7	28	434	7	82
mod 6, aggregated	1	9	3	1	8	77	1	27

Fig. 9. Operation compactification by aggregation for residue classes modulo 5 and 6

the expression. Within a *Coord* construct, it is tested whether a standard function (we use identity and inverse within the given residue class) satisfies mappings between the elements of the lists of constants. Then a single index is sufficient for a pair of such lists (see the first line in Figure 8). Otherwise, all pairs of constants (n-tupels, in general), are enumerated. The mathematical formulas for the running example are listed besides the corresponding *Coord* and *Permut* constructs in Figure 8.

For the puzzle, the 128 original propositions are expressed by 15 sentences, which highlight relations among variants and degrees of choices and restriction. For the residue class categorizations, Figure 9 indicates the degrees of compactification obtained for each of the categories (there are no non-abelian groups and monoids). This Figure shows considerable reductions, reducing up to about 30 formulas into a handful ones, while a few 100 formulas are reduced by factors between 3 and 7.

9 Conclusion and Discussion

In this paper, we have described a presentation method that is applicable to solutions of problems encoded as sets of ground atoms. We achieve this result through adapting linguistically motivated aggregation techniques to specificities of formal problems, to express predications in natural language text, and in terms of formulas. We have defined novel constructs that can express sets of propositions with highly regular alternations on argument values concisely, including special forms of disjunctions. The application of the procedure defined on top of the constructs is demonstrated for model generation and for categorization proofs, including additions to the basic method. In an earlier paper [8], we have described presentations of unintended models satisfying incomplete specifications to the Steamroller problem [18] – not necessarily all solutions that satisfy given definitions. Our system is reasonably efficient – the aggregation process is linear with the number of data records, apart from sorting.

The method is implemented in CommonLisp, running on a Pentium 3 PC with 550 MHz. For the largest set of data, the residue classes modulo 6 categorized as magma (434 formulas), the overall running time is less than 5 seconds, including reordering and the subformula merging operations as described in Section 7.2. The system is set up as as a configurable tool, offering several ordering functions; choices among ordering criteria and uses of multiple passes and constructs (e.g., whether or not using disjunctions) can be specified with minimal effort. Currently, the system is interfaced with $\Omega MEGA$ for the categorization proofs and with KIMBA [10] for model generation with simple dedicated procedures, mostly consisting of calls to a string editor. The effect for aggregating sets of formulas can still be increased by some generalizations. When aggregation is not only performed over individual parts, but also over subformulas, two formulas G_1 and G_2, which are identical except to some subformula F_1 resp. F_2, that is, $G_1 \equiv G[F_1|F]$ and $G_2 \equiv G[F_2|F]$ can be jointly expressed by $G(x)$, $x = F_1, F_2$. Moreover, exceptions can be generalized to "regular" omissions, as in the form $(x+i)*(y+j)$, $i \neq j$, which aggregates 6 *Coord* constructs for the residue classes modulo 6 categorized as magmas. For these algebraic structures, the two extensions outlined would lead to a further compactificaction by a factor 2.

References

1. S. Busemann. Best-First Generation. In Proc. of the *8th International Workshop on Natural Language Generation*, pp. 101–110, Hearstmonceaux, UK, 1996.
2. Simon Colton, Alan Bundy, Toby Walsh. Automatic Concept Formation in Pure Mathematics. In Proc. of IJCAI-99, pp. 786–793, Stockholm, 1999.
3. Yann Coscoy, Gilles Kahn, Laurent Théry. Extracting Text from Proof. In *Typed Lambda Calculus and its Application*, 1995.
4. Ingo Dahn. Using ILF as a User Interface for Many Theorem Provers. In *Proc. of User Interfaces for Theorem Provers*, Eindhoven, 1998.
5. H. Dalianis. Aggregation in Natural Language Generation. *Computational Intelligence* 15(4), 1999.
6. Hakim Freihat. Realisierung aggregierter Ausdrücke in mehreren Sprachen und mit Formeln. Master thesis, University of the Saarland, forthcoming.
7. F. Giunchiglia, A. Villafiorita, T. Walsh. Theories of Abstrction. In *AI Communications* 10(3-4), pp. 167–176, 1997.
8. H. Horacek and K. Konrad. Presenting Herbrand Models with Linguistically Motivated Techniques, In Proc. of CIMCA-99, Vienna, 1999.
9. X. Huang and A. Fiedler. Proof Verbalization as an Application of NLG. In *15th International Conference on Artificial Intelligence*, pp. 965–970, Nagoya, Japan, 1997.
10. K. Konrad and D. Wolfram. System Description: Kimba, A Model Generator for Many-Valued First-Order Logics. In *16th Proc. of CADE*, pp. 282–286, Trento, Italy, 1999.
11. B. Mann and J. Moore. Computer as Author – Results and Prospects. Research Report ISI/RR-79-82, Univ. of Southern California, Information Sciences Institute, 1980.
12. B. Mann and J. Moore. Computer Generation of Multiparagraph English Text. *American Journal of Computational Linguistics* 8(2), pp. 17–29, 1981.
13. A. Meier, M. Pollet and V. Sorge. Comparing Approaches to Explore the Domain of Residue Classes. *Journal of Symbolic Computation*, 34(4), pp. 287–306, 2002.
14. M. Reape and C. Mellish. What is Aggregation Anyhow? In Proc. of *7th European Workshop on Natural Language Generation*, Toulouse, France, 1999.
15. J. Shaw. Segregatory Coordination and Ellipsis in Text Generation. In Proc. of the *36th ACL and the 17th COLING*, pp. 1220–1226, 1998.
16. J. Shaw. Clause Aggregation Using Linguistic Knowledge. In Proc. of the *9th International Workshop on Natural Language Generation*, pp. 138–147,1998.
17. J. Siekmann, C. Benzmüller, V. Brezhnev, L. Cheikhrouhou, A. Fiedler, A. Franke, H. Horacek, M. Kohlhase, A. Meier, E. Melis, M. Moschner, Immanuel Normann, Martin Pollet, V. Sorge, C. Ullrich, C.-P. Wirth, and J. Zimmer. Proof Development with $\Omega MEGA$. In *Proc. of the* 18th *CADE-02*, pp. 144–149, Kopenhagen, 2002.
18. M. Stickel. Schubert's Steamroller Problem: Formalisation and Solutions. In *Journal of Automated Reasoning* 2(1), pp. 89–101, 1986.

Automatic Document Categorization
Interpreting the Perfomance of Clustering Algorithms

Benno Stein and Sven Meyer zu Eissen

Paderborn University
Department of Computer Science
D-33095 Paderborn, Germany {stein,smze}@upb.de

Abstract. Clustering a document collection is the current approach to automatically derive underlying document categories. The categorization performance of a document clustering algorithm can be captured by the F-Measure, which quantifies how close a human-defined categorization has been resembled.

However, a bad F-Measure value tells us nothing about the reason why a clustering algorithm performs poorly. Among several possible explanations the most interesting question is the following: Are the implicit assumptions of the clustering algorithm admissible with respect to a document categorization task?

Though the use of clustering algorithms for document categorization is widely accepted, no foundation or rationale has been stated for this admissibility question. The paper in hand is devoted to this gap. It presents considerations and a measure to quantify the sensibility of a clustering process with regard to geometric distortions of the data space. Along with the method of multidimensional scaling, this measure provides an instrument for accessing a clustering algorithm's adequacy.

Keywords: Document Categorization, Clustering, F-Measure, Multidimensional Scaling, Information Visualization

1 Introduction

Clustering is a key concept in automatic document categorization and means grouping together texts with similar topics [5, 42]. It can serve several purposes:

1. Enhance the retrieval performance in terms of query relevance [13].
2. Enhance the retrieval performance in terms of response time [13].
3. Improve the user interface by facilitating navigation, inspection, and organization of document collections.
4. Automate text generation by providing the basis for a further processing like summarization.

Document clustering is a collective term for a complex data processing procedure that includes several model formation tasks: elimination of stop words, application of stemming algorithms, syntactic indexing based on term frequencies, semantic indexing based on term document correlations, or computation of similarity matrices [28]. For

A. Günter et al. (Eds.): KI 2003, LNAI 2821, pp. 254–266, 2003.

each of these tasks exist different approaches and several parameters, and different clustering algorithms behave differently sensitive to a concrete document representation model.

The various number of published experiments give an idea of what clustering algorithms can afford with respect to document categorization—but a justification, or a clear intuition why an algorithm performs well or poorly in a particular setting is hardly presented. This is in the nature of things: Aside from their computational complexity, clustering algorithms are primarily assessed by geometrical properties of the data space they are working on.

The categorization performance of a clustering algorithm can be quantified, for instance by the F-Measure. In a successful situation, say, for a high F-Measure value, one can argue that the chosen algorithm is adequate; with a bad F-Measure value, however, the following questions come up:

– Are the geometrical assumptions of the clustering algorithm admissible for the data at hand?
– Does noisy data disguise the underlying category structure?
– Is there an underlying structure at all?

These and similar questions can be answered easily by visual inspection.

1.1   Contributions of the Paper

The contributions of this paper are based on the hypothesis that a visual analysis of the data space is indispensable to understand the behavior of a clustering algorithm.

Note that visualizing a document collection is bound up with the question of dimensionality: The interesting data are documents which are abstracted towards feature vectors of several thousand dimensions. To become interpretable for a human beholder the objects must be embedded in a two or three-dimensional space. I. e., the document similarity, whose computation is based on all features in the original term space, has to be resembled by the geometrical object distance in the Euclidean embedding space. Although the singular value decomposition of large term document matrices shows that this reduction in degrees of freedom appears more drastic than it really is, the embedding implies a noticeable distortion of document similarities.

Stress measures are used to judge this distortion in the embedding space. Nevertheless, they tell us only little about the impact of the distortion with respect to a clustering algorithm. This is where the paper sets in. It contrasts an algorithm's clustering behavior in the high-dimensional term space and the low-dimensional Euclidean space and quantifies the degree of clustering coherence by a so-called "relative F-Measure". This measure can be regarded as a stress measure from the clustering algorithm perspective. In particular the paper shows

1. that a high embedding stress may or may not affect the performance of a clustering algorithm, and
2. how the relative F-Measure is used as a tool to interpret visualizations of the data space.

Moreover, the relative F-Measure can be used to compare clustering algorithms with respect to their robustness against geometric distortion.

2   Related Work and Background

Document clustering is a popular subject of research, and there are many publications on this topic dealing with performance experiments. E. g., Yang and Pedersen present a comparative study of feature selection methods [41], Salton presents a comparative study of term weighting models [33], and Aggarwal investigates the correlation between dimension reduction and Nearest Neighbor search [1]. The majority of the investigations employ a standard document representation method and analyze the categorization performance with respect to different clustering algorithms (strategies) [12, 42, 11, 37, 4].

Some of the recent results are quoted in the next subsection, while the subsections 2.2 and 2.3 are devoted to approaches for document space visualization.

2.1   Document Clustering

Let D be a set of objects each of which representing a document. An element $d \in D$ comprises a parsimonious but significant vector of term-number-pairs that characterize the document associated with d. Often, the terms in d are counted according to the approved $tf \cdot idf$-scheme, and the similarity computation between each two elements in D follows the cosine-measure. The construction of D from a document collection is called indexing and is not treated in this place; details can be found in [33].

An exclusive clustering of a set of documents D is a collection $\mathcal{C}$ of disjoint sets with $\bigcup_{C_i \in \mathcal{C}} C_i = D$. Most clustering algorithms can be assigned to one of the following classes.

- Iterative algorithms, which strive for a successive improvement of an existing clustering, such as k-Means, k-Medoid, Kohonen, or Fuzzy-k-Means [25, 19, 20, 40].
- Hierarchical algorithms, which create a tree of node subsets by successively merging or subdividing the objects, such as k-Nearest-neighbor, linkage, Ward, or Min-cut methods [10, 34, 16, 24, 39].
- Density-based algorithms, which separate a similarity graph into subgraphs of high connectivity values, such as DBSCAN, MAJORCLUST, or CHAMELEON [36, 8, 18].
- Meta-search algorithms, which treat clustering as a generic optimization task where a given goal criterion is to be minimized [3, 30, 31, 30].

The runtime of iterative algorithms is $\mathcal{O}(nkl)$, where n, k and l designate the number of documents, clusters, and necessary iterations to achieve convergence. Hierarchical algorithms construct a complete similarity graph, which results in $\mathcal{O}(n^2)$ runtime. When applied to non-geometrical data, the runtime of density-based algorithms is in the magnitude of hierarchical algorithms or higher.

The different clustering algorithms are differently sensitive with respect to noisy data, outliers, cluster dilations, non-convex cluster shapes, etc., and different statements can be found in the literature on this subject. Altogether, a trade-off can be observed between an algorithm's runtime complexity and its capability to detect clusters of complex shape. k-Means [25], for example, provides a simple mechanism for minimizing the sum of squared errors with k clusters. Moreover, aside from its efficiency, it provides a robust behavior, say, it rarely fails completely with respect to the quality of the clusters found.

Table 1. Characterization of selected clustering algorithms with respect to geometrical and geometry-related properties [2, 18, 19].

Agglomeration characteristic	
dilative (cluster number over size)	Complete Link
contractive (cluster size over number)	Single Link
conservative (balanced behavior)	Group Average Link, k-Means, variance-based methods (Ward)
Type of detected clusters	(+) good in (o) to some extent (−) unqualified
spherical clusters	k-Means (+), k-Medoid (+), Group Average Link (o),
arbitrarily shaped	Single Link (+), k-Means (−), k-Medoid (−), DBSCAN (+)
small clusters	Group Average Link (o)
equally sized	Ward (+), Complete Link (+)
different density	CHAMELEON (+), MAJORCLUST (+)

On the other hand, k-Means is not able to identify clusters that deviate much from a spherical shape. Table 1 lists typical geometrical properties of prominent clustering algorithms.

2.2 Document Space Visualization

Document space visualization is a collective term for approaches that prepare relations within a document collection D in order to make D amenable for human visual inspection. The result of such a preparation may be a thematic landscape, an information terrain, a rendered text surface, a hyperbolic graph layout, or an interaction graph [6, 7, 9, 17, 21, 26, 27, 29, 32, 35, 38].

Since documents are represented by high-dimensional term vectors, many visualization approaches employ a dimension reduction like multidimensional scaling (MDS) along with a cluster analysis as essential preprocessing steps when rendering D. To the interplay of these document abstraction steps, however, only less attention is payed.

A clustering in the reduced two- or three-dimensional embedding space may deviate significantly from a clustering in the original n-dimensional document space, $n \in [1000..5000]$. The developers of the WebRat visualization system "solve" this problem by performing the cluster analysis in the embedding space: *"Our algorithm returns labels for the clusters the user sees."* [32]. This strategy obviously entails the risk of pretending clusters that may not exist in the original data; Figure 3 in Section 4 gives an example for such a situation (which is easily uncovered by computing the relative F-measure).

Navarro also reports on the sensitivity of the MDS with respect to the quality (= separability) of a document collection [27]: *"... MDS produces very good visualizations for higher quality data, but very poor visualizations of lower quality data."*

Other visualization approaches rate cluster quality over layout quality. I.e., the cluster analysis is performed in the original space, while the visualization capabilities are limited to an approximate, say locally reasonable cluster placement. The systems BiblioMapper, Blobby-Texts, and AISEARCH follow this paradigm [35, 29, 26].

Note that the impact of an MDS on the clustering performance in the embedding space can hardly be judged by a classical MDS stress value: The typical size of the visualized collection D, $|D| \in [100..1000]$, along with the drastic dimension reduction results in stress values that exceed the worst case of Kruskal's application-independent rules of thumb in the very most cases [22].

2.3 Multidimensional Scaling

Multidimensional scaling (MDS) is a class of techniques for the analysis of dissimilarity data. MDS is used to find representations in $\mathbf{R}^k$ of objects for which only pairwise dissimilarities are given. The dissimilarities need not to be correct in the sense of a metric—they may be biased or estimated by humans. MDS techniques aim to reflect the inter-object dissimilarities through the distances of their representatives in $\mathbf{R}^k$ as good as possible. For $k = 2$ or $k = 3$ the representation can serve to visualize the objects. In general, the k real values per object can be considered as abstract features that can be used for further analysis.

Stress functions are used to measure how good a set of representatives $x_1, \ldots, x_n \in \mathbf{R}^k$ approximates the dissimilarities $\delta_{i,j}$ of the embedded objects. A candidate stress function is the residual sum of squares

$$S(x_1, \ldots, x_n) = \left(\sum_{i<j} (\delta_{i,j} - d_{i,j})^2 \right)^{1/2}$$

where $d_{i,j} = ||x_i - x_j||$ is the distance between x_i and x_j measured by a norm which is induced by an arbitrary metric on $\mathbf{R}^k$: High stress values are interpreted as a high degree of misfit of the representation.

Note that this stress function has several drawbacks. First, the stress value of an arbitrary representation is not normalized and hence is not comparable to stress values of other representations. Second, the relation between $\delta_{i,j}$ and $d_{i,j}$ is absolute; for the underlying model it might be useful or even necessary to relate the dissimilarities to the distances by a function. As a consequence, transformed dissimilarities, called disparities $\hat{\delta}_{i,j} = f(\delta_{i,j})$ are used, where the function f is derived from the underlying model. Note that f can be used to map ordinal data onto real values. In this case we speak of ordinal or non-metric MDS. To eliminate the mentioned drawbacks, stress measures called Stress-1 and Stress-2 are used [22], which are given by

$$S_1(x_1, \ldots, x_n) = \left(\frac{\sum_{i<j} \left(\hat{\delta}_{i,j} - d_{i,j} \right)^2}{\sum_{i<j} d_{i,j}^2} \right)^{1/2}$$

and

$$S_2(x_1, \ldots, x_n) = \left(\frac{\sum_{i<j} \left(\hat{\delta}_{i,j} - d_{i,j} \right)^2}{\sum_{i<j} (d_{i,j} - \bar{d})^2} \right)^{1/2}$$

where $\bar{d}$ is the average value of all distances $d_{i,j}$. Aside from measuring the goodness of fit, stress functions are employed as optimization criterion for MDS algorithms. A question which remains open is up to which stress value a representation can be judged valid with respect to the disparities. Kruskal provided rules of thumb for Stress-1 values, which are listed in Table 2.

Table 2. Kruskal's rules of thumb for the goodness of fit with respect to a stress value.

Stress	Goodness of fit
0	perfect
0.025	excellent
0.05	good
0.1	fair
0.2	poor

3   Interpreting Clustering Performance

The categorization performance of a clustering algorithm can be analyzed with external, internal, or relative measures [15]. External measures use statistical tests in order to quantify how well a clustering matches the underlying structure of the data. In absence of an external judgment, internal clustering quality measures must be used to quantify the validity of a clustering. Relative measures can be derived from internal measures by evaluating different clusterings and comparing their scores [19].

In our context, the underlying structure is the known categorization of a document collection as provided by a human editor, and external measures can be used.

3.1   The F-Measure

The F-Measure quantifies how well a clustering matches a reference partitioning of the same data; it hence is an external validity measure. The F-Measure combines the precision and recall ideas from information retrieval [23] and constitutes a well-accepted and commonly used quality measure for automatically generated document clusterings.

Let D represent the set of documents and let $\mathcal{C} = \{C_1, \ldots, C_k\}$ be a clustering of D. Moreover, let $\mathcal{C}^* = \{C_1^*, \ldots, C_l^*\}$ designate the reference partitioning. Then the recall of cluster j with respect to partition i, $rec(i,j)$, is defined as $|C_j \cap C_i^*|/|C_i^*|$. The precision of cluster j with respect to partition i, $prec(i,j)$, is defined as $|C_j \cap C_i^*|/|C_j|$. The F-Measure combines both values as follows:

$$F_{i,j} = \frac{2}{\frac{1}{prec(i,j)} + \frac{1}{rec(i,j)}}$$

Based on this formula, the overall F-Measure of a clustering C is:

$$F = \sum_{i=1}^{l} \frac{|C_i^*|}{|D|} \cdot \max_{j=1,\ldots,k}\{F_{i,j}\}$$

A perfect clustering matches the given partitioning exactly and leads to an F-Measure value of 1. In Figure 1 (left hand side) a cluster with a high precision and a low recall value is shown. Note that although the precision value is close to the maximum value of 1, the F-Measure value is rather low at 0.4. A high F-Measure value can only be achieved if both precision and recall are high, as exemplary shown in Figure 1 on the right hand side.

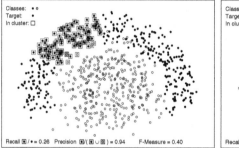 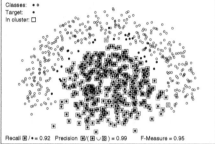

Fig. 1. A cluster with high precision and low recall values (left), and a cluster with both high precision and high recall values (right).

3.2   The Relative F-Measure

Let $\mathcal{A}_1, \ldots, \mathcal{A}_{t_A}$ be the sequence of clusterings generated by a clustering algorithm in the original space, and let $\mathcal{B}_1, \ldots, \mathcal{B}_{t_B}$ be the sequence of clusterings generated by the same clustering algorithm in the embedding space. To measure the effect of the MDS distortion on the clustering process we compare the clusterings $\mathcal{A}_i$ to the corresponding clusterings $\mathcal{B}_j$, where $\mathcal{A}_1$ corresponds to $\mathcal{B}_1$, $\mathcal{A}_{t_A}$ corresponds to $\mathcal{B}_{t_B}$ and an equidistant mapping is applied in between.

For each pair of clusterings $\mathcal{A}_i$, $\mathcal{B}_j$, the clustering $\mathcal{A}_i$ defines the reference classification to which the clustering $\mathcal{B}_j$ is compared using the F-Measure. We denote the resulting value as the *relative* F-Measure value. If a clustering algorithm behaves identically in both the original space and the embedding space, the relative F-Measure value will always be 1. Typically, the comparison delivers a curve that starts with 1 and that oscillates between $1/k$ and 1, depending on the MDS distortion and the sensitivity of the clustering algorithm.[1] Note that if the relative F-Measure is high at the end of the clustering process, the algorithm found a clustering in the embedding space that is similar

---

[1] If k defines an upper bound for the number of clusters, $1/k$ defines a lower bound of possible F-Measure values.

to the clustering found in the original space. I. e., the distortion error of the embedding is without impact on the clustering algorithm, and we can use the MDS projection for visual inspection.

4   Illustration

This section illustrates the presented ideas with a collection D based on 800 objects. With respect to feature number (dimension), feature distribution, and object similarity each element in D resembles a document which falls into one of two classes.[2]

Figure 1, presented already in the previous section, shows the MDS projection of D in the two-dimensional space. This embedding has an error (stress value) of 31%, which is typical for embeddings of mid-sized document collections D, and which is not acceptable according to Kruskal's rules of thumb.

To get an idea of how the MDS distortion influences the performance of k-Means, MajorClust, Single Link, and Group Average Link, we clustered the points in the original space as well as in the embedding space and computed the relative F-Measure in each clustering step. For convenience, the figures depict also the F-Measure curves for both the original and the embedded data in each clustering step.

4.1   k-Means Clustering

Figure 2 (top) shows the development of the relative F-Measure during the k-Means clustering process. The first part of the curve shows that cluster assignments differ noticeably for the original and the embedding space. This is a consequence of the MDS projection error—however, at the end of the clustering process the relative F-Measure value is high (0.9).

I. e., the MDS projected data in the embedding space appears to k-Means like the data in the original space, and, consequently, one can accept the found clusters: k-Means performs poorly here because the data contains entwined clusters.

4.2   Linkage-Based Clustering

The behavior of Group Average Link (cf. Figure 3, top) differs substantially from k-Means. In the original space, a high F-Measure value is achieved (0.9), while the performance in the two-dimensional embedding space is poor. Consequently, the relative F-Measure at the end of the agglomeration process is also low (0.6).

Figure 3 (bottom left) shows the found cluster in the embedding space, but it cannot serve as a basis for an analysis of the performance of Group Average Link in the original space, since the relative F-Measure is low at the end of the clustering process, indicating that the algorithm gets misleaded by the MDS projection. To get an idea of the cluster quality in the original space, Figure 3 (bottom right) shows this cluster in the embedding space.

---

[2] Various experiments have been conducted with the new Reuters Corpus Volume 1, English Language http://about.reuters.com/researchandstandards/corpus/. This corpus contains about 34.000 single topic documents that fall into more than hundred classes. For illustration purposes only figures of the binary classification situation are shown in this section.

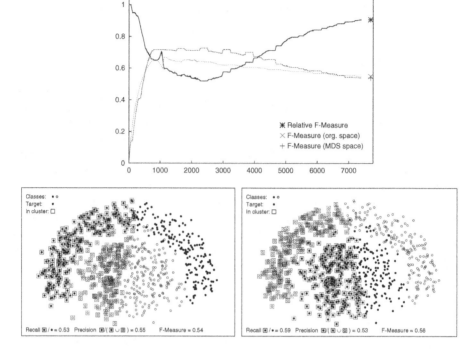

Fig. 2. The development of the relative F-Measure during the k-Means clustering process (top), a cluster found by k-Means in the embedding space (bottom left), and the cluster found in the original space (bottom right). The x-axis and y-axis of the top figure displays the number iterations of k-Means and the F-Measure values respectively.

4.3   MajorClust Clustering

MAJORCLUST shows a good and robust F-Measure development during the clustering process (cf. Figure 4). Since the final relative F-Measure values are fairly high, the MDS projection can be used to analyze the performance of MAJORCLUST in the original space. The cluster which is found was already shown in Figure 1.

The reason why MAJORCLUST's F-Measure values in both of the spaces are not higher is that the algorithm assigns the remaining points to three clusters (cf. Figure 1), which lead to high precision but lower recall values and consequently to an overall F-Measure value of approximately 0.8.

Discussion

As already pointed out by other authors, clustering algorithms often contain implicit assumptions about the clusters' shapes, sizes, or density distributions [14, cf. page 268]. While humans perform competitively with clustering algorithms in two dimensions, it is difficult to obtain an intuitive interpretation of data in high-dimensional spaces.

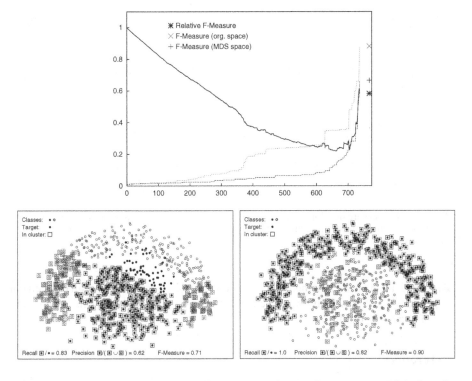

Fig. 3. The development of the relative F-Measure during the Group Average Link clustering process (top), a cluster found by Group Average Link in the embedding space (bottom left), and the cluster found in the original space (bottom right). The x-axis and y-axis of the top figure displays the agglomeration level of Group Average Link and the F-Measure values respectively.

Documents are represented in the high-dimensional vector space model, and an embedding of the data for visual interpretation purposes is usually performed by multi-dimensional scaling. The stress values involved with an MDS are typically significantly above Kruskal's suggestions [22], which raises the question of interpretability of the resulting scatter plots.

The key idea of the paper in hand is the following: If a cluster algorithm behaves similar in both the original data space and the embedding space, then the latter is amenable to geometrical interpretation. For this purpose we have introduced the relative F-Measure which quantifies the coherence of two clusterings during the clustering process.

We conducted several experiments in the field of automatic document categorization. It becomes clear that Kruskal's commonly accepted leveling rule for the interpretation of MDS stress values cannot be applied to detect an inadmissible distortion in the low-dimensional space. The relative F-Measure, however, provides a means to distinguish between admissible and inadmissible embeddings.

There is the question whether certain clustering algorithms behave more sensitive than others with respect to geometric distortion. Although our experiments included

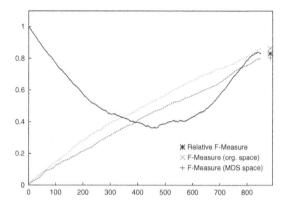

Fig. 4. The F-Measure development during the MAJORCLUST clustering process. The x-axis and y-axis displays the number of iterations (node reassignments) of MAJORCLUST and the F-Measure values respectively.

algorithms from each class mentioned in Subsection 2.1, they allow no final statement respecting distortion sensitivity or even a sensitivity-runtime tradeoff. This issue is subject of current research.

References

[1] Charu C. Aggarwal. Hierarchical subspace sampling: a unified framework for high dimensional data reduction, selectivity estimation and nearest neighbor search. In *Proceedings of the ACM SIGMOD international conference on Management of data*, pages 452–463. ACM Press, 2002.

[2] K. Backhaus, B. Erichson, W. Plinke, and R. Weiber. *Multivariate Anaylsemethoden.* Springer, 1996.

[3] Thomas Bailey and John Cowles. Cluster Definition by the Optimization of Simple Measures. *IEEE Transactions on Pattern Analysis and Machine Intelligence*, September 1983.

[4] Andrei Z. Broder, Steven C. Glassman, Mark S. Manasse, and Geoffrey Zweig. Syntactic Clustering of the Web. In *Selected papers from the sixth international conference on World Wide Web*, pages 1157–1166. Elsevier Science Publishers Ltd., 1997.

[5] Heide Brücher, Gerhard Knolmayer, and Marc-Andre Mittermayer. Document classification methods for organizing explicit knowledge. In *Third European Conference on Organizational Knowledge, Learning, and Capabilities*, 2002.

[6] A. Buja, D. F. Swayne, M. Littman, N. Dean, and H. Hofmann. XGvis: Interactive Data Visualization with Multidimensional Scaling. *Journal of Computational and Graphical Statistics*, 2001.

[7] Matthew Chalmers. Using a landscape metaphor to represent a corpus of documents. In *Proc. European Conference on Spatial Information Theory*, volume 716 of *LNCS*, pages 377–390, 1993. URL citeseer.nj.nec.com/chalmers93using.html.

[8] M. Ester, H.-P. Kriegel, J. Sander, and X. Xu. A Density-Based Algorithm for Discovering Clusters in Large Spatial Databases with Noise. In *Proceedings of the 2nd International Conference on Knowledge Discovery and Data Mining (KDD96)*, 1996.

[9]   Sara Irina Fabrikant. Visualizing Region and Scale in Information Spaces. In *The 20th International Cartographic Conference*, pages 2522–2529, Beijing, China, August 2001.

[10] K. Florek, J. Lukaszewiez, J. Perkal, H. Steinhaus, and S. Zubrzchi. Sur la liason et la division des points d'un ensemble fini. *Colloquium Methematicum*, 2, 1951.

[11] Eui-Hong Han and George Karypis. Centroid-Based Document Classification: Analysis and Experimental Results. Technical Report 00-017, Univercity of Minnesota, Department of Computer Science / Army HPC Research Center, March 2000.

[12] Taher H. Haveliwala, Aristides Gionis, Dan Klein, and Piotr Indyk. Evaluating strategies for similarity search on the web. In *Proceedings of the eleventh international conference on World Wide Web*, pages 432–442. ACM Press, 2002.

[13] Makoto Iwayama and Takenobu Tokunaga. Cluster-based text categorization: a comparison of category search strategies. In Edward A. Fox, Peter Ingwersen, and Raya Fidel, editors, *Proceedings of SIGIR-95, 18th ACM International Conference on Research and Development in Information Retrieval*, pages 273–281, Seattle, USA, 1995. ACM Press, New York, US.

[14] A. K. Jain, M. N. Murty, and P. J. Flynn. Data Clustering: a Review. *ACM Computing Surveys (CSUR)*, 31(3):264–323, 2000. ISSN 0360-0300.

[15] Anil K. Jain and Richard C. Dubes. *Algorithm for Clustering in Data*. Prentice Hall, Englewood Cliffs, NJ, 1990. ISBN 0-13-022278-X.

[16] S. C. Johnson. Hierarchical clustering schemes. *Psychometrika*, 32, 1967.

[17] Eser Kandogan. Visualizing multi-dimensional clusters, trends, and outliers using star coordinates. In *Proceedings of the seventh ACM SIGKDD international conference on Knowledge discovery and data mining*, pages 107–116. ACM Press, 2001.

[18] G. Karypis, E.-H. Han, and V. Kumar. Chameleon: A hierarchical clustering algorithm using dynamic modeling. Technical Report Paper No. 432, University of Minnesota, Minneapolis, 1999.

[19] Leonard Kaufman and Peter J. Rousseuw. *Finding Groups in Data*. Wiley, 1990.

[20] T. Kohonen. *Self Organization and Assoziative Memory*. Springer, 1990.

[21] T. Kohonen, S. Kaski, K. Lagus, J. Salojrvi, V. Honkela, V. Paatero, and A. Saarela. Self organization of a massive document collection. In *IEEE Transactions on Neural Networks*, volume 11, may 2000. URL citeseer.nj.nec.com/378852.html.

[22] J. B. Kruskal. Multidimensional Scaling by Optimizing Goodness of Fit to a Nonmetric Hypothesis. *Psychometrika, Vol. 29, No. 1,*, March 1964.

[23] Bjornar Larsen and Chinatsu Aone. Fast and Effective Text Mining Using Linear-time Document Clustering. In *Proceedings of the KDD-99 Workshop San Diego USA*, San Diego, CA, USA, 1999.

[24] Thomas Lengauer. *Combinatorical Algorithms for Integrated Circuit Layout*. Applicable Theory in Computer Science. Teubner-Wiley, 1990.

[25] J. B. MacQueen. Some Methods for Classification and Analysis of Multivariate Observations. In *Proceedings of the Fifth Berkeley Symposium on Mathematical Statistics and Probability*, pages 281–297, 1967.

[26] Sven Meyer zu Eißen and Benno Stein. The AISEARCH Meta Search Engine Prototype. In Amit Basu and Soumitra Dutta, editors, *Proceedings of the 12th Workshop on Information Technology and Systems (WITS 02), Barcelona Spain*. Technical University of Barcelona, December 2002.

[27] Daniel J. Navarro. Spatial Visualization of Document Similarity. Defence Human Factors Special Interest Group Meeting, 2001.

[28] M. F. Porter. An algorithm for suffix stripping. *Program*, 14(3):130–137, 1980.

[29] Randall M. Rohrer, David S. Ebert, and John L. Sibert. The Shape of Shakespeare: Visualizing Text using Implicit Surfaces. In *IEEE Symposium on Information Visualization*, pages 121–129, North Carolina, USA, October 1998.

[30] Tom Roxborough and Arunabha. Graph Clustering using Multiway Ratio Cut. In Stephen North, editor, *Graph Drawing*, Lecture Notes in Computer Science, Springer, 1996.

[31] Reinhard Sablowski and Arne Frick. Automatic Graph Clustering. In Stephan North, editor, *Graph Drawing*, Lecture Notes in Computer Science, Springer, 1996.

[32] V. Sabol, W. Kienreich, M. Granitzer, J. Becker, K. Tochtermann, and K. Andrews. Applications of a Lightweight, Web-Based Retrieval, Clustering and Visualisation Framework. In *4th International Conference on Practical Aspects of Knowledge Management*, volume 2569 of *LNAI*, pages 359–368, 2002.

[33] G. Salton. *Automatic Text Processing: The Transformation, Analysis and Retrieval of Information by Computer*. Addison-Wesley, 1988.

[34] P. H. A. Sneath. The application of computers to taxonomy. *J. Gen. Microbiol.*, 17, 1957.

[35] Min Song. BiblioMapper: A Cluster-based Information Visualization Technique. In *IEEE Symposium on Information Visualization*, pages 130–136, North Carolina, USA, October 1998.

[36] Benno Stein and Oliver Niggemann. *25. Workshop on Graph Theory*, chapter On the Nature of Structure and its Identification. Lecture Notes on Computer Science, LNCS. Springer, Ascona, Italy, July 1999.

[37] Michael Steinbach, George Karypis, and Vipin Kumar. A comparison of document clustering techniques. Technical Report 00-034, Department of Computer Science and Egineering, University of Minnesota, 2000.

[38] Edgar Weippl. Visualizing Content-based Relations in Texts. In *Proceedings of the 2nd Australasian conference on User interface*, pages 34–41. IEEE Computer Society Press, 2001. ISBN 0-7695-0969-X.

[39] Zhenyu Wu and Richard Leahy. An optimal graph theoretic approach to data clustering: Theory and its application to image segmentation. *IEEE Transactions on Pattern Analysis and Machine Intelligence*, November 1993.

[40] J. T. Yan and P. Y. Hsiao. A fuzzy clustering algorithm for graph bisection. *Information Processing Letters*, 52, 1994.

[41] Yiming Yang and Jan O. Pedersen. A comparative study on feature selection in text categorization. In Douglas H. Fisher, editor, *Proceedings of ICML-97, 14th International Conference on Machine Learning*, pages 412–420, Nashville, US, 1997. Morgan Kaufmann Publishers, San Francisco, US.

[42] Ying Zaho and George Karypis. Criterion Functions for Document Clustering: Experiments and Analysis. Technical Report 01-40, Univercity of Minnesota, Department of Computer Science / Army HPC Research Center, Feb 2002.

A Logical Approach to Data-Driven Classification

Rainer Osswald[1] and Wiebke Petersen[2]

[1] Praktische Informatik VII, FernUniversität Hagen,
Universitätsstraße 1, 58084 Hagen, Germany,
rainer.osswald@fernuni-hagen.de,

[2] Institut für Sprache und Information,
Abteilung Computerlinguistik, Heinrich-Heine-Universität Düsseldorf,
Universitätsstraße 1, 40225 Düsseldorf, Germany,
wiebke.petersen@uni-duesseldorf.de

Abstract. We present a flexible approach for extracting hierarchical classifications from data, which employs the logic of affirmative assertions. The basic observation is that each set of rules induced by the data canonically determines a classificational hierarchy. We give a characterization of how the chosen rule type affects the structure of the induced hierarchy. Moreover, we show how our approach is related to Formal Concept Analysis. The framework is then applied to the induction of hierarchical classifications from an amino acid database. Based on this example, the pros and cons of several types of hierarchies are discussed with respect to criteria such as compactness of representation, suitability for inference tasks, and intelligibility for the human user.

1 Introduction

The logic of affirmative assertions, which has its origins in domain theory and program semantics [16,1], has proved useful for the study of formal classification as well [10,11]. Its close connection with Formal Concept Analysis [4] has already been observed in [13], where the emphasis was on the classification of linguistic data; see also [15,14]. In this paper, the framework is illustrated by inducing hierarchical classifications from biochemical data. Another potential area of application is the generation of ontologies for the Semantic Web.

The key observation underlying our approach is that, first, any set of implicational statements which correctly describe a given classification table uniquely determines a hierarchical classification of that data, and, second, restrictions on the form of the statements systematically correspond to structural properties of the induced classificational hierarchy. For instance, if only atomic attributes are allowed as premise and conclusion, then the resulting hierarchy is a distributive lattice. Viewed from another perspective, our approach helps to clarify the relation between a theory and its *information domain* [2], where the latter is the ordered universe of admissible combinations of atomic attributes.

A. Günter et al. (Eds.): KI 2003, LNAI 2821, pp. 267–281, 2003.

The rest of the paper is organized as follows: In Section 2, each theory consisting of universally quantified Boolean predicates is shown to determine an information domain. In addition, it is shown how the information domain of a theory depends on the class the theory belongs to. This result is used in Section 3 for inducing different types of conceptual hierarchies from classification tables. In the case of Λ-free Horn theories, the induced hierarchies essentially coincide with the concept lattices of Formal Concept Analysis.[1] In Section 4, we give an illustration of how our framework can be used to generate hierarchical classifications from biochemical data. We discuss the effects of varying the underlying theory class. Moreover, we consider the selective addition of disjunctive rules.

2   Theories and Information Domains

2.1   Terms and Theories

Let Σ be a set of *atomic* one-place predicates. The logical framework employed in the following is a small fragment of first-order predicate logic. We will frequently make use of a variable-free notation. For instance, if ϕ and ψ are one-place predicates, then $\phi \wedge \psi$ is their logical conjunction. In addition, we introduce two special one-place predicates V and Λ that are respectively satisfied by everything and nothing of the universe of discourse. Moreover, $\forall \phi$ stands for $\forall x(\phi x)$, where ϕ is a one-place predicate. Finally, let $\preceq$ and $\equiv$ be two binary term operators such that $\phi \preceq \psi$ and $\phi \equiv \psi$ are $\forall(\phi \rightarrow \psi)$ and $\forall(\phi \leftrightarrow \psi)$, respectively.

As the attentive reader will notice, we could equally well make use of plain propositional logic instead. The reason for adopting the predicational viewpoint is conceptual clarity. For, in classification tasks, we basically have to deal with ascriptions of certain properties or attributes to certain entities, i.e., with predications. Furthermore, we are concerned with statements of the sort that everything with property ϕ also has property ψ, that is, with universally quantified conditionals. An additional point in favor of the predicational view is the fact that every theory consisting of such universal conditionals naturally defines a universal model of that theory, the elements of whose universe can be regarded as the "generic entities" classified by the theory (see also [12]).

Definition 1 (Term/Statement/Theory). *A Boolean term over Σ is inductively built by $\wedge$, $\vee$, $\neg$, and $\rightarrow$ from elements of Σ plus V and Λ. A Boolean term is* affirmative *if it is free of $\neg$ and $\rightarrow$. A universal statement over Σ is a statement of the form $\forall \phi$, with ϕ a Boolean term. A theory Γ over Σ is a set of universal statements over Σ.*

Given two theories Γ and Γ' over Σ, we say that Γ *entails* Γ', in symbols, $\Gamma \vdash \Gamma'$, if Γ entails Γ' by any sound and complete inference calculus for first-order predicate logic. The theories Γ and Γ' are said to be *equivalent* if they entail each other.

---

[1] The results of Section 2 and 3 are to a large part adapted from [11].

Definition 2 (Conditional Form). *A statement has* conditional (or bicondi-tional) *form if it is of the form* $\phi \preceq \psi$ *(or* $\phi \equiv \psi$*), with* ϕ *and* ψ *affirmative. A theory over* Σ *has* conditional (or biconditional) *form if its statements are of this form. The conditional form is* normal, *if* ϕ *is purely conjunctive (or* V*) and* ψ *is purely disjunctive (or* Λ*).*[2] *The conditional normal form is* reduced, *if* ϕ *and* ψ *have no atom in common.*

Proposition 1. *Every theory is logically equivalent to a theory in reduced con-ditional normal form and to one in biconditional form.*

Proof. By applying the standard transformations of propositional logic, every Boolean predicate has an equivalent conjunctive normal form. So every universal statement is equivalent to a finite set of statements of the form $\phi \preceq \psi$, with ϕ, ψ affirmative. Finally notice that $\phi \preceq \psi$ is equivalent to $\phi \equiv \phi \wedge \psi$.

Definition 3 (Horn/Simple Inheritance/Exclusion). *A conditional state-ment* $\phi \preceq \psi$ *is a* Horn *statement if* ϕ *and* ψ *are free of disjunctions; it is a* simple inheritance *statement if* ϕ *and* ψ *are atomic; it is an* exclusion *statement if* ψ *is* Λ*. A* Horn theory *is a theory consisting of Horn statements, etc.*

Remark 1 (Nonredundant Basis). A *nonredundant basis* of a theory Γ is a *min-imal* subset of Γ that entails Γ. For finite Σ, [3] presents a construction of a nonredundant basis, which generalizes the approach of [6].

Interpretations and models of theories are defined as usual in standard first-order predicate logic.

Definition 4 (Interpretation/Satisfaction). *A* (set-valued) interpretation *of* Σ *consists of a* universe U *and an* interpretation function M *from* Σ *to* $\wp(U)$*. The function* M *uniquely corresponds to a* satisfaction relation $\vDash$ *from* U *to* Σ*, with* $x \vDash p$ *iff* $x \in M(p)$*.*

An interpretation M can be inductively extended to all Boolean terms by $M(V) = U$, $M(\Lambda) = \varnothing$, $M(\phi \wedge \psi) = M(\phi) \cap M(\psi)$, $M(\neg\phi) = U \setminus M(\phi)$, etc.

Definition 5 (Truth/Model). *A statement* $\forall\phi$ *is* true *with respect to an in-terpretation if* ϕ *is satisfied by all elements of the universe. A* model *of a theory* Γ *over* Σ *is an interpretation of* Σ *with respect to which all statements of* Γ *are true.*

Definition 6 (Specialization). *Given an interpretation* M *of* Σ *with universe* U *and two elements* x *and* y *of* U*, then* x *is* specialized by y *(with respect to* M*), in symbols,* $x \sqsubseteq_M y$*, if* y *satisfies every element of* Σ *that is satisfied by* x*.*[3]

The specialization relation $\sqsubseteq$ is reflexive and transitive, i.e. a preorder. If $\sqsubseteq$ is antisymmetric and thus a partial ordering, we say that the interpretation satisfies *identity of indiscernibles*. It should be noticed that by stressing the importance of the specialization relation, we distinguish affirmative terms from Boolean terms in general. For one shows easily by term induction that $x \sqsubseteq y$ iff y satisfies every affirmative term over Σ that is satisfied by x.

---

[2] Notice that a statement in normal conditional form is essentially one in *clausal* form.

[3] In case M is clear from context, we drop the subscript.

2.2   Information Domains

We now show how to associate with each theory a *canonical model*. The ordered universe of that model, called the *information domain* of the theory, can be regarded as a conceptual hierarchy induced by the theory. We give a characterization of how the structure of these hierarchies depends on the type of the theory, and vice versa.

Definition 7 (Canonical Interpretation/Model). *The* canonical interpretation *of Σ has universe $\wp(\Sigma)$ and takes each $p \in \Sigma$ to the set $\{X \subseteq \Sigma \mid p \in X\}$, that is, $X \vDash p$ iff $p \in X$. Given a theory Γ over Σ, let $C(\Gamma)$ be the set of all $X \subseteq \Sigma$ which, under the canonical interpretation, satisfy ϕ for every statement $\forall\phi$ of Γ. The* canonical model *$M(\Gamma)$ of Γ takes $p \in \Sigma$ to $\{X \in C(\Gamma) \mid p \in X\}$.*

We call the elements of $C(\Gamma)$ the *consistently Γ-closed subsets* of Σ. Specialization on $C(\Gamma)$ is set inclusion and hence a partial order. Adapting the terminology of [2], we refer to $C(\Gamma)$, partially ordered by specialization, as the *information domain* of Γ.

For each interpretation M of Σ with universe U let ε_M be the function from U to $\wp(\Sigma)$ that takes x to $\{p \in \Sigma \mid x \vDash_M p\}$. By definition of specialization, $x \sqsubseteq y$ iff $\varepsilon_M(x) \subseteq \varepsilon_M(y)$. So ε_M is an order embedding of U into $\wp(\Sigma)$ if M satisfies identity of indiscernibles. Moreover, it follows by term induction that $x \vDash_M \phi$ iff $\varepsilon_M(x) \vDash \phi$. Consequently, if M is a model of a theory Γ then ε_M is a homomorphism of models from M to $M(\Gamma)$. The canonical model is thus the "largest" Γ-model satisfying identity of indiscernibles in the sense that every other such model M is embedded in $M(\Gamma)$ via ε_M (see also [12]). Another consequence is that $M(\Gamma)$ is *universal* in the sense that a statement is true in $M(\Gamma)$ iff it is true in all models of Γ, i.e., iff it is entailed by Γ.

Depending on the class of Γ, the information domain $C(\Gamma)$ can be characterized as a subset system as follows (see [11] for a proof):

Theorem 1. *If a theory Γ over a finite set Σ belongs to one of the classes listed on the left of Table 1 then its information domain $C(\Gamma)$ is closed with respect to the properties listed in the same row on the right. Conversely, if a subset system $\mathcal{U}$ over Σ has closure properties that are listed in the right column then $\mathcal{U}$ is the information domain of a theory over Σ of the corresponding class on the left.*

Remark 2. The finiteness of Σ in Theorem 1 is essential. If Σ is infinite then, e.g., closure with respect to directed union has to be added in the case of Horn theories. Moreover, it should be noted that the information domains of the various classes of theories can also be characterized order-theoretically. The information domains of Horn theories, for instance, are precisely the *Scott domains*. For both topics see [10,11].

Definition 8 (Canonical Theory). *Let $\mathcal{C}$ be a class of statements over Σ and $\mathcal{U}$ a subset system over Σ. The* canonical $\mathcal{C}$-theory *$\Gamma_{\mathcal{C}}(\mathcal{U})$ associated with $\mathcal{U}$ is the set of all $\mathcal{C}$-statements $\forall\phi$ such that $\forall X \in \mathcal{U}\,(X \vDash \phi)$.*

Table 1. Relationship between Γ and $C(\Gamma)$

Class of Γ	Closure properties of $C(\Gamma)$
unrestricted	none
Horn	nonempty intersection
Λ-free Horn	intersection
simple inheritance	intersection + union
exclusion	subsets + bounded union
binary exclusion	subsets + pairwise bounded union
simple inheritance + exclusion	nonempty intersection + bounded union

Let us say that $\mathcal{U}$ is C-*definable* if $\mathcal{U}$ is the information domain of a C-theory (which is the case, for instance, if C is the class of Horn statements and $\mathcal{U}$ is closed with respect to nonempty intersection). It is easy to see that $\mathcal{U}$ is C-definable just in case $\mathcal{U} = C(\Gamma_C(\mathcal{U}))$. In general, $\Gamma_C(\mathcal{U})$ is the *least C-definable subset system containing* $\mathcal{U}$. Consequently, by Theorem 1:

Theorem 2. *The information domain of $\Gamma_C(\mathcal{U})$ is the closure of $\mathcal{U}$ with respect to the properties of Table 1 that correspond to class C.*

3   Induction of Theories from Data

3.1   Complete Theories of Classification Tables

Consider the situation that a certain set U of objects is classified with respect to a set Σ of properties (or attributes). In other words, we are given a satisfaction relation $\models$ from U to Σ, i.e. an interpretation function M from Σ to $\wp(U)$. The triple $\langle U, \Sigma, \models \rangle$ is henceforth called a *classification table*. Given a classification table one can ask for a theory that explains the data. To make this precise, we need to fix the type of theory we are interested in. For example, one can ask for a simple inheritance theory with or without exclusions, a Horn theory with or without Λ, or a theory in general.

Definition 9 (Complete Theory). *Let C be a class of statements over Σ and M an interpretation of Σ. A C-theory Γ is a complete C-theory of M if, first, every statement of Γ is true with respect to M, i.e. M is a model of Γ, and, second, Γ entails every C-statement that is true in M.*

It is an immediate consequence of definitions that a complete C-theory of M is unique up to equivalence. Moreover, there is a trivial way to get a complete theory by taking the set $\Gamma_{C,M}$ of all C-statements that are true with respect to M.

Let us explore more closely the relation between a given classification table and the information domain of its complete C-theory. As shown in Section 2,

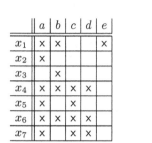

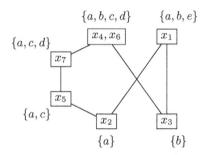

	a	b	c	d	e
x_1	X	X			X
x_2	X				
x_3		X			
x_4	X	X	X	X	
x_5	X		X		
x_6	X	X	X	X	
x_7	X		X	X	

Fig. 1. Classification table and induced specialization order

a classification table, i.e. a satisfaction relation $\vDash$ from U to Σ, determines a specialization relation $\sqsubseteq$ on U. Let $\mathcal{U}_M$ be the image $\{\varepsilon_M(x) \mid x \in U\}$ of the (pre)order-preserving function ε_M from U to $\wp(\Sigma)$ that takes $x \in U$ to $\{p \in \Sigma \mid x \vDash p\}$. In general ε_M is not one-to-one because there is no guarantee of *identity of indiscernibles*, i.e. different elements of U may satisfy exactly the same elements of Σ. We have $\mathcal{U}_M \simeq U/{\sim}$, with $x \sim y$ iff $\varepsilon_M(x) = \varepsilon_M(y)$.

Now notice that the canonical $\mathcal{C}$-theory $\Gamma_\mathcal{C}(\mathcal{U}_M)$ associated with $\mathcal{U}_M$ coincides with $\Gamma_{\mathcal{C},M}$, because $\varepsilon_M(x) \vDash \phi$ iff $x \vDash \phi$. So we can apply Theorem 2 to characterize the information domain of a complete $\mathcal{C}$-theory of M. For instance, if Γ is a complete Horn theory of M then $C(\Gamma)$ is the closure of $\mathcal{U}_M$ with respect to nonempty intersection; similarly, if Γ is a complete simple inheritance theory of M then $C(\Gamma)$ is the closure of $\mathcal{U}_M$ with respect to intersection and union.

Example 1. Let Σ be $\{a, b, c, d, e\}$. Suppose U consists of the seven elements $x_1, x_2, \ldots, x_7$ which are classified according to the table of Figure 1. In addition, the figure shows the specialization order on $U/{\sim}$ induced by the given classification table (where x_4 and x_6 are indiscernible, i.e. $x_4 \sim x_6$), as well as the corresponding subset system $\mathcal{U}_M$ over Σ. Figure 2 provides an overview of the information domains of several complete $\mathcal{C}$-theories of M, with varying $\mathcal{C}$. At the top of the Figure there is the information domain of a complete simple inheritance theory of M; it is the closure of $\mathcal{U}_M$ with respect to intersection and union. A (nonredundant) complete simple inheritance theory of M is given by the statements $d \preceq c$, $c \preceq a$, $e \preceq a$, and $e \preceq b$. The diagram below the top on the left depicts the closure of $\mathcal{U}_M$ with respect to intersection of nonempty subsets and union of bounded subsets. It is the information domain of the extension of the above simple inheritance theory by the exclusion statement $c \wedge e \preceq \Lambda$. Addition of the Horn statement $b \wedge c \preceq d$ further weakens the closure properties of the associated information domain. If the statement $b \wedge c \preceq d$ is added to the simple inheritance theory before the exclusion statement $c \wedge e \preceq \Lambda$, the resulting effect on the respective information domains is as depicted by the right branch of Figure 2. Finally, adding the statements $V \preceq a \vee b$ and $a \wedge b \preceq c \vee e$ leads to a complete theory of M, whose information domain consequently is $\mathcal{U}_M$.

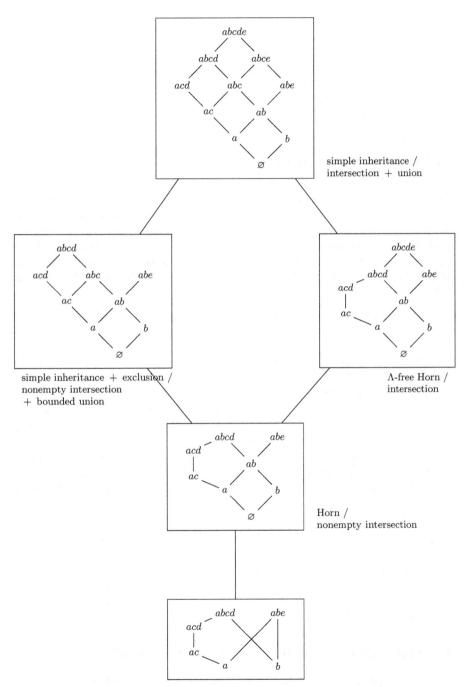

Fig. 2. Information domain of complete $\mathcal{C}$-theory with varying $\mathcal{C}$

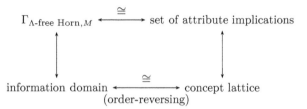

Fig. 3. Information domain approach vs. Formal Concept Analysis

3.2   Formal Concept Analysis

Formal Concept Analysis ([4]) associates with each classification table $\langle U, \Sigma, \models \rangle$ a (complete) lattice of formal concepts. (In the terminology of *Formal Concept Analysis*, a classification table is called a *formal context*.) A *formal concept* of $\langle U, \Sigma, \models \rangle$ is a pair $\langle V, X \rangle$ consisting of a set $V \subseteq U$ of objects (the *extent*) and a set $X \subseteq \Sigma$ of attributes (the *intent*) such that X is the set of those attributes that are shared by all objects of V, whereas V consists of all objects that have all attributes of X. So $\langle V, X \rangle$ is a formal concept just in case $V^{\blacktriangleright} = X$ and $X^{\blacktriangleleft} = V$, where

$$V^{\blacktriangleright} = \{p \in \Sigma \,|\, \forall x \in V \,(x \models p)\} = \bigcap\{\varepsilon_M(x) \,|\, x \in V\},$$

$$X^{\blacktriangleleft} = \{x \in U \,|\, \forall p \in X \,(x \models p)\} = \bigcap\{M(p) \,|\, p \in X\},$$

and M is the interpretation function associated with the classification table. Clearly $\langle (V^{\blacktriangleright})^{\blacktriangleleft}, V^{\blacktriangleright} \rangle$ is a formal concept for each $V \subseteq U$. Furthermore, every formal concept is of the form $\langle (V^{\blacktriangleright})^{\blacktriangleleft}, V^{\blacktriangleright} \rangle$. Within Formal Concept Analysis, a concept $\langle V_1, X_1 \rangle$ is said to be a *subconcept* of a concept $\langle V_2, X_2 \rangle$, notation: $\langle V_1, X_1 \rangle \leq \langle V_2, X_2 \rangle$, iff $V_1 \subseteq V_2$ or, equivalently, iff $X_1 \supseteq X_2$. The set of formal concepts ordered by $\leq$ forms a complete lattice, the so-called *concept lattice*. Notice that the subconcept ordering is reverse to the specialization ordering.

By definition, the set $\{V^{\blacktriangleright} \,|\, V \subseteq U\}$ of intents is the closure of $\{\varepsilon_M(x) \,|\, x \in U\}$, i.e. of $\mathcal{U}_M$, with respect to intersection. Hence Theorem 2 gives us the following characterization:

Theorem 3. *There is an order-reversing one-to-one correspondence between the concept lattice of a (finite) classification table and the information domain of the complete Λ-free Horn theory of that table.*

The diagram of Figure 3 summarizes the relation between (finite) concept lattices and information domains of Λ-free Horn theories. For the rest of the paper, we take up the convention of Formal Concept Analysis to graphically depict more special elements *below* less special ones.

4   Application: Classification of Amino Acids

4.1   Conceptual Hierarchies via Formal Concept Analysis

The automatic induction of hierarchies is desirable both from a practical and a theoretical point of view. On the one hand, it makes the processing of large

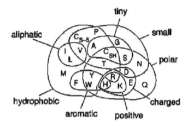

Fig. 4. Venn diagram taken from [7]

amounts of data possible and provides fast results. On the other hand, it is of theoretical interest to compare an automatically induced classification with existing descriptions, in order to reveal the assumptions made by the human expert. Furthermore, an automatically induced hierarchy can guide the human expert in analyzing new data. To this end, the induced hierarchy should exhibit as much of the implicitly given information as possible, and the original data should always be reconstructible from the induced hierarchy.

We discuss these issues by means of an example from an amino acid data base. Proteins are essentially built from 20 different amino acids that are specified by the genetic code. The amino acids can be classified by physico-chemical properties. Often this classification is represented in form of a Venn diagram (see Figure 4). Table 2 shows a classification table of those nine polar amino acids which tend to be at the surface of proteins; they are characterized by 17 physico-chemical properties.[4] It covers the properties: acidic, basic, neutral, charged, positive, negative, polar, hydrophobic, aliphatic, aromatic, buried, surface, acyclic, cyclic, large, medium, small.[5] Details about the properties of amino acids can be found in any introductory book on biochemistry (e.g. [9]).

Classifying the example data with Formal Concept Analysis results in the concept lattice shown in Figure 5.[6] As usual, only the attribute and the object concepts are labeled.[7] The concept lattice represents a monotonic multiple inheritance hierarchy, where a node inherits all the attributes labeled to its supernodes. Notice that conflicting attributes cannot be inherited, since the hierarchy is constructed on the base of the subset relation of concept intents. Compared to Venn diagrams, which are frequently used in biochemistry books, the hierarchical representation by the concept lattice is in our view easier to access for human beings. Questions like 'what are the common attributes of two amino

---

[4] See http://www.rrz.uni-hamburg.de/biologie/b_online/d16/16j.htm

[5] "Buried", in contrast to "surface", classifies amino acids that tend to be buried inside proteins. The three attributes of size refer to the number of atoms in the molecule.

[6] The drawing was done by the software tool "Concept Explorer" written by Sergey Yevtushenko; see http://www.sourceforge.net/projects/conexp.

[7] The *attribute concept* associated with an attribute p is the greatest concept whose intent contains p and the *object concept* of an object x is the smallest concept whose extent contains x.

Table 2. Classification of several amino acids by their physico-chemical properties

	acidic	basic	neutral	charged	negative	positive	polar	hydrophobic	aliphatic	aromatic	buried	surface	acyclic	cyclic	large	medium	small
Arg:R		×		×		×	×					×	×		×		
Asn:N			×				×					×	×			×	
Asp:D	×			×	×		×					×	×			×	
Glu:E	×			×	×		×					×	×		×		
Gln:Q			×				×					×	×		×		
His:H		×	×	×		×	×			×		×		×	×		
Lys:K		×		×		×	×					×	×		×		
Ser:S			×				×					×	×				×
Thr:T			×				×					×	×			×	

acids?' can be answered simply by looking at the smallest node above the amino acids.

Let us focus more closely on the six unlabeled nodes of the example concept lattice. The nodes of an inheritance hierarchy have essentially two roles: first, they can introduce new information, which will be inherited by subnodes and second, they "collect" information from their supernodes and transmit it "bundled up" to their subnodes. Unlabeled nodes are nodes which only perform information bundling and not information introduction. Nodes that do not bundle up information are necessarily labeled. Altering the hierarchy by varying the underlying theory which models the data of the classification table changes the proportion between the information introducing and the information bundling nodes.

4.2 Varying the Theory Class

Among the different hierarchical representations of a given data set there is none which is optimal in every respect. Rather, the question is to find the most appropriate representation depending on the task for which the hierarchy is built. Two criteria must be met by any reasonable representation: it must be complete and consistent with respect to the data. Furthermore, a good representation is maximally informative, maximally compact, and avoids redundancies by capturing generalizations. Unfortunately, it is not possible to construct an inheritance hierarchy which is optimal with respect to each of these criteria.

What does it mean to say that an hierarchical representation is maximally informative? In principle, every hierarchy which is consistent and complete with

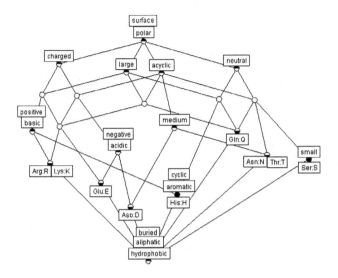

Fig. 5. Concept lattice corresponding to Table 2

respect to the data is equally informative in the sense that the original classification table can be reconstructed from the hierarchy. But the information domain of the complete (unrestricted) theory of the example data consists only of seven attribute sets which are pairwise incommensurable. They correspond to the seven elements of the concept lattice of Figure 5 that are immediately above the bottom element. For the observer the resulting flat hierarchy is less informative than the concept lattice, although from the viewpoint of the underlying theories, the Horn theory is a subtheory of the unrestricted one and therefore less informative. Switching to a less restricted theory class and looking at the rules gives the possibility to gain extra information. For example, the complete Horn theory of our example data only expresses that amino acids which are "positive" (or "negative") are also "charged". But it fails to point out the connection that every amino acid which is "charged" is either "positive" or "negative".

Since we are interested in the induction of hierarchical representations, we record that hierarchies differ with regard to the amount of information they exhibit explicitly. If the hierarchy is designed to be viewed by human beings it should maximize this amount of information. The compactness of a network can be measured in several respects, but in what follows we will only look at the number of nodes. The compactness criterion clearly favors the network of the unrestricted theory. A good representation avoids redundancy by capturing generalizations. In the case of the flat information domain of the unrestricted theory no generalizations are captured and therefore, most attributes have to be stated more than once (e.g. "charged"). In other words, the unrestricted theory leads to "overfitting". In the concept lattice (see Figure 5) all generalizations

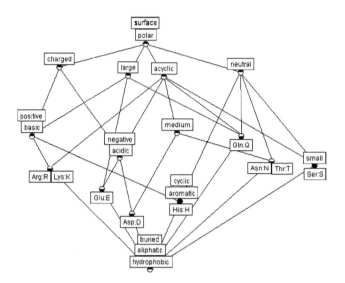

Fig. 6. AOC-poset corresponding to Table 2

are captured and every attribute and every object occurs exactly once; such a representation is said to be free of redundancy.

Is there any representation that has this desirable property but is more compact than the concept lattice? According to the results of Section 2 and 3, such a representation is the information domain of an extension of a complete Λ-free Horn theory by disjunctive rules that are consistent with respect to the data. Recalling the two different roles of nodes in inheritance hierarchies we can dispense with the six nodes which only bundle up information. This results in the inheritance network in Figure 6, which is the partially ordered set of the attribute and object concepts (*AOC-poset*).[8] A theory of the data whose information domain coincides with the AOC-poset can be obtained by taking all rules of the complete Λ-free Horn theory and by adding for each concept to be pruned from the concept lattice a rule whose premise is the conjunction of the intent X of the concept and whose conclusion is the disjunction of the conjunctions of its subconcept intents minus X. For example, to eliminate the node with intent {acyclic, neutral} (the unlabeled node on the right of Figure 5), we can add the rule

$$\text{acyclic} \wedge \text{neutral} \preceq \text{small} \vee \text{medium} \vee \text{large},$$

which is clearly true with respect to Table 2. Then {acyclic, neutral} is not consistently closed with respect to the extended theory and thus not an element of its information domain. Notice also that by definition the rule does no eliminate any other nodes.

---

[8] AOC-posets are also known as *pruned concept hierarchies* [5]. The present terminology has been introduced in [15].

Compared to the concept lattice, the AOC-poset is more compact and also free of redundancy. But it is not as informative as the concept lattice, since the information about common attributes is not captured in single nodes anymore. In the worst case, the AOC-poset has only two levels: the level of the attribute nodes and the level of the object nodes. This happens if, first, all objects intents and, second, all attribute extents are pairwise incomparable with respect to set inclusion. Nevertheless, the AOC-poset is more informative than the flat hierarchy since it simplifies the access to the information to which objects an attribute applies and it shows the hierarchical relations between the attributes.

The number of nodes in an AOC-poset is bounded by the sum of the number of attributes and the number of objects. In realistic data sets the difference in compactness between AOC-posets and concept lattices can be dramatic. For instance, take the lexical database CELEX, compiled by the Dutch Center for Lexical Information, which consists of three large electronic databases and provides users with detailed English, German and Dutch lexical data. The German database, which serves us as a test database, holds 51.728 lemmas with 365.530 corresponding word forms. Focusing at the stored derivational information of German lemmas, the number of nodes in the corresponding concept lattice is greater than 72.000, whereas the number of nodes in the AOC-poset is less than 4.000. (The underlying classification table consists of 9.567 objects and 2.032 attributes.) Hence, switching to the AOC-poset reduces the memory requirements. Moreover, since the AOC-poset is just the partial order of the attribute and object concepts, there is an efficient construction algorithm. To summarize, compared to concept lattices, AOC-posets provide a very simple method to induce redundancy-free inheritance hierarchies from huge databases. Inference tasks, however, are better supported by concept lattices, due to the explicit representation of shared attributes.

Having discussed the case of adding rules to a complete Horn theory, it remains to consider the omission of rules. Switching to the complete simple inheritance theory without exclusions seems to be overdone, because for the example data of Table 2 the resulting lattice has 100 concepts. Since many of the attributes of the example are incompatible, it makes sense to take the complete simple inheritance theory with exclusions instead. The corresponding hierarchy has 25 elements, witness Figure 7, and is hence less compact than the concept lattice. The simple inheritance theory is weaker than the one describing the AOC-poset or the concept lattice; it is thus more likely that a new object can be inserted without serious changes to the structure of the lattice.[9]

5   Outlook

A natural task to pursue is to analyze the presented approach from the viewpoint of *machine learning* (e.g. [8]). The problem of inducing theories from classifica-

---

[9] In biology, as well as in other sciences, hierarchical classifications are often presented in form of *taxonomic trees*. In [13], it is indicated how to "cut out" classification trees from concept lattices by adding appropriate disjunctive rules.

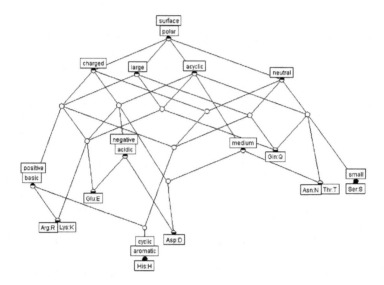

Fig. 7. Simple inheritance hierarchy with exclusions

tion tables can be characterized as follows: A given class $\mathcal{C}$ of theories constitutes the *hypothesis space* $\mathcal{H}$ of the learning problem, whereas the *version space* with respect to $\mathcal{H}$ and M consists of all $\mathcal{C}$-theories with model M. The commitment to statement type $\mathcal{C}$ determines the *inductive bias*: one can fit the data only as well as $\mathcal{C}$ permits. On the other hand, if $\mathcal{C}$ is too expressive, *overfitting* can occur: the induced theory explains the given data perfectly but does not allow generalizations. In addition to such general considerations, it seems worth to spell out the precise relation to *concept learning* and *inductive logic programming*.

A possible application of the presented approach is to allow disjunctive rules in attribute exploration tasks.[10] As discussed in Section 4.2, the problem is to avoid accepting too many disjunctive rules, since otherwise, in the case of incommensurable objects the exploration would always end in a flat hierarchy. One way to prevent this could be to introduce two steps: first, the standard attribute exploration is performed and second, each concept which is not yet an attribute or an object concept is tested to determine whether there is any object in the universe to which exactly the attributes of its intent apply. If so, the object is added to the context and if not, a disjunctive rule is added which excludes the concept from the information domain. In an exploration tool the concept could be tested by presenting the corresponding disjunctive rule (see Section 4.2) and asking if there is any known counter example.

---

[10] Attribute Exploration allows to determine a typical set of objects given a set of classifying attributes. An interactive procedure presents implications to the user, who can either accept them or deny them by giving a counterexample. For more details see [3].

Furthermore it would be interesting to explore possible ways to automatically shift from one theory to another, based on parameters like compactness monitored during incremental construction of the inheritance hierarchy.

References

1. Samson Abramsky. Domain theory in logical form. *Journal of Pure and Applied Logic*, 51:1–77, 1991.
2. Manfred Droste and Rüdiger Göbel. Non-deterministic information systems and their domains. *Theoretical Computer Science*, 75:289–309, 1990.
3. Bernhard Ganter. Attribute exploration with background knowledge. *Theoretical Computer Science*, 217(2):215–233, 1999.
4. Bernhard Ganter and Rudolf Wille. *Formal Concept Analysis. Mathematical Foundations*. Springer, Berlin, 1999.
5. Robert Godin, Hafedh Mili, Guy W. Mineau, Rokia Missaoui, Amina Arfi, and Thuy-Tien Chau. Design of class hierarchies based on concept (Galois) lattices. *Theory and Application of Object Systems*, 4(2):117–134, 1998.
6. J.-L. Guigues and Vincent Duquenne. Familles minimales d'implications informatives resultant d'un tableau de données binaires. *Mathématiques et Sciences Humaines*, 95:5–18, 1986.
7. Rainer Merkl and Stephan Waack. *Bioinformatik Interaktiv – Algorithmen und Praxis*. Wiley-VCH, Weinheim, 2003.
8. Tom M. Mitchell. *Machine Learning*. McGraw-Hill, New York, 1997.
9. David L. Nelson and Michael M. Cox. *Lehninger Principles of Biochemistry*. Worth Publishers, New York, 3rd edition, 2000.
10. Rainer Osswald. Classifying classification. In Geert-Jan Kruijff, Larry Moss, and Dick Oehrle, editors, *Proceedings of the Joint Conference on Formal Grammar and Mathematics of Language (FG/MOL-01)*, Electronic Notes in Theoretical Computer Science 53, 2001.
11. Rainer Osswald. *A Logic of Classification – with Applications to Linguistic Theory*. PhD thesis, FernUniversität Hagen, Praktische Informatik VII, 2002.
12. Rainer Osswald. Generic ontology of linguistic classification. In Benedikt Löwe, Wolfgang Malzkorn, and Thoralf Räsch, editors, *Foundations of the Formal Sciences II – Applications of Mathematical Logic in Philosophy and Linguistics*, Trends in Logic, pages 203–212. Kluwer, Dordrecht, 2003.
13. Rainer Osswald and Wiebke Petersen. Induction of classifications from linguistic data. In *Proceedings of the ECAI-Workshop on Advances in Formal Concept Analysis for Knowledge Discovery in Databases*, Lyon, July 23 2002.
14. Wiebke Petersen. *Induction of linguistic classifications – supported by Formal Concept Analysis*. PhD thesis, Heinrich-Heine-Universität Düsseldorf, Institut für Sprache und Information, in preparation.
15. Wiebke Petersen. A set-theoretic approach for the induction of inheritance-hierarchies. In Geert-Jan Kruijff, Larry Moss, and Dick Oehrle, editors, *Proceedings of the Joint Conference on Formal Grammar and Mathematics of Language (FG/MOL-01)*, Electronic Notes in Theoretical Computer Science 53, 2001.
16. Steven Vickers. *Topology via Logic*. Cambridge Tracts in Theoretical Computer Science 5. Cambridge University Press, Cambridge, 1989.

Spatial Inference – Combining Learning and Constraint Solving

Carsten Gips and Fritz Wysotzki

Berlin University of Technology
{cagi, wysotzki}@cs.tu-berlin.de

Abstract. In our approach to spatial reasoning we use a metric description, where relations between objects are represented by parameterised homogeneous transformation matrices with nonlinear constraints on the parameters. For drawing inferences we have to multiply the matrices and to propagate the constraints. We improve a machine learning algorithm (proposed in [1]) for solving these constraints. Thereafter we present the results of combining the advantages of this enhanced machine learning approach and interval arithmetics based constraint solving.

1 Introduction

The capability of understanding spatial descriptions and drawing inferences is self-evident and important for humans. We use this capability for almost everything, e.g. when reading texts, for navigation or design tasks. In the field of cognitive research this is subject to many investigations, where the concept of the Mental Model ([2]) plays an important part.

It is our aim to model the processes of understanding texts and drawing inferences using methods of artificial intelligence. In contrast to qualitative approaches to spatial reasoning ([3]) we use a metric approach for the inference procedure ([4]), which is based on Mental Models. From descriptions of spatial scenes we try to construct a corresponding Mental Model, which represents the described scene. Therefore we use a labelled digraph, where the nodes represent the objects and the edges represent the given spatial relations, resp. This graph can be used to draw inferences, i.e. to infer relations between pairs of objects, which were not initially mentioned in the text. Furthermore we can use the model for generating appropriate depictions of the described scene.

The semantics of the spatial relations is given by homogeneous transformation matrices and constraints on the variables. We associate a coordinate system with each object. As shown in [4], inference of a relation between two objects is done by searching a path in the graph connecting these objects, multiplying the matrices on the this path, and propagating the constraints. These constraints contain trigonometric functions and inequalities. Thus, we can solve them analytically only in rare cases. In [1] we proposed a cooperating constraint solver approach and a machine learning algorithm to solve the constraints.

A. Günter et al. (Eds.): KI 2003, LNAI 2821, pp. 282–296, 2003.

In this paper we show how the machine learning approach can be improved. Furthermore we demonstrate the combination of both, the cooperating constraint solver system and the (improved) machine learning algorithm. In the remainder, we first introduce the spatial descriptions and inferences in Sect. 2. After this, we sketch the cooperating constraint solver approach (Sect. 3) and recapitulate shortly the machine learning algorithm (Sect. 4). Then, we demonstrate in Paragraph 4.2, how the results of the machine learning algorithm can be improved using some background knowledge. In Sect. 5 we present a combination of both approaches, the constraint solver approach and the improved machine learning algorithm. Finally, we state conclusions (Sect. 6).

Note, the work presented in Sect. 2 to Sect. 4 is fundamental for the combination presented in Sect. 5. So we discuss it shortly, even though parts of the material are already published ([4,1]).

2   Constructing Mental Models from Texts

For a given text containing spatial descriptions, we want to create a cognitive model, which represents the described situation. Using the model we can draw inferences and generate appropriate depictions. For simplification, we consider 2D scenes only.

2.1   Spatial Descriptions

We start with textual descriptions of spatial scenes. It is known from psychology that humans create a suitable mental representation while reading spatial descriptions ([2]). Using these Mental Models, one can answer questions on the text, i.e. draw inferences. It is our aim to transform the spatial description given in the text into a formalised "Mental Model". For this formalisation we use digraphs, where the nodes represent the objects mentioned in the text and the edges between the nodes represent the spatial relations of the objects. Starting from an empty graph, it is constructed by sequentially checking, whether the relations are compatible or not with the so far generated model. If the current relation is compatible with the model, a corresponding edge is inserted into the graph. The text from Example 1 leads to the graph shown in Fig. 1(b).

Example 1. Given the following spatial description:

> *Steffi is standing in the room. She is looking around. There is a fridge in front of her. The nice new lamp is standing left to the fridge and right to the antique cupboard. It was a gift of her mother.*

Beside other informations, this spatial description contains the spatial relations `front(steffi, fridge)`, `left(fridge, lamp)`, and `right(cupboard, lamp)`. Since we use an *intrinsic* interpretation, in Fig. 1(a) an appropriate (and possibly intended) scene is shown. Note, the lamp is left to the fridge in the intrinsic system of the fridge. However, this is not the only possible scene. The question whether a scene is actually a representation of the given set of relations, depends of course on the intended meaning of the relations.

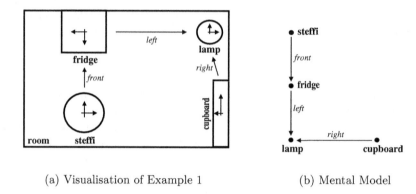

(a) Visualisation of Example 1   (b) Mental Model

Fig. 1. Example scene and resulting Mental Model (using an intrinsic reference system)

2.2 Expressing Spatial Relations

As mentioned above, in contrast to qualitative techniques for spatial reasoning we use a metric approach known from the area of robotics. With every object we associate a coordinate system, its shape and size. Relations between pairs of objects are represented by their transformation matrices. Thus, the current coordinates of an object depend on its relation, i.e. orientation and distance, to its relatum, which may be different in different constraints. That implies, that we need to transform the coordinates of an object using the corresponding matrix when changing its relatum. A point $\mathbf{s}_k$, expressed wrt. system j, is transformed to the new reference system i using the homogeneous transformation matrix $\mathbf{P}_j^i$:

$$\mathbf{s}_k^i = \mathbf{P}_j^i \mathbf{s}_k^j \qquad \text{where} \qquad \mathbf{P}_j^i = \begin{pmatrix} \cos\theta_j^i & -\sin\theta_j^i & \Delta x_j^i \\ \sin\theta_j^i & \cos\theta_j^i & \Delta y_j^i \\ 0 & 0 & 1 \end{pmatrix}.$$

The parameter θ_j^i describes the rotation angle of system j and system i. The distances of object j in the x- and y-directions from the relatum i are denoted by Δx_j^i and Δy_j^i, resp. At this, the lower index denotes the object and the upper index its reference system (the relatum).

A relation is defined by the transformation matrix with constraints on the parameters of the matrix, i.e. restrictions to the relative positions and rotations of the objects. Let us consider the relation `right/2` in detail[1]. The relation `right(cupboard, lamp)` places the lamp right wrt. the cupboard. The cupboard is the origin of the relation. The lamp can be placed within the bisectors of the right angles of the cupboard. This is shown in Fig. 2, whereas the lamp is represented by a circle and the cupboard by a rectangle.

---

[1] In the remainder we will write shortly `right` instead of `right/2`.

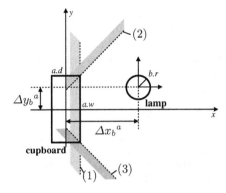

Fig. 2. The relation `right(cupboard, lamp)` in detail

We can describe the relation `right`(a, b) mathematically by the following inequalities, whereby in the above example the parameter a stands for the cupboard and b for the lamp, resp.:

$$\Delta x_b{}^a \geq a.w + b.r \tag{1}$$

$$\Delta x_b{}^a \geq \Delta y_b{}^a + a.w - a.d + \sqrt{2}\, b.r \tag{2}$$

$$\Delta x_b{}^a \geq -\Delta y_b{}^a + a.w - a.d + \sqrt{2}\, b.r. \tag{3}$$

At this, $a.w$ and $a.d$ represent the width and the depth of the rectangle, i.e. the cupboard, and $b.r$ stands for the radius of the lamp. The parameter $\Delta x_b{}^a$ and $\Delta y_b{}^a$ describe, as explained above, the relative position of object b wrt. object a. Each parameter belongs to a real valued interval. This is due to the ambiguousness of the given texts. Usually there is no information on the exact extents of the objects. So we have to deal with intervals, e.g. the radius of the lamp may range in the interval $[0.1, 0.5]$.

The other needed spatial relations, like `left`, `front`, and `behind` are defined analogous. Note, that for the relation `right`, like for every spatial relation, the formulae differ depending on the shape of the relata and referents.

2.3 Drawing Inferences

Using the Mental Model we can draw inferences, i.e. answer questions on relations between objects which where not initially given in the text. As shown in [4], this is done by propagating the constraints (i.e. (1) to (3) when considering `right(cupboard, lamp)`). The homogeneous transformation matrices are used for changing the reference system.

Example 2. We want to verify, whether the relation front(steffi, lamp) is consistent with the text given in Example 1. Therefore we have to search for a path in the graph connecting the objects steffi and lamp, to multiply the transformation matrices $\mathbf{P}_j{}^i$ on the found path, to propagate the constraints on them, and to compare the result with the defining constraints for the relation front. In Fig. 1(b) there is a path from steffi to the lamp via the fridge (front(steffi, fridge) and left(fridge, lamp)). Thus we have to calculate

$$\mathbf{P}_{\text{lamp}}{}^{\text{steffi}} = \mathbf{P}_{\text{fridge}}{}^{\text{steffi}} * \mathbf{P}_{\text{lamp}}{}^{\text{fridge}}$$

and to compare the resulting matrix $\mathbf{P}_{\text{lamp}}{}^{\text{steffi}}$ and its constraints with the defining constraints for front. For instance we have to check, whether

$$\Delta x_{\text{lamp}}{}^{\text{steffi}} = \cos\theta_{\text{fridge}}{}^{\text{steffi}} * \Delta x_{\text{lamp}}{}^{\text{fridge}} - \sin\theta_{\text{fridge}}{}^{\text{steffi}} * \Delta y_{\text{lamp}}{}^{\text{fridge}} + \Delta x_{\text{fridge}}{}^{\text{steffi}}$$

meets the definition of front, which is similar to the definition of right (Fig. 2). In very rare cases ([4]) we can do the comparison analytically. Thus we have to use numerical methods to solve and check the constraints. Since each parameter belongs to the interval algebra domain we use appropriate methods ([5]).

This inference mechanism is analogous to the propositional-qualitative inference using transitive chains. In contrast to the qualitative approaches we do not need a set of basic relations nor a composition table like the Allen calculus. We can prove relations between objects by calculating the corresponding matrices and constraints, which results in a system of complicated nonlinear inequalities. Since there are up to now no general methods to solve the constraints analytically, we use numerical methods of constraint solving. In the following sections we address this problem using two different approaches. In Sect. 3 we present a direct approach using cooperating constraint solvers, whereas the second approach, presented in Sect. 4, employs machine learning methods to solve the constraints. To benefit from the advantages of both approaches we combine them in Sect. 5 to a new method for solving constraints in the spatial domain.

3   Cooperative Constraint Solver

A direct approach to the problem of spatial reasoning is to use a constraint solver appropriate for this kind of problem. As mentioned in the last section, it is appropriate to use an interval constraint solver, like the Brandeis Constraint Solver ([6]), which handles basic operations, like addition and multiplication on rational intervals, as well as trigonometric functions. Note, that this solver is incomplete. That means, it may not detect every unsatisfiable constraint. So it is useful to employ other solvers for parts of the constraints. In [1] we introduced the use of cooperating constraint solvers. This concept, which was proposed in [7], allows the integration of arbitrary black box solvers. A meta solver coordinates the different solvers and the information exchange between them. Using such a system of cooperating constraint solvers it is possible to deal with hybrid constraints over different constraint domains.

For applying the meta solver to Example 1 we have to specify the problem using the algebraic representation for each relation (part (2) in Fig. 3). The intervals of the object extent parameters must be known (part (1)). Furthermore we add the needed transformations as additional constraints (part (3)). Part (4) expresses the background knowledge, i.e. each object must be located in the room. At this, $room.w$, $room.d$, and $lamp.r$ represent the extents of the room and the lamp. The parameters $\Delta x_{\text{lamp}}^{\text{room}}$, $\Delta y_{\text{lamp}}^{\text{room}}$, $\Delta x_{\text{lamp}}^{\text{cupboard}}$, and $\Delta y_{\text{lamp}}^{\text{cupboard}}$ denote the position of the lamp wrt. the room and the cupboard.

```
# extents of the objects                                              (1)
room.w ∈ [4.0, 5.0];      room.d ∈ [4.5, 5.0];      lamp.r ∈ [0.1, 0.5];
cupboard.w ∈ [0.4, 1.0];  cupboard.d ∈ [0.2, 0.5];  ...
# constraints for relations                                          (2)
```

$\Delta x_{\text{lamp}}^{\text{cupboard}} >= \text{cupboard}.w + \text{lamp}.r;$

$\Delta x_{\text{lamp}}^{\text{cupboard}} >= \Delta y_{\text{lamp}}^{\text{cupboard}} + \text{cupboard}.w - \text{cupboard}.d + \sqrt{2}\,\text{lamp}.r;$

$\Delta x_{\text{lamp}}^{\text{cupboard}} >= -\Delta y_{\text{lamp}}^{\text{cupboard}} + \text{cupboard}.w - \text{cupboard}.d + \sqrt{2}\,\text{lamp}.r;$

. . .

```
# transformations, abbreviations: room = r, cupboard = c, lamp = l   (3)
```

$\Delta x_{\text{l}}^{\text{c}} = \cos\theta_{\text{c}}^{\text{r}} * \Delta x_{\text{l}}^{\text{r}} + \sin\theta_{\text{c}}^{\text{r}} * \Delta y_{\text{l}}^{\text{r}} - \cos\theta_{\text{c}}^{\text{r}} * \Delta x_{\text{c}}^{\text{r}} - \sin\theta_{\text{c}}^{\text{r}} * \Delta y_{\text{c}}^{\text{r}};$

$\Delta y_{\text{l}}^{\text{c}} = -\sin\theta_{\text{c}}^{\text{r}} * \Delta x_{\text{l}}^{\text{r}} + \cos\theta_{\text{c}}^{\text{r}} * \Delta y_{\text{l}}^{\text{r}} + \sin\theta_{\text{c}}^{\text{r}} * \Delta x_{\text{c}}^{\text{r}} - \cos\theta_{\text{c}}^{\text{r}} * \Delta y_{\text{c}}^{\text{r}};$

. . .

```
# additional extents (needed for transformation)                     (4)
```

$\Delta x_{\text{cupboard}}^{\text{room}} \in [-\text{room}.w, \text{room}.w];$ $\Delta y_{\text{cupboard}}^{\text{room}} \in [-\text{room}.d, \text{room}.d];$

. . .

Fig. 3. Parts of the constraint system describing Example 1

Parts of the computed solution region are given in Tab. 1. The objects must not overlap. Thus, there is e.g. for the lamp at least a distance of 0.3 in x-direction of the cupboard. However, the lamp is also argument of other spatial relations, so the minimal distance to the cupboard with regard to the complete scene is 0.5 (as shown in Tab. 1). On the other hand, the calculated solution region is slightly to large. Due to the radius of the lamp, its position in the room can be at most the maximal extent of the room minus the minimal radius of the lamp, i.e. $\Delta x_{\text{lamp}}^{\text{room}}, \Delta y_{\text{lamp}}^{\text{room}} \in [-4.9, 4.9]$. Similar reasons lead to $\Delta x_{\text{lamp}}^{\text{cupboard}} \in [0.5, 14.2]$ and $\Delta y_{\text{lamp}}^{\text{cupboard}} \in [-14.2, 14.2]$.

Using the described system of cooperating constraint solvers allows to specify the spatial constraints and the transformations directly by using the defining sets of inequalities. The system determines automatically the appropriate solvers for certain constraints and propagates the solution of one solver to the others. The approach provides a fast and convenient method for solving constraints in the spatial domain. However, the used solvers are often incomplete, which is in

Table 1. Parts of the solution region for the problem given in Fig. 3

room.$w \in [4.0, 5.0]$	$\Delta x_{\mathrm{lamp}}{}^{\mathrm{room}} \in [-5.0, 5.0]$	$\Delta x_{\mathrm{lamp}}{}^{\mathrm{cupboard}} \in [0.5, 20.0]$
room.$d \in [4.5, 5.0]$	$\Delta y_{\mathrm{lamp}}{}^{\mathrm{room}} \in [-5.0, 5.0]$	$\Delta y_{\mathrm{lamp}}{}^{\mathrm{cupboard}} \in [-20.0, 20.0]$
lamp.$r \in [0.1, 0.5]$	cupboard.$w \in [0.4, 1.0]$	cupboard.$d \quad \in [0.2, 0.5]$

general taken over by the over-all system. Thus, the meta solver may not detect every unsatisfiable constraint or it cannot properly narrow the solution region.

We consider in the following Sect. 4 another approach for solving spatial scenes. In Sect. 5 we combine the advantages of both approaches.

4   Machine Learning

Instead of solving the constraints directly we try to learn a decision function $C(\mathbf{x})$ which decides whether a vector $\mathbf{x} = (x_1, \ldots, x_n)$ of the configuration space belongs to a region where the predicate C is true, i.e. the corresponding constraints are satisfied. Afterwards we use the result from the learning step for solving the constraints and generating depictions. We introduced this idea in [1] as an alternative approach for solving spatial constraints. For each relation and each tuple of object types, e.g. circles or rectangles, an appropriate classifier must be learned. Therefore we construct a training set by exploiting the given constraints for the relation. The datasets consist of classified feature vectors, where each variable of the constraints represents an attribute. The ranges of the extent parameters of the objects are given by background knowledge. Thus the learned classifier generalises on the possible objects of the given types. Points satisfying all constraints of a spatial relation are denoted with class symbol 'A', class 'B' otherwise.

Using these training data sets, machine learning algorithms construct classifiers. We have chosen the decision tree learning algorithm CAL5 ([8]) for learning the spatial relations. It uses axis-parallel hyperplanes for approximating the class boundaries piecewise linearly. Due to the approximation of the decision boundary between the A- and B-regions there is a small generalisation error. This error can be reduced by increasing the number of training data and by simultaneously increasing a certain parameter of CAL5. In the limit of an infinite set of training data the error becomes zero. For a more detailed survey on the learning process and its results refer to [1,9]. Note, the learned decision trees contain all generalisations for a given tuple of object types. So we can use the same tree for different input objects of a relation, as long as the objects have proper types.

4.1   Deciding Constraints by Generating Depictions

The aim is to solve spatial constraints in order to draw inferences in the Mental Model and to generate depictions. Therefore it is sufficient to decide the constraints, in contrast to the cooperating constraint solvers, which compute the complete solution region. Subsequently we sketch an algorithm (Fig. 4), which decides a spatial scene by generating an appropriate depiction, i.e. it delivers a solution of the constraint system. It uses the learned decision trees. For a more detailed explanation of the algorithm please refer to [1].

Since every valid depiction is a point in the solution region of the configuration space, we can represent them using feature vectors similar to the one we used for the training data. The vectors have to contain all variables of the whole problem now. The algorithm processes the relations sequentially. Because our relations are binary, we get for each relation three cases:

1. Both objects are 'unknown'. The relation does not contain any information on the first argument, so we place it randomly in the room (lines 09 and 10).
2. One object is already placed. Thus we have to place the other object wrt. the relation. Therefore we pick a class-A-leaf of the tree (describing a hyper cube, where the relation holds) and compute the size, and the relative position and orientation of the object by randomly assigning values to its remaining variables within the intervals of the chosen leaf (lines 11 and 12).
3. Both objects are placed. We have to check, whether the values of the parameters of the two objects can be classified as class A by the corresponding decision tree (lines 05 and 06). If not, the current vector does not satisfy the constraints and is rejected.

We repeat this procedure up to k times (block between lines 08 and 14), as long as the collision check in line 13 fails. If we do not have admissible values after the kth attempt (line 15), we suppose that the current relation cannot hold in combination with the others and we reject the depiction generated so far. However, there may exist solutions. Actually we cannot distinguish between the case "no solution possible" and "disadvantageous values". So if we reject the current vector, we have to start again with the first relation. For practical reasons we work instead on a number of object constellations in parallel. This means, we are starting with v empty vectors and apply the algorithm to each vector. Thus, we obtain in each step at most v depictions (valid for the relations processed so far).

This procedure is repeated for every relation. Finally we obtain up to v depictions according to the given spatial description. In the case that we have found no depiction, we have to assume that the constraints are not satisfiable. For some typical results refer to Tab. 3.

In this basic version of our approach we used uniformly distributed data for training. Thus we have no natural criterion for selecting a leaf (line 11 in Fig. 4). Following the idea, that small boxes[2] are located near the decision boundary and hence are rather unreliable with regard to the classification, we preferred larger areas for the placement of the second object. However, larger areas are located rather far away from the origin of a relation (Fig. 5(a)). So it may be difficult to find suitable values in these areas because the probability of collisions of the just

---

[2] Each leaf of the decision tree corresponds to a (hyper) box in the configuration space.

```
Depiction generation algorithm

INPUT: number v of initial vectors and number k of attempts
       relations r that have to hold
OUTPUT: up to v depictions, where all relations r hold
ALGORITHM:
 01  foreach relation r:
 02     identify objects and object types by object descriptions
 03     load the corresponding (pruned) decision tree
 04     foreach vector v:
 05       if both objects were placed
 06       then check whether relation r holds (classification)
 07       else
 08         repeat up to k times:
 09           if both objects are new
 10           then place first object randomly in room
 11             pick area (randomly according to weight of leaf)
 12             assign values to object parameters within intervals of leaf
 13             check non-overlapping with other objects and walls
 14         until check passes
 15       if no success
 16       then reject vector v
 17   show remaining vectors (depictions)
```

Fig. 4. Algorithm for generating depictions using decision trees

placed object with the walls or other objects increases. In combination with the large number of class-A-leafs (Tab. 2) this leads to a large number of attempts needed and thus to rather large computation times. This problem is subject of the improvement of our algorithm which is presented below.

Furthermore we cannot distinguish between the case "no solution" and "disadvantageous values". So if the algorithm does not find a solution we can only state with some probability, that there might be no solution. This problem and a further improvement is proposed in Sect. 5.

4.2   Improving the Algorithm Using Preferred Areas

As stated in the previous paragraph, the selection of the leafs is important in relation to the computation times. A students project at the TU Berlin investigated this question ([9]).

Preferring larger areas seems to be a good decision at first. However, usually these boxes are located far away from the origin of the relation (Fig. 5(a)). But when an object is placed in the selected area, this increases the probability of collisions with other objects and the walls of the rooms. This leads to the idea to use regions located near the origin for placement. But as shown in Fig. 5(a), the boxes near the origin are, like all leafs near the decision boundary, rather small. Hence the volume of the boxes is no reliable measure for selecting a leaf. The number of training data in a region is also no real criterion because we used an uniformly distributed data set. Thus we have to change the distribution of the training data.

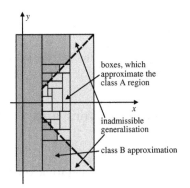

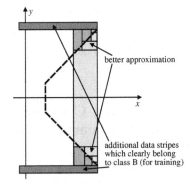

(a) Approximation of the decision boundary for `right`

(b) Additional stripes for class B added to the training data to avoid inadmissible generalisations

Fig. 5. Approximation and additional data stripes for a slice of the configuration space

In [9] several different distributions for the training data were tested. The best results are obtained using the data distribution shown in Fig. 6. A small region near the origin contains very much data. In order to avoid inadmissible generalisations (Fig. 5(a)), we have to add two small stripes with more data along the x-direction, which belongs clearly to class B (Fig. 5(b) and Fig. 6(b)). As a result, we can use the density of data in a box as selection criterion, since almost all data are located near the origin. For details refer to [9].

The results are very promising. Table 3 shows the quotient v per valid depiction, i.e. the number of vectors needed per solution found for the constraint satisfaction problem. The larger this quotient, the more tests we have to perform in order to solve the problem. That means, lower values for that quotient indicate a better and faster approach. The difference to the basic algorithm using uniformly distributed training data is obvious. We can even lower the values of the parameters v and k by an order of magnitude, which considerably lowers the calculation times. As shown in Tab. 2 the number of the class-A-leafs shrinks dramatically. This side effect also increases the speed of the algorithm, as already mentioned.

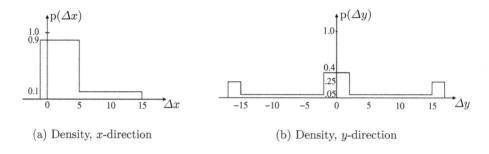

(a) Density, x-direction   (b) Density, y-direction

Fig. 6. Distribution density used for generating training data for the relation `right`

5   Combining Cooperative Constraint Solvers and Machine Learning Methods

In this Section we will combine the advantages of the cooperating constraint solvers and the (improved) machine learning approach.

As explained in Sect. 3, the system of cooperating constraint solvers represents a very fast approach for solving spatial constraints. It operates directly on a given set of constraints and narrows the solution region. However, due to the incompleteness of individual solvers the solver system may not detect unsolvable constraints. Likewise, the computed solution region may be too large. On the other hand, we sketched in Sect. 4 an alternative approach, which uses well interpretable decision trees for deciding spatial scenes. The approximation of the decision boundary may be (at least in principle) arbitrary high. As already mentioned, the algorithm may not find a solution, although one does exist. In this case we have to increase the runtime parameters and thus to increase the computation time. This leads to the following idea: We use the cooperating constraint solvers for a fast precomputation of the solution region of a spatial description. We safely can stop, if this step does not yield a solution. Otherwise we have to proceed: Due to the mentioned incompleteness of the system, the computed solution may be not properly narrowed or there may even be no solution. At this point we can use the machine learning approach. The decision trees approximate the region, where a relation individually holds. But when combined with other relations, the satisfaction region of a certain relation in this context is in general only a subset of its solution region. Thus we intersect the intervals computed by the constraint solvers and those of the decision trees. Thereby we prune every path in a tree, where the intersection yields the empty interval. This procedure has two advantages: At first, the resulting decision trees are much smaller than the original ones and describe the solution region of a relation wrt. the combination of several relations. Secondly, if we get non empty sets from the constraint solvers, even though there is no real solution, this intersection yields empty decision trees. Thus we know, that the description is inconsistent and we can stop.

Otherwise we start the machine learning algorithm (Fig. 4) using the new trees now. This step is quite fast now, because the intersection usually pruned many of the leafs and adjusted the trees wrt. the set of relations.

Example 3. As already mentioned, the first step is applying the cooperating constraint solver system to the problem. Thus the text from Example 1 leads to the configuration for the solver system shown in Fig. 3. Now the system uses its different solvers to narrow the solution region, which usually takes only parts of a second, depending on the number of constraints. We get intervals for each parameter, like shown in Tab. 1 for the parameters of right(cupboard, lamp).

The result of the solver system may be too large intervals, but it considers the dependences on the set of relations, whereas a decision tree describes the region, where a single relation individually holds. Thus the solution region computed by the solvers should be a subset of the solution region if a single relation is considered. We intersect the intervals of the parameters computed by the solvers and those of the corresponding decision trees. Whenever an intersection yields an empty interval, the path in the tree is pruned. This is shown in Fig. 7 for right(cupboard, lamp), which affects the parameters $\Delta x_{\text{lamp}}^{\text{cupboard}}$, $\Delta y_{\text{lamp}}^{\text{cupboard}}$, and the extents of both objects.[3]

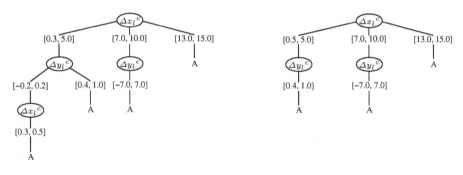

(a) Decision tree for right (artificial example)

(b) Tree after intersection with intervals shown in Tab. 1

Fig. 7. Intersecting the decision tree with the results of the constraint solvers

The number of the class-A-leafs of the obtained trees for this example are shown in Tab. 2. Now we use the machine learning approach (Fig. 4) in combination with the new trees for deciding the constraints. The promising results are shown in Tab. 3 (combination A).

---

[3] We use an artificial decision tree, because the real tree is to large for displaying it. For the same reason we show only the paths to class-A-leafs.

For some spatial relations the results of the combined approach are shown in Tab. 2 and Tab. 3. At first, the trees obtained from the intersection are much smaller, i.e. they contain fewer class-A-leafs. Furthermore the new trees are adjusted to the complete scene. This reduces the computation time, as already mentioned. For the description from Example 1 the number of the class-A-leafs are shown in Tab. 2. We used for the intersection the trees learned with the new data distribution (Sect. 4.2). The improvement is significant: The new tree for right(cupboard, lamp) contains only 24 class-A-leafs, which is nearly a factor 100 smaller than the original tree used in the basic algorithm.

Table 2. Number of class-A-leafs for Example 1 after intersection vs. the original trees

Relation	Number of class-A-leafs		
	original	using new distribution	after intersection
front	1.984	46	16
left	832	38	17
right	2.079	101	24

Some evaluation of the algorithm is shown in Tab. 3. We compare the original algorithm (Sect. 4.1), its improved variant (Sect. 4.2), and the combined approach (Sect. 5). Therefore we tested several descriptions with different numbers of relations, whereas combination A corresponds to Example 1 and consists of the relations front(steffi, fridge), left(fridge, lamp), and right(cupboard, lamp). Combination B augments combination A by right(steffi, cupboard). For combination C the relation atwall(wall1, cupboard) is added to combination B. Up to now we considered solvable scenes only. Recall, the parameter v stands for the number of (empty) depictions we start with. The parameter k quantifies the number of retries, if the collision check after placing an object fails. As a measure of complexity we introduce in the third column the quotient "number v per valid depiction". This parameter indicates the average number of needed initial (empty) depictions for generating just one depiction, i.e. the amount of backtracking down to the first relation for deciding the constraints and the scene. As this parameter also indicates the speed of the algorithm, lower values for it imply a faster solution. The value of this quotient is also independent of the implementation language or the testing machine. Compared to the basic algorithm, the improved variant is much faster. The combined approach yields for spatial scenes consisting of three relations similar results. However, for scenes with more relations it benefits from the smaller decision trees. We can also lower the values for v and k for an order of magnitude for surely getting at least one depiction.

Table 3. Some test runs and typical results of our algorithms

Combination of relations	Suitable v/k	Number v per valid depiction (average)	Method
Combination A (three relations)	1.000/100	125	original (Sect. 4.1)
	100/10	1.9	improved (Sect. 4.2)
	100/10	1.2	combined (Sect. 5)
Combination B (four relations)	1.000/100	375	original (Sect. 4.1)
	100/10	43	improved (Sect. 4.2)
	100/10	16	combined (Sect. 5)
Combination C (five relations)	10.000/1.000	638	original (Sect. 4.1)
	1.000/100	49	improved (Sect. 4.2)
	1.000/100	27	combined (Sect. 5)

6 Conclusions and Future Work

In this paper we presented several approaches to solve the constraints, which appear when reasoning in our metric model. We sketched a direct approach using systems of cooperating constraint solvers. Also, we improved a machine learning algorithm for solving the spatial constraints. Furthermore we combined the advantages of both approaches into a new, promising method.

The advantages of the cooperating constraint solving approach are obvious. It is a direct approach, which uses different solvers for different domains. It works directly on the algebraic definition of the constraints and narrows the solution region as much as possible. Thus it is comfortable in use. However, the disadvantage of the system is the possible incompleteness of the used solvers, and, thus, of the over-all system. Due to this fact the system may not detect unsolvable, i.e. inconsistent descriptions. The second approach is a machine learning algorithm. We transformed the problem by learning the decision boundary and used the decision trees learned by CAL5, because the trees are very well interpretable. The approximation of the decision boundary, and thus, of the solution region, may be (under certain conditions) arbitrary high. The algorithm decides the constraints by generating depictions of the described scene. Using background knowledge we can improve both, the speed of the algorithm and the quality of the depictions. We do this by using specific data distributions for the training step. The search is controlled by the two heuristic parameters v and k. Thus we may find no solution, although there is one. In this case we do not know, whether there is really no solution or, due to the stochastic nature of the search, not all class-A-leafs were inspected.

Combining both approaches yields very promising results. We use the direct solving approach for a more large-grain precomputation of the scene. If the solver does not find a solution, we can stop. Otherwise the precomputed solution may be to wide, due to the incompleteness of the used interval algebra solver. Particularly there may be no real solution even though the solver computed a non empty solution. Therefore we intersect this precomputed scene with the corresponding decision trees for the individual relations, which results in pruned decision trees. We can stop if the intersection is empty, because the solution of the complex scene must be a subset of the set of individual solution regions of the single relations, which are represented by the decision trees. Otherwise we use the pruned decision trees, which represent now the solution region of the relations wrt. the complete scene, in our (improved) machine learning algorithm and try to generate a depiction for the spatial description. If we succeed, we can state, that the constraints are solvable.

Future work includes a further analysis of behaviour of the combined solver when processing more complex scenes, which includes predictions on the scalability of our new algorithm. Therefore we have to re-implement the current prototype using a speed optimised language. Last not least, we plan to investigate the applicability of other methods of machine learning on the problem of spatial reasoning. DIPOL, which is a combination of a neural net and a clustering approach, approximates the solution region using much fewer training data than CAL5 and reaches nevertheless a higher accuracy. However, the result is not as easy interpretable as the CAL5 decision trees. Furthermore there are plans to employ genetic algorithms for searching for a solution.

References

1. Gips, C., Hofstedt, P., Wysotzki, F.: Spatial Inference – Learning vs. Constraint Solving. In Jarke, M., Köhler, J., Lakemeyer, G., eds.: KI2002: Advances in AI. LNAI 2479, Springer (2002)
2. Johnson-Laird, P.N.: Mental Models: Towards a Cognitive Science of Language, Inference and Consciousness. Cambridge University Press, Cambridge (1983)
3. Cohn, A., Hazarika, S.: Qualitative spatial representation and reasoning: An overview. Fundamenta Informaticae **46** (2001) 2–32
4. Wiebrock, S., Wittenburg, L., Schmid, U., Wysotzki, F.: Inference and Visualization of Spatial Relations. In Freksa, C., Brauer, W., Habel, C., Wender, K., eds.: Spatial Cognition II. LNAI 1849. Springer (2000)
5. Hickey, T., van Emden, M., Wu, H.: A Unified Framework for Interval Constraints and Interval Arithmetic. In Maher, M., Puget, J.F., eds.: Principles and Practice of Constraint Programming – CP'98. LNCS 1520, Springer (1998)
6. Hickey, T.: The Brandeis Interval Arithmetic Constraint Solver (2002) Available from http://www.cs.brandeis.edu/~tim/.
7. Hofstedt, P., Godehardt, E., Seifert, D.: A Framework for Cooperating Constraint Solvers – A Prototypic Implementation. In Monfroy, E., Granvilliers, L., eds.: Workshop on Cooperative Solvers in Constraint Programming – CoSolv. (2001)
8. Nakhaeizadeh, G., Taylor, C.C., eds.: Machine Learning and Statistics – The Interface. Wiley (1997)
9. Kirsch, D., Bärmann, T., Cissée, R., Rapoport, T.: Berücksichtigung präferierter Gebiete bei der Depiktion räumlicher Relationen. In Wiebrock, S., ed.: Anwendung des Lernalgorithmus CAL5 zur Generierung von Depiktionen und zur Inferenz von räumlichen Relationen. Report No. 2000–14, TU Berlin, ISSN 1436–9915 (2000)

Hybrid Approaches for Case Retrieval and Adaptation

Claudio A. Policastro, Andre C.P.L.F. Carvalho, and Alexandre C.B. Delbem

Institute of Mathematical and Computer Sciences – University of Sao Paulo.
Av. Trabalhador Sao-Carlense, 400 – 13560-970 – Sao Carlos, Sao Paulo, Brazil.
{capoli, andre, acbd}@icmc.usp.br

Abstract. The number of researches on hybrid models has been grown significantly in the last years, both in the development of intelligent systems and in the study of cognitive models. The integration of Case Based Reasoning and Artificial Neural Networks has received large attention by the area of neurosymbolic models. This paper proposes a new Case Based Reasoning approach using hybrid mechanisms for case retrieval and adaptation.

1 Introduction

The research interest on hybrid models (HMs) is increasing. This research involve both the development of intelligent systems and the study of cognitive models. The main motivations for the researches on HMs are [18]:

- Cognitive processes are not homogeneous, consequently, a large variety of representations and modelling techniques can be used;
- The performance of intelligent systems can be improved by the combination of different Artificial Intelligence (AI) techniques. Therefore, may effectively solve several real-world problems.

The integration of Case Based Reasoning (CBR) and Artificial Neural Networks (ANNs) has received large attention by researchers in the neurosymbolic area [2]. Several approaches integrating CBR systems with ANNs have been proposed in the last years [22,17,18,24]. A hybrid approach can be composed of two independent CBR and ANN modules or consisted of an unique structure combining characteristics from both paradigms [4].

CBR is a reasoning methodology that can be implemented using several techniques. The use of AI techniques, specially ANNs, to compose the CBR mechanisms may result in more efficient and robust systems for real-world problem solving than usual CBR mechanisms [17].

This paper proposes a new CBR approach using hybrid mechanisms for case retrieval and adaptation. Section 2 briefly introduces the CBR paradigm. Section 3 describes the case adaptation strategies. Section 4 presents an overview of hybrid CBR systems. Section 5 discusses the proposal for case retrieval and the adaptation. Section 6 shows the evaluation of the proposed system. Section 7 presents final considerations.

A. Günter et al. (Eds.): KI 2003, LNAI 2821, pp. 297–311, 2003.

2   Case Based Reasoning

CBR is a methodology for problem solving based on past experiences. This technique tries to solve a new problem by employing a process of retrieval and adaptation of previously known solutions of similar problems. CBR systems are usually described by a reasoning cycle (also named CBR CYCLE) with four main phases [1]:

1. *Retrieval*: according to a new problem provided by the user, the CBR system retrieves, from a Case Base (CB), previous cases that are similar to the new problem;
2. *Reuse*: the CBR system adapts a solution from a retrieved case to fit the requirements of the new problem. This phase is also named *case adaptation*;
3. *Revision*: the CBR system revises the solution generated by the *reuse* phase;
4. *Retention*: the CBR system may learn the new case by its incorporation in the CB, which is named *case learning*. The fourth phase can be devided into the following procedures: relevant *information selection* to create a new case, *index composition* for this case and *case incorporation* into the CB.

CBR is not a technology developed for specific proposes, its a general methodology of reasoning and learning [13,1,27], differing in important aspects from other AI paradigms [1]:

- CBR can use specific knowledge from previous problems;
- The reasoning from previous problems is a powerful strategy of problem solving, which is frequently applied by the human beings.
- The CBR paradigm is based on psychological principles.

The CBR paradigm is supported by two main principles [15]. The first says that the world is regulate: similar problems have similar solutions. Consequently, the solutions of similar problems are a good starting point for the solution of new problems. The second states that problems tend to repeat. Thus, new problems tend to be similar to previous problems.

CBR possesses also characteristics of Machine Learning (ML). It allows unsupervised and incremental learning by updating the CB when a solution for a new problem is found [1].

3   Case Adaptation Strategies

When CBR systems are applied to real-world problems, the retrieved solutions rarely can be straight forward used as proper solution for a new problem. Retrieved solutions in general require adaptations (second phase of the CBR CYCLE) in order to be applied to new contexts. The adaptation process may be either as simple as the substitution of a component from the retrieved solution or as complex as a complete change of the solution structure. The adaptation

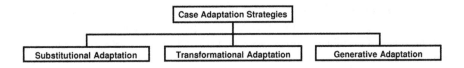

Fig. 1. Classification of case adaptation strategies.

can occur by the inclusion, removal, substitution or transformation of the components of a previous solution.

Several strategies for case adaptation have been proposed in the literature [14, 23]. They can be classified in three main groups (see Fig. 1): substitutional adaptation, transformational adaptation and generative adaptation.

The strategies for substitutional adaptation exchange solution attribute values of the retrieved solution by appropriate values, producing a new solution. The strategies for transformational adaptation modify the solution structure by including or removing components of the retrieved solution in order to satisfy the requirements of the new problem. The strategies for generative adaptation constructs a new solution from problem data using a predefined procedure. When a new problem is presented, an adapted solution is directly obtained by applying the procedure.

4   Hybrid CBR Systems

CBR and ANNs have been successfully combined, producing neurosymbolic systems [22,17,2,18,24]. This combination has been particularly successful in situations that require a functional integration among differents techniques [2]. The integration of CBR and ANNs can be carried out by two basic approaches [18]:

- *Separate components*: CBR and ANN are combined as completely distinct components that contribute equally to problem solving. Three types of processing can be distinguished: *co-processing*, *meta-processing* and *chained processing* [12];
- *ANN incorporated into the CBR CYCLE*: ANNs are used in one or more phases of the CBR CYCLE. This approach can also be named *sub-processing*.

Several approaches for integration of CBR and ANN employs neural networks in particular stages of the CBR CYCLE, specially, in the case retrieval.

In [17], an incremental ANN is used for case learning and retrieval. The network is composed by three layers: the input layer, whose units receive the problem attributes, the output layer, which contains a neuron for each case, and the internal layer, where each neuron represents a cluster of similar cases (also named prototype). The main idea is the construction of a simple system of case organization with two levels of memory: one containing prototypes of cases and another comprising instances of real cases.

Corchado et al. [6] use an ANN based on *Radial Basis Function* (RBF) model [20] for case adaptation. When a new problem is presented to the CBR system, a set of similar previous cases is retrieved. These cases are then used to train the RBF network. After the training, the new problem description is presented to the network, which works as a function mapping the current problem to a solution.

It must be highlighted that the use of another AI techniques to compose the CBR CYCLE may result in more efficient and robust systems for real-world problem solving than usual CBR mechanisms [17].

In this context, a system architecture that uses ANNs - and other ML algorithms - into the CBR CYCLE was developed.

5   Proposed Hybrid System

This work proposes a hybrid CBR system that uses an ANN for case retrieval, combined with other ML algorithms for case adaptation. The architecture of the proposed CBR system contains:

- A case retrieval mechanism composed by an ANN based on the *Adaptative Resonance Theory* (ART2) model [5];
- A case adaptation mechanism composed by one of the following ML algorithms:
  - an ANN based on the *Multi Layer Perceptron* (MLP) model [4];
  - a symbolic learning algorithm M5 [26];
  - an algorithm based on the statistical learning theory named *Support Vector Machine* (SVM) [25].

The ART2 networks are in a class of ANNs following the unsupervised learning paradigm. ART2 supports online learning, being able to learn a new pattern without forgetting patterns previously learned. Moreover, this technique supports inputs with continuous or binary values. [5].

MLP is the most commonly used ANN model for pattern recognition. A MLP usually presents one or more hidden layers with nonlinear activation functions (generally sigmoidal) that carry out successively nonlinear transformations on the input patterns. In this way, the intermediate layers can change nonlinearly separable problems into linearly separable ones [4].

M5 is a learning algorithm that generates models on the form of regression trees combined with regression equations (Model Tree) [26]. This model works similarly as a regression tree. However, the leaves contain linear expressions instead of predicted values. The Model Tree is constructed by a divide-and-conquer approach that recursively creates new nodes. The approach applies a standard deviation test to divide the remaining data into subsets and associates the test results to this new node. This process is done for all data subsets, creating an initial model. Afterward, a linear model is calculated for each inner node of the tree using a standard regression process. Then, the tree is pruned by evaluating the linear model of each node and its sub-trees [21].

SVM is a class of learning algorithms based on the statistical learning theory. It combines generalization control with a technique that deals with the dimensionality problem[1] [25]. This technique basically uses hyperplanes as decision surface, maximizing the separation borders between positive and negative classes. In order to achieve this, SVM follows a statistical principle named *structural risk minimization* [25]. Another central idea on SVM algorithms is the kernel of support vectors produced from a training data set. Different classifiers type can be constructed depending on how these vectors are generated.

5.1   Case Retrieval and Incorporation Approach

Previous Works. CBR solve new problems by retrieving and adapting known problems and their solution. Obviously as more the retrieval phase is efficient more the performance of the system increases.

In a flat memory system, cases are retrieved by applying similarity metrics to each case in the memory. The addition of a new case in a flat memory is computationally cheap, but the case retrieval becomes more expensive as the system CB increases [17].

In a hierarchical memory organization, cases sharing many features are grouped together. This organization is very efficiently for case retrieval, but the addition of a new case requires complex procedures. Moreover, it is in general difficult to keep an optimal structure when adding new cases [17].

Case Retrieval Proposal. This work proposes an approach for retrieval (first phase of the CBR CYCLE) and case incorporation (fourth phase of the CBR CYCLE) that keeps a simple memory organization. Moreover, this approach improves the case retrieval process by reducing the search space. The proposed strategy contains two levels of memory organization (see Fig. 2):

- The first level is composed by the output layer of an ART2 network, which creates and also indicates clusters with similar cases, reducing the search space and the retrieval time.
- The second consists of a simple flat memory that stores case instances grouped into the similarity clusters of the first memory level.

It must be highlighted that this approach may be integrated with an usual retrieval mechanism, like KNN [9] or Case Retrieval Nets (CRN) [16]. In this way, after the determination of a cluster by the ART2, an usual mechanism can be used for retrieve the most similar cases in that cluster, reducing the retrieval time.

---

[1] Machine Learning algorithms can have a poor performance when working on data sets with a high number of attributes. Techniques of attribute selection can reduce the dimensionality of the original data set. SVM is a ML Algorithm capable of keeping a good generalization even for large data sets.

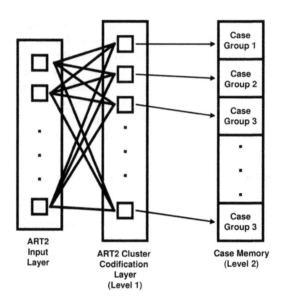

Fig. 2. Architecture of the case index and retrieval mechanism.

Case Retrieval Process. The case retrieval mechanism proposed (first phase of the CBR CYCLE) allows the retrieval of one or more similar cases according to the system requirements. The memory organization employed allows the division of the search space, reducing the retrieval time. This process is shown in the Algorithm 1.

Algorithm 1 Case Retrieval

---

function Retrieve (Description, CasesNumber)
    ClusterCode $\Leftarrow$ PresentPatternART2 (PreProcess(Description))
    SelectedCases $\Leftarrow$ RetrieveCluster (ClusterCode)
    SimilarCases $\Leftarrow$ SimilarityCalc (SelectedCases, Description)
    RetrievedCases $\Leftarrow$ MakeRanking (SimilarCases, CasesNumber)
    return RetrievedCases
end function

When the CBR system needs to retrieve similar cases for a new problem, it extracts the corresponding description and sends it to the retrieval mechanism as an attribute-value vector (*Description*). This mechanism, in turn, pre-processes this vector to form an input pattern that is presented to the ART2 network, which indicates the most similar cluster to the input pattern (*ClusterCode*). The retrieval mechanism selects the stored cases from the cluster indicated by the ART2 network (*SelectedCases*). Then, the similarity between each retrieved case and the new problem is calculated (*SimilarCases*) by using an usual mechanism like KNN [9] or Case Retrieval Nets [16].

The retrieval mechanism ranks the most similar cases (*RetrievedCases*) and returns them. The number of cases retrieved is indicated by *CasesNumber*.

Case Incorporation Process. The case incorporation mechanism proposed supports the storage of new cases at any time (fourth phase of the CBR CYCLE). The memory organization used by this mechanism makes possible the storage of new cases without the eliminating cases previously stored. The incorporation process is shown in the Algorithm 2.

Algorithm 2 Case Incorporation

---

function NewCaseStore (NewCase)
    Description ⇐ DescriptionExtract (NewCase)
    ClusterCode ⇐ ART2Train (PreProcess(Description))
    SaveNewCase (NewCase, ClusterCode)
end function

When the system needs to learn a new case (*NewCase*), the case is sent to the incorporation mechanism, which extracts the description of the problem (*Description*), and saves it in an attribute-value vector. Then, this vector is converted (*PreProcess*) in an input pattern for the ART2 network to be trained. Afterward, the ART2 network indicates the cluster to which the new case is belong (*ClusterCode*). The incorporation mechanism stores the new case in the flat memory (level 2) associated with the similarity cluster (level 1).

5.2 Case Adaptation Approach

Previous Works. The retrieved solution can not be directly applied to solve real or complex problems. In general, it needs to be adapted to fit new requirements (third phase of the CBR CYCLE). One of the major challenges in designing CBR systems is the acquisition and modelling of appropriate adaptation knowledge.

An alternative to overcome difficulties in acquiring adaptation knowledge has been the use of automatic learning. Nevertheless, there are few investigations in automatic learning adaptation knowledge on the literature.

Hanney [11] proposed an algorithm that acquires automatically adaptation knowledge as a set of adaptation rules made from the system CB. This set is generalized by joining similar rules and selecting appropriate ones for application in the adaptation process. Hanney also developed her own algorithm for rule generation and application instead a ML technique based on AI. This particular procedure may result in specific domain and computational complex processes.

Wiratunga et al. [28] proposed an inductive method for automatic acquisition of adaptation knowledge from system CB. The adaptation knowledge extracted from CB is used to train a committee of Rise algorithms [8] by applying Boosting [10] to generate different classifiers. The knowledge generation process proposed may also result in a complex computational process, since the adaptation rule generation demands many comparisons among solution components. Moreover, it is specific for certain design domains.

Case Adaptation Proposal. The approach for case adaptation employs two modules. The first module (data set generation module) generates a data set of patterns for case adaptation. This data set is then used by the second module (case adaptation mechanism), which trains a ML approach to automatically perform case adaptations.

The data set generation constructs the patterns adaptation data set. Let x be a problem stored in the CB and y_i a case retrieved by the CBR retrieval mechanism when x is presented. A pattern is obtained by calculating the differences between the solution stored in x and the solution stored in each retrieved case y_i. The adaptation patterns are used in the training of the adaptation mechanism. Afterward, the adaptation mechanism is used as a heuristic to adapt the attribute values of an retrieved solution.

This approach assumes that a CB is representative, i.e. all future problems in the current domain are covered by the CB. Therefore, no training of the adaptation mechanism is required when the system creates new cases during the reasoning process.

Adaptation Pattern Generation Process. The data set generation module proposed is capable of extracting implicit knowledge from a CB. This module uses an algorithm that is an extension of the algorithms proposed in [11,28]. The extended algorithm possesses some simplifications in the format of the patterns generated and in the manipulation of the patterns by the case adaptation mechanism (see Algorithm 3).

Initially, the pattern generation algorithm extracts a case from the original CB and uses it as a new problem ($ProofCase$) to be presented to the CBR system. Next, the algorithm extracts the attributes of the problem and its solution from the proof case ($ProofDescrpt$ and $ProofSolution$). The remaining cases compose a new CB without the proof case. Then, from the $ProofDescrpt$, the module returns the N most similar cases of the retrieved cluster ($RetrievedCases$), where N is a predefined value. For each retrieved case, the attributes of the problem and the components of the corresponding solution are extracted ($RetDescrpt$ and $RetSolution$). Then, the differences between the retrieved and the proof case solutions are calculated ($Diferences$).

Afterward, the algorithm generates the adaptation patterns using:

- Input attributes:
  - The problem stored in the proof case;
  - The problem stored in the retrieved case;
  - The solution stored in the retrieved case.

Algorithm 3 Adaptation Pattern Generation

---

function AdaptationPatternGenerate (CasesNumber)
   for all case from the original case base **do**
      ProofCase ⇐ ProofCaseExtract ()
      ProofDescrpt ⇐ DescriptionExtract (ProofCase)
      ProofSolution ⇐ SolutionExtract (ProofCase)
      RetrievedCases ⇐ Retrieve (ProofDescrpt, CasesNumber)
      for all RetrievedCases **do**
         RetDescrpt ⇐ DescriptionExtract (RetrievedCases(i))
         RetSolution ⇐ SolutionExtract (RetrievedCases(i))
         Differences ⇐ DifferencesExtract(ProofSolution, RetSolution)
         MakeAdaptationPattern (ProofDescrpt, RetDescrpt, RetSolution, Diferences)
      end for
   end for
end function

- Output attribute:
  - Differences between the proof case and the retrieved case solutions.

Finally, the generated patterns are used to train a ML algorithm (MLP, M5 or SVM) using the generated patterns. The training process is a component of the case adaptation mechanism.

Case Adaptation Process. The case adaptation mechanism proposed allows the learning of the modifications that must be performed in the components values of the retrieved solutions to reach an adequate solution for a new problem. The most important characteristic of this mechanism is the employment of the implicit knowledge inside the system CB with a minimum effort for the knowledge acquisition. The case adaptation process is shown in the Algorithm 4.

Algorithm 4 Case Adaptation

---

function Adaptation (Description, RetrievedCase)
   RetDescription ⇐ DescriptionExtract (RetrievedCase)
   RetSolution ⇐ SolutionExtract (RetrievedCase)
   InputPattern ⇐ MakeInputPattern (Description, RetDescription, RetSolution)
   Acts ⇐ AdaptationMechanism (PreProcess(InputPattern))
   NewSolution ⇐ ApplyActs (RetSolution, Acts)
   return NewSolution
end function

When a new problem is presented to the CBR system, the most similar stored case of the CB is obtained by a retrieval mechanism. This case is sent to the adaptation mechanism together with the problem description (*Description* and *RetrievedCase*). The adaptation algorithm extracts the problem and solution attributes of the retrieved case (*RetDescription* and *RetSolution*). Then, the adaptation algorithm generates the input pattern for the ML algorithm. Next the ML algorithm performs modifications in the attributes of the retrieved solution (*Acts*). Finally, these modifications are applied to the retrieved solution in order to obtain the solution for the new problem (*NewSolution*).

Fig. 3 shows the general architecture of the proposed hybrid approach, highlighting each proposed algorithm into the CBR CYCLE.

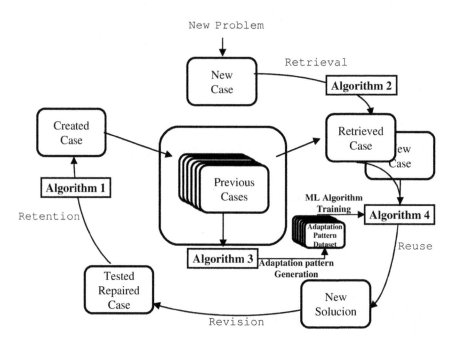

Fig. 3. The CBR Cycle and the hybrid approach architecture (Algorithms 2, 1, 3 and 4).

6   Test Results

The CBR system proposed employs an ART2 neural network as case retrieval mechanism. For the case adaptation mechanism, the following ML techniques were investigated: MLP neural network; M5 algorithm and SVM. In order to evaluate the proposed approaches, several tests were carried out to compare them which te performance of the ML techniques alone (MLP, M5 and SVM).

For the evaluation of the knowledge extraction algorithm, a data set available in the repository from the Machine Learning Group of the University of California, Irvine (UCI) (http://www.ics.uci.edu) was used. The selected domain constitutes of servomechanism data. This data set has been used in previous approaches case adaptation [11], which have shown that this domain corresponds to an extremely non-linear phenomenon. The servomechanism data set is composed of 167 cases, containing 4 discrete input attributes and 1 continuous class attribute (see Table 1).

Table 1. Servomechanism case structure.

	Attribute	Values
	Motor	A,B,C,D,E
Problem	Screw	A,B,C,D,E
	PGain	3,4,5,6
	VGain	1,2,3,4,5
Solution	Class	Continuous

A sample of the adaptation pattern generated is shown in the Fig. 4:

Proof Case		Retrieved Case	
Motor	E	Motor	E
Screw	E	Screw	E
PGain	5	PGain	3
VGain	4	VGain	1
Class	1,118	Class	0,700

Adaptation Pattern

Input Attributes									Class Attributes
E	E	5	4	E	E	3	1	0,700	-0,418

Fig. 4. Adaptation Pattern Sample.

The topology of the MLP network developed contains 2 layers: 25 input units, a hidden layer with 13 neurons and an output layer with 1 neuron. The network was trained using backpropagation with the momentum algorithm, using moment term 0.2 and learning rate 0.3. The M5 algorithm was trained using Model Tree and pruning factor equal to 2.0. The SVM Algorithm was trained using Radial Basis Function kernel.

The MLP network and M5 algorithm were simulated using the WEKA library, version 3.2 - a set of algorithms of machine learning[2]. The SVM algorithm was simulated using the LIBSVM library[3].

---

[2] Available in http://www.cs.waikato.ac.nz/ml/weka/index.htm
[3] Available in http://www.csie.ntu.edu.tw/c̃jlin/libsvm

For the tests, three different strategies for the adaptation pattern generation were analyzed:

- Strategy I - only the most similar case is retrieved for a given proof case. Then, one adaptation pattern is created for each proof case;
- Strategy II - the three most similar cases are retrieved for a given proof case. Thus, three adaptations are created for each proof case.
- Strategy III - the five most similar cases are retrieved for a given proof case. Thus, five adaptation are created for each proof case.

The pre-processing of the data (see *PreProcess* in Algorithm 2, Algorithm 1 and Algorithm 3) is only performed if the retrieval and adaptation mechanisms requires it. The cases were stored in the CB in their original format. The symbolic values were transformed into orthogonal vectors of binary values. The numerical values were normalized for the interval $[0 \ldots 1]$. The class attribute was also normalized.

The tests for the CBR system followed the *10-fold-cross-validation* strategy [3]. The patterns were randomly divided into 10 groups (*folds*) with similar size. One *fold* was used as a *test-fold* (a set of new problems to be presented to the system) and the remaining 9 *folds* were considered as a *training-fold* (a set of previously stored cases). After the training of the adaptation mechanisms using the *training-fold*, the *test-fold* was presented to the system and the average absolute error was calculated. This process was repeated for the remaining 9 *folds*. Afterward, the average and standard deviation of the absolute error for each training stage were calculated.

Table 2 shows the results of the tests carried out with the hybrid CBR systems using the three strategies of adaptation pattern generation. Moreover, the results of the ML techniques alone (MLP, M5 and SVM), i.e. directly applied to the problem, are also shown:

In order to confirm the performance of the proposed approach, the authors used the t test for bilateral procedures which 99% of certainty [7,19]. The results are shown in Table 3.

The results of the RBC employing a SVM with strategies I, II and III as adaptation mechanism are similar (see Table 2). Nevertheless, the performance of CBR systems increases according to the number of retrieved cases in each strategy of pattern generation (strategies I, II and III respectively). This result occurs possibly due to, in general, a large number of cases produce a high number of adaptation rules.

In addition, the results have shown that the hybrid approaches proposed have learned better the adaptation rules than the ML algorithms applied directly to the problem (ML techniques alone). This suggest that the set of adaptation rules extracted from CB of the systems is consistent. Therefore this approach of adaptation knowledge learning may be a potencial technique for real-world problem solving.

Table 2. Average error rates for the proposed approach.

Model	Average Absolute Error
RBC (M5-I)	0.038 ± 0.017
RBC (M5-II)	0.028 ± 0.018
RBC (M5-III)	0.023 ± 0.016
RBC (MLP-I)	0.042 ± 0.015
RBC (MLP-II)	0.030 ± 0.014
RBC (MLP-III)	0.026 ± 0.014
RCB (SVM-I)	0.018 ± 0.012
RBC (SVM-II)	0.019 ± 0.013
RBC (SVM-III)	0.019 ± 0.012
M5	0.351 ± 0.187
MLP	0.358 ± 0.198
SVM	0.523 ± 0.349

Table 3. Results for the t Test.

Compared Methods	Conclusion
MLP and SVM (Method I)	SVM better than MLP
MLP and SVM (Method II)	Similar Performance
MLP and M5 (Method III)	MLP better than M5
MLP and SVM (Method III)	MLP better than SVM
M5 and SVM (Method III)	Similar Performance

7   Conclusions

In this work, a CBR system that uses hybrid approaches for case retrieval and adaptation was presented.

The proposed memory organization and case retrieval mechanisms enable a search space reduction, decreasing the retrieval time required. This approach may also be integrated with an usual retrieval mechanism, like KNN [9] or CRN [16]. Any of this integrated approach should present a better performance than KNN or CRN alone, since the hybrid approaches would only search in the space corresponding to the cluster obtained by the ART2 network (see Subsection 5.1).

When CBR is applied to real-world problem solving, the retrieved solutions can not be directly used for a new problem. In general, they need to be adapted to fit new requirements. One of the major challenges in designing CBR systems is the acquisition and modelling of appropriate adaptation knowledge [11]. The case adaptation approach proposed employs a process of adaptation pattern generation that can reduce the effort for knowledge acquisition in domains that require substitutional adaptation (see Section 3).

The hybrid system proposed is computationally cheap, since the generation of the adaptation patterns demands few solution components comparisons and the ART2 training for a pattern demands only one cycle. Moreover, the process to obtain an adaptation pattern data set is fully integrated with the case retrieval mechanism and can be implemented employing usual retrieval approaches.

The results obtained suggest that the set of adaptation rules extracted from CB of the systems is consistent and that this approach of adaptation knowledge learning may be a potencial technique for real-world problem solving.

In order to continue the performance investigation of the hybrid system proposed, new researches should be carried out involving tests with other and more complex domains, including also symbolic attributes.

Acknowledgments. The authors would like to thank CNPq, a Brazilian Research Agency, for the support received.

References

1. Aamondt,A., Plaza,E.: Case based reasoning: Foundational issues, methodological variations, and systems approaches. AI Communications. **7** (1994) 39–59
2. Alexandre,F., Labbi,A., Lallement,Y., Malek,M.: A common architeture for integrating case-based reasoning and neural networks. Technical report, MIX/WP2/IMAG-INRIA/S3. (1996)
3. Bailey,T. Elkan,C.: Estimating the Accuracy of Learned Concepts. 13th International Joint Conference on Artificial Intelligence, Chambéry, France. Bajcsy,R. eds. Morgan Kaufmann. (1993) 895–901
4. Braga,A., Ludermir,T. Carvalho,A.: Sistemas neurais híbridos. Redes Neurais Artificiais: Teoria e aplicacoes. Livros Tecnicos e Cientificos. (2000)
5. Carpenter,G., Grossberg,S.: ART 2 : Self-organization of stable category recognition codes for analog input paterns. Applied Optics. **26:23** (1987) 4919–4930
6. Corchado,J., Lees,B., Fyle,C., Ress,N., Aiken,J.: Neuro-adaptation method for a case-based reasoning system. Computing and Information Systems Journal. **5** (1998) 15–20
7. Cristmann,R.: Estatística aplicada. Edgard Blücher. (1978)
8. Domingos,P.: Unifying Instance-Based and Rule-Based Induction. Machine Learning. **24** (1996) 141–168
9. Duda,R., hart,P., Stork,D.: Pattern Classification. Wiley-Interscience. (2001)
10. Freund,Y. and Schapire,R.: Experiments with a New Boosting Algorithm. 13th. International Conference on Machine Learning, Bari, Italy. Saitta, L. eds. Morgan Kaufmann. (1996) 148–156
11. Hanney,K.: Learning adaptation rules from cases. Master's thesis. University College Dublin. (1996)
12. Hilario,M.: An Overview Of Strategies For Neurosymbolic Integration. Connectionist-Symbolic Integration: From Unified to Hybrid Approaches. Chapter 2. Lawrence Earlbaum Associates, Inc. (1997)
13. Kolodner,J.: An introduction to case based reasoning. AI Review. **6** (1992) 3–34.
14. Kolodner,J.: Adaptation methods and strategies. Case-Based Reasoning. Chapter 11. Morgan Kaufmann. (1993)

15. Leake,D.: CBR in context: The present and future. Case-Based Reasoning: Experiences, Lessons and Future Directions. Chapter 1. AAAI Press/MIT Press. (1996)
16. Lenz,M., Burkhard,H.-D.: Case Retrieval Nets: Basic Ideas and Extensions. 4th. German Workshop on Case-Based Reasoning: System Development and Evaluation, Berlin, German. Burkhard,H.-D. and Lenz,M. eds. (1996) 103–110
17. Malek,M.: A connectionist indexing aproach for CBR systems. 1st International Conference on Case-Based Reasoning. Sesimbra, Portugal. Veloso,M., Aamodt,A. eds. Springer Verlag (1995) 520–527
18. Malek,M.: Hybrid approaches for integrating neurai networks and case-based reasoning: From loosely coupled to tightly coupled models. Soft Computing in Case Based Reasoning. Chapter 4. Springer Verlag. (2001)
19. Mason,R., Gunst,R., Hess,J.: Statistical design and analysis of experiments. John Wiley & Sons. (1989)
20. Orr,M.: Introduction to radial basis function networks, Technical report. Centre for Cognitive Science. University of Edinburgh. (1996).
21. Quinlan,R.: Learning with Continuous Classes. 5th. Australian Joint Conference on Artificial Inteligence, Hobart, Tasmania, World Scientific, Singapore. (1992) 343–348
22. Reategui,E., Campbell,J.: A classification system for credit card transaction. 2th European Workshop on Case-Based Reasoning. Chantilly, France. Keane, M. ed. Springer Verlag. (1994) 280–291
23. Smyth,B., Cunningham,P.: Complexity of adaptation in real-world case-based reasoning systems. 6th Irish Conference on Artificial Intelligence and Cognitive Science. Belfast, Ireland. (1993)
24. Sovat,R., Carvalho,A.: Retrieval and adaptation of cases using an neural network. 4th International Conference on Case-Based Reasoning. Workshop. Vancouver, Canada. (2001) 196–200
25. Vapnik,V.: Statistical learning theory. John Wiley & Sons. (1998)
26. Wang,Y., Witten,I.: Induction of model trees for predicting continuous classes. 9th European Conference on Machine Learning. Prague, Czech Republic. Someren,M., Widmer,G. eds. Springer Verlag. (1997) 128–137
27. Watson,I.: CBR is a methodology not a technology. Knowledge-Based Systems. **12**(1999) 303–308
28. Wiratunga,N., Craw,S., Rowe,R.: Learning to adapt for case-based design. 6th European Conference on Case-Based Reasoning. Aberdeen, Scotland, Uk. Craw,S., Preece,A. eds. Springer Verlag. (2002) 421–435

Applied Connectionistic Methods in Computer Vision to Compare Segmented Images

S. Bischoff[1], D. Reuss[2], and F. Wysotzki[2]

[1] Fraunhofer Institute for Telecommunications, Heinrich-Hertz-Institut,
Einsteinufer 37, 10587 Berlin, Germany,
bischoff@hhi.de,
http://www.hhi.de
[2] Technical University Berlin, Franklinstr. 28/29, 10587 Berlin, Germany,
wysotzki@cs.tu-berlin.de,
http://www.tu-berlin.de

Abstract. Two similarity measures to compare whole and parts of images are proposed. These measures consider the color, shape and texture properties of image segments as well as their relative positions mutually. After image segmentation MPEG-7 descriptors are computed for each segment. Now the information reduced images will be represented by labeled graphs.

To compute the first similarity measure it is necessary to solve the Maximum Weight Clique Problem in an extended compatibility graph. This problem is solved by a connectionistic method.

The second similarity measure needs to solve a special kind of Consistent Labeling Problem. This is done by a connectionistic method too.

Both measures may be used to improve the similarity measurement of images for instance in image and video retrieval, object recognition, stereo and many other Computer Vision tasks.

Keywords: Image Retrieval, Similarity Measures, Image Indexing, Image Segmentation, MPEG-7 Descriptors, Graph Metric, Maximum Weight Clique Problem, Consistent Labeling Problem, Hopfield-Style Neural Network, WTA-Net, Mean Field Annealing

1 Introduction

Retrieval of digital images based on image features rather than text descriptions has been subject of considerable research efforts over the last years. Within this framework the MPEG-7 standard (Moving Picture Experts Group) attempts to standardize suitable descriptors to allow many image search engines to access as many distributed images as possible. Various image descriptors are currently under consideration in the MPEG video group, such as color and color distribution descriptors, texture and shape descriptors [5].

Unfortunately, most descriptors are integral quantities and depend strongly on the integration area. Calculation on the whole image or on bad areas may misrepresent them. In addition, the typical user searches for images in which

A. Günter et al. (Eds.): KI 2003, LNAI 2821, pp. 312–326, 2003.

semantical objects like cars, houses or persons occur. That cannot be described by feature vectors calculated from the whole image. An adequat description rather needs both: a suitable representation of the visual properties of semantic image parts and their mutual positions, too.

Graphs are an appropriate tool to represent image parts with respect to translation and rotation invariance. In the following we describe our approach to transform an image into a labeled graph. The nodes present features of the segments and the edges relative positions, respectively. This graph is then the basis of fast recognition procedures using special Neuronal Nets.

2   Image Segmentation

In most computer vision applications image segmentation constitutes a crucial initial step before performing high level tasks such as object recognition and scene interpretation. Automatic image segmentation is well known as one of the hardest low-level vision problems. It is not guaranteed that a coherent cluster in feature space corresponds to a coherent image region. Several algorithms are known like [1] [12] [14]. We chose "Edge Flow" [4], which utilizes a predictive coding model to identify the direction of change in color and texture at each image location at a given scale, and constructs an edge flow vector. By iteratively propagating the edge flow, the boundaries can be detected. After boundary detection, disjoint boundaries are connected to form closed contours.

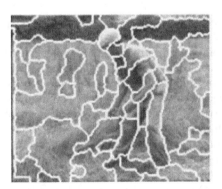

Fig. 1. Segmented Image

Today, no system is able to segment any image into semantic meaningful parts without additional information. Furthermore the segmentation result depends strongly on illumination conditions, camera position and algorithm parameters.

In the next section we describe which visual properties are extracted for each segment.

3   Extraction of MPEG-7 Descriptors

Scalable Color Descriptor (SCD): The Scalable Color Descriptor describes the color distribution in the segment. The MPEG-7 generic SCD is a color histogram in the HSV (Hue, Saturation, Value) colorspace, which is a three dimensional RGB colorspace in cylinder coordinates. The color histogram is based on the definition of uniform colorspace quantization with 16 bins in hue and 4 bins in both saturation and value.

Homogenous Texture Descriptor (HTD): The Homogenous Texture Descriptor describes directionality, coarseness and regularity of patterns in the segment. In order to describe the segment texture, energy and energy deviation values are extracted from a frequency layout. Suitable descriptions are obtained in the frequency domain by computing mean and standard variation of frequency coefficients [11]. To handle the dependence on the segment shape, only higher frequencies were taken into account. The descriptor is based on convolution with a filter bank consisting of 12 2d Gabor wavelets (3 scales and 4 directions). This can be quickly done by filtering with fourier transformed 2d Gabor wavelets in the fourier domain.

Edge Histogram Descriptor (EHD): The Edge Histogram Descriptor represents the spatial distribution of five types of edges. The edge types are a horizontal, a vertical, two different diagonal and a non-directional edge type. The non-directional edge type describes, if there are edges, but if no direction is dominant. So the edge histogram with 5 bins forms a feature vector with 5 components. For more details see [5] and [11].

4   Image Representation by Labeled Graphs (RAG)

Labeled graphs are an appropriate and popular representation of structured objects in many domains. To transform an image into a labeled graph the centroid for each segment was calculated. The set of all centroids is the set of nodes. Every node is labeled with an MPEG-7 feature vector. Edges, labeled with distances between centroids, are introduced for each pair of nodes. The distances are normalized with respect to the image diagonal. The neighbourhood relation is one additional component of the edge feature vector. So the RAG (Region Adjacency Graph) is included. Now we formalize.

Let be $G_1 := (N_{G_1}, V_{G_1}, l_{G_1}, e_{G_1}, \theta_{G_1})$ the Region Adjacency Graph of image 1 and $G_2 := (N_{G_2}, V_{G_2}, l_{G_2}, e_{G_2}, \theta_{G_2})$ the RAG of image 2. G_1 and G_2 are two complete undirected graphs with finite node sets N_{G_1}, N_{G_2} and (finite) edge sets $V_{G_1} = N_{G_1} \times N_{G_1}$, $V_{G_2} = N_{G_2} \times N_{G_2}$. With $l_{G_i} : N_{G_i} \rightarrow \mathbb{R}^n$ (MPEG-7 feature vector) and $e_{G_i} : V_{G_i} \rightarrow \mathbb{R}$ (normalized euclidean distance) we denote the node and edge label functions for $i \in \{1,2\}$, respectively. Let be $\sigma_L : \mathbb{R}^n \times \mathbb{R}^n \rightarrow [0,1]$ a scalar function of two vector valued arguments and $\sigma_E : \mathbb{R} \times \mathbb{R} \rightarrow [0,1]$ a scalar function of two scalar valued arguments, which measure the similarity of nodes and edges respectively ($[0,1] \simeq$ [not similar,identical]). With θ we describe the adjacency relation. If two segments $x_1, x_2 \in N_{G_1}$ are adjacent, then $(x_1, x_2) \in \theta$. By definition always $(x,x) \in \theta$, too.

5   The First Image Distance

Images are considered to be similar, if the distance between their representation by a configuration of features is small. Caused by the graph representation used here it is necessary to compute a graph distance. Most graph distances need a unique node assignment. But the segmentation results depend strongly on illumination conditions, camera position and algorithm parameters. Different graph representations of one image are possible.

To compare two segmented images in the first step a graph normalization is computed for both RAG1 and RAG2. This is an iteration process to achieve similar segmentation results for similar images. In the second step the computation of a graph metric between the normalized RAG1 and RAG2 defines the image similarity. We describe the first step in the next section.

5.1   Graph Normalization

The graph normalization step is an iteration process which tries to unify such neighbouring segments in the first image and vice versa, which correspond to one segment in the second one and which have suitable topological relations to all other segments.

For this purpose let be F, G the set of mappings

$$F := \{f : N_{G_1} \to N_{G_2} \mid f(x_i) = f(x_j) \Rightarrow (x_i, x_j) \in \theta \}$$

$$G := \{g : N_{G_2} \to N_{G_1} \mid g(y_i) = g(y_j) \Rightarrow (y_i, y_j) \in \theta \}$$

and

$$Q(f) := \sum_{x \in N_{G_1}} \sigma_L(l_{G_1}(x), l_{G_2}(f(x))) + \sum_{(x_i, x_j) \in V_{G_1}} \sigma_E(e_{G_1}(x_i, x_j), e_{G_2}(f(x_i), f(x_j)))$$

$$Q(g) := \sum_{y \in N_{G_1}} \sigma_L(l_{G_2}(y), l_{G_1}(g(y))) + \sum_{(y_i, y_j) \in V_{G_2}} \sigma_E(e_{G_2}(y_i, y_j), e_{G_1}(g(y_i), g(y_j))).$$

We unify 2 segments x_i and x_j of image 1, if $(x_i, x_j) \in \theta$ and $f^\star(x_i) = f^\star(x_j)$ with $f^\star := \arg\max_{f \in F} Q(f)$. For $(y_i, y_j) \in \theta$ we do the same, if $g^\star(y_i) = g^\star(y_j)$ and $g^\star := \arg\max_{g \in G} Q(g)$. Now we calculate a new RAG1 and RAG2 and iterate, until no more segments can be unified. We appply a connectionistic method to compute $f^\star$ and $g^\star$. This connectionistic method is declared in next section in detail to determine a best mapping $\Phi^\star$ from G_1 into G_2. Computation of $f^\star$ and $g^\star$ is similar.

5.2   A New Graph Metric and Its Computation

Provided a one to one match between the normalized RAG1 and RAG2, so that a unique node assignment has been given, we generalize and prove a metric property for abstract graphs with node label set L and egde label set E. In the context of image retrieval there is $L = \mathbb{R}^n$ and $E = \mathbb{R}$. Segmented images are considered as similar, if this graph metric between the Region Adjacency Graphs is small.

Definition 1. *A mapping* $\Phi : N_{G_1} \to N_{G_2}$ *is called* generalized graph isomorphism :$\Longleftrightarrow$

1. Φ *is without consideration of node and edge labels a graph isomorphism.*
2. $\forall x_i, x_j \in N_{G_1} : \sigma_L(l_{G_1}(x_i), l_{G_2}(\Phi(x_i))) > 0 \wedge$
$$\sigma_E(e_{G_1}(x_i, x_j), e_{G_2}(\Phi(x_i), \Phi(x_j))) > 0 \ .$$

Then G_1 *and* G_2 *are called* g-isomorph.

Definition 2. *A mapping* $\Phi : N_{G_1} \to N_{G_2}$ *is called* generalized subgraph isomorphism :$\Longleftrightarrow$ $\exists$ *an induced subgraph* G_1' *of* G_1 *and* $\exists$ *an induced subgraph* G_2' *of* G_2 *and* $\Phi \mid_{N_{G_1'}} : N_{G_1'} \to N_{G_2'}$ *is a generalized isomorphism.*

Definition 3. *Let* Φ *be a generalized subgraph isomorphism.* G_1' *and* G_2' *being the g-isomorphic induced subgraphs. We define as* support of Φ *$\mathrm{supp}\Phi := \{x \in N_{G_1} : x \in N_{G_1'}\}$ the set of all nodes of* G_1 *mapped g-isomorph.*

Now consider the following functional d which measures the distance of two labeled graphs G_1 and G_2:

$$d(G_1, G_2) := \min_{\left\{\Phi \,:\, \Phi \, \substack{g-subgraph-\\isomorphism}\right\}} \alpha \left(\mu(\mu - 1) - v_\Phi\right) + \beta(\mu - n_\Phi)$$

with

$$\mu := \max\{\mid N_{G_1} \mid, \mid N_{G_2} \mid\}$$
$$n_\Phi := \sum_{x \in \mathrm{supp}\Phi} \sigma_L(l_{G_1}(x), l_{G_2}(\Phi(x)))$$
$$v_\Phi := \sum_{(x_i, x_j) \in (\mathrm{supp}\Phi)^2} \sigma_E(e_{G_1}(x_i, x_j), e_{G_2}(\Phi(x_i), \Phi(x_j)))$$

$\alpha, \beta \in [0, 1]$ and $\alpha + \beta = 1$ measuring the relative contribution of edges and nodes, respectively. This function is well defined except for nodes and edges with similarity zero. Then the following proposition holds:

Proposition 1. *d is a metric in the space of isomorphic classes of labeled graphs with the same label sets L, E.*

Proof. For a sketch of the proof see appendix. $\square$

Zelinka defined a metric for unlabeled graphs G_1 and G_2 with same number of nodes $|N|$ without loops and without multiple edges: $d(G_1, G_2) := |N| - |N_U|$. $|N_U|$ is the number of nodes of maximum common induced subgraph [15]. Kaden [2] generalized to unlabeled graphs with different number of nodes:

$$d(G_1, G_2) := \max\{|N_{G_1}|, |N_{G_2}|\} - |N_U|.$$

Proposition 2. *d is a generalization of the "Kaden Distance".*

Proof. $\qquad \alpha = 0,\ \beta = 1,\ l_{G_1} = l_{G_2} = e_{G_1} = e_{G_2} = 1$

$$\sigma_E(x,y) = \begin{cases} 1 & x = y = 1 \\ 0 & \text{else} \end{cases}$$

$$\sigma_L(\boldsymbol{x},\boldsymbol{y}) = \begin{cases} 1 & \boldsymbol{x} = \boldsymbol{y} \\ 0 & \text{else} \end{cases}$$

$\square$

To quantify d, it is necessary to specify the best mapping $\Phi^* = \arg\max(\alpha v_\Phi + \beta n_\Phi)$ among all possible g-subgraph isomorphisms from G_1 into G_2. If we enumerate all nodes of G_1 and G_2, every mapping from G_1 into G_2 can be described by a matrix $o \in \{0,1\}^{|N_{G_1}| \times |N_{G_2}|}$ where $o_{ik} = 1$ if $\Phi(x_i) = y_k$ and $o_{ik} = 0$ else. So we can formulate this problem as an optimization problem:

$$o^* = \arg\max_o \left(\alpha \sum_{i,j,k,l} o_{ik} s_{ij,kl} o_{jl} + \beta \sum_{i,k} o_{ik} s_{ik} \right)$$

with $s_{ij,kl} = \sigma_E(e_{G_1}(x_i,x_j), e_{G_2}(y_k,y_l))$ and $s_{ik} = \sigma_L(l_{G_1}(x_i), l_{G_2}(y_k))$ with uniqueness restriction $o_{ik}o_{il} = o_{ik}o_{jk} = 0 \ \forall i \neq j$, $k \neq l$ and induced subgraph restriction $\prod_{i,j,k,l} s_{ij,kl} \neq 0$. These restrictions can be included by means of a penalty term *pen*. So we can rewrite with minimal node and edge similarities Θ_N, Θ_V:

$$o^* = \arg\max_o \left(\alpha \sum_{i,j,k,l} o_{ik} \hat{s}_{ij,kl} o_{jl} + \beta \sum_{i,k} o_{ik} \hat{s}_{ik} \right)$$

with

$$\hat{s}_{ik} = \begin{cases} s_{ik} & s_{ik} \geq \Theta_N \\ 0 & \text{else} \end{cases}$$

and

$$\hat{s}_{ij,kl} = \begin{cases} \frac{s_{ij,kl} + s_{ji,lk}}{2} & i \neq j \wedge k \neq l \ \wedge \frac{s_{ij,kl} + s_{ji,lk}}{2} \geq \Theta_V \\ -pen & i = j \vee k = l \\ -pen & \frac{s_{ij,kl} + s_{ji,lk}}{2} < \Theta_V. \end{cases}$$

Solving this optimization problem is equal to find this common generalized induced subgraph with maximum summarized nodes and edges similarity. This can be regarded as maximum weight clique problem in the generalized compatibility graph (ECG) [9] [8], which will be described now.

Definition 4. *The generalized compatibility graph* $ECG = (N, V, l, e)$ *of two graphs* $G_1 = (N_{G_1}, V_{G_1}, l_{G_1}, e_{G_1})$ *and* $G_2 = (N_{G_2}, V_{G_2}, l_{G_2}, e_{G_2})$ *is constructed as follows:*

1. $N := \{(x_i, y_k) : x_i \in N_{G_1} \wedge y_k \in N_{G_2} \wedge \sigma_L(l_{G_1}(x_i), l_{G_2}(y_k)) \geq \Theta_N\}$
2. $l((x_i, y_k)) := \hat{s}_{ik}$
3. $V := N \times N$
4. $e((x_i, y_k), (x_j, y_l)) := \hat{s}_{ij,kl}.$

The maximum weight clique problem is a generalization of the maximum clique problem which is well known to be NP-complete. To solve this problem we use a Winner-Takes-All Net (WTA-Net), which is a Hopfield style Neural Network with excitatory and inhibitory connections. The WTA-Net is constructed directly from ECG by using the following rules:

1. For every node $(x_i, y_k) \in N$ with label $\hat{s}_{ik}$ create a unit $u(x_i, y_k)$ of the net.
2. For every edge $((x_i, y_k), (x_j, y_l)) \in V$ with positive label $\hat{s}_{ij,kl}$ create a (symmetric) connection $(u(x_i, y_k), u'(x_j, y_l))$ with positive initial weight $\omega_{ij,kl} \sim \hat{s}_{ij,kl}$ (excitatory connection).
3. For every edge $((x_i, y_k), (x_j, y_l)) \in V$ with the label -pen create a (symmetric) connection $(u(x_i, y_k), u'(x_j, y_l))$ with negative initial weight $\omega_{ij,kl} \sim -pen$ (inhibitory connection).
4. Every unit $u(x_i, y_k)$ gets a bias input $I_{ik} \sim \hat{s}_{ik}$.

The units are updated synchronously, according to the rule:

$$p_{ik}(t+1) = (1-d)p_{ik}(t) + I_{ik} + \sum_{(j,l) \neq (i,k)} \omega_{ij,kl} o_{jl}(t)$$

$$o_{ik}(t+1) = \begin{cases} 0 & p_{ik}(t+1) < 0 \\ p_{ik}(t+1) & p_{ik}(t+1) \in [0,1] \\ 1 & p_{ik}(t+1) > 1. \end{cases}$$

A steady state of the net defines a mapping between the two original graphs. The distance measure d can be calculated based on this mapping.

6   The Second Image Similarity Measure

In this chapter we describe our approach to measure the similarity of segmented images as a special kind of Consistent Labeling Problem. Segmented images are considered as similar, if the similarity measure S between the Region Adjacency Graphs is high. For this purpose let be $G_1 := (N_{G_1}, V_{G_1}, l_{G_1}, e_{G_1}, \theta_{G_1})$ the Region Adjacency Graph (RAG) of image 1 and $G_2 := (N_{G_2}, V_{G_2}, l_{G_2}, e_{G_2}, \theta_{G_2})$ the RAG of image 2 like defined in chapter 4. With r, r' we now denote the nodes of G_1 and with α, β the nodes of G_2 respectively. Every node $r \in N_{G_1}$ may be stay in some state k from a finite set of states K. A mapping $f : N_{G_1} \to K$ assigning each node $r \in N_{G_1}$ its state $f(r)$ is called a labeling. Suppose the labeling f satisfies some restrictions given by a local conjunctive predicate χ of second order. This is a function $\chi : N_{G_1} \times N_{G_1} \times K \times K \to \{0,1\}$. The value $\chi_{(r,r')}(\alpha, \beta)$ determines whether the node r may stay in the state α while the node r' stays in the state β.

The whole labeling $f : N_{G_1} \to K$ is called consistent if

$$\bigwedge_{(r,r') \in \theta_{G_1}} \chi_{(r,r')}(f(r), f(r')) = 1.$$

The Consistent Labeling Problem (CLP) consists in answering the question, whether there exists a consistent labeling f_c or not [7] [10].

To measure the similarity of two segmented images we regard the following Consistent Labeling Problem:

$$K = N_{G_2}$$
$$\chi_{(r,r')}(\alpha, \beta) = 1 - Adj\,A_{r,r'}(1 - Adj\,B^{\alpha\beta})$$

with

$$Adj\,A_{r,r'} = \begin{cases} 1 & (r,r') \in \theta_{G_1} \\ 0 & \text{else} \end{cases}$$

and

$$Adj\,B^{\alpha,\beta} = \begin{cases} 1 & (\alpha,\beta) \in \theta_{G_2} \\ 0 & \text{else}. \end{cases}$$

Among all possible consistent labelings f_c we search this one which maximizes the cost function $C_{1\to2}(f_c) := \frac{1}{|N_{G_1}|} \sum_{r \in N_{G_1}} \sigma_L(l_{G_1}(r), l_{G_2}(f_c(r)))$. The best consistent labeling $f_{bc} := \arg\max_{f_c} C_{1\to2}$ is called Best Match. The Best Match Problem (BMP) consists in determining the Best Match and is a generalization of the Consistent Labeling Problem which is well known to be NP-complete. To solve the BMP we formulate the BMP as an Optimization Problem. Then we use a connectionistic method to solve it:

$$E_c := -\frac{1}{2} \sum_{r=1}^{|N_{G_1}|} \sum_{r'=1,r'\neq r}^{|N_{G_1}|} \sum_{\alpha=1}^{|N_{G_2}|} \sum_{\beta=1,\beta\neq\alpha}^{|N_{G_2}|} F_{rr'}^{\alpha\beta} x_{r\alpha} x_{r'\beta} \longrightarrow \text{Min.}$$

under restriction

$$F_{rr'}^{\alpha\beta} = \begin{cases} \frac{1}{2}(S_r^\alpha + S_{r'}^\beta) & \chi_{(r,r')}(\alpha, \beta) = 1 \\ -\text{penalty} & \chi_{(r,r')}(\alpha, \beta) = 0 \\ 0 & r = r' \end{cases}$$

$$S_r^\alpha := \sigma_L(l_{G_1}(r), l_{G_2}(\alpha))$$
$$S_{r'}^\beta := \sigma_L(l_{G_1}(r'), l_{G_2}(\beta))$$

$$x_{r\alpha}, x_{r'\beta} \in \{0,1\}$$

$$\sum_{\alpha=1}^{|N_{G_2}|} x_{r\alpha} = 1.$$

To solve the Minimization Problem we use a Mean Field Annealing. In the Mean Field Annealing approximation the binary spin variables $x_{r\alpha} \in \{0,1\}$ are replaced by their expectation values which are continuous variables with $0 \leq x_{r\alpha} \leq 1$. Instead of minimizing the energy directly, the function to be minimized is the mean field free energy given by

$$E^F = -\frac{1}{2} \sum_{r\alpha} \sum_{r'\beta} F_{rr'}^{\alpha\beta} x_{r\alpha} x_{r'\beta} + T \sum_{r\alpha} x_{r\alpha} \log x_{r\alpha}$$

subject to the constraints $\sum_{\alpha} x_{r\alpha} = 1$. At high temperature T the free energy is dominated by the convex entropy term and has a unique minimum. The convex term serves to smooth out local minima. By gradually lowering T more and more structure of the original energy at $T = 0$ is recovered. A local minimum solution satisfies

$$x_{r\alpha} = \frac{\exp(-(\sum_{r'\gamma} F_{rr'}^{\alpha\gamma} x_{r'\gamma})/T)}{\sum_{\beta} \exp(-(\sum_{r'\gamma} F_{rr'}^{\beta\gamma} x_{r'\gamma})/T)}.$$

A mean field algorithm works by parallel or iteratively solving these mean field equations together with a gradual lowering of the temperature T [13]. A solution defines a mapping $f : N_{G_1} \to N_{G_2}$ which is a approximation of f_{bc}.

Finally we can define the similarity S of image 1 and image 2:

$$S := \frac{1}{2}(C_{1\to 2}(f_{bc}) + C_{2\to 1}(g_{bc}))$$

with $g_{bc} := \arg \max_{g_c} C_{2\to 1}$ and $C_{2\to 1}(g_c) := \frac{1}{|N_{G_2}|} \sum_{\alpha \in N_{G_2}} \sigma_L(l_{G_1}(g_c(\alpha)), l_{G_2}(\alpha))$ and $\chi_{(\alpha,\beta)}(r, r') = 1 - AdjB^{\alpha,\beta}(1 - AdjA_{rr'})$ and $K = N_{G_1}$.

7   Results

Image retrieval makes great demands on fast matching as well as suitable retrieval results. Taking color and edge histograms for the whole image like QBIC and PicToSeek or for fixed subimages like C-bird [3], FOCUS, Mars [6] and PicHunter is an often used way to represent visual information. The retrieval is fast, but the results are not so satisfactory (Fig. 2).

Fig. 2. Classical search request. First image is query image.

There are images retrieved which exhibit no similarity with the query image. Our first distance measure considers the visual properties of image segments as well as their relative mutual positions. The user has the choice to search for a whole image or only for special image parts. Fig. 3 shows a segmented query image.

Fig. 3. Query image. Segments which are searched for are outlined black.

Segments which are searched for are outlined black. For the corresponding labeled graph, graph normalization and distance measure d to all other graph representations of database images are calculated. The images (unsegmented) with the shortest graph distance to image in Fig. 3 are shown in Fig. 4. The first pictures shown in Fig. 4 have another background than the last image in Fig. 4. The position of the farmer in the last picture is a little bit translated as well. The high similarity is caused by the rotation and translation invariant graph representation used here.

Fig. 4. Result of search request for distance 1. Image in Fig. 3 is query image.

Image segmentation, graph normalization and maximum weight clique finding are iterative processes. So it is difficult to estimate, how the whole algorithm scales. A request for the image in Fig. 3 for instance needs 33 seconds computation time on P4/2.4GHz and 100 database images. In general the computation time depends on the order of graph representation and quantity of database images.

Fig. 5.

Fig. 9.

Fig. 6.

Fig. 10.

Fig. 7.

Fig. 11.

Fig. 8.

Fig. 12.

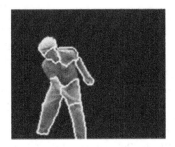

Fig. 13.

The second image similarity measure is able to measure the similarity of segmented images too. Table 1 shows the similarity of images shown in Fig. 5 to Fig. 13 :

Table 1. Image Similarity

	Fig. 5	Fig. 6	Fig. 7	Fig. 8	Fig. 9	Fig. 10	Fig. 11	Fig. 12	Fig. 13
Fig. 5	1.000	0.337	0.110	0.120	0.097	0.093	0.101	0.088	0.199
Fig. 6	0.337	1.000	0.143	0.115	0.059	0.078	0.107	0.091	0.161
Fig. 7	0.110	0.143	1.000	0.296	0.062	0.050	0.119	0.103	0.059
Fig. 8	0.120	0.115	0.296	1.000	0.040	0.028	0.085	0.082	0.066
Fig. 9	0.097	0.059	0.062	0.040	1.000	0.474	0.072	0.071	0.063
Fig. 10	0.093	0.078	0.050	0.028	0.474	1.000	0.072	0.078	0.054
Fig. 11	0.101	0.107	0.119	0.085	0.072	0.072	1.000	0.400	0.066
Fig. 12	0.088	0.091	0.103	0.082	0.071	0.078	0.400	1.000	0.068
Fig. 13	0.199	0.161	0.059	0.066	0.063	0.054	0.066	0.068	1.000

The similarity between each image and itself has value 1. The second most similar image is the other picture of each image pair. The pictures shown in Fig. 5 and Fig. 6 have another background than the image in Fig. 13. The position of the farmer in picture 13 is a little bit translated as well. But image 5 and 6 are the most similar images to picture 13 except for itself.

Computation time takes 1 second for one image comparison on P4/2.4GHz.

References

1. C.S. Fuh, S.W. Cho, and K. Essig. Hierarchical color image region segmentation for content based image retrieval system. *IEEE TRANSACTIONS ON IMAGE PROCESSING*, 9(1), January 2000.
2. F. Kaden and F. Sobik. Beiträge zur angewandten Graphentheorie. *ZKI-Information*, 1982.

324   S. Bischoff, D. Reuss, and F. Wysotzki

3. Z.N. Li, O.R. Zaiane, and Z. Tauber. Illumination invariance and object model in content-based image and video retrieval. *Journal of Visual Communication and Image Representation*, 10(3):219–244, September 1999.
4. W.Y. Ma and B.S. Manjunath. Edge flow: a framework of boundary detection and image segmentation. *Proc. of CVPR*, 1997.
5. T. Meiers, I. Keller, and T. Sikora. Image visualization and navigation based on MPEG-7 descriptors. *Conference on Augmented, Virtual Environments and 3D Imaging, EUROIMAGE 2001*, May 2001.
6. M. Ortega, Y. Rui, K. Chakrabarti, S. Mehrotra, and T.S. Huang. Supporting similarities queries in MARS. In *Proceedings of the 5th ACM International Multimedia Conference ,Seattle,Washington,8-14 Nov. '97*, pages 403–413, 1997.
7. A. Rosenfeld, R. Hummel, and S. Zucker. Scene labeling by relaxation operation. *IEEE Trans. Syst. Man. and Cybern*, pages 420–433, 1976.
8. K. Schaedler. *Die Ermittlung struktureller Ähnlichkeiten und struktureller Merkmale bei komplexen Objekten: Ein konnektionistischer Ansatz und seine Anwendungen*. PhD thesis, Technische Universität Berlin, 1999.
9. K. Schaedler and F. Wysotzki. Comparing structures using a hopfield-style neural network. *Applied Intelligence*, 11:15–30, 1999.
10. M.I. Schlesinger and B. Flach. Some solvable subclasses of structural recognition problems. *Czech Pattern Recognition Workshop 2000*.
11. T. Sikora. The MPEG-7 visual standard for content description-An Overview. *IEEE TRANSACTIONS ON CIRCUITS AND SYSTEMS FOR VIDEO TECHNOLOGY*, 11(6), June 2001.
12. J. Weickert. *Mustererkennung 1998*, chapter Fast segmentation methods based on partial differential equations and the watershed transform, pages 93–100. Springer Verlag, 1998.
13. H. Wersing. *Spatial Feature Binding and Learning in Competitive Neural Layer Architectures*. PhD thesis, Technische Fakultät der Universität Bielefeld, 2000.
14. A. Winter and C. Nastar, editors. *Differential Feature Distribution Maps for Image Segmentation and Region Queries in Image Databases*, Ft Collins, Colorado, June 1999. IEEE CVPR'99 workshop on Content Based Access of Images and Video Libraries.
15. B. Zelinka. On a certain distance between isomorphism classes of graphs. *Casopis pro pestovani matematiky*, 100:371–373, 1975.

Appendix:

Proof. We only give a sketch of proof for Proposition 1. To simplify matters let be $\alpha = \beta = 1$:

1. $d(G_1, G_2) \geq 0$, because $\mu(\mu - 1) \geq v_\Phi$ and $\mu \geq n_\Phi$.
2. $G_1 \cong G_2 \Rightarrow d(G_1, G_2) = 0$.
3. $d(G_1, G_2) = 0 \Rightarrow \mu(\mu - 1) - v_\Phi + \mu - n_\Phi = 0 \Rightarrow \mu^2 = n_\Phi + v_\Phi \Rightarrow n_\Phi = \mu$ and $v_\Phi = \mu(\mu - 1)$ because $n_\Phi \leq \mu$ and $v_\Phi \leq \mu(\mu - 1) \Rightarrow \forall x_i, x_j$: $\sigma_L(l_{G_1}(x_i), l_{G_2}(\Phi(x_j))) = 1$ and $\sigma_E(e_{G_1}(x_i, x_j), e_{G_2}(\Phi(x_i), \Phi(x_j))) = 1 \Rightarrow G_1 \cong G_2$.
4. $d(G_1, G_2) = d(G_2, G_1)$
5. Proof that triangle inequality holds is more difficult:

Let Φ_{GH}^* and Φ_{HL}^* be these g-subgraphisomorphisms defined by $d(G, H)$ and $d(H, L)$: $N_G \xrightarrow{\Phi_{GH}^*} N_H \xrightarrow{\Phi_{HL}^*} N_L$. $\text{Dom}(\Phi_{GH}^*)$, $\text{range}(\Phi_{GH}^*)$, $\text{dom}(\Phi_{HL}^*)$, $\text{range}(\Phi_{HL}^*)$ let be the Φ_{GH}^* and Φ_{HL}^* g-isomorph mapped induced subgraphs. $\text{Range}(\Phi_{GH}^*)$ $\cap \text{dom}(\Phi_{HL}^*)$ describes the subgraph which includes that nodes and edges, which contained in $\text{range}(\Phi_{GH}^*)$ as well as in $\text{dom}(\Phi_{HL}^*)$. Thus $\text{range}(\Phi_{GH}^*) \cap \text{dom}(\Phi_{HL}^*)$ is an induced subgraph. $\text{Range}(\Phi_{GH}^*) \setminus \text{dom}(\Phi_{HL}^*)$ describes that subgraph of H, which arised from $\text{range}(\Phi_{GH}^*)$ by removing all nodes of $\text{dom}(\Phi_{HL}^*)$ and all edges joined with that nodes. $\text{Range}(\Phi_{GH}^*) \setminus \text{dom}(\Phi_{HL}^*)$ is an induced subgraph of H, because if $x_i, x_j \in \text{range}(\Phi_{GH}^*) \setminus \text{dom}(\Phi_{HL}^*) \Rightarrow x_i, x_j \in \text{range}(\Phi_{GH}^*)$ and hence x_i, x_j adjacent $\Longleftrightarrow (x_i, x_j) \in V_H$. $\text{Dom}(\Phi_{HL}^*) \setminus \text{range}(\Phi_{GH}^*)$ is an induced subgraph analogicaly. Triangle inequality holds, if

$$
\begin{aligned}
& (\mu_{GH}(\mu_{GH} - 1) - v_{\Phi_{GH}^*}) + (\mu_{GH} - n_{\Phi_{GH}^*}) \\
+ \ & (\mu_{HL}(\mu_{HL} - 1) - v_{\Phi_{HL}^*}) + (\mu_{HL} - n_{\Phi_{HL}^*}) \\
- \ & (\mu_{GL}(\mu_{GL} - 1) - v_{\Phi_{GL}^*}) - (\mu_{GL} - n_{\Phi_{GL}^*}) \\
& \geq 0 \ .
\end{aligned}
\tag{1}
$$

It must be distinguished between three cases:

$$
\begin{aligned}
& 1. \ \max\{|N_G|, |N_H|, |N_L|\} = |N_H| \\
& 2. \ \max\{|N_G|, |N_H|, |N_L|\} = |N_G| \\
& 3. \ \max\{|N_G|, |N_H|, |N_L|\} = |N_L| \ .
\end{aligned}
$$

We regard only first case:

$$
\begin{aligned}
(1) \ = \ & (|N_H|(|N_H| - 1) - v_{\Phi_{GH}^*}) + (|N_H| - n_{\Phi_{GH}^*}) \\
+ \ & (|N_H|(|N_H| - 1) - v_{\Phi_{HL}^*}) + (|N_H| - n_{\Phi_{HL}^*}) \\
- \ & ((\mu_{GL}(\mu_{GL} - 1) - v_{\Phi_{GL}^*}) + (\mu_{GL} - n_{\Phi_{GL}^*})) \\
= \ & [\ |N_H|(|N_H| - 1) - v_{\Phi_{GH}^*} - v_{\Phi_{HL}^*} + |N_H| - n_{\Phi_{GH}^*} - n_{\Phi_{HL}^*} \ ] \ + \\
& \{ \ |N_H|(|N_H| - 1) + |N_H| - ((\mu_{GL}(\mu_{GL} - 1) - v_{\Phi_{GL}^*}) + (\mu_{GL} - n_{\Phi_{GL}^*})) \ \}.
\end{aligned}
$$

$\{ \ |N_H|(|N_H| - 1) + |N_H| - ((\mu_{GL}(\mu_{GL} - 1) - v_{\Phi_{GL}^*}) + (\mu_{GL} - n_{\Phi_{GL}^*})) \ \} \geq 0$ because case 1 holds. So 2 cases must also distinguished:

1.a: $\text{range}(\Phi_{GH}^*) \cap \text{dom}(\Phi_{HL}^*) = \{\oslash\}$. Then $[\ |N_H|(|N_H|-1) - v_{\Phi_{GH}^*} - v_{\Phi_{HL}^*} + |N_H| - n_{\Phi_{GH}^*} - n_{\Phi_{HL}^*} \ ] \geq 0$ and triangle inequality holds.

1.b: $\text{range}(\Phi_{GH}^*) \cap \text{dom}(\Phi_{HL}^*) \neq \{\oslash\}$. Consider $\Phi_{GHL} := \Phi_{HL}^* \circ \Phi_{GH}^*$. Following unequation holds:

$$
v_{\Phi_{GL}^*} + n_{\Phi_{GL}^*} \geq v_{\Phi_{GHL}} + n_{\Phi_{GHL}}.
\tag{2}
$$

With assumption that σ_L descends from a metric, (2) can be estimated downwards. For this purpose consider $n_{\Phi_{GHL}} + |N_H|$:

$$n_{\Phi_{GHL}} + |N_H| \quad \geq \quad n_{\Phi_{GHL}}$$
$$+ \sum_{y \in \, range(\Phi_{GH}^*) \backslash dom(\Phi_{HL}^*)} \sigma_L(l_G(\Phi_{GH}^{*-1}(y)), l_H(y))$$
$$+ \sum_{y \in \, dom(\Phi_{HL}^*) \backslash range(\Phi_{GH}^*)} \sigma_L(l_H(y), l_L(\Phi_{HL}^*(y)))$$
$$= \sum_{y \in \, range(\Phi_{GH}^*) \cap dom(\Phi_{HL}^*)} \sigma_L(l_G(\Phi_{GH}^{*-1}(y)), l_L(\Phi_{HL}^*(y)))$$
$$+ \sum_{y \in \, range(\Phi_{GH}^*) \backslash dom(\Phi_{HL}^*)} \sigma_L(l_G(\Phi_{GH}^{*-1}(y)), l_H(y))$$
$$+ \sum_{y \in \, dom(\Phi_{HL}^*) \backslash range(\Phi_{GH}^*)} \sigma_L(l_H(y), l_L(\Phi_{HL}^*(y)))$$
$$\geq \sum_{y \in \, range(\Phi_{GH}^*) \cap dom(\Phi_{HL}^*)} \sigma_L(l_G(\Phi_{GH}^{*-1}(y)), l_H(y))$$
$$+ \sum_{y \in \, range(\Phi_{GH}^*) \cap dom(\Phi_{HL}^*)} \sigma_L(l_H(y), l_L(\Phi_{HL}^*(y)))$$
$$+ \sum_{y \in \, range(\Phi_{GH}^*) \backslash dom(\Phi_{HL}^*)} \sigma_L(l_G(\Phi_{GH}^{*-1}(y)), l_H(y))$$
$$+ \sum_{y \in \, dom(\Phi_{HL}^*) \backslash range(\Phi_{GH}^*)} \sigma_L(l_H(y), l_L(\Phi_{HL}^*(y)))$$
$$= \quad n_{\Phi_{GH}^*} + n_{\Phi_{HL}^*}.$$

Summarizing:

$$n_{\Phi_{GHL}} + |N_H| \geq n_{\Phi_{GH}^*} + n_{\Phi_{HL}^*}. \tag{3}$$

It follows analogously for the edges:

$$v_{\Phi_{GHL}} + |N_H|(|N_H| - 1) \geq v_{\Phi_{GH}^*} + v_{\Phi_{HL}^*}. \tag{4}$$

From (2), (3) and (4) follows:

$$v_{\Phi_{GL}^*} + n_{\Phi_{GL}^*} \geq v_{\Phi_{GH}^*} + v_{\Phi_{HL}^*} - |N_H|(|N_H| - 1)$$
$$+ n_{\Phi_{GH}^*} + n_{\Phi_{HL}^*} - |N_H|. \tag{5}$$

Now we are able to proof case 1.b:

$$[\, |N_H|(|N_H| - 1) - v_{\Phi_{GH}^*} - v_{\Phi_{HL}^*} + |N_H| - n_{\Phi_{GH}^*} - n_{\Phi_{HL}^*}]$$
$$+ \{|N_H|(|N_H| - 1) + |N_H| - (\mu_{GL}(\mu_{GL} - 1) - v_{\Phi_{GL}^*}) + (\mu_{GL} - n_{\Phi_{GL}^*})\}$$
$$\geq_{(5)} \qquad\qquad -v_{\Phi_{GL}^*} - n_{\Phi_{GL}^*}$$
$$+ \{|N_H|(|N_H| - 1) + |N_H| - (\mu_{GL}(\mu_{GL} - 1) - v_{\Phi_{GL}^*}) + (\mu_{GL} - n_{\Phi_{GL}^*})\}$$
$$= \qquad |N_H|(|N_H| - 1) + |N_H| - (\mu_{GL}(\mu_{GL} - 1) + \mu_{GL})$$
$$\geq \qquad\qquad 0 \, .$$

$\square$

Sequential Learning Algorithm of Neural Networks Systems for Time Series

O. Valenzuela[1], I. Rojas[2], and F. Rojas[2]

[1]Department of Applied Mathematic, University of Granada. Spain.
[2]Department of Architecture and Computer Technology. University of Granada. Spain.

Abstract. This article describes a new structure to create a RBF neural network that uses regression weights to replace the constant weights normally used. These regression weights are assumed to be functions of input variables. In this way the number of hidden units within a RBF neural network is reduced. A new type of nonlinear function is proposed: the pseudo-gaussian function. With this, the neural system gains flexibility, as the neurons possess an activation field that does not necessarily have to be symmetric with respect to the centre or to the location of the neuron in the input space. In addition to this new structure, we propose a sequential learning algorithm, which is able to adapt the structure of the network; with this, it is possible to create new hidden units and also to detect and remove inactive units. We have presented conditions to increase or decrease the number of neurons, based on the novelty of the data and on the overall behaviour of the neural system, (for example, pruning the hidden units that have lowest relevance to the neural system using Orthogonal Least Squares (OLS) and other operators), respectively. The feasibility of the evolution and learning capability of the resulting algorithm for the neural network is demonstrated by predicting time series.

1 Introduction

Time series are ordered sequences of numbers relating to some observed or measured entity, where the ordering of the sequence is typically done based on the time of the observation or measurement. Typical examples in business and economics are daily closing stock prices, weekly interest rates, and yearly earnings. Contrary to the ease with which we can come up with examples of time series in finance, however, there is a remarkable lack of the use of systematic time series analysis techniques in finance. For instance, very simple models (e.g. constant or first order linear models) are sometimes used to predict future values of important company attributes such as sales, but little use is made of higher order models.

Forecasting in time series is a common problem. Using a statistical approach, Box and Jenkins have developed the integrated autoregressive moving average (ARIMA) methodology for fitting a class of linear time series models. Statisticians in a number of ways have addressed the restriction of linearity in the Box-Jenkins approach. Robust versions of various ARIMA models have been developed. In addition, a large amount of literature on inherently nonlinear time series models is available. The stochastic approach to nonlinear time series outlined by can not only fit non-linear models to time series data, but again provides measures of uncertainty in the estimated model parameters as well as forecasts generated by these models. It is

A. Günter et al. (Eds.): KI 2003, LNAI 2821, pp. 327–341, 2003.

the stochastic approach that again enables the specification of uncertainty in parameter estimates and forecasts. On the other hand, Artificial Neural Networks have been studied as an alternative to these nonlinear model-driven approaches.

In this paper, a Radial Basis Function Neural Network will be used to forecast time series. Existing learning strategies for RBF neural networks can be classified as follows: (a) RBF networks with a fixed number of radial basis function centres selected randomly from the training data [9]; (b) RBF networks employing unsupervised procedures for selecting a fixed number of radial basis function centres [15] (e.g., k-means clustering of Kohonen's self-organizing maps [12]), which offer computational efficiency and convergence speed; (c) RBF networks employing supervised procedures for selecting a fixed number of radial basis function centres, using for example orthogonal least-squares [20] or the Kalman filter [5]; (d) Methods combining supervised and unsupervised learning techniques [10]; (e) Algorithms that add hidden units to the network based on the "novelty" of the input data [18][23].

A different approach is proposed in this paper to reduce the complexity of the RBF networks. It comprises a sequential learning algorithm, which is able to adapt the structure of the network; thus, it is possible to create new hidden units and also to detect and remove inactive units. The task of sequential learning highlights the "stability / plasticity dilemma". Ideally the representations developed by a learning system should be stable enough to preserve important information over time, but plastic enough to incorporate new information when necessary. The use of variable connection weights as a medium for encoding information leads most ANNs to err on the side of excessive plasticity - new learning changes the weights and thus disrupts any old information (items previously learned by the network). Grossberg [8] suggests the analogy of a human trained to recognise the word "cat", and subsequently to recognise the word "table", being then unable to recognise "cat". This effect has been identified in many guises in the ANN literature under headings such as catastrophic forgetting, catastrophic interference, or the serial learning problem. It is this underlying problem that limits most ANN learning algorithms to concurrent learning, items cannot be learned in a sequence because later items will disrupt or eliminate earlier items.

A special RBF network architecture is presented; instead of using constant weights in the output layer of the network, regression weights, which are functions of the input variables, are considered. It will be seen in the simulation results that this modification significantly reduces the size of the hidden layer. Based on the analysis made of the principal functions required to design the neural network, which determine the variables that are most influential in the response of an RBF [19], a modification in the definition of the nonlinear function within the hidden neurons is introduced.

2   RBF System Structure

The output of the networks is defined as t the weighted average $\widetilde{F}_{RBF}^{*}$ of the radial basis function with the addition of lateral connections between the radial neurons, as follows:

$$\tilde{F}_{RBF}^{*}(\mathbf{x}_n) = \sum_{i=1}^{K} w_i \phi_i (\mathbf{x}_n, \mathbf{c}_i, \sigma_i) \tag{1}$$

We propose to use a pseudo-gaussian function for the nonlinear function within the hidden unit. The output of a hidden neuron is computed as:

$$\phi_i(x) = \prod_v \varphi_{i,v}(x^v)$$

$$\varphi_{i,v}(x^v) = e^{-\frac{\left(x^v - c_i^v\right)^2}{\sigma_{i,-}^v}} U(x^v; -\infty, c_i^v) + e^{-\frac{\left(x^v - c_i^v\right)^2}{\sigma_{i,+}^v}} U(x^v; c_i^v, \infty) \tag{2}$$

$$where \ : \ U(x^v; a, b) = \begin{cases} 1 & if \ a \leq x^v < b \\ 0 & otherwise \end{cases}$$

The index i runs over the number of neurons (K) while v runs over the dimension of the input space ($v0[1,D]$). The weights connecting the activation of the hidden units with the output of the neural system, instead of being single parameters, are functions of the input variables. Therefore, the w_i are given by:

$$w_i = \sum_v b_i^v x^v + b_i^0 \tag{3}$$

where b_i^v are single parameters.

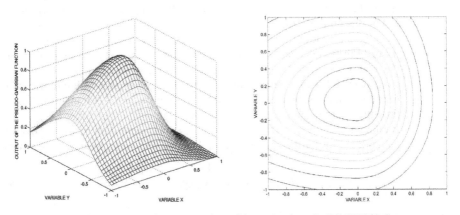

Fig. 1. a) Tri-dimensional representation of the activation of a PG-RBF b) Contour

3   Prunnig Strategy for the Pg-Rbf Network

Learning in the RBF consists of determining the minimum necessary number of rules and adjusting the mean and variance vectors of individual hidden neurons as well as the weights that connect these neurons with the output layer. A sequential learning algorithm is presented to adapt the structure of the network, in which it is possible to create new hidden units and also to detect and remove inactive units.

One drawback of the algorithm for growing RBF proposed in the bibliography [16],[18] is that once a hidden neuron is created it can never be removed. The algorithms basically increase the complexity of the neural model in order to achieve a better approximation of the problem, whereas in some problem domains a better approximation may result from a simplification (e.g. pruning) of the model. This is very important in order to avoid overfitting.

Therefore, we propose a pruning strategy that can detect and remove hidden neurons, which although active initially, may subsequently end up contributing little to the network output. Then a more streamlined neural network can be constructed as learning progresses. Because, in general, we do not know the number of hidden nodes, the algorithm starts with only one hidden node and creates additional neurons based on the novelty (innovation) in the observations which arrive sequentially. The decision as to whether a datum should be deemed novel is based on the following conditions:

$$e_n = \left| y_n - \widetilde{F}^*_{RBF} \right| > \xi$$
$$\beta_{max} = \underset{i}{Max}(\phi_i) < \zeta \tag{4}$$

If both conditions are satisfied, then the data is considered to have novelty and therefore a new hidden neuron is added to the network, until a maximum number, MaxNeuron, is reached. The parameters > and . are thresholds to be selected appropriately for each problem. When all the input vectors have been presented in an iteration, it is necessary to determine whether there exist any neurons that can be removed from the neural system, without unduly affecting its performance (pruning operation). For this purpose, four cases will be considered:

(a)   Pruning the hidden units that have lowest relevance to the neural system using Orthogonal Least Squares (OLS). This method can be used to prune the leat relevant RBFs in the neural network systems, thus obtaining a simpler model whose approximation error is as close as possible to the error of the original net. A more detailed discussion of the OLS transformation is presented in the next seccion.

(b)   Pruning the hidden units that make very little contribution to the overall network output for the whole data set. Pruning removes a hidden unit i when

$$\theta_i = \left[\sum_{n=1}^{N} \phi_i(x_n) \right] < \chi_1 \tag{5}$$

where χ_1 is a threshold.

(c)   Pruning hidden units which have a very small activation region. These units obviously represent an overtrained learning. A neuron i having very low values of $\sigma^v_{i,+} + \sigma^v_{i,-}$ in the different dimensions of the input space will be removed.

$$\sum_{v} \left(\sigma_{i,+}^{v} + \sigma_{i,-}^{v} \right) < \chi_2 \tag{6}$$

(d)   Pruning hidden units which have a very similar activation to other neurons in the neural system. To achieve this, we define the vector $\psi_i \, 0 \, \aleph^N$, where N is the number of input/output vectors presented, such that:

$$\psi_i = \left[\phi_i(x_1), \phi_i(x_2), ..., \phi_i(x_n) \right] \tag{7}$$

As a guide to determine when two neurons present similar behaviour, this can be expressed in terms of the inner product $\psi_i \bullet \psi_j$. If the inner product is near one then ψ_i and ψ_j are both attempting to do nearly the same job (they possess a very similar activation level for the same input values). In this case, they directly compete in the sense that only one of these neurons is selected and therefore the other one is removed. On the other hand, if $\psi_i \bullet \psi_j$ is close to zero, then the two neurons are being activated for different input vectors and thus make a relatively independent contribution to the overall behaviour of the neural system. In this case, it would not make sense for the hidden neurons ϕ_i, ϕ_j to compete as they are performing two different functions and both are necessary to construct the neural system.

If any of these conditions are fulfilled for a particular neuron, it is automatically removed.

4 Orthogonal Least Squares (Ols) for Pruning the Rbf Network

Once the parameters concerning the RBFs have been fixed, their associated weights can be optimally calculated using a linear systems solver. Equation (1) can be seen as a special case of linear regression:

$$\widetilde{F}_{RBF}^{*}(x_n) = \sum_{i=1}^{K} w_i \phi_i(x_n, c_i, \sigma_i) + e_n \tag{8}$$

In this regression model, $\phi_i(x_n, c_i, \sigma_i)$ are the regressors, w_i the parameters, and e_n are the residual errors for each input vector x_n. Given N input-output samples, equation (8) can be expressed as:

$$\widetilde{F} = Pw + e \tag{9}$$

Where:

$$\widetilde{F} = \left[\widetilde{F}_1, ..., \widetilde{F}_N \right]^T \in \Re^N \tag{10}$$

is the column vector containing all the expected outputs, $P=[p_1,...,p_K]\in \Re^{NxK}$ is a matrix whose columns $p_j= [\phi_j(x_1,c_j,\sigma_j),...,\phi_j(x_N,c_j,\sigma_j)]^T$ represent the output of the j-th basis function for all the input vectors. The vector $e = [e_1,...,e_N]^T$ contains all the errors committed by the model (assumed to be uncorrelated), and w is a vector containing the net weights. Henceforth in this paper P will be the activation matrix of the RBFNN and Pw will be the predictor of the model. The number of training samples N is usually greater than the number of RBFs K, and so we only have to solve the following overdetermined linear system:

$$\widetilde{F} = Pw \tag{11}$$

to minimize the approximation error of the net and find the optimal weights (in the least squares sense). There are several ways to solve overdetermined linear systems, and we will use the OLS method.

This method was originally employed in [3] to calculate the optimum weights of an RBFNN. It also estimates the relevance of each RBF $\phi_j(x_1,c_j,\sigma_j)$ in the output of the net by assigning it an error reduction ratio $[err]_j$. OLS transforms the columns of the activation matrix P into a set of orthogonal vectors u_j. This transformation is performed by applying the Gram-Schmidt orthogonalization method [7] and produces:

$$P = UR \tag{12}$$

Note that (12) gives the same information as the ``standard" QR decomposition of P (P=QR) [7]. Substituting (12) in (9) we obtain

$$\widetilde{F} = URw + e = Ug + e \tag{13}$$

where g =Rw. As u_j and u_l are orthogonal $\forall j \neq l$, the sum of squares of $\widetilde{F}_n$ ($\widetilde{F}^T\widetilde{F}$) can be written as:

$$\widetilde{F}^T\widetilde{F} = \sum_{j=1}^{K} g_j^2 u_j^T u_j + e^T e \tag{14}$$

Dividing both sides of equation (14) by N, it can be seen how the model variance ($\widetilde{F}^T\widetilde{F}/N$) is decomposed into explained and residual variances:

$$\frac{\widetilde{F}^T\widetilde{F}}{N} = \frac{\sum_{j=1}^{K} g_j^2 u_j^T u_j}{N} + \frac{e^T e}{N} \tag{15}$$

So, $\dfrac{\sum_{j=1}^{K} g_j^2 u_j^T u_j}{N}$ as is the contribution of u_j to the total output variance, we can define the *error reduction ratio* of u_j as [3]

$$[err]_j = \frac{g_j^2 u_j^T u_j}{\tilde{F}^T \tilde{F}}; \forall j = 1,...,m \tag{16}$$

This ratio can be used to rank the RBFs according to their contribution to the reduction of the approximation error. If we want to keep the r most relevant RBFs (r<K), we will select the r basis functions that have the highest error reduction ratios. This method can be used to prune the least relevant RBFs in the net, thus obtaining a simpler model whose approximation error is as close as possible to the error of the original net.

5 Optimization the Parameters of the Rbf

A simple approach to minimizing the merit function χ^2 is to use information about the gradient of the function to step along the surface of the function "downhill" towards a minimum, i.e. update the parameters a at each iteration using the rule:

$$\delta w = -\varepsilon \nabla \chi^2(w) \tag{17}$$

where the gradient $\nabla \chi^2(a)$ is composed of the p first derivatives $\dfrac{\delta \chi^2(w)}{\delta w}$ and ε is a small positive constant. In our RBF model, this equation are the following:

$$\Delta c_i^v = -\frac{\partial E}{\partial c_i^v} = -\frac{\partial E}{\partial \tilde{F}_{RBF}^*} \frac{\partial \tilde{F}_{RBF}^*}{\partial \phi_i} \frac{\partial \phi_i}{\partial c_i^v} =$$

$$= (y_n - \tilde{F}_{RBF}^*)(w_i - y_n)*$$

$$\left[2\frac{x_n^v - c_i^v}{\sigma_{i,-}^v} e^{-\frac{(x_n^v - c_i^v)^2}{\sigma_{i,-}^v}} U(x_n^v; -\infty, c_i^v) + 2\frac{x_n^v - c_i^v}{\sigma_{i,+}^v} e^{-\frac{(x_n^v - c_i^v)^2}{\sigma_{i,+}^v}} U(x_n^v; c_i^v, \infty) \right] \tag{18}$$

$$\Delta \sigma_{i,+}^v = -\frac{\partial E}{\partial \sigma_{i,+}^v} = -\frac{\partial E}{\partial \tilde{F}_{RBF}^*} \frac{\partial \tilde{F}_{RBF}^*}{\partial \phi_i} \frac{\partial \phi_i}{\partial \sigma_{i,+}^v} =$$

$$= (y_n - \tilde{F}_{RBF}^*)(w_i - y_n)\left[2\left(\frac{x_n^v - c_i^v}{\sigma_{i,+}^v}\right)^2 e^{-\frac{(x_n^v - c_i^v)^2}{\sigma_{i,+}^v}} U(x_n^v; c_i^v, \infty) \right] \tag{19}$$

$$\Delta \sigma_{i,-}^v = (y_n - \tilde{F}_{RBF}^*)(w_i - y_n)\left[2\left(\frac{x_n^v - c_i^v}{\sigma_{i,-}^v}\right)^2 e^{-\frac{(x_n^v - c_i^v)^2}{\sigma_{i,-}^v}} U(x_n^v; -\infty, c_i^v) \right]$$

$$\Delta b_i^v = -\frac{\partial E}{\partial b_i^v} = (y_n - \widetilde{F}_{RBF}^*)\phi_i(x_n)x_n^v$$

$$\Delta b_i^0 = -\frac{\partial E}{\partial b_i^0} = (y_n - \widetilde{F}_{RBF}^*)\phi_i(x_n)$$

(20)

The problem with the gradient descent approach is in choosing ε: we'd like it to be small, so that we stay on the χ^2 surface and thus ensure we make progress moving downhill, but we'd also like it to be big so that we converge to the solution quickly. Solutions to this dilemma include varying ε in response to how well previous steps worked, or iteratively finding the minimum in the direction of the gradient (i.e. "minimization").

The Levenberg-Marquardt method takes a different approach, by recognizing that the curvature of the function gives us some information about how far to move along the slope of the function. It approximates the χ^2 function with a second order Taylor series expansion around the current point w_0:

$$\chi^2(w) \approx \chi^2(w_0) + \nabla\chi^2(w_0)^T w + \frac{1}{2}w^T Hw$$

(21)

where H is the Hessian matrix evaluated at w_0:

$$[H]_{kl} \equiv \frac{\delta\chi^2}{\delta w_k \delta w_l}\bigg|_{w_0}$$

(22)

Since the approximating function is quadratic its minimum can easily be moved to using step size

$$\delta w = -H^{-1}\nabla\chi^2(w_0)$$

(23)

However, this approximation will not always be a good one (especially early in the estimation process), and thus the Levenberg-Marquardt method allows the user to adopt any combination of the simple gradient descent rule and the inverse Hessian rule by multiplying the diagonal of H with a constant λ (i.e. $H_{kk}^{'} \equiv H_{kk}(1+\lambda)$). Thus a typical iterative strategy is to use more of a gradient descent step by increasing λ when the previous δw doesn't work (i.e. increases χ^2), and use more of an inverse Hessian step by decreasing λ when the previous δw does work (i.e. decreases χ^2).

The final algorithm is summarized below:

Step 1: Initially, no hidden neuron exists.
Step 2: Set n=0, K=0, h=1, where n, K and h are the number of patterns presented to the network, the number of hidden neurons and the number of learning cycles, respectively. Set the effective radius .. Set the maximum number of hidden neurons MaxNeuron.
Step 3: For each observation (x_n, y_n) compute:
a) the overall network output:

$$\widetilde{F}^{*}_{RBF}(\mathrm{x_n}) = \sum_{i=1}^{K} w_i \phi_i(\mathrm{x_n}, \mathrm{c_i}, \sigma_i) \tag{24}$$

b) the parameter required for the evaluation of the novelty of the observation; the error $e_n = \left| y_n - \widetilde{F}^{*}_{RBF} \right|$ and the maximum degree of activation β_{max} .

If ($(e_n > >)$ and ($\beta_{max} < .$) and K<MaxNeuron) allocate a new hidden unit:

$$K = K + 1$$

$$b^{v}_K = \begin{cases} y_n - \widetilde{F}^{*}_{RBF} & \text{if } v = 0 \\ 0 & \text{otherwise} \end{cases} \tag{25}$$

$$c_K = x_n(c^{v}_K = x^{v}_n, \forall v \in [1, D]$$

$$\sigma^{v}_{K,+} = \sigma^{v}_{K,-} = \gamma \sigma_{init} \underset{i=1,\dots,K-1}{Min} \left\| x_n - c_i \right\|$$

Else apply the parameter learning for all the hidden nodes
Step 4: If all the training patterns are presented, then increment the number of learning cycles (h=h+1), and check the criteria for pruning hidden units:

$$\theta_i = \left[\sum_{n=1}^{N} \phi_i(x_n) \right] < \chi_1$$

$$\sum_{v} \left(\sigma^{v}_{i,+} + \sigma^{v}_{i,-} \right) < \chi_2 \tag{26}$$

$$\psi_i \bullet \psi_j < \chi_3 \quad , \forall j \neq i$$

Pruning the hidden units that have lowest relevance to the neural system using

Orthogonal Least Squares (OLS).

Step 5: If the network shows satisfactory performance (NRMSE<Π^{*}) then stop. Otherwise go to Step 3

6 Simulation Results

6.1 Real Time Serie: Lake Eriel

First, we will discuss the obtained results from a real time series. We will use a time series from the Time Series Data Library (http://www-personal.buseco.monash.edu.au/ ~hyndman/TSDL/hydrology.html). The Time series Erie is a file of 600 data of the Levels of the lake Eriel (Monthly Lake Erie Levels 1921 – 1970).

Fig. 2 shows the behavior of the time series. presents the comparison between the real time series and that predicted by the algorithm, using 3 input variables, in order to predict the value of the time series (1 step), using 8 neurons in the hidden layer. The error indices, the root mean square error for traing and test, and the correlation coefficient, for this simulation were 0.5717 0.78784 and 0.88, respectively

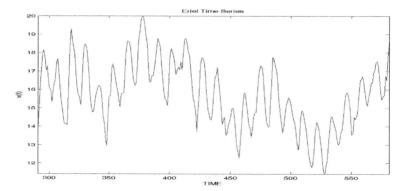

Fig. 2. Detail presentation of the original time series

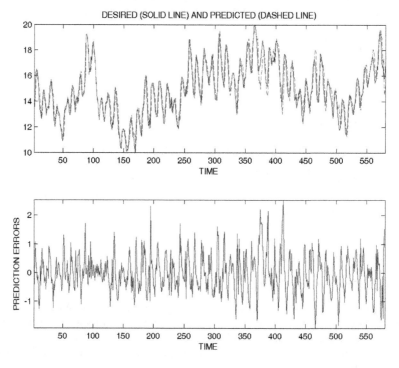

Fig. 3. Behaviour of the PG-RBF system using a prediction step=1; a) Comparison of the original and predicted time series b) prediction errors

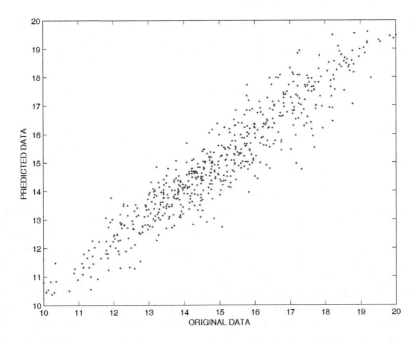

Fig. 4. Result of correlation for prediction at 1 step ahead for the Eriel time series

Fig. 5 shows the results of the prediction of the Eriel time series when the prediction step changes (RMSE and Correlation Coefficient).

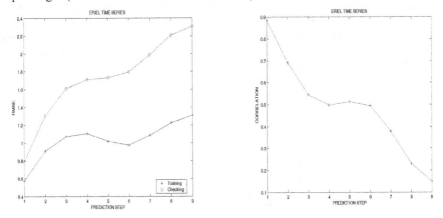

Fig. 5. a) Evolution of the RMSE of the prediction of the Eriel time series when the prediction step is modified b) Evolution of the Correlation coeficient

6.2 Simulated Time Series: Lorenz Attractor

In this subsection we attempt a short-term prediction by means of the algorithm presented in the above subsection with regard to the Lorenz attractor time series. The Lorenz attractor time series was generated by solving the Lorenz equations:

$$\frac{dx_1(t)}{dt} = \sigma(_2(t) - x_1(t))$$

$$\frac{dx_2(t)}{dt} = \rho \cdot x_1(t) - x_2(t) - x_1(t)x_3(t) \qquad (27)$$

$$\frac{dx_3(t)}{dt} = -x_3(t)\beta + x_1(t)x_2(t)$$

where the parameters are set at the standard values $\sigma = 10$, $\rho = 28$ and $\beta = 8/3$. Solutions to this system of three differential equations exhibit the sensitive dependence on initial conditions which is characteristic of chaotic dynamics. In realistic situations, knowledge of the true state of a system can be done only in finite precision. In such cases, sensitivity to initial conditions rules out long-term prediction. On the other hand, short-term prediction is possible to the extent that the current position can be estimated and that the dynamics can be approximated. A long trajectory of the Lorenz attractor (1000 points) was generated using a differential equation solver (Runge-Kutta method) with step size of 0.05 to create a univariate time series ($x_1(t)$). The data was split into 2 parts: 500 points were used for training and the remaining 500 for assessing the generalization capability of the network. Fig. 6 shows a characterization of this time series (its phase diagram)

Fig. 7 presents the comparison between the real time series and that predicted by the algorithm, using 3 input variables, in order to predict the value of the time series (1 step), using 8 neurons in the hidden layer. The error indices, the root mean square error and the correlation coefficient, for this simulation were 0.091 and 0.99. It is important to note that other approaches appeared in the bibliography, for example T.Iokibe et.al [6] obtain an RMSE of 0.244, J.S.R.Jang et. al [9] an RMSE of 0.143, using fuzzy and neuro-fuzzy systems.

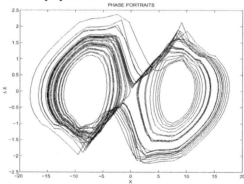

Fig. 6. *The characterization of the Lorenz time series; the phase diagram*

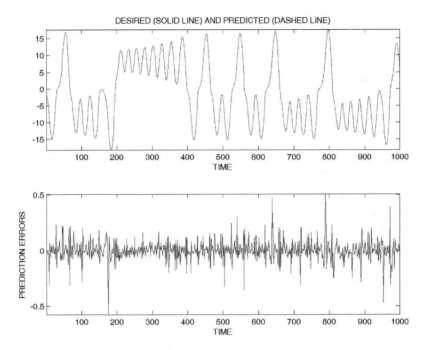

Fig. 7. Behaviour of the PG-RBF system using a prediction step=1; a) Comparison of the original and predicted time series b) prediction errors

7 Conclusions

This paper proposes a framework for constructing and training a radial basis function (RBF) neural network, which is an example of fuzzy system. For this purpose, a sequential learning algorithm is presented to adapt the structure of the network, in which it is possible to create a new hidden unit (rule) and also to detect and remove inactive units. The structure of the gaussian functions (membership functions) is modified using a pseudo-gaussian function (PG) in which two scaling parameters Φ are introduced, which eliminates the symmetry restriction and provides the neurons in the hidden layer with greater flexibility with respect to function approximation. Other important characteristics of the proposed neural system is that instead of using a single parameter for the output weights, these are functions of the input variables which leads to a significant reduction in the number of hidden units compared with the classical RBF network. Finally, we examine the result of applying the proposed algorithm to time series prediction.

Acknowledgement. This work has been partially supported by the CICYT Spanish Project DPI2001-3219.

References

[1]   F.Anouar, F.Badran, S.Thiria, "Probabilistic self-organizing maps and radial basis function networks", Neurocomputing, vol.20, pp.83–96, 1998.

[2]   M.Benaim, "On functional approximation with normalized Gaussian units", Neural Comput. Vol.6, 1994

[3]   S. Chen, C. F. N. Cowan, and P. M. Grant. "Orthogonal Least Squares Learning Algorithm for Radial Basis Functions". IEEE Trans. Neural Networks, 2:302–309, 1991.

[4]   K.B.Cho, B.H.Wang "Radial basis function based adaptive fuzzy systems and their applications to system identification and prediction", Fuzzy Sets and Systems, vol.83, pp.325–339, 1995.

[5]   S.Haykin, Neural Networks- A Comprehensive Foundation, IEEE Press, New York, 1994.

[6]   T.Iokibe, Y.Fujimoto, M.Kanke, S.Suzuki, "Short-Term prediction of chaotic time series by local fuzzy reconstruction method", Journal of Intelligent and Fuzzy Systems, vol.5, pp.3–21, 1997.

[7]   G. H. Golub and C. F. Van Loan. Matrix Computations. Johns Hopkins University Press, Baltimore, 3rd edition, 1996.

[8]   S. Grossberg, "Competitive Learning: From Interactive Activation to Adaptive Resonance", Cognitive Science, 11, 23–63, (1987).

[9]   J.S.R.Jang, C.T.Sun, E.Mizutani, "Neuro-Fuzzy and soft computing", Prentice Hall, ISBN 0-13-261066-3, 1997.

[10]   N.B.Karayiannis, G.Weiqun Mi, "Growing Radial Basis Neural Networks: Merging Supervised and Unsupervised Learning with Network Growth Techniques", IEEE Transaction on Neural Networks, vol.8, no.6, pp.1492–1506, November 1997.

[11]   D.Kim, C. Kim, "Forecasting time series with genetic fuzzy predictor ensemble", IEEE Transactions on Fuzzy Systems, vol.5, no.4, pp.523–535, November 1997.

[12]   T.Kohonen, Self-Organization and Associative Memory, Springer, New York, 1988.

[13]   S.Lee, R.M. Kil, "A Gaussian potential function network with hierarchically self-organizing learning", Neural Network, vol.2, pp.207–224, 1991.

[14]   S.-H. Lee, I.Kim, "Time series analysis using fuzzy learning", in Proc. Int. Conf. Neural Inform. Processing, Seoul, Korea, , pp.1577–1582, vol.6, Oct. 1994.

[15]   J.E.Moody, C.J.Darke, "Fast learning in networks of locally-tuned processing units", Neural Computa., vol.1, pp.281–294, 1989.

[16]   M.T.Musavi, W.Ahmed, K.H.Chan, K.B.Faris, D.M.Hummels, "On the training of radial basis function classifier", Neural Networks, vol.5, pp.595–603, 1992.

[17]   S.Nowlan, "Maximum likelihood competitive learning", Proc. Neural Inform. Process. Systems, pp.574–582, 1990.

[18]   J.Platt, "A resource allocating network for function interpolation", Neural Computa., vol.3, pp.213–225, 1991.

[19]   I.Rojas, M.Anguita, E.Ros, H.Pomares, O.Valenzuela, A.Prieto,: "What are the main factors involved in the design of a Radial Basis Function Network ?", 6th European Symposium on Artificial Neural Network, ESANN'98, pp.1-6, April 22–24, 1998.

[20]   A.Sherstinsky, R.W.Picard, "On the efficiency of the orthogonal least squares training method for radial basis function networks", IEEE Trans. Neural Networks vol.7, no.1, pp.195–200, 1996.

[21]   L.X.Wang, J.M.Mendel, "Generating fuzzy rules by learning from examples", IEEE Trans. On Syst. Man and Cyber, vol.22, no.6, November/December, pp.1414–1427, 1992.

[22]   B.A.Whitehead, Tinothy.D.Choate, "Cooperative-Competitive Genetic Evolution of Radial Basis Function Centers and Widths for Time Series Prediction", IEEE Transaction on Neural Networks, vol.7,no.4, pp.869–880, July, 1996.

[23]   L.Yingwei, N.Sundarajan, P.Saratchandran, "Performance Evaluation of a Sequential Minimal Radial Basis Function (RBF) Neural Network Learning Algorithm", IEEE Transactions on Neural Networks, vol.9, no.2, pp.308–318, March 1998.

A k-Winner-Takes-All Classifier for Structured Data

Brijnesh J. Jain and Fritz Wysotzki

Dept. of Electrical Engineering and Computer Science
Technical University Berlin, Germany

Abstract. We propose a *k-winner-takes-all* (KWTA) classifier for structures represented by graphs. The KWTA classifier is a neural network implementation of the *k*-nearest neighbor (KNN) rule. The commonly used comparator for identifying the *k* nearest neighbors of a given input structure is replaced by an inhibitory winner-takes-all network for *k*-maximum selection. Due to the principle *elimination of competition* the KWTA classifier circumvents the problem of determining computational intensive structural similarities between a given input structure and several model structures. In experiments on handwritten digits we compare the performance of the self-organizing KWTA classifier with the canonical KNN classifier, which uses a supervising comparator.

1 Introduction

Let $\mathcal{Y} = \{Y_1, \dots, Y_N\} \subseteq \mathcal{X}$ be a set of N models each representing a class or category. Suppose that σ is a problem dependent similarity measure[1] on $\mathcal{X}$. Given an input data $X \in \mathcal{X}$ a *nearest-neighbor* (NN) classifier first computes N similarities $\sigma(X, Y_i)$. Then a *comparative maximum selector* identifies the model

$$Y_{i^*} = \arg \max_{Y_i} \sigma\big(X, Y_i\big),$$

which is nearest to X. Finally, the *nearest-neighbor rule* assigns X to the category associated with Y_{i^*}. An obvious extension of the nearest-neighbor classifier is the *k-nearest-neighbor* (KNN) classifier. A *comparative k-maximum selector* picks the k models nearest to X. The decision is made by examining the categories associated with the k nearest models and taking a vote.

KNN classifiers for graphs, in particular for $k = 1$, have been applied in various classification, pattern recognition, and clustering tasks by using similarity measures based on the common maximal structural overlap of the graphs under consideration [9], [8], [18], [23], [25]. The problem of computing a similarity between graphs by means of structural overlaps belongs to the class of *graph matching problems*. Since the graph matching problem is well known to be NP complete [6], exact algorithms, which guarantee an optimal solution, are useless in a practical setting for all but the smallest graphs. Therefore, due to its applicability in various fields, many heuristics have been devised to approximately solve the graph matching problem within a *reasonable* amount of time

---

[1] For convenience of representation we consider similarity-based classification rather than distance-based classification. This is no severe restriction, since each distance function can be transformed to a similarity function in several ways.

A. Günter et al. (Eds.): KI 2003, LNAI 2821, pp. 342–354, 2003.

[4], [5], [7], [20], [24], [28]. As well as various other heuristics, artificial neural networks and related methods have been successfully employed to graph matching problems [21], [23], [26], [27], [29]. Nevertheless, in contrast to computing similarities of real valued feature vectors, computation of approximate similarities between graphs remains still a computational intensive procedure. Since decision making of a KNN classifier relies on a maximum selector, the computational effort is linearly dependent on the number N of models. Therefore classifying a large number of unseen input data by a KNN classification procedure may be computational intractable.

In this paper we propose a two layer *k-winner-takes-all* (KWTA) classifier for graphs. To circumvent the high computational effort of an 1:N matching task, possibly at the expense of classification accuracy, we replace the comparative k-maximum selector by an inhibitory k-winner-takes-all network for identifying the k largest of N real numbers. The basic procedure of the KWTA classifier simultaneously matches the input data X with the N models Y_i by using N Hopfield networks $\mathcal{H}_i$, called *subnets*. During evolution the subnets $\mathcal{H}_i$ participate in a winner-takes-all competition. Following the principle *elimination of competition* the KWTA classifier focuses on promising subnets and disables unfavorable subnets until k subnets win the competition and all other subnets are disabled. The input X is then classified according to the k-nearest-neighbor rule with respect to the k winners of the competition. This procedure aims to select k winners without completing the computation of a single subnet.

This paper is structured as follows: Section 2 reviews basic components, which will be assembled to a KWTA classifier for structures. Section 3 introduces the KWTA classifier. Section 4 presents and discusses experiments. Finally, Section 5 concludes this contribution.

2   Foundations

This section provides the prerequisites for describing the KWTA classification algorithm.

2.1   The Graph Matching Problem

Let V be a set. With $V^{\{k\}}$ we denote the set of all k-element subsets $\{i_1, \ldots, i_k\} \subseteq V$ where $k \leq |V|$. If $V = \{1, \ldots, N\}$ we sometimes write $\mathcal{I}_N$ and $\mathcal{I}_N^{\{k\}}$ instead of V and $V^{\{k\}}$.

A *weighted graph* is a pair $X = (V, \mu)$ consisting of a finite set $V \neq \emptyset$ of *vertices* and a mapping $\mu : V^{\{2\}} \to \mathbb{R}_+$ assigning each pair $\{i, j\} \in V^2$ a non-negative real valued weight. The elements $\{i, j\} \in V^{\{2\}}$ with positive weight $\mu(\{i, j\}) > 0$ are the *edges* of X. The vertex set of a graph X is referred to as $V(X)$, its edge set as $E(X)$, and its weight mapping as μ_X. A *binary graph* is a weighted graph $X = (V, \mu)$ with $\mu(V^{\{2\}}) \subseteq \{0, 1\}$. A binary graph assigns the weight 1 for its edges and the weight 0 for non-edges. The *adjacency matrix* of a graph X is a matrix $A(X) = (x_{ij})$ with entries $x_{ij} = \mu_X(\{i, j\})$. The number $|X| = |V(X)|$ of vertices of X is called the order of X.

Let X be a graph. A graph Z is an *induced subgraph* of X $(Z \subseteq X)$, if $V(Z) \subseteq V(X)$ and $E(Z) = E(X) \cap V(Z)^{\{2\}}$. A subset C_m of $V(X)$ with m vertices is called *clique* of X if $C_m^{\{2\}} \subseteq E(X)$. Thus the graph $X[C_m]$ induced by the vertex set $C_m \subseteq V(X)$ is a fully connected induced subgraph of X. A *maximal clique* is a clique which is not properly contained in any larger clique. A *maximum clique* is a clique with maximum number of vertices.

Let X and Y be graphs. An *isomorphism* between X and Y is a bijective mapping

$$\phi : V(X) \to V(Y), \quad i \mapsto i^\phi$$

with $\{i, j\} \in E(X) \Leftrightarrow \{i^\phi, j^\phi\} \in E(Y)$ for all $i, j \in V(X)$. If there is an isomorphism between X and Y then X and Y are said to be *isomorphic*. In this case we also write $\phi : X \to Y$ instead of $\phi : V(X) \to V(Y)$. An *overlap* of X and Y is an isomorphism $\phi : X' \to Y'$ between induced subgraphs $X' \subseteq X$ and $Y' \subseteq Y$. By $|\phi| = |X'|$ we denote the *order* of ϕ. A *maximal overlap* is an overlap $\phi : X' \to Y'$, which can not be extended to an overlap $\pi : X'' \to Y''$ with $X' \subset X''$. A *maximum overlap* of X and Y is an overlap $\phi : X' \to Y'$ of maximum order $|\phi|$. By $\mathcal{O}(X, Y)$ we denote the set of all overlaps of X and Y.

The problem of determining a maximum overlap of X and Y is more generally referred to as a *graph matching problem*. Solving that graph matching problem is equivalent to compute a similarity measure

$$\sigma(X, Y) = \max \left\{ f(|\phi|) \ : \ \phi \in \mathcal{O}(X, Y) \right\}. \tag{1}$$

where f is a monotonously increasing function of $|\phi|$. Examples for f are

$$f_1(|\phi|) = \frac{|\phi|}{n} \tag{2}$$

$$f_2(|\phi|) = \frac{|\phi|^2 - |\phi|}{n^2 - n} \tag{3}$$

where n is a scaling factor.

2.2   Graph Matching as Maximum Clique Search

Let X and Y be graphs with adjacency matrices $A(X) = (x_{ij})$ and $A(Y) = (y_{ij})$, respectively. The detection of a maximum overlap of X and Y can be transformed to the problem of finding a maximum clique in an association graph $X \diamond Y$. This concept apparently has been first suggested by Ambler [1], Barrow and Burstall [2], and Levi [16]. Since then it has been applied in several graph matching problems [20], [23], [22]. An association graph $X \diamond Y$ of X and Y is a binary graph with

$$V(X \diamond Y) = \left\{ (i, j) \in V(X) \times V(Y) \ : \ x_{ii} = y_{jj} \right\}$$

$$E(X \diamond Y) = \left\{ \{(i, k), (j, l)\} \in V(X \diamond Y)^{\{2\}} \ : \ x_{ij} = y_{kl}, i \neq j, k \neq l \right\}.$$

Theorem 1 justifies to cast graph matching problems to the problem of finding a maximum clique in an association graph.

Theorem 1. *Let $X \diamond Y$ be the association graph of X and Y. Then the maximum (maximal) cliques of $X \diamond Y$ are in 1-1 correspondence to the maximum (maximal) overlaps of X and Y.*

Proof. We first construct a bijective mapping $\Phi : C(X \diamond Y) \rightarrow \mathcal{O}(X, Y)$ between the set $C(X \diamond Y)$ of cliques in $X \diamond Y$ and the set $\mathcal{O}(X, Y)$ of overlaps of X and Y.

Let $C_m = \{(i_1, j_1), \dots, (i_m, j_m)\} \in C(X \diamond Y)$ be a clique and $X' \subseteq X, Y' \subseteq Y$ the subgraphs induced by $\{i_1, \dots, i_m\} \subseteq V(X)$ and $\{j_1, \dots, j_m\} \subseteq V(Y)$, respectively. We define $\Phi(C_m)$ to be the bijective mapping $\phi : V(X') \rightarrow V(Y')$ with $i_k^{\phi} = j_k$ for all $1 \leq k \leq m$. By definition of $X \diamond Y$ the mapping ϕ is an isomorphism between X' and Y' and therefore an overlap of X and Y. By construction Φ is well defined.

In order to show that Φ is a bijection, we construct a mapping $\Phi' : \mathcal{O}(X, Y) \rightarrow C(X)$ as follows: Let $\phi : X' \rightarrow Y'$ be an isomorphism between induced subgraphs $X' \subseteq X$ and $Y' \subseteq Y$. Define $\Phi'(\phi) = \{(i, i^{\phi}) : i \in V(X)\} \subseteq V(X \diamond Y)$. By definition of $X \diamond Y$ the set $\Phi'(\phi)$ forms a clique in $X \diamond Y$. Then Φ is a bijection, since $\Phi \circ \Phi' = id_{\mathcal{O}(X,Y)}$ and $\Phi' \circ \Phi = id_{C(X)}$.

From the definitions of Φ and Φ' directly follows the assertion, that the restriction of Φ to the subset of all maximum (maximal) cliques in $X \diamond Y$ is a bijection onto the subset of all maximum (maximal) overlaps. $\qquad\square$

In order to cope with noise in the case of weighted graphs we slightly modify the definition of an association graph according to an approach proposed in [13]. Let $\varepsilon \geq 0$. Then $(i, j) \in V(X \diamond Y)$ if $|x_{ii} - y_{jj}| \leq \varepsilon$. Similarly, $\{(i, k), (j, l)\} \in E(X \diamond Y)$ if $|x_{ij} - y_{kl}| \leq \varepsilon$. Searching a maximum clique in $X \diamond Y$ corresponds to searching a *noisy* maximum overlap of X and Y where the weights of matched vertices and edge differs at most by ε.

2.3   Solving Maximum Clique with Hopfield-Clique Networks

Several different neural network approaches and related techniques have been proposed to solve the maximum clique problem [3], [11]. Following the seminal paper of Hopfield and Tank [10], the general approach to solve combinatorial optimization problems by using neural networks maps the objective function of the optimization problem onto an energy function of the network. The constraints of the problem are included in the energy function as penalty terms, such that the global minima of the energy function correspond to the solutions of the combinatorial optimization problem. Here the combinatorial optimization problem is the problem of finding a maximum clique in an association graph. As in [11] we refer to the term *Hopfield-Clique Network* (HCN) as a generic term for any variant of the Hopfield model for solving the maximum clique problem. As a representative and reference model we consider the HCN described in [12].

Let X be a graph with $|X| = n$. A HCN $\mathcal{H}_X$ associated with X is composed of n fully interconnected units. The synaptic weight w_{ij} between distinct units i and j is $w_E > 0$, if the corresponding vertices are connected by an edge $\{i, j\} \in E$ and $w_I \leq 0$, if $\{i, j\} \notin E$. Connections with weight w_E (w_I) are said to be *excitatory* (*inhibitory*). Thus a graph X uniquely determines the topology of $\mathcal{H}_X$ (up to isomorphism). For this reason we identify units and excitatory connections of $\mathcal{H}_X$ with vertices and edges of X. The dynamical rule of $\mathcal{H}_X$ is given by

$$x_i(t + 1) = x_i(t) + \sum_{j \neq i} w_{ij} o_j(t) \qquad (4)$$

where $x_i(t)$ denotes the activation of unit i at time step t. The output $o_i(t)$ of unit i is a piecewise linear limiter transfer function of the form

$$o_i(t) = \begin{cases} 1 & : \quad x_i(t) \geq \tau_t \\ 0 & : \quad x_i(t) \leq 0 \\ x_i(t)/\tau_t & : \quad \text{otherwise} \end{cases} \tag{5}$$

where $\tau_t > 0$ is a control parameter called *pseudo-temperature* or *gain*. Starting with a sufficient large initial value τ_0 the pseudo-temperature is decreased according to an *annealing-schedule* to a final value τ_f.

Provided an appropriate parameter setting is given, the following Theorem is a direct consequence of the results proven in [12]. It states that the dynamical rule (4) performs a gradient descent with respect to the energy function

$$E(t) = -\frac{1}{2} \sum_i \sum_{j \neq i} w_{ij} o_i(t) o_j(t) \tag{6}$$

where the minima of E correspond to the maximal cliques of X. To simplify the formulation of Theorem 2 we introduce some technical terms: Let $\deg_E(i)$ be the number of excitatory connections incident to unit i. We call

$$\deg_E = \max\{\deg_E(i) \mid 1 \leq i \leq n\}$$
$$\deg_I = \max\{n - \deg_E(i) \mid 1 \leq i \leq n\}$$

the *excitatory* and *inhibitory degree* of $\mathcal{H}_X$, respectively.

Theorem 2. *Let $\mathcal{H}_X$ be a HCN associated with a graph X. Suppose that $\deg_E > 0$ and $\deg_I > 0$. If*

$$w_E < \frac{2\tau_t}{\deg_I(n - \deg_E)} \tag{7}$$
$$w_I > \deg_E w_E \tag{8}$$

then the dynamical system (4) performs a gradient descent of the energy function $E(t)$ where the global (local) minima of $E(t)$ are in a 1-1 correspondence with maximum (maximal) cliques of X.

Given a parameter setting satisfying the bounds of Theorem 2 the HCN operates as follows: An initial activation is imposed on the network. Finding a maximum clique then proceeds in accordance with the dynamical rule (4) until the system converges to a stable state $o(t) \in \{0,1\}^n$. During evolution of the network any unit is excited by all active units with which it can form a clique and inhibits all other units. After convergence the stable state corresponds to a maximal clique of X. The size of a maximal clique can be read out by counting the units with output $o_i(t) = 1$.

2.4   A KNN Classifier for Graphs

Let $X \in \mathcal{X}$ be a data graph and $\mathcal{Y} = \{Y_1, \ldots, Y_N\}$ be the set of model graphs. In most classification and pattern recognition tasks of graphs reported in the literature KNN classifiers are used. Here we consider a KNN classifier based on a structural similarity measure as given in (1), which is directly related to the KWTA classifier proposed in Section 3.

The KNN classifier first computes the similarities $\sigma(X, Y_i)$ by means of HCNs applied on $X \diamond Y_i$ for all $i \in \{1, \dots, N\}$. Then a comparative k-maximum selector identifies the k models Y_i with

$$\sigma(X, Y_i) > \sigma(X, Y_j)$$

for all $i \in \mathcal{I}_N^{\{k\}}$ and all $j \in \mathcal{I}_N \setminus \mathcal{I}_N^{\{k\}}$ for some k-element subset $\mathcal{I}_N^{\{k\}} \subseteq \mathcal{I}_N$.

A drawback of this approach is that each classification task requires the computational intensive calculation of N similarities $\sigma(X, Y_i)$ for $1 \le i \le N$. Therefore this approach may be intractable in a practical setting. To circumvent this problem, possibly at the expense of classification accuracy, we replace the comparative k-maximum selector by an inhibitory winner-takes-all network for k-maximum selection. Inhibitory winner-takes-all networks are the subject-matter of the following Subsection 2.3.

Here we consider a KNN classifier based on a structural similarity measure as given in (1), which is directly related to the KWTA classifier proposed in Section 3.2.

2.5   Winner-Takes All Networks for k-Maximum Selection

This section first describes *winner-takes-all* (WTA) networks as a neural network implementation of a maximum selector. A slight modification of the termination criterion yields a KWTA network for k-maximum selection. For a pure self-organizing dynamical system of a KWTA network we refer to [19].

Let $\mathcal{V} = \{v_1, \dots, v_N\}$ be a set consisting of distinct values $v_i \in \mathbb{R}$. One way to select the maximum from $\mathcal{V}$ within a connectionist framework are *winner-takes-all* (WTA) networks. The WTA net consists of N mutually inhibitory connected units. The activation $z_i(t)$ of unit c_i is initialized with v_i. After initialization the WTA network updates its state according to

$$z_i(t+1) = z_i(t) - w \cdot \sum_{j \neq i} \left[z_j(t) \right]_0 + I_i(t) \tag{9}$$

where $-w < 0$ represents the synaptic weight of the inhibitory connections and $I_i(t)$ is the external input of unit c_i. For $z \in \mathbb{R}$ the function

$$[z]_0 := \begin{cases} z & : \quad z > 0 \\ 0 & : \quad z \le 0 \end{cases}$$

denotes the linear threshold function with lower saturation 0.

The next result is due to [17], [14]. It shows, that under some assumptions, the WTA network converges to a feasible solution within finite time.

Theorem 3. *Let* $I(t) = \mathbf{0} \in \mathbb{R}^N$ *and* $z(0) \in \mathbb{R}^N$ *be the initial activation of the dynamical system (9). Suppose that* $z(0)$ *has a unique maximum* $z_{i^*}(0) > z_j(0)$ *for all* $j \neq i$. *If*

$$0 < w < \frac{1}{N-1}$$

then $z(t)$ *converges after a finite number of update steps to a state* z *with* $z_{i^*} > 0$ *and* $z_j \le 0$ *for all* $j \neq i^*$.

For selecting the maximum of a given set $\mathcal{V}$ of input values it does not matter how the winner-takes-all character is implemented. In a practical setting one prefers a simple search algorithm for finding the maximum. However, a neural network implementation of the winner-takes-all selection principle is a fundamental prerequisite to accelerate decision making in classification and pattern recognition tasks of structures.

Extension to KWTA Networks: The KWTA network for k-maximum selection operates like the WTA network for maximum selection as long as there are more than k active units c_i with activation $z_i(t) > 0$. We terminate the KWTA network if the following condition is satisfied:

Termination criterion. Let $\mathcal{I}_N^{\{\kappa_t\}} \subseteq \mathcal{I}_N$ denote the κ_t-element subset of $\mathcal{I}(N)$ at time step t with

1. $z_i(t) > 0$ for all $i \in \mathcal{I}_N^{\{\kappa_t\}}$
2. $z_j(t) > 0$ for all $j \in \mathcal{I}(N) = \backslash \mathcal{I}_N^{\{\kappa_t\}}$.

Terminate the KWTA network, if $\kappa_t > k$ and $\kappa_{t+1} \leq k$.

The termination criterion takes into account that the dynamical system (9) not necessarily passes a state $z(t)$ with $\kappa_t = k$, since two or more units can be inhibited at the same time. If the KWTA network terminates after t update steps with $\kappa_t \leq k$, we reset the k largest activations to a positive value, regardless if some of them have a negative activation. In the following we refer to these k units as the *winners* of the competition.

3   The KWTA Classifier for Graphs

Let $X \in \mathcal{X}$ be a data graph, $\mathcal{Y} = \{Y_1, \ldots, Y_N\}$ be the set of model graphs, and σ the similarity measure given in (1).

A KWTA classifier is a neural network consisting of two layers of neural networks, a matching layer and an output layer. The matching layer has N subnets $\mathcal{H}_i = \mathcal{H}_{X \diamond Y_i}$, each of which is a HCN for matching an input X with model Y_i. The output layer is a competitive KWTA network for k-maximum selection consisting of N inhibitory connected units c_i. Each subnet $\mathcal{H}_i$ is connected to output c_i. Notice that the term KWTA classifier refers to the overall system and the term KWTA network solely to the inhibitory network in the output layer.

The KWTA classifier proceeds first by initializing the inhibition w of the KWTA network and the subnets $\mathcal{H}_i$ with respect to the graphs X and Y_i of consideration. Once the classifier has been initialized, the KWTA classifier repeatedly executes three basic steps, *similarity matching*, *competition*, and *adaption* until k output units win the competition and all other output units are inhibited:

1. *Similarity Matching.* The classifier simultaneously updates the current state vector $x_i(t)$ of each subnet $\mathcal{H}_i$ according to the dynamical rule (4) giving $x_i(t + 1)$ as the new state of $\mathcal{H}_i$. Subsequently the classifier computes *interim values* $\sigma_i(t + 1)$ of the target similarities $\sigma(X, Y_i)$ to be calculated by the subnets $\mathcal{H}_i$ for all i. An interim value $\sigma_i(t + 1)$ is an approximation of the target similarity $\sigma(X, Y_i)$ given the current state $x_i(t + 1)$ of $\mathcal{H}_i$ at any one time $t + 1$.

2. *Competition.* The interim values $\sigma_i(t+1)$ provide the basis for competition among the subnets via the KWTA network. The classifier updates the current state $z(t)$ of the KWTA network according to the dynamical rule (9) giving $z(t+1)$ as its new state vector. The external input $I_i(t)$ applied to unit c_i is of the form

$$I_i(t) = I(\sigma_i(t+1))$$

where I is a function transforming the interim values in a suitable form for further processing by the KWTA network.

3. *Adaption* The KWTA classifier disables all subnets $\mathcal{H}_i$ for which $z_i(t+1) \leq 0$. Once a subnet is disabled it is excluded from the competition. A disabled subnet, which has not converged, aborts its computation and terminates before reaching a stable state.

Intertwined execution of the three basic steps, similarity matching, competition, and adaption implements the principle *elimination of competition*. This principle is based on the policy that a large similarity $\sigma(X, Y_i)$ emerges from a series of increasing large interim values $\sigma_i(t)$ at an early stage of the computation of $\mathcal{H}_i$. In detail the KWTA classifier proceeds as follows:

ALGORITHM: Let X be a data graph and $\mathcal{Y} = \{Y_1, \ldots, Y_N\}$ a set of model graphs. Choose a value for the inhibition $w \in]0, \frac{1}{N-1}[$.

1. Enable all subnets $\mathcal{H}_i$. Each subnet can be *enabled* or *disabled*.
2. Set $t = 0$.
3. **Repeat**
   a) **For** each enabled subnet $\mathcal{H}_i$ **do**
      i. Update $\mathcal{H}_i$ according to the dynamical rule (4) giving $x_i(t+1)$.
      ii. Compute an interim value $\sigma_i(t+1)$ of $\sigma(X, Y_i)$.
      iii. Compute the external input $I_i(t) = \sigma_i(t+1) + \varepsilon_i(t)$ of output unit c_i.
   b) Update the KWTA network according to the dynamical rule (9) giving $z(t+1)$.
   c) Disable and terminate all subnets $\mathcal{H}_i$ for which the activation $z_i(t+1) \leq 0$.
   d) Set $t = t+1$. steps
   until $z_i(t) > 0$ for at most k output units c_i.
4. Assign X to the category most frequently represented among the k winners.

Suppose that $k = 1$. Figure 1 depicts a functional diagram of the KWTA network for $N = 3$. Excitatory connections are represented by solid lines and inhibitory connections by dotted lines. The subnets $\mathcal{H}_1$, $\mathcal{H}_2$, and $\mathcal{H}_3$ in the matching layer are excitatory connected to the output units c_1, c_2, and c_3 via on-off switches. The switches enable or disable a subnet for or from further computation. The subnets $\mathcal{H}_1$ and $\mathcal{H}_3$ are enabled, while $\mathcal{H}_2$ is disabled. The shading of an output unit c_i indicates its activation $z_i(t)$. Brighter shading corresponds to lower activation and vice versa. A white shading represents output units c_i with activation $z_i(t) \leq 0$. Thus unit c_1 has the largest activation and unit c_2 the lowest. The white shading of unit c_2 indicates that $z_2(t) \leq 0$. In this case subnet $\mathcal{H}_2$ is disabled as illustrated by the off-position of the corresponding switch. In contrast the switches connecting $\mathcal{H}_1$ and $\mathcal{H}_3$ with c_1 and c_3, resp., are in an on-position. Thus the subnets $\mathcal{H}_1$ and $\mathcal{H}_3$ are enabled and further participate in the competition. This instantaneous state of the KWTA classifier is consistent with the results we would expect if the subnets $\mathcal{H}_i$ converge to optimal solutions corresponding to maximum cliques. For each subnet a maximum clique of the associated graph is highlighted.

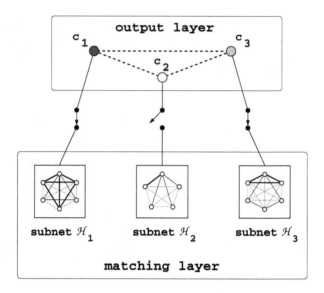

Fig. 1. Architecture of a KWTA classifier.

Computing Interim Values

The task of each subnet $\mathcal{H}_i$ is to approximate the similarity

$$\sigma_i = \sigma(X, Y_i) = \max\left\{ f(|\phi|) \;:\; \phi \in \mathcal{O}(X, Y_i) \right\}.$$

between X and Y_i as defined in (1) where the particular choice of a monotonously increasing function f does not effect the class decision. An interim value $\sigma_i(t)$ reports the current degree of similarity between X and Y_i as perceived by $\mathcal{H}_i$ at time step t. In other words, $\sigma_i(t)$ can be regarded as a preliminary estimate of σ_i given the state of $\mathcal{H}_i$ at time step t, where congruency with σ_i gradually emerges with the time spent on the matching process. We define an interim value $\sigma_i(t)$ of the target similarity σ given in (1) by

$$\sigma_i(t) = \frac{1}{n_i^2 - n_i} \sum_{\{k,l\} \in C_i^+} \mathrm{sgn}(w_{kl}) \left(o_k^i(t) + o_l^i(t) \right)$$

where $n_i = |X \diamond Y_i|$ is the number of units of $\mathcal{H}_i$, and $C_i^+ \subseteq V_i^{\{2\}}$ is the set of all connections $\{i, j\}$ between active units k, l of $\mathcal{H}_i$. An unit k of $\mathcal{H}_i$ is an *active unit* if $o_k^i(t) > 0$. The function $sgn(.)$ with

$$sgn(w_{ij}) = \begin{cases} 1 & : \quad w_{ij} = w_E \\ -1 & : \quad w_{ij} = w_I \end{cases}$$

denotes the signum function.

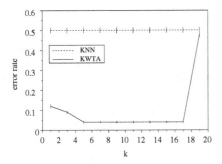

Fig. 2. Comparison of the KWTA and KNN classifier. Plotted is the error rate versus k. The error bars indicate the 95% confidence intervals.

If a stable state $\mathcal{H}_i$ corresponds to a maximum clique in $X \diamond Y_i$, then

$$\sigma_i(t) = \sigma(X, Y_i) = \max_\phi \left\{ f_2(|\phi|) \right\} = \max_\phi \left\{ \frac{|\phi|^2 - |\phi|}{n_i^2 - n_i} \right\}$$

where $n_i^2 - n_i$ is the scaling factor of f_2 in (3).

Computing the External Input

The external input $I_i(t) = I(\sigma_i(t + 1))$ applied to output unit c_i wraps the interim value $\sigma_i(t + 1)$ in a form suitable to the KWTA network in the output layer. If $\sigma_i(t)$ is directly applied to output unit c_i as external input, two problems may occur: (1) The KWTA classifier disables subnets $\mathcal{H}_i$ with $\sigma_i(1) \leq 0$ in the first iteration step without giving them a *fair* chance to participate in the competition. (2) In order to classify an input X according to the k-nearest-neighbor rule, the k winners must be unique. In general there is no guarantee that the interim values determine a unique set of k winners.

To guard against premature disabling and ambiguities we define the external input $I_i(t)$ applied to the respective output unit c_i by

$$I_i(t) = [\sigma_i(t + 1)]_\theta^1 + \varepsilon_i(t) \tag{10}$$

where $[\,.\,]_\theta^1$ is the piecewise linear limiter function with lower saturation $\theta > 0$ and upper saturation 1, respectively. The function $\varepsilon_i(t) \in [-\varepsilon, +\varepsilon]$ with $\varepsilon > 0$ is a small random noise with mean zero. The positive constant θ with $1 \gg \theta > \varepsilon$ prevents a premature disabling. Imposing noise on the output units dissolves ambiguities almost surely.

4   Experimental Results

In this experiment we compare the performance of the KWTA and KNN classifier. Both classifier use a mean-field annealing algorithm described in [11] as HCN. The algorithms are implemented in Java using JDK 1.2. All experiments were run on a Sparc SUNW Ultra-4.

We used the training set $\mathcal{T}$ of the well-known MNIST database containing 60,000 gray-level images of handwritten digits [15]. Both classifiers were tested on a subset of $\mathcal{T}$ to classify 11,774 images of '0' and '8'.

We randomly rotated each image of number $'0'$ and $'8'$, respectively. Then from each image we selected all pixels with a gray-level exceeding a threshold $\theta \geq 150^2$. From the set of pixels with gray-level $\gamma \geq \theta$ we selected distinguishing pixels to transform the rotated image to a weighted graph. The set of chosen pixels comprises the centroid pixel (if it exists), the most distant pixels, and 4 randomly selected pixels, which are equidistant to all other selected pixels. The vertices of the weighted graph represent the pixels and the edges the normalized distances between two pixels. Thus each graph is a representation of one of the numbers $'0'$ and $'8'$, resp., which is invariant to rotation, translation, and scaling.

In order to obtain representatives of the numbers $'0'$ and $'8'$, we randomly selected 10 samples of $'0'$ and 10 samples of $'8'$ giving a well-balanced set of 20 models. We classified all $11,774$ images of $'0'$ and $'8'$ using the KWTA and KNN classifier for $k = 1, 3, 5, \ldots, 19$.

In Figure 2 we plotted the error rate of both classifiers as a function of k. The results show that the KWTA classifier outperforms the canonical KNN classifier. The poor classification accuracy of the KNN is due to the similar representation of the numbers $'0'$ and $'8'$ by weighted graphs. Therefore the subnets $\mathcal{H}_i$ often converged to local minima giving suboptimal approximations of the similarities $\sigma(X, Y_i)$. In contrast the KWTA classifier is independent from the actual similarity of the input X and the models Y_i. It performs well, if the subnets $\mathcal{H}_i$ corresponding to the true category of X are the most promising at an early stage of the computation.

Figure 3 shows the average times required by the classifiers as a function of k. Figure 3(a) and Figure 3(b) measure the average times in *msec* and by the total amount of iteration steps of all 20 subnets, respectively. As expected, the KWTA classifier outperforms the KNN classifier. The KNN classiffier is in average about 3 times slower with respect to clock time and requires in average about 6 times more iteration steps than the KWTA classifier. The different ratios of clock time and number iteration steps between both classifiers is due to the computation of interim values in the case of the KWTA classifier. For each subnet of the KWTA classifier the time complexity of computing an interim value is of the same order as the time complexity for performing one iteration step of that subnet. This doubles the time complexity of one iteration step of a subnet in the KWTA classifier giving half the gain in clock time. As can be seen from the plots the computational effort of the KNN classifier is independent from k. In contrast the average time required by the KWTA classifier slightly decreases with increasing k. Thus an appropriate choice of k is a trade-off between speed and classification accuracy.

5   Conclusion

We proposed a KWTA classifier for structures. A distinguishing feature of KWTA classification is elimination of competition. The k winners of the competition determine the category the input structure is assigned to. In contrast to the commonly used KNN classifier no similarity must be computed. In experiments on handwritten digits we have shown that the KWTA classifier is capable to outperform the KNN classifier. In forthcoming papers we extend the KWTA classifier to competitive learning in the domain of structures.

---

[2] An entry with gray level 0 represents a white pixel and an entry with gray level 255 a black pixel.

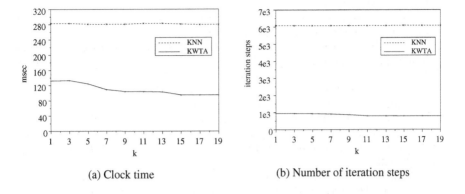

(a) Clock time   (b) Number of iteration steps

Fig. 3. Average times required by the KWTA and KNN classifier as a function of *k*.

References

1. A.P. Ambler, H.G. Barrow, C.M. Brown, R.M. Burstall, and R. J. Popplestone. A versatile computer-controlled assembly system. In *International Joint Conference on Artificial Intelligence*, pages 298–307. Stanford University, California, 1973.
2. H. Barrow and R. Burstall. Subgraph isomorphism, matching relational structures and maximal cliques. *Information Processing Letters*, 4:83–84, 1976.
3. I.M. Bomze, M. Budinich, P.M. Pardalos, and M. Pelillo. The maximum clique problem. In D.-Z. Du and P.M. Pardalos, editors, *Handbook of Combinatorial Optimization*, volume 4, pages 1–74. Kluwer Academic Publishers, Boston, MA, 1999.
4. W.J. Christmas, J. Kittler, and M. Petrou. Structural matching in computer vision using probabilistic relaxation. *IEEE Transactions on Pattern Analysis and Machine Intelligence*, 17(8):749–764, 1995.
5. M.A. Eshera and K.S Fu. An image understanding system using attributed symbolic representation and inexact graph-matching. *IEEE Transactions on Pattern Analysis and Machine Intelligence*, 8(5):604–618, 1986.
6. M. Garey and D. Johnson. *Computers and Intractability: A Guide to the Theory of NP-Completeness*. W.H. Freeman and Company, New York, 1979.
7. S. Gold and A. Rangarajan. A graduated assignment algorithm for graph matching. *IEEE Transactions on Pattern Analysis and Machine Intelligence*, 18(4):377–388, 1996.
8. S. Günter and H. Bunke. Adaptive self-organizing map in the graph domain. In H. Bunke and A. Kandel, editors, *Hybrid Methods in Pattern Recognition*, pages 61–74. World Scientific, 2002.
9. S. Günter and H. Bunke. Self-organizing map for clustering in the graph domain. *Pattern Recognition Letters*, 23:401–417, 2002.
10. J.J. Hopfield and D.W. Tank. Neural computation of decisions in optimization problems. *Biological Cybernetics*, 52:141–152, 1985.
11. A. Jagota. Approximating maximum clique with a Hopfield network. *IEEE Trans. Neural Networks*, 6:724–735, 1995.
12. B.J. Jain and F. Wysotzki. Fast winner-takes-all networks for the maximum clique problem. In *25th German Conference on Artificial Intelligence*, pages 163–173. Springer, 2002.

13. B.J. Jain and F. Wysotzki. A novel neural network approach to solve exact and inexact graph isomorphism problems. In *Proc. of the International Conference on Artificial Neural Networks (ICANN 2003)*. Springer-Verlag, 2003.

14. K. Koutroumbas and N. Kalouptsidis. Qualitative analysis of the parallel and asynchronous modes of the hamming network. *IEEE Transactions on Neural Networks*, 15(3):380–391, 1994.

15. Y. LeCun. The MNIST Database of Handwritten Digits. NEC Research Institute, Princeton, NJ. URL = http://yann.lecun.com/exdb/mnist/, 2003.

16. G. Levi. A note on the derivation of maximal common subgraphs of two directed or undirected graphs. *Calcolo*, 9:341–352, 1972.

17. R.P. Lippman. An introduction to computing with neural nets. *IEEE ASSP Magazine*, pages 4–22, April 1987.

18. A. Lumini, D. Maio, and D. Maltoni. Inexact graph matching for fingerprint classification. *Machine GRAPHICS and VISION, Special issue on Graph Transformations in Pattern Generation and CAD*, 8(2):231–248, 1999.

19. E. Majani, R. Erlanson, and Y. Abu-Mostafa. On the k-winner-take-all network. *Advances in Neural Information Processing Systems*, 1:634–642, 1989.

20. M. Pelillo, K. Siddiqi, and S.W. Zucker. Matching hierarchical structures using association graphs. *IEEE Transactions on Pattern Analysis and Machine Intelligence*, 21(11):1105–1120, 1999.

21. A. Rangarajan, S. Gold, and E. Mjolsness. A novel optimizing network architecture with applications. *Neural Computation*, 8(5):1041–1060, 1996.

22. J.W. Raymond, E.J. Gardiner, and P. Willett. Heuristics for similarity searching of chemical graphs using a maximum common edge subgraph algorithm. *Journal of Chemical Information and Computer Sciences*, 42(2):305–316, 2002.

23. K. Schädler and F. Wysotzki. Comparing structures using a Hopfield-style neural network. *Applied Intelligence*, 11:15–30, 1999.

24. L.G. Shapiro and R.M. Haralick. Structural descriptions and inexact matching. *IEEE Transaction on Pattern Analysis and Machine Intelligence*, 3:514–519, 1981.

25. K. Siddiqi, A. Shokoufandeh, S. Dickinson, and S. Zucker. Shock graphs and shape matching. *International Journal of Computer Vision*, 35:13–32, 1999.

26. A. Sperduti and A. Starita. Supervised neural networks for the classification of structures. *IEEE Transactions on Neural Networks*, 8(3):714–735, 1997.

27. P. Suganthan, E. Teoh, and D. Mital. Pattern recognition by graph matching using potts mft networks. *Pattern Recognition*, 28:997–1009, 1995.

28. A. Wong and M. You. Entropy and distance of random graphs with application to structural pattern recognition. *IEEE Transactions on Pattern Analysis and Machine Intelligence*, 7(5):599–609, 1985.

29. S.-S. Yu and W.-H. Tsai. Relaxation by the hopfield neural network. *Pattern Recognition*, 25(2):197–209, 1992.

Continuity of Semantic Operators in Logic Programming and Their Approximation by Artificial Neural Networks

Pascal Hitzler[1] and Anthony K. Seda[2]

[1] Department of Computer Science, Dresden University, 01062 Dresden, Germany
phitzler@inf.tu-dresden.de, http://www.wv.inf.tu-dresden.de/~pascal

[2] Department of Mathematics, University College Cork, Cork, Ireland
a.seda@ucc.ie, http://euclid.ucc.ie/pages/staff/seda/tseda.htm

Abstract. One approach to integrating first-order logic programming and neural network systems employs the approximation of semantic operators by feedforward networks. For this purpose, it is necessary to view these semantic operators as continuous functions on the reals. This can be accomplished by endowing the space of all interpretations of a logic program with topologies obtained from suitable embeddings. We will present such topologies which arise naturally out of the theory of logic programming, discuss continuity issues of several well-known semantic operators, and derive some results concerning the approximation of these operators by feedforward neural networks.

1 Introduction

The area of neuro-symbolic integration has received growing attention in the recent past. It would be highly desirable to enhance the very adaptable and robust neural networking machinery with the ability to handle structured, symbolic knowledge expressed, for example, as first-order logic programs.

Several attempts to obtain such an integration have been made, and we refer to [1] for a recent survey and to [2] for an overview of the recent challenges in this area. However, most of these attempts have stayed within the context of propositional logic and they are unlikely to carry over to full first-order logic. One exception to this statement is due to Hölldobler, Störr and Kalinke in [3] who employed a general approximation theorem due to Funahashi [4] which states that every continuous function on the real numbers can be uniformly approximated by 3-layer feedforward neural networks. Hölldobler et al. investigated a syntactically restricted class of logic programs (acyclic normal with injective level mapping) and showed that for these a semantic operator (the immediate consequence operator) can, via suitable embeddings, be viewed as a continuous function on the real line. It follows then that the immediate consequence operator can be approximated by neural networks due to Funahashi's theorem. It even turned out in this case that the approximating function is a contraction on

A. Günter et al. (Eds.): KI 2003, LNAI 2821, pp. 355–369, 2003.

the reals, when endowed with the usual metric, and that iterations of the approximating function are well-behaved, in a certain specific sense. We also note that such methods and techniques are quite closely related to the overall aims of the programme of research being undertaken by Blair et al. [5] relating logic programming to continuous models of computation.

In this paper, we will examine the topological content of the results of Hölldobler, Störr and Kalinke, and set out to generalize some of their results. We present our results in two sections, Sections 2 and 3. In the first of these, Section 2, we study continuity issues of semantic operators in logic programming. Then, in Section 3, we relate this discussion to the results of Hölldobler et al. and Funahashi already alluded to.

2   Continuity of Semantic Operators

A (*normal*) *logic program* is a finite set of *clauses* of the form

$$\forall(A \leftarrow L_1 \wedge \cdots \wedge L_n),$$

where $n \in \mathbb{N}$ may differ for each clause, A is an atom in a first order language $\mathcal{L}$ and $L_1, \ldots, L_n$ are literals, that is, atoms or negated atoms, in $\mathcal{L}$. As is customary in logic programming, we will write such a clause in the form

$$A \leftarrow L_1, \ldots, L_n,$$

in which the universal quantifier is understood. Then A is called the *head* of the clause, each L_i is called a *body literal* of the clause and their conjunction $L_1, \ldots, L_n$ is called the *body* of the clause. We allow $n = 0$, by an abuse of notation, which indicates that the body is empty; in this case the clause is called a *unit clause* or a *fact*. We will occasionally use the notation $A \leftarrow \mathsf{body}$ for clauses, so that body stands for the conjunction of the body literals of the clause. If no negation symbol occurs in a logic program, the program is called a *definite* logic program. The Herbrand base underlying a given program P will be denoted by B_P and the set of all Herbrand interpretations by I_P, and we note that the latter can be identified simultaneously with the power set of B_P and with the set $\mathbf{2}^{B_P}$ of all functions mapping B_P into the set $\mathbf{2}$ consisting of two distinct elements. By ground(P), we will denote the set of all ground instances of clauses in P. Finally, we refer the reader to [6] for general background concerning logic programming.

Throughout the rest of the paper, we will impose the standing condition on the language $\mathcal{L}$ that it contains at least one constant symbol and at least one function symbol with arity greater than 0. If this is not done, ground(P) may be a finite set of ground instances of clauses, and can be treated essentially as a propositional program, for which methods other than those propounded here seem more appropriate.

In logic programming semantics, it has turned out to be both useful and convenient to use many-valued logics. Our investigations will therefore begin by studying suitable topologies on spaces of many-valued interpretations. We assume we have given a finite set $\mathcal{T} = \{t_1, \ldots, t_n\}$ of truth values containing at least the two distinguished values t_1 and t_n, which are interpreted as being the truth values for "false", and "true", respectively. We also assume that we have truth tables for the usual connectives $\vee$, $\wedge$, $\leftarrow$, and $\neg$. Given a logic program P, we denote the set of all (Herbrand) *interpretations* or *valuations* in this logic by $I_{P,n}$; thus $I_{P,n}$ is the set $\mathcal{T}^{B_P}$ of all functions $I : B_P \to \mathcal{T}$. If n is clear from the context, we will use the notation I_P instead of $I_{P,n}$ and we note that this usage is consistent with the one given above for $n = 2$. As usual, any interpretation I can be extended, using the truth tables, to give a truth value in $\mathcal{T}$ to any variable-free formula in $\mathcal{L}$.

Throughout the paper we will make substantial use of elementary notions and results from the mathematical area called *Topology*, our standard reference being [7].

Definition 1. *Given any logic program P, the* generalized atomic topology $\mathcal{Q}$ *on $I_P = I_{P,n}$ is defined to be the product topology on $\mathcal{T}^{B_P}$, where $\mathcal{T} = \{t_1, \ldots, t_n\}$ is endowed with the discrete topology.*

We note that these topologies can be defined analogously for the non-Herbrand case. For $n = 2$, the generalized atomic topology $\mathcal{Q}$ specializes to the query topology of [8] (in the Herbrand case), or to the atomic topology Q of [9] (in the non-Herbrand case). The following results follow immediately since $\mathcal{Q}$ is a product topology of the discrete topology on a finite set, and hence is a topology of pointwise convergence.

Proposition 1. *For $A \in B_P$ and t_i a truth value, let $\mathcal{G}(A, t_i) = \{I \in I_{P,n} \mid I(A) = t_i\}$. The following hold.*

(a) *$\mathcal{Q}$ is the topology generated by the subbase $\mathcal{G} = \{\mathcal{G}(A, t_i) \mid A \in B_P, i \in \{1, \ldots, n\}\}$.*
(b) *A net (I_λ) in I_P converges in $\mathcal{Q}$ if and only if for every $A \in B_P$ there exists some λ_0 such that $I_\lambda(A)$ is constant for all $\lambda \geq \lambda_0$.*
(c) *$\mathcal{Q}$ is a second countable totally disconnected compact Hausdorff topology which is dense in itself. Hence, $\mathcal{Q}$ is metrizable and homeomorphic to the Cantor topology on the unit interval of the real line.*

We note that the second countability of $\mathcal{Q}$ rests on the fact that B_P is countable, so that this property does not in general carry over to the non-Herbrand case.

The study of topologies such as $\mathcal{Q}$ comes from our desire to be able to control the iterative behaviour of semantic operators. Topologies which are closely related to order structures, as common in denotational semantics [10], are of limited applicability since nonmonotonic operators frequently arise naturally in the logic programming context. See also [11,12] for a study of these issues.

We proceed next with studying a rather general notion of semantic operator, akin to Fitting's approach in [13], which generalizes standard notions occurring in the literature.

Definition 2. *An operator T on I_P is called a* consequence operator *for P if for every $I \in I_P$ the following condition holds: for every ground clause $A \leftarrow \textbf{body}$ in P, where $T(I)(A) = t_i$, say, and $I(\textbf{body}) = t_j$, say, we have that the truth table for $t_i \leftarrow t_j$ yields the truth value t_n, that is, "true".*

It turns out that this notion of consequence operator relates nicely to $\mathcal{Q}$, yielding the following result which was reported by us in [11,14]. If T is a consequence operator for P and if for any $I \in I_P$ we have that the sequence of iterates $T^m(I)$ converges in $\mathcal{Q}$ to some $M \in I_P$, then M is a model, in a natural sense, for P. Furthermore, continuity of T yields the desirable property that M is a fixed point of T.

Intuitively, consequence operators should propagate "truth" along the implication symbols occurring in the program. From this point of view, we would like the outcome of the truth value of such a propagation to be dependent only on the relevant clause bodies. The next definition captures this intuition.

Definition 3. *Let $A \in B_P$ and denote by $\mathcal{B}_A$ the set of all body atoms of clauses with head A that occur in ground(P). A consequence operator T is called (P-)local if for every $A \in B_P$ and any two interpretations $I, K \in I_P$ which agree on all atoms in $\mathcal{B}_A$, we have $T(I)(A) = T(K)(A)$.*

It is our desire to study continuity in $\mathcal{Q}$ of local consequence operators. Since $\mathcal{Q}$ is a product topology, it is reasonable to expect that finiteness conditions will play a role in this context, and indeed conditions which ensure finiteness in the sense of Definition 4 below, due to [9], have made their appearance in this context.

Definition 4. *Let C be a clause in P and let $A \in B_P$ be such that A coincides with the head of C. The clause C is said to be of* finite type *relative to A if C has only finitely many different ground instances with head A. The program P will be said to be of* finite type *relative to A if each clause in P is of finite type relative to A, that is, if the set of all clauses in ground(P) with head A is finite. Finally, P will be said to be of* finite type *if P is of finite type relative to A for every $A \in B_P$.*

A *local variable* is a variable which appears in a clause body but not in the corresponding head. Local variables appear naturally in practical logic programs, but their occurrence is awkward from the point of view of denotational semantics, especially if they occur in negated body literals since this leads to the so-called floundering problem, see [6].

It is easy to see that, in the context of Herbrand-interpretations, and if function symbols are present, then the absence of local variables is equivalent to a program being of finite type.

Proposition 2. *Let P be a logic program of finite type and let T be a local consequence operator for P. Then T is continuous in $\mathcal{Q}$.*

Proof. Let $I \in I_P$ be an interpretation and let $G_2 = \mathcal{G}(A, t_i)$ be a subbasic neighbourhood of $T(I)$ in $\mathcal{Q}$, and note that G_2 is the set of all $K \in I_P$ such that $K(A) = t_i$. We need to find a neighbourhood G_1 of I such that

$T(G_1) \subseteq G_2$. Since P is of finite type, the set $\mathcal{B}_A$ is finite. Hence the set $G_1 = \bigcap_{B \in \mathcal{B}_A} \mathcal{G}(B, I(B))$ is a finite intersection of open sets and is therefore open. Since each $K \in G_1$ agrees with I on $\mathcal{B}_A$, we obtain $T(K)(A) = T(I)(A) = t_i$ for each $K \in G_1$ by locality of T. Hence, $T(G_1) \subseteq G_2$.

Now, if P is not of finite type, but we can ensure by some other property of P that the possibly infinite intersection $\bigcap_{B \in \mathcal{B}_A} \mathcal{G}(B, I(B))$ is open, then the above proof will carry over to programs which are not of finite type. Alternatively, we would like to be able to disregard the infinite intersection entirely under conditions which ensure that we have to consider finite intersections only, as in the case of a program of finite type. The following definition is, therefore, quite a natural one to make.

Definition 5. *Let P be a logic program and let T be a consequence operator on I_P. We say that T is (P-)locally finite for $A \in B_P$ and $I \in I_P$ if there exists a finite subset $S = S(A, I) \subseteq \mathcal{B}_A$ such that we have $T(J)(A) = T(I)(A)$ for all $J \in I_P$ which agree with I on S. We say that T is (P-)locally finite if it is locally finite for all $A \in B_P$ and all $I \in I_P$.*

It is easy to see that a locally finite consequence operator is local. Conversely, a local consequence operator for a program of finite type is locally finite. This follows from the observation that for a program of finite type the sets $\mathcal{B}_A$, for any $A \in B_P$, are finite. But a much stronger result holds.

Theorem 1. *A local consequence operator is locally finite if and only if it is continuous in $\mathcal{Q}$.*

Proof. Let T be a locally finite consequence operator, let $I \in I_P$, let $A \in B_P$, and let $G_2 = \mathcal{G}(A, T(I)(A))$ be a subbasic neighbourhood of $T(I)$ in $\mathcal{Q}$. Since T is locally finite, there is a finite set $S \subseteq \mathcal{B}_A$ such that $T(J)(A) = T(I)(A)$ for all $J \in \bigcap_{B \in S} \mathcal{G}(B, I(B))$. By finiteness of S, the set $\bigcap_{B \in S} \mathcal{G}(B, I(B))$ is open, which suffices for continuity of T.

For the converse, assume that T is continuous in $\mathcal{Q}$ and let $A \in B_P$ and $I \in I_P$ be chosen arbitrarily. Then $G_2 = \mathcal{G}(A, T(I)(A))$ is a subbasic open set, so that, by continuity of T, there exists a basic open set $G_1 = \mathcal{G}(B_1, I(B_1)) \cap \cdots \cap \mathcal{G}(B_k, I(B_k))$ with $T(G_1) \subseteq G_2$. In other words, we have $T(J)(A) = T(I)(A)$ for each $J \in \bigcap_{B \in S'} \mathcal{G}(B, I(B))$, where $S' = \{B_1, \ldots, B_k\}$ is a finite set. Since T is local, the value of $T(J)(A)$ depends only on the values $J(A)$ of atoms $A \in \mathcal{B}_A$. So if we set $S = S' \cap \mathcal{B}_A$, then $T(J)(A) = T(I)(A)$ for all $J \in \bigcap_{B \in S} \mathcal{G}(B, I(B))$ which is to say that T is locally finite for A and I. Since A and I were chosen arbitrarily, we obtain that T is locally finite.

The following corollary was communicated to us by Howard A. Blair in the two-valued case. A *level mapping* for a program P is a mapping $l : B_P \to \alpha$ for some ordinal α; we always assume that l has been extended to all literals by setting $l(\neg A) = l(A)$ for each $A \in B_P$. An *ω-level mapping* for P is a level mapping $l : B_P \to \mathbb{N}$.

Corollary 1. *Let P be a program, let T be a local consequence operator and let l be an injective ω-level mapping for P with the following property: for each $A \in B_P$ there exists an $n_A \in \mathbb{N}$ such that $l(B) < n_A$ for all $B \in \mathcal{B}_A$. Then T is continuous in $\mathcal{Q}$.*

Proof. It follows easily from the given conditions that $\mathcal{B}_A$ is finite for all $A \in B_P$, which implies that T is locally finite.

We next take a short detour from our discussion of continuity to study the weaker notion of measurability [15] for consequence operators. For a collection M of subsets of a set X, we denote by $\sigma(M)$ the smallest σ-algebra containing M, called the σ-algebra *generated by* M. Recall that a function $f : X \to X$ is measurable with respect to $\sigma(M)$ if and only if $f^{-1}(A) \in \sigma(M)$ for each $A \in M$. If β is the subbase of a topology τ and β is countable, then $\sigma(\beta) = \sigma(\tau)$. It turns out that local consequence operators are always measurable with respect to the σ-algebra generated by a generalized atomic topology. The following result generalizes a theorem from [16].

Theorem 2. *Local consequence operators are measurable with respect to* $\sigma(\mathcal{G}) = \sigma(\mathcal{Q})$.

Proof. Let T be a local consequence operator. We need to show that for each subbasic set $\mathcal{G}(A, t_i)$ we have $T^{-1}(\mathcal{G}(A, t_i)) \in \sigma(\mathcal{G})$.

Let $A \in B_P$ and let $t \in \mathcal{T}$ both be chosen arbitrarily. Let F be the set of all functions from $\mathcal{B}_A$ to $\mathcal{T}$, and note that F is countable since $\mathcal{B}_A$ is countable and $\mathcal{T}$ is finite. Let F' be the subset of F which contains all functions f with the following property: whenever an interpretation I agrees with f on $\mathcal{B}_A$, then $T(I)(A) = t$. Then, $\bigcap_{B \in \mathcal{B}_A} \mathcal{G}(B, f(B)) \in T^{-1}(\mathcal{G}(A, t))$ for each $f \in F'$.

We obtain by locality of T, that whenever I is an interpretation for which $T(I)(A) = t$ holds, then there exists a function $f_I \in F'$ such that f_I and I agree on $\mathcal{B}_A$, and this yields $T^{-1}(\mathcal{G}(A, t)) = \bigcup_{f_I \in F'} \bigcap_{B \in \mathcal{B}_A} \mathcal{G}(B, I(B))$. Since F' and $\mathcal{B}_A$ are countable, the set on the right hand side is measurable as required.

We turn now to the study of the continuity of a particular operator introduced by Fitting [13] to logic programming semantics. To this end, we associate a set P^* with each logic program P by the following construction. Let $A \in B_P$. If A occurs as the head of some unit clause $A \leftarrow$ in ground(P), then replace it by the clause $A \leftarrow t_n$, where by a slight abuse of notation we interpret t_n to be an additional atom which we adjoin to the language $\mathcal{L}$ and always evaluate to $t_n \in \mathcal{T}$, that is, it evaluates to "true". If A does not occur in the head of any clause in ground(P), then add the clause $A \leftarrow t_0$, where t_0 is interpreted as an additional atom which again we adjoin to $\mathcal{L}$ and always evaluate to $t_0 \in \mathcal{T}$, that is, it evaluates to "false". The resulting (ground) program, which results from ground(P) by the changes just given with respect to every $A \in B_P$, will be denoted by P'. Now let P^* be the set of all *pseudo clauses* of the form $A \leftarrow C_1 \vee C_2 \vee \ldots$, where the C_i are exactly the bodies of the clauses in P' with head A. We call A the *head* and $B_A = C_1 \vee C_2 \vee \ldots$ the *body* of the resulting pseudo clause, and we note that each $A \in B_P$ occurs in the head of exactly one pseudo clause in P^*. Bodies of pseudo clauses are possibly infinite disjunctions, but this will not pose any particular difficulty with respect to the logics which we are going to discuss. We note that a program P is of finite type if and only if all bodies of all pseudo clauses in P^* are finite.

Now, if we are given (suitable) truth tables for negation, conjunction and disjunction, we are able to evaluate the truth values of bodies of pseudo clauses relative to given interpretations.

Definition 6. *Let P be a logic program. Define the mapping $F_P : I_{P,n} \rightarrow I_{P,n}$ relative to a given (suitable) logic with n truth values by $F_P(I) = J$, where J assigns to each $A \in B_P$ the truth value $I(B_A)$.*

We call operators which satisfy Definition 6 *Fitting operators*. If we impose the mild assumption that $t_j \leftarrow t_j$ evaluates to "true" for every j with respect to the underlying logic, then we easily obtain that every Fitting operator is a local consequence operator. This will always be the case in the remaining section.

The virtue of Definition 6, due to Fitting [13], lies in the fact that several operators known from the theory of logic programming can be derived from it in a very concise way, and we refer to [13,17] for a discussion of these matters, see also [14]. We will now investigate some of these operators in the light of Theorem 1. In the following, we will denote the "true" truth value by **t** and the "false" truth value by **f**.

If the chosen logic is classical two-valued logic, then the corresponding Fitting operator is the *single-step* or *immediate consequence operator* T_P (for a given program P). Now, if $T_P(I)(A) = \mathbf{t}$, then there exists a clause $A \leftarrow$ body in ground(P) such that $I($body$)$ is true, and we obtain $T_P(J)(A) = \mathbf{t}$ whenever $J($body$) = \mathbf{t}$. The observation that bodies of clauses are finite conjunctions leads us to conclude the following lemma.

Lemma 1. *If $T_P(I)(A)$ is true, then T_P is locally finite for A and I. Furthermore, T_P is continuous if and only if it is locally finite for all A and I with $T_P(I)(A) = \mathbf{f}$.*

A body $\bigvee C_i$ of a pseudo clause is false if and only if all C_i are false. Since T_P is a Fitting operator, we obtain $T_P(I)(A) = \mathbf{f}$ if and only if all C_i are false. If we require T_P to be locally finite for A and I, then there must be a finite set $S \subseteq \mathcal{B}_A$ such that any $J \in I_P$ which agrees with I on S renders all C_i to be false. These observations now easily yield the following theorem from [9].

Theorem 3. *Let P be a normal logic program. Then T_P is continuous if and only if, for each $I \in I_P$ and for each $A \in B_P$ with $T_P(I)(A) = \mathbf{f}$, either there is no clause in P with head A or there exists a finite set $S(I,A) = \{A_1, \ldots, A_k, B_1, \ldots, B_{k'}\} \subseteq \mathcal{B}_A$ with the following properties:*

(i) $A_1, \ldots, A_k$ are true in I and $B_1, \ldots, B_{k'}$ are false in I.
(ii) Given any clause C with head A, at least one $\neg A_i$ or at least one B_j occurs in the body of C.

In the case of Kleene's strong three-valued logic, with set of truth values $\mathcal{T} = \{t, u, f\}$ and logical connectives as in Table 1, the associated Fitting operator was introduced in [18] and is denoted by Φ_P, for a given program P. As in the case of classical two-valued logic, we obtain the following lemma.

Table 1. Connectives for Kleene's strong three-valued logic.

p	q	$p \wedge q$	$p \vee q$	$\neg p$
t	t	t	t	f
t	u	u	t	f
t	f	f	t	f
u	t	u	t	u
u	u	u	u	u
u	f	f	u	u
f	t	f	t	t
f	u	f	u	t
f	f	f	f	t

Lemma 2. *If $\Phi_P(I)(A) = t$, then Φ_P is locally finite for A and I. Furthermore, Φ_P is continuous if and only if it is locally finite for all A and I with $\Phi_P(I)(A) \in \{u, f\}$.*

Obtaining a theorem analogous to Theorem 3 is now straightforward, but tedious, and we omit the details. Similar considerations apply to the operator Ψ on Belnap's four-valued logic [13] and to the operators from [19].

We mention in passing the nonmonotonic Gelfond-Lifschitz operator [20] in classical two-valued logic, whose fixed points yield the stable models of the program in question. It turns out that this operator is not a consequence operator in the sense discussed in this paper, and attempts to characterize continuity of it will involve different methods, e.g. by means of the results from [21].

3   Approximation by Artificial Neural Networks

A *3-layer feedforward network* (or *single hidden layer feedforward network*) consists of an *input layer*, a *hidden layer*, and an *output layer*. Each layer consists of finitely many *computational units*. There are connections from units in the input layer to units in the hidden layer, and from units in the hidden layer to units in the output layer. The input-output relationship of each unit is represented by *inputs* x_i, *output* y, *connection weights* w_i, *threshold* θ, and a function ϕ as follows:

$$y = \phi \left(\sum_i w_i x_i - \theta \right).$$

The function ϕ, which we will call the *squashing function* of the network, is usually non-constant, bounded and monotone increasing, and sometimes also assumed to be continuous. We will specify the requirements on ϕ that we assume in each case.

We assume throughout that the input-output relationships of the units in the input and output layer are linear. The output function of a network as described above is then obtained as a mapping $f : \mathbb{R}^r \to \mathbb{R}$ with

$$f(x_1, \ldots, x_r) = \sum_j c_j \phi \left(\sum_i w_{ji} x_i - \theta_j \right),$$

where r is the number of units in the input layer, and the constants c_j correspond to weights from hidden to output layers. See also Figure 1. We refer to [22] for background concerning artificial neural networks.

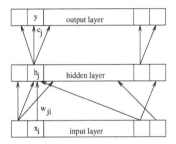

Fig. 1. 3-Layer Feedforward Neural Network.

It is our aim to obtain results on the approximation of consequence operators by input-output functions of 3-layer feedforward networks. Our first result rests on the following theorem, which is due to Funahashi, see [4].

Theorem 4. *Suppose that $\phi : \mathbb{R} \to \mathbb{R}$ is non-constant, bounded, monotone increasing and continuous. Let $K \subseteq \mathbb{R}^n$ be compact, let $f : K \to \mathbb{R}$ be a continuous mapping and let $\varepsilon > 0$. Then there exists a 3-layer feedforward network with squashing function ϕ whose input-output mapping $\bar{f} : K \to \mathbb{R}$ satisfies $\max_{x \in K} d(f(x), \bar{f}(x)) < \varepsilon$, where d is a metric which induces the natural topology on $\mathbb{R}$.*

In other words, each continuous function $f : K \to \mathbb{R}$ can be uniformly approximated by input-output functions of 3-layer networks. For our purposes, it will suffice to assume that K is a compact subset of the set of real numbers, so that our network architecture can be depicted as in Figure 2.

The Cantor set $\mathcal{C}$ is a compact subset of the real line and the topology which $\mathcal{C}$ inherits as a subspace of $\mathbb{R}$ coincides with the Cantor topology on $\mathcal{C}$. Also, the Cantor space $\mathcal{C}$ is homeomorphic to $I_{P,n}$ when the latter is endowed with a generalized atomic topology $\mathcal{Q}$. Hence, if a consequence operator T is continuous in $\mathcal{Q}$, we can identify it with a mapping $\iota(T) : \mathcal{C} \to \mathcal{C} : x \mapsto \iota(T(\iota^{-1}(x)))$ which is continuous in the subspace topology of $\mathcal{C}$ in $\mathbb{R}$, as follows.

Theorem 5. *Let P be a program, let T be a consequence operator which is locally finite and let ι be a homeomorphism from $(I_{P,n}, \mathcal{Q})$ to $\mathcal{C}$. Then T (more precisely $\iota(T)$) can be uniformly approximated by input-output mappings of 3-layer feedforward networks.*

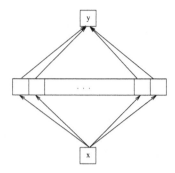

Fig. 2. Network architecture used in this paper.

Proof. Under the conditions stated in the theorem, the operator T is continuous in $\mathcal{Q}$. Using the homeomorphism ι, the resulting function $\iota(T)$ is continuous on the Cantor set $\mathcal{C}$, which is a compact subset of $\mathbb{R}$. Applying Theorem 4, $\iota(T)$ can be uniformly approximated by input-output functions of 3-layer feedforward networks.

The restriction to programs with continuous consequence operator is unsatisfactory. There is another approximation theorem due to [23], which requires only measurable functions:

Theorem 6. *Suppose that ϕ is a monotone increasing function from $\mathbb{R}$ onto $(0,1)$. Let $f : \mathbb{R}^r \to \mathbb{R}$ be a Borel-measurable function and let μ be a probability Borel-measure on $\mathbb{R}^r$. Then, given any $\varepsilon > 0$, there exists a 3-layer feedforward network with squashing function ϕ whose input-output function $\bar{f} : \mathbb{R}^r \to \mathbb{R}$ satisfies*

$$\varrho_\mu(f, \bar{f}) = \inf\{\delta > 0 : \mu\{x : |f(x) - \bar{f}(x)| > \delta\} < \delta\} < \varepsilon.$$

In other words, the class of functions computed by 3-layer feedforward neural nets is dense in the set of all Borel measurable functions $f : \mathbb{R}^r \to \mathbb{R}$ relative to the metric ϱ_μ defined in Theorem 6.

By means of Theorem 2, we can now view a local consequence operator T as a measurable function $\iota(T)$ on $\mathcal{C}$ by identifying $I_{P,n}$ with $\mathcal{C}$ via a homeomorphism ι. Since $\mathcal{C}$ is measurable as a subset of the real line, this operator can be extended[1] to a measurable function on $\mathbb{R}$ and we obtain the following result.

Theorem 7. *Given any program P with local consequence operator T, the operator T (more precisely $\iota(T)$) can be approximated in the manner of Theorem 6 by input-output mappings of 3-layer feedforward networks.*

---

[1] E.g. as a function $T : \mathbb{R} \to \mathbb{R}$ with $T(x) = \iota(T_P(\iota^{-1}(x)))$ if $x \in \mathcal{C}$ and $T(x) = 0$ otherwise.

This result is somewhat unsatisfactory since the approximation stated in Theorem 6 is only *almost everywhere*, that is, pointwise with the exception of a set of measure zero. The Cantor set, however, is a set of measure zero. In [16], the present authors were able to strengthen this result in the case of classical logic by giving an explicit extension of T to the real line.

We want to return now to the case discussed earlier in Theorem 5. In [3], the following recurrent neural network architecture was considered: we assume that the number of output and input units is equal and that, after each propagation through the network, the output values are fed back without changes into input values. For the case which we consider it will again be sufficient to suppose that the input layer consists of one unit only, so that the architecture can be depicted as in Figure 3.

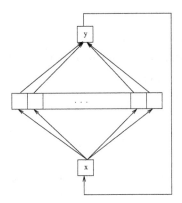

Fig. 3. Recurrent Network.

We will show in the following that iterates of locally finite local consequence operators can be approximated arbitrarily closely by iterates of suitably chosen networks. This is in fact a consequence of the uniform approximation obtained from Theorem 4 and the compactness of the unit interval.

Let P be a logic program, let T be a locally finite local consequence operator for P and let $\iota : I_P \to \mathcal{C}$ be a homeomorphism. Let F be a continuous extension of $\iota(T)$ onto the unit interval $[0, 1]$ in the reals, let d be the natural metric on $\mathbb{R}$, and let $\varepsilon > 0$. By Theorem 5, there exists a three-layer feedforward network with input-output mapping f such that $\max_{x \in [0,1]} d(f(x), F(x)) < \varepsilon$. Since $[0, 1]$ is compact, and F is continuous, we obtain that F is Lipschitz-continuous, that is, there exists $\lambda \geq 0$ such that for all $x, y \in [0, 1]$ we have $d(F(x), F(y)) \leq \lambda d(x, y)$. For $x, y \in [0, 1]$ we therefore obtain

$$d(f(x), F(y)) \leq d(f(x), F(x)) + d(F(x), F(y)) \leq \varepsilon + \lambda d(x, y). \qquad (1)$$

Now let $x \in [0,1]$ be arbitrarily chosen. By Equation (1) we obtain

$$d(f^2(x), F^2(x)) \leq \varepsilon + \lambda d(f(x), F(x)) \leq \varepsilon + \lambda \varepsilon. \tag{2}$$

Inductively, we can prove that for all $n \in \mathbb{N}$ we have

$$d(f^n(x), F^n(x)) \leq \varepsilon + \lambda \varepsilon + \cdots + \lambda^{n-1} \varepsilon = \varepsilon \left(\sum_{i=0}^{n-1} \lambda^i \right) = \varepsilon \frac{1 - \lambda^n}{1 - \lambda}. \tag{3}$$

Thus we obtain the following bound on the error produced by the recurrent network after n iterations.

Theorem 8. *With the notation and hypotheses above, for any $I \in I_P$ and any $n \in \mathbb{N}$ we have*

$$|f^n(\iota(I)) - \iota(T^n(I))| \leq \varepsilon \frac{1 - \lambda^n}{1 - \lambda}.$$

Proof. Note that $\iota(T^n(I)) = F^n(\iota(I))$, and the assertion follows from Equation (3) since d is the natural metric on $\mathbb{R}$.

We derive a few corollaries from this result.

Corollary 2. *If F is a contraction on $[0,1]$, so that $\lambda < 1$, then $(F^k(\iota(I)))$ converges for every I to the unique fixed point x of F and there exists $m \in \mathbb{N}$ such that for all $n \geq m$ we have*

$$|f^n(\iota(I)) - x| \leq \varepsilon \frac{1}{1 - \lambda}.$$

Proof. The convergence follows from the Banach contraction mapping theorem. The inequality follows immediately from Theorem 8 using the well-known equation for limits of geometric series.

If F is a contraction on $[0,1]$, then T is a contraction on the complete subspace $\mathcal{C}$, and also has a fixed point M, and $\iota(M) = x$. However, it seems difficult to guarantee the hypothesis of Corollary 2, although Hölldobler et al. have achieved in [3] a similar result for acyclic programs with injective level mappings in classical logic. The following result may be more promising.

Corollary 3. *If for some $I \in I_P$, $T^n(I)$ converges in $\mathcal{Q}$ to a fixed point M of T, then for every $\delta > 0$ there exists a network with input-output function f, and some $n \in \mathbb{N}$ such that $|f^n(\iota(I)) - \iota(M)| < \delta$.*

Proof. The hypothesis implies that $F^n(\iota(I))$ converges to $\iota(M)$ in the natural metric on $\mathbb{R}$. Given $\delta > 0$, there exists $n \in \mathbb{N}$ such that $|F^m(\iota(I)) - \iota(M)| < \frac{\delta}{2}$ for all $m \geq n$. Since F is fixed, we know the value of λ. Now, by the approximation results above, we choose a network with input-output function f such that $\varepsilon \frac{1 - \lambda^n}{1 - \lambda} < \frac{\delta}{2}$. Then using Theorem 8 and the triangle inequality we obtain

$$|f^n(\iota(I)) - \iota(M)| \leq |f^n(\iota(I)) - F^n(\iota(I))| + |F^n(\iota(I)) - \iota(M)|$$

$$< 2 \cdot \frac{\delta}{2} \leq \delta.$$

We will close by describing a class of programs for which the additional hypothesis from Corollary 3 is satisfied. The result is well-known for the case of classical two-valued logic and the immediate consequence operator in this case. The following definition is due to [24].

Definition 7. *A logic program P is called* acyclic *if there exists an ω-level mapping l such that for each clause $A \leftarrow L_1, \ldots, L_n$ in ground(P) we have $l(A) > l(L_i)$ for all $i = 1, \ldots, n$.*

In the following, let P be acyclic with level mapping l, and let T be a local consequence operator for P. We next define a mapping $d : I_P \times I_P \to \mathbb{R}$ by $d(I, J) = 2^{-n}$, where n is least such that I and J differ on some atom A with $l(A) = n$. It is easily verified that d is a complete metric on I_P, see [25].

Proposition 3. *With the stated hypotheses, T is a contraction with respect to d.*

Proof. Suppose $d(I, J) = 2^{-n}$. Then I and J coincide on all atoms of level less than n. Now let $A \in B_P$ with $l(A) = n$. Then by acyclicity of P we have that all atoms in $\mathcal{B}_A$ are of level less than n, and by locality of T we have that $T(I)(A) = T(J)(A)$. So $d(T(I), T(J)) \leq 2^{-(n+1)}$.

We finally obtain the following theorem.

Theorem 9. *Let P be an acyclic program and let T be a local consequence operator for P. Then for any $I \in I_P$ we have that $T^n(I)$ converges in $\mathcal{Q}$ to the unique fixed point M of T.*

Proof. By Proposition 3, and since d is a complete metric, we can apply the Banach contraction mapping theorem which yields convergence of $T^n(I)$ in d to a unique fixed point M of T. By definition of d, the convergence of the sequence of valuations $T^n(I)$ to M must be pointwise, hence is also convergence in $\mathcal{Q}$.

Theorem 9 is remarkable since the existence of a fixed point of the semantic operator can be guaranteed without any further knowledge about the underlying multi-valued logic.

4   Conclusions

The contribution of this paper is twofold.

(1) We have motivated the study of local consequence operators in multi-valued logic from an abstract and topological point of view. So far, semantic operators in multi-valued logic have been monotonic, to our knowledge, in order to circumvent problems related to nonmonotonicity of semantic operators in the study of declarative semantics. However, it is becoming clearer and clearer that nonmonotonic semantic operators in logic programming can be controlled using topological methods, see [11,12]. By merging multi-valued logics and nonmonotonicity the arsenal of tools available to researchers working on the declarative semantics of logic programming becomes considerably larger.

(2) We have generalized substantially some results from [3] concerning the approximation of semantic operators by artificial neural networks. However, many questions remain. We have not yet found a way to actually construct the approximating network. Very recent results [26] indicate that in order to do this, it will be necessary to find ways of obtaining good bounds on Lipschitz constants of semantic operators. Also, alternative methods of extending the results for continuous operators are needed, since the approach based on measurability seems unsatisfactory. One may get better results by using different homeomorphisms or even by using p-adic numbers[2] for representing I_P as a subspace of $\mathbb{R}$.

Acknowledgement. We would like to thank Howard A. Blair, Steffen Hölldobler, and Hans-Peter Störr for discussions on the subject matter.

References

1. Browne, A., Sun, R.: Connectionist inference models. Neural Networks **14** (2001) 1331–1355
2. Hölldobler, S.: Challenge problems for the integration of logic and connectionist systems. In Bry, F., Geske, U., Seipel, D., eds.: Proceedings 14. Workshop Logische Programmierung. Volume 90 of GMD Report., GMD (2000) 161–171
3. Hölldobler, S., Störr, H.P., Kalinke, Y.: Approximating the semantics of logic programs by recurrent neural networks. Applied Intelligence **11** (1999) 45–58
4. Funahashi, K.I.: On the approximate realization of continuous mappings by neural networks. Neural Networks **2** (1989) 183–192
5. Blair, H.A., Dushin, F., Jakel, D.W., Rivera, A.J., Sezgin, M.: Continuous models of computation for logic programs. In Apt, K.R., Marek, V.W., Truszczyński, M., Warren, D.S., eds.: The Logic Programming Paradigm: A 25-Year Persepective. Springer, Berlin (1999) 231–255
6. Lloyd, J.W.: Foundations of Logic Programming. Springer, Berlin (1988)
7. Willard, S.: General Topology. Addison-Wesley, Reading, MA (1970)
8. Batarekh, A., Subrahmanian, V.: Topological model set deformations in logic programming. Fundamenta Informaticae **12** (1989) 357–400
9. Seda, A.K.: Topology and the semantics of logic programs. Fundamenta Informaticae **24** (1995) 359–386
10. Abramsky, S., Jung, A.: Domain theory. In Abramsky, S., Gabbay, D., Maibaum, T.S., eds.: Handbook of Logic in Computer Science. Volume 3. Clarendon, Oxford (1994)
11. Hitzler, P.: Generalized Metrics and Topology in Logic Programming Semantics. PhD thesis, Department of Mathematics, National University of Ireland, University College Cork (2001)
12. Hitzler, P., Seda, A.K.: Generalized metrics and uniquely determined logic programs. Theoretical Computer Science (200x) to appear
13. Fitting, M.: Fixpoint semantics for logic programming — A survey. Theoretical Computer Science **278** (2002) 25–51

---

[2] Suggested by Howard A. Blair.

14. Hitzler, P., Seda, A.K.: Semantic operators and fixed-point theory in logic programming. In: Proceedings of the joint IIIS & IEEE meeting of the 5th World Multiconference on Systemics, Cybernetics and Informatics, SCI2001 and the 7th International Conference on Information Systems Analysis and Synthesis, ISAS2001, Orlando, Florida, USA, International Institute of Informatics and Systemics: IIIS (2001)

15. Bartle, R.G.: The Elements of Integration. John Wiley & Sons, New York (1966)

16. Hitzler, P., Seda, A.K.: A note on relationships between logic programs and neural networks. In Gibson, P., Sinclair, D., eds.: Proceedings of the Fourth Irish Workshop on Formal Methods, IWFM'00. Electronic Workshops in Comupting (eWiC), British Computer Society (2000)

17. Denecker, M., Marek, V.W., Truszczynski, M.: Approximating operators, stable operators, well-founded fixpoints and applications in non-monotonic reasoning. In Minker, J., ed.: Logic-based Artificial Intelligence. Kluwer Academic Publishers, Boston (2000) 127–144

18. Fitting, M.: A Kripke-Kleene-semantics for general logic programs. The Journal of Logic Programming **2** (1985) 295–312

19. Hitzler, P., Seda, A.K.: Characterizations of classes of programs by three-valued operators. In Gelfond, M., Leone, N., Pfeifer, G., eds.: Logic Programming and Non-monotonic Reasoning, Proceedings of the 5th International Conference on Logic Programming and Non-Monotonic Reasoning, LPNMR'99, El Paso, Texas, USA. Volume 1730 of Lecture Notes in Artificial Intelligence., Springer, Berlin (1999) 357–371

20. Gelfond, M., Lifschitz, V.: The stable model semantics for logic programming. In Kowalski, R.A., Bowen, K.A., eds.: Logic Programming. Proceedings of the 5th International Conference and Symposium on Logic Programming, MIT Press (1988) 1070–1080

21. Wendt, M.: Unfolding the well-founded semantics. Journal of Electrical Engineering, Slovak Academy of Sciences **53** (2002) 56–59 (Proceedings of the 4th Slovakian Student Conference in Applied Mathematics, Bratislava, April 2002).

22. Bishop, C.M.: Neural Networks for Pattern Recognition. Oxford University Press (1995)

23. Hornik, K., Stinchcombe, M., White, H.: Multilayer feedforward networks are universal approximators. Neural Networks **2** (1989) 359–366

24. Cavedon, L.: Acyclic programs and the completeness of SLDNF-resolution. Theoretical Computer Science **86** (1991) 81–92

25. Fitting, M.: Metric methods: Three examples and a theorem. The Journal of Logic Programming **21** (1994) 113–127

26. Bader, S.: From logic programs to iterated function systems. Master's thesis, Department of Computer Science, Dresden University of Technology (2003)

Bayesian Metanetworks for Modelling User Preferences in Mobile Environment

Vagan Terziyan[1] and Oleksandra Vitko[2]

[1] Department of Mathematical Information Technology, University of Jyvaskyla,
P.O. Box 35 (Agora), FIN-40014 Jyvaskyla, Finland
vagan@it.jyu.fi
http://www.cs.jyu.fi/ai/vagan/index.html
[2] Department of Artificial Intelligence, Kharkov National University of
Radioelectronics, Lenin Avenue 14, 61166 Kharkov, Ukraine
vitko@kture.kharkov.ua

Abstract. The problem of profiling and filtering is important particularly for mobile information systems where wireless network traffic and mobile terminal's size are limited comparing to the Internet access from the PC. Dealing with uncertainty in this area is crucial and many researchers apply various probabilistic models. The main challenge of this paper is the multilevel probabilistic model (the Bayesian Metanetwork), which is an extension of traditional Bayesian networks. The extra level(s) in the Metanetwork is used to select the appropriate substructure from the basic network level based on contextual features from user's profile (e.g. user's location). Two models of the Metanetwork are considered: C-Metanetwork for managing conditional dependencies and R-Metanetwork for modelling feature selection. The Bayesian Metanetwork is considered as a useful tool to present the second order uncertainty and therefore to predict mobile user's preferences.

1 Introduction

Filtering the Web content is an emerging problem at the age of information overload. Delivering relevant information to a particular user is one of the key tasks in many information systems. The promising application area for the development of new filtering techniques is mobile information systems. The small secure mobile terminal is rapidly evolving into the Personal Trusted Device [20], which allows users to access mobile Internet services and run applications at any time and any place. Advances in wireless network technology and continuously increasing number of users of mobile terminals make the latter a possible channel for offering personalised services to mobile users and give space to the rapid development of the Mobile Electronic Commerce (m-commerce). As a result, the huge market for user profiling is open in the mobile communication environment.

Information filtering is the task of splitting a large-volume data stream into substreams according to some selection criterion [14]. Selection for a substream is based on criteria describing its profile, which might be "an interest to a given

A. Günter et al. (Eds.): KI 2003, LNAI 2821, pp. 370–384, 2003.

user" or "a relation to a certain topic". The profile usually consists of a set of representative items, filter rules or description of the content of the stream in terms of items features. Whenever information is being filtered for a user, exploiting user's profile is important.

We consider profiling just as a data mining process for efficient and automated construction of the presentation of user's filtering preferences. Profiles are used to target the audience of particular products. Personal information that user provides on registration, his behaviour and history are combined to create user's personal profile. The profile is then used to target certain products or services for this user. XML-based and emerging Semantic Web technologies allow to present data in such a way that both the content and semantics of it including context descriptions are presented. Additionally, attributes allow us to provide metadata regarding that context.

Many filtering techniques have been developed in the last years. Generally filtering methods are divided into two main classes - content-based and collaborative filtering. In modern adaptive systems content-based and collaborative filtering are combined [6], [8].

Each filtering task has a set of variables (predictive attributes) that influence in some way the choice or the preference (target attribute) of a customer. It is evident that one cannot avoid dealing with uncertainty when predicting user's preferences. A Bayesian network has proved to be a valuable tool for encoding, learning and reasoning about probabilistic (casual) relationships. The Bayesian network for a set of variables $X = X_i, \ldots, X_n$ is a directed acyclic graph with the network structure S that encodes a set of conditional independence assertions about variables in X, and the set P of local probability distributions associated with each variable [10]. Bayesian networks as well as other probabilistic techniques are widely used for prediction of user's preferences. Once learned, the Bayesian network can support probabilistic inference including prediction of user's preferences.

The foundation for the use of Bayesian networks and Markov models for user profiling in the information retrieval was given by Wong and Butz in [23]. They implemented an idea of using probabilistic mixture models as a flexible framework for modelling user's preferences. In Cadez et al. [4] an application of probabilistic mixture models was studied for representing an individual's behaviour as a linear combination of his transactions. The works [2], [11] on probabilistic model-based collaborative filtering introduce a graphical model for probabilistic relationships - an alternative to the Bayesian network - called the dependency network. Kuenzer et al. [13] presented the empirical study of dynamic Bayesian Networks for user modelling. They evaluate six topologies of the dynamic BN for predicting the future user's behaviour: Markov Chain of order I, Hidden Markov Model (HMM), autoregressive HMM, factorial HMM, simple hierarchical HMM, and tree structured HMM. Hoffman [12] proposed an aspect model - a latent class statistical mixture models, and Popeskul et al. extended the aspect model to a three-way aspect model to incorporate three-way co-occurrence data among users, items and item content.

In [3] Butz exploited contextual independencies (see also Boutiler et al. [1]) for user profiling based on assumption that while conditional independence must exist in all contexts, a contextual independence need only exist in one particular context. He shows how contextual independencies can be modelled using multiple Bayesian networks.

A recursive Bayesian multinet was introduced by Pena et al. [15] as a decision tree with component Bayesian networks at the leaves and was applied to a geographical data-clustering problem. The key idea was to decompose the learning Bayesian network problem into learning component networks from incomplete data.

As our main goal in this paper, we are presenting another view to the Bayesian "multinets" towards making them to be really "metanetworks", i.e. by assuming that interoperability between component Bayesian networks can be also modelled by another Bayesian network. Such models suit well to user profiling applications where different probabilistic interrelations within predictive features from user's profile can be controlled by probabilistic interrelations among the contextual features.

As a new market for user profiling has appeared in the mobile communication systems, probabilistic models for modelling of user's preferences should take into account all the features of profiling in the mobile Internet.

Thus another goal of this work was to consider the use of sophisticated probabilistic networks in the context of prediction of user's preferences in mobile environment taking into account special features and constraints of mobile environment.

The rest of the paper is organised as follows. In Sect. 2 we first provide some features of the mobile information environment as an application area for advanced probabilistic modelling. In Sect. 3 we introduce the Bayesian Metanetwork to deal with modelling user's preferences in mobile environment. There we also provide two models of the Metanetwork. We conclude in Sect. 4.

2   Features and Constrains of Mobile Environment

Advances in wireless network technology and continuously increasing number of users of hand-held terminals make such Personal Trusted Devices (PTD) [20] a possible channel for offering personalised services to mobile users, and enables the rapid development of the mobile electronic commerce (m-commerce). The emergence of five different types of m-commerce can be identified: banking, Internet e-commerce over wireless access networks, location-based services, ticketing applications, and retail shopping [21]. The public commerce (p-commerce) in the mobile environment was introduced in [19]. P-commerce operates partially in a different environment than the traditional e-commerce due to the special characteristics and constraints of the terminals and wireless networks and due to the different context and circumstances where people use their PTDs. As a result the huge market for user profiling is open in mobile communication environment. The problem of profiling and filtering is urgent particularly for the mobile information systems where wireless network traffic and terminal space are limited comparing to the Internet access from the PC.

The mobile environment imposes the set of constraints and requirements on a filtering technique, among which there are:

- restrictions on computational resources of a portable device;
- restrictions on time of a connection and amount of data transferred (a customer pays for every additional second or byte of information during a connection);
- limitations on size of a mobile terminal.

One of the most distinguishing features of mobile environment is *mobility*. The evaluation of mobility lies in satisfying the needs of immediacy and location [22]. The mobile network infrastructure is able now to determine the position of the terminal precisely enough. This gives the basis for the new class of services called the Location Based Services (LBS) [5]. If a user wants to go to the theatre, for example, he should be able to use the LBS to find a nearby show, to book a reservation, to get navigational directions to an event, to receive relevant traffic information and to use micro-payments to pay for all this [17].

Combining positional mechanisms with information about location of various objects can develop very powerful and flexible personal information services [16]. Suppose there is some geographical area that contains a certain number of objects (points of interests [9]). Each point of interest is assumed to have its virtual representation or, rather, a source of relevant information. A user of this information is expected to be mobile. The aim of the location-aware service is providing the user with information about the objects taking into account spatial relationships between him and the objects. One of the main input parameters is user's location. It is obvious that the system should have information about all objects with their spatial location and links to their information sources. If the system has this information, it is able to find the near objects. Note that for mobile objects the system has to update periodically the location information via the location service or to request it directly from the objects. The first could be done automatically if we have an access to the location service. In the second case, the user can input his location by himself, for instance the street address or the name of the region. After that, the service is able to provide a geographical description of his surroundings. These data act an auxiliary role of a navigator or a guide in order to connect real objects with their virtual representations. The next client's function is providing customers with the information from the sources associated with surrounding objects. The user can either directly receive the information from the chosen object or charge the server to find the needed information. In the last case, the server performs the whole work: it analyses information sources according to user's directives and sends the results of his query to him [24].

The attribute "location of mobile user" is constantly changing its values. We hardly can say that such an attribute is "predictive" in the full meaning of the word, although it has an influence on user's choice. Better to say that this is a "contextual" attribute. Location, among other highly dynamic attributes such as e.g. time, forms a context in which a mobile customer makes his decisions. Filtering and profiling techniques for mobile environment should be specified to take into account the difference between predictive and contextual attributes. Thus we should require from our model to process separately predictive and contextual variables in order to improve performance of modelling and prediction tools for mobile information systems.

Taking into account the specifics of a mobile environment we suggest to distinguish several classes of attributes. Usually, when constructing the Bayesian network, every attribute is treated in a similar way. The typical task in learning Bayesian networks from data is model selection [10]. The set of models-candidates is evaluated according to some criterion that measures the degree to which the network structure fits the prior knowledge and data. Then the best structure (model) is selected or several good structures are processed in model averaging. Each attribute in ordinary Bayesian network has the same status, so they are just combined in possible models-candidates to encode possible conditional dependencies.

We propose the following classes and their inclusions into probabilistic model for modelling user's preferences:

Class 1. Target attributes. Possible members: best offering, type of goods, relevant information, user's cluster (user group to which he belongs), user's next transaction, etc. Characteristics: ordinary target nodes of the Bayesian network.

Class 2. Predictive attributes. Possible members: personal data about user (age, occupation, gender, etc.), observations of user's behavior (what he/she has bought before). Characteristics: ordinary nodes of the Bayesian network, which can form some structure according to casual dependencies among them. We call them "predictive" because of task definition - prediction of user's desires.

Class 3. Contextual attributes. Possible members: user's current location, time, weather, current user's mood, etc. Mobile user's coordinates together with the knowledge of the surrounding area can produce several location variables (e.g. distance to the nearest hotel, settlement scale - city, town or village, etc.). Depending on user's location different sets of predictive attributes will form user's preference. Characteristics: these attributes are conditionally independent of predictive attributes. They influence the dependencies in the predictive model, influence relevance of predictive attributes. But the knowledge of the state of variables at the predictive level doesn't have impact on the belief of the contextual variables. Contextual attributes can be dependent of other contextual variables.

Class 4. Metacontextual attributes. Possible members: parameters that define weakness or strength of some casual relationships between predictive and target attributes, relevance of location or time variables, etc. Characteristics: these attributes are independent of predictive and contextual attributes. They influence the conditional dependencies in the contextual model or influence relevances of contextual attributes.

Conceptual model of the domain should be build after the domain analysis is done and available variables are classified as target, predictive, contextual or even metacontextual. There might be a situation, when some attributes belong to the predictive class in one case (one context) and to the contextual class in another case (another context). The parameters, which define the class membership, can be classified as metacontextual attributes.

3   The Bayesian Metanetwork and Its Modifications

We define the Bayesian Metanetwork implementing the basic intuition we had while defining a Semantic Metanetwork few years ago. The Semantic Metanetwork [17], [18] was defined as a set of semantic networks, which are put on each other in such a way that the links of every previous semantic network are at the same time the nodes of the next network. In the Semantic Metanetwork every higher level controls the semantic structure of the lower level. Controlling rule might be, for example, as such: in what contexts certain link of the semantic structure can exist and in what context it should be deleted from the semantic structure.

Definition. The Bayesian Metanetwork is a set of Bayesian networks, which are put on each other in such a way that the elements (nodes or conditional dependencies) of every previous probabilistic network depend on the local probability distributions associated with the nodes of the next level network.

The Bayesian Metanetwork is a triplet:

$$MBN = (BN, R, P),\tag{1}$$

where $BN = \{BN_1, BN_2, \ldots BN_n\}$ is a set of Bayesian networks representing a set of levels; $R = \{R_{1,2}, R_{2,3}, \ldots R_{n-1,n}\}$ is a set of sets of interlevel links; P is a joint probability distribution over the Metanetwork.

Each $R_{i,i+1}$ is a set of interlevel links between i and $i+1$ levels. We have defined 2 types of links:

- R_{v-e} is a link "vertex-edge" meaning that stochastic values of vertex $v_{i,k}$ in the network BN_i correspond to the different conditional probability tables $P_k(v_{i-1,j}|v_{i-1,pj})$ in the network BN_{i-1};
- R_{v-v} is a link "vertex-vertex" meaning that stochastic values of vertex $v_{i,r}$ in the network BN_i correspond to the different relevance values of vertex $v_{i-1,r}$ in the network BN_{i-1}.

According to the introduced two types of interlevel links we consider two models of the Bayesian Metanetwork:

- C-Metanetwork having interlevel links of R_{v-e} type – for managing conditional dependencies (Conditional dependencies Metanetwork);
- R-Metanetwork having interlevel links of R_{v-v} type – for modelling relevant feature selection (Relevances Metanetwork).

3.1   C-Metanetwork – The Bayesian Metanetwork for Managing Conditional Dependencies

First consider the two-level Bayesian C-Metanetwork with interlevel links of R_{v-e} type (Fig. 1). Context variables in it are considered to be on the second (contextual) level to control the conditional probabilities associated with the predictive level of the network.

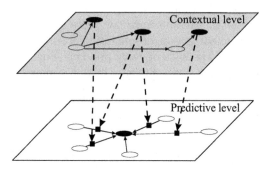

Fig. 1. The two-level Bayesian C-Metanetwork for managing conditional dependencies

We will consider each arc separately. The possible dependence between causal influences of two parents is processed on the second level of Metanetwork. Each arc in the ordinary Bayesian network corresponds to the conditional dependence between two variables. Standard Bayesian inference is applied in the Bayesian network of each level. The samples of C-Metanetwork (for simplicity projected to 2-D space) are presented in Fig. 2, Fig. 3.

The C-Metanetwork in Fig. 2 has the following parameters:

- the attributes on the predictive level: A, B, X, Y with their possibble values;
- the probabilities on the predictive level: $P(A)$, $P(X)$;
- the conditional probabilities on the predictive level (and at the same time attributes on the contextual level):
  - $P(B|A)$ which is a random variable with the set of values $\{p_k(B|A)\}$. It's important to note that this parameter serves as an ordinary conditional probability in the predictive level of the Bayesian Metanetwork and in the same time it is an attribute node on the contextual level of it;
  - $P(Y|X)$ which is a random variable with the possible values $\{p_r(Y|X)\}$ and is also considered as an attribute node on the contextual level of the Bayesian Metanetwork;
- the conditional probability on the contextual level: $P(P(Y|X), P(B|A))$, which defines Bayesian conditional probability between two contextual attributes $P(B|A)$ and $P(Y|X)$.

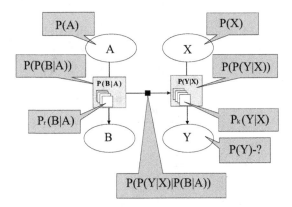

Fig. 2. The example of the Bayesian C-Metanetwork. The nodes of the 2nd-level network correspond to the conditional probabilities of the 1st-level network $P(B|A)$ and $P(Y|X)$. The directed arc in the 2nd-level network corresponds to the conditional probability $P(P(Y|X)|P(B|A))$. The inference is given in equation (2)

The probability of the target attribute $P(Y)$ can be computed by applying basic Bayesian inference on both levels of the C-Metanetwork as follows:

$$P(Y = y_j) = \sum_i \sum_k (p_k(Y = y_j | X = x_i) \cdot P(X = x_i) \cdot \\ \sum_r (P(P(Y|X) = p_k(Y|X) | P(P(B|A) = p_r(Y|X)) \cdot \\ \cdot P(P(B|A) = p_r(B|A))))).$$ (2)

Such model of the Bayesian Metanetwork can be implemented for predicting mobile user's preferences in the following way. Mobile user's profile has some predictive and contextual features. Predictive features (learned or defined within user's preferences) will be placed on the basic predictive network level and they will be used to predict user's behaviour to be able to push him carefully selected and wanted filtered products and services. Contextual features will be placed on the control network level. They will be used to predict appropriate conditional dependencies between preference features of user's profile (the basic network level) regarding the current context.

In the location-based services the main contextual feature will be current mobile user's location. When the user changes his location some conditional dependencies between his preferences are probably also changed and after applying the Bayesian inference technique a mobile service provider is able to suggest and deliver the most preferable products/services regarding current location context.

The two-level Metanetwork can be easily extended for the multilevel (multicontext) Metanetwork [18]. In principle we can assume that the Bayesian Metanetwork might have as many levels as necessary. Fig. 4 shows an example of the three-level Bayesian C-Metanetwork.

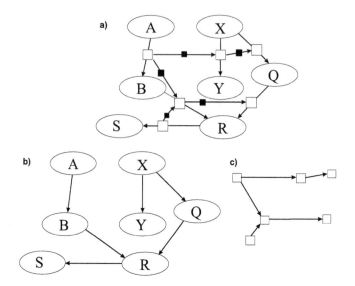

Fig. 3. The example of the Bayesian C-Metanetwork. The Metanetwork (a) actually consists of two Bayesian networks (b) and (c), and nodes of the network (c) correspond to the arcs of the network (b). The network (b) is the 1st-level predictive network, and it is controlled by the 2nd-level contextual network (c)

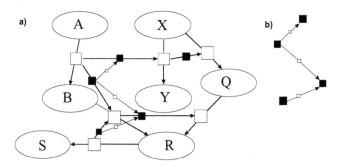

Fig. 4. The example of the three-level Bayesian C-Metanetwork. The 3rd level network (b) controls the conditional dependencies of the 2nd level network, which controls the conditional dependencies of the 1st level as shown in (a)

3.2   R-Metanetwork − The Bayesian Metanetwork for Modelling Relevant Feature Selection

Feature selection methods try to pick a subset of features that are relevant to the target concept. Each of these methods has its strengths and weaknesses based on data types and domain characteristics. It is well known that there is no single feature selection method that can be applied to all applications. The choice of the feature selection method depends on various data set characteristics: data types, data size, and noise. In [7] some guidelines were given to a potential user which method to select for a particular application based on different criteria. The Bayesian Metanetwork can be also used as a tool for modelling of relevant feature selection. Let's consider the two-level Bayesian R-Metanetwork with interlevel links of R_{v-v} type. Context variables are considered again as the control higher level to the level of network with predictive variables. Values of context variables influence the relevances of the variables on the predictive level as shown in Fig. 5.

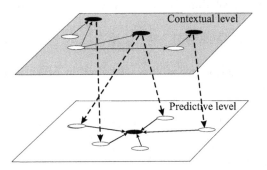

Fig. 5. The two-level Bayesian R-Metanetwork for modelling relevant feature selection

We consider relevance value as a probability of importance of the variable to the inference of target attribute in the given context (see Fig. 6).

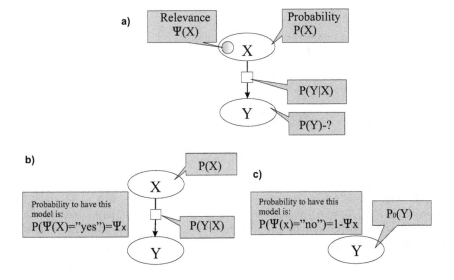

Fig. 6. The relevance definition for Bayesian R-Metanetwork. Bayesian inference is shown in equations (3), (4) and (5)

The Bayesian R-Metanetwork in Fig. 6 has the following parameters:

- the attributes: X and with the values $\{x_1, x_2, \ldots x_n\}$; Y with the values $\{y_1, y2, \ldots y_m\}$;
- the probabilities: $P(X)$, $P(Y|X)$;
- the relevance predicate: $\Psi(X) = $ "yes", if parameter X is relevant; $\Psi(X) = $ "no", if parameter X is not relevant;
- the relevance value: $\Psi_X = P(\Psi(X) = $ "yes").

The conditional probability of Y given X and $\Psi(X)$ will be the following:

$$P(Y|X, \Psi(X)) = \begin{cases} P(Y|X); \Psi(X) = \text{"yes"} \\ P_0(Y); \Psi(X) = \text{"no"} \end{cases}, \tag{3}$$

where $P_0(Y)$ is the prior probability distribution of Y. The possible way to calculate $P_0(Y)$ is:

$$P_0(Y = y_j) = \frac{1}{n} \cdot \sum_{i=1}^{n} P(Y = y_j | X = x_i), \tag{4}$$

where n is the number of values of X. So, the probability of the target attribute Y can be estimated as follows:

$$P(Y) = \frac{1}{n} \cdot \sum_{X} (P(Y|X) \cdot (n \cdot \Psi_X \cdot P(X) + (1 - \Psi_X))). \tag{5}$$

Contextual relevance network can be defined over the given predictive probabilistic network as it shown in Fig. 7. It encodes the conditional dependencies over the relevances.

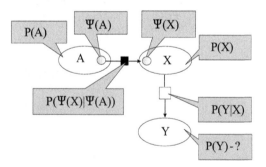

Fig. 7. The simple relevance network with attributes $\Psi(A)$, $\Psi(X)$ and conditional probability $P(\Psi(X)|\Psi(A))$ defined over the predictive network with attributes A, X, Y and conditional probability $P(Y|X)$. Inference of the target attribute is shown in equation (6)

In the relevance network the relevances are considered as random variables between which the conditional dependencies can be learned. The probability of target attribute Y can be computed as follows:

$$P(Y) = \frac{1}{n} \cdot \sum_X (P(Y|X) \cdot (n \cdot P(X) \cdot \sum_{\Psi_A} (P(\Psi_X|\Psi_A) \cdot P(\Psi_A) + (1 - \Psi_X))). \quad (6)$$

Considering such definition of the relevance network over the predictive network one can see that the strict correspondence between nodes of both networks exists but the arcs do not need to correspond. Relevances of two variables can be dependent, although their values are conditionally independent and vice versa (as it is shown in Fig. 8). More complicated example of the Bayesian R-Metanetwork completed from the predictive and relevance networks is shown in Fig. 8.

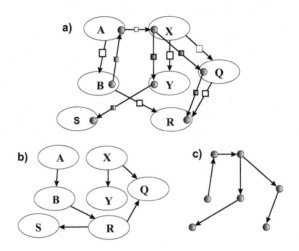

Fig. 8. The example of the Bayesian R-Metanetwork (a), consisting of the predictive network (b) and relevance network (c). The predictive and relevance networks have corresponding nodes, but different topologies

Modelling the relevant features selection with Bayesian R-Metanetwork can be implemented also in mobile applications, where applications should process only relevant information because of system resource restrictions. Mobile user's profile has predictive (user's preferences) and contextual features (user's location etc.). Contextual features will be used to decide which subset of predictive features is relevant in the recent context. Evidence about some contextual features should give us hints to extract appropriate Bayesian substructure with the limited amount of attributes from the basic level. In location-based services the main contextual feature will be the current mobile user's location. When some user changes his location probably some preferences become probabilistically irrelevant and we can extract smaller subnetwork from basic level and process it. In such effective way a mobile service provider is able to suggest and deliver the most preferable products/services regarding current location context.

4   Conclusion

Filtering the Web content is an emerging technology at the age of information overload. The problem of profiling and filtering is important particularly for mobile information systems where wireless network traffic and mobile terminal's size are limited comparing to the Internet access from the PC. Mobile user modelling accounts not only user's profile features and collected user's experiences but also user's location, which can be tracked. Dealing with uncertainty in this area is crucial and many researchers apply various probabilistic models.

The main challenge of this paper is the multilevel probabilistic model (the Bayesian Metanetwork), which is the extension of traditional Bayesian networks and is also considered as a useful tool to predict a mobile user's preferences. The extra level(s) in the Metanetwork is used to select the appropriate substructure from the basic network level based on contextual features from user's profile (e.g. location). Two models of the Metanetwork are considered. C-Metanetwork considers conditional dependencies of the Bayesian network as random variables and assumes conditional dependencies between conditional dependencies. R-Metanetwork assumes that the relevances of predictive variables in the Bayesian network might be random variables themselves and provides a tool to reason based not only on probabilities of predictive variables but also on their relevances. The advantages of proposed multilevel models comparing with the ordinary Bayesian networks are:

- flexibility (you don't need to relearn the whole model when some changes occur, it can be enough to relearn the one level);
- reduction of computational complexity (in the case when complex one-level model can be decomposed on two or more easy structures, Naive Bayes for instance) and increase of processing speed;
- the accuracy of the Metanetwork will be higher than the accuracy of the traditional Bayesian network when the environment indirectly affects the probabilistic process, which is modelled by predictive network. We gain in the accuracy because use more precise models in every context and do not use averaging through all the contexts.

The Bayesian Metanetwork is considered as a useful tool to present the second order uncertainty and therefore to predict mobile user's preferences. The general formalism of the Bayesian Metanetwork can be applied for such modelling task formulations: modelling conditional dependencies in the user's profile (by C-Metanetwork) and modelling relevant feature selection (by R-Metanetwork). As location of mobile user is being considered as a very important determinative attribute in modelling of user's decision making, the applications of Bayesian Metanetworks for mobile location-based systems and particularly to mobile and public commerce location aware services are viewed as relevant.

References

1. Boutiler, C., Friedman, N., Goldszmidt, M., Koller, D.: Context-Specific Independence in Bayesian Networks. In: Proc. of the 12-th Conference on Uncertainty in Artificial Intelligence UAI'96 (1996) 115–123
2. Breese, J.S., Heckerman D., Kadie C.: Empirical Analysis of Predictive Algorithms for Collaborative Filtering. In: Proc. of the 14-th Conference on Uncertainty in Artificial Intelligence. Madison WI: Morgan Kauffman (1998)
3. Butz, C.J.: Exploiting Contextual Independencies in Web Search and User Profiling. In: Proc. of the World Congress on Computational Intelligence (2002) 1051–1056
4. Cadez, I.V., Smyth, P., Mannila, H.: Probabilistic Modeling of Transaction Data with Applications to Profiling, Visualization, and Prediction. In: Proc. of the KDD'2001 (2001) 37–46
5. Chadha, K.: Location-Based Services: The Next Differentiator. Mobile Internet and Inf. Services (2000) Available in:
   http://www.the-arc-group.com/ebrief/2000/mobileinternetis/
   executive_summary.htm
6. Claypool, M., Phong, L., Waseda, M., Brown, D.: Implicit Interest Indicators. In: Proc. of ACM Intelligent User Interfaces Conference IUI'2001. Santa Fe, New Mexico (2001)
7. Dash, M., Liu, H.: Feature selection for classification. Intelligent Data Analysis **1** (3) (1997)
8. Delgado, J., Ishii, N.: Multi-Agent Learning in Recommender Systems for Information Filtering on the Internet. Int. J. CIS **10** (1–2) (2001) 81–100
9. Garmash, A.: A geographical XML-based format for the mobile environment. In: Proc. of HICSS Conference. Hawaii (2001)
10. Heckerman, D.: A tutorial on learning with Bayesian networks. Technical Report MSR-TR-95-06, Microsoft Research (1995)
11. Heckerman, D., Chickering, D., Meek, C., Rounthwaite, R., Kadie, C.: Dependency Networks for Inference, Collaborative Filtering, and Data Visualization. J. Machine Learning Research **1** (2000) 49–75
12. Hoffman, T.: Probabilistic latent semantic indexing. In: Proc. of the ACM SIGIR Conference.New York: ACM Press (1999) 50–57
13. Kuenzer, A., Schlick, C., Ohmann, F., Schmidt, L., Luczak, H.: An empirical study of dynamic Bayesian networks for user modeling. In: Schafer, R., Muller, M. E., Macskassy, S. A. (eds.): Proc. of the UM'2001 Workshop on Machine Learning for User Modeling (2001) 1–10
14. Kutschinski, E., Poutre, H.L.: Scientific techniques for interactive profiling. Technical Report (ASTA project). Telematica Instituut, Enschede (2001)
15. Pena, J., Lozano, J.A., Larranaga, P.: Learning Bayesian Networks for Clustering by Means of Constructive Induction. Machine Learning, **47** (1) (2002) 63–90
16. Swedberg, G.: Ericsson's Mobile Location Solution. Ericsson Review (1999)
17. Terziyan, V.: Multilevel Models for Knowledge Bases Control and Automated Information Systems Applications. Doctor of Technical Sciences Degree Thesis. Kharkov State Technical University of Radioelectronics, Kharkov (1993)
18. Terziyan, V., Puuronen, S.: Reasoning with Multilevel Contexts in Semantic Metanetworks. In: P. Bonzon, M. Cavalcanti, R. Nossun (eds.): Formal Aspects in Context. Kluwer Academic Publishers (2000) 107–126

19. Terziyan, V.: Architecture for Mobile P-Commerce: Multilevel Profiling Framework. In: Proc. of the IJCAI'2001 International Workshop "E-Business and the Intelligent Web". Seattle (2001)
20. The MeT Initiative – Enabling Mobile E-Commerce. Met Overview White Paper (2000) Available in:
    http://www.mobiletransaction.org/pdf/MeT_White_Paper.pdf
21. Veijalainen, J., Terziyan, V.: Transaction Management for M-Commerce at a Mobile Terminal. In: Proc. of the International Workshop on Reliable and Secure Applications in Mobile Environment in conjunction with SRDS'2001. New Orleans (2001)
22. Wassum, B.: Mobile Data Service Models for Mobile Network Operators, Mobile Internet and Inf. Services (2000) Available in:
    http://www.the-arc-group.com/ebrief/2000/mobileinternetis/
    executive_summary.htm
23. Wong, S.K.M., Butz, C.J.: A Bayesian Approach to User Profiling in Information Retrieval. Technology Letters, **4** (1) (2000) 50–56
24. Virrantaus, K., Veijalainen, J., Markkula, J., Katasonov, A., Garmash, A., Tirri, H., Terziyan, V.: Developing GIS-Supported Location-Based Services. In: Proc. of WGIS'2001 – First International Workshop on Web Geographical Information Systems. Kyoto, Japan (2001) 423–432

On Identifying Tree-Structured Perfect Maps

Christian Borgelt

Dept. of Knowledge Processing and Language Engineering
School of Computer Science
Otto-von-Guericke-University of Magdeburg
Universitätsplatz 2, 39106 Magdeburg, Germany
`borgelt@iws.cs.uni-magdeburg.de`

Abstract. It is well known that tree-structured perfect maps can be uniquely identified by computing a maximum weight spanning tree with mutual information providing the edge weights. In this paper I generalize the edge evaluation measure by stating the conditions such a measure has to satisfy in order to be able to identify tree-structured perfect maps. In addition, I show that not only mutual information, but also the well-known χ^2 measure satisfies these conditions.

1 Introduction

At the core of the theory of graphical models [10,6,9,2,1], that is, of Bayes networks and Markov networks, is the notion of a so-called *conditional independence graph* or *independence map* for a given multidimensional probability distribution. It allows us to determine the conditional independence statements obtaining in the probability distribution by applying a simple graph theoretic criterion, which is based on node separation.

The exact form of this criterion depends on whether the graph is directed (Bayes network) or undirected (Markov network). If it is undirected, so-called *u-separation* is defined as follows: Let X, Y, and Z be three disjoint sets of nodes of a graph G. Then Z *u*-separates X and Y iff all paths from a node in X to a node in Y contain a node in Z. If the graph is directed, the slightly more complicated notion of *d-separation* is used [10]: Here Z *d*-separates X and Y iff there is no path, i.e., no sequence of consecutive edges (of any directionality) along which the following two conditions hold:

1. every node, at which edges of the path converge (i.e., both edges are directed towards the node), either is in Z or has a descendant in Z,
2. every other node is not in Z.

As already stated above, a graph G is called a *conditional independence graph* or an *independence map* [10] iff all conditional independences that can be read from it using these criteria actually hold in the associated probability distribution p, or formally

$$\langle X \mid Z \mid Y \rangle_G \quad \Rightarrow \quad X \perp\!\!\!\perp_p Y \mid Z,$$

A. Günter et al. (Eds.): KI 2003, LNAI 2821, pp. 385–395, 2003.

where $\langle X \mid Z \mid Y \rangle_G$ denotes that Z separates X and Y in the graph G and $X \perp\!\!\!\perp_p Y \mid Z$ means that

$$\forall x \in \mathrm{dom}(X) : \forall y \in \mathrm{dom}(Y) : \forall z \in \mathrm{dom}(Z) :$$
$$P(X = x, Y = y \mid Z = z) = P(X = x \mid Z = z) \cdot P(Y = y \mid Z = z).$$

However, there may be additional conditional independences holding in the distribution that are not captured by the graph.

The dual concept is a so-called *conditional dependence graph* or *dependence map* [10], which captures all conditional dependences holding in the distribution, or—stated the other way round—all conditional independences obtaining in the distribution are represented in the graph. Formally, we have

$$X \perp\!\!\!\perp_p Y \mid Z \quad \Rightarrow \quad \langle X \mid Z \mid Y \rangle_G.$$

The graph may represent additional conditional independences that do not hold in the distribution, but wherever it indicates a conditional dependence, this dependence holds in the distribution.

If a graph is both an independence map as well as a dependence map, that is, if it captures exactly the conditional independence statements holding in the distribution, no more and no less, it is called a *perfect map* [10].

In this paper I consider tree-structured perfect maps and examine how they can be determined by constructing a maximum weight spanning tree for given edge weights. While it is well-known that tree-structured perfect maps can be uniquely determined if mutual information is used to compute the edge weights, I state here more generally what conditions the edge evaluation measure has to satisfy for this task. Furthermore, I show that not only mutual information, but also the well-known χ^2 measure satisfies these conditions.

2   Identifying Tree-Structured Perfect Maps

The best-known greedy approach to induce a graphical model—and at the same time the oldest—is *optimum weight spanning tree construction* and was first suggested in [3]. All possible (undirected) edges over the set $U = \{A_1, \ldots, A_n\}$ of attributes used to describe the multidimensional domain under consideration are evaluated with an evaluation measure (in [3] *mutual information* was used). Then an optimum weight spanning tree is constructed with either the (well-known) Kruskal algorithm [7] or the (somewhat less well-known) Prim algorithm [12] (or any other greedy algorithm for this task).

I am interested in this approach here, because if the probability distribution, for which a graphical model is desired, has a perfect map that is a tree, optimum weight spanning tree construction is guaranteed to find this perfect map, provided the evaluation measure used has a certain property.

However, before I state the corresponding theorem, I should introduce the notion of *symmetry* (although it is, of course, canonical): An evaluation measure $m : U \times U \to \mathbb{R}$ is called *symmetric* iff $\forall A, B : m(A, B) = m(B, A)$.

Theorem 1. *Let m be a symmetric evaluation measure satisfying*

$$\forall A, B, C: \quad m(C, AB) \geq m(C, B),$$

with equality obtaining only if the attributes A and C are conditionally independent given B. (AB is a pseudo-attribute with values in $\mathrm{dom}(A) \times \mathrm{dom}(B)$.) Let G be a singly connected (or tree-structured) undirected perfect map of a probability distribution p over a set U of attributes. Then constructing a maximum weight spanning tree for the attributes in U with m (computed from p) providing the edge weights uniquely identifies G.

In order to prove this theorem, it is convenient to prove first the following lemma, by which an important property of the measure m is established:

Lemma 1. *Let m be a symmetric evaluation measure satisfying*

$$\forall A, B, C: \quad m(C, AB) \geq m(C, B)$$

with equality obtaining only if the attributes C and A are conditionally independent given B. Furthermore, let p be the probability distribution from which m is computed. If A, B, and C are three attributes satisfying $A \perp\!\!\!\perp_p C \mid B$, but neither $A \perp\!\!\!\perp_p B \mid C$ nor $C \perp\!\!\!\perp_p B \mid A$, then

$$m(A, C) \; < \; \min\{m(A, B), m(B, C)\}.$$

Proof. From the facts that m is symmetric and $A \perp\!\!\!\perp_p C \mid B$ we know that

$$m(C, AB) = m(C, B) \qquad \text{and} \qquad m(A, CB) = m(A, B).$$

Since it is $A \not\perp\!\!\!\perp_p B \mid C$ and $C \not\perp\!\!\!\perp_p B \mid A$, we have

$$m(C, AB) > m(C, A) \qquad \text{and} \qquad m(A, CB) > m(A, C).$$

Consequently, $m(C, A) < m(C, B)$ and $m(C, A) < m(A, B)$. $\qquad\qquad\square$

Proof. (of Theorem 1)
Let C and A be two arbitrary attributes in U that are not adjacent in G. Since the graph G is singly connected there is a unique path connecting C and A in G. I show that any edge connecting two consecutive nodes on this path has a higher weight than the edge (C, A).

Let B be the successor of C on the path connecting C and A in G. Then it is $C \perp\!\!\!\perp_p A \mid B$, but neither $C \perp\!\!\!\perp_p B \mid A$ nor $A \perp\!\!\!\perp_p B \mid C$, because G is a perfect map. Consequently, it is $m(C, A) < m(C, B)$ and $m(C, A) < m(B, A)$. If B is the predecessor of A on the path, we already have that all edges on the path have a higher weight than the edge (C, A). Otherwise we have that the edge (C, B) has a higher weight than the edge (C, A). For the remaining path, i.e., the path that connects B and A, the above argument is applied recursively.

Therefore any edge between two consecutive nodes on the path connecting any two attributes C and A has a higher weight than the edge (C, A). From this it is immediately clear, for example by considering how the Kruskal algorithm [7] works, that constructing the optimum weight spanning tree with m providing the edge weights uniquely identifies G. $\qquad\qquad\square$

In the next section I show in Theorems 3 and 4 that at least mutual information and the χ^2 measure have the property presupposed in this theorem.

It is clear that the above theorem holds also for directed trees, since any undirected conditional independence graph that is a tree can be turned into an equivalent directed tree by choosing an arbitrary root node and (recursively) directing the edges away from this node. However, with an additional requirement, it can also be extended to polytrees.

Theorem 2. *Let* m *be a symmetric evaluation measure satisfying*

$$\forall A, B, C: \quad m(C, AB) \geq m(C, B)$$

with equality obtaining only if the attributes A *and* C *are conditionally independent given* B *and*

$$\forall A, C: \quad m(C, A) \geq 0$$

with equality obtaining only if the attributes A *and* C *are (marginally) independent. Let* G *be a singly connected directed perfect map of a probability distribution* p *over a set* U *of attributes. Then constructing a maximum weight spanning tree for the attributes in* U *with* m *(computed from* p*) providing the edge weights uniquely identifies the so-called* skeleton *of* G, *i.e., the undirected graph that results if all edge directions are discarded.*

Proof. Let C and A be two arbitrary attributes in U that are not adjacent in G. Since the graph G is singly connected, there is a unique path connecting C and A. Suppose first that this path does not contain a node with converging edges (from its predecessor and its successor on the path). In this case the proof of Theorem 1 can be transferred, because, according to d-separation, we have $C \perp\!\!\!\perp_p A \mid B$, but neither $C \perp\!\!\!\perp_p B \mid A$ nor $A \perp\!\!\!\perp_p B \mid C$ (because G is a perfect map). Therefore the value of m must be less for the edge (C, A) than for any pair of consecutive nodes on the path connecting C and A.

Suppose next that the path connecting C and A in G contains at least one node with converging edges (from its predecessor and its successor on the path). According to the d-separation criterion (see Section 1 for the definition), C and A must be marginally independent and hence it is $m(C, A) = 0$. However, no pair (B_i, B_j) of consecutive nodes on the path is marginally independent (since G is a perfect map) and thus $m(B_i, B_j) > 0$.

Therefore any edge between two nodes on a path connecting two nonadjacent nodes in the perfect map G has a higher weight than the edge connecting them directly. From this it is immediately clear, for example by considering how the Kruskal algorithm [7] works, that constructing the maximum weight spanning tree with m providing the edge weights uniquely identifies the skeleton of G. □

Note that the above theorem is an extension of a theorem shown in [14,10], where it was proven with mutual information providing the edge weights. Note also that the edges of the skeleton found with the above approach may be directed with an algorithm presented in [14,10], although the result may not be unique, because often the direction of some edges can be chosen arbitrarily.

3   Edge Evaluation Measures

The theorems in the preceding section are formulated in a general way with an evaluation measure m that has to satisfy certain properties. In this section I show that at least *mutual information* [8,3], which is also known under the names of *cross entropy* or *information gain* [13], and the χ^2 measure satisfy these conditions, so both can be used to identify tree-structured perfect maps.

3.1   Notation

In the following I will use the following notation: Let A, B, and C be three attributes with domains $\mathrm{dom}(A) = \{a_1, \ldots, a_{n_A}\}$, $\mathrm{dom}(B) = \{b_1, \ldots, b_{n_B}\}$, and $\mathrm{dom}(C) = \{c_1, \ldots, c_{n_C}\}$, respectively. Furthermore, let P be a strictly positive probability measure defined on the joint domain of A, B, and C. In order to make the formulae easier to read, I introduce the following abbreviations:

$$
\begin{aligned}
p_{i..} &= P(C = c_i), & p_{ij.} &= P(C = c_i, A = a_j), \\
p_{.j.} &= P(A = a_j), & p_{i.k} &= P(C = c_i, B = b_k), \\
p_{..k} &= P(B = b_k), & p_{.jk} &= P(A = a_j, B = b_k), \quad \text{and} \\
& & p_{ijk} &= P(C = c_i, A = a_j, B = b_k),
\end{aligned}
$$

i.e., the index i always refers to the attribute C, the index j always refers to the attribute A, and the index k always refers to the attribute B. If a formula refers only to two attributes C and A, the third index k is dropped.

3.2   Mutual Information

The *mutual information* of two attributes C and A w.r.t. P can be defined in different ways. In the first place, it can be defined as a pointwise comparison of the actual joint distribution, as it is described by p_{ij}, to a hypothetical independent distribution, as it can be computed by $p_{i.}p_{.j}$. That is,

$$
I_{\mathrm{mut}}(C, A) = \sum_{i=1}^{n_C} \sum_{j=1}^{n_A} p_{ij} \log_2 \frac{p_{ij}}{p_{i.}p_{.j}}.
$$

Alternatively, one may draw on the notion of the *Shannon entropy* H of a probability distribution [15], which leads to

$$
\begin{aligned}
I_{\mathrm{mut}}(C, A) &= H(C) + H(A) - H(CA) \\
&= -\sum_{i=1}^{n_C} p_i \log_2 p_i - \sum_{j=1}^{n_A} p_j \log_2 p_j + \sum_{i=1}^{n_C} \sum_{j=1}^{n_A} p_{ij} \log_2 p_{ij},
\end{aligned}
$$

which can be interpreted intuitively as measuring the reduction of the expected number of yes/no questions one has to ask in order to determine the obtaining value combination, or the reduction of the expected binary code length for transmitting the value tuple [1]. Obviously, the two definitions are equivalent.

The following theorem shows that mutual information satisfies the prerequisites of Theorem 1. Although the property of mutual information stated in it is well-known and the proof is merely a technical task, I provide a full proof (derived from a proof in [11] that mutual information is always nonnegative), because it is rarely spelled out clearly and thus is difficult to find.

Theorem 3. *Let A, B, and C be three attributes with finite domains and let their joint probability distribution be strictly positive, i.e., let $\forall a \in \mathrm{dom}(A) : \forall b \in \mathrm{dom}(B) : \forall c \in \mathrm{dom}(C) : P(A = a, B = b, C = c) > 0$. Then*

$$I_{\mathrm{mut}}(C, AB) \geq I_{\mathrm{mut}}(C, B),$$

with equality obtaining only if the attributes C and A are conditionally independent given B.

Proof. Since it makes the proof much simpler, I show that

$$I_{\mathrm{mut}}(C, B) - I_{\mathrm{mut}}(C, AB) \leq 0,$$

from which the original statement follows trivially.

$$
\begin{aligned}
& I_{\mathrm{mut}}(C, B) - I_{\mathrm{mut}}(C, AB) \\
&= H(C) + H(B) - H(CB) - (H(C) + H(AB) - H(CAB)) \\
&= -H(CB) - H(AB) + H(CAB) + H(B) \\
&= \sum_{i=1}^{n_C}\sum_{k=1}^{n_B} p_{i.k} \log_2 p_{i.k} + \sum_{j=1}^{n_A}\sum_{k=1}^{n_B} p_{.jk} \log_2 p_{.jk} \\
&\quad - \sum_{i=1}^{n_C}\sum_{j=1}^{n_A}\sum_{k=1}^{n_B} p_{ijk} \log_2 p_{ijk} - \sum_{k=1}^{n_B} p_{..k} \log_2 p_{..k} \\
&= \sum_{i=1}^{n_C}\sum_{j=1}^{n_A}\sum_{k=1}^{n_B} p_{ijk} \log_2 \frac{p_{i.k} p_{.jk}}{p_{ijk} p_{..k}} \\
&= \frac{1}{\ln 2}\sum_{i=1}^{n_C}\sum_{j=1}^{n_A}\sum_{k=1}^{n_B} p_{ijk} \ln \frac{p_{i.k} p_{.jk}}{p_{ijk} p_{..k}} \\
&\leq \frac{1}{\ln 2}\sum_{i=1}^{n_C}\sum_{j=1}^{n_A}\sum_{k=1}^{n_B} p_{ijk} \left(\frac{p_{i.k} p_{.jk}}{p_{ijk} p_{..k}} - 1 \right) \\
&= \frac{1}{\ln 2}\left[\sum_{i=1}^{n_C}\sum_{j=1}^{n_A}\sum_{k=1}^{n_B} \frac{p_{i.k} p_{.jk}}{p_{..k}} - \underbrace{\sum_{i=1}^{n_C}\sum_{j=1}^{n_A}\sum_{k=1}^{n_B} p_{ijk}}_{=1} \right] \\
&= \frac{1}{\ln 2}\left[\left(\sum_{k=1}^{n_B} \frac{1}{p_{..k}} \sum_{i=1}^{n_C}\sum_{j=1}^{n_A} p_{i.k} p_{.jk} \right) - 1 \right]
\end{aligned}
$$

$$= \frac{1}{\ln 2} \left[\left(\sum_{k=1}^{n_B} \frac{1}{p_{..k}} \underbrace{\left(\sum_{i=1}^{n_C} p_{i.k} \right)}_{=p_{..k}} \underbrace{\left(\sum_{j=1}^{n_A} p_{.jk} \right)}_{=p_{..k}} \right) - 1 \right]$$

$$= \frac{1}{\ln 2} \left(\underbrace{\left(\sum_{k=1}^{n_B} \frac{p_{..k}^2}{p_{..k}} \right)}_{=1} - 1 \right)$$

$$= \frac{1}{\ln 2} (1 - 1) \; = \; 0,$$

where the inequality follows from the fact that

$$\ln x \leq x - 1,$$

with equality obtaining only for $x = 1$. (This can most easily be seen from the graph of $\ln x$.) As a consequence, $I_{\text{gain}}(C, AB) = I_{\text{gain}}(C, B)$ only if

$$\forall i, j, k : \frac{p_{i.k} p_{.jk}}{p_{ijk} p_{..k}} = 1 \quad \Leftrightarrow \quad \forall i, j, k : p_{ij|k} = p_{i.|k} p_{.j|k},$$

where $p_{ij|k} = P(C = c_i, A = a_j \mid B = b_k)$ and $p_{i.|k}$ and $p_{.j|k}$ likewise. That is, $I_{\text{gain}}(C, AB) = I_{\text{gain}}(C, B)$ only holds if the attributes C and A are conditionally independent given attribute B.   □

Note that with the above theorem it is easily established that mutual information is always nonnegative and zero only for independent attributes: Assume that attribute B has only one value. In this case it is $I_{\text{gain}}(C, B) = 0$, since the joint distribution on the values of the two attributes clearly coincides with the distribution on the values of C. In addition, the combination of the attributes A and B is obviously indistinguishable from A alone and thus we get $I_{\text{gain}}(C, AB) = I_{\text{gain}}(C, A)$. Consequently, we have as a corollary:

Corollary 1. *Let C and A be two attributes with finite domains and let their joint probability distribution be strictly positive, i.e. $\forall c \in \text{dom}(C) : \forall a \in \text{dom}(A) : P(C = c, A = a) > 0$. Then*

$$I_{\text{gain}}(C, A) \; \geq \; 0,$$

with equality obtaining only if C and A are (marginally) independent.

Therefore mutual information also satisfies the prerequisites of Theorem 2.

3.3 χ^2 Measure

As mentioned above, one way to define mutual information relies on a pointwise comparison of the actual joint distribution, as it is described by p_{ij}, to a hypothetical independent distribution, as it can be computed by $p_i p_j$. The χ^2 *measure*, which is well known in statistics, does the same, but instead of the pointwise quotient (as mutual information does) it computes the pointwise squared difference of the two distributions. It is usually defined as

$$\chi^2(C, A) = \sum_{i=1}^{n_C} \sum_{j=1}^{n_A} \frac{(E_{ij} - N_{ij})^2}{E_{ij}} \qquad \text{where } E_{ij} = \frac{N_{i.}\, N_{.j}}{N_{..}}$$

$$= \sum_{i=1}^{n_C} \sum_{j=1}^{n_A} \frac{N_{..}^2 \left(\frac{N_{i.}}{N_{..}} \frac{N_{.j}}{N_{..}} - \frac{N_{ij}}{N_{..}} \right)^2}{N_{..} \frac{N_{i.}}{N_{..}} \frac{N_{.j}}{N_{..}}}$$

$$= N_{..} \sum_{i=1}^{n_C} \sum_{j=1}^{n_A} \frac{(p_{i.}\, p_{.j} - p_{ij})^2}{p_{i.}\, p_{.j}},$$

where the N's are counters for the occurrence of certain value combinations in a sample. From these counters the probabilities are estimated by simple maximum likelihood estimation (i.e. as relative frequencies).

With the above transformation it is obvious that the numerator of the fraction is the squared difference of the actual joint distribution and the hypothetical independent distribution. The denominator serves to weight these pointwise differences. In order to render this measure independent of the number of sample cases, the factor $N_{..}$ (the size of the sample) is often discarded.

For the χ^2 measure we have a direct analog of Theorem 3. That is, the χ^2 measure also satisfies the prerequisites of Theorem 1 and may thus also be used to identify tree-structured perfect maps. The proof is also mainly a technical task, although it is slightly more complicated than the proof of Theorem 3.

Theorem 4. *Let A, B, and C be three attributes with finite domains and let their joint probability distribution be strictly positive, i.e. let $\forall a \in \text{dom}(A):$ $\forall b \in \text{dom}(B): \forall c \in \text{dom}(C): P(A = a, B = b, C = c) > 0$. Then*

$$\chi^2(C, AB) \geq \chi^2(C, B),$$

with equality obtaining only if the attributes C and A are conditionally independent given B.

Proof. Since it makes the proof much simpler, I show

$$\frac{1}{N_{..}} \left(\chi^2(C, AB) - \chi^2(C, B) \right) \geq 0,$$

from which the original statement follows trivially.

$$\frac{1}{N_{..}} \left(\chi^2(C, AB) - \chi^2(C, B) \right)$$

$$= \sum_{i=1}^{n_C} \sum_{j=1}^{n_A} \sum_{k=1}^{n_B} \frac{(p_{ijk} - p_{i..}p_{.jk})^2}{p_{i..}p_{.jk}} - \sum_{i=1}^{n_C} \sum_{k=1}^{n_B} \frac{(p_{i.k} - p_{i..}p_{..k})^2}{p_{i..}p_{..k}}$$

$$= \sum_{i=1}^{n_C} \sum_{k=1}^{n_B} \left(\sum_{j=1}^{n_A} \frac{p_{ijk}^2 - 2p_{ijk}p_{i..}p_{.jk} + p_{i..}^2 p_{.jk}^2}{p_{i..}p_{.jk}} - \frac{p_{i.k}^2 - 2p_{i.k}p_{i..}p_{..k} + p_{i..}^2 p_{..k}^2}{p_{i..}p_{..k}} \right)$$

$$= \sum_{i=1}^{n_C} \sum_{k=1}^{n_B} \left(\sum_{j=1}^{n_A} \left(\frac{p_{ijk}^2}{p_{i..}p_{.jk}} - 2p_{ijk} + p_{i..}p_{.jk} \right) - \frac{p_{i.k}^2}{p_{i..}p_{..k}} + 2p_{i.k} - p_{i..}p_{..k} \right)$$

$$= \sum_{i=1}^{n_C} \sum_{k=1}^{n_B} \left(\sum_{j=1}^{n_A} \frac{p_{ijk}^2}{p_{i..}p_{.jk}} - 2p_{i.k} + p_{i..}p_{..k} - \frac{p_{i.k}^2}{p_{i..}p_{..k}} + 2p_{i.k} - p_{i..}p_{..k} \right)$$

$$= \sum_{i=1}^{n_C} \sum_{k=1}^{n_B} \frac{1}{p_{i..}p_{..k}} \left(p_{..k} \sum_{j=1}^{n_A} \frac{p_{ijk}^2}{p_{.jk}} - p_{i.k} \sum_{j=1}^{n_A} p_{ijk} \right)$$

$$= \sum_{i=1}^{n_C} \sum_{k=1}^{n_B} \frac{1}{p_{i..}p_{..k}} \left[\left(\sum_{j_1=1}^{n_A} p_{.j_1 k} \right) \left(\sum_{j_2=1}^{n_A} \frac{p_{ij_2k}^2}{p_{.j_2k}} \right) - \left(\sum_{j_1=1}^{n_A} p_{ij_1k} \right) \left(\sum_{j_2=1}^{n_A} p_{ij_2k} \right) \right]$$

$$= \sum_{i=1}^{n_C} \sum_{k=1}^{n_B} \frac{1}{p_{i..}p_{..k}} \left(\sum_{j_1=1}^{n_A} \sum_{j_2=1}^{n_A} \frac{p_{.j_1k} p_{ij_2k}^2}{p_{.j_2k}} - \sum_{j_1=1}^{n_A} \sum_{j_2=1}^{n_A} p_{ij_1k} p_{ij_2k} \right)$$

$$= \sum_{i=1}^{n_C} \sum_{k=1}^{n_B} \frac{1}{p_{i..}p_{..k}} \left(\sum_{j_1=1}^{n_A} \sum_{j_2=1}^{n_A} \frac{p_{.j_1k}^2 p_{ij_2k}^2 - p_{ij_1k} p_{ij_2k} p_{.j_1k} p_{.j_2k}}{p_{.j_1k} p_{.j_2k}} \right)$$

$$= \sum_{i=1}^{n_C} \sum_{k=1}^{n_B} \frac{1}{2p_{i..}p_{..k}} \sum_{j_1=1}^{n_A} \sum_{j_2=1}^{n_A} \frac{(p_{.j_1k} p_{ij_2k} - p_{ij_1k} p_{.j_2k})^2}{p_{.j_1k} p_{.j_2k}}$$

$$= \sum_{i=1}^{n_C} \sum_{k=1}^{n_B} \sum_{j_1=1}^{n_A} \sum_{j_2=1}^{n_A} \frac{(p_{.j_1k} p_{ij_2k} - p_{ij_1k} p_{.j_2k})^2}{2p_{i..}p_{..k} p_{.j_1k} p_{.j_2k}} \geq 0,$$

where the semi-last step follows by duplicating the term in parentheses and then interchanging the indices j_1 and j_2 in the second instance (which is possible, because they have the same range). From the result it is immediately clear that $\chi^2(C, AB) \geq \chi^2(C, B)$: Since each term of the sum is a square divided by a product of (positive) probabilities, each term and thus the sum must be non-negative. It also follows that the sum can be zero only if all of its terms are zero, which requires their numerators to be zero:

$$\forall i, j_1, j_2, k : p_{.j_1k} p_{ij_2k} - p_{ij_1k} p_{.j_2k} = 0 \Leftrightarrow \forall i, j_1, j_2, k : \frac{p_{ij_2k}}{p_{.j_2k}} = \frac{p_{ij_1k}}{p_{.j_1k}}$$

$$\Leftrightarrow \forall i, j_1, j_2, k : p_{i|j_2k} = p_{i|j_1k},$$

where $p_{i|j_\alpha k} = P(C = c_i \mid A = a_{j_\alpha}, B = b_k)$ with $\alpha \in \{1,2\}$. As a consequence we have that $\chi^2(C, AB) = \chi^2(C, B)$ only holds if the attributes C and A are conditionally independent given attribute B. $\qquad \square$

Note that no corollary is needed in this case, because from the definition of the χ^2 measure it is already obvious that $\chi^2(C, A) \geq 0$. Therefore the χ^2 measure also satisfies the prerequisites of Theorem 2 and thus may also be used to identify the skeleton of a polytree.

4   Conclusions

In this paper I provided a general statement of the conditions an edge evaluation measure has to satisfy in order to be able to identify a tree-structured perfect map or the skeleton of a polytree that is a perfect map. This generalizes the well-known fact that applying maximum weight spanning tree construction with mutual information providing the edge weights solves these tasks. In addition I showed that not only mutual information, but also the well-known χ^2 measure satisfies these conditions, so that it may be used for the same task. However, for mutual information also a stronger statement holds, namely that if there is no tree-structured perfect map, constructing a maximum weight spanning tree yields the best tree-structured approximation w.r.t. the Kullback-Leibler information divergence [8] between the original distribution and the distribution represented by the tree [3,10]. This result even generalizes to the construction of tree-augmented naive Bayes classifiers, where the star-like structure of such a classifier is augmented by edges that form a tree [5,4]. To find out whether a similar result can be obtained for the χ^2 measure, for example, w.r.t. the difference between the original distribution and the approximation as it can be measured by an adapted χ^2 measure itself, remains as future work.

References

1. C. Borgelt and R. Kruse. *Graphical Models — Methods for Data Analysis and Mining.* J. Wiley & Sons, Chichester, United Kingdom 2002
2. E. Castillo, J.M. Gutierrez, and A.S. Hadi. *Expert Systems and Probabilistic Network Models.* Springer-Verlag, New York, NY, USA 1997
3. C.K. Chow and C.N. Liu. Approximating Discrete Probability Distributions with Dependence Trees. *IEEE Trans. on Information Theory* 14(3):462–467. IEEE Press, Piscataway, NJ, USA 1968
4. N. Friedman and M. Goldszmidt. Building Classifiers using Bayesian Networks. *Proc. 13th Nat. Conf. on Artificial Intelligence (AAAI'96, Portland, OR, USA)*, 1277–1284. AAAI Press, Menlo Park, CA, USA 1996
5. D. Geiger. An entropy-based learning algorithm of Bayesian conditional trees. *Proc. 8th Conf. on Uncertainty in Artificial Intelligence (UAI'92, Stanford, CA, USA)*, 92–97. Morgan Kaufmann, San Mateo, CA, USA 1992
6. F.V. Jensen. *An Introduction to Bayesian Networks.* UCL Press, London, United Kingdom 1996
7. J.B. Kruskal. On the Shortest Spanning Subtree of a Graph and the Traveling Salesman Problem. *Proc. American Mathematical Society* 7(1):48–50. American Mathematical Society, Providence, RI, USA 1956

8. S. Kullback and R.A. Leibler. On Information and Sufficiency. *Annals of Mathematical Statistics* 22:79–86. Institute of Mathematical Statistics, Hayward, CA, USA 1951

9. S.L. Lauritzen. *Graphical Models.* Oxford University Press, Oxford, United Kingdom 1996

10. J. Pearl. *Probabilistic Reasoning in Intelligent Systems: Networks of Plausible Inference.* Morgan Kaufmann, San Mateo, CA, USA 1988 (2nd edition 1992)

11. W.H. Press, S.A. Teukolsky, W.T. Vetterling, and B.P. Flannery. *Numerical Recipes in C — The Art of Scientific Computing (2nd edition).* Cambridge University Press, Cambridge, United Kingdom 1992

12. R.C. Prim. Shortest Connection Networks and Some Generalizations. *The Bell System Technical Journal* 36:1389-1401. Bell Laboratories, Murray Hill, NJ, USA 1957

13. J.R. Quinlan. *C4.5: Programs for Machine Learning.* Morgan Kaufmann, San Mateo, CA, USA 1993

14. G. Rebane and J. Pearl. The Recovery of Causal Polytrees from Statistical Data. *Proc. 3rd Workshop on Uncertainty in Artificial Intelligence (Seattle, WA, USA)*, 222–228. USA 1987.

15. C.E. Shannon. The Mathematical Theory of Communication. *The Bell System Technical Journal* 27:379–423. Bell Laboratories, Murray Hill, NJ, USA 1948

Bayesian Treatment of Incomplete Discrete Data Applied to Mutual Information and Feature Selection

Marcus Hutter and Marco Zaffalon

IDSIA, Galleria 2, CH-6928 Manno-Lugano, Switzerland [*]
{marcus,zaffalon}@idsia.ch,
http://www.idsia.ch/~{marcus,zaffalon}

Abstract. Given the joint chances of a pair of random variables one can compute quantities of interest, like the mutual information. The Bayesian treatment of unknown chances involves computing, from a second order prior distribution and the data likelihood, a posterior distribution of the chances. A common treatment of incomplete data is to assume ignorability and determine the chances by the expectation maximization (EM) algorithm. The two different methods above are well established but typically separated. This paper joins the two approaches in the case of Dirichlet priors, and derives efficient approximations for the mean, mode and the (co)variance of the chances and the mutual information. Furthermore, we prove the unimodality of the posterior distribution, whence the important property of convergence of EM to the global maximum in the chosen framework. These results are applied to the problem of selecting features for incremental learning and naive Bayes classification. A fast filter based on the distribution of mutual information is shown to outperform the traditional filter based on empirical mutual information on a number of incomplete real data sets.

1   Introduction

Let π_{ij} be the joint chances of a pair of random variables (i,j). Many statistical quantities can be computes if π is known; for instance the *mutual information* $I(\pi)$ used for measuring the stochastic dependency of i and j. The usual procedure in the common case of *unknown chances* π_{ij} is to use the *empirical probabilities* $\hat{\pi}_{ij} = n_{ij}/n$ as if they were precisely known chances. This is not always suitable: (*a*) The point estimate $\hat{\pi}_{ij}$ does not carry information about the reliability of the estimate. (*b*) Samples (i, j) may be incomplete in the sense that in some samples the variable i or j may not be observed.

The *Bayesian* solution to (*a*) is to use a (second order) prior distribution $p(\pi)$ over the chances π themselves, which takes account of uncertainty about π. From the prior $p(\pi)$ and the likelihood $p(D|\pi)$ of data D one can compute

---

[*] This work was supported in parts by the NSF grants 2000-61847.00 and 2100-067961.02.

A. Günter et al. (Eds.): KI 2003, LNAI 2821, pp. 396–406, 2003.

the posterior $p(\boldsymbol{\pi}|\boldsymbol{D})$. The traditional solution to (b) is to assume that the data are *missing at random* [12]. A (local) maximum likelihood estimate for $\hat{\boldsymbol{\pi}}$ can then be obtained by the *expectation-maximization* (EM) algorithm [2].

In this work we present a full Bayesian treatment of incomplete discrete data with Dirichlet prior $p(\boldsymbol{\pi})$ and apply the results to *feature selection*. This work is a natural continuation of [16], which focused on the case of complete data and, by working out a special case, provided encouraging evidence for the extension of the proposed approach to incomplete data. Here we develop that framework by creating a very general method for incomplete discrete data, providing the complete mathematical derivations, as well as experiments on incomplete real data sets. In particular, Section 2 derives expressions (in leading order in $1/n$) for $p(\boldsymbol{\pi}|\boldsymbol{D})$. In the important case (for feature selection) of missingness in one component of (i, j) only, we give closed form expressions for the mode, mean and covariance of $\boldsymbol{\pi}$. In the general missingness case we get a self-consistency equation which coincides with the EM algorithm, that is known to converge to a local maximum. We show that $p(\boldsymbol{\pi}|\boldsymbol{D})$ is actually unimodal, which implies that in fact *EM always converges to the global maximum*. We use the results to derive in Section 3 closed-form leading order expressions of the distribution of mutual information $p(I|\boldsymbol{D})$. In case of complete data, the mean and variance of I have been approximated numerically in [10] and analytically in [8]. The results are then applied to feature selection in Section 4. A popular *filter approach* discards features of low empirical mutual information $I(\hat{\boldsymbol{\pi}})$ [11,1,3]. We compare this filter to the two filters (introduced in [16] for complete data and tested empirically in this case) that use *credible intervals* based on $p(I|\boldsymbol{D})$ to robustly estimate mutual information. The filters are empirically tested in Section 5 by coupling them with the *naive Bayes classifier* [5] to incrementally learn from and classify incomplete data. On five real data sets that we used, one of the two proposed filters consistently outperforms the traditional filter.

2   Posterior Distribution for Incomplete Data

Missing data. Consider two discrete random variables, class i and feature[1] j taking values in $\{1, ..., r\}$ and $\{1, ..., s\}$, respectively, and an i.i.d. random process with samples $(i, j) \in \{1, ..., r\} \times \{1, ..., s\}$ drawn with joint probability π_{ij}. In practice one often has to deal with incomplete information. For instance, observed instances often consist of several features plus class label, but some features may not be observed, i.e. if i is a class label and j is a feature, from the pair (i, j) only i is observed. We extend the contingency table n_{ij} to include $n_{i?}$, which counts the number of instances in which only the class i is observed ($=$ number of $(i, ?)$ instances). Similarly, $n_{?j}$ counts the number of $(?, j)$ instances, where the class label is missing. We make the common assumption that the missing-data mechanism is ignorable (missing at random and distinct) [12], i.e.

---

[1] The mathematical development is independent of the interpretation as class and feature, but it is convenient to use this terminology already here.

the probability distribution of class labels i of instances with missing feature j is assumed to coincide with the marginal $\pi_{i+} := \sum_j \pi_{ij}$. Similarly, given an instance with missing class label, the probability of the feature being j is assumed to be $\pi_{+j} := \sum_i \pi_{ij}$.

Maximum likelihood estimate of π. The likelihood of a specific data set D of size $N = n + n_{+?} + n_{?+}$ with contingency table $N = \{n_{ij}, n_{i?}, n_{?j}\}$ given π, hence, is $p(D|\pi, n, n_{+?}, n_{?+}) = \prod_{ij} \pi_{ij}^{n_{ij}} \prod_i \pi_{i+}^{n_{i?}} \prod_j \pi_{+j}^{n_{?j}}$. Assuming a uniform $p(\pi) \sim 1 \cdot \delta(\pi_{++} - 1)$, Bayes' rule leads to the posterior[2]

$$p(\pi|D) = p(\pi|N) = \frac{1}{\mathcal{N}(N)} \prod_{ij} \pi_{ij}^{n_{ij}} \prod_i \pi_{i+}^{n_{i?}} \prod_j \pi_{+j}^{n_{?j}} \, \delta(\pi_{++} - 1), \qquad (1)$$

where the normalization $\mathcal{N}$ is chosen such that $\int p(\pi|N) d\pi = 1$. With missing features and classes there is no exact closed form expression for $\mathcal{N}$.

In the following, we restrict ourselves to a discussion of leading-order (in N^{-1}) expressions, which are as accurate as one can specify one's prior knowledge [8]. In leading order, the mean $E[\pi]$ coincides with the mode of $p(\pi|N)$ (=the maximum likelihood estimate) of π. The log-likelihood function $\log p(\pi|N)$ is

$$L(\pi|N) = \sum_{ij} n_{ij} \log \pi_{ij} + \sum_i n_{i?} \log \pi_{i+} + \sum_j n_{?j} \log \pi_{+j} - \log \mathcal{N}(N) - \lambda(\pi_{++} - 1),$$

where we have replaced the δ function by a Lagrange multiplier λ to take into account the restriction $\pi_{++} = 1$. The maximum is at $\frac{\partial L}{\partial \pi_{ij}} = \frac{n_{ij}}{\pi_{ij}} + \frac{n_{i?}}{\pi_{i+}} + \frac{n_{?j}}{\pi_{+j}} - \lambda = 0$. Multiplying this by π_{ij} and summing over i and j we obtain $\lambda = N$. The maximum likelihood estimate $\hat{\pi}$ is, hence, given by

$$\hat{\pi}_{ij} = \frac{1}{N} \left(n_{ij} + n_{i?} \frac{\hat{\pi}_{ij}}{\hat{\pi}_{i+}} + n_{?j} \frac{\hat{\pi}_{ij}}{\hat{\pi}_{+j}} \right). \qquad (2)$$

This is a non-linear equation in $\hat{\pi}_{ij}$, which, in general, has no closed form solution. Nevertheless (2) can be used to approximate $\hat{\pi}_{ij}$. Eq. (2) coincides with the popular expectation-maximization (EM) algorithm [2] if one inserts a first estimate $\hat{\pi}_{ij}^0 = \frac{n_{ij}}{N}$ into the r.h.s. of (2) and then uses the resulting l.h.s. $\hat{\pi}_{ij}^1$ as a new estimate, etc.

Unimodality of $p(\pi|N)$. The $rs \times rs$ Hessian matrix $H \in \mathbb{R}^{rs \cdot rs}$ of $-L$ and the second derivative in direction of the rs dimensional column vector $v \in \mathbb{R}^{rs}$ are

$$H_{(ij)(kl)}[\pi] := -\frac{\partial L}{\partial \pi_{ij} \partial \pi_{kl}} = \frac{n_{ij}}{\pi_{ij}^2} \delta_{ik} \delta_{jl} + \frac{n_{i?}}{\pi_{i+}^2} \delta_{ik} + \frac{n_{?j}}{\pi_{+j}^2} \delta_{jl},$$

---

[2] Most (but not all) non-informative priors for $p(\pi)$ also lead to a Dirichlet posterior distribution (1) with interpretation $n_{ij} = n'_{ij} + n''_{ij} - 1$, where n'_{ij} are the number of samples (i, j), and n''_{ij} comprises prior information (1 for the uniform prior, $\frac{1}{2}$ for Jeffreys' prior, 0 for Haldane's prior, $\frac{1}{rs}$ for Perks' prior, and other numbers in case of specific prior knowledge [7]). Furthermore, in leading order in $1/N$, any Dirichlet prior with $n''_{ij} = O(1)$ leads to the same results, hence we can simply assume a uniform prior. The reason for the $\delta(\pi_{++} - 1)$ is that π must be constrained to the probability simplex $\pi_{++} := \sum_{ij} \pi_{ij} = 1$.

$$\boldsymbol{v}^T \boldsymbol{H} \boldsymbol{v} = \sum_{ijkl} v_{ij} \boldsymbol{H}_{(ij)(kl)} v_{kl} = \sum_{ij} \frac{n_{ij}}{\pi_{ij}^2} v_{ij}^2 + \sum_i \frac{n_{i?}}{\pi_{i+}^2} v_{i+}^2 + \sum_j \frac{n_{?j}}{\pi_{+j}^2} v_{+j}^2 \geq 0.$$

This shows that $-L$ is a convex function of $\boldsymbol{\pi}$, hence $p(\boldsymbol{\pi}|\boldsymbol{N})$ has a single (possibly degenerate) global maximum. L is strictly convex if $n_{ij} > 0$ for all ij, since $\boldsymbol{v}^T \boldsymbol{H} \boldsymbol{v} > 0 \ \forall \boldsymbol{v} \neq 0$ in this case[3]. This implies a unique global maximum, which is attained in the interior of the probability simplex. Since EM is known to converge to a local maximum, this shows, that in fact *EM always converges to the global maximum.*

Covariance of $\boldsymbol{\pi}$. With

$$\boldsymbol{A}_{(ij)(kl)} := \boldsymbol{H}_{(ij)(kl)}[\hat{\boldsymbol{\pi}}] = N \left[\frac{\delta_{ik}\delta_{jl}}{\rho_{ij}} + \frac{\delta_{ik}}{\rho_{i?}} + \frac{\delta_{jl}}{\rho_{?j}} \right],$$

$$\rho_{ij} := N \frac{\hat{\pi}_{ij}^2}{n_{ij}}, \quad \rho_{i?} := N \frac{\hat{\pi}_{i+}^2}{n_{i?}}, \quad \rho_{?j} := N \frac{\hat{\pi}_{+j}^2}{n_{?j}}. \tag{3}$$

and $\boldsymbol{\Delta} := \boldsymbol{\pi} - \hat{\boldsymbol{\pi}}$ we can represent the posterior to leading order as an $rs - 1$ dimensional Gaussian:

$$p(\boldsymbol{\pi}|\boldsymbol{N}) \sim e^{-\frac{1}{2}\boldsymbol{\Delta}^T \boldsymbol{A}\boldsymbol{\Delta}} \delta(\Delta_{++}). \tag{4}$$

The easiest way to compute the covariance (and other quantities) is to also represent the δ-function as a narrow Gaussian of width $\varepsilon \approx 0$. Inserting $\delta(\Delta_{++}) \approx \frac{1}{\varepsilon\sqrt{2\pi}} \exp(-\frac{1}{2\varepsilon^2} \boldsymbol{\Delta}^T \boldsymbol{e}\boldsymbol{e}^T \boldsymbol{\Delta})$ into (4), where $e_{ij} = 1$ for all ij (hence $\boldsymbol{e}^T \boldsymbol{\Delta} = \Delta_{++}$), leads to a full rs-dimensional Gaussian with kernel $\tilde{\boldsymbol{A}} = \boldsymbol{A} + \boldsymbol{u}\boldsymbol{v}^T$, $\boldsymbol{u} = \boldsymbol{v} = \frac{1}{\varepsilon}\boldsymbol{e}$. The covariance of a Gaussian with kernel $\tilde{\boldsymbol{A}}$ is $\tilde{\boldsymbol{A}}^{-1}$. Using the Sherman-Morrison formula $\tilde{\boldsymbol{A}}^{-1} = \boldsymbol{A}^{-1} - \boldsymbol{A}^{-1} \frac{\boldsymbol{u}\boldsymbol{v}^T}{1+\boldsymbol{v}^T \boldsymbol{A}^{-1}\boldsymbol{u}} \boldsymbol{A}^{-1}$ [14, p73] and $\varepsilon \to 0$ we get

$$\mathrm{Cov}_{(ij)(kl)}[\boldsymbol{\pi}] := E[\Delta_{ij}\Delta_{kl}] \simeq [\tilde{\boldsymbol{A}}^{-1}]_{(ij)(kl)} = \left[\boldsymbol{A}^{-1} - \frac{\boldsymbol{A}^{-1}\boldsymbol{e}\boldsymbol{e}^T \boldsymbol{A}^{-1}}{\boldsymbol{e}^T \boldsymbol{A}^{-1}\boldsymbol{e}} \right]_{(ij)(kl)}, \tag{5}$$

where $\simeq$ denotes $=$ up to terms of order N^{-2}. Singular $\boldsymbol{A}$ are easily avoided by choosing a prior such that $n_{ij} > 0$ for all ij. $\boldsymbol{A}$ may be inverted exactly or iteratively, the latter by a trivial inversion of the diagonal part $\delta_{ik}\delta_{jl}/\rho_{ij}$ and by treating $\delta_{ik}/\rho_{i?} + \delta_{jl}/\rho_{?j}$ as a perturbation.

Missing features only, no missing classes. In the case of missing features only (no missing classes), i.e. for $n_{?j} = 0$, closed form expressions for $\mathrm{Cov}[\boldsymbol{\pi}]$ can be obtained. If we sum (2) over j we get $\hat{\pi}_{i+} = \frac{N_{i+}}{N}$ with $N_{i+} := n_{i+} + n_{i?}$.

---

[3] Note that $n_{i?} > 0 \ \forall i$ is not sufficient, since $v_{i+} \equiv 0$ for $\boldsymbol{v} \neq 0$ is possible. Actually $v_{++} = 0$.

Inserting $\hat{\pi}_{i+} = \frac{N_{i+}}{N}$ into the r.h.s. of (2) and solving w.r.t. $\hat{\pi}_{ij}$ we get the explicit expression

$$\hat{\pi}_{ij} = \frac{N_{i+}}{N}\frac{n_{ij}}{n_{i+}}. \tag{6}$$

Furthermore, it can easily be verified (by multiplication) that $\boldsymbol{A}_{(ij)(kl)} = N[\delta_{ik}\delta_{jl}/\rho_{ij} + \delta_{ik}/\rho_{i?}]$ has inverse $[\boldsymbol{A}^{-1}]_{(ij)(kl)} = \frac{1}{N}[\rho_{ij}\delta_{ik}\delta_{jl} - \frac{\rho_{ij}\rho_{kl}}{\rho_{i+}+\rho_{i?}}\delta_{ik}]$. With the abbreviations

$$\tilde{Q}_{i?} := \frac{\rho_{i?}}{\rho_{i?}+\rho_{i+}} \quad \text{and} \quad \tilde{Q} := \sum_i \rho_{i+}\tilde{Q}_{i?} \tag{7}$$

we get $[\boldsymbol{A}^{-1}\boldsymbol{e}]_{ij} = \sum_{kl}[\boldsymbol{A}^{-1}]_{(ij)(kl)} = \frac{1}{N}\rho_{ij}\tilde{Q}_{i?}$ and $\boldsymbol{e}^T\boldsymbol{A}^{-1}\boldsymbol{e} = \tilde{Q}/N$. Inserting everything into (5) we get

$$\text{Cov}_{(ij)(kl)}[\boldsymbol{\pi}] \simeq \frac{1}{N}\left[\rho_{ij}\delta_{ik}\delta_{jl} - \frac{\rho_{ij}\rho_{kl}}{\rho_{i+}+\rho_{i?}}\delta_{ik} - \frac{\rho_{ij}\tilde{Q}_{i?}\rho_{kl}\tilde{Q}_{k?}}{\tilde{Q}}\right]. \tag{8}$$

Expressions for the general case. The contribution from unlabeled classes can be interpreted as a rank s modification of $\boldsymbol{A}$ in the case of no missing classes. One can use Woodbury's formula $[\boldsymbol{B} + \boldsymbol{U}\boldsymbol{D}\boldsymbol{V}^T]^{-1} = \boldsymbol{B}^{-1} - \boldsymbol{B}^{-1}\boldsymbol{U}[\boldsymbol{D}^{-1}+\boldsymbol{V}^T\boldsymbol{B}^{-1}\boldsymbol{U}]^{-1}\boldsymbol{V}^T\boldsymbol{B}^{-1}$ [14, p75] with $\boldsymbol{B}_{(ij)(kl)} = \delta_{ik}\delta_{jl}/\rho_{ij}+\delta_{ik}/\rho_{i?}$, $\boldsymbol{D}_{jl} = \delta_{jl}/\rho_{?j}$, and $\boldsymbol{U}_{(ij)l} = \boldsymbol{V}_{(ij)l} = \delta_{jl}$ to reduce the inversion of the $rs \times rs$ matrix $\boldsymbol{A}$ to the inversion of only a *single* s-dimensional matrix. The result (which may be inserted into (5)) can be written in the form

$$[\boldsymbol{A}^{-1}]_{(ij)(kl)} = \frac{1}{N}\left[F_{ijl}\delta_{ik} - \sum_{mn}F_{ijm}[\boldsymbol{G}^{-1}]_{mn}F_{kln}\right], \tag{9}$$

$$F_{ijl} := \rho_{ij}\delta_{jl} - \frac{\rho_{ij}\rho_{kl}}{\rho_{i?}+\rho_{i+}}, \qquad G_{mn} := \rho_{?n}\delta_{mn} + F_{+mn}.$$

3   Distribution of Mutual Information

Mutual information I. An important measure of the stochastic dependence of $\imath$ and $\jmath$ is the mutual information

$$I(\boldsymbol{\pi}) = \sum_{i=1}^{r}\sum_{j=1}^{s} \pi_{ij}\log\frac{\pi_{ij}}{\pi_{i+}\pi_{+j}} = \sum_{ij}\pi_{ij}\log\pi_{ij} - \sum_i \pi_{i+}\log\pi_{i+} - \sum_j \pi_{+j}\log\pi_{+j}.$$

The point estimate for I is $I(\hat{\boldsymbol{\pi}})$. In the Bayesian approach one takes the posterior (1) from which the posterior probability density of the mutual information can, in principle, be computed:[4]

---

[4] $I(\boldsymbol{\pi})$ denotes the mutual information for the specific chances $\boldsymbol{\pi}$, whereas I in the context above is just some non-negative real number. I will also denote the mutual information *random variable* in the expectation $E[I]$ and variance $\text{Var}[I]$. Expectations are *always* w.r.t. to the posterior distribution $p(\boldsymbol{\pi}|\boldsymbol{N})$.

$$p(I|\boldsymbol{N}) = \int \delta(I(\boldsymbol{\pi}) - I)p(\boldsymbol{\pi}|\boldsymbol{N})d^{rs}\boldsymbol{\pi}.^5 \qquad (10)$$

The $\delta(\cdot)$ distribution restricts the integral to $\boldsymbol{\pi}$ for which $I(\boldsymbol{\pi}) = I$. For large sample size, $N \to \infty$, $p(\boldsymbol{\pi}|\boldsymbol{N})$ is strongly peaked around the mode $\boldsymbol{\pi} = \hat{\boldsymbol{\pi}}$ and $p(I|\boldsymbol{N})$ gets strongly peaked around the frequency estimate $I = I(\hat{\boldsymbol{\pi}})$. The (central) moments of I are of special interest. The mean

$$E[I] = \int_0^\infty I \cdot p(I|\boldsymbol{N}) \, dI = \int I(\boldsymbol{\pi})p(\boldsymbol{\pi}|\boldsymbol{N})d^{rs}\boldsymbol{\pi} \; = \; I(\hat{\boldsymbol{\pi}}) + O(N^{-1}) \qquad (11)$$

coincides in leading order with the point estimate, where $\hat{\boldsymbol{\pi}}$ has been computed in Section 2. Together with the variance $\mathrm{Var}[I] = E[(I - E[I])^2] = E[I^2] - E[I]^2$ (computed below) we can approximate (10) by a Gaussian[6]

$$p(I|\boldsymbol{N}) \sim \exp\left(-\frac{(I - I(\hat{\boldsymbol{\pi}}))^2}{2\mathrm{Var}[I]}\right) \sim \exp\left(-\frac{(I - E[I])^2}{2\mathrm{Var}[I]}\right) \qquad (12)$$

In a previous work we derived higher order central moments (skewness and kurtosis) and higher order (in N^{-1}) approximations in the case of complete data [8].

Variance of I. The leading order variance of the mutual information $I(\boldsymbol{\pi})$ has been related[7] in [8] to the covariance of $\boldsymbol{\pi}$:

$$\mathrm{Var}[I] \simeq \sum_{ijkl} \log \frac{\hat{\pi}_{ij}}{\hat{\pi}_{i+}\hat{\pi}_{+j}} \log \frac{\hat{\pi}_{kl}}{\hat{\pi}_{k+}\hat{\pi}_{+l}} \mathrm{Cov}_{(ij)(kl)}[\boldsymbol{\pi}] \qquad (13)$$

Inserting (8) for the covariance into (13) we get for the variance of the mutual information in leading order in $1/N$ in the case of missing features only, the following expression:

$$\mathrm{Var}[I] \simeq \frac{1}{N}[\tilde{K} - \tilde{J}^2/\tilde{Q} - \tilde{P}], \qquad \tilde{K} := \sum_{ij} \rho_{ij} \left(\log \frac{\hat{\pi}_{ij}}{\hat{\pi}_{i+}\hat{\pi}_{+j}}\right)^2, \qquad (14)$$

$$\tilde{P} := \sum_i \frac{\tilde{J}_{i+}^2 Q_{i?}}{\rho_{i?}}, \qquad \tilde{J} := \sum_i \tilde{J}_{i+}\tilde{Q}_{i?}, \qquad \tilde{J}_{i+} := \sum_j \rho_{ij} \log \frac{\hat{\pi}_{ij}}{\hat{\pi}_{i+}\hat{\pi}_{+j}}.$$

---

[5] Since $0 \le I(\boldsymbol{\pi}) \le I_{max}$ with sharp upper bound $I_{max} = \min\{\log r, \log s\}$, the domain of $p(I|\boldsymbol{n})$ is $[0, I_{max}]$, and integrals over I may be restricted to $\int_0^{I_{max}}$.

[6] For $I(\hat{\boldsymbol{\pi}}) \ne 0$ the central limit theorem ensures convergence of $p(I|\boldsymbol{N})$ to a Gaussian. Using a Beta distribution instead of (12), which also converges to a Gaussian, has slight advantages over (12) [16].

[7] $\hat{\boldsymbol{\pi}}$ was defined in [8] as the mean $E[\boldsymbol{\pi}]$ whereas $\hat{\boldsymbol{\pi}}$ has been defined in this work as the ML estimate. Furthermore the Dirichlet priors differ. Since to leading order both definitions of $\boldsymbol{\pi}$ coincide, the prior does not matter, and the expression is also valid for incomplete data case, the use of (13) in this work is permitted.

A closed form expression for $\mathcal{N}(\mathbf{N})$ also exists. Symmetric expressions for missing classes only (no missing features) can be obtained. Note that for the complete case $n_{?j} = n_{i?} \equiv 0$, we have $\hat{\pi}_{ij} = \rho_{ij} = \frac{n_{ij}}{n}$, $\rho_{i?} = \infty$, $\tilde{Q}_{i?} = 1$, $\tilde{J} = J$, $\tilde{K} = K$, and $\tilde{P} = 0$, consistent with [8] (where J and K are defined and the accuracy is discussed).

There is at least one reason for minutely having inserted all expressions into each other and introducing quite a number definitions. In the so presented form all expressions involve at most a double sum. Hence, the overall computation time of the mean and variance is $O(rs)$ in the case of missing features only.

Expression for the general case. The result for the covariance (5) can be inserted into (13) to obtain the variance of the mutual information to leading order.

$$\mathrm{Var}[I] \simeq \boldsymbol{l}^T \boldsymbol{A}^{-1} \boldsymbol{l} - (\boldsymbol{l}^T \boldsymbol{A}^{-1} \boldsymbol{e})^2 / (\boldsymbol{e}^T \boldsymbol{A}^{-1} \boldsymbol{e}) \quad \text{where} \quad l_{ij} = \log \frac{\hat{\pi}_{ij}}{\hat{\pi}_{i+}\hat{\pi}_{+j}}$$

Inserting (9) and rearranging terms appropriately we can compute $\mathrm{Var}[I]$ in time $O(rs)$ plus the time $O(s^2 r)$ to compute the $s \times s$ matrix $\boldsymbol{G}$ and time $O(s^3)$ to invert it, plus the time $O(\#\cdot rs)$ for determining $\hat{\pi}_{ij}$, where $\#$ is the number of iterations of EM. Of course, one can and should always choose $s \leq r$. Note that these expressions converge for $N \to \infty$ to the exact values. The fraction of data with missing feature or class needs not to be small.

In the following we apply the obtained results to feature selection for incomplete data. Since we only used labeled data we could use (11) with (6), and (14) with (7) and (3).

4   Feature Selection

Feature selection is a basic step in the process of building classifiers [1]. We consider the well-known filter (F) that computes the empirical mutual information $I(\hat{\pi})$ between features and the class, and discards features with $I(\hat{\pi}) < \varepsilon$ for some threshold ε [11]. This is an easy and effective approach that has gained popularity with time.

We compare F to the two filters introduced in [16] for the case of complete data, and extended here to the more general case. The *backward filter* (BF) *discards* a feature if its value of mutual information with the class is less than or equal to ε with high probability $\bar{p}$ (discard if $p(I \leq \varepsilon | \mathbf{N}) \geq \bar{p}$). The *forward filter* (FF) *includes* a feature if the mutual information is greater than ε with high probability $\bar{p}$ (include if $p(I > \varepsilon | \mathbf{N}) \geq \bar{p}$). BF is a conservative filter, because it will only discard features after observing substantial evidence supporting their irrelevance. FF instead will tend to use fewer features, i.e. only those for which there is substantial evidence about them being useful in predicting the class.

For the subsequent classification task we use the naive Bayes classifier [4], which is often a good classification model. Despite its simplifying assumptions (see [6]), it often competes successfully with much more complex classifiers, such

Table 1. Incomplete data sets used for the experiments, together with their number of features, instances, missing values, and the relative frequency of the majority class. The data sets are available from the UCI repository of machine learning data sets [13]. Average number of features selected by the filters on the entire data set are reported in the last three columns. FF always selected fewer features than F; F almost always selected fewer features than BF. Prediction accuracies where significantly different only for the Hypothyroidloss data set.

Name	#feat.	#inst.	#m.v.	maj.class	FF	F	BF
Audiology	69	226	317	0.212	64.3	68.0	68.7
Crx	15	690	67	0.555	9.7	12.6	13.8
Horse-colic	18	368	1281	0.630	11.8	16.1	17.4
Hypothyroidloss	23	3163	1980	0.952	4.3	8.3	13.2
Soybean-large	35	683	2337	0.135	34.2	35	35

as C4.5 [15]. Our experiments focus on the incremental use of the naive Bayes classifier, a natural learning process when the data are available sequentially: the data set is read instance by instance; each time, the chosen filter selects a subset of features that the naive Bayes uses to classify the new instance; the naive Bayes then updates its knowledge by taking into consideration the new instance and its actual class. Note that for increasing sizes of the learning set the filters converge to the same behavior, since the variance of I tends to zero (see [16] for details).

For each filter, we are interested in experimentally evaluating two quantities: for each instance of the data set, the average number of correct predictions (namely, the prediction accuracy) of the naive Bayes classifier up to such instance; and the average number of features used. By these quantities we can compare the filters and judge their effectiveness.

The implementation details for the following experiments include: using the Gaussian approximation (12) to the distribution of mutual information with the mean (11) using (6), and the variance (14) using (7) and (3); using natural logarithms everywhere; and setting the level $\bar{p}$ of the posterior probability to 0.95, and the threshold ε to 0.003 as discussed in [16].

5   Experimental Analysis

Table 1 lists five data sets together with the experimental results. These are real data sets on a number of different domains. The data sets presenting non-nominal features have been pre-discretized by MLC++ [9], default options (i.e., the common entropy based discretization). This step may remove some features judging them as irrelevant, so the number of features in the table refers to the data sets after the possible discretization. The instances have been randomly sorted before starting the experiments.

The last three columns of Table 1 show that FF selects lower (i.e. better) number of features than the commonly used filter F, which in turn, selects lower

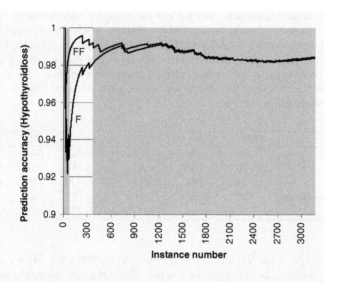

Fig. 1. Prediction accuracies of the naive Bayes with filters F and FF on the Hypothy-roidloss data set. BF is not reported because there is no significant difference with the F curve. The differences between F and FF are significant in the range of observations 71–374 (white area). The maximum difference is achieved at observation 71, where the accuracies are 0.986 (FF) vs. 0.930 (F).

number of features than the filter BF. We used the *two-tails paired t test* at level 0.05 to compare the prediction accuracies of the naive Bayes with different filters, in the first k instances of the data set, for each k. On four data sets out of five, both the differences between FF and F, and the differences between F and BF, were never statistically significant, despite the different number of used features, as indicated in Table 1. The reduction can be very pronounced, as for the Hypothyroidloss data set. This is also the only data set for which the prediction accuracies of F and FF are significantly different, in favor of the latter. This is displayed in Figure 1. Similar (even stronger) results have been found for 10 complete data sets analyzed in [16].

The most prominent evidence from the experiments is the better performance of FF versus the traditional filter F. In the following we look at FF from another perspective to exemplify and explain its behavior. FF includes a feature if $p(I > \varepsilon | n) \geq \bar{p}$, according to its definition. Let us assume that FF is realized by means of the Gaussian (as in the experiments above), and let us choose $\bar{p} \approx 0.977$. The condition $p(I > \varepsilon | n) \geq \bar{p}$ becomes $\varepsilon \leq E[I] - 2 \cdot \sqrt{\mathrm{Var}[I]}$, or, in an approximate way, $I(\hat{\pi}) \geq \varepsilon + 2 \cdot \sqrt{\mathrm{Var}[I]}$, given that $I(\hat{\pi})$ is the first-order approximation of $E[I]$ (cf. (11)). We can regard $\varepsilon + 2 \cdot \sqrt{\mathrm{Var}[I]}$ as a new threshold ε'. Under this interpretation, we see that FF is approximately equal to using the filter F with the bigger threshold ε'. This interpretation makes it also clearer why FF can be better suited than F for sequential learning tasks. In sequential learning, $\mathrm{Var}[I]$

decreases as new units are read; this makes ε' to be a self-adapting threshold that adjusts the level of caution (in including features) as more units are read. In the limit, ε' is equal to ε. This characteristic of self-adaptation, which is absent in F, seems to be decisive to the success of FF.

6 Conclusions

We addressed the problem of the reliability of empirical estimates for the chances π and the mutual information I in the case of incomplete discrete data. We used the Bayesian framework to derive reliable and quickly computable approxima-tions for the mean, mode and the (co)variance of π and $I(\pi)$ under the posterior distribution $p(\pi|D)$. We showed that $p(\pi|D)$ is unimodal, which implies that EM always converges to the global maximum. The results allowed us to effi-ciently determine credible intervals for I with incomplete data. Applications are manifold, e.g. to robustly infer classification trees or Bayesian networks. As far as feature selection is concerned, we empirically showed that the forward filter, which includes a feature if the mutual information is greater than ε with high probability, outperforms the popular filter based on empirical mutual informa-tion in sequential learning tasks. This result for incomplete data is obtained jointly with the naive Bayes classifier. More broadly speaking, obtaining the dis-tribution of mutual information when data are incomplete may form a basis on which reliable and effective uncertain models can be developed.

References

1. A. L. Blum and P. Langley. Selection of relevant features and examples in machine learning. *Artificial Intelligence*, 97(1–2):245–271, 1997. Special issue on relevance.
2. T. T. Chen and S. E. Fienberg. Two-dimensional contingency tables with both completely and partially cross-classified data. *Biometrics*, 32:133–144, 1974.
3. J. Cheng, C. Hatzis, H. Hayashi, M. Krogel, S. Morishita, D. Page, and J. Sese. KDD cup 2001 report. *ACM SIGKDD Explorations*, 3(2), 2002.
4. R. O. Duda and P. E. Hart. *Pattern classification and scene analysis*. Wiley, New York, 1973.
5. R. O. Duda, P. E. Hart, and D. G. Stork. *Pattern classification*. Wiley, 2001. 2nd edition.
6. P. Domingos and M. Pazzani. On the optimality of the simple Bayesian classifier under zero-one loss. *Machine Learning*, 29(2/3):103–130, 1997.
7. A. Gelman, J. B. Carlin, H. S. Stern, and D. B. Rubin. *Bayesian Data Analysis*. Chapman, 1995.
8. M. Hutter. Distribution of mutual information. In T. G. Dietterich, S. Becker, and Z. Ghahramani, editors, *Advances in Neural Information Processing Systems 14*, pages 399–406, Cambridge, MA, 2002. MIT Press.
9. R. Kohavi, G. John, R. Long, D. Manley, and K. Pfleger. MLC++: a machine learning library in C++. In *Tools with Artificial Intelligence*, pages 740–743. IEEE Computer Society Press, 1994.
10. G. D. Kleiter. The posterior probability of Bayes nets with strong dependences. *Soft Computing*, 3:162–173, 1999.

11. D. D. Lewis. Feature selection and feature extraction for text categorization. In *Proc. of Speech and Natural Language Workshop*, pages 212–217, San Francisco, 1992. Morgan Kaufmann.

12. R. J. A. Little and D. B. Rubin. *Statistical Analysis with Missing Data*. John-Wiley, New York, 1987.

13. P. M. Murphy and D. W. Aha. UCI repository of machine learning databases, 1995. http://www.sgi.com/Technology/mlc/db/.

14. W. H. Press, B. P. Flannery, S. A. Teukolsky, and W. T. Vetterling. *Numerical Recipes in C: The Art of Scientific Computing*. Cambridge University Press, Cambridge, second edition, 1992.

15. J. R. Quinlan. *C4.5: Programs for Machine Learning*. Morgan Kaufmann, San Mateo, 1993.

16. M. Zaffalon and M. Hutter. Robust feature selection by mutual information distributions. In A. Darwiche and N. Friedman, editors, *Proceedings of the 18th International Conference on Uncertainty in Artificial Intelligence (UAI-2002)*, pages 577–584, San Francisco, CA., 2002. Morgan Kaufmann.

Fusing Probabilistic Information on Maximum Entropy

Gabriele Kern-Isberner[1] and Wilhelm Rödder[2]

[1] FernUniversität Hagen, Depart. of Computer Science
58084 Hagen, Germany
`Gabriele.Kern-Isberner@fernuni-hagen.de`

[2] FernUniversität Hagen, Depart. of Economics,
58084 Hagen, Germany
`Wilhelm.Roedder@fernuni-hagen.de`

Abstract. We present a method to fuse pieces of probabilistic information stemming from different sources which is based on information theoretical optimization techniques. We use the well-known principle of maximum entropy to process information most faithfully, while interactions between the different knowledge bases are precluded. The so-defined fusion operator satisfies basic demands, such as commutativity and the Pareto principle. A detailed analysis shows it to merge the corresponding epistemic states. Furthermore, it induces a numerical fusion operator that computes the information theoretical mean of probabilities.

1 Introduction

The problem of combining different pieces of information is not new. Actually, already when designing the first expert systems, it had to be implicitly dealt with in the knowledge acquisition process, in order to build up a consistent and expressive knowledge base from opinions provided by different experts. It is also closely related to belief change theory [1], the aim of which is to make a belief state compatible with a new piece of information.

The increasing popularity and relevance of multi-agent and distributed systems in recent years, however, made information fusion a major topic in Artificial Intelligence. Its principal concern is to merge information stemming from different sources in order to make this merged information usable for purposes such as query answering, or decision making (for a profound discussion of this notion and a broad overview, cf. [2]). Although information fusion has many facets, and the methods depend highly on the respective application and context, its basic problems can be described as solving conflicting beliefs and handling inconsistencies.

This paper is concerned with information fusion in a classical multi-agent scenario: The sources providing information are intelligent agents, each agent doing so to the best of their knowledge. Also information extracted from statistical data or from literature is considered as being stated by a virtual agent

A. Günter et al. (Eds.): KI 2003, LNAI 2821, pp. 407–420, 2003.

and can be taken into account. These pieces of information may state complete or incomplete knowledge, but in any case, they are assumed to be a consistent projection of the epistemic state of the corresponding agent. Conflicts that may arise are not necessarily caused by mistakes but are due to differences in background knowledge, or different points of view of the agents. A typical example for such an information fusion problem is to build up a consistent knowledge base from information provided by different medical experts.

As to the complexity of belief, it must be noted that many of the papers that address information fusion only deal with information expressed by classical formulas. Similar to the situation in belief revision theory [3], preferential relations may serve to guide reasonable fusion processes in this case [4]. Maynard-Reid II and Lehmann [5] consider binary relations as general representations of belief states and present operators to combine such relations. Also work has been done on fusing possibilistic degrees of belief [6]. In this paper, we are working in a most complex environment: The pieces of information we are going to combine are probabilistic rule bases, i.e. consistent sets of probabilistic conditionals. Knowledge bases of this kind are often used in probabilistic expert systems ([7, 8]; see also [9,10]); they are also a basic ingredient in probabilistic networks [11].

The methodology we build upon is directly derived from information theory: We fuse probabilistic information with the help of the *principle of maximum entropy*, abbreviated in the following as the *ME-principle*. This well-known principle [12,13,14] handles information most faithfully. In various papers, the relevance and usefulness of the ME-principle and of its generalization, the *principle of minimum cross-entropy*, for inductive knowledge representation and belief change operations has been shown [15,16,17,18]. Its crucial features are the unbiased way in which it processes incomplete probabilistic information, and its appropriateness for dealing with conditional relationships. Thus, it also provides an ideal framework for fusing probabilistic rule bases. We take up the idea from [19], but show that a straightforward approach yields possibly undesired, weakening effects. We fix this problem and define an *ME-fusion-operator* that computes kind of mean value from probabilities describing degrees of belief, given by different experts. In particular, if all experts agree on a certain probability, ME-fusion returns this same probability. It should be emphasized that the ME-fusion operator introduced in this paper is not apt to combine values of attributes, such as "colours" or "diseases", but fuses (probabilistic) degrees of beliefs on which value is the correct one. Such fusion operators may be called *epistemic*. Indeed, we will show that actually not knowledge bases, but complete epistemic states (here represented by probability distributions) are merged under ME-fusion. As a direct application of our methods, we derive a fusion operator for probabilities that yields an *information theoretical mean value* for a set of probabilities. In particular, this numerical fusion operator may be used to offer precise probabilities suitable for ME-propagation, when the agents are only able to state imprecise, interval-valued probabilities.

This paper is organized as follows: Section 2 starts with useful preliminaries, and Section 3 briefly recalls the maximum entropy methodology, as far as it is needed here. Section 4 states some basic postulates for probabilistic information fusion, and shows how the ME-approach can be used to realize fusion in accordance with these postulates. In Section 5, we go into details and make clear how ME-fusion actually works, whereas in Section 6, we present a numerical fusion operator for probabilities. Section 7 concludes this paper.

2 Logical and Probabilistic Background

Let $\mathcal{L}$ be a propositional logical language, finitely generated by propositional variables from an alphabet $\mathcal{V} = \{a, b, c, \ldots\}$. Formulas from $\mathcal{L}$ are well-formed in the usual way by use of the junctors $\wedge$ (*and*), $\vee$ (*or*), and $\neg$ (*not*), and will be denoted by uppercase letters, $A, B, C, \ldots$. To simplify notation, we will omit the $\wedge$-junctor in conjunctions and simply juxtapose conjuncts, i.e. $AB = A \wedge B$. Moreover, instead of $\neg A$, we will write $\overline{A}$. Ω is the set of all classical-logical interpretations of $\mathcal{L}$.

This Boolean frame is extended by a binary, non-Boolean conditional operator, $|$. Formulas of the form $(B|A)$ are called *conditionals*, or *rules*. In a second extension step, propositional and conditional formulas are assigned a real number $x \in [0, 1]$, representing a probability. Propositional formulas $A \in \mathcal{L}$ are identified with the conditional $(A|\top)$, where $\top$ is any tautology. So, the syntactical objects we will consider in this paper have the form $(B|A)[x]$, $A, B \in \mathcal{L}, x \in [0, 1]$.

As to the semantics, the models are probability distributions, P, over the propositional variables $\mathcal{V}$. P *satisfies* a conditional $(B|A)[x]$, $P \models (B|A)[x]$, iff $P(A) > 0$ and $P(B|A) = \frac{P(AB)}{P(A)} = x$. This satisfaction relation generalizes to sets of conditionals in a straightforward way. Our probabilities will be subjective probabilities, so the elements $\omega \in \Omega$ should be taken as possible worlds, rather than statistical elementary events.

A set $\mathcal{R} = \{(B_1|A_1)[x_1], \ldots, (B_m|A_m)[x_m]\}$ of probabilistic conditionals is *consistent* iff it has a model P, i.e. iff there is a distribution P with $P \models \mathcal{R}$. Otherwise, it is called *inconsistent*. For a propositional formula W, we define the *conditioning of $\mathcal{R}$ by W* via

$$\mathcal{R}|W := \{(B_1|A_1 W)[x_1], \ldots, (B_m|A_m W)[x_m]\}$$

3 Probabilistic Reasoning on Maximum Entropy

The principle of maximum entropy is a well-known technique to represent (mostly incomplete) probabilistic knowledge inductively (cf. e.g. [12]). Entropy is a notion stemming from information theory, and it quantifies the indeterminateness inherent to a distribution P by $H(P) = -\sum_\omega P(\omega) \log P(\omega)$. Given a consistent set $\mathcal{R} = \{(B_1|A_1)[x_1], \ldots, (B_m|A_m)[x_m]\}$ of probabilistic conditionals, the *principle of maximum entropy (ME-principle)*

$$\max H(Q) = -\sum_\omega Q(\omega) \log Q(\omega) \tag{1}$$

s.t. Q is a probability distribution with $Q \models \mathcal{R}$

solves (uniquely) the problem of representing $\mathcal{R}$ by a probability distribution without adding information unnecessarily [20]. The resulting distribution is denoted by $ME(\mathcal{R})$. The ME-approach follows the paradigm of *informational economy* and is particularly well-behaved, as has been proved by several authors [13, 21,15,22]. Using well-known Lagrange techniques, we may represent $ME(\mathcal{R})$ in the form

$$ME(\mathcal{R})(\omega) = \alpha_0 \prod_{\substack{1 \leqslant i \leqslant n \\ \omega \models A_i B_i}} \alpha_i^{1-x_i} \prod_{\substack{1 \leqslant i \leqslant n \\ \omega \models A_i \overline{B_i}}} \alpha_i^{-x_i}, \tag{2}$$

with the α_i's being exponentials of the Lagrange multipliers, one for each conditional in $\mathcal{R}$, and α_0 simply arises as a normalizing factor. Since, by construction, $ME(\mathcal{R})$ satisfies all conditionals in $\mathcal{R}$, $\alpha_1, \ldots, \alpha_n$ are solutions of the nonlinear equations

$$\alpha_i = \frac{x_i}{1 - x_i} \frac{\displaystyle\sum_{\omega \models A_i \overline{B_i}} \prod_{\substack{j \neq i \\ \omega \models A_j B_j}} \alpha_j^{1-x_j} \prod_{\substack{j \neq i \\ \omega \models A_j \overline{B_j}}} \alpha_j^{-x_j}}{\displaystyle\sum_{\omega \models A_i B_i} \prod_{\substack{j \neq i \\ \omega \models A_j B_j}} \alpha_j^{1-x_j} \prod_{\substack{j \neq i \\ \omega \models A_j \overline{B_j}}} \alpha_j^{-x_j}}, \tag{3}$$

$$\text{with} \quad \alpha_i \begin{cases} > 0 & : \quad x_i \in (0,1) \\ = \infty & : \quad x_i = 1 \\ = 0 & : \quad x_i = 0 \end{cases} , \ 1 \leqslant i \leqslant n, \tag{4}$$

using the conventions $\infty^0 = 1$, $\infty^{-1} = 0$ and $0^0 = 1$ (cf. [22]). Each α_i symbolizes the impact of the corresponding rule in $\mathcal{R}$ in the resulting distribution $ME(\mathcal{R})$. The representation (2) is crucial to understand the fundamental meaning of the ME-approach for processing conditional information [15,22], even in more qualitative environments [17].

All ME-calculations in this paper have been carried out with the system shell SPIRIT [9,8].

4   Information Fusion via the ME-Approach

When building up knowledge bases, one often is presented with the problem to fuse knowledge coming from different experts, or to combine expert knowledge with knowledge from statistical data. In the framework dealt with in this paper, information is provided by sets $\mathcal{R}_1, \ldots, \mathcal{R}_n$ of probabilistic conditionals. We assume each of these sets $\mathcal{R}_i$ to be consistent; inconsistent rule bases have to be split up into consistent subbases. The union $\bigcup_{i=1}^n \mathcal{R}_i$, however, may be inconsistent, or even plainly contradictory in that identical formulas may be assigned different probabilities.

In the following, we will explain how to use ME-methodology for information fusion in this case; in detail, we will

- merge the rule bases $\mathcal{R}_1, \ldots, \mathcal{R}_n$ into one (consistent) rule base $\mathcal{R} := \mathcal{R}_1 \odot \ldots \odot \mathcal{R}_n$, and then

- apply the principle of maximum entropy to build up a complete probability distribution $F_{ME}(\mathcal{R}_1, \ldots, \mathcal{R}_n) = ME(\mathcal{R}_1 \odot \ldots \odot \mathcal{R}_n)$ which can be used for further inferences.

Note that, although the terms *merging* and *fusion* are often used synonymously, in our two-step approach we will use *merging* for the combination of *knowledge bases* $\mathcal{R}_1, \ldots, \mathcal{R}_n$, and *fusion* for the overall aggregation of knowledge in one (ideal) belief state, which will be denoted by $F(\mathcal{R}_1, \ldots, \mathcal{R}_n)$ and is assumed to be represented by a probability distribution here.

The basic idea is to consider each set $\mathcal{R}_i$ of probabilistic rules as describing the world from a certain point of view, W_i, provided by an intelligent agent i, and to condition the rules accordingly. This eliminates inconsistencies between the rule bases. So, for each agent $i, 1 \leqslant i \leqslant n$, a new binary variable W_i is introduced representing their point of view. Then the union $\mathcal{R}_1|W_1 \cup \ldots \cup \mathcal{R}_n|W_n$ is consistent. The following simple example shows, however, that this first, straightforward approach to merge probabilistic rule bases yields undesired effects when combined with ME-methodology.

Example 1. We consider the following sets $\mathcal{R}_1$, $\mathcal{R}_2$ of probabilistic rules specified by two different experts: $\mathcal{R}_1 = \{A[0.7]\}$, $\mathcal{R}_2 = \{A[0.8]\}$. The experts disagree on the probability of the fact A, so $\mathcal{R}_1 \cup \mathcal{R}_2$ is obviously inconsistent. Conditioning each fact on the corresponding expert, however, makes both pieces of knowledge compatible – $\mathcal{R}_1|W_1 \cup \mathcal{R}_2|W_2$ is consistent, where $\mathcal{R}_1|W_1 = \{(A|W_1)[0.7]\}$, $\mathcal{R}_2|W_2 = \{(A|W_2)[0.8]\}$. Thus, $P^* := ME(\mathcal{R}_1|W_1 \cup \mathcal{R}_2|W_2)$ can be computed (e.g., by using SPIRIT [8]), and $P^*(A)$ is to reflect the fused information. But we find $P^*(A) = 0.6613$ – a disappointingly low value. We might have expected kind of average between 0.7 and 0.8, the information, however, got weakened. On the other hand, referring explicitly to the agents yields a reinforcing effect: $P^*(A|W_1W_2) = 0.8270$, a value which is likewise not within the interval $[0.7, 0.8]$.

These unexpected effects become even more evident when we assume that both experts agree and specify the same degree of belief for A: $\mathcal{R}_1' = \mathcal{R}_2' = \{A[0.7]\}$. Here, the most intuitive result of a fusion process would be to assign A the probability 0.7. Constructing a distribution $P^{*\prime} := ME(\mathcal{R}_1'|W_1 \cup \mathcal{R}_2'|W_2)$ in the same way as above, however, yields the probabilities $P^{*\prime}(A) = 0.6325$ and $P^{*\prime}(A|W_1W_2) = 0.7598$.

Although there may be good reasons for such a weakening or reinforcement, such effects should be controlled and not appear as unexpected by-products. Moreover, it should also be able to model the general case of non-interfering knowledge bases $\mathcal{R}_i$, each providing an independent piece of information. Our main focus is on a proper definition of the merging operator $\odot$ to combine rule bases $\mathcal{R}_1, \ldots \mathcal{R}_n$. As outlined above, the actual fusion work will be done by ME-technology in a straightforward way.

But before going into details, we will first make explicit what we expect from the resulting distribution by a very basic postulate:

$$\text{For } \mathcal{R}_1 = \{A[x_1]\}, \ldots, \mathcal{R}_n = \{A[x_n]\},$$
$$\min_{1 \leqslant i \leqslant n} x_i \leqslant F(\mathcal{R}_1, \ldots, \mathcal{R}_n)(A) \leqslant \max_{1 \leqslant i \leqslant n} x_i \tag{5}$$

This postulate ensures that the fused probabilities are kind of mean values, so that the resulting distribution reflects average degrees of belief as a compromise. In particular, such counterintuitive effects as in Example 1 are precluded. As a straightforward consequence, it also guarantees that a simple probabilistic *Pareto principle* (from *Social Choice Theory*, see e.g. [23,5]) is satisfied:

$$\text{For } \mathcal{R}_1 = \ldots = \mathcal{R}_n = \{A[x]\},$$
$$F(\mathcal{R}_1, \ldots, \mathcal{R}_n)(A) = x \tag{6}$$

Moreover, we expect the result of the fusion to be independent of the order of the inputs used, i.e. if $\pi : \{1, \ldots, n\} \to \{1, \ldots, n\}$ is any permutation, then

$$F(\mathcal{R}_1, \ldots, \mathcal{R}_n) = F(\mathcal{R}_{\pi(1)}, \ldots, \mathcal{R}_{\pi(n)}) \tag{7}$$

After these preliminary considerations, we will focus on how to define probabilistic rule base merging appropriately. The problems in Example 1 arise from unwanted interactions between the (different) sources of knowledge. So, further probabilistic information has to be added to ensure that the W_i provide comprehensive but non-interfering views of the world. This gives rise to the following definition of knowledge base merging:

$$\mathcal{R}_1 \odot \ldots \odot \mathcal{R}_n := \quad \mathcal{R}_1|W_1 \cup \ldots \cup \mathcal{R}_n|W_n \tag{8}$$
$$\cup \{W_1 \vee \ldots \vee W_n[1], W_i W_j[0], 1 \leqslant i, j \leqslant n, i \neq j\}$$

The ME-fusion operation is now realized in a straightforward way:

$$F_{ME}(\mathcal{R}_1, \ldots, \mathcal{R}_n) := ME(\mathcal{R}_1 \odot \ldots \odot \mathcal{R}_n) \tag{9}$$

$F_{ME}(\mathcal{R}_1, \ldots, \mathcal{R}_n)$ yields the desired ideal probabilistic belief state representing the fused pieces of information.

First, we check whether the so-defined fusion operation yields more intuitive results in Example 1.

Example 2. Let $\mathcal{R}_1$ and $\mathcal{R}_2$ be as in Example 1, and let $P_1^* := F_{ME}(\mathcal{R}_1, \mathcal{R}_2)$. Now the fused information concerning A is computed as $P_1^*(A) = 0.7472$, indeed kind of mean value between 0.7 and 0.8.

Let us consider again the case that both experts agree, i.e. $\mathcal{R}_1 = \mathcal{R}_2 = \{A[0.7]\}$. ME-fusion, as defined in (9), yields $F_{ME}(\mathcal{R}_1, \mathcal{R}_2)(A) = 0.7$, as desired.

These probabilities can be computed via SPRIT [8]. In Sections 5 and 6, further explanations on how these values arise will be given.

The following example illustrates the method in a more complex case.

Example 3. Two physicians argue about the relevance of a symptom, A, for diseases B, C, D. They both agree that A is a good indicator of disease B, although they disagree on its estimated degree of relevance: One physician specifies his corresponding belief as $(B|A)[0.9]$, whereas the other physician considers $(B|A)[0.8]$ more appropriate. In case that B can definitely be excluded, however, the first physician holds strong belief in C $((C|A\overline{B})[0.8])$, whereas the second physician thinks D to be a most probable diagnosis $((D|A\overline{B})[0.9])$.

So, the two packages of information to be fused are

$$\mathcal{R}_1 = \{(B|A)[0.9], (C|A\overline{B})[0.8]\}$$
$$\mathcal{R}_2 = \{(B|A)[0.8], (D|A\overline{B})[0.9]\}$$

Merging these set of rules yield

$$\mathcal{R}_1 \odot \mathcal{R}_2 = \{(B|AW_1)[0.9], (C|A\overline{B}W_1)[0.8],$$
$$(B|AW_2)[0.8], (D|A\overline{B}W_2)[0.9],$$
$$W_1 \vee W_2[1], W_1 W_2[0]\},$$

and the final result of the fusion process is represented by $P^* := ME(\mathcal{R}_1 \odot \mathcal{R}_2)$. From P^*, we obtain the following probabilistic answers for the queries listed below:

query	probability	query	probability
$(B|A)$	0.85	$(D|A\overline{B}W_1)$	0.50
$(C|A)$	0.51	$(C|A\overline{B}W_2)$	0.50
$(D|A)$	0.54	$(C|A\overline{B})$	0.59
		$(D|A\overline{B})$	0.78

This table shows that although both experts favor one of C and D in case that $A\overline{B}$ is present, no unjustified bias as to the respective other diagnosis has been introduced by the ME-approach $(P^*(D|A\overline{B}W_1) = P^*(C|A\overline{B}W_2) = 0.50)$. If only A is known, then P^* reflects the expected high probability for disease B $(P^*(B|A) = 0.85)$, whereas the probabilistic belief in C or D, respectively, is quite low $(P^*(C|A) = 0.51, P^*(D|A) = 0.54)$. The probabilities attached to $(C|A\overline{B})$ and $(D|A\overline{B})$ can be used to find a proper diagnosis if symptom A is present, but diagnosis B can be excluded. In this case, a clear vote for diagnosis D can be derived from the fused knowledge of both experts $(P^*(D|A\overline{B}) = 0.78$ vs. $P^*(C|A\overline{B}) = 0.59)$. This can be explained as follows: The first physician establishes quite a strong connection between A and B by stating $(B|A)[0.9]$. This connection gets lost when it becomes obvious that A, but not B, is present. In that case, diagnosis D is assigned the higher probability, so $P^*(D|A\overline{B}) > P^*(C|A\overline{B})$ should be expected. The significant difference in both probabilities can be attributed to a bias towards the second physician $(P^*(W_2|A\overline{B}) = 0.69)$ who held, a priori, a weaker belief in B, given A, and thus is taken to be more reliable under those circumstances.

F_{ME} is obviously commutative, hence satisfies postulate (7). We will investigate further formal properties of our fusion operation in the following section. In particular, we will show that F_{ME} satisfies the mean value postulate (5), and hence also the Pareto principle (6).

5   How ME-Fusion Works

Example 3 above gives a nice illustration and application of the ME-fusion operator. In this section, we will be concerned with revealing its underlying techniques, in order to make ME-fusion more transparent and intelligible. A formal analysis [22] of the ME-fusion distribution will prove to be helpful. The following proposition relates the ME-fused probability distribution to the ME-representations of each rule base.

Proposition 1. *Let $\mathcal{R}_1, \ldots, \mathcal{R}_n$ be consistent sets of probabilistic conditionals. Let $P^* = F_{ME}(\mathcal{R}_1, \ldots, \mathcal{R}_n)$ be the probability distribution obtained by ME-fusion, and let $P_i^* = ME(\mathcal{R}_i)$ be the ME-representation of rule base $\mathcal{R}_i$, $1 \leqslant i \leqslant n$. Then there are positive real numbers $\lambda_1, \ldots, \lambda_n$ with $\sum_{i=1}^n \lambda_i = 1$ such that, for all $\omega \in \Omega$,*

$$P^*(\omega) = \lambda_1 P_1^*(\omega) + \ldots + \lambda_n P_n^*(\omega)$$

More exactly, $\lambda_i = P^*(W_i)$ for all $i, 1 \leqslant i \leqslant n$.

Proof. In order to cut down technical details to a tolerable amount, we will focus on the case $n = 2$, i.e. the case of fusing two knowledge bases. The idea will become clear, and the general case can be dealt with analogously.

Let

$$\mathcal{R}_1 = \{(B_1|A_1)[x_1], \ldots, (B_k|A_k)[x_k]\}$$
$$\mathcal{R}_2 = \{(D_1|C_1)[y_1], \ldots, (D_m|C_m)[y_m]\}$$

be two sets of probabilistic conditionals reflecting consistent views on the world, or situation under consideration, respectively, and let $P^* = F_{ME}(\mathcal{R}_1, \mathcal{R}_2) = ME(\mathcal{R}_1 \odot \mathcal{R}_2)$ be the probability distribution resulting by ME-fusion.

From (2), we obtain for possible worlds over $\mathcal{V} \cup \{W_1, W_2\}$ the following representations (where ω is a possible world over $\mathcal{V}$):

$$P^*(\omega W_1 W_2) = P^*(\omega \overline{W_1}\, \overline{W_2}) = 0,$$
$$P^*(\omega W_1 \overline{W_2}) = \alpha_0 \prod_{\substack{1 \leqslant i \leqslant k \\ \omega \models A_i B_i}} \alpha_i^{1-x_i} \prod_{\substack{1 \leqslant i \leqslant k \\ \omega \models A_i \overline{B_i}}} \alpha_i^{-x_i},$$
$$P^*(\omega \overline{W_1} W_2) = \alpha_0 \prod_{\substack{1 \leqslant j \leqslant m \\ \omega \models C_j D_j}} \beta_j^{1-y_j} \prod_{\substack{1 \leqslant j \leqslant m \\ \omega \models C_j \overline{D_j}}} \beta_j^{-y_j},$$

with $\alpha_1, \ldots, \alpha_k, \beta_1, \ldots, \beta_m$ being solutions of a system of equations of type (3), and a normalizing constant α_0. The way in which the rule bases $\mathcal{R}_1, \mathcal{R}_2$ are merged by forming $\mathcal{R}_1 \odot \mathcal{R}_2$ ensures that the impacts exerted on P^* by the two rule bases are kept apart, that is to say, the α_i's do not interfere with the β_j's. Indeed, a closer investigation of the equation system (3) would show that it consists of two equation systems, one for the α_i's, and one for the β_j's. So let us denote system (3) for P^* by $(\mathcal{A};\mathcal{B})$ where $\mathcal{A}$ and $\mathcal{B}$ specify the α_i's and the β_j's, respectively. Using the approach provided by (2) and (3) to set up P_1^* and P_2^*, one finds that the equation systems $\mathcal{A}$ and $\mathcal{B}$ may also serve to yield the corresponding factors for P_1^* and P_2^*, respectively, that is, we have

$$P_1^*(\omega) = \gamma_0 \prod_{\substack{1 \leqslant i \leqslant k \\ \omega \models A_i B_i}} \alpha_i^{1-x_i} \prod_{\substack{1 \leqslant i \leqslant k \\ \omega \models A_i \overline{B_i}}} \alpha_i^{-x_i},$$

$$P_2^*(\omega) = \delta_0 \prod_{\substack{1 \leqslant j \leqslant m \\ \omega \models C_j D_j}} \beta_j^{1-y_j} \prod_{\substack{1 \leqslant j \leqslant m \\ \omega \models C_j \overline{D_j}}} \beta_j^{-y_j},$$

with suitable normalizing constants γ_0, δ_0, satisfying $\gamma_0^{-1} + \delta_0^{-1} = \alpha_0^{-1}$. In summary, we obtain

$$P^*(\omega) = P^*(\omega W_1 \overline{W_2}) + P^*(\omega \overline{W_1} W_2)$$
$$= \frac{\alpha_0}{\gamma_0} P_1^*(\omega) + \frac{\alpha_0}{\delta_0} P_2^*(\omega)$$

with $\frac{\alpha_0}{\gamma_0} = P^*(W_1), \frac{\alpha_0}{\delta_0} = P^*(W_2)$ and $\frac{\alpha_0}{\gamma_0} + \frac{\alpha_0}{\delta_0} = 1$. This proves the proposition.

Proposition 1 reveals that in the ME-fusion process as defined by (9), the information provided by the rule bases $\mathcal{R}_1, \ldots \mathcal{R}_n$ are actually processed independently and are glued together in a weighted sum, each component being weighted by the probability of the respective W_i. Note that, although we did not specify priorities among the agents, or knowledge bases, respectively, now automatically weight factors are introduced, giving more emphasis to some pieces of information than to others.

So under ME-fusion, complete epistemic states are combined. This also implies, however, that not only the information made explicit by stating the conditionals in each set $\mathcal{R}_i$ is used in the fusion process, but also the implicit information obtained by ME-inferences from $\mathcal{R}_i$. In particular, even in the case when the union of the rule bases $\mathcal{R}_1 \cup \ldots \cup \mathcal{R}_n$ is consistent, we have in general $F_{ME}(\mathcal{R}_1, \ldots, \mathcal{R}_n) \neq ME(\mathcal{R}_1 \cup \ldots \cup \mathcal{R}_n)$, as is illustrated in the following example.

Example 4. Let a, b, c, d be pairwise different propositional variables of our alphabet. The rule bases $\mathcal{R}_1 = \{(b|a)[0.7]\}$ and $\mathcal{R}_2 = \{(d|c)[0.9]\}$ are obviously consistent with one another. Let $P^* = F_{ME}(\mathcal{R}_1, \mathcal{R}_2)$ be the distribution resulting from ME-fusing $\mathcal{R}_1$ and $\mathcal{R}_2$, and let $P_1^* = ME(\mathcal{R}_1)$ and $P_2^* = ME(\mathcal{R}_2)$ be the ME-representations of $\mathcal{R}_1$ and $\mathcal{R}_2$, respectively. Then we find $P^*(b|a) = 0.6042$ and $P^*(d|c) = 0.6675$, so the knowledge made explicit in $\mathcal{R}_1$ and $\mathcal{R}_2$ is not fully reflected in $F_{ME}(\mathcal{R}_1, \mathcal{R}_2)$. This can be explained by the probabilities in P_1^* and P_2^*, since we have $P_1^*(d|c) = P_2^*(b|a) = 0.5$.

Proposition 1 shows that ME-fused probabilities actually arise as mean values, thus verifying our basic postulates (5) and (6). In the next section, we continue our investigations to set up a formula for what can be called the *information theoretical mean value* for probabilities.

6   An Induced Fusion Operator for Probabilities

In this section, we apply the techniques of ME-fusion to the problem, that a compromise probability of different probabilities has to be found in an information theoretical way. This problem arises, for instance, if a user is uncertain about the actual probability and only is able to give an interval of possible probability values. The result of applying plain ME-techniques to such imprecise probabilities is unsatisfactory: If the user specifies the probability of A to lie within the interval $[x, y]$, then ME-propagation chooses the one[1] value out of x or y which is closest to 0.5 unless interactions with other constraints make this impossible. This is justified by information cautiousness, but does not fit the idea the user possibly has in mind: The unknown probability value is "something in between x and y".

This problem can be solved in our framework by modelling two experts, a cautious one specifying the probability closest to 0.5, and a bold one specifying the more expressive value. Of course, this idea can be applied to sets of conditionals as well, or also can be generalized to handle several different probabilities by modelling more than two experts. In the following, we will focus on the case that a compromise value "somewhere in between" conflicting probabilities is searched for.

First, we will deal with the fusion of two probabilistic rule bases $\mathcal{R}_1 = \{A[x]\}, \mathcal{R}_2 = \{A[y]\}, A \in \mathcal{L}, x, y \in [0, 1]$, to make clear what actually happens to probability values under ME-fusion. This basic case of fusing two simple knowledge bases will provide us with important insights into the fusion process.

In the first step, $\mathcal{R}_1$ and $\mathcal{R}_2$ are merged according to (8):

$$\mathcal{R}_1 \odot \mathcal{R}_2 = \{(A|W_1)[x], (A|W_2)[y], W_1 \vee W_2[1], W_1 W_2[0]\}$$

Let $P^* = F_{ME}(\mathcal{R}_1, \mathcal{R}_2) = ME(\mathcal{R}_1 \odot \mathcal{R}_2)$. From (2) and (3), P^* can be easily computed as follows:

ω	$P^*(\omega)$	ω	$P^*(\omega)$
AW_1W_2	0	$\overline{A}W_1W_2$	0
$AW_1\overline{W_2}$	$\alpha_0\alpha_1^{1-x}$	$\overline{A}W_1\overline{W_2}$	$\alpha_0\alpha_1^{-x}$
$A\overline{W_1}W_2$	$\alpha_0\alpha_2^{1-y}$	$\overline{A}\,\overline{W_1}W_2$	$\alpha_0\alpha_2^{-y}$
$A\overline{W_1}\,\overline{W_2}$	0	$\overline{A}\,\overline{W_1}\,\overline{W_2}$	0

with

---

[1] If $|0.5 - x| = |0.5 - y|$, then 0.5 is taken by ME-propagation.

$$\alpha_1 = \frac{x}{1-x}, \quad \alpha_2 = \frac{y}{1-y}$$

$$\alpha_0 = (\alpha_1^{1-x} + \alpha_1^{-x} + \alpha_2^{1-y} + \alpha_2^{-y})^{-1}$$

P^* fuses the information given by the two experts to yield

$$P^*(A) = \alpha_0(\alpha_1^{1-x} + \alpha_2^{1-y})$$
$$= \frac{x^{1-x}(1-x)^{x-1} + y^{1-y}(1-y)^{y-1}}{x^{-x}(1-x)^{x-1} + y^{-y}(1-y)^{y-1}}$$

The right hand side of this equation defines an operator, also denoted with $\odot$, to combine two probabilities $x, y \in [0, 1]$:

$$x \odot y := \frac{x^{1-x}(1-x)^{x-1} + y^{1-y}(1-y)^{y-1}}{x^{-x}(1-x)^{x-1} + y^{-y}(1-y)^{y-1}} \tag{10}$$

The following proposition gives some basic properties of $\odot$.

Proposition 2. *Let $x, y \in [0, 1]$, $\odot$ as defined in (10). Then the following properties hold:*

1. *Commutativity: $x \odot y = y \odot x$.*
2. *Idempotence: $x \odot x = x$.*
3. *Mean Value Property (MVP): If $x < y$, then $x < x \odot y < y$.*
4. *Symmetry I (Sym1): $x \odot (1 - x) = 0.5$.*
5. *Symmetry II (Sym2): $(1 - x) \odot (1 - y) = 1 - x \odot y$.*

The proof of this proposition is done by straightforward calculations.

Commutativity, Idempotence, and *Mean Value Property, MVP* correspond to the postulates (7), (6), and (5), respectively. It should be emphasized that $\odot$ does not combine information in the way *t-norms* do – actually, $\odot$ is *not* a t-norm since it lacks associativity. This is not a drawback, since associativity is in conflict with idempotence and the Mean Value Property (MVP). This can be seen as follows: If both associativity and idempotence were assumed to hold, we would have $(x \odot y) \odot y = x \odot (y \odot y) = x \odot y$. On the other hand, from MVP we would obtain $x < x \odot y < y$ for $x < y$, and further $x \odot y < (x \odot y) \odot y < y$, so in particular $x \odot y \neq (x \odot y) \odot y$, a contradiction.

Rather, Proposition 2 shows $x \odot y$ to be a probabilistic mean value, respecting the extreme probabilities of 0 and 1 as special values, observing 0.5 as a point of complete indeterminateness, and satisfying intuitive probabilistic symmetry properties.

Another interesting point is to make the effect of indeterminate knowledge ($x = 0.5$) in a fusion process explicit:

Proposition 3. *For $y \in [0, 1]$,*

$$0.5 \odot y = \frac{1 + y^{1-y}(1-y)^{y-1}}{2 + y^{-y}(1-y)^{y-1}}$$

For instance, $0.5 \odot 1 = \frac{2}{3}$. The following tabular shows some more examples of ME-fused probabilities $x \odot y$.

x	y	$x \odot y$	x	y	$x \odot y$
0.2	0.3	0.2528	0.5	0.9	0.6636
0.2	0.6	0.4172	0.7	0.8	0.7472
0.4	0.9	0.6069	0.8	0.9	0.8456
0.5	0.7	0.5959	0.8	1.0	0.8755

We will now consider the general case, that more than two probabilities have to be fused. As we have already pointed out above, $\odot$ as defined in (10) is not associative, so a straightforward generalization by repeated application of $\odot$ does not make sense. Instead, we have to deal with a more general fusion problem, namely the fusion of n knowledge bases $\mathcal{R}_1 = \{A[x_1]\}, \ldots, \mathcal{R}_n = \{A[x_n]\}$ in order to find an n-ary (numerical) fusion operator $\odot_n$ that generalizes $\odot$. Similar to the case n=2 dealt with above, by a closer look at the corresponding ME-distribution $P^* = F_{ME}(\mathcal{R}_1, \ldots, \mathcal{R}_n)$, we obtain

$$P^*(A) = \frac{x_1^{1-x_1}(1-x_1)^{x_1-1} + \ldots + x_n^{1-x_n}(1-x_n)^{x_n-1}}{x_1^{-x_1}(1-x_1)^{x_1-1} + \ldots + x_n^{-x_n}(1-x_n)^{x_n-1}}$$
$$=: \odot_n(x_1, \ldots, x_n) \tag{11}$$

The numerical fusion operator $\odot_n$ for n probabilities defined by (11) satisfies similar properties as stated in Proposition 2 above; more exactly, the n-ary versions of *Commutativity*, *Idempotence*, *MVP*, and *Sym2* can easily be shown to hold.

7   Conclusion

This paper presented a new method to fuse different pieces of probabilistic information by making use of the principle of maximum entropy. First, global consistency is established by conditioning each knowledge base on a new variable, representing explicitly the corresponding agent's point of view. Before applying the ME-principle to the union of all these conditioned knowledge bases, further probabilistic information is added to exclude interferences between the information stated by different agents. So each knowledge base is processed and completed independently by ME-methodology, and finally, the resulting probability distributions are merged to yield one ideal probabilistic belief state. The ME-fusion operator introduced in this paper proved to be quite well-behaved, in particular, it satisfies basic demands such as commutativity, and the Pareto principle. Its probabilities arise as mean values. As an application of our method, we defined a numerical fusion operator computing the information theoretical mean of probability values.

In this paper, we proposed a method for non-prioritized information fusion. However, priorities that emphasize the information provided by some agents more than that of others may be introduced by adding suitable probabilistic information. The elaboration of these ideas is part of our ongoing work.

References

1. Alchourrón, C., Gärdenfors, P., Makinson, P.: On the logic of theory change: Partial meet contraction and revision functions. Journal of Symbolic Logic **50** (1985) 510–530
2. Bloch, I., Hunter, A., et al.: Fusion: General concepts and characteristics. International Journal of Intelligent Systems **16** (2001) 1107–1134
3. Katsuno, H., Mendelzon, A.: Propositional knowledge base revision and minimal change. Artificial Intelligence **52** (1991) 263–294
4. Konieczny, S., Pino-Perez, R.: On the logic of merging. In: Proceedings Sixth International Conference on Principles of Knowledge Representation and Reasoning, KR'98. (1998) 488–498
5. Maynard-Reid II, P., Lehmann, D.: Representing and aggregating conflicting beliefs. In: Proceedings Seventh International Conference on Principles of Knowledge Representation and Reasoning, KR'2000. (2000)
6. Dubois, D., Lang, J., Prade, H.: Dealing with multi-source information in possibilistic logic. In: Proceedings ECAI'92. (1992) 38–42
7. Schramm, M., Ertel, W.: (PIT) www.pit-systems.de.
8. Rödder, W., Meyer, C.H.: (SPIRIT) www.fernuni-hagen.de/BWLOR/forsch.html.
9. Rödder, W., Meyer, C.H.: Coherent knowledge processing at maximum entropy by SPIRIT. In Horvitz, E., Jensen, F., eds.: Proceedings 12th Conference on Uncertainty in Artificial Intelligence, San Francisco, Ca., Morgan Kaufmann (1996) 470–476
10. Schramm, M., Ertel, W.: Reasoning with probabilities and maximum entropy: the system PIT and its application in LEXMED. In: Symposium on Operations Research, SOR'99. (1999)
11. Cowell, R., Dawid, A., Lauritzen, S., Spiegelhalter, D.: Probabilistic networks and expert systems. Springer, New York Berlin Heidelberg (1999)
12. Jaynes, E.: Where do we stand on maximum entropy? In: Papers on Probability, Statistics and Statistical Physics. D. Reidel Publishing Company, Dordrecht, Holland (1983) 210–314
13. Shore, J., Johnson, R.: Axiomatic derivation of the principle of maximum entropy and the principle of minimum cross-entropy. IEEE Transactions on Information Theory **IT-26** (1980) 26–37
14. Paris, J., Vencovská, A.: A note on the inevitability of maximum entropy. International Journal of Approximate Reasoning **14** (1990) 183–223
15. Kern-Isberner, G.: Characterizing the principle of minimum cross-entropy within a conditional-logical framework. Artificial Intelligence **98** (1998) 169–208
16. Kern-Isberner, G.: The principle of conditional preservation in belief revision. In: Proceedings of the Second International Symposium on Foundations of Information and Knowledge Systems, FoIKS 2002, Springer LNCS 2284 (2002) 105–129
17. Kern-Isberner, G.: Handling conditionals adequately in uncertain reasoning and belief revision. Journal of Applied Non-Classical Logics **12** (2002) 215–237

18. Rödder, W., Kern-Isberner, G.: From information to probability: an axiomatic approach. International Journal of Intelligent Systems **18** (2003) 383–403
19. Rödder, W., Xu, L.: Entropy-driven inference and inconsistency. In: Proceedings Artificial Intelligence and Statistics, Fort Lauderdale, Florida (1999) 272–277
20. Csiszár, I.: I-divergence geometry of probability distributions and minimization problems. Ann. Prob. **3** (1975) 146–158
21. Paris, J.: The uncertain reasoner's companion – A mathematical perspective. Cambridge University Press (1994)
22. Kern-Isberner, G.: Conditionals in nonmonotonic reasoning and belief revision. Springer, Lecture Notes in Artificial Intelligence LNAI 2087 (2001)
23. Sen, A.: Social choice theory. In Arrow, K., Intriligator, M., eds.: Handbook of Mathematical Economics. Volume III. Elsevier Science Publishers (1986) 1073–1181

A Probabilistic Approach for Dynamic State Estimation Using Visual Information

Alvaro Soto[1] and Pradeep Khosla[2]

[1] Pontificia Universidad Catolica de Chile
Santiago 22, Chile
asoto@ing.puc.cl
[2] Carnegie Mellon University
5000 Forbes Avenue, Pittsburgh, Pa, 15213, USA
pkk@ece.cmu.edu

Abstract. This work presents a computational framework for the adaptive integration of information from different visual algorithms. The approach takes advantage of the richness of visual information by adaptively considering a variety of visual properties such as color, depth, motion, and shape. Using a probabilistic approach and uncertainty metrics, the resulting framework makes appropriate decisions about the most relevant visual attributes to consider. The framework is based on an agent paradigm. Each visual algorithm is implemented as an agent that adapts its behavior according to uncertainty considerations. These agents act as a group of experts, where each agent has a specific knowledge area. Cooperation among the agents is given by a probabilistic scheme that uses Bayesian inference to integrate the evidential information provided by them. To deal with the inherent no linearity of visual information, the relevant probability distributions are represented using a stochastic sampling approach. The estimation of the state of relevant visual structures is performed using an enhanced version of the particle filter algorithm. This enhanced version includes novel methods to adaptively select the number of samples used by the filter, and to adaptively find a suitable function to propagate the samples. We show the advantages of our approach by applying it to the task of tracking targets in a real video sequence.

1   Introduction

In the robotics domain the problem of understanding sensing information from the environment is highly relevant. In particular, visual perception is a very attractive option to equip a robot with suitable perceptual capabilities. The robustness and flexibility exhibited by most seeing beings is a clear proof of the advantages of a sophisticated visual system. Evolution has managed to provide biological creatures with the timely visual perception needed to interact with a dynamic world.

Insects provide one of the most basic examples of a robust visual system able to successfully operate in a natural environment. Insects are able to navigate

A. Günter et al. (Eds.): KI 2003, LNAI 2821, pp. 421–435, 2003.

around a 3D cluttered world, avoiding obstacles, recognizing paths, landing in many places, taking off to avoid capture, and so on. Several studies [1] show that insects, such as bees, move around their environment using a set of visual skills based on simple visual cues such as color, position, orientation, and relative change of size from different points of view. They can find food using the salient color of flowers or they can find their way home using the visual changing size of relevant natural landmarks.

In the case of the human visual system, people usually characterize objects using distinctive visual features [2]. For example, most people are comfortable with instructions such as "Go straight until you see the tall round building, then turn right and go until you see the red sign... " .

The previous examples show the richness of visual information. In contrast to other sensor modalities, vision provides information about a large number of different features of the environment such as color, shape, depth, or motion. This multidimensionality provides strong discriminative capabilities to eliminate ambiguities being one of the key strength that explains the great robustness observed in most advanced biological visual systems.

Unfortunately, the state of the art of artificial visual perception is still far behind that of its biological analogue. Currently, most successful applications of machine vision demonstrate a robust operation only under constrained conditions. The typical approach relies on simplifications of the environment or on good engineering work to identify relevant visual attributes to solve a specific visual task. As an example, consider the case of a robot localization system based on artificial landmarks. In this case, the use of distinctive visual features in the landmarks provides strong constraints to construct algorithms especially designed to detect the key visual attributes [3]. In the same way, recent successful vision systems to detect people or cars are examples of specific visual applications where good engineering work provides an off-line identification of key visual attributes [4,5,6].

The previous strategy lacks the flexibility needed to account for the variability of most natural scenarios. Problems such as partial occlusion, changes in illumination, or different postures constantly modify the amount of information of the different visual attributes. As a consequence, the most adequate set of attributes to complete a given task is highly variable.

This paper presents a computational framework for the adaptive integration of information from different visual algorithms. The basic scenario is a mobile robot embedded in a dynamic environment and processing visual information. As new information arrives, the goal is to use the most adequate set of information sources in order to update the knowledge about relevant visual structures. The central idea is to deal with the ambiguity and dynamics of natural environments by adapting the operation of the system. The adaptive integration of visual information aims to achieve two desirable attributes of an engineering system: *robustness* and *efficiency*. By combining the outputs of multiple vision modules the assumptions and constraints of each module can be factored out to result in a more robust system overall. Efficiency can be kept through the on-line selection and specialization of the algorithms according to the relevant conditions present at each time in the visual scene.

The computational framework is based on an intelligent agent paradigm. Each visual algorithm is implemented as an agent that adapts its behavior according to uncertainty considerations. These agents act as a group of experts, where each agent has a specific knowledge area. Cooperation among the agents is given by a probabilistic scheme that uses Bayesian inference to integrate the evidential information provided by them. To deal with the inherent no linearity of visual information, the relevant probability distributions are represented using a stochastic sampling approach. The estimation of the state of relevant visual structures is performed using an enhanced version of the particle filter algorithm. This enhanced version includes novel methods to adaptively select the number of samples used by the filter, and to adaptively find a suitable function to propagate the samples.

This paper is organized as follows section 2 presents the main components of the framework. Section 3 describes the adaptation mechanisms used to select the visual agents. Section 4 discusses the details of our probabilistic approach. Section 5 shows the results of applying our methodology to tracking targets in a real video sequence. Finally, Section 6 presents the main conclusions of this work.

2   A Multimodal Probabilistic Agent Based Approach

The goal of the approach presented here is to keep track of a joint probability density function (joint-pdf) over a set of state variables that characterizes the state of the world. For example, for the case of visual tracking of a single target, the state of the system is represented by four state variables (x, y, w, h), which determine a bounding box surrounding the target: (x, y) represent the center of the box in the image plane, w its width, and h its height. Each instance of the state corresponds to a hypothesis of the possible position of a target.

The level of uncertainty in the state estimation is the key element used by the system to implement the adaptation mechanisms that select the most adequate visual agent. For example, if the system is tracking a target using color information but similarities with respect to the color of the background or other target produce a high level of uncertainty, the system automatically activates new visual modalities such as texture or stereovision to reduce the current ambiguities.

Figure 1 shows an example of the basic probabilistic architecture used in this work. This can be considered as a Bayes net. Agent nodes correspond to the visual algorithms that directly process the incoming images. Inference nodes keep track of the state estimation represented by a set of sample hypotheses and their probabilities. Inference nodes provide the integration of information and the representation of relevant visual structures. Also, inference nodes introduce conditional independence relations among the visual algorithms. This decoupling of information facilitates the construction of probabilistic models for applying Bayesian inference and provides a high degree of modularity to reconfigure the system.

A practical difficulty of using Bayesian inference is to find adequate pdfs. The problem is even more difficult in the dynamic case, where one also needs to find

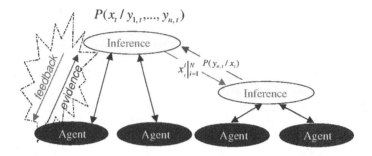

Fig. 1. Typical Bayes net and information flow for the probabilistic architecture used in this work.

a time propagation model. This work uses a sequential Monte Carlo technique commonly known as particle filter as the basic stochastic sampling algorithm to perform Bayesian inference. As opposed to alternative techniques such as the Kalman Filter, the particle filter is able to approximate any functional non-linearity of the pdfs. The key idea is to represent a posterior distribution by samples (particles) that are continually re-allocated after each new estimation of the state.

Figure 1 can be considered as a hierarchical representation of the simpler case of just one inference node. In this case the posterior distribution of the estimation of the state can be expressed as:

$$P(x_t/\boldsymbol{y}_{1,t}...\boldsymbol{y}_{n,t}) = \beta\, P(y_{1,t}/x_t)...P(y_{n,t}/x_t) \sum_{x_{t-1}} P(x_t/x_{t-1})\, P(x_{t-1}/(\boldsymbol{y}_{1,t-1}...\boldsymbol{y}_{n,t-1})$$

(1)

where x_t corresponds to a hypothesis of the state of the system at time t; $\boldsymbol{y}_{i,t}$ contains the historic evidence provided by agent i until time t; n corresponds to the number of independent sources of information; and β is a normalization factor.

Equation (1) shows the decoupling between the evidence provided by each agent through a likelihood function, and the state updating performed by an inference node. The process is as follows. Agent nodes provide evidential information to an inference node. Using this information the inference node keeps track of a probability density function (pdf) that represents its beliefs about the state of the system. According to these beliefs, the inference node sends high-level feedback to its active descending agent nodes. This feedback consists of a list of hypotheses that need further consideration and a signal to the agents that need to be active. The idea is that, according to the level of ambiguity, the inference node decides which of its potential descending nodes to activate, and which hypotheses are worth being considered. The agent nodes use this feedback to efficiently allocate their resources and as a reference about the quality of their own performance. The active agents evaluate the set of hypotheses and send this evidence back to the inference node starting a new cycle of the adaptive state estimation. Eventually, an inference node can send feedback to a descending node that is also an inference node. This can happen in problems that require higher levels of inference, such as the case of considering occlusion in a multiple target tracking application.

3   Adaptation

The adaptation mechanisms are based on the evaluation of the level of uncertainty present in the state estimate and the evaluation of the quality of the information provided by each agent in terms of uncertainty reduction. The goals are to perform robust estimation keeping uncertainty low, and also to perform efficient estimation avoiding the processing of irrelevant, misleading, or redundant information. In order to achieve these goals, we introduce two performance indexes.

The first index, called uncertainty deviation (UD), is intended to evaluate the level of ambiguity in the state representation.

$$UD = \sum_{x_i} d^2(x_i, MAP) P(x_i) \tag{2}$$

where d denotes a distance metric and x_i denotes a generic hypothesis of the state of the system. In this work we use Euclidean distance and state variables (x, y, w, h).

The second index is intended to evaluate the quality of the information provided by each agent in terms of uncertainty reduction. The intuition behind it is that, if an agent is providing good information, its local likelihood should be close to the state-pdf maintained by the inference node. Thus, the problem reduces to quantifying similarity between probability distributions. This work compares probability distributions using the Kullback-Leibler divergence (KL-divergence). The KL-divergence between two probability distributions is given by Equation (3),

$$KL(f, g) = \sum_i f(i) \ln(\frac{f(i)}{g(i)}). \tag{3}$$

In this case, $f(i)$ corresponds to the pdf of the state and $g(i)$ corresponds to the local normalized agent likelihood.

Using the described performance indexes, this work introduces two adaptation schemes to the state estimation. The first scheme is performed by inference nodes. An inference node measures the level of ambiguity in its state representation using the UD index. If the value of the index exceeds some desired level, the inference node sends an activation signal to any inactive agent asking for supporting evidence that can eventually reduce the current ambiguities. If the value of the UD index is lower than some desired level, the inference node stops the less informative agent in order to increase the efficiency of the state estimation.

The selection of the less informative agent is performed based on the relative values of the KL-divergence among the active agents.

The second adaptation scheme is carried out locally by each agent using the UD index. In this case, given that each agent calculates a likelihood function, the MAP in Equation (2) is replaced by the maximum likelihood hypothesis (ML). Using this index each agent evaluates the local level of uncertainty in its estimation. If this value exceeds some desired level, the agent modifies its own local actions in order to improve its performance. In the case that, after a number of cycles, the agent is still not able to improve its performance, the agent stops processing information, becoming inactive.

4   Probabilistic Inference

Besides the adaptive allocation of prominent hypotheses, the standard formulation of a particle filter lacks of further tools that take into account the varying complexity of the shape and dynamics of the hypothesis space. As the state of a system evolves the standard implementation of the particle filter keeps a fixed number of samples and a fixed propagation function to track the evolution of the state. The next two sections present mechanisms to overcome these limitations. Section 4.1 presents a method that can be used to adaptively estimate a suitable size for the sample set used at each iteration of the particle filter. Section 4.2 presents a method to improve the allocation of samples by updating the importance function using the most recent observation.

4.1   Adaptive Selection of the Number of Particles

The regular implementation of the particle filter uses a fixed number of samples. In most situations this is highly inefficient. The dynamics of most processes usually produces great variability in the complexity of the posterior distribution. As a consequence, the initial estimation of the number of particles can be much larger than the real number needed to perform a good estimation or, even worse, at some point the number can be too low causing the filter to diverge. This section shows a technique that can be used to adaptively estimate a suitable number of particles that, with a certain level of confidence, limits the maximum error in the approximation.

At NIPS'01, Fox introduces KLD-Sampling [7], a novel technique to adaptively estimate the number of particles that bound the error in the estimation of the true posterior. The error is measured by the Kullback-Leibler divergence (KL-divergence) between the true posterior distribution and the empirical distribution, which is a well known nonparametric maximum likelihood estimate [8]. The method is based on the assumption that the true posterior distribution can be represented by a discrete piecewise constant distribution consisting of a set of multidimensional bins. Using this representation, Fox finds a relation connecting the likelihood ratio to the KL-divergence.

The problem with KLD-Sampling is the derivation of the bound using the empirical distribution, which has the implicit assumption that the samples comes from the true distribution. This is not the case for particle filters. In particle filters the samples come from an importance function, moreover, the quality of the match between this function and the true distribution is one of the main elements that determines the accuracy of the filter, hence a suitable number of particles.

To fix the problem of KLD-Sampling one needs a way to quantify the degradation in the estimation using samples from the importance function. The goal is to find the equivalent number of samples from the importance and the true densities that captures the same amount of information about $p(x)$. In the context of MC integration, Geweke [9] introduces the relative numerical efficiency (RNE), which provides an index to quantify the influence of sampling from an importance function. The idea behind RNE is to compare the relative accuracy of solving an integral using samples coming from either the true or the importance function. Accuracy is measured according to the variance of the estimator of the integral.

In the case that the integral corresponds to the estimation of the mean value of the state, the variance of the estimator corresponds to the variance of MC integration, which is given by [10]:

$$Var[E_{MC}^N(x)] = Var_p(x)/N \qquad (4)$$

where N is the number of samples coming from the true distribution [1].

Now, in the case where the samples come from an importance function $q(x)$, the variance of the estimator corresponds to the variance of importance sampling, which is given by [9]:

$$Var[E_{IS}^N(x)] = E_q((x - E_p(x))^2\, w(x)^2)/N_{IS} = \sigma_{IS}^2/N_{IS}, \qquad (5)$$

where $w(x) = p(x)/q(x)$ corresponds to the weights of importance sampling and N_{IS} is the number of samples coming from the importance function.

To achieve similar levels of accuracy, the variance of both estimators should be equal. This relation provides a way to quantify the equivalence between samples from the true and the proposal density:

$$N = \frac{N_{IS}\,Var_p(x)}{\sigma_{IS}^2} \qquad (6)$$

Replacing (6) in the bound given by KLD-Sampling, it is possible to obtain (7) which takes into account the case that the samples do not come from the true distribution but from an importance function (See [11] for details):

$$N_{IS} > \frac{\sigma_{IS}^2}{Var_p(x)}\frac{1}{2\epsilon}\chi_{k-1,1-\delta}^2. \qquad (7)$$

---

[1] The rest of this section concentrates on one iteration of the particle filter and the t subscripts are dropped.

4.2   Adaptive Propagation of the Samples

The regular implementation of the particle filter uses the dynamic prior $p(x_t/\boldsymbol{y}_{t-1})$ [10] as the importance function to obtain the set of hypotheses that are sent to the agent nodes. This has the advantage of allowing a computational complexity of $O(N)$ in the operation of the filter, where N is the number of hypotheses. However, the use of this importance function has the limitation of allocating the samples without considering the most recent observation y_t. This section shows a new algorithm that improves this situation by incorporating the current observation in the generation of the samples, and also keeping the computational complexity of $O(N)$.

Consider the following expression for the dynamic prior:

$$p(x_t/\boldsymbol{y}_{t-1}) = \int p(x_t/x_{t-1})\,p(x_{t-1}/\boldsymbol{y}_{t-1})dx_{t-1}. \tag{8}$$

Using the method of composition the samples from the dynamic prior are obtained by sampling from $p(x_{t-1}/\boldsymbol{y}_{t-1})$ and then propagating each of these samples x_{t-1}^k by $p(x_t/x_{t-1}^k)$. From an MC perspective, it is possible to achieve a more efficient allocation of the samples by including y_t in the generation of the samples that are propagated by $p(x_t/x_{t-1}^k)$. The intuition is that the incorporation of y_t increases the number of samples drawn from mixture components $p(x_t/x_{t-1}^k)$ associated with areas of high probability under the likelihood function.

Under importance sampling it is possible to sample from $p(x_{t-1}/\boldsymbol{y}_t)$ instead of $p(x_{t-1}/\boldsymbol{y}_{t-1})$ and then adding to each particle x_t^i a correcting weight given by,

$$w_t^i = \frac{p(x_{t-1}^k/\boldsymbol{y}_{t-1})}{p(x_{t-1}^k/\boldsymbol{y}_t)}, \quad \text{with } x_t^i \sim p(x_t/x_{t-1}^k) \tag{9}$$

The resulting set of weighted samples $\{x_t^i, w_t^i\}_{i=1}^n$ still comes from the dynamic prior, so the computational complexity of the resulting filter is still $O(N)$. The extra complexity of this operation comes from the need to evaluate and to draw samples from the importance function $p(x_{t-1}^i/\boldsymbol{y}_t)$. Fortunately, the calculation of this function can be obtained directly from the operation of the regular particle filter. To see this clearly, consider the following:

$$\begin{aligned}
p(x_t, x_{t-1}/\boldsymbol{y}_t) &\propto p(y_t/x_t, x_{t-1}, \boldsymbol{y}_{t-1})\,p(x_t, x_{t-1}/\boldsymbol{y}_{t-1}) \\
&\propto p(y_t/x_t)\,p(x_t/x_{t-1}, \boldsymbol{y}_{t-1}) \\
&\quad \times p(x_{t-1}/\boldsymbol{y}_{t-1}) \\
&\propto p(y_t/x_t)p(x_t/x_{t-1}) \\
&\quad \times p(x_{t-1}/\boldsymbol{y}_{t-1}) \tag{10}
\end{aligned}$$

Equation (10) shows that, indeed, the regular steps of the particle filter generate an approximation of the joint density $p(x_t, x_{t-1}/\boldsymbol{y}_t)$. After re-sampling from $p(x_{t-1}/\boldsymbol{y}_{t-1})$, propagating these samples with $p(x_t/x_{t-1})$, and calculating the weights $p(y_t/x_t)$, the set of resulting sample pairs (x_t^i, x_{t-1}^i) with correcting weights $p(y_t/x_t^i)$ forms a valid set of samples from the joint density $p(x_t, x_{t-1}/\boldsymbol{y}_t)$. Considering that $p(x_{t-1}/\boldsymbol{y}_t)$ is just a marginal of this joint distribution, the set of weighted-samples x_{t-1}^i are valid samples from it.

5   Application

This section illustrates the main features of the work presented here, when used to track targets in real video sequences. The main focus is to show the operation of the different adaptation mechanisms introduced for the activation of visual algorithms, the selection of the number of particles, and the propagation function used by the particle filter. See [11] for further examples and comparison with alternative existing techniques. The system operates using visual agents based on color and stereo vision.

Figure 2 shows a set of frames of the video sequence used to test our approach. This sequence consists of two children playing with a ball. In this case, the goal is to keep track of the positions of the ball and the left side child.

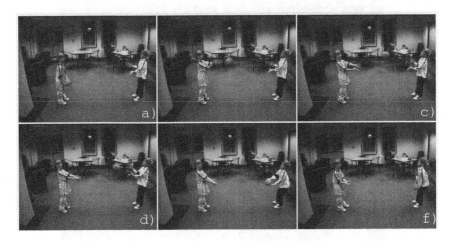

Fig. 2. a) Frame 1. b) Frame 4. c) Frame 5. d) Frame 6. e) Frame 7. f) Frame 14. A set of representative frames of the video sequence used to illustrate the advantages of the approach presented in this work.

In this application each hypothesis about the position of a target is given by a bounding box defined by height, width, and the coordinates of its center. The motion model used for the implementation of the particle filter corresponds to a Gaussian function of zero mean and known diagonal covariance matrix with standard deviations set to 20 for the center of each hypothesis and to 0.5 for its width and height.

The first test considers tracking using visual algorithms based on color and stereovision. In this case, the particle filter used to estimate the pdf of the state of each target considers an adaptive number of particles, but a fixed importance function to generate the samples. Figure 3 shows the tracking results at different time instants. The left figures show all the hypotheses used to estimate the state of each target, while the right side figure shows only the hypothesis with the highest probability (MAP hypothesis).

The system starts the tracking of both targets using the color and stereovision agents. After three frames, the system automatically decides to track the child using only the information provided by the stereovision agent and the ball using only the information provided by the color agent. In the case of the child, lack of hue information in his pants and similarities between the hue of his t-shirt and the carpet make the color information unreliable, and the system decides to use the clear depth features provided by the stereovision agent. In the case of the ball its small size and abrupt motion produce a very poor information from the stereovision agent, and the system decides to use the clear orange color to perform the tracking.

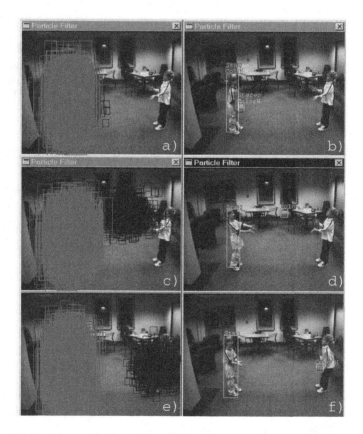

Fig. 3. a-b) Frame 1. c-d) Frame 5. e-f) Frame 14. a-c-e) Hypotheses representing the posterior distribution of each state at different time instants. b-d-f) The MAP hypothesis is marked with a bounding box.

Figure 4 shows the number of particles used at each frame to estimate the posterior distribution of the targets. The number of particles is obtained using a desired error of 0.1 and a confidence level of 95%. In the calculation of the number of particles only the x and y dimensions are considered, assuming independence to facilitate the use of Equation (7). At each iteration, the number of particles selected to run the filter corresponds to the greater value between the estimates obtained in the x and y dimensions. Given that the results in Equation (7) are asymptotic, in practice a minimum number of 1000 samples is always used to ensure that convergence has been achieved.

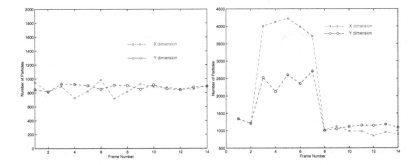

Fig. 4. Number of particles at each iteration of the particle filter using Equation (7) with desired error of 0.1 and a confidence level of 95%. Left: Left side child. Right: Orange Ball

As expected, in the case of the child, the number of particles is roughly constant during the entire sequence. In this case the motion model is highly accurate because the child has only a small and slow motion around a center position. Then, the performance is similar to the case of using a regular particle filter with a constant number of particles. In the case of the ball the motion model is a poor approximation of the real motion, because the ball has a large and fast motion traveling from one child to the other. Then, the number of particles needed to achieve the desired error level has a large increment during this period (Frames 3 to 7). Also, during this period the mismatch between the dynamic prior and the posterior produces an inefficient allocation of the samples. This is clear in Figure 5, which shows the resulting posterior distribution at different time instants. For clarity only the (x, y) coordinates of the center of each hypothesis are shown in the graphs.

In Figure 5, at Frame 1 the ball is mostly static in the hands of the left-side child. As a consequence, the motion model is adequate, and most of the samples from the important function are allocated in areas of high likelihood. In contrast, Figures 5(b), (c), and (d) show the situation when the ball travels from one child to the other. In this case, most of the samples are allocated in the tails of the posterior distribution, having a low likelihood. As a consequence, the estimate needs a larger set of samples to populate the relevant part of the posterior.

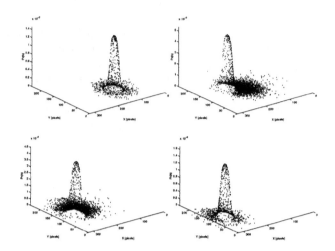

Fig. 5. Estimate of the posterior distribution of the position of the center of the ball at different time instants. From top to bottom: Frames 1, 5, 7, and 12.

In the next test we add to the previous example the algorithm that enables the adaptation of the importance function used by the particle filter. Again, the estimate of the number of particles is performed using Equation (7). The decision to adapt the importance function is based on the estimate of the KL-divergence between the dynamic prior and the posterior distribution (See [11] for details). Figure 6 shows the evolution of the KL-divergence calculated before adapting the importance function. The Figure shows how the value of the KL-divergence has a large increment during the period that the ball travels from one child to the other. Setting a value of 2 for the threshold on the KL-divergence, the system decides to

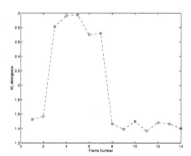

Fig. 6. KL-divergence between the dynamic prior and the posterior distribution.

adapt the importance function at all the frames where the ball travels from one child to the other (Frames 3-7). Figure 7 shows the location of the resulting set of samples used to estimate the posterior distribution. Comparing Figure 7 with

Figure 5, it is possible to observe the gain in efficiency by a better allocation of the samples. The update of the importance function by using information from the current observation produces a re-allocation of the samples towards areas of high likelihood, reducing the number of samples needed to estimate the posterior distribution with a desired error level.

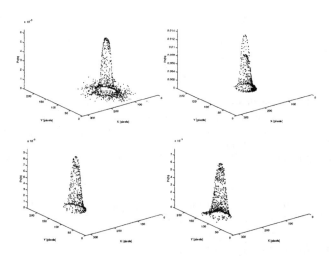

Fig. 7. Estimate of the posterior distribution of the position of the center of the ball at different time instants for the case of using an updated version of the dynamic prior as the importance function.

Figure 8 shows the number of particles predicted by Equation (7) to estimate the posterior distribution of the position of the ball. During Frames 3 to 7 it is possible to observe a reduction in the number of samples needed to achieve the desired level of accuracy in the estimate. This is the result of the compact representation of the estimate of the posterior that is influenced by accurate new observation given by a peaked likelihood function.

6   Conclusions

Using a synergistic combination of standard and innovative tools from computer vision, probabilistic reasoning, agent technology, and information theory, we presented a computational framework for the adaptive integration of visual information.

By taking into account the uncertainty in the information provided by a set of visual agents, the system was able to take appropriate decisions about the information sources that were worth processing. Furthermore, our enhanced version of the particle filter provided an adaptive mechanism to determine a suitable number of samples and a suitable position for them. Given that the

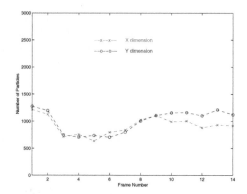

Fig. 8. Number of particles at each iteration of the enhanced version of the particle filter for tracking the orange ball. Between Frames 3 to 7 the importance function is updated including information from the last observation. The number of particles is adaptively selected using Equation (7). In this equation the error is set to 0.1 and the confidence level to 95%.

selection of the number of particles and the importance function are one of the main factors that determine the efficiency and accuracy of a particle filter, it is expected that the enhanced version presented in this work has an impact well beyond the application presented here.

The implementation of the system for the case of target tracking showed encouraging results. Using highly general visual algorithms and motion models, the system was able to simultaneously track targets with very different motions and visual features. In this test the application of the enhanced version of the particle filter produced a considerable reduction in the number of samples needed to estimate the state of the system.

References

1. Collett, T.: Insect navigation en route to the goal: Multiple strategies for the use of landmarks. Journal of Experimental Biology **235** (1996) 199–227
2. Zeki, M.: A Vision of the Brain. Oxford, Blackwell scientific publications (1993)
3. Nourbakhsh, I., Bobenage, J., Grange, S., Lutz, R., Meyer, R., Soto, A.: An affective mobile educator with a full-time job. Artificial Intelligence **114** (1999) 95–124
4. Darrell, T., Gordon, G., Harville, M., Woodfill, J.: Integrated person tracking using stereo, color, and pattern detection. In: IEEE Computer Vision and Pattern Recognition, Santa Barbara (1998) 601–609
5. Kanade, T., Collins, R., Lipton, A., Burt, P., Wixson, L.: Advances in cooperative multisensor video surveillance. In: Darpa Image Understanding Workshop, Morgan Kaufmann (1998) 3–24
6. Lipton, A., Fujiyoshi, H., Patil, R.: Moving target classification and tracking from real-time video. In: Proceedings of the 1998 DARPA Image Understanding Workshop. (1998)

7. Fox, D.: KLD-Sampling: Adaptive particle filters. In: Advances in Neural Information Processing Systems 14 (NIPS). (2001)
8. Owen, A.: Empirical Likelihood. Monographs on Statistics and Applied Probability, Stanford University, California, USA (2001)
9. Geweke, J.: Bayesian inference in econometric models using Monte Carlo integration. Econometrica **57** (1989) 1317–1339
10. Doucet, A., de Freitas, N., Gordon, N.: An introduction to sequential Monte Carlo methods. In: Sequential Monte Carlo Methods in Practice, Springer (2001) 3–14
11. Soto, A.: A probabilistic approach for the adaptive integration of multiple visual cues using an agent framework. Tech report CMU-RI-TR-02-30, Carnegie Mellon University (2002)

Approaches to Semi-supervised Learning of Fuzzy Classifiers

Aljoscha Klose

Department of Knowledge Processing and Language Engineering
University of Magdeburg, School of Computer Science
D-39106 Magdeburg, Germany
`aljoscha.klose@cs.uni-magdeburg.de`

Abstract. Recently, semi-supervised classifier learning has received a lot of attention. The idea of semi-supervised learning is to learn not only from the labeled training data, but to exploit also the structural information in additionally available unlabeled data. In this paper we propose two such approaches suited to learn fuzzy if-then classifiers. They are both based on evolutionary algorithms. We observed good performance on artificial and "real world" datasets compared to other algorithms proposed in literature.

1 Introduction

Fuzzy *if-then* rules have become a popular basis for classifiers. Especially in applications where transparency is of importance, it can be advantageous if the rule base is readable and interpretable for a human expert. Automatic induction of fuzzy rules from data is therefore an interesting topic. A variety of techniques has been proposed for this task, e.g. neuro-fuzzy systems, evolutionary algorithms, or decision tree based methods. These approaches have in common that they solve a *supervised learning* task, i.e. they induce the rules from a database of examples with known class labels.

Getting the labels for the data is, however, a problem in many practical applications. Often, training samples have to be labeled manually, which can be a tedious task when there are many objects. Typical examples of such domains are image processing or document retrieval. If only unlabeled data is available for learning, i.e. if the class labels of all sample data are unknown, *unsupervised learning* algorithms can be used. This is a task for cluster analysis, which tries to find groups of similar objects in data. Fuzzy extensions of cluster analysis represent the clusters by multidimensional fuzzy sets and can be used to extract fuzzy if-then rules from data [13]. The main drawback of unsupervised learning is that it strongly depends on the given distance measures. It has usually problems in finding the right number of clusters. Usually, we cannot guarantee that the clusters in the data space correspond to meaningful classes of the objects.

As unsupervised learning without any guidance does in many cases not yield satisfactory results, in practice supervised learning is much more common. If it

A. Günter et al. (Eds.): KI 2003, LNAI 2821, pp. 436–449, 2003.

is not possible to label all objects, one usually confines the examples to a certain — hopefully representative — fraction of the data and leaves the unlabeled data aside. However, though unlabeled, the additional data might still bear valuable information on the true distribution of the objects in the input space. Thus, it is an appealing idea to use the remaining, otherwise discarded, data to support the learning of a classifier. Such *semi-supervised* learning could thus be expected to yield better generalization on unseen data with much less labeled examples.

There have been some efforts to combine supervised and unsupervised learning. In Sect. 2 we briefly review previous work on semi-supervised learning. However, there are only few approaches to the semi-supervised induction of more convenient models like fuzzy rules from data. This, however, was our intention. As exploitation of structural information from unlabeled data is the focus of cluster analysis, it is not surprising that a number of semi-supervised learning methods have been established as extensions of cluster algorithms. Due to the closeness of fuzzy clustering and fuzzy rule-based classification, it would be straight-forward to use such an algorithm. However, as we will discuss in section 4 and empirically show in section 5, they have certain weaknesses and are not fully suited for our needs. We thus present an alternative approach, based on evolutionary learning and specialized fitness functions that allows learning of more flexible rule bases and overcomes some of the shortcomings of the existing algorithms. Our system is described in Sect. 4. We propose two different fitness functions in Sect. 4.1 and Sect. 4.2. The results of applying the classifiers on example data are presented in Sect. 5. Sect. 6 summarizes our results.

2   Semi-supervised Learning

The classical paradigms of machine learning can be separated into supervised and unsupervised approaches. Unsupervised learning techniques like cluster analysis seek for inherent structure in the distribution of the data, whereas supervised techniques try to generalize the regularities given by some sample data.

There have been some proposals how to combine and thus exploit the benefits of both approaches. In most publications, Pedrycz's approach from 1985 [22] is cited as the first work in the area of semi-supervised clustering. Since then, there have been a number of different ideas how to combine the information of labeled and unlabeled data in a semi-supervised learning algorithm. The underlying ideas include:

- Use the class information of the labeled points as seed points, and incrementally label the unlabeled points (e.g. [26]),
- learn prototypes from the labeled data and adjust their exact positions to fit labeled *and* unlabeled data (e.g. [3,22]),
- learn prototypes from the unlabeled data and determine their labels from the labeled (e.g. [2,16]),
- learn from the labeled points, use low densities between classes to optimize class borders (e.g. [1,9]),

  – use the abundance of unlabeled data for more reliable estimation of the
    probability density function of all the data in the input space (e.g. [24]).

Successful applications of semi-supervised approaches are reported e.g. in the
field of image processing [3] or text classification [18].

3   Semi-supervised Extension of Fuzzy C-Means

Not all of the ideas listed in the last section can be used for the induction of fuzzy
rules. Some of them rely on special characteristics of a certain model like, for
example, support vector machines. Due to the relationships between fuzzy clustering and fuzzy classification, we considered two extended cluster approaches
as benchmark for our own approach, namely the semi-supervised fuzzy c-means
(ssFCM) as proposed by Bensaid [3], and the semi-supervised point-prototype
clustering (ssPCM) devised by the same authors as an improvement of the first
algorithm [2,16]. We will briefly outline the ideas of the algorithms in the next
paragraphs. In section 4, we will explain which drawbacks we see with these
algorithms and why we devise our own semi-supervised fuzzy rule learner.

In [3], Bensaid *et al* propose a semi-supervised fuzzy clustering algorithm (**ss-
FCM**) that is based on the—originally unsupervised—fuzzy c-means algorithm.
The idea of this algorithm is that the labeled examples can help to control the
cluster–class relationship. The ssFCM uses one cluster per class. The cluster
centers are initialized from the coordinates of the labeled examples. The clusters are modified with the usual alternating optimization scheme, i.e. repeatedly
cluster centers are determined using the fixed membership degrees of objects to
clusters, followed by updating of the membership degrees with new prototype
positions. In ssFCM, the membership update step is modified such that the labeled examples always have a membership degree of 1 to their corresponding
cluster, and 0 to the other clusters. Thus cluster learning is directed towards the
labeled examples.

One drawback of this algorithm is the restriction of one cluster per class. The
semi-supervised point-prototype clustering algorithm (**ssPPC**), also proposed
by Bensaid *et al* [2], overcomes this weakness. It is also based on the fuzzy c-
means algorithm. The idea of ssPPC is to initially *overpartition* the unlabeled
input patterns in a fully unsupervised manner, where the number of cluster
prototypes is set to the number of labeled examples. Thus classes can be split
into several clusters. The resulting clusters are then labeled based on the labeled
examples. Several alternative strategies have been proposed to find the cluster
labels (improved version of the labeling strategies can be found in [16]). All of
them use the distances of clusters to labeled examples. The class for an unlabeled
tuple is computed by aggregating the prototype labels and the tuples' cluster
membership degrees. If necessary, crisp labels are generated by winner-takes-all
defuzzification.

4 An Evolutionary Algorithm for Semi-supervised Fuzzy Classification

In the last section, we outlined two approaches that extract fuzzy cluster descriptions in a partially supervised manner. So, where do we see the need to propose another algorithm? There are several reasons. First, the algorithms are not aimed at inducing fuzzy classifiers that are satisfying when interpreted as rule bases. The strict cluster-class correspondence of ssFCM wastes much of the flexibility of fuzzy classifiers. The extreme overpartitioning of ssPPC, on the other hand, degrades interpretability and readability of the rule base. We would like to have an algorithm that exploits the expression ability of fuzzy rule bases (including, for example, flexible cluster shapes, or "don't cares" in the antecedents), and still preserves interpretability and readability. Secondly, as we will see in the experimental section 5, neither of the approaches is very good in learning when the labeled examples are less representative for the prototypes. However, these are the cases where semi-supervised learning could be most powerful (if the labeled examples were representative, supervised methods would also perform well).

In this section we present two alternative approaches to the induction of fuzzy rules from partially labeled data. Although the approaches are rather different in their details, they share a similar basic idea how to incorporate labeled and unlabeled examples into an objective function. One advantage of using an evolutionary algorithm for fuzzy rule learning is that it can directly use these quite different quality measures. Apart from this convenient aspect, there are several other reasons that speak for evolutionary rule learning in comparison to other search techniques like, for example, alternating optimization. It allows to learn structure and incorporate constraints to maintain interpretability. It is less sensitive to premature convergence in local minima, which can be a problem in semi-supervised learning due to the "strong" guidance from the labeled and the "weak" guidance from the unlabeled examples. And, last but not least, it also works with non-differentiable objective functions, as those presented in sections 4.1 and 4.2. In this section, we briefly discuss implementation aspects of our evolutionary rule learner.

A fuzzy classification system [13] consists of a fuzzy rule base and an inference engine, which evaluates the rule base for the datum to be classified. The rule base contains a set of fuzzy classification rules of the form:

> **if** x_1 is μ_1 **and** x_2 is μ_2 **and** ... **and** x_n is μ_n
> **then** pattern $(x_1, x_2, \ldots, x_n)$ belongs to class c,

where the μ_k are fuzzy sets describing regions in the corresponding dimensions. We use Gaussian functions, and calculate the rule activation as the product of the individual membership degrees in the antecedent. Additionally, we allow "don't cares" in the antecedents, i.e. fuzzy sets $\mu_{DC} \equiv 1$. Especially in higher dimensional datasets "don't cares" are important to make the fuzzy rules more readable, the rule bases more compact and improve generalization ability.

Fuzzy membership functions in fuzzy rule base systems can be defined either locally or globally. Globally means that a set of membership functions is defined for the rule base, and that they are referred to by the antecedents of the rules. In the local case, each rule might have its own fuzzy set definitions. Globally partitioning the axes into fuzzy sets makes it easier to assign linguistic labels to them. The global definition is thus more commonly used. However, in our implementation we chose to use locally defined fuzzy sets for two reasons. First, locally defined fuzzy sets allow more degrees of freedom, where rules with globally defined fuzzy sets often yield only axis parallel separation borders between classes (see, e.g., [19]). Secondly, the rule-wise definition eases the genetic operations like crossover and thus enables synchronous optimization of rules and fuzzy sets. By applying repair mechanisms we try to ensure linguistic interpretability of the resulting fuzzy sets.

In the implementation of the evolutionary learning we roughly follow the "Pittsburgh-style" [25] approach described in [5]. Opposed to "Michigan-style" [12] approaches, one chromosome represents a complete rule base (instead of cooperating individual rules).

As selection operator we chose the tournament selection [10], i.e. we randomly choose two chromosomes from the pool and take the fitter of the two. This operator is more robust compared to fitness proportional approaches, as it does not depend on the scaling of the fitness function, and computationally cheaper than rank based selection, which implies sorting the chromosomes by fitness.

According to the *building block theorem* [11], a good recombination operator should produce valid offsprings that preserve good partial solution from their parents. In our case, reasonable building blocks are obviously the rules, or combinations of them. In a former implementation [15], we used the so-called *one-point ordered crossover* [5]. It chooses a split point on every axis and thus separates the rule space into two subspaces. In the child's rule base we copy the rules of one parent falling in one, and of the other parent falling in the other subspace. The resulting rule base of the child chromosome is covered with rules from the whole rule space, and neighboring rules have a higher probability to survive together. The number of rules may change by this procedure. However, the subspaces can show some peculiarities[1] if dimensionality is high. We thus perform the split differently by defining a random hyperplane and choose the rules that have their center on one or the other side.

The mutation operator changes structure as well as parameters of the fuzzy sets. Thus rules might be deleted or added, dimensions might be set to "don't care", and the fuzzy set parameters are overlaid with small Gaussian distributed noise.

To enable linguistic interpretation of the fuzzy sets after learning, a minimum requirement is that they are ordered. In that way we can assign the usual labels (e.g. *small, medium, large*) or mixtures of them (e.g. *small to medium*). We

---

[1] The exchanged subspace is actually a corner of a hypercube. If the split point is uniformly drawn, the hypervolume of the corner will in average be much smaller than that of the remainder, especially with high dimensionality.

implemented a repair mechanism that checks the fuzzy sets of every dimension after crossover and mutation. If the constraints are violated, the fuzzy sets are appropriately shifted to restore them.

4.1   A Fitness Function Based on Impurity and Dispersion

The fitness function for the evolutionary rule learner must take labeled and unlabeled examples into account. One way to do this is by combining measures of cluster impurity and cluster dispersion. Cluster impurity measures, how the known samples are distributed to the clusters (i.e. the influence regions of the rules). A very simple measure of impurity would be the number of misclassifications. However, more sophisticated measures take the distribution of misclassification into account, and prefer configurations where the misclassifications are concentrated in few clusters. Inspired by [7], we used the Gini-Index, which is well known in the decision tree community [4]. Let X_{ij}^d denote the labeled examples of class j assigned to rule i (i.e. rule i yields the maximal activation), and let X_i^d be the total number of labeled examples assigned to rule i. Then the Gini-index for a rule i is defined as

$$\text{gini}_i = 1 - \sum_{j=1}^{c} \left(\frac{|X_{ij}^d|}{|X_i^d|} \right)^2 .$$

The impurity measure is combined from the k rules' Gini-indexes:

$$\text{impurity} = \sum_{i=1}^{k} \frac{|X_i^d|}{|X^d|} \cdot \text{gini}_i$$

A dispersion measure is calculated from all tuples $X^d \cup X^u$, ignoring the known labels U^d. Its purpose is to measure, how well the rules cover the tuples in the input space. A simple dispersion measure is, for example, the sum of squared distances between points x and corresponding (closest) rule centers v_{i_x}

$$E = \sum_{x \in X^d \cup X^u} \| x - v_{i_x} \|^2 .$$

BTW, this dispersion measure is minimized by c-means clustering. Demiriz *et al* proposed the inverse Davies-Bouldin index [6,14] as dispersion measure for semi-supervised point-prototype classification. The Davies-Bouldin index measures the relation of inner-cluster to inter-cluster distances. Inter-cluster distance is the squared Euclidean distance between two cluster centers v_i and $v_{i'}$

$$D_{ii'} = \| v_i - v_{i'} \|^2,$$

and inner-cluster distance is defined as the average distance of the tuples X_i assigned to a cluster center i

$$e_i = \frac{1}{|X_i|} \sum_{x \in X_i} \| x - v_i \|^2 .$$

The inner-inter-cluster ratio for two clusters is defined as

$$R_{ii'} = \frac{e_i + e_{i'}}{D_{ii'}}.$$

The Davies-Bouldin index is calculated from the ratios of the k clusters as

$$DB = \frac{1}{k} \sum_{i=1}^{k} \max_{i' \neq i} R_{ii'}.$$

As we wanted to induce fuzzy rules instead of just point prototypes, we could not use this measure directly, as it considers only the centers and not the size of the cluster. As we use Gaussian membership functions and $\top_{prod}$-inference, there is an obvious relationship between distance and (negative logarithm of) rule activation. Thus, we define the average activation of a rule i' for tuples assigned to rule i as

$$\hat{e}_{ii'} = -\frac{1}{|X_i|} \sum_{x \in X_i} \ln \text{act}_{i'}(x).$$

We replace the inner cluster distance e_i by $\hat{e}_{ii}$, and approximate the intra cluster distance $D_{ii'}$ by $\frac{1}{2}(\hat{e}_{ii'} + \hat{e}_{i'i})$. From this we get an alternative dispersion measure

$$\text{dispersion} = \widehat{DB} = \frac{2}{k} \sum_{i=1}^{k} \max_{i' \neq i} \frac{\hat{e}_{ii} + \hat{e}_{i'i'}}{\hat{e}_{ii'} + \hat{e}_{i'i}}.$$

The fitness function for the evolutionary algorithm is simply a linear combination of the two measures:

$$\text{fitness} = \alpha \cdot \text{impurity} + (1 - \alpha \cdot \text{dispersion})$$

4.2 A Fitness Function Based on the MDL Principle

The fitness function described in this section can also be seen as a combination of impurity and dispersion measure. However, the measure is based on the Minimum Description Length Principle (MDL), which gives us the appealing opportunity to derive both parts of the fitness function in the same theoretic context [23]. Additionally it allows to compare models of different complexity and has a rather objective mechanism of punishing over-complex models.

The idea of MDL is that the data has to be transmitted from an (imaginary) sender to an (imaginary) receiver. Structure in the data can be used for more efficient codes that result in shorter messages. However, both sender and transmitter need to know the encoding scheme of the data. Thus the message is compound by first transmitting the coding scheme, and then the data, encoded using this scheme. Complex models need a longer coding scheme, as more free parameters have to be transmitted. However, the resulting data part of the message will usually be shorter. The model with the shortest overall message length is assumed to fit the data best and is chosen. MDL is equivalent to maximum likelihood for the estimation of models with a fixed number of free parameters, but additionally offers a possibility to compare objectively between models of different complexity.

To apply the MDL principle to our problem, we have to define an appropriate encoding scheme. The message consists of the following parts:

- **the rule base (the** *code***)**, e.g. the number of dimensions, the number of rules, the fuzzy sets used in a rule. This information is then used to encode
- **the data tuples (the** *data* **itself)**, e.g. the index of the rule that is used to encode this tuple, the exact values of the tuple using a rule specific code, and the class labels.

According to Shannon's coding theorem, the lengths in bits of parts of a message are calculated as $- \log p_i$, where p_i is the probability of an instantiation i within all possible alternatives over some appropriately chosen probability distribution. To illustrate this, we present the equations for the message length for data tuples below.

If the t-norm $\top_{\mathrm{prod}}$ is used and some restrictions are placed on the fuzzy sets and rule weights, (neuro-) fuzzy classification systems can be seen as Naive Bayes classifiers [20]. We can use this interpretation of the fuzzy membership values as probability densities to transmit the tuple coordinates. Let x be a tuple, r the rule which is used to encode it, i.e. the rule with the highest activation, and w_r the appropriate normalizing rule weight. Then the part of the message that transmits the coordinates of the d dimensions of a tuple has a length of

$$l(\mathbf{x}) = - \log_2 w_r - \sum_{i=1}^{d} \log_2 \mu_{r,i}(x_i).$$

This part measures cluster dispersion. It is used for encoding both, labeled and unlabeled tuples. The closer a tuple lies to the center of the membership functions of its rule (i.e. the better the rule is adapted to the data), the higher the probabilities and thus the shorter the code length is.

Additionally, we have to transmit the class labels of the tuples. We associate each rule with the majority class of the tuples covered by it. Thus we can use the (already transmitted) information which rule is used to encode a tuple. However, there might be tuples of several classes covered by one rule. Therefore, we have also to transmit the exceptions from the rule. We have to encode the class distribution in a rule and the explicit class labels for the tuples. Let X_i denote the tuples covered by a rule i, and within those let X_{ij} denote the tuples of class j. Let c be the number of classes in the dataset. In that part of the message the X_i^u unlabeled points play a role. We consider them as belonging to the majority class $j_{\max}$ in that rule and thus transmit this class (the most probable class yields the shortest message length). For the encoding of the class information for all tuples covered by one rule i we thus get a length of

$$l(r) = \log_2 \frac{(|X_i| + c - 1)!}{|X_i|!(c-1)!} + \log_2 \frac{|X_i|!}{(\prod_{j=1, j \neq j_{\max}}^{c} |X_{ij}|!)|X_{ij_{\max}} \cup X_i^u|!}.$$

	ID3	QP	ssPPC: A, B, C			ssFCM	G/DB, G/DB fix.		MDL, MDL fix.	
Avg										
10%	13.30	23.80	10.77	9.50	8.27	12.60	23.17	12.90	6.57	7.90
20%	11.17	29.35	6.13	7.47	7.20	12.47	13.30	9.77	6.33	5.27
30%	9.33	25.30	4.77	5.94	3.73	12.27	7.43	7.33	5.23	4.70
40%	9.77	17.15	3.23	4.20	3.30	11.23	6.20	6.53	3.83	3.23
50%	8.47	17.25	2.60	3.33	2.97	11.23	4.27	6.13	3.13	2.90
60%	7.47	14.90	2.53	3.20	2.20	11.80	3.30	3.37	2.30	2.77
70%	7.37	10.60	1.80	1.70	1.47	11.60	3.30	2.87	2.43	1.83
Std										
10%	6.56	6.56	7.13	5.77	4.22	3.48	11.83	3.97	2.53	3.81
20%	4.40	4.40	2.23	2.59	3.81	2.81	8.95	4.21	3.29	2.85
30%	2.78	2.78	1.71	2.58	1.15	2.19	3.87	3.29	2.25	2.12
40%	3.73	3.73	1.33	1.56	1.37	1.93	5.60	2.66	1.23	1.61
50%	2.23	2.23	1.25	1.42	1.25	1.73	2.13	2.83	1.61	1.52
60%	1.20	1.20	1.56	1.87	0.87	1.51	1.42	1.54	2.09	1.43
70%	1.33	1.33	1.05	1.32	1.15	1.36	2.29	1.38	1.10	0.99
Min										
10%	7	3	5	4	3	5	6	3	3	3
20%	7	5	3	3	3	6	5	4	2	2
30%	6	3	2	3	2	8	3	2	3	1
40%	6	3	0	2	1	8	2	2	2	1
50%	6	2	0	1	0	8	1	1	0	0
60%	6	2	0	0	1	9	0	1	0	0
70%	6	2	0	0	0	10	1	1	1	0
Max										
10%	28	55	30	29	20	17	51	22	13	15
20%	21	49	10	12	16	16	43	23	18	13
30%	16	39	9	12	7	17	20	16	14	10
40%	20	30	6	7	7	15	32	13	6	7
50%	16	35	5	6	7	15	10	12	7	6
60%	10	20	6	8	4	15	7	7	11	6
70%	11	15	4	6	5	14	13	6	4	5

Fig. 1. Experimental results on Iris data (the first 6 columns are cited from [16]).

Misclassified labeled tuples make that part of the message longer, as the probability distribution of a rule becomes more heterogeneous, and thus this part of the measure quantifies cluster impurity.

One problem of this measure is that the relation of the lengths of the code part and the data part of the message depends on the number of tuples and the number of dimensions. It can therefore be important to weight the individual parts of the message. This can be interpreted as adjusting the precision of the transmitted tuple coordinates.

5   Empirical Results

We compared the performance of the algorithms on two examples: the "real world" Iris dataset with randomly hidden labels, and an artificial dataset where the labeled examples are less representative for the cluster prototypes.

In [2,16] the algorithms of Sect. 3 have been extensively tested on the well-known Iris data from the UCI machine learning repository [17]. We will cite these results here and compare them to the algorithms we proposed in Sect. 4.

For each algorithm (or variant thereof) 210 runs have been performed: The fraction of presented labels was chosen from 10% to 70% in steps of 10%, and for each the data was 30 times randomly split into labeled and unlabeled examples. We performed transduction, i.e. we learned the classifiers on labeled and unlabeled data and used it to assign labels to the same set of unlabeled data. For each percentage, we report mean, standard deviation, minimum and maximum of the error rates over the 30 runs.[2] The compared algorithms are (cf. Fig. 1):

- ID3: a decision tree learner [21]. This algorithm is fully supervised, thus only the labeled fraction is used for learning. The results are quoted from [16].
- QP: another fully supervised algorithm: a Quickprop neural network [8] with 4-3-3 structure (results quoted from [16]).
- ssPPC A/B/C: the semi-supervised point-prototype classifier from section 3, with the three labeling variants described in [16] (results quoted from there: A, B, and C correspond to Eq. (8), Eq. (9), and Eq. (12), respectively).
- ssFCM: the semi-supervised point-prototype classifier described in Sect. 3 (results quoted from [2]).
- G/DB: our proposed algorithm based on the Gini- and modified Davies-Bouldin-index (see Sect. 4.1).
- G/DB fix.: same, but with fixed widths of the fuzzy sets.
- MDL: proposed algorithm based on the minimal description length principle (see Sect. 4.2).
- MDL fix.: same, but with fixed widths of the fuzzy sets.

The two supervised algorithms perform rather poor on this dataset. This is what we expected for a small number of presented labels, but it is rather surprising for the runs with 70% of the labels presented. The percentage of labeled examples least affects ssFCM. We assume, that (unsupervised) clustering prevails. The results of the remaining semi-supervised approaches do not differ so much. Only the fitness function based on Gini-index and Davies-Bouldin-index

---

[2] The error rates reported in [16] are calculated by reclassification, i.e. the classifier is induced from labeled fraction plus remaining unlabeled data, and then applied to all data. It would certainly be preferable to estimate the error rates on an independent test dataset. However, as the Iris data has only 150 instances, the authors of [16,2] decided to use the reclassification rates. To be comparable, we also use the reclassification rates. As the true labels of the unlabeled data are not used during induction, the danger of overfitting is rather small. For few labeled examples, the error rates produced on them will in most cases be (at least close to) 0, and thus the reported mixed error should be reasonably fair.

is significantly worse. The evolutionary algorithm tends to find solutions with rules rather degenerated (the extent in one dimension is almost zero). The runs with fixed widths of the fuzzy sets ("GI/DB fix.") thus perform much better.

The two MDL based approaches are slightly ahead the other approaches. Especially when extremely few labeled examples are presented to the learner (10% means 5 tuples per class), the results are significantly better than that of ssFCM, ssPPC and Gini/DBI-approaches. When many labeled examples are presented to the semi-supervised approaches, the estimated performances are probably over-optimistic. Especially ssPPC will more or less "memorize" the labeled points (with 70% labeled examples it uses 105 cluster prototypes!). This at least partially explains, why ssPPC outperforms the other, less flexible supervised and semi-supervised models in the runs with many labeled examples.

Fig. 2a shows the second considered dataset. It has 1000 cases in two classes, "△" and "○". The data comes from three normal distributions, two of them form class "△". From the 1000 examples, only 40 labels are shown to the learner (bigger+colored points). Obviously the examples of class "○" only cover the bottom region of the cluster. This could, for example, be a realistic situation if the data had been manually labeled: the expert chose examples of class "○" such that they are different from class "△". Thus, they may be "typical", however they are not representative for the clusters.

The algorithms mentioned in this paper have been applied to this dataset. The resulting classifiers have been applied to an independent test dataset with 1000 examples of the same distribution. The results are shown in Fig. 2b-f. The shaded background visualizes the decision boundaries of the classifiers. Wrongly classified examples are drawn with their correct shape, but bigger and in red.

Fig. 2b shows the result of ssFCM. Obviously, the two prototypes (for the two classes) are not enough to model the distribution adequately. Interestingly, although the right cluster of class o is lower than the left, the decision boundary is slightly tilted to the left. There is no mechanism in ssFCM that could compensate this. Fig. 2c depicts the result of ssPPC. Faintly, one can see the positions of the 40 cluster centers. The used labeling algorithm is C, i.e. Eq. (12) in [16]. The algorithm produces a smooth decision boundary, and it would certainly have the expression ability to model a rather good boundary. However, all proposed labeling algorithm use only the distance of the clusters to the labeled examples. Thus, the result is rather disappointing and not very different from what could be expected from, e.g., a nearest neighbor classifier. The deficiencies of the two presented existing algorithms can be clearly seen on this dataset.

The result of our proposed semi-supervised MDL-based evolutionary learner is shown in Fig. 2d. The decision boundary is very close to the optimal boundary, i.e. the boundary that would result from supervised learning with all labels given (remember that we presented only 4% of the training data!). The distribution is modeled with four rules, two for each class.

The last two figures 2e and 2f depict the results from the evolutionary algorithm with the Gini and Davies/Bouldin index. The Davies/Bouldin index is known to prefer small numbers of clusters. If flexible widths of the fuzzy sets are

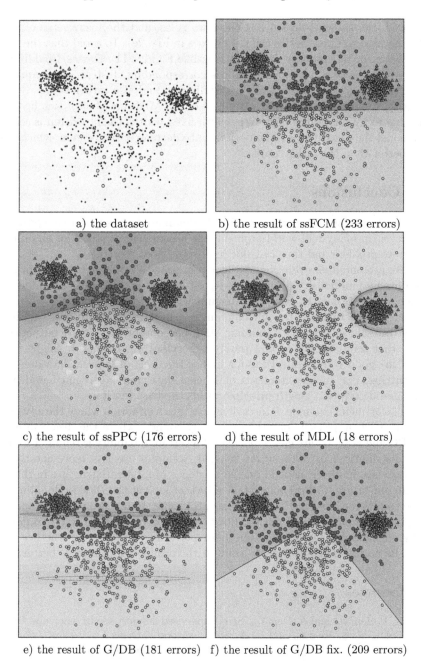

a) the dataset

b) the result of ssFCM (233 errors)

c) the result of ssPPC (176 errors)

d) the result of MDL (18 errors)

e) the result of G/DB (181 errors) f) the result of G/DB fix. (209 errors)

Fig. 2. Experimental results on artificial dataset.

allowed, the shown solution has only two rules, and the fuzzy sets are almost degenerated to lines (notice the flat ellipses in Fig. 2e). To avoid this, the widths can be fixed. In that case the result look like Fig. 2f. The Davies/Bouldin index leads to a choice of three rules. As the corresponding clusters are of equal size, the result is poorly adapted to the distribution and also rather weak.

One could argue, that the advantage of the MDL-based approach lies in the flexible fuzzy set widths. However, width fixed widths the algorithm is still able to model the distribution. The performance decreases to 43 errors, which is still far better than the other results.

6   Conclusions

The state of the art in data mining is dominated by supervised approaches. However, in many real-world problems the assignment of labels for all objects is a severe problem and thus calls for semi-supervised methods.

We presented an evolutionary algorithm to induce fuzzy rules, and proposed two fitness functions that allows to exploit labeled and unlabeled training data. We compared them to existing semi-supervised algorithms that have been proposed for the related—though different—task of fuzzy clustering. On the Iris data, Bensaid *et al*'s ssPPC and our MDL based approach clearly outperformed the other semi-supervised and purely supervised algorithms. It might well be that the good results of ssPPC for higher fractions of labeled data are due to overfitting. For smaller fractions of labeled data, our algorithm based on the minimal description length principle yields the best results.

The artificial example dataset demonstrates a situation where the advantages of our MDL approach (or—the other way round—where the disadvantages of ssPPC and ssFCM) are clearly visible: If a certain flexibility is required to model the distribution, or if the given labeled examples are less representative. All approaches, however, depend on the existence of inherent structure in the data.

In our future work we might take a further look at the Davies/Bouldin index. The results reported in [7] were rather promising. Hence, we might compare the original approach against our modified approach. We might also try to find out, why our modified Davies/Bouldin index performed so bad, and whether it can, e.g., be normalized such that learning with variable widths works better.

References

1. K. P. Bennett and A. Demiriz. Semi-supervised support vector machines. In D. A. Cohn, M. S. Kearns, and S. A. Solla, editors, *Advances in Neural Information processing Systems*, pages 368–374, MIT Press, Cambridge, MA, 1998.
2. A. M. Bensaid and J. C. Bezdek. Semi-Supervised point prototype clustering. *Pattern Recognition and Artificial Intelligence*, 12(5):625–643, 1998.
3. A. M. Bensaid, L. O. Hall, J. C. Bezdek, and L. P. Clarke. Partially supervised clustering for image segmentation. *Pattern Recognition*, 29(5):859–871, 1996.
4. L. Breiman, J. H. Friedman, J. A. Olshen, and C. J. Stone. *Classification and Regression Trees*. Belmont, CA: Wadsworth , 1984.

5. B. Carse, T. C. Fogarty, and A. Munro. Evolving fuzzy rule based controllers using genetic algorithms. *Fuzzy Sets and Systems*, 80:273–293, 1996.
6. D. L. Davies and D. W. Bouldin. A cluster separation measure. *IEEE Transactions on Pattern Analysis and Machine Intelligence*, 1(2):224–227, 1979.
7. A. Demiriz, K. P. Bennett, and M. J. Embrechts. Semi-supervised clustering using genetic algorithms. In *Proc. Artificial Neural Networks in Applications*, 1999.
8. S. Fahlman. Fast Learning Variations on Backpropagation: an Empirical Study. In *Proc. Connectionist Models Summer School*, 1988.
9. G. Fung and O. L. Mangasarian. Semi-Supervised Support Vector Machines for Unlabeled Data Classification. *Data Mining Institute, TR 99–05*, 1999.
10. D. E. Goldberg and K. Deb. A comparative analysis of selection schemes used in genetic algorithms. In G. Rawlins, editor, *Foundations of Genetic Algorithms*. Morgan Kaufmann, 1991.
11. J. H. Holland. *Adaptation in natural and artificial Systems*. The University of Michigan Press, Ann Arbor, MI, 1975. (reprint by MIT Press, 1992)
12. J. H. Holland and J. S. Reitman. Cognitive systems based on adaptive algorithms. In D. A. Waterman and F. Hayes-Roth (eds.): *Pattern-Directed Inference Systems*, Academic Press, pp. 313–329, 1978.
13. F. Höppner, F. Klawonn, R. Kruse, and T. Runkler. *Fuzzy Cluster Analysis*. Kluwer Verlag, 1998.
14. A. K. Jain and R. C. Dubes. *Algorithms for clustering data*. Prentice Hall, Englewood Cliffs, N.J., 1988.
15. A. Klose and R. Kruse. Enabling Neuro-Fuzzy Classification to Learn From Partially Labelled Data. In *Proc. FUZZ-IEEE'02*, IEEE, Piscataway, 2002.
16. T. Labzour, A. Bensaid, and J. Bezdek. Improved Semi-Supervised Point-Prototype Clustering Algorithms. In *Proc. of Intl. Conf. on Fuzzy Systems*, pages 1383–1387, 1998.
17. C. J. Merz and P. M. Murphy. UCI Repository of Machine Learning Databases. Department of Information and Computer Science, University of California, Irvine, CA. [Online]. Available: http:// www.ics.uci.edu/ mlearn/MLRepository.html.
18. K. Nigam, A. McCallum, S. Thrun, and T. Mitchell. Text classification from labeled and unlabeled documents using EM. *Machine learning*, 39(2/32): 103–134, 2000.
19. A. Nürnberger, A. Klose, and R. Kruse. Effects of Antecedent Pruning in Fuzzy Classification Systems In *Proc. KES'00*, pages 154–157, IEEE, Piscataway, 2000.
20. A. Nürnberger, C. Borgelt, and A. Klose. Improving naive Bayes classifiers using neuro-fuzzy learning. In *Proc. ICONIP'99*, pages 154–159, Perth, Australia, 1999.
21. J. R. Quinlan. *Induction of decision trees*. Machine Learning, 1:81–106, 1986.
22. W. Pedrycz. Algorithms of fuzzy clustering with partial supervision. *Pattern Recognition Letters*, 3:13–20, 1985.
23. J. Rissanen. A universal prior for integers and estimation by minimum description length. *Annals of Statistics*, 11:416–431, 1983.
24. A. Skabar. Augmenting supervised neural classifier training using a corpus of unlabeled data. In *Proceedings of 25th German Conference on Artificial Intelligence (KI-2002)*, pages 174–185, Aachen, Germany, 2002.
25. S. F. Smith. *A learning system based on genetic adaptive algorithms*. PhD thesis, Department of Computer Science, University of Pittsburgh, 1980.
26. A. Verikas, A. Gelzinis, and K. Malmquist. Using Unlabeled Data for Learning Classification Problems. In L. C. Jain and J. Kacprzyk, editors, *New Learning Paradigms in Soft Computing*, pages 368–403, Physica, Heidelberg, 2002.

Instance-Based Learning of Credible Label Sets

Eyke Hüllermeier

Informatics Institute, Marburg University, Germany
eyke@mathematik.uni-marburg.de

Abstract. Even though instance-based learning performs well in practice, it might be criticized for its neglect of uncertainty: An estimation is usually given in the form of a predicted label, but without characterizing the confidence of this prediction. In this paper, we propose an instance-based learning method that allows for deriving "credible" estimations, namely set-valued predictions that cover the true label of a query object with high probability. Our method is built upon a formal model of the heuristic inference principle underlying instance-based learning.

1 Introduction

The name instance-based learning (IBL) stands for a family of machine learning algorithms, including well-known variants such as memory-based learning, exemplar-based learning and case-based reasoning [14,10,8]. As the term suggests, in instance-based algorithms special importance is attached to the concept of an *instance* [2]. An instance, also called a case, an observation or an example, can be thought of as a single experience, such as a pattern (along with its classification) in pattern recognition or a problem (along with a solution) in case-based reasoning.

As opposed to inductive, model-based machine learning methods, IBL provides a simple means for realizing *transductive* inference [15], that is inference "from specific to specific": Rather than inducing a general model (theory) from the data and using this model for further reasoning, the data itself is simply stored. The processing of the data is deferred until a prediction (or some other type of query) is actually requested, a property which qualifies IBL as a *lazy* learning method [1]. Predictions are then derived by combining in one way or the other the information provided by the stored examples, especially by those objects which are *similar* to the new query.

In fact, the concept of similarity plays a central role in IBL whose underlying inference principle corresponds to the well-known *nearest-neighbor* rule, suggesting that "similar objects have similar labels". This assertion, which we shall occasionally call the "IBL assumption", is apparently of *heuristic* nature: It is a rule of thumb that works in most situations but is not guaranteed to do so in every case. This clearly reveals the necessity of taking the aspect of *uncertainty* in IBL into account [4]. Especially, this is true for sensitive applications such as medical diagnosis or legal reasoning and all the more if decisions (classifications) must be made on the basis of sparse experience.

A. Günter et al. (Eds.): KI 2003, LNAI 2821, pp. 450–464, 2003.

In this paper, we shall propose an instance-based learning method that allows for deriving "credible" predictions. The way in which this approach takes the aspect of uncertainty into account takes its inspiration from statistical methods: The basic idea is to derive a kind of *credible set*[1] for the value (label) to be estimated, that is a subset of values which is likely to contain the true one.

The remaining part of the paper is organized as follows: After some preliminaries, we introduce the concepts of a *similarity profile* and a *similarity hypothesis* (Sections 3–4). These concepts will allow us to propose a formal model of the IBL assumption as well as an instance-based inference scheme that derives predictions in the form of a set of potential labels. Then, a method for learning similarity hypotheses from a memory of cases will be presented, along with theoretical and empirical results on the validity of predictions derived from such hypotheses (Section 5). Finally, in Section 6, we consider the problem of adapting the involved similarity measures so as to optimize our algorithm's performance.

2   Preliminaries

Throughout the paper we proceed from the following setting: $\mathcal{X}$ denotes the instance space, where an instance corresponds to the description x of an object (usually in attribute–value form). $\mathcal{X}$ is endowed with a reflexive and symmetric similarity measure, $\sigma_{\mathcal{X}}$. $\mathcal{L}$ is a set of labels, also endowed with a reflexive and symmetric similarity measure, $\sigma_{\mathcal{L}}$. We assume that $\sigma_{\mathcal{X}}$ and $\sigma_{\mathcal{L}}$ are normalized such that both measures return similarity degrees between 0 and 1, where 1 stands for complete similarity. $\mathcal{D}$ denotes a sample (memory, case base) that consists of n labeled instances (cases) $\langle x_i, \lambda_{x_i} \rangle \in \mathcal{X} \times \mathcal{L}$, $1 \leq i \leq n$. Finally, a novel instance $x_0 \in \mathcal{X}$ (a query) is given, whose label λ_{x_0} is to be estimated.

We do not make any assumptions on the cardinality of the label set $\mathcal{L}$. In fact, we do not even distinguish between the performance tasks of classification (estimating one among a finite set of class labels) and regression (estimating a real-valued output), which means that $\mathcal{L}$ might even be infinite. As concerns classification, however, it deserves mentioning that our method is more suitable for problems involving many labels. This does hardly diminish its practical relevance, since there are enough problems of this type. For example, consider case-based problem solving where an instance corresponds to a problem description, e.g. a set of requirements a technical system has to meet, and the label corresponds to a solution of that problem, e.g. the assemblage of primitive components into a complete technical system [5]. Having to build a new system, one will usually try to exploit experience that has been gained from building systems for similar requirements, relying on the assumption that "similar problems have similar solutions". As another example, consider a problem somewhat more difficult than classification: Rather than predicting one among n labels, we seek a full *ranking* of these labels, that is a complete order relation [3]. Since n "ba-

---

[1] This term is also common in Bayesian statistics. A related concept in classical statistics is that of a confidence region.

sic" labels can be arranged to $n!$ different rankings, the actual set of potential predictions can be huge.

Finally, note that no kind of transitivity is assumed for the similarity measures, which means that the structure of $\mathcal{X}$ and $\mathcal{L}$ is weaker than that of a metric space. This excludes the application of several standard methods from statistics.

3   Similarity Profiles

A basic idea of our approach is to proceed from a formal model of the heuristic IBL assumption, that is a formalization of this otherwise vague principle. As will be seen later, this formalization provides the basis of a sound inference procedure and will allow us to make assertions about the confidence of predictions.

To begin, suppose that the IBL hypothesis has the following concrete meaning:

$$\forall x_1, x_2 \in \mathcal{X} : \sigma_{\mathcal{X}}(x_1, x_2) \leq \sigma_{\mathcal{L}}\left(\lambda_{x_1}, \lambda_{x_2}\right). \tag{1}$$

In words: The similarity between two labels is always lower-bounded by the similarity between the corresponding instances, or, roughly speaking, the more similar two instances are, the more similar are the corresponding labels.

If the similarity constraint (1) does indeed hold true for the application at hand, then one can reason as follows: Given a query x_0 and an observed case $\langle x_1, \lambda_{x_1} \rangle$ such that x_1 is α_1-similar to x_0, the unknown label λ_{x_0} must be an element of the α_1-neighborhood of the label λ_{x_1}, i.e., of the set of labels λ such that $\sigma_{\mathcal{L}}(\lambda, \lambda_{x_1}) \geq \alpha_1$. Moreover, given a second case $\langle x_1, \lambda_{x_1} \rangle$, the same kind of reasoning applies, and we can conclude that λ_{x_0} must be an element of a certain α_2-neighborhood of λ_{x_2}. And we can even come up with a more precise prediction by combining the two constraints: λ_{x_0} must belong to the intersection of the two neighborhoods (see Fig. 1).

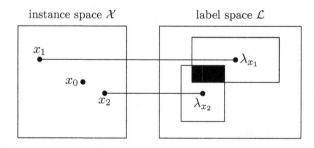

Fig. 1. Each case puts a constraint on the label λ_{x_0} by virtue of property (1).

Needless to say, the similarity constraint (1) will usually not be satisfied for a practical application (and given similarity measures $\sigma_{\mathcal{X}}, \sigma_{\mathcal{L}}$). Therefore, let us consider a relaxation of this constraint:

$$\forall x_1, x_2 \in \mathcal{X} : \zeta\left(\sigma_{\mathcal{X}}(x_1, x_2)\right) \leq \sigma_{\mathcal{L}}(\lambda_{x_1}, \lambda_{x_2}), \tag{2}$$

where ζ is a function $\mathcal{A} \to [0, 1]$ with $\mathcal{A} =_{\text{def}} \{\sigma_{\mathcal{X}}(x, x') \mid x, x' \in \mathcal{X}\}$. This function assigns to each similarity degree between two instances, α, the largest similarity degree $\beta = \zeta(\alpha)$ such that the following property holds:

$$\forall x_1, x_2 \in \mathcal{X} : \sigma_{\mathcal{X}}(x_1, x_2) = \alpha \Rightarrow \sigma_{\mathcal{L}}(\lambda_{x_1}, \lambda_{x_2}) \geq \zeta(\alpha).$$

We call ζ the *similarity profile* of the application at hand. More formally, ζ is defined as follows: For all $\alpha \in \mathcal{A}$,

$$\zeta(\alpha) =_{\text{def}} \inf_{x, x' \in \mathcal{X}, \sigma_{\mathcal{X}}(x, x') = \alpha} \sigma_{\mathcal{L}}(\lambda_x, \lambda_{x'}).$$

Note that the similarity profile conveys a precise idea of the extent to which the application at hand actually meets the IBL assumption. Roughly speaking, the larger ζ is, the better this assumption is satisfied.

Using the relaxed constraint (2), we can perform the same kind of reasoning as before. We only have to replace the α_i-neighborhoods of the known labels λ_{x_i} by the corresponding β_i-neighborhoods, where $\beta_i = \zeta(\alpha_i)$. Thus, the following inference scheme is obtained: $\lambda_{x_0} \in C(x_0)$ with $C(x_0) =_{\text{def}} \mathcal{L}$ if $\mathcal{D} = \emptyset$ and

$$C(x_0) =_{\text{def}} \bigcap_{i=1}^{n} \mathcal{N}_{\zeta(\sigma_{\mathcal{X}}(x_i, x_0))}(\lambda_{x_i}) \tag{3}$$

otherwise, where the β-neighborhood of a label λ is given by

$$\mathcal{N}_{\beta}(\lambda) =_{\text{def}} \{\lambda' \in \mathcal{L} \mid \sigma_{\mathcal{L}}(\lambda, \lambda') \geq \beta\}. \tag{4}$$

This inference scheme is obviously correct in the sense that $C(x_0)$ is guaranteed to cover λ_{x_0}, a property that follows immediately from the definition of the similarity profile ζ. We call $C(x_0)$ a *credible label set*, or simply a *credible set*.

Note that taking the intersection over $k < n$ of the cases in $\mathcal{D}$ comes along with a loss of precision but preserves correctness of the prediction (3). Since less similar instances will often hardly contribute to the precision of predictions, it might indeed be reasonable to derive $C(x_0)$ from the $k \ll n$ instances maximally similar to x_0, all the more if computing the intersection of neighborhoods (4) is computationally complex.

An apparent disadvantage of a similarity profile concerns its sensitivity toward outliers or, say, "exceptional" cases. In fact, recall that $\zeta(\alpha)$ is a *lower bound* to the similarity of labels that belong to α-similar instances. Thus, the existence of only one pair of α-similar instances having rather dissimilar labels entails a small lower bound $\zeta(\alpha)$. Small bounds in turn will obviously have a negative effect on the precision of (3).

One way to avoid this problem is to maintain an individual similarity profile for each case in the memory $\mathcal{D}$. This approach is somehow comparable to the use of *local metrics* in kNN algorithms and IBL, e.g., metrics which allow feature weights to vary as a function of the instance [11]. The *local similarity profile* of the ith case $\langle x_i, \lambda_{x_i} \rangle$ is defined as follows:

$$\zeta_i(\alpha) =_{\text{def}} \inf_{x \in \mathcal{X}, \sigma_{\mathcal{X}}(x, x_i) = \alpha} \sigma_{\mathcal{L}}\left(\lambda_x, \lambda_{x_i}\right),$$

where $\inf \emptyset = 1$ by definition. Thus, $\zeta_i(\alpha)$ is a lower bound on the similarity between λ_{x_i} and the label λ_{x_0} of an instance x_0 which is α-similar to x_i. A local profile indicates the validity of the IBL assumption for *individual* cases. The inference scheme (3) now becomes

$$C(x_0) =_{\text{def}} \bigcap_{i=1}^{n} \mathcal{N}_{\zeta_i(\sigma_{\mathcal{X}}(x_i, x_0))}(\lambda_{x_i}). \tag{5}$$

As can be seen, a case with a poorly developed profile hardly contributes to precise predictions. The local similarity profile might hence serve as a (perhaps complementary) criterion for selecting "competent" cases to be stored in the memory $\mathcal{D}$ [13].

4   Similarity Hypotheses

The application of the inference scheme (3) requires the similarity profile ζ to be known, a requirement that will usually not be fulfilled. This motivates the related concept of a *similarity hypothesis*, which is thought of as an approximation of a similarity profile. A similarity hypothesis can thus be seen as a formal model of the IBL assumption, adapted to the application under consideration.

Formally, a similarity hypothesis is identified with a function $h : \mathcal{A} \to [0, 1]$. The intended meaning of the hypothesis h is that

$$\forall x_1, x_2 \in \mathcal{X} : \sigma_{\mathcal{X}}(x_1, x_2) = \alpha \implies \sigma_{\mathcal{L}}(\lambda_{x_1}, \lambda_{x_2}) \geq h(\alpha). \tag{6}$$

A hypothesis h is called *stronger* than a hypothesis h' if $h' \leq h$ and $h \not\leq h'$. We say that h is *admissible* if $h(\alpha) \leq \zeta(\alpha)$ for all $\alpha \in \mathcal{A}$.

It is obvious that using an admissible hypothesis h in place of the true similarity profile ζ within the inference scheme (3) leads to correct predictions. That is, the estimation

$$C^{est}(x_0) =_{\text{def}} \bigcap_{i=1}^{n} \mathcal{N}_{h(\sigma_{\mathcal{X}}(x_i, x_0))}(\lambda_{x_i}) \tag{7}$$

is guaranteed to cover the unknown label λ_{x_0}. Indeed, $h \leq \zeta$ implies

$$\mathcal{N}_{\zeta(\sigma_{\mathcal{X}}(x_i, x_0))}(\lambda_{x_i}) \subseteq \mathcal{N}_{h(\sigma_{\mathcal{X}}(x_i, x_0))}(\lambda_{x_i})$$

for all cases $\langle x_i, \lambda_{x_i} \rangle$ and, hence, $C(x_0) \subseteq C^{est}(x_0)$.

Yet, assuming the profile ζ to be unknown, one cannot guarantee the admissibility of a hypothesis h and, hence, the correctness of (7). In other words, it might happen that $\lambda_{x_0} \notin C^{est}(x_0)$. In fact, we might even have $C^{est}(x_0) = \emptyset$ (in which case the prediction is definitely incorrect). Nevertheless, taking for granted that h is indeed a good approximation of ζ, it seems reasonable to derive $C^{est}(x_0)$ according to (7) as an approximation of $C(x_0)$, that is, to realize instance-based learning as a kind of *approximate* reasoning. Our results in the next section, showing how to derive a suitable hypothesis from the data given and how to estimate the probability that predictions obtained from such hypotheses are correct, will provide a formal justification for this approach.

Before proceeding, let us note that an approximate version of the local inference scheme (5) can of course be realized as well. In this case, an individual hypothesis h_i has to be specified (or induced from data) for each case $\langle x_i, \lambda_{x_i} \rangle$.

5   Learning Similarity Hypotheses

Our discussion so far has left open the question of how to specify a similarity hypothesis in an appropriate way. An obvious idea in this connection is to induce such a hypothesis from the observed cases. Before going into detail, note that the method thus obtained can be seen as a combination of instance- and model-based learning. In fact, adapting the similarity hypothesis is a kind of model-based learning, since a similarity hypothesis is a model of the IBL assumption, whereas storing new cases in the memory corresponds to instance-based learning.

Given a hypothesis space $\mathcal{H}$, i.e. a class of functions $h : \mathcal{A} \rightarrow [0,1]$, learning amounts to choosing one among these hypotheses on the basis of the given data. But which of the hypotheses are interesting candidates? Of course, first of all a hypothesis h should be consistent with the data given, that is, (6) should be satisfied for all cases in $\mathcal{D}$:

$$\forall\, x, x' \in \mathcal{D}\, :\, \sigma_{\mathcal{X}}(x, x') = \alpha \;\Rightarrow\; \sigma_{\mathcal{L}}(\lambda_x, \lambda_{x'}) \geq h(\alpha). \tag{8}$$

Denote by $\mathcal{H}_C \subseteq \mathcal{H}$ the set of hypothesis that are consistent in this sense. Among two consistent hypothesis h and h', where h is stronger than h', we should prefer the former since it leads to more precise predictions.[2] Thus, we call a hypothesis h_* optimal if $h_* \in \mathcal{H}_C$ and if there is no hypothesis $h \in \mathcal{H}_C$ such that h is stronger than h_*. The following observation is very simple to prove:

Observation 1 *Suppose the hypothesis space $\mathcal{H}$ to satisfy $h \equiv 0 \in \mathcal{H}$ and $(h, h' \in \mathcal{H}) \Rightarrow (h \vee h' \in \mathcal{H})$, where $h \vee h'$ is the pointwise maximum $x \mapsto \max\{h(x), h'(x)\}$. Then, a unique optimal hypothesis $h_* \in \mathcal{H}$ exists, and $\mathcal{H}_C$ is given by the set $\{h \in \mathcal{H} \mid h \leq h_*\}$.* □

Given the assumptions of this observation, IBL can be realized as a *candidate-elimination* algorithm [9], where h_* is a compact representation of the *version space*, i.e., the subset $\mathcal{H}_C$ of hypotheses from $\mathcal{H}$ which are consistent with the training examples.

---

[2] Note that the extreme hypothesis $h \equiv 0$ is always consistent but leads to the trivial prediction $C^{est}(x_0) = \mathcal{L}$.

Note that (8) guarantees consistency in the "empirical" sense that $\lambda_{x_i} \in C^{est}(x_i)$ for all $\langle x_i, \lambda_{x_i} \rangle \in \mathcal{D}$. One might think of further demanding a kind of "logical" consistency, namely $C^{est}(x) \neq \emptyset$ for all $x \in \mathcal{X}$. Of course, this additional requirement makes the testing of consistency more difficult and would greatly increase the complexity of learning.

5.1   Hypotheses as Step Functions

A very simple representation of hypotheses, that will nevertheless turn out to be very useful, is a step function

$$h : x \mapsto \sum_{k=1}^{m} \beta_k \cdot \mathbb{I}_{A_k}(x), \tag{9}$$

where $A_k = [\alpha_{k-1}, \alpha_k)$ for $1 \leq k \leq m-1$, $A_m = [\alpha_{m-1}, \alpha_m]$, and $0 = \alpha_0 < \alpha_1 < \ldots < \alpha_m = 1$ defines a partition of $[0, 1]$. The class $\mathcal{H}_{step}$ of functions (9), defined for a fixed partition, does obviously satisfy the assumptions of Observation 1. The optimal hypothesis h_* is defined by the values

$$\beta_k =_{def} \min \left\{ \sigma_{\mathcal{L}}(\lambda_x, \lambda_{x'}) \mid \langle x, \lambda_x \rangle, \langle x', \lambda_{x'} \rangle \in \mathcal{D}, \sigma_{\mathcal{X}}(x, x') \in A_k \right\} \tag{10}$$

for $1 \leq k \leq m$, where $\min \emptyset = 1$ by definition. We call h_* the *empirical similarity profile*.

Now, suppose that the case base is to be extended, i.e. that a newly observed case $\langle x_{n+1}, \lambda_{x_{n+1}} \rangle$ is to be added to the current sample $\mathcal{D}$. Updating the empirical similarity profile h_* can then be accomplished by passing the iteration

$$\beta_{\kappa(x_{n+1}, x_j)} \leftarrow \min \left\{ \beta_{\kappa(x_{n+1}, x_j)}, \sigma_{\mathcal{L}}(\lambda_{x_{n+1}}, \lambda_{x_j}) \right\} \tag{11}$$

for $1 \leq j \leq n = |\mathcal{D}|$. The index $1 \leq \kappa(x, x') \leq m$ is defined for instances $x, x' \in \mathcal{X}$ by $\kappa(x, x') = k \Leftrightarrow \sigma_{\mathcal{X}}(x, x') \in A_k$. As can be seen, the time complexity of updating the empirical profile is linear in the size of the memory.

5.2   The Learning Process

The updating scheme (11) suggests a process in which prediction and learning are repeated alternately in the style of incremental supervised learning:

- At each point of time, we dispose of a sample $\mathcal{D}$ with an associated empirical similarity profile h_*.
- Having to predict the label of a new instance x_0, an estimation $C^{est}(x_0)$ is derived from $\mathcal{D}$ and h_* according to (7).
- The system learns the correct label λ_{x_0} from the teacher.
- $\langle x_0, \lambda_{x_0} \rangle$ is added as the $(n+1)$th case $\langle x_{n+1}, \lambda_{x_{n+1}} \rangle$ to the memory and the empirical profile h_* is updated.

Needless to say, the strategy of simply adding all observations to the current case base $\mathcal{D}$ will usually not be efficient. In fact, much more sophisticated strategies for maintaining a case base are often used in practice, including the possibility of removing or replacing stored cases [12]. Still, the strategy above is sufficient for our purpose here. Besides, it simplifies a theoretical analysis of the prediction performance, as will be seen below.

For obvious reasons we call $h^* \in \mathcal{H}_{step}$ defined by the values

$$\beta_k^* =_{\text{def}} \inf \{ \zeta(x) \,|\, x \in \mathcal{A} \cap A_k \},\qquad(12)$$

$1 \leq k \leq m$, the *optimal admissible* hypothesis. Since admissibility implies consistency, we have $h^* \leq h_*$. This inequality suggests that the empirical similarity profile h_* will usually overestimate the true profile ζ and, hence, that h_* might not be admissible. And indeed, the constraints imposed by the observed cases will usually not "press" the step function h_* below the profile ζ (see Fig. 2 for an illustration). Of course, the fact that admissibility of h_* is not guaranteed seems to conflict with the objective of providing correct predictions and, hence, gives rise to questions concerning the actual quality of the empirical profile as well as the quality of predictions derived from that hypothesis. In the sequel, we shall present first answers to these questions.

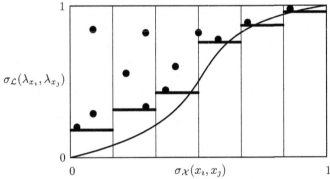

Fig. 2. Similarity profile (solid line) and empirical similarity profile (step function). Each point is induced by a pair of observed cases. By the definition of the similarity profile, all points are located above the graph of that function.

5.3   Properties of the Learning Process

We make the simplifying assumption that the instance space $\mathcal{X}$ is countable. Further, we make the standard assumption that the query instances x_0 (resp. the new cases $\langle x_0, \lambda_{x_0} \rangle$) are chosen at random according to a fixed (not necessarily known) probability distribution μ. In other words, the observed cases are independent and identically distributed (*i.i.d*) random variables, i.e. $\mathcal{D}$ is an *i.i.d* sample. Note that we can assume $\mu(x) > 0$ for all $x \in \mathcal{X}$ without loss of generality.

Now, denote by $\mathcal{D}_n$ the case base in the nth step of the above learning process, that is the sample $\mathcal{D}$ such that $|\mathcal{D}| = n$, and by h_n the empirical similarity profile derived from that sample. Since, according to our assumption, the observed cases are random variables, the induced hypotheses h_n are random variables (random functions) as well. As a first important property of the above learning process we can prove that the sequence of hypotheses $h_1, h_2, \ldots$ converges stochastically toward the optimal admissible hypothesis h^*.[3]

Theorem 2 *For the sequence $(h_n)_{n \geq 1}$ of empirical similarity profiles it holds true that $h_n \searrow h^*$ stochastically as $n \to \infty$. That is, $h_n \geq h^*$ for all $n \in \mathbb{N}$ and $\Pr(|h_N - h^*|_\infty \geq \varepsilon) \to 0$ for all $\varepsilon > 0$.* □

As concerns the quality of estimations, we are first of all interested in the probability of incorrect predictions. Denote by

$$q_{n+1} =_{\text{def}} \Pr\left(\lambda_{x_0} \notin C^{est}(x_0) \mid \mathcal{D}_n, h_n\right) \tag{13}$$

the probability that the $(n + 1)$th prediction, i.e. the prediction derived from $\mathcal{D}_n$ and h_n, is incorrect. In this connection, it should be noted that a prediction might well be correct even if the involved empirical profile h_* is not admissible: Recall that the estimation (7) is derived from a *limited* number of constraints (4), namely the β_i-neighborhoods associated with known labels λ_{x_i}. As we cannot exclude that $\beta_i = h_n(\sigma_{\mathcal{X}}(x_i, x_0)) > \zeta(\sigma_{\mathcal{X}}(x_i, x_0))$, it is true that each of these neighborhoods might be "too small" and, hence, might remove some labels from the credible set $C(x_0)$. Still, this unjustified removal does not necessarily concern the correct label λ_{x_0}. An indeed, we can show the following interesting result:

Theorem 3 *The following estimation holds true for the probability (13):*

$$q_{n+1} \leq 2m/(1+n), \tag{14}$$

where m is the size of the partition underlying $\mathcal{H}_{step}$. □

Corollary 4 *The expected proportion of incorrect predictions in connection with the above learning scheme converges toward 0.* □

According to the above results, the probability of an incorrect prediction becomes small for large memories, even if the hypotheses h_n are not admissible. In fact, this probability tends toward 0 with a convergence rate of order $O(1/n)$. In a statistical sense, the predictions $C^{est}(x_0)$ can indeed be seen as *credible sets*, a justification for using this term not only for $C(x_0)$ but also for $C^{est}(x_0)$. Note that the level of confidence guaranteed by $C^{est}(x_0)$ depends on the number of observed cases and can hence be controlled.

---

[3] All proofs, omitted here due to reasons of space, can be found in [6].

The upper bound established in Theorem 3 might suggest decreasing the probability of an incorrect prediction by reducing the size m of the partition underlying $\mathcal{H}_{step}$. Observe, however, that this will also lead to a less precise approximation of ζ and, hence, to less precise predictions of labels. "Merging" two neighbored intervals A_k and A_{k+1}, for instance, means to define a new hypothesis h with $h|(A_k \cup A_{k+1}) \equiv \min\{\beta_k, \beta_{k+1}\}$.

It is interesting to note that the confidence of a prediction does not depend on the similarity measures $\sigma_\mathcal{X}$ and $\sigma_\mathcal{L}$. In other words, our method works for *any* pair of such measures. Yet, the similarity measures will strongly influence the *precision* of predictions. Indeed, one cannot expect precise predictions if $\sigma_\mathcal{X}$ and $\sigma_\mathcal{L}$ are not suitably defined (in which case the IBL hypothesis is hardly satisfied). Therefore, the adaptation of these measures to the application at hand is clearly advised. In this connection, an interesting idea is to take the empirical similarity profile induced by the measures as an indicator of their suitability: Define $\sigma_\mathcal{X}$ and $\sigma_\mathcal{L}$ such that the induced profile becomes "large" in a certain sense, since large profiles yield precise predictions. This problem will be discussed in more detail in Section 6 below.

Let us finally mention that results similar to the above theorems can also be obtained for the case of *local* similarity profiles [6]. Usually, local profiles yield predictions that are more precise but less confident. This finding can also be grasped intuitively: The level of confidence decreases since one has to learn more similarity profiles from the same amount of data, and the precision increases because local profiles are much more tolerant toward outliers.

5.4   Examples

This section is meant to convey a first idea of the practical performance of our method, without laying claim to providing an exhaustive experimental evaluation. (As an aside, let us note that a comparison with standard IBL, or machine learning methods in general, is difficult anyway. The main reason is that our method provides a different type of prediction, namely credible label sets rather than point-estimations.)

Artificial data. As a first example, let us consider a simple regression problem.[4] More specifically, let the function to be learned be given by the polynomial $x \mapsto x^2$. Moreover, suppose n training examples $\langle x_i, \lambda_{x_i} \rangle$ to be given, where the x_i are uniformly distributed in $[0, 1]$, and the λ_{x_i} are normally distributed with mean $(x_i)^2$ and standard deviation $1/10$. As a similarity measure for both instances (inputs) and labels (outputs) we employ the function $(u, v) \mapsto \exp(-2|u - v|)$. Given a random sample $\mathcal{D}$, we first induce a similarity hypothesis for an underlying equi-width partition of size $m = 5$. Using this hypothesis and the sample $\mathcal{D}$, we derive a prediction λ_x for all instances x (resp. for

---

[4] Strictly speaking, since our theoretical results above assume a countable instance space, they do not apply to regression proper. They can be generalized to this case, however.

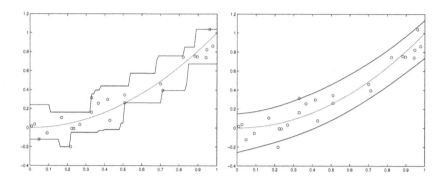

Fig. 3. Approximation of the function $x \mapsto x^2$ in the form of a "confidence band"; left: our instance-based approach, right: linear regression.

the discretization $\{0, 0.01, 0.02, \ldots, 1\}$). Note that such a prediction is simply an interval. Hence, what we obtain is a lower and an upper approximation of the true mapping $x \mapsto x^2$.

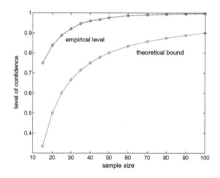

Fig. 4. Confidence levels of predictions: Theoretical bound and empirical level for different sample sizes.

Fig. 3 (left) shows a typical inference result for $n = 25$. According to our estimation (14), the degree of confidence for $n = 25$ is $16/26$. This, however, is only a lower bound, and empirically (namely by averaging over 1,000 experiments) we found that the level of confidence is almost 0.9 (see Fig. 4).

To draw a comparison with standard statistical techniques, Fig. 3 (right) shows the 0.9-confidence band obtained from a linear regression estimation for the same sample. In general, it turned out that linear regression yields slightly more precise predictions. However, in this connection one should realize that this method makes much more assumptions than our instance-based approach. Especially, the type of function to be estimated must be specified in advance: Knowing that this function is a polynomial of degree 2, we estimated the coefficients β_i in the mapping $x \mapsto \beta_0 + \beta_1 x + \beta_2 x^2$ in our example, but usually such knowledge will not be available (results already become worse when estimating a polynomial of degree $k > 2$). Moreover, the confidence band is valid only if the error terms follow a normal distribution (as they do in our case).

The housing data. We also applied our method to several real-world data sets, not fully discussed here due to reasons of space. For example, in connection with the HOUSING DATABASE,[5] the problem is to predict the price of houses which are characterized by 13 attributes. To apply our method, we simply defined similarity as an affine-linear function of the distance between (real-valued) attribute values (see Section 6 below for the acquisition of such similarity measures). For 30 randomly chosen sample cases we have learned corresponding local similarity hypotheses, using 450 cases as training examples. Using these (local) hypotheses, we derived predictions for the prices of the 56 houses that remain of the complete data. The precision of the predictions was approximately 10,000 dollars with a confidence level of 0.85. Taking the center of an interval as a point-estimation, one thus obtains predictions of the form $x \pm 5,000$ dollars. As can be seen, these estimations are quite reliable but not extremely precise (the average price of a house is approximately 22,500 dollars). In fact, this example clearly points out the practical limits of an inference scheme built upon the IBL assumption: A similarity-based prediction of prices cannot be confident and extremely precise at the same time, simply because the housing data meets the IBL assumption but moderately. Our approach takes these limits into account and makes them explicit.

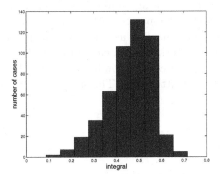

Fig. 5. Distribution of the quality of cases for the housing data, measured in terms of the integral of similarity profiles.

In connection with the housing data, let us recall that a local similarity profile can serve as an indicator of the "quality" of a case. For example, suppose that we measure this quality by means of the integral of the profile (which is easy to compute since the latter is a step-function, see Section 6 below). Fig. 5 shows the distribution of this quality measure for the housing data in the form of a histogram. As can be seen, there are a few cases of rather high

---

[5] Available at http://www.ics.uci.edu/~mlearn.

quality. The corresponding houses are "typical" in the sense that their prices are representative of the prices for similar houses, and deriving predictions based on these cases will usually be better than gathering a case base at random.

6   Adaptation of Similarity Measures

As already mentioned above, an intuitively reasonable principle for adapting the similarity measures $\sigma_{\mathcal{X}}$ and $\sigma_{\mathcal{L}}$ is to define these functions such that the induced (empirical) similarity profile becomes "large" in some sense. Of course, in order to realize this idea one first has to clarify the meaning of "large".

Recall that empirical profiles are specified as step functions for a given partition of $[0, 1]$. This partition is determined through $m + 1$ points $0 = \alpha_0 < \alpha_1 < \ldots < \alpha_m = 1$. Since no complete order is defined on the class of step functions $\mathcal{H}_{step}$ in a natural way, such an order has to be imposed somehow. For example, one possibility is to associate with each function h, specified through coefficients $\beta_1, \ldots, \beta_m$, its integral. We thus obtain the optimization criterion

$$I(h) =_{\text{def}} \sum_{k=1}^{m} (\alpha_k - \alpha_{k-1}) \cdot \beta_k \quad \to \quad \max \quad (15)$$

Instead of the width $\alpha_k - \alpha_{k-1}$ of the interval $A_k = [\alpha_{k-1}, \alpha_k)$ other weights could be used as well. For instance, a reasonable idea is to weigh β_k by the probability that the similarity between two instances lies in the interval A_k. This probability can be estimated from the sample $\mathcal{D}$ by the corresponding relative frequency.

Needless to say, a suitable method for adapting similarity measures can be developed only on the basis of some assumptions concerning the structure of these measures. Here, we proceed from the following assumption which is often satisfied in practice: Instances x are characterized by means of a fixed number of attribute values, and the similarity $\sigma_{\mathcal{X}}$ is a convex combination of individual similarity measures defined for the different attributes. The same assumption is made for the measure $\sigma_{\mathcal{L}}$:

$$\sigma_{\mathcal{X}} = v_1 \sigma_{\mathcal{X}}^1 + v_2 \sigma_{\mathcal{X}}^2 + \ldots + v_p \sigma_{\mathcal{X}}^p,$$
$$\sigma_{\mathcal{L}} = w_1 \sigma_{\mathcal{L}}^1 + w_2 \sigma_{\mathcal{L}}^2 + \ldots + w_q \sigma_{\mathcal{L}}^q.$$

The task of adapting $\sigma_{\mathcal{X}}$ and $\sigma_{\mathcal{L}}$ can then be specified as determining the coefficients v_i and w_j in an optimal way.

Now, consider a sample $\mathcal{D}$ consisting of n cases $\langle x_i, \lambda_{x_i} \rangle$. We denote by $\alpha_{ij}^k = \sigma_{\mathcal{X}}^k(x_i, x_j)$ the similarity degree between the kth attribute values of x_i and x_j. Likewise, $\beta_{ij}^k = \sigma_{\mathcal{L}}^k(\lambda_{x_i}, \lambda_{x_j})$ denotes the similarity degree between the kth attribute values of the labels λ_{x_i} and λ_{x_j}.

For the time being, suppose the measure $\sigma_{\mathcal{X}}$ to be given. The optimal adaptation of $\sigma_{\mathcal{L}}$ can then be formulated as a linear optimization problem: Choose $\beta_1, \ldots, \beta_m$ and the coefficients $w_1, \ldots, w_q$ so as to maximize (15) subject to the constraints

$$\beta_{\kappa(x_\imath,x_\jmath)} \leq w_1\beta_{\imath\jmath}^1 + w_2\beta_{\imath\jmath}^2 + \ldots + w_q\beta_{\imath\jmath}^q, \qquad (1 \leq \imath,\jmath \leq n)$$

$$w_1 + w_2 + \ldots + w_q = 1$$

$$w_1 \geq 0, \ldots, w_q \geq 0$$

Again, the index $\kappa(x_\imath, x_\jmath)$ specifies the interval of the underlying partition that covers the similarity degree between $x_\imath$ and $x_\jmath$: $\sigma_\mathcal{X}(x_\imath, x_\jmath) \in A_{\kappa(x_\imath,x_\jmath)}$. This coefficient must be known for writing down the linear inequalities above, which is the main reason why $\sigma_\mathcal{X}$ and $\sigma_\mathcal{L}$ cannot be optimized simultaneously. As can be seen, however, an optimal $\sigma_\mathcal{L}$ can be found in a quite efficient way once $\sigma_\mathcal{X}$ is given.[6] This suggests an optimization procedure in which the adaptation of $\sigma_\mathcal{L}$ is embedded as a sub-routine. For example, one could apply any local search method that searches the space of similarity measures $\sigma_\mathcal{X}$, that is the space of admissible coefficients $v_1, \ldots, v_p$. The quality of a measure $\sigma_\mathcal{X}$, e.g. the fitness in genetic algorithms, can then be computed by solving the above linear program, i.e. by deriving the measure $\sigma_\mathcal{L}$ that complements $\sigma_\mathcal{X}$ in an optimal way.

7 Summary

We have proposed an instance-based learning method that allows for deriving an estimation in the form of a *credible label set* rather than a single label. This set provably covers the true label with high probability. Bearing in mind that the IBL assumption might apply to an application in a limited scope, our inference scheme does not pretend a precision or credibility of instance-based predictions which is actually not justified. At a formal level, uncertainty is expressed by supplementing (set-valued) predictions with a level of confidence.

From a statistical point of view, our method can be seen as a non-parametric approach to estimating confidence regions, which makes it also interesting for statistical inference (cf. the comparison with linear regression in Section 5.4). In [7], an instance-based prediction method has been advocated as an alternative to linear regression techniques. By deriving set-valued instead of point estimations, our approach somehow combines advantages from both methods: Like the instance-based approach it requires less structural assumptions than (parametric) statistical methods. Still, it allows for specifying the uncertainty related to predictions by means of confidence regions.

A main concern in this paper was aimed at the *correctness* of predictions (3). Still, it is also possible to obtain results related to the *precision* of predictions. In [6], for instance, a result similar to the one in [7] has been shown: Provided that the function $x \mapsto \lambda_x$ mapping instances to labels satisfies certain continuity assumptions, it can be approximated to any degree of accuracy. That is, for each $\epsilon > 0$ one can find a finite memory of cases $\mathcal{D}$ such that $\lambda_x \in C^{est}(x)$ for all $x \in \mathcal{X}$ and $\sup_{x \in \mathcal{X}} \text{diam}(C^{est}(x)) < \epsilon$.

---

[6] Despite its theoretical complexity, linear programming is rather efficient in practice.

Without going into detail, we have proposed the use of *local* similarity profiles in order to overcome the problem that globally admissible hypotheses might be too restrictive for some applications. In this connection, let us also mention a further idea of weakening the concept of globally valid similarity bounds, namely the use of *probabilistic* similarity hypotheses [4].

References

1. D.W. Aha, editor. *Lazy Learning*. Kluwer Academic Publ., 1997.
2. D.W. Aha, D. Kibler, and M.K. Albert. Instance-based learning algorithms. *Machine Learning*, 6(1):37–66, 1991.
3. W.W. Cohen, R.E. Schapire, and Y. Singer. Learning to order things. *Journal of Artificial Intelligence Research*, 10, 1999.
4. E. Hüllermeier. Toward a probabilistic formalization of case-based inference. In *Proceedings* IJCAI–99, pages 248–253, Stockholm, Sweden, 1999.
5. E. Hüllermeier. Focusing search by using problem solving experience. In W. Horn, editor, *Proceedings* ECAI–2000, *14th European Conference on Artificial Intelligence*, pages 55–59, Berlin, Germany, 2000. IOS Press.
6. E. Hüllermeier. Similarity-based inference: Models and applications. Technical Report 00-28 R, IRIT – Institut de Recherche en Informatique de Toulouse, Université Paul Sabatier, October 2000.
7. D. Kibler and D.W. Aha. Instance-based prediction of real-valued attributes. *Computational Intelligence*, 5:51–57, 1989.
8. J.L. Kolodner. *Case-based Reasoning*. Morgan Kaufmann, San Mateo, 1993.
9. T.M. Mitchell. Version spaces: A candidate elimination approach to rule learning. In *Proceedings* IJCAI-77, pages 305–310, 1977.
10. S. Salzberg. A nearest hyperrectangle learning method. *Machine Learning*, 6:251–276, 1991.
11. R. Short and K. Fukunaga. The optimal distance measure for nearest neighbor classification. IEEE *Transactions on Information Theory*, 27:622–627, 1981.
12. B. Smyth and T. Keane. Remembering to forget. In C.S. Mellish, editor, *Proceedings International Joint Conference on Artificial Intelligence*, pages 377–382. Morgan Kaufmann, 1995.
13. B. Smyth and E. Mc Kenna. Building compact competent case-bases. In *Proceedings* ICCBR-99, *3rd International Conference on Case-Based Reasoning*, pages 329–342, 1999.
14. C. Stanfill and D. Waltz. Toward memory-based reasoning. *Communications of the ACM*, pages 1213–1228, 1986.
15. V.N. Vapnik. *Statistical Learning Theory*. John Wiley & Sons, 1998.

Self Learning or How to Make a Knowledge Base Curious about Itself

Wilhelm Rödder[1] and Gabriele Kern-Isberner[2]

[1] FernUniversität in Hagen, Fachbereich Wirtschaftswissenschaft, Lehrstuhl für BWL, insb. Operations Research, Postfach 9 40, 58084 Hagen, Germany
wilhelm.roedder@fernuni-hagen.de

[2] FernUniversität in Hagen, Fachbereich Informatik, Lehrstuhl für Praktische Informatik VIII, Postfach 9 40, 58084 Hagen, Germany
gabriele.kern-isberner@fernuni-hagen.de

Abstract. The inference process in a probabilistic and conditional environment under minimum relative entropy, is briefly repeated following the steps knowledge acquisition, query and response. In general, acquired knowledge suffers from first and second order uncertainty. First order uncertainty is missing information in the knowledge base; second order uncertainty is the vagueness or non-reliability of the system's response to a query. Both, first and second order uncertainty can be reduced by adequate additional information. In the present paper we develop the idea of a self learning knowledge base. Once the system detects a not justifiable vagueness in a recent answer it informs the user about the second order uncertainty and requires additional information in an intelligible syntactical form. This communication reduces both, first and second order uncertainty in general. Suitable examples accompany the theoretical considerations; they are modelled and calculated by means of the expert system shell SPIRIT.

1 Introduction

Minimum Relative Entropy (MinREnt) inference in a probabilistic conditional environment enjoys a growing popularity. Since the axiomatic foundations of the MinREnt principle ([1], [2], [3], [4]) and the communication tool of three-valued conditionals ([5], [6], [7]) were combined and implemented in the expert system shell SPIRIT ([8], [9]), even large scale decision problems' solutions can be supported by the shell ([10], [11]).

In [9] the author relates on the MinREnt inference process following the steps knowledge acquisition, query and response, which will be briefly repeated in Section 2. In [12] the process is shown to be measurable in that it allows to quantify the (missing) knowledge or first order uncertainty in an epistemic state, among others. How this first order uncertainty can be reduced is repeated in Section 3, so as to prepare the concept of second order uncertainty or non-reliability in the system's answer to a query.

A. Günter et al. (Eds.): KI 2003, LNAI 2821, pp. 465–474, 2003.

There should be a strong desire to complete missing knowledge and to reduce non-reliability once they are detected during the communication process between man and machine. Both, knowledge improvement and non-reliability reduction come from further information supplied to the knowledge base.

What makes an agent intelligent – besides of plausibly concluding facts from learned facts – is his ability to independently ask for further information about the knowledge domain, we feel. And this claimed information should be relevant in that it augments knowledge and decreases vagueness. In the present paper we hope to proceed a little step in that direction.

A first naïve idea to enrich knowledge might be the detection and the removal of (conditional probabilistic) independence among variables in the domain. Is it really true that weight does not influence height? And if it does influence, can you provide conditional probabilities? Unfortunately such naïve procedure might cause uneasiness due to a missing link to the semantic background. The user certainly is not amused by permanently being asked questions like 'are big objects green?' or even worse 'is the sex of airplanes male?'. A minimal semantic structure could be of *categories* and *attributes*, such that attributes describe categories. For a first course in representation methods for categorial structures – propositional and semantic networks, among others – see [13], Section 5, for instance. If two categories show identical patterns of attributes, the system cannot discriminate between them and so must ask for additional facts. If two categories show similar patterns this should cause the question for a hierarchical super-category. Like craws and songbirds have a bill, have wings and fly. The additional ability 'sing' discriminates between them and there is the super-category bird. Such a semantics based learning is promising but needs a costly semantic organisation in the knowledge base. We leave this for further research.

If an expert system's *user* asks the question 'is a student mother young?' there should be no problem with the semantic compatibility like was the sex of an airplane. If now the answer to such a question is little reliable, the reason is not semantic misuse but yet missing information. How to detect such relevant information, is the subject of the present paper.

After preliminaries and the MinREnt inference process in Section 2, in Section 3 we show what first and second order uncertainty is about and then develop the idea of self learning by factorisation in Section 4. The paper is concluded by a summary and by some remarks concerning future research.

2   MinREnt Inference

Let $\mathcal{L}$ be a propositional language, built from a finite set of finite-valued variables $V = \{V_1, ..., V_n\}$ with values v_j of V_j. Elements of $\mathcal{L}$ are well-formed by literals $V_j = v_j$, by the junctors $\wedge$ (and), $\vee$ (or), $^-$ (not) and by respective parentheses; such elements are denoted by upper case letters A, B, C,... and called facts. To simplify notation we juxtapose conjuncts, i.e. $AB = A \wedge B$. If A is implicant of B this reads $A \subset B$. Complete or simple conjunctions of literals we write as unordered tuples such as $v = v_1...v_n$ or v_I , v_J , v_K, respectively, with I, J, K being subsets of $\{1,...,n\}$. Note that such a v_I is a special fact which can be true or false for respective interpretations of $\mathcal{L}$. $\mathcal{V}$ is the set of all complete conjunctions v and $|\mathcal{V}|$ its cardinality.

Consider a binary conditional operator, $|$. Formulas of the form $B|A$ are called conditionals or rules. Note again that $v_J|v_I$ is a special conditional which can be true, false or inapplicable for respective interpretations of $\mathcal{L}$ [7]. Without loss of generality we assume $I \cap J = \emptyset$ for such special conditionals. Propositions $A \in \mathcal{L}$ are identified with conditionals $A|T$ where T is any tautology.

To facts and conditionals we assign real numbers $x \in [0,1]$, representing probabilities. As to the semantics, a model is a probability distribution P on $\mathcal{L}$. P satisfies a conditional $B|A$ $[x]$, $P \models B|A$ $[x]$, iff $P(BA) = x \cdot P(A)$.

Let $\mathcal{R} = \{B_1|A_1[x_1], ... , B_m|A_m[x_m]\}$ be a consistent set of such probabilistic conditionals, i.e. there exists a distribution P satisfying all conditionals $B_i|A_i[x_i]$. The following optimisation problem generates a distribution P^* obeying the Min-REnt principle, in that it respects the desired conditional probabilities without adding any unnecessary information to this epistemic state:

$$P^* = \arg \min R(Q, P^0), \quad \text{s.t.} \, Q \models \mathcal{R}, \tag{1}$$

here P^0 is the uniform distribution and R is the relative entropy or cross-entropy, respectively. P^* is the epistemic state derived from $\mathcal{R}$ and from the prior P^0, it is the knowledge base. For a deep justification of (1) see [2], [3], [4]. This is what *knowledge acquisition* is concerned with.

A *query* consists of three parts: the *focus*, the *question* and finally the *answer*. The focus is temporarily conditioning the whole epistemic state P^* with respect to a certain fact F. Focus a situation where F is true, so to speak:

$$P^{**} = \arg \min R(Q, P^*), \quad \text{s.t.} \, Q \models F[1.0]. \tag{2}$$

This is what the focus is concerned with.

The question is a conditional $H|G[?]$ which the user wants to be evaluated under the focus F $[1.0]$.
$$P^{**}(H|G) \tag{3}$$
is the respective answer. $P^{**}(H|G)$ is the probability of the conditional $H|G$ inferred from basic knowledge and from a given focus. This is what question and response is concerned with.

(1), (2), (3) we call the MinREnt inference process. Focussing several, even uncertain conditions instead of one certain F, only, is possible but not considered here ([9]). Please note that evaluating $H|G$ under a certain focus F is equivalent to evaluating $H|GF$. Such a simplification does not apply to the general case, however. SPIRIT ([14]) is an expert system shell which supports this process of knowledge acquisition, general focussing and response even for knowledge bases with umpteen variables and hundreds of rules.

3   First and Second Order Uncertainty

3.1   Lea Sombé

In the remainder of this paper time and again we shall refer to a little knowledge base about Lea Sombé, a member of a fictitious society which first was presented in [15] and has been frequently studied in the context of uncertain reasoning in general and MinREnt inference in particular ([12]). We briefly repeat the society's characteristics, then develop first and second order uncertainty measures and exemplify them for the little knowledge base.

Example 1. (Lea Sombé)
In the fictitious society members have the properties: to be a student or not $S = s/\overline{s}$; to be young or not $Y = y/\overline{y}$; to have the marital status single, married or corporate life $M = si, m, c$; to be parent or not $P = p/\overline{p}$. With the conditionals $\mathcal{R} = \{y|s[.9], si|y[.8], y|si[.7], s|y[.3], y|c[.8], \overline{si}|sp[.9]\}$ we inform the system about respective conditional probabilities from which P^* is calculated solving (1). Then focussing $sp[1.0]$, solving (2) for $F \equiv sp$ and evaluating $P^{**}(y) = .81$ provides the result: Under MinREnt inference the unconditioned question $y[?]$ in the focussed situation, that a member of the society is a parent student, yields an 81% estimated probability to be young.

In the next two sections we define first and second order uncertainty and their reduction, exemplified again by the little knowledge base around Lea Sombé.

3.2   First Order Uncertainty and Its Reduction

Once we solved (1) of Section 2, P^* is the epistemic state about the domain, including *all* conditional probabilistic structure. In [16] the author develops that the divergence $R(P^*, P^0)$ measures this intrinsic conditional probabilistic structure relative to that in P^0. Mind the fact that $R(P^*, P^0)$ assumes its maximum $ld|\mathcal{V}|$ if in P^* the probability of one v is 1 and 0 for the other configurations. The intrinsic conditional probabilistic structure is knowledge − the more facts condition each other, the higher $R(P^*, P^0)$. Missing knowledge or first order uncertainty is $ld|\mathcal{V}| − R(P^*, P^0)$. Without proof we mention that any rule $B|A[x]$ with $x \neq P^*(B|A)$ increases knowledge and decreases first order uncertainty, when added to $\mathcal{R}$. The considerations so far give rise to the following definition.

Definition 1.   (Knowledge, first order uncertainty and its reduction)

1. Let P^* be the solution of (1) with respect to the rule set $\mathcal{R}$. $R(P^*, P^0)$ is the (amount of) knowledge acquired in P^* from $\mathcal{R}$, $ld|\mathcal{V}| − R(P^*, P^0)$ is the first order uncertainty. Both measure in [bit].
2. Let $P^*(\mathcal{R})$ and $P^*(\mathcal{R} \cup \mathcal{R}_1)$ be the solution of (1) with the rule set $\mathcal{R}$ and with the enriched rule set $\mathcal{R} \cup \mathcal{R}_1$, respectively. Then $R(P^*(\mathcal{R} \cup \mathcal{R}_1), P^0) − R(P^*(\mathcal{R}), P^0)$ is the first order uncertainty reduction or knowledge gain. It measures in [bit].

Example 2. (Lea Sombé, knowledge and knowledge gain)
With the notation of Example 1, we have $ld|\mathcal{V}| = 4.58$ [bit], since the set of all configurations v counts 24. $R(P^*, P^0) = 1.05$ [bit] indicates little knowledge in the base and $ld|\mathcal{V}| - R(P^*, P^0)$ shows a considerable first order uncertainty of 3.53 [bit]. If now $\mathcal{R}_1 = \{p|ys[.01]\}$ and $\mathcal{R} = \mathcal{R} \cup \mathcal{R}_1$, we receive an enriched epistemic state, for which the first order uncertainty reduces to 3.48 [bit]. Hence the knowledge gain amounts to .05 [bit].

3.3   Second Order Uncertainty and Its Reduction

Once we solved (2) of Section 2 and evaluate $P^{**}(H|G)$ we get a unique number as an answer to the question $H|G$ [?] under the focus F [1.0]. Usually this number might change with future knowledge acquisition and hence is not always reliable.

Example 3. (Lea Sombé, second order uncertainty)
In Example 2, $\mathcal{R}_1 = \{p|ys[.01]\}$ enriched the epistemic state by modest .05 [bit]. Now focussing $sp[1.0]$ and evaluating $P^{**}(y)$ results in an 18% probability of being young, quite different from the original 81% in Example 1.

Example 3 shows that the system's answer to a question under a certain focus might be little reliable, due to missing information about the domain. Fortunately the non-reliability or second order uncertainty can be measured. There is an interval in which the answer, even after future knowledge acquisition, must fall and this interval can be calculated. As an information theoretic measure for the width of this interval we propose the maximum difference of uncertainty reduction if we come to know the answer to be true. And this is the difference of the interval 's boundaries' logarithm, see below.

Second order uncertainty needs reduction, as did first order uncertainty. This time additional rules $\mathcal{R}_1$ must be relevant for the question under the given focus. Sometimes these additional rules also reduce first order uncertainty, sometimes they don't. Before studying a suitable example we write down the above explained relations as a definition. First and second order uncertainty for the first time were studied in [17].

Definition 2.   (Relevance, second order uncertainty and its reduction)

1. Let $\mathcal{R}, F, H|G$ [?] be given as in (1), (2), (3).
   $[l, u]$ is the second order uncertainty interval and $m = -ld\, l - (-ld\, u)$ the answer's second order uncertainty, it measures in [bit]. Here

$$l = \min Q(H|GF) \quad s.t. Q \models \mathcal{R} \text{ and} \tag{4}$$
$$u = \max Q(H|GF) \quad s.t. Q \models \mathcal{R}. \tag{5}$$

2. Let m be the second order uncertainty with respect to $\mathcal{R}, F, H|G[?]$. Let m_1 be the corresponding second order uncertainty with respect to $F, H|G[?]$ under the enriched $\mathcal{R} \cup \mathcal{R}_1$.
   Then $m - m_1$ is the relevance of $\mathcal{R}_1$ for $H|G[?]$ under the focus F, relevance measures in [bit].

The reader must be aware that each restriction in (1), $Q \models B_i|A_i[x_i]$, is equivalent to $Q(B_iA_i) \cdot (1 - x_i) - Q(A_i) \cdot x_i = 0$, a linear equation in Q-space. So (4) and (5) are linear fractional optimisation problems which can be solved by suitable software. Most of the ideas developed here become more transparent with the following example.

Example 4. (Lea Sombé, relevance, second order uncertainty reduction)
For $\mathcal{R}$ as in Example 1, the focus $F \equiv sp$ and the question y [?], the second order uncertainty interval is $[l, u]=[0,1]$ with $m = -ld\,0 - (-ld\,1)= \infty$ [bit]. The calculated 81% are little reliable; with future information these 81% can change significantly, cf. Example 3. Note that $P^*(p|s)= .225$; so enriching $\mathcal{R} = \mathcal{R} \cup \mathcal{R}_1=\{p|s[.225]\}$ does not change P^* at all, as $\mathcal{R}_1$ is redundant information. Consequently the 81% probability of a student parent to be young does not change, either. But what changes significantly is the second order uncertainty; we get $[l, u]=[.56, 1]$ and $m = .84$ [bit]. If we even come to know that over and above 20% of young students have children, a further broadening $\mathcal{R} = \mathcal{R} \cup \{p|sy[.20]\}$ makes the vagueness disappear. Now $[l, u]=[.8, .8]$ with $m=0$ [bit].

Example 4 shows that relevant additional information might reduce an answer's vagueness significantly. But which additional information? How to detect the conditionals $p|s$ and $p|sy$? This is the subject of the next section.

4 Self Learning by Factorisation

4.1 Logical Factorisation

In [7] the author considers a three-valued logic and then proposes a Boolean extension for conditionals, thus allowing an arbitrary composition of conditionals by the junctors $\wedge$, $\vee$, $^-$, $|$. In [12], p. 386, this extension is slightly modified when conditioning conditionals. In either extension it can be shown that composed conditionals always are reducible to simple ones, i.e. not composed conditionals. In the actual contribution we need the conjunction and the conditioning of conditionals, only. For the following equations consult again [7],[12]: $(B|A) \wedge (D|C)=[(B \vee \overline{A})(D \vee \overline{C})]\,|(A \vee C)$ and $(B|A)|(D|C) = B|ACD$, respectively. Please verify $(B|A)|A=B|A$ and $(B|A)\wedge A=BA$. With these preliminaries the authors in [12] define c-independence which will be repeated here. Note that c-independence is a logical rather than a probabilistic concept.

Definition 3. (c-independence)
$B|A$ is conditionally or c-independent of $D|C$ iff $(B|A)|(D|C) = B|A$.

It is straightforward to prove that $B|A$ is c-independent of $D|C$ iff $A \subset DC$. This kind of independence is directed and it induces a partial order $\sqsubseteq$ for rules: $D|C \sqsubseteq B|A$ iff $A \subset DC$. If in some rule set $D|C \sqsubseteq B|A$ holds and if there is no $F|E$ such that $D|C \sqsubseteq F|E \sqsubseteq B|A$, $B|A$ is called a successor of $D|C$ and $D|C$ a predecessor of $B|A$, respectively.

Definition 4. (Factorisation)

Let $D_k|C_k$, k=1...l, be a sequence of conditionals with $D_k|C_k \sqsubseteq D_{k+1}|C_{k+1}$, $C_{k+1} = D_kC_k$, all k, and $C_1 = T$.

Then $D_lC_l = \bigwedge_{k=1}^{l} D_k|C_k$ and is called a (logical) factorisation of the proposition D_lC_l, and the $D_k|C_k$ are called the factorising conditionals.

Observation: As it is convenient we sometimes also say: $\bigwedge_{k=1}^{l} D_k|C_k$ is a factorisation of $D_l|C_l$ rather than of D_lC_l. There should be no problem with this diction.

If $D_1|C_1 \sqsubseteq ... \sqsubseteq D_l|C_l$ like in the definition but $C_{k+1} \not\sqsubset D_kC_k$, some k, make $K_kD_kC_k = C_{k+1}$ for a suitable K_k, make $D_{i+1}|C_{i+1} := D_i|C_i$, i=1...$k+1$, and insert $D_{k+1}|C_{k+1} := K_k|D_kC_k$. So any sequence of c-independent conditionals can be completed to a factorisation. Note that $C_1 = T$ is not restrictive; add $C_1|T$ if $C_1 \neq T$.

Please verify $v_2|v_3 \sqsubseteq v_4|v_3v_2v_1$ for arbitrary but fixed values v_j and the factorisation $v_4v_3v_2v_1 = v_3|T \wedge v_2|v_3 \wedge v_1|v_2v_3 \wedge v_4|v_3v_2v_1$, for instance.

The idea now is to close any set $\mathcal{S}$ of conditionals under factorisation. More precisely: Find a set $\mathcal{C}(\mathcal{S}) \supseteq \mathcal{S}$ so that for each $B|A \in \mathcal{C}(\mathcal{S})$, its factorising conditionals also are in $\mathcal{C}(\mathcal{S})$. The following procedure obviously generates $\mathcal{C}(\mathcal{S})$.

Procedure 1 (Factorising rule set)

1. $\mathcal{C}(\mathcal{S}) := \mathcal{S}$.
2. Choose a pair $D|C \sqsubseteq B|A$ with $B|A$ successor of $D|C$ and $A \not\sqsubset DC$. Make $KDC = A$ for a suitable K, $\mathcal{C}(\mathcal{S}): = \mathcal{C}(\mathcal{S}) \cup \{K|DC\}$, until $\mathcal{C}(\mathcal{S})$ is closed under this operation.
3. For all $B|A \in \mathcal{C}(\mathcal{S})$ with $A \neq T$ and without a predecessor make $\mathcal{C}(\mathcal{S}) := \mathcal{C}(\mathcal{S}) \cup \{A|T\}$.

Sometimes there are two factorisations of different propositions and for whatever reason we would benefit from supplementing either proposition in such a way that both of them become equal. This is what Procedure 2 is about.

Procedure 2 (Completion of factorisations)

Let $D_lC_l = \bigwedge_{k=1}^{l} D_k|C_k$ and $B_nA_n = \bigwedge_{m=1}^{n} B_m|A_m$ be two non-exclusive factorised propositions and let $D_lC_l \neq B_nA_n$. Make $D_{l+1} = B_nA_n = A_{n+1}$ and $C_{l+1} = D_lC_l = B_{n+1}$. Then $D_lC_lB_nA_n$ has the factorisations $\bigwedge_{k=1}^{l+1} D_k|C_k$ and $\bigwedge_{m=1}^{n+1} B_m|A_m$.

This is what logical factorisation is concerned with. In the next section we consider its probabilistic counterpart.

4.2   Probabilistic Factorisation and Self Learning

For each factorisation $D_lC_l = \bigwedge_{k=1}^{l} D_k|C_k$ and a distribution P on $\mathcal{L}$ we have the probabilistic factorisation $P(D_lC_l) = \prod_{k=1}^{l} P(D_k|C_k)$, cf. the definition of a conditional's probability in Section 2 and the remarks at the beginning of Section 4.1.

So if a proposition has two different factorisations like the proposition generated in Procedure 2, last section, the respective probabilistic factorisations can be equated as

$$\prod_{k=1}^{l+1} P(D_k|C_k) = P(D_l C_l B_n A_n) = \prod_{m=1}^{n+1} P(B_m|A_m).$$

If now in $\mathcal{S} = \mathcal{R} \cup \{q\}$, $\mathcal{R}$ is the set of conditionals forming a knowledge base according to (1), if $q = H|GF$ is the respective query conditional like in (2), (3), if $\mathcal{C}(\mathcal{S})$ is the closure of $\mathcal{S}$ in accordance with Procedure 1 of the last section, and if two completed factorisations of $HGFA_iB_i$ for some rule $A_i|B_i[x_i]$ are given, then they can be equated:

$$\prod_{k=1}^{l+1} P(D_k|C_k) = P(HFGA_iB_i) = \prod_{m=1}^{n+1} P(B_m|A_m), \text{ say.} \tag{6}$$

Some of the involved probabilities are known as the respective rules are in $\mathcal{R}$, some of the probabilities are unknown and one probability is desired, namely that of $H|GF[?]$. Now resolve (6) for the desired $H|GF[?]$ to get

$$H|GF[?] = f \cdot \frac{\prod_m P(B_m|A_m)}{\prod_k P(D_k|C_k)}. \tag{7}$$

f is a quotient of known probabilities from $\mathcal{R}$ and the rest contains conditionals with unknown probabilities, only. We call the respective conditionals a *missing link* between the question $H|GF[?]$ and the rules $\mathcal{R}$. They must be estimated to reduce the non-reliability of the system's answer. Once all unknown probabilities are estimated by the user, they determine the question's probability. The answer's vagueness disappeared.

To facilitate the duty of estimating the unknown probabilities,

- equal expressions in the nominator and denominator should be cancelled, (8)
- put $\dfrac{P(B_m|A_m)}{P(D_k|C_k)} = P(A_m|C_k)$ for $B_m A_m = D_k C_k$ and $A_m \subset C_k$, (9)
- put $\dfrac{P(B_m|A_m)}{P(D_k|C_k)} = P(B_m A_m|D_k C_k)$ for $A_m = C_k$ and $B_m A_m \subset D_k C_k$. (10)

With these observations we get a rudimentary self learning procedure.

Procedure 3 (Self Learning)

1. Solve (4) and (5) in Section 3.3, calculate m, the second order uncertainty. Is the uncertainty 'small', STOP.
2. Generate $\mathcal{C}(\mathcal{S})$ for $\mathcal{S} = R \cup \{q\}$, following Procedure 1.
3. Choose a 'good' $A_i | B_i [x_i] \in \mathcal{R}$ to generate a missing link. Complete following Procedure 2, equate like (6) and resolve for $H|GF[?]$ like in (7). Simplify following (8), (9), (10).
4. Ask the user for estimations of the remaining unknown probabilities. Add the corresponding rules and their probabilities to $\mathcal{R}$. Go to 1.

To implement Procedure 3 there remains a lot of work to do. Not only the 'good' choice must be specified but also the user's personal affection for or dislike to special questions must be taken into account. Besides of these restrictions we demonstrate self learning for the little knowledge domain about Lea Sombé.

Example 5. (Lea Sombé, self learning)
For the question $y|ps[?]$ one (!) factorisation is $yps = ps \wedge y|ps$, for the base rule $y|s[.9]$ the factorisation reads $ys = s \wedge y|s$. Since the propositions yps and ys are not equal complete $yps = s \wedge y|s \wedge p|ys$ for the latter. Equating the probabilities like in (6), resolving for the question like in (7) and simplifying we get

$$y|ps[?] = y|s[.9] \cdot \frac{P(s) \cdot P(p|ys)}{P(ps)} = f \cdot \frac{P(p|ys)}{P(p|s)}.$$

The probabilities of $p|ys$ and $p|s$ must be estimated. They are a missing link between the question and the rule base. Exactly these rules were added to $\mathcal{R}$ in Example 4 to eliminate vagueness.

5   Summary and Further Research

In the present paper we showed how a knowledge base's first order uncertainty can be measured in [bit], as can the second order uncertainty of a given answer. Additional information about the domain reduces them both, if provided suitably. To detect such a missing information link between the vague answer and the knowledge so far acquired, the sketched factorisation method seems to be efficient and effective. This method must be developed further so as to permit an automatic generation of missing information and integrate it into a permanent communication interplay between man and machine. Until now the expert system shell SPIRIT provides first and second order uncertainty, only.
The reader interested in the shell is invited to visit our homepage
http://www.xspirit.de.

References

1. J. B. Paris and A. Vencovská: A note on the inevitability of maximum entropy, Int. J. of Approximate Reasoning, 14 (1990) 183–223

2. J. B. Paris and A. Vencovská: In defence of the maximum entropy inference process, Int. J. of Approximate Reasoning, 17 (1997) 77–103

3. J. E. Shore and R. W. Johnson: Axiomatic Derivation of the Principle of Maximum Entropy and the Principle of Minimum Cross Entropy, IEEE Trans. Information Theory, 26 (1) (1980) 26–37

4. G. Kern-Isberner: Characterising the principle of minimum cross-entropy within a conditional-logical framework, Artificial Intelligence, Vol. 98 (1998) 169–208

5. B. de Finetti: Induction and Statistics, Wiley, New York (1972)

6. P. G. Calabrese: Deduction and Inference Using Conditional Logic and Probability, in: Conditional Logic in Expert Systems, I. R. Goodman, M. M. Gupta, H.T. Nguyen and G. S. Rogers (editors). Elsevier Science Publishers B. V. (1991) 71–100

7. P. G. Calabrese: Reflections on Logic and Probability in the Context of Conditionals, Proc. Conditionals, Information and Inference, Workshop May 13–15 2002, Hagen (2002) 27–45

8. W. Rödder and C.-H. Meyer: Coherent knowledge processing at maximum entropy by SPIRIT, Proceedings 12th Conference on Uncertainty in Artificial Intelligence, E. Horvitz and F. Jensen (editors), Morgan Kaufmann, San Francisco Cal. (1996) 470–476

9. W. Rödder: Conditional Logic and the Principle of Entropy, Artificial Intelligence, 117 (2000) 83–106

10. F. Kulmann: Wissen und Information in konditionalen Modellen – Zur Entscheidungsvorbereitung im Anfrage- und Auftragsmanagement, Deutscher Universitäts-Verlag, Wiesbaden (2002)

11. F. Kulmann and E. Reucher: Computergestützte Bonitätsprüfung bei Banken und Handel, DBW – Die Betriebswirtschaft, 60 (2000) 113–122

12. W. Rödder and G. Kern-Isberner: From Information to Probability, an Axiomatic Approach, Int. J. of Intelligent Systems, 18 (4) (2003) 383–403

13. J. R. Anderson: Cognition psychology and its implications, W. H. Freeman Co. (2000)

14. SPIRIT-Version 3.1, http://www.xspirit.de (2002)

15. L. Sombé: Schließen bei unsicherem Wissen in der Künstlichen Intelligenz, Vieweg, Braunschweig, Wiesbaden (1992)

16. W. Rödder: Knowledge Processing under Information Fidelity, Proc. 12th Int. Joint Conf. on AI (IJCAI – 2001), Seattle (2001) 749–754

17. W. Rödder and E. Reucher: Wissen uund Folgern aus relevanter Information, Diskussionsbeitrag Nr. 301, FB Wirtschaftswissenschaft, FernUniversität in Hagen (2001)

Tolerance Spaces and Approximative Representational Structures[*]

Patrick Doherty[1], Witold Łukaszewicz[1,2], and Andrzej Szałas[1,2]

[1] Department of Computer Science, University of Linköping, Sweden,
patdo@ida.liu.se
[2] The College of Economics and Computer Science, Olsztyn, Poland
{witlu,andsz}@ida.liu.se

Abstract. In traditional approaches to knowledge representation, notions such as tolerance measures on data, distance between objects or individuals, and similarity measures between primitive and complex data structures are rarely considered. There is often a need to use tolerance and similarity measures in processes of data and knowledge abstraction because many complex systems which have knowledge representation components such as robots or software agents receive and process data which is incomplete, noisy, approximative and uncertain. This paper presents a framework for recursively constructing arbitrarily complex knowledge structures which may be compared for similarity, distance and approximativeness. It integrates nicely with more traditional knowledge representation techniques and attempts to bridge a gap between approximate and crisp knowledge representation. It can be viewed in part as a generalization of approximate reasoning techniques used in rough set theory. The strategy that will be used is to define tolerance and distance measures on the value sets associated with attributes or primitive data domains associated with particular applications. These tolerance and distance measures will be induced through the different levels of data and knowledge abstraction in complex representational structures. Once the tolerance and similarity measures are in place, an important structuring generalization can be made where the idea of a *tolerance space* is introduced. Use of these ideas is exemplified using two application domains related to sensor modeling and communication between agents.

1 Introduction

In traditional approaches to knowledge representation, notions such as tolerance measures on data, distance between objects or individuals, and similarity measures between primitive and complex data structures such as properties and relations, elementary and complex descriptors, decision rules, information systems, and relational databases, are rarely considered. This is unfortunate because

---

[*] Supported in part by the WITAS project grant under the Wallenberg Foundation, Sweden and KBN grant 8 T11C 009 19.

A. Günter et al. (Eds.): KI 2003, LNAI 2821, pp. 475–489, 2003.

many complex systems which have knowledge representation components such as robots or software agents receive and process data which is incomplete, noisy, approximative and uncertain. There is often a need to use tolerance and similarity measures in processes of data and knowledge abstraction and in communication between agents.

This is a particular problem in the area of cognitive robotics where data input by sensors has to be fused, filtered and integrated with more traditional qualitative knowledge structures. A great many levels of knowledge abstraction and data reduction must be used as one tries to integrate newly acquired raw data with existing data which has previously been abstracted and represented explicitly in the form of more qualitative data and knowledge structures. It is also a problem for software agents on the world wide web where knowledge structures are continually required to be compared and merged and agents are obligated to communicate with each other using similar, but unidentical ontologies or vocabularies.

This paper presents a framework for recursively constructing arbitrarily complex knowledge structures which may be compared for similarity, distance and approximativeness. It integrates nicely with more traditional knowledge representation techniques and attempts to bridge a gap between approximate and crisp knowledge representation [2]. It can be viewed in part as a generalization of approximate reasoning techniques used in rough set theory [5] where an approximate relation is represented as having both an upper and lower approximation represented as classical sets and an individual in a domain of discourse has additional structure in terms of attribute/value pairs. It also has connections to recent work by Gärdenfors with conceptual spaces [4].

Ontologically, the world is viewed as consisting of individual elements with associated sets of attribute/value pairs. Each attribute has a value set and tolerance relations will be associated with each value set inducing a neighborhood relation. Arbitrarily complex data structures and representational systems are constructed recursively from the primitive notions of individual, attribute and value. Consequently, notions of tolerance and similarity can be induced through these structures via the tolerance and similarity measures placed on primitive data or value sets. For example, a set of values for each attribute associated with an individual may be viewed as a tuple. A set of one-tuples is a property, a set of k-tuples is a k-relation, sets of relations are associated with relational structures. In regard to relations, upper and lower approximations to these can be derived through use of the individual tolerance relations.

The representational structures constructed in this manner are viewed as information granules and have a great deal of representational fluidity. They can be combined, compared for tolerance and similarity, reasoned about approximatively, and often represented using traditional database techniques. The latter is especially important for integration with legacy knowledge structures and logical inferencing techniques. Use of the framework will be exemplified using two fundamentally important potential applications: sensor to symbolic data conversions and communication between software agents. The techniques are currently being applied to real-world applications in both the cognitive robotics and software agents application domains.

Let us begin with the notion of tolerance and tolerance measures. Webster's dictionary defines tolerance as "the amount of variation allowed from a standard, accuracy, etc."

For example, suppose a system receives data about an attribute a from two sources, where source one asserts that that $a = 1.04$ and source two asserts that $a = 0.98$. Depending on the context, the system might want to consider the values 1.04 and 0.98 as the same relative to some tolerance measure since their distance is only 0.06. In another application this difference may have serious repercussions on system safety, so it is important to make sure that tolerance measures are contextual and can be tuned either automatically or manually relative to the application and context at hand.

The strategy that will be used is to define tolerance and distance measures on the value sets associated with attributes or primitive data domains associated with particular applications. These tolerance and distance measures will be induced through the different levels of data and knowledge abstraction in complex representational structures. The representational structures will in some sense inherit the tolerance measures from the primitive data domains and value sets used in these structures at lower levels of abstraction and taken into account when comparing for similarity or reasoning. By defining parameterized measures of tolerance via distance measurements on values sets and primitive domains, one can cluster sets of values into tolerance neighborhoods and view the clusters as individual elements. Similarly, individuals whose identities are dependent on sets of attribute/value pairs can also be clustered into tolerance neighborhoods and viewed as indiscernible entities to a particular degree of tolerance when used in other data structures.

The basic primitive in the ideas presented is that of a tolerance function. Let's begin with a value set V and two elements $x, y \in V$. A tolerance function τ provides us with a distance measure between x and y normalized to the real interval $[0, 1]$ where the higher the value, the closer in tolerance the two elements are. Given a parameter $p \in [0, 1]$, a tolerance relation τ^p is then introduced among individuals with a threshold p which tunes the tolerance to be within a certain degree. If $\tau(x, y) \geq p$ then the pair $\langle x, y \rangle$ is in the relation τ^p. Both the tolerance function and the parameter p must be provided by a knowledge engineer or must be machine learned. One can continually refine these values.

Once this is done for individual value sets or primitive data domains, it can be generalized to tuples of values and tolerance can be measured between two tuples $\langle x_1, \ldots, x_k \rangle$ and $\langle y_1, \ldots, y_k \rangle$ using pairwise comparison of associated tolerance relations.

Given a value set V with associated tolerance measures, we can then take subsets $V_1, V_2 \subseteq V$ and induce tolerance measures and neighborhood functions on the subsets. Likewise, given a set T of k-tuples with associated tolerance measures, we can then take subsets $T_1, T_2 \subseteq T$ and induce tolerance measures and neighborhood functions on the subsets. Subsets of V can be viewed as properties or concepts and subsets of T can be viewed as k-argument relations.

These ideas can be generalized further to sets of sets and sets of sets of tuples, where the tolerance and similarity measures between these structures is induced from the primitive tolerance measures in the base value sets. Once the tolerance and similarity measures are in place, an important structuring generalization can be made where the idea of a *tolerance space* is introduced.

Given a universe U of objects in a tolerance space with the associated tolerance measures, we can provide a generalization of the notions of upper and lower approximations on sets used in rough set theory to subsets of U. The lower and upper approximations will again be induced from the particular tolerance measures provided by the tolerance space in question. Rather than using equivalence classes of individuals constructed from subsets of attributes as in rough set theory, one would work instead with neighborhoods generated from neighborhood functions of individuals.

There is an interesting connection between the idea of tolerance spaces proposed in this chapter and the work of Gärdenfors with conceptual spaces (see, e.g., [4]). Conceptual spaces are built up using multi-dimensional spaces of quality dimensions (attributes) and providing geometric constraints between these dimensions in order to model distance measures and similarity. However, we use the notion of semi-distances rather than of distances. Tolerance spaces contribute to a generalization of conceptual spaces in the sense that concepts can be generalized to approximate concepts based on tolerance measures and the geometric constraints used are less rigid than with conceptual spaces. In order to place tolerance spaces in the proper context with conceptual spaces, we define a simple version of conceptual spaces and show how tolerance spaces may be integrated in this framework.

In the remainder of the paper, the basic framework will be presented and then exemplified using two applications.

2   Conceptual Spaces

A *semi-metric space* is a pair $\langle A, \delta \rangle$, where A is a set and δ is a function

$$\delta : A \times A \longrightarrow \mathcal{R}$$

which, for all $x, y \in A$, satisfies:
$$\delta(x,y) \geq 0,\ \delta(x,x) = 0 \text{ and } \delta(x,y) = \delta(y,x).$$

Any function δ satisfying the above properties is called a *semi-metric* for A and $\delta(x,y)$ is called the *semi-distance* between x and y.

Definition 1. *Let U be a finite nonempty set of objects. By a* quality dimension *over U we understand any semi-metric space $\langle U, \delta \rangle$. By a* conceptual space *over U we mean any pair $\langle U, Q \rangle$, where Q is a finite set of quality dimensions over U.* ∎

Quality dimensions usually correspond to attributes of objects together with a semi-distance defined on the attributes value domains. For example, if one measures colors of objects, quality dimensions can correspond to hue, chromaticity and brightness. The concept "fruit" may have dimensions corresponding to weight, taste, color, etc.

Usually, with any quality dimension one associates a relational structure representing a domain of values corresponding to the quality dimension, together with functions and relations allowing one to calculate (semi-)distances.

For instance, with the quality dimension "weight" one can associate a relational structure defining arithmetic on the real numbers.

3   Tolerance and Inclusion Functions

We begin by defining a tolerance function on individuals. From this a parameterized tolerance relation follows naturally.

Definition 2. *By a tolerance function on a set U we mean any function $\tau :$ $U \times U \longrightarrow [0,1]$ such that for all $x, y \in U$,*

$$\tau(x, x) = 1 \quad and \quad \tau(x, y) = \tau(y, x). \qquad \blacksquare$$

Given a conceptual space $\langle U, Q \rangle$ and a quality dimension $\langle U, \delta \rangle \in Q$, a *tolerance function τ, based on the quality dimension* can be defined as follows:

$$\tau(u, u') \stackrel{\text{def}}{=} 1 - \frac{\delta(u, u')}{\max\{\delta(x, y) : x, y \in U\}}. \tag{1}$$

Of course, the same approach could be used for an attribute a and its value set V_a in a complex knowledge structure, provided δ is given, without appeal to conceptual spaces.

Definition 3. *For $p \in [0, 1]$ by a tolerance relation to a degree at least p based on τ, we mean the relation τ^p given by*

$$\tau^p \stackrel{\text{def}}{=} \{\langle x, y \rangle \mid \tau(x, y) \geq p\}.$$

The relation τ^p is also called the parameterized tolerance relation. $\blacksquare$

In the rest of the paper, $\tau^p(x, y)$ is used to denote the characteristic function for the relation τ^p.

Intuitively, $\tau(x, y)$ provides a degree of similarity between x and y, whereas $\tau^p(x, y)$ states that the degree of similarity between x and y is at least p. In what follows we limit ourselves to tolerance relations where it is assumed that the parameter p has been provided and is tuned to fit particular applications.

Often one considers objects to be similar if a given distance between them is not greater than a given threshold, say d. Given a quality dimension $\langle U, \delta \rangle$ and a threshold $d \geq 0$, one can define the parameter p from Definition 3 to be

$$p \stackrel{\text{def}}{=} 1 - \frac{d}{\max\{\delta(x, y) : x, y \in U\}}. \tag{2}$$

A parameterized tolerance relation is used to construct tolerance neighborhoods for individuals.

Definition 4. *By a* neighborhood function wrt τ^p *we mean a function given by*

$$n^{\tau^p}(u) \stackrel{\text{def}}{=} \{u' \in U \mid \tau^p(u, u') \ holds\}.$$

By a neighborhood of u wrt τ^p *we mean the value* $n^{\tau^p}(u)$. ∎

4   Tolerance Spaces

The concept of tolerance spaces plays a fundamental rôle in our approach.

Definition 5. *A* tolerance space *is defined as the tuple* $TS = \langle U, \tau, p \rangle$, *which consists of*

- *a nonempty set U, called the* domain *of TS;*
- *a tolerance function τ*
- *a tolerance parameter $p \in [0, 1]$.*

The parameterized tolerance relation τ^p is defined as in Definition 3. ∎

Given a universe U of individuals, a set of attributes A and a set $X \subseteq U$, one often considers the lower and upper approximation of X as defined in terms of a partitioning of the universe U in indiscernibility classes relative to a subset of the attributes A. Given a tolerance space $TS = \langle U, \tau, p \rangle$, rather than considering an individual's indiscernibility class as a basis for defining the lower and upper approximation of $X \subseteq U$, we can instead use the neighborhood of an individual induced by the tolerance function/parameter pair(s) provided by the tolerance space. In addition, we can tune our definition of upper approximation via a parameter q which determines how much of a neighborhood must be part of X in order for it to be included in the upper approximation.[1]

Below, for any set X, by $|X|$ we mean the cardinality of X.

Definition 6. *Let $U_1, U_2 \subseteq U$. By the* standard inclusion function *we mean the function given by*

$$\mu(U_1, U_2) \stackrel{\text{def}}{=} \begin{cases} \dfrac{|U_1 \cap U_2|}{|U_1|} & \text{if } U_1 \neq \emptyset \\ 1 & \text{otherwise.} \end{cases}$$

---

[1] A different approach, based on a notion of approximation spaces, object neighborhoods and rough inclusion, has been introduced in [6].

Let $TS = \langle U, \tau, p \rangle$ be a tolerance space and $X \subseteq U$. The lower and upper approximations of X wrt TS to a degree $q \in [0,1]$, X_{TS+}^q and $X_{TS\oplus}^q$, are defined by

$$X_{TS+}^q = \{u \in U : \mu(n^{\tau^p}(u), X) = 1\}, X_{TS\oplus}^q = \{u \in U : \mu(n^{\tau^p}(u), X) > q\}.$$

The approximations $X_{TS+}^0, X_{TS\oplus}^0$ are called the lower and upper approximations of X wrt TS and are often denoted by $X_{TS+}, X_{TS\oplus}$, respectively.   ∎

5   Defining Tolerance on Complex Representational Structures

In this section we show how to induce a tolerance relation on complex structures on the basis of a tolerance relation defined on domain elements.

Consider a tolerance space $TS = \langle U, \tau, p \rangle$. First, we would like to extend the tolerance and neighborhood functions induced by TS to deal with subsets of U. We shall need a notion of generalized inclusion function ν^{τ^p} which will be used as a basis for measuring similarity between complex information structures.

One of the important motivations behind the definition provided is that we require a generalized inclusion function to coincide with the standard inclusion function in the case of a trivial tolerance space (identifying equal elements and distinguishing elements that are not equal).[2]

Definition 7. Let U be a set and $U_1, U_2 \subseteq U$. By the generalized inclusion function induced by τ^p we mean the function given by

$$\nu^{\tau^p}(U_1, U_2) \stackrel{\text{def}}{=} \begin{cases} \dfrac{|\{u_1 \in U_1 : \exists u_2 \in U_2 [u_1 \in n^{\tau^p}(u_2)]\}|}{|U_1|} & \text{if } U_1 \neq \emptyset \\ 1 & \text{otherwise.} \end{cases}$$

For $q \in [0,1]$, we say that U_1 is included in U_2 to a degree at least q wrt ν^{τ^p} iff $\nu^{\tau^p}(U_1, U_2) \geq q$.

In the case of tuples[3] $U_1 = \langle u_1, \ldots, u_n \rangle$ and $U_2 = \langle u'_1, \ldots, u'_n \rangle$, by the generalized inclusion function over tuples, induced by τ^p we mean the function given by

$$\nu_o^{\tau^p}(U_1, U_2) \stackrel{\text{def}}{=} \begin{cases} \dfrac{|\{u_i : 1 \leq i \leq n \text{ and } u_i \in n^{\tau^p}(u'_i)\}|}{|U_1|} & \text{if } n \neq 0 \\ 1 & \text{otherwise.} \end{cases} \quad \blacksquare$$

In the sequel we write $\nu_{TS}^{\tau p}$ and $n_{TS}^{\tau p}$, respectively, to denote $\nu^{\tau p}$ and n^{τ^p}, where τ^p is a tolerance relation induced from a tolerance space TS.[4]

---

[2] We also require such "continuity" in other definitions. Namely, the trivial tolerance space should always lead to standard notions that are accepted when tolerance is not considered.

[3] I.e., ordered sets of the same cardinality.

[4] We often drop the superscripts and subscripts when the tolerance spaces and relations are known from context.

Definition 8. *Let* $TS = \langle U, \tau, p \rangle$ *be a tolerance space. By a* power tolerance space *induced by* TS *we mean* $T^{TS} = \langle U^{TS}, \tau^{TS}, s \rangle$, *where*

- $U^{TS} \stackrel{\text{def}}{=} 2^U$, *is the set of all subsets of* U
- *for* $U_1, U_2 \in U^{TS}$, $\tau^{TS}(U_1, U_2) \stackrel{\text{def}}{=} \min\left\{ \nu^{\tau^p}(U_1, U_2), \nu^{\tau^p}(U_2, U_1) \right\}$
- $s \in [0, 1]$ *is a tolerance parameter.*   ∎

We define tolerance and neighborhood functions on tuples of elements in a similar manner.

Definition 9. *Let* $TS = \langle U, \tau, p \rangle$ *be a tolerance space. By a* k-tuple tolerance space *induced by* TS *we mean* $T^{TS^k} = \langle U^{TS^k}, \tau^{TS^k}, s \rangle$, *where*

- $U^{TS^k} \stackrel{\text{def}}{=} \underbrace{U \times \ldots \times U}_{k-times}$, *is the set of all* k-tuples of U
- *for* $U_1, U_2 \in U^{TS^k}$, $\tau^{TS^k}(U_1, U_2) \stackrel{\text{def}}{=} \nu_o^{\tau^p}(U_1, U_2) = \nu_o^{\tau^p}(U_2, U_1),$[5]
- $s \in [0, 1]$ *is a tolerance parameter*[6].   ∎

Let us summarize the methodology we propose:

- we start with a quantitative representation of the similarity of considered concepts given by semi-distance or tolerance functions (see Definitions 1 and 2)
- the definition of tolerance spaces (Definition 5) and neighborhoods (Definition 4) allows us to transform the quantitative representation of the similarity into a qualitative representation of the concepts. Such a transformation can also be applied to complex representational structures using Definitions 8 and 9. Tolerance parameters allow us to tune the similarities to fit particular application domains
- the approximations provided in Definition 6 allow us to isolate objects that surely satisfy a given property and that might satisfy the property. In consequence, we also obtain a characterization of objects that surely do not satisfy the property
- finally one can apply various deduction mechanisms to reason about the considered concepts (see, e.g., [2]).

6   An Example

In the following example we will use the data in Table 1 to exemplify the definition and use of tolerance spaces, where objects (birds) are characterized by attributes Length, Wingspan, Weight and Color.

For simplicity of presentation, below we use a separate domain for each of the attributes. Of course, the domains can simply be encoded by a single domain.

---

[5] The equality between $\nu_o^{\tau^p}(U_1, U_2)$ and $\nu_o^{\tau^p}(U_2, U_1)$ follows from the symmetry of τ.

[6] The tolerance paramter s specified in definitions 8 and 9 is not used in this paper.

Table 1. Description of birds.

Object	Length (cm)	Wingspan (cm)	Weight (g)	Color
blue jay	28	41	85	blue and grey
gray jay	29	46	70	grey with white and black
rusty blackbird	23	36	60	black
brewer's blackbird	23	39	63	black
european starling	22	41	82	black to brown

Let $\delta(x, y) \overset{\text{def}}{=} abs(x - y)$ be a distance function, where $abs(z)$ stands for the absolute value of z.

We first define a tolerance space for the integer value domain V_L of the attributes Length and Wingspan. We use a threshold of 5cm. The corresponding tolerance space $TS_L = \langle V_L, \tau_L, p_L \rangle$ is defined by:

$$V_L = \{x : 20 \leq x \leq 50\}, \ \tau_L(x, y) = 1 - \frac{\delta(x, y)}{\delta(20, 50)}, \ p_L = 1 - \frac{5}{\delta(20, 50)}.$$

Now $n^{\tau_L^{P_L}}(x) = \{y \in V_L : abs(x - y) \leq 5\} = \{y \in V_L : \tau_L^{P_L}(x, y)\}$.

Similarly one can define a tolerance space for the integer value domain V_W of the attribute Weight. We use a threshold of 10g. The tolerance space $TS_W = \langle V_W, \tau_W, p_W \rangle$ is defined by:

$$V_W = \{x : 60 \leq x \leq 90\}, \ \tau_W(x, y) = 1 - \frac{\delta(x, y)}{\delta(60, 90)}, \ p_W = 1 - \frac{10}{\delta(60, 90)}.$$

Now $n^{\tau_W^{P_W}}(x) = \{y \in V_L : abs(x - y) \leq 10\} = \{y \in V_L : \tau_W^{P_W}(x, y)\}$.

We define a tolerance space for the symbol value domain V_C of the attribute Color to be $TS_C = \langle V_C, \tau_C, p_C \rangle$, where:

- V_C consists of colors listed in the column of Table 1 labelled by Color
- for any color c, $\tau_C(c, c) = 1$. We also assume that

$$\tau_C(\text{black, black to brown}) = \tau_C(\text{black to brown, black}) = 0.9$$

- $p_C = 0.85$.

Assuming such tolerance spaces, we can conclude that rusty blackbird is similar to brewer's blackbird, since the first one is characterized by attributes $\langle 23, 36, 60, \text{black} \rangle$ and the second by attributes $\langle 23, 39, 63, \text{black} \rangle$. By Definition 9,

$$\tau^{TS^4}(\langle 23, 36, 60, \text{black} \rangle, \langle 23, 39, 63, \text{black} \rangle) = 4/4 = 1,$$

since $23 \in n^{\tau_L^{P_L}}(23)$, $36 \in n^{\tau_L^{P_L}}(39)$, $60 \in n^{\tau_L^{P_L}}(63)$ and black $\in n^{\tau_C^{P_C}}(\text{black})$.

For blue jay and grey jay we can conclude that:

$$\tau^{TS^4}(\langle 28, 41, 85, \text{blue and grey}\rangle, \langle 29, 46, 70, \text{grey with white and black}\rangle) = 2/4,$$

since $28 \in n^{\tau_L{}^{P_L}}(29)$, $41 \in n^{\tau_L{}^{P_L}}(46)$, $85 \notin n^{\tau_L{}^{P_L}}(70)$ and
blue and grey $\notin n^{\tau_C{}^{P_C}}$ (grey with white and black).

For rusty blackbird and european starling we can conclude that:

$$\tau^{TS^4}(\langle 23, 36, 60, \text{black}\rangle, \langle 22, 41, 82, \text{black to brown}\rangle) = 3/4,$$

since $23 \in n^{\tau_L{}^{P_L}}(22)$, $36 \in n^{\tau_L{}^{P_L}}(41)$, $60 \notin n^{\tau_L{}^{P_L}}(82)$ and
black $\in n^{\tau_C{}^{P_C}}$ (black to brown).

One can further define tolerance spaces on collections of birds, using Definition 8, relations defined on birds, etc.

7   Applications

7.1   Sensor Models and Tolerance Spaces

In this section, we provide a simple sensor model[7] and one method for modeling uncertainty in sensor data which integrates well with tolerance spaces. We also discuss the construction of virtual sensors from combinations of actual and other virtual sensors.

A sensor is used to measure one or more physical attributes in an environment E. The value sets associated with a physical attribute might be the real numbers, as in the case of measurement of the temperature or velocity of an object; Boolean values, as in the measurement of the presence or absence of an object such as a red car; integer values, as in the case of measurement of the number of vehicles in a particular intersection; or scalar values, such as the specific color of a vehicle. An environment E can be viewed as an abstract entity containing a collection of physical attributes that are measurable. Vectors or n-dimensional arrays of attribute/value pairs could be used to represent a particular environment. One may want to add a temporal argument to E, so the current state of the environment is dynamic and changes with time.

We denote a sensor S_i as a function of the environment E and time point t, $S_i(E, t)$. S_i is a function which returns a pair of functions,

$$S_i(E, t) = \{V_i(t), \epsilon_i(t)\}.$$

Depending on the type of sensor being modeled, $V_i(t)$ will be a function that returns the values of the physical attributes associated with the sensor. V_i might return a single value, as in the case of a single temperature sensor, or a vector or array of values for more complex sensors.

For any physical attribute measured, explicit accuracy bounds will be supplied in the form of $\epsilon_i(t)$. The temporal argument is supplied since the accuracy of a

---

[7] This model is based on a generalization of that in [1].

sensor may vary with time. As in the case of V_i, ϵ_i might return a single accuracy bound or a vector or array of accuracy bounds.

For example, suppose S_{temp} is a sensor measuring the temperature of a PC104 box on an unmanned aerial vehicle. Let a_{temp} be the physical attribute associated with temperature in the environment, where the actual temperature is $E(t)(a_{temp})$ and the value returned by the sensor is $V_i(t)(a_{temp})$. The following constraint holds:

$$E(t)(a_{temp}) \in [V_i(t)(a_{temp}) - \epsilon_i(t), V_i(t)(a_{temp}) + \epsilon_i(t)].$$

By using tolerance spaces, accuracy bounds for a physical attribute can be represented equivalently as tolerance relations to degree p on the value set for the attribute. In this manner, we can use neighborhood functions to reason about the tolerance or accuracy neighborhoods around individual sensor readings and combine these into neighborhoods for more complex virtual sensors.

In the following, we will drop the temporal argument for ϵ and assume the accuracy bounds for attributes do not change with time. Let $TS_{S_{ik}} = \langle V_{S_{ik}}, \tau_{s_{ik}}, p_{s_{ik}} \rangle$ be a tolerance space for the kth physical attribute, a_{i_k} associated with the sensor S_i, where,

- $V_{S_{ik}} = \{x \mid lb \leq x \leq ub, x \in D\}$, where D is a value domain such as the reals or integers. It is assumed that the legal values for a physical attribute have a lower and upper bound, lb, ub. We associate a distance measurement $\delta(x) = \mid x - y \mid$ with the value set $V_{S_{ik}}$, which includes all the values that can be read from the sensor S_i.
- Both the tolerance function $\tau_{s_{ik}}$, and the tolerance parameter $p_{s_{ik}}$ are defined as follows,

$$\tau_{s_{ik}}(x, y) = 1 - \frac{\delta(x, y)}{\delta(lb, ub)}, \quad p_{s_{ik}} = 1 - \frac{\epsilon_i}{\delta(lb, ub)}.$$

The neighborhood function can be used to compute the possible actual values of a physical attribute in the environment, given a sensor reading, under the assumption that the accuracy bounds have been generated correctly for a particular sensor and the sensor remains calibrated. For example, if $V_i(a_{temp})$ is the current value measured by the sensor S_i then we would know that $E(a_{temp}) \in n^{p_{s_{ik}}}(V_i(a_{temp}))$. So, the tolerance neighborhood around a sensor reading always contains the actual value of the physical attribute in the environment E and it would be correct to reason with the neighborhoods of sensor values, rather than the sensor value itself.

We can then use these physical attributes and their associated tolerance spaces to construct more complex attributes and knowledge structures in terms of these. These new attributes and knowledge structures would inherit the accuracy (inaccuracy) of the primitive sensor data used in their construction.

7.2   Mutual Understanding between Tolerance Agents

Consider a multi-agent application in a complex environment such as the world wide web for software agents, or a natural disaster in an urban area for physical robots. Each agent will generally have its own view of its environment due to a number of factors such as the use of different sensor suites, knowledge structures, reasoning processes, etc. Agents may also have different understandings of the underlying concepts which are used in their respective representational structures and will measure objects and phenomena with different accuracy. How then can agents with different knowledge structures and perceptive accuracies understand each other and effect meaningful communication and how can this be modeled? In this section, both tolerance spaces and upper and lower approximations on agent concepts and relations are used to define a means for agents to communicate when different sensor capabilities and different levels of accuracy in knowledge structures are assumed.

We begin with a broad definition of a *tolerance agent*.

Definition 10. *By a* tolerance agent *we shall understand any pair* $\langle Ag, TS \rangle$*, where Ag is an agent and TS is a tolerance space.*   ■

The assumption is that the Ag part of an agent consists of common functionalities normally associated with agents such as planners, reactive and other methods, knowledge bases or structures, etc. The knowledge bases or structures are also assumed to have a relational component consisting of approximate relations which are derived and viewed through the agents limited sensor capabilities. When the agent introspects and queries its own knowledge base these limited perceptive capabilities should be reflected in any answer to a query.

The following definition will be used to provide a tolerance limited semantics for queries in the context of a particular tolerance space.

Definition 11. *Let* $TS = \langle U, \tau, p \rangle$ *be a tolerance space. Consider a pair of sets,* $Z = \langle X, Y \rangle$ *, such that* $X \subseteq Y$.[8] *By a* lower *and* upper *approximation of Z wrt TS we mean*

$$Z_{TS+}^{\tau^p} \overset{\text{def}}{=} \{ u \in U : n_{TS}^{\tau^p}(u) \subseteq X \}$$
$$Z_{TS\oplus}^{\tau^p} \overset{\text{def}}{=} \{ u \in U : n_{TS}^{\tau^p}(u) \cap Y \neq \emptyset \}.$$

$Z_{TS-}^{\tau^p}$ *is defined as* $-Z_{TS\oplus}^{\tau^p}$.   ■

To keep the exposition concise, simple queries, such as $R(\mathsf{a})$ will be used, where R is a relation symbol and a is a constant symbol. Due to its limited perceptive capabilities, one can assume that the agent may not recognize the difference between a and other objects in the neighborhood of a. Thus, the agent can be sure that $R(\mathsf{a})$ holds only if all elements in the neighborhood of a satisfy R. The agent also can not exclude the possibility that $R(\mathsf{a})$ holds if there is at least one element in the neighborhood of a satisfying R. Consequently, it is clear that R can be viewed as a set such that:

---

[8] Intuitively, X and Y correspond to a lower and upper approximation of a set.

- its lower approximation only contains elements that, together with all elements in their neighborhood, satisfy R
- its upper approximation contains elements for which there is at least one element in their neighborhood that satisfies R.

Moreover, the set itself is given only via its approximations.

The following example illustrates this approach.

Example 1. Let *TA* be a tolerance agent with the following domain of discourse: Mary, lR, mR, dR, where the latter three elements denote "light red", "medium red" and "dark red", respectively. *TA*'s knowledge base contains the following three facts:

$$Likes(\text{Mary}, \text{lR}),\ Likes(\text{Mary}, \text{mR}),\ \neg Likes(\text{Mary}, \text{dR}),$$

Assume further that the single tolerance relation associated with the tolerance space of *TA* identifies lR with mR and mR with dR.

Suppose agent *TA* is given the task of verifying whether Mary likes a color it directly senses as being lR. Based on the agent's tolerance relation, its sensors are not capable of recognizing the difference between lR and mR. However, Mary likes both colors, so *TA* can be sure that she likes the color sensed by *TA* with certainty.

If *TA* directly sensed the color as mR then it could not be sure whether Mary likes this color or not, since it does not perceive any difference between mR and dR. The sensed color might actually be dR which Mary does not like. On the other hand, *TA* could not exclude the alternative that Mary likes this color, as it could equally well be mR.

In summary, lR is in the lower approximation of the (unary) relation $likes(\text{Mary}, x)$ and mR and dR are in the upper approximation of the relation. The agent *TA* would use these approximations of the relation together with its knowledge and associated tolerance space when answering questions about Mary's likes or dislikes. ∎

These intuitions are formalized in the following definition.

Definition 12. *Let* TA $= \langle Ag, TS \rangle$ *be a tolerance agent. Then the semantics of a relation R wrt* TA *is given by:*

$$R_{TA+} \stackrel{\text{def}}{=} R_{TS+},\ R_{TA\oplus} \stackrel{\text{def}}{=} R_{TS\oplus}\ \text{and}\ R_{TA-} \stackrel{\text{def}}{=} R_{TS-},$$

where R_{TS+}, $R_{TS\oplus}$ and R_{TA-} are as defined in Definition 11. ∎

Remark 1. It is important to note that Definition 12 refers to an arbitrary relation. Since any first-order or fixpoint query to a RDB returns a relation as its result, the definition also provides us with the semantics of queries asked to and answered by tolerance agents. ∎

Example 2. Consider the tolerance agent *TA* again, with the same tolerance space and facts given in Example 1. The answer returned by agent *TA* to the sample query, $Likes(\mathsf{Mary}, x)$, will be computed using Definition 12.

According to Example 1,

$$Likes = \{\langle \mathsf{Mary}, \mathsf{IR} \rangle, \langle \mathsf{Mary}, \mathsf{mR} \rangle\}.$$

Consequently, *Likes* is approximated by *TA* as follows:

$$Likes_{TA^+} \stackrel{\text{def}}{=} Likes_{TS^+} = \{u \mid u \in \{\langle \mathsf{Mary}, \mathsf{IR} \rangle, \langle \mathsf{Mary}, \mathsf{mR} \rangle, \langle \mathsf{Mary}, \mathsf{dR} \rangle\}$$
$$\text{and } n_{TS}(u) \subseteq Likes\} = \{\langle \mathsf{Mary}, \mathsf{IR} \rangle\}$$

$$Likes_{TA^\oplus} \stackrel{\text{def}}{=} Likes_{TS^\oplus} = \{u \mid u \in \{\langle \mathsf{Mary}, \mathsf{IR} \rangle, \langle \mathsf{Mary}, \mathsf{mR} \rangle, \langle \mathsf{Mary}, \mathsf{dR} \rangle\}$$
$$\text{and } n_{TS}(u) \cap Likes \neq \emptyset\} = \{\langle \mathsf{Mary}, \mathsf{IR} \rangle, \langle \mathsf{Mary}, \mathsf{mR} \rangle, \langle \mathsf{Mary}, \mathsf{dR} \rangle\}.$$

Thus,the following facts hold:

$$Likes(\mathsf{Mary}, \mathsf{IR})_{TA^+}, \ Likes(\mathsf{Mary}, \mathsf{IR})_{TA^\oplus},$$
$$Likes(\mathsf{Mary}, \mathsf{mR})_{TA^\oplus}, \ Likes(\mathsf{Mary}, \mathsf{dR})_{TA^\oplus}.$$

These results reflect the intuitions described in Example 1.   ∎

Given that two tolerance agents have different tolerance spaces it becomes necessary to define the meaning of queries and answers relative to the two tolerance agents. As advocated before, a tolerance agent, when asked about a relation, answers by using the approximations of the relation wrt its tolerance space. On the other hand, the agent that asked the query has to understand the answer provided by the other agent wrt to its own tolerance space. The dialog between agents, say TA_1 (query agent) and TA_2 (answer agent), conforms then to the following schema:

1. TA_1 asks a query Q to TA_2
2. TA_2 computes the answer approximating it according to its tolerance space and returns as an answer the approximations $QA = \langle Q_{TA_2^+}, Q_{TA_2^\oplus} \rangle$
3. TA_1 receives QA as input and approximates it according to its own tolerance space. The resulting approximations provide the answer to the query, as understood by TA_1.

In order for the schema to work properly, it has to be assumed that the two agents operate with a common vocabulary when communicating. This does not imply that the agents need to have the same vocabulary, simply that there is some overlap.

The definition describing this interaction now follows.

Definition 13. *Let* TA_1, TA_2 *be tolerance agents and let* Q *be a query, expressed in a logic, which is asked by* TA_1 *and answered by* TA_2. *Then the meaning of the query is given by the following approximations:*

$$\langle \langle Q_{TA_2^+}, Q_{TA_2^\oplus} \rangle_{TA_1^+}, \langle Q_{TA_2^+}, Q_{TA_2^\oplus} \rangle_{TA_1^\oplus} \rangle. \tag{3}$$

∎

The notion of mutual understanding used by communicating agents of this type is developed in full in [3].

8   Summary

This paper presents a framework for recursively constructing arbitrarily complex knowledge structures which may be compared for similarity, distance and approximativeness. The techniques used attempt to bridge a gap between quantitative representations of data in terms of attribute/value pairs and their use in qualitative knowledge representations at different levels of abstraction. The qualitative representations inherit the approximativeness of their component structures through the use of neighborhoods of objects and upper and lower approximations induced through their use. Tolerance spaces provide a structured means of constructing complex representational structures. These ideas have been exemplified by using the techniques for sensor modeling and signal to symbol conversions and for representing approximate queries between agents with heterogenous perceptive capabilities.

References

1. R. R. Brooks and S.S. Iyengar. *Multi-Sensor Fusion*. Prentice-Hall, 1998.
2. P. Doherty, W. Łukaszewicz, A. Skowron, and A. Szałas. Combining rough and crisp knowledge in deductive databases. In *Rough-Neuro Computing: Techniques for Computing with Words*. 2003.
3. P. Doherty, W. Łukaszewicz, and A Szałas. On mutual understanding among communicating agents. In B. Dunin-Keplicz and R. Verbrugge, editors, *Proceedings of Workshop on Formal Approaches to Multi-agent Systems (FAMAS'03)*, pages 83–97, 2003.
4. P. Gärdenfors. *Conceptual spaces: the geometry of thought*. MIT Press, Cambridge, Mass., 2000.
5. Z. Pawlak. *Rough Sets. Theoretical Aspects of Reasoning about Data*. Kluwer Academic Publishers, Dordrecht, 1991.
6. A. Skowron and J. Stepaniuk. Tolerance approximation spaces. *Fundamenta Informaticae*, 27:245–253, 1996.

Planning in Answer Set Programming Using Ordered Task Decomposition

Jürgen Dix[1*], Ugur Kuter, and Dana Nau[2]

[1] The University of Manchester
Dept. of CS, Oxford Road
Manchester M13 9PL, UK
dix@cs.man.ac.uk
http://www.cs.man.ac.uk/~jdix
[2] University of Maryland
Dept. of CS, A.V. Williams Building
College Park, MD 20752, USA
{ukuter,nau}@cs.umd.edu

Abstract. In this paper we introduce a formalism for solving *Hierarchical Task Network* (HTN) Planning using *Answer Set Programming* (ASP). We consider the formulation of HTN planning as described in the *SHOP* planning system and define a systematic translation method from *SHOP*'s representation of the planning problem into logic programs with negation. We show that our translation is *sound* and *complete*: answer sets of the logic program obtained by our translation correspond exactly to the solutions of the planning problem. We compare our method to (1) similar approaches based on non-HTN planning and (2) *SHOP*, a dedicated planning system. We show that our approach outperforms non-HTN methods and that its performance is better with ASP systems that allow for nonground programs than with ASP systems that require ground programs.

Keywords: HTN planning, nonmonotonic reasoning, ASP systems, benchmarks

1 Introduction

In the past few years, the availability of very fast nonmonotonic systems based on logic programming (LP) made it possible to attack problems from other, non-LP areas, by translating these problems into logic programs and running a fast prover on them. One of the first such system was *smodels* [1] and one of the early applications [2] was to transform planning problems in a suitable way and to run *smodels* on them (see also [3]).

Since then more implemented systems with different properties for dealing with logic programs have become available: *DLV* [4], *XSB* [5,6] to cite the

---

* This paper is an extended abstract of a paper that is currently submitted as a regular paper for *Theory and Practice of Logic Programming*.

A. Günter et al. (Eds.): KI 2003, LNAI 2821, pp. 490–504, 2003.

most well-known. In addition, the paradigm of Answer Set Programming (ASP) emerged [7] is based on the following two key ideas: (1) solving problems by computing models for logic programs rather than by evaluating queries against logic programs (as used to be done in conventional logic programming), (2) addressing the problems located on the second level of the polynomial hierarchy which seem to be well suited to be tackled with the machinery of answer sets. In particular many planning problems fit in this picture. Indeed, the problems on the first two levels of polynomial time hierarchy are covered by the current ASP implementations.

In this paper, we investigate the ways of formulating and solving Hierarchical Task Network (HTN) planning problems using nonmonotonic logic programs under the ASP semantics. HTN planning [8,9,10,11] is an AI-planning paradigm in which the goals of the planner are defined in terms of activities (tasks) and the planning process is accomplished by using the techniques of task decomposition. There are several well-known HTN planning systems such as *Universal Method Composition Planner (UMCP)* [9], *Simple Hierarchical Ordered Planner (SHOP)* [11], and *SHOP2* (a total-order planner with partially ordered subtasks) [12]. In this work, we focus on the *SHOP* planning system, which is a domain-independent HTN planning system that is built around the concept called *ordered task decomposition.*

We describe a systematic translation method $\mathfrak{Trans}(\cdot)$ which transforms HTN-planning problems as formalised in *SHOP* into logic programs with negation. Our basic goal is that an appropriate semantics of the logic program should correspond to the solutions (plans) of the planning problem. We have adapted the syntax of the *smodels* software for our transformation, although we are also experimenting with other systems like *DLV* and *XSB*.

Our experimental results suggest that both (1) encodings using HTN planning are better than other encodings, because the HTN control knowledge can be used very naturally to prune irrelevant branches of the search space; and (2) running an ASP system on non-ground programs (obtained from planning problems) results in a drastic performance relative to *smodels*, thus bringing our method closer to dedicated planning systems like *SHOP*.

This paper is organised as follows. In the following section, we present the related work. In Section 2, we describe the basic HTN Planning concepts as they are defined in *SHOP*. In Section 3, we first present our causal theory for HTN planning and then our translation methodology to transform HTN-planning problems into logic programs with negation. Section 4 contains our theoretical and experimental results. Our main theorem states that our translation method is correct and complete with respect to *SHOP*. Finally, we conclude with Section 5 and provide our future research directions.

1.1   Related Work

There are many efforts in the literature for formulating actions in logic programs and solving planning problems by using formulations such as [13,14,15,16,17]. The idea in all these works is that representing a given computational problem by a logic program whose models correspond to the solutions for the original problem. This idea was the main inspiration for our work presented here.

[18] proposes a declarative language, called the K language, for planning with incomplete information. The K language makes it possible to describe transitions between knowledge states, which may not be complete, regarding the world. This language is implemented as a front-end to the *DLV* logic programming system.

[19] presents a language about actions using causal laws to reason in probabilistic settings and solves the planning problems in such settings. The language resembles similarities to those described above, but the action theory incorporates probabilities and probabilistic reasoning techniques to solve the planning problems with uncertainty.

Dimopoulos, Nebel and Köhler ([2]) were the first to present a framework for encoding planning problems in logic programs with negation-as-failure and implementing it using an ASP engine. In this work, the idea is the same as ours, that is, the models of the logic program correspond to the plans. However, their work considers action-based planning problems and incorporates ideas from such planners *GRAPHPLAN* and *SATPLAN*. In terms of the underlying assumptions and methods presented in [2], our approach is completely different. Both methods complement each other.

[20] discusses solving planning programs by logic programs. The difference between this work and the one described above is that [20] incorporates domain-dependent control knowledge to improve the performance of the planning. In this respect, this work is similar to HTN planning algorithms. However, the encoding provided in this work is conceptually not an HTN planner.

2   Definitions for HTN Planning: Syntax and Semantics

A *term* is either a constant or a variable symbol. A *state* S is a set of ground atoms. An *axiom* is an expression of the form $a \leftarrow l_1, \dots, l_n$, where a is an atom and the l_i are literals. Axioms need not be ground. We assume that the set of axioms does not contain cycles through negation.

A task is an expression of the form $(h t_1 t_2 \dots t_n)$, where h (the task's name) is a task symbol, and $t_1, t_2, \dots, t_n$ (the task's arguments) are terms. A task can be either primitive or composite. A task list is a list of tasks.

An *operator* is an expression of the form $\mathsf{Op} = (\mathbf{Op}\ h\ \chi_{del}\ \chi_{add})$, where h (the *head*) is a primitive task and χ_{add} and χ_{del} are lists of atoms (called the *add-* and *delete-lists*). The set of variables in the atoms in χ_{add} and χ_{del} is a subset of the set of variables in h. Let t be a primitive task, $\mathsf{Op} = (\mathbf{Op}\ h\ \chi_{del}\ \chi_{add})$ be an operator, and S be the current state of the world. Suppose that u is a unifier for h and t. Then the operator instance Op^u is *applicable* to t in S and the result of applying it to t in S is a new state $\mathrm{result}(\mathsf{Op}^u, S)$ that is created by first deleting every ground atom in χ_{del}^u from S and then by adding every ground atom in χ_{add}^u to S.

A *method* is an expression of the form $(\mathbf{Meth}\ h\ \chi\ \mathbf{t})$ where h (the method's *head*) is a compound task, χ (the method's *preconditions*) is a conjunct and $\mathbf{t}$ is a totally ordered list of subtasks, called the *task list*. Let t be a compound task, $\mathcal{S}$ be the initial state, $Meth = (\textbf{Meth } h \, \chi \, \textbf{t})$ be a method, and $\mathcal{AX}$ be an axiom set. Suppose that u is a unifier for h and t, and that v is a unifier that unifies χ^u with respect to $\mathcal{S} \cup \mathcal{AX}$. Then the method instance $(Meth^u)^v$ is *applicable* to t in $\mathcal{S}$, and the result of applying it to t is the task list $\textbf{r} = (\textbf{t}^u)^v$. The task list $\textbf{r}$ is a *simple reduction* of $\textbf{t}$ by $Meth$ in $\mathcal{S}$.

A *plan* is a list of heads of ground operator instances. If $P = (p_1 p_2 \ldots p_n)$ is a plan and $\mathcal{S}$ is a state (a set of ground atoms a), then the *result* of applying P to $\mathcal{S}$ is the state result$(\mathcal{S}, P) =$ result(result($\ldots$ (result$(\mathcal{S}, p_1), p_2), \ldots), p_n)$. A plan P is called a *simple plan* when $n = 1$.

A *planning domain* is a set of axioms, operators and methods. A planning domain can contain more than one method applicable to a particular compound task, but it must have only one operator applicable to a particular primitive task. A *planning problem* is a triple $(\mathcal{S}, \textbf{t}, \mathcal{D})$, where $\mathcal{S}$ is a state, $\textbf{t} = (t_1 t_2 \ldots t_k)$ is a task list, and $\mathcal{D}$ is a planning domain.

Suppose $(\mathcal{S}, \textbf{t}, \mathcal{D})$ is a planning problem and $P = (p_1 p_2 \ldots p_n)$ is a plan. We say that P solves $(\mathcal{S}, \textbf{t}, \mathcal{D})$, or equivalently, that P *achieves* $\textbf{t}$ from $\mathcal{S}$ in $\mathcal{D}$ (we will omit the phrase "in $\mathcal{D}$" if the identity of $\mathcal{D}$ is obvious) if any of the following cases is true: (1) $\textbf{t}$ and P are both empty, (i.e., $k = 0$ and $n = 0$); (2) t_1 is a primitive task, p_1 is a simple plan for t_1, $(p_2 \ldots p_n)$ achieves $(t_2 \ldots t_k)$ from result$(\mathcal{S}, p_1)$; and (3) t_1 is a composite task, and there is a simple reduction $(r_1 \ldots r_j)$ of t_1 in $\mathcal{S}$ such that P achieves $(r_1 \ldots r_j t_2 \ldots t_k)$ from $\mathcal{S}$. The planning problem $(\mathcal{S}, \textbf{t}, \mathcal{D})$ is *solvable* if there is a plan that solves it. We define $\textbf{Sol}(\mathcal{S}, \textbf{t}, \mathcal{D})$ as the set of all possible plans that can be found given $(\mathcal{S}, \textbf{t}, \mathcal{D})$ as a solution during planning. Note that $\textbf{Sol}(\mathcal{S}, \textbf{t}, \mathcal{D})$ is a *multi set*: it can contain the same plan in a number of copies. This is because the same plans may be generated during the planning process due to the fact that there may be different method applicable to a particular compound task, thus creating a branching point in the search space of the planner, and different branches may end up with same plans.

3   Encoding HTN Planning in Nonmonotonic LP

Our approach of encoding HTN-planning problems as logic programs is based on *SHOP*'s representation of a planning problem.[1] In this section, we present first steps of a causal theory of HTN planning based on the *SHOP* formalism. The reason for presenting this causal theory is not to give a formal semantics, but to give some motivations for the more technical aspects of the translation methodology presented in the later in this section.

Definition 1 (Causable Tasks). *For a planning problem* $(\mathcal{S}, \textbf{t}, \mathcal{D})$, *the notion of an ordered list of tasks to be causable* **wrt.** $(\mathcal{S}, \mathcal{D})$ *comes in 3 steps.*

---

[1] *SHOP* is a domain-independent HTN-planning system that plans for tasks in the same order that they will later be executed. This provides the planner with a significant inferencing and reasoning power, including the ability to call external programs and the ability to perform numeric computations. Due to the lack space, we cannot go into the details of *SHOP* in this paper; for more information please see [11,21].

Literals: *A literal l is caused by* $(\mathcal{S}, \mathcal{AX})$ *if l is true in all answer sets of* $\mathcal{S} \cup \mathcal{AX}$, *where* $\mathcal{AX}$ *is the set of axioms in* $\mathcal{D}$. *A literal l is causable* wrt. $(\mathcal{S}, \mathcal{D})$ *if it is caused by* $(\mathcal{S}, \mathcal{AX})$ *A conjunction of literals is causable* wrt. $(\mathcal{S}, \mathcal{D})$ *if every conjunct is causable* wrt. $(\mathcal{S}, \mathcal{D})$.

Primitive tasks: *An ordered list of primitive tasks* $t_1, \ldots, t_n$ *is* causable wrt. $(\mathcal{S}, \mathcal{D})$ *if the following holds:*

> *For each* t_i, *there exists an operator* **(Op** h χ_{del} χ_{add}**)** $\in \mathcal{D}$ *such that there is a unifier u for h and* t_i.
>
> *This includes that the empty list* [] *is causable.*

Composite tasks: *An ordered list of tasks* $t_1, \ldots, t_j, \ldots, t_n$, *where* t_j *is a composite task and all tasks* $t_1, \ldots, t_{j-1}$ *are primitive tasks, is* causable wrt. $(\mathcal{S}, \mathcal{D})$ *if the following holds:*

1. *there exists a method* **(Meth** h χ $\{t_{j_1}, \ldots, t_{j_m}\}$**)** $\in \mathcal{D}$ *for* t_j *such that there is a unifier u for h and* t_j,
2. *the preconditions-list* χ^u, *which is a list of literals representing a conjunction, is causable* wrt. $(result(\mathcal{S}, t_1, \ldots t_{j-1}), \mathcal{D})$, *and*
3. *the ordered list* $(t_1, \ldots, t_{j-1}, t_{j_1}, \ldots, t_{j_m}, t_{j+1}, \ldots t_n$ *is causable* wrt. $(\mathcal{S}, \mathcal{D})$.

Theorem 1. *Let a planning problem* $(\mathcal{S}, \mathbf{t}, \mathcal{D})$ *be given, where* $\mathcal{S}$ *is the initial state,* $\mathbf{t}$ *is the list of tasks to be achieved and* $\mathcal{D}$ *is the domain description.*

There is a solution to $(\mathcal{S}, \mathbf{t}, \mathcal{D})$ *if and only if the list* $\mathbf{t}$ *is causable* wrt. $(\mathcal{S}, \mathcal{D})$.

Using this causal theory as an intermediate step, we developed a systematic translation method for mapping planning problems to logic programs with negation which we illustrate now.

Translating a planning problem $(\mathcal{S}, \mathbf{t}, \mathcal{D})$ to its logic program counterpart $\mathfrak{Trans}((\mathcal{S}, \mathbf{t}, \mathcal{D}))$ requires encoding the methods, the operators, and the axioms as logic program segments as well as the underlying ordered task decomposition characteristics of *SHOP*.

Definition 2 ($\mathfrak{Trans}((\mathcal{S}, \mathbf{t}, \mathcal{D}))$: **Translation for the Planning Problem).**
The logic program $\mathfrak{Trans}((\mathcal{S}, \mathbf{t}, \mathcal{D}))$ *that solves the planning problem* $(\mathcal{S}, \mathbf{t}, \mathcal{D})$ *is defined as*

$$\mathfrak{Trans}((\mathcal{S}, \mathbf{t}, \mathcal{D})) = \mathfrak{Trans}(G) \cup \mathfrak{Trans}(\mathcal{S}) \cup \mathfrak{Trans}(\mathbf{t}) \cup \mathfrak{Trans}(\mathcal{AX}) \cup$$
$$\mathfrak{Trans}(F) \cup \mathfrak{Trans}(\mathcal{OP}) \cup \mathfrak{Trans}(\mathcal{METH}), \cup \mathfrak{Trans}(ST),$$

where each $\mathfrak{Trans}(\ldots)$ *is a logic program segment as defined in the following subsections.*

Encoding the Grounding Rules. Given a planning problem, these rules encode all of the objects that may be used in solving the planning problem, the type descriptions of those objects, and all of the atoms that may appear to be true in some state of the planner during the planning process. The reason that we need these rules are the following important distinction between *SHOP* and most nonmonotonic systems: *SHOP* allows using variables in the domain descriptions of the planning problems and all variables are implicitly universally quantified. However, unlike most nonmonotonic systems, *SHOP* searches over the original formulas without expanding the ground representation before search.

Definition 3 ($\mathfrak{Trans}(G)$: Translation for the Grounding Rules).
Given a planning problem $(\mathcal{S}, \mathbf{t}, \mathcal{D})$, *we define* $\mathfrak{Trans}(G)$ *as the logic program segment that consists of the following set of rules:*

- *For each object o:* $[type](o) : -$
- *For each atom A:* $atom(A) : -$

Encoding the Initial State. The initial state $\mathcal{S}$ is a set of ground atoms.
Definition 4 ($\mathfrak{Trans}(\mathcal{S})$: Translation for Initial State).
Given a planning problem $(\mathcal{S}, \mathbf{t}, \mathcal{D})$, *for each ground atom* $a \in \mathcal{S}$, *the logic program segment* $\mathfrak{Trans}(\mathcal{S})$ *contains the rule "$in\_state(a, 0) : -$", where 0 indicates the initial time.*

Encoding the Goal Task(s). In *SHOP*-like HTN planning, a task is accomplished if and only if it is *causable* with respect to the initial state and the domain description given in the planning problem. This is due to the Definition 1 and a direct consequence of Theorem 1. We denote the fact that whether a task is causable by the following definition.

Definition 5 (CAUSABLE).
  Given a task t, we define $CAUSABLE(t, T_{selected}, T_{accomplished})$ as follows:

$$\begin{cases} false & \text{if } t \text{ is a primitive task and} \\ & \text{there is no operator for it in } \mathcal{D}, \text{ or} \\ & \text{if } t \text{ is a compound task and} \\ & \text{there is no method for it in } \mathcal{D}, \\ currentTask(t, T_{selected}), & \text{if } t_k \text{ is a primitive task and} \\ & \text{there is an operator for it in } \mathcal{D}, \\ causable(t, T_{selected}, T_{accomplished}) & \text{if } t_k \text{ is a compound task and} \\ & \text{there is a method for it in } \mathcal{D}, \end{cases}$$

where the predicate $currentTask(t, T)$ encodes the fact that the task t is selected as the "current task" – i.e., the task that the planner will try to accomplish next – at time T.

  We are now ready to define the logic program that encodes the goal task list of a given planning problem.

Definition 6 ($\mathfrak{Trans}(\mathbf{t})$: Translation for Goal Tasks).
Given a planning problem $(\mathcal{S}, \mathbf{t}, \mathcal{D})$, *let* $\mathbf{t} = h_1, h_2, \ldots, h_n$ *be the ordered sequence of goal tasks. Then, $\mathfrak{Trans}(\mathbf{t})$ is the logic program segment that contains one rule for each goal task h_i, where $i = 1, 2, \ldots, n$, as follows:*

$$currentTask(h_1, 0) \ : -$$
$$currentTask(h_i, T_i) : - CAUSABLE(h_{i-1}, T_{i-1}, T_i), T_i > T_{i-1}.$$

Note that if there exists only one goal task to be accomplished for the problem in hand, then only defining the first rule will suffice. Definition 6 enforces the fact that a goal task h_i is designated as the current task to be accomplished if the previous goal task h_{i-1} in $\mathbf{t}$ is causable. This is a direct consequence of our Theorem 1. The planning process terminates successfully when all of the goal tasks are accomplished (i.e., caused) in the order they are given in the planning problems. The following definition is given to encode the successful termination of the planning process.

Definition 7 ($\mathfrak{Trans}(ST)$: Successful Termination).
Given a planning problem $(S, \mathbf{t}, \mathcal{D})$, the logic program segment $\mathfrak{Trans}(ST)$ that encodes the successful termination of the planning process (i.e., the fact that a solution to the given planning problem is found) is defined as follows:

$$plan\_found : - \ CAUSABLE(h_n, T_n, T_{n+1}).$$
$$: - \ not \, plan\_found.$$

Encoding the Domain Control Structures. Given a planning problem $(S, \mathbf{t}, \mathcal{D})$, the domain description $\mathcal{D}$ contains axioms, operators and methods as described in the previous section. For each of these constructs, we present a translation procedure.

Definition 8 (Translation for Literals).
Given a literal, l, we define $C(l, T)$, the translation of l at time T (a is an atom):

$$C(l, T) := \begin{cases} in\_state(a, T) \text{ if } l = a, \\ not \ in\_state(a, T) \text{ if } l = \neg a. \end{cases}$$

Definition 9 ($\mathfrak{Trans}(\mathcal{AX})$: Translation for Axioms).
Given a planning problem $(S, \mathbf{t}, \mathcal{D})$, for all "$a \leftarrow l_1, \dots, l_n$" $\in \mathcal{AX}$, the logic program segment $\mathfrak{Trans}(\mathcal{AX})$ contains the following rule

$$in\_state(a, T) \ : - \ C(l_1, T), C(l_2, T), \dots, C(l_n, T),$$

where $C(l_i, T)$ is the translation of a literal as defined in Definition 8 above.

Definition 10 ($\mathfrak{Trans}(\mathcal{OP})$: Translation for Operators).
Given a planning problem $(S, \mathbf{t}, \mathcal{D})$, for all $Op \in \mathcal{OP}$, $\mathfrak{Trans}(Op)$ is the logic program segment that contains the following rules:

for all $a \in Del(Op)$: $out\_state(a, T + 1) \ : - \ currentTask(h, T).$
and for all $a \in Add(Op)$: $in\_state(a, T + 1) \ : - \ currentTask(h, T).$

Note that an operator only describes the *change* it causes to occur in the current state. Therefore, we still need to address the famous *Frame Problem* as follows.

Definition 11 ($\mathfrak{Trans}(F)$: Keeping Track of the State S). *The logic program segment $\mathfrak{Trans}(F)$ that encodes the frame axiom is defined as follows:*

$$in\_state(A, T + 1) : - \ atom(A), in\_state(A, T), not \, out\_state(A, T + 1).$$

Definition 12 ($\mathfrak{Trans}(\mathcal{METH})$: Translation for Methods). *Given a planning problem $(\mathcal{S}, \mathbf{t}, \mathcal{D})$, let h be a compound task that needs to be accomplished in the solution of the given planning problem. Suppose the domain description $\mathcal{D}$ contains N methods whose heads unify with h; namely, $m_1, m_2, \ldots, m_N$. Let $\text{Pre}(h)_i$ be the label for the precondition list of the method m_i. Then, the logic program segment that encodes these methods is defined as follows:*

1. The nondeterministic choice of which method to apply to the task h:

$$method_1(h, \text{Pre}(h)_1, T) \quad : - \; currentTask(h, T),$$
$$not\, method_2(h, \text{Pre}(h)_2, T), ...,$$
$$not\, method_N(h, \text{Pre}(h)_N, T)$$

$$\vdots \qquad\qquad \vdots \qquad\qquad \vdots$$

$$method_N(h, \text{Pre}(h)_N, T) : - \; currentTask(h, T),$$
$$not\, method_1(h, \text{Pre}(h)_1, T), ...,$$
$$not\, method_{N-1}(h, \text{Pre}(h)_{N-1}, T)$$

2. The precondition list χ_i of each method m_i: *For each precondition $p \in \chi_i$, we have one of the following two cases:*

   a) *p is a positive literal and it contains free variables: The free variables in a precondition literal are the variable symbols that do not appear in the head of the method m_i. We denote p as $p = p(Y_1, Y_2, \ldots, Y_f)$, where $Y_1, Y_2, \ldots, Y_f$ are the free variables in p.[2] Let R_j denote the range of the free variable Y_j – i.e. the set of all possible values for the variable Y_j –, and for each such variable Y_j, let $Y_{j,k}$ be a new variable symbol such that $k = 1, \ldots, R_j$. Then, $\mathfrak{Trans}(\mathcal{METH})$ contains the following rule to encode the precondition $p \in \chi_i$:*

$$checked\_state(p(Y_{1,1}, Y_{2,1}, \ldots, Y_{f,1}), T) \; : -$$
$$method_i(h, \text{Pre}(h)_i, T),$$
$$in\_state(p(Y_{1,1}, Y_{2,1}, \ldots, Y_{f,1}), T),$$
$$not\, checked\_state(p(Y_{1,1}, Y_{2,1}, \ldots, Y_{f,2}), T),$$
$$not\, checked\_state(p(Y_{1,1}, Y_{2,1}, \ldots, Y_{f,3}), T),$$

$$\vdots$$

$$not\, checked\_state(p(Y_{1,R_1}, Y_{2,R_2}, \ldots, Y_{f,R_f}), T),$$
$$\bigwedge_{j=1}^{f} Y_{j,1}! = Y_{j,2}! = \ldots! = Y_{j,R_j}.$$

   b) *Otherwise: The logic program segment $\mathfrak{Trans}(\mathcal{METH})$ contains the rule "$checked\_state(p, T) \; : - \; C(p, T), method_i(h, \text{Pre}(h)_i, T)$" (where $C(p, T)$ is as defined in Definition 8) to encode the precondition $p \in \chi_i$.*

---

[2] Note that p may also contain variable symbols that do appear in the head of the particular method. However, those variables are not relevant for the discussion above, so we omitted them for the sake of simplicity. Normally, those variables appear in the translated logic programs.

3. The decomposition list $\{t_1, t_2, \ldots, t_n\}$ for m_i: Let $p_1, p_2, \ldots, p_{|\chi_i|}$ be the list of preconditions of the method m_i. Then, the logic program segment $\mathfrak{Trans}(\mathcal{METH})$ contains the following rules to encode the decomposition list of m_i (note that the time variable T_1 in the following rule definitions in this item denote the same value as the time variable T in the rule definitions presented in other items does):

$$currentTask(t_1, T_1) : - method_i(h, \mathsf{Pre}(h)_i, T_1),$$
$$\bigwedge_{k=1}^{|\chi_i|} checked\_state(p_k, T_1).$$
$$currentTask(t_2, T_2) : - method_i(h, \mathsf{Pre}(h)_i, T_1),$$
$$\bigwedge_{k=1}^{|\chi_i|} checked\_state(p_k, T_1),$$
$$CAUSABLE(t_1, T_1, T_2),$$
$$T_2 > T_1.$$
$$\vdots \qquad \vdots \qquad \qquad \vdots$$
$$currentTask(t_n, T_n) : - method_i(h, \mathsf{Pre}(h)_i, T_1)$$
$$\bigwedge_{k=1}^{|\chi_i|} checked\_state(p_k, T_1),$$
$$CAUSABLE(t_{n-1}, T_{n-1}, T_n),$$
$$T_n > T_{n-1}.$$

4. The accomplishment (i.e., causation) of h by the method m_i:

$$causable(h, T_1, T_{n+1}) : - method_i(h, T_1),$$
$$\bigwedge_{k=1}^{|\chi_i|} checked\_state(p_k, T_1),$$
$$CAUSABLE(t_n, T_n, T_{n+1}),$$
$$T_{n+1} > T_n.$$

4 Results: Theory and Practice

In this section, we present our theoretical results on the correctness of our translation method and the soundness and the completeness of the resulting logic programs as planning systems as well as the experiments we have undertaken. Due to space limitations, we will not present the whole proofs here, the basic ideas behind them can be found in [22].

4.1 Soundness and Completeness

Given an HTN-planning problem $(\mathcal{S}, \mathbf{t}, \mathcal{D})$ for *SHOP*, let $\mathfrak{Trans}((\mathcal{S}, \mathbf{t}, \mathcal{D}))$ be the translated logic problem with negation as described in the previous section. We are interested in the relationship between the models (or answer sets) of $\mathfrak{Trans}((\mathcal{S}, \mathbf{t}, \mathcal{D}))$ and the solutions to the planning problem.

Soundness and completeness are the two important requirements for any planning system. Soundness means that all of the plans that are generated by the planner are actually true solutions to the given planning problem; that is, no plan, which is not solution to the problem, should be generated. Completeness means that the planning system must be able to generate all of the possible plans (solutions) for the given problem.

Theorem 2 (Soundness and Completeness of ASP using $\mathfrak{Trans}(\cdot)$).

Given a planning problem $(\mathcal{S}, \mathbf{t}, \mathcal{D})$, where $\mathcal{S}$ is the initial state, $\mathbf{t}$ is the list of tasks to be achieved and $\mathcal{D}$ is the domain description, let $\mathfrak{Trans}((\mathcal{S}, \mathbf{t}, \mathcal{D}))$ be the corresponding logic program with negation. Furthermore, let $\mathbf{Sol}(\mathcal{S}, \mathbf{t}, \mathcal{D})$ be the set of solutions of the planning problem.

Then, the answer sets of $\mathfrak{Trans}((\mathcal{S}, \mathbf{t}, \mathcal{D}))$ correspond exactly to the plans in $\mathbf{Sol}$ (S,t,D). There is a bijection between these two sets and each plan in $\mathbf{Sol}$ (S,t,D) can be reconstructed from its corresponding answer set in $\mathfrak{Trans}((\mathcal{S}, \mathbf{t}, \mathcal{D}))$ and vice versa.

4.2   Experimental Study

In our experiments, we used three different planning domains:

The Travelling Domain: This domain is the one of the domains included in the distribution of SHOP planning system. The scenario for the domain is that we want to travel from one location to another in a city. There are three locations: downtown, uptown, and park. There are three possible means of transportation: taxi, bus and foot. The planning problem is to generate a sequence of actions that needs to be taken in a trip from our original location to our destination by using the available transportation means. More detailed description of this domain is given in [22]

The Miconic-10 Elevator Domain: This domain was introduced as an official benchmark domain during the AIPS-2000 competition (see [23] and http://www.cs.toronto.edu/aips2000). Its simplest version (the one referred to as the "first track" version at http://www.informatik.uni-freiburg.de/~koehler/elev/elev.html) was one of the test cases in [20], and we used the same version in our experiments. In this version, the planner simply has to generate plans to serve a group of passengers of whom the origin and destination floors are given. There are no constraints such as satisfying space requirements of passengers or achieving optimal elevator controls.

The Zeno-Travel Domain: The Zeno-Travel problem was one of the domains that were introduced as recent benchmarks in International Planning Competition (IPC-2002).[3] This domain is again a transportation domain that involves transporting people from their original locations to their destinations via planes using two different modes of movement: namely fast and slow. There were four versions of the domain in the competition. In our experiments we used the simplest version. For more information on IPC-2002, please see <http://www.dur.ac.uk/d.p.long/competition.html>. For more information about the ZenoTravel planning problem, please see <http://www.cs.washington.edu/ai/zeno.html>.

We prepared two sets of experiments: the first set aimed for investigating the time performance of the logic programs generated by our translation

---

[3] IPC-2002 was organised within the Sixth International Conference on AI Planning and Scheduling 2002 (AIPS-2002).

methodology and the second set was for investigating the effects of grounding on their performance. We ran our experiments on an HP OmniBook 6000 Laptop with 128MB RAM and an Intel Pentium III 600 Mhz processor. We used both the software package *smodels* v2.7—which is available at http://www.tcs.hut.fi/Software/smodels/—and the *DLV* system—which is available at http://www.dbai.tuwien.ac.at/proj/dlv/—as testing environments for our logic program encodings.

Efficiency of Encoding HTN Control Knowledge. In this set of experiments, we compared the time performance of the logic programs produced by using our translation methodology with that of the logic-program encodings presented in [20]. In their paper, Son et al., showed that encoding control knowledge has increased the time performance of the logic programs for solving planning problems. The encoding methods proposed in [20], however, does not use actual HTN control knowledge, rather they make use of only a few properties of HTNs —as they are introduced in [9]— for implementing control knowledge in logic programs that perform action-based planning.

In our experiments, we aimed to investigate the impact of using HTN control knowledge as used in *SHOP* on the performance of logic programs that perform planning, and we compared our results with those of [20]. The problems that we used in these experiments are from http://www.CS.NMSU.Edu/~tson/asp_planner. Table 1 shows both our results and the results from [20], which were obtained on the *smodels* system.

Table 1. Comparison of HTN Encoding, $\mathfrak{Trans}(\cdot)$, on *smodels* and *DLV* with on Miconic-10 problems. All times are in CPU seconds.

Problem	smodels	DLV	[20]
S1-0	0.050	0.040	0.520
S2-0	0.330	0.060	12.410
S3-0	1.390	0.080	121.810
S4-0	4.540	0.260	883.700
S5-0s1	19.530	0.640	no solution
S5-0s2	20.630	0.680	no solution
S6-0	23.150	0.980	no solution

Table 2. Comparison of HTN Encoding, $\mathfrak{Trans}(\cdot)$, on *smodels* and *DLV* with *SHOP* on Travelling problems. All times are in CPU seconds.

Problem	smodels	DLV	SHOP
P1	3.23	0.20	0.026
P2	2.23	0.12	0.002
P3	2.19	0.22	0.003
P4	2.08	0.10	0.002
P5	2.20	0.19	0.004
P6	2.18	0.11	0.009
P7	2.21	0.19	0.003
P8	2.15	0.08	0.003

The results clearly show that the logic programs produced by our translation methodology outperform the logic programs produced in [20]. Our encoding was even able to solve a problem, for a solution could not be found by [20]. In this respect, these results that *SHOP*-like HTN planning is an effective way of solving planning problems.

Table 3. Comparison of *DLV* with *SHOP* on ZenoTravel Domain. All times are in CPU seconds.

Problem	smodels	DLV	SHOP	Performance Ratio(*DLV* / *SHOP*)
P2	no-solution	0.670	0.010	67.00
P4	no-solution	0.320	0.010	32.00
P8	no-solution	26.180	0.030	872.67
P9	no-solution	38.390	0.070	548.43
P12	no-solution	22.930	0.020	1146.50
P13	no-solution	16.560	0.060	276.00
P16	no-solution	78.060	0.090	867.34
P19	no-solution	146.030	0.120	1216.92
P20	no-solution	168.630	0.130	1297.15
P23	no-solution	4275.25	12.250	349.00
P24	no-solution	3612.96	7.980	452.75

The Effects of Grounding. We hypothesise that our translation methodology provides more efficient logic programs with ASP semantics if the system on which those programs are implemented allows the usage of variables in the programs– that is, if the ASP systems do not require solely ground programs as input, but can work with variables in the programs and ground those variables as the search progresses. Most of the recent planning systems—such as *SHOP* [11], *TALPlanner* [24], etc.—can work on planning-problem descriptions with variables and these systems are proven to be faster than those which require ground descriptions.

As we described earlier, the *smodels* system cannot work on the logic programs with variables. To test our hypothesis, we applied our translation methodology to our elevator and travelling examples to produce logic programs on a different system called *DLV*. *DLV* is a deductive database system, and can be used as a logic programming system as well. It implements stable model semantics and it supports the usage of variables in the input logic programs to some extent.

Table 2 show our results on the problems of the Simple-Travel domain. As it can be seen, our programs are much more faster on *DLV*, than on *smodels*. Like *smodels*, *DLV* also imposes a safeness restriction on the input programs, but since it allows the usage of variables in the input programs, we do not have to specify the ranges of the variables as long as they do not violate the safeness restrictions required by the system, which is an important characteristic of *DLV*'s approach to grounding.

On the elevator problems, however, the performances of our programs are almost the same (see Table 1). This is because the encodings for these problems are mostly ground; they did not require using variables. Thus, we were not able to observe the effect of grounding techniques used by the two systems on the performance of our programs for these problems.

On the problems from the Zeno-Travel domain, *smodels* was not able to solve any of the problems because of memory limitations. Table 3 shows our results on *DLV* as well as on *SHOP*. In these experiments, we investigated the ratio between the amount of time that our logic programs require and the time required by *SHOP*. If the average-case time complexity of our programs were worse than that of *SHOP*, then we would expect this ratio would get worse with increasing problem size. However, it did not seem to be the case, as it can be seen in Table 3. Although there is not enough data to say so conclusively, our results suggest that the average-case time complexity of our programs may be roughly the same as that of *SHOP*. This gives reason to hope that future improvements in our programs and in ASP solvers may make it possible to get performance competitive with planning systems such as *SHOP*.

5   Conclusions and Future Research Directions

In this paper, we have described a way to encode HTN-planning problems as logic programs under the answer set semantics. This transformation is sound and complete, and it corresponds to HTN-planning systems that generate plans by using ordered task decomposition. In the view of the latter, our method differs from the previous approachesÊfor encoding planning problems as logic programs (as first introduced in [2] and further investigated in [20] by encoding control knowledge to increase the performance of the logic programs).

Our overall aim was to investigate to what extent state-of-the-art nonmonotonic theorem provers can compete with dedicated planners (in particular those based on HTN) and what lessons we could learn from the different translation methods. In our experiments, we used our approach to create both *smodels* and *DLV* logic programs on three different AI planning domains: the Simple-Travel Domain, the "first track" version of the Miconic 10 Elevator Planning Domain, and the simplest version of the ZenoTravel Domain. Here is a summary of our experimental results and what we believe they signify:

1. Although the experiments we have done so far were on relatively simple planning domains, the results were encouraging since they showed the possibility that encoding the HTN control knowledge in ASP programs may provide efficient solutions to planning problems. In the near future, we are planning to conduct further experiments on more complicated HTN planning domains to test this hypothesis.
2. Our experiments suggests that the average-case time complexity of our programs may be roughly the same as that of *SHOP*. Although we do not have enough data to say so conclusively, this gives reason to hope that future improvements in our programs and in ASP solvers may make it possible to get performance competitive with planning systems such as *SHOP*.
3. Our experiments showed that the way that ASP systems perform grounding is an important factor on the performance of the logic programs. In our experiments, our ASP programs were slower than *SHOP*. Our explanation

for this difference in performance is the following: *SHOP*, like most planners, can work on planning-problem descriptions with variables. However, the ASP systems we used requires safeness constraints and they are creating ground instances of clauses that are irrelevant for the planning process in order to meet these constraints.

As a byproduct, like [2], we believe our method can be easily used as transferring benchmarks from the planning community to benchmarks for comparing nonmonotonic systems based on computing answer sets.Furthermore, our method complements the technique described in [2] as it enables to transfer benchmarks for HTN-planning problems. In the near future, we will conduct more experiments on translating more complicated HTN domains than the ones presented in this paper.

Acknowledgments. This work was supported in part by the following grants, contracts, and awards: Air Force Research Laboratory F30602-00-2-0505, Army Research Laboratory DAAL0197K0135, and Naval Research Laboratory N00173021G005. The opinions expressed in this paper are those of authors and do not necessarily reflect the opinions of the funders.

References

1. Niemelä, I., Simons, P.: Efficient Implementation of the Well-founded and Stable Model Semantics. In Maher, M., ed.: Proceedings of the Joint International Conference and Symposium on Logic Programming, Bonn, Germany, The MIT Press (1996) 289–303
2. Dimopoulos, Y., Nebel, B., Koehler, J.: Encoding Planning Problems in Nonmonotonic Logic Programs. In Steel, S., Alami, R., eds.: Proceedings of the Fourth European Conference on Planning, Toulouse, France, Springer-Verlag (1997) 169–181
3. Dix, J., Furbach, U., Niemelä, I.: Nonmonotonic Reasoning: Towards Efficient Calculi and Implementations. In Voronkov, A., Robinson, A., eds.: Handbook of Automated Reasoning. Elsevier-Science-Press (2001) 1121–1234
4. Eiter, T., Leone, N., Mateis, C., Pfeifer, G., Scarcello, F.: The KR System dlv: Progress Report, Comparisons and Benchmarks. In Cohn, A.G., Schubert, L., Shapiro, S.C., eds.: Proceedings Sixth International Conference on Principles of Knowledge Representation and Reasoning (KR'98), Morgan Kaufmann (1998) 406–417
5. Chen, W., Warren, D.S.: Tabled Evaluation with Delaying for General Logic Programs. Journal of the ACM **43** (1996) 20–74
6. Rao, P., Sagonas, K., Swift, T., Warren, D.S., Freire, J.: XSB: A System for Efficiently Computing Well-Founded Semantics. In Dix, J., Furbach, U., Nerode, A., eds.: Logic Programming and Non-Monotonic Reasoning, Proceedings of the Fourth International Conference. LNAI 1265, Berlin, Springer (1997) 430–440
7. Apt, K.R., Marek, V., Truszczynski, M., Warren, D.S., eds.: The Logic Programming Paradigm: Current Trends and Future Directions, Berlin, Springer (1999)
8. Sacerdoti, E.: A Structure for Plans and Behavior. American Elsevier Publishing (1977)

9. Erol, K., Hendler, J., Nau, D.: UMCP: A Sound and Complete Procedure for Hierarchical Task-Network Planning. In Hammond, K., ed.: Proceedings of AIPS-94, Chicago, IL, AAAI Press (1994) 249–254

10. Wilkins, D.: Practical Planning – Extending the Classical AI Planning Paradigm. Morgan Kaufmann (1988)

11. Nau, D., Cao, Y., Lotem, A., Muñoz-Avila, H.: SHOP: Simple Hierarchical Ordered Planner. In Dean, T., ed.: Proceedings of IJCAI-99, Morgan Kaufmann (1999)

12. Nau, D., Cao, Y., Lotem, A., Muñoz-Avila, H., Mitchell, S.: Total-Order Planning with Partially Ordered Subtasks. In Nebel, B., ed.: Proceedings of IJCAI-01, Seattle, Washington, Morgan Kaufmann (2001) 425–430

13. Gelfond, M., Lifschitz, V.: Action Languages. Electronic Transactions on AI **2** (1998) 193–210

14. Turner, H.: Representing Actions in Logic Programs and Default Theories: A Situation Calculus Approach. The Journal of Logic Programming **31** (1997) 245–298

15. Lifschitz, V.: Action Languages, Answer Sets and Planning. In Apt, K.R., Marek, V.W., Truszczynski, M., Warren, D.S., eds.: The Logic Programming Paradigm: A 25-Year Perspective, Springer-Verlag (1999) 357–373

16. McCain, N., Turner, H.: Causal Theories of Action and Change. In: Proceedings of the 14th National Conference on Artificial Intelligence (AAAI-97), Menlo Park, CA, AAAI Press (1997) 460–465

17. McCain, N.: Using Causal Calculator with the C Input Language. Technical report, University of Texas at Austin (1999)

18. Eiter, T., Faber, W., Leone, N., Pfeifer, G., Polleres, A.: The DLV-K Planning System: Progress Report. In Ianni, G., Flesca, S., eds.: Proceedings of Journees Europeens de la Logique en Intelligence Artificielle (JELIA '02). LNCS 2424, Springer (2002) 541–544

19. Baral, C., Tran, N., Tuan., L.: Reasoning about Actions in a Probabilistic Setting. In: AAAI/IAAI 2002, AAAI Press (2002) 507–512

20. Son, T., Baral, C., McIlraith., S.: Planning with domain-dependent knowledge of different kinds – an answer set programming approach. In Eiter, T., Truszczyński, M., Faber, W., eds.: Logic Programming and Non-Monotonic Reasoning, Proceedings of the Sixth International Conference. LNCS 2173, Berlin, Springer (2001) 226–239

21. Nau, D., Au, T.C., Ilghami, O., Kuter, U., Murdock, W., Wu, D., Yaman, F.: SHOP2: an HTN planning system. Journal of Artificial Intelligence Research (2003) To appear.

22. Dix, J., Kuter, U., Nau, D.: HTN Planning in Answer Set Programming. Technical Report CS TR 4336, University of Maryland (2002) Submitted for publication.

23. Bacchus, F.: AIPS'00 Planning Competition. AI Magazine **22** (2001) 47–56

24. Kvarnström, J., Doherty, P.: TALplanner: A Temporal Logic Based Forward Chaining Planner. Annals of Mathematics and Articial Intelligence **30** (2001) 119–169

The Process Semantics Based Reasoning about Continuous Change

Chunping Li

School of Software, Tsinghua University, Peking 100084, China
cli@tsinghua.edu.cn

Abstract. In this paper, we realize a formal method of integrating the process semantics with the situation calculus to reason about continuous change. Our aim is to overcome some of limitations of the earlier works. We present a general translation of the process semantics into the situation calculus. Furthermore, we prove the soundness and completeness of the situation calculus with respect to the process semantics. Finally, related works are discussed.

1 Introduction

In the real world a vast variety of applications need logical reasoning about physical properties in dynamic, continuous systems, e.g., specifying and describing physical systems with continuous actions and changes. The early research work on this aspect was encouraged to address the problem of representing continuous change in a temporal reasoning formalism.

The standard approach is equidistant, discrete time points, namely to quantify the whole scenario into a finite number of points in time at which all system parameters are presented as variables. If there were infinitely many points at infinitely small distance, this might be sufficient, even though impossible to calculate. But, since discretization is always finite, a problem arises when an action or event happens in between two of these points. For instance, consider two balls moving at a certain speed into two different directions but their courses cross each other (Billiard Scenario in [14]). Assume that these two balls will collide on their courses at a certain point in time. If the discretization does not take into account this very point in time, then the collision is not detected and the balls seem to be moving on into their original directions, which results in an entirely wrong prediction of the final positions of the balls. To solve this problem, some work has been done to extend specific action calculi in order to deal with continuous processes and change.

It is known that logical reasoning aims at solving problems, or proving validity. Calculi provide a way of testing the validity of formulas in a purely mechanical way [1]. In the aspect of reasoning about dynamic, continuous systems, the research stand point concentrated on specialized logical formalisms, typically of the situation calculus and their extensions [9,10,11].

Whereas these previously described formalisms have directly focused on creating new or extending already existing specialized logical formalisms, the other

A. Günter et al. (Eds.): KI 2003, LNAI 2821, pp. 505–519, 2003.

research direction consists in the development of an appropriate semantic [2, 13,16] as the basis for a general theory of action and change, and successfully applied to concrete calculi [14,4,15]. In [2], the *Action Description Language* was developed which is based on the concept of single-step actions, and does not include the notion of time. In [13], the duration of actions is not fixed, but an equidistant discretization of time is assumed and state transitions only occur when actions are executed. In [16], it is allowed for user-independent events to cause state transitions. Again equidistant discretization is assumed. But these formalisms are not suitable for calculi dealing with continuous change.

Herrmann and Thielscher [3] proposed a new semantics for reasoning about continuous change which allows for varying temporal distances between state transitions, and a more general notion of a *process* is proposed as the underlying concept for constructing state descriptions. In this high-level process semantics, a state transition may cause existing processes to disappear and new processes to arise. State transitions are either triggered by the execution of actions or by interactions between processes, which both are specified by transition laws.

In this paper, we realize a formal method of integrating process semantics with the situation calculus to reason about continuous change. Our aim is to overcome some of limitations of the earlier works. We present the general transformation rules from the process semantics into the situation calculus, and furthermore, prove the soundness and completeness of the situation calculus with respect to the process semantics. In section 2, the process semantics for reasoning about continuous change, its relevant concepts and transition laws are given in detail. In section 3, the situation calculus and its extension with the branching time are introduced. In section 4, we represent the process semantics in the situation calculus. In section 5, we prove the soundness and completeness of the situation calculus with respect to the process semantics. In section 6, we have a conclusion for this work, and related works are discussed.

2   Semantics of Process Describing Continuous Change

In this section, we introduce a formal, high-level semantics proposed by C. Herrmann and M. Thielscher [3] in detail, for reasoning about continuous processes, their interaction in the course of time, and their manipulation.

In the semantics of processes, a general concept of *process* is used as a basic entity for constructing state descriptions, in contrast to the concept *fluent* in the situation calculus. It allows for varying temporal distances between state transitions.

Definition 1. *A* process scheme *is a pair* $\langle C, F \rangle$ *where C is a finite, ordered set of symbols of size $l > 0$ and F is a finite set functions f: $\mathbb{R}^{l+2} \to \mathbb{R}$.*

From the definition as above, a process scheme actually specifies two kinds of parameters: the static parameters C which do not change as long as the process is in progress, and the dynamic parameters F whose actual values vary with time. Components of the dynamic description part are formally represented as functions in which the arguments are static parameters with two time points, e.g., the initial time of the process and the actual time.

Example 1. Let $\langle C, F \rangle$ be a process scheme describing continuous movement of an object on a line as follows: $C = \{l_0, v\}$ and $F = \{f(l_0, v, t_0, t) = l_0 + v \cdot (t - t_0)\}$, where l_0 denotes the initial location coordinate, v the velocity, t_0 and t the initial and the actual time, and we denote $l = f(l_0, v, t_0, t)$ as the actual location of the object at time t.

Definition 2. *Let N be a set of symbols (called* names*). A process is a 4-tuple* $\langle n, \tau, t_0, \boldsymbol{p} \rangle$ *where*

1. $n \in N$;
2. $\tau = \langle C, F \rangle$ *is a process scheme where C is of size m;*
3. $t_0 \in \mathbb{R}$; *and*
4. $\boldsymbol{p} = (p_1, \ldots, p_m) \in \mathbb{R}^m$ *is an m-dimensional vector over* $\mathbb{R}$.

In the process semantics, the notion of process serves as the basic entity of situation descriptions for continuous change. Any concrete process is an instance of the correspondong process scheme. The description components of a process are determined with its process scheme.

Example 2. Let τ_{move} denote the example scheme from above then

$$\langle TrainA, \tau_{move}, 1{:}00pm, (0mi, \ 25mph) \rangle$$
$$\langle TrainB, \tau_{move}, 1{:}30pm, (80mi, \ -20mph) \rangle \tag{PS1}$$

are two processes describing two trains moving toward each other with different speeds at different starting times.

Definition 3. *A* situation *is a pair* $\langle S, t_s \rangle$ *where S is a set of processes and* t_s *is a time-point which denotes the time when S started.*

Definition 4. *An* event *is a triple* $\langle P_1, t, P_2 \rangle$ *where* P_1 *(the precondition) and* P_2 *(the effect) are finite sets of processes and* $t \in \mathbb{R}$ *is the time at which the event is expected to occur.*

In general, an event causes some processes to end and at the same time some new processes to start. For instance, an inelastic collision between two moving objects terminates their movements and initiates two new processes where both objects move side by side, possibly in a new direction and with changed velocity.

Definition 5. *An event* $\langle P_1, t, P_2 \rangle$ *is* potentially applicable *in a situation* $\langle S, t_s \rangle$ *iff* $P_1 \subseteq S$ *and* $t > t_s$. *If* ε *is a set of events then an event* $\langle P_1, t, P_2 \rangle \in \varepsilon$ *is* applicable *to* $\langle S, t_s \rangle$ *iff it is potentially applicable and for each potentially applicable* $\langle P'_1, t', P'_2 \rangle \in \varepsilon$ *we have* $t \leq t'$.

Example 3. Let S denote the two processes of Example 2. Further, let $t_s = 3{:}00\text{pm}$, then the following event, which describes an inelastic collision which is interpreted as a coupling of trains, is applicable to $\langle S, t_s \rangle$:

$$\begin{aligned} \langle P_1 &= \{\langle \mathit{TrainA}, \tau_{move}, \mathit{1{:}00pm}, (\mathit{0mi}, \mathit{25mph})\rangle, \\ &\quad \langle \mathit{TrainB}, \tau_{move}, \mathit{1{:}30pm}, (\mathit{80mi}, \mathit{-20mph})\rangle\} \\ t &= \mathit{3{:}00pm} \qquad\qquad\qquad\qquad\qquad\qquad\qquad\qquad\text{(PS2)} \\ P_2 &= \{\langle \mathit{TrainA}, \tau_{move}, \mathit{3{:}00pm}, (\mathit{50mi}, \mathit{5mph})\rangle, \\ &\quad \langle \mathit{TrainB}, \tau_{move}, \mathit{3{:}00pm}, (\mathit{50mi}, \mathit{5mph})\rangle\}\rangle \end{aligned}$$

In fact, concrete events are instances of general *transition laws* which contain variables and constraints to guide the process of instantiation, and the event's time is usually determined by the instances of other variables. We can describe the transition law for inelastic collisions of two continuously moving objects as follows.

$$\begin{aligned} \langle P_1 &= \{\langle N_A, \tau_{move}, T_{A0}, (X_{A0}, V_A)\rangle, \langle N_B, \tau_{move}, T_B, (X_{B0}, V_B)\rangle\} \\ t &= T \qquad\qquad\qquad\qquad\qquad\qquad\qquad\qquad\qquad\qquad\text{(PS3)} \\ P_2 &= \{\langle N_A, \tau_{move}, T, (X_{new}, V_A + V_B)\rangle, \langle N_B, \tau_{move}, T, (X_{new}, V_A + V_B)\rangle\}\rangle \end{aligned}$$

where it is required that $N_A \neq N_B$, $V_A - V_B \neq 0$, and $x_A = x_B = X_{new}$ at time T. Suppose that the two movement differentials are $x_A = X_{A0} + V_A \cdot (T - T_{A0})$ and $x_B = X_{B0} + V_B \cdot (T - T_{B0})$; then the result is:

$$T = \frac{X_{A0} - X_{B0} - V_A \cdot T_{A0} + V_B \cdot T_{B0}}{V_B - V_A} \quad and \quad X_{new} = X_{A0} + V_A \cdot (T - T_{A0}) \quad \text{(PS4)}$$

Definition 6. *Let ε be a set of events and $\langle S, t_s \rangle$ a situation, then the successor situation $\Phi(\langle S, t_s \rangle)$ is defined as follows.*

1. *If no applicable event exists in ε then $\Phi(\langle S, t_s \rangle) = \langle S, \infty \rangle$;*
2. *if $\langle P_1, t, P_2 \rangle \in \varepsilon$ is the only applicable event then $\Phi(\langle S, t_s \rangle) = \langle S', t_s \rangle$ where $S' = (S \setminus P_1) \cup P_2$ and $t_{s'} = t$;*
3. *Otherwise $\Phi(\langle S, t_s \rangle)$ is undefined, i.e., events here are not allowed to occur simultaneously.*

In words, if no applicable event exists then the system has reached a stable state, which is assumed to hold forever; else the result of an applicable event is obtained by exchanging processes according to the event's description and adjusting the initiating time point of the new situation accordingly.

Definition 7. *An observation is an expression of the form $[t] \propto (n) = r$ where*

1. *$t \in I\!R$ is the time of the observation;*
2. *$\propto$ is either a symbol in C or the name of a function in F for some process scheme $\langle C, F \rangle$;*
3. *n is a symbol denoting a process name; and*
4. *$r \in I\!R$ is the observed value.*

Example 4. The observation $[2:15\text{pm}]\,l(\,TrainB) = 65mi$ is true in Example 3, while the observation $[3:15\text{pm}]\,l(\,TrainB) = 45mi$ is not true since the latter does not take into account the train collision.

Definition 8. *A model for a set of observations* Ψ *(under given sets of names* $\mathcal{N}$ *and events* $\mathcal{E}$ *) is a system development* $\langle S_0, t_0 \rangle$, $\Phi(\langle S_0, t_0 \rangle)$, $\Phi^2(\langle S_0, t_0 \rangle)$, ... *which satisfies all elements of* Ψ. *Such a set* Ψ *entails an (additional) observation* ψ *iff* ψ *is true in all models of* Ψ.

Furthermore, the concept of executing actions in a system of continuous processes can be easily integrated into the model by viewing actions as events as well. For example, the following event describes the action of starting *Train B* at time 1:30pm:

$$\begin{aligned} \langle P_1 &= \{\langle TrainB, \tau move, \, 1{:}00pm, (80mi, 0mph)\rangle\}, \\ t &= 1{:}30pm && \text{(PS5)} \\ P_2 &= \{\langle TrainB, \tau move, \, 1{:}30pm, (80mi, -20mph)\rangle\}\rangle \end{aligned}$$

Such events can be instances of more general transition laws whose applicability is triggered by executing some action. An interesting feature for the representation of action is that the time of their execution may depend on the situation itself. For example, *Train B* starts to move with velocity $-20mph$ as soon as *Train A* passes the $12.5mi$ mark. The specification can be represented by the transition law:

$$\begin{aligned} \langle P_1 &= \{\langle TrainA, \tau move, T_{A0}, (X_{A0}, V_A)\rangle, \ \langle TrainB, \tau move, T_B, (X_{B0}, 0mph)\rangle\} \\ t &= T && \text{(PS6)} \\ P_2 &= \{\langle TrainA, \tau move, T_{A0}, (X_{A0}, V_A)\rangle, \ \langle TrainB, \tau move, T, (X_{B0}, -20mph)\rangle\}\rangle \end{aligned}$$

where it is required that $V_A \neq 0$ and $X_{A0} + V_A \cdot (T - T_{A0}) = 12.5mi$. In fact, the action described in (PS5) is an instance of the translation law (PS6) considering the case that *Train A* is continuously unchanged.

All definitions concerning successor situations, developments, and observations carry over to the case where a set of actions, which are to be executed (external events), and interactions between processes (internal events) are given.

3   Situation Calculus and Its Extension with the Branching Time

The situation calculus is the most popular formalism designed to represent dynamically changing worlds. The formalism has its origins in the early work of John McCarthy and P. Hayes [8]. The intuition behind the situation calculus is that there is an initial situation, and that the world changes from one situation to next when actions are performed. We here discuss the situation calculus as a sorted first-order language extended with a second-order induction axiom to characterize the space of situations [12].

There are three domain independent sorts $\mathcal{A}$, $\mathcal{S}$ and $\mathcal{F}$ for action types, situations and propositional fluents (we take a fluent to be a property of the world that may or may not hold at any situation). Variables are denoted by lower case letters and constants are denoted by upper case letters (with or without subscripts). For example, letters a, s, f, d (A, S, F, D) are used for variables (constants) of sorts $\mathcal{A}$, $\mathcal{S}$, $\mathcal{F}$, $\mathcal{D}$ respectively. We will have a single 1-place predicate variable φ which ranges over properties of situations. A special constant S_0 of sort $\mathcal{S}$ denotes the initial situation.

3.1   Basic Axioms

In the situation calculus, the primary intuition about situations that we wish to capture axiomatically is that they are finite sequences of actions. We are also able to say that a certain sequence of actions precedes another one. The four basic axioms are presented to capture these two properties of situations.

$$(\forall \varphi) \; [\varphi(S_0) \wedge (\forall s, a) \; (\varphi(s) \rightarrow \varphi(do\,(a, s)))] \rightarrow (\forall s)\varphi(s), \tag{SC1}$$

$$(\forall a_1, a_2, s_1, s_2) \; do\,(a_1, s_1) = do\,(a_2, s_2) \rightarrow a_1 = a_2 \wedge s_1 = s_2, \tag{SC2}$$

$$(\forall s_1, s_2, a) \; s_1 \subset do\,(a, s_2) \equiv s_1 \subseteq s_2, \tag{SC3}$$

$$(\forall s) \; \neg s \subset S_0, \tag{SC4}$$

3.2   Axiomatizing Actions in the Situation Calculus

The first observation we can make about actions is that they have preconditions, i.e., requirements that must be satisfied whenever they can be executed in the current situation. The predicate $Poss\,(a, s)$ is used to describe the preconditions of an action and means that it is possible to execute the action a in the situation s.

Action precondition axiom

$$Poss\,(a, s) \equiv \Pi_a(s)$$

where $\Pi_a(s)$ is a first order formula with a free situation variable s which is distinguished from the other variables.

For example, in the blocks world, we might have the following action precondition axiom for the action *pickup* by a robot.

$$Poss\,(pickup\,(r, x), s) \equiv [(\forall y) \; \neg holding\,(r, y, s)] \wedge clear\,(x, s) \wedge \neg heavy\,(x, s).$$

Successor state axiom

$$Poss\,(a, s) \rightarrow [holds\,(f, do\,(a, s)) \equiv \gamma_f^+(a, s) \vee holds\,(f, s) \wedge \neg \gamma_f^-(a, s)]$$

where $\gamma_f^+(a, s)$ is a formula stating the conditions in which the fluent f is made to hold as a result of action a, and $\gamma_f^-(a, s)$ is a formula stating the conditions under which the fluent f is made not to hold as a result of action a.

For example, in the blocks world, we have the following successor state axiom for the fluent *inHand*.

$$Poss\,(a, s) \rightarrow holds\,(inhand\,(Block), do\,(a, s))$$
$$\equiv a = pickup\,(Block) \vee holds\,(inHand\,(Block), s)$$
$$\wedge \neg(a = drop\,(Block)).$$

3.3   Extension of the Situation Calculus with Branching Time

Pinto and Reiter proposed the concept of a time line to extend the original situation calculus by incorporating the basic elements of a linear temporal logic [10,11]. For reasoning about time in the situation calculus, a predicate *actual* is incorporated. A situation is actual if it lies on the path that describes the world's real evolution. The axioms for actual are

$$actual\,(S_0), \tag{ESC1}$$

$$(\forall a, s)\ actual\,(do\,(a, s)) \rightarrow actual\,(s) \wedge Poss\,(a, s), \tag{ESC2}$$

$$(\forall a_1, a_2, s)\ actual\,(do\,(a_1, s)) \wedge actual\,(do\,(a_2, s)) \rightarrow a_1 = a_2. \tag{ESC3}$$

a new sort $\mathcal{T}$ is incorporated into the situation calculus, interpreted as a continuous time line. The sort $\mathcal{T}$ is considered isomorphic to the non-negative reals. Intuitively, each situation has a starting time and an ending time. Also, two functions *start* from $\mathcal{S}$ to $\mathcal{T}$ and *end* from $\mathcal{S} \times \mathcal{A}$ to $\mathcal{T}$ are defined. Actions occur at the ending time of situations. This is captured by the following axioms.

$$(\forall s, a)\ end\,(s, a) = start\,(do\,(a, s)) \tag{ESC4}$$

$$(\forall s, a)\ start\,(s) < start\,(do\,(a, s)) \tag{ESC5}$$

$$start\,(S_0) = 0 \tag{ESC6}$$

The predicate *occurs* is introduced as describing a relation between action types and situations. For example, *occurs* (*pickup* (*Block*), s) denotes that the action of picking up a block occurred in situation S. Occurrences are defined in terms of the actual path as follows.

$$occurs\,(a, s)\ \equiv\ actual\,(do\,(a, s)) \tag{ESC7}$$

To establish the relation between actions that occur and the time at which they occur, a relation $occurs_{\mathcal{T}} \subseteq \mathcal{A} \times \mathcal{T}$ is defined as

$$occurs_{\mathcal{T}}(a, t)\ \equiv\ (\exists s)\ occurs\,(a, s) \wedge start\,(do\,(a, s)) = t \tag{ESC8}$$

Similarly, a relation $holds_{\mathcal{T}}$ between fluents and time points and a relation *during* between time points and situations are defined as

$$holds_{\mathcal{T}}(f, t)\ \equiv\ (\exists s)\ actual\,(s) \wedge during\,(t, s) \wedge holds\,(f, s) \tag{ESC9}$$

$$during\,(t, s)\ \equiv\ actual\,(s) \wedge start\,(s) < t \wedge \tag{ESC10}$$
$$(\forall a)\ [occurs\,(a, s) \rightarrow end\,(s, a) \geq t]$$

Furthermore, in this approach, the concept of a *natural event (action)* is defined for dealing with the continuous change of an object in time. Here all events whose occurrences are dictated by physical laws are called *natural*. Natural events are distinguished from the other events (actions) by introducing the predicate *natural* $\subseteq \mathcal{A}$. The important characteristic of natural events is that when the conditions for their occurrence arise, they must occur.

A new predicate $\Pi_t \subseteq \mathcal{A} \times \mathcal{S} \times \mathcal{T}$ which is domain dependent is introduced. $\Pi_t(a, s, t)$ is true whenever the conditions at time $start(s)$ are such that at time t action a would occur. Therefore, some properties of natural events are described as follows.

$$Poss(a, s) \equiv [\Pi_t(a, s, end(s, a)) \wedge$$
$$\Pi_t(a', s, t') \wedge start(s) < t' \leq end(s, a)].$$

4   Representing Process Semantics in the Situation Calculus

4.1   General Axiomatization for the Process Semantics

In the process semantics, the domain description consists of two parts: a set of *processes* and a sequence of *events*. In the situation calculus, we define a fluent $P(n, F, R, C)$ representing the concept of a process, where P is a 4-ary function symbol: n denotes the name for a process, R and C the set of dynamic and static parameters for the process n, and F a finite set of functions describing the relationship between the dynamic and static parameters. Here a *state* in the situation calculus is regarded as a set of processes. If neither an interaction between the given processes nor actions take place, then the individual processes are assumed to continue eternally and the *state* does not change. We write a deliberative action as $A(n, C)$ in which n denotes the process name and C the set of static, unchanged parameters in the process n.

Specially, processes may interact by means of executing actions without manipulating the ongoing processes. Interaction giving rise to change within a collection of processes and causing a discontinuity in the state of affairs is described as an *event* in the process semantics. In general, an *event* causes some running processes to end and some new processes to hold at a particular time point. We write it as $E(\hat{n}, \hat{C}, t)$ in the situation calculus to represent the interaction between processes, where $\hat{n}$ denotes a *name set* of the processes which interact, $\hat{C}$ a collection for the set of static parameters of new processes produced by the interaction, and t the time at which the interaction or the event occurs. We represent the process semantics in the situation calculus in form of the general rules as follows.

Action Precondition Axioms:

$$Poss(A(n, C), s) \equiv occurs_T(A(n, C), t_0) \wedge start(s) < t_0 \tag{GPS1}$$

$$Poss(E(\hat{n}, \hat{C}, t), s) \equiv (n_1, \ldots, n_k \in \hat{n}) \wedge (C_1, \ldots, C_k \in \hat{C}) \wedge$$
$$(P(n_1, F_1, R_1, C_1), \ldots, P(n_k, F_k, R_k, C_k) \in s) \wedge$$
$$g(F_1(C_1, t), \ldots, F_k(C_k, t)) = 0 \wedge \tag{GPS2}$$
$$start(s) < t$$

Successor State Axioms:

$$Poss\,(a,s) \rightarrow holds\,(P(n,F,R,C),do\,(a,s)) \equiv$$
$$((a = A(n,C) \;\wedge\; occurs_T(a,t_0) \wedge R = F(C,t,t_0)) \vee$$
$$(\exists \hat{n},\hat{C})\;(a = E(\hat{n},\hat{C},t) \wedge occurs_T(a,t)\; \wedge$$
$$R = F(C,t,t_0) \wedge n \in \hat{n}\; \wedge\; C \in \hat{C}) \wedge \qquad\qquad\text{(GPS3)}$$
$$\vee\;(holds\,(P(n,F,R,C),s)\;\wedge\;\neg(a = A(n,C))\;\wedge$$
$$\neg(a = E(\hat{n},\hat{C},t) \wedge n \in \hat{n}))$$

4.2   Example: Trains Moving Scenario

We consider that two trains start at different times and move towards each other with different speed. At the time t_s a collision happens after which they continue to move as a couple with a common speed together.

In the situation calculus, the moving of train can be represented as a process, which we describe by the fluent $P(n,F,R,C)$. In this example, the static parameter set C includes two elements: initial location l_0 and velocity vel. The dynamic parameter set has only one element, the actual location l varying with time t_s, and an equation describes the process of moving as F: $l = l_0 + vel \cdot (t_s - t_0)$ where t_0 and t_s denote the start and actual time of the moving of a train.

In this example, we need to define two kinds of actions (events): *engineOn* and *collision*, which represent the occurrence of the trains movement and the occurrence of a collision of two trains. We formalize these actions (events) with the action precondition axioms as follows.

$$Poss\,(engineOn\,(train_A,(l_{A0},vel_A)),s)\;\equiv$$
$$holds\,(moving\,(train_A,f,l_A,(l_{A0},vel_A)),s)\;\wedge$$
$$occurs_T(engineOn\,(train_A,(l_{A0},vel_A)),T_{A0}) \wedge start\,(s) < T_{A0}\;\wedge$$
$$T_{A0} = \textit{1:00} \wedge l_{A0} = 0 \wedge vel_A = 25$$

$$Poss\,(engineOn\,(train_B,(l_{B0},vel_B)),s)\;\equiv$$
$$holds\,(moving\,(train_B,f,l_B,(l_{B0},vel_B)),s)\;\wedge$$
$$occurs_T(a,T_{B0}) \wedge start\,(s) < T_{B0}\;\wedge$$
$$T_{B0} = \textit{1:30} \wedge l_{B0} = 80 \wedge vel_A = -20$$

$$Poss\,(collision\,((train_A,train_B),((l'_{A0},vel'_{A0}),(l'_{B0},vel'_{B0})),t),s)\;\equiv$$
$$holds\,(moving\,(train_A,f,l_A,(l_{A0},vel_A)),s)\;\wedge$$
$$holds\,(moving\,(train_B,f,l_B,(l_{B0},vel_B)),s)\;\wedge$$
$$t = (l_{B0} - l_{A0} + vel_A \cdot T_{A0} - vel_B \cdot T_{B0})/(vel_A + vel_B)\;\wedge$$
$$l'_{A0} = l'_{B0} = l_{A0} + vel_A \cdot (t - T_{A0})\;\wedge$$
$$vel'_{A0} = vel'_{B0} = vel_A + vel_B\;\wedge$$
$$start\,(s) < t$$

Two fluents are defined, *Moving* and *MovingTogether*, and with the successor state axioms we have the general rules to describe the property of the fluents as follows.

$$Poss\,(a,s) \rightarrow holds\,(moving\,(train_A,f,l_A,(l_{A0},vel_A)),do\,(a,s))\;\equiv$$
$$(a = engineOn\,(train_A,(l_{A0},vel_A))\;\wedge$$
$$occurs_T(a,T_{A0}) \wedge l_A = F(l_{A0},vel_A,t,T_{A0})\;\wedge$$
$$\vee\;(holds\,(moving\,(train_A,f,l_A,(l_{A0},vel_A)),s) \wedge$$
$$\neg(a = engineOn\,(train_A,(l_{A0},vel_A))))$$

$Poss\,(a,s) \rightarrow holds\,(moving\,(train_B, f, l_B, (l_{B0}, vel_B)), do\,(a,s)) \equiv$
$\qquad (a = engineOn\,(train_B, (l_{B0}, vel_B)) \wedge$
$\qquad occurs_T(a, T_{B0}) \wedge l_B = f(l_{B0}, vel_B, t, T_{B0}) \wedge$
$\qquad \vee\ (holds\,(moving\,(train_B, f, l_B, (l_{B0}, vel_B)), s) \wedge$
$\qquad \neg(a = engineOn\,(train_B, (l_{B0}, vel_B))))$

$Poss\,(a,s) \rightarrow holds\,(movingTogether\,(train_A, f, l_A, (l'_{A0}, vel'_{A0})), do\,(a,s)) \equiv$
$\qquad a = collision\,(\hat{n}, \hat{C}, T_{AB}) \wedge$
$\qquad train_A \in \hat{n} \wedge (l'_{A0}, vel'_{A0}) \in \hat{C} \wedge$
$\qquad l'_A = f(l'_{A0}, vel'_{A0}, t, T_{AB}) \wedge occurs_T(a, t) \wedge$
$\qquad \neg((\exists a')\ occurs\,(a', do\,(a,s)) \rightarrow end\,(a', do\,(a,s)) < t)$

$Poss\,(a,s) \rightarrow holds\,(movingTogether\,(train_B, f, l_B, (l'_{B0}, vel'_{B0})), do\,(a,s)) \equiv$
$\qquad a = collision\,(\hat{n}, \hat{C}, T_{AB}) \wedge$
$\qquad train_B \in \hat{n} \wedge (l'_{B0}, vel'_{B0}) \in \hat{C} \wedge$
$\qquad l'_B = f(l'_{B0}, vel'_{B0}, t, T_{AB}) \wedge occurs_T(a, t) \wedge$
$\qquad \neg((\exists a')\ occurs\,(a', do\,(a,s)) \rightarrow end\,(a', do\,(a,s)) < t)$

We suppose here that *trainA* (initial location is 0mi) starts to move at time 1:00 pm with the velocity 25mph, while *TrainB* at time 1:30pm with the velocity -20mph, then the occurrence axioms $\mathcal{T}_{occ}$ can be described as follows.

$occurs_T(engineOn\,(train_A, (l_{A0}, vel_A)), 1{:}00) \wedge$
$occurs_T(engineOn\,(train_B, (l_{B0}, vel_B)), 1{:}30)$

and equivalently

$occurs\,(engineOn\,(train_A, (l_{A0}, vel_A)), S_1) \wedge$
$occurs\,(engineOn\,(train_B, (l_{B0}, vel_B)), S_2)$
where
$start\,(S_1) = 1{:}00 \wedge start\,(S_2) = 1{:}30$, and $S_0 < S_1 < S_2$.

The only event which happens in this scenario is *collision*. We have

$$a = collision\,((train_A, train_B), ((l'_{A0}, vel'_{A0}), (l'_{B0}, vel'_{B0})), t)$$

We suppose that the initial facts and the equality constraint for the continuous movements of train as follows.

$vel_A = 25mph \wedge t_{A0} = 1{:}00 \wedge l_A = 0mi \wedge vel_B = -20mph \wedge t_{B0} = 1{:}30 \wedge l_B = 80mi$
$f : l = l_0 + vel \cdot (t - t_0)$

Our objective is to determine that the process *movingTogether* holds (i.e. two trains move together with the same speed) after an inelastic collision. Let *AXIOMS* be the all axioms of (SC1) – (SC4) and (ESC1) – (ESC10) plus the action precondition and successor state axioms given in this example. It is easy to see that for any model $\mathcal{M}$ of *AXIOMS* there is

$\mathcal{M} \models S_1 = do\,(engineOn\,(train_A, (l_{A0}, vel_A)), S_0) \wedge$
$\qquad\quad S_2 = do\,(engineOn\,(train_A, (l_{A0}, vel_A)), S_1).$

It follows that $\mathcal{M}$ satisfies

$\mathcal{M} \models (\exists t_1, t_2)\ occurs_T(enginOn\,(train_A, (l_{A0}, vel_A)), t_1) \wedge$
$\qquad\quad occurs_T(enginOn\,(train_B, (l_{B0}, vel_B)), t_2) \wedge t_1 < t_2.$

The only event *collision* will occur in the time t_3 which the following equation will be true.

$$t_3 = (l_{B0} - l_{A0} + vel_A \cdot T_{A0} - vel_B \cdot T_{B0})/(vel_A + vel_B)$$

Thus,

$$occurs_T(natural(a), t_3) \; \wedge \; a = collision((train_A, train_B), ((l'_{A0}, vel'_{A0}), (l'_{B0}, vel'_{B0})), t_3)$$

will hold in the model $\mathcal{M}$. By using the successor state axiom for *movingTogether* and the action precondition axioms, we obtain

$$\mathcal{M} \models holds(movingTogether(train_A), \mathcal{S}_\ni) \; \wedge \; holds(movingTogether(train_B), \mathcal{S}_\ni) \; \wedge$$
$$\mathcal{S}_3 = do(collision(train_A, train_B), \mathcal{S}_2).$$

It follows that the process in which the two trains move together holds in S_3.

5   Soundness and Completeness Theorem

Definition 9. *Let Σ be a theory of action with occurrences and continuous processes. It should include:*

- *a set of basic axioms (SC1)–(SC4);*
- *a set of axioms based on the actual time line (ESC1)–(ESC10),*
- *a set of axioms formalizing the process semantics (GPS1)–(GPS3), in which successor state axioms and action precondition axioms are included.*

The problem of reasoning about actions and continuous processes is: given an incomplete description of the actions that occur in time, what are the actions that actually will occur, especially in regard of the implicit events in the process semantics? Here we choose models that contain minimal sets of occurring actions and events. This can be formalized using circumscription.

In order to simplify the presentation of circumscription, we consider the predicates *occurs*, $holds_T$, *during* and the function *end* to be abbreviations. By doing this, we need not include these elements in the list of symbols whose interpretation is made variable in the circumscription policy.

The circumscription policy is as follows.

$$CIRC(\Sigma; occurs_T; actual, start)$$

We select the models that satisfy Σ with a minimal extension for the predicate $occurs_T$. The predicate *actual* and the function *start* are variable elements in circumscription. Clearly, these elements need to vary since $occurs_T$ is defined in terms of them. Notice that the situation tree is fixed except for the elements that determine what the actual line looks like. A property of this policy is that if we know all the actions that occur, and if it is consistent to believe that they are all that occurred, then the circumscription will select those models in which the actual line of situation contains all and only those actions.

Based on Lifschitz's results [7], we present the model-theoretic meaning of the above circumscription.

Let $\mathcal{D} = (\mathcal{P}, \mathcal{E})$ be a consistent domain description for the process semantics, where $\mathcal{P}$ is a set of initial processes and $\mathcal{E}$ is a set of events. We write $\mathcal{P} = (p_1, p_2, \ldots, p_m)$ and $\mathcal{E} = (e_1, e_2, \ldots, e_n)$.

Let π denote the translation from the domain description of the process semantics into the formalism of the situation calculus. The following symbols are used: situation variables $s, s', \ldots$, time variables $t, t', \ldots$, action (event) variables $a, a', \ldots$, *fluent* representing process $P(n, F, R, C)$, action $A(n, C)$ and event $E(\hat{n}, \hat{C}, t)$.

Furthermore, let $OBS(P, \alpha, t_s)$ denote an observation of the process with name n at time t_s in the process semantics, where α is a symbol in C or R for some process scheme (C, F) and $\alpha = r$ (r is an observed value). In the situation calculus we describe an observation in the form

$$holds_{\mathcal{T}}(P(n, F, R, C), t_s) \wedge \alpha = r$$

where α is a variable name in R or C.

Lemma 1. *Let $\mathcal{D}$ be a domain description for process semantics, for any process P from $\mathcal{D}$ if $CIRC[\pi\mathcal{D} \wedge \Sigma_{proc}] \models holds_{\mathcal{T}}(P(n, F, R, C), t_s) \wedge \in (R \cup C) \wedge \alpha = r$, then $\mathcal{D}$ entails $OBS(P, \alpha, t_s) \wedge \alpha = r$.*

Proof Assume that a process $P(n, F, R, C)$ in $CIRC[\pi\mathcal{D} \wedge \Sigma_{proc}]$ holds at time t_s. For some parameter α and $\alpha \in R \cup C$, there exists an observed value which we denote by r. Since $CIRC[\pi\mathcal{D} \wedge \Sigma_{proc}] \models holds_{\mathcal{T}}(P(n, F, R, C), t_s)$, there must exist the actual occurrences of a set of actions and events in some order such that the process $holds_{\mathcal{T}}(P(n, F, R, C), t_s)$ holds at time t_s. Σ_{proc} is a theory in which the set $\mathcal{T}_{occ}$ contains an axiom of the form

$$(\exists s_1, \ldots, s_n) \; occurs(A_1, s_1) \wedge \ldots \wedge occurs(A_n, s_n) \wedge \mathcal{O}_<(s_1, \ldots, s_n) \equiv$$
$$(\exists t_1, \ldots, t_n) \; occurs_{\mathcal{T}}(A_1, t_1) \wedge \ldots \wedge occurs_{\mathcal{T}}(A_n, t_n) \wedge \mathcal{O}_<(t_1, \ldots, t_n)$$

where $\mathcal{O}_<$ is an ordering formula.

Thus, every model in $CIRC[\pi\mathcal{D} \wedge \Sigma_{proc}]$ satisfies

$$occurs(a, s) \equiv a = A_1 \wedge s = S_1 \vee \ldots \vee a = A_n \wedge s = S_n, \tag{a}$$

correspondingly,

$$occurs_{\mathcal{T}}(a, t) \equiv a = A_1 \wedge t = T_1 \vee \ldots \vee a = A_n \wedge t = T_n, \tag{b}$$

where $T_1 < \ldots < T_n < t_s$.

Then, every model of $CIRC[\pi\mathcal{D} \wedge \Sigma_{proc}]$ will satisfy (a) and (b) and also satisfy

$$S_n = do(A_{n-1}, S_{n-1}) \wedge \ldots \wedge S_2 = do(A_1, S_1) \wedge S_1 = S_0. \tag{c}$$

$$t_n = start(do(A_{n-1}, S_{n-1})) \wedge \ldots \wedge t_2 = start(do(A_1, S_1)) \wedge t_1 = start(S_0). \tag{d}$$

Thus, for all models in $CIRC[\pi\mathcal{D} \wedge \Sigma_{proc}]$, there must exists the time points t_i and t_{i+1} where $1 \leq i < n$, so that the process $P(n, F, R, C)$ holds in the time period $[t_i, t_{i+1}]$, and it is concluded that for $t_s \in [t_i, t_{i+1}]$, $\alpha \in (R \cup C) \wedge \alpha = r$ must be true.

We need to prove that $\mathcal{D} \models OBS(P, \alpha, t_s) \wedge \alpha = r$ under the condition mentioned above. We prove this by contradiction. Suppose that the observation of the process $OBS(P, \alpha, t_s)$ with the observation value $\alpha = r$ is not entailed from the domain description $\mathcal{D}$. Then there exists a model of $\mathcal{D}$, in which the value of the observation $\alpha = r$ is false. Thus, a corresponding system development of this model (under the domain description $\mathcal{D}$ with initial processes and events) satisfies that the observation $OBS(P, \alpha, t_s)$ which its value $\alpha = r$ is false. In the process semantics, since a system development $\langle S_0, t_0 \rangle$, $\Phi(\langle S_0, t_0 \rangle)$, $\Phi^2(\langle S_0, t_0 \rangle)$, ... is regarded as an infinite sequence of situations which are transformed by the events and actions, the state of the system at the particular time-point t_s can be described by the collection of processes S where $\langle S, t_i \rangle = \Phi^i(\langle S_0, t_0 \rangle)$ and $\langle S', t_{i+1} \rangle = \Phi^{i+1}(\langle S_0, t_0 \rangle)$ such that $t_i \leq t_s < t_{i+1}$. Corresponding to the situation calculus paradigm, it follows that the observation which its value $\alpha = r$ for $OBS(P, \alpha, t_s)$ at the time t_s does not hold. In this case, the contradiction between this assumption and the premise takes place. Thus, it follows that $\mathcal{D}$ entails the observation $OBS(P, \alpha, t_s) \wedge \alpha = r$.

Theorem 1. [Soundness Theorem] *Let $\mathcal{D}$ be a domain description for process semantics, for any process P if $\pi \mathcal{D}$ entails πP, then $\mathcal{D}$ entails P.*

Proof. By Lemma 1, an observation $OBS(P, \alpha, t_s) \wedge \alpha = r$ is entailed by $\mathcal{D}$, if $CIRC[\pi \mathcal{D} \wedge \Sigma_{proc}] \models \pi OBS$. Suppose that $\pi \mathcal{D}$ entails πP, since the observation is made during a development of the system being modeled and involved in some concrete process at time t_s, the observed process holds under the development of the system (given the set of initial processes and the set of events), if $holds_T(P(n, F, R, C), t_s)$ is true in all the models of $CIRC[\pi \mathcal{D} \wedge \Sigma_{proc}]$. It follows that $\mathcal{D}$ entails P.

Theorem 2. [Completeness Theorem] *Let $\mathcal{D}$ be a domain description for process semantics, for any process P if $\mathcal{D}$ entails P, then $\pi \mathcal{D}$ entails πP.*

Proof. Given a process P and $\mathcal{D}$ entails P; then in the process semantics, there must be a system development satisfying a set of observations Ψ for the process P under $\mathcal{D}$. We assume that a model for the observations Ψ is represented as a system development $\langle S_0, t_0 \rangle, \ldots, \langle S_n, t_n \rangle$ which satisfies all elements of Ψ (where $\langle S_i, t_i \rangle$ is defined as a *situation* at the start time t_i, and there exists a successor situation function Φ such that we can yield an infinite sequence of situation: $\langle S_{i+1}, t_{i+1} \rangle = \Phi(\langle S_i, t_i \rangle)$ see [3]). Let $OBS(P, \alpha, t_s)$ represent an observation for the process P at time t_s and the observed value $\alpha = r$, then $OBS(P, \alpha, t_s) \in \Psi$ and $OBS(P, \alpha, t_s)$ is true in all models of Ψ.

By the definition of the system development, it is consistent to assume that all the events (actions) are only those that occur during the system development and the events (actions) are totally ordered. Let $\mathcal{M}$ be a model for $OBS(P, \alpha, t_s)$. Thus, there is a corresponding model $\pi \mathcal{M}$ of the theory Σ_{proc} in the situation calculus that satisfies

$$occurs(a, s) \equiv a = A_1 \wedge s = S_1 \vee \ldots \vee a = A_n \wedge s = S_n,$$

and also

$$occurs_{\mathcal{T}}(a, t) \equiv a = A_1 \wedge t = T_1 \vee \ldots \vee a = A_n \wedge t = T_n.$$

Since Σ_{proc} is a theory in which $\mathcal{T}_{occ}$ contains the form

$$occurs\,(A_1, S_1) \wedge \ldots \wedge occurs\,(A_n, S_n) \wedge \mathcal{O}_<(S_1, \ldots, S_n)$$

where $\mathcal{O}_<$ is an ordering formula, therefore, $\pi\mathcal{M}$ is a model of $CIRC[\pi\mathcal{D} \wedge \Sigma_{proc}]$. By (ESC9)–(ESC10) and the general rules (GPS1)–(GPS3), $holds_{\mathcal{T}}\,(P(n, F, R, C)) \wedge \alpha \in (R \cup C) \wedge \alpha = r$ is true in all models of $CIRC[\pi\mathcal{D} \wedge \Sigma_{proc}]$. It follows that $\pi\mathcal{D}$ entails πP.

6   Related Work and Concluding Remarks

The situation calculus is the most popular formalism designed to represent theories of action and change. It is included in the standard material of every introductory course on artificial intelligence, and it is the language of choice for investigations of various technical problems that arise in theorizing about actions and their effects. As it does not yet provide a very rich temporal ontology, it makes it hard to represent time, events, and continuous change. To overcome these shortcomings, some techniques have been presented by the means of further extending the expressivity and temporal reasoning capability. Pinto and Reiter [10] proposed the temporal concepts in the situation calculus for representing the time and simultaneous event. Furthermore, Reiter [12] developed a framework to specify the properties of continuous change in his temporal situation calculus. We drew on the works of them and proposed the general axioms to represent the process semantics in the temporal situation calculus.

Our method carried on some important properties of Reiter's temporal situation calculus, and implemented the reasoning about continuous change. The main difference is that our method adopted a more general concept of a process, which is more appropriate to the semantic description in the case of continuous change [5,6]. The advantage is that our method integrates high-level semantics with logical calculi. On this basis, we further consider to realize a formal justification of different calculi and their comparison, and an assessment of the range of their applicability, yet this is left as future work.

Acknowledgments. I would like to thank Prof. W. Bibel and Prof. M. Thielscher for their insightful comments on an earlier version of this paper. This work was supported by German Academic Exchange Service and China 863 Research Project.

References

1. Bibel, W., Eder, E.: Methods and calculus for deduction. Handbook of Logic in Artificial Intelligence and Logic Programming, Volume 1, Clarendon Press, Oxford (1993) 68–184
2. Gelfond, M., Lifschitz, V.: Representing action and change by logic programs. Journal of Logic Programming **17** (1993) 301–321

3. Herrmann, C., Thielscher, M.: Reasoning about continuous change. In Proc. of AAAI, Portland, U.S.A. (1996) 639–644.
4. Kartha, F., Lifschitz, V.: Soundness and completeness theorem for three formalization of actions. In Proc. International Joint Conference on Artificial Intelligence, France (1993) 724–729.
5. Li, C.: Reasoning about processes and continuous change: analysis and implementation. Shaker-Verlag, Aachen (1999)
6. Li, C.: Representing the Process Semantics in the Event Calculus. In Proc. Logic in Artificial Intelligence,Vol. 1919 of LNCS, Springer-Verlag (2000) 118–132
7. Lifschitz, V.: Circumscription. The Handbook of Logic in Artificial Intelligence and Logical Programming, Vol 3, Oxford Science Publication (1994) 297–352
8. McCarthy, J., Hayes, P.: Some philosophical problems from the standpoint of artificial intelligence. Machine Intelligence **4**, Edinburgh University Press (1969) 463–502
9. Miller, R.: A case study in reasoning about action and continuous change. In Proc. ECAI, Budapest, Hungary (1996) 624–628.
10. Pinto, J., Reiter, R.: Adding a time line in the situation calculus. In 2th Symposium on Logical Formalizations of Commonsense Reasoning (1993) 172–177
11. Pinto, J., Reiter, R.: Reasoning about time in the situation calculus. Annals of Mathematics and Artificial Intelligence **14** (1995) 251–268
12. Reiter, R.: Natural actions, concurrency and continuous time in the situation calculus. In Proceedings of the 5th International Conference on Principles of Knowledge Representation and Reasoning. Cambridge, Massachusetts, U.S. (1996) 2–13
13. Sandewall, E.: The range of applicability and non-monotonic logics for the inertia problem. In Proc. International Joint Conference on Artificial Intelligence, France (1993) 738–743.
14. Shoham, Y., McDermott, D.: Problems in formal temporal reasoning. Artificial Intelligence **36** (1988) 49–61
15. Thielscher, M.: Representing actions in equational logic programming. In Proc. International Joint Conference on Logic Programming, Italy (1994) 207–224
16. Thielscher, M.: The logic of dynamic system. In Proc. International Joint Conference on Artificial Intelligence, Montreal, Canada (1995) 639–644

A Flexible Meta-solver Framework for Constraint Solver Collaboration

Stephan Frank[1], Petra Hofstedt[1], and Pierre R. Mai[2]

[1] Berlin University of Technology
{sfrank, ph}@cs.tu-berlin.de
[2] PMSF IT Consulting
pmai@pmsf.de

Abstract. The solving of multi-domain constraint problems with the help of collaborating solvers has seen extended interest in recent years. We describe the implementation (Meta-S) and extension of a previously proposed theoretical framework of cooperating constraint solvers. Meta-S allows the dynamic integration of arbitrary external (stand-alone) solvers to enable the collaborative processing of constraints. The modular structure allows the easy experimentation with different cooperation strategies. This is further amplified by an integrated strategy description language which supports the adaption of general strategies for problem specific needs to reduce the incurred cooperation overhead.

1 Introduction

Constraint solving has seen active research and application during the last decades. The computational costs were reduced by the introduction of advanced heuristics and sophisticated solving algorithms. However, constraint solvers are limited to restricted domains for efficient processing. Many interesting problems, on the other hand, are intuitively expressed as multi-domain descriptions. The effort for developing new constraint solvers that are able to handle such multi-domain problems is significant. A different approach, researched actively during the last years, is the employment of meta-solvers that handle the overall solving process by managing the collaboration of a number of individual (preexisting) constraint solvers.

The theoretical meta-solver framework developed by Hofstedt [1] provides a sound architecture for the cooperation of arbitrary constraint solvers. In this approach mixed-domain constraint problems are split into their single-domain subproblems which can be tackled by the individual solvers. Such multi-domain problems can then be solved cooperatively while none of the individual participating solvers would be able to handle the problem on their own.

The system architecture consists of a global pool associated with the meta-solver and any number of pluggable arbitrary (external) constraint solvers. Initially the pool contains a constraint conjunction which is to be solved. The meta-solver then takes constraints of this conjunction and propagates them to the individual participating solvers. This is done via the interface function *tell*.

A. Günter et al. (Eds.): KI 2003, LNAI 2821, pp. 520–534, 2003.

The solvers put these propagated constraints into their stores and derive new information (i.e. new constraints). These newly derived constraints are then in return requested by the meta-solver via the function *project* in order to add them to the global pool. This *tell – project* cycle continues until either a failure occurs, i.e. the constraint problem is unsatisfiable, or the pool eventually is emptied, i.e. no contradiction could be found.

A previous proof of concept implementation [2] worked quite satisfactorily. However, due to the monolithic structure it was difficult to experiment with changing solver collaboration and constraint propagation strategies to decrease the inherent communication overhead of the meta-solver approach. Taking aboard the lessons learned we developed an enhanced and revised framework which provides the ability to easily define generic and problem-specific solving strategies. This task was well supported by the dynamic features of the Common Lisp (CL) programming language.

The remainder of the paper is organized as follows. The next section introduces related work of the constraint community. After that, Sect. 3 describes the overall system architecture thereby focusing on internal details necessary for later explanations. This is followed by the illustration of an actual constraint problem definition in Sect. 4. General solving strategies influence the behavior of the overall meta-solving process. Section 5 focuses on the development of such strategies with special emphasis on the termination conditions and general approaches. This part is completed by the introduction of a specialized strategy specification language in Sect. 5.3 which supports the user to easily express more sophisticated algorithms. Finally, Sect. 6 focuses on the problem of value conversion to ensure broader information flow. The paper is concluded in Sect. 7.

2   Related Work

Active research within the field of constraint programming during the last decades has yielded many interesting directions of sophisticated solving algorithms as well as approaches of collaborating solvers to join the capabilities of different solvers. Hong [3] was one of the first to suggest the basic scheme cooperative solvers operate on. Each individual subsolver is repeatedly applied until a fixed-point is reached and hence no further changes occur. Hong especially focuses on the confluence of his cooperation system. The termination and confluence suppositions for Meta-S are extensively elaborated in [4].

Rueher [5] presents an agent-based concurrent cooperation scheme with a fixed set of collaborating solvers and only a single predefined cooperation strategy. All solver functions are defined on the same type (particularly real numbers).

Like our architecture the BALI environment for executing constraint solver combinations by Monfroy [6] provides a glass box mechanism to link a (predefined) set of (heterogeneous) black box solvers. BALI provides a fixed set of three cooperation primitives: sequential, concurrent and parallel; it is integrated into a logic host language. Formulation of BALI's cooperation operations within our framework is discussed in [4]. Meta-S provides a more fine-grained control for strategy development. New cooperation strategies can be easily defined and plugged in, just like additional solvers (cf. Sect. 5). Different host languages can be integrated into the framework by treating them as constraint solvers [7]. In [8] Castro and Monfroy extend the ideas of BALI. Compared to Meta-S the available fixed strategy-operator set is more abstract though allows a similar strategy description. Our explicit distinction of propagation and projection phases enables a more fine-grained strategy definition and optimization. The strategy operators of [8] could be provided as predefined core functions in our system.

OpenCFLP by Kobayashi *et al.* [9] is a system for solving *equations* by collaborating solvers. It allows the plug-in like integration of arbitrary solvers in conjunction with a declarative strategy definition basing upon a set of basic operators. However, we believe the presented strategy language of Meta-S combined with the structural pattern-matching and optional rewriting facilities provide finer and more intuitive control for strategy development.

3   Architecture

Since Meta-S was intended to serve as a test-bed for cooperation strategy experimentation the whole architecture was designed in a highly modular way to allow even radical changes without interfering with other parts of the framework. As illustrated in Fig. 1 *Base* and *Meta* are the two main modules representing the meta-solver system, together with any number of pluggable constraint solvers. The special role of the CL-solver will be illustrated in Sect. 6. Note that Fig. 1 only depicts the overall module structure, not the class structure as some CL Object System features are not easily describable graphically (e.g. in UML).

3.1   System Decomposition

The Base module contains the basic data structures and fundamental functionality of the framework. This includes the external and internal representations of constraints and the ability to translate between those representations.

A pattern language provides positional pattern expressions for matching constraints depending on their structure and contents. Combined with a template mechanism this enables (sub)constraint selection and rewriting of constraints.

Here also resides the abstract interface providing the connection between the meta-solver framework and the attached solvers. Using this solver interface we have connected a number of constraint solvers from several domains: a solver for linear arithmetic, finite domain (FD) solvers for different domain types (floats, strings and rationals), and an interval arithmetic solver.

The *Meta* module contains the meta-solver proper and additional user facilities to support the command-line interface as well as programming constructs for the integration within other applications. Furthermore, here the strategy framework for basic and enhanced strategy development resides.

Instances of the class *meta-solver*, which is at the core of the module, represent each an actual meta-solver system consisting of an initial constraint disjunction branch (usually only a conjunction is given initially), defined variables with

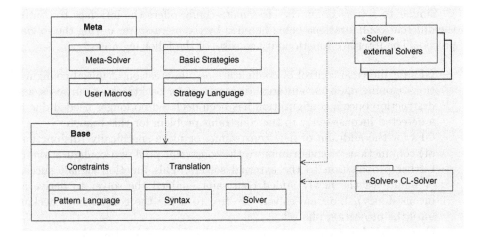

Fig. 1. The overall module structure of the Meta-S framework

associated types and the participating solvers. They each represent a complete constraint problem with associated state and solver information that is to be solved or simplified.

3.2   A Closer Look inside

In [4] a *configuration* is defined as the state of the architecture for one constraint conjunction. Such configurations are cloned when a disjunction is encountered during projection – one copy for each disjunction part. The *meta-solver* class keeps track of state information common to all configurations whereas another class *meta-config* corresponds to the above configurations where each instance represents a possible solution set, similar to the branches of a search-tree. State information of a configuration covers the set of pending constraints (the constraint pool), the individual (external) solver states and strategy-specific information like pending disjunctions and the current projection mode (see below).

The state information for each solver is tracked by instances of the *solver-config* class which are referenced by the according *meta-config* states. The *solver-config* class implements the minimal interface to enable control and access of external solvers by the superior meta-solver. The abstract solver interface consists of a number of generic functions (GFs) that need to be realized by an actual solver implementation/bridge:

- GFs for the creation, initialization, cloning and destruction of configurations. The ability to clone the solver states (including its associated store) is required to implement backtracking along different branches of a disjunction.
- Two GFs for propagation of constraint conjunctions and projection of disjunctions of constraint conjunctions respectively.

Similar to *solver-config*, the class *meta-config* offers the interface to control the different configurations being handled by the meta-solver during the solving process. The interface functionality consists of the following areas:

- GFs for life-time control of configurations, i.e. creation of initial configurations, cloning upon encountering disjunctions for backtracking purposes, and destruction once a configuration has been declared no longer needed due to a detected inconsistency in the constraint problem for this branch.
- GFs for the addition of new constraints, or more specifically (disjunctions of) conjunctions of constraints, to the constraint pool of a configuration for further propagation to the external solvers. This function signals success or failure (if the newly added constraint enabled the solver to derive an inconsistency). External solvers are free to delay the consistency checking until the projection phase.[1]
- One generic function (*meta-config-run*) that implements the solving process for a particular configuration. This function will be invoked by the meta-solver and continues until the configuration is solved or declared unsatisfiable by any of the cooperating solvers. In the latter case the configuration is destroyed, otherwise "success" is signaled.

  Furthermore it is possible to suspend the solving process of a configuration, yielding control back to the meta-solver. This might be useful to limit processing depth/time per configuration for certain strategies, especially when the task is not to find all but only one solution. Suspended configurations can be restarted again at any time.
- A GF is provided to extract the final constraints and variable bindings of a successfully solved configuration for further processing and presentation.

One optimization we included is the delayed instantiation of disjunction branches since heavy cloning can lead to quite dramatic space requirements. This obvious *disjunction parking* space optimization technique creates only one additional copy of the current configuration and continues to use this newly cloned configuration for one single part of the disjunction. The other backup copy is used to spawn additional clones step by step when the remaining, parked disjunction branches are processed. Since earlier branches and their configurations may have already failed and are consequently destroyed this can lead to noticeable memory savings.

A second, optional optimization to reduce the number of life configurations taken over from [2] is the distinction of two different projection categories: *weak* and *strong projection* which can be easily integrated into the solver connection interface. Weak projection tries to reduce the number of disjunctions by rewriting constraints of the form $X = 1 \lor X = 2 \lor X = 3$ to the disequations $X \geq 1 \land X \leq 3$ whereas strong projection simply returns the unaltered disjunction, i.e. weak

---

[1] This also enables solvers to delay constraints internally. Such techniques are often used in linear arithmetic solvers to process nonlinear constraints – these constraints are delayed until enough variables are bound to exact values such that the constraint becomes linear and can be processed eventually.

projection always returns conjunctions only, whereas strong projection can also yield disjunctions. Incorporation of a weak projection phase thus delays (and potentially reduces) the occurence of constraint disjunctions. Weak projection is optional and it is obviously necessary to ensure that a strong projection phase is always initiated eventually (cf. the discussion of termination in Sect. 5.1).

Before going into detail how the described interface functions can be applied and enhanced for (meta-)solving strategy development, we will shed some light on the actual definition of constraint problems.

4   Defining Constraint Problems

Since we were using Common Lisp as the implementation language it was deemed sensible to use an s-expression[2] based input syntax as basis for our constraint problem definition language. While the reservoir of defined operators and relations that are usable as part of the problem specification is *only* dependent on (and dynamically inherited from) the applied/currently connected constraint solvers, using s-expressions, which are fully parenthesized, had the additionally benefit of avoiding any issues with operator precedence.

However the simple nature of s-expressions might not be appropriate for certain domains. Hence we provide a syntax extension facility, based on CL reader macros, that allows the definition of specialized (sub)syntaxes for the input description, while retaining the benefits of s-expressions. An example for one such syntax-extension would be the introduction of an optional infix-notation for mathematical expressions. The set-notation for the domain elements (using braces – {}) in the example in Fig. 2 (lines 9–16) is another application of extended syntax. Here, the underlying general s-expression syntax would require nested calls to the add-to-domain and empty-domain constructor operators provided by the FD-solver, because of the fixed arity of constructors in Meta-S.

Figure 2 displays a (simple) complete example of a (row-wise) definition of the well-known SEND-MORE-MONEY crypto-arithmetic problem. An equivalent column-wise description is also possible, where the columns are added to temporary variables which are then multiplied by a ten-power factor depending on their position. Line 1 initiates the loading of the finite domain specific syntax extensions. Line 3 starts the problem description assigning it the name *smm-row*. The meta-solver will use the *eager* strategy (line 4, cf. Sect. 5) with the given preferred variable ordering for projections. Lines 6–7 state the used solvers (fd-rational, a FD-solver on rational numbers and cllin – a linear-arithmetic solver) and assign names to the solver instances to enable access by name later on. The following line 8 declares constraint variables of type rational. The remainder of the example specifies the actual constraint conjunction for the SEND-MORE-MONEY problem: First the possible domain values (lines 9–16), the demanded inequalities between all one-letter variables (line 17), and finally the sums to compute the values for the variables send, more, and

---

[2] s-expressions are the textual presentation of complex tree-structures used e.g. by Lisp-like languages

```
 1 (with-file-syntax :finite-domain)          ;; load domain specific syntax
 2
 3 (define-meta-solver *smm-row*               ;; problem definition
 4     (meta-solver eager-strategy             ;; select the eager strategy
 5                 :variable-ordering '(send more money m o n e y r s d))
 6   ((my-fd-rational fd-rational)             ;; employ a FD and a linear arith-
 7    (my-linar cllin))                        ;; metic solver
 8   ((rational s e n d m o r y send more money)) ;; declare variable types
 9   (((in s #{0 1 2 3 4 5 6 7 8 9})           ;; define the problem conjunction
10     (in e #{0 1 2 3 4 5 6 7 8 9})
11     (in n #{0 1 2 3 4 5 6 7 8 9})           ;; in and all-different are provi-
12     (in d #{0 1 2 3 4 5 6 7 8 9})           ;; ded by the FD-Solver, = by both,
13     (in m #{0 1 2 3 4 5 6 7 8 9})           ;; and the +, * operators by
14     (in o #{0 1 2 3 4 5 6 7 8 9})           ;; our linear-arithmetic solver cllin
15     (in r #{0 1 2 3 4 5 6 7 8 9})
16     (in y #{0 1 2 3 4 5 6 7 8 9})
17     (all-different {s e n d m o r y})
18     ((= my-linar) send (+ (* (+ (* (+ (* s 10) e) 10) n) 10) d))
19     (= more (+ (* (+ (* (+ (* m 10) o) 10) r) 10) e))
20     (= money (+ (* (+ (* (+ (* (+ (* m 10) o) 10) n) 10) e) 10) y))
21     (= (+ send more) money))))
```

Fig. 2. Sample code for the Meta-S problem description of the SEND-MORE-MONEY variant with 25 solutions (i.e. leading zeros are allowed). It utilizes two cooperating constraint solvers: a finite-domain and a linear arithmetic solver.

money (lines 18–21). The possibility to refer to specific constraint solver instances is used in line 18 where the constraint relation '=' is annotated such that this constraint will only be propagated to the solver instance named my-linar. It enables *ad hoc* control of constraint propagation on the problem definition level. This mechanism is useful when several of the participating solvers overlap on the constraint/function capabilities but we know at the same time that one specific solver can handle certain input constraints comparatively better than the other collaborating solvers. It would be thus advantageous to restrict the constraint propagation to one or more specific solvers. Such concepts are of course also expressible within a specific strategy definition (cf. Sect. 5.3).

5   Strategy Development

The meta-solver based architecture causes some inherent communication over-head but provides the advantage of letting constraint solvers of different domains cooperate via the implementation of a simple interface. Solutions are derived as follows: Propagate constraints from the global pool to the external solvers. All solvers signaling a change are marked *dirty*. All dirty solvers are then re-quested to project their information. These constraints are then again added to the pool. This cycle ends when the pool is emptied or a solver signals a conflict which marks the current setting unsatisfiable. The flow of information (i.e. newly derived constraints and assignments) between the participating solvers greatly influences the overall efficiency. Unfortunately, an effective cooperation strategy depends on the problem (and its modeling) as well as on the number and capabilities of the cooperating solvers and can thus not be generally formulated.

Meta-S provides the user and strategy developer with facilities to develop solving strategies within different levels of abstraction and detail.

The class *meta-config* (cf. Sect. 3.2) is the natural place to implement different solving strategies by providing complete implementations of the generic function *meta-config-run*, each representing a different solving strategy. However, using this approach much code would be duplicated by the different strategy implementations. Recognition of this fact led to the introduction of the abstract *strategy* class which provides a more specific interface and default implementations for a number of generic functions, thus allowing the developer of strategies to override default code at a much finer granularity.

5.1   Termination Conditions

For the creation of the strategy class it was vital to encapsulate the essential termination conditions which can be traced independently and without particular assistance by the strategy proper. Thus the strategy developer can concentrate on the information flow only, without having to keep track of the termination conditions explicitly.

The state information of a configuration as managed by *meta-config* like described in Sect. 3.2 can be used to formulate the termination criteria which correspond to the conditions described and proven in [4]. Termination of the solving process of a particular configuration eventually ensues when:

1. there are no pending constraints left in the pool, i.e. all constraints have been propagated to the external solvers,
2. there are no parked disjunction left,
3. none of the solvers is marked *dirty*, i.e. there are no changes that have not been requested yet by projection,
4. the current projection mode is *strong projection*.

Tests for these criteria can be run independently and are easily outsourced from the solving strategy itself. Updating the individual criteria states is done when the actual actions changing them are performed. We can thus describe strategies without explicit checks for termination and without extra update code for the termination states. Consequently any strategy that takes care to eventually empty the pool, project all propagated variables and switch to strong projection will terminate and not exit prematurely. Otherwise a strategy is essentially free to do whatever it wants by using the full power of Common Lisp. It is of course still possible to write non-terminating strategies, e.g. by implementing endless loops or by never propagating any constraints from the pool.

The solving process for a configuration now essentially consists of the following actions:

1. Check if there are pending constraints and/or dirty solvers. If "not", then we are finished, otherwise
2. Invoke *strategy-step* (cf. Sect. 5.2) for a single solving step where constraint propagation and projection to/from the external solvers is handled.
3. Repeat step 1, if *strategy-finish* does not succeed, i.e. not all termination conditions are met.

strategy-finish provides expanded termination checking since strategies may employ optimizations that delay or suppress the addition of constraints to the global pool, like e.g. the above mentioned disjunction parking technique. The time needed to meet the termination criteria is highly dependent on the overall collaboration method. Providing efficient collaboration methods is vital for acceptable performance. This problem will be addressed in the next sections.

5.2   General Strategies

To provide easy access points for strategy development the *strategy* class extends the interface of *meta-config* with fine-grained action-oriented hooks where the user can add and replace code by deriving new classes. We provide default implementations for these generic interface functions that form the base for all strategies. Interface functions are divided into the following categories:

- delaying and undelaying of constraints,
- constraint propagation and projection of individual or all (dirty) solvers,
- rewriting and conversion of projected constraints from the originating solver to other solvers (cf. Sect. 6), and
- additional termination testing (*strategy-finish*) and restart actions when awaking suspended configurations (*strategy-restart-actions*).
- The function *strategy-run* that constitutes the *overall* control loop of the whole strategy. It installs the hooks to allow dynamic exits and terminates by indicating success, failure or suspension, depending on the solver return states and strategy actions. It is invoked by the meta-solver action loop.
- *strategy-step* represents the processing of a single control loop run and is thus repeatedly invoked. It is the most natural place for strategies to establish variations of ordering, classification or form of propagation and projection actions (cf. Sect. 5.3).

In order to utilize the flexibility of the abstract *strategy* class, three generic strategies were implemented. They are all realized by defining replacements of the default methods for disjunction adding and for extended termination testing (in *strategy-finish*), thus the main strategy loop was left unaltered. All strategies could be realized in under 50 lines of code combined. The implemented strategies currently all emphasize on the handling of returned disjunction within the projection phase:

eager. This strategy propagates all constraint information as early as possible in the solving process. Returned disjunctions (during projection) lead to immediate spawning of cloned configurations for the individual disjunction branches. The partition into two projection stages (weak and strong projections, cf. Sect 3.2) can be applied advantageously as it delays and potentially reduces the number of live configurations. The *parked disjunction* technique (cf. Sect. 3.2) helps to further reduce the memory requirements.

lazy. This strategy is comparable to *eager* with the major difference that the backtrack-branches of disjunctions (returned by projections) are not created immediately but possibly remaining constraint conjunctions are propagated first to the solvers. This is done in the hope that it will help to reduce the lifetime of dead-end backtracking branches. Once all conjunctions are processed the cloning actions for the disjunction branches are initiated. The deferred handling of disjunction obviously clashes with our weak/strong-projection partitioning scheme. For solver plug-ins that adhere the optional *weak* option, this strategy is thus inferior to *eager*. However, in cases where the (optional) weak projection phase is ignored by the solver interface, this strategy might prove advantageous over our eager strategy.

heuristic. This last strategy integrates the previous two and additionally implements a heuristic element commonly known as *fail first* [10]. Here, the disjunction that is most likely to lead to an inconsistency (i.e. the one with the least branches) is processed first to keep the backtracking graph lean. This comes at the additional cost of more strong projections since disjunctions are requested from the solvers to decide which one (disjunction) to choose next, depending on the number of branches. After the strong projection round, the disjunction with the least number of elements is used for processing; the remaining disjunctions are discarded as their validity might be already obsolete at a later time. However, despite the greater number of strong projections it turns out that this strategy provides better results for most of our example problems.

The implemented example strategies have been tested with several different constraint problems exercising variations of constraint solver cooperation sets. Results for the SEND-MORE-MONEY problem runs behave representatively and are displayed in the upper half of Table 1. The strategies provide an optional parameter to allow the definition of a variable order that should be used for projection. This consequently also influences the order for the propagation of derived constraints and thus is essential for the overall runtime. Rows tagged *ordered* are the runs where we provided the strategies with a beneficial variable order whereas the other rows operated on an arbitrary projection order.[3]

The table emphasizes the important role of the projection order and shows that the heuristic strategy is able to derive a good order without the need for additional user supplied information. This is important as such an order is usually not known *a priori* nor easily derivable.

---

[3] Care was taken that the orders were identical for the different strategy runs.

Table 1. Benchmarking results for generic and problem-specific strategies for the SEND-MORE-MONEY crypto-arithmetic puzzle (column-wise definition; 25 solutions, i.e. leading zeros are allowed)

strategy	time in s	# of clones	# of propagates	# of projections weak	strong
lazy	79.0	3521	44918	18909	16126
lazy, ordered	27.7	5269	36539	2761	25366
eager	91.2	2502	49891	20933	2068
eager, ordered	9.2	253	6368	2717	858
heuristic	10.2	73	6097	3829	1276
heuristic, ordered	8.4	45	4850	2915	1012
domain-eq-first	9.1	253	6149	2728	858
once-domain-eq-first	9.2	253	6149	2728	858
solver-flow	6.3	253	4763	2013	858
heuristic-solver-flow	5.4	45	3808	2123	1012

5.3 Problem-Specific Strategies

It is obvious that control of information flow can gain important performance increases. Despite the comfortable performance of the different base strategies (eager, lazy and heuristic) it should be possible to influence strategy actions at a higher level. Such a feature allows the incorporation of problem and domain specific knowledge that would help speeding up the solving process. To support the user in this important task we developed a strategy language that allows to devise new more efficient strategies by extending generic strategies with additional control flow specifications.

Figure 3 presents one example strategy called heuristic-solver-flow. It was derived by extending the general heuristic strategy with a more optimized information flow. The :step clause initiates the inner strategy control loop definition. We start by partitioning all the constraints of the global pool into three groups based on their structure using the pattern matching facility (lines 4–6):

eq-constraints are constraints with an equality relation (=),
in-constraints match constraints with the in relation,
rest match all other constraints. This is expressed by the wildcard t.

The classified constraints are then propagated to the external solvers in the order of the groups given in lines 7–9. This is supported by our knowledge that this order helps the FD-solver and the linear arithmetic solver to populate their internal data structures more effectively. In the next step the linear arithmetic solver instance my-linar is requested to project its knowledge (line 10). The received constraints are again removed from the pool and propagated to the other solvers (line 11). Finally, the remaining solvers are requested to project their derived constraints (line 12). This solving step is repeatedly initiated by the controlling strategy until the termination conditions are satisfied.

```
1   (define-strategy heuristic-solver-flow
2       (heuristic-strategy)                    ;; use heuristic as base strategy
3    (:step
4       (select ((eq-constraints (= t t))       ;; patterns for eq/in constraints
5                 (in-constraints (in t t))
6                 (rest t))
7        (tell-all in-constraints)              ;; first propagate in
8        (tell-all eq-constraints)              ;; and eq constraints
9        (tell-all rest)                        ;; then all others
10       (project-one my-linar)                 ;; project from my-linar
11       (tell-all)                             ;; and propagate, then
12       (project-all)))))                      ;; project from all other solvers
```

Fig. 3. Strategy specification for the heuristic-solver-flow strategy

The lower part of Table 1 shows the performance data for four different specific strategies. The individual strategies all prioritize different types of constraints and/or different solver instances and clearly show the advantage of problem-tailored strategies for our setting.

The design of our strategy language anticipates that the user wants to control the exact order of constraint propagations, basing on different criteria like the target solver and/or the structure/properties of constraints. Additionally optional rewriting of returned constraints and influence on the projection sequencing should be possible.

Founded on these considerations the strategy language provides the following set of constructs and properties:

- We provide a set of support functions and macros, but the language is not limited to them. Due to the integration into the CL environment, all normal Common Lisp constructs can be applied.
- The execution of strategies is at the core of the meta-solving process and should thus run with high efficiency. This is ensured by automatically compiling the strategy language (on invocation) to native code (via CL). Therefore no interpretation overhead is carried into the inner execution loop.
- The integrated pattern language allows the classification/selection, destructuring (i.e. splitting into sub-parts matching specified patterns) and rewriting of constraints based on their structure by using positional pattern expressions. Destructuring of constraints is supported in pattern expressions by binding local (strategy) variables to matched subexpressions. Partitioning a set of constraints (like the set of pending constraints in the global pool) is possible as well. Creation of new constraints within the rewriting process is supported by a template mechanism.
  The matching expressions of the pattern language are compiled to native code, like the whole strategy language.
- Primitives for propagation of sets of constraints, as well as projection of specific or all solvers against a given set of variables and terms, support a detailed information flow control.

6   Conversions and the CL-Solver

Since we are working on different domains and solver types, the underlying relations, operators and types may be different. The meta-solver will split initial problems such that every participating solver only receives subproblems it is able to manage. However, to ensure efficient processing of the overall constraint problem, additional information flow between different solver types is desirable. Hofstedt [4] introduces the function $conv_{\nu \to \mu}$ which converts disjunctions of constraint conjunctions between the languages of two solvers ν and μ.

Such conversions are present in Meta-S at two different places. First, conversion of constraint conjunctions and disjunctions can be seen as a way of rewriting. Such rewriting can be applied as an intermittent step in the projection phase, using the built-in rewriting capabilities. Here, the solver-returned constraints are rewritten, before they are seen by the meta-solver and before being added to the global pool. Only the then rewritten constraints are considered for further processing. Another possibility is the application of an external rewriting solver, e.g. one implementing CHR [11]. This solver will participate in the overall problem solving process like any other cooperating solver. The original constraint conjunction of appropriate type is propagated to the rewriting solver and then the rewritten constraints are returned during the projection phase.

A second type of interesting conversion common to many (multi-domain) applications, is the transformation between disjoint though still fairly compatible value types. Consider two solvers, one operating on floating point numbers, the other on rationals (like our interval and linear arithmetic solvers). Since these number types are disjoint, ordinarily no information interchange (like value bindings) would happen between the two solvers. The CL-solver offers a residuation [12] based approach to define conversion operators using the functions of the underlying CL system. Figure 4 shows the extract of a constraint problem definition that defines a CL-solver instance `my-conversions` with two operators `to-dfloat` and `to-rat` which convert from double-floats to rationals and vice versa respectively using the standard Common Lisp functions `coerce` and `rationalize`. Additionally the appropriate equality relations are declared. These ensure that the CL-solver receives all bindings and can thus react on all variables captured in `to-dfloat` and `to-rat` applications. Note that such conversions are not necessary for existing subtype relations, like e.g. within the standard numeric tower of CL, where information flow will be propagated automatically by the meta-solver in the direction of the subtype relation because there is no type mismatch.

Of course this approach is fraught with problems when the coercions involved are imprecise, i.e. result in loss of information, which is the case with the numeric types mentioned. Invoking such conversions several times during a meta-solver run can quickly lead to a significant information loss. This is all the more problematic, because common techniques for analyzing the numerical accuracy of algorithms are hard to apply in the setting of a meta-solver system, where the overall algorithm is fairly involved and dynamic in nature, making the exact flow of numeric information hard to discover. We are convinced that further investigation of the general problem of conversion between representations is needed.

```
1  (my-conversions cl-solver
2                  :operators '((to-dfloat (rational) double-float
3                                (lambda (x) (coerce x 'double-float)))
4                               (to-rat (double-float) rational rationalize))
5                  :relations '((= (rational rational) =)
6                               (= (double-float double-float) =)))
```

Fig. 4. Definition of a conversion solver instance `my-conversion` for converting *double-float* to *rational* numbers (and *vice versa*) by applying the CL-solver

Nevertheless, putting aside the numeric problems while converting numbers, the easy conversion of more abstract data types (when possible) is still an interesting option.

Even though the CL-solver works on the principle of residuation and thus represents a quite strong barrier of information flow, conversion worked surprisingly well in our experiments. It additionally provides a simple way to integrate the meta-solver system within larger Common Lisp applications.

The ability to operate on arbitrary CL functions provides the additional benefit of simple Meta-S integration into larger applications. Variable bindings for dynamically created or statically described constraint systems are established by simple function calls within the CL-solver when a variable value is requested (which can e.g. issue GUI input actions by the user).

A possible option to reduce the information flow barrier posed by the residuation principle used by the CL-solver would be the application of a specific, more intelligent conversion solver. Especially the knowledge about possible inverse relations and operators would provide a more flexible information propagation.

7   Conclusion

The research described in this paper was motivated to provide a usable implementation of the theoretical framework by Hofstedt [1,4]. Integrating the lessons learned in a previous proof of concept implementation [2], one of the goals was to provide a flexible architecture to allow the easy exchange of core modules without interfering the rest of the system. This supports experimentation with different strategy approaches to cushion the inherent collaboration overhead and resulting performance problems of meta-solver systems originating from the necessary communication between the participating solvers (and the meta system).

The paper started with a description of the overall module structure (Sect. 3), highlighting implementation details where necessary. The notion of *configurations* and their resemblance in the implementation as *meta/solver-configs* was introduced to hold the state of a computation branch thus allowing backtracking. Section 4 continued with an illustration of the problem definition facilities.

Section 5 opens the strategy part of the paper. By encapsulating the termination conditions we were able to ease the task of implementing different collaboration strategies since state and termination condition tracking could be outsourced to a lower part of the system and maintained automatically. We continued with the development of three different cooperation strategies, each focusing on a different part of the overall information flow (Sect. 5.2). Observing that propagation and projection orders are essential for acceptable performance and appropriate heuristics vary for different problems and settings, we introduced a strategy description language in Sect. 5.3. With the help of a positional pattern language it was possible to easily alter the core solving steps of existing strategies for problem specific needs. The effect has been verified on a number of multi-domain constraint problems. We believe that current performance barriers are imposed by (speed) limitations of the plugged-in solvers (particularly the linear-arithmetic solver). A future work will be the integration of more sophisticated solvers and the study of the effects of a stronger multi-domain mix.

Finally, Sect. 6 discussed the problem of constraint value conversion to support a stronger information flow. Such handling is quite delicate for numerical issues though necessary to provide a stronger information interchange between the individual solvers. It is certainly useful for non-numeric values. However, more experimentation is needed in this area to further reduce barriers for value/constraint propagation (of disjoint types).

References

1. Hofstedt, P.: Better Communication for Tighter Cooperation. In Lloyd, J., ed.: First Int'l Conf. on Computational Logic – CL'00. Volume 1861 of LNCS. (2000)
2. Godehardt, E., Hofstedt, P., Seifert, D.: A Framework for Cooperating Constraint Solvers. In: CoSolv Workshop. At the 7th Int'l Conf. on Principles and Practice of Constraint Programming. (2001)
3. Hong, H.: Confluency of Cooperative Constraint Solvers. Technical Report 94-08, Research Institute for Symbolic Computation, Linz, Austria (1994)
4. Hofstedt, P.: Cooperation and Coordination of Constraint Solvers. PhD thesis, Technische Universität Dresden (2001) Shaker Verlag, Aachen.
5. Rueher, M.: An Architecture for Cooperating Constraint Solvers on Reals. In Podelski, A., ed.: Constraint Programming: basics and trends. Châtillon Spring School 1994. selected papers. Volume 910 of LNCS. (1995)
6. Monfroy, E.: Solver Collaboration for Constraint Logic Programming. PhD thesis, Université Henri Poincaré – Nancy I (1996)
7. Hofstedt, P.: A general Approach for Building Constraint Languages. In McKay, B., Slaney, J., eds.: AI 2002: Advances in AI. Volume 2557 of LNCS. (2002)
8. Castro, C., Monfroy, E.: Basic Operators for Solving Constraints via Collaboration of Solvers. In: Proceedings of AISC. Volume 1930 of LNAI., Springer-Verlag (2000)
9. Kobayashi, N., Marin, M., Ida, T., Che, Z.: Open CFLP: An Open System for Collaborative Constraint Functional Logic Programming. In: 11th Int'l Workshop on Functional and (Constraint) Logic Programming (WFLP 2002). (2002)
10. Bitner, J., Reingold, E.M.: Backtrack Programming Techniques. Communications of the ACM (CACM) 18 (1975)
11. Frühwirth, T.: Constraint Handling Rules. In Podelski, A., ed.: Constraint Programming: Basics and Trends. Volume 910 of LNCS. (1995)
12. Aït-Kaci, H., Nasr, R.: Integrating logic and functional programming. Lisp and Symbolic Computation 2 (1989)

Tripartite Line Tracks – Bipartite Line Tracks

Björn Gottfried

Artificial Intelligence Group, TZI, University of Bremen
Universitätsallee 21-23, 28359 Bremen, Germany, `bg@tzi.de`

Abstract. Theories of shapes are important for object recognition and for reasoning about the behaviour of objects, both tasks strongly constrained by shape. Whereas the extraction of shape properties has extensively been studied in vision, there is still a lack of qualitative shape descriptions which allow reasoning about shapes with AI techniques in a flexible manner.

In this paper we present a qualitative shape description. This description is based on a set of qualitative relations which can be combined to construct arbitrary polygonal shapes. As we are interested in demonstrating how qualitative reasoning approaches can be applied to shape descriptions, our theory is confined to stylised shape representations which are obtainable by applying conventional image processing techniques. We will show how to qualitatively reason about shapes.

1 Introduction

Shape descriptions have extensively been studied in vision. Traditionally, such descriptions resort to quantitative methods that often give rise to high dimensional feature spaces which are useful for classification tasks. However, these representations are inappropriate for symbolic reasoning and do not provide for dealing flexibly with shapes. But this becomes important in more sophisticated reasoning tasks when studying the behaviour of objects, for example, their change in shape, motion in space, and interaction with other objects.

Qualitative abstractions allow reducing information in order to obtain descriptions which are more tractable than quantitative descriptions. A qualitative shape description is investigated which represents a kind of qualitative abstraction which permits application of reasoning techniques to shapes that have been devised for qualitative spatial reasoning, especially in the context of navigation.

For any qualitative shape description, there exist several conceivable differences to be considered. Shape descriptions can be classified as either two-dimensional or three-dimensional, as either can be related to regions or just confined to outlines. These may loosely be the two most important distinctions. For an overview of qualitative shape approaches see [2]. Our description will be restricted to two-dimensional polygonal outlines since we are mainly interested in demonstrating how shape descriptions can be devised by considering orientation information and navigation tasks. For that purpose, we will confine ourselves to one single approach from Freksa and Zimmermann which is described in [5], and which we will adopt to shape reasoning problems.

A. Günter et al. (Eds.): KI 2003, LNAI 2821, pp. 535–549, 2003.

2   Obtaining Shapes by Navigation

With qualitative descriptions, objects are often regarded in relation to other objects. This concerns particularly navigation tasks where the position of objects are described with respect to landmarks. One example is a simple localisation task, stated by [5]:

> *Walk down the road. You will see a church in front of you on the left. Before you reach the church turn down the path that leads forward to the right. The question one might ask on his way down the path is, where is the church with respect to me?*

When recording the path someone walks along we obtain a trajectory. Any trajectory can simultaneously be accounted for being part of a shape's outline. Necessarily, we will get something of the kind of a shape description by considering how the localisation task can be solved. That is to say, we will learn something about properties of trajectories which are made up of landmarks and points between which movements take place. More precisely, we are interested in the representation which has been used to solve such tasks, rather than in the solution itself.

The representation that Freksa and Zimmermann have introduced is based on what they call an *orientation grid*. This grid is aligned to the orientation determined by two points, i.e. the start-point and the end-point of a movement (see Fig. 1.a). A third point can then be considered to be on the left, on the right, or straight on this movement-vector, and furthermore, it can be before the start-point, behind the end-point, or in between (see Fig. 1.b). Eventually, it can be on one of the two lines separating the three consecutive regions (the dotted lines in Fig. 1.b). We are then able to distinguish fifteen different positions, as shown in Fig. 1.c, and the localisation task can now simply be stated by asking where a landmark c is with respect to a vector $a \rightarrow b$ (see Fig. 1.d).

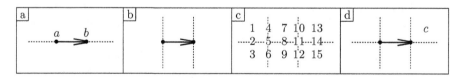

Fig. 1. The orientation grid introduced by one continuously drawn vector distinguishes fifteen positions

Freksa and Zimmermann demonstrate how to reason about positions with respect to landmarks by using the orientation grid. In contrast, we will consider different possible trajectories put up by means of landmarks, and we will show how to describe the outlines of shapes with the aid of the orientation grid.

3   Bipartite Line Tracks

We will introduce our approach for qualitatively describing shapes. For this description, the orientation grid is adapted in order to represent shape primitives. These primitives are made up of two connected lines according to the localisation task which was described in the previous section. In addition to a movement-vector, a line is considered which connects the end-position of this movement to a landmark. In this way, each primitive corresponds to a bipartite path which is described by the start-position of a movement, a, its end-position, b, and additionally by a landmark, c.

$\mathcal{BLT}(1)$	$\mathcal{BLT}(2)$	$\mathcal{BLT}(3)$	$\mathcal{BLT}(4)$	$\mathcal{BLT}(5)$	$\mathcal{BLT}(6)$

Fig. 2. Six distinguishable classes of Bipartite Line Tracks; the orientation of the horizontal line corresponds to the vector $a \to b$

In order to construct shape primitives only general positions are considered, i.e. the six positions which do not lie on the orientation grid: $1, 3, 7, 9, 13$, and 15 in Fig. 1.c. The other nine positions lying directly on the orientation grid are called singular positions. We will discuss later how to deal with singular positions. As there exist six general positions with respect to a vector $a \to b$, we obtain six bipartite relations, shown in Fig. 2. We will call these primitives *Bipartite Line Tracks*, and the i-th relation can be accessed by $\mathcal{BLT}(i)$, for $i \in \{1, 2, 3, 4, 5, 6\}$.

3.1   Polygons

A closed polygon with $k \geq 2$ lines is described as a vector of k $\mathcal{BLT}$s, an open polygon as a vector of $k - 1$ $\mathcal{BLT}$s: $\mathcal{BLT}(i, j, ...), i, j \in \{1, 2, 3, 4, 5, 6\}$. In order to be able to treat each arbitrary polygon with k lines, and not only those which consist of a multiple of two lines, a vector of $\mathcal{BLT}$s describes a polygon in such a way that two consecutive $\mathcal{BLT}$s share one line.

For closed polygons, different $\mathcal{BLT}$ descriptions will be obtained depending on where one starts to enumerate a polygon. Any description can be converted into another equivalent description by means of a cyclic permutation of the $\mathcal{BLT}$s involved. For a given polygon we choose the description that comes first in the ordering with respect to the $\mathcal{BLT}$ numbers. We define an anticlockwise orientation regarding the two-dimensional plane, i.e. we describe any contour anticlockwise. Fig. 3 shows an example.

3.2   Neighbourhood Graph

Fig. 4 shows the neighbourhood graph adopted from [4]. In this graph, two relations are connected if they are just separated by one of the lines of the

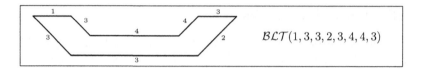

Fig. 3. Example of a polygon described by Bipartite Line Tracks anticlockwise

orientation grid. In other words, two relations are neighbours if one relation can be transformed into the other relation by continuously moving one endpoint to another position whilst crossing the orientation grid exactly once. This graph will be used for reasoning tasks, and at first we will show how to deal with singular positions with the aid of the neighbourhood graph.

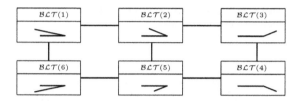

Fig. 4. Neighbourhood graph of the $\mathcal{BLT}$-relations

3.3 Singular Line Tracks

To be more precise, $\mathcal{BLT}$s which have been considered so far would have been better denominated as *General Bipartite Line Tracks* because singular positions were disregarded. Line Tracks that comprise inter alia singular positions are of special interest with respect to the boundaries of artificial objects which often have perpendicular sides. Orthogonality corresponds to relations in singular position.

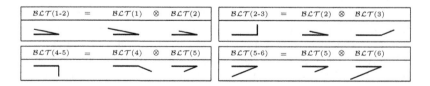

Fig. 5. Singular Bipartite Line Tracks

A *Singular Bipartite Line Track* is referred to as $\mathcal{BLT}(a\text{-}b)$, i.e. $\mathcal{BLT}(a\text{-}b)$ refers to an edge in the neighbourhood graph, whereby a and b are the relations which are connected by this edge. As an example, consider $\mathcal{BLT}(1\text{-}2)$ in Fig. 5. This singular position is in between the two general positions $\mathcal{BLT}(1)$ and $\mathcal{BLT}(2)$.

Singular line tracks with the endpoints lying on the positions 2, 5, 8, 11, or 14 (see Fig. 1) are in accordance with degenerated cases where we only perceive a single line. These positions are denoted in the following way: $\mathcal{BLT}(3\text{–}4)$ (position 14 in Fig. 1.c), $\mathcal{BLT}(2\text{–}3\text{–}4\text{–}5)$ (position 11), $\mathcal{BLT}(2\text{–}5)$ (position 8), $\mathcal{BLT}(1\text{–}2\text{–}5\text{–}6)$ (position 5), and $\mathcal{BLT}(1\text{–}6)$ (position 2). This notation allows us to consider all those general positions between which there is uncertainty regarding the position of a point or line, respectively. Uncertainty arises whenever one perceives any position somewhere near the transition between two or more general positions. In most cases, a singular position will not definitely be recognised as beeing singular. One will simply have doubts regarding a general position which lies near the transition to another general position. All in all, singular positions are mainly treated in a way that is related to the question of how one has to cope with uncertainty regarding the positions near boundaries of two or more neighbouring regions.

3.4 Non-oriented Primitives

With Bipartite Line Tracks we introduced a shape description which consists of six oriented shape primitives. Oriented primitives allow us to discriminate contour parts that are oriented to the shape of an object from those which are mirror-symmetrical to the former parts, i.e. parts which are oriented to the background. Hence, we distinguish $\mathcal{BLT}(1)$ and $\mathcal{BLT}(6)$, $\mathcal{BLT}(2)$ and $\mathcal{BLT}(5)$, as well as $\mathcal{BLT}(3)$ and $\mathcal{BLT}(4)$ (see Fig. 4). In ambiguous cases we write more precisely $\mathcal{BLT}_6$ in order to refer to these six relations.

Fig. 6. Different polygons described by $\mathcal{BLT}_3(3,3)$, thus not distinguishable by $\mathcal{BLT}_3$

In the context of vision we often have to deal with incomplete shape information. As a consequence, partial shape information has to be described. But frequently nothing can be said concerning the orientation of shape parts since in most instances it is not known on which side of any contour-part the figure or the ground is. As such, it seems reasonable to consider primitives which are not oriented and we obtain only three relations, i.e. one obtuse angled primitive, like $\mathcal{BLT}_6(3)$, and two kinds of acute angled primitives, like $\mathcal{BLT}_6(1)$ and $\mathcal{BLT}_6(2)$. These three relations will be referred to as $\mathcal{BLT}_3$. Such non-oriented primitives have the disadvantage that it is not possible to distinguish some shapes anymore, as, for example, the two polygonal parts in Fig. 6. In order to distinguish more complex non-oriented primitives line tracks made up of three lines will be considered in the next section.

4   Tripartite Line Tracks

We now consider three end-point-connected lines, also described by the orientation grid, as shown by the example on the right of Fig. 7. The medial line determines the orientation grid and the two endpoints are described with respect to the medial line by considering their position with regard to the orientation grid.

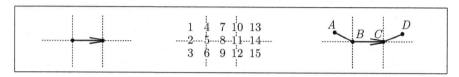

Fig. 7. Left: The orientation grid introduced by one continuously drawn vector, distinguishes fifteen positions (Middle); Right: A line track $(\overline{AB}, \overline{BC}, \overline{CD})$ which consists of three connected lines

4.1 $\mathcal{TLT}_{36}$

Both endpoints of one line track can be in six different general positions, generating a variation of $6^2 = 36$ different relations, as outlined in Fig. 8. These line tracks are called *Tripartite Line Tracks*, in short $\mathcal{TLT}$, since they are made up of three lines. The i-th relation is accessed by $\mathcal{TLT}(i)$. The medial line is considered to be oriented, for instance, from left to right, i.e. from a to b as exemplified for $\mathcal{TLT}_{36}(1)$.

Consider, for instance, $\mathcal{TLT}_{36}(1)$, $\mathcal{TLT}_{36}(15)$, $\mathcal{TLT}_{36}(22)$, and $\mathcal{TLT}_{36}(36)$. These relations look quite similar since in each case the two endpoints are lying in the same corner-area of the orientation grid. That is, the medial line was originally considered as an oriented vector and in one of these four relations both endpoints are at the top left of the vector, whereas in the other three cases they are at different positions with respect to the medial vector. Similar symmetrical relationships hold for all other relations. But we are interested in non-oriented shape primitives. Hence, in the next paragraph relations are considered with the medial line being oriented not anymore.

4.2 $\mathcal{TLT}_{12}$

The orientation of a shape can be considered with respect to any global frame of reference. The same holds for the parts of any shape. But for shape descriptions

Orientation of the medial line: $\longrightarrow$

$\mathcal{TLT}_{36}(1)$	$\mathcal{TLT}_{36}(2)$	$\mathcal{TLT}_{36}(3)$	$\mathcal{TLT}_{36}(4)$	$\mathcal{TLT}_{36}(5)$	$\mathcal{TLT}_{36}(6)$
$\mathcal{TLT}_{36}(7)$	$\mathcal{TLT}_{36}(8)$	$\mathcal{TLT}_{36}(9)$	$\mathcal{TLT}_{36}(10)$	$\mathcal{TLT}_{36}(11)$	$\mathcal{TLT}_{36}(12)$
$\mathcal{TLT}_{36}(13)$	$\mathcal{TLT}_{36}(14)$	$\mathcal{TLT}_{36}(15)$	$\mathcal{TLT}_{36}(16)$	$\mathcal{TLT}_{36}(17)$	$\mathcal{TLT}_{36}(18)$
$\mathcal{TLT}_{36}(19)$	$\mathcal{TLT}_{36}(20)$	$\mathcal{TLT}_{36}(21)$	$\mathcal{TLT}_{36}(22)$	$\mathcal{TLT}_{36}(23)$	$\mathcal{TLT}_{36}(24)$
$\mathcal{TLT}_{36}(25)$	$\mathcal{TLT}_{36}(26)$	$\mathcal{TLT}_{36}(27)$	$\mathcal{TLT}_{36}(28)$	$\mathcal{TLT}_{36}(29)$	$\mathcal{TLT}_{36}(30)$
$\mathcal{TLT}_{36}(31)$	$\mathcal{TLT}_{36}(32)$	$\mathcal{TLT}_{36}(33)$	$\mathcal{TLT}_{36}(34)$	$\mathcal{TLT}_{36}(35)$	$\mathcal{TLT}_{36}(36)$

Fig. 8. 36 oriented classes of line tracks with three connected lines

it is sometimes useful to consider in the first place the relationships between parts, and not the orientation of a single part with regard to a global frame of reference. This also holds when we have to cope with incomplete shapes as mentioned in the previous section when we introduced $\mathcal{BLT}_3$. Therefore, it is more expedient to consider parts which are invariant with respect to rotation and reflection. Rotational and reflectional differences are primarily relevant concerning the whole shape.

After removing all symmetrical relations of $\mathcal{TLT}_{36}$ there remain twelve distinguishable relations, as depicted in Fig. 9. The dotted lines outline those areas where the endpoints are allowed to lie in order to satisfy the denoted relation. For simplification, in unambiguous situations we write $\mathcal{TLT}$ instead of $\mathcal{TLT}_{12}$.

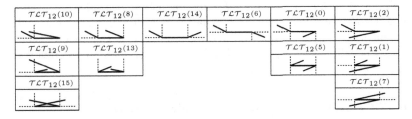

Fig. 9. Twelve non-oriented boundary primitives distinguished by $\mathcal{TLT}_{12}$

4.3 Polygons

A closed polygon with $k \geq 3$ lines is described as a vector of k $\mathcal{TLT}$s, an open polygon as a vector of $k - 2$ $\mathcal{TLT}$s:

$$\mathcal{TLT}_{12}(i, j, ...), i, j \in \{0, 1, 2, 5, 6, 7, 8, 9, 10, 13, 14, 15\}.$$

In order to be able to treat each arbitrary polygon with k lines, and not only those consisting of a multiple of three lines, a vector of $\mathcal{TLT}$s describes a polygon in such a way that two consecutive $\mathcal{TLT}$s share two lines. In this way, there exist $\mathcal{TLT}$s which are incompatible. For example, $\mathcal{TLT}_{12}(5)$ and $\mathcal{TLT}_{12}(6)$ cannot be combined since as a combination they would have to share two adjacent lines or one angle, respectively. But the angles of $\mathcal{TLT}_{12}(5)$ are both acute whereas the angles of $\mathcal{TLT}_{12}(6)$ are both obtuse. A compatible combination consists of four lines or two entwined $\mathcal{TLT}$s, respectively.

As for Bipartite Line Tracks, for a given polygon, we choose that description which comes first in the ordering with respect to the $\mathcal{TLT}$ numbers and all possible cyclic permutations.

Fig. 10. Example polygon described by Tripartite Line Tracks anticlockwise

Running around the contour of a shape it is reasonable to use $\mathcal{TLT}_{36}$ for a description. In this way, we define an orientation as, for example, anticlockwise regarding the two-dimensional plane, and we are able to distinguish the two sides of the contour. Fig. 10 shows an example shape with both the $\mathcal{TLT}_{12}$ and the $\mathcal{TLT}_{36}$ description. While $\mathcal{TLT}_{36}$ distinguishes both sides of the contour as well as a front-back dichotomy for any part, $\mathcal{TLT}_{12}$ distinguishes parts which are invariant with respect to rotation and reflection. From this follows that similar parts are equally characterised by $\mathcal{TLT}_{12}$, though oriented in different ways with respect to the two-dimensional plane.

4.4 $\mathcal{TLT}$ Neighbourhood and Singular Line Tracks

We define the neighbourhood graph and singular line tracks in a manner similar to that used for $\mathcal{BLT}$s. Fig. 11 shows the $\mathcal{TLT}_{12}$ neighbourhood graph. A *Singular Tripartite Line Track* is referred to as $\mathcal{TLT}(a\text{-}b)$ with one sideline in general position and the other sideline in singular position. In this way, $\mathcal{TLT}(a\text{-}b)$ refers to an edge in the neighbourhood graph, whereby a and b are the nodes which are connected by this edge. Consider the examples in Fig. 12. $\mathcal{TLT}(13\text{-}8\text{-}14)$

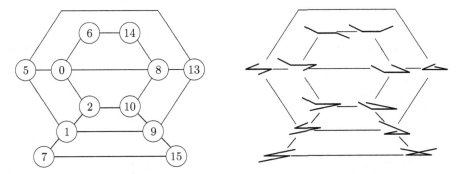

Fig. 11. Left: the neighbourhood graph; Right: example instantiations; the numbers refer to the $\mathcal{TLT}_{12}$-relations

$\mathcal{TLT}(13\text{-}8\text{-}14)$	$\mathcal{TLT}(8\text{-}9\text{-}10\text{-}13)$	$\mathcal{TLT}(13\text{-}9\text{-}15)$	$\mathcal{TLT}(5\text{-}0\text{-}6)$	$\mathcal{TLT}(0\text{-}1\text{-}2\text{-}5)$	$\mathcal{TLT}(5\text{-}1\text{-}7)$

$\mathcal{TLT}(8\text{-}13)=\mathcal{TLT}(8)\otimes\mathcal{TLT}(13)$	$\mathcal{TLT}(8\text{-}14)=\mathcal{TLT}(8)\ \otimes\ \mathcal{TLT}(14)$	$\mathcal{TLT}(13\text{-}8\text{-}14)=\mathcal{TLT}(8\text{-}13)\otimes\mathcal{TLT}(8\text{-}14)$

Fig. 12. Upper row: all *Singular Tripartite Line Tracks* with both sidelines in singular position; Lower row: the construction of $\mathcal{TLT}(13\text{-}8\text{-}14)$

denotes a line track with both sidelines in singular position. Singular line tracks with the endpoints lying on the positions 2, 5, 8, 11, or 14 (see Fig. 1) correspond to degenerated cases. Concerning $\mathcal{TLT}_{12}$ descriptions we are only interested in visually distinguishable line tracks.

5   Reasoning about Shapes

Reasoning tasks for shapes are important by all means: shapes are occluded, nonetheless we want to state something about occluded parts; shapes have to be compared and we are interested in their similarity; shapes may get deformed and physically possible deformation processes have to be described.

5.1   Deformation

Physically possible deformation processes of single $\mathcal{BLT}$s can be described by means of the neighbourhood graph. For instance, $\mathcal{BLT}(1)$ can be directly transformed to $\mathcal{BLT}(2)$ but not to $\mathcal{BLT}(3)$. In order to transform $\mathcal{BLT}(1)$ to $\mathcal{BLT}(3)$ a way through the neighbourhood graph has to be found. More interesting are polygons made up of more than two lines.

We consider change in shape locally, i.e. given any polygon with n lines, a single transformation step consists in changing the position of only one line segment. Such local changes always modify the description of two consecutive $\mathcal{TLT}$s, as exemplified on the right of Fig. 13. On the other hand, regarding the $\mathcal{BLT}$-description only one $\mathcal{BLT}$ is changed. Thus, the $\mathcal{BLT}$-description reflects more appropriately the locality of change, whereas the $\mathcal{TLT}$-description reflects more precisely the effect which a local change has on neighbouring relations.

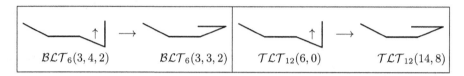

$$\mathcal{BLT}_6(3,4,2) \qquad \mathcal{BLT}_6(3,3,2) \quad\Big|\quad \mathcal{TLT}_{12}(6,0) \qquad \mathcal{TLT}_{12}(14,8)$$

Fig. 13. Changing one line segment changes only one $\mathcal{BLT}$ but two consecutive $\mathcal{TLT}$s; the upward-pointing arrows depict the direction for the deformation process

5.2   Similarity

Deformations and similarity measures are closely related, provided only continuous deformation processes are considered, and this relationship is inversely proportional. The less the deformation applied to any shape, the higher the similarity between the original shape and its deformed complement. Thus, we employ the neighbourhood graph for a measure of similarity likewise describing deformations.

We write $\mathcal{BLT}$ if $\mathcal{BLT}_3$ and $\mathcal{BLT}_6$ are to be treated equally. The distance $\delta(\mathcal{BLT}(i), \mathcal{BLT}(j))$ between $\mathcal{BLT}(i)$ and $\mathcal{BLT}(j)$ is defined as the length of the shortest path between these $\mathcal{BLT}$s in the neighbourhood graph. For their similarity S it holds:

$$S(\mathcal{BLT}(i), \mathcal{BLT}(j)) = \frac{1}{1+\delta(\mathcal{BLT}(i),\mathcal{BLT}(j))}.$$

Two line tracks which represent the same $\mathcal{BLT}$ relation have the highest similarity value of one since their distance is zero. For example, it holds

$$S(\mathcal{BLT}_6(1), \mathcal{BLT}_6(2)) > S(\mathcal{BLT}_6(1), \mathcal{BLT}_6(3)).$$

That is, $\mathcal{BLT}_6(1)$ and $\mathcal{BLT}_6(2)$ are more similar than $\mathcal{BLT}_6(1)$ and $\mathcal{BLT}_6(3)$. In contrast, $\mathcal{BLT}_6(1)$ and $\mathcal{BLT}_6(2)$ are equally similar as $\mathcal{BLT}_6(1)$ and $\mathcal{BLT}_6(6)$:

$$S(\mathcal{BLT}_6(1), \mathcal{BLT}_6(2)) = S(\mathcal{BLT}_6(1), \mathcal{BLT}_6(6)).$$

These relations hold, provided that the similarity between all neighbouring relations in the neighbourhood graph are weighted equally. Traversing through the neighbourhood graph towards a relation $\mathcal{BLT}(i)$, the similarity between $\mathcal{BLT}(i)$ and any passed relation $\mathcal{BLT}(j)$ increases the more in strength the less the distance between $\mathcal{BLT}(i)$ and $\mathcal{BLT}(j)$.

We now consider the similarity between two n-partite polygons

$P_0 = \mathcal{BLT}(x_0, x_1, ..., x_{n-1})$ and $P_1 = \mathcal{BLT}(y_0, y_1, ..., y_{n-1})$.

Provided that P_0 and P_1 are aligned in such a way that x_i is aligned to y_j, for their distance we write

$$\delta_{i,j}(P_0, P_1) \qquad = \qquad \delta_{i,j}(\mathcal{BLT}(x_i, ..., x_{(n-1+i) \bmod n}),$$
$$\mathcal{BLT}(y_j, ..., y_{(n-1+j) \bmod n})).$$

The similarity of two polygons, $S(P_0, P_1)$, is based on the most similar alignment of the relations involved. That is, from all possible alignments the one with the smallest distance determines the similarity between two polygons:

$$S(P_0, P_1) = \frac{1}{1 + \min_{k=0}^{n-1}\{\delta_{0,k}(P_0, P_1)\}}.$$

While we keep hold of the position of P_0 we consider all possible cyclic permutations of P_1 in order to find the best alignment. The index k represents those cyclic permutations.

For one alignment, the distance between the polygons equals the summation of all distances between two aligned $\mathcal{BLT}$ relations:

$$\delta_{0,k}(\mathcal{BLT}(x_0, ...), \mathcal{BLT}(y_k, ...)) = \sum_{i=0}^{n-1} \delta(\mathcal{BLT}(x_i), \mathcal{BLT}(y_{(i+k) \bmod n})).$$

For any similarity measurement, the sizes of differently sized polygons have to be taken into account as well. But it depends on the application as to how the difference in size influences the similarity between these polygons.

Weights at the edges of the neighbourhood graph may determine more appropriate similarities between single $\mathcal{BLT}$s since some neighbours may be considered more similar than others. For instance, perceptually it holds

$$S(\mathcal{BLT}_6(1), \mathcal{BLT}_6(2)) > S(\mathcal{BLT}_6(2), \mathcal{BLT}_6(3)).$$

When dealing with singular line tracks singular positions have to be considered like general relations when computing any distance. The same considerations on measuring the similarity between polygons hold for $\mathcal{TLT}$s.

As an example, in Fig. 14, there are all possible convex quadrilaterals made up of $\mathcal{BLT}_3(2)$ and $\mathcal{BLT}_3(3)$, i.e. only the distinction between acute and obtuse angles has been considered along with rectangular angles which correspond to $\mathcal{BLT}_3(2\text{-}3)$. Even so, we are able to distinguish many different quadrilaterals. However, we cannot distinguish some of those simple convex polygons from other concave polygons. For those distinctions we have to use $\mathcal{BLT}_6$. The relationship between deformation and similarity is illustrated in Fig. 14. Two quadrilaterals are connected if a local deformation step transforms one of them into the other one. Simultaneously, two quadrilaterals are more similar regarding our similarity measurement the less deformation steps are necessary for such transformations.

[7] demonstrates how to distinguish different object categories by describing salient contour parts with the aid of $\mathcal{TLT}_{12}$. The $\mathcal{TLT}_{12}$ neighbourhood graph is used as a measure of similarity between an object-instance and possible categories. In this way, even the complex shapes of similar natural objects such as

cats and dogs, which are represented in a stylised manner by simple polygons, can be discriminated. Each category is adequately described by typical tuples and triples of $\mathcal{TLT}$ relations. Tuples or triples of $\mathcal{TLT}$ relations at special positions, characterise object categories and constitute salient object-specific spatial structures. When replacing $\mathcal{TLT}$s in such structures with neighbouring relations, similar spatial structures are obtainable.

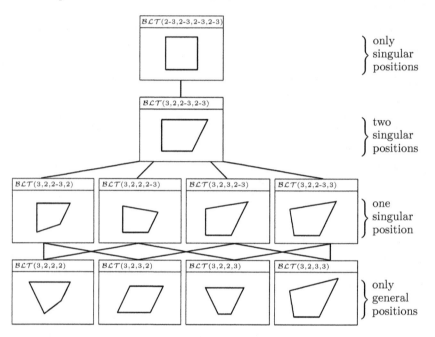

Fig. 14. Simple convex quadrilaterals described by $\mathcal{BLT}_3$; for comparisons the anticlockwise encodation starts always with the bottom line

5.3   Occlusion

Among other reasoning tasks, [5] considered the problem of specifying a short cut from a position a to another position c, given the position of c with respect to the path $a \to b$. More formally, the idea is to deduce a position b relative to a vector $a \to c$, provided that position c with respect to the vector $a \to b$ is known. This task can be cast into the following shape reasoning problem:

> We see a partly occluded object and notice two arbitrary parts, a and b, as illustrated on the left of Fig. 15. The object moves and suddenly one of these two parts is occluded, for example, b as shown on the right of Fig. 15. Then, we would like to know where the occluded part is now, with respect to a and another visible part c.

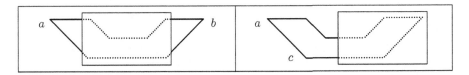

Fig. 15. A polygon being partly occluded in two different ways, at two different times

Table 1. Given (c w.r.t. $a \to b$) (left column) derive (b w.r.t. $a \to c$) (middle column), and derive (c w.r.t. $b \to a$) (last column) - encoded by $\mathcal{BLT}_6$

c w.r.t. $a \to b$	b w.r.t. $a \to c$	c w.r.t. $b \to a$
$\mathcal{BLT}(1)$	$\mathcal{BLT}(6)$	$\mathcal{BLT}(4)$
$\mathcal{BLT}(2)$	$\mathcal{BLT}(4) \vee \mathcal{BLT}(4\text{-}5) \vee \mathcal{BLT}(5)$	$\mathcal{BLT}(5)$
$\mathcal{BLT}(3)$	$\mathcal{BLT}(5)$	$\mathcal{BLT}(6)$
$\mathcal{BLT}(4)$	$\mathcal{BLT}(3)$	$\mathcal{BLT}(1)$
$\mathcal{BLT}(5)$	$\mathcal{BLT}(2) \vee \mathcal{BLT}(2\text{-}3) \vee \mathcal{BLT}(3)$	$\mathcal{BLT}(2)$
$\mathcal{BLT}(6)$	$\mathcal{BLT}(1)$	$\mathcal{BLT}(3)$
$\mathcal{BLT}(1\text{-}2)$	$\mathcal{BLT}(5\text{-}6)$	$\mathcal{BLT}(4\text{-}5)$
$\mathcal{BLT}(2\text{-}3)$	$\mathcal{BLT}(4\text{-}5)$	$\mathcal{BLT}(5\text{-}6)$
$\mathcal{BLT}(4\text{-}5)$	$\mathcal{BLT}(2\text{-}3)$	$\mathcal{BLT}(1\text{-}2)$
$\mathcal{BLT}(5\text{-}6)$	$\mathcal{BLT}(1\text{-}2)$	$\mathcal{BLT}(2\text{-}3)$
$\mathcal{BLT}(3\text{-}4)$	$\mathcal{BLT}(2\text{-}5)$	$\mathcal{BLT}(1\text{-}6)$
$\mathcal{BLT}(2\text{-}3\text{-}4\text{-}5)$	$\mathcal{BLT}(2\text{-}3\text{-}4\text{-}5)$	$\mathcal{BLT}(1\text{-}2\text{-}5\text{-}6)$
$\mathcal{BLT}(2\text{-}5)$	$\mathcal{BLT}(3\text{-}4)$	$\mathcal{BLT}(2\text{-}5)$
$\mathcal{BLT}(1\text{-}2\text{-}5\text{-}6)$	every position is possible	$\mathcal{BLT}(2\text{-}3\text{-}4\text{-}5)$
$\mathcal{BLT}(1\text{-}6)$	$\mathcal{BLT}(1\text{-}6)$	$\mathcal{BLT}(3\text{-}4)$

We assume that one is able to retain coarsely the vector $a \to b$ after b has been occluded, at least for a short moment. Thus, when realising c, it can be described with respect to $a \to b$, and this relationship is easier to keep in mind than the single position of b, which gradually diminishes. But later, it is absolutely possible to state where the position of b is with respect to the vector $a \to c$. In this way, Table 1 allows us to deduce the position of b regarding $a \to c$, given c with respect to $a \to b$.

For $\mathcal{BLT}(2)$ and $\mathcal{BLT}(5)$, there exist three possible positions of b with respect to $a \to c$. Hence, these relations are not unambiguously deducible. Consider $\mathcal{BLT}(4)$ and $\mathcal{BLT}(5)$. These two cases are different since the position of b in the former case is doubtlessly $\mathcal{BLT}(3)$. In contrast, the situation is uncertain for $\mathcal{BLT}(5)$ since both positions, $\mathcal{BLT}(2)$ and $\mathcal{BLT}(3)$, are possible. This uncertainty arises because the position in question may be near the transition between $\mathcal{BLT}(2)$ and $\mathcal{BLT}(3)$. For $\mathcal{BLT}(1\text{-}2\text{-}5\text{-}6)$ the situation is highly ambiguous since every position is a possible position for b.

As an example consider again Fig. 15. When the object moves to the right, the position of c with respect to $a \to b$ is $\mathcal{BLT}(5)$. When we rotate Fig. 15 in order to describe b with respect to $a \to c$, we learn that b is somewhere on the left-middle or left front of the vector $a \rightarrow c$, and thus we obtain the relations $\mathcal{BLT}(2)$, $\mathcal{BLT}(2-3)$, and $\mathcal{BLT}(3)$.

It seems inappropriate to rotate the image first in order to describe the position of the occluded part b. This rotation is necessary because c is below a regarding the image plane, and because we want to describe b with respect to $a \rightarrow c$. It would be more appropriate to describe b with respect to $c \rightarrow a$. For such cases, we describe the inverse relation in the rightmost column of Table 1 and we are then able to derive b with respect to $a \rightarrow c$. Freksa and Zimmermann show that in contrast to the first operation the inversion operation always yields precise results. Let us consider how this especially concerns singular positions. We treat singular positions as positions about which uncertainty exists regarding neighbouring general positions. The inverse relations of singular positions correspond to such uncertain positions, too. At this, imprecision and uncertainty must not be confused. The inversion operation is precise in the sense that we do not have any disjunction in the right column of Table 1, i.e. any inverse relation is unambiguously deducible regardless of whether it corresponds to a singular position or a general position.

6   Related Work

There exist a vast amount of quantitative shape descriptions but only a few qualitative approaches. In [2] there is a short overview of some qualitative shape descriptions, and we will only mention those which are mostly related to our own approach.

Closely related to our approach is [10], who describes polygons by considering triangle orientations of vertices. Not restricted to polygons, but also confined to two-dimensional outlines is the approach of [6]. They consider seven different curvature types and propose a grammar for their combination. In contrast, [1] investigates a topological approach for shape descriptions. He distinguishes different concave regions by considering the notion of connection of regions and their convex hulls. [8] shows that $\mathcal{TLT}$s are more expressive than the approach of [10], and further comparisons with other descriptions have to be accomplished.

7   Discussion

Four sets of relations have been presented, namely $\mathcal{BLT}_3$, $\mathcal{BLT}_6$, $\mathcal{TLT}_{12}$, and $\mathcal{TLT}_{36}$. The relationships between these sets have to be investigated more thoroughly. For now, a kind of cooperation between these relations can be reconciled with a strategy of least commitment, which is frequently recommended in vision. This means that any description is only allowed to be as precise as the available conditions allow. Particularly shape descriptions in earlier stages of object recognition should not be over-constrained. Fuzziness and incompleteness require shape descriptions which are, among other things, invariant with respect to orientation. For instance, it may not be clear how single contour parts are oriented with respect to a shape's region, when the region could not be detected because of noisy image data. In this case, an invariant description like $\mathcal{TLT}_{12}$ may be useful, and for less complex shapes, even $\mathcal{BLT}_3$. In contrast, $\mathcal{BLT}_6$ and $\mathcal{TLT}_{36}$ are more appropriate for descriptions in later stages of object recognition. For example, when the distinction between figure and ground is already established, and hence the orientation of any contour part. Cutting matter short, the more knowledge obtained, the more constrained is any description allowed to be.

From the data acquisition point of view, it seems appropriate to deal with polygonal structures like in the present paper. 58% of almost one hundred papers reviewed by [3], apply thinning techniques and polygonal approximations to shapes. Moreover, there exist a lot of algorithms for polygonal approximations and [9] even develops several measures to assess the stability of such algorithms.

Generally speaking, we demonstrated how qualitative spatial reasoning techniques can be adopted for reasoning about shapes. This concerns particularly orientation information applied in the context of navigation. The relationship between navigation and shape is quite obvious since outlines of shapes and trajectories which are related to navigation, are identical from a geometrical point of view. As one can imagine, other spatial reasoning methods may be similarly suitable in order to better manage the complexity of shapes in the future.

References

1. A. G. Cohn. A hierarchical representation of qualitative shape based on connection and convexity. In A. M. Frank and W. Kuhn, editors, *COSIT 1995, Spatial Information Theory*, Lecture Notes in Computer Science, pages 311–326. Springer-Verlag, 1995.
2. A. G. Cohn and S. M. Hazarika. Qualitative spatial representation and reasoning: An overview. *Fundamenta Informaticae*, 43:2–32, 2001.
3. L. P. Cordella and M. Vento. Symbol recognition in documents: a collection of techniques? *International Journal on Document Analysis and Recognition*, 3:73–88, 2000.
4. C. Freksa. Temporal reasoning based on semi-intervals. *Artificial Intelligence*, 94:199–227, 1992.
5. C. Freksa and K. Zimmermann. On the utilization of spatial structures for cognitively plausible and efficient reasoning. In *IEEE International Conference on Systems, Man and Cybernetics*, Chicago, 1992.
6. A. Galton and R. C. Meathrel. Qualitative outline theory. In *IJCAI-99*, pages 1061–1066, Stockholm, Sweden, 1999.
7. B. Gottfried. Tripartite Line Tracks. In K. Wojciechowski, editor, *International Conference on Computer Vision and Graphics*, pages 288–293, Zakopane, 2002.
8. B. Gottfried. Tripartite Line Tracks, Qualitative Curvature Information. In W. Kuhn, M. Worboys, and S. Timpf, editors, *COSIT 2003, Spatial Information Theory*, Lecture Notes in Computer Science. Springer-Verlag, 2003.
9. P. L. Rosin. Assessing the behaviour of polygonal approximation algorithms. *Pattern Recognition*, 36:505–518, 2003.
10. C. Schlieder. Qualitative shape representation. In P. Burrough and A. M. Frank, editors, *Geographic objects with indeterminate boundaries*, pages 123–140, London, 1996. Taylor & Francis.

Consistent 3D Model Construction with Autonomous Mobile Robots

Andreas Nüchter, Hartmut Surmann, Kai Lingemann, and Joachim Hertzberg

Fraunhofer Institute for Autonomous Intelligent Systems (AIS)
Schloss Birlinghoven, D-53754 Sankt Augustin, Germany
{nuechter|surmann|lingemann|hertzberg}@ais.fraunhofer.de

Abstract. Digital 3D models of the environment are needed in facility management, architecture, rescue and inspection robotics. To create 3D volumetric models of scenes, rooms or buildings, it is necessary to gage several 3D scans and to merge them into one consistent 3D model. This paper presents a system, composed of a fast and robust, autonomous mobile robot, a precise, cost effective, high quality 3D laser scanner, and reliable scan matching algorithms for measuring and reconstructing environments, capable of matching two 3D scans within a fraction of a second.

The proposed new software modules for scan matching are fast variants of the iterative closest point algorithm (ICP) for consistent alignment. Two applications are presented: First, the reconstruction of an office environment, second, the fitting of sewer pipes into 3D data to detect deviations from the spatial geometry.

1 Introduction

3D digitalization of environments without occlusions requires multiple 3D scans. Autonomous mobile robots equipped with a 3D laser range finder are well suited for gaging the 3D data. Due to odometry errors, the self localization of the robot is an unprecise measurement and therefore cannot be relied on for registration of the 3D scans in a common coordinate system. The geometric structure of overlapping 3D scans has to be considered. Our approach uses a newly developed, fast version of the well known Iterative Closest Point (ICP) algorithm, a method for aligning three dimensional models purely based on the geometry.

To build complete volumetric models, multiple 3D scans have to be registered. Most published registration methods concentrate on pairwise alignment of two 3D scans. Pulli concludes that extending these pairwise methods for a multiview case has proven not to be straightforward, since simply chaining pairwise registration over all scans seldom works [13]. The goal of the work presented here is to develop a method that does work. To acquire the multiple 3D scans a robot equipped with the AIS 3D laser range finder explores the world and creates reliably a precise and consistent 3D volumetric representation, in real-time.

Instead of using 3D scanners, which yield consistent 3D scans in the first place, some groups have attempted to build 3D volumetric representations of

A. Günter et al. (Eds.): KI 2003, LNAI 2821, pp. 550–564, 2003.

environments with 2D laser range finders. Thrun et al. [10,21], Früh et al. [8] and Zhao et al. [23] use two 2D laser range finder for acquiring 3D data. One laser scanner is mounted horizontally, the other vertically. The latter one grabs a vertical scan line which is transformed into 3D points using the current robot pose. Since the vertical scanner is not able to scan sides of objects, Zhao et al. use two additional vertical mounted 2D scanner shifted by 45° to reduce occlusion [23]. The horizontal scanner is used to compute the robot pose. The precision of 3D data points depends on that pose and on the precision of the scanner.

A few other groups use 3D laser scanners [16,1]. The RESOLV project aimed at modeling interiors for virtual reality and tele-presence [16]. They used a RIEGL laser range finder on robots and the ICP algorithm for scan matching [4, 6,22]. The AVENUE project develops a robot for modeling urban environments [1], using a CYRAX laser scanner and a feature-based scan matching approach for registration of the 3D scans in a common coordinate system [18]. The research group of M. Hebert has reconstructed environments using the Zoller+Fröhlich laser scanner and aims to build 3D models without initial position estimates, i.e., without odometry information [11].

The paper is organized as follows. Sections 2 and 3 describe the used 3D laser range finder and the mobile robots. Section 4 presents the scan matching, followed by the application of matching sewer pipes in section 5. Section 6 concludes.

2   The AIS 3D Laser Range Finder

The AIS 3D laser range finder (Fig. 1) [19] is built on the basis of a 2D range finder by extension with a mount and a small servomotor. The 2D laser range finder is attached in the center of rotation to the mount for achieving a controlled pitch motion. A standard servo is connected on the left side (Fig. 1) and is controlled by the computer running RT-Linux, a real-time operating system which runs LINUX as a task with lowest priority [19,20]. The 3D laser scanner operates up to 5h (Scanner: 17 W, 20 NiMH cells with a capacity of 4500 mAh, Servo: 0.85 W, 4.5 V with batteries of 4500 mAh) per battery pack.

The area of 180°(h) × 120°(v) is scanned with different horizontal (181, 361, 721) and vertical (128, 256) resolutions. A plane with 181 data points is scanned in 13 ms by the 2D laser range finder (rotating mirror device). Planes with more data points, e.g., 361, 721, duplicate or quadruplicate this time. Thus a scan with 181 × 256 data points needs 3.4 seconds. In addition to the distance measurement the 3D laser range finder is capable of quantifying the amount of light returning to the scanner. Fig. 2 (top row) shows an example of a reflectance image of the GMD-Robobench, a standard office environment for the evaluation of autonomous robots. The left image gives an distorted view of the scene: One scan line of the figure corresponds to a slice of the 2D scanner, the rotation of the scanner is not considered. The right image shows the scene with the distortions corrected.

Fig. 1. The AIS 3D laser range finder. Its technical basis is a SICK 2D laser range finder (LMS-200).

The basis of the scan matching are algorithms for reducing points and detecting lines. Next we give a brief description of these algorithms. Details can be found in [19,20].

The scanner emits the laser beams in a spherical way, such that the data points close to the source are more dense. The first step is to reduce the data. Therefore, data points located close together are joined into one point. The number of these *reduced points* is one order of magnitude smaller than before (Fig. 6 (right)). Furthermore noise within the data is reduced [20].

Second a simple length comparison is used as a line detection algorithm. Given that the anticlockwise ordered data of the laser range finder (points $a_0, a_1, \ldots, a_n$) are located on a line, then for a_{j+1} the algorithm has to check if $\|a_i, a_{j+1}\| \,/\, \sum_{t=i}^{j} \|a_t, a_{t+1}\| < \epsilon(j)$ to determine if a_{j+1} is on line with a_j.

3   The Autonomous Mobile Robots

The Ariadne Robot. (Fig. 3, left) is based on a commercial DTV and is about 80 cm × 60 cm large and 90 cm high. The mobile platform can carry a payload of 200 kg at speeds of up to 0.8 m/s (about half the speed of a pedestrian). The right and left driving wheels are mounted on a suspension on the center line of the mobile platform. Passive castors on each corner of the chassis ensure stability. The core of the robot is a Pentium-III-800 MHz with 384 MB RAM and real-time Linux. One embedded PC-104 system is used to control the motor, internal display and numerical keyboard and radio link of the robot. The platform is

Fig. 2. Two persons standing in a corridor of an office building (GMD Robobench). Top left: Reflectance image (distorted). Top right: Corrected reflectance image with distant points clipped. Bottom left: All points. Bottom right: Result of line detection with orientation.

rigged with two 2D safety laser scanners as bumper substitutes, one on the front and the other on the rear of the robot. Each laser scans a horizontal plane of 180° of the environment. The robot has a weight of 250 kg and operates for about 8 hours with one battery charge.

KURT2. (Fig. 3, left) is a mobile robot platform with a size of 45 cm (length) × 33 cm (width) × 26 cm (hight) and a weight of 15.6 kg. Equipped with the 3D laser range finder the height increases to 47 cm and weight increases to 22.6 kg. KURT2's maximum velocity is 5.2 m/s (autonomously controlled 4.0 m/s). Two 90W motors are used to power the 6 wheels, whereas the front and rear wheels have no tread pattern to enhance rotating. KURT2 operates for about

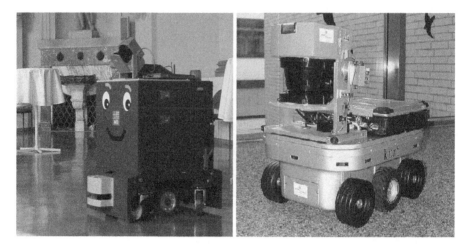

Fig. 3. Left: The Ariadne robot platform. Right: KURT2. Both systems can be equipped with the the AIS 3D laser range finder.

4 hours with one battery (28 NiMH cells, capacity: 4500 mAh) charge. The core of the robot is a Pentium-III-600 MHz with 384 MB RAM and real-time Linux. An embedded 16-Bit CMOS microcontroller is used to control the motor.

4   Range Image Registration

Multiple 3D scans are necessary to digitalize environments without occlusions. To create a correct and consistent model, the scans have to be merged into one coordinate system. This process is called registration. If the localization of the robot with the 3D scanner were precise, the registration could be done directly by the robot pose. However, due to the unprecise robot sensors, the self localization is erroneous, so the geometric structure of overlapping 3D scans has to be considered for registration.

Scan matching approaches can be classified into two categories:

Matching as an optimization problem uses a cost function for the quality of the alignment of the scans. The range images are registered by determining the rigid transformation (rotation and translation) which minimizes the cost function.

Feature based matching extracts distinguishing features of the range images and uses corresponding features for calculating the alignment of the scans.

The matching of 3D scans can either operate on the whole three-dimensional scan point set or can be reduced to the problem of scan matching in 2D by extracting, e.g., a horizontal plane of fixed height from both scans, merging these 2D scans and applying the resulting translation and rotation matrix to all points of the corresponding 3D scan.

Matching of complete 3D scans has the advantage of having a larger set of attributes (either pure data points or extracted features) to compare the scans. This results in higher precision and lowers the possibility of running into a local minimum of the cost function. Furthermore, using three dimensions enables the robot control software to recognize and take into account changes of height and roll, yaw and pitch angles of the robot. This is essential for robots driving cross country and in pipes.

4.1 Matching as an Optimization Problem

The following method for registration of point sets is part of many publications, so only a short summary is given here. The complete algorithm was invented in 1991 and can be found, e.g., in [4,6,22]. The method is called *Iterative Closest Points (ICP) algorithm*.

Given two independently acquired sets of 3D points, M (model set, $|M| = N_m$) and D (data set, $|D| = N_d$) which correspond to a single shape, we want to find the transformation consisting of a rotation $\mathbf{R}$ and a translation $\mathbf{t}$ which minimizes the following cost function:

$$E(\mathbf{R}, \mathbf{t}) = \sum_{i=1}^{N_m} \sum_{j=1}^{N_d} w_{i,j} \left\| \mathbf{m}_i - (\mathbf{R}\mathbf{d}_j + \mathbf{t}) \right\|^2. \tag{1}$$

$w_{i,j}$ is assigned 1 if the i-th point of M describes the same point in space as the j-th point of D. Otherwise $w_{i,j}$ is 0. Two things have to be calculated: First, the corresponding points, and second, the transformation $(\mathbf{R}, \mathbf{t})$ that minimize $E(\mathbf{R}, \mathbf{t})$ on the base of the corresponding points.

The ICP algorithm calculates iteratively the point correspondences. In each iteration step, the algorithm selects the closest points as correspondences and calculates the transformation $(\mathbf{R}, \mathbf{t})$ for minimizing equation (1). Besl et al. proves that the method terminates in a minimum [4]. The assumption is that in the last iteration step the point correspondences are correct.

In each iteration, the transformation is calculated by the quaternion-based method of Horn [12]. A unit quaternion is a 4 vector $\dot{q} = (q_0, q_x, q_y, q_z)^T$, where $q_0 \geq 0, q_0^2 + q_x^2 + q_y^2 + q_z^2 = 1$. It describes a rotation axis and an angle to rotate around that axis. A 3×3 rotation matrix $\mathbf{R}$ is calculated from the unit quaternion according the the following scheme:

$$\mathbf{R} = \begin{pmatrix} (q_0^2 + q_x^2 - q_y^2 - q_z^2) & 2(q_x q_y + q_z q_0) & 2(q_x q_z + q_y q_0) \\ 2(q_x q_y + q_z q_0) & (q_0^2 - q_x^2 + q_y^2 - q_z^2) & 2(q_y q_z - q_x q_0) \\ 2(q_z q_x - q_y q_0) & 2(q_z q_y + q_x q_0) & (q_0^2 - q_x^2 - q_y^2 + q_z^2) \end{pmatrix}.$$

To determine the transformation, the mean values (centroid vectors) $\mathbf{c}_m$ and $\mathbf{c}_d$ are subtracted from all points in M and D, respectively, resulting in the sets M' and D'. The rotation expressed as quaternion that minimizes equation (1) is the largest eigenvalue of the cross-covariance matrix

$$N = \begin{pmatrix} (S_{xx} + S_{yy} + S_{zz}) & (S_{yz} + S_{zy}) & (S_{zx} + S_{xz}) & (S_{xy} + S_{yx}) \\ (S_{yz} + S_{zy}) & (S_{xx} - S_{yy} - S_{zz}) & (S_{xy} + S_{yx}) & (S_{zx} + S_{xz}) \\ (S_{zx} + S_{xz}) & (S_{xy} + S_{yx}) & (-S_{xx} + S_{yy} - S_{zz}) & (S_{yz} + S_{zy}) \\ (S_{xy} + S_{yx}) & (S_{yz} + S_{zy}) & (S_{zx} + S_{xz}) & (-S_{xx} - S_{yy} + S_{zz}) \end{pmatrix},$$

with $S_{\alpha\beta} := \sum_{i=1}^{N_m} \sum_{j=1}^{N_d} w_{i,j} m'_{i\alpha} d'_{j\beta}$. After the calculation of the rotation $\mathbf{R}$, the translation is $\mathbf{t} = \mathbf{c}_m - \mathbf{R}\mathbf{c}_d$ [12]. Fig. 4 shows three steps of the ICP algorithm in registering two 3D scans in our GMD Robobench environment[1].

The time complexity of the algorithm mainly depends on determination of the closest points (brute force search $O(n^2)$ for 3D scans of n points). Several enhancements have been proposed [4,17]. We have implemented kd-trees as proposed by Simon et al., combined with the above-described *reduced points*. Table 1 summarizes the results of different experiments on a Pentium-III-800. The starting point for optimization is given by the robot odometry.

Table 1. Computing time of the different 3D scan matching implementations for two scans of the GMD Robobench (Fig. 4). The number of all points is 46336 (181 × 256) and the number of the *reduced points* is 4910.

points used	time	# iter.
all points & brute force	3 hours 47 min	27
reduced points & brute force	3 min 6 sec	25
all points & kD–tree	6 sec	27
reduced points & kD–tree	<1.4 sec	25

4.2 Matching Multiple 3D Scans

To digitalize environments without occlusions, multiple 3D scans have to be registered. After registration, the scene has to be globally consistent. A straightforward method for aligning several 3D scans is *pairwise matching*, i.e., the new scan is registered against the scan with the largest overlapping areas. The latter one is determined in a preprocessing step. Alternatively, Chen and Medioni [6] introduced an *incremental matching* method, i.e., the new scan is registered against a so-called *metascan*, which is the union of the previously acquired and registered scans. Each scan matching has a limited precision. Both methods accumulate the registration errors such that the registration of many scans leads to inconsistent scenes (Fig. 5) and to problems with the robot localization.

Pulli presents a registration method that minimizes the global error and avoids inconsistent scenes [13]. This method distributes the global error while the registration of one scan is followed by registration of all neighboring scans. Other matching approaches with global error minimization have been published, e.g., by Benjemaa et. al. [2] and Eggert et. al. [7].

---

[1] For an animation of this result please refer to the following website:
http://www.ais.fhg.de/ARC/3D/videos.

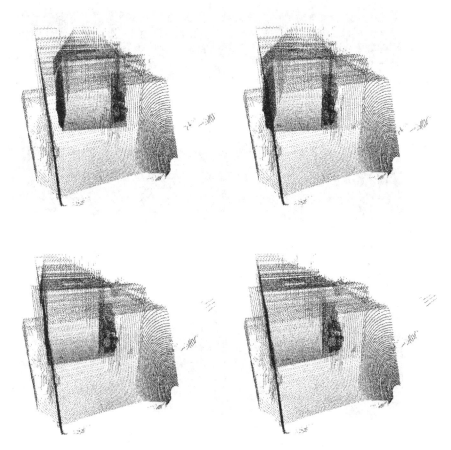

Fig. 4. Registration of two 3D-scans of an office environment with the ICP algorithm. Top left: Initial alignment based on odometry. Top right: Alignment after 2 iterations. Bottom left: after 5 iterations. Bottom right: Final alignment after 25 iterations. The scans correspond to Fig. 2. The number of sampled 3D points is 46336 per 3D scan and the number of *reduced points* is 4910.

Based on the idea of Pulli we have designed a method called *simultaneous matching*. Here, the first scan is the masterscan and determines the coordinate system. This scan is fixed. The following steps register all scans and minimize the global error:

1. Based on the robot odometry, pairwise matching is used to find a start registration for each new scan. This step speeds up computation.
2. A queue is initialized with the new scan.
3. Three steps are repeated until the queue is empty:

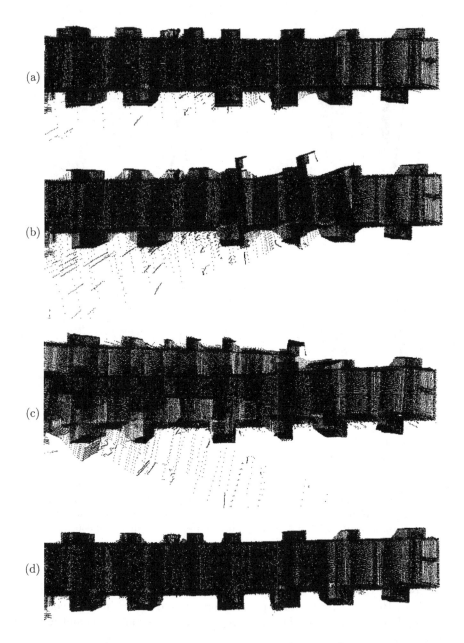

Fig. 5. Results of the scan matching of 20 scans (top view). All 3D scans were taken in an office environment, the GMD Robobench, the first one corresponds to Fig. 2. (a) Pairwise matching, (b) incremental matching, (c) 3D scan matching with edge points and (d) simultaneous matching. 3D animations can be found at http://www.ais.fhg.de/ARC/3D/videos.

a) The current scan is the first scan of the queue. This scan is removed from the queue.
b) If the current scan is not the master scan, then a set of neighbors (set of all scans that overlap with the current scan) is calculated. This set of neighbors form one point set M. The current scan forms the data point set D and is aligned with the ICP algorithm.
c) If the current scan changes its location by applying the transformation, then each single scan of the set of neighbors that is not in the queue, is added to the end of the queue.

Note: One scan overlaps with another, iff more than 250 corresponding point pairs exist. To speed up the matching, kD trees and *reduced points* are used (see Table 1).

In contrast to Pulli's approach, the proposed method is totally automatic and no interactive pairwise alignment needs to be done. Furthermore the point pairs are not fixed [13]. Fig. 5 shows results of the scan matching using 20 scans taken in the GMD Robobench. Pairwise matching (a) works sufficient, incremental matching shows most outliers (b), and simultaneous matching (d) reconstructs the corridor perfectly.

4.3 Feature Based Matching

Sappa et al. suggest to extract edge points and use them for the creating point pairs [15]. Based on our line representation of the scene (Fig. 2, bottom right) the end points of every line are used to create an edge base representation. Fig. 6 (left) shows an edge-based representation in comparison with the *reduced points* (right). Fig. 5 (c) shows the result of the registration process with the edge points (pairwise matching). The registration speed is good due to the lower number of points. Unfortunately, the matching results are insufficient for office environments, because of the simple structure of the scanned scene. The office environment (corridors) mainly consists of floor, ceiling and walls.

4.4 Scanning in Dynamic Environments

Dynamic objects lead to errors in the resulting 3D volumetric model with artefacts or misalignments. Misalignments result in an incorrect self localization of the mobile robot. To eliminate these errors, the robot monitors the environment with its other sensors, e.g., the horizonal mounted 2D laser range finders or cameras. If the sensors detect dynamic objects with the method of the differential frames, the robot simply repeats the 3D scan. Data points belonging to dynamic objects are not yet isolated and removed.

5 Mapping Shapes with Scan Matching

Another application of the ICP algorithm is the mapping of arbitrary shapes into a scanned scene. For a given shape, the model set M is computed by calculating

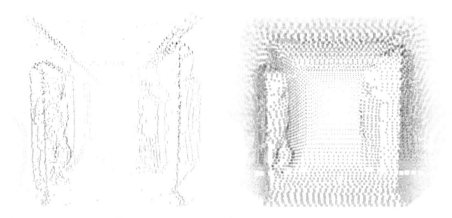

Fig. 6. Left: The scanned scene of the GMD Robobench (see Fig. 2) in an edge based representation using the simple line detection routine. Right: 4910 *reduced points* (enlarged).

the closest points from an abstract description of the shape, e.g., a plane for mapping a wall, or a cuboid for mapping an office cubicle. Similar to minimizing the total error between two sets of points, the selected shape is being transformed (rotated & translated) in order to match it into the given scene.

5.1 Matching Sewerage Pipes

Inspecting communal sewer systems is a potential application for mobile robots[3,14]. Two basic problems of such inspection robots are self localization and the reconstruction of the sewerage pipe system. These problems are addressed in this section. Similar to matching sewerage pipes is the problem of mapping cylinders in 3D data, which is well known in the reconstruction of industrial environments with pipes and tubes [5]. State of the art is semi-automatic reconstruction [9].

For matching tubes into scanned pipes, the closest point on the pipe surface is calculated as follows: Given a scan point $\mathbf{x} \in \mathbb{R}^3$ and a pipe, described by two points $\mathbf{a}$ and $\mathbf{b}$ ($\mathbf{a}, \mathbf{b} \in \mathbb{R}^3$) and the radius r (Fig. 7), the closest point $\mathbf{c}$ to $\mathbf{x}$ on the pipe surface is

$$\mathbf{n} = \frac{\mathbf{a} - \mathbf{b}}{\|\mathbf{a} - \mathbf{b}\|} , \qquad s = \frac{< \mathbf{x} - \mathbf{a}, \mathbf{n} >}{< \mathbf{n}, \mathbf{n} >} \qquad (2)$$

$$\mathbf{c} = s \cdot \mathbf{n} + r \cdot \frac{\mathbf{x} - s \cdot \mathbf{n}}{\|\mathbf{x} - s \cdot \mathbf{n}\|} \qquad (3)$$

with $\mathbf{n}$ the norm vector between $\mathbf{a}$ and $\mathbf{b}$ and s the projection of $\mathbf{x}$ to $\mathbf{n}$.

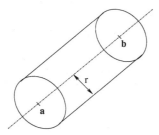

Fig. 7. A sewerage pipe is modeled by two points **a** and **b** and the radius r.

The following steps match pipes with the pipe model:

1. A default tube is inserted into the 3D scan to initialize the matching (Fig. 8 top left).
2. An optimal rotation and translation matrix is calculated with the ICP algorithm (Fig. 8 top right).
3. The radius of the tube is gradually enlarged or reduced until the tube matches the 3D points, i.e., until the error function of the ICP algorithm is minimal (Fig. 8 bottom).

At the beginning, the last two steps are iterated with a reduced number of points to rapidly calculate the transformations. Finally the matching is refined with all points. The result is given in Fig. 8 and 9.[2]

With the proposed matching, a pipe is reconstructed. Due to the exact matching of the tube and the high precision of the scanner, deviations and abnormalities like pipe deformations are also detected. Furthermore obstacles, e.g., a brick as given in the middle picture of Fig. 9 are found. The self localization of the robot is improved, because the transformations calculated by the matching process is applied inversely to the robot pose.

6 Conclusions

3D digitalization of environments without occlusions requires multiple 3D scans. This paper has presented a system, composed of an autonomous mobile robot, a 3D laser scanner, and scan matching algorithms for measuring and reconstructing of environments. Basic scan matching algorithms based on the ICP algorithm have been accelerated and extended to consistent multiview scan registration. A sophisticated reduction of scan points enables to maintain soft real time constraints in 3D scan matching. Multiview registration (simultaneous matching) based on the mutually alignment of a 3D scan with its neighbors generate overall consistent scenes.

---

[2] For an animation of the matching process please visit:
http://www.ais.fhg.de/ARC/3D/tube.gif.

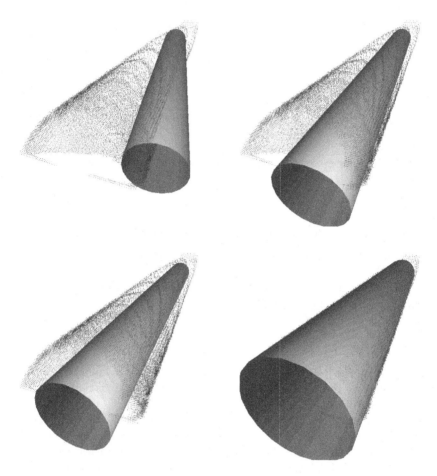

Fig. 8. Matching of a tube into a scanned sewerage pipe (first the tube is being rotated & translated into the correct position, then the size is being adapted)

Several applications, namely, the 3D reconstruction and modeling, deviation and deformation detection and 3D obstacle detection, have been presented. The algorithms have been tested in two different environments, i.e., in indoor, office environments and sewerage pipes. Further applications, e.g., deformation detection in sewer pipes have to be tested. An additional advantage of the proposed systems is that the AIS 3D laser range finder measures actively distances and reflections. Vision-based approaches for sewerage pipes need additional power consuming light sources.

Future work will concentrate on more experiments in sewerage pipes, on scene interpretation, view point planning and on sensor fusion with camera images for office environments.

Fig. 9. Distances between scanned points and ideal tube. Left: A tube with point-to-tube vectors and *without* adjusted radius. Middle: Fully processed tube with an obstacle (a brick). Right: KURT2 inside of a test sewer network.

References

1. P. Allen, I. Stamos, A. Gueorguiev, E. Gold, and P. Blaer. AVENUE: Automated Site Modelling in Urban Environments. In *Proceedings of the Third International Conference on 3D Digital Imaging and Modeling (3DIM '01)*, Quebec City, Canada, May 2001.
2. R. Benjemaa and F. Schmitt. Fast Global Registration of 3D Sampled Surfaces Using a Multi-Z-Buffer Technique. In *Proceedings IEEE International Conference on Recent Advances in 3D Digital Imaging and Modeling (3DIM '97)*, Ottawa, Canada, May 1997.
3. K. Berns, Th. Christaller, R. Dillmann, J. Hertzberg, W. Ilg, M. Kemmann, E. Rome, and H. Stapelfeldt. LAOKOON – lernfähige autonome kooperierende Kanalroboter. *KI*, 11(2):28–32, 1997.
4. P. Besl and N. McKay. A method for Registration of 3–D Shapes. *IEEE Transactions on Pattern Analysis and Machine Intelligence*, 14(2):239–256, February 1992.
5. Th. Chaperon and F. Goulette. Extracting Cylinders in Full 3-D Data Using a Random Sampling Method and the Gaussian Image. In *Proceedings of the of the 6th International Fall Workshop Vision, Modeling, and Visualization (VMV '01)*, Stuttgart, Germany, November 2001.
6. Y. Chen and G. Medoni. Object Modelling by Registration of Multiple Range Images. In *Proceedings of the IEEE Conferenc on Robotics and Automation (ICRA '91)*, pages 2724–2729, Sacramento, CA, USA, April 1991.
7. D. Eggert, A. Fitzgibbon, and R. Fisher. Simultaneous Registration of Multiple Range Views Satisfying Global Consistency Constraints for Use In Reverse Engineering. *Computer Vision and Image Understanding*, 69:253–272, March 1998.
8. C. Früh and A. Zakhor. 3D Model Generation for Cities Using Aerial Photographs and Ground Level Laser Scans. In *Proceedings of the Computer Vision and Pattern Recognition Conference (CVPR '01)*, Kauai, Hawaii, USA, December 2001.
9. F. Haertl and Chr. Fröhlich. Semi-Automatic 3D CAD Model Generation of As-Built Conditions of Real Environmentsusing a Visual Laser Radar. In *Proceedings of the 10th IEEE International Workshop on Robot-Human Interactive Communication (ROMAN '01)*, Paris, France, September 2001.

10. D. Hähnel, W. Burgard, and S. Thrun. Learning Compact 3D Models of Indoor and Outdoor Environments with a Mobile Robot. In *Proceedings of the fourth European workshop on advanced mobile robots (EUROBOT '01)*, Lund, Sweden, September 2001.

11. M. Hebert, M. Deans, D. Huber, B. Nabbe, and N. Vandapel. Progress in 3–D Mapping and Localization. In *Proceedings of the 9th International Symposium on Intelligent Robotic Systems, (SIRS '01)*, Toulouse, France, July 2001.

12. B. Horn. Closed–form solution of absolute orientation using unit quaternions. *Journal of the Optical Society of America A*, 4(4):629–642, April 1987.

13. K. Pulli. Multiview Registration for Large Data Sets. In *Proceedings of the 2nd International Conference on 3D Digital Imaging and Modeling (3DIM '99)*, pages 160–168, Ottawa, Canada, October 1999.

14. E. Rome, J. Hertzberg, Th. Christaller, F. Kirchner, and U. Licht. Towards Autonomous Sewer Robots: The MAKRO Project. *Journal Urban Water*, 1:57–70, 1999.

15. A. Sappa, A. Restrepo-Specht, and M. Devy. Range Image Registration by using an Edge–based Representation. In *Proceedings of th 9th International Symposium on Intelligent Robotic Systems, (SIRS '01)*, Toulouse, France, July 2001.

16. V. Sequeira, K. Ng, E. Wolfart, J. Goncalves, and D. Hogg. Automated 3D reconstruction of interiors with multiple scan–views. In *Proceedings of SPIE, Electronic Imaging '99, The Society for Imaging Science and Technology /SPIE's 11th Annual Symposium*, San Jose, CA, USA, January 1999.

17. D. Simon, M. Hebert, and T. Kanade. Real–time 3–D pose estimation using a high–speed range sensor. In *Proceedings of IEEE International Conference on Robotics and Automation (ICRA '94)*, volume 3, pages 2235–2241, San Diego, CA, USA, May 1994.

18. I. Stamos and P. Allen. 3-D Model Construction Using Range and Image Data. In *Proceedings of the Conference on Computer Vision and Pattern Recognition (CVPR '00)*, USA, June 2000.

19. H. Surmann, K. Lingemann, A. Nüchter, and J. Hertzberg. A 3D laser range finder for autonomous mobile robots. In *Proceedings of the of the 32nd International Symposium on Robotics (ISR '01)*, pages 153–158, Seoul, Korea, April 2001.

20. H. Surmann, K. Lingemann, A. Nüchter, and J. Hertzberg. Fast acquiring and analysis of three dimensional laser range data. In *Proceedings of the of the 6th International Fall Workshop Vision, Modeling, and Visualization (VMV '01)*, pages 59–66, Stuttgart, Germany, November 2001.

21. S. Thrun, D. Fox, and W. Burgard. A real-time algorithm for mobile robot mapping with application to multi robot and 3D mapping. In *Proceedings of the IEEE International Conference on Robotics and Automation (ICRA '00)*, San Francisco, CA, USA, April 2000.

22. Z. Zhang. Iterative point matching for registration of free–form curves. Technical Report RR-1658, INRIA–Sophia Antipolis, Valbonne Cedex, France, 1992.

23. H. Zhao and R. Shibasaki. Reconstructing Textured CAD Model of Urban Environment Using Vehicle-Borne Laser Range Scanners and Line Cameras. In *Second International Workshop on Computer Vision System (ICVS '01)*, pages 284–295, Vancouver, Canada, July 2001.

Who Can Connect in RCC?

Mehmet Giritli

Arbeitsgruppe Grundlagen der Künstlichen Intelligenz
Institut für Informatik, Albert-Ludwigs-Universität
Georges-Köhler-Allee Geb. 52, 79110 Freiburg, Deutschland
`mgiritli@informatik.uni-freiburg.de`

Abstract. We provide a method for integrating de Laguna's geometry of solids into the region connection calculus (RCC). de Laguna's geometry of solids is concerned with solid-based (rather than point-based) comparative distance representations using the triadic primitive relation "can-connect". No formalization is given to the theory in the original version by de Laguna and his work is mainly in the form of a philosophical text. Our main contribution with this work is to give a formalization for de Laguna's theory within the framework of RCC. Although de Laguna's notions from the original version are kept intact, some modifications are made as the embedding procedure requires. Furthermore, we make use of the combined strength of the resulting theory to add representations into our formalism which can characterize notions of boundedness/unboundedness and finiteness/infiniteness.

1 Introduction

Qualitative spatial reasoning (QSR) can be described as the method of efficiently reasoning about physical space by omitting the out-of-context information [1,2]. Qualitative abstraction is necessary for our understanding and reasoning of the physical space since a purely quantitative representation of space can not be adequately representative. Spatial reasoning that occurs in our every day life is mostly based on qualitative abstractions, making QSR a promising field of research. QSR has impressively developed in last ten years by researchers in the fields ranging from geography to computer science. Specific improvements have been achieved in topological aspects of the theory as the region connection calculus (RCC) developed, attracting most of the attention [3,4]. Other aspects of QSR like distance and orientation have also received remarkable attention [1, 2,5,6,7].

Mathematics has developed several geometries which contribute to the science of spatial measurement. But when it comes to computer science, it is very hard to directly import the achievements of mathematics based on set-theoretical concepts. Related problems are not so hard to see: Direct import of mathematical structures give birth to untractable algorithms in computer science. Instead of adapting highly expressive quantitative methods from mathematics, what useful in real applications is a good compromise between expressiveness and efficiency. Fortunately mathematics still has something to offer to us: Topology.

A. Günter et al. (Eds.): KI 2003, LNAI 2821, pp. 565–579, 2003.

On the other hand, since most of the mathematical structures are based on the abstract entity of "point", besides the issue of computational costs some philosophical dilemmas arise when it comes to modelling the physical space. In the mathematical sense, point is a dimensionless fundamental entity which has location but no magnitude. Points do not exist in our surrounding physical space and nobody has ever perceived one. In this case, should we take points as a fundamental entity in QSR, a science that aims to model our physical surrounding space?

Summing it all up, what we get is the topologically oriented and region-based spatial theories in computer science. We will be particularly interested in the RCC calculus [8,9,10] and de Laguna's geometry of physical solids [11,12, 13].

RCC is a topologically oriented calculus based on the "connection" primitive C and the basic ontological entity of "region". Under a topological interpretation that can be attached to C, $C(x, y)$ holds true whenever the regions x and y share a common point. A number of relations can be defined using merely C. A special group of eight relations form a jointly exhaustive and pairwise disjoint set of "base relations", called the RCC-8.

Although it has proved to be surprisingly expressive [14,15,16] since RCC-8 is a topologically-oriented calculus, its expressiveness can be unsatisfactory in the situations where there is a need for more detailed distance information [17,1] than RCC supplies with[1]. There have been studies on qualitative distance [18,5, 6] but these are generally developed distinctly from the RCC. Moreover, most of the available studies about qualitative distance are based on points rather than regions which makes them incompatible to use with the RCC.

In [12] de Laguna constructs a variant of classical metrical geometry based on the ontology of "solids" and the triadic primitive relation of "can-connect", $CC(x, y, z)$[2]. The primitive $CC(x, y, z)$ holds true whenever the solid x can be brought into simultaneous contact with the solids y and z. If $CC(x, y, z)$ holds true and in addition if $\neg CC(x, p, q)$ also holds true then we know that the solids p and q are farther apart from each other than the solids y and z are.

Although we are interested in region-based theories and not point-based, there are some well regarded profits that one can have by admitting such an ontological entity. In de Laguna's original work, points are defined in the theory as special-case solids: A solid whose length is equal to the distance between two other solids which are in contact exists, and it is called a point.

Besides giving a formalization for de Laguna's geometry of solids, we also characterize the notions of boundedness/unboundedness and finite-

---

[1] RCC can supply very basic distance information: One can take the distance between two regions to be null iff they are connected.

[2] The variation in the vocabulary used separately for RCC and de Laguna's theory should not confuse the reader. We will regard de Laguna's "solids" and RCC's "regions" as the same ontological primitive. Moreover, the meaning of "connection" between regions in RCC is equivalent to the meaning of "contact" between solids in de Laguna's system.

ness/infiniteness in this formalism. These concepts have not been seriously addressed in the spatial reasoning literature that I know of. [19] refers to the problem of a lacking axiomatization for the characterization of bounded and unbounded regions (in particular about the universe which itself is a region) for RCC and its importance.

Boundedness can not be defined or characterized using purely topological tools and it requires some sort of an underlying metric for its definition unless we are going to introduce it as a primitive. Therefore, two regions one of which is bounded and the other is not, can be topologically equivalent! Topology can not detect boundedness. de Laguna's system will be used to achieve exactly this.

The structure of the rest of paper is as follows: Sections two and three are the overviews of the RCC theory and de Laguna's geometry of solids respectively. Section four is dedicated to the technical formalization steps of de Laguna's theory within the framework of RCC theory. In section five, we show how to represent points in the new theory and later in section six we give a characterization for the notions of boundedness/unboundedness and finiteness/infiniteness. Finally, in section seven we give the conclusion and summarize the achievements.

2   The Region Connection Calculus

RCC is originally developed upon Clarke's calculus of individuals based on connection [20]. RCC's formalism is based on the many sorted logic of LLAMA [21] which details fall far outside the scope of this paper. Nevertheless, the fundamental primitive sorts of the theory that we will be explicitly referring are REGION and NULL. While the sort REGION refers to the primitive ontology of the theory, the necessity for the sort NULL is explained in the forthcoming paragraphs of this section.

We use the usual font in uppercase when mentioning the sorts (eg. REGION), where as the variables for regions are written in lowercase single letters of the italic font (eg. x, y, z). The relations are written in uppercase of the sans font (eg. $\mathsf{NTPP}(x, y)$) and the functions of the theory are written in lowercase of the sans font (eg. $\mathsf{sum}(x, y)$). Finally, we use the symbol $\mathcal{U}$ to represent the universe we are working in, which is assumed to be the two-dimensional plane unless otherwise is stated.

Points are not assumed as an ontological primitive in the RCC theory as it preserves the feature of being based on individuals (i.e. regions), inheriting from Clarke's calculus. Nevertheless, with a point-set topological interpretation that can be attached to regions, a region is a set which is identical to the interior of its closure and also such that its closure is identical to the closure of its interior. That is, regions can be interpreted as regular closed sets.

RCC assumes a single primitive dyadic relation $\mathsf{C}(x, y)$ which is interpreted as holding true whenever the regions x and y share a common point. Then, we say that regions x and y are connected. The relation C is axiomatized to be reflexive and symmetric.

(Cref) $\forall x[C(x,x)]$
(CSym) $\forall xy[C(x,y) \rightarrow C(y,x)]$

By using C, we can derive a useful set of dyadic relations expressing the "type of connection" between two regions: $DC(x,y)$ (x is disconnected from y), $P(x,y)$ (x is a part of y), $PP(x,y)$ (x is a proper part of y), $PO(x,y)$ (x partially overlaps y), $EQ(x,y)$ (x is equal to y), $O(x,y)$ (x overlaps with y), $EC(x,y)$ (x is externally connected with y), $TPP(x,y)$ (x is a tangential proper part of y), $NTPP(x,y)$ (x is a non-tangential proper part of y).

Definitions of the above relations based on C are given below and more can be found in [3,16]:

$$DC(x,y) \equiv_{df} \neg C(x,y)$$
$$P(x,y) \equiv_{df} \forall z[C(z,x) \rightarrow C(z,y)]$$
$$PP(x,y) \equiv_{df} [P(x,y) \wedge \neg P(y,x)]$$
$$EQ(x,y) \equiv_{df} [P(x,y) \wedge P(y,x)]$$
$$O(x,y) \equiv_{df} \exists z[P(z,x) \wedge P(z,y)]$$
$$DR(x,y) \equiv_{df} \neg O(x,y)$$
$$PO(x,y) \equiv_{df} [O(x,y) \wedge \neg P(x,y) \wedge \neg P(y,x)]$$
$$EC(x,y) \equiv_{df} [C(x,y) \wedge \neg O(x,y)]$$
$$TPP(x,y) \equiv_{df} PP(x,y) \wedge \exists z[EC(x,z) \wedge EC(y,z)]$$
$$NTPP(x,y) \equiv_{df} PP(x,y) \wedge \neg \exists z[EC(x,z) \wedge EC(y,z)]$$

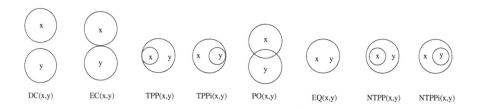

DC(x,y)   EC(x,y)   TPP(x,y)   TPPi(x,y)   PO(x,y)   EQ(x,y)   NTPP(x,y)   NTPPi(x,y)

Fig. 1. RCC-8 base relations

RCC-8 is the set of eight binary relations DC, EQ, EC, PO, TPP, $NTPP$, TPP^{-1}, $NTPP^{-1}$ of RCC which together form a jointly exhaustive and pairwise disjoint set of base relations[3]. This means that, always one and only one of these eight relations must hold between any given two regions. Figure 1 shows the two-dimensional illustration of the RCC-8 base relations.

Apart from the relations defined above, it is also possible to define a set of boolean functions such that we can obtain new regions given the existing ones. In what follows we define: $compl(x)$ (complement of x), $sum(x,y)$ (the sum or

---

[3] The notation $^{-1}$ stands for the converse of a relation. Thus, $TPP^{-1}(x,y) \equiv TPP(y,x)$.

union of x and y), $\mathsf{prod}(x,y)$ (the product or intersection of x and y), $\mathsf{diff}(x,y)$ (the difference of x and y). These functions are made total by introducing a new sort called NULL and also axiomatizing that sorts REGION and NULL are disjoint.

(BFcompl) $\forall xy[[\mathsf{C}(y, \mathsf{compl}(x)) \leftrightarrow \neg\mathsf{NTPP}(y,x)] \wedge [\mathsf{O}(y, \mathsf{compl}(x)) \leftrightarrow \neg\mathsf{P}(y,x)]]$
(BFsum) $\forall xyz[\mathsf{C}(z, \mathsf{sum}(x,y)) \leftrightarrow [\mathsf{C}(z,x) \vee \mathsf{C}(z,y)]]$
(BFprod) $\forall xyz[\mathsf{C}(z, \mathsf{prod}(x,y)) \leftrightarrow \exists w[\mathsf{P}(w,x) \wedge \mathsf{P}(w,y) \wedge \mathsf{C}(z,w)]]$
(BFdiff) $\forall xyz[\mathsf{C}(z, \mathsf{diff}(x,y)) \leftrightarrow [\mathsf{C}(z, \mathsf{compl}(\mathsf{prod}(x,y)))]]$

Finally, a further set of standard axioms for RCC exists [3]. These are the following:

(Univ) $\forall x[\mathsf{C}(x, \mathcal{U})]$,
(Discr) $\forall xy[\mathsf{NULL}(\mathsf{prod}(x,y)) \leftrightarrow \mathsf{DR}(x,y)]$,
(NoAtm) $\forall x \exists y[\mathsf{NTPP}(y,x)]$.

The first axiom stipulates that the universe $\mathcal{U}$ is connected with every region where as second axiom says that if the product of two regions is NULL then these regions are discrete. Finally, in the third axiom it is required that every region has a NTPP, which means that there are no "atomic" regions and every region has infinitely many sub-regions.

In this work, we only consider self-connected regions, the regions that are not divided into a number of DC parts. Such a definition can be easily given in RCC to check whether a given region is self-connected:

$$\mathsf{CON}(x) \equiv_{\mathrm{df}} \forall yz[\mathsf{EQ}(x, \mathsf{sum}(y,z)) \rightarrow \mathsf{C}(y,z)].$$

3   de Laguna's Geometry of Solids

Classical geometry has gone through many stages of development until it reached to its current state as a major mathematical branch. It is without question that the role of the introduction of point as an ontological entity has been the biggest contribution in those stages. Without points, the scientists lacked answers to many questions which are obvious to us in today's geometry. Although geometry owes its well respected current state to points, some scientists have argued that the assumption of an entity which does not exist in physical space is a philosophical mistake. The argument is simple to understand. Point, by its assumed nature, is an entity that has location but no magnitude [11]. It can not be broken into any other sub components and it does not have any. Objects with such properties are not familiar to us in our surrounding physical space. Every object that we know of can be broken into pieces, given that we have the right tools for the type of object. Although it might be very small, even imperceivable by our senses, we know that every object has a certain magnitude.

These questions have urged some scientists to look for geometries which are not based on points but individuals[4]. How would a geometry without points look

---

[4] Different authors have used different terms in the literature which includes: individuals, regions, solids and bodies.

like? In his work of [12], de Laguna constructs a variant of metrical geometry in which the distance relation ranges over "solids" instead of points as it is the case with classical metrical geometry. In his theory, solids are assumed to be rigid bodies and the only primitive ontology.

The notions that he derives from our common-sense conceptions are made to be fundamental to his theory. These notions are primarily *solid* and then *motion, contact* and *simultaneity*. Thus, "Geometry is a science of measurement which involves the observation of occurrence or non-occurrence of simultaneous contact of one solid with two others" [11].

When we observe that a solid is in simultaneous contact with two others at some certain moment in time, we know for sure that the distance between two solids which are in simultaneous contact with a third one, is no greater than the length of the third one. Moreover, if we are unable to bring a third solid in simultaneous contact with two others then we also know that the distance between the two solids must be greater than the length of the third one.

Moving on forward from this point, the principle of measurement is assumed as a fundamental induction. This is the main assumption that de Laguna's theory sits on:

"If the solids A,B,C and D are at rest, and if there is at least one solid X which can be brought into simultaneous contact with A and B, but can not in any way be brought into simultaneous contact with C and D, then there is no solid that can-connect[5] C and D but can not connect A and B."

The above statement can be brought into a more general setting by allowing a "chain of solids" to realize the contact between two solids. One can include any solid into a chain in any number of times and moreover, this can be done in an efficient way by repeatedly using the same solids to construct a chain. A chain may also contain only one solid.

Finally there is the relationship between distance and length that has to be addressed. Distance is a relation between two solids and length is a property of a single solid. These two notions are in an interesting relationship that we shall follow carefully. The question that whether there is a distance for every length and a length for every distance is an important one that we shall attempt to answer in the coming sections.

4   A Formalization of de Laguna's Theory within the RCC Framework

As we noted in Sect. 3, de Laguna's theory sits on the triadic primitive relation can-connect and the basic ontology of solid. As we are integrating his theory into the RCC, the ontology of region will replace de Laguna's solid. As to the can-connect primitive, it is admitted as the second primitive relation into the RCC besides the dyadic primitive C. We call this new primitive $CC(x, y, z)$ and interpret it as follows: $CC(x, y, z)$ holds true iff there is a region or a chain of regions x which can be brought into simultaneous contact with regions y and

---

[5] The term can-connect is the primitive triadic relation that is used in de Laguna's theory. It is to be understood for "being in simultaneous contact with".

z. In de Laguna's system, the first parameter x is also allowed to be a chain of solids for maximum generalization and flexibility. Given that we added this concept into our interpretation of CC, we also add it into our formalization. When we write $CC(x, y, z)$ then it is to be understood that there is one region called x that realize the contact between y and z. On the other hand, we will write $CC([x], y, z)$ to mean that the contact between y and z is realized by a chain of regions called x and we are not interested in what particular regions are included in the chain x. Finally, we will write $CC([a, b, c, ...], y, z)$ to mean that the contact between y and z is realized by a chain of regions which consists of regions $a, b, c, ...$.

Firstly we axiomatize a general property of CC that it is symmetric with respect to the second and the third arguments. That is, if a region x can-connect regions y and z then it also can-connect z and y:

(CCSym) $\forall xyz[CC(x, y, z) \rightarrow CC(x, z, y)]$.

Secondly, there is the principal of measurement that has to be axiomatized. If region x can-connect regions y and z but can not connect v and w, then there is no region which can-connect v and w but not y and z:

(CCPri) $\forall xyzwv[CC(x, y, z) \wedge \neg CC(x, w, v) \rightarrow \neg \exists q[CC(q, w, v) \wedge \neg CC(q, y, z)]]$.

Thirdly there is the link between two primitives C and CC. The question arises whether we can always find a region or chains of regions to connect any given two regions. If two regions are connected then any region can-connect them. Thus,

(CC-C) $\forall xyz[C(y, z) \rightarrow CC(x, y, z)]$.

Let us postpone the case when the same question applies to two disconnected regions until Sect. 6.

Fourthly, we axiomatize that for any region x there can be found two other regions y and z such that x can-connect y and z:

(CCExt) $\forall x \exists yz[DC(y, z) \wedge CC(x, y, z)]$.

Finally, the following two axioms establish the necessary links between parthood relations and distance:

(CC-P) $\forall xy[P(x, y) \wedge REGION(x) \rightarrow \forall zq[CC(x, z, q) \rightarrow CC(y, z, q)]]$,

(CC-PP) $\forall xy[NTPP(x, y) \wedge REGION(x) \rightarrow \exists zq[CC(y, z, q) \wedge \neg CC(x, z, q)]]$.

Now we are ready to give some basic definitions about distances.

The first definition based on the CC primitive is $FAT(x, y, z, w)$ (x and y are farther apart than z and w): If x, y, z and w are regions and also there is a region q such that it can-connect z and w but not x and y then we say that regions x and y are farther apart than regions z and w. Likewise we define $LT(p, q)$ (p is longer than q): A region p is longer than another region q iff there can be found regions z and w such that p can-connect and q can not. Thus,

$$FAT(x, y, z, w) \equiv_{df} \exists q[CC(q, z, w) \land \neg CC(q, x, y)]$$
$$LT(p, q) \equiv_{df} \exists zw[CC(p, z, w) \land \neg CC(q, z, w)]$$

We continue with two other definitions for $JAFA(x, y, z, w)$ (x and y are just as far apart as z and w) and $JALA(p, q)$ (p is just as long as q). Formalization is as follows:

$$JAFA(x, y, z, w) \equiv_{df} \neg FAT(x, y, z, w) \land \neg FAT(z, w, x, y)$$
$$JALA(p, q) \equiv_{df} \neg LT(p, q) \land \neg LT(q, p)$$

For $JAFA$, if x and y are not farther apart than z and w and z and w are not farther apart than x and y then z and w must be just as far apart as x and y. For $JALA$, if neither p is longer than q nor q is longer than p then p is just as long as q.

de Laguna explicitly gives a definition for distance between regions x and y as the set of all pairs of regions which are just as far apart as x and y. He also mentions the possibility to define distance as a property: Distance between x and y is the property of being just as far apart as x and y. Unfortunately neither of de Laguna's options is desirable in our case. Keeping in mind that we have primarily qualitative concerns, we do not really want to know what distance between a pair of regions is but instead we want to know how does the distance between a pair of regions compares to the distance between another pair of regions. Thus, we carry on by defining $DGT(x, y, z, w)$ (distance between x and y is greater than the distance between z and w) and $LGT(p, q)$ (length of p is greater than the length of q). Note that the following two definitions are only a matter of notational harmony with de Laguna's system:

$$DGT(x, y, z, w) \equiv_{df} FAT(x, y, z, w)$$
$$LGT(p, q) \equiv_{df} LT(p, q)$$

The following definitions $DETL(x, y, p)$ (distance between x and y is equal to the length of p), $LETD(x, y, p)$ (length of p is equal to the distance between x and y), $DGTL(x, y, p)$ (distance between x and y is greater than the length of p), $LGTD(x, y, p)$ (length of p is greater than the distance between x and y) establish the necessary links between lengths and distances. The symmetry between the definitions of distance-predicates and the length-predicates continues as before.

$$DETL(x, y, p) \equiv_{df} CC(p, x, y) \land \forall zw[FAT(z, w, x, y) \rightarrow \neg CC(p, z, w)]$$
$$LETD(x, y, p) \equiv_{df} CC(p, x, y) \land \neg \exists q[LT(p, q) \land CC(q, x, y)]$$
$$DGTL(x, y, p) \equiv_{df} \exists zw[DGT(x, y, z, w) \land DETL(z, w, p)]$$
$$LGTD(x, y, p) \equiv_{df} \exists zwq[LGT(p, q) \land LETD(x, y, q)]$$

Some basic theorems that follows in the theory are as follows:

(T1) $\forall xyzw[FAT(x, y, z, w) \rightarrow \neg FAT(z, w, x, y)]$
(T2) $\forall xyzwpq[FAT(x, y, z, w) \land FAT(z, w, p, q) \rightarrow FAT(x, y, p, q)]$
(T3) $\forall xyp[DETL(x, y, p) \rightarrow LETD(x, y, p)]$
(T4) $\forall xyp[LETD(p, x, y) \rightarrow DETL(x, y, p)]$

Next, I demonstrate how to work with the sum of lengths and sum of distances. de Laguna uses a chain of regions to define the sum of two lengths: "The sum of the lengths of x and y is the length of the chain consisting of x and y". With the chain-version of the CC primitive, we can easily adapt de Laguna's method here as well. So the statement "the distance between x and y is greater than the sum of lengths of z and w" can be formalized as: $\neg CC([z,w],x,y)$. Hence, leaving the qualitative nature of our formalism intact.

Now, what can we say about the sum of two distances? There is a conceptual difference between distances and lengths. There are no chains of regions that correspond to the sum of multiple distances as it is the case with lengths. Length is a property of a single region whereas distance is always between two regions. But we know that there is a length which corresponds to the distance between two regions establishing a direct relationship between distances and lengths. Thus, the sum of distances between x and y and between z and w is the sum of lengths that are equal to those distances. Thus, the statement "the sum of the distances between x and y and between y and z is not greater than the length of w" can be formalized as: $\exists pq[DETL(p,x,y) \wedge DETL(q,y,z) \rightarrow LT([p,q],w)]$, where as $LT([p,q],w) \equiv \exists uv[CC([p,q],u,v) \wedge \neg CC(w,u,v)]$.

5 Regions to Points

So far, our work exhibited parallel progress for distances and lengths. Now, the question arises whether there is a length for every distance and a distance for every length. The fruitful discussion which is going to take place in this section will yield a very useful theoretical result: Points. This discussion takes place in de Laguna's work but we will focus more on the formalization of the concepts that take place in that discussion. Moreover, our primary interests lies within the integration process of de Laguna's system in the RCC framework. Now, let us start by asking whether there is a distance for every length.

Given an arbitrary length we ask whether there is a distance that is equal to this length. But the axiom of CCExt refers exactly to this: For every region x (so, for any length), there are regions y and z such that $CC(x,y,z)$. Now, we can always choose y and z such that for any other pair of regions p and q which $FAT(p,q,y,z)$ we have that $\neg CC(x,p,q)$. From here it follows that $DETL(y,z,x)$. That is, the distance between y and z is equal to the length of x. Thus, for every given length an equal distance can be found.

Now the same question applies conversely: For any given distance, is there a length that is equal to this distance? Let x and y be two disconnected regions, $DC(x,y)$. Also, let p be an arbitrary region whose length is not equal to the distance between x and y.

If p is longer than the distance between x and y then we can always divide p into two parts one of which is just as long as the distance between x and y. There is no reason to think otherwise. On the other hand, if p is shorter than the distance between x and y then we can always combine other regions with p to form a chain of regions whose length is equal to the distance between x and y.

Thus, we conclude that for every length there is an equal distance and conversely for every distance subsisting between two disconnected regions, there is an equal length. Now it remains to consider the case whether there is a length corresponding to the distance between two connected regions.

First let us remember this: A region p has a length equal to the distance between x and y iff p can-connect to x and y and for every other region q if $LT(p, q)$ is true then $\neg CC(q, x, y)$ is true.

Let x and y be two regions such that $C(x, y)$ holds true. Now, assume that there is a region p whose length is equal to the distance between the regions x and y. Now, pick a region q such that $LT(p, q)$ (i.e. take one of the NTPPs of p as q). By axiom CC-C it follows that $CC(q, x, y)$ holds. Hence, the length of p is not equal to the distance between x and y; This is a contradiction. Thus, there is no region whose length is equal to the distance between two connected regions.

de Laguna constructs points by abstractly assuming that, regions whose length is equal to the distance between two connected regions exists. In our framework, the axioms of CC-C and CCExt prevents the existence of such a region. To allow such regions, we need to remove the axiom C-CC and the axiom CCExt can be relaxed by the following version of it:

(CCExt') $\forall x \exists yz[CC(x, y, z)]$.

Unfortunately the manipulations above are not adequate to prevent inconsistencies in the calculus. One source of problem is the non-atomic axiom[6].

Conclusively, a more fundamental method is required to introduce points. A number of solutions have been already proposed in [3] regarding such methods in the original version of RCC. With a slight addition, we safely import one of those methods in here as well. A new primitive sort for points is introduced besides the primitive sorts (that we explicitly refer to) NULL and REGION. Let us call the new primitive sort as POINT. Note that in [3] the new sort is referred to as ATOM but I prefer to use the name POINT to preserve the harmony. Given that we assume POINT as a primitive sort its properties are axiomatized as follows:

(PntAx1) $\forall xy[POINT(x) \rightarrow JALA(y, \mathsf{sum}(y, x))]$,
(PntAx2) $\forall xy[POINT(x) \wedge POINT(y) \wedge O(x, y) \rightarrow EQ(x, y)]$,
(PntAx3) $\forall x[POINT(x) \rightarrow \exists y[PARTICLE(y) \wedge PP(y, x)]]$,
(PntAx4) $\forall x[\neg POINT(x) \wedge \neg PARTICLE(x) \rightarrow \exists y[P(y, x) \wedge POINT(y)]]$.

Where as,

$PARTICLE(x) \equiv_{df} \exists y[POINT(y) \wedge PP(x, y)]$.

The first axiom means that the length of a region remains unchanged when a point is summed with it. The second axiom stipulates that two overlapping points must be equal. Third axiom is about the fact that a POINT must contain a PARTICLE. Finally, fourth axiom forces every region to contain a POINT. Hence, any region contains infinitely many points.

---

[6] Also look in [3] for a more detailed discussion of this problem.

Finally, we summarize the benefits of admitting points in the theory:

1. Points, being entities without a magnitude, are useful instruments for negligible distances. This is especially the case when a comparison is made between two objects which the difference in their sizes is so great that the magnitude of the smaller one can be neglected. This simplifies our calculations without any reasonable loss in the result.
2. One major effect of this simplification is that it allows us to have chains of distances just like we have chains of lengths. Thus, we can add distances up like we do with the lengths.

6 Boundedness

In de Laguna's geometry of solids, his entities "solids" are flatly assumed to be bounded. It is also the case with RCC that such an assumption exists with regions. There is no study that I am aware of which tackles this problem. The main aim of this section is to supply RCC with a necessary set of tools such that the difference between bounded and unbounded entities can be characterized.

Before we go any further I give the classical definition of bounded set from mathematics so that the term boundedness has a clear meaning. A set in a metric space (X, d) is bounded if it has a finite generalized diameter, i.e., there is an $r < \infty$ such that $d(x, y) \leq r$ for all $x, y \in X$. A set in $\mathbb{R}^n$ is bounded if it is contained inside some ball $x_1^2 + ... + x_n^2 \leq R^2$ of finite radius R [22].

It is noteworthy to make some comments at this point. RCC is a topologically oriented calculus based on the primitive dyadic relation of $C(x, y)$. On the other hand, boundedness is not an invariant property under topological transformations. This means that a topological set of tools is not sufficient to distinguish between bounded and unbounded objects. Figure 2 demonstrates this failure of topological tools.

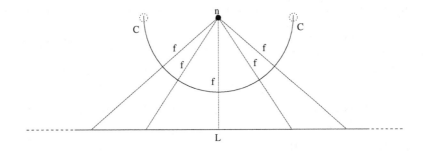

Fig. 2. Topological tools can not distinguish between bounded and unbounded sets.

Figure calls for some comments. First, we recall the definition of a homeomorphism. If a function f is bijective and moreover, if f and f^{-1} are continuous functions, then the function f is called a homeomorphism[7]. The notion of topological homeomorphism is analogous to the notion of isomorphism in algebra. Finally, a topological homeomorphism between two sets entails that these sets are topologically indistinguishable.

Now, if we return to the Fig. 2, the function denoted by f is a homeomorphism between the bounded set of points on a half-circle C and the unbounded set of points on an infinitely long line L. f maps every point x on C to a point y on L where the extension of the line segment connecting points n and x intersects L. Obviously, the function f is a homeomorphism and the sets C and L are homeomorphic to each other, in other words they are topologically indistinguishable despite one set is bounded and the other one is not.

The concept of boundedness requires the existence of some underlying metric in order to define it. So, how can we introduce boundedness into a topological calculus like RCC? As the reader might guess with no surprise, we will use the formalization of de Laguna's theory in RCC.

Before we go deep into the discussion about abstract notions like unbounded regions, we need to fix the meanings underlying such notions. Firstly, nobody has ever perceived an object which has an infinite length or two objects that are infinitely farther apart from each other. But there is one thing that we know for sure: Some objects are so greatly farther apart from each other that we know for certain, we can not travel from one to another. This can happen because it takes an enormous effort to realize it which we can not deliver. Therefore, for us there is not much difference between the abstract definition of infinite distance and a very long distance which we can not handle. Hence, both kind of distances are inaccessible for us.

Firstly, assume that there are two regions x and y and that there is no region which can be brought into simultaneous contact with x and y. The reasons why this situation might occur can be summarized as follows:

1. If the universe $\mathcal{U}$ is not self-connected. In this case we can find regions p and q such that $p + q = \mathcal{U}$ and $\mathsf{DC}(p, q)$. Moreover, if $\mathsf{P}(x, p)$ and $\mathsf{P}(y, q)$ then there is no region which can-connect x and y.
2. If there are some other rules which prevents the existence of a region that can-connect x and y (eg. size).
3. If the distance between regions x and y is inaccessible. If none of the above is the case and we still not can-connect x and y with a third one then we interpret this situation that the distance between x and y is inaccessible.

Now, let us assume that the first two items are not the case. Hence, assume that the distance between x and y is inaccessible. We begin by formalizing the notion of inaccessible distance:

$$\mathsf{INAC}(x, y) \equiv_{\mathrm{df}} \neg \exists z [\mathrm{REGION}(z) \wedge \mathsf{CC}(z, x, y)].$$

$\mathsf{INAC}(x, y)$ holds true iff there can be found no region which can-connect x and y. Then, we say that the distance between x and y is inaccessible or simply x and y are inaccessible.

---

[7] The notation $^{-1}$ stands for the inverse of a function. A function is bijective iff it is surjective (onto) and injective (one-to-one).

Next, there is the question of the length which corresponds to an inaccessible distance. Given two regions x and y such that $\mathsf{INAC}(x, y)$ is true, what is the length that corresponds to the distance between x and y? In order to determine the length which corresponds to the distance between x and y, we first need to find a region which can-connect x and y. On the other hand, INAC relation mentions exactly this problem that no such region exists. Hence, it follows that there is no region whose length is equal to an inaccessible distance. Just like we did for the points, we can simply assume regions of inaccessible length. Thus, we introduce a primitive sort INFINITE and axiomatize its properties as follows:

(InfAx1) $\forall xyz[\mathrm{INFINITE}(x) \rightarrow \mathsf{CC}(x, y, z)]$,
(InfAx2) $\forall xy[\mathrm{INFINITE}(x) \wedge \mathrm{INFINITE}(y) \rightarrow \mathsf{JALA}(x, y)]$,
(InfAx3) $\forall xy[\mathrm{INFINITE}(x) \rightarrow \mathrm{INFINITE}(\mathsf{sum}(x, y))]$,
(InfAx4) $\forall x \exists yz[\mathrm{INFINITE}(x) \wedge \mathsf{EQ}(x, \mathsf{sum}(y, z)) \rightarrow$
$\qquad\qquad [\mathrm{INFINITE}(y) \vee \mathrm{INFINITE}(z)]]$.

An INFINITE object can-connect any two objects and there is nothing longer than an INFINITE object. Also, the sum of an INFINITE object with any other object must be INFINITE. Finally, if we split an INFINITE object into two parts then one of the parts must be INFINITE.

It is noteworthy that, if there are two regions which are inaccessible then it follows that the universe $\mathcal{U}$ is INFINITE. Hence, the traditional case that $\mathcal{U}$ is always a REGION, is not valid anymore.

7 Conclusion

The lack of a metric component in the topologically oriented RCC calculus and a component to fill this gap is mainly addressed in this work. The main contribution that we have supplied is the formalization of de Laguna's "can-connect" based system [11,12]. de Laguna's system has the feature of being a rare example of qualitative distance system which is based on solids (i.e. regions) rather than points. Unfortunately, the original work of de Laguna is in the form of a philosophical text. We have supplied the necessary formalization with related set of axioms and modified de Laguna's methods as necessary to "patch" his system onto the RCC.

This work did not aim to measure the strength of the triadic CC primitive but rather has been a starting point for such a research by giving the needed formalization for it.

We have also showed how it can be possible to introduce points in the RCC framework by exploiting the features of new theory.

The bigger contribution to both RCC and de Laguna's system is the introduction of a characterization for boundedness/unboundedness and finiteness/infiniteness. Instead of sharply strict definitions for abstract notions of infinity or boundedness, I proposed a weaker notion that should be of greater help in understanding the nature of such concepts. In this sense, I introduced inaccessible distances. An inaccessible distance refers to two regions that there is no other region which can-connect them.

References

1. Cohn, A.G., Hazarika, S.M.: Qualitative spatial representation and reasoning: An overview. Fundamenta Informaticae **46** (2001) 1–29
2. Cohn, A.G.: Qualitative spatial representation and reasoning techniques. In Brewka, G., Habel, C., Nebel, B., eds.: Proceedings of KI-97. Volume 1303 of LNAI., Springer Verlag (1997) 1–30
3. Randell, D.A., Cui, Z., Cohn, A.G.: A spatial logic based on regions and connection. In: Proc. 3rd Int. Conf. on Knowledge Representation and Reasoning, San Mateo, Morgan Kaufmann (1992) 165–176
4. Randell, D.A., Cohn, A.G.: Modelling topological and metrical properties in physical processes. In Brachman, R., Levesque, H., Reiter, R., eds.: Proceedings 1st International Conference on the Principles of Knowledge Representation and Reasoning, Los Altos, Morgan Kaufmann (1989) 55–66
5. Hernández, D., Clementini, E., Felice, P.D.: Qualitative distances. In Kuhn, W., Frank, A., eds.: Spatial Information Theory: a theoretical basis for GIS. Volume 988 of LNCS., Berlin, Springer Verlag (1995) 45–58
6. Liu, J.: A method of spatial reasoning based on qualitative trigonometry. Artificial Intelligence **98** (1998) 137–168
7. Clementini, E., Felice, P.D., Hernández, D.: Qualitative representation of positional information. Artificial Intelligence **95** (1997) 317–356
8. Gotts, N.M.: Toplogy from a single primitive relation: defining topological properties and relations in terms of connection. Technical report, Report 96.23, School of Computer Studies, University of Leeds (1996)
9. Renz, J., Nebel, B.: Spatial reasoning with topological information. Lecture Notes in Computer Science **1404** (1998) 351–??
10. Gotts, N.M., Gooday, J.M., Cohn, A.G.: A connection based approach to commonsense topological description and reasoning. The Monist **79** (1996) 51–75
11. de Laguna, T.: The nature of space–I. The journal of Philosophy **19** (1922) 393–407
12. de Laguna, T.: The nature of space–II. The journal of Philosophy **19** (1922) 421–440
13. de Laguna, T.: Point, line and surface as sets of points. The journal of Philosophy **19** (1922) 449–461
14. Cohn, A.G.: A hierarchical representation of qualitative shape based on connection and convexity. In Frank, A.M., ed.: Proc COSIT95. LNCS, Springer Verlag (1995) 311–326
15. Cohn, A.G., Randell, D.A., Cui, Z., Bennett, B.: Qualitative spatial reasoning and representation. In Carreté, N.P., Singh, M.G., eds.: Qualitative Reasoning and Decision Technologies, Barcelona, CIMNE (1993) 513–522
16. Cohn, A.G., Randell, D.A., Cui, Z.: Taxonomies of logically defined qualitative spatial relations. Journal of Human-Computer Studies (1994)
17. Clementini, E., Felice, P.D.: A global framework for qualitative shape description. GeoInformatica **1** (1997) 1–17
18. Worboys, M.: Metrics and topologies for geographic space. In Kraak, M.J., Molenaar, M., eds.: Advances in Geographic Information Systems Research II: Proceedings of the International Symposium on Spatial Data Handling, Delft (1996) 7A.1–7A.11
19. Bennett, B.: Carving up space: existential axioms for logical theories of spatial regions. In: Proceedings of IJCAI95 workshop on Spatial and Temporal Reasoning. (1995)

20. Clarke, B.L.: Individuals and points. Notre Dame Journal of Formal Logic **26** (1985) 61–75
21. Cohn, A.G.: A more expressive formulation of many sorted logic. Journal of Automated Reasoning **3** (1987) 113–200
22. Adams, R.A.: Calculus: A Complete Course. Addison-Wesley, MA (1994)

An Arrangement Calculus, Its Complexity, and Algorithmic Properties

Marco Ragni

Albert-Ludwigs-Universität Freiburg,
Lehrstuhl für Grundlagen der Künstlichen Intelligenz,
Georges-Köhler-Allee Geb. 52,
79110 Freiburg im Breisgau, Germany
ragni@informatik.uni-freiburg.de

Abstract. We define a calculus for spatial reasoning on a grid structure, present a logical calculus, investigate the complexity of the satisfiability problem, we prove its NP completeness and specify additionally a concrete algorithm for solving it.

1 Introduction

1.1 Psychological Motivation

If A is left of B and C is right of B then A is left of C. This easy (transitive) conclusion would be easily accepted by everybody. Two major theoretical positions have emerged in cognitive psychology how people reason about such problems.

On the one hand, proponents of the theories based on formal rules claim that people solve reasoning problems with a set of formal rules that are applied to the information given in the premises. [9]

On the other hand, the theory based on mental models assumes that the main strategy employed in reasoning is the successive construction of a simulation or model of the "state of affairs" which contain all the information given in the premises in an integrated representation. Psychologists try to discern the theories by constructing problems with a small number of inference rules, but many models to construct (which are called indeterminate problems) and vice versa. The indeterminate problems (with a small number of inference rules) would be harder if we reason with mental models. On the other side, the problems with a high number of inference rules (but a small number of models) would be harder if we reason with a set of inference rules. The investigated problems are schematically illustrated in (a) and (b):

> (a)The hammer is to the right of the pliers.
> The screwdriver is to the left of the pliers.
> The wrench is in front of the screwdriver.
> The saw is in front of the hammer.

A. Günter et al. (Eds.): KI 2003, LNAI 2821, pp. 580–590, 2003.

(b) The hammer is to the right of the pliers.
The screwdriver is to the left of the hammer.
The wrench is in front of the screwdriver.
The saw is in front of the hammer.

Obviously, for problems of type (a) there is only one possible arrangement:

screwdriver pliers hammer
wrench   saw

From this arrangement follows the conclusion "the wrench is to the left of the saw", and there is no other possibility that refutes this conclusion.

For problem (b), in contrast, there are two alternative arrangements:

screwdriver pliers hammer   pliers screwdriver hammer
wrench   saw   wrench   saw

Cognitive testing will show an answer which of these two theories is the favoured one. Results of Johnson-Laird shows that the mental model based approach is the most probable one [9].

1.2   The AI Perspective

The major task from the computational perspective is to analyse the experimental data created to discern the both theories in an abstract framework.

Our approach is based on a grid whose size is context dependent and which overlaps a subset of the discrete 2-dimensional physical space. The grid will be used to have an easy unambigous description for terms of orientation to avoid problems [11] and [5]. As a result of psychological experiments we know that the reasoning of humans is predominantly qualitative [10]. Therefore we use a qualitative description. There are several useful but very general qualitative calculi like Frank's Cardinal Direction System, Escrig and Toledo's DRS [4] but no known calculus satisfies our requirements with respect to granularity, smallest number of relation and the particularities of the underlying discrete space.

This paper has two parts. The first part is about a representation of such tasks by a certain representation algebra and a logical calculus to model the rule-based reasoning, the second part gives us the complexity of the satisfiability problem and an algorithm to solve it. The first part has a subtle subproblem. Defining a calculus has to confront two things. First of all you have to choose all the relations in a way that they describe everything you want to (also in the sense of granularity), but otherwise the structure should be chosen small enough that it can be easily handled.

2   Qualitative Vocabulary

First of all we give here a small overview about the definition of finite concrete relational algebras. In the following section we define a related concept - a representation algebra.

Definition 1 (Binary Relation) *Let M be a set. A subset R of the cartesian product $M \times M$ is called a binary relation on M.*

We will investigate only binary relations because they have not only the advantage of having two kinds of compact visual representation, tables and graphs, but they have a natural notion of *transitivity*. Which we hold for the most important property of relations in spatial reasoning. The following definition is based on [1]. With $\mathcal{R}$ we will always mean a finite set of relations.

Definition 2 (Finite Concrete Relational Algebra) *A finite concrete relational algebra $(\mathcal{R}, \sqcup, \sqcap, \circ, {}^{-}, {}^T)$ (over finitely many relations) over a finite universe M where the relations are interpreted on, consists of*

1) A Boolean algebra for $(\mathcal{R}, \sqcup, \sqcap, {}^{-}, 0, 1)$ with the usual semantics.
2) An involuted semigroup $(\mathcal{R}, \circ, {}^T)$, i.e.

$$(x \circ y) \circ z = x \circ (y \circ z)$$
$$(x \circ y)^T = y^T \circ x^T$$
$$(x^T)^T = x.$$

3) Both structures are connected in such a way that they form a normal Boolean Algebra with operators

$$(x \sqcup y) \circ z = (x \circ z) \sqcup (y \circ z)$$
$$(x \sqcup y)^T = x^T \sqcup y^T$$
$$0 \circ x = 0, \quad 0^T = 0.$$

4) ^{T} is a Boolean isomorphism and $x \mapsto 1 \circ x$ is a complemented closure operation, i.e.

$$\overline{(x^T)} = (\overline{x})^T$$
$$x \leq 1 \circ x$$
$$\overline{(1 \circ x)} = 1 \circ \overline{(1 \circ x)}.$$

Remember that $x \leq y \Leftrightarrow x \sqcup y = y$.

Definition 3 (Logical Characterization of Operators) *Let $a, b, c \in M$ and R, S be relations of M.*

$$R \sqcup S = \{(a, b) | (a, b) \in R \vee (a, b) \in S\}$$
$$R \sqcap S = \{(a, b) | (a, b) \in R \wedge (a, b) \in S\}$$
$$\overline{R} = \{(a, b) | (a, b) \notin R\}$$
$$R \circ S = \{(a, c) \in M \times M \mid \exists b \in M (a, b) \in R$$
$$\wedge (b, c) \in S\}$$

For every relation R a converse relation R^T is given by:

Definition 4 (Converse Relation) *Let* $a, b \in M$ *and* R *a relation on* M. *Then*

$$R^T := \{(a, b) | (b, a) \in R\}$$

is called the converse relation of R. *We will call a relation that is self-convers* $(R = R^T)$ *symmetric.*

For a relational algebra of a finite set of disjoint relations a typical representation is given by $(2^M, \sqcup, \sqcap, \circ, ^{-T}, \emptyset, EQ, ALL)$. Where $ALL = M \times M$ is the *allrelation*. One particularity of relational algebras is that the relations are definitly more important than the actual objects. Therefore the objects are in the literature often handled as points   [4]. But this point is up to further research from the cognitive viewpoint.

A union of relations holds if at least one relation holds for two objects. Exactly one relation from a relational partition $\mathcal{R}$ holds for each pair of objects taken from the ground set M.

Definition 5 (Relational Partition) *A set of relations* $\mathcal{R} = \{R_i\}_{i \in \mathcal{I}}$ *is called a relational partition of* $M \times M$, *iff*:

$$\bigsqcup_{i \in \mathcal{I}} R_i = M \times M \qquad (cover)$$
$$R_k \sqcap R_l = \emptyset \qquad \forall k \neq l; \ k, l \in \mathcal{I} \ (pairwise \ disjoint).$$

relations are called *atomic* or *base*.

Definition 6 (Basis of a Concrete Relational Algebra) *A smallest set of relations* $\mathcal{R}$ *is called a basis of a concrete relational algebra* $\mathcal{A}$ *(on* M*), iff* $\mathcal{R}$ *is a relational partition of* $M \times M$ *and it is closed under composition.*

We have further the following theorem:

Theorem 1 (Uniqueness of Basis Relations) *All elements from a concrete finite relational algebra* $\mathcal{R}$ *can be written as unions of basis elements* R_i *in* $\mathcal{R}$:

$$\forall S \in \mathcal{R} \quad S = R_1 \sqcup R_2 \sqcup \cdots \sqcup R_m$$
$$\{R_i\}_{i \in \{1, ..., m\}} \in \mathcal{R}.$$

We call S *a linear combination of* R_i *for* $i = 1, ..., m$.

Since every element from a concrete finite relational algebra can be written by basis elements - we can easily compute composition from the basis elements in the following way:

$$(R_1 \sqcup R_2) \circ R_3 = R_1 \circ R_3 \sqcup R_2 \circ R_3$$

Composition   tables allows fast computation by table lookup. The composition operation corresponds directly with the use of path consistency algorithm by repeated application of

$$P_{i,j} := P_{i,j} \sqcap (P_{i,k} \circ P_{k,j})$$

for given $P_{i,j}, P_{i,k}, P_{k,j}$. We will see in the following that we have to modify slightly the concept of relational algebra to describe more accurate the given psychological tasks.

3   Defining the $\mathcal{AC}$-Calculus

In the following we define and investigate a new calculus. This calculus has two levels of granularity, which means that we can discern between next-neighborhood and longer distance.

We base our approach on the definition of a grid $G_n(\mathbb{N}^2)$ (of size $n \times n$) of the discrete 2-dimensional physical space, which is a subset of $\mathbb{N}^2$. We give now a more precise definition. Structures for this language consist of a finite linear order $(M, <, S, min, max)$ and we have in addition to the ordering axioms:

- $S^M ab$ iff $(a <^A b$ and for all c, if $a <^A c$ then $b <^A c$ or $b = c)$.
- $min^A <^A a$ or $min^A = a$.
- $a < max^A$ or $max^A = a$.

With the successor relation we can easily define the operations $+1, -1$. Two dimensional valuations for atoms are made at ordered pairs of $M \times M$. We can think of one $(M, <, S, min, max)$ as lying horizontally and another (copy) lying vertically on a cartesian grid. For this grid (of $n = |M|$) we write $G_n(\mathbb{N}^2)$.

3.1 $\mathcal{AC}$

A **Constraint Satisfaction Problem** (CSP) is characterised by

- a set V of n variables $\{v_1, ..., v_n\}$
- the possible values D_i of variables v_i
- constraints (sets of relations) over subsets of variables.

A *spatial* object is an ordered pair (x, y) where x and y are interpreted as the x coordinate and y coordinate points in the grid $G_n(\mathbb{N}^2)$. This means that an object in the cell $(x, y), (x + 1, y), (x, y + 1), (x + 1, y + 1)$ will be represented by the coordinate (x, y). We norm $(min, min) = (0, 0)$. Given two concrete spatial points (on a grid) the relative positions (with respect to a given grid) can be described by exactly one of the elements of the set $\mathcal{AC}$ of the thirteen binary relations $\{EQ, AR, DR, AL, DL, AF, DF, AB, DB, FR, BR, FL, BL\}$. The relations are abreviated, e.g. AR stands for *AdjacentRight* and DF stands for *DistantLeft* and so on.

Definition 7 (Basis Relations of $\mathcal{AC}$ on a Grid Structure) *We define the relations of an object z_1 $(= (x_1, y_1) \in G_n(\mathbb{N}^2))$ with an object z_2 $(= (x_2, y_2) \in G_n(\mathbb{N}^2))$ in the following way:*

$$EQ z_1 z_2 := (x_1 = x_2) \qquad \wedge (y_1 = y_2)$$
$$AR z_1 z_2 := (x_1 + 1 = x_2) \wedge (y_1 = y_2)$$
$$DR z_1 z_2 := (x_1 + 1 < x_2) \wedge (y_1 = y_2)$$
$$AL z_1 z_2 := (x_1 = x_2 + 1) \wedge (y_1 = y_2)$$
$$DL z_1 z_2 := (x_1 > x_2 + 1) \wedge (y_1 = y_2)$$
$$AF z_1 z_2 := (x_1 = x_2) \qquad \wedge (y_1 + 1 = y_2)$$
$$DF z_1 z_2 := (x_1 = x_2) \qquad \wedge (y_1 + 1 < y_2)$$
$$AB z_1 z_2 := (x_1 = x_2) \qquad \wedge (y_1 = y_2 + 1)$$
$$DB z_1 z_2 := (x_1 = x_2) \qquad \wedge (y_1 > y_2 + 1)$$
$$FR z_1 z_2 := (x_1 < x_2) \qquad \wedge (y_1 < y_2)$$
$$FL z_1 z_2 := (x_1 > x_2) \qquad \wedge (y_1 < y_2)$$
$$BR z_1 z_2 := (x_1 < x_2) \qquad \wedge (y_1 > y_2)$$
$$BL z_1 z_2 := (x_1 > x_2) \qquad \wedge (y_1 > y_2)$$

We see immediately that this calculus is a partition $G_n(\mathbb{N}^2)$ for every $n \in \mathbb{N}$.

FL	FL	FL	DF	FR	FR	FR
FL	FL	FL	DF	FR	FR	FR
FL	FL	FL	AF	FR	FR	FR
DL	DL	AL	EQ	AR	DR	DR
BL	BL	BL	AB	BR	BR	BR
BL	BL	BL	DB	BR	BR	BR
BL	BL	BL	DB	BR	BR	BR

Fig. 1. Table of $\mathcal{AC}$ relations

The problem is that we have not a closed relational algebra, in spite of our natural definition of relations, because of $DL \circ DL \neq DL$. So we split the former structure in a representation structure and in a logical calculus, where the reasoning take place. So we are nearer on structures of a more modeltheoretic nature.

Definition 8 (Representation Algebra) *A representation algebra is a structure $(\mathcal{R}, \sqcup, \sqcap, \bar{\ }^T)$ (over finitely many relations) over a finite universe M where the relations are interpreted on, consists of*

1) $\mathcal{R}$ is a relational partition on $M \times M$.
2) A Boolean algebra for $(\mathcal{R}, \sqcup, \sqcap, \bar{\ }, 0, 1)$ with the usual semantics.
3) $(\mathcal{R}, ^T)$ is closed under ^{T} and $(x^T)^T = x$ holds.
4) Both structures are connected in a way that they form a normal Boolean Algebra with operators

$$(x \sqcup y)^T = x^T \sqcup y^T$$
$$0^T = 0$$

5) ^{T} is a Boolean isomorphism $\overline{(x^T)} = (\bar{x})^T$

A representation algebra is a finite concrete relational algebra without the compose operator. The advantage is clear, we can split the relational algebra in a "representation part"(which we call representation algebra) and a "reasoning part" (which will be described by a logical calculus).

Proposition 1 $\mathcal{AC}$ *is a representation algebra.* $\square$

The terms of basis and uniqueness are transferable. One task of the project is to model background knowledge. Background kowledge in sense of reasoning rules for specific domains can be given as deductive rules of a (logical) calculus.

We have to give the "rules" of the human reasoning process in a syntactic way.

In a grid we have for instance some rules like:

$$\forall x \forall y \quad AR^T xy \quad = ALxy \qquad (AR^T)^T xy = ARxy$$
$$ARxy \quad = ALyx \qquad AB^T xy \quad = AFxy$$
$$(AB^T)^T xy = ABxy \qquad ABxy \quad = AFyx$$

We have also some transitive rules.

$$\forall w \forall x \forall y \forall z \quad AR^T xy \wedge ABzy \wedge ARwz \rightarrow ABxw$$
$$\forall w \forall x \forall y \forall z \quad AF^T xy \wedge ARzy \wedge AFwz \rightarrow ARxw$$

So we have to define in our logical calculus the following rules:
For $X \in \{AL, AR\}$ and $Y \in \{AF, AB, DF, DB\}$ or
$X \in \{AF, AB\}$ and $Y \in \{AL, AR, DL, DR\}$ or
$X \in \{AL, AR, AF, AB, DL, DR, DF, DB\}$ and $Y = EQ$

$$\forall x \forall y \forall w \forall z \frac{Xxy, Yyz, X^T zw}{Yxw}$$

And for $Z \in \{EQ, AL, AR, AB, AF, DL, DF, DB, DF, FR, FL, BR, BL\}$ we have

$$\forall x \forall y \frac{Zxy}{Z^T yx}$$
$$\forall x \forall y \frac{(Z^T)^T xy}{Zxy}$$

and again another rule for $(A, D) \in \{(AR, DR), (AL, DL), (AF, DF), (AB, DB)\}$

$$\forall x \forall y \forall z \frac{Axy, Ayz}{Dxz}$$

and $X \in \{DR, DL, DF, DB\}$

$$\forall x \forall y \forall z \frac{Xxy, Xyz}{Xxz}$$

$X \in \{AR, AL, AF, AB\}$

$$\forall x \forall y \forall z \frac{X x y, X^T y z}{EQ x z}$$

It is immediately clear that we can model all syntactic ("rule-based") reasoning of the given psychological examples by such rules and further we have a more precise representation of the human reasoning. It can easily be verified that the given logical calculus is sound, but not complete with respect to intended grid models, because

$$\theta := \{\{x_1 AF x_2\}, \{x_2 AF x_3\}, \{x_3 AR x_4\}, \{x_4 AR x_5\},$$
$$\{x_1 FR x_6\}, \{x_5 BL x_6\}\}.$$

Then we have:

$$\theta \models \{x_2 AR x_6\}$$
$$\not\vdash \{x_2 AR x_6\}.$$

The incompleteness has no importance for our needs.

x_3	x_4	x_5
x_2	x_6	
x_1		

Fig. 2. The model of θ

A *spatial configuration* can be described by a set θ of spatial formulas. One important computational problem is deciding *consistency* of θ, i.e. deciding whether it is possible to assign points (of a grid) to the spatial variables in a way that all relations holds. We call this problem **ACSAT**.

Whenever we have a solution of a spatial configuration in n variables in a grid of size bigger than $(2n)^2$ we can do the following: Remove for two empty adjacent rows or colums one of them. Therefore we have:

Theorem 2 (Assigned Grid Structure) *For a given* **ACSAT** *problem θ of n spatial variables the problem of satisfiability can be answered in a grid of size $(2n)^2$.*   □

Theorem 3 (ACSAT) *The satisfiability problem of $\mathcal{AC}$ is NP-complete.*

Proof. With the previous theorem we have: The problem θ of n variables is satisfiable $\Leftrightarrow$ it is satisfiable in a grid of size $(2n)^2$. That it is in NP is immediately clear: The NP-Machine guesses for every spatial variable the right assignment (coordinates of $G_{2n}(\mathbb{N}^2)$) which means it guesses a tuple of length $2n$. The checking is in PTIME.

The NP-hardness: Reduction from 3-colorability on ACSAT. Let $G = (V, E)$, $V = \{v_1, ..., v_n\}$ be an instance of 3-colorability. Then we use the points (of $G_{2(n+3)}(\mathbb{N}^2))$ $\{v_1, ..., v_n, c_1, c_2, c_3\}$ with the following constraints:

$$
\begin{array}{ccc}
c_1 & \{AL\} & c_2 \\
c_2 & \{AL\} & c_3 \\
v_i & \{EQ, AR, DR\} & c_1 \\
v_i & \{EQ, AL, DL\} & c_3 \\
v_i & \{AL, DL, AR, DR\}\, v_j & \forall (v_i, v_j) \in E
\end{array}
$$

It is immediately clear that the mapping is in P. Now it is obvious that the constraint system is satisfiable *iff* G can be colored with 3 colors. Therefore the problem is NP-complete.   □

We will give at the end of the paper a more practical nondeterministic polynomial time algorithm for this problem. It consists of three parts:

– Guessing Part
– Relation Transformation Program
– Linear Program Solver.

3.2   The Base Relation Algorithm

We will see that the following is true:

Theorem 4 (ACSAT of Base Relations) *The **ACSAT** problem of Base Relations is in PTIME.*

We suppose that θ consists only of base relations. In the next step we substitute the constraints in θ in the following way:

```
Program RelationTransformation
 For i := 1 to n do
  Replace (object variable) zᵢ  by a tuple (xᵢ, yᵢ)
  Replace in θ
```

$$
\begin{array}{rclcl}
EQ z_1 z_2 &= (x_1 &=& x_2) & \wedge\ (y_1\ =\ y_2) \\
AR z_1 z_2 &= (x_1 + 1 &=& x_2) & \wedge\ (y_1\ =\ y_2) \\
DR z_1 z_2 &= (x_1 + 2 &\le& x_2) & \wedge\ (y_1\ =\ y_2) \\
AL z_1 z_2 &= (x_1 &=& x_2 + 1) & \wedge\ (y_1\ =\ y_2) \\
DL z_1 z_2 &= (x_2 + 2 &\le& x_1) & \wedge\ (y_1\ =\ y_2) \\
AF z_1 z_2 &= (x_1 &=& x_2) & \wedge\ (y_1 + 1\ =\ y_2) \\
DF z_1 z_2 &= (x_1 &=& x_2) & \wedge\ (y_1 + 2\ \le\ y_2) \\
AB z_1 z_2 &= (x_1 &=& x_2) & \wedge\ (y_1\ =\ y_2 + 1) \\
DB z_1 z_2 &= (x_1 &=& x_2) & \wedge\ (y_2 + 2\ \le\ y_1) \\
FR z_1 z_2 &= (x_1 + 1 &\le& x_2) & \wedge\ (y_1 + 1\ \le\ y_2) \\
FL z_1 z_2 &= (x_2 + 1 &\le& x_1) & \wedge\ (y_1\ + 1\le\ y_2) \\
BR z_1 z_2 &= (x_1 + 1 &\le& x_2) & \wedge\ (y_2 + 1\ \le\ y_1) \\
BL z_1 z_2 &= (x_2 + 1 &\le& x_1) & \wedge\ (y_2 + 1\ \le\ y_1)
\end{array}
$$

Now we have transformed the original problem in a problem of solving inequalities.

3.3   The Main Algorithm

When in θ are not only base relations but combined relations respective $\sqcup$ we have to modify the program with the following: We write $\theta(R_1, ..., R_m)$ for all relations R_i for $1 \leq i \leq m$ in θ. Every non base relation is a disjunction of base relations, e.g. $\{FR, AR, DR, BR\}$ we represent also every base relation by the set which unique element is this relation. So we can define

$$|R| := \begin{cases} 1, & \text{if } R \text{ is a base relation} \\ n, & \text{if } R \text{ consists of } n \text{ base relations} \end{cases}$$

We define for all relations R in θ a function $\sigma : \{1, ..., |R|\} \to R$ with $\sigma(i) \in R$ for $1 \leq i \leq |R|$. Remember that $\mathcal{R}$ stands for the set of all relations of a representational algebra. With these definitons we can describe all relations of a CSP θ over n objects by a function $\sigma_j : \{1, ..., |R_j|\} \to \mathcal{R}$ for $1 \leq j \leq n$.

```
Algorithm ACSAT
  For j:=1 to n do
   Replace in θ(R₁, ..., Rₘ) every relation Rⱼ
            by  σⱼ
  od
  Guess (nondeterministically)
        a value  (i₁, ..., iₘ)
  Program RelationTransformation θ(σ₁(i₁), ..., σₘ(iₘ))
  Test for cycles
  if yes than write the
         problem is infeasible
    else
     use a Linear Program Solver
     with bounds of variables in {0, ..., 2n}
     minimizing the function x₁ + ... + xₙ
               and  y₁ + ... + yₙ.
```

With the minimizing function and the given constraints we get only solutions of natural numbers, which are the coordinates of the objects. So we get not only a solution but a minimal one. It is immediately clear that the algorithm is running in nondeterministic polynomial time.   □

This program is complete because of the completeness of the Linear Program Solver. Why do we use such a strong algorithm like a Linear Program Solver ? Because this algorithm will be generalized in the future to an algorithm on real structures. If ACSAT consists only of base relations, we have not to guess and so we have the following:

Corollary 1 (ACSAT for baserelations) *ACSAT for base relations is in PTIME.*

4   Conclusions

We have presented a calculus for arrangement and a logical calculus to simulate the "rule-based" approach. This calculus can be used for further test design and for a representation of the "rule-based" inferences of the test candidates. Then we analysed the appropriate satisfiability problem **ACSAT**, found out that it lies in the same complexity class as many others satisfiability problems like Allen's ISAT, RSAT (of RCC-8 or RCC-5) [12] and RISAT [7]. It is up to further research to find the determining factors. At last we presented a nondeterministic polynomial time algorithm. This is not a problem for psychological testing, because the problems consists only of a small number of objects.

References

1. Gabbay,D. (eds.): Andreka,H., Nemeti,I.,Sain,I. Algebraic Logic Handbook of Philosophical Logic Kluwer,1997
2. Brewka,G., Habel,C., Nebel,B. (eds.) KI-97: Cohn,A.G.:Qualitative Spatial Reasoning Advances in Artificial Intelligence, LNAI No.1303, Springer (1997) 1–30
3. Escrig, M.T., Toledo,F: Qualitative Spatial Reasoning: Theory and Practice Application to Robot Navigation. Frontiers in AI and Applications,Volume 47, IOS Press, Amsterdam,(1998)
4. Escrig, M.T., Toledo,F: A Framework Based on CLP Extended with CHRs for Reasoning with Qualitative Orientation and Positional Information. Journal of Visual Languages and Computing,9,(1998) 81–101
5. Freksa,C. and Zimmermann,K.: On Utilization of Spatial Structures for Cognitively Plausible and Efficient Reasoning, Proc. IEEE Intl. Conf. on Systems, Man and Cybernetics, (1992) 18–21
6. Mark,D.M., Frank, A.U.(eds.): Cognitive and linguistic aspects of geographic space Freksa,C.: Qualitative Spatial Reasoning Dordrecht:Kluwer (1991)
7. A. Gerevini, B. Nebel: Qualitative Spatio-Temporal Reasoning with RCC-8 and Allen's Interval Calculus: Computational Complexity, Proceedings of ECAI 2002, pp. 312–316, IOS Press.
8. Hernandez,D.: Qualitative representation of spatial knowledge Berlin, Springer (1994)
9. Shapiro, S.C. (eds.): Johnson-Laird,P.N.: Mental models. Encyclopedia of artificial intelligence (2nd ed.) New York,NY:John Wiley & Sons.(1992) 932–939
10. Knauff,M., Rauh,R., Renz,J.: A Cognitive Assessment of Topological Spatial Relations: Results from Empirical Investigation. Cosit97,(1997)
11. Knauff,M., Rauh,R., Schlieder,C.: Prefered mental models in qualitative spatial reasoning: A cognitive assessment of Allen's Calculus. In Proceedings of the Seventeenth Annual Conference of the Cognitive Science Society (1995) 200–205 Mawah,NJ:Lawrence Erlbaum Associates.
12. Renz,J.: Maximal Tractable Fragments of the RCC: A complete Analysis IJCAI'99.

Multimodal User State Recognition in a Modern Dialogue System

J. Adelhardt, R. Shi, C. Frank, V. Zeißler, A. Batliner, E. Nöth, and
H. Niemann

Martensstraße 3., 91058 Erlangen, Germany
{adelhardt, shi, batliner, frank, noeth, zeissler,
niemann}@informatik.uni-erlangen.de,
http://www5.informatik.uni-erlangen.de/

Abstract. A new direction in improving automatic dialogue systems
is to make a human-machine dialogue more similar to a human-human
dialogue. A modern system should be able to recognize the semantic
content of spoken utterances but also to interpret some paralinguistic or
non-verbal information — as indicators of the *internal user state* — in
order to detect success or trouble in communication. A common problem
in a human-machine dialogue, where information about a users internal
state of mind may give a clue, is, for instance, the recurrent misunder-
standing of the user by the system. This can be prevented if we detect
the anger in the users voice. In contrast to anger, a joyful face combined
with a pleased voice may indicate a satisfied user, who wants to go on
with the current dialogue behavior, while a hesitant searching gesture
of the user reveals his unsureness. This paper explores the possibility of
recognizing a user's internal state by using facial expression classification with eigenfaces and a prosodic classifier based on artificial neural
networks combined with a *discrete Hidden Markov Model* (HMM) for gesture analysis in parallel. Our experiments show that all the three input
modalities can be used to identify a users internal state. However, a user
state is not always indicated by all three modalities at the same time;
thus a fusion of the different modalities seems to be necessary. Different
ways of modality fusion are discussed.

1 Introduction

Dialogue systems nowadays are intended to be used by laymen, i.e., naive users.
Neither are these users familiar with "drag and drop" nor are they willing to read
a bunch of manuals describing numerous unnecessary functionalities. Modern
dialogue systems try rather to behave similar to a human-human dialogue in
order to be used by such naive users. But what does a human-human dialogue
look like?

Human beings use much more input information than the spoken utterances
during a conversation with another human being: their ears listen to the tone
of the voice and interpret the sounds, they use gesture to deliver information,

A. Günter et al. (Eds.): KI 2003, LNAI 2821, pp. 591–605, 2003.

their eyes recognize movements of the body and the facial muscles, and their skin recognizes physical contact. All that belongs to the category of non-verbal communication and provides a lot of additional information besides the textual content of spoken phrases.

Another aspect in communication is the users internal state of mind that influences the progression of a human-machine dialogue. Internal state here does not only refer to standard emotions like hate, love and fear. It covers all states affecting the interaction with a dialogue system, e.g. helplessness or irritation, which we will call "user states"; this concept is discussed in more detail in [1]. Vocal expression of user states can be detected by analyzing the prosody of a spoken utterance, facial expression by analyzing the eyes and the mouth of the user. To detect the gesture expression we can analyze the dynamics of hand movements.

Different approaches are described in the literature to improve modern dialogue systems. The ETUDE system in [2], e.g., enlarges a dialogue manager with backing up. Now this dialogue manager is able to return to a previous dialogue state when a resolved ambiguity turns out to be wrong.

Another possibility is the combination of more modalities like a human being does. That is what [3] does in his dialogue manager which implements a dynamic information state model. This dialogue manager handles speech commands as well as deictic commands from a human user to control a robot.

The dialogue system *SmartKom* [4], funded by the BMBF[1], is one of these new powerful dialogue systems. It is a multimodal multimedia system using speech, gesture and facial expression as input channels for a human-machine dialogue. The output of the system is a combination of images, animation and speech synthesis.

The idea of user state recognition is to get as soon as possible a hint for an angry user in order to modify the dialogue strategies of the system and to give more support. This prevents the users from getting disappointed up to such an extent that they break off interaction and never use the system again.

In the following we will concentrate on facial expressions, gesture analysis, and prosody.

2   Facial Expression

If a system wants to know about the users internal state by observing the face, it first has to localize the face and then it has to recognize the facial expression. Face localization aims to determine the image position of a single face [5], [6], [7], [8]. The task of facial expression recognition is to determine the persons internal state of mind, the user state. A common method is to identify facial action units (AU). These AU were defined by Paul Ekman in [9]. In [10] a neural-network is used to recognize AU from the coordinates of facial features like lip corners

---
[1] This research is being supported by the German Federal Ministry of Education and Research (*BMBF*) in the framework of the SmartKom project under Grant 01 IL 905 K7. The responsibility for the contents of this study lies with the authors.

or the curve of eye brows. To determine the muscle movement from the optical flow when showing facial expressions is the task in [11]. It is supplemented by temporal information to form a spatial-temporal motion energy model which can be compared to different models for the facial expressions. In this paper, we only deal with the second task, the analysis of an already found face.

2.1   Introduction to Eigenspaces

The method proposed by us for the recognition of facial expressions is a modification of a standard eigenspace classification for user identification. Eigenspace methods are well known in the field of face recognition ([12], [13], [14]). In a standard face recognition system, one eigenspace for each person is created using different face images. The set of face images for each person is used to create a probability distribution or a representative for this person in face space. Later, when classifying a photo of an unknown person, this image is projected to the face spaces. The probability distribution or representative which best matches the new image is chosen as the searched class.

To create an eigenspace with training images, a partial Karhunen-Loéve transformation, also called principal component analysis (PCA), is used. This is a dimensionality reduction scheme that maximizes the scatter of all projected samples, using N sample images of a person $\{x_1, x_2, \ldots, x_N\}$ with values in an n-dimensional feature space. Let μ be the mean image of all feature vectors. The total scatter matrix is then defined as

$$S_T = \sum_{k=1}^{N} (x_k - \mu)(x_k - \mu)^T \tag{1}$$

In PCA, the optimal projection W_{opt} to a lower dimensional subspace is chosen to maximize the determinant of the total scatter matrix of the projected samples,

$$W_{opt} = \arg\max_{W} |W^T S_T W| = [w_1, w_2, \ldots, w_m] \tag{2}$$

where $\{w_i | i = 1, 2, \ldots m\}$ is the set of n-dimensional eigenvectors of S_T corresponding to the set of decreasing eigenvalues. These eigenvectors have the same dimension as the input vectors and are referred to as Eigenfaces. In Figure 1 the first 5 eigenfaces of the *anger* eigenspace are shown.

In the following sections we assume that high order eigenvectors correspond to high eigenvalues. Therefore high order eigenvectors contain more relevant information.

An advantage and as well a disadvantage of eigenspace methods is their capability of finding the significant differences between the input samples which need not to be significant for the classification problem. This feature enables eigenspace methods to model a given sample of a n-dimensional feature space in an optimal way using only an m-dimensional space.

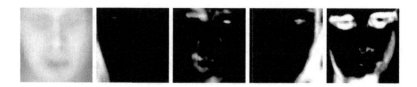

Fig. 1. The left image is the average image, the following images are the first 4 eigenvectors of the *anger* eigenspace.

2.2 Recognition of Facial Expressions Using Eigenspaces

Our classification procedure of facial expressions does not correspond to the one mentioned above. Preliminary results showed that a class of facial expression is less comparable to a class build of faces from one person than to the face class *per se*. That means one eigenspace per facial expression is necessary. For face classification a new image is projected to each eigenspace and the eigenspace which best describes the input image is selected. This is accomplished by calculating the residual description error.

Imagine we have training sets F_κ of l samples $\boldsymbol{y}_i$ with similar characteristics for each class Ω_κ, $\kappa \in 1, \ldots k$. Thus there is different illumination, different face shape etc. in each set F_κ. Reconstructing one image $\boldsymbol{y}_i$ with each of our eigenspaces results in k different samples $\boldsymbol{y}^\kappa$. The reconstructed images do not differ in characteristics like illumination, because this is modeled by each eigenspace. But they differ in the facial expression of specific regions, such as the mouth or the eyes area.

With a set of eigenspaces for each class Ω_κ we receive distances ν_κ of a test image $\boldsymbol{y}_i$ to each class

$$\nu_\kappa = ||\boldsymbol{y}_i - \boldsymbol{y}^\kappa||^2 \tag{3}$$

$$k = \arg \min_{j \in 0 \ldots k} \nu_\kappa \tag{4}$$

An image is attributed to a class k with minimum distance as criterion.

3 Prosody

Another way to recognize user state is by analyzing prosodic characteristics. Many studies have shown that vocal expression of emotions can be recognized more or less reliably in the case of simulated emotions produced by trained speakers or actors ([15,16,17]).

3.1 Feature Extraction

For prosodic analysis we use the prosody module described in [18]. First, we compute frame-wise basic prosodic features such as normalized energy, duration and fundamental frequency F0. We use a forced time alignment of the spoken word chain to get the word segmentation [19]. Then, based on these data the full feature set consisting of 91 *word-based* features, 30 linguistic features (PartOf-Speech, POS) and 39 *global* features is computed.

The word-based features were computed on the speech signal segments corresponding to the single words in spoken word chain. For each word in the word hypothesis graph (WHG), a set of different characteristics describing word duration, energy and F0 is extracted: mean/maximum/minimum values and their positions, regression coefficient and regression error. To incorporate the word context information as well these features are augmented by coefficients which correspond to the two adjacent words to the left and to the right.

In analogy six different POS-flags for each word in a five word context are used; thus we get a set of 30 linguistic features. The 39 global features were computed on the whole utterance and include the averaged Mel-cepstral-coefficients, averaged jitter/shimmer characteristics and some statistics over the distribution of voiced and unvoiced segments. For a detailed description of the feature set, cf. [17].

3.2 Classification

For the classification we use an MLP (Multi-Layer-Perceptron), a special kind of neural networks. To find an optimal training configuration, we need to know the following parameters: network topology, training weight for the rprop training algorithm [20], and random seed for the initialization. In preliminary tests we found out that complex topologies with two or more hidden layers do not improve the results for our data set than a simple three layer perceptron. Hence, we restrict the number of hidden layers to one and look only for the optimal number of nodes in the hidden layer. We evaluate then different combinations of these parameters and choose the configuration with the best result on the validation set.

As primary classification method we used the word-wise classification. For each word ω_i we compute a probability $P(s \mid \omega_i)$ to belong to one of the given user states s. The probability maximum determines then the classification result. Further we used these probabilities to classify the whole utterance assuming the conditional independence between word classification events [21]. The utterance probabilities were computed with the following equation:

$$P(s \mid \omega_1, \omega_2, \ldots, \omega_n) \approx \prod_{i=1}^{n} P(s \mid \omega_i) . \tag{5}$$

4 Gesture

As mentioned above, the user can communicate with SmartKom not only via speech and facial expression but also by gesture, which is recorded by the embedded SiVit (Siemens Virtual Touchscreen) unit introduced by C. Maggioni in [22]. The user state influences to some degree the way of gesturing, e.g., if the user gets annoyed, his gesture tends to be quick and iterating, while it becomes short and determined if the user is satisfied with the service and the information provided by the system. Both gesture and speech indicate the user state and both complement each other. Thus, we will base our experiment on a joint sample set of speech and gesture. Since we deal with the ever-changing user states, it is clear that the central point of this issue is concentrated on the dynamics of the gesture and its interpretation, instead of focusing on its segmentation from background.

4.1   Gesture in SmartKom

Figure 2 shows the setup of an intended SmartKom system with an integrated SiVit unit at the top of the machine [2]. A similar version of this system was used to collect the gesture data in the Wizard-of-Oz experiments. The SiVit unit consists of a video projector, an infrared camera and a virtual touch screen, which is not sensitive. The system works in the following manner: the video projector projects all the graphical user interface (GUI) information onto the display, where the user can use her hand to select or search objects. The infrared camera captures the trajectory of her hand for the gesture analysis. Gestures are captured together with the recording of the face via video camera, and speech through a microphone array. The position of these components are pointed out in Figure 2.

4.2   Hidden Markov Model and Gesture Analysis

HMMs are a suitable model to incorporate temporal continuity. Temporal continuity here means that a pixel of the gesture trajectory belongs to a certain category (state) for a period of time. If a pixel moves at a high speed at a given time, it is likely that this pixel will still keep moving fast at the next time step. HMMs are able to learn the observation distributions for different categories (hidden states) from the trajectory of the gesture. The training data are recorded in a system similar to the one depicted in Figure 2. In this paper, each observation will be classified into one of four different categories: *ready* (R), *stroke* (S), *pause* (P) and/or *end* (E) (see subsection 4.5).

We use the standard Baum–Welch re-estimation algorithm for the training, which is based on the EM algorithm (See [23] by Rabiner *et al*), and the standard Forward-Algorithm to solve the classification problem. A detailed description of these algorithms can be found in [23,24], an example of how to apply these algorithms can be found in [25]. Here we use discrete HMMs due to their simplicity.

4.3   Feature Extraction

In order to incorporate the temporal continuity, we choose trajectory variance, instantaneous speed, instantaneous acceleration, and kinetic energy as the feature vector, which best represents the motion and the dynamics of the gesture.

---

[2] http://w3.siemens.ch/td/produkte/multimedia/multimedia.htm

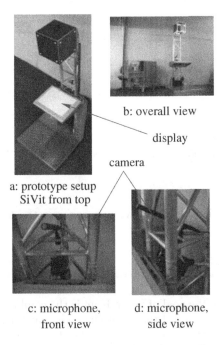

b: overall view

display

camera

a: prototype setup
SiVit from top

c: microphone,   d: microphone,
front view   side view

Fig. 2. Siemens Virtual Touchscreen for Gesture Data Recording

The continuous two-dimensional coordinates (trajectories) plus the time stamp, which are recorded by the SiVit unit, are the most important information on the dynamics of the gesture. The reason for computing the instantaneous velocity v over time is for the system to learn from the behavior of the user's gesture. That is, with simple data-analysis, it would be possible to determine trends and anticipate future moves of the user. The next set of data-points is the acceleration a of the gestures, which is easily computed by approximating the second derivative of the position coordinate. Kinetic energy K is also a significant factor which is just the square of the velocity while the mass is neglected. In our feature set, the trajectory variance is also included. This is the geometric variation or oscillation of the gestures with respect to their moving direction. A large value of this variance can indicate that the user gesticulates hesitantly and moves his hand around on the display, while a determined gesture leads to a small variance. Figure 3 shows how the trajectory variance D is computed. So we have a feature vector

$$f = (v, a, K, D). \tag{6}$$

The vector D can be computed every N points along the gesture trajectory. Other possible features are, e.g., the number of pauses of a gesture, the transient time before and after a pause, the transient time of each pause relative to the begin of the gesture, average speed, average acceleration or change of moving

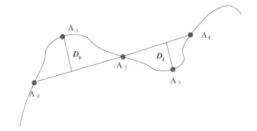

Fig. 3. Calculation of Geometric Variance of A Gesture

direction. However, in this study we just consider the feature vector shown in Eq. 6.

4.4   Modification of User States Category

As mentioned above, the goal of SmartKom is the combination of all three input modalities. Gesture, as one of the input channels, must define its own output, to contribute to the fusion of the analysis of the three inputs. In contrast to facial analysis, where four user states are defined, *neutral, angry, joyful,* and *hesitant,* we define in gesture analysis only three user states: *determined, negative,* and *hesitant.* There are two reasons for making this kind of mapping: the intuitive reason is that normally people cannot tell if the user is angry or joyful by alone observing his gesture. Furthermore, we have tested an HMM with this topology, which gave unsatisfactory results and we decided thus in favor of the three states topology. The user state *determined* is given if the user knows what he wants from SmartKom, e.g., if he decides to zoom in a part of a city map on the GUI by pointing to it. If the user gets confused by SmartKom and does not know what to choose, his gesture will probably ponder around or zigzag among different objects presented on the SmartKom GUI. Finally, if he feels badly served by SmartKom, if the information given is not correct, he can use gestures in such a way as to show a strong negative expression like a windshield wiper, which corresponds to the user state *angry* in facial expression.

4.5   Choice of Different Topologies

For the HMMs, we evaluated different topologies; an HMM with 3 or 4 states gave the best results. Besides using simple ergodic HMMs, we suppose that a gesture consists of some basic states such as *ready, stroke, end* and/or *pause.* The user moves his hand to a start position, and then makes a gesture consisting of several strokes, probably with pauses in between, and finally ends his gesture. An alternative is to merge *pause* and *ready.* We also tried different connection schemata; the easiest one is an ergodic HMM, while a partially connected HMM better corresponds to the correct physical order of each state (see Figure 4).

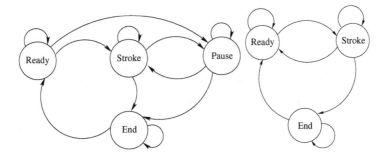

Fig. 4. Non-Ergodic HMM with Different Numbers of Hidden States for Gesture Analysis

5 Audio, Video, and Gesture Data

For our study we collected data from 63 more or less naive subjects (41m/22f). They were instructed to act as if they had asked the SmartKom system for the TV-program and felt content/discontent/helpless or neutral with the system answers. Different genres as, e.g., news, daily soap, or science reports, were projected onto the display to select from. The subjects were prompted with an utterance displayed on the screen and should then indicate their internal state through voice and gesture, and at the same time, through different facial expressions. Facial expression, gesture and speech were recorded simultaneously; this made it possible to combine all three input modalities afterwards. The user states were equally distributed. The test persons read 20 sentences per user state. The utterances were taken in random order from a large pool of utterances. About 40 % out of them were repetitions of a TV-genre or special expressions, not actually depending on the given user state, like *"tolles Programm!"* (*"nice program!"*). In other words we choose expressions one could produce in each of the given user states. (Note that a prima facie positive statement can be produced in a sarcastic mood and by that, turned into a negative statement.) All the other sentences were multi-word expressions, where the user state could be guessed from the semantics of the sentence. The test persons should keep close to the given text, but minor variations were allowed.

From all collected data we picked up 4848 sentences (3.6 hours of speech) with satisfying signal quality and used them for further experiments. For the experiments with prosodic analysis, we chose randomly 4292 sentences for the training set and 556 for the validation set.

For the facial analysis video sequences of 10 persons were used. These persons where selected because their mouth area was not covered by facial hair or the microphone.

As training images, we used image sequences of these persons without wearing the headset. In the images of the test sequences, there is a headset.

Some of the training images can be seen in Figure 5. For gesture analysis there are all in all 5803 samples of all three user states (note that there are only

Fig. 5. Samples data from left to right *hesitant, anger, joy* and *neutral*

three user states for gesture as mentioned above), 2075 of them are accompanied by speech. As we are interested in the combination of all three modalities, we concentrate on this subset. 1891 are used for training and the other 184 are used for testing. Since the samples were recorded according to the user states categories in facial expression and speech, we merge the data of the corresponding user states *neutral* and *joyful* into the user state category *determined* for gesture.

6   Results of User State Classification

6.1   Facial Expression

For facial expression classification, the sequences of the 10 persons were used in a leave one out manner. The whole face is used to create four eigenspaces for four facial expression classes. The classification of faces with internal movements according to speech is very difficult; recent methods have not been adapted yet. We achieve a low recognition rate of 32 %. The confusion matrix is shown in Table 1. A problem is the user state *angry*. Anger is that facial expression, which is shown in many ways by different users. As opposed to this, a friendly face has always risen lip corners.

Table 1. Confusion Matrix of User State Recognition with Facial Expression Data (in %)

reference	results			
user state	neutral	joy	angry	hesitant
neutral	**7**	23	36	33
joy	5	**54**	22	20
angry	4	62	**17**	16
hesitant	6	12	35	**48**

The same procedure applied to a data set (presented in [26]) of mugshots yields 59 % for a four class problem. Reasons for the big difference in classification rates for both data sets could be that, e.g., not each image in an angry sequence shows anger. There are also neutral and other facial expressions which are attributed to the angry training subset. An other reason is the movement of the face not belonging to facial expressions but to speaking and playing around with the muscles.

6.2 Prosody

For the prosodic user state classification, we had first to find out the optimal feature set. We tried different subset combinations of F0-based features, all prosody features, linguistic POS features and global features (Glob.) in both context dependent and independent form. In context independent feature sets we used only the features computed for the word in question. For all configurations we trained the neural networks and tested them on the validation set. To ensure that we really recognize user states and not the different syntactic structures of the sentences, we additionally tested each configuration on the test set consisting only of utterances with the same syntactic structure (see section 5 and cf. the results of vali vs. test in Table 2). The class-wise averaged recognition rates for the 4-class problems (in percent) are shown in Table 2. We computed both word-wise and sentence-wise recognition rates as indicated in the second column.

Table 2. Recognition Results on Different Feature Sets (in %)

test set	type	without context			with context		
		F0 feat. 12 feat.	all pros. 29 feat.	pros.+POS 35 feat.	all pros. 91 feat.	pros.+POS 121 feat.	pros.+Glob. 130 feat.
vali	word	44.8	61.0	65.7	**72.1**	86.6	**70.4**
	sentence	53.8	64.7	72.1	**75.3**	81.4	**66.6**
test	word	37.0	46.8	46.5	**54.6**	52.7	**53.3**
	sentence	39.8	47.6	48.1	**55.1**	54.3	**55.4**

In Table 2 we notice that the POS features bring great improvement only on the validation set; the results on the test set get worse (cf. col. 3 and 5). That means they reflect to a great extent the sentence structure and therefore could not be properly applied for the user state recognition in our case. The best results were achieved with the 91 prosody feature set (75.3 % vali, 55.1 % test sentence-wise) and with extended 130-feature set (prosody + global features: 66.6 % vali 55.4 % test). To verify these results with the speaker independent tests we additionally conducted one *"leave one out"* (LOO) training using the 91-feature set. Here we achieve an average recognition rate of 67.0 % word-wise and 68.2 % sentence-wise. The confusion matrix of this test is given in Table 3.

Table 3. Confusion Matrix of User State Recognition with Prosody Features using LOO (in %)

reference	word-wise				sentence-wise			
user state	neutral	joy	angry	hesitant	neutral	joy	angry	hesitant
neutral	**62.3**	12.5	12.6	6.6	**67.6**	12.1	16.5	3.8
joy	13.8	**65.8**	10.6	9.8	14.3	**66.3**	14.0	5.4
angry	14.5	11.3	**64.7**	9.5	13.7	9.3	**70.8**	6.2
hesitant	10.0	10.8	9.9	**69.3**	9.9	6.5	15.4	**68.2**

6.3   Gesture

Tables 4, 5 and 6 show the results of the gesture analysis (see subsection 4.5 for choice of topology). We can see that the user state *hesitant* is sometimes mismatched with *negative*. The reason is that some users, whose gestures are used in the training set, made similar gestures like those in *negative* state, in that the windshield wiper movement has the same zigzag only with different dynamics and speed. Probably, some persons gesticulate slowly while indicating anger, thus their recorded gestures may have similar properties like those of a *hesitant* state. Another reason for a false classification is that the training data for the user state *determined* consists of those from *joyful* and *neutral*; the latter of them makes the HMM for *determined* biased towards *hesitant* (See Table 6 with 4 states). In general, the classification has a class-wise averaged recognition rate of 72 % for 3 states and 76.3 % for 4 states, while LOO achieves 73 % for 3 states and 67 % for 4 states.

Table 4. Confusion Matrix of User State Recognition with Gesture Data (in %)

reference	3 HMM states			4 HMM states		
user state	determined	hesitant	negative	determined	hesitant	negative
determined	**61**	5	34	**80**	15	5
hesitant	5	**72**	23	15	**77**	8
negative	10	6	**84**	10	18	**72**

Table 5. Confusion Matrix of User State Recognition with Gesture Data using LOO (in %)

reference	3 HMM states			4 HMM states		
user state	determined	hesitant	negative	determined	hesitant	negative
determined	**62**	5	33	**75**	7	18
hesitant	5	**74**	21	13	**74**	13
negative	8	8	**84**	30	8	**62**

Table 6. Confusion Matrix of User State Recognition with Gesture Data using Non-Ergodic HMM (in %)

reference user state	3 HMM states			4 HMM states		
	determined	hesitant	negative	determined	hesitant	negative
determined	**72**	16	12	**40**	49	11
hesitant	32	**45**	23	2	**70**	28
negative	60	12	**28**	2	24	**74**

6.4 Fusion of Modalities

The recognition of user states in a multimodal dialog system such as SmartKom will most likely have better classification performance, if different input modalities are combined during analysis. This is also reflected in our daily life, where people communicate with others through speech, gesture and facial expression in an automatic, coordinated and complementary way.

In the following, we discuss modality fusion in more detail only for prosody and gesture since the coincidence of speech with facial expression can severely hamper classification due to its interfering property: if, for instance, a confused user says "Ah", this might be incorrectly interpreted as "joyful" because for this vowel, the mouth angle is wide open. The classifier for gestures (3 classes) yields a recognition rate of 77 % and the classifiers for prosody (4 classes) result in 76 % (See Table 7) recognition rate, respectively. 60 % of both cases are correctly recognized by all modalities and 7 % recognized by none of the modalities. A possible and promising way of combining all three modalities which has an optimal configuration for the user state, is to combine the recognition rates of all three modalities separately. A new neural network can be trained with all these rates as input. The combination of user states in gesture and speech analysis during training can be realized in such a way that a "neutral" from gesture and a "joyful" from speech is always mapped onto "joyful" since there are only three user state classes in gesture. However, this method demands more computing time since all the training data must also be used to generate data for the training of the new neural network. A more elegant alternative is to combine the feature vectors of the modalities to train a new neural network, which will not increase the training cycles but only use some training time, since we just only need to train a single neural network.

Other possible fusion methods are a weighted sum over the training data from different modalities, and probability multiplication. Moreover, if the interference could be solved in a robust way, the majority decision can be used to merge all three modalities.

7 Conclusion

The single modalities speech (with prosody), gesture and facial expression are able to recognize a users internal state when using a modern dialogue system. But only a very small number of persons always show their internal state in all these modalities.

Table 7. Possible Fusion on Classwise User State Recognition Rate (in %)

Recognition	Gesture	Prosody
60	recognied correctly	recognied correctly
7	recognied incorrectly	recognied incorrectly
76	recognied correctly	recognied incorrectly
77	recognied incorrectly	recognied correctly

All in all, the recognition rates, esp. for facial expressions, are not yet satisfactory. Possible reasons have been discussed in the respective sections above. Another reason might be that quite a few of the subjects were not able to indicate their – supposed – user state, i.e., to act *as if* they were in such a state. Note that no pre-selection of "good" vs. "bad" actors took place.

We have observed many cases where only some of above mentioned modalities were available, e.g. only facial expression and gesture with non-verbal input or only speech input if the user looks aside. Especially in this situation, the benefit of multimodality is evident. If the interference problem among modalities can be solved, their fusion can improve classification.

References

1. Batliner, A., Fischer, K., Huber, R., Spilker, J., Nöth, E.: How to Find Trouble in Communication. Speech Communication **40** (2003) 117–143
2. Pieraccini, R., Caskey, S., Dayanidhi, K., Carpenter, B., Phillips, M.: Etude, A Recursive Dialog Manager with Embedded User Interface Patterns. In: Automatic Speech Recognition and Understanding Workshop. (2001)
3. Lemon, O., Bracy, A., Gruenstein, A., Peters, S.: Information States in a Multimodal Dialouge System for Human–Robot Conversation Bi–Dialog. In: 5th Workshop on Formal Semantics and Pragmatics of Dialogue. (2001) 57–67
4. Wahlster, W., Reithinger, N., Blocher, A.: Smartkom: Multimodal Communication with a Life–Like Character. In: Eurospeech 2001. (2001) 1547–1550
5. Chai, D., Ngan, K.: Locating Facial Regions of a Head–and–Shoulders Color Image. In: Automatic Face and Gesture Recognition 2000. (1998) 124–129
6. Heisele, B., Poggio, T., Pontil, M.: Face Detection in Still Gray Images. In: MIT AI Memo, AIM–1687. (2000)
7. Yang, M., Ahuja, M., Kriegman, D.: Face Detection using a Mixture of Factor Analyzers. In: Proceedings of the International Conference on Image Processing. Volume 3. (1999) 612–616
8. Jones, M., Rehg, J.: Statistical Color Models with Application to Skin Detection. In: Proceedings of Computer Vision and Pattern Recognition. (1999) I:274–280
9. Ekman, P., Friesen, W.: The Facial Action Coding System: A technique for the measurement of facial movement. In: Consulting Psychologists Press, Palo Alto, CA. (1978)
10. Tian, Y., Kanade, T., Cohn, J.: Recognizing Action Units for Facial Expression Analysis. IEEE Transactions on Pattern Analysis and Machine Intelligence (PAMI) **23** (2001) 97–115

11. Essa, I., Pentland, A.: Facial Expression Recognition Using a Dynamic Model and Motion Energy. In: Proceedings of the Fifth International Conference on Computer Vision. (1995) 360–367
12. Turk, M., Pentland, A.: Face Recognition Using Eigenfaces. In: Proceedings of Computer Vision and Pattern Recognition. (1991) 586–591
13. Yambor, W., Draper, B., Beveridge, J.: Analyzing PCA–based Face Recognition Algorithms: Eigenvector Selection and Distance Measures. In: Second Workshop on Empirical Evaluation Methods in Computer Vision. (2000)
14. Moghaddam, B., Pentland., A.: Face Recognition Using View–Based and Modular Eigenspaces. In: Vismod, TR-301. (1994)
15. Li, Y., Zhao, Y.: Recognizing Emotions in Speech Using Short-term and Long-term Features. In: Proceedings of the International Conference on Spoken Language Processing. Volume 6., Sydney (1998) 2255–2258
16. Paeschke, A., Kinast, M., Sendlmeier, W.F.: F_0-Contours in Emotional Speech. In: Proc. 14th Int. Congress of Phonetic Sciences. Volume 2., San Francisco (1999) 929–932
17. Batliner, A., Huber, R., Niemann, H., Nöth, E., Spilker, J., Fischer, K.: The Recognition of Emotion. [27] 122–130
18. Batliner, A., Buckow, A., Niemann, H., Nöth, E., Warnke, V.: The Prosody Module. [27] 106–121
19. Kompe, R.: Prosody in Speech Understanding Systems. Lecture Notes for Artificial Intelligence. Springer–Verlag, Berlin (1997)
20. Riedmiller, M., Braun, H.: A Direct Adaptive Method for Faster Backpropagation Learning: The RPROP Algorithm. In: Proc. of the IEEE Intl. Conf. on Neural Networks, San Francisco, CA (1993) 586–591
21. Huber, R., Nöth, E., Batliner, A., Buckow, A., Warnke, V., Niemann, H.: You BEEP Machine – Emotion in Automatic Speech Understanding Systems. In: TSD98, Brno (1998) 223–228
22. Maggioni, C.: Gesture computer–new ways of operating a computer. In: Proceedings of the International Conference on Automatic Face and Gesture Recognition. (1995) 166–171
23. Rabiner, L., Juang, B.: An Introduction to Hidden Markov Models. ASSP **3** (1986) 4–16
24. Rabiner, L., Juang, B.: Fundamentals of Speech Recognition. first edn. Prentice Hall PTR (1993)
25. Rabiner, L.: A Tutorial on Hidden Markov Models and selected applications in speech recognition. In: Proceedings of IEEE. Volume 77. (1989) 257–286
26. Martinez, A., Benavente., R.: The AR Face Database. In: CVC Technical Report Nr. 24. (1998)
27. Wahlster, W., ed.: Verbmobil: Foundations of Speech-to-Speech Translations. Springer, Berlin (2000)

Tailoring the Presentation of Plans to Users' Knowledge and Capabilites

Detlef Küpper[1] and Alfred Kobsa[2]

[1] University of Applied Science Aalen, Beethovenstr. 1, 73433 Aalen, Germany
detlef.kuepper@fh-aalen.de
[2] Dept. of Information and Computer Science, University of California,
Irvine, CA 92697-3425, U.S.A.
kobsa@ics.uci.edu

Abstract. Tailoring advice to a user means finding a plan by which she can reach her goal, and supplying the missing knowledge that she needs to successfully execute the plan. The paper presents a method to determine the kind and amount of this missing knowledge for an already generated domain plan. We show that both a user's knowledge and his capabilities to perform actions must be taken into account when deciding on a plan presentation that is suitable for him. We also argue that it may be useful to consider issues of plan presentation already during the planning process, and show how this can be accomplished in a planning system.

1   Introduction

The effectiveness of advice-giving systems essentially hinges on users' ability to take advantage of given advice to reach their goals. The problem of whether a user can *understand* advice has already received considerable attention in the research literature (see, e.g. [19] for a survey). However, the user must also be able to execute the advice, i.e. have the *capabilities* to perform each step of the advice. Capability in this sense means the user's personal abilities and her authorization to perform the actions that occur in the advice.

Küpper and Kobsa [9] presented a plan generation approach for achieving the user's goals that considers the user's capabilities. The resulting plans are then *in principle* executable by the user. In order to perform the plan, she may however need additional information. In this paper, we describe our approach to identify this missing user knowledge, starting with a plan that the user can in principle execute and that is suitable for reaching her goals. We will show that the additional knowledge that must still be communicated depends not only on the user's existing knowledge but again also on her capabilities.

In the remainder of this paper, we will first summarize central characteristics of the user model that we employ and introduce some terminology. The next section discusses the different types of knowledge that users must possess to be able to perform a plan. We then present an algorithm that determines this knowledge for a plan

A. Günter et al. (Eds.): KI 2003, LNAI 2821, pp. 606–617, 2003.

generated for the current user. This algorithm also calculates the "presentation cost" of the plan to be communicated, which is proportional to the structural complexity of the presentation and can be regarded as a coarse estimate of the user's comprehension efforts. Afterwards, we re-integrate our results into the plan generation process to ascertain that plans will preferably be generated that the user is not only capable of performing but also have the lowest presentation costs. We also discuss other measures besides presentation cost for rating plan presentations, which take user skills, user preferences, and the likelihood of success into account. Finally we describe some related research, and outline future work to decide which parts of the missing knowledge identified by our algorithm should be presented explicitly or may be omitted, depending on inferences that the user may draw.

2   Elements of Our Approach

For representing assumptions about the user, we employ an enhanced version of the user model in [9], which separates system assumptions about users' knowledge and their capabilities. User capabilities are modeled as *plan operators* that a user is in principle able and authorized to perform. They have a terminological representation in the user model, the so-called *plan concepts*. Their preconditions and effects are represented by attributes of their plan concepts. Plan operators/concepts can be instantiated for the generation of user-tailored plans, and become the *steps* of the plans. Plan concepts are also used for modeling (the system's assumptions about) the user's planning knowledge, and the system's own planning knowledge. Since plan steps are instances of plan concepts, assumptions about the user's knowledge about plan steps are inherited from the assumptions about his knowledge about plan concepts. The same holds true for user capabilities.

Each plan concept can also be associated with one or more *decompositions* in the models of the system's and the user's knowledge. Such decompositions are sets of partially ordered plan steps and thus (simplified) plans. Steps of decompositions are again instantiations of plan concepts. This is roughly comparable to decompositions in hierarchical planning [15, 3], except that plan concepts in our decompositions usually do not possess preconditions and effects and cannot be used for planning any more. Instead, decompositions are canned recipes of how to perform the associated plan concept. This is justified since we require the plan generation process that precedes plan presentation to consider all relevant conditions and dependencies.

Küpper and Kobsa [9] describe this planning process for generating plans that the user is able to perform. While its exact nature is irrelevant for presentation purposes (we use UCPOP [12]), we require that the resulting plan not only contain steps but also *causal links*, which are by-products of the planning process. A causal link (s, l, r) is a relation between a step s, a condition represented by literal l that is satisfied by s, and a step r that requires l for its executability. The recognition of user's capabilities and plan knowledge is not directly part of this work since it is highly domain-dependent (see [13, 9, 14] for relevant work).

3   Identifying the Contents for Plan Presentation

Plan presentation should enable users to perform the generated plan and thereby reach their goals. A plan for a user should not be decomposed to the lowest possible level (e.g., down to finger movements). This would considerably increase the communication and comprehension efforts, and lower users' acceptance of the resulting lengthy advice (from a technical point of view, the domain modeling effort and the planning complexity would also soar). Instead, plan presentation should rely on users' ability to further elaborate received plans [21]. Such plans still include, e.g., abstract plan concepts that need to be refined, and abstract object descriptions that need to be replaced by identified objects. When such a plan becomes presented to the user, she is expected to continue decomposing plan steps into a sequence of more primitive executable actions (which may even be well beyond the system's domain model). If unforeseen obstacles hinder the successful execution of a more abstract plan, the user still has a chance to modify it. Besides a listing of the plan steps in correct order, the user therefore needs knowledge about the *properties* of and *interrelations* between the plan steps, and she must know how to *perform*, i.e. further decompose, the steps of the plan.[1]

3.1   Knowing Plan Steps and Their Interrelations

Information about the role of each step in a plan is provided by the causal links of the plan. They describe what step satisfies which precondition for what other step. This knowledge is important for modifying the plan when unexpected obstacles occur, since each modification of the plan must take care not to threaten a causal link. If a plan contains a causal link (s, l, r), no modifications between step s and step r are allowed that negate l since otherwise the precondition of step r is not satisfied anymore and the plan will fail.

3.2   Knowing How to Perform a Step of a Plan

Users may need additional advice for decomposing plan steps if their knowledge is insufficient or even wrong. A plan concept is marked as *atomic* in the user model if the user does not need further information about it (such plan concepts may be directly executable, or the user may have extensive competence for further plan decomposition that goes beyond the system's domain model). For non-atomic plan concepts, the decision on what to explain to the user will hinge on her presumed knowledge how to execute the plan concept. Such knowledge is represented by the presence of one or more decompositions of the plan concept in the user's knowledge model. But even when the user has such knowledge, it may be wrong, or not usable

---

[1] Furthermore, she may require referential descriptions and properties of objects that play a role in the plan [16, 17].

since the user is unable to perform it. Therefore we provide explanations of all presented plan concepts except when the user's knowledge about how to perform the concept is assumed to be *reliable*. We call a plan concept *reliable* if

    a) none of its decompositions in the user's knowledge model is false, and
    b) at least one of them is *usable single-handedly* by the user.

The first condition aims at preventing that the user will consider wrong execution alternatives. The reference point for judging correctness is the system's domain model: a decomposition of a plan concept in the user's knowledge model is correct only if it is also part of the system's knowledge. Assumptions about such user misconceptions may stem from knowledge about typical errors of certain user groups, or from the recognition of individual user misconceptions [14]. A decomposition is usable *single-handedly* (by the current user) if he can in principle perform all its steps and has reliable knowledge about how to perform them if they are non-atomic. Note that the steps of a decomposition may in turn be instantiations of non-atomic plan concepts which the user must know how to perform as well (in the domains that we investigated so far, the nesting was found to be fairly shallow though).

For plan concepts that are not reliable (and which therefore require further explanation of how they can be executed), the system must select one of the plan's decompositions from its own knowledge. Different decompositions generally do not lead to equally good explanations (more on this in the next subsection), and some of them may not even be usable by the current user. We call a decomposition *usable* (by the current user) if he can in principle carry out all its steps and, for each non-atomic step, the system knows at least one decomposition that is usable by the current user. For an example, consider the plan concept *shutdown-windows-computer* with the following two decompositions:

    (1) push keys <Ctrl>, <Alt> and <Del> simultaneously,
        then select <shutdown-button>;
    (2) select <Start> from the task bar, then <Shutdown>.

Although both recipes will shut down a computer under Windows, the former will not be usable for someone who cannot hit three keys simultaneously.

If the system knows several usable decompositions of a plan concept, it should select the "best". The presentation algorithm described below computes a valuation of each available alternative. The rating of an alternative is a function of the ratings of the components of its decomposition and, if the components are plan concepts that require further explanation, the valuation of the decompositions that will be used for these explanations.

3.3   The Presentation Algorithm

The pseudo code of Fig. 1 summarizes the algorithm for determining the knowledge that a user needs to successfully execute a plan *p*. The task is distributed among three

---

present-plan (p:plan, cs:set-of-plan-concepts)

(p1) set *cost* initially to (| *steps* (p) | + 2 * | *causal-links* (p) |) * k_{pres}

(p2) set *presentation* initially to *linearize* (p)

(p3) for each *s* ∈ *steps* (p)

add the name of *plan-concept* (s) to *s* in *presentation*

(p4) for each *pc* ∈ *plan-concepts* (p) \ *cs*

(p5)   add results of *present-plan-concept* (pc, cs) to *presentation, cost*

(p6)   add *pc* and all *plan-concepts* of

presentation (*present-plan-concept* (pc, cs)) to *cs*

present-plan-concept (pc:plan-concept, cs:set-of-plan-concepts)

(c1) set *presentation* initially to { }

set *cost* initially to 0

(c2) if user doesn't know *pc*

(c3)   set *presentation* to descript (pc)

set *cost* to *cost*(descript (pc))

(c4) if not (pc is atomic or user has reliable knowledge of pc)

(c5) add results of present-recipe-for-plan-concept (pc, cs) to

presentation, cost

present-recipe-for-plan-concept (pc:plan-concept, cs:set-of-plan-concepts)

(r1) let *ec* be the set of usable decompositions of *pc* according to system's knowledge

(r2) if *ec* = { } → set *cost* to ∞ (plan presentation fails)

(r3) else set *presentation, cost* to results of *present-plan* (d, cs) where

(r4)   *d* ∈ *ec* ∧

$cost(present\text{-}plan\,(d,\,cs)) = \min_{(d' \in ec)} cost(present\text{-}plan\,(d',\,cs))$

Fig. 1. Pseudo code of the plan presentation algorithm

functions which return two values, namely a data structure that represents the contents of the presentation, and a numerical value *cost* that represents the rating of this presentation. We use the auxiliary functions *presentation* and *cost* to access these two results.

The function *present-plan* processes generated plans as well as decompositions of plan concepts. It starts with a linearization[2] of the plan (p2) and adds the name of the corresponding plan concept for each plan step (p3). This should enable the user to identify the steps. Function *present-plan-concept* determines whether the user needs information on plan concepts, and what kind of information. The function is called for each plan concept unless it had already been processed (the bookkeeping parameter *cs* will be described below). An explanation of a plan concept may consist of

---

[2] The plan generation process may result in a plan that is only partially ordered.

a canned description if the user does not know the concept (c2,c3), and user-specific information about how to perform it if the plan concept is non-atomic and the user does not have reliable knowledge (c4,c5). User-specific information about how to perform a plan concept is determined by the function *present-recipe-for-plan-concept*. It selects the decomposition with the minimal cost (r4) from the set of usable decompositions of the plan concept (r1). The presentations of these decompositions are recursively computed by the function *present-plan*. Line (r2) handles the case in which the system cannot give an explanation that is *usable* by the current user. The subsequent enhanced plan generation process excludes such *unexplainable* plan concepts from further consideration and thus produces plans only for which the algorithm can come up with an adequate presentation.

Let us now discuss some more details of the presentation algorithm. We use the auxiliary functions *steps*, *causal-links* and *plan-concepts,* which return the set of steps, causal-links and plan concepts of a plan, respectively. The function *plan-concept* of a plan step yields the plan concept of which the step is an instantiation.

To avoid multiple explanations of the same concept, the loop starting at line (p4) excludes plan concepts that are in *cs*, the set of already processed plan concepts. This set is passed on in all subsequent function calls as their second argument. Since an explanation of a plan concept may contain explanations of other plan concepts that are also used later in the plan, the set is updated after each call of *present-plan-concept* (p6).

Besides its main task of determining the missing knowledge that the user needs for successful plan execution, the algorithm also computes the *presentation-cost*. Each component of the presentation contributes to this value: steps and causal links in line (p1), and descriptions of plan concepts in line (c3). Following the propositional theory of text comprehension [5, 6], this may be seen as a rough estimation of the user's effort to comprehend the presentation since all components carry new information that must be processed by the user if they are presented explicitly. In (p1), we use the factor k_{pres} as a unit for the presentation cost. If we use it to estimate the user's comprehension effort, k_{pres} stands for the effort that is caused by the presentation of one plan step. Since causal links are more complex components, each contributes two units to the presentation cost.

3.4   An Example

This example demonstrates the behavior of our algorithm for different system assumptions about users' knowledge and capabilities. Users download files through FTP by first selecting the file and then initiating the transfer. Fig. 2 shows three possible decompositions of the corresponding plan concept *ftp-dnload-bin*:

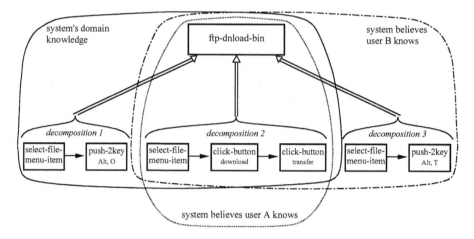

Fig. 2. Different planning knowledge of the system and two users

1. *select-file-menu-item* and *push-2key (Alt,O)*:
   users select the file and hit *<Alt>-<O>* to start the transfer.
2. *select-file-menu-item*, *click-button (download)* and *click-button (transfer)*:
   users select the file, chose the transfer direction, and initiate the transfer.
3. *select-file-menu-item* and *push-2key(Alt,T)*:
   same as (1), except *<Alt>-<T>* is hit instead of *<Alt>-<O>*.

(1) and (2) are correct decompositions of *ftp-dnload-bin* while (3) models a frequently occurring mistake. The former are therefore included in the system's domain model while the latter is not (see Figure 2). Assume that user A knows decomposition 2, is able to perform all its steps, and that all steps are atomic for him. The respective plan concepts are therefore contained both in the knowledge and the capabilities part of A's user model, and marked as atomic in the knowledge part. User A therefore has reliable knowledge about *ftp-dnload-bin* and does not need further explanations thereon. Function *present-plan-concept* in line (p5) of Fig. 1 yields an empty presentation for this plan-concept, and 0 for the *presentation-cost*.

Assume that user B believes that *ftp-dnload-bin* can be decomposed into decompositions 2 and 3. Both are therefore contained in the knowledge part of B's user model. From the system's point of view, B believes in both correct and incorrect decompositions. Since her beliefs about *ftp-dnload-bin* are thus not reliable, the system must provide its own decomposition. To this end, function *present-plan-concept* calls *present-recipe-for-plan-concept* (c5), which must decide between the presentation of decompositions 1 or 2. If B is able to perform all steps of either decomposition and if all are atomic, both decompositions are *usable*. The decision between them in (r3,r4) is made by applying *present-plan* to both alternatives and opting for the one with the lower returned presentation costs. In (p1-p3), a presentation is constructed consisting of two steps for decomposition 1 and three steps for decomposition 2, respectively. The costs are calculated as $2 * k_{pres}$ and $3 * k_{pres}$, (lines (p4-p6) add no extra costs since all plan steps are atomic), and decomposition 1 is thus preferred in (r3,r4).

If user B would not know how to perform *push-2key (Alt, O)*, then *present-plan-concept* (p5) would generate a decomposition of this concept as well (via recursive calls of *present-recipe-for-plan-concept* and *present-plan*), and add its costs to $2 * k_{pres}$. The total *presentation-cost* of decomposition 2 will be lower in this case. Decomposition 2 will also be selected if the user is not able to perform *push-2key (Alt, O)* since, say, these keys are relatively far apart. In this case, decomposition 1 would not be in the set of usable decompositions and hence is not considered any further.

4   Plan Valuation during Plan Generation

Up to now, our discussion separated the two phases of user-tailored advice (i.e., plan generation and plan presentation), in order to work out more clearly the processes and knowledge sources that support them. A generation process that completely disregards the need for subsequent plan presentation may however end up with a plan that requires tedious explanations or, in the worst case, does not have an acceptable presentation at all.

We can identify two starting points for considering presentation aspects during plan generation without curtailing the solution space of the presentation component. First, we exclude unexplainable non-atomic plan concepts from the planning process, because their occurrence in a plan always leads to a rejection of the presentation. The second onset exploits a planning control feature in UCPOP. Gerevini and Schubert [4] investigate several search control strategies to speed up the planning process. We use some of their results to bias the planning process to prefer "good" plans, i.e. plans for which the presentation algorithm will compute a low presentation-cost. The UCPOP algorithm works on several plan candidates in parallel. Before each processing step, it rates all candidates and selects the candidate with the best rating to process next. We use a rating function that considers the presentation-cost of the plan candidate. UCPOP will therefore first operate on the plan candidate with the lowest presentation-cost. If UCPOP adds steps or causal links to the plan candidate, the presentation-cost of this candidate increases and UCPOP may work on another candidate in the next step if it has a better rating. The first solution found has the lowest presentation-cost. This means that plans with a low presentation-cost are preferred, but no solution is lost. Similar control mechanisms are available in most practical plan generators.

For efficiency reasons we do not use the function *present-plan* to calculate the presentation-cost. Instead, we compute the *direct presentation-cost* and the *explanation set* of each plan concept before the planning process starts. The *direct presentation-cost* of a plan concept is determined by the cost of its description if the user does not know the concept, and by the number of (direct) steps of an explanation if the user does not know how to perform it. The *explanation set* of a plan concept is the set of plan concepts that would be (indirectly) used in an explanation of how to perform the plan concept if the user would need such an explanation, and the empty set otherwise. Thus the rating of a plan candidate p can be computed as the sum of

a) $(\mid steps(p) \mid + 2 * \mid causal\text{-}links \ (p) \mid) * k_{pres}$ plus
b) the direct presentation-cost of each plan concept $pc \in$

$$(plan\text{-}concepts(p) \ \cup \ \bigcup\nolimits_{pc' \in \ plan\text{-}concepts(p)} explanation\text{-}set(pc')).$$

This value is a close approximation of the value that would be computed by the function *present-plan*. However, the plan concepts for a plan in the presentation algorithm may influence the decision between alternative explanations of plan concepts that are used later in the plan. This may result in a lower presentation-cost than the value computed for the plan candidate.

We use this technique of biasing the planning process in the way described above only, but also see three other applications scenarios in user-tailored plan presentation:

1. Users may prefer performing certain plan concepts over other plan concepts.
2. Users may have more practice performing certain plan concepts than others [13].
3. Certain plan concepts may have a lower risk of failure for certain users.

User preferences, user practice and likelihood of failure can be expressed by appropriate cost factors that will be taken into account in the planning process. These cost factors can be assigned to the respective plan concept in the capability part of the user model. In contrast to presentation-cost, they relate to the execution of a plan, and not its presentation or comprehension. The recursive combination function for determining these costs therefore will have to consider the complete plan, i.e. not only those plan structures that become explicitly communicated to the user but also those that the user will still expand.

5   Related Work

An early piece of work on plan presentation was the system of Mellish and Evans [11] that produced a natural language description of plans generated by the planner NONLIN [18]. However, this approach neglected the users' needs and characteristics, and usually yielded descriptions that contained too much detail to be useful for user advice. Subsequent work on the generation of instructional text [10, 13] and multimedia presentation [20, 1] considered user characteristics, but did not take users' capabilities to perform plan steps into account nor a further elaboration of the plan by the user. Young's approach [22] is closely related to ours in that he also generated descriptions from the result of a planning process. He focused on curtailing descriptions by removing information that the user can easily infer, but did not take individual differences in the planning knowledge of users into account.

While our approach tries to identify the missing knowledge that users need for successful plan execution, other research [19] focuses on the surface structure of the presentation. The goal in this case is that users should be able to comprehend the presentation, i.e. be able to incorporate all intended information into their internal knowledge structures. We view these approaches as complementary to ours since the knowledge determined by our algorithm still needs to be passed on to the user in an adequate communicative manner.

Other related research includes negotiations with the user about the system's proposal, like in collaborative dialog systems [2]. In this approach, a user may reject advice of the system if he believes it is inadequate. This may especially be the case if the user has wrong assumptions about how to perform plan steps.

6   Summary and Further Development

This work dealt with the problem of determining the missing knowledge that the current user needs for being able to successfully execute an already generated domain plan. Additionally we demonstrated that it may be useful to consider issues of plan presentation during the planning process already, and showed how this can be accomplished in a planning system.

Our approach was guided by the idea that plan descriptions for human users are generally not immediately executable, but need further elaboration by the recipient. This requires a description that enables the user to comprehend not only the sequence of steps that must be executed, but also the internal structure and functionality of the plan. Further knowledge is required if the user does not know, or has wrong assumptions about, how to carry out some plan steps. We showed the knowledge that is required for these tasks, and analyzed how properties of the user influence the kind and amount of this knowledge. Particularly the presentation of knowledge about how to perform plan steps benefited from a user model that separates the user's knowledge from his capabilities. However, even the best plan from a plan generation point of view is useless if there is no good way to explain it to the user. This motivated the improvement of the planning process by taking presentation issues into account.

Additional work is required to generate presentations that are adequate for a user. One important question is, what subset of the knowledge to be communicated (as identified by our algorithm) should be explicitly presented to the user, since presenting the complete knowledge usually leads to lengthy descriptions. Young [22] showed that users make fewer errors during plan execution if the plan description does not contain information that they can easily infer. He proposed to omit such information from a plan presentation. For deciding which plan components should be omitted, he simulated the user's inferences by a user-specific planning algorithm. Currently, we also work on this problem. Our approach is similar to Young's, in that it is also based on the assumption that a user will continue the planning process when she obtains an incomplete plan from the system. However, we do not postulate a user-specific planning algorithm but rather believe that the user's planning *knowledge* has the most impact on his ability to infer missing plan components. The decision whether or not a component of the plan should be presented explicitly is made on the basis of a comparison between the user's effort to comprehend and memorize a description of this component and the his effort to infer it. Details of this work can be found in [8, ch. 4.4].

Whereas most assumptions in our model are based on studies in (text and discourse) comprehension (e.g., [6, 7]), a new line of research will be to find empirical answers through experiments to a number of questions that remained open so far. For instance, in the example of Section 3.4 the system decided to explain the shortest but unknown decomposition, rather than referring to the longer but known decomposition, or even correcting the user's misconception once and forever. We foresee user experiments in environments where users' plan knowledge and abilities can be highly controlled (e.g., computer games with first-person player) to determine additional factors besides explanation length that may influence the choice between these explanatory options.

7   Implementation

A prototype of the system described here has been implemented in CommonLisp and is available from http://linux2.image.fh-aalen.de/kuepper/Diss-CD/.

References

1. André, E.: *A plan-based approach to the generation of multi-modal presentations* (in German). INFIX-Verlag, Sankt Augustin, Germany (1995)
2. Chu-Carroll, J. and Carberry, S.: Collaborative response generation in planning dialogues. *Computational Linguistics 24*(3) (1998) 355–400
3. Erol, K.; Hendler, J. and Nau, D.: Semantics for hierarchical task-network planning. Techn. Report CS-TR-3239, Computer Science Dept., Univ. of Maryland (1994)
4. Gerevini, A. and Schubert, L.K.: Accelerating partial-order planners: Some techniques for effective search control and pruning. *Journal of Artificial Intelligence Research 5* (1996) 95–137
5. Kintsch, W. and van Dijk, T.A.: Toward a model of text comprehension and production. *Psychological Review 85* (1978) 363–394
6. Kintsch, W. and Vipond, D.: Reading comprehension and readability in educational practice and psychological theory. In *Perspectives on memory research*, Nilsson, L.-G. ed., Erlbaum, Hillsdale, NJ (1979) 329–365
7. Kintsch, W.: *Comprehension: A Paradigm for Cognition.* Cambridge University Press, Cambridge (1998)
8. Küpper, D.: *User modeling for user-tailored plan generation and presentation* (in German). Academic Publishing Corporation / IOS Press, Berlin, Amsterdam, forthcoming (2003)
9. Küpper, D. and Kobsa, A.: User-tailored plan generation. In *User Modeling: Proc. of the 7th International Conference, UM'99*. Springer, Wien (1999) 45–54
10. McKeown, K.R.; Elhadad, M.; Fukumoto, Y.; Lim, J.; Lombardi, C.; Robin, J. and Smadja, F.: Natural language generation in COMET. In *Current Research in Natural Language Generation*, Dale, R.; Mellish, C. and Zock, M. eds., Academic Press, London, UK (1990)

11. Mellish, C. and Evans, R.: Natural language generation from plans. *Computational Linguistics 15*(4) (1989) 233–249

12. Penberthy, J.S. and Weld, D.S.: UCPOP: A sound, complete, partial order planner for ADL. In *Principles of Knowledge Representation and Reasoning: Proc. of 3rd International Conference (KR'92)*. Morgan Kaufmann, San Mateo, CA (1992) 103–114

13. Peter, G. and Rösner, D.: User-model-driven generation of instructions. *User Modeling and User-Adapted Interaction 3*(4) (1994) 289–319

14. Pollack, M.E.: Plans as complex mental attitudes. In *Intentions in Communication*, Cohen, P.R.; Morgan, J.; Pollack, M.E., MIT Press, Cambridge, MA (1990) 77–103

15. Sacerdoti, E.D.: *A Structure for Plans and Behavior*. Elsevier/North-Holland, Amsterdam (1977)

16. Sarner, M. and Carberry, S.: Generating tailored definitions using a multifaceted user model. *User Modeling and User-Adapted Interaction 2*(3) (1992) 181–210

17. Schmauks, D. and Reithinger, N.: Generating multimodal output: Conditions, advantages and problems. In *Proc. of 12th International Conference on Computational Linguistics*. North-Holland, Amsterdam (1988) 584–588

18. Tate, A.: Project planning using a hierarchic non-linear planner. Research Report 25, Univ. of Edinburgh, Department of Artificial Intelligence (1976)

19. van Mulken, S.: *User Modeling for Multimedia Interfaces: Studies in Text and Graphics Understanding*. Dt. Univ.-Verlag, Wiesbaden, Germany (1999)

20. Wahlster, W.; André, E.; Finkler, W.; Profitlich, H.-J. and Rist, T.: Plan-based integration of natural language and graphics generation. *Artificial Intelligence 63* (1993) 387–427

21. Webber, B.; Badler, N.; Di Eugenio, B.; Geib, C.; Levison, L. and Moore, M.: Instructions, Intentions and Expectations. *Artificial Intelligence 73*(1-2) (1995) 253–269

22. Young, R.M.: Using Grice's maxim of quantity to select the content of plan descriptions. *Artificial Intelligence 115*(2) (1999) 215–256

An Agents' Definition Framework and a Methodology for Deriving Agents' Taxonomies

Silke Höppner

Cork Institute of Technology, Dept. of Mathematics and Computing, Rossa Avenue, Cork, Ireland
silke@hoeppner.com
http://www.cit.ie

Abstract. This paper presents a proposal for defining software agents and for deriving taxonomies of agents. It also extends [5]. First a theoretical framework is established as foundation giving a new abstract and set-based definition of agents. Based on this definition, a methodology is presented which takes a new approach to derive taxonomies treating software agents.

1 Introduction

Originally the term *agent* (agentis[1]) means somebody who leads or who acts upon somebody else's behalf. Several attempts to define agents have been made e.g. by Franklin and Graesser [8], Wooldridge and Jennings [26], Huhns and Singh [9], Maes [13], Nwana [15] and others, although the lack of a generally accepted definition caused a lot of researchers to define their agents aligned with their applications as was shown by Franklin and Graesser [8].

In the beginning of the nineties a general revival of agents took place, not only in the research society: The concept of individual user support and delegation provided by software programs with a touch of personality grew quickly popular, rebirthing old science fiction visions of artificial intelligence. The result was an overwhelming emergence of pseudo- agents everywhere in the Internet. Many companies advertised their programs as agents or assistants, no matter which functionality was actually provided. Wayner & Joch placed it cynically in [24]:

> *"...the metaphor has become so pervasive that we're waiting for some enterprising company to advertise its computer switches as empowerment agents"*.

The response of many researchers was to invent new synonyms and new definitions, leading to a large variety of newly defined "agents", lacking systematics and standards, although agent standards were provided and are permanently further developed [comp.[7]].

---

[1] (Agent) a. [L. agens, agentis, p. pr. of agere to act; akin to Gr. to lead, Icel. aka to drive, Skr. aj. √2.] Acting; — opposed to patient, or sustaining, action. [Archaic] "The body agent." Bacon [25].

A. Günter et al. (Eds.): KI 2003, LNAI 2821, pp. 618–632, 2003.

1.1   Agent Taxonomies: State of the Art

The lack of a standardised agent definition shows consequences when it comes to ordering the different agent types into a taxonomy: Various taxonomies are used simultaneously, depending on different approaches and project-related applications of the responsible researchers. This section gives a short overview on presented taxonomies for agents.

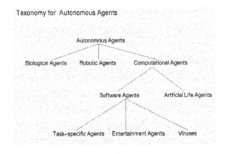

Fig. 1a. Decision tree approach by Franklin and Graesser [8].

Fig. 1b. Set-based taxonomy suggested by Nwana [15].

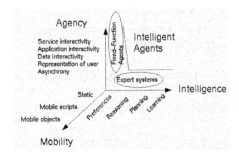

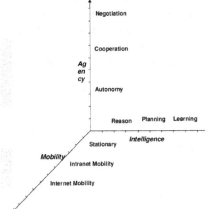

Fig. 1c. Dimension-based taxonomy by Bradshaw [3].

Fig. 1d. Similar taxonomy by Schwehm for mobile agents [19].

Franklin and Graesser were probably the first to offer the definition of an agent taxonomy [8]. After establishing an overview on the variety of agent definitions, they attempted to classify them by creating a taxonomy. The result (Figure 1a) represents the status quo of the agent definitions in 1996 and is now obsolete, since so many new agent types have been created which cannot be found in or covered by this taxonomy.

Reacting to the emerging amount of different agent types, Nwana's taxonomy (Figure 1b) follows the union of only three types of properties: Autonomy, Learning and Cooperation [16]. This offers a large granularity leading to the distinction of only a few types of abstract agents. It is arguable if this represents the current situation in the IT environment.

Another taxonomy is from Bradshaw (Figure 1d) [3]. He suggests the terms *intelligence*, *mobility* and *agency* as properties for agent classification, where agency ranges from asynchronous behaviour and the interaction of first data, then applications and finally services. This taxonomy gives the impression that it tries to fit more than three properties into one three-dimensional graph: Already the term *agency* in itself holds a whole variety of terms, which could serve as an independent property (e.g. collabo ration, sociability or autonomy). The graph implies that expert systems can only reach an agency state of asynchrony, but are never used in e.g. application interaction. But since it is known from societies of planning agents which collaborate as distributed systems or applications [i.e. 4, 20], this part of the taxonomy is also found to be arguable. A quite similar taxonomy for mobile agents, perhaps based on the one from Bradshaw is presented by Schwehm [19].

Huhns and Singh offered an approach to solve the problem of large granularity by offering many dimensions with large attribute ranges. This seems to cover a huge range of possible agent types. However, because of the amount of possibilities it offers, the taxonomy seems complex, making it difficult to keep the overview.

Table 1. Attributes of Huhns' and Singh's Taxonomy [9]

Intrinsic characteristics	
Property	*Range of Values:*
Life-span	Transient to long-lived
Level of Cognition	Reactive to Deliberate
Construction	Declarative to Procedural
Mobility	Stationary to Itinerant
Adaptability	Fixed to Teachable to Auto-didactic
Modelling	of environments, themselves, or other agents
Extrinsic characteristics	
Property	*Range of Values:*
Locality	Local to Remote
Social Autonomy	Independent to Controlled
Sociability	Autistic, Aware, Responsible, Team player
Friendliness	Co-operative to Competitive to Antagonistic
Interactions	Logistics: direct or via facilitators, mediators, or non-agents
	Style/Quality/Nature: with agents/world/both
	Semantic Level: declarative or procedural communications

Probably because of the difficulty of ordering such a variety of agents which all lack definitions and which differ in so many aspects, all taxonomies presented in this section seem to be suffering from some sort of trade-off: Either they define a constrained agent field and can not be applied to the whole agent society; or they are structured in a large and/or fuzzy granularity, leading to superficiality or not enough types of properties are presented, which prevents the subsumption of different types of agents. Taxonomies that try to represent a whole set of agent properties loose the ability to give an overview of agent types. Therefore a new attempt to create an agent taxonomy is made, which seeks to introduce a finer, more specific and labelled granularity in order to help clarify the status quo of the agent community.

2 Deriving a Component-Based Methodology for Creating Agent Taxonomies

As was shown above the term *agent* has come to be a widely used term. In order to base the derivation of a taxonomy on such a term, a foundational framework must be defined first. Therefore the following paragraphs give a derivation of a new definition of software agents. Since the framework to be defined is used as a foundation for further definitions, each definition used in the framework should fullfill two requirements:

- A systematic and formal context must exist, to which each term can be related to and
- A clear empirical meaning of each term exists.

This leads us to use a theory of science [2] approach in order to derive the foundational base:

If the term *agent* is to be introduced, then it must be defined first, which formal contextual frame of the term exists. Then an empirical relation to the term *agent* must be created. Therefore empirical theories which already deal with agent-like systems must be found, the foundations they have established concerning agents must be sorted and combined.

Which empirical theories deal with »actor«? In the variety of empirical sciences the following can be listed: Biology, psychology and sociology. These sciences deal with agent-like systems which all incorporate the same basic fact: they are alive. Liveliness implies the ability to change, especially when it comes to endogenous changes. Revisiting contemporary learning theories, the smallest common denominator between all the currently accepted theories can be found in systems, where autonomous changes can be observed over certain time intervals. In lifelike systems it can be differentiated between observable specific and unspecific changes.

In order to be able to make general statements about lifelike and learning systems in environments, the above-mentioned empirical sciences need to introduce formal structures for deriving explanations. In the presented approach, the long-standing concepts of systems theory [11] combined with set theoretic notations are used. The central term *system* shall be used for formalising the structures of the above-mentioned empirical sciences.

2.1 Basic Definitions

The following sections will give a number of definitions in order to establish the theoretical framework of agency used in this thesis. If not otherwise stated, the reader may assume that the author takes the following presumptions:

Elements of sets are described by small letters $(x \in N)$, functions are described by small letters $(func(x))$, sets are described by capital letters $(NUM = \{x \mid ...\})$,

i.   Let D be the set of dimensions d_x with $D \neq \{\,\}$ and $D = \{d_x \mid x, d_x \in IN\}$, where each element consists of a unit of measurement (dimension).

ii. Let P be the set of ordered pairs, where each pair consists of a unit of measurement (dimension) and a value and each pair represents a state. P is a subset of the set of dimensions D associated with the set of values IR with

$$P \subseteq D \times IR, P = \{\langle d_1, v_1 \rangle, \langle d_i, v_i \rangle, ..., \langle d_n, v_n \rangle \mid d_i \in D, v_i \in IR, n \in IN\}.$$

Let TR be a set of transitions, which represent actions that result in state changes. Transition functions are separated in first order and second order transition functions. First order transition functions map sets of values on sets of values while second order transition functions map sets of fist order transition functions and sets of values onto sets of first order transition functions.

2.2 Agent Definition Framework

In order to generate an underlying concept for agents, the theoretical framework is started by defining a general term, which is *object*.

Definition 1: An *object* $o = \langle Q, S, E, TR \rangle$ is a tuple consisting of sets of states and a set of transition functions, where

i. Q is the finite set of states q_i of the object with $Q = \{s_0, s_1, ..., s_i, q_0, q_1, ...q_j, e_0, e_1, ...e_k \mid i, j, k \in N\}$ and $Q \subset P$,

ii. S is the finite set of start states s_i with $S = \{s_i \mid i \in N\}$ and $S \subset Q$

iii. E is the finite set of end states e_i with $E = \{e_i \mid i \in N\}$ and with $E \subset Q$ is the finite set of first order transition functions $TR = \{tr_i \mid i \in N\}$, where the following state transitions apply:

$$\begin{array}{ccccc} tr_i & tr_{i+1} & & tr_{n-1} & tr_n \\ s_i \rightarrow & q_i \rightarrow & q_{i+1} .. \rightarrow & q_n \rightarrow & e_i \end{array}$$

Variables or constants, which are part of the object and hold some values, are considered properties of the object's states, meaning they are used for representing the current state of the object.

For interaction an object needs an environment. Therefore it must be defined:

Definition 2: An *environment* $v = \langle \hat{Q}, \hat{S}, \hat{E}, \hat{TR}, O \rangle$ is a tuple consisting of sets of states, a set of transition functions between these states and a set of objects which are situated in this environment, where

i. $\hat{Q}$ is the finite set of states

$$\hat{Q} = \left\{\hat{s}_0, \hat{s}_1..., \hat{s}_i, \hat{q}_0, \hat{q}_1,..., \hat{q}_j, \hat{e}_0, \hat{e}_1,..., \hat{e}_k \mid i, j, k \in N \right\} \text{ with}$$

$$\hat{Q}(v) = Q(v) \cup Q(o_0) \cup Q(o_1)... \cup Q(o_i)... \cup Q(o_n), i, n \in N,$$

where the set of states $\hat{Q}$ consists of the subset of environmental own states (e.g. properties, variables, constants) $Q(v)$ and the subsets $Q(o_i)$ of the states of the objects o_i, which belong to the surrounding environment, since they are incorporated by it.

ii. $\hat{S}$ is the finite set of start states $\hat{S} = \left\{\hat{s}_i \mid i \in N \right\}$ with $\hat{S} \subseteq \hat{Q}$

iii. $\hat{E}$ is the finite set of end states $\hat{E} = \left\{\hat{e}_i \mid i \in N \right\}$ with $\hat{E} \subseteq \hat{Q}$

iv. $\hat{TR}$ is the finite set of first order transition functions

$$\hat{TR} = \left\{\hat{tr}_0, \hat{tr}_1,..., \hat{tr}_i \mid i \in N \right\} \text{ with}$$

$$\hat{TR}(v) = TR(v) \cup TR(o_0) \cup ...TR(o_i) \cup ...TR(o_n), i, n \in N \text{ where the}$$

set of transition functions $\hat{TR}$ consists of the subset of environmental own transition functions (e.g. inter-object transition functions) $TR(v)$ and the subsets $TR(o_i)$ of the transition functions of objects (e.g. intra-object transition functions) that belong to the surrounding environment.

v. O is the set of objects, which the environment holds with $O = \left\{o_i \mid i \in N \right\}$.

Comparing objects and environment, the similarity structure becomes obvious. It can be proved that each object can simultaneously be an environment. For describing hierarchical structures consisting of objects including objects etc. over multiple layers, a more generalised term is introduced, fulfilling both conditions of objects and environments, representing an abstract and perspective-independent level.

Definition 4: A *system* s is a tuple consisting of objects, states and transition functions. $s = \langle Q, S, E, TR, O \rangle$, where

i. Q is the finite set of states q_i with $Q = \{q_i \in IN\}$,

ii. S is the finite set of start states s_i with $S = \{s_i \mid i \in IN\}$ with $S \subseteq Q$,

iii. E is the finite set of end states e_i with $E = \{e_i \mid i \in IN\}$ with $E \subseteq Q$,

iv. TR is the finite set of first order transition functions tr_i with
$TR = \{tr_i \mid i \in IN\}$ and

v. O is the finite set of objects o_i with $O = \{o_i \mid i \in IN\}$

If the term *system* is generalised further in order to incorporate lifelike systems, as defined in empirical sciences, two perspectives of system can be found:
According to the presented theoretical framework an *environment* is perceived as an instance of system, as well as *object* is an instance of system. For describing the relationship between the environment and an individual object inside of this environment a means of interaction/communication between the objects and their environment needs to be derived: The interfacing and interaction between objects and their environment seemingly takes place through the surface of the objects. An environmental event causes a state change to happen, this state change is perceived by the object through sensing functions provided by the surface. The transformation of the perception into an internal format leads to state changes inside of the object. The object may – following a certain state change - then perform some action in the environment, as reaction to the former environmental event. This reaction or event causes a new environmental state change, possibly provoking reactions from other objects. This leads to the next definition:

Definition 5: A *surface* surf is a tuple consisting of a set SS of internal states, a set IS of input states, a set OS of output states and a set IT consisting of transition functions mapping the input states onto the internal states of a system and of transition functions which map internal states onto output states.

$surf = \langle SS, IS, OS, STI, ST, STO \rangle$, where:

i. SS is the finite set of internal states $SS = \{ss_i \mid i \in IN\}$, consisting of property states of the surrounded system (e.g. properties, variables, constants) - which influence the perception and action of the surface - and the subsets of input and output states of the surface itself (states which are reached while sensing or acting in the environment). SS is a subset of the set of states Q of the surrounded system ($SS \subseteq Q$).

ii. IS is the finite set of input states is_i with $IS = \{is_i \mid i \in IN\}$ and $IS \subseteq SS$ and therefore $IS \subseteq Q$.

iii. OS is the finite set of output states os_i with $OS = \{os_i \mid i \in IN\}$ and $OS \subseteq SS$ and therefore $OS \subseteq Q$.

iv. STI is the finite set of surface input transition functions sti_i with $STI = \{sti_i \mid sti_i : f(is_j) \rightarrow q_k, i, j, k \in IN\}$, which map surface input states onto internal states and $STI \subseteq TR$,

v. ST is the finite set of surface transition functions st_i with $ST = \{st_i \mid st_i : f(ss_j) \rightarrow ss_k, i, j, k \in IN\}$, which map internal surface states ss_i onto internal surface states and $ST \subseteq TR$,

vi. STO is the finite set of surface transition functions sto with $STO = \{sto_i \mid sto_i : f(ss_j) \rightarrow os_k, i, j, k \in IN\}$, which map internal states onto output states $os_k \in OS$ and $STO \subseteq TR$.

Definition 6: A surface of a system can exist, if in the environment, which surrounds the system, a set of stimulating and acting functions exist which enable an interaction with the surface. A system does not need to interact with its environment, therefore $STI = STO = SS = \{\ \}$ is valid.

Definition 7: A lifelike *system* or a system, which simulates livelikeness, is a system that incorporates a set IT of transition functions, which map internal states onto internal states. A lifelike system must have a surface. If acting as environment, it must also incorporate transition functions for mapping internal states onto surfaces of internal objects and vice versa. Considering this, the following tuple applies:

$lls = \langle Q, S, E, SS, IS, INS, OS, TR, STI, ST, STO, IT, O \rangle$, where

i. INS is the finite subset of internal system states $INS = \{ins_i \mid i \in IN\}$, which refer to the kernel of a system and are not included in the surface with $INS \subseteq Q, SS \cap INS = \{\ \}$.

ii. IT is the finite set of first order transition functions with $IT : INS^n \rightarrow INS^m$ which map internal states onto internal states.

For simplicity the tuple is reduced to the supersets which leads to $lls = \langle Q, TR, O \rangle$ with $IT \subseteq TR$, where

i. Q is the finite set of states q_i with $Q = \{q_i \mid i \in IN\}$, $Q = SS \cup IS \cup OS \cup INS \cup S \cup E$,

ii. TR is the finite set of first order transition functions tr_i with $TR = \{tr_i \mid i \in IN\}$, $TR = STI \cup STO \cup ST \cup IT$,

iii. O is the finite set of objects o_i with $O = \{o_i \mid i \in IN\}$.

A lifelike system can only exist, if all sets in its tuple besides O are not empty ($E \neq \{\ \}, S \neq \{\ \}, INS \neq \{\ \}$ and therefore $Q \neq \{\ \})(IS \neq \{\ \}, OS \neq \{\ \}$ and therefore $SS \neq \{\ \}, STI \neq \{\ \}, STO \neq \{\ \}, IT \neq \{\ \}$ and therefore $TR \neq \{\ \}$). This means that lifelike systems incorporate functions, which allow them to change their internal states through some sort of behaviour. These systems will always repeat the same behaviour in the same situation. The main difference between a lifelike system and a learning system is the ability to evaluate its situation-dependent behaviour and to change its behaviour accordingly. Therefore a learning system is defined as follows:

Definition 8: A *learning system* is a lifelike system, which incorporates a set LT of learning functions and a set ET of evaluation functions et_b. Learning functions LT map functions onto functions, therefore they represent a finite set of second order transition functions with $TR \cap LT = \{\ \}$. Evaluation functions map ordered groups of perceived environmental states $\hat{Q}$ onto a set of internal evaluation states $es_b \in ES$ with

$$ET = \{et_0, et_1, ..., et_b, ..., et_h \mid et_b : \hat{Q} \to ES, b, h \in IN, ES \subseteq Q\},$$
$$ET \subseteq TR.$$

A learning system can therefore be described as a tuple $lrs = \langle Q, S, E, SS, IS, OS, INS, ES, TR, STI, STO, ST, IT, ET, LT, O \rangle$. For simplicity the tuple is reduced to the supersets, leaving $lrs = \langle Q, TR, LT, O \rangle$, with

i. Q is the finite set of states q_i with $Q = \{q_i \mid i \in IN\}$ and $Q = SS \cup IS \cup OS \cup INS \cup S \cup E \cup ES$.

ii. TR is the finite set of first order transition functions tr_i with $TR = \{tr_i \mid i \in IN\}$ and $TR = STI \cup STO \cup ST \cup IT$

iii. LT is the finite set of second order transition functions lt_i with
$$LT = \{lt_j \mid lt_j : f(it_i^{t_0}) \to it_i^{t_{0+1}}, i, j \in IN\} \quad \text{and}$$
$$LT : Q \times TR_{t_0} \to TR_{t_0+1},$$

iv. O is the finite set of objects o_i with $O = \{o_i \mid i \in IN\}$

A non-learning system may incorporate a set ET of evaluation functions as well as a set ES of evaluation states, but it lacks the ability to learn from those evaluated experiences and therefore does not incorporate a set of learning functions LT. Using all the above defined capabilities, an agent can now be defined as follows:

Definition 9: An agent in its simplest form is a lifelike system. An adaptive agent is a learning system.

If the agent is a lifelike or learning system, then it must interact with its environment through its surface. IS denotes the input states, therefore the stimuli received from the environment, to which it reacts. The surface input transitions STI transfer the input state into the kernel, where it is processed. The surface output transitions STO transfer the reaction of the agent onto the output states OS, with effects to the environment.

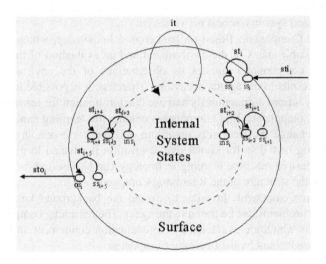

Fig. 2. Structure of a learning system

2.3 Agent Architectural Components

Taking a technical view for a moment, it should be noticed that most software agents consist of either a set of software modules or a set of software objects. How can this fact be mapped onto the above given definitions ? By defining the components, of which agents may consist:

Definition 10: A component is a tuple consisting of one or more sets of states and one or more sets of first or second order transition functions, where every component is responsible for the fullfillment of certain tasks. Therefore a component is a system. Following from there, each lifelike or learning system consists of a set of components and the difference between learning and lifelike agents lies in the omittance of the component that includes the ability to learn.

As defined in Definition 8 and 9, lifelike and learning systems are composed by sets of states and sets of transition functions. The structure of the system is defined by the way these subsets are composed in componentes. Considering and comparing the structural overviews of software agents given in [12], [17] and [6] – and keeping in mind that a component in the most simple case may consist of one state and one transition function and in a complex structure of various sets of functions and states – then all software agents include the following components:

- Kernel Component: This component incorporates the overall algorithm which describes the agent's behaviour., a means to store the data which is needed for the algorithm and the abstract machine which executes the algorithm.
- Reasoning Component: The agent uses the existing amount of background knowledge in order to decide how to react to the received input. Here any knowledge representations with their corresponding means of deduction can be found, e.g. rule based systems, neural networks, etc..
- Evaluation Component: Based on background knowledge, which describes the various possible states of the environment and an evaluation of these states, the evaluation component evaluates its observations of the environmental states caused as results to the agents behaviour. Therefore it is possible for the agent to evaluate its actions autonomously and use this information for learning.
- Learning Component: This component contains the learning function, that is a means to change the reasoning algorithm and the corresponding data. Also a means to log new data for knowledge acquisition is situated in this component. Here any desired machine learning technology can be inserted, as long as it accords with the structure of the Reasoning Component.
- Exploration Component: In order to extend the background knowledge of an agent, new problems can be posed to the agent. The reasoning component will offer solutions which are evaluated by the evaluation component and – in case of success – are learned by the Learning Component.
- Surface Component: Depending on the internal structure of the kernel component, this component incorporates as many interfaces as necessary to map information from the outside to the kernel component, but also to the learning, reasoning and evaluation component.

As shown above, a variety of taxonomies were built upon the concept of behaviour, functional abilities or images of agents. Using the above given definitions, a mapping can be performed between structures of agents, their behaviour and their image, based on transition functions and states, structured in components. Using those components as features in a feature vector for the description of each agent type allows a comparison and therefore the creation of an agent taxonomy. This is described in the following section.

2.4 Software Agent Taxonomy

As defined above, all agents consist of sets of transition functions and states as well as a surface. In addition to that, agents may consist of combinations of a kernel component, a learning component, an evaluation component and an exploration component. The first two mandatory and the four optional components build a solution space of 2^6 possible combinations. The above listed components represent functionalities and therefore behaviour of the agents. As the above given examples of other researchers show, it is extremely difficult to create a taxonomy based on behaviours. But a classic type of taxonomy can be created by sets and subsets of components. Through the mapping of components onto behaviours it is possible to describe most agent types: If the different types of agents can be matched to component combinations (or component vectors), they can be integrated into a taxonomy. Such a taxonomy, which is created from single examples of concrete agent types and their corresponding definitions depensds very much on the amount of examples used and on the conformance of the single example definitions. In order to achieve a complete and thorough taxonomy, all agent definitions used must first be adapted onto the same feature vector. Because of time constraints this was not possible in the scope of this work. Instead, this was performed for 36 concrete agents, which were found in the internet and interpreted by the author concerning their abstract architecture from the information given with these agents. A taxonomy following this approach can therefore only represent the given set of agents and the interpretations of its author. However, considering these constraints, the resulting overlapping agent sets show the potential of such an approach. Based on the variety and fuzziness of the term agent, the used examples are problematic: Various agent terms, as they appear in research publications and the Internet, were collected and mapped onto component vectors. The given list (presented in Table 2) holds groups of agent types, which overlap strongly. Also the list is by far not complete. As many agent groups overlapped to a certain degree a set-based graphical presentation of the resulting sets was chosen: The resulting sets are illustrated in the appendix. After each agent type was mapped onto the feature vectore, similar agent types could be grouped. The feature vectors of the found agent type groups were combined and ordered into a decision tree (3a). From there, for illustration purposes, overlapping sets of agent type groups could be extracted (3b).

The taxonomy presents various groups of agents, growing more intelligent from the right to the left, when imagined on a horizontal axis and decreasing in adaptability from the top to the bottom. The agent groups are situated in sets and subsets, where a set represents a wider definition than the incorporated subset. So for example the set of adaptive agents ranges from learning autonomous agents, which truly perform learning, to adaptive reactive agents which are mobile and just adapt a few parameters since they cannot afford to carry large knowledge structures with them through networks. Further (non-learning) autonomous agents are found to be a subset of emotional autonomous agents, which again are a subset of emotional agents.

3   Summary and Evaluation

This paper formulated a new agent definition framework and described the resulting agent structure and taxonomy structure on an abstract level. The agent theory was developed using formal set theory and following a theory of science- approach, which is a traditional and established approach to the creation of theories based on logic [1].

From the presented definitions and their degree of abstraction on one hand combined with a recursive element (each object can contain other objects) which enables the formulation of any desired granularity on the other hand, it follows that this framework should be able to map all existing agent definitions. This enables a common expression of varying agent architectures and allows an ordering of those agents into a corresponding taxonomy.

Summarising, the derived definition framework is general, can take on every degree of granulation and complexity, enabling its potential use for an extension of agent standards with respect to the internal structuring of agents. It also enables the set-up of a type of taxonomy. Empirical proof was established through the application to a set of 36 agent types found in research papers or in the internet.

However, applying the agent theory has one drawback: Its application is difficult and expensive. Therefore, to increase user friendliness, the theory should be further extended with predefined components. The finer granulated such components are, the better the resulting taxonomies may become.

References

1.   Agents 97 Online Proceedings: http://sigart.acm.org/proceedings/agents97
2.   Bhaskar, R.: A Realist Theory of Science. New Edition: Verso Books, London (1997). Originally Edt. Leeds Books Ltd. (1975)
3.   Bradshaw, J.: Introduction to Software Agents, in: Bradshaw, Jeff (Ed.): Software Agents, AAAI / MIT-Press (1997) 3–46
4.   Bouchefra, F. / Maurin, T. / Auge, P. / Rozoy, B. / Reynaud, R.: Multi-Agent Based Architecture Specification and Verification. In: Proceedings of the Eleventh Workshop on Knowledge Acquisition, Modelling and Management. Banff Alberta (1998)
5.   Doeben-Henisch, G. and Hoeppner, S. : Defining Agency. In: Proceedings of the 3rd International Conference on Interactive Systems. Ulyanovsk, Russia (1999)
6.   Ferber, J.: Les Systeme Multi-Agents. Vers une intellligence collective. InterEditions, Paris (1995, 1997)
7.   Foundation for Intelligent Physical Agents, FIPA '98 Specification Part 12: Ontology Service, FIPA Specification '98 Version 1.0. FIPA, Geneva (1998)
8.   Franklin, S. and Graesser, A.: Is it an Agent, or just a Program? A Taxonomy for Autonomous Agents, in: Proceedings of the Third International Workshop on Agent Theories, Architectures, and Languages, Springer-Verlag (1996)
9.   Huhns, M. N. / Singh, M. P.: Agents and Multiagent Systems: Themes, Approaches and Challenges, in: Huhns, M. N. / Singh, M.P. (Eds.): Readings in Agents, Morgan Kaufmann Publishers Inc., San Francisco (1997)
10.   Janson, Sverker: Swedish Institute of Computer Science: Agent-Based Systems, http://www.agentbase.com/survey-mobile.html
11.   Klir, G. J.: Facets of Systems Science, in: IFSR International Series on Systems Science and Engineering, Volume 7, Plenum Press, New York (1991)
12.   Klügl, F.: Multiagenten-simulation, Konzepte, Werkzeuge, Anwendung. Addison-Wesley, München Boston San Francisco Harlow Don Mills, Ontario Sydney Mexico City Madrid Amsterdam (2001)

13. Maes, P.: Artificial Life Meets Entertainment: Life like Autonomous Agents, in: Communications of the ACM Magazine, Vol. 38, No. 11 (1995) 108–114
14. MIT Media Lab Software Agents Projects Home Page,
    http://agents.www.media.mit.edu/groups/agents/projects/
15. Nwana, S. Hyacinth: Software Agents: An Overview, in: Knowledge Engineering Review, Vol 11, No 3 (1996) 1–40
16. Nwana, S. H. / Ndumu, D.T.: A Brief Introduction to Software Agent Technology, in: Jennings, N. / Wooldridge, M. (Eds.): Agent Technology: Foundations, Applications and Markets, Springer Verlag, New York (1998)
17. Russel, S. / Norvig, P.: Artificial Intelligence – A Modern Approach, Prentice Hall, New Jersey (1995)
18. Second International Conference on Autonomous Software Agents,
    http://www.cis.udel.edu/agents98
19. Schwehm, M.: Mobile Softwareagenten, in: ObjektSpektrum 6 (1998) 19–23
20. Shen, W. / Norrie, D. H.: A Hybrid Agent-Oriented Infrastructure for Modelling Manufacturing Enterprises, in: Proceedings of the Eleventh Workshop on Knowledge Acquisition, Modelling and Management, Banff, Alberta (1998)
21. Third International Conference on Autonomous Agents:
    http://www.cs.washington.edu/research/agents99/
22. UMBC Agent Weg: http://agents.umbc.edu/
23. User Modelling 2001 Proceedings,
    http://bistrica.usask.ca/UM/UM01/Proceedings01.html
24. Wayner, P. / Joch, A.: Agents of Change, in: Byte, March (1995) 94–95
25. Webs13, Webster: Webster's Unabridged Dictionary, 1913,
    http://www.bibliomania.com/Reference/Webster/
26. Wooldrige, M. J. / Jennings, N. R.: Intelligent Agents: Theory and Practice, in: Knowledge Engineering Review, 10(2) (1995) 115–152

Appendix: Example Taxonomy

Table 2 lists the used agent types ordered by an empirically found taxonomy (Figure 3). Listed are number, name and source (S.) of the agent types. Please note that in Table 2 the sources present the references where certain agent types can be found instead of listing every single source, which would have extended the paper too much.

Table 2. List of agent types found in the internet by the author

No.	Name	S.	No.	Name	S.	No.	Name	S.
1	Autonomous Agents	[14,21]	2	Adaptive Autonomous Agents	[14]	3	Autonomous Emotional Agents	[18]
4	Autonomous Mobile Robots	[18,21]	5	Animated Learning Creatures	[18]	6	Autonomous Scientific Agents	[18]
7	Believable Agents	[14]	8	Believable Social Agents	[1]	9	Collaborative Agents	[14]
10	Collaborative Mobile Agents	[14]	11	Collaborative User Interface Agents	[14]	12	Co-operating Mobile Robots	[18]
13	Decision Supporting Agents	[18]	14	Domain adaptive Agents	[18]	15	Emotional Agents	[14,18]
16	Intelligent User Interface Agents	[14]	17	Enactio nal and Adaptive Agents	[18]	18	Entertainment Agents	[14,18]
19	Entertainment Robots	[18]	20	Exploring Agents	[14]	21	Game Playing Agents (e.g. RoboCup)	[1]
1	Intelligent Agents	[14]	23	Intelligent Mobile Agents	[14]	24	Matchmaking Agents	[14]
25	Knowbots	[23]	26	Learning Agents	[14]	27	Adaptive Reactive Agents	[22]
28	Lifecycle Consultant Agents	[1]	29	Messenger Agents	[10]	30	Mobile Agents	[14,10]
31	Pedagogical Agents	[18]	32	Planning Agents	[14]	33	Presentation Agents	[18]
34	User Modelling Agents	[23]	35	Search Agents	[1]	36	Shopping Agents	[1]
37	Social Agents	[1]	38	Storyboard Agents	[1]	39	Story-Telling Agents	[14]

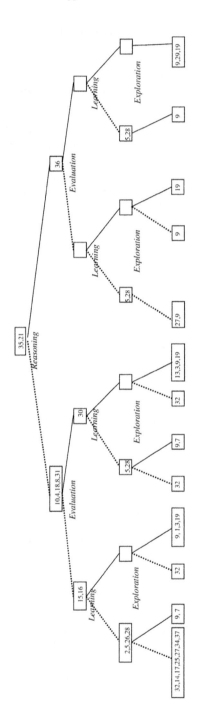

Fig. 3. The resulting sets of overlapping agents: The decision tree sorting the feature vector (3a), the sets, showing the overlaps (3b).

A Multimodal Fission Approach with a Presentation Agent in the Dialog System SmartKom

Jochen Müller, Peter Poller, and Valentin Tschernomas

German Research Center for Artificial Intelligence GmbH Stuhlsatzenhausweg 3,
D-66123 Saarbrücken
{jmueller,poller,tscherno}@dfki.de

Abstract. One of the major scientific goals of SmartKom is to design a new human-machine interaction metaphor for a multimodal dialog system that combines speech, gesture, and mimics input with speech, gesture, mimics and graphics output. In SmartKom an animated life-like character, serves as the communication partner of the user.

In this paper we focus on the multimodal output of SmartKom, performed by MMoPaD (Multi Modal Presentation and Display), showing how these highly ambitious tasks of the SmartKom system are managed and realized on the output side, i.e., how the communication assistant adapts its behavior to the available output media and modalities with respect to the current dialog situation.

Depending on them presentations are split in parts (fission), which are output in different ways. An important task is the synchronization of gestures, mimics and speech of the presentation agent Smartakus which enriches the presentation and makes it more lively. The system is used on standard and mobile devices.

1 Introduction

SmartKom (www.smartkom.org) is a multimodal dialog system that supports the situated understanding of possibly imprecise, ambiguous or partial multimodal input and the generation of coordinated, cohesive, and coherent multimodal presentations. Interactions in SmartKom are managed based on representing, reasoning and exploiting models of the user, the domain, the task, the context, the media and modalities themselves. SmartKom is based on the situated delegation-oriented dialog paradigm (SDDP) [13], in which the user delegates a task to a virtual communication assistant, visualized as a life-like artificial character on a graphical display. The presentation manager of the SmartKom system generates dynamically a multimodal and multimedia presentation undertaking the task of fission. The system uses speech, graphic, gesture and mimic on the output side as well as on the input side. Unlike the traditional desktop interaction metaphor, that is based on WIMP (windows, icons, mouse pointer) interaction, the content of the graphical user interface is radically reduced to

A. Günter et al. (Eds.): KI 2003, LNAI 2821, pp. 633–645, 2003.

only those elements (e.g., graphics) that are relevant to the user. The presentation agent Smartakus guides the user and presents tools and objects as needed. During the multimodal presentation speech, mimics and gestures of the agent are synchronized.

2   Overview of SmartKom

As shown in figure 1, there are three different application scenarios of SmartKom.

SmartKom PUBLIC: In this scenario, SmartKom represents a multimodal information kiosk. The gestures of the user are tracked by the Siemens Virtual Touch screen (SIVIT) and the display is projected on the table surface or on a tablet.

SmartKom HOME: Here, the system acts as an intelligent information system at home, e.g., as an EPG and for device control (TV set, video cassette recorder). The visual output is shown on a Tablet PC.

SmartKom MOBILE: This instance of the SmartKom system with its display on a PDA is used for providing mobile tourist information and navigation (car and pedestrian). Here the presentation agent Smartakus acts as a tour guide which show the user interesting sights.

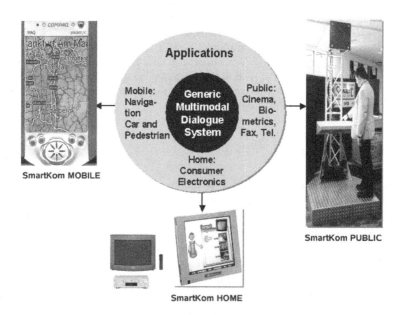

Fig. 1. *SmartKom backbone and scenarios*

The multimodal dialog backbone, a set of modules that are responsible for analysis, dialog management and presentation, works independently of the current scenario. The output of SmartKom is controlled mainly by the components Presentation Manager, Display Manager and Character Animation Module (figure 2).

The *Presentation Manager* gets his task specification from the Action Planning component. The task specification (presentation goal) defines, what should be presented to the user. The Presentation Manager, decides how that is done which also includes the distribution of presentations to the available output media and modalities.

Another source of presentation goals can be the Dynamic Help and the Watchdog modules, which permanently supervise the global state of the overall system. In case of problems, e.g. speech recognition difficulties or incomplete user intentions, they also produce presentation goals, which are intended to give hints to the user about what the problem was and possibly how it can be solved by sending appropriate presentation goals for that to the presentation planner [9].

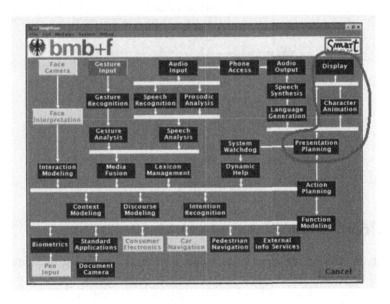

Fig. 2. *Presentation Modules in SmartKom (control screen of the system)*

The *Display Manager* and the *Character Animation Module* perform the multimodal presentation on the selected output devices. The animated life-like character is included in the user interface. A special task hereby is the synchronization of the speech output (generated by the Text Generator and the Speech Synthesizer) with the gesture and lip animation. Since the Gesture Analysis module of SmartKom needs a representation of all objects that are currently visible on the screen in order to relate gesture input of the user to the current presentation on the screen, a representation of all objects on the screen, including coordinates of their bounding boxes and links to the world objects they represent is generated. This document is finally sent to the gesture analysis module.

Figure 3 shows a simplified data flow architecture of the output modules of SmartKom focusing on the Presentation Planner and the Display Manager.

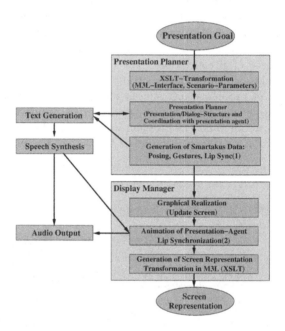

Fig. 3. *Presentation Pipeline in the SmartKom System*

3   Presentation Planning and Media Fission

The main task of the Presentation Manager is the planning of a multimodal presentation that consists of 2 parts: static gesture-sensitive graphical elements and a corresponding multimodal animation of Smartakus including gestures referring to objects with aligned audiovisual speech output. All information that flows between modules is represented as an XML-document conforming to the schema-based "Multi-Modal Markup Language - M3L" which was developed in SmartKom [5]. The input of the Presentation Planner consists of a M3L-document which is sent by the Action Planner or the Dynamic Help component. It contains an abstract representation of the system intention to be presented multimodally to the user.

The first computational step being performed on the M3L input document is a transformation of the document into the special input format of the core planning component PrePlan [1,12] by application of an appropriate XSLT-stylesheet. The use of stylesheets ensures flexibility with respect to the input structure of the Presentation Planner. Similarly, different situation-dependent XSLT-stylesheets, that reflect different dialog situations are used (one stylesheet per situation). A dialog situation is defined by the set of parameter for the Presentation Planner.

Some examples for the presentation parameters are the current scenario (SmartKom MOBILE, SmartKom HOME, SmartKom PUBLIC), the display size (SIVIT and Tablet PC have a resolution of 1024x768 pixel, the PDA has 240x320 pixels), language (German, English), available user interface elements (e.g., lists for TV or cinema movies, seat-maps, virtual phone or fax devices), user preferences (preference for spoken output while using SmartKom MOBILE in a car), available output modalities (graphic, gesture, speech) and design styles (e.g. different background colors for MOBILE and PUBLIC, figure 5 and figure 4).

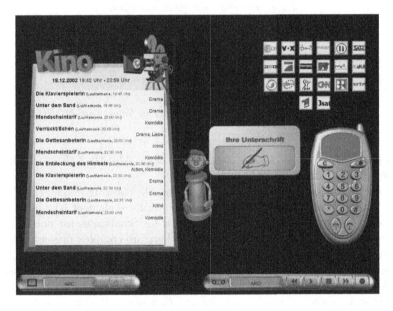

Fig. 4. *Presentation in SmartKom HOME*

The stylesheet transformations additionally add scenario-specific or language-specific data to the knowledge base of the presentation planner. For example, translations for labels and a logical description of available screen-layout elements are inserted.

Then, the Presentation Planner starts the planning process by applying a set of so-called presentation strategies, which define how the facts are presented in the given scenario. Based on constraints, the strategies decompose the complex presentation goal into primitive tasks and at the same time they do the media fission step depending on available modalities, which means they decide which part of the presentation should be instantiated as spoken output, graphics

Fig. 5. *Presentation of touristic sights in SmartKom MOBILE*

or gestures of our presentation agent Smartakus. Also they choose appropriate graphical elements like lists or slide-shows.

For example on simple presentation tasks, like showing phone, the Presentation Planner creates commands for a simple graphical element (the phone itself), simple speech comment and a gesture script for Smartakus for pointing at the phone. In contrast to simple presentations there are complex presentation tasks, which depend on some more input and modality parameters. For example while planning of a TV-program the Presentation Planner chooses the appropriate graphical element depending on amount and type of input data. Is only one broadcast to show, so much more information about it can be presented (like directors, actors and description). The Presentation Planner must take into account, what the user likes (i.e. if the user likes action films and does not like channel ARD, all found action films will be shown first and all broadcasts of ARD will be shown at the end or not shown at all). If some information parts are not available the place reserved for this information can be used to extend other information parts (i.e. if there is a film description, only some actors are shown, but if there is no description available, all actor names are presented. In MOBILE on absence of pictures for a sight description the whole place is used for text).

After choosing of graphical presentation appropriate speech and gesture presentations are generated. The gesture and speech form is chosen depending on the graphically shown information. I.e. if the graphically presented information is in focus of a presentation, only a comment is generated for speech output. The goal of the gesture presentation is then to focus on the appropriate graphical element. If there is no graphical presentable information or it is insufficient, so more speech is generated. In SmartKom HOME, there is a special mode (called lean-backward mode) where the user turns away from the screen, e.g., watches TV. Since the visual modality is not available, the Presentation Planner uses speech output to inform the user. In this case, only the presentation agent remains visible on screen just to indicate that the system is still active.

The Presentation Planner takes also the size of the graphical display into account. While in SmartKom HOME and in SmartKom PUBLIC several graphical elements can be shown on the screen at the same time, in SmartKom MOBILE only one graphical object is shown on the screen due to the small screen size.

In order to solve a presentation task, the Presentation Planner uses a top-down approach with declarative knowledge bases: one static and one dynamic knowledge base. The static knowledge base describes for example available presentation possibilities and dictionaries for text translations. The dynamic knowledge base is built from Presentation Planner input on every presentation task. The Presentation Planner decomposes automatically the presentation task into subtask, subsubtasks and so on.

An important sub-task of this planning process is the generation of animation scripts for the presentation agent Smartakus, that have to be related and coordinated with the graphical presentations. The main task of the Presentation Planner here is the selection of gestures that appropriately supplement the graphical output. The Presentation Planner constructs a special script for Smartakus that is based on the script-language of the PERSONA system [6] on an abstract level. In order to generate speech output, a speech generation request is sent to the text generator [3], which produces the utterance. The speech synthesis module [11] reads this representation and generates the audio data and viseme sequence for lip synchronization.

The result of this planning process is a hierarchical plan, which reflects the structure of the presentation (figure 6). This resulting planning tree is evaluated in order to create a presentation script that is finally passed on to the Display Manager which renders the resulting presentation on the available output media and modalities.

4 Display Management

After the presentation script is generated, it is sent to the Display Manager. The Display Manager evaluates this script and performs the planned actions as follows.

The Display Manager first chooses the appropriate graphical layout elements from his knowledge base. According to the planned presentation, these layout elements are dynamically filled with actual data (e.g. movie titles, channel logos, maps) with respect to space restrictions of the choosen graphical elements. This also includes the update of status information that is graphically on screen like

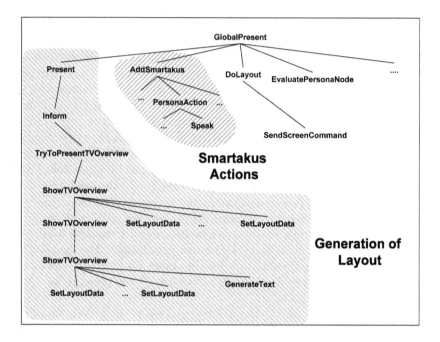

Fig. 6. *Presentation Plan in SmartKom*

the display of the virtual cellular phone or the virtual console for tv and video devices.

Since in SmartKom many graphical objects can be shown at the same time, a layout manager must be used to arrange the objects on the screen and to remove unnecessary objects of preceding presentation. For that purpose, all layout elements are classified with constraints as follows:

MUST-objects: Objects which must be shown in the current context
SHOULD-objects: Objects which are not essential but useful in the current context
CAN-Objects: Objects which are currently placed on screen, but already out of the context

The decision of the object classification is done by the Presentation Planner while generating the presentation tree (see 3). The Presentation Planner defines MUST- and SHOULD-objects. Other objects which are already on the screen become CAN-objects.

Additionally, constraints for every graphical object can contain boundary information for one up to four sides. So, some objects can be placed fix or floating within a region. This is e.g. useful during the document scanning application, in which the scanning camera has only a limited rotation angle, so documents must be placed inside predefined area. In the document scanning application, a video camera is used in order to scan a document. After this, the document data is sent via e-mail or a fax machine.

For some objects like status bar for tv and video it is useful to exclude them from the layout process, because they must always be visible at the same position independent from other objects. This feature can also be set through layout constraints.

Finally, the Display Manager computes a screen representation in M3L-format that is published to the SmartKom system in order to permit the gesture analysis component to relate gestures on screen objects to the world objects they represent.

5   Presentation Agent Smartakus

Life-like characters offer great promise for a wide range of applications [10,4,8,7, 2] since they make presentations more lively and entertaining and allow for the emulation of conversation styles common in human-human communication. In virtual environments, animated agents may help users learn to perform procedural tasks by demonstrating them. Furthermore, they can also serve as a guide through a presentation and release the user from orientation and navigation problems.

The presentation agent Smartakus acts as a dialogue partner and represents the whole SmartKom system for the user. Smartakus has the role of a real presenter. He points to objects, speaks to the user and shows mimics.

The presentation agent Smartakus is based on the PERSONA-system [6]. He is instructed by the Presentation Planner at an abstract level. Abstract complex commands are dynamically converted to the simple agent scripts, which are used to control the animated character. While converting constraints are used to generate special so-called BETWEEN-gestures if needed. BETWEEN-gestures are automatically generated gestures for a smooth transition between two agent postures. These gestures are used to combine different gestures in one fluently animation.

The knowledge source for the behaviors and gestures of Smartakus is a large catalog of predefined GIF images. Smartakus is statically modeled with 3D-Studio-Max as a 3D-life-like character. But for efficiency reasons the deeply 3D-modeled gestures are rendered as single GIF files. These categorized GIF files form the behavior knowledge base of the presentation sub-system of SmartKom.

During runtime, the animation of Smartakus is dynamically generated from the elements of this catalog by combining the elementary gestures to larger animation sequences. All deictic gestures have to be synchronized with the displaying of the corresponding graphical output they are related to. Also the acoustic speech output has to be synchronized by appropriate lip movements of the communication assistant Smartakus.

The Display Manager is responsible for the realization of visible output while the Audio Output module realizes speech output. Thus, audio output and visual output are performed independently from each other and can even be processed and realized on different machines. When presenting both modalities, we have to merge them to get lip synchronized output.

The lip synchronization is based on an underspecified mapping between acoustic and visual units (so called phonemes and visemes). In our system a viseme is defined as a specific mouth position picture. Due to the cartoon-like character of Smartakus (neither tongue nor teeth are visible) only a limited variety of mouth/jaw positions or movements are possible at all (figure 7). Consequently, the only parameters that we found relevant to describe mouth positions are the lip rounding and the jaw opening.

Fig. 7. *Possible visemes for lip synchronization*

We found that almost every phoneme has a corresponding viseme, while only a few of them (plosives and diphtongues) have to be mapped to at least two visemes to visualize their articulation appropriately [11]. Thus, in such cases the mapping partly becomes a one-to-many mapping in the sense that one phoneme can be mapped to more than one viseme. Furthermore, the mapping has to be partly underspecified in lip rounding and jaw opening as well to be able to take articulation effects into account. Since the Audio Output module and Display Manager are two separate modules in SmartKom that in principle work independently from each other, the idea to synchronize lip movements with speech output is to synchronize the individual time points at which corresponding acoustic and visual events occur as exactly as possible.

The speech synthesis module in SmartKom does not only produce audio data but also a detailed representation of the phonemes and their exact time points (in milliseconds) inside the audio signal. Based on this representation and the phoneme-viseme mapping mentioned above, the Character Animation Module generates a lip animation script for Smartakus, which is then executed during speech output.

The animation script is generated by a stepwise procedure iterating over the phonemes that consecutively specifies the concrete viseme(s) and their exact time points at which they have to be shown in one stream. In terms of figure 7 the procedure always tries to select a viseme that has a common borderline with the previous viseme whenever possible (also by inserting intermediate visemes if necessary).

During presentation, Smartakus often points to graphical objects on the screen to focus the user attention on them. To make such presentations more lively Smartakus is pointing while speaking. For this purpose the body animation is separated from head (and visemes) animation. Additionally heads with visemes for left, front and right side exist. During pointing the body often gets a stance in which the head must be moved horizontally or vertically to synchronize the agent move. For this purpose for every body posture and every head posture an image with a one ground point is generated to be able to calculate body and head coordinates. Such point images can be easily generated from the 3D model of the Smartakus, such that the synchronization of heads and bodies can be done fully automatically at run time.

Since the Display Manager with the Character Animation Module and the Audio Device of the SmartKom system may run on different computers, the start of the output of the audio data and the start of the lip animation must be synchronized in a special manner. A fixed time point at which the audio signal has to start is defined dynamically and at exactly this time point the animation is started by the PERSONA player.

Fig. 8. *Some behaviors of Smartakus*

In order to increase the liveliness of the character, the character shows idle-time actions like breathing or waving. Another job of the presentation agent is to show the actual system state to the user (figure 8). For example if the system is expecting spoken input from the user, Smartakus looks to the user expectantly. While the system is searching for information in a database, Smartakus takes a notebook and works on it. This symbolizes that the system is currently processing the input and the user can not speak with the system.

6   Conclusions

In this paper, we presented the components of the SmartKom system, which are responsible for the presentation generation. The system provides a plan-based generation of multimodal presentations (fission) with a life-like character which guides the user through the presentation. The modules provide an interface based on XML, which makes it possible to use MMoPaD in a wide range of applications apart from SmartKom. Since the system is implemented in the Java programming language, it is possible to use the system under Windows, Linux and Sun Solaris operating systems.

Acknowledgements. This work was funded by the German Federal Ministry of Education, Science, Research and Technology (BMBF) in the framework of the SmartKom project under Grant 01 IL 905 K7. The responsibility for the contents lies with the authors.

References

1. E. André. *Ein planbasierter Ansatz zur Generierung multimedialer Präsentationen.* PhD thesis, Universität des Saarlandes, 1995.
2. G. Ball, D. Ling, D. Kurlander, J. Miller, and D. Pugh. Lifelike computer characters: The persona project at microsoft. In J. M. Bradshaw, editor, *Software Agents.* AAAI Press/The MIT Press, Menlo Park, CA, 1997.
3. T. Becker. Practical, template–based natural language generation with tag. In *Proceedings of TAG+6*, Venice, Italy, May 2002.
4. J. Cassell, J. Sullivan, S. Prevost, and E. Churchill. *Embodied Conversational Agents.* The MIT Press, Cambridge, MA, USA, 2000.
5. Gerd Herzog, Heinz Kirchmann, Stefan Merten, Alassane Ndiaye, Peter Poller, and Tilman Becker. MULTIPLATFORM Testbed: An Integration Platform for Multimodal Dialog Systems. In Hamish Cunningham and Jon Patrick, editors, *HLT-NAACL 2003 Workshop: Software Engineering and Architecture of Language Technology Systems (SEALTS)*, pages 75–82, Edmonton, Alberta, Canada, 2003. Association for Computational Linguistics.
6. J. Müller. *Persona: Ein anthropomorpher Präsentationsagent für Internet-Anwendungen.* PhD thesis, Universität des Saarlandes, Saarbrücken, 2000.
7. T. Noma and N.I. Badler. A Virtual Human Presenter. In *Proc. of the IJCAI-97 Workshop on Animated Interface Agents: Making them Intelligent*, pages 45–51, Nagoya, 1997.
8. K. Perlin and A. Goldberg. Improv: A System for Scripting Interactive Actors in Virtual Worlds. *Computer Graphics*, 28(3), 1996.
9. P. Poller and M. Streit. Improving error handling by inferring the system´s processing state. In *submitted to ISCA workshop on Error handling in dialogue systems 2003*, 2003.
10. T. Rist, E. André, and J. Müller. Adding animated presentation agents to the interface. In *Proceedings of the 1997 International Conference on Intelligent User Interfaces*, pages 79–86, Orlando, Florida, 1997.

11. A. Schweitzer, G. Dogil, and P. Poller.   Gesture-speech interaction in the smartkom project. Poster presented at the 142nd meeting of the Acoustical Society of America (ASA), 2001. Ft. Lauderdale, FA, USA, *http://www.ims.uni-stuttgart.de/~schweitz/documents.shtml.*

12. V. Tschernomas. *PrePlan Dokumentation (Java-Version).* Deutsches Forschungszentrum für Künstliche Intelligenz, Saarbrücken, 1999.

13. W. Wahlster, N. Reithinger, and A. Blocher. Smartkom: Multimodal communication with a life-like character. In *Proceedings of Eurospeech 2001, 7th European Conference on Speech Communication and Technology,* volume 3, pages 1547 – 1550, Aalborg, Denmark, 2001.

Monitoring Agents Using Declarative Planning*

Jürgen Dix[1], Thomas Eiter[2], Michael Fink[2], Axel Polleres[2], and Yingqian Zhang[1]

[1] Department of Computer Science, University of Manchester, M13 9PL, UK
{dix,zhangy}@cs.man.ac.uk
[2] Institut für Informationssysteme, TU Wien, A-1040 Wien, Austria
{eiter,fink,polleres}@kr.tuwien.ac.at

Abstract. We present an *agent monitoring* approach, which aims at refuting from (possibly incomplete) information at hand that a multi-agent system (*MAS*) is implemented properly. In this approach, agent collaboration is abstractly described in an action theory. Action sequences reaching the collaboration goal are determined by a planner, whose compliance with the actual *MAS* behavior allows to detect possible collaboration failures. The approach can be fruitfully applied to aid offline testing of a *MAS* implementation, as well as online monitoring.
Keywords: knowledge representation, multi agent systems, planning

1 Introduction

Multi-Agent systems have been recognized as a promising paradigm for distributed problem solving, and numerous multi-agent platforms and frameworks have been proposed, which allow to program agents in languages ranging from imperative over object-oriented to logic-based ones [16]. A major problem which agent developers face with many platforms is verifying that a suite of implemented agents collaborate well to reach a certain goal (e.g., in supply chain management). Tools for automatic verification[1] are rare. Thus, common practice is geared towards extensive agent testing, employing tracing and simulation tools (if available).

In this paper, we present a *monitoring* approach which aids in automatically detecting that agents do not collaborate properly. In the spirit of Popper's *principle of falsification*, it aims at refuting from (possibly incomplete) information at hand that an agent system works properly, rather than proving its correctness. In our approach, agent collaboration is described at an abstract level, and the single steps in runs of the system are examined to see whether the agents behave "reasonable," i.e., "compatible" to a sequence of steps for reaching a goal.

Even if the internal structure of some agents is unknown, we may get hold of the messages exchanged among them. A given message protocol allows us to draw conclusions about the correctness of the agent collaboration. Our monitoring approach hinges on this fact and involves the following steps:

---

* This work was supported by FWF (Austrian Science Funds), projects P14781 and Z29-N04, and partially funded by the Information Society Technologies programme of the European Commission, Future and Emerging Technologies under the IST-2001-37004 WASP project.

[1] By well-known results, this is impossible in general but often also in simple cases if details of some agents (e.g., in a heterogenous environment) are missing.

A. Günter et al. (Eds.): KI 2003, LNAI 2821, pp. 646–660, 2003.
© Springer-Verlag Berlin Heidelberg 2003

(1) The intended collaborative behavior of the agents is modelled as a planning problem. More precisely, knowledge about the agent actions (specifically, messaging) and their effects is formalized in an *action theory*, T, which can be reasoned about to automatically construct *plans* as sequences of actions to reach a given goal.

(2) From T and the collaborative goal G, a set of intended plans, *I-Plans*, for reaching G is generated via a planner.

(3) The observed agent behavior, i.e., the message actions from a message log, is then compared to the plans in *I-Plans*.

(4) In case an incompatibility is detected, an error is flagged to the developer resp. user, pinpointing to the last action causing the failure so that further steps might be taken.

Steps 2-4 can be done by a special *monitoring agent*, which is added to the agent system providing support both in testing, and in the operational phase of the system. Among the benefits of this approach are the following:

- It allows to deal with collaboration behavior regardless of the implementation language(s) used for single agents.
- Depending on the planner used in step 2, different kinds of plans (optimal, conformant, ...), might be considered, reflecting different agent attitudes and collaboration objectives.
- Changes to the agent messaging by the system designer may be transparently incorporated to the action theory T, without further need to adjust the monitoring process.
- Furthermore, T adds to a formal system specification, which may be reasoned about and used in other contexts.
- As a by-product, the method may also be used for automatic *protocol generation*, i.e., determine the messages needed and their order, in a (simple) collaboration.

In the following, we detail the approach and illustrate it on an example derived from an implemented agent system. The next section describes the basic agent framework that we build upon and presents a (here simplified version) of a multi-agent system in the postal services domain. After that, in Section 3 we describe how to model the intended behavior of a multi-agent system as an abstract planning problem, and instantiate this for our example system using the action language $\mathcal{K}$ [5,4]. Our approach to agent monitoring is then discussed in Section 4, where we also investigate some fundamental properties. After a brief discussion of the implementation in Section 5 and a review of related work in Section 6, we conclude in Section 7 with an outlook on further research.

2   Message Flow in a Multi-agent System

In a multi-agent system (*MAS*), a set of autonomous agents are collaborating to reach a certain goal. Our aim is to monitor (some aspects of) the behavior of the agents in order to detect inconsistencies and help debugging the whole system.

As opposed to verification, monitoring a *MAS* does not require a complete specification of the behavior of the particular agents. Rather, we adopt a more general (and in practice much more realistic) view: We do not have access to the (entire) internal state of a single autonomous agent, but we are able *to observe the communication be-tween agents* of the system. By means of its communication capabilities, an agent can potentially control another agent. Our aim is to draw conclusions about the state of a multi-agent system by monitoring the message protocol.

2.1 Basic Framework

We consider multi-agent systems consisting of a finite set $A = \{a_1, \dots, a_n\}$ of col-laborating agents a_i. Although agents may perform a number of different (internal) actions, we assume that only one action is externally observable, namely an action called $\mathtt{send\_msg}(m)$, which allows an agent to send a message, m, to another agent in the system. Every $\mathtt{send\_msg}$ action is given a timestamp and recorded in a message-log file containing the history of messages sent. The following definitions do not assume a sophisticated messaging framework and apply to almost any *MAS*. Thus, our framework is not bound to a particular *MAS*.

Definition 1 (Message, $\mathcal{M}_{log}$ file). *A message is a quadruple* $m = \langle s, r, c, d \rangle$, *where* $s, r \in A$ *are the identifiers of the* sending *and the* receiving *agents, respectively;* $c \in C$ *is from a finite set* C *of message commands;* d *is a list of constants representing the* message data. *A message-log file is an ordered sequence* $\mathcal{M}_{log} = t_1{:}m_1, t_2{:}m_2, \dots, t_k{:}m_k$ *of messages* m_i *with timestamps* t_i, *where* $t_i \leq t_{i+1}$, $i < k$.

The set C constitutes a set of message *performatives* specifying the intended meaning of a message. In other words, it is the type of a message according to speech act theory: the illocutionary force of an utterance. These commands may range from **ask/tell** primitives to application specific commands fixed during system specification.

Often, an agent a_i will not send every kind of message, but use a message repertoire $C_i \subseteq C$. Moreover, only particular agents might be message recipients (allowing for simplified formats). Given that the repertoires C_i are pairwise disjoint and each message type c has a unique recipient, we use $\langle c, d \rangle$ in place of $m = \langle s, r, c, d \rangle$.

Finally, we assume a fixed bound on the time within the next action should happen in the *MAS*, i.e., a timeout for each action (which may depend on previous actions), which allows to see from $\mathcal{M}_{log}$ whether the *MAS* is stuck or still idle.

2.2 *Gofish* Post Office

We consider an example *MAS* called *Gofish Post Office* for postal services. Its goal is to improve postal product areas by mail tracking, customer notifications, and advanced quality control. The following scenario is our running example:

Example scenario: Pat drops a package, p_1, for a friend, Sue, at the post office. In the evening, Sue gets a phone call that a package has been sent. The next day, Sue decides to pick up the package herself at the post office on her way to work. Unfortunately, the clerk has to tell her that the package is already on a truck on its way to her home.

The overall design of the *Gofish MAS* is depicted in Figure 1. An *event dispatcher agent* (disp) communicates system relevant (external) events to an *event management agent* (em) which maintains an event database. Information about packages is stored

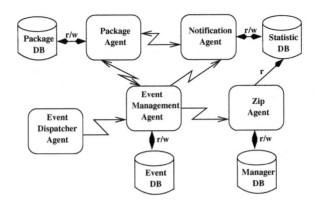

Fig. 1. The *Gofish* post office system.

in a package database manipulated by a *package agent* (pa). The *notification agent* ($notify$) notifies customers about package status and expected delivery time, for which it maintains a statistics database. Finally, a *zip agent* (zip) informs responsible managers, stored in a manager database, about zip codes not being well served.

Example 1 (Simple Gofish). For space reasons and to keep things simple and illustrative, we restrict the *Gofish MAS* to the package agent, pa, the event management agent, em, and the event dispatcher agent, $disp$; thus, $A = \{pa, em, disp\}$.

The event dispatcher informs the event manager agent about the drop off of a package (identified by a unique identifier), its arrival at the distribution center, its loading on a truck, its successful delivery, or when a recipient shows up at the distribution center to pick up a package by herself: $C_{disp} = \{\mathsf{dropOff}, \mathsf{distCenter}, \mathsf{truck}, \mathsf{delivery}, \mathsf{pickup}\}$. The event manager agent instructs the package agent to add a package to the package database after drop off, as well as to update the delivery time after delivery or customer pickup: $C_{em} = \{\mathsf{addPackage}, \mathsf{setDelivTime}\}$. The package agent here only receives messages, thus $C_{pa} = \{\}$.

Running scenario: The message-log $\mathcal{M}_{log}$ contains the messages $m_1 = \langle \mathsf{dropOff}, p_1 \rangle$, $m_2 = \langle \mathsf{addPackage}, p_1 \rangle$, $m_3 = \langle \mathsf{distCenter}, p_1 \rangle$, $m_4 = \langle \mathsf{truck}, p_1 \rangle$, and $m_5 = \langle \mathsf{pickup}, p_1 \rangle$. The entries are $0{:}\langle disp, em, \mathsf{dropOff}, p_1 \rangle$, $5{:}\langle em, pa, \mathsf{addPackage}, p_1 \rangle$, $13{:}\langle disp, em, \mathsf{distCenter}, p_1 \rangle$, $19{:}\langle disp, em, \mathsf{truck}, p_1 \rangle$, and $20{:}\langle disp, em, \mathsf{pickup}, p_1 \rangle$.

3   Modelling Agent Behavior via Declarative Planning

We now discuss how to formalize the intended collaborative agent behavior as an action theory for planning, which encodes the legal message flow. In it, actions correspond to messages and fluents represent assumptions about the current state of the world.

Under suitable encodings, we could use planning formalisms like STRIPS [8], PDDL [9] or HTN [7] based planners to model simple agent environments. In fact, HTN planning has recently been incorporated in a *MAS* [3] and formulated as action theories in logic programming [2]. Another powerful language suitable for modeling control knowledge and plans for agents is GOLOG [15]. However, due to its high expressive power (loop, conditionals) automated plan generation is limited in this formalism. In Subsection 3.1 we give a generic formulation of our approach, independent of a particular planning mechanism. Then, in Subsection 3.2 we instantiate this high-level description using the action language $\mathcal{K}$ [5,4]. While our approach does not rely on $\mathcal{K}$, we have chosen it because of its declarative nature and its capabilities to deal with incomplete knowledge and nondeterminism.

3.1   Modelling Intended Behavior of a *MAS*

Our approach to formalize the intended collaborative behavior of a *MAS* consisting of agents $A = \{a_1, \dots, a_n\}$ as a planning problem $\mathcal{P}$ comprises three steps:

Step 1: *Actions (Act).* Declare a corresponding *action* for each message $m = \langle s, r, c, d \rangle$ in our domain, i.e., we have $c(s, r, d) \in Act$ (see Def. 1). Again, if the message repertoires C_i are pairwise disjoint and each message type c has a unique recipient, we use in short $c(d)$. These actions might have effects on the states of the agents involved and will change the properties that hold on them.

Step 2: *Fluents (Fl).* Define properties, *fluents*, of the "world" that are used to describe action effects. We distinguish between the sets of *internal* fluents, Fl_a, of a particular agent a^2 and *external* fluents, Fl_{ext}, which cover properties not related to specific agents. These fluents are often closely related to the message performatives C_i of the agents.

Step 3: *Theory (T)* and *Goal (G).* Using the fluents and actions from above, state various axioms about the collaborative behavior of the agents as a *planning theory* T. The axioms describe how the various actions change the state and under which assumptions they are executable. Finally, state the ultimate *Goal* G (in the running scenario: to deliver the package) suitable for the chosen planning formalism.

We end up with a *planning problem* $\mathcal{P} = \langle Act, Fl, T, G \rangle$, where $Fl = \bigcup_{a \in A} Fl_a \cup Fl_{ext}$, whose *solutions* are a set of $\mathcal{P}$-*Plans*. Note that the precise formulation of these notions depends on the underlying planning formalism. For example, in HTN planning one has to specify *operators* and *methods* and their effects (this is closely related to *Act* and *Fl* above), as well as a domain description and a task list (which corresponds to T and G above): we refer to [2] for a full discussion. The above is a generic formulation suitable for many planning frameworks.

3.2   Using Action Language $\mathcal{K}$

In this section, we instantiate the planning problem $\mathcal{P}$ described above to a problem $\mathcal{P}^{\mathcal{K}}$ formulated in the action language $\mathcal{K}$. Due to space constraints, we only give the key features and refer to [5,4] for further details.

Declarations of the type $p(\overline{X})$ $requires$ $bk_1(\overline{Y_1}), \dots, bk_m(\overline{Y_m})$ define *actions* and *fluents* p in $\mathcal{K}$ ($\overline{X} = X_1, \dots, X_n$ are parameters that must be *typed* by some predicates $bk_1, \dots, bk_m$ defined in the so called *background knowledge BK*, which specifies a

---

[2] Internal fluents especially can describe private values which might be inaccessible by an external observer.

finite set of static facts in a function-free first-order language). In addition, $\mathcal{K}$ allows to state axioms of the following form:[3]

(1)   caused f if α after β.
(2)   total f if α after β.
(3)   inertial f.
(4)   executable a if β.
(5)   nonexecutable a if β.

(1) means that fluent f is caused whenever α holds after β. (2) simulates nondeterministic effects: its meaning is that fluent f is either true or false if α holds after β. (3) models inertia of a fluent f: it is a macro for caused f if not $\neg.f$ after f, where not is default negation and $\neg$ is strong negation. Furthermore, with (4) and (5) we can express under which circumstances an action is *executable* or *nonexecutable*.

A planning problem $\mathcal{P}^{\mathcal{K}}$ may then be formalized as a tuple $\langle Act, Fl, T, G \rangle$, where Act defines the actions, Fl the fluents, T comprises BK and all axioms (of the sort introduced above), and G is the goal, i.e. a set of ground fluent literals.

The semantics of $\mathcal{K}$ is defined through *legal transitions* $t = \langle s, A, s' \rangle$ from states s to states s' by simultaneous execution of actions A, where a *state* s is any consistent set of ground fluent literals.[4] A *trajectory* Tr is any initial state s_0 or sequence $t_1, \dots, t_n$ of legal transitions $t_i = \langle s_{i-1}, A_i, s_i \rangle$, $i \in \{1, \dots, n\}$, starting in an initial state s_0. An *(optimistic) plan* for goal G is $P = \langle \rangle$, resp. the projection $P = \langle A_1, \dots, A_n \rangle$ of a trajectory Tr, such that G holds in s_0 resp. s_n.

Example 2 (Simple Gofish cont'd). In the *Gofish* example, the following $\mathcal{K}$ actions (corresponding to the possible messages) and fluents are defined (in DLV$^{\mathcal{K}}$ notation [4]):

```
actions : dropOff(P) requires pkg(P).
          addPkg(P) requires pkg(P).
          distCenter(P) requires pkg(P).
          truck(P) requires pkg(P).                  }  Act
          delivery(P) requires pkg(P).
          pickup(P) requires pkg(P).
          setDelivTime(P) requires pkg(P).

fluents : pkgAt(P,Loc) requires pkg(P),loc(Loc).
          delivered(P) requires pkg(P).
          recipAtHome(P) requires pkg(P).            }  Fl
          added(P) requires pkg(P).
          delivTimeSet(P) requires pkg(P).
```

The first three external fluents describe the current location of a package, whether it has successfully been delivered, and whether its recipient is at home, respectively. The last two fluents are internal fluents about the state of agent pa; whether the package has already been added to the package database resp. whether the delivery time has been set properly.

---

[3] In all the statements below, f is a fluent literal, a is an action, α is a set of (possibly default negated) fluent literals, and β is a set of (possibly default negated) actions and fluent literals.

[4] Note that in $\mathcal{K}$ states are not "total", i.e., a fluent f can be neither true nor false in a state.

A possible package (e.g., a generic p_1) and its locations are background knowledge represented by the set of facts $BK=\{pkg(p_1), loc(drop), loc(dist), loc(truck)\}$. Now we specify further axioms for T (in DLV$^\mathcal{K}$ notation) as follows:

```
initially : recipAtHome(p₁).
always :    noConcurrency.
  inertial pkgAt(P, L).        inertial delivered(P).
  inertial recipAtHome(P).  inertial added(P).

  executable dropOff(P) if not added(P).
  caused pkgAt(P, drop) after dropOff(P).
  nonexecutable dropOff(P) if pkgAt(P, drop).

  executable addPkg(P) if pkgAt(P, drop), not added(P).
  caused added(P) after addPkg(P).

  executable distCenter(P) if added(P), pkgAt(P, drop).
  caused pkgAt(P, dist) after distCenter(P).
  caused -pkgAt(P, drop) after distCenter(P).

  executable truck(P) if pkgAt(P, dist), not delivered(P).
  caused pkgAt(P, truck) after truck(P).
  caused -pkgAt(P, dist) after truck(P).

  executable delivery(P) if pkgAt(P, truck), not delivered(P).
  caused delivered(P) after delivery(P), recipAtHome(P).

  executable setDelivTime(P, DTime) if delivered(P).
  caused delivTimeSet(P) after setDelivTime(P).

  executable pickup(P) if pkgAt(P, dist), not delivered(P).
  executable pickup(P) if pkgAt(P, truck), not delivered(P).
  caused delivered(P) after pkgAt(P, dist), pickup(P).
  total recipAtHome(P) after pickup(P).
```

Most of the theory is self-explanatory. The recipient is at home initially. The keyword noConcurrency specifies that concurrent actions are disallowed. An important aspect is modelled by the final `total` statement. It expresses uncertainty whether after a pickup attempt at the distribution center, the recipient will be back home, in particular in time before the truck arrives to deliver the package, if it was already on the way. Finally, the goal is $G = $ delivTimeSet(p_1).

The following (optimistic) plans reach G:

$$P_1 = \langle \text{dropOff}(p_1); \text{addPkg}(p_1); \text{distCenter}(p_1); \text{truck}(p_1);$$
$$\text{pickup}(p_1); \text{delivery}(p_1); \text{setDelivTime}(p_1) \rangle$$
$$P_2 = \langle \text{dropOff}(p_1); \text{addPkg}(p_1); \text{distCenter}(p_1); \text{truck}(p_1);$$
$$\text{delivery}(p_1); \text{setDelivTime}(p_1) \rangle$$
$$P_3 = \langle \text{dropOff}(p_1); \text{addPkg}(p_1); \text{distCenter}(p_1); \text{pickup}(p_1); \text{setDelivTime}(p_1) \rangle$$

In P_1, the recipient shows up at the distribution center after the package is loaded on the truck and the truck is on its way. In P_2, the package is successfully delivered before the recipient comes to pick it up herself, whereas in P_3, she picks up the package before it has been loaded on the truck.

Running scenario: According to the message history in $\mathcal{M}_{log}$, we see that plan P_2 is infeasible, as well as P_3 since the package can not be handed over to Sue at the distribution center. Thus, only P_1 remains for successful task completion.

4   Agent Monitoring

The overall aim of adding a monitoring agent (monitor) is to *aid debugging a given MAS*. We can distinguish between two principal types of errors: *(1) design errors*, and *(2) implementation (or coding) errors*. While the first type means that the model of the system is wrong (i.e., the *MAS* behaves correctly to the model of the designer of the *MAS*, but this model is faulty and does not yield the desired result in the application), the second type points to more mundane mistakes in the actual code of the agents: the code does not implement the formal model of the system (i.e., the actions are not implemented correctly).

Note that often it is very difficult, if not impossible at all, to distinguish between design and implementation errors. But even before the system is deployed, the planning problem $\mathcal{P}$ can be given to a planner and thus the overall existence of a solution can be checked. If there is no solution, this is clearly a design error and the monitoring agent can pinpoint where exactly the planning fails (assuming the underlying planner has this ability). If there are solutions, the agent designer can check them and thus critically examine the intended model.

However, for most applications the bugs in the system become apparent only at runtime. Our proposed monitoring agent has the following structure.

Definition 2 (Structure of the monitoring agent). *The agent* monitor *loops through the following steps:*

1. *Read and parse the message log $\mathcal{M}_{log}$. If $\mathcal{M}_{log} = \emptyset$, the set of plans for $\mathcal{P}$ may be cached for later reuse.*
2. *Check whether an action timeout has occurred.*
3. *If this is not the case, compute the current* intended plans *(according to the planning problem description and additional info from the designer) compatible with the actions as executed by the* MAS.
4. *If no compatible plans survive, or the system is no more idle, then inform the agent designer about this situation.*
5. *Sleep for some pre-specified time.*

We now elaborate more deeply into these tasks.

Checking *MAS* behavior: monitor continually keeps track of the *messages sent between the agents*. They are stored in the message-log, $\mathcal{M}_{log}$, which is accessible by monitor. Thus for monitor, the behavior of the *MAS* is completely determined by $\mathcal{M}_{log}$. We think this is a realistic abstraction from internal agent states. Rather than describing all the details of each agent (which might be unknown, e.g. if legacy agents are involved), the kinds of messages sent by an agent can be chosen so as to give a declarative high-level view of it. In the simplified *Gofish* example, these messages for agents em, disp, pa are given by C_{em}, C_{disp}, and C_{pa} (see Section 2).

Intended behavior and compatibility: The desired collaborative *MAS* behavior is formalized as a planning problem $\mathcal{P}$ (e.g., in language $\mathcal{K}$, cf. Section 3). Thus, even before the *MAS* is in operation, problem $\mathcal{P}$ can be fed into a planner which computes potential plans to reach a goal. Agent $monitor$ is exactly doing that.

In general, not all $\mathcal{P}$-Plans may be admissible, as constraints may apply (derived from the intended collaborative behavior). [5] E.g., some actions ought to be taken in fixed order, or actions may be penalized with costs whose sum must stay within a limit. We thus distinguish a set *I-Plans*($\mathcal{P}$) $\subseteq \mathcal{P}$-*Plans* as *intended plans* (of the *MAS* designer).

It is perfectly possible that the original problem has successful plans, yet after some actions executed by the *MAS*, these plans are no longer valid. This is the interesting case for the agent designer since it clearly shows that something has gone wrong: $monitor$ can pinpoint to the precise place indicating which messages have when caused the plan to collapse. Because these messages are related to actions executed by the agents, information about them will help to debug the *MAS*. In general, it is difficult to decide whether the faulty behavior is due to a coding or design error. However, the info given by $monitor$ will aid the agent designer to detect the real cause.

Messages from $monitor$**:** Agent $monitor$ continually checks and compares the actions taken so far for compatibility with all current plans. Once a situation has arisen in which no successful plan exists (detected by the planner employed), $monitor$ writes a message into a separate file containing (1) the first action that caused the *MAS* to go into a state where the goal is not reached, (2) the sequence of actions taken up to this action, and (3) all the possible plans *before* the action in 1) was executed (these are all plans compatible with the *MAS* behavior up to it).

In the above description, we made heavily use of the notion of a *compatible* plan. Before giving a formal definition, we consider our running scenario. In *Gofish*, all three plans P_1, P_2, P_3 generated from the initial problem coincide on the first three steps: dropOff(p_1), addPkg(p_1), and distCenter(p_1).

Running scenario (coding error): Suppose on a preliminary run of our scenario, $\mathcal{M}_{log}$ shows m_1=dropOff(p_1). This is compatible with each plan P_i, $i \in \{1, 2, 3\}$. Next, m_2=distCenter(p_1). This is incompatible with each plan; $monitor$ detects this and gives a warning. Inspection of the actual code may show that the command for adding the package to the database is wrong. While this doesn't result in a livelock (the *MAS* is still idle), the database was not updated. Informed by $monitor$, this is detected at this stage already.

After correction of this coding error, the *MAS* may be started again and another error shows up:

Running scenario (design error): Instead of waiting at home (as in the "standard" plan P_2), Sue shows up at the distribution center and made a pickup attempt. This "external" event may have been unforeseen by the designer (problematic events could also arise from *MAS* actions). We can expect this in many agent scenarios: we have no complete knowledge about the world, unexpected events may happen, and action effects may not fully determine the next state.

---

[5] This might depend on the capabilities of the underlying planning formalism to model constraints such as cost bounds or optimality wrt. resource consumption etc.

Only plan P_1 remains to reach the goal. However, there is *no guarantee of success*, if Sue is not back home in time for delivery. This situation can be easily captured in the framework of [5,4]. There, we have the notion of a *secure* plan. An (optimistic) plan is *secure* (or *conformant* [11]), if regardless of the initial state and the outcomes of the actions, the steps of the plan will always be executable one after the other and reach the goal (i.e., in all trajectories). As can be easily seen, P_1 is not secure. Thus, a design error is detected, if delivering the package must be guaranteed under any circumstances. Based on a generic planning problem $\mathcal{P}$, we now define compatible plans as follows.

Definition 3 ($\mathcal{M}_{log}$ **compatible plans**). *Let the planning problem $\mathcal{P}$ model the intended behavior of a MAS, which is given by a set I-Plans($\mathcal{P}$) $\subseteq$ $\mathcal{P}$-Plans. Then, for any message log $\mathcal{M}_{log} = t_1{:}m_1, \ldots, t_k{:}m_k$, we denote by C-Plans($\mathcal{P}, \mathcal{M}_{log}, n$), $n \geq 0$, the set of plans from I-Plans($\mathcal{P}$) which comply on the first n steps with the actions $m_1, \ldots, m_n$.*

Respecting that the $\mathcal{K}$ planner, DLV$^{\mathcal{K}}$, is capable of computing optimistic and secure plans, we denote for any $\mathcal{K}$ planning problem $\mathcal{P}^{\mathcal{K}}$ by X-Plans^o($\mathcal{P}^{\mathcal{K}}, \mathcal{M}_{log}, n$) (resp. X-Plans^s ($\mathcal{P}^{\mathcal{K}}, \mathcal{M}_{log}, n$) the set of all optimistic (resp. secure) plans for $\mathcal{P}^{\mathcal{K}}$ with the above property, $X \in \{I, C\}$.

Definition 4 (**Culprit**($\mathcal{M}_{log}, \mathcal{P}$)). *Let $t_n{:}m_n$ be the first entry of $\mathcal{M}_{log}$ such that either (i) C-Plans($\mathcal{P}, \mathcal{M}_{log}, n$) $= \emptyset$ or (ii) a timeout is detected. Then, Culprit($\mathcal{M}_{log}, \mathcal{P}$) is the pair $\langle t_n{:}m_n, idle \rangle$ if (i) applies and $\langle t_n{:}m_n, timeout \rangle$ otherwise.*

Initially, $\mathcal{M}_{log}$ is empty and thus C-Plans($\mathcal{P}$) $=$ I-Plans($\mathcal{P}$). As more and more actions are executed by the *MAS*, they are recorded in $\mathcal{M}_{log}$ and the set C-Plans($\mathcal{P}$) shrinks. *monitor* can thus compare at any point in time whether C-Plans($\mathcal{P}, \mathcal{M}_{log}, n$) is empty or not. Whenever this happens, Culprit($\mathcal{M}_{log}, \mathcal{P}$) is computed and pinpoints to the problematic action.

Running scenario: Under guaranteed delivery (i.e., secure planning), *monitor* writes Culprit($\mathcal{M}_{log}, \mathcal{P}$)$=\langle 20{:}m_5, idle \rangle$ (the *pickup*(p_1) message) on a file, and thus clearly points to a situation missed in the *MAS* design. Note that there are also situations where everything is fine; if pickup would not occur, agent *monitor* would not detect a problem at this stage.

4.1 Properties

We can show that the agent monitoring approach has desirable properties. The first result concerns its soundness.

Theorem 1 (**Soundness**). *Let the planning problem $\mathcal{P}$ model the intended collaborative MAS behavior, given by I-Plans($\mathcal{P}$) $\subseteq$ $\mathcal{P}$-Plans. Let $\mathcal{M}_{log}$ be a message log. Then, the MAS is implemented incorrectly if Culprit($\mathcal{M}_{log}, \mathcal{P}$) exists.*

Semantically, the intended collaborative *MAS* behavior (described in any formalism) may manifest in a set of trajectories as described for $\mathcal{K}$ planning problems, where trajectories correspond to possible runs of the *MAS* (sequences of states and executed actions). On the other hand, optimistic plans for a $\mathcal{K}$ planning problem $\mathcal{P}^{\mathcal{K}}$ are projected trajectories. We say that a set OP of such plans *covers* the intended collaborative *MAS* behavior, if each run of the *MAS* corresponds to some trajectory whose projection is in OP. For example, this holds if OP is the set of all optimistic plans for $\mathcal{P}^{\mathcal{K}}$ and the intended collaborative *MAS* behavior is given by a secure plan, or, more liberally, by a conditional plan. We have:

Theorem 2 (Soundness of $\mathcal{P}^{\mathcal{K}}$ Cover). *Let $\mathcal{P}^{\mathcal{K}}$ be a $\mathcal{K}$ planning problem, such that I-Plans$^o(\mathcal{P}^{\mathcal{K}})$ covers the intended collaborative* MAS *behavior. Let $\mathcal{M}_{log}$ be a message log. Then,* MAS *is implemented incorrectly if* Culprit$(\mathcal{M}_{log}, \mathcal{P}^{\mathcal{K}})$ *exists.*

As for completeness, we need the assertion that plans can not grow arbitrarily long, i.e., have an upper bound on their length.

Theorem 3 (Completeness). *Let the planning problem $\mathcal{P}$ model the intended collaborative* MAS *behavior, given by I-Plans$(\mathcal{P}) \subseteq \mathcal{P}$-Plans where plans are bounded. If the* MAS *is implemented incorrectly, then there is some message log $\mathcal{M}_{log}$ such that either (i)* C-Plans$(\mathcal{P}, \mathcal{M}_{log}, 0) = \emptyset$*, or (ii)* Culprit$(\mathcal{M}_{log}, \mathcal{P})$ *exists.*

In (i), we can conclude a design error, while in (ii) a design or coding error may be present. There is no similar completeness result for $\mathcal{P}^{\mathcal{K}}$ covers; note that in our running scenario, a design error is detected for secure plans as *MAS* collaborative behavior formalism. However, the culprit vanishes if the cover contains plan P_1, which is compatible with $\mathcal{M}_{log}$.

As for complexity, we mention that in expressive planning formalisms like $\mathcal{K}$, deciding whether C-Plans$(\mathcal{P}, \mathcal{M}_{log}, n) \neq \emptyset$ or Culprit$(\mathcal{M}_{log}, \mathcal{P})$ exists from $\mathcal{P}$, $\mathcal{M}_{log}$ and n is NP-hard in general, which is inherited from expressive planning language. We remind that, like for satisfiability (SAT), this is a theoretical worst-case measure, though, and still solutions for many instances can be found quickly. Moreover, there are instance classes which are polynomial time solvable and for which DLV$^{\mathcal{K}}$ is guaranteed to compute plans in polynomial time.

5   Implementation

To demonstrate the proposed approach, a running example has been implemented. The *Gofish MAS* and Agent $monitor$ is developed within IMPACT (*Interactive Maryland Platform for Agents Collaborating Together*). Note that in principle our approach is completely independent of any specific agent system. We refer to [17] for the details of IMPACT.

Each agent consists of a set of *data types*, *API functions*, *actions*, and an *agent program* that includes some rules prescribing its behaviors. Since we use DLV$^{\mathcal{K}}$ [4] as the planner, a new connection module has been created within Agent $monitor$ so that $monitor$ can access the DLV$^{\mathcal{K}}$ planner. In this way, before the *Gofish MAS* operates, we feed $\mathcal{P}^{\mathcal{K}}_{Gofish}$ into $monitor$, which then exploits DLV$^{\mathcal{K}}$ to compute all potential plans including both secure and optimistic plans.

Running scenario: The *Gofish* post office guarantees the package delivery within 24 hours of dropOff (time 0). Consider the case that Sue wanted to pick up her package

(p_1=0x00fe6206c.1) at the distribution center. Unfortunately, it has been loaded on the truck. Sue did not come back home in time, therefore the package wasn't delivered in time. Thus after the "pickup" action at time 20, the *MAS* was keeping idle till a timeout (24 in this example) was detected by $monitor$. In the end, $monitor$ generated a log file as follows (see also the project webpage [6]):

> Problematic action:
> 20:pickup($0x00fe6206c.1$), timeout

> Actions executed:
> 0:dropOff($0x00fe6206c.1$); 5:addPkg($0x00fe6206c.1$);
> 13:distCenter($0x00fe6206c.1$); 19:truck($0x00fe6206c.1$)

> Possible plans before problematic action:
> ⟨dropOff(p_1); addPkg(p_1); distCenter(p_1); truck(p_1);
>   pickup(p_1); delivery(p_1); setDelivTime(p_1)⟩
> ⟨dropOff(p_1); addPkg(p_1); distCenter(p_1); truck(p_1);
>   delivery(p_1); setDelivTime(p_1)⟩

6   Related Work

Monitoring problem has been raised in Robotics literature. [10] presented a situation calculus-based account of execution monitoring for robot programs. A situation calculus specification is given for the behavior of a Golog program. The interpretation of Golog programs is combined with an execution monitor, which detects and recovers from discrepancies. Similar to our method, their approach is formal and works for monitoring arbitrary programs. While we focus on monitoring the collaboration of multiple agents, they address the problem of a single agent acting in an uncertain environment.

Another interesting monitoring approach is based on multi-agent *plan-recognition*, by Tambe [18], Intille and Bobick [12], Devaney and Ram [1], Kaminka et al. [13,14]. In this approach, an agent's intentions (goals and plans), beliefs or future actions are inferred through observations of another agent's ongoing behavior.

Devaney and Ram [1] describe the plan recognition problem in a complex multi-agent domain involving hundreds of agents which act over large space and time scales. They use pattern matching to recognize team tactics in military operations. The team-plan library stores several strategic patterns which the system needs to recognize during the military operation. In order to make computation efficient, they utilize representations of agent-pair relationships for team behaviors recognition.

Intille and Bobick [12] constructed a probabilistic framework that can represent and recognize complex actions based on visual evidence. Complex multi-agent action is inferred using a multi-agent belief network. The network integrates the likelihood values generated by several visual goal networks at each time and returns a likelihood that a given action has been observed. The network explicitly represents the logical and temporal relationships between agents, and its structure is similar to a naive Bayesian classifier network structure, reflecting the temporal structure of a particular complex

---

[6] http://www.cs.man.ac.uk/~zhangy/project/monitor/

action. Their approach relies on all *coordination constraints* among the agents. Once an agent fails, it may not be able to recognize the plans.

Another line of work has been pursued in ISI. Gal Kaminka et al. [13,14] developed the *OVERSEER* monitoring system, which builds upon work on multi-agent plan-recognition by [12] and [18]. They address the problem of many geographically distributed team members collaborating in a dynamic environment. The system employs plan recognition to infer the current state of agents based on the observed messages exchanged between them. The basic component is a *probabilistic plan-recognition algorithm* which underlies the monitoring of a single agent and runs separately for each agent. This algorithm is built under a Markovian assumption and allows linear-time inference. To monitor multiple agents, they utilize social knowledge, i.e. relationships and interactions among agents, to better predict the behavior of team members and detect coordination failures. *OVERSEER* supports reasoning about *uncertainty* and *time*, and allows to answer queries related to the likelihood of current and future team plans.

Comparison: While our objective is (1) to debug *offline* an implemented MAS, and (2) to monitor *online* the collaboration of multiple agents, the approaches described above mainly aim to inferring (sub-)team plans and future actions of agents. They do not address the MAS debugging issue. Furthermore, we point out that our method might be used in the MAS design phase to support *protocol generation*, i.e., determine at design time the messages needed and their order, for a (simple) agent collaboration. More precisely, possible plans $P = \langle m_1, \dots, m_k \rangle$ for a goal encode sequences of messages $m_1, \dots, m_k$ that are exchanged in this order in a successful cooperation achieving the goal. The agent developer may select one of the possible plans, e.g. according to optimality criteria such as least cost, P^*, and program the individual agents to obey the corresponding protocol. In subsequent monitoring and testing, P^* is then the (single) intended plan.

Plan recognition, which is adopted for multi-agent monitoring by the above approaches, is suitable for various situations: if communication is *not* possible, agents exchanging messages are not reliable, or communications must be secure.

The above methods significantly differ from our approach in the following points:

(1) If a multi-agent system has already been deployed, or it consists of legacy code, the plan-recognition approach can do monitoring without modifications on the deployed system. Our method entirely relies on an agent message log file.

(2) The algorithms developed in [14] and [1] have low computational complexity. Especially the former is a linear-time plan recognition algorithm.

(3) Our model is not yet capable of reasoning about uncertainty, time and space.

(4) In some tasks, agents do not frequently communicate with others during task execution. In addition, communication is not always reliable and messages may be incorrect or get lost.

We believe the first three points can be taken into account in our framework. (1) Adding an agent actions log file explicitly for a given MAS should not be too difficult. (2) While the developed algorithms are of linear complexity, the whole framework needs to deal with uncertainty or probabilistic reasoning which can be very expensive. While our approach is NP-hard in the worst case, we did not encounter any difficulties in the scenarios we have dealt with. (3) Although IMPACT does not yet have implemented capabilities for dealing with probabilistic, temporal and spatial reasoning, such extensions have been developed and are currently being implemented.

Among the advantages of our method are the following:

- Our method can be more easily extended to do *plan repair* than the methods above. Merely Kaminka et al. mentioned the idea of dealing with failure actions.
- The approach we have chosen includes protocol generation in a very intuitive sense relying on the underlying planner while the cited approaches model agent behavior at an abstract level which can not be used to derive intended message protocols directly.
- Since ascertaining the intentions and beliefs of the other agents will result in uncertainty with respect to that information, some powerful means of reasoning under uncertainty are required for the plan recognition method.

7   Conclusion

We have described a method to support testing of a multi-agent system, based on monitoring their message exchange using planning methods. This can be seen as a very useful debugging tool for detecting coding and design errors. We also presented some soundness and completeness results for our approach, and touched its complexity.

Our approach works for arbitrary agent systems and can be tailored to any planning formalism that is able to express the collaborative behavior of the *MAS*. We have briefly discussed (and implemented) how to couple a specific planner, $DLV^{\mathcal{K}}$, which is based on the language $\mathcal{K}$, to a particular *MAS* platform, viz. IMPACT. A webpage for further information and detailed documentation has been set up (see footnote 6).

There are many extensions to our approach. We mention just some:

(1) Cost based planning: Can the goal still be reached with a certain bound on the overall costs, given that actions which the agents take have costs attached? And, what is the optimal cost and how does a corresponding behavior look like? This would allow us to assess the quality of an actual agents behavior and to select cost-effective strategies. To keep the exposition simple, we have omitted that $DLV^{\mathcal{K}}$ is also capable of computing admissible plans (plans within a cost bound) and, moreover, optimal plans over optimistic and secure plans, respecting that each action has certain declared cost [6]. For instance, in the *Gofish* example we might prefer plans where the customer picks up the package herself, which is cheaper than sending a truck. Thus, in the realization of our approach, also economic behavior of agents in a *MAS* under cost aspects can be easily monitored, such as obedience to smallest number of message exchanges or least total communication cost.

(2) Dynamic planning: We assumed an *a priori* chosen collaboration plan for $\mathcal{M}_{log}$ compatibility. This implies C-Plans$(\mathcal{P}, \mathcal{M}_{log}, n') \subseteq$ C-Plans$(\mathcal{P}, \mathcal{M}_{log}, n)$, for all $n' \geq n \geq 0$. However, this no longer holds if the plan may be dynamically revised. Checking $\mathcal{M}_{log}$ compatibility then amounts to a new planning problem whose initial states are the states reached after the actions in $\mathcal{M}_{log}$.

(3) At the beginning of monitoring, all potentially interesting plans for the goal are generated, and they can be cached for later reuse. We have shown the advantages of this

method. However, if a very large number of intended plans exists up front, the method may become infeasible. In this case, we might just check, similar as above, whether from the state reached and the actions in $\mathcal{M}_{log}$, the goal can be reached.

Investing the above issues is part of ongoing and planned future research.

References

1. M. Devaney and A. Ram. Needles in a haystack: Plan recognition in large spatial domains involving multiple agents. In *Proc. AAAI-98*, pp. 942–947, 1998.
2. J. Dix, U. Kuter, and D. Nau. HTN planning in answer set programming. Tech. Rep. CS-TR-4332, CS Dept., Univ. Maryland, 2002. Submitted to *Theory and Practice of Logic Programming*.
3. J. Dix, H. Munoz-Avila, and D. N. and Lingling Zhang. Theoretical and empirical aspects of a planner in a multi-agent environment. In G. Ianni and S. Flesca, editors, *Proc. European Conference on Logic and AI (JELIA '02)*, LNCS 2424, pp. 173–185. Springer, 2002.
4. T. Eiter, W. Faber, N. Leone, G. Pfeifer, and A. Polleres. A logic programming approach to knowledge-state planning, II: the DLV$^{\mathcal{K}}$ system. *Artificial Intelligence*, 144(1-2):157–211, 2003.
5. T. Eiter, W. Faber, N. Leone, G. Pfeifer, and A. Polleres. A logic programming approach to knowledge-state planning: Semantics and complexity. *ACM Transactions on Computational Logic*, 2003. To appear.
6. T. Eiter, W. Faber, N. Leone, G. Pfeifer, and A. Polleres. Answer Set Planning under Action Costs. *Journal of Artificial Intelligence Research*, 2003. To appear.
7. K. Erol, J. A. Hendler, and D. S. Nau. UMCP: A sound and complete procedure for hierarchical task-network planning. In K. J. Hammond, editor, *Proc. 2nd Int'l Conference on Artificial Intelligence Planning Systems (AIPS-94)*, pp. 249–254. AAAI Press, 1994.
8. R. E. Fikes and N. J. Nilsson. STRIPS: A new approach to the application of theorem proving to problem solving. *Artificial Intelligence*, 2(3-4):189–208, 1971.
9. M. Ghallab, A. Howe, C. Knoblock, D. McDermott, A. Ram, M. Veloso, D. Weld, and D. Wilkins. PDDL — The Planning Domain Definition Language. Technical report, Yale Center for Computational Vision and Control, October 1998. Available at http://www.cs.yale.edu/pub/mcdermott/software/pddl.tar.gz.
10. G.D. Giacomo, R. Reiter and M. Soutchanski. Execution Monitoring of High-Level Robot Programs. In *Principles of Knowledge Representation and Reasoning*, pp. 453–465, 1998.
11. R. Goldman and M. Boddy. Expressive planning and explicit knowledge. In *Proc. AIPS-96*, pp. 110–117. AAAI Press, 1996.
12. S. S. Intille and A. F. Bobick. A framework for recognizing multi-agent action from visual evidence. In *Proc. AAAI-99*, pp. 518–525, 1999.
13. G. Kaminka, D.V.Pynadath, and M. Tambe. Monitoring deployed agent teams. In *Proc. Fifth International Conference on Autonomous Agents (Agents-2001)*, pp. 308–315. ACM, 2001.
14. G. A. Kaminka and M. Tambe. Robust agent teams via socially-attentive monitoring. *Journal of Artificial Intelligence Research*, 12:105–147, 2000.
15. H. J. Levesque, R. Reiter, Y. Lespérance, F. Lin, and R. B. Scherl. GOLOG: A Logic Programming Language for Dynamic Domains. *Journal of Logic Programming*, 31(1–3):59–83, 1997.
16. M. Luck, P. McBurney, C. Preist, and C. Guilfoyle. The Agentlink agent technology roadmap draft. Available at http://www.agentlink.org/roadmap/index.html, 2002.
17. V.S. Subrahmanian, P. Bonatti, J. Dix, T. Eiter, S. Kraus, F. Ozcan, and R. Ross. *Heterogeneous Agent Systems: Theory and Implementation*. MIT Press, 2000.
18. M. Tambe. Tracking dynamic team activity. In *Proc. AAAI-96*, pp. 80–87, 1996.

Author Index

Lecture Notes in Artificial Intelligence (LNAI)

Lecture Notes in Computer Science